WYCLIFFE
HISTORICAL GEOGRAPHY
of BIBLE LANDS

WYCLIFFE
HISTORICAL GEOGRAPHY
of BIBLE LANDS

Howard F. Vos

WYCLIFFE HISTORICAL GEOGRAPHY OF BIBLE LANDS, Revised Edition, 2003

Howard F. Vos

ISBN 1-56563-349-0

Manufactured in the United States of America

Color maps arranged by Hendrickson Publishers

Drawings by Ben Wood

PICTURES ON TITLE PAGE

A human headed bull (about 30 tons) from palace of Sargon II at Khorsabad, now in the Louvre in Paris. Sargon claimed to have destroyed the northern kingdom of Israel.

The church of the Nativity, Nazareth

Photographs in this book for which credit is not given were taken by author.

CONTENTS

INTRODUCTION:
THE REASON FOR THIS BOOK

The reason for this book in the year 2003 is essentially the same as it was for the first edition in 1967. There was then no single book that discussed the history and geography of all the eleven Bible lands. And that situation still holds true. In the minds of many writers of books, articles, and travel advertisements, and perhaps of the general public, Palestine is *the* land of *the* Bible. Few have recognized that such widely separated places as Iran, Egypt, Greece, Turkey, and Italy also provided a geographical stage on which the biblical drama unfolded. So a survey of the history and geography of all the Bible lands is very much needed today.

In recent years Bible dictionaries, encyclopedias, and atlases have appeared in increasing numbers. While they have often provided information on several or all of the Bible lands, their approach has been either topical or very largely geographical. The present volume brings together historical, geographical, biblical, and archaeological material on all eleven areas of the Near Eastern and Mediterranean world that might properly be called "Bible Lands."

Separate chapters describe each of these lands, and the areas are discussed in the order in which they figure most significantly in the biblical narrative. Unquestionably, the earliest events occurred in Mesopotamia. Then, although the Patriarchs lived in Palestine for a while, the Children of Israel were rather firmly anchored in Egypt for a more extended period of time. Thus, the chapter on Egypt appears second. Then, the spotlight focused on Palestine for most of a millennium—hence the third chapter. Of course develop-

ments in Phoenicia and Syria were closely entwined with Palestinian history, but intimate relations between Phoenicia and Palestine came during the United Monarchy, a little earlier than those between Palestine and Syria. So the chapter on Phoenicia appears fourth. Then, because Syrian and Palestinian affairs were most closely linked during the days of the separate history of Judah and Israel, the chapter on Syria comes next. Not long after the fall of the Northern Kingdom to the Assyrians and the Southern Kingdom to the Babylonians (Mesopotamian powers), Persia (Iran) won control of the whole Near East and held it for some two hundred years. It ruled the area at the close of the Old Testament narrative. Hence the chapter on Biblical Iran appears sixth.

When the curtain rose on the New Testament, Palestine again figured prominently during the life of Christ, but the territory was not free to initiate action. Rome was in control. Soon a new message of salvation through Christ was being proclaimed, the church was founded, and missionary crusades were launched. The apostle Paul led in these church-expansion movements under Roman auspices. Cyprus, Asia Minor, Greece, Malta, and Italy, in that order, assumed prominence in his missionary endeavors. So these five lands constitute the subject matter of the final chapters of the book.

As to arrangement of material within the chapters, treatment varies. Commonly, a brief geographical survey appears first, followed by an historical outline. Thereafter, divergence frequently occurs because of differing subject matter. In some instances historical developments receive greater prominence, in others geographical concern predominate. Sometimes the large number of biblical references throws the spotlight there.

In the first edition of this book Dr. Charles Pfeiffer was co-author, writing four of the main chapters. Then during the more than fifteen years that the book was in print, it gradually grew out of date and Dr. Pfeiffer passed away. In the present edition I have replaced all of Dr. Pfeiffer's sections and have completely rewritten the rest of the book, resulting is an up-to-date discussion of the historical geography of all the Bible lands.

But some will ask, "What is the good of a historical geography to someone who just wants to study the Bible?" The answer is simple. A study of the history, archaeology, and geography of the Bible lands sheds light upon the biblical text, giving understanding to it. Also, it helps, to give a sense of reality to the life and times of the Bible. By this means the people and the events of the Bible may emerge from a dusty past to assume current factuality. Sometimes it helps us to have a sense of "you are there." Moreover, a study of this sort helps to confirm the accuracy or authenticity of the Bible. A whole new plausibility of the biblical message may dawn upon us.

The actual facade of Nebuchadnezzar's throne room, now in the Staaliche Museen, Berlin.
(To see this picture in color turn to the color insert in this book.)

1

MESOPOTAMIA

Mesopotamia as a Bible Land

Mesopotamia holds special interest for the modern Bible student. There civilization began. Such is the claim of the Bible, and modern scholarship agrees. The Garden of Eden was located in this general area; the Euphrates and the Hiddekel, or Tigris, flowed through the Garden or past it (Genesis 2:14). Noah's ark came to rest on the "Mountains of Ararat" (Genesis 8:4) at the northern fringe of the region. And after the Flood, descendants of Noah established such biblical cities as Erech, Nineveh, Calah, and Babylon in Mesopotamia (Genesis 10:10–11).

Later on, Abraham was born in Ur, one of the greatest cities of the region. Subsequently, he moved to Haran in northern Mesopotamia. At Haran some of Abraham's relatives remained; there Abraham sought a wife for his son Isaac (Genesis 24); there Jacob married Leah and Rachel (Genesis 29); and there all of the progenitors, or forefathers, of the twelve tribes of Israel were born except Benjamin.

Many centuries later, Assyria conquered the kingdom of Israel and carried off thousands of Hebrews into captivity in Mesopotamia. About a century after that, Babylon destroyed the kingdom of Judah and also deported large numbers of Hebrews to Mesopotamia. There they remained until the Persians took over the area and permitted the Hebrews to go back home. As the restoration progressed, the population of restored Jerusalem and its environs came largely from Mesopotamia.

Geographical Features

The Meaning of Mesopotamia

In order to think intelligently about Mesopotamia, we need to discover what it was. The literal meaning of the term is "land between the rivers" (the Tigris and Euphrates), but that does not spell out the territory specifically. Apparently Jewish scholars in Alexandria, Egypt, coined the word when they translated Genesis from Hebrew into Greek (the version called the Septuagint) probably about 250 B.C. Their word "Mesopotamia" in Genesis 24:10 translates a Hebrew term, which literally means "Aram of the two rivers" and seems to apply to the small area between the Euphrates and the Khabur river in the northwestern part of what we now call Mesopotamia.

The Greek historian Polybius (second century B.C.) and the Greek geographer Strabo (first century B.C.) applied it to the land extending southward from the Armenian highlands to modern Baghdad. This is the equivalent of the territory that Arab geographers call *al Jazira* or *Gezirah* (the island). It is almost an island because the Tigris and Euphrates begin close together in

the north and again flow close together near Baghdad.

Acts 7:2 puts Abraham's hometown of Ur (220 miles south of Baghdad) in Mesopotamia; and Acts 2:9 seems to refer to Jewish residents of Babylonia as "dwellers in Mesopotamia." So by New Testament times the term Mesopotamia had come to apply to the whole region between the Tigris and Euphrates from the Armenian Mountains in the north to the Persian Gulf in the south.

Since Roman times, the name Mesopotamia has applied to the entire Tigris-Euphrates valley from the mountains of the north to the marshlands at the head of the Persian Gulf and includes some modern land to the east of the Tigris and west of the Euphrates. Modern Iraq occupies most of the territory of ancient Mesopotamia, which stretched some 600 miles from northwest to southeast and 300 miles from east to west.

Both the Tigris and Euphrates originate in the mountains of Armenia, less than 20 miles apart. The rivers flow in greatly divergent channels in a southeasterly direction until at one point they are 290 miles apart. Then they converge and near Baghdad flow about 25 miles apart. About 100 miles north of the Persian Gulf they join and spill their waters as one river (the Shatt-al-Arab) into the Gulf.

The Tigris

The more easterly of the two rivers is the Tigris, called *Hiddekel* in some versions of the Old Testament (Genesis 2:14; Daniel 10:4). It rises on the southern slopes of the Taurus Mountains in present-day Turkey and cuts a bed 1,180 miles long on its way to the Persian Gulf. On its journey it is joined by several tributaries (including Great Zab, Little Zab, and Diyala) flowing from the mountains to the east. Although there is no evidence of any great change in the upper course of the Tigris, its lower course to the south of Baghdad was very unstable. During Old Testament times that part of the river flowed a considerable distance to the west of where it is now located.

The Tigris floods annually. Its rise begins about the first of March; the waters reach their height in May and recede in June or July. At Baghdad the river is about a quarter of a mile wide, with a depth at high water of 26 feet and at low water of 4.5 feet. The speed of the current in flood is about 4 miles per hour and at low water one mile per hour. The river is full of obstructions; the upper

The Euphrates River near Babylon.

part of the river is navigable only by native rafts, but from Baghdad approximately to a point where the Tigris joins the Euphrates, it is navigable by boats of some size.

Since the Tigris lies in a fairly deep bed, it was difficult for ancient peoples to raise its waters for irrigation as easily as they could those of the Euphrates. In fact, most of the course of the Tigris lies at a lower altitude than that of the Euphrates, so in ancient times irrigation canals were dug from the Euphrates to the Tigris, the latter receiving the tailings of canals between the rivers. Apparently the Tigris did not carry as much silt as the Euphrates.

The Tigris was the great river of Assyria; on its banks stood most of the important Assyrian cities; those mentioned in the Bible include Nineveh, Calah, and Ashur.

The Euphrates

The Euphrates is mentioned in Genesis 2:14 as one of the rivers of Eden and appears frequently in the Old Testament (in eight books) and in Revelation (9:14; 16:12) because it is the river of Mesopotamia closer to Palestine and Syria. It rises on the northern slopes of the Taurus Mountains and winds its way over a meandering 2,235-mile path to the Persian Gulf. As it flows from the mountains, it first goes in a southwesterly course toward the Mediterranean, coming to

within 90 miles of that sea; then it bends sharply toward the southeast. In Syria it has two tributaries from the east or north: the Balikh and the Khabur. Like the Tigris, its lower course has changed considerably during historical times: the ancient channel flowed past Kish and Nippur in the south. Now remains of those cities stand far to the east of the Euphrates. As its bed has moved westward, the river has been less useful to cities of the area. Since a majority of irrigation canals led from the east bank to the Tigris, the increasing distance put a heavy strain on the labor force of the area.

Also, like the Tigris, the Euphrates floods annually. The waters begin to rise about the middle of March, continue to rise until June, and recede to ordinary levels in September. The flooding of the rivers of Mesopotamia did not prove to be the blessing to the area that the flooding of the Nile was in Egypt. The flood came while crops were growing, and dikes were required to protect the land. Late flooding increased salinization of the soil (see discussion below) because of rapid evaporation in increasingly high temperatures. Mud suspended in the swollen rivers was less fertile than mud carried by the Nile and could not be immediately deposited on fields. As a result, it clogged the irrigation canals that carried the water inland and required that

Modern Iraqis still sometimes weave reeds to make boats (coracles) and caulk them with bitumen. Here is one of these boats on the Tigris near Bagdad.

miles per hour at low water. Much of the river is interrupted by rapids, and navigation is difficult except at high water.

Most of the biblical cities of Babylonia—Babylon, Ur, Erech, and many others—were located along the Euphrates. This was true, of course, because the river was necessary for irrigation—for the sustaining of life. Not only did the river make possible the development of cities, it necessitated urbanization.

The reason for this is easy to understand: because the river came to flood stage while crops stood in the fields, it was necessary to build dikes along the banks. And since the river carried so much silt in its waters, some of which it deposited, it tended to raise the level of its bed, forcing the dikes to be built ever higher. Thus, during part of its course, the riverbed stood at some height above the surrounding land. Tapping of the river for irrigation purposes therefore required large irrigation canals with dikes of their own and a vast system of subsidiary canals. Only in this way could the tremendous pressure of flood waters be handled.

canals be redredged or replaced by new ones.

In the neighborhood of Hit in the Middle Euphrates northwest of Baghdad are extensive bitumen lakes, which supplied the ancients with material for cementing bricks and caulking boats. From Hit to where the Tigris and Euphrates join lies broad, flat alluvium. At Hit the river is 250 yards across and then decreases in size because there are no tributaries and its water is used for irrigation. The current of the Euphrates is 5 miles per hour at high water and 1.5

The development and maintenance of this system required a massive amount of organized labor. Individual farmers could not do the job. So, as peoples of the Mesopotamian plain sought to harness the river for their livelihood, they had to collect

Ancient Assyrians often used reed boats. Here a platoon of soldiers crosses the Tigris. A coracle carries a dismantled chariot, horses swim; soldiers swim, helped along by inflated goatskins. From Nimrud, about 865 B.C. *British Museum*

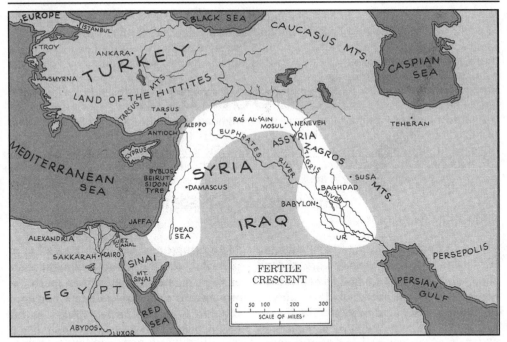

Mesopotamia within the Fertile Crescent

themselves together into city-states to get the job done.

Stretching northwestward from the Persian Gulf is a narrow strip of land that skirts the Arabian and Syrian deserts and descends to the border of Egypt. Early in the twentieth century James H. Breasted, eminent Egyptologist of the University of Chicago named this region "The Fertile Crescent," and the name has stuck. Along its northern boundary lie the 3,000-foot-high tablelands of Anatolia and Iran, separated from each other by the mountains of Armenia, the Urartu of ancient cuneiform inscriptions and the Ararat of the Bible (Genesis 8:4).

South and east of the Fertile Crescent are the desert areas that forbid access to the merchant and the soldier alike. The famous trek of Abraham from Ur of the Chaldees through Haran to Canaan approximates the way by which people have journeyed from southern Mesopotamia to Palestine since the beginning of history.

As human beings moved from either the mountains or the desert into river valleys of the Fertile Crescent, they became a part of the culture that early produced separate

city-states and later on the Assyrian and Babylonian empires. In these valleys of the Tigris and the Euphrates rivers –two of the four rivers of Eden (Genesis 2:14)—were found the earliest evidences of complex civilization.

As the Fertile Crescent turns southwestward along the coasts of Syria and Palestine, rainfall diminishes and cultivated land gradually passes into desert. Along the Mediterranean Sea the desert begins at Gaza (cf. Acts 8:36), and this technically speaking, also marks the end of the Fertile Crescent. The Fertile Crescent has historically been the connecting road between the nations of the Nile and of the Tigris-Euphrates valleys. It connects Asia to Africa, which dangles from Asia by a mere thread of less than one hundred miles of land north of the Gulf of Suez. The Suez Canal has eliminated even that tenuous connection.

Mesopotamian Prosperity

As the valley people harnessed the river, they became prosperous and built an advanced civilization. Their success stirred envy in the hearts of the mountain peoples along the eastern fringes of Mesopotamia and the desert peoples of the Arabian peninsula to the west and south. Envy and at times dire necessity led to periodic invasion, against which there were no natural barriers. These infusions of new ethnic stock and new cultural elements created in the Mesopotamian valley a heterogeneous or mixed culture. In the Nile Valley, on the other hand, barriers to invasion permitted the maintenance of a relatively homogeneous culture—one without extensive outside influence.

The degree of wealth and cultural sophistication of ancient Mesopotamia becomes quite surprising when we consider the area's lack of natural resources. Ancient Mesopotamians were singularly a "have-not" people. Since the soil of much of the region was waterlaid, it had no mineral deposits, no stone or great timber resources. The people had little more than sun, soil, and water to work with. In a very real sense they became people of the soil.

On the soil they grew their foodstuffs (dates, wheat, emmer, millet, sesame, and especially barley were among key items) and from it they produced their clothing (wool from sheep and linen from flax). From the clay they made pottery used for storage and preparation of food and for eating meals. From the clay they also made bricks (baked and unbaked) for construction of houses and public buildings, and tablets on which to keep their records and do their school assignments. Reeds caulked with bitumen and inflated animal skins provided materials for boats and rafts and thus a means of traveling on the rivers. Agricultural surplus could be traded abroad for metals, timber, and other necessities and luxuries.

Climate

The importance of the Tigris and Euphrates to the maintenance of life in Mesopotamia is clear from even a brief look at the climate and rainfall pattern of the area. In Baghdad, temperatures hit 120°–140° in the sun and about 108° in the shade during July and August. Even higher temperatures occur in southern Iraq near the Persian Gulf. Some regions there, baked under cloudless skies, are among the hottest places on earth. At least in most of the southern part of Mesopotamia there is rarely ever rain in the summer. Even in the rainy season there is commonly not more than six or seven inches. And, unfortunately, this meager amount is not constant, for Baghdad has been known to receive as much as twenty-two inches or as little as two inches per year. In the hill country of the north, the annual average is about sixteen inches; the mountains receive double that amount. Under such conditions, the waters of the Tigris and Euphrates are a necessity for the maintenance of life.

Unfortunately, however, the rivers prove to be a mixed blessing. Low waters mean drought and famine. Excessive flooding brings catastrophe when rivers break through their embankments, submerge land, and sweep away mud houses. Although flood control projects make this a less likely threat today, ancient Mesopotamia hovered between a state of swamp and desert.

Geographical Divisions

As indicated, there are regional differences in Mesopotamia. The southern part, from the area around Baghdad (where the rivers come closest together) to the Persian Gulf, is flat, alluvial or waterlaid soil, and is commonly called Babylonia. What the earliest peoples called it is not known, but by 2000 B.C. inhabitants were calling it Sumer and Akkad, after the Sumerians and Akkadians who lived there. Sumer was the region just north of the Persian Gulf and Akkad the area around ancient Babylon or modern Baghdad. Southern Mesopotamia was called Chaldea after the Chaldeans who came into it about 1000 B.C. In several passages the Old Testament speaks of Shinar, which clearly applies to Babylonia, though efforts to equate Shinar and Sumer linguistically now have been abandoned.

Assyria occupied northern Mesopotamia and was composed of land that was sometimes hilly and even mountainous in the far north. So Assyria had greater supplies of stone and some timber in the early days. She also had districts that enjoyed enough rainfall to practice dry farming. It was therefore not so necessary to band together in the north to maintain the agricultural system as it was in the south, and Assyria had a substantial class of small farmers. The boundaries of Assyria were more fluid than those of Babylonia, depending on the relative strength of peoples living in Syria and Asia Minor.

Coastline of the Persian Gulf

That the Tigris and Euphrates have carried billions of tons of soil southward in their muddy waters and deposited it somewhere is certain. The old standard view subscribed to in many textbooks is that the rivers dropped this soil at their mouths and pushed the coastline of the Persian Gulf ever southward. In fact, the entire area below Babylon is supposed to have been formed in that way. Presumably, the Tigris and Euphrates did not join in earlier days, but flowed as separate streams into the gulf.

On the basis of newer studies in geology, however, that view is being seriously questioned. It is argued that, although the rivers bring down much silt, some 90 percent apparently is deposited before reaching the gulf. Tremendous deposits, up to more than thirty feet in depth, have been laid in southern Mesopotamia. But the rise of the land level has not been marked in this area. So the theory has been advanced that the Tigris and Euphrates drop their sediment in a slowly subsiding basin. Without question, the subterranean water level has risen over the centuries, because, for example, the Babylon of Hammurabi (about 1800 B.C.) is now under water and cannot be excavated. The gradual sinking of the land level supposedly has prevented the land elevation or the coastline from changing significantly since Old Testament times, and the two Mesopotamian rivers are believed always to have flowed into the gulf as a single stream.

While many geologists have followed the new theories, archaeologists and some geologists haven't been quick to do so. Excavations and textual information indicate that Ur and Eridu, for instance, had easy access to the sea in Old Testament times. Ur had two seaports, and, at the minimum, the 150 miles of waterway between Ur and the Persian Gulf must have been more open than at present. Moreover, recent geological investigations in southern Iraq indicate that even into historic times the shore of the Persian Gulf may have run anywhere from 80-to-175 miles northwest of its present line.[1] The changing position of the shoreline is connected not only to sediment deposit but also to fluctuations in sea level. Apparently the sea level was higher in the period 4000–2000 B.C. than it is today. Further study of textual, archaeological, geological, and hydrographical data is necessary in order to solve this knotty problem.

The Decline of Mesopotamia

In the Old Testament times, Mesopotamia was fertile and prosperous. Today it is possible to look for miles across the flat plains and see nothing but brown and barren land. What has happened? For one thing, the Euphrates River has shifted its course westward, leaving numerous southern Mesopotamian cities without the life-giving waters necessary for their existence and making the whole irrigation system more difficult to maintain. Second, the ancient empires that gave so much attention to maintaining the irrigation system passed off the scene, and the system fell into decay. Third, the destructiveness of the Mongol Tamerlane's invasion at the end of the fourteenth century was of a magnitude and cruelty that is unimaginable. Dikes and canals wrecked at that time were never restored under the long Turkish occupation that followed, and the region has fallen into utter ruin. But the real enemy of prosperity in this region is salinization of the soil.

Today one can see in many places a coat of salt on the surface of the soil. Even in other areas where no such extreme situation exists, crops cannot be grown. Barley, with a high salt toleration, will not bear fruit if the soil contains more than one percent salt. The date palm will not yield fruit if salt content is more than two percent. Because of salinization of the soil, population began to drift out of Southern Mesopotamia to the northern regions in the third century B.C.

Salinization comes from two sources: irrigation and the water table. Irrigation waters from the Tigris and Euphrates were slightly saline (containing a combination of calcium, magnesium, and sodium). When they stood on the land and evaporated under the hot sun of the area, the cumulative effect of the deposit they left could be damaging. Extensive rains that might wash salts from the soil did not exist. Over the centuries these salts have accumulated in the groundwater. In some places saline groundwater rose to the roots of growing crops; this often occurred because new waters, added as a result of excessive irrigation, rains, or floods, can raise the level of the water table considerably when drainage systems are poor. Although the salinization problem is acute in large areas of southern Mesopotamia today, making it virtually impossible to restore former productivity, the situation is not so severe in the north, where the water table does not rise dangerously close to the roots of growing crops.

Neolithic Beginnings, c. 8000–6000 B.C.

Rise of village life

Domestication of wild grains

Domestication of animals

Making of pottery

Working of stone into useful forms

The Beginnings of Village Life and Civilization

Very early in human history village life began. Scripture says that Adam's son Cain "was . . . building a city" (Genesis 4:17, NIV). Evidently this means that his numerous children and then grandchildren and great-grandchildren lived together in an extended family arrangement. Many generations later his descendant Jabal became the "father" or "ancestor" of those who raise livestock (Genesis 4:20). Jabal's brother Jubal became the "father" or "ancestor" of those who play the harp and flute (4:21). Jabal and Jubal had a cousin, Tubal-Cain, "who forged all kinds of tools out of bronze and iron" (4:22).

In other words, village life came very early as a natural result of an extended family's living together. Much later, perhaps thousands of years later, some of the real trappings of civilization—widespread domestication of livestock, the development of musical instruments, and the working of metal—came into existence.

Thus the development of village life and civilization are not synonymous and did not happen at the same time. The rise of village life is usually associated with a Neolithic stage, when human beings learned how to domesticate wild grains and produce their own food, to domesticate animals, to make pottery, and to work stone into useful forms (axes, arrow heads, and the like). Civilization, on the other hand, involves the development of writing, monumental architecture, the decorative arts, the wheel, and metallurgy.

There seems to be no hope of dating these events of Genesis 4 by working out a genealogy of early humankind from Scripture. Biblical scholars now commonly believe that there are gaps in the early biblical chronology and that it is therefore impossible to establish a chronological development from Adam to Abraham. We have in the early chapters of Genesis, then, representative names in the line of the Redeemer and a passing of an indefinitely long period of time.[2]

Scripture is clear, however, in its assertion that both village life and civilization began in Mesopotamia. Now the question arises as to what modern scholarship has to say about either of these matters. A new stage in early Mesopotamian studies came with the work of Professor Robert Braidwood of the University of Chicago at Jarmo, thirty miles east of the modern oil town of Kirkuk in Iraq. In three seasons there (1943–51) he excavated what he claimed to be the earliest known site of "the village-farming era," and reported a carbon-14 date of about 6,750 B.C. for materials uncovered there.[3]

Braidwood believes that the beginnings of village life will be found in northern

Mesopotamia and adjacent regions, and that those early villages will date somewhere between 10,000 and 7000 B.C. Of course the Bible student recognizes that such discoveries probably will have nothing to do with any early cities of Genesis 4. The Genesis flood was extremely destructive; presumably these discoveries will relate more to urban development following the landing of the ark at the northern edge of Mesopotamia (Genesis 8:4) and may give some indication of the date of the Flood.

While reports of Braidwood's work at Jarmo were circulating in scholarly circles, Kathleen Kenyon was directing a British School of Archaeology in Jerusalem dig at Jericho (1952–58). She especially concentrated her attention on the preliterary levels of the site. On the basis of carbon-14 tests, she assigned an approximate date of 8000 B.C. to the early village culture there.[4] Subsequently it became fashionable to claim that Jericho was the oldest town site in the world.

But that is not the end of the matter. Materials subsequently recovered in village remains at Abu Hureyra in the bend of the Euphrates east of Aleppo, Syria, have yielded carbon-14 dates before 9000 B.C. And a few miles west of Abu Hureyra, also in the bend of the Euphrates, stood Mureybit. The village there dated to before 8000 B.C., according to carbon-14 dating.[5]

EARLIEST KNOWN VILLAGES

Abu Hureyra, in the bend of the Ephrates east of Aleppo, c. 9500 B.C.

Mureybit, just east of Abu Hureyra on the Euphrates, c. 8200 B.C.

Jericho in the Jordan Valley, c. 8000 B.C.

Çayönü, located between where the Tigris and Euphrates rivers originate, c. 8000–7500 B.C.

Another very early Mesopotamian village site is Çayönü, located between where the Tigris and Euphrates rivers originate in northern Mesopotamia. Carbon-14 dates assigned there go back to about 7500 B.C.[6] and may even be pushed to an earlier date. It seems clear that Mesopotamia need not cede primacy of urban development to Palestine, or to any other part of the world for that matter.

As to the beginnings of civilization, this involved, as noted above, the invention of writing and the wheel and the development of metallurgy, monumental architecture, and the decorative arts. All these achievements appeared first in Mesopotamia during the fourth millennium B.C., and the Sumerians of the southern part of the region normally are given credit for them. Comments on the Sumerians appear later in this chapter.

The Earliest Mesopotamian Cultures

Thousands of years before the beginning of Hebrew history several peoples developed distinctive cultures in Mesopotamia. If we are to place the biblical patriarchs in a meaningful setting, it is useful to outline at least briefly the long historical development of which they were in some degree the heirs. The period from Jarmo to the advent of writing (c. 6500–3500 B.C.) is sometimes called "prehistoric," but that is an unwise choice because in the minds of many it conjures up pictures of cave men and other Stone Age developments. Technically, prehistoric denotes a period prior to the writing of history. Others prefer the term "proto-history," which signifies the time not long before the invention of writing and the recording of history. The term "proto-literate" may be even more acceptable because it indicates the stage just before the invention of writing. In actuality, the writing of what might properly be called history came long after people learned to write.

Hassuna

The first of these early cultures we identify is called Hassuna. Like other culture periods, it gets its name from the place where it was first found, at Hassuna, twenty-two miles south of Mosul in northern

Iraq. Though typical Hassuna culture turned up elsewhere (as is true of the other cultures noted below), such as at Nineveh, of particular significance is that this earliest culture and the one that follows it should appear in northern Mesopotamia. This fact is appropriate from a biblical standpoint because they are closer to where the ark landed (on the mountains of Ararat, Genesis 8:4). It is also appropriate from a geographical standpoint because places in the south would need to wait for marshy areas to solidify and for the population to be large enough to develop either irrigation or flood control systems. The Hassuna culture may be dated about 6000 to 5000 B.C. But if one classifies Samarra as a separate culture instead of a sub-period of Hassuna, Hassuna would date 6000 to 5500 and Samarra 5500 to 5000 B.C.

Hassuna was excavated by the Iraqi Directorate of Antiquities under the leadership of Seton Lloyd and Fuad Safar in 1943 and 1944. What they found was a Neolithic farming community using flint sickleblades for reaping and stone hoes and hand axes for a variety of agricultural chores. These people had domesticated the ox, ass, and sheep. Their houses consisted of six or seven rooms arranged in two blocks around a courtyard; one block served as living quarters, the other as a kitchen and storage area. The earlier house walls were made of pressed mud but later of cigar-shaped mud bricks plastered with clay or gypsum. Much of their pottery was painted and some both painted and incised. Alabaster bowls, beautifully carved and polished, have appeared at some sites. Wheat and barley were among the main crops. The antecedent of the stamp seal also appeared during this period. These small engraved stone or clay discs were impressed as a mark of ownership on lumps of clay fastened to baskets or jar stoppers.

Halaf

Halaf, on the Turkish-Syrian border about halfway between the Tigris and Euphrates, gives its name to the second culture period. The home of this culture was probably in the Nineveh area. This period dates about 5000 to 4500 B.C., but some

would start it earlier or continue it later. Halaf excavations were especially the work of Max von Oppenheim, who worked there from 1911 to 1913 and again in 1927 and 1929. Halafian culture dates to the Chalcolithic or copper-stone era; copper and stone tools were used side by side. Homes were made of pressed mud (adobe) or mud-brick, but rectangular houses were smaller than during the previous period and round houses become predominant. Some of them rested on stone foundations. A special achievement of the Halafians was their remarkable painted pottery, the finest of Mesopotamian antiquity. Made by hand, this elegant, thin painted pottery was fired at an intense heat and had an almost porcelain-like finish. Some patterns were geometric; but birds, flowers, animals, and human representations also appear.

A clay tablet and cylinder seal from Uruk, about 3000 B.C. *Courtesy Staatliche Museen, Berlin*

Ubaid (Obeid)

Ubaid (four miles northwest of Ur) gave its name to a culture that lasted for perhaps a millennium, from about 4500 to 3500 B.C. At Ubaid in 1923 and 1924 C. Leonard Woolley documented this first great culture in southern Mesopotamia. But actually, as excavations at Eridu (twelve miles southwest of Ur, the earliest site known in the south) demonstrate, a people probably related to the Samarra folk had occupied large parts of southern Mesopotamia before the Ubaid period. It is now clear that during the Ubaid period the population of the south had expanded and become powerful enough to dominate the whole of

Writing cuneiform. Courtesy Oriental Institute, *University of Chicago*

Mesopotamia culturally, and perhaps politically. Pottery was now made by hand or on a slow hand-turned wheel. Animal motifs were rare on pottery but many animal and human figurines were hand-modeled in clay. Houses in the south were made from reeds plastered with mud, and some buildings were made of sundried bricks. Houses in the north were commonly made of brick. Builders often pressed small clay cones, painted red or black or left plain, into the wet plaster of a wall to form a design.

A striking achievement of the Ubaid period appeared at Tepe Gawra, just northeast of Nineveh. There three monumental temple buildings stood on three sides of an open court. Built of sun-baked brick, they were plastered and painted; one was red, a second reddish-brown, and a third white. The existence of such an acropolis indicated the combined efforts of a large community and extensive social organization. The construction of large and well-built temples as the dominant feature of several towns during the period anticipated the later Sumerian focus on religion in the city-state.

Ubaid culture also appeared at Susa (biblical Shushan) in the 4000 B.C. level. There

copper mirrors and fragments of fine linen indicate a new degree of sophistication.

Commerce during the Ubaid period was evidently widespread and included India, the Syrian coast, and the Arabian shores of the Persian Gulf.[7] The Ubaid period possibly represented the first stage in the development of Sumerian culture

Uruk (biblical Erech, modern Warka)

The Uruk (biblical Erech, Genesis 10:10) period was an exciting time in world history, for then (3500–3100 B.C.) civilization began. At least the inventions or developments that characterize civilization occurred during this period. The wheel came into use and was especially employed to good advantage in the making of pottery, which was now produced on a spinning potter's wheel; the ware was highly polished but left unpainted. Four-wheeled chariots are known. Writing, too, first appeared during the Uruk period. Hundreds of flat clay tablets dating soon after 3500 B.C. turned up in the temple of E-Anna at Uruk. Written in crude pictograms, these later lost their pictographic character and became the wedge-shaped cuneiform. Cuneiform was written in soft clay by a wooden stylus with a triangular end and sharp edges. Thus it was possible to create combinations of wedges and tailings (using the end or the edge of the stylus) to represent the many syllables of ancient Mesopotamian languages. The tablets were then either sun-dried or baked.

Presumably the early tablets of Uruk were written in Sumerian. They primarily employed a number system based on sixty, but a decimal system also appeared.[8] Thus they figured in terms of twelve hours in the day (1/5 of 60) and thirty minutes in an hour (1/2 of 60), and they understood a circle to have 360° (6 x 60).

BEGINNINGS OF CIVILIZATION

True civilization is generally thought to have begun around 3500 B.C., during the Uruk period with

• the invention of writing

- invention of the wheel

- monumental architecture

- the decorative arts

- large scale metallurgy

Another feature of the development of civilization during this period was monumental architecture. The ziggurat had its birth at this time. The one at Uruk was simply a large platform thirty feet high and measuring 150 by 140 feet at the base and oriented toward the points of the compass. The shrine on it was 65 feet long and 50 feet wide. Ziggurats became a characteristic feature of southern Mesopotamian cities, and with the passage of time rose several levels or stages into the air, always with a temple on top. Here the peoples of Mesopotamia sought to provide a home for their gods and to meet them there. Back in 1954 André Parrot compiled a list of thirty-three of these sacred towers that had either been excavated or alluded to in ancient literature.[9] His list would probably be even longer if he were to construct it today.

Critical scholars frequently make a connection between the ziggurat (especially the Tower of Babylon) and the biblical Tower of Babel. But a connection between the two doesn't seem plausible for at least three reasons. First, the development of high ziggurats to consist of several stages came fairly late, perhaps around 2000 B.C., long after the advent of numerous languages. Second, the biblical Tower of Babel (Genesis 11) was not a worship center with a temple on top. Rather, it was a rallying center or a defense bastion to prevent dispersion of people over the earth. Third, the Tower of Babel was a structure that represented defiance against God, not respect for or worship of Him.

The monumental architecture of the Uruk period involved more than building ziggurats. The organized effort of a substantial population also produced numerous large and impressive temples, one of them 26-by-100 feet and built on a lime-

stone foundation. Of course the limestone had to be imported. The use of the pillar in construction also dates to this period. For example, in a courtyard between two temples at Uruk stood a portico of eight massive mudbrick columns, eight feet in diameter and arranged in two rows.[10] Thus the pillar as a weight-carrying device antedated the invention of the arch in Mesopotamia.

Clay decorative cones pressed into the side of a building at Uruk.
Courtesy Staatliche Museen, Berlin

Domestic architecture of the Uruk period has not yet been well documented at Uruk itself, but we can know something about it from two other sites. In both cases, the town had a sort of grid plan with a main street intersected by smaller streets at right angles. Houses built of oblong bricks consisted of three units of two-to-four spacious rooms each arranged around a hall or courtyard. The private houses present a near-luxurious quality.[11]

Fairly sophisticated artistic production also appeared during the Uruk period. It was common to press into the wet clay of the exterior of a building small clay cones with their ends painted in various colors. Thus a sort of mosaic design could be achieved. Thousands of these clay cones still litter the site of Uruk. An example of what might be seen in Uruk-age temples comes from Tell 'Uqair, about fifty miles south of Baghdad. Temple walls still stand several yards high and have their inner

A cylinder seal rolled out in soft clay. *Courtesy Staatliche Museen, Berlin*

faces covered with mural paintings in several colors. There was a band of geometrical ornament, above which was a frieze of human and animal figures. On the altar were painted two spotted guardian leopards in red and black.[12]

Yet another important aspect of Uruk's artistry was the cylinder seal. These consisted of stone cylinders one-to-three inches long, with a hole drilled through them so they could be worn around the neck on a cord. On the seal's surface was cut a design that became a distinctive mark of the owner. When rolled across wet clay it could serve as a signature or a sign of ownership. These first appeared in the White Temple at Uruk and date to 3500 B.C. or earlier, thus antedating the earliest writing. Cylinder seals were used for about 3000 years, to the Persian period, when the stamp seal came to predominate. These cylinder seals were commonly quite well made and are important not only for art history but for social history, for they picture war, religious and agricultural scenes, and numerous other aspects of everyday life.

Excavation at Uruk, thirty-five miles up the Euphrates from Ubaid, has been a major project of the German Oriental Society, which worked there 1912–1913, 1928–1939, and 1954–1960. The earliest culture found at Uruk (3500–3100 B.C.) shows no clear-cut break with the Ubaid development that preceded it and involved a blossoming of Sumerian culture and the urbanization of southern Mesopotamia. Northern Mesopotamia now evidently lagged behind the south in cultural development.

At least by 3500 B.C. agricultural and climatic conditions apparently approximated conditions known during more recent millennia. Thus, if people were to prosper there they had to band together to maintain irrigation and flood control systems. Such banding together required a government to manage this concentration of population and resulted in a division of labor as farmers engaged in agriculture and industries arose to meet the needs of an urban population.

Moreover, social stratification occurred as rulers, managers, and priests fulfilled special functions. The temple with its priestly class was especially powerful in early Sumer. Its control of large tracts of land and production systems gave it extensive clout in both economic and political spheres. In time military establishments were also required to defend a city or a small empire that it might control.

Jemdet (Jemdat) Nasr

There is no fundamental difference in culture between Uruk and Jemdet Nasr (c. 3100–2900 B.C.). But Jemdet Nasr (just northeast of later Babylon) had a distinctive pottery, was marked by a boom in the production of sculpture in stone, used bronze commodities, and generally enjoyed an amazing advance in civilization. Surviving sculptures in relief and in the round are numerous and run the gamut in quality from poor to excellent. Subject matter is varied too, including violent scenes of heroes overcoming lions or lions attacking bulls, peaceful scenes of rams and ewes, and statuettes of worshipers. The first use of bronze indicated that the Bronze Age had come to Mesopotamia. The growth in population, wealth, communication and commerce, the development of writing, and the development of the canal system were all rapid. There was also a wider use of metal and several new cities were founded.

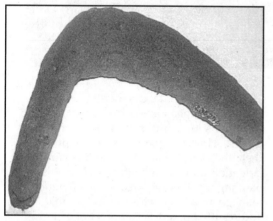

A clay sickle of the Jemdet Nasr period in the *Chicago Museum of Natural History*

Northern Mesopotamia does not seem to have kept up with the south in cultural development during the Uruk and Jemdet Nasr periods and never appears to have caught up with it at a later time. The Third Dynasty of Ur and Hammurabi of Babylon implied in their inscriptions that the north was culturally inferior. And after the rise of Assyria, the Babylonians never willingly accepted rule by those "barbarians."[13]

Sumerian City-States

The Sumerians were one of the most important peoples in all of world history. They get credit for the invention of writing and the wheel; the development of monumental architecture (including the employment of the pillar and arch as weight-carrying devices); the city-state; one of the first calendars (lunar); a number system (sexagesimal—based on 60—as well as decimal); the codification of law, and more. In short, the Sumerians appear to be responsible for the beginnings of civilization in the world. Moreover, they launched what may properly

be called a Mesopotamian civilization. The cast they gave to life in the valley remained with little basic modification until Alexander the Great introduced Hellenistic culture there in the fourth century B.C.

SUMERIAN CONTRIBUTIONS

Earliest writing (Cuneiform)

The wheel (for transportation and pottery making)

Development of monumental architecture (including the pillar and the arch as weight carrying devices)

The city-state

Codification of law

A lunar calendar

A number system based on 60 (including the knowledge of 360° in the circle)

The Sumerian Question

Reference to the Sumerians immediately raises what is called the Sumerian question. Who were the Sumerians? When did they come into Mesopotamia and from where did they come? First, it is important to note that there were two major linguistic groupings in ancient Mesopotamia: Sumerians just north of the Persian Gulf and Semites (in the central area, around ancient Babylon or modern Baghdad). Georges Roux reminds us that Sumerians should signify "Sumerian-speaking people" and Semites "those who spoke a Semitic dialect"; there was no such thing as a Sumerian race.[14] Scholars generally don't claim to know what the Sumerians were ethnically.

It is tempting from a biblical intimation, however, to suggest that they may have been Hamites. At least the Table of Nations (Genesis 10) states that descendants of Ham built Babylon, Erech (Uruk) and Akkad in the land of Shinar (v. 10). The Table of Nations also mentions Calneh in the King James Version and the American Standard

Version, but the Hebrew for Calneh is not understood to be a proper noun in the New Revised Standard Version and Revised English Bible, where it is translated "all of them" in the land of Shinar. Thus it could imply that Hamites originally populated the whole southern part of Mesopotamia, including the Sumerian city of Ur. It is interesting that Genesis 10:11 views southern Mesopotamian developments as giving rise to Assyrian cultural developments. To be sure, Sumerians did indeed influence all of Mesopotamian culture until the days of Alexander the Great.

Reconstruction of a Sumerian Chariot, c. 2700 B.C.
Courtesy Oriental Institute, University of Chicago

As to when the Sumerians came into southern Mesopotamia, something has already been said. The Uruk period was certainly a time of Sumerian achievement, and there is no debate about Sumerian presence by the middle of the fourth millennium B.C. Also, there was no great cultural break between the Ubaid and Uruk periods, and many feel that cultural developments during the Ubaid era were largely Sumerian-inspired. In fact, some believe they were the original settlers of southern Mesopotamia. Arguing against such a claim is the indication that nearly all the oldest cities of Sumer have non-Sumerian names. Hence the Sumerians must have taken control of them after their founding.[15]

The original home of the Sumerians is as much debated as the other questions about the Sumarians. Kramer argues that they came from the region of the Caspian Sea.[16] Others suggest that they came from the mountain region just east of Sumer. Those who hold that they were the original inhabitants of southern Mesopotamia see the glorious Sumerian civilization as slowly evolving in the region as a synthesis of indigenous and foreign elements.

Classical Sumerian Culture

Thus scholars have no final answers as to who the Sumerians were, or whether they invaded Mesopotamia or were the original settlers who gradually developed their superior culture there. However, we do know much about them. The period of classical Sumerian culture is commonly dated from about 2800 B.C. to about 2360, though chronologies vary somewhat. This is also known as the Early Dynastic Period. It was a time when the irrigation culture of southern Mesopotamia spawned numerous city-states, which, in the nature of the case, gave rise to political, social, religious, and military organization. Babylonia, an area some 100–150 miles east and west and 150–200 miles north and south, was divided into at least fourteen tiny states, each centered around a city.

A visitor to one of these city-states would see a city center surrounded by a mudbrick wall guarded by numerous towers. Inside were mudbrick flat-roofed houses standing along twisting, narrow blank-walled streets. The houses faced inner

The Sumerians get credit for the invention of the Arch. Here an arch appears above a doorway of the treasury or court building of Ur, c. 2000 B.C.

An early Sumerian priest. Pergamon
Museum, Berlin

THE URBAN DEVELOPMENT IN
MESOPOTAMIA IN THE BRONZE AGE

Map of urban development in the Bronze Age.
Numerous Sumerian city states rose in southern
Mesopotamia by around 2500 B.C.

in advance of Jethro Tull's seed drill of A.D. 1701. These have been documented by cylinder seals of the period. This is how the planter worked. A yoke of oxen drew a seeder, their driver beside them. Behind the seeder followed a farmer holding it by two handles. The pointed instrument made a shallow trench in the soil. Rising from the frame of the seeder was a tube with a funnel on top. A third man walked beside the seeder and dropped grain into this funnel with one hand, while holding a sack of grain over his shoulder with the other. The grain dropped through the tube and fell into the trench made by the seeder. Barley, wheat, and vegetables were the main crops. Sheep and cattle grazed here and there, and groves of date palms and fruit trees dotted the landscape.

Excavations have now taken place at numerous Sumerian sites, but the initial

courtyards and got their light and ventilation from that source, rather than from windows. In one part of the city was the ziggurat with its temple and living quarters for priests and servants to the temple. Nearby was the king's palace. In another part of the city lived artisans, potters, metal workers, and other craftsmen. Outside the city small villages remained, but the city proper dominated.

As visitors moved outside the city, they would walk on a relatively straight main road with fields carefully marked out on both sides by means of relatively advanced surveying techniques. Here and there irrigation canals appeared. Most of the farming was done with stone hoes and wooden plows drawn by oxen.

With a surprising twist of modernity, seeders, or machine planters, are in evidence,[17] far

A plow with a seeder attachment, from a Kassite seal, second millennium B.C. A man drives the team of oxen while a farmer holds the plow and opens a furrow. An attendant drops seed into the funnel, through which it drops into the ground.

Queen Puabi's headdress, *British Museum*

discovery of Sumerian culture was especially the work of Sir C. Leonard Woolley, who excavated at Ur from 1922 to 1934.[18] Woolley found materials dating to various eras at Ur, but he was especially interested in what are called the Ur I and Ur III periods. The first, dating to about 2500 B.C., took place during classical Sumerian times; he connected the second, dating to about 2100 B.C., with the days of Abraham at Ur. The Abrahamic period at Ur is commonly classified as a time of Neo-Sumerian revival.

The information about the earlier period especially came from the great shaft tombs of the wealthy, who evidently believed "You can take it with you." Since those ancient people had a strong belief in the afterlife, royalty was provided with all that might make such existence more pleasant. Musical instruments (especially lyres made of wood or silver, with expensive inlay of gold and mother of pearl), jewelry, clothing, utensils of various kinds, wagons and beasts of burden, weapons, and even servants were placed in their tombs. King A-bar-gi's grave

included sixty-five people besides himself; Queen Puabi's (formerly rendered Shubad) contained twenty-five.[19] No evidence of violent death suggests that servants were either poisoned or drugged and buried alive.

It is impossible to describe all the tombs excavated or the richness of the contents. The gold vases of Queen Puabi (e.g., a fluted vase, a fluted bowl, and a vase shaped like an ostrich egg), the gold helmet of Meskalumdug (evidently ceremonial), the elaborate headdresses of valuable metals and precious stones, the copper weapons and utensils all bespeak a high point of development in the civilization of Ur long before the days of Abraham.

Gold vases of Queen Puabi, *British Museum*

In his summary on the Ur I period, Woolley commented, "The contents of the tombs illustrate a very highly developed state of society of an urban type... the craftsman in metal possessed a knowledge of metallurgy and a technical skill which few peoples ever rivaled; the merchant carried on a far-flung trade and recorded his transactions in writing; the army was well organized and victorious; agriculture prospered"[20] Among the Sumerian inventions developed during this historical period was the arch as a weight-carrying device.

The Old Akkadian Period (c. 2360–2180 B.C.)

While the Sumerian city-states were flourishing in the region just north of the Persian Gulf, Semites occupied the area of Akkad, the northern part of Babylonia

Sargon of Akkad

empire had collapsed as rapidly as it had been built up. Its rise and fall offer a pattern for subsequent Mesopotamian empires: rapid expansion followed by rebellions, frontier wars, and a final blow by highlanders—in this case the Guti.

Culturally the Akkadians fell under the spell of the Sumerians and only slightly modified what they inherited from them. They evidently could not read or write during their earlier history, so they adopted the cuneiform script. Their linguistic development became the parent of Babylonian and Assyrian, which are only dialects of Akkadian. Mesopotamia was fundamentally altered by the Old Akkadian period. Henceforth the small city-state passed out of fashion with the rise of large centralized kingdoms. Henceforth there was also a blending of the Sumero-Akkadian culture, the influence of which spread beyond the borders of Mesopotamia and was enriched by contacts and contributions from abroad.

Ur III and Abraham

As the great excavator of Ur, Sir C. Leonard Woolley especially brought to light the city of the Ur III period and popularized the idea that this was indeed the city Abraham knew. To deal with this subject intelligently, it would seem useful, first, to trace the historical development from Sargon's empire to the glory of Ur, then to look at the questions of when to date Ur III and Abraham, and finally to draw a picture of Ur and Abraham's possible place in it.

Rise and Fall of Ur III

The people who finally toppled the remnant of Sargon's empire were a little known

where the Tigris and Euphrates flow fairly close together. Subsequently the Akkadians took center stage. The dynamic figure of this period was Sargon of Akkad, who built his new capital, Agade, on the banks of the Euphrates. He soon conquered the Sumerians down to the Persian Gulf, next advanced into Elam and built up the city of Susa (biblical Shushan), and then conquered northward to the Taurus Mountains and west through Syria to the Lebanese coast. Thus he controlled all the territory from the Persian Gulf to the Mediterranean. So in his some fifty-five years of reign (c. 2334–2279 B.C.) Sargon had built the first empire in the Mesopotamian valley.

Like his grandfather Sargon, Naram Sin (2254–2218 B.C.) was a great warrior and did much to shore up his empire. But soon after his death it began to disintegrate. Several Sumerian cities became independent. By about 2190 B.C. the Akkadian

A game from an Ur I tomb, *British Museum*

Pottery of the Akkadian period from Ur.
British Museum

Cuneiform as it was written during the Ur III
period

Caucasian group from the eastern mountains, "semi-anonymous barbarians" known at Guti. They seem to have ravaged the country and to have ruled a few strategic centers for about a century. Finally Utuhegal of Uruk rallied princes of Sumer and Akkad to expel the hated foreigners. But after Utuhegal had ruled for only seven years, one of his officials, Ur-Nammu, governor of Ur, rebelled against him successfully and established himself as king of Ur and king of Sumer and Akkad. Thus Ur-Nammu had founded the Third Dynasty of Ur.

Apparently very early in his seventeen-year reign, Ur-Nammu was able to establish control over the whole of Mesopotamia, though his inscriptions do not provide details of his conquests. He also soon eliminated brigandage from the countryside and then proclaimed the earliest known law code in the world, hundreds of years earlier than Hammurabi's famous Code (see discussion below). Unlike Hammurabi's Code, Ur-Nammu's provided that at least in some cases a criminal was to compensate a victim for losses sustained. Ur-Nammu is also known for his construction, which included digging a number of canals to improve agriculture and communications, fortifying towns, and especially building ziggurats and temples in Ur and several other cities.

After Ur-Nammu died on the battlefield, his son Shulgi ruled for forty-seven years. A peaceful and effective administrator during the first half of his reign, he subsequently launched an annual series of military campaigns in the region at the northeast of Mesopotamia, for reasons not now known. He was worshiped as a god during and after his lifetime. Shulgi's son Amar-Sin (who ruled nine years) was also deified and also fought campaigns in the region where his father had.

Under Shulgi and Amar-Sin the government was centralized as never before: city-states became administrative districts. Fortresses staffed by police forces were maintained along the main roads. The empire was stable and prosperous. This high level of power continued into the fourth year of Amar-Sin's successor Shu-Sin, who then experienced some trouble with the Amorites. Of course there were Amorites living in villages in Syria, but the Amorites the Sumerians were worried

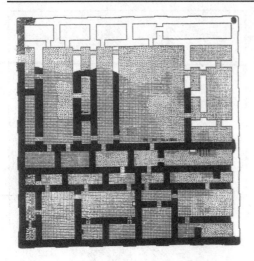

Floor plan of the Ekhursag at Ur.
The Ekhursag was evidently a shrine that served as a temple of the deified king Ur-Nammu and his son Shulgi. The 190-foot square structure had walls of burnt brick and floors of burnt brick set in bitumen. The exterior was buttress and recess in form. The kings probably conducted the actual affairs of state here. For security, there was one entrance on the left. The two large rooms in the upper part of the plan were open courts.

about were nomadic bands who pressed against the borders of the empire and disrupted prosperity, communications, and administrative efficiency.

At length, after eighty-four years of virtually undisputed Sumerian reign, the last Ur III king, Ibbi-Sin, came to the throne. Hardly had he done so when the eastern provinces began to declare their independence. In his fifth year, Amorites cut through the western defenses and penetrated deep into the empire. Invaders were defeated with great difficulty and at great cost. Finally the Elamites invaded from the East and in Ibbi-Sin's twenty-fourth year they took Ur, sacked it and burned it, taking the king prisoner to Iran where he died. The glorious Ur III empire had come to an end.

The Chronology of Ur III

There is no general agreement on exactly when the Ur III period occurred. Jack Finegan has popularized a date of 2070–1960 B.C.[21] Carl Roebuck of Northwestern University put the period between 2135 and 2027 B.C.[22] The chronology used at the

University of Chicago is 2112–2004 B.C.[23] (a date that the French scholar Roux also uses,[24] as does Amélie Kuhrt of University College, London.[25] But McGuire Gibson of the Oriental Institute of the University of Chicago pushes the beginning of the Ur III period back to 2200 B.C.[26] A chronology followed by some of the scholars at the Louvre Museum in Paris begins the period around 2150 B.C. The tendency among scholars in both America and Europe is to regard the minimal chronology of Finegan to be too late. It is likely that Ur III began prior to 2100 B.C.

The Date of Abraham

The date of Abraham's birth and move from Ur is quite another matter. There are differences of opinion about that too, but I anchor the chronological system to the Masoretic. or Hebrew, text of the Old Testament. Of course that chronology is established by working backward from a known point. The Hebrew text puts the date of the dedication of Solomon's temple in the fourth year of Solomon's reign. If we conclude that he began his reign in 970 B.C., his fourth year would have been 966 B.C. First Kings 6:1 states that the Exodus took place 480 years before that, or in 1446 B.C.

The Hebrews had by that time been in Egypt for 430 years (Exodus 12:40), entering in about 1876 B.C.; and the patriarchs had lived in Canaan for 215 years before going to Egypt.[27] So the patriarchal period in Canaan began in 2091 B.C., when Abraham came from Haran at the age of seventy-five. His birth in Ur then would have occurred in 2166 B.C. How old he was when he moved

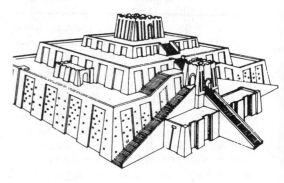

A reconstruction of the Ziggurat at Ur.

from Ur to Haran is nowhere intimated. But if we accept the chronology used by almost any of the scholars mentioned above except Finegan, it is possible to conclude that Abraham knew Ur during her golden age and left it then for Haran.

ESTABLISHING A DATE FOR ABRAHAM

To establish a date for Abraham, we must work backwards. Solomon began to build the temple in his fourth year, 966 B.C.; the Exodus took place 480 years before that, in 1446 B.C. (1 Kings 6:1). The Hebrews entered Egypt 430 years earlier, in 1876 B.C. (Exodus 12:40). By that time the patriarchs had lived in Canaan for 215 years. This we discover from the fact that Abraham was seventy-five when he entered Canaan and one hundred when Isaac was born. Isaac was sixty when Jacob was born and Jacob was 130 when he entered Egypt (see Genesis 12:4; 21:5; 25:26; 47:9). Thus it was 2091 B.C. when Abraham entered Canaan at age seventy-five. And his birth should be dated to 2166 B.C.

Abraham's Identity

If Abram (later Abraham) may have known Ur during her golden age, it is in order to ask who he really may have been and what sort of position he had in the city. To put these questions in context, it is useful to make some generalizations on the social and economic structure of Mesopotamia at the time. The old traditional view of the ancient Mesopotamian economy is that among the Sumerians in theory the state was viewed as an earthly estate of the gods, and its economic activities were focused on the temple. The land, which the gods owned, was partly farmed directly for the temple. The rest was allotted to individual farmers, who paid a large percentage of their produce to temple granaries. The temple also owned great numbers of livestock,

many date orchards, and even its own boats and plows.

Now some scholars suggest that this generalization is based on scattered evidence and it may not have been the usual economic situation. Also they observe that while this may have been valid for some places in Sumer, there was more of a feudal society in Akkad, where great nobles owned large tracts of land; and there was a larger percentage of small, independent farmers in Assyria to the north. Even in Sumer, however, over time there were marked changes in economic conditions and thus of the social structure. For example, the conquests of Sargon of Akkad tended to secularize much land formerly held by the temples. Then at the end of the Ur III period, the Amorite conquest put an end to the temple and royal monopoly of land. There was still crown and temple land, but its extent declined as the amount of land in private hands increased.

As to the Ur III period itself, there was a major economic reorientation. By conquest, the royal government owned the lands formerly held by local rulers. It also operated factories (much like modern factories, sometimes with hundreds of workers, mass-producing goods for domestic and foreign competition), workshops, and trading centers in Mesopotamia and abroad. Therefore it employed a vast army of laborers, civil servants to run the government, and military personnel to ensure protection. The temples also still had their own estates, factories, workers, and administrations. Thus there was a landless working class of state and temple workers, an aristocracy of top officials who managed the affairs of religion and state, and a growing middle class of merchants engaged in state or private business. Just below them was an unknown number of small land owners and farmers.

Now how did Abraham fit into this picture? To be sure he was a patriarch, the head of an extended family. But there is no hint that he started out as a nomadic chieftain wandering about from place to place. He came from a sophisticated commercial center where the urban and rural population was almost totally sedentary. Nor is

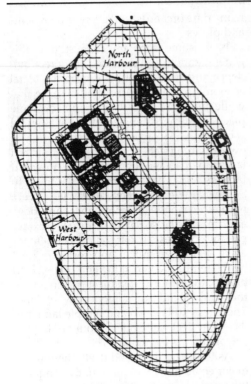

A map of Ur in about 2000 B.C. The enclosed area in the center is the great worship center with its ziggurat

there evidence that economic, political, or military conditions forced him to leave Ur. He responded to the call of God. First God appeared to him in Ur (Acts 7:2–3) and told him to go to another land that God would show the patriarch. So the patriarchal family moved to Haran, where Abraham's father Terah died. Then God appeared to him again and told him to leave the land of his fathers, and Abraham moved on to the land of Canaan (Genesis 12:1). Some have suggested that Haran was the ancestral home city of Terah and Laban and surmise that Terah had taken his family from Haran to Ur for business purposes, and was then willing to accompany Abraham as far as Haran to die there (see Genesis 27:43; 28:2, 6; 29:4; cf. Genesis 11:32; 12:4–5).

It makes good sense to think of Abraham as a member of the rising commercial class. As such, he would have been free to leave the city, as members of the royal or temple aristocracy or men in the army or the vast proletariat were not. He may even have been a member of a business house with trade representatives in Haran, so he would have had good contacts in this commercial capital of the north.

When Abraham came into Canaan, he was described as being "rich in gold and silver" (Genesis 13:2; 24:35), not merely in flocks and herds. When Sarah died and he bought the cave of Machpelah from Ephron the Hittite as a burial plot, he paid 400 shekels of silver, seemingly without batting an eye, and did not haggle over how many sheep or other commodities to give for the property. This payment is called "current money with the merchant" (Genesis 23:16 KJV).

Moreover, Abraham had a very large entourage in Canaan. For the battle recorded in Genesis 14 he was able to field 318 armed "retainers," who with their families would have constituted a community of at least a thousand. Subsequently, and presumably following in the steps of Abraham, Jacob's household won from the Shechemites permission to "dwell and trade" and "acquire real estate" in their territory (Genesis 34:10). On the basis of these and other intimations, many have concluded that Abraham was a "merchant prince."[28] Certainly he was not merely an ignorant sheikh living in a nomadic state, and it did mean a great deal for him to move from Ur to Haran and then on to Palestine, following God by faith.

Ur As Abraham May Have Known It

If Abraham lived in Ur during the city's golden age, we may wonder what sort of place the patriarch would have known. Ur under the leadership of Ur-Nammu had created an empire which encompassed all of Mesopotamia. The city-state itself was a prosperous commercial and agricultural center with a population of some 360,000, according to Woolley's estimates,[29] though some scholars would now reduce the figure to about 200,000. The city center was enclosed by a wall about 2.5 miles in circumference and 77 feet thick. The thickness of the wall was not so much an indication of the need for formidable fortifications as a reminder that the area had no stone, so it was necessary to erect an earthen rampart

A street scene in Ur with house walls dating to Abraham's time. The presence of Iraqi workers shows how narrow the streets were

or embankment. Within the wall lived about 25,000 people.

The streets were winding and narrow; one could frequently touch the buildings on either side with outstretched arms. It was a tight squeeze when two individuals passed carrying large bundles or when a loaded donkey and a pedestrian met. To prevent the populace from getting hurt on sharp edges, corners of buildings were rounded off at intersections.

The streets were windowless. Only doors opened into houses that were constructed around a central courtyard open to the sky. The houses of the middle class commonly measured 40-by-50 feet or more and were divided into ten-to-twenty rooms. Normally two stories, houses had a kitchen and eating area, guest room, lavatory, servants' quarters, and storage on the first floor and bedrooms on the second floor.[30]

Dominating the northwest part of Ur was the sacred enclosure of the moon god Nanna (see accompanying city plan), which measured about 400 yards long and 200 yards wide. Inside this enclosure rose the great brick ziggurat or stage-tower of Nanna, measuring about 200 feet in length, 150 feet in width, and 70 feet in height. Each of the three stages of the tower was smaller than the one below, and on the topmost level stood the temple of the god. Gardens beautified the terraces. (Note the black dots on the accompanying reconstruction; they represent drainage holes.) The core of the ziggurat was of mudbrick, and the face was a skin of burnt or oven baked bricks set in bitumen mortar, about eight feet thick.

As noted, Ur was a great commercial center. The accompanying map of the city shows north and west harbors, where riverboats and oceangoing vessels could dock. Business houses of the city had their agents working all over the Euphrates and Tigris valleys to the north and along the Persian Gulf to the southeast. Their accounting departments maintained elaborate records of all their transactions, including bills of lading, invoices, letters of credit, court cases, and tax records. They practiced double-entry bookkeeping.[31]

Education seems to have been fairly widespread at Ur in Abraham's day. A substantial percentage of the upper-class boys went to school. The social positions of fathers of hundreds of the students are known and include governors, ambassadors, temple administrators, accountants, tax officials, and others. Students paid tuition, and presumably the teachers' salary came from that source. Originally the goal of these schools was to train scribes for temple and palace and later to meet business needs. The curriculum included botanical, zoological, mineralogical, geographical, and theological texts, along with Sumerian grammar and mathematics. Students were able to extract square and cube roots and to do exercises in practical geometry.[32]

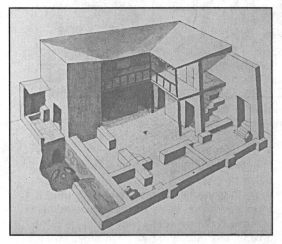

Half section of a private house at Ur in Abraham's day. The main entrance is on the right. On the extreme left is the domestic chapel and family burial ground.

With the widespread availability of education at Ur in Abraham's day, there is no reason why Abraham could not have known how to read and write. Or at least, as a wealthy man he could have employed scribes. This fact alters the traditional view of the early chapters of the Old Testament. Abraham or his scribes could have written the accounts of such famous events as the visit of the angels to predict the birth of Isaac (Genesis 18:1–15), the sacrifice of Isaac (Genesis 22:1–19), or the destruction of Sodom and Gomorrah (Genesis 18:16–19:38). It is unnecessary to believe that the early stories of Genesis were passed down only by word of mouth and

therefore subjected to the possibility of extensive corruption (as some believe), protected only by miraculous preservation through the centuries. Nor is it necessary to claim that God dictated those stories to Moses, thus guaranteeing accuracy. Abraham's originals or early copies could have been passed on to Moses who included them in the book of Genesis.

If Abraham had walked outside the city of Ur, he would have seen a countryside very similar to what appeared during the classical Sumerian period. The vast tracts of farmland were still marked out by means of fairly accurate surveying techniques. But in Abraham's day, much more land was under cultivation, not only around Ur but throughout the lower Mesopotamian valley. And of course there were more irrigation canals, maintained by a more efficient central government.

Some farmers were still using stone hoes, though bronze hoes were now the tool of choice. The seeder or machine planter was still in common use and would be for centuries to follow. Everywhere there was an aura of prosperity. Even though life for the slaves and poorest classes was very hard, and efficient bureaucrats exacted all they could from a highly regulated public, everyone had sufficient food and clothing. And the army and police force maintained peace and security in the countryside.

Bolstering the economy was a "far-flung trade," to which Woolley referred earlier. This especially included exchange of goods along the rivers of Mesopotamia, but also commerce along the Persian Gulf and with Syria, Anatolia, Elam, and through the Zagros Mountains into Iran.

The Patriarchs in Northern Mesopotamia

When the biblical account resumed in Mesopotamia the setting was far different from what it had been in Abraham's day. Instead of taking place in an urban setting, the action occurred in the countryside. Instead of engaging in commercial pursuits, the actors were tending flocks. Instead of in the surroundings of the highly populated waterlaid plains of the south, the story unfolded in the sparsely-populated rolling hills of northern Mesopotamia. The time was a generation later. Isaac was forty years old and still unmarried (Genesis 25:20).

Concerned that Isaac would marry a Canaanite (a descendant of Ham, Genesis 24:3), Abraham sent his servant to find a bride for Isaac among his own people (Semites) left behind in the Haran area. Genesis 24 tells the touching story of how the servant found Rebekah, presumably paid the bride-price for her (Genesis 24:53), and brought her back to Isaac. Rebekah's brother Laban was a principal party to all the negotiations for Rebekah's hand. He would be heard from again.

As it turned out, Isaac, like his father Abraham, had to wait in faith for an heir. Rebekah did not give birth to a child for twenty years, when Isaac was sixty (Genesis 25:26); and then she bore twins— Jacob and Esau. The account of Genesis soon throws the spotlight on Mesopotamia again when Jacob flees from Esau to the Haran area to find refuge with his uncle Laban. Before Jacob leaves, Isaac charges him to find a wife in Laban's household instead of among the Canaanites of Palestine (Genesis 28:1–2).

Apparently Esau had broken his parents' hearts by marrying Hittite (Canaanite) wives. Jacob was over forty when he went to Mesopotamia (his twin was forty when he took Hittite wives, Genesis 26:34). There he served Laban for twenty years as a bride-price for Laban's daughters Leah and Rachel and for the flocks and herds and other possessions he gained from Laban. This is, of course, an important time in Hebrew history, for all the forefathers of the twelve tribes of Israel except Benjamin were born in the Haran area.

What was going on in the wider world is not at all clear from the Genesis narrative, which focuses narrowly on the personal concerns of the patriarchal development. A full 125 years[33] elapsed between Abraham's entrance into Canaan (c. 2091 B.C.) and Jacob's arrival in Laban's household. So Jacob's stay of twenty years occurred between about 1965 and 1945 B.C. By this time certainly the golden age of Ur was over and probably Mesopotamia was going through the confused time of the so-called

Isin and Larsa period, which lasted for over 125 years after the fall of Ur. During those years numerous city-states, the more powerful of which were Isin and Larsa, vied for the ascendancy. The intimation from the Jacob-Laban narrative is that some city-state was maintaining a degree of stability and security in the area of Haran at the time.

Whatever was going on politically in northern Mesopotamia in the early centuries of the second millennium B.C., social customs were developing that are reflected in the Genesis narrative. One of these permitted or even required a barren wife to present a slave girl to her husband to bear an heir for him. Thus Sarah gave Hagar to Abraham and she bore him Ishmael (Genesis 16); and Rachel and Leah gave Bilbah and Zilpah to Jacob (Genesis 30:1–13), resulting in the birth of several of Jacob's numerous children. This practice, with the provision that slaves would not rank with the wife after bearing an heir, is described in the Code of Hammurabi of Babylon (c. 1800–1700 B.C.; laws #144–147).

Several other events of the patriarchal narrative have interesting parallels in Mesopotamia. For example, Esau sold his birthright to his brother Jacob (Genesis 25:29–34), who then went on to trick his father Isaac into giving him an oral blessing rightfully belonging to Esau (Genesis 27). Jacob later bestowed an oral blessing on his sons, giving headship of the family to Judah (Genesis 49). Laban apparently adopted Jacob as his son and heir; then when natural sons were born to Laban, his attitude toward Jacob changed (Genesis 31:1–2).

Light on some of these patriarchal actions comes especially, but not exclusively, from Nuzi, about nine miles southwest of the modern oil town of Kirkuk in the eastern hill country of northern Iraq. Of special interest among the discoveries were some four thousand cuneiform tablets dating to about 1500 B.C. and consisting largely of family archives revealing social and legal customs resembling those of the patriarchal period. Though these texts date long after the days of Abraham and Jacob, that is not a problem, for most socio-legal customs of the ancient Near East were in use in various forms for hundreds of years.

THE CODE OF HAMMURABI AND PATRIARCHAL CONDUCT

The Code of Hammurabi, Law 145, states:

"If a man takes a priestess and she does not present him with children and he sets his face to take a concubine, that man may take a concubine and bring her into his house. That concubine shall not rank with the wife."

Thus, Sarah gave Hagar to childless Abraham (Genesis 16). And Rachel and Leah gave Bilhah and Zilpah to Jacob (Genesis 30:1–13).

In the event that the concubine bore children, she might tend to lord it over her mistress and make life miserable for her.

The Code of Hammurabi, Law 146 deals with such a situation:

"If a man takes a priestess and she gives to her husband a maidservant and she bears children, and afterward that maidservant would take rank with her mistress; because she has borne children her mistress may not sell her for money, but she may reduce her to bondage and count her among the female slaves."

This law is closely parallel to the account of the treatment of Hagar in Genesis 16:5–7 and 21:9–10.

These laws or customs decrease the notion or implication that Abraham was merely acting lustfully concerning Hagar, and that Sarah (and Abraham) were acting purely out of self-will in their treatment of Hagar and Ishmael.

We need to be careful how we use the Nuzi material, however. Some supposed parallels between customs there and the book of Genesis, long held, have now been modified or abandoned. For example, the supposed parallel between Esau's sale of his birthright to Jacob (Genesis 25:27–34) has now been abandoned. Though there are several examples of part of an inheritance being transferred from one brother to another, there is no known case of an eldest son selling his inheritance rights to a younger brother.

Also, the view that in Nuzi the possession of family gods or house gods served as symbols or tokens of inheritance rights has been discarded. Thus possession of them would not have given family headship to Jacob instead of the natural sons of Laban (see Genesis 31:19). Each new household normally made new house-god images.

Moreover, it appears that neither Jacob nor Rachel had any desire to inherit Laban's estate or to stay in Mesopotamia and manage it. We are left only with suppositions about Rachel's actions. Possibly she was not yet as fully weaned from the old paganism as Bible students would like to believe. The fertility and good fortune of the family were the responsibility of the family gods.

A parallel between the Nuzi tablets and the Genesis account that still holds is that if one adopted another who became his heir, that heir would have to step aside if a natural heir was subsequently born. Apparently Laban had sons born to him after Jacob's marriage to Leah and Rachel (compare Genesis 29:16; 31:1).[34]

Hammurabi and His Empire

Out of the confusion of the Isin and Larsa period a new empire finally arose. As noted earlier, it was Amorites who especially contributed to the destruction of Ur's empire. Now an insignificant Amorite, Samu-abu, established his dynasty at Babylon, an insignificant town east of Kish, around the middle of the nineteenth century B.C. Gradually Babylon and Larsa became the two chief cities in southern Mesopotamia; and in the days of Hammurabi, Babylon's sixth king, the Babylonians defeated Larsa and all Sumer fell under control of the Babylonians. Finally, in his thirty-second year of reign,

Hammurabi

attention to the details of government and his ability to handle political and economic problems. Another indication of his acumen was his codification of law.

What might be called Hammurabi's propaganda sense was also sound. In this connection, he sought to strengthen his political position by establishing Babylon's chief deity, Marduk, as supreme over the Sumerian gods. A religious document describing creation and the establishment of order out of chaos, the *Enuma Elish*,[36] was rewritten to give Marduk credit for these achievements. This account was made to suggest that Marduk and his earthly representative, Hammurabi, had been especially chosen by the older gods to be responsible for the welfare of humanity. Hammurabi sought to equip Babylon with buildings suitable for the capital of an empire.

The Old Babylonian period was distinguished for its literary and scientific activity. Many of the literary compositions of the time were inspired by Sumerian originals, but the authors managed to infuse them with a new spirit and character that secured their recognition as classics in future ages. Most of the cuneiform mathematical texts that have survived were written in the age of Hammurabi. Dating to his time are tables of multiplication, square roots, and problem texts such as the computation of areas of fields and volumes of cisterns or ovens. In algebra, Babylonians of the era were able to solve quadratic equations in a variety of ways. They also knew and used the Pythagorean theorem twelve hundred

Hammurabi also defeated the kingdom of Mari in the north and fully established the Old Babylonian Empire.

With the Amorite conquest of Mesopotamia came tremendous economic and social changes, though revolution may be too strong a term. First there was a secularization of land ownership. Crown and temple land still existed, but its extent declined as the amount of land in private hands expanded. Increasingly private persons participated in trade and industry too. Second, the population seems to have grown considerably under the Amorites, with more land brought under cultivation. There was also expanded commerce, with metals more commonly used than barter as a medium of exchange.

The prime mover in the development of the Old Babylonian Empire was Hammurabi himself. Since he ruled for about forty-three years,[35] he lived long enough to consolidate his territorial gains and to demonstrate his administrative genius. His correspondence with royal officials reveals his

OLD BABYLONIAN EMPIRE (UNDER HAMMURABI)

The Code of Hammurabi. *Louvre Museum, Paris*

pieces of the stele in December of 1901 and January of 1902, it was the oldest and longest law code in the world. Hammurabi was given the credit he claimed for the brilliant achievement of having composed it. But then, in 1947, a Sumerian code of Lipit-Ishtar surfaced at Isin. Dating before 1850 B.C., it was a century and a half earlier than Hammurabi's code. The similarity of some laws in the two codes showed that Hammurabi did not concoct all of his laws. Some took the position that he was bringing up to date the common law of Mesopotamia.

Then in the very next year (1948) at Eshnunna (modern Tell Asmar) in southern Mesopotamia, an Akkadian code of King Bilalama came to light. This dated some seventy years earlier than Lipit-Ishtar's. Four years later, in 1952, archaeologists found the Sumerian code of Ur-Nammu at Ur, dating perhaps 2100–2050 B.C. Of course no one can predict whether other earlier codes are still to be found in Mesopotamia, but if they are, the assumption is that they will be Sumerian in origin because Sumerians were the people given credit for inventing writing.

The Code of Hammurabi is the longest and best-preserved of all these codes. Inscribed on a black diorite shaft almost eight feet high and six feet in circumference, it has 3600 lines of cuneiform text arranged in 44 columns. A total of 282 laws appear in the text. On the top front of the stele is a low relief of Hammurabi standing before the sun god Shamash, the god of justice, and presumably receiving the text of the code from him. The code was originally set up in the great Temple to Marduk in Babylon during the second year of Hammurabi's reign, but the Elamites carted it off to Susa around 1200 B.C. as a trophy of war. The code is now in the Louvre Museum in Paris.

When the Code of Hammurabi was found, scholars began to notice similarities between it and the Mosaic laws in the Old Testament, and many professed to find a dependence of Moses on the earlier code. But on more sober reflection, direct dependence or borrowing cannot be defended. The attitude of the two codes is very different.

years before Pythagoras. Moreover, they calculated the value of *pi* to about six places. One text dating to Hammurabi's day can only be interpreted as a table of logarithms.

The Code of Hammurabi

When the name Hammurabi surfaces, usually people think first, and almost exclusively, of his law code. This wide-ranging Akkadian legal text covers so many topics that students of business, medicine, law and law enforcement, religion, sociology, and many other fields pay attention to its provisions. When the French excavators at Susa (biblical Shushan) found the three

Hammurabi's code is polytheistic, civil, and commercial, and punishments are geared to class distinctions. Moreover, though Hammurabi wants to pay lip service to the god of justice in artistic representation, he clearly claims in the preamble and the epilogue of the code that he was the wise law-giver who composed his code.

The Mosaic code, on the other hand, is monotheistic, civil, and religious, and does not recognize class distinctions in meting out punishments. Moses claims no credit for formulating his code; this was God's set of requirements for His people. Similarities between the codes may rise from their Semitic antecedents and the fact that to be called a law code at all or to meet the basic requirements of society, certain similar items would have to be included— control of murder, theft, and false testimony in the courts.

The top of the Code of Hammurabi. Hammurabi stands before Shamash, god of justice, to receive the laws of his code. *Louvre Museum*

COMPARISON OF THE CODE OF HAMMURABI AND THE MOSAIC CODE

Hammurabi's

Polytheistic

Civil and commercial

Punishments geared to class distinctions

Hammurabi claimed to be the wise law-giver who composed his code

Moses'

Monotheistic

Civil and religious

Punishments fell on all alike

Moses claimed no credit for composition; this was God's set of requirements

We must be careful how we use any law code (including the Mosaic) to write social history. Law codes are, after all, only an indication of how a certain element in society (or God) wants things to go. We can never be sure to what degree legal systems were enforced. Because of some repetition of laws or legal principles in these ancient Mesopotamian codes, we may assume that they to some degree reflect the common law of ancient Mesopotamia, perhaps analogous to some of the Anglo-Saxon common law that grew up in England in the late Middle Ages.[37] So the code of Hammurabi may be more indicative of what really happened in society than are some other law codes in history.

Assyrian Expansion

The first glimpses we have of Assyrian expansion date back to 2000 B.C. or earlier. At that time the Assyrians came out of their hills along the Tigris to establish merchant colonies in Cappadocia in eastern Asia Minor and in the region of Kirkuk in the eastern hills of Mesopotamia. What led to either the beginning of this development or the end of it we do not now know. But donkey caravans

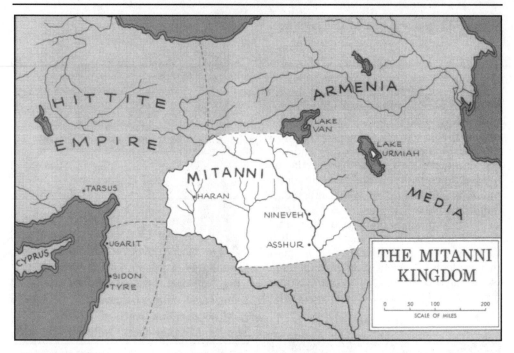

THE MITANNI
KINGDOM

SCALE OF MILES

periodically trekked the some 750 difficult and dangerous miles from Ashur in Assyria to Kanesh and elsewhere in Cappadocia. They especially carried tin (obtained from the Zagros Mountains in the east) and fabrics (from Babylonia) and presumably obtained copper and silver and other commodities from Cappadocia.[38]

Political Beginnings

Well-documented political developments in Assyria began just before 1800 B.C., when Shamshi-Adad I, an Amorite prince, established himself in Ashur and for the first time brought the other major cities of Assyria—Nineveh and Erbil—into a single domain. Eventually he controlled a kingdom about 300 miles north and south and an equal distance east and west. His administrative efficiency, political skill, and military prowess all contributed to his success. He even developed the Assyrian siege warfare, formerly thought to date to the first millennium B.C.[39] After the death of Shamshi-Adad, his son lost control of the larger Assyrian kingdom and maintained sovereignty over only the Assyrian heartland. Subsequently, for approximately three centuries, kings of Ashur ruled a very limited area.

The Mitanni

While Amorites had been moving into Mesopotamia from the Syrian desert, Hurrians were coming from the area of Armenia. A particularly powerful Hurrian kingdom, known as the Mitanni, established itself in northern Mesopotamia east of the Euphrates by about 1550 B.C. The Mitanni fought and negotiated on relatively equal terms with the Hittites and Egyptians, and about the middle of the fifteenth century Thutmose III of Egypt fought successfully against them in Syria. A Mitanni princess was even married to Thutmose IV before 1400 B.C. Soon after the Mitanni fought Thutmose III, they turned eastward and forced the Assyrian kingdom into vassal status. This servile relationship continued for over a half century.

Early Assyrian Empire

Having established their independence from the Mitanni after 1400 B.C., the Assyrians were once more free to build an empire. Some would assign the beginnings to Ashur-Uballit I (1365–1330 B.C.) and others to Adad-Nirari I (1307–1275 B.C.). Under successive kings the Assyrians first established their power over the region between the Tigris and Euphrates. Then they advanced northward against the peoples of Urartu in the Lake Van region in the far north (the area of the mountains of Ararat, Genesis 8:4) and subsequently came to control the last vestiges of the Kingdom of Mitanni. With the passage of time the city of Nineveh gained in power and significance. By about 1220 B.C. the Assyrians had also defeated the peoples of the mountains east of the Tigris.

Next they fought and defeated the Babylonians, sacking the city of Babylon and holding it for seven years. This conquest had considerable significance for Assyria because it was now wide open to Babylonian cultural influence. For much of the next century (c. 1200–1115 B.C.) Assyria was in decline politically. Her kings were relatively inactive and therefore made few grandiose claims in their inscriptions.

Middle Assyrian Empire and Hebrew Developments

Conditions were finally favorable to the expansion of Assyrian power once again. The Hittite Empire came to an end in Asia Minor and in north Syria around 1200 B.C. The Egyptian Empire ceased to exist shortly after 1100 B.C., and so the Egyptians offered no competition in Phoenicia and Palestine. The Old Babylonian Empire had declined soon after Hammurabi's day and dissolved by 1550 B.C. at the latest. The able Tiglath-Pileser I (1115–1077 B.C.) took advantage of the political and military vacuum and launched the Middle Assyrian Empire. He was an intrepid campaigner (especially invading territories north of the Tigris and fighting the Aramaeans west of the Euphrates) and an effective administrator.

But unfortunately for Assyria, Tiglath-Pileser's successors were not of his caliber, and the Aramaeans kept infiltrating Assyria in small groups, becoming a serious threat to the whole of Mesopotamia. Meanwhile, in Syria the Aramaeans were establishing stable kingdoms with central authorities by 1000 B.C. so David could defeat those powers and gain control of the area west of the Euphrates. But the Aramaeans of Mesopotamia continued to be an assortment of unruly groups and clans with no central authority through which to work until after about 950 B.C. At that point the Assyrian kings also had a chance to subdue the Aramaean intruders.

HOW COULD DAVID BUILD AN EMPIRE?

The question is sometimes raised as to how David could build an empire around 1000 B.C. when there were so many powerful states in the Eastern Mediterranean world.

The answer is fundamentally simple. The Hittite Empire came to an end shortly after 1200 B.C. and the Egyptian Empire about a century later. Assyrian power was down between about 1050 and 935 B.C. And over in the Aegean world, the Mycenaean centers at Mycenae, Pylos, and elsewhere had suffered destruction by 1100 B.C.

Thus there was a power vacuum between Greece and the Zagros Mountains east of Mesopotamia around 1000 B.C. Nothing stood in the way of David's expansion. He might have built an even bigger kingdom if he had chosen to do so.

As a matter of fact, for over a century before 935 B.C., not only were the Aramaeans a serious threat to the Assyrians, but also the central administration in Assyria was virtually nonexistent. What this means is that between about 1050 and 935 B.C. there was a power vacuum at the eastern end of the Mediterranean. As noted, the Hittite and Egyptian empires were gone. Therefore, nothing stood in the way of David's building the substantial Hebrew kingdom (ruled 1010–970 B.C.) or Solomon's maintaining it (ruled 970–931 B.C.). Likewise, nothing prevented Hiram of Tyre from developing his city-state and advancing the fortunes of Phoenicia.

Ashurnasirpal II enthroned, from Nimrud.
Ashurnasirpal (883–859 B.C.) was the real founder
of the Assyrian Empire. *British Museum*

The New Assyrian Empire

Just at the point when Solomon was about to pass off the scene and when the idolatry of his reign was about to incur the judgment of God, Ashur-Dan II (934–912 B.C.) launched the New Assyrian Empire. It is important to note also that the Hebrew kingdom split in two early in Ashur-Dan's reign (931 B.C.). Thus the sovereign working of God may be seen in history as He raised up a pagan power to bring judgment on His people. Isaiah described Assyria as the "rod of My anger" (10:5). Ashur-Dan restored the virtually non-existent central administration of Assyria, reestablished Assyrian military control within Assyria's natural borders, and improved the economic base of the kingdom. His four able successors built effectively on the solid foundation he laid, and within a century Assyria became *a*, if not *the*, major world power. (There was nothing in India or China or the West that compared with it.) Ashur-Dan's son and grandson greatly expanded Assyrian holdings to the north, south, east, and west.

But Ashurnasirpal II (883-859 B.C.) usually gets credit for being the real founder of the Neo-Assyrian Empire. He converted Assyria into a ruthless fighting machine, and his voluminous records boast of the

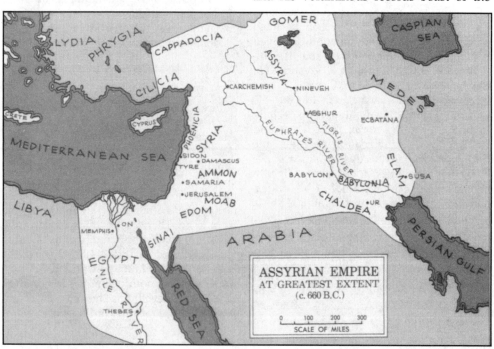

ASSYRIAN EMPIRE
AT GREATEST EXTENT
(c. 660 B.C.)

0   100   200   300
SCALE OF MILES

merciless cruelty of his campaigns. The fierceness of the king's countenance, as preserved on his statues and bas reliefs in the British Museum in London, supports the image conveyed in his inscriptions. Some have argued that the Assyrians may not have been more cruel than other ancient people but allege that their cruelty is just better documented. Admittedly, reliefs on Egyptian temple walls show piles of body parts of enemy warriors, and the Hebrews also engaged in mutilation of their enemies (e.g., 1 Samuel 18:25, 27).

Possibly Assyrian brutality resulted not so much from their bloodthirsty nature as from their desire to intimidate their enemies so thoroughly that they would surrender without a fight. A case in point is the treatment of Tur Abdin, northwest of Nineveh. When the vassal ruler of that territory rebelled and attacked an Assyrian garrison town, Ashurnasirpal responded with such terrible atrocities that other petty kingdoms in the area submitted without resistance.

In any case, Ashurnasirpal had considerable military success. First he secured a hold on territory to the north of Assyria, then subdued the region to the northwest and subjugated lands to the northeast. Then, after a show of force in the south, which secured the border with Babylonia, he conquered the region in the bend of the Euphrates in the west. Finally he pushed west to the Mediterranean, winning submission of all the kings of north Syria and receiving tribute from some of the Phoenician city-states.

As a further display of his prowess, he moved the capital of Assyria from Ashur to Calah (Genesis 10:11), or Nimrud, twenty miles south of Nineveh. There he built a magnificent palace covering six acres, which is the best preserved of Assyrian royal dwellings. Extensive reliefs from the palace now line the walls of the Assyrian rooms of the British Museum in London. The Museum also has wonderful pieces of ivory inlay from the palace.

Though A. H. Layard excavated at Calah from 1845 to 1848, Sir Max Mallowan (husband of British detective story author Agatha Christie) led the main dig there for the British School of Archaeology in Iraq

On his Monolith Inscription, badly weathered and covered with cuneiform writing, Shalmaneser III tells of meeting King Ahab and his allies at Qarqar (853 B.C.). *British Museum.*

from 1949 to 1961. Sir Max completed excavation of Ashurnasirpal's palace, worked at the palace of Shalmaneser III there, and largely excavated Shalmaneser's great fort, eighteen acres in size, which lay just inside the city wall at its southeast edge. This is the most extensive military installation yet discovered in ancient Assyria.

King Jehu of Israel is shown paying tribute to Shalmaneser III of Assyria on the Black Obelisk, now in the *British Museum*

Shalmaneser III (858–824 B.C.) effectively continued the expansionist program of his father. He secured the Mediterranean coast, and Phoenician city-states paid him tribute. But when he tried to move into inner Syria, the story was different. At Qarqar on the Orontes (853 B.C.) he met a powerful coalition of Syrian and Palestinian kings, including Hadadezer of Damascus and Ahab of Israel. His monolith inscription (now in the British Museum) says that Ahab contributed ten thousand men and two thousand chariots to the joint effort. Though it is not at all certain that Shalmaneser won the great victory at Qarqar that he claimed, he was eventually successful in the region.

A few years later, Ahab's successor, Jehu, became a vassal to Shalmaneser; Shalmaneser's Black Obelisk (a victory monument he set up in the public square in Calah, now in the British Museum) portrays Jehu bowing before him and paying tribute. Neither of these events is referred to in Scripture. Shalmaneser also moved across the Amanus Mountains into Cilicia, thus securing the principal source of iron in the Near East and important trade connections with Cyprus and Greece. In other campaigns he crossed the Zagros Mountains to the east and reduced the Medes to client status.

Assyria in Decline

Near the end of Shalmaneser's reign a power struggle developed between two of his sons. This was accompanied by widespread revolt from which Shamshi-Adad V (823–811 B.C.) emerged victorious and completely restored order. Subsequently he settled some scores with the Babylonians and wrought havoc in the cities of northern Babylonia. His wife was Sammurammat, the famous Semiramis of Greek medieval tradition. She was the power behind the throne not only during the reign of her husband but also her son Adad-Nirari III (810–783 B.C.). Adad-Nirari had trouble with more than his domineering mother; the kingdom of Urartu arose to the north of Assyria and expanded into North Syria at the expense of the

Tiglath-Pileser of Assyria, *British Museum*

Assyrian Empire. Urartu continued to gain power during the reign of Adad-Nirari's three successors (Shalmaneser IV, 782–773 B.C.; Ashur-Dan III, 772–755 B.C.; and Ashur-Nirari V, 754–745 B.C.).

These Assyrian kings mounted only minimal military campaigns, and provincial governors tended to assert increasing amounts of independence. Under these circumstances, Aramaean states of Syria tried to build alliances against Assyria, and Israel and Judah were free to enlarge their holdings. Uzziah of Judah (782–740 B.C.) and Jeroboam II of Israel (793–753 B.C.) benefited from the changed international situation and together controlled territory almost equal to the Hebrew kingdom under Solomon. With Assyria in decline, the Hebrews grew a little careless and many doubted that the judgment predicted by the prophets would occur.

Tiglath-Pileser and Assyrian Resurgence

Then the governor of Calah took the throne and assumed the name Tiglath-Pileser III. It is not clear whether he was a usurper, but he was certainly of royal blood. Tiglath-Pileser (744–727 B.C.) came on the scene with a burst of energy, carried out an administrative reorganization that gave him effective control of the empire and set up an efficient communications network and an intelligence system. His personal name was Pul or Pulu, and that is the way he is referred to in the Old Testament (2 Kings 15:19; 1 Chronicles 5:26). Critics used to claim that Scripture was in error in calling him by this name.

Tiglath-Pileser's reign launched a century of great imperial expansion. He campaigned effectively against Urartu in the north, took control of most of Babylonia in the southeast, and gradually overwhelmed the coalitions pitted against him in Syria and Palestine. On one occasion, probably in 743 B.C., he put Menahem of Israel to tribute (2 Kings 15:19–20). Later, Pekah of Israel and Rezin of Damascus allied against Assyria and tried to force King Ahaz of Judah to join them (2 Kings 16:5–9). In order to stop their attacks, Ahaz appealed to Tiglath-Pileser for relief.

In this inscription Tiglath-Pileser III tells of his conquests, including the putting to tribute of Ahaz of Judah (2 Kings 16). *British Museum*

The Assyrian was only too happy to oblige. He descended on Damascus, killed Rezin (2 Kings 16:9), and annexed his kingdom in 732 B.C. About the same time he annexed the northern part of Israel and carried off thousands of captives (2 Kings 15:29). With Samaria and Judah in tributary status (2 Kings 16:7), Tiglath-Pileser had gained control of the Palestine coast as far south as Gaza, and by the time he died he controlled an empire that extended from the Persian Gulf to the Sinai Peninsula and through Syria to Cilicia.

Assyria and the Fall of Samaria

Shalmaneser V (726–722 B.C.) followed his able father, and like his father, faced trouble in Israel. Hoshea rebelled against Assyria in 725 B.C. and Shalmaneser launched a three-year siege of the city of Samaria. The reference in 2 Kings 17:3–6 implies but does not state that Shalmaneser lived to complete the siege and to destroy the city of Samaria and the Northern Kingdom. Evidence seems to point to the fall of the city during the summer of 722 B.C., and Shalmaneser lived almost to the end of the year.[40] After the fall of Samaria, the Assyrians deported many Hebrews—some to northern Mesopotamia and some to "the towns of the Medes" (2 Kings 17:6). This helps to explain the presence of Jews in the Medo-Persian city of Susa (biblical Shushan) in the days of Esther. But Esther 2:6 specifically states that Mordecai descended from a Jew taken in Nebuchadnezzar's deportation of thousands of Jews in 597 B.C.(the exile of Jeconiah or Jehoiachin). So Jews in Shushan had come from both the northern and southern kingdoms.

ASSYRIAN CONTACTS WITH ISRAEL

- Shalmaneser III met Ahab at the Battle of Qarqar in 853 B.C.

- Shalmaneser III exacted tribute from Jehu shortly thereafter.

- Tiglath-Pileser III annexed the northern part of Israel in 732 B.C. (2 Kings 15:29).

- Shalmaneser V launched the final siege of Samaria in 725 B.C. and probably took the city in 722 B.C.

- His son and successor, Sargon II, mopped up after the victory and carried off captives to Assyria.

- Sennacherib invaded Judah in 701 B.C. and besieged Jerusalem. A plague kept him from destroying the kingdom (Isaiah 36–37).

The primary reason for any debate over which Assyrian king took Samaria arises from the claim of Sargon (721–705 B.C.) in his inscriptions that he took Samaria. In fact, he claimed not only to have taken the city but to have hauled off 27,290 inhabitants and then to have resettled the area with other non-Hebrew peoples.[41] Presumably he conducted the mopping-up activities after Shalmaneser's victory. The number carried off into captivity seems too large to have come from the small city of Samaria alone and therefore probably includes those from the surrounding region. His resettlement activities help to provide background for the later half-Jewish or quasi-Jewish Samaritan religion which in Jesus' day was such an

anathema to good Jews. As is clear from John 4, Jews and Samaritans had little contact with each other or little respect for each other's religious convictions or institutions.

As for Sargon himself, he was not the legitimate successor of Shalmaneser but came to power as the result of a revolution at the end of Shalmaneser's reign. It is important to note the apparent reason for the revolt because it seems to relate to treatment of the Hebrews. The catalyst for the uprising was an attempt to impose forced labor on the people of the city of Ashur, contrary to precedent.[42]

What seems to have been happening was this. Constant Assyrian warfare overburdened the populace as it took them away from gainful employment and in time reduced the citizen roster as soldiers were killed off. With so many men away on military duty or with the reduction of the number of able-bodied Assyrians, it was increasingly necessary to force people to do urgent civilian tasks.

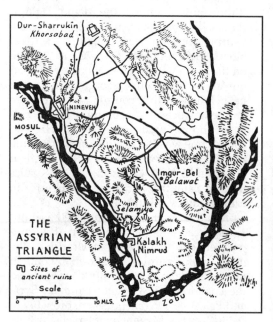

In the Assyrian Triangle, the area where the Zab (Zabu) and Tigris rivers joined, three Assyrian capitals were located: Khorsabad in the north, Nineveh in the center, and Nimrud or Calah in the south. Though Nineveh is the most famous capital of Assyria, the capital moved around at the wishes of the King.

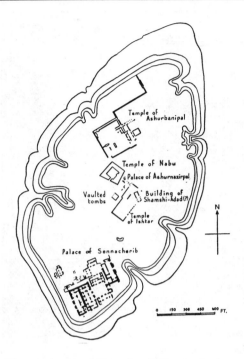

Assyrian army. The religious barrier to such employment was absent as the Hebrew populace generally subscribed to pagan worship practices. And of course men needed ways to support themselves and their families. The surest way to guarantee one's economic well-being at that point in time was to take service in the Assyrian army.

Sargon's other military actions were extensive. About seven years after the fall of Samaria he crippled Urartu on the north following a fierce contest with that inveterate enemy. Shortly thereafter, he faced serious difficulties in Babylonia. There he finally forced Merodach-Baladan, a Chaldean who had overwhelmed much of the earlier Semitic population, out of his capital city of Babylon into his base in the marshes of southern Babylonia. Sargon established his control of Babylon just in time to meet a new wave of Indo-Europeans from the north, the Cimmerians (Gomer of the Bible, Genesis 10:2–3; Ezekiel 38:6;), and possibly he died in battle fighting them. Along the

The monuments of Nineveh, with the great palace of Sennacherib at the south of the mound of Kouyunjik (after A. Parrot)

If the Assyrians could not get enough work, or military duty, out of their own people, they would have to turn to others. From the days of Tiglath-Pileser III on there was less talk in the Assyrian inscriptions about killing large numbers of the enemy in battle and more tabulation of the large numbers of captives taken and periodically deported to Assyria. We have already seen that Shalmaneser V and Sargon II took Hebrews as captives to Assyria. In fact, Hebrews seem to have been used on construction gangs involved in building Sargon's new capital of Khorsabad, fourteen miles northeast of Nineveh.[43]

Not only were foreigners increasingly deported to Assyria to swell the labor force, but they were also used to contribute to the military establishment. A case in point is Sargon's incorporation into his army of a corps of fifty chariots and their teams from the Hebrew exiles after the fall of Samaria.[44] Presumably it would not have been too difficult for destitute warriors of the Northern Kingdom to become mercenaries in the

Sargon II, who claimed to have destroyed Samaria in 722 B.C.

The Jerwan Aqueduct that brought water to Nineveh

way, in 709 B.C., he conquered the last of the Hittite city-states of north Syria.

Sennacherib and the Greatness of Nineveh

Those who talk about the terror Assyria struck in the hearts of peoples of Western Asia associate the terrible power of Assyria with the greatness of its capital of Nineveh. Actually Assyria had several capitals during its long history (Calah, or Nimrud; Ashur; Khorsabad; and Nineveh), but from Sennacherib's reign on (704–681 B.C.), Nineveh was permanently the capital. To Sennacherib goes credit for the great city wall, the Jerwan aqueduct (which brought water a distance of about thirty miles), and a great palace.

The ruins of Nineveh now lie about 220 miles northwest of Baghdad on the east bank of the Tigris opposite the modern city of Mosul. They cover an 1,800-acre area surrounded by remains of a brick wall almost eight miles in length and still standing at a height of ten-to-twenty feet. Within this perimeter rise two great mounds—Kouyunjik and Nebi Yunus—and a number of smaller ones. Kouyunjik is unoccupied

and the site of most of the archaeological work at Nineveh; Nebi Yunus has a village on top, so little excavation can be done there.[45]

Archaeologists have worked along the city wall and on stretches of the Jerwan aqueduct. They extensively excavated the great palace of Sennacherib at the southern edge of Kouyunjik. It had more than seventy rooms decorated with sculptured stone slabs for a total of almost two miles of reliefs. In the middle of Kouyunjik stood Sennacherib's temple to Nabu (god of writing) where Sennacherib deposited his royal library (found by Layard). At the northern edge of the mound was the palace of Ashurbanipal (Osnappar of Ezra 4:10 RSV), where Rassam found the rest of the royal library (totaling tens of thousands of texts, including Babylonian accounts of creation and the Flood). Palaces of several other Assyrian kings came to light on Kouyunjik and a palace of Esarhaddon on Nebi Yunus. The site of Nineveh is so huge that work there has hardly begun.

The fact that the walls of Nineveh were only eight miles in circumference has led some critics to argue against the accuracy of

The site of Nineveh today, with a clear outline of the 8–mile circuit of the ancient wall.

Jonah 3:3. There Nineveh is described as "an exceeding great city of three days' journey," with the assumption that it would take three days to walk around it or through it. One way of dealing with the problem is to view the reference as including greater Nineveh, which with its suburbs may have stretched several miles to the north and more than twenty miles to the southeast, to Calah (Nimrud). Measured from end to end, that whole urban area would have extended over thirty miles. To go around it would have required a journey of more than sixty miles, or a three-day journey, at the rate of twenty miles a day. If the reference to 120,000 who did not know their right hand from their left (Jonah 4:11) had in view young children, then a total population of the built-up area may have been as much as 600,000, as is often asserted.

An alternate view is that Nineveh proper was such a large city that it would have taken three days to stop at its major centers to proclaim the judgment of God. On this supposition, the 120,000 might include the entire population, whose not knowing their right hand from their left is taken to indicate spiritual ignorance. Scholars commonly estimate that 170,000 people lived within the walls of Nineveh at the height of Assyria (c. 650 B.C.). Jonah's indication that there were over 120,000 in his day (c. 760 B.C.) who did not know their right hand from their left seems to apply to virtually the entire population. If so, it would be the only inspired population figure we have for a biblical city, and the population of Nineveh would then have grown about fifty thousand between about 750 and 650 B.C. Certainly Nineveh was a much smaller and less significant place in Jonah's day, before Sennacherib made it the capital of the empire and carried on significant construction there.

Though building his new capital at Nineveh was Sennacherib's ongoing project, he was forced to meet several enemies on the battlefield. The Cimmerian threat, which had surfaced during his father's reign, led him to a friendship of sorts with Urartu in order to use them as a buttress against the new and more dangerous enemy. Then in 703 B.C. Merodach-Baladan again organized a Chaldean insurrection in Babylonia, with Elamite support. Sennacherib's response was to force Merodach-Baladan out of Babylon, to set up a puppet king in the city, and to devastate southern Babylonia. Two years later Sennacherib had to deal with Hezekiah's bid for independence in Judah.

The account of what happened appears in Isaiah 36–37 and 2 Kings 18:13–19:36. In Hezekiah's fourteenth year (701 B.C.), Sennacherib launched a full-scale invasion of Judah, taking all the fortified cities of the kingdom and finally besieging the city of Jerusalem. Isaiah was the court prophet, serving at the right hand of the king to steady him in his hour of distress. Fortunately for Hezekiah, Sennacherib overreached himself. As he taunted Hezekiah's defenders on the walls, he bragged about all the other peoples he had conquered. Then he said, in effect, "Their gods could not save them and yours can't either." Such an allegation challenged God

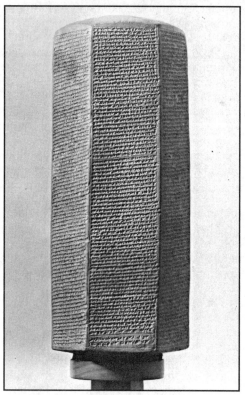

An inscription of Sennacherib (701 B.C.) in which he tells of taking Lachish and shutting up Hezekiah like a "bird in a cage" in Jerusalem. *Courtesy Oriental Institute, University of Chicago*

of the city (now on display in the British Museum, with a cast at the Oriental Institute in Chicago). Conquest of Jerusalem and destruction of the Judean kingdom no doubt would have prompted a much more grandiose artistic celebration. Incidentally, Sennacherib's enumeration of captured cities and prisoners may be fairly accurate. The Assyrian bureaucracy was quite efficient and meticulous in record keeping, and scribes appear everywhere on palace bas reliefs—certainly at the battle-front—tabulating and recording.

Merodach-Baladan, Hezekiah, and Sennacherib

While Sennacherib and his army were busy in Judah, Assyrian pressure on Babylonian disaffection was lifted and rebellion smoldered there once more. Isaiah 39 records an enigmatic account of the coming of a delegation from Merodach-Baladan to Hezekiah of Judah. Hezekiah's reception of the embassy drew severe rebuke of the prophet Isaiah. The situation was this. Merodach-Baladan had been engaged in a running battle with the Assyrians for some thirty years, and now evidently was encouraged by the report of Hezekiah's ability to stand up to Sennacherib to believe that an alliance with the Judean might be advantageous to his own cause. Perhaps he thought that the two of them, located at opposite ends of the Assyrian Empire, could in alliance contribute to the demise of the empire.

A clue to the severity of God's, and therefore the prophet's, condemnation of Hezekiah's civility toward the Babylonians appears in the king's admission that he had showed them "his treasures" and "all his armory" (Isaiah 39:2). That is, he showed them what strength he could bring to an alliance, and in his armory indicated the basis on which he had been able to defeat Sennacherib—when in fact it was God who had really given the victory. From a non-spiritual standpoint the alliance was to be criticized because Merodach-Baladan was a known double-crosser.

In any case, when Sennacherib was free to deal with Merodach-Baladan, in 700 B.C.

to act. The text says that just at the right moment God intervened, apparently by bringing a plague on Sennacherib's army, and the Assyrian broke off the siege and went home.

Sennacherib's own account of his campaign into Judah tells of taking forty-six fortified cities, 200,150 captives, and countless spoil, and then shutting up Hezekiah in Jerusalem "like a bird in a cage."[46] Obviously something happened at Jerusalem to keep him from capturing the city, for his statement intimates he did not take it. Nowhere did he claim conquest of Jerusalem.

On this same invasion of Judah, Sennacherib was, however, successful in taking Lachish, Judah's second city. He memorialized the fact by devoting a couple of walls of his palace in Nineveh to a pictorial representation of the siege and capture

Sennacherib's forces carrying away Hebrew captives from Lachish. *British Museum*

the rebel fled to Elam and was heard from no more. That was not the end of insurrection in Babylonia, however. After several more years of warfare, finally in 689 B.C., Sennacherib's patience ran out and he "ruthlessly wrecked the city," giving license to his troops to loot and destroy. Eight years later (681 B.C.) factionalism within the royal family led to Sennacherib's murder by two of his sons in Nineveh (2 Kings 19:37).

Assyrian Conquest of Egypt

Esarhaddon (690–669 B.C.) was a son of Sennacherib, who had no part in his father's assassination and whom his father had designated as crown prince. Under the circumstances, however, Esarhaddon was forced to fight for the throne against troops raised by the regicides. After establishing himself in office, he reversed his father's policies toward Babylon. Presumably he was of the pro-Babylonian faction in Assyria and sought to gain the goodwill of the Babylonian populace; therefore he decided to restore the ruined city. He

helped to rebuild the walls and the temple to Marduk and resettled many of the people who had fled Assyrian attack.

Next, he established an alliance with Medes in Iran and renewed the alliance with Urartu, evidently in an effort to marshal forces against Elam and the Cimmerians and Scythians, who were pushing south out of the area of modern Russia. In the northwest, Syria and Palestine remained generally loyal to Assyria; only Sidon rebelled, and Esarhaddon dealt sternly with her. With the corridor to Egypt firmly under control, Esarhaddon decided to conquer that land. Presumably the reason was to head off the dynamic threat of Pharaoh Taharka, or Tirhaka (a Nubian ruler of the Twenty-Fifth Dynasty), against Assyrian holdings in Palestine and Syria (see 2 Kings 19:9). After incredible difficulties with desert conditions, he took Memphis in 671 B.C. and secured the submission of the delta region soon thereafter. But no sooner had Esarhaddon left the country than the Egyptians rebelled and Taharka retook Memphis.

Sennacherib besieging Lachish. His troops ascend a ramp with a battering ram. *British Museum*

Ashurbanipal (668–627 B.C.) had to take up the sword against Egypt to complete his father's conquests there. First he recaptured Memphis and then moved south against Taharka's successor Tanutamun, conquering Thebes and thoroughly looting it in 663 B.C. (see Nahum 3:8–19). Thus the Assyrian Empire had come to its greatest extent in the southwest. But Assyrian control in Egypt was short-lived. Psamtik I established the Twenty-Sixth Dynasty and cleared the Assyrians from Egypt by 651 B.C.

Ashurbanipal was unable to maintain control of Egypt because of trouble with Elam in the east. There King Teuman mustered a powerful force but Ashurbanipal worsted him, and the Elamite king met death in battle. Elam continued to be a threat to Assyria, however (in part as a supporter of the rebellious forces in Babylonia), and Ashurbanipal eventually totally devastated Elam and even deported some of the Elamites to Samaria (Ezra 4:9–10). He was also forced to put down rebellion in Babylonia. In dealing with all uprisings or opposition he was harsh, ruthless, and vindictive—devoid of human kindness or statesmanlike qualities.

Assyrians flaying (skinning alive) Hebrew officials captured at Lachish. *British Museum*

The Great Nineveh Library and Genesis Accounts

But Ashurbanipal had another side to him. The Osnapper (NKJV) or Osnappar (RSV) of Ezra 4:10, he had a passion for building the great Assyrian library. His was probably the first systematically collected library in the ancient Near East, and it was the first to be found by archaeologists. Though a library of sorts had been in existence at the Temple of Nabu at Nineveh for some fifty years, it was Ashurbanipal who sent scribes all over Assyria and Babylonia to copy and translate Sumerian, Akkadian, Babylonian, and Assyrian texts containing historical, scientific, and religious literature, official and business documents, and private communications "as precious possessions of my royalty." Nearly all these found their way to the British Museum in London as a result of Hormuzd Rassam's excavations at Nineveh in 1852 and 1853. But George Smith of the museum staff discovered additional tablets in 1872.

This horde of literature is significant, first because it provides abundant material for the study of Assyria and the establish-ment of its grammar and the meaning of words. Second, many tablets contain dated references and thus help to refine the chronology of Mesopotamia. Third, the variety of material representing many aspects of life contributes to an understanding of the context in which the biblical narrative developed.

And finally, there were in the library parallels to the Old Testament. For example, the library contains a creation account (the *Enuma Elish*) and a flood account (the *Gilgamesh Epic*). These texts have numerous similarities to the biblical record, although they also contain many marked differences. It used to be fashionable for critics to claim that these accounts furnished the basis for the biblical narratives, which, primarily, removed the polytheistic elements and introduced a monotheistic approach. But careful study has rather effectively answered many of the earlier critical arguments. In particular, Alexander Heidel of the University of Chicago dealt with the problem of the relationship of these texts to Scripture in *The Babylonian Genesis* (2nd ed., 1959) and *The Gilgamesh Epic* (2nd ed., 1949) and concluded

Ashurbanipal feasting with his queen. *British Museum*

Whatever repentance took place at that time must have been partial and temporary. A generation later, under Tiglath-Pileser III (after 744 B.C.) they were again on the attack against the Hebrews. Subsequently Sennacherib had railed against the Hebrews and against their God as he besieged Jerusalem, declaring God to be powerless to save them (Isaiah 36).

So the prophets predicted woe against Assyria. Through Isaiah God said (all quotations from NKJV), "I will punish the fruit of the arrogant heart of the king of Assyria, and the glory of his haughty looks" (Isaiah 10:12); "I will break the Assyrian in My land, And on My mountains tread him underfoot" (Isaiah 14:25); "Assyria will be beaten down" (Isaiah 30:31); "The Assyrian shall fall by a sword not of man, And a sword not of mankind shall devour him" (Isaiah 31:8).

Nahum prophesied more specifically against Nineveh "Woe to the bloody city!" (3:1); "Nineveh is laid waste!" (Nahum 3:7); "The gates of your land are wide open for your enemies" (Nahum 3:13); "The fire will devour you, The sword will cut you off" (Nahum 3:15); "Your shepherds slumber, O

that neither the biblical nor the Babylonian accounts borrowed from the other, but that similarities derived from the fact that both arose from the same general context or source. Unfortunately, some popular books still claim that the biblical accounts had their origin in the Mesopotamian texts.

Prophecies Against Assyria and Their Fulfillment

The prophets had much to say about Assyria in general and Nineveh in particular. First they foretold Assyrian punishment of the Hebrews for their idolatry and their general waywardness (see, for example, Isaiah 10:5–6; cf. 2 Kings 17:7–23). That fulfillment came with the fall of Samaria in 723/22 and the terrible attacks on Judah in 701 B.C. Second, they predicted the destruction of Assyria and her capital Nineveh.

This pronouncement came because of Assyrian treatment of the Jews (those who curse Abraham's descendants, Genesis 12:1–3) and their idolatry and pride (see 2 Chronicles 32:12–17, 19; cf. Isaiah 10:7–14). After the Battle of Qarqar in 853 B.C., when Ahab had sought to stop the Assyrian advance into Palestine and after Jehu had been forced to pay tribute to Assyria (perhaps a couple of decades later) God had specifically given Assyria a chance to avoid judgment by sending Jonah to preach there (c. 760 B.C.).

A flood account from Ashurbanipal's library at Nineveh. *British Museum*

king of Assyria; your nobles rest in the dust. Your people are scattered on the mountains, And no one gathers them" (3:18). Finally, Zephaniah predicted, "And He will . . . destroy Assyria, And make Nineveh a desolation, As dry as the wilderness. The herds shall lie down in her midst" (Zephaniah 2:13–14 NKJV).

Soon after Zephaniah's pronouncement and soon after Ashurbanipal's death in 627 B.C. the judgment fell. Nabopolassar, a Chaldean and possible descendant of Merodach-Baladan, established an independent state in Babylonia at the end of 626 B.C. Meanwhile the Medes had moved into Elam and had begun to infiltrate Assyria proper. The Babylonians and Medes made a treaty of alliance late in 614 B.C., and evidently the Scythians joined them later. These confederates then laid siege to Nineveh in 612 B.C. The Assyrian capital fell in the amazingly short time of three months, and it was thoroughly sacked and looted. The survivors fled westward to Haran, where the last flicker of Assyrian resistance was extinguished by 609 B.C. The prophecy had been fulfilled. Unlike many other great cities of antiquity, Nineveh was destroyed, never to be rebuilt. Modern visitors to the site may see herds lying down in her midst (Zephaniah 2:14).

The Babylon of Nebuchadnezzar and Daniel

After Nabopolassar of Babylon and Cyaxares the Mede destroyed Nineveh in 612 B.C., they divided the Assyrian Empire, the Medes taking territory to the north and east of the Tigris River and the Babylonians taking the region to the south and west of the Tigris. Nabopolassar consumed his energies on consolidating his power and establishing his empire. He left it to his famous son Nebuchadnezzar to expand the empire and build up the capital city.

The Magnificence of the City

"Is not this the great Babylon I have built as the royal residence, by my mighty power and for the glory of my majesty?" (Daniel 4:30, NIV), asked Nebuchadnezzar as he walked in his garden one day. To a large degree his boast was true. Although

Hammurabi (c.1800–1700 B.C.) had raised the status of Babylon from that of an insignificant village to the position of foremost city of Babylonia, and though he had engaged in building activities proportionate to her prestige, the city had fallen on evil days before the time of Nebuchadnezzar.

In an effort to stop the constant rebellion of the Babylonians, Sennacherib of Assyria had sacked the city in 690–89 B.C. and destroyed a large part of it. Esarhaddon (680–669 B.C.), son of Sennacherib, believed that he could best placate his southern province by rebuilding Babylon. But it was Nabopolassar (626–605 B.C.) and his son Nebuchadnezzar (605–562 B.C.), who reconstructed the entire city along grander lines.

The location of Babylon (54 miles south of modern Baghdad) was never completely forgotten, as was the case with many other biblical sites. Numerous visitors went there, but C. J. Rich in 1811 and 1818 measured the various mounds that encased the ruins and made the first accurate plan of the site. Of the several others who worked there during the nineteenth century, most important was

An altar from an Assyrian temple. *British Museum*

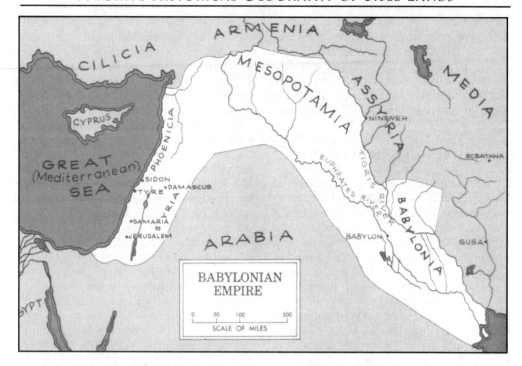

Hormuzd Rassam, who in 1879 unearthed a large collection of business documents and the famous Cyrus cylinder with Cyrus's account of his conquest of Babylon.

Most important of all the expeditions to Babylon was that of Robert Koldewey, who led the German Oriental Society dig there between 1899 and 1917, and brought to light the city of Nebuchadnezzar's day. German excavators returned to Babylon in 1956 and worked for several years in the area of the Greek theater. And since 1955 the Iraqi Department of Antiquities has partially restored several important structures.

The city itself, roughly rectangular, sat astride the Euphrates. The new city, on the west bank, was joined to the older section by a bridge that was truly magnificent for its day. The span was supported by boat-shaped piers built of brick and set in asphalt. The piers measured sixty-nine feet in length and twenty-eight feet in width and they were spaced at twenty-eight foot intervals. The wall, eleven miles long and eighty-five feet thick, was protected by a moat filled with water from the Euphrates. Actually the wall was double; the outer wall was twenty-five feet thick and the inner one twenty-three feet thick with an

intervening space filled with rubble. Watchtowers stood sixty-five feet apart on the walls. There were eight gates in the wall; of these Koldewey excavated four and identified the rest.

Of these, the most famous was the Ishtar Gate, which entered the city from the north on the east side of the river. It was a double gate flanked by forty-foot towers of blue enameled brick decorated with alternating rows of yellow and white bulls and dragons, executed in enameled brick. Through the gate passed Procession Street which sometimes reached a width of sixty-five feet. In honor of Marduk, this roadway was paved with imported limestone and was bordered with sidewalks of red breccia. Walls on either side of the road were faced with blue enameled brick and decorated with life-size yellow and white lions and dragons.

Surely this street was the scene of many great spectacles. Here trooped the captives, including Hebrews, whom Nebuchadnezzar took in war. Along this street, too, at the annual New Year festival, the image of Marduk was carried, and ritual acts were performed at each of the sacred buildings passed en route. A diminutive Ishtar Gate

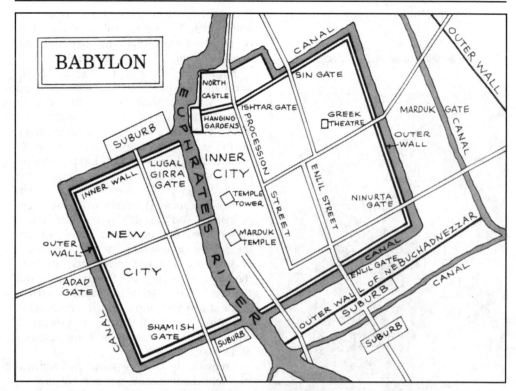

and part of Procession Street have been recreated in the Staatliche Museen in Berlin with original materials taken from Babylon. Fortunately the display has survived the vicissitudes of war. As I have walked this roadway, I have wondered what went through Daniel's mind as he passed this way in 605 B.C.

The city's major structures opened on Procession Street. One of these was the temple tower or ziggurat, which measured about 300 feet on a side at the base; but it was impossible to determine the nature of the superstructure. Some have conjectured a reconstruction based on the ziggurats at Ur or elsewhere. Another structure opening on Procession Street was Nebuchadnezzar's main palace. It was a huge complex of buildings protected by a double wall; rooms of the palace surrounded five courtyards. The white-plastered throne room (55 by 170 feet) had a great central entrance flanked by smaller side doors. The enameled colored brick façade is also on display in Berlin (see color insert in this book).

A third major structure on Procession Street was the great Marduk temple, one of five temples excavated in the city. Each of these was surrounded by a walled precinct, and in each case temple gates opened on inner courts flanked by buildings. The shrine room with a raised dais for a cult statue was approached through an antechamber. The famous hanging gardens of Babylon used to be located near the Ishtar Gate, but at present there's no absolute certainty as to their location.

BABYLONIANS AND HEBREWS

- Nebuchadnezzar invaded Judah and carried off Daniel and other captives in 605 B.C.

- Nebuchadnezzar sacked Jerusalem in 597 B.C., deporting King Jehoiachin, Ezekiel, and thousands of others and plundering the temple.

- Nebuchadnezzar besieged Jerusalem in 588 B.C. and took the city in 586 B.C., destroying the city and temple and killing or deporting the ruling classes.

The Ishtar Gate recreated in the Staatliche Museen, Berlin, with original materials taken from Babylon

Destruction of the Kingdom of Judah

Bible students are especially interested in Babylon and Nebuchadnezzar because of their connection with the destruction of the Southern Kingdom of Judah. In order to understand what happened in Judah, it is necessary to make a quick reference to the international situation. After the destruction of Nineveh in 612 B.C. and the move of the Assyrian court to Haran in the west, Pharaoh Necho of Egypt went north to aid the Assyrians against Babylon. King Josiah of Judah sought to prevent the Egyptians from marching north through his territory to help his inveterate foe. For his efforts Josiah paid with his life (609 B.C., 2 Kings 23:29). Then, evidently not merely interested in helping the Assyrians, Necho estab-

lished control over Palestine and Syria as he went north. He put Josiah's son Jehoiakim on the throne of Judah and expected subservience from him (2 Kings 23:34).

For a few years Egypt dominated Syria and Palestine, but in 605 B.C. the aging and perhaps infirm Nabopolassar turned over control of the armed forces to his able son Nebuchadnezzar, and a new dynamic came on the scene. The Babylonian army made mincemeat of the Assyrian-Egyptian army at the battle of Carchemish in Syria in the spring of 605 B.C. The remnants of Assyrian power disappeared forever from the pages of history, and Necho's Syrian empire collapsed like a house of cards. Jones explains the demise of Assyria in part by the failure of Assyrians to participate meaningfully in the economic structure of their empire and the gradual extinction in constant warfare of the sturdy peasantry, which served as the recruiting base for the army. Assyria could not get the same results with mercenaries and subject levies.[47]

Immediately after the battle of Carchemish, Nebuchadnezzar took control of all Syria and Palestine. Jehoiakim of Judah, who had been a vassal of Necho, now submitted to Nebuchadnezzar, and some Jews, including the prophet Daniel, were carried off as captives or hostages to Babylon (Daniel 1:1–7).[48] In the midst of this campaign on August 15/16, 605 B.C., Nabopolassar died in Babylon. Receiving word of the death of his father, Nebuchadnezzar rushed back to the capital, arrived in the city on September 6/7, and immediately took the throne. During the following three years Nebuchadnezzar made a show of force in Syria and Palestine, evidently in an effort to establish firm control of territory through which military supply lines would have to pass when he launched an attack on Egypt.

Finally, in his fourth year (601/600 B.C.), Nebuchadnezzar was ready for the Egyptian offensive. After a fiercely fought battle in which casualties were heavy on both sides, Nebuchadnezzar and his army "turned back and returned to Babylon"[49] (his words), apparently admitting defeat. With this evidence of weakness on the part of Babylon, Jehoiakim seemed to have thought he could get away with a move for independence. He

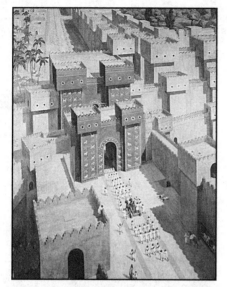

Artist's conception of Babylon. Courtesy Oriental Institute, *University of Chicago*

with the Egyptians. All during his reign, the pro-Egyptian faction pressured Zedekiah to rebel against Babylon, and in his ninth year he decided to do so. The forces of Nebuchadnezzar advanced against Jerusalem (2 Kings 25:1) and began the siege on January 15, 588 B.C., and it continued until July 18, 586 B.C.[50]

About a month after the fall of the city, Nebuzaradan, commander of the guard, came to take charge of liquidating the Judean state and reorganizing the government there. The Babylonians looted the city, destroyed its main buildings, broke down the walls, destroyed the Temple, depopulated the city, and then deported the upper classes from the countryside. And so were fulfilled the many warnings of the prophets that captivity in a foreign land would result from Judah's idolatry and other waywardness.

Prophecies Against Babylon and Their Fulfillment

But God also had a score to settle with Babylon. Long passages in Isaiah and

rebelled against Nebuchadnezzar in that very year (601/600 B.C., 2 Kings 24:1). Nebuchadnezzar did not respond in person immediately, largely because he was busy rebuilding his shattered military establishment, but he evidently sent "raiding bands," lightly armed mercenaries from the east of the Jordan (Syrians, Moabites, and Ammonites), to engage in guerrilla activities and weaken the state (2 Kings 24:2).

Jehoiakim ruled for eleven years (609–598 B.C.) and apparently died in December 598 B.C., about the time Nebuchadnezzar finally sent an army to deal with rebellious Judah. As the siege began, Jehoiakim died and his eighteen-year-old son Jehoiachin came to the throne. The Babylonians must have begun the siege of the city in January of 597 B.C.; apparently it did not last much more than two months. Then the Babylonians helped themselves to the spoils of war, thoroughly looting the treasuries of the temple and palace and deporting the king, his mother, wives, and officials, and all those capable of mounting an effective rebellion and running a viable war effort (2 Kings 24:12–17).

Nebuchadnezzar then installed Jehoiachin's uncle Zedekiah as king, on the condition that he would keep the kingdom for Nebuchadnezzar and make no alliance

Artist's conception of Babylon viewed from the Euphrates, with the ziggurat and the great Temple of Marduk in the foreground. Courtesy Oriental Institute, *University of Chicago*

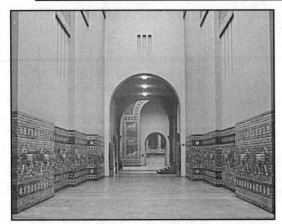

Procession Street, Babylon, as recreated in Berlin with original materials from Babylon. *Staatliche Museen, Berlin*

Jeremiah predict the downfall of her empire and the desolation of the city. Especially specific are Isaiah 13:17–22 and 45:1–3 and Jeremiah 25:12–14 and all of chapters 50 and 51 (note especially Jeremiah 50:9–10, 14–15, 26, 30, 32, 39–40; 51:4, 11, 26, 28, 37, 59).

Seven distinct prophecies against Babylon outlined in these passages include: (1) her enemies will be nations from the north; (2) more specifically, the Medes shall come against the city; (3) to Cyrus it was said that nations would be subdued before him; gates would not be shut before him; and he would be given the treasures and hidden riches of secret places; (4) the specific time of overthrow of Babylon would occur when the seventy-year captivity of the Jews was accomplished; (5) Babylon will be as when God overthrew Sodom and Gomorrah; (6) her foundations would fall and walls would be thrown down, (7) and she should not be dwelt in from generation to generation.

Jeremiah detailed the primary reason for God's judgment on Babylon: their rejoicing over Israel's troubles and their destruction of Israel:

"Because you were glad, because you rejoiced, You destroyers of my heritage (Jeremiah 50:11 NKJV); "Israel is like scattered sheep; The lions have driven him away. First the king of Assyria devoured him; Now at last

this Nebuchadnezzar king of Babylon has broken his bones. Therefore thus says the LORD of hosts, the God of Israel: 'Behold, I will punish the king of Babylon and his land, As I have punished the king of Assyria'" (Jeremiah 50:17–18 NKJV).

Jeremiah further elaborated: "And I will repay Babylon And all the inhabitants of Chaldea For all the evil they have done in Zion in your sight, says the Lord" (Jeremiah 51:24 NKJV). In taking up the cause of Israel against Babylon, God said, "Behold, I will plead your case and take vengeance for you' . . . Babylon shall become a heap, A dwelling place for jackals" (Jeremiah 51:36–37 NKJV).

The beginning of the judgment against Babylon came with the death of Nebuchadnezzar in 561 B.C. His successors had little of the political and military genius that characterized his forty-three year reign. After this internal decline, the forces of Cyrus the Great of Persia took the city of Babylon without a fight on October 12, 539 B.C.; Cyrus himself entered the city on October 29. Cyrus did not destroy Babylon; it only slowly declined. Later the city surrendered without a blow to Alexander the Great, who voiced the desire of making it his eastern capital. But with the death of Alexander, the hopes of the inhabitants were dashed and Babylon continued its decline. (The account of Alexander's campaigns in Mesopotamia appears in chapter 9 on Greece).

Babylon became part of the Seleucid Empire in 312 B.C. From then on the decay of the area gradually became apparent as the irrigation system was neglected and as political and religious interests were centered on Mediterranean shores. It is not necessary to trace the history of Babylon during Parthian, Roman, and Arab occupations. But the final blow came during the Mongol conquest. In 1258 A.D. a grandson of Genghis Khan captured Baghdad and wrought terrible devastation in the area; most of the vast irrigation system that had supported the land since the beginning of civilization ceased to function. Babylon became an uninhabited waste.

Specific prophecies against Babylon have been fulfilled. Cyrus of Persia led the Medo-Persian forces from the north to bring an end to Nebuchadnezzar's empire in 539 B.C., at the end of the seventy years of Babylonian captivity. Shapeless heaps of rubbish cover many acres where the powerful and glorious city used to stand. The uninhabited ruins give much the same appearance as when God overthrew Sodom and Gomorrah.

Unfortunately modern Americans, whether Bible students or not, have little knowledge of or appreciation for Mesopotamia. Almost all they seem to know about it is that the Gulf War was fought there in 1991, that Saddam Hussein continued to be a problem for the West, and that Iraq sits on a tremendous deposit of oil.

But we need to remember that at the north of the region Noah's ark rested in the Mountains of Ararat and from there the world was repopulated after the Flood.

Later civilization began there, including the inventions of writing and the wheel, law codes, the earliest mathematical systems, the arch, and much more. Then as we think of the history of the Jews, we need to remember that nearly all the original ancestors of the twelve tribes of Israel were born there. Later Assyrians and Babylonians destroyed the Hebrew state and carried off large numbers of her citizens into captivity there. Also subsequently the restoration of the Jews to their homeland was launched from Mesopotamia.

But that was not the end of Jewish life in Mesopotamia. Many Jews continued to live there after the days of Ezra and Nehemiah, and it became a center for Jewish life and culture. The Babylonian Talmud originated there, Jews from Mesopotamia were present in Jerusalem on the day of Pentecost (Acts 2:9), and archaeologists have uncovered a third century A.D. synagogue at Dura-Europos, with its magnificent frescoes, as well as an early Christian church.[51]

So Mesopotamia is of vital importance to the history of culture, to the history of the Jews, as well as to the early church and to the understanding and appreciation of the Bible.

NOTES

1. Leonard Woolley, *Ur of the Chaldees*, ed. P. R. S. Moorey, rev. ed. (London: Herbert, 1981), See also Moorey's bibliographical notes on p. 35.

2. For a discussion of gaps in the biblical chronology, see Oswald T. Allis, *The Five Books of Moses* (Philadelphia: Presbyterian and Reformed, 1943), 261–64; Gleason L. Archer Jr., *A Survey of Old Testament Introduction*, 2nd rev. ed. (Chicago: Moody Press, 1973), 185–89, and updated ed. (1994), 209-12; Merrill F. Unger, *Introductory Guide to the Old Testament* (Grand Rapids: Zondervan, 1951), 192–94; and B. B. Warfield, *Studies in Theology* (New York: Oxford, 1932), 235–58.

3. Robert Braidwood, *Prehistoric Men*, 7th ed. (Glenview, IL: Scott Foresman, 1967), 116–20.

4. Kathleen Kenyon, *Archaeology in the Holy Land*, 3rd ed. (London: Ernest Benn, 1970), 331.

5. Moore, A. M. T. and others, *Village on the Euphrates* (New York: Oxford University Press , 2000), 104; James Mellaart, *The Neolithic of the Near East* (New York: Scribner's, 1975), 44–45. See also Hans J. Nissen, *The Early History of the Ancient Near East 9000–2000 B.C.* (Chicago: University of Chicago Press, 1988).

6. Mellaart, *Neolithic*, 52.

7. Georges Roux, *Ancient Iraq*, 3rd ed. (New York: Penguin, 1992), 64–65.

8. Jack Finegan, *Light from the Ancient Past*, 2nd ed. (Princeton: Princeton University Press, 1959), 26.

9. André Parrot, *The Tower of Babel* (New York: Philosophical Library, 1954), 26.

10. Roux, *Ancient Iraq*, 69.

11. Ibid., 70.

12. Seton Lloyd, *The Archaeology of Mesopotamia* (London: Thames and Hudson, 1978), 52.

13. Roux, *Ancient Iraq*, 80.

14. Ibid., 81.

15. Tom B. Jones, ed., *The Sumerian Problem* (New York: John Wiley & Sons, 1969), 99.

16. Samuel N. Kramer, *The Sumerians* (Chicago: University of Chicago Press, 1963), 42.

17. Harriet Crawford, *Sumer and the Sumerians* (Cambridge: Cambridge University Press, 1991), 44.

18. See especially, C. Leonard Woolley, *The Sumerians* (New York: W. W. Norton, 1965).

19. Finegan, *Ancient Past*, 41.

20. Leonard Woolley, *Ur of the Chaldees* (Harmondsworth, England: Penguin Books, 1950), 67–68.

21. Finegan, *Ancient Past*, 49.

22. Carl Roebuck, *The World of Ancient Times* (New York: Scribner's, 1966), 33.

23. A. Leo Oppenheim, *Ancient Mesopotamia*, rev. ed. (Chicago: University of Chicago Press, 1977), 336.

24. Roux, *Ancient Iraq*, 162.

25. Amélie Kuhrt, *The Ancient Near East* (New York: Routledge, 1995), 1, 56.

26. McGuire Gibson, *The Oriental Institute 1981–82 Annual Report*, 41.

27. From a study of Genesis 12:4; 21:5; 25:26; and 47:9, it is clear that Abraham entered Canaan at seventy-five; Isaac was born to him at age 100; Isaac was 60 when Jacob was born; and Jacob was 130 when he stood before Pharaoh. A total of 215 years (25 + 60 + 130) elapsed, then, between Abraham's entrance into Canaan and Jacob's entrance into Egypt.

28. See Cyrus Gordon, "Abraham and the Merchants of Ura," *Journal of Near Eastern Studies* (January 1958): 28–30; William F. Albright, *Yahweh and the Gods of Canaan* (Garden City, NY: Double Day, 1968), 51, 62–73; D. J. Wiseman, "Abraham Reassessed," *Essays on the Patriarchal Narratives*, ed. A. R. Millard and D. J. Wiseman (Winona Lake, IN: Eisenbrauns, 1983), 141–53. The French Assyriologist Georges Roux observes that silver, "used as a standard for exchanges," was "hoarded by high officials and did not circulate unless authorized by the Palace" (Roux, *Ancient Iraq*, 173). Did Abraham get his hands on a quantity of silver as an official in the employ of the government of Ur? Was he possibly a favorite of the court? Perhaps we should note that Gordon in his 1958 article, "Abraham and the Merchants of Ura" noted above, located Ur in northern Mesopotamia. That idea never caught on with scholars, but it surfaced again in the January/February 2000 issue of *Biblical Archaeology Review*. Observe, however, that references to Ur in Scripture locate it in southern Mesopotamia: "Ur of the Chaldees" (Genesis 11:31; 15:7; Nehemiah 9:7; Acts 7:4).

29. C. L. Woolley, *History of Mankind*, vol. 1 (New York: New American Library, 1965), 2:123–35.

30. C. L. Woolley, *Abraham* (New York: Scribner's, 1936), 111–15.

31. Ibid., 118–33.

32. Ibid., 103.

33. Abraham was 75 when he entered Canaan and 100 when Isaac was born; Isaac was 60 years old when Jacob was born; and Jacob was over 40 when he went to Haran.

34. For a discussion of old and current views of the relation between the Nuzi tablets and Genesis, see Cyrus Gordon, "Biblical Customs and the Nuzu Tablets," *The Biblical Archaeologist:* (February 1940) 1–12; M. J. Selman, "Comparative Customs and the Patriarchal Age," *Essays on the Patriarchal Narratives*, ed. A. R. Millard and D. J. Wiseman (Winona Lake, IN: Eisenbrauns, 1983), 91–139; Martha A. Morrison, "The Jacob and Laban Narrative in Light of Near Eastern Sources," *Biblical Archaeologist*,

(Summer 1983): 155–164; Howard F. Vos, *Nelson's New Illustrated Bible Manners & Customs* (Nashville: Thomas Nelson, 1999), 38–42.

35. *The Minimal Chronology* dates Hammurabi's reign 1728–1686, Finegan, *Ancient Past*, 57; but others, such as Roebuck, *Ancient Times*, 42, and Roux, *Ancient Iraq*, 184, put the date at 1792–1750. This latter date is probably the most widely accepted.

36. See Alexander Heidel, *The Babylonian Genesis*, 2nd ed. (Chicago: University of Chicago Press, 1951).

37. The texts of the Lipit-Ishtar, Eshnunna, and Hammurabi codes appear in James B. Pritchard, ed., *Ancient Near Eastern Texts*, 2nd ed. (Princeton: Princeton University Press, 1955), 159–180. For a useful comparison of the Hammurabi and Mosaic codes and a translation of the Hammurabi code, see George A. Barton, *Archaeology and the Bible*, 7th ed. (Philadelphia: American Sunday-School Union, 1937), 378–406.

38. H. W. F. Saggs, *The Might That Was Assyria* (London: Sidgwick & Jackson, 1984), 28–34.

39. Ibid., 36–37.

40. Finegan, *Ancient Past*, 208.

41. Pritchard, *Ancient Past*, 284–85

42. Saggs, *Ancient Past*, 92.

43. Though a grandiose project, and though excavations there provided magnificent displays at the Louvre in Paris and the Oriental Institute of the University of Chicago, Khorsabad was never completed and never served as Assyria's capital.

44. Pritchard, *Ancient Near Eastern Texts*, 284–85.

45. Most of the archaeological work at Nineveh has been done by British expeditions: A. H. Layard (1845); H. Rassam (1852–54); George Smith (1872–73, 1876); H. Rassam (1878–82); E. A. W. Budge (1888–91); L. W. King and R. Campbell Thompson (1903–1905); Thompson and M. E. L. Mallowan (1927–32); and the Iraq Department of Antiquities (1954). Thompson was especially responsible for bringing a degree of order out of the chaos created by previous campaigns at the site. He cut down to virgin soil and established the history from 612 B.C. (when the Babylonians destroyed the city) back to almost 5000 B.C.

46. Pritchard, *Ancient Near Eastern Texts*, 288.

47. Tom B. Jones, *Ancient Civilization*, rev. ed. (Chicago: Rand McNally, 1964), 135.

48. Donald J. Wiseman, *Chronicles of Chaldaean Kings* (London: British Museum, 1961), 26.

49. Ibid., 71.

50. Edwin R. Thiele, *The Mysterious Numbers of the Hebrew Kings*, rev. ed. (Grand Rapids: Zondervan, 1983), 190.

51. Finegan, *Ancient Past*, 497–501.

BIBLIOGRAPHY

Adams, Robert McC. *Heartland of Cities.* Chicago: University of Chicago Press, 1981.

Adams, Robert McC, and Hans J. Nissen. *The Uruk Countryside.* Chicago: University of Chicago Press, 1972.

Beaulieu, Paul-Alain. *The Reign of Nabonidus King of Babylon 556–539 B.C.* New Haven: Yale University Press, 1989.

Beek, Martin A. *Atlas of Mesopotamia.* New York: Thomas Nelson and Sons, 1962.

Black, Jeremy, and Anthony Green. *Gods, Demons, and Symbols of Ancient Mesopotamia.* London: British Museum Press, 1992.

Bottéro, Jean. *Everyday Life in Ancient Mesopotamia.* Baltimore: Johns Hopkins, 2001.

Bottéro, Jean. *Mesopotamia.* Chicago: University of Chicago Press, 1992.

Crawford, Harriet. *Sumer and the Sumerians.* Cambridge: Cambridge University Press, 1991.

Curtis, J. E., and J. E. Reade, eds. *Art and Empire.* New York: Metropolitan Museum of Art, 1995.

Finer, S. E. *The History of Government,* Vol. 1. Oxford: Oxford University Press, 1997.

Grayson, A. Kirk. *Assyrian and Babylonian Chronicles.* Winona Lake, IN: Eisenbrauns, 2000.

Hawkes, Jacquetta. *The First Great Civilizations.* New York: Alfred A. Knopf, 1973.

Jacobsen, Thorkild. *The Treasures of Darkness.* New Haven: Yale University Press, 1976.

Kern, Paul B. *Ancient Siege Warfare.* Bloomington: Indiana University Press, 1999.

Kramer, Samuel N. *History Begins at Sumer* 3rd ed. Philadelphia: University of Pennsylvania Press, 1981.

Kramer, Samuel N. *The Sumerians.* Chicago: University of Chicago Press, 1963.

Kuhrt, Amelie. *The Ancient Near East c. 3000–330 B.C.* 2 vols. New York: Routledge, 1995.

Larsen, Mogens T. *The Conquest of Assyria.* New York: Routledge, 1994.

Larue, Gerald A. *Babylon and the Bible.* Grand Rapids: Baker, 1969.

Lloyd, Seton. *The Archaeology of Mesopotamia.* London: Thames & Hudson, 1978.

Lloyd, Seton. *Foundations in the Dust.* Rev. ed. London: Thames & Hudson, 1980.

Luckenbill, Daniel D. *Ancient Records of Assyria and Babylonia.* 2 vols. Chicago: University of Chicago Press, 1926.

Macqueen, James G. *Babylon.* London: Robert Hale, 1964.

Moorey, P. R. S. *Ancient Mesopotamian Materials and Industries.* Oxford: At the Clarendon Press, 1994.

Moorey, P. R. S. *The Origins of Civilization.* Oxford: Clarendon Press, 1979.

Moortgat, Anton. *The Art of Ancient Mesopotamia.* London: Phaidon Press, 1969.

Oates, Joan. *Babylon.* Rev. ed. London: Thames & Hudson, 1986.

Olmstead, A. T. *History of Assyria.* Chicago: University of Chicago Press, 1951.

Oppenheim, A. Leo. *Ancient Mesopotamia.* Rev. ed. Chicago: University of Chicago Press, 1977.

Oppenheim, A. Leo, and others. *Glass and Glassmaking in Ancient Mesopotamia.* Corning, NY: The Corning Museum of Glass Press, 1970.

Parker, Richard A., and Waldo H. Dubberstein. *Babylonian Chronology 626 B.C.–A.D.45.* Rev. ed. Chicago: The Oriental Institute, 1946.

Parrot, André. *Nineveh and the Old Testament.* New York: Philosophical Library, 1955.

Pollock, Susan. *Ancient Mesopotamia.* Cambridge: Cambridge University Press, 1999.

Postgate, J. N. *Early Mesopotamia.* New York: Routledge, 1992.

Potts, D. T. *Mesopotamian Civilization.* Ithaca: Cornell University Press, 1997

Reade, Julian. *Assyrian Sculpture.* London: British Museum Press, 1983.

Roaf, Michael. *Cultural Atlas of Mesopotamia.* New York: Facts on File, 1990.

Roux, Georges. *Ancient Iraq.* 3rd. ed. New York: Penguin Books, 1992.

Russell, John M. *Sennacherib's Palace Without Rival at Nineveh.* Chicago: University of Chicago Press, 1991.

Saggs, H. W. F. *Babylonians.* Norman, OK: University of Oklahoma Press, 1995.

Saggs, H. W. F. *Everyday Life in Babylonia and Assyria.* New York: G. P. Putnam's Sons, 1965.

Saggs, H. W. F. *The Greatness That Was Babylon.* 2nd ed. London: Sidgwick & Jackson, 1988.

Snell, Daniel C. *Life in the Ancient Near East 3100–332 B.C.E.* New Haven: Yale University Press, 1997.

Van DeMieroop, Marc. *The Ancient Mesopotamian City.* New York: Oxford University Press, 1998.

Wellard, James. *Babylon.* New York: Saturday Review Press, 1972.

Whitehouse, Ruth. *The First Cities.* Oxford: Phaidon, 1977.

Wiseman, D. J. *Chronicles of the Chaldaean Kings.* London: British Museum, 1961.

Woolley, C. Leonard, *The Sumerians.* New York: Norton, 1965.

Woolley, C. Leonard, *Ur 'of the Chaldees'.* Rev. by P.R.S. Moorey. London: The Herbert Press, 1982.

"The World of Ur," *Expedition.* 40, no. 2, (1998).

Zettler, Richard L. and Lee Horne, eds. *Treasures from the Royal Tombs of Ur.* Philadelphia: University of Pennsylvania Museum, 1998.

The papyrus (left) and lotus, symbols of Lower and Upper Egypt.

2

EGYPT

Egypt as a Bible Land

Ancient Egypt exerts a magnetic pull on modern peoples of the West. Perhaps it is the mysterious character of the civilization on the Nile, or the grandiose architecture, or the artistic beauty of objects from Tutankhamon's tomb, or the personal attractiveness of Cleopatra. Whatever it is, something elusive draws hosts of people to buy the latest "coffee table" book on Egypt, to see a traveling collection of Egyptian antiquities, to visit the Egyptian rooms of a major museum, or to go in person to see the astounding remains still standing in the land of the Pharaohs.

Grandiosity is as good a word as mystery to describe the magnetism of ancient Egypt. The great pyramid, with its some 2,300,000 blocks of limestone weighing an average of 2.5 tons each and covering thirteen acres, is the only one of the seven wonders of the ancient world to survive to the present. In fact, we are not even sure what most of the rest of the seven wonders looked like.

Attractive though ancient Egypt may be to the average person on the street, it holds special interest for the Bible student. Time and time again the biblical narrative intersects with Egyptian history. Early in the history of humankind, soon after the Flood, descendants of Noah went down into Egypt. Genesis 10:6 mentions a son of Ham (Noah's son), Mizraim, who was the forefather of a large clan of people. *Mizraim* is the Hebrew word for Egypt and must here indicate that this descendant of Noah was father of the Egyptian people. Many centuries later, Abraham briefly went to Egypt to escape a famine in Canaan (probably during the twenty-first century B.C. (Genesis 12:10–20). Subsequently Sarah, Abraham's wife, when she proved unable to bear children, gave him an Egyptian servant girl named Hagar as a concubine. From this union was born Ishmael, forefather of the Arabs (Genesis 16).

The major period of Hebrew involvement came when Joseph was sold into slavery in Egypt and the great famine occurred; following that the Hebrews entered and remained in Egypt for 430 years (Exodus 12:40, probably 1876–1446 B.C.), much of that time in bondage. Of course the plagues and the Exodus took place at the end of that period of bondage.

EGYPT AS A BIBLE LAND

Egypt qualifies as a Bible land, especially because the Hebrews lived there 430 years (Exodus 12:40) and because the great plagues and the

Exodus occurred there. Then during New Testament times, Joseph and Mary took the baby Jesus to Egypt to escape the long arm of Herod the Great.

Again and again affairs of the Hebrews intertwined with those of the Egyptians. For example, Abraham took as a concubine the Egyptian Hagar and fathered the ancestor of the Arab peoples. Solomon married an Egyptian wife and received as a dowry a Palestinian town captured by the Egyptians. Solomon's son and successor Rehoboam suffered an Egyptian invasion and humiliation at their hands. A century later the good king Josiah met defeat and death at the hands of Necho of Egypt. And the list goes on.

After the Hebrews established themselves in Palestine and prospered during the united monarchy under David and Solomon, the kingdom split into two parts: Israel and Judah. In a somewhat weakened condition these two kingdoms were subjected to the invasions or intrigues of several Egyptian monarchs. Probably in the year 925 B.C. Shishak I (Sheshonk I) of Egypt invaded the kingdom of Judah during the fifth year of Rehoboam, the son and successor of Solomon, carrying off much booty (1 Kings 14:25–27). He even marched into the territory of Israel, as archaeological discoveries show.

Around 700 B.C., in the days of King Hezekiah and the prophet Isaiah, Tirhakah of Egypt led an army into Palestine to help the Hebrews against the invading Assyrians (2 Kings 19:9). Then in 609 B.C., Pharaoh Necho of Egypt led an army through Judah to come to the aid of weakened Assyria. When King Josiah of Judah tried to stop the Egyptian, he lost his life in battle (2 Kings 23:29) and Necho dominated Judean affairs for about three years. The next brush the Hebrews had with the Egyptians was more positive, however. During the final Babylonian siege of Jerusalem (588–586 B.C.), Pharaoh Hophra,

or Apries, entered Palestine in support of the Judean Zedekiah, causing the Babylonians to lift the siege briefly (Jeremiah 37:5; 44:30). This generous act was not motivated by love for the Hebrews but by fear of the Babylonians, who had invaded Egypt a few years earlier and suffered defeat there.

The Rosetta Stone, key to the decipherment of Egyptian hieroglyphics. Jean François Champollion gets credit for deciphering Egyptian hieroglyphics. *British Museum*

After the destruction of Jerusalem in 586 B.C., a group of Jews forced Jeremiah to go with them into Egypt (Jeremiah 43:6–7). During the centuries that elapsed between the Old and New Testaments, the Egyptians controlled Palestine in the days of the Ptolemies (301–198 B.C.), and a very large and prosperous Jewish community arose in Egypt, especially in Alexandria. When the New Testament opens, Egypt again figures in the biblical narrative as the place of refuge for the holy family. There Joseph, Mary, and Jesus fled to escape the assassination attempt by Herod the Great (Matthew 2:13–23), after which he killed the infants in Bethlehem.

The biblical narrative is also often concerned with prophecies against Egypt. Ezekiel 29–32 details one of the most extended prophecies against Egypt; but Isaiah, Jeremiah, Daniel, Hosea, Joel, and Zechariah also condemn the Egyptians. All prophecies concerning Egypt are not negative, however. In the midst of woe appears the glorious prediction that Egypt will be redeemed. In a future day a great spiritual revival will sweep this land (Isaiah 19:19–25).

Next to Palestine, more years of biblical history took place in Egypt than in any other country (a total of more than 430 years). And the influence of Egypt on Hebrew life crops up periodically, such as in the worship of the golden calf at Sinai (Exodus 32) and the calf worship that Jeroboam I of Israel instituted at Dan and Bethel after his brief exile in Egypt (1 Kings 12:23–30).

Egyptian influence less evident to the reader of the English Bible than these historical references includes the numerous Egyptianisms in the Hebrew text. There are loanwords from Egyptian and a large number of idioms and figures of speech that are characteristically Egyptian in origin but translated into Hebrew. Abraham S. Yahuda's *Language of the Pentateuch in Its Relationship to Egyptian* extensively discusses the Egyptian background of the Joseph and Moses narratives. His more popular work is *The Accuracy of the Bible*.

Geographical Features

The Nile River

A vast desert plateau stretches across the entire width of North Africa from the Atlantic to the Red Sea and then continues on into central Asia. Two great river valleys interrupt this desert: the Tigris-Euphrates and the Nile. Of course, the focus here is on the Nile valley. In fact, Egypt is the gift of the Nile, as the Greek historian Herodotus said in the fifth century B.C. Someone else has said that Egypt is the biggest and greenest oasis in the world. The absolute necessity of Nile waters to the existence of life in Egypt becomes clear from a quick glance at the rainfall statistics for the country. Along

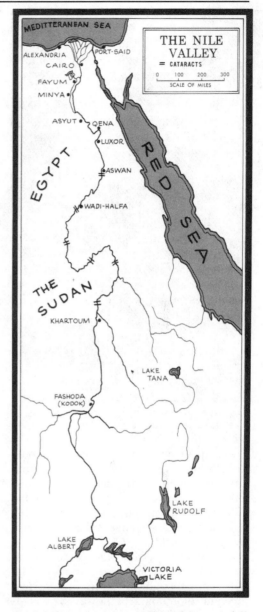

the Mediterranean at Alexandria, rainfall totals 6-to-8 inches per year and at Cairo 1 1/2-to-2 inches; south of Cairo rainfall totals less than an inch.

The Nile originates in equatorial Africa in the Mountains of the Moon (Mt. Ruwenzori), which pour their waters northward into Lakes Victoria, Albert, and Edward; these in turn become the sources of the Nile. The main source of the Nile is Lake Victoria, which is supplied by tropical rains that fall almost daily. This huge lake covers about

The ancient nilometer on the island of Elephantine at Aswan, used for measuring the Nile flood.

The Nile flood was significant for the ancient Egyptian. It softened and watered the soil, washed salts out of it, and deposited a new layer of rich black loam. That had a considerable amount of humus already worked in, because the river torrents carried down vegetation from the Ethiopian highlands. It is estimated that the Nile has deposited at least ten feet of silt over the whole valley since 3000 B.C.

THE NILE FLOOD

Before construction of the first Aswan Dam in 1902, the Nile flood came predictably every year. Between July 15 and 20 the river rose rapidly and continued to swell until the end of September. Then it remained at a crest for 20-to-30 days, rising again in October and reaching its greatest height. After that the river gradually fell, and in January, February, and March the fields dried off. So the Nile flood controlled the Egyptian calendar and dictated the pace of life in the valley.

But very importantly, the flood made possible the abundant life in this corner of Africa. It watered the soil, cleansed the soil of salts, and deposited a new layer of rich black loam with a considerable amount of humus already worked in. Now the land is deprived of those benefits.

27,000 square miles and is second in size only to Lake Superior among world lakes. From Lake Victoria to the Mediterranean, the distance is 2,450 miles in a straight line, but the Nile actually travels a distance of about 4,160 miles in a winding course and is the longest river in the world.

The branch of the Nile coming from these lake reservoirs is called the White Nile, even though its waters are grayish-green in color. It is light, however, by comparison with the Blue Nile, which is dark or turbid and carries much loose soil. The Blue Nile descends from the highlands of Ethiopia and joins the White Nile at Khartoum, capital of modern Sudan, about 1,350 miles in a straight line from the Mediterranean. Approximately 140 miles north of the union of the White and Blue Niles, the river receives its only other tributary, the Atbara. Both the Blue Nile and the Atbara are comparatively insignificant streams except in flood season.

The flood could be depended on to come at the same time every year. At the beginning of June, the river began to swell; between July 15 and 20 the increase was rapid and continued until the end of September. At that time, it ceased to rise and remained at a crest for 20-to-30 days. In October it rose again and reached its greatest height. Thereafter it gradually fell, and in January, February, and March, the fields dried off. Before the Aswan Dam was built in 1902 and arrested the flood, a low inundation meant famine; a high inundation would sweep away dikes and

Part of the first cataract at Aswan is still visible, but much of it has been submerged by the first Aswan dam.

the beginning of the twentieth century) and had a gradual fall of 16½ feet. The distance between the first and second cataracts is 214 miles; the second cataract, under the water of Lake Nasser since construction of the high dam, was 124 miles long with a fall of 216 feet. From the second to the third cataract is a distance of 73 miles, and the third cataract is 45 miles long with a drop of 36 feet. Two miles farther upstream is the fourth cataract, the most difficult of all to navigate, which is 80 miles long and has a drop of 110 feet. In another 60 miles occurs the fifth cataract, which is 100 miles long and has a drop of about 80 feet. Then it is necessary to travel 188 miles to reach the sixth cataract, which is 8 miles long and has a fall of 2 feet. North of Aswan the river is unimpeded because it no longer flows through sandstone; the limestone of Egypt itself is not as hard for the Nile to cut through.

Egypt is currently excavating the New Valley Canal west of the Nile (some say "cloning the Nile"), which is supposed to suck 3.6 billion gallons of water per day from Lake Nasser and to create a million acres of new farmland. There is considerable debate over the wisdom and value of the project and over the effects on the land of Egypt. Readers can watch the progress of this venture as history renders its own verdict.

the mud-brick villages. An average rise at the turn of the century was twenty-six feet; only twenty-one feet would cause suffering or famine; thirty feet brought danger of a flood. So Egypt was precariously perched along the Nile.

There are six places in the Nile between Aswan and Khartoum where the river has failed to cut a clear channel and rocks are piled in irregular masses in the streambed. These cataracts, as they are called, have no great or sudden falls as at Niagara; but they do present serious hindrances to navigation. It is difficult to get any idea of their nature or importance without some detail.

The first cataract, at Aswan, was 3 miles long before construction of the low dam (at

Lower Egypt

Egypt consists of two lands: the trough or Nile valley of upper Egypt in the south and the spreading delta of lower Egypt in the north. The delta is a pie-shaped region

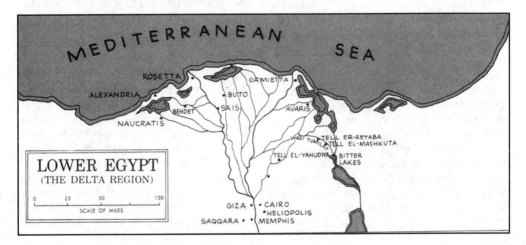

LOWER EGYPT
(THE DELTA REGION)

0   25   50   100
SCALE OF MILES

MEDITERRANEAN SEA

ROSETTA
ALEXANDRIA
DAMIETTA
BEHDET
BUTO
SAIS
NAUCRATIS
AVARIS
WADI TUMILAT
TELL ER-RETABA
TELL EL-MASHKUTA
TELL EL-YAHUDIYA
BITTER LAKES
GIZA
CAIRO
HELIOPOLIS
SAQQARA
MEMPHIS

Here, just south of Cairo, Egypt is about
ten miles wide.

fields to the north of the Wadi Tumilat are among the richest in Egypt. Pithom was probably a town in the Wadi Tumilat region, and *Ramses* (Rameses, Exodus 1:11) was probably the rebuilt city of Avaris.

The Nile Valley

The Nile valley is a tube, shut in on either side by cliffs and corked up at the southern end by the cataracts. Egypt proper extended north from the first cataract at Aswan. From Aswan to Cairo at the base of the delta is a distance of approximately 600 miles, and from Cairo to the Mediterranean is another 125 miles, making the country approximately 725 miles long. If we include the valley south to the fourth cataract, which Egypt ultimately conquered, the length of the country was about 1,100 miles. The part of the valley between the first and sixth cataracts was known as Nubia (now Sudan).

From cliff to cliff the Nile valley ranges from about 10-to-31 miles in width between Cairo and Aswan. But the cultivated area is only about 6-to-10 miles wide along that stretch of the river and narrows to 1 or 2 miles in width around Aswan. This cultivated tract is only about 5,000 square miles. If we add the most heavily populated southern part of the delta, ancient Egypt would be approximately 10,000 square miles, roughly equal to the state of Maryland or a little less than the area of the country of Belgium. Thus the inhabited part of Egypt is and always has been one of the most densely populated places on the earth.[1]

We should not conclude that irrigation or land reclamation projects could add unlimited tracts of land to the cultivated area, for beyond the deposit of black loam (33-to-38 feet in depth) the soil is marginal in quality. An elaborate system of irrigation canals and reservoirs made possible a profitable agricultural program, and the wealth of Egypt became chiefly agricultural.

The valley is flanked on the west by cliffs of the Libyan tableland, which rise to approximately 1,000 feet. Beyond that rolls the Libyan desert, part of the great Sahara.

formed by silt deposits of the Nile over the millennia. Roughly the equivalent of lower Egypt, it is about 125 miles from north to south and about 115 miles from east to west. In ancient times there were seven branches of the Nile in the delta, but these gradually silted up. Today two branches remain, the western is known as the Rosetta, and the eastern as the Damietta. In pharaonic times, Egyptians did not live in the northern delta in very large numbers. There were no important towns along the coast. Edfu, considered to be Egypt's most northerly town, was thirty miles inland. Before Alexander the Great founded the city to which he gave his name (332 B.C.), only a small market town stood on the site. Greeks considered the Egyptian seaboard far from hospitable. At a very early period the Egyptians established observation posts there to prevent pirates from entering the river mouths.

Along the eastern edge of the delta the Egyptians built defenses against Asiatic invaders. In the vicinity of these fortresses they established store cities or granaries with sufficient supplies for the Egyptian garrisons. During the years that the Egyptians enslaved the Israelites, they forced the Israelites to build store cities in this area (Ezekiel 1:11). No doubt the land of Goshen, where the Israelites lived (Genesis 46:28–47:31), was located in the eastern delta in the area around Wadi Tumilat, a valley about forty miles long, connecting the Nile valley with Lake Timsah—now a part of the Suez Canal. The

West of the Nile extend a chain of oases, the largest of which is the Fayum, about 55 miles southwest of Cairo. In the center of the Fayum is Lake Qarun, Egypt's only large inland lake, which today covers 90 square miles and is about 17 feet deep. It is surrounded by slightly less than a half million acres of good farmland. That area was especially developed during the Middle Kingdom (c. 2000–1800 B.C.) and under the Ptolemies (305–30 B.C.). On the east of the Nile, between the river and the Red Sea, rise granite mountains (to a height of 6,500 feet) with gold-bearing quartz veins and deposits of alabaster and semiprecious stones.

South of Aswan the granite mountains of Nubia (the hardest in the world) confine the river. The quarries of Syene at Aswan are famous for their extremely hard and durable red granite. In Nubia the valley is only 5-to-9 miles wide, and the cultivated area is very narrow, often consisting of only a melon patch. The river itself in the 200 miles between the first and second cataracts had an average breadth of about 1,650 feet. Most of that area is now completely changed by the construction of the High Dam at Aswan and the creation of Lake Nasser (about 200 miles long) behind it.

DISEASE IN ANCIENT EGYPT

The Nile and the sun, blessings and essentials for life in ancient Egypt, also became a curse. Bilharzia, tape worms, and guinea worms were parasites *widely* transmitted in the waters of the Nile, irrigation ditches, and stagnant pools. People waded in the water, tended cattle in the water, worked in papyrus glens, worked in water and mud when making bricks, and went fishing. Moreover, they got much of their drinking water from the Nile.

A few years ago, during one of my trips to Egypt, I went sailing in a small boat on the Nile in southern Egypt. Along the way we saw scores of men and boys taking a group bath in the Nile. Then we came upon a herd of water buffalo splashing about as their owners watched them. A little later we saw several Coptic women with their waterpots drawing water from the Nile. Before sailing we had passed a man making sundried brick with mud he had collected from the banks of an irrigation ditch. It was an excellent display of how ancient Egyptians must have constantly run the risk of parasite infection.

Though the sun caused the crops to grow and provided additional Vitamin D for a people with dietary deficiency, it kept the country warm and without frost that could kill off insects. Flies and other insects swarmed everywhere. Flies especially brought on eye infections, and blindness was common. Stagnant waters provided breeding places for mosquitoes. We do not know how widespread malaria was, but lice infection was endemic. Rats ran everywhere in decaying garbage and must have been responsible for plagues. The goddess Sekhmet was known as the Lady of Plague; she could bring them on and also help to protect against them.

When we look at the disease rampant in the Nile valley, we recognize what a blessing it was that God in His sovereign care arranged for the Hebrews to live in the grasslands of Goshen in the eastern Delta. Though the Hebrews still depended on the Nile and sometimes worked in it, their occupation as shepherds kept them from the degree of exposure to the parasites that afflicted the native Egyptians of the valley.

Evidently Ancient Egypt was not a healthful place. Probably the average lifespan for men was thirty-five years and for women thirty.[2] By way of contrast, in 2001 lifespan for Egyptian males was about sixty-one and for females sixty-five.

Egypt As a Gift of the Nile

In a sense, Egypt is the gift of the Nile. The Nile provided water to sustain life on a day-by-day basis, irrigating crops as well as

Near the step pyramid it is easy to see that Egypt is a gift of the Nile. Beyond the black loam that the Nile has deposited over the centuries there is desert as far as the eye can see.

Onions, garlic, beans, lentils, and lettuce were common vegetables. Oil came from castor oil plants and sesame, rather then from the olive as in other Mediterranean lands. Honey was the chief sweetener, and barley beer the typical alcoholic drink. Grape wine was a luxury commodity.

Domesticated animals included oxen, cattle, sheep, goats, donkeys, and horses. Among the fowl raised were pigeons, ducks, geese, and chickens (beginning in the Empire or New Kingdom period around 1500 B.C.) Linen clothing came from flax, likewise grown on the soil. Along the Nile grew papyrus reeds from which a kind of paper was made for writing purposes. And along the Nile was clay from which was made pottery and sundried bricks for building.

The river itself was an incredible all-weather highway. It was possible to float northward with the current and sail southward against the weak current (three miles per hour) by means of the prevailing northerly winds.[4] Boats were made of papyrus bundles and sycamore wood. Trees from the Nubian wadis gave the ancient Egyptians the wood for the barges that carried the huge loads of stone for construction of pyramids, temples, palaces, and other magnificent structures of the ancient period. Cedars of Lebanon also were imported for construction of Egyptian ships.

laying alluvial silt on which to grow them.[3] The chief crops were barley, emmer, wheat, and other grains not yet identified. The "corn" of which the King James Bible speaks must be understood as an earlier English word for cereals and should not be confused with the Indian corn that came from the New World to the Old in the sixteenth century.

The boat with hoisted sail shown in this picture is able to sail south against the weak current of the Nile. Without the use of this sail, it could float northward with the current.

Relief of the Nile god Hapi at Abu Simbel.
Lehnert & Landrock, Cairo

Because the Nile did so much for them, the ancient Egyptians considered it to be a sacred river. Several of their gods were associated with the river and its productivity. For example, the spirit of the Nile was deified as Hapi. Also, the waters of the river were considered to be the bloodstream of Osiris, god of the underworld. It is clear, then, that the first of the ten plagues, which turned the Nile to blood, was more than a nuisance to the Egyptians. It was an attack on their gods and demonstrated the superiority of Yahweh, the true God of heaven (Exodus 7:16–20).

Egyptian Isolation

The ancient Egyptians lived in comparative isolation and peace in their valley home. The cataracts on the south, the deserts on east and west, and the harborless coast of the Mediterranean protected them from invasion and left them free to develop a uniform or homogeneous culture. Chiefly at the two northern corners of the Delta, outside influences could sift in. There were Semitic incursions from the east and Libyans, possibly of European origin, from the west. Defenses were erected to protect against both.

The security of their valley home and the regular provision of the sun and the Nile gave the Egyptians a sense of confidence and well-being that was not the lot of other peo-

ples of the ancient Near East. They built their great capitals at Memphis (biblical Noph, near modern Cairo) and at Thebes (biblical No or No-Amon, 440 miles south of Cairo, at modern Luxor) and had no great upset of their way of life until the Hyksos domination around 1730 B.C. Though life was not destined to be quite the same thereafter, they gained a new sense of power and importance during the Empire period (c. 1580–1100 B.C.) when Egypt ruled the East.

The Sinai

Egypt dominated the Sinai during most of her ancient history. This area was important for its copper and turquoise resources, the mining of which was apparently a government monopoly. But the Sinai has special significance in Scripture as the scene of Israel's wilderness wanderings and receipt of the law, the sacrificial system, the priesthood, and pattern for building the Tabernacle—later to serve as a pattern for Solomon's Temple.

The Sinai is shaped like a wedge that juts down into the Red Sea and divides between Africa and Arabia. The Gulf of Suez separates it from Africa, the Gulf of Aqaba separates it from Arabia. Its northern shore fronts on the Mediterranean, and at the northeast it abuts on the land of Canaan. The peninsula is about 140 miles long.

Sinai is a rugged, waste region with a landscape of wild beauty and grandeur. The barren mountain ranges, made of red and gray granite and gneiss, often have colorful veins of stone that look almost unreal. There is little settled population and there are few oases to sustain human life. Less than one-tenth of one percent of the peninsula is currently under cultivation, and probably no more than that was farmed in ancient times.[5] Grazing grounds are also sparse. A population estimate of the early 1980s concluded that around 200,000 people were living in the Sinai, and the Egyptian government was laying plans to increase that to one million by shortly after the year 2000. Informed observers doubted the feasibility of this effort, however.

Traditionally Mount Sinai, where Moses received the law, is identified with Jebel Musa (mountain of Moses) in the southwest

The traditional springs of Elim, where the Israelites camped (Exodus 15:27)

corner of the peninsula. This 7,519-foot peak is one of the three major peaks that dominate a region of mountains at the southern tip of Sinai. There is an adjacent plain where the Israelites could have camped and where Bedouin today obtain water by digging shallow wells.

The location of Mount Sinai is explored at length in Emmanuel Amati's *The Mountain of God* (1986) and Joseph J. Hobbs' *Mount Sinai* (1995). Paul's reference to Mount Sinai as being in Arabia (Galatians 4:25) should not confuse the modern reader. It does not locate Mount Sinai in the Arabian peninsula. The Arabia referred to here is Arabia Nabataea, the area around Damascus then controlled by the Nabataean king Aretas IV. It extended eastward from the Nile and included the Sinai and the territory east and south of the Dead Sea. (Map on p. 129).

Actually the Bible itself indicates the existence of substantial quantities of water in the Sinai, and modern research estimates the extent of the supply. The books of Exodus and Numbers speak of springs at Marah (Exodus 15:23) and Elim (Exodus 15:27) in the western Sinai and Kadesh on the northeastern edge of Sinai (Numbers 20:10–13). And of course the Israelites found adequate supplies of water for themselves and their animals during the forty years of wandering in the wilderness.

For some time hydrogeologists have been studying the existence of a huge aquifer, or underground fossil water, under the Sinai and the Negev. This water collected there in millennia past and is non-renewable, once it is tapped and used up. Hydrogeologists now calculate that the aquifer under the Sinai and the Negev of southern Israel holds 200 billion cubic meters of water, 70 billion of which is under the Negev. Israelis are now using about 25 million cubic meters of water per year from the aquifer under the Negev for industrial and agricultural purposes.[6]

In addition, at the Wadi el-'Arish (the traditional boundary between Egypt and Israel) Oasis and at other oases along the ancient travel routes in the northern Sinai there are shallow groundwater tables under the sand dunes. Here rain water collects and may be reached by digging shallow wells. What happens in these cases is that the scanty rains quickly seep through the sand, and the water accumulates on a rocky substructure which it cannot penetrate.[7] Thus travelers can dig shallow wells to find an adequate supply of water for immediate needs.

Historical Developments

The Structure of Ancient Egyptian History

Modern historians of ancient Egypt who look for an ordering of events in this ancient land take their cue from an Egyptian priest named Manetho, who around 300 B.C. wrote a history of ancient Egypt in Greek. Though only fragments of his work remain, the structure he developed serves as a framework for modern historians. He divided the Egyptian rulers from the earliest King Menes to Alexander the Great into thirty dynasties.[8] Some related dynasties fall together in groups, and in time these groupings have achieved a high degree of permanence. Thus the Third to the Sixth Dynasty have become known as the Old Kingdom, the Seventh to the Eleventh as the First Intermediate Period, the Twelfth Dynasty as the Middle Kingdom, the Thirteenth to the Seventeenth Dynasty as the Second Intermediate Period, and the Eighteenth to the Twentieth as the New Kingdom or Empire.

The tendency among earlier scholars was to treat all of Manetho's dynasties as consecutive, with the result that very early dates were assigned to the earliest dynasties. But more recent scholarship recognizes that some of the dynasties were at least partially contemporary. With the passage of time, considerable refinement of Egyptian chronology has taken place so that today most Egyptologists put the date for the unification of Egypt at about 3000 B.C. Many follow the eminent John A. Wilson of the University of Chicago (*The Burden of Egypt*) in assigning the date 3100 B.C.; but an increasing number seem to follow the minimal chronology school, which puts the date of unification around 2900 B.C. (see, e.g., Jack Finegan, *Light from the Ancient Past*). Of course refinement of chronology involves more than a date for the unification of ancient Egypt. Other chronological issues appear subsequently.

OUTLINE OF EGYPTIAN HISTORY

Historians commonly divide ancient Egyptian history into three major periods: Old, Middle, and New Kingdoms; or the Old Kingdom, Middle Kingdom, and Empire periods. The Old Kingdom is dated about 2700–2200 B.C.; the Middle Kingdom about 2000–1780 B.C.; and the Empire 1570–1080 B.C. Intermediate periods are seen as taking place before and after the Middle Kingdom. And a Post-Empire Period stretches for many centuries after the fall of the Empire. Thus there is a fairly simple and manageable ordering of the ancient Egyptian past.

Egypt Before the Pharaohs

Egypt had a long history before its unification took place, before Manetho's first dynasty. Known cultures or village sites date between about 5000 and 3000 B.C. A beginning student of the period may quickly be confused by the fairly large number of place names and cultures that the scholars talk about. Moreover, scholars seem to differ considerably in their conclusions about this period. For a clear understanding of Egyptian history, it is important first to note that publications written within the last decade or two generally agree, and they tend to differ in many ways from the older literature.

Second, it is useful to generalize about the information available. The period should be divided into two phases: c. 5000–3500 B.C. and 3500 B.C.–3100/3000 B.C. The earlier phase was essentially Neolithic; that is, the people used polished (or worked) stone tools and weapons, lived in village sites, domesticated animals, and produced their food.

By the end of this phase, however, they were producing copper tools and weapons alongside the stone implements; and the subsequent culture (3500–3000 B.C.) is dubbed Chalcolithic, meaning copper-stone. The sites of cultures belonging to the Neolithic period are the Merimdian (from Merimda in the Delta), Fayumic, and Tasian (from Tasa). The cultures belonging to Chalcolithic are the Badarian (from Badari) and Amratian (from Amra). The latter part of the Chalcolithic is also called Naqada I, the early stages at the important site of Naqada in southern Egypt.

The people of the Naqada I period grew wheat and barley; domesticated dogs, goats, sheep, cattle, pigs, and geese; and made most of their tools and weapons of stone or flint. They had distinctive styles of pottery, including polished red ware, often with black rims. Their expertise in the weaving of baskets and of linen had attained fairly high levels. Their cosmetic arts showed advancement too— they produced eye paint from green malachite and cleansing oils from the castor plant. These were important in the hot, dry, fly-bitten Egyptian summer and helped sooth or prevent eye and skin disorders. They also developed a throw-stick or a kind of boomerang, probably for use in fowling. Moreover, during that period there was considerable attention to burials, some in separate cemeteries. This fact illustrates the increasing interest in preparation for the afterlife which ultimately led to the practice of mummification.

The buttress and recess style of architecture of Zoser's temple at the Step Pyramid is thought to reflect Mesopotamian influence.

Naqada II, or the later materials at Naqada, date to the latter part of the predynastic period, 3500–3100 B.C. This is also the time of the Gerzean culture (at el Girza). Considerable advancements in technology occurred throughout Egypt during this period—in the production of fine flint tools and copper implements, the widespread use of the cranked borer or wobbly drill, and the development of a fine buff pottery decorated with purple paint.

Some give credit for the rapid advance in Egypt during this time to contacts with western Asia, especially with the Jemdet Nasr culture of Mesopotamia. The rectangular sundried mudbrick, the buttress and recess style of architecture (see design of the later temple of Zoser at Saqqara), and the first attempts at a pictographic system of writing are all attributed to Mesopotamian influences. Certainly the occasional use of non-Egyptian materials such as lapis lazuli show trade contacts with Asia. There was a rapid increase in population during these centuries too.

Politically, during the early predynastic period, Naqada seems to have been the center of power in the south, with the storm god Seth as chief deity; and Behdet as the center of power in the north, with the falcon god Horus as chief deity. In the late predynastic period Buto, the city of the cobra goddess Edjo, was the capital in the Delta; and Hierakonpolis, with its vulture goddess as protectress, was capital in the south. During this latter period two confedera-

tions became more clearly defined, one organized in the north and the other in the south. The king of Lower Egypt (in the north and lower in altitude) wore the red crown, and the king of Upper Egypt (in the south, higher in altitude and farther up the Nile) wore the white crown. After a long time of continuous struggle, the south conquered the north and Menes (according to Manetho) brought about the unification of Egypt. He is usually identified with the powerful Narmer (thought to be an alternate name) whose shield-shaped victory palette is now in the Cairo Museum.[9]

This magnificent palette turned up in the excavation of a temple at his capital of Hierakonpolis. On one side of the palette Narmer (wearing the white crown of Upper Egypt) sacrifices a captive before the falcon god Horus, which offers the captive Delta to the king. In a register below lie two fallen Asiatics, symbolizing fortified villages. On the other side, the king (wearing the red crown of Lower Egypt) and his retinue

The victory palette of king Narmer.
Lehnert and Landrock

inspect a battlefield with rows of victims. In a register below the king is depicted as a wild bull that breaks into a fortified town and tramples its fallen Asiatic chieftain.

The division of Egypt was never quite forgotten, however, and it was referred to as the "Two Lands" throughout ancient history. The pharaohs wore a double crown, a combination of the red crown of Lower Egypt and the white crown of Upper Egypt. The king's palace was called the "double palace" and even the royal granary was double. The Hebrews also recognized this duality, for throughout the Old Testament they called Egypt *Misrayim*—a word with a dual ending.

The village at modern Memphis.

MEMPHIS IN HISTORY

Memphis, located about a dozen miles southwest of Cairo, was once the sprawling capital of Egypt; now for all practical purposes it does not exist. A mudbrick village has risen at the edge of the site, however, because the expanding population of Egypt makes it impossible to allow any good land to remain vacant indefinitely.

When the city was founded around 3000 B.C., it was known as "white wall" and was later called Men-nefru-Mine, or Menfe in Egyptian. From the latter the Greeks got the name Memphis. Though one Hebrew reference follows the Greek (Hosea 9:6), Memphis is commonly called Noph in the Old Testament (Isaiah 19:13; Jeremiah 2:16; 44:1, 46:14, 19; Ezekiel 30:13, 16). Presumably this is a corruption of the middle part of the Egyptian name.

Memphis served as the capital of Egypt during the Old Kingdom period (C. 2700–2200 B.C.). And Memphis, or the nearby city of It-Towy, continued as capital during much of the Middle Kingdom (about 2050–1775 B.C.).

During the Empire period (C. 1570–1100 B.C.) the capital was moved to Thebes. But Memphis was Egypt's second capital during most of that period, and some rulers lived there because of its central geographical location. Though Rameses II moved his residence to Tanis in the Delta during the thirteenth century B.C., he built a number of new structures at Memphis and engaged in large-scale renovation and restoration of old structures. As early as the sixteenth or fifteenth century B.C. Memphis began to take on a cosmopolitan character. Syrians, Phoenicians, Greeks, and Jews eventually established separate residential quarters there.

Though some decline set in at Memphis during the invasions and uncertainties of the first millennium B.C., the city remained virtually intact. Even after the founding of Alexandria in the fourth century B.C., the city maintained its greatness; some of the Ptolemies were crowned there instead of at the primary capital of Alexandria.

Memphis lost its importance as a religious center after the Christian emperor Theodosius closed its temples and ordered them torn down in the fourth century A.D. Then in the seventh century the Muslims began to build Cairo nearby and used Memphis as a stone quarry. But even as late as the twelfth and thirteenth centuries, Arab writers were amazed at the magnificence of the ruins there. These continued to disappear until there is now virtually nothing left at the site.

A column base lies in a cornfield at Memphis

A small sphinx of Ramses II stands in a little clearing at the site

Some sacrificial altars have been excavated in the temple of Ptah at Memphis

A 40-foot fallen statue of Ramses II lies under a protection erected by the Department of Antiquities

Early Dynastic Period (3100–2700 B.C.)

Kings of the first two dynasties ruled at This or Thinis, some three hundred miles south of Cairo; but they built Memphis as another administrative center. Tradition has it that Menes was responsible for building this new capital, which was erected on ground reclaimed from the Nile by diverting its course. The site was also neutral ground between the kingdoms of Upper and Lower Egypt. At first the city was known as White Walls because it was connected with the White Kingdom, whose victorious power it represented. From the

Sixth Dynasty on it held the name Menfe, from which is derived the Greek name Memphis. The Hebrews called the place Noph.[10] Though the First Dynasty kings were buried in the Thinis Abydos area, the Second Dynasty moved the royal cemetery to Saqqara, just west of Memphis.

Important developments of the period include advances in hieroglyphic writing and the perfection of the pottery wheel, increased foreign relations, and the establishment of the god-king idea. Throughout the period Egypt was involved in extensive

Mastaba of Mereruka at Saqqara

contact with the outside world—especially with Palestine, Syria, and Mesopotamia. Influences from Mesopotamia continued to be pronounced. Cedar was imported from Phoenicia and exploitation of the copper and turquoise of the Sinai began. The idea that the king was divine developed soon

A guide shows the method of quarrying large stones

after Egyptian unification and continued throughout ancient Egyptian history. After the pharaohs, Alexander the Great, the Ptolemies, and Roman emperors were also worshiped there.

Another important development of the period was the creation of the mastaba, an Arabic word meaning bench. A mastaba was a tomb, with the burial chamber and adjacent rooms for prized possessions below ground and a bench-like structure (from the side, appearing as a parallelogram) above ground, which had rooms as in the house that the deceased had enjoyed when alive. These rooms were filled with objects that the dead might use in the next life. One of the rooms was used for worship of the dead man and had a false door facing the entrance. In front of this door was an offering table where offerings to the dead might be put. The mastaba should face east, toward the rising sun; Re, the sun god, was ruler of the underworld and of the dead. The whole structure was originally built of brick. Stone masonry was first employed in the burial pit and later in the superstructure.

The attention of ancient Egyptians to preparing tombs and the body for burial does not mean that the Egyptians were a morbid people. On the contrary, they enjoyed life and sought to defy death and to

The Step Pyramid of King Djoser. *Lehnert & Landrock*

The Step Pyramid and its adjacent temple for worship of the divine king.

project as much of the enjoyment of this life as possible into the afterlife. Thus, as time went on, mummification developed, tombs became increasingly elaborate, and the number of objects deposited for the use of the dead in the next life increased rapidly. "You can take it with you" was a belief that seemed to motivate all who could afford to put things aside for enjoyment in the next life.

As an example of the amount of stuff stored with the kings in their "eternal homes," over forty thousand stone vessels, probably royal heirlooms of the Archaic period, were housed in the tomb complex of King Djoser (Zoser), builder of the step

The Mukattam quarries, now in the middle of Cairo, where stone for the pyramids was quarried.

pyramid.[11] These were in addition to all the objects with intrinsic value that tomb robbers had carried off.

The Old Kingdom, Dynasties 3 to 6 (c. 2700–2200 B.C.)

The Old Kingdom is especially known as the pyramid age. Construction of the pyramids began soon after 2700 B.C., with Djoser, (Zoser), second king of the dynasty, who gets credit for construction of the Step Pyramid.

Such a project was possible because by 2700 B.C. the Egyptians had developed techniques for cutting stones from the quarry. Usually they used copper chisels and wooden mallets to cut stones away from the rock on all sides except the bottom, where wedges were employed. Sometimes they drilled holes or cut a groove along a line where a block was to be split off. Then they drove in wedges of dry wood and wetted them to swell the wood and split off the block. Occasionally they lit a fire along the groove to heat the stone and then poured water over it to split it away from

the main rock. Bronze saws and other bronze implements were used in the finishing process, and abrasive materials such as quartz sand helped to smooth surfaces.

Some stone for the pyramids was cut on the spot. Much of the stone for the great pyramids of the Third and Fourth Dynasties came from the Mukattam quarries, now located in the middle of modern Cairo on the east bank of the Nile. These quarries had plenty of reasonably soft limestone that could be split out of the quarry and floated across the Nile at flood stage to the edge of the western desert.

The step pyramid was an experimental form, a transitional structure between the earlier mastaba and the later true pyramid. Djoser intended to build a moderate-sized mastaba. Then, as excavations at the site show, he moved to a three-stepped mastaba, then four, and finally a six stage structure. When completed, the step pyramid rose 207 feet high and measured 411 feet (east to west) by 358 feet (north to south) at the base. This, still fairly well preserved, is the oldest large structure of stone known in antiquity. Adjacent to the pyramid were a magnificent temple and other structures surrounded by a large sacred enclosure. The pyramid was solid; the burial chamber was below ground level under the pyramid.

Of course Djoser did not build his own tomb. The person who deserves all the credit as architect was his vizier, or prime

The Great Pyramid.

The Great Pyramid and other great stone pyramids had a smooth casing that stone robbers have removed. Some of The Great Pyramid's casing may still be seen at one corner.

tions about the pyramids are in order.

1. The Great Pyramid is not the only pyramid, even at Giza. There are ten pyramids there and at least seventeen other pyramid fields (places where pyramids are located) scattered throughout Egypt, with a total of 110 pyramids known to date.

2. Pyramids were not isolated items. For each there was at least a roadway from the wharf where stone-carrying barges docked to the pyramid itself, a lower temple where all could worship the deceased pharaoh, an upper temple where the royal family could worship, mastabas for the nobility (who sought to be near the king in death as they had been in life), and barracks for the workmen.

3. The pyramids were tombs, and it is totally unacceptable to hold that one of them, the Great Pyramid, was designed to be a revelation of God.[12]

4. The pyramids were not built by Hebrew slaves, as is often popularly believed, but by native Egyptians. The pyramids of the Old

minister, Imhotep, who at a later date was also credited with the beginnings of architecture, literature, and medicine. He was eventually deified and identified by the Greeks with their god of medicine, Asklepios.

The best-known pyramids of ancient Egypt date to the Fourth Dynasty and were constructed at Giza. And the best known of these is the Great Pyramid—the only one of the seven wonders of the ancient world surviving at present. Because so many know about only one pyramid of ancient Egypt or focus on one pyramid, some generaliza-

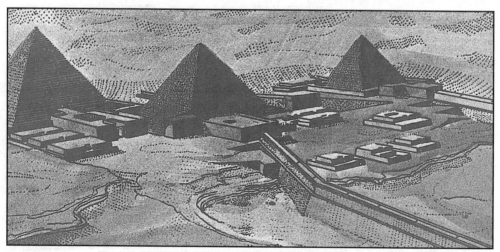

The fully-developed pyramid complex with roadways and mastabas

An air view of the Giza pyramid field

wealthy avoided that duty by hiring substitutes. So it was the peasants who really provided this labor. In addition, there were craftsmen and architects who performed the more specialized aspects of the construction.[13] Entire villages where these pyramid builders lived have been found.

5. The pyramids were not family mortuaries but only tombs for the pharaohs. Their queens were buried in separate tombs.

6. The reason for adoption of the pyramid form or at least for its continued use is a subject of considerable research and speculation. James H. Breasted, eminent Egyptologist at the University of Chicago, early in the twentieth century concluded that pharaohs used the pyramid as a symbol of the sun god, which stood in the holy of holies in the sun-temple at Heliopolis.[14] Edwards has shown that the stone symbol was originally conical instead of pyramidal, but he believes the ancient Egyptian architects turned the cone into the pyramid form. Moreover, he argues cogently that the pyramid represents the rays of the sun shining down on earth and observes that the rays of the sun in Egypt strike downward at about the same angle as the slope of the Great Pyramid. Additionally, he notes that, "The Pyramid Texts often describe the king as mounting to heaven on the rays of the

and Middle Kingdoms were constructed long before the Hebrews arrived. As noted subsequently, the Hebrews probably entered Egypt in 1876 B.C. as guests of the pharaoh. There were only seventy of them at the time (Exodus 1:5), and it took generations for the Hebrews to multiply to the point that they could provide a significant labor force. Pyramid construction passed out of fashion centuries before the Hebrews were made to do forced labor for the Egyptians.

Rosalie David has shown that most of the labor force that built the pyramids consisted of conscripted Egyptian peasants. Though in theory every Egyptian was obliged to work for the state a certain number of days each year, the

Sneferu, first king of the Fourth Dynasty, built the Bent Pyramid (c. 2600 B.C.) at Dahshur, about seven miles south of the Step Pyramid

sun."[15] So if the pyramid represents the sun's rays, it provides a means whereby the dead king could ascend to heaven.

The Great Pyramids at Giza

The Fourth Dynasty pharaohs were the great pyramid builders. After the first of the dynasty, Sneferu built a pyramid at Dahshur, and the second king, Khufu (Cheops), launched the Giza construction. The three great pyramids there date between about 2500 and 2400 B.C. Khufu's own pyramid, the Great Pyramid, covers thirteen acres; it originally rose to a height of 481 feet (still 451 feet high) and contains some 2,300,000-to-2,500,000 blocks of limestone: averaging 2.5 tons each. The angle of the sides is 51° 50°; stones are set together within the tiniest fraction of an inch. Someone has said the pyramid involves surfaces equal to optician's work on a scale of acres.

SOLAR BOATS

Why did the Egyptians build a wooden ship about 140 feet long and bury it in a pit next to the Great Pyramid?

The answer seems to lie in the ancient Egyptian myth of the journey of the Sun-god around the heavens in his Reed Float. Of course it would not do to bury a papyrus boat because it would quickly perish. A Lebanese cedarwood replica would be long-lasting. Though scholars do not really know the significance of the solar boat, they have suggested that it was meant to carry the dead king on his journey with the Sun-god. A good discussion appears in Nancy Jenkins' *The Boat Beneath the Pyramid* (New York: Holt, Rinehart & Winston, 1980).

Around the pyramid are five boat-shaped pits for ceremonial solar boats. One of these boats, 143 feet long and found in an excellent state of preservation in 1954 (disassembled into 1,224 pieces), has now been reassembled and installed in its own museum adjacent to the pyramid. Adjacent to Khufu's pyramid are three small pyramids for his wives. Even though almost all the casing stone was removed from the pyramid for construction in medieval Cairo, the Great Pyramid is still truly magnificent.

The second pyramid, that of Khafre (Chephren), stands to its original height of 447 feet because the upper fourth of the structure retains its original casing of smooth limestone. The angle of the sides is 52° 20°. Unlike the Great Pyramid, which has its burial chamber up inside the structure, the burial chambers of the second and third pyramids are below ground; this is usually the case with other pyramids. Accompanying the second pyramid is the Sphinx, which is a couchant lion with the head of Khafre. The Sphinx consists of a sculpted spur of rock standing up out of the desert floor and a lower body and paws built up with blocks of stone. It stands 66 feet high and 240 feet long. The third pyramid, that of Menkaure (Mycerinus), is now 204 feet high; it was originally 219.

The Great Pyramid, cross section looking west

1. entrance to descending corridor
2. unfinished chamber
3. ascending corridor
4. Grand Gallery
5. Queen's Chamber
6. unfinished shafts
7. shafts leading to surface from King's Chamber
8. shaft leading to descending corridor
9. King's Chamber

The interior of the Great Pyramid. The other pyramids were solid, with the burial chamber below the ground. The burial chamber is no. 9.

The second pyramid and the Sphinx

The Pyramid texts from an inner wall of the Sixth Dynasty pyramid of Unas at Saqqara
Lehnert & Landrock

Coffin text on the coffin of Amenhotep II, possible Pharoah of the Exodus.

On the walls of Fifth and Sixth Dynasty pyramids appear the pyramid texts, carved and painted inscriptions, magical spells, and hymns which were all supposed to facilitate the transit of the deceased to the afterlife and aid him there. When the pyramids passed out of fashion, the pyramid texts became the coffin texts during the Middle Kingdom and the *Book of the Dead* during the New Kingdom or Empire period.

Of course much more than pyramid construction took place during the Old Kingdom. Commercial contacts, established centuries earlier, continued unabated during this period. Especially heavy was the traffic between Egypt and Byblos in Phoenicia, and the Egyptians learned to construct ships for these longer hauls— ships that came to be known as "Byblos travelers."[16] Though the Egyptians imported numerous commodities from the north, they especially sought cedar and a variety of forest products of Lebanon. In exchange they sent large quantities of papyrus. By 2700 B.C. the Egyptians had learned how to make this "paper" by criss-crossing strips cut from the pith of the papyrus plant and

forming them into sheets.[17] So heavy was Egyptian involvement in Phoenicia, that some think Egypt actually maintained outposts of empire there during the Old Kingdom. Such scholars speak of an Old Empire, a Middle Empire, and a New Empire.

The artistic standards of Egypt were established during the Old Kingdom. The king and the gods were portrayed in a rather stiff and stylized form. Art tended to be conceptual rather than perceptual; that is, instead of reproducing what one sees, the artist painted what he knew to be there. For example, a school of fish became individual fish painted whole instead of being pictured naturally with one fish obscuring part of the fish next to it. In the same vein, a donkey with saddle bags was shown with the one facing the viewer reproduced in a natural way; the other one, known to be behind the donkey's back, was flipped up in the air above the donkey's back.

The importance of an individual determined his or her size in a pictorial representation. In a battle scene the pharaoh would be the largest figure, his commanding officers

The Egyptian artist reproduced what he knew was present, rather than what he saw. Thus he painted individual fish in a garden pool or individual trees around it as in this picture from the British Museum.

The importance of an individual determined size. Here the noble Nakht is largest, his wife next in size, and the children smallest yet—even though the wife and children might be about equal to him in size.
Lehnert & Landrock

Often art was more like a motion picture than a shapshot. Here wine-making from the tomb of Nakht (c. 1425 B.C.) shows stages in the process. *Lehnert & Landrock*

next in size, the common soldiers smaller yet, and the enemy troops smallest of all.

Egyptian art was intended to tell a story; much of it was more like a motion picture than a snapshot. A wine-making scene might include picking the grapes, treading out the juice (normally done by stomping with the bare feet), and storing the juice in jars.

Ancient Egyptian artists also observed a law of frontality. That is, they could not show the face and upper body naturally in profile but showed the eye wide open as in a frontal view with the rest of the face in profile. The torso was also twisted into a frontal view, while the lower body appeared in profile.

Evidently Egyptian medical knowledge was also developing during the Old Kingdom. Though the sources of knowledge of Egyptian medicine are the great papyri of the Middle Kingdom, there is some indication that medical knowledge claims far greater antiquity. Numerous archaic expressions appear in the Middle Kingdom texts. Perhaps Egyptians knew something of the circulation of the blood; they talked about feeling the "voice of the heart." Egyptian medical practice combined a hodgepodge of home remedies, charms and incantations, and scientific expertise.

MEDICAL KNOWLEDGE IN ANCIENT EGYPT

The use of magic or charms by doctors in ancient Egypt should not obscure the fact that physicians had a certain amount of scientific knowledge and administered some treatment reasonably effectively. Our sources of knowledge about their medical practice are especially the Ebers, Edwin Smith, Chester Beatty VI, Hearst, and the Berlin papyri.

Physicians understood that the pulse was the "voice of the heart," that there was a relationship between the nervous system and voluntary movements and between "vessels" and various parts of the body. That is, what we call veins, arteries, muscles, and tendons were known to transfer blood and other fluids, as well as disease, to other parts of the body and to control its functioning. The Egyptians had a good practical knowledge of the structure of the body.

Using diagnostic procedures, they decided whether an injury or disease was treatable and, if so, how they should proceed. They were especially effective in treating bone fractures with wooden splints and body casts. They knew how to pack wounds and treat sores or surgical incisions. Though they did not undertake internal surgery, they did perform brain surgery or skull repair with some success, as examinations of mummies reveal. They had numerous pharmaceuticals, including astringents, laxatives, diuretics, sedatives, and antacids. The medical papyri include careful instructions for the dispensing of medicines—as to exact dosage and the manner in which the medicine was to be taken internally, as well as external applications.

During the Sixth Dynasty the Old Kingdom began to break up. Scholars used to say this was almost solely a result of internal weakness, a combination of poor rulers, aggressive nobles, fiscal difficulties, Nubian incursions in the south and Asiatic attacks in the northeast. But more recent research has shown that a fundamental climatic change was especially responsible. Lack of rainfall in central Africa resulted in low levels of the annual flood of the Nile. Hot winds also scorched the crops and caused terrible dust storms.[18] The drought and famine brought repudiation of the divine pharaohs who could not maintain prosperity, and nobles who could protect their people and provide for them became supreme in their districts. The central government broke down.

Egypt in the Development of Culture

Achievements of Egypt in cultural development raise a question about her contribution to world culture in general. In recent years, in the spirit of multiculturalism, Afrocentrism, and the desire to give recognition to the black peoples of the earth, there has been a whole new emphasis on Egypt as the seedbed of world cultural development. In part, this approach has come in reaction to the supposedly racist view that Classical Greece provided the basis of Western Civilization. A flood of publication in books and journals, pro and con, has now appeared on this subject. Of special importance are Martin Bernal's *Black Athena: The Afroasiatic Roots of Classical Civilization*, Volume 1 (1987), Volume 2 (1991); Mary A. Lefkowitz and Guy M. Rogers, eds., *Black Athena Revisited* (1996); and Mary Lefkowitz, *Not Out of Africa* (1996). The claim that the Theban conquerors who established the Middle Kingdom or the much later Cleopatra were black is not substantiated. The Middle Kingdom rulers were native Egyptians, and Cleopatra was a Greek princess, the last of the Ptolemies to rule Egypt.[19] Aristotle could not, as charged, have gotten some of his ideas from the famous library in Alexandria, Egypt, because it was founded after his death.

What should be our reaction to this issue and the literature in the field?

First, that ancient Egypt had a high civilization has no real bearing on the subject of Afrocentrism or black history. Classicists in the past recognized the influence of Egypt on the Greek world; now that influence is better understood.

Second, Bernal and others have tried to show a great influence of Near Eastern culture on the West. That is clear. But we have known all along that Mesopotamia and Syria had influenced Egypt (as well as Greece and the West). The eminent John A. Wilson of the University of Chicago made the point in 1951.[20]

BLACK AFRICANS FROM CUSH

Black soldiers from Cush or the Sudan appear frequently in affairs of the ancient Near East. There are fifty-four references to Cush and the Cushites in the Bible. Cushites served in the Israelite army (2 Samuel 18:19–33). Conversely, Zerah the Cushite fought against Judah during the reign of Asa (2 Chronicles 14:10). The Assyrians got chariot horses from Cush in the days of Tiglath-Pileser III. Ebedmelech, a Cushite, was an official in Jerusalem in the days of Jeremiah and rescued the prophet after the Judean king Zedekiah had thrown him into a pit (Jeremiah 38:7–13; 39:16–18). J. Daniel Hays has made a useful study of the place of black Africans from Cush in the Bible and more broadly in the ancient Near East (See *Bible Review*, August 1998).

Third, we need to observe that ancient Egyptians, residents of Africa, were Hamitic and darker skinned (depicted in tomb paintings as dark yellowish-brown) but not black. The Egyptians understood that they were different from the Nubians to the south. And during part of their history ancient Egyptians dominated the black Nubians and used them as mercenaries in their armies. There was no considerable fusion of the two peoples. Unfortunately, all this investigation does not include a proper investigation of the early black cultures of Africa and their contributions to civilization. A better knowledge of ancient Egypt does not significantly contribute to Afrocentrism.

Fourth, one of the most glorious periods of Egyptian history occurred during the Hellenistic and Roman eras when the Greek Ptolemies ran the country and when Alexandria became one of the great cities of the world. Alexandria was the second city of the Roman Empire and a great center of Jewish and Christian thought. Obviously the Greco-Roman influence extending from Alexandria has nothing to do with the impact of black cultures on world civilization.

First Intermediate Period, Dynasties seven to eleven (c. 2200–2050 B.C.)

During the Old Kingdom there was political stability and prosperity. The Nile flood came predictably, not devastatingly. There was enough for all to eat. If one behaved himself, worked hard, and studied diligently in school, he could count on the proper promotions and general success in life. Familiar social, political, economic, and religious institutions remained constant and could be counted on to assume their regular place in the rhythm of life.

But now, during the First Intermediate Period, the old aristocracy had fallen. The central government had broken down; nobles ruled many districts and took the title of kings. Manetho's Seventh and Eighth Dynasties continued to rule weakly at Memphis. The Ninth and Tenth Dynasties arose at Herakleopolis (77 miles south of Cairo).

It was no longer true that if one did certain things he could count on success. The collapse of the whole philosophy of life of the Old Kingdom had brought a spiritual upset and spawned attempts at re-evaluation of life. Some of the literature of the time advocated the hedonistic approach of drowning one's problems in pleasure; some recommended a stoical approach—to steel one's self against the hardships of life; and some anticipated the coming of a messiah or deliverer who would right the wrongs of society and become the ideal shepherd of all.

The Middle Kingdom, Twelfth Dynasty (c. 2000–1780 B.C.)

Late in the Eleventh Dynasty, princes of Thebes (440 miles south of Memphis) struggled to restore order and royal control and were partially successful. Mentuhotep was especially victorious in uniting the country

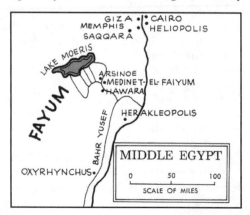

The god Amon, from a Theban temple relief

the hands of the nobles, he was promised it at the hands of the king. Thus there came an approach to a concern for human rights that was out of character for the region and the time. Their propaganda program also portrayed the pharaoh as concerned with responsible leadership instead of merely exercising authority. The pharaoh was the shepherd of his people. The art of the time represented the king with a worn look on his face—a result of constantly bearing the burdens of his people.

Kings were wise enough not to exhaust the treasury on great pyramids but undertook public works such as a massive effort to increase cultivable acreage in the Fayum, construction of a defensive wall across the Isthmus of Suez, or systematic working of the Sinai copper mines. Trade was extensive with Crete, Lebanon, Syria, and even Malta, and with the legendary land of Punt.

Scholars debate whether Middle Kingdom pharaohs dominated Palestine and Syria by means of military action or as part of their economic imperialism. It appears that invasion of Palestine was designed to deter Asiatic intrusion into Egypt and to protect Egyptian interests in the region. In fact, foreign involvement generally seems to have been designed to protect the flourishing arts and crafts and commerce of Egypt during the period. There does appear to have been some political control in Phoenicia during the Middle Kingdom, however, and there is no debate about Egyptian conquest and control of Nubia south to the second cataract. So in some sense it may be appropriate to speak of a Middle Empire instead of merely a Middle Kingdom.

The Middle Kingdom was a time when Amon began to emerge as the great god of Egypt. He was grafted onto the sungod Re as Amon-Re and came to supercede the gods who had formerly stood for Thebes. As god of the nation, he was to become the great imperial god under the Empire and thus to assume a universal quality.

A literary flowering occurred during the Middle Kingdom. Scientific literature is represented by such outstanding works as the Rhind Mathematical Papyrus and the Smith Surgical and Ebers Medical Papyrus.

once more, though he was destined to face further rebellion. Ultimately his vizier, Amenemhet, established the Twelfth Dynasty and the Middle Kingdom itself. Rulers of this dynasty were native Thebans who made their capital at Lisht in the Fayum and at Itj-towy near Memphis.

The six rulers of this dynasty took the names of Amenemhet and Senwosret (Sesostris). Each of them ruled some thirty years and most of them placed their eldest son on the throne as co-regent before their own death. Thus the danger of a usurper was eliminated. Since these kings did not dare to deprive the nobles of their largely independent power, a feudal condition existed during much of the period.

Unable to function as absolute kings, these pharaohs had to rule by persuasion and the development of good will. Their demonstration or exercise of ma'at, or social justice, was constantly emphasized. And if a person could not obtain ma'at at

The *Instructions of Merikare* portrays something of the wisdom literature of the period; and the *Tale of Sinuhe* introduces the genre or category of entertainment literature.

PAPYRUS

Papyrus was the writing material developed in very early times in ancient Egypt. Unfortunately there is much we do not know about the plant or its processing. For example, we do not know to what degree modern plants differ from the ancient variety. Nor is there much detailed information on how the Egyptians made papyrus.

We do know that Papyrus was a fresh water plant that especially grew along the banks of the Nile or one of the numerous river branches and channels in the Delta. Propagation came especially by root-stock division in spring or summer, but plants can be and have been grown from seeds.

For production of "paper" the stem of the plant (triangular in cross-section) was cut into segments, exposing the white pith. Next the rind was peeled away. Then the pith was thinly sliced into strips longitudinally. These were laid on a board side by side, just touching or slightly overlapping, to form the first layer. Then a second layer of strips was placed over them at right angles. Finally the two layers were pressed together or beaten with a wooden mallet and allowed to dry.

Apparently there was enough adhesive quality in the papyrus to serve as a glue to form a solid sheet. But it was necessary to moisten the material prior to pressing in order to cause the layers to stick together. We don't know much more about the ancient processes.

When sheets were dry, they were joined to form a roll, usually of twenty sheets. Joining was achieved by overlapping sheets slightly and applying a paste made from fine flour. Joins were secured and flattened with a mallet. Papyrus was not kept or supplied in the form of separate sheets. Only letters or short documents appear to have been kept single or folded as small packets.

Overall, the Middle Kingdom was a time when Egypt enjoyed increasing political stability, international reputation, commercial success, and artistic achievement. Though the monarchy began the period in a weakened position, it gradually overcame the power of the nobles and established the supremacy of the central government once more.

Papyrus plant

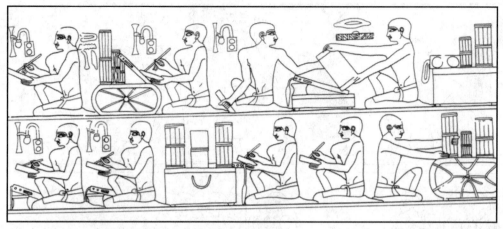

A scene from the tomb of Ti at Saqqara, c. 2400 B.C. It shows scribes writing on papyrus; one takes a roll from the keeper of rolls, another moves a bound stock of rolls; the papyri are stored in chests and oval containers.

The Joseph Narrative in Historical Context[21]

In a book on historical geography of Bible lands, it is always important to ask how or whether the biblical narrative intersects with secular history and whether in the process we find enrichment of our biblical understanding. Based on 1 Kings 6:1, we've pinpointed the Exodus to have occurred about 1446 B.C. The Hebrews had been in Egypt 430 years by that time (Exodus 12:40). Thus they would have entered the country in 1876 B.C., during the Middle Kingdom. By that year the famine was biting deep in Egypt and adjacent lands, and the seven years of plenty and Joseph's rise to power would have preceded that date.

With regard to the Egyptians in this biblical drama, the Bible does not say who was ruling at the time but only that the pharaoh accepted his dream of seven fat cows and seven lean cows as a revelation from God that there would be seven prosperous years followed by seven years of famine. He then decided to make Joseph a high official, perhaps vizier (a sort of prime minister) of Egypt, to prepare for the bad years ahead and to administer distribution of supplies when famine struck (Genesis 41:1–44). If we accept the year 1876 B.C. as the time Jacob and his extended family arrived, Sesostris III (1878–1840 B.C.) would have been ruling

at the time, according to a fairly well established chronology.

That means the years of bumper crops and the appointment of Joseph as administrator would have taken place during the reign of the ruling king's father, Sesostris II (1897–1878 B.C.). Although the Bible indicates no change of administration in the middle of the Joseph story, it is possible that such an event occurred. As crown prince, Sesostris III presumably would have agreed to the policies inaugurated by his father and would have continued them when he became king.

In exploring how biblical and Egyptian accounts interweave, it makes sense to question whether there is any evidence that Asiatics came to Egypt or were welcome there in Joseph's day or whether Egypt was fairly well sealed off from the outside world. Interestingly, a noble in the days of Sesostris II, Khnumhotep by name, painted a scene in his tomb of thirty-seven Asiatics (Semites) who he said came to do business with him in the sixth year of Sesostris II (1892).[22] The coming of this delegation is reminiscent of the band of Ishmaelites who came to sell Joseph into slavery in Egypt, and their visit would have roughly coincided with Joseph's arrival in Egypt. We also now know that Hyksos (see subsequent discussion) began to infiltrate the delta from Canaan during the twentieth century B.C.

A scene from the tomb of Khnumhotep (c. 1892) showing Semites coming to do business with him.

and came in increasing numbers during subsequent centuries.

Another relevant discussion includes the administration of Sesostris II. Did any of his actions relate to the Genesis account? Sesostris II was involved in a massive effort to improve the irrigation system in the Fayum and to increase farmland there. What he began his son and grandson continued, with the result that they added some 27,000 acres of arable land in and around the area of Fayum.[23] It is possible that the effort resulted from Joseph's encouragement to produce more heavily during the years of plenty to prepare for the famine.

The actions or involvement of Sesostris III offer far more correlation with the Genesis account than those of his father. Sesostris III was one of the most powerful pharaohs of ancient Egypt. First, he established and maintained Egyptian power in the south, effectively controlling the area to the second cataract. Significantly, one of his border patrols at the second cataract made a cryptic report in his third year, 1876 B.C., that "the desert is dying from hunger."[24] This appears to indicate famine conditions

and dates to the very year that Jacob and his extended family came into Egypt from Canaan because of drought there. Moreover, it appears that conditions in the south were so bad at this time that hungry and unemployed Sudanese sought mercenary service in the Egyptian army and police force. The use of Sudanese at this time "marked the beginning of the dependence of the Egyptians on foreign troops,"[25] and this dependence continued right on through the Empire period.

SESOSTRIS III AND JOSEPH

Sesostris III (1878–1840 B.C.) took the helm in Egypt during the Middle Kingdom when the position of the ruler was relatively weak. Nobles in various places exercised a high degree of independence. But Sesostris reestablished the absolute power of the pharaoh and also enjoyed success on the battlefield, especially in the South. Moreover, he considerably expanded acreage under cultivation in the Fayum area, south-west of Memphis.

If we have the biblical chronology correct, Joseph would have been a Vizier or Prime Minister during the reign of Sesostris III (Senwosret, Sen-Usert), and his activities may have been useful in the pharaoh's effort to increase his power (see Genesis 47:13–26). Moreover, his expansion of acreage in the Fayum may have been connected with efforts to prepare for the famine and recovery from it.

Second, Sesostris III, like those before him, sought to reverse the decentralization of the First Intermediate Period and restore the absolute control of the central government once more. But where others had tried and failed, he had been successful. All the literature on Sesostris III gives him credit for destroying the power of the provincial nobles and reducing them to the status of "political nonentities." It is interesting to note that Sesostris' resurgence of power coincided with the years of famine. Thus we may speculate that Joseph's action in

using the famine to buy up the land of Egypt and establish control over all its people (no doubt under Pharaoh's direction, see Genesis 47:13–26) was instrumental in Sesostris' success.

After the famine years, Sesostris III's exploits continued to be noteworthy. To facilitate commerce and military action in the South, he cut a channel through a granite barrier at the first cataract —260 feet long, 34 feet wide, and 26 feet deep. He also launched a campaign up into Palestine and seems to have been victorious in the area of Shechem, but we do not have his official account of the foray. One of his officers did leave a record of the battle, however.[26] Absence of evidence to the contrary, it does not appear that Sesostris had plans to build an empire in Palestine.

A final connection between Egyptian life and the Joseph narrative concerns the embalming of Jacob and Joseph.[27] After Jacob died, Joseph gave orders for the physicians to embalm his father. They took forty days to complete the process, and Jacob was mourned for seventy days. When Joseph died he also was embalmed according to the practice of the Egyptians (Genesis

Anubis, god of the dead, watches over a mummy. *Lehnert & Landrock*

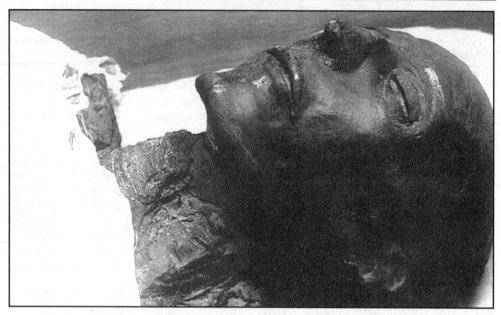

Mummified head of Seti I, Cairo Museum.
Lehnert & Landrock

50:2–3, 26). This immediately raises the question of how the Egyptians embalmed or mummified their dead.

Mummification in ancient Egypt was well underway by the Third Dynasty. Since practices varied considerably over the centuries, comments here center on the Middle Kingdom (the days of Joseph) and the Empire (the days of Moses and the Exodus). In trying to preserve the body, the Egyptians obviously sought to remove the liquid, about 75 percent of the body weight. This they did by use of a dehydrating agent, natron (composed of sodium bicarbonate and sodium chloride), available in considerable quantities in Egypt.

In the Middle Kingdom they coated the body with dry natron. But first they commonly cut an abdominal incision and removed the liver, lungs, stomach, and intestines, which were separately treated and put in four canopic jars, each with the head of a deity as a stopper. The heart and brain were left in place. When the body was ready for burial, it was washed with a natron bath and anointed with cedar oil and other ointments. It was customary to stuff the chest and abdominal cavities with linen soaked in resin. Then the body was

wrapped with endless yards of linen strips soaked in resin, and often resin was poured over the mummy when it was partially

A canopic jar with the head of the jackal god Duamutef, one of the sons of Horus, who watched over the stomach

A cartonnage coffin, normally gilded and painted to provide a portrait of the corpse, from the Empire Period

wrapped. Finally the body was placed in a painted wooden coffin inscribed with religious formulae.

During the Empire period several more details were added. At that time the brain was now extracted, through the nose. There was more attention to packing the abdominal cavity and inserting packing between the skin and bones to fill out the body. Thimbles were used to hold the nails in place, the body was covered with a thick coating of molten resin to prevent moisture from entering the pores, and the outside of the wrapped mummy was normally painted.

So it was in mummified condition that Joseph was to take Jacob's body for burial in Palestine. And it was in the mummified state that the children of Israel ultimately carried Joseph's body out of Egypt at the time of the Exodus. But hundreds of years were to elapse before his corpse was to accompany them out of Egyptian slavery to the land promised as an everlasting possession to their great forebear Abraham, father of the faithful.

Second Intermediate Period, Thirteenth through Seventeenth Dynasties (c. 1780–1570 B.C.)

The Egyptian state collapsed fairly suddenly soon after 1800 B.C. Scholars are still puzzled as to why it happened. Perhaps it was because the monarchy had lost its ability to rule; the last sovereign of the Twelfth Dynasty was a woman and the line may have been dying out. There was unrest in the eastern Mediterranean world and Egypt may have been losing some of the benefits of its cultural and commercial imperialism; its commercial prosperity declined. Also, Nubians were constricting Egyptian power in the South and Asiatics were moving into the northeast. All of these factors may have played a part, but we still do not understand why the Middle Kingdom came to an end when it did.

Historical details and the chronology of the Second Intermediate Period are hard to unscramble. Evidently the Thirteenth Dynasty continued to maintain itself weakly at Thebes. In fact, Thebans continued to rule throughout the period. During the Thirteenth Dynasty a line established its independence as the Fourteenth Dynasty and ruled at Xois in the western delta until about 1600 B.C. Meanwhile, a powerful line of Hyksos kings, six in number, ruled as the Fifteenth Dynasty from around 1720 to around 1570 B.C. from their capital at Avaris in the eastern delta. They were successful in dominating most of Egypt and enjoyed far-flung commercial ventures—from Mesopotamia to Crete. Concurrently, a Sixteenth Dynasty of

The Hyksos get credit for introducing the vertical loom (as shown in this scene of women weaving and washing) and such musical instruments as the lyre, long-necked lute and tambourine, to Egypt (as shown). From Egyptian tomb paintings

Hyksos kinglets controlled minor territories wherever the Hyksos kings could not squelch them. Meanwhile the Seventeenth Dynasty (native Egyptians), though subservient to the Hyksos, governed much of the Nile valley for several hundred miles north of the first cataract at Aswan.

All this sounds confusing and several of Manetho's dynasties were contemporaneous. To summarize, the situation was something like this. The Thirteenth and Seventeenth Dynasties ruled at Thebes, while the Fourteenth ruled in the western delta and the Fifteenth and Sixteenth ruled in the eastern delta. Of all these, the Fifteenth is especially important as a Hyksos dynasty that dominated most of the country, even if it did not directly rule it.

The old view is that the Hyksos invaded Egypt and in a violent conquest took over the country. Now it appears that the Hyksos infiltrated the eastern delta in increasing numbers between about 1950 and 1720 B.C. and about the latter date

defeated the Egyptians in battle and established their dynasty and capital at Avaris in the eastern delta. This they were able to do with minimal military action because they were already a large element in society, because the Egyptians were comparatively weak in the north, and because they had superior weapons. Though they never ruled southern Egypt directly, the Theban kings were puppets under their control. The Hyksos controlled Egypt until Thebans were able to throw off their shackles around 1570 B.C.

Those who assign late dates to the patriarchs and the Exodus commonly place Joseph and Jacob's entrance into Egypt during the period of Hyksos rule, c. 1700–1570 B.C. They argue that it would be natural for other Asiatics to welcome Hebrews into the general area they had come to dominate. Those who hold the early chronology say that the Hebrews and the Hyksos were entering Egypt and multiplying there about the same time. When the Hyksos came to

Upper Egypt with the cities of Thebes and Amarna, important during the Empire Period

from the Egyptian historian Manetho in the third century B.C., who said that it meant "shepherd kings." Now we know that the ancient Egyptian terminology really meant "rulers of foreign lands" and that the Egyptians often referred to them simply as *Aamu,* meaning "Asiatics." This still does not specify who the Hyksos were. Hitti spoke of them as "a horde, an unclassified goulash of humanity which the melting pot of the eastern Mediterranean had spilled over the edge and washed down into Egypt." He continued by observing that among them were Semites and non-Semitic peoples—including Hurrians, Hittites, and possibly several other minor peoples.[28] The predominant element among them was certainly Semitic. At the height of their power the Hyksos controlled the Delta of Egypt and much of southern Egypt, all of Palestine, and at least part of Syria. They left extensive remains at various biblical sites (e.g., Hazor).

power, the Hebrews, who had been welcomed by native Egyptians, continued to find a congenial atmosphere under the domination of other Semites.

Conversely, when the native Egyptians reasserted their power and tossed out the Hyksos or oppressed or enslaved those remaining (c. 1570 B.C), the Hebrews fell into bondage along with other Asiatics. The biblical statement that "there arose a new king over Egypt, who did not know Joseph" (Exodus 1:8 NKJV) is commonly taken to mean that there rose up a new king of the native Egyptian or Theban line that not only literally did not know Joseph but was not sympathetic to the interests of Joseph's people and was determined to assert Egyptian interests over those of Asiatics.

Placing the Hyksos in history does not identify who they were. We get the name

The papyrus (left) and lotus, symbols of Lower and Upper Egypt

Obelisks in the Temple of Karnak at Luxor. The one on the left, Hatshepsut's, 97 feet tall, is the highest in Egypt and weighs about 700,000 pounds. Thutmose I erected the one on the right.

The Hyksos did not leave us an account of their doings and of their times. This partly is because they ruled in the Delta, where the heavy moist soil is not conducive to preservation of antiquities[29] and partly because of the efforts of the Egyptians to erase any memory of them. When the Egyptians did choose to talk about them at a later time, it was to record victories over them. Also they painted a picture of the Hyksos with "black borders," as merciless tyrants who imposed a harsh rule, and as cultural barbarians.

Actually the picture that archaeologists are able to paint is far different. The Hyksos do not appear to have been tyrants, and they made numerous contributions to Egyptian life that fundamentally changed life along the Nile. Of special importance in overthrowing Hyksos control and in establishing the Egyptian Empire thereafter was their introduction of the horse and chariot (the ancient equivalent of a tank as far as psychological effects are concerned), the powerful composite bow, new types of daggers and swords, and a war helmet. Their contributions to peaceful arts were numerous too. New techniques in bronzeworking, an improved potter's wheel, improved methods of spinning and weaving (including the vertical loom), new breeds of cattle, new vegetable and fruit crops, and new musical instruments (including a lyre, oboe, tambourine, and long-necked lute) are among Hyksos contributions to Egyptian life.

Whatever good we can say for the Hyksos, they were still hated foreigners to the Egyptians. And their ability to conquer and rule over the Egyptians for an extended period of time had rudely dashed the proud superiority of the Egyptians. Finally pharaohs of the Seventeenth Dynasty at Thebes started the war for liberation—actually using Hyksos weapons against them. Probably Sekenenre and certainly Kamose and his successor Ahmose led the fight against the Hyksos. Ahmose succeeded in capturing the Hyksos capital of Avaris, in driving the Hyksos rulers from the country, and in effectively pursuing them up into Palestine. With him began the Eighteenth Dynasty and the New Kingdom or Empire.

The New Kingdom, Eighteenth through Twentieth Dynasties (c. 1570–1080 B.C.)

The New Kingdom or Empire period of Egyptian history holds tremendous interest for tens of millions of people all over the world. For the Jew it is the time when Passover originated in connection with the redemption and escape from Egypt. For Christians Passover is of course connected with the Last Supper and the sacrament of Communion. Both Jews and Christians are also interested in discovering who the pharaoh of the Exodus may have been and when the Exodus may have occurred. This glorious period "when Egypt ruled the East," when it built tremendous monuments all over the country, and when it deposited its divine pharaohs in tombs in the Valley of the Kings holds great attraction for historians

Temple of Hatshepsut at Deir el Bahri

Atlas of Ancient Egypt; and on the basis of their conclusions it is hard to work out a correlation with the biblical account.

Ahmose (1570–1546 B.C.) gets credit for launching the Eighteenth Dynasty and the Empire or New Kingdom as well. Riding a wave of nationalistic enthusiasm, he inaugurated a policy of aggression in Western Asia, initially aimed at Hyksos holdings there. After a three-year siege of the Hyksos stronghold of Sharuhen in southern Palestine, he was successful in taking that bastion. Ahmose was even more determined to advance Egyptian power in Nubia, however, and recovered the country as far as the second cataract. He was also successful in subduing nobles who had managed to gain independence from the central government during the Hyksos era.

Amenhotep I (1546–1525 B.C.) continued Egyptian advances against the Nubians in the south, conquering beyond the third cataract. He also campaigned victoriously against the Libyans at the northwest edge of the Delta. Dying without a son to succeed him, Amenhotep I was followed on the throne by his sister Ahmose, who married a Thutmose (Thutmose I), probably a relative. Thutmose I (1525–1508 B.C.) also

and tourists alike. And people never seem to tire of hearing about the boy-king Tutankhamon (Tut) and looking at books that portray the magnificent art works from his tomb. In short, there is a general fascination with the New Kingdom of Egypt.

In order to think in any meaningful way about the New Kingdom, it is necessary to have a chronological framework. I have generally followed the dates advocated in George Steindorff and Keith C. Seele (of the University of Chicago) in *When Egypt Ruled the East*. This is essentially the same chronological system used by T. G. H. James and the staff of the Department of Egyptian Antiquities at the British Museum, in *An Introduction to Ancient Egypt*. A very neat correlation with the biblical account can be worked out on the basis of the Steindorff and Seele dating system.

John A. Wilson (also of the University of Chicago) in *The Burden of Egypt* and Jack Finegan (Pacific School of Religion) in *Light from the Ancient Past* modify the foregoing systems slightly, and on their basis we would produce a different pharaoh of the Exodus from the conclusions derived from Steindorff and Seele. It is important to note, however, that other scholars modify the chronology even further, for example, John Baines and Jaromir Malek in

A ship of Hatshepsut of the type used in trading expeditions to the Land of Punt

A statue of Thutmose III in the Cairo Museum
Lehnert & Landrock

marry his daughter Merytre to a son by a minor wife (Thutmose III, 1504–1450 B.C.). Rehearsing the details of Egyptian sovereigns is necessary to discover how the biblical account of the Exodus may fit into the Egyptian context.

When the sickly Thutmose II died in 1504 B.C., his wife Hatshepsut[30] took over as regent for her young stepson, Thutmose III. In a year or two she or a group of powerful officials arranged for her coronation, and she ruled Egypt as sovereign in her own right until 1482 B.C. (according to Steindorff and Seele) or 1486 B.C. (according to John A. Wilson).

It should be noted that many have suggested that Hatshepsut was the daughter of Pharaoh who rescued Moses and brought him up. If so, Moses' birth must have occurred during the reign of Thutmose I, whose daughter Hatshepsut was. If the Exodus took place in 1446 B.C. and Moses was about eighty at the time, his birth took place in 1526 B.C. or possibly 1525 B.C.—the first year of the reign of Thutmose I. Some speculate that with no son of her own, Hatshepsut could have had in mind grooming Moses, her adopted son (Exodus 2:10), as her successor as pharaoh of Egypt.

But Moses did not stay around to become pharaoh. He identified with his own people and fled from Egypt at the age of forty, in around 1486 B.C. If John A. Wilson's chronology is right in concluding that Hatshepsut died in that year and the dynamic Thutmose took the throne, there could be special reasons why Moses left the country. Perhaps Thutmose would have disposed of him if he had stayed around.

Of course all this discussion of Hatshepsut is merely interesting speculation. Probably Hatshepsut was only a young child when Moses was born, hardly old enough to have thoughts about adopting a baby, ruling Egypt, or having a successor. In fact Moses may have been born before Hatshepsut was. The daughter of Pharaoh who rescued Moses may have been no special person; pharaohs had numerous concubines and numerous daughters. And she need have no ulterior motive in bringing him up. The important

expanded Egypt's Nubian holdings and mounted an offensive in Syria. Thus he could claim an empire that stretched from the third cataract of the Nile to the Euphrates. Thutmose I began the practice of carving out royal tombs in the Valley of the Kings west of Thebes, a practice that continued throughout the New Kingdom. It is possible that Moses was born at the very beginning of his reign.

Evidently the only surviving child of the union of Thutmose and Ahmose was a daughter, Hatshepsut, who was married to Thutmose II (1508–1504 B.C.), a son of Thutmose I by a secondary princess. Thutmose II had to quell rebellious Nubians but little else is known of his reign. Since his marriage to Hatshepsut produced two daughters but no sons, he decided to thing is that Moses was rescued and that he was given a superior education that prepared him to lead his people and to write the Pentateuch. That education at court would have included reading and writing hieroglyphic and hieratic scripts of Egyptian, and studying foreign languages of the Near East (Akkadian and Canaanite dialects, among others), mathematics, possibly music, and rhetoric. Rigorous physical and military training would also have been included.[31]

Whether or not Hatshepsut had any connection with Moses, she was a remarkable woman, ruling Egypt with a firm hand for almost twenty years (1504–1482 B.C.) in what was clearly a man's world. She dressed as a king, took all the male royal titles except one—"the Mighty Bull," which was hardly applicable to her—and even wore the ceremonial false beard, as smooth-shaven Egyptian kings did. During her reign Egypt enjoyed economic prosperity for the first time since the Middle Kingdom. Her building activities were considerable, including her magnificent mortuary temple at Deir el-Bahri near Thebes and the erection of two great obelisks at the Temple of Karnak at Luxor. The one remaining shaft of rose granite from far away Aswan stands to a height of 97½ feet and weighs about 700,000 pounds. She also conducted trade expeditions to the land of Punt on the Somali coast. She owed much of her success to her very capable vizier Senenmut.

Whether Hatshepsut died a natural death or met an untimely end at the hands of Thutmose III (1482–1450 B.C.) is unknown but she probably died a natural death. In any event, Thutmose promptly took over the realm and within seventy-five days had assembled an army and was leading it north into Palestine-Syria to subjugate rebellious princes there. A confederation of 330 princelings of the region decided to make a stand near Megiddo in northern Palestine. Such a diverse host was no match for Thutmose's army when he sprung a surprise attack. But while the Egyptian army was plundering the enemy camp, the king of Megiddo and his forces managed to retreat behind his almost impregnable fortifications.

THUTMOSE III, NAPOLEON OF ANCIENT EGYPT

Thutmose III (c. 1482–1450 B.C.) strode across the landscape of the eastern Mediterranean world as a great conqueror. Many have called him the Napoleon of ancient Egypt. He conducted seventeen campaigns north into Palestine and Syria, as well as forays south of Aswan into Nubia. In the process he built the Egyptian Empire. Its continuance he assured by carrying hostage to Egypt the sons of defeated princes. Thoroughly brainwashed, they were later sent home to take the thrones of their fathers and to be loyal subjects of Egypt.

It took Thutmose III a seven-month siege, from our May to December, to starve out the defenders. When he did, he showed remarkable political skill or wisdom. Instead of killing the princes holed up there and taking large numbers of captives, as normally would occur, he took plunder, forced the princelings to swear an oath of loyalty to him and sent them home—winning a certain amount of goodwill in the process. On this occasion and subsequently he carried off sons of local chiefs as hostages and trained them at court. Brainwashed in this way, they later returned home to take their fathers' thrones and tended to be reasonably loyal subjects of the Egyptian pharaoh.

Though Thutmose's great initial victory at Megiddo cowed the northern Canaanites, it did not break their will to resist. Thutmose found himself campaigning in Canaan almost annually during the next two decades for a total of seventeen expeditions. Thutmose also campaigned in Nubia late in his reign and controlled territory beyond the fourth cataract of the Nile. Thus the Egyptian Empire came to extend from the fourth cataract of the Nile to the Euphrates. Increased contacts to the north required improved roads from Egypt across

A modern Egyptian making bricks

Semitic slaves making bricks, as pictured in the tomb of Rekmire, Vizier of Thutmos III, possibly Pharaoh of the Oppression.

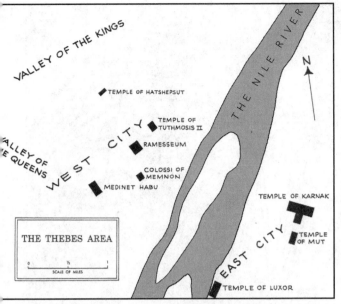

THE THEBES AREA

glorify the pharaoh as sportsman, athlete, and warrior that
was to last for several generations; he had the powers of a
god in conducting the affairs of
men.

If one accepts the early date
of the Exodus, Thutmose III is
often considered to have been
the pharaoh of the great
oppression of the Hebrews.
Reminiscent of the biblical
account of Hebrew slaves
being forced to make bricks
without straw (Exodus 5:6–19)
is a brickmaking scene in the
tomb of Rekhmire, vizier for
Upper Egypt during the reign
of Thutmose III.[32] The painting
shows bearded Asiatic foreigners making bricks. The process
involved breaking up Nile mud with mat-
tocks, moistening it with water, mixing it
with sand and chopped straw, forming it in
wooden molds, and baking it in the sun.

the northern Sinai and more extensive
naval activity in the Mediterranean. A
whole new bureaucracy developed under
Thutmose's rule to provide the infrastruc-
ture to maintain the empire.

What started out as an Egyptian impulse
to punish the Hyksos had turned into a
spirit of imperialism, which enjoyed a sense
of power in victory. As the frontiers
expanded, there was almost always a peril
to attend to somewhere during subsequent
generations; some of them were real and
some remote. Thus the sense of security
that Egyptians had enjoyed during earlier
centuries when they were shut up in their
valley home gave way to a feeling of insecurity. And as the god Amon-Re smiled on
Egyptian military efforts, he was rewarded
with spoils of war and handsome gifts. In
time the temples gained so much wealth
and power that they came to exercise great
clout in political and economic circles.
Especially great was the power of the
priesthood of Amon at the Temple of
Karnak.

Thutmose III was one of the greatest of
Egypt's ancient pharaohs. A conqueror and
empire builder, he is often called the
"Napoleon of ancient Egypt." Moreover,
there was hardly a city of any size in the
kingdom where he did not engage in building activities. With him began an effort to

If Thutmose III was the pharaoh of the
great oppression, his son, Amenhotep II
(1452–1425 B.C.), should have been the
pharaoh of the Exodus. Serving briefly as
co-regent with his father, he enjoyed an
easy transition to sole ruler over the empire.
Unusually tall and strong for an ancient
Egyptian king, he sought to be known for
his prowess as a sportsman and his ruth-
lessness as a warrior. He had a chance to
prove himself on the battlefield in two
major campaigns into western Asia. In the
first he marched all the way to the
Euphrates to subdue rebellious towns.
During the second, in his ninth year, he confined his activities to Palestine, where he
took about 90,000 captives, including 127
Asiatic princes.[33] The fact that such a large
number could be absorbed in Egyptian
enterprises shows the expansion of
Egyptian manufactures and crafts at the
time. He also penetrated far south into the
Sudan, extending Egypt's control to the
fourth cataract, about 800 miles upstream
from Aswan.

Amenhotep was buried in the Valley of
the Kings and his body was undisturbed
until his sarcophagus was opened in 1898.

Amenhotep II granted life by the god Osiris, from his tomb in the Valley of the Kings.
Lehnert & Landrock

The fact that we have his mummy (now in the Cairo Museum) does not prove he was not the pharaoh of the Exodus. Some have claimed that if he were the pharaoh of the Exodus, he should have drowned in the Red Sea, but the Exodus narrative says only that some Egyptian troops who followed the Israelites were drowned. There is no direct reference to Pharaoh in that context (Exodus 14:26–28).

As noted above, Egyptian chronology is not absolute. If we should follow the chronology of John A. Wilson, Thutmose III would have reigned from 1468 to 1436 B.C. and therefore could have been both the pharaoh of the great oppression and the Exodus. Though the position is taken here that Amenhotep II was the pharaoh of the Exodus, the great plagues occurring at the time would have been the same during either reign. Also the route of the Exodus and the crossing of the Red Sea would have been the same. Of course they would also have been the same if one subscribes to the late date of the Exodus (c. 1274 B.C.).

The Plagues and the Exodus

When Moses came to rescue the Hebrews from Egypt, he had no illusions about the difficulty of the task. He had lived at the court for forty years and knew the iron grip with which Pharaoh ruled the land. Moreover, God had told him He would harden[34] Pharaoh's heart (Exodus 4:21). What's more, no sooner had Moses started to appeal to Pharaoh than the Hebrews blamed Moses for their increased oppression (Exodus 5:20–23).

THE PLAGUES AND EGYPTIAN RELIGION

The ten plagues were a frontal attack on Egyptian theology and on Egyptian religious beliefs and practices. Particularly, turning the Nile River to blood in the first plague, attacked the very basis of all Egyptian life and the gods of the Nile. Without

Amenhotep II, warrior and sportsman, engaged in target practice.

the Nile there could have been no Egypt.

The fifth plague involved an affliction of the cattle of the land—the whole bovine family was worshiped: the bull, the cow, and the calf. This plague rendered those animals helpless, sick and dying.

The ninth plague blotted out the face of the sun and brought intense darkness over the land. The sun, along with the Nile, was recognized as the source of all life and during the Empire (when the plagues occurred) was primarily worshiped as Amon-Re.

The tenth plague, the most terrifying of all, brought the death of the firstborn—of all Egyptians, including the firstborn of the divine pharaoh and the priests. It demonstrated that the gods of Egypt could not protect their priests or their people.

While all of the plagues affected the religion of the Egyptians in some capacity, the first, fifth, ninth, and tenth plagues struck especially close to home.

Pharaoh found it difficult to grant the demands of Moses—to permit the Hebrews to leave Egypt to offer sacrifice or for Pharaoh to pay tribute to the God of heaven as the only God worthy of praise. Pharaoh was, after all, supposed to be a living god himself and to have sole rule over his people. The process of bringing the king to terms is called the ten plagues, and it involved a complete discrediting of the gods of Egypt.

The first plague—turning the Nile waters to blood (Exodus 7:14–21)—attacked the very life of the nation, for Egypt was the gift of the Nile. Hapi was worshiped as the spirit of the Nile; and the river waters, considered to be the bloodstream of Osiris, god of the underworld, became a plague to them.

Frogs became totally repulsive to Egyptians during the second plague (Exodus 8:1–15). This was particularly poignant because Heket or Heqt, a goddess with a frog's head, was the symbol of resurrection and an emblem of fertility and was believed to assist women in childbirth.

The third plague—(almost invisible gnats with a painful sting (Exodus 8:16–19) does not as specifically relate to the theology of Egypt, but the gnats certainly would

A pharaoh in a festival robe, from an Empire period relief

that were worshiped. Several bulls and cows were considered sacred. The Apis bull was the sacred animal of the god Ptah. Hathor, goddess of love, beauty, and joy, was represented by the cow. Commonly she appeared in human form wearing on her head the sun-disc flanked by a cow's horns. This goddess is often portrayed as a cow suckling the king and giving him divine nourishment. Mnevis, a sacred bull worshiped at Heliopolis, was associated with the sun god Re. It appeared with the solar disc and the sacred uraeus serpent between its horns.

In the sixth plague (Exodus 9:8–11) Moses threw ashes into the air in the sight of Pharaoh, and they caused a terrible plague of boils that apparently became open and running sores. The magicians were infected and could not stand before Pharaoh, either to duplicate or stop the miracle. Presumably the priesthood were afflicted along with the rest of the populace, and the Egyptian gods of healing, such as Sekhmet (represented as a lioness or a woman with a lion's head), were powerless to protect the Egyptians.

Entrance to the Serapeum at Memphis, where mummified Apis bulls were buried.

have greatly irritated the king, the royal family, and the priesthood and therefore would have affected the national religion in that way.

Swarms (Exodus 8:20–32) are not identified in the Hebrew text describing the fourth plague, but they are often considered to involve flies; and the translation of the Septuagint (produced in Egypt around 250 B.C.) identified them as the blood-sucking dogfly, which again would have greatly annoyed the divine pharaoh and the priesthood, along with everyone else.

The fifth plague involved some sort of affliction of cattle and other domestic animals (Exodus 9:1–7). The judgment resulted in a widespread loss of personal property, including animals used for agriculture, warfare, and members of the bovine family

Likewise during the seventh plague, when fire and hail destroyed crops (flax and barley) and cattle (Exodus 9:12–35), gods that were supposed to protect the crops were unable to do so. Especially the sky-goddess Nut was powerless to help—or even became a plague to them.

The eighth plague—the plague of locusts (Exodus 10:1–20)—brought terrible suffering on the mass of Egyptians, destroying their farm income and bringing many to the verge of starvation with the loss of their food supply. The gods of agriculture were powerless to protect the crops. By this time the patience of the Egyptians was wearing thin, and some even dared to question Pharaoh's wisdom in dealing with the Hebrews (Exodus10:7).

The gods of Egypt were especially discredited by the ninth plague (Exodus 10:21–29)—three days of darkness so thick it could be "felt" (Exodus 10:21). We might say, "The darkness was so heavy or thick one could almost cut it with a knife." One day of darkness might have been manageable. But three days of darkness in a society where there was no public lighting and little oil available for oil lamps meant that people simply could not stir from their homes to work or even to fill their water jugs.

The sun was especially revered in Egypt, where it almost always shone brightly, and along with the Nile was recognized as the source of all life. The sun was primarily worshiped as Amon-Re (the god of empire during the Eighteenth Dynasty) and as Aton (the sun disc), the deity of the Amarna Age. Of course deities connected with worship of the moon and stars also lost face in the ninth plague. After this catastrophe Pharaoh told Moses to leave his presence forever and to return only on pain of death (Exodus10:28).

The tenth plague (Exodus 12:29–36) involved the death of the firstborn of the Egyptians, including the firstborn of Pharaoh (v. 29) and of all the priests of the land, and of all the livestock. This judgment humiliated the "divine" pharaoh and demonstrated that various gods of Egypt could not protect their priests or their people. God had achieved the release of His people after 430 years in Egypt (Exodus 12:40).

An epitaph for a sacred bull at the Serapeum at Memphis.

Those who reject the miraculous often try to explain the ten plagues as simply heightened natural phenomena. But the miraculous nature of the plagues is supported in at least five ways: (1) *Intensification*—far beyond ordinary occurrence; (2) *Prediction*—specific times set for the coming or removal of some of the plagues (Exodus 8:23; 9:5; 9:18; 10:4; 8:10; 9:29); (3) *Discrimination*—some of the plagues affected Egyptians but not the Hebrews in Goshen (Exodus 8:22; 9:4; 9:26); (4) *Orderliness*—orderly increase in severity until the death of the firstborn; and (5) *Moral or spiritual purpose*—to discredit the gods of Egypt (Exodus 12:12), to persuade Pharaoh that Yahweh is God (Exodus 9:27; 10:16), and to reveal God as Savior in rescuing Israel from the Egyptians (Exodus 14:30).[35]

Egyptian records tell us nothing about the plagues and the Exodus. At that time in Egyptian history records consisted largely

The sun was worshipped as Aton during the Amarna Age. The Aton is represented by the sun disc with life-giving rays extending from it, pictured here on the back of Tutankhamon's throne. Cairo Museum.
Lehnert & Landrock

of things like inscriptions on the walls of tombs, monuments describing the victories of kings in battle, medical and mathematical texts, and myths connected with the worship of the gods and the afterlife. The kings did not record anything uncomplimentary to themselves. They as gods were always supposed to be victorious in battle, and the scribes did a good job of portraying them as victorious and invincible. The

The goddess Hahor, goddess of love and beauty, wearing on her head the sun-disc flanked by cow's horns

nobles painted scenes on their tomb walls of waving fields of grain, healthy herds of cattle, and abundance of every sort that could somehow set them up for a prosperous afterlife.

The situation was a little different in New Testament times when men away in the Roman army and boys away at school wrote letters home commenting on all sorts of personal and social matters. Some of these papyrus items have been found in Egyptian "rubbish heaps."

The plagues were only a brief episode in the history of Egypt, not designed to destroy the country nor punish it on a continuing basis, but only to spring the Hebrews from Egyptian bondage and to bring recognition of God's power and glory. The rich land of Egypt was resilient and no doubt soon returned to normal.

Route of the Exodus and Crossing of the Red Sea

The route of the Exodus appears in Exodus 12–19 and Numbers 11–12, 33. From the town of Rameses in the eastern delta they went south to Succoth in the Wadi Tumilat and then farther south. Since

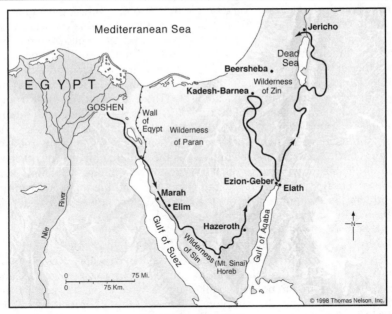

The Route of the Exodus
Courtesy Thomas Nelson

this is not an archaeological study, it is not necessary to deal with the pros and cons of identifying the sites that are named.[36]

An important reason why they went south instead of east from the Wadi Tumilat, we now know, was the existence of a wide canal that ran from the Mediterranean to Lake Timsah in the Bitter Lakes region. This canal was dug not for irrigation purposes but as a defense against Asiatics and for containment of runaway slaves. Well over two hundred feet wide at the water level, it was an effective deterrent.[37] Hoffmeier surmises that this canal is hinted at in Exodus 14:3. There Pharaoh is quoted as saying of the Israelites, "They are wandering aimlessly in the land; the wilderness [desert] has closed in on them" (NRSV). He is suggesting that the desert boundary has hemmed them in and Egyptian chariots may now pursue and mow down the fleeing captives.[38]

Scripture says that at that point God worked a miracle and they were able to walk across the Red Sea and into the Sinai. The older, traditional view is that they crossed the Red Sea near the northern end of the Gulf of Suez in the neighborhood of the modern city of Suez.

But in recent decades a fundamentally different view has developed. The words translated Red Sea, *Yam suph*, are commonly translated "Reed Sea" or "Sea of Reeds," *suph*, presumably being a loan word from Egyptian, referring to papyrus or other kinds of reeds (e.g., Exodus 2:3, 5, where the baby Moses was hidden among the *suph*). Of course there are no reeds, papyrus or otherwise, in the salty waters of the Red Sea. So it was concluded that the Israelites must have gone through the Bitter Lakes region (the "Sea of Reeds") in the southern part of the Isthmus of Suez, where there are reeds in abundance. It is now virtually an article of faith that the route of the Exodus moved southeast at this point and into the Sinai peninsula. Nearly all recent Bible versions translate references in Exodus 13:18 and 15:4, for instance, as "Reed Sea" or "Sea of Reeds"; or at least they put the alternate translation in a footnote.

But this does not provide a simple solution. By way of defense of the traditional view I argue, first, that in many places *yam suph* clearly refers to the Red Sea. For example, this is certainly true in 1 Kings 9:26 and Jeremiah 49:21 and apparently in Numbers 14:25; 21:4; and 33:10– 11. We may ask, on what basis should we translate *yam suph* "Reed Sea" in one place and "Red Sea" in another?

Second, the Greek translation of the Old Testament, the Septuagint, was produced in Alexandria, Egypt, only some 150 miles from the "Reed Sea." It usually translated *yam suph* as "Red Sea." The book of Exodus was translated around 250 B.C., and the translators should have known what they were doing. Third, Acts 7:36 and Hebrews 11:29 also understand *yam suph* to refer to the Red Sea. Fourth, The Latin Vulgate agrees with the Septuagint. Lastly, at the end of the plague of locusts, according to Exodus 10:19, God caused a strong northwest wind to blow all the locusts into the Red Sea. Seemingly the Gulf of Suez rather than one of the lakes of the Suez region would have been required to hold them all.

Offering a solution to the problem, Bernard F. Batto[39] and John Currid[40] conclude that *suph* comes not from Egyptian but from the Hebrew word *sôph*, literally meaning "sea of the end," and referring to waters to the south at the end of the land— the Red Sea. Batto notes that the Greeks applied the name Red Sea to the Red Sea, the Indian Ocean, and even the Persian Gulf, "the sea at the end of the world." And he observes that the Dead Sea Scrolls *Genesis Apocryphon* and the Jewish historian Josephus included in the designation "Red Sea" (*yam suph*) the Persian Gulf and everything to the south.[41] That is, for Greeks and Jews it included the extensive waters to the south and east that formed a continuous sea, beginning with the Red Sea.

I personally conclude that the Hebrews journeyed southward to the west of the present canal system and crossed the Red Sea just south of the modern port of Suez. If indeed the Israelites did cross the north end of the Red Sea, some will ask how plausible was such a feat? Exodus 14:21 says a strong east wind blew all night and parted the waters so the Israelites could cross over.

A few years ago two oceanographers investigated that plausibility. Doron Nof, professor of oceanography at Florida State University, and Nathan Paldor, an expert in atmospheric sciences at Hebrew University in Jerusalem, produced a study that shows how strong winds in the region of the north end of the Red Sea do lower the water level and could have allowed the Israelites to cross. They also identified an undersea ridge that could have provided a temporary bridge for the Israelites to pass over.[42]

These scholars were not trying to prove the accuracy of the Exodus narrative but merely sought to discover whether this crossing was scientifically plausible. If this is the explanation, the miracle comes in the timing and the intensity, for such winds do not blow all the time, and certainly do not periodically lower the water level very much.

The Sinai Journey

As the Israelites crossed over into the Sinai and moved toward Canaan, they might have taken any one of three routes across the peninsula. Skirting the Mediterranean is the Via Maris, "the way of the sea," which the armies of Egypt used when they campaigned in Asia. Scripture calls it "the way of the land of the Philistines" (Exodus 12:17–18), and asserts that the Israelites avoided this road at God's direction. The former slaves of Pharaoh were in no condition to wage full-scale warfare, which would have been unavoidable had the route of the Exodus followed the coastal road.

South of the Via Maris was the "way to Shur" (Genesis 16:7), the road that Hagar took as she fled from her mistress Sarah. Hagar, an Egyptian, was evidently on the way to her homeland when an angel stopped her and told her to return to the home of Abraham. The Egyptian end of this road seems to have been in the region of modern Ismailia on the Suez Canal. In southern Canaan the "way to Shur" connected with roads leading northward to Beersheba, Hebron, and Jerusalem.

A third route, the biblical "way of the wilderness," known in modern times as the Darb el-Haj, "the pilgrim's way," runs across the Sinai Peninsula from the head of the Gulf of Suez to Ezion-geber at the head of the Gulf of Aqaba.

The Exodus did not take Israel along any of the well-traveled roads eastward. Instead they turned southward into the Sinai

Peninsula, taking a route parallel to the Gulf of Suez. They made brief stops at Marah (possibly at Ain Hawara, approximately 7 miles east of the Red Sea), where the bitter waters were made sweet (Exodus 15:25–26), and at the oasis of Elim (perhaps in the Wadi Gharandel) with its twelve springs and seventy palm trees (Exodus 15:27).

In the heart of the Sinai Peninsula, south of the Wilderness of Shur, is the region known as the Wilderness of Sin, in which Dophkah was located (Numbers 33:12). Dophkah is thought to have been situated near the famed copper and turquoise mines that were operated by the pharaohs from early dynastic times. In the center of the mining region was the famed temple to the goddess Hathor at Serabit el-Khadem. Hundreds of inscriptions have been identified at the temple and at the entrances to the mines. Although most of them are in hieroglyphic Egyptian characters, about forty are in the so-called Proto-Sinaitic alphabetic script from the fifteenth century B.C. They represent one of the earliest attempts at developing a purely alphabetic means of writing.

The last stop before Mount Sinai was at Rephidim (Exodus 17:1), possibly modern Wadi Refayid in the southwestern part of the peninsula. Here Moses smote the rock (Exodus 17:1–7) in order to obtain water to supply the demands of his people. Shortly thereafter the Israelites met their first enemies, the Amalekites, and gained a victory after a difficult battle (Exodus 17:8–16).

Since the fourth century A.D., tradition has located Mount Sinai in the southern part of the Sinai Peninsula, at Jebel Musa (Mountain of Moses), a 7,500-foot peak. On the northwest slope of this mountain is the monastery of St. Catherine, founded about A.D. 527 under the emperor Justinian, who established it on the site where Helena, mother of Constantine, had erected a small church two centuries earlier.

Near Jebel Musa is a fairly wide valley called er-Raha, two miles long and ⅓–⅔ of a mile wide. This would be the natural place for Israel to have encamped (Exodus 19:1–2; Numbers 33:15). Towering above the plain are three summits: Ras es-Safsaf to the

northwest; Jebel Musa to the southeast; and, still higher, Jebel Katarin, rising 8,500 feet to the southwest. While Jebel Musa (meaning "mount of Moses") is the traditional location, where Moses met God, we cannot be positive concerning the identification. Other identifications have been suggested.

After traveling at length through the Sinai (see Numbers 33 itinerary), the Hebrews ultimately arrived at Kadesh-Barnea, from which spies advanced into Canaan to scout out the land prior to conquest. After that, failure to move forward by faith condemned them to wander in the wilderness for about forty years (see Numbers 13–14).

During the years that modern Israel occupied the Sinai (A.D. 1967–1982), Israeli archaeologists and explorers excavated in and studied the region. Unfortunately, however, they did not find any concrete remains of stations on the Exodus route, or even small encampments that could be attributed to the Israelites.[43] An argument from silence is no proof that they were not there, however. The lack of permanent debris, stone walls, and potsherds at campgrounds can be explained in that the Israelites were continually on the move. Moreover, they probably used goatskins for waterbags instead of pottery water jugs and made other substitutions that would have left no remains for archaeologists to excavate.

The Empire Prosperous and Declining—Amenhotep III and His Successors

After the rather uneventful reign of Thutmose IV (1425–1417 B.C.), Egypt entered the long, prosperous, and stable reign of Amenhotep III (1417–1379 B.C.). His great-grandfather, Thutmose III, had laid the foundations of the empire with his extensive campaigning into Palestine and Syria. After a few years of vigorous rule, Amenhotep III gave himself to luxurious living, his growing harem, and construction projects. The country was wealthy, primarily as a result of international trade and the plentiful supply of gold. Gold came especially from the Wadi Hammamat (which

Thutmose IV in battle with the Syrians (from his chariot in the Cairo Museum)

extended from the Nile north of modern Luxor to the Red Sea) and Kush to the south.

The quality of Amenhotep's construction appears in the great colonnaded court of the Temple of Luxor. But he built several other temples, including a mortuary temple at Thebes, to which were attached the famous Colossi of Memnon, seated statues of the king about 65 feet high. The temple itself was used as a stone quarry a century or so later and has disappeared. Though dutiful priests represented Amenhotep as a great conqueror on temple walls, he seems

The colonnade of Amenhotep III with its seven pairs of columns forms the central feature of the Temple of Luxor

The Colossi of Memnon, 65 feet high, are all that remain of Amenhotep III's mortuary temple at Thebes

to have engaged in stifling only one uprising in Nubia and probably never set foot in Palestine or Syria.

Just as Amenhotep III made no effort to maintain the empire, neither did his son Amenhotep IV (1379–1362 B.C.). Of a mystical bent, he devoted himself to the establishment of the cult of the sungod Aton (represented by the sun's disc) at a new capital named Amarna, halfway between Memphis and Thebes. He changed his name to Akhenaton (meaning "Servant of Aton"). His capital he called Akhetaton, "the place of the effective glory of Aton." Sometimes he is given credit for instituting monotheism, but if we have the chronology

Portraits of Amenhotep IV. *Lehnert & Landrock*

Nefertiti, famous queen of Amenhotep IV.
Lehnert & Landrock

brand new, however, because it had been accepted as early as the reign of Thutmose IV.

Akhenaton paid no attention to maintenance of the empire and certainly not to numerous appeals in the Amarna Letters, which were sent by loyal princes of Palestine and Syria for Egyptian help to repel invaders. As a result the empire disintegrated. Acceptance of the early date of the Exodus would place the Hebrew conquest and subsequent settling in process under Joshua and the first Judges (c. 1400–1350 B.C.) during the reigns of Amenhotep III and IV, precisely when Egyptian power over Palestine virtually disappeared. We should be careful, however, not to identify the Habiru, which some of these appeals name as attackers, as Hebrews. Much of what is said about them could not have been true of the Israelite Hebrews. The Habiru were merely marauding plunderers. Launching sporadic forays in which they looted and burned towns, they quickly withdrew with their booty. The point to be made here is that Egyptian power did not stand in the way of Hebrew entrance into Palestine under Joshua and subsequent brush fires set by individual Hebrew (Israelite) tribal groups as they tried to extend their holdings.

correct, Moses came earlier, and of course the biblical view is that monotheism was the original faith. Long before Amenhotep IV and Moses, Abraham was also a monotheist. Moreover, Amenhotep was no real monotheist; the king was worshiped along with the god. The new faith had few adherents outside the court. Sometimes it is suggested that the approach to monotheism in the days of Amenhotep IV might have been influenced by the memory of the impact of the plagues at court. But the great plagues would have taken place some seventy years earlier and probably had nothing to do with this religious development.

Religious changes, political changes connected with the move of the capital, and artistic changes constituted three of the main elements of the so-called Amarna Revolution. The new loose naturalism in art, almost bordering on caricature, was not

The new naturalism in art at Amarna is reflected in this picture of a daughter of Amenhotep IV sitting on a cushion and eating a duck
Lehnert & Landrock

Limestone bust of Tutankhamon.
Lehnert & Landrock

The gold death mask of Tutankhamon.
Cairo Museum. *Lehnert & Landrock*

Egyptian imperial weakness continued during the reign of Tutankhamon (1361–1352 B.C.). A young boy of eight or nine when he came to the throne, he was under the direct care and influence of Ay. When Tutankhamon died nine years later, Ay con- tinued to rule until 1348 B.C. When Tutankhamon became king he was known as Tutankhaton, but very soon his name was changed to Tutankhamon and he was returned to Thebes, where the old Amon worship was reestablished. Interestingly, on

The chariot of Tutankhamon. Cairo Museum.
Lehnert & Landrock

The tomb of Tutankhamon in the floor of the Valley of the Kings where its entrance was long buried by stone excavated from the tomb of Ramses IX above

from an accident or foul play it is impossible to say. Some informed scholars in Egypt and abroad and a number of the less informed believe he may have been murdered. At any rate, when he died, Ay married his widow Ankhesenamun. Ay lasted only four years, and by the time of his death Ankhesenamun was gone too.[46]

The Empire Resurgent: Harmhab and the Ramessides

When Ay died, Harmhab, or Horemheb, commander-in-chief of the army, succeeded to the throne and ruled from 1348 to 1320 B.C. He was a career officer who first served under Amenhotep III and became commander of the army under Amenhotep IV and King's Deputy during the rule of Tutankhamon. As soon as Harmhab took the throne he began restoration of the status quo, reopening the temples closed during the Amarna age and conducting necessary repairs. To make sure that the old Amon priesthood did not pose a threat to his rule, however, he appointed loyal army men to priesthoods in the official cult. He spent his reign of almost thirty years in consolidation, not yet really in a position to rebuild the empire. Ramesside kings of the Nineteenth Dynasty honored him as the founder of their line.

Dying childless, Harmhab designated as his successor Rameses I, commander of the army and vizier or prime minister. Rameses lasted only two years (1320–1318 B.C.) and was succeeded by his son, Seti I, who had held the same positions as his father. Their family came from the northeast Delta area of Avaris, which had been the capital of the Hyksos.

Seti I (1318–1304 B.C.) launched the monarchy on a path to power and glory once more. At home this involved a major building program. Abroad it involved military efforts to restore the empire. Among his constructions, pride of place goes to the great hypostyle hall of the Temple of Karnak at modern Luxor. Covering an area of 335 by 174 feet, it could com-

the back of his throne the Aton name remained where it would not be seen. On the front it was changed to Amon.

Because of the relatively unrifled[44] condition of Tutankhamon's tomb when Howard Carter opened it in 1922, the boy king has received attention out of proportion to his significance in antiquity. The large number of objects in his tomb illustrate the wealth, grandeur, and artistic achievements of ancient Egypt and help to demonstrate what it meant for Moses to turn his back on the riches of Egypt (Hebrews 11:26). If this young lad had so much wealth at his disposal, what must older kings have enjoyed?

The Cairo Museum Guide lists 1,703 objects from the tomb on display there. But it held many more than that. Numerous pieces have disappeared. While some Egyptians declared that there may have been as many as 5,000 objects in the tomb, there is no way of confirming that.

As an example of how some of the objects may have been spirited away, over 300 objects from the tomb came to light in Lord Carnarvon's castle, when a retired butler revealed their hiding place in 1988.[45] Lord Carnarvon had sponsored Howard Carter's excavation in the Valley of the Kings.

Tutankhamon died at about age eighteen. The cause of death was not tuberculosis as once thought. But whether it resulted

The Hypostyle Hall at the Temple of Karnak at Luxor

fortably hold Notre Dame cathedral in Paris. The 134 gigantic columns (the tallest in the ancient world) are arranged in sixteen rows. The double row of central columns is slightly higher than the others and stands to a height of about seventy-five feet. One hundred men could stand on the capitals of each of the columns. Although Rameses I had planned and begun the construction and Rameses II finished it, Seti I was responsible for the major part of the project. At Abydos Seti built the most remarkably decorated temple of ancient Egypt, and his tomb in the Valley of the Kings was the longest and deepest of them all (each measurement over 300 feet). Its decoration is superb.

RAMESES II, BIGGER THAN LIFE

Rameses II did everything on the grand scale. He was a great builder. Remains of his building activity stand all over Egypt—at Memphis, Thebes, Aswan, and elsewhere. He also laid out a new capital in the Delta. Great statues of the king, several over 60 feet high, stand or lie in various places around the land. To enhance his own reputation for building, Rameses II sometimes shamelessly erased the dedication inscription of another Pharaoh and had his own name inserted.

Rameses II was also a warrior and reestablished the Egyptian Empire in Palestine and Syria after the weakness of the Amarna Period. If we are correct in placing the Exodus and Conquest of the Hebrews around 1446–1400 B.C., they should have been in Palestine when Rameses marched through. Hebrews and Egyptians need not have met, however, because Rameses campaigned primarily along the coastal plain; the Hebrews occupied the hill country of Judea, Samaria, and Galilee. Rameses was especially proud of his fight with the

Hittites and victory over them in Syria. His scribes dutifully embellished the account and inscribed it on several temple walls.

On the personal level, Rameses ruled for a long time (c. 1299–1232 B.C.) and had numerous wives and concubines. We know that he had more than a hundred sons, plus many daughters. Many assume that he was the pharaoh of the Exodus.

A head of Ramses II from the Luxor Temple

Probably during his first year Seti led an army into Syria. This he kept up almost annually for the next several years. His approach was the same as Thutmose III's: swift movement through the Gaza Strip and along the Palestinian coast, with the use of the navy to cover his flank and supply his forces. He also tangled with the Libyans in the western desert several times. And he captured Kadesh in Syria. There for the first time Egyptians met Hittites in battle.

Seti's son and successor, Rameses II (1304–1237 or 1299–1232 B.C.) did everything on the grand scale. He enjoyed a long reign of sixty-seven years. He had over a hundred sons as well as daughters. He built more temples and erected more colossal

statues and obelisks than any other pharaoh. And he was a great conqueror, if we are to believe the repeated inscriptions of his victory over the Hittites.

He was a great builder. Even though he simply erased the names of some of his predecessors and substituted his name as responsible for construction, he also did

The great temple of Ramses II at Abu Simbel is fronted by four great seated statues 66 feet high

Ramses II was also responsible for the pylon entrance to the Luxor Temple with its two obelisks and huge statues of Ramses

much in his own name, including completion of the great hypostyle hall at the Temple of Karnak and carving his great temple out of the rock at Abu Simbel, south of the High Dam. His four great seated statutes in front of that temple stand 66 feet high. This was too much for the world to let submerge under the waters of Lake Nasser when the High Dam was built. So UNESCO rescued the complex and moved it to higher ground in a truly great modern engineering feat. Almost 1,500 figures of soldiers are carved and painted on the temple walls in connection with Rameses' conquest of his Hittite enemies at the great battle of Kadesh. Interestingly, in 1995 Kent Weeks of the American University in Cairo announced discovery of the tomb of Rameses' fifty sons in the Valley of the Kings at Luxor.

Rameses continued the effort to restore Egyptian control in Palestine. In his fifth year he met the Hittites in battle at Kadesh on the Orontes in Syria (20,000 Egyptians faced 37,000 Hittites) and narrowly missed destruction of his forces. His dutiful and resourceful scribes turned the confrontation into a great victory. Actually the outcome of the battle was a draw and neither empire

had the strength or resources to destroy the other. Subsequently Rameses II fought battles all the way from southern Palestine to northern Syria. Finally, in his twenty-first year, he made a peace treaty with the Hittites and kept it to the end of his days.

If the Hebrews were then in the land, as an early date of the Exodus requires, they probably never made contact with the Egyptians because they were shepherds and vinedressers in the hills of Palestine. The Egyptians campaigned mainly along the coastal plain and into Lebanon and Syria.

It is a common view that Rameses II was the pharaoh of the Exodus. The argument is that as he tried to maintain the capital in the Delta and to reestablish the Egyptian Empire in Palestine and Syria, he needed store cities for the war effort. Hence the construction of those cities (Pithom and Rameses) and the enslavement and oppression of the Hebrews (Exodus 1:11). Under this view, the Exodus would have taken place somewhere around 1275 B.C. or a little before. Let's look at the pros and cons.

First Kings 6:1 dates the Exodus 480 years before the fourth year of Solomon's reign, when he dedicated the Temple. If his reign began in 970 B.C., his fourth year would have been 967 or 966 B.C. When we add 480 years to that time of dedication, we arrive at a date of about 1447–46 for the Exodus. And, of course, subtracting forty years for wandering in the wilderness, we arrive at about 1400 B.C. for the conquest.

Two other biblical references support that general date. In Judges 11:26, the judge Jephthah reminds the Amorites that the Israelites have been in possession of the land for 300 years. Jephthah's date would have been about 1100 B.C., and 300 years before that, about 1400 B.C. (the time of the Conquest). Further, Acts 13:19–20 gives a figure of 450 years that covered the time from the Exodus to the conquest of Jerusalem (c.1000 B.C.), thus resulting in a date of about 1450 B.C. for the Exodus.[47]

It is interesting to note that the Egyptians bonded together huge blocks of stone in the various temples (here the Temple of Karnak) with bronze or iron dowels.

Support for the early date of the Exodus was provided by the excavations of John Garstang at Jericho (1930–1936). He reported that the Canaanite city fell around 1400 B.C.[48] and when allowance is made for a forty-year wandering in the wilderness, the date of the Exodus approximates 1440. In spite of opposition to his conclusions, Garstang reiterated his earlier contention in a postwar work produced in collaboration with his son.[49] At that point he was able to get his records out of storage and reevaluate them.

When Kathleen Kenyon conducted her excavations at Jericho (1952–58), she concluded that the city fell to Joshua somewhere between 1350 and 1325 B.C. and thought she would probably satisfy neither the holder of the early or of the late date of the Exodus.[50] Miss Kenyon's excavation reports, published posthumously, have received careful analysis by Bryant Wood, a specialist on Jericho. On the basis of these reports, Wood argued that all evidence pointed to an approximate 1400 B.C. date for the fall of the city.[51]

The early date of the Exodus is objected to by such scholars as William F. Albright, who pointed out that Nelson Glueck's explorations in Edomite territory revealed that this area had no sedentary population until the thirteenth century B.C.[52] Therefore, the Israelites could not have been stopped by them on their way to Palestine at the beginning of the fourteenth century B.C. In recent years Glueck's chronology for the region has been greatly modified. And Archer notes numerous discoveries that confirm existence of a settled society in Transjordan during the period in question.[53]

Also, Yigael Yadin, eminent excavator of Hazor, claimed that Hazor did not fall to the Israelites until the second third of the thirteenth century B.C.[54] But Scripture indicates that Hazor fell to the Israelites twice: in the days of Joshua (Joshua 11:10–11), when Jabin I ruled; and in the days of Deborah and Barak (Judges 4:2, 23–24), when another Jabin ruled. Yadin assumed that Joshua's conquest is to be related to thirteenth-century destruction in the lower city of Hazor. There was, however, evidence of destruction at the site around 1400 B.C., or a little later, in Areas H and K of the lower city.[55] What is more natural than to conclude that the earlier destruction dates

Eventually the temples of Luxor and Karnak were joined by a causeway lined with ram-headed sphinxes.
Lehnert & Landrock

to Joshua's day and the thirteenth-century destruction to the period of the Judges?

Further, it is argued that the palace's accessibility to Moses militates against the early date of the Exodus. The reasoning is that such accessibility indicates the palace was in the Delta region, where the Israelites lived, and the periods when the palace was located in the Delta were the days of Joseph and during the thirteenth century B.C. It may be pointed out, however, that the pharaoh of the Exodus could have met Moses at a secondary palace or administrative center. The argument is not conclusive proof for the late date of the Exodus. Moreover, Thutmose III, Amenhotep II, and Rameses II were all active in building projects in the Delta and all three also moved through there as they conducted military actions to the north.

Actually, the presence of the palace and the capital and large numbers of Egyptians in the Delta in the days of the Exodus does not fit the biblical narrative. For example, several of the plagues did not affect the Hebrew communities. If Hebrews and Egyptians were thoroughly mixed, as they would be under the late date scenario, it would have been impossible to keep the Hebrews from being affected by the plagues.

In somewhat the same vein, Beno Rothenberg saw the implications of his archaeological work in the Timna Valley (c. 15 miles north of the Gulf of Aqaba) between 1964 and 1970. What he discovered was that during the days of Rameses II such swarms of Egyptian miners and troops were busy working the copper mines in this region where the Israelites had to pass that it seemed quite unthinkable that the Israelites could have been there then. Rothenberg felt that his discoveries would require a "reconsideration" of the thirteenth-century date of the Exodus.[56]

Supposedly, strong evidence for the late date of the Exodus is the destruction of Bethel, Lachish, and Debir around 1230 B.C.[57] But a second glance puts the matter in a different light. True, those cities fell about the same time and near the beginning of the conquest, according to the Joshua narrative. But certainly the conquest did not occur as late as 1230 B.C., because the inscription on the Stele of Pharaoh Merneptah (see following discussion) represents the Hebrews as settled in Canaan when Merneptah's armies attacked them around 1230 B.C. If

117

adjustment in the dates assigned to the destruction of those sites needs to be made, how effective is the use of evidence in establishing the date of the Exodus?

It is also important to note that while Joshua captured Bethel, Lachish, and Debir, the Bible says nothing about destroying them. He burned only Ai, Jericho, and Hazor (Joshua 6:24; 8:19; 11:13). Some of Joshua's conquests were not permanent. We know that Debir had to be recaptured later (Joshua 15:13–17), and possibly the others did also. If dates of destruction at Bethel, Lachish, and Debir are correct, they may well refer to attacks during the days of the judges instead of to Joshua's conquests.

We need to keep in mind that the Israelites did not engage in a scorched earth policy in Joshua's day. God had said in Exodus 23:29–30: "I will not drive them out from before you in one year, lest the land become desolate and the beasts of the field become too numerous for you. Little by little I will drive them [the inhabitants of the land] out before you, until you have increased, and you inherit the land"(NKJV). And Numbers 21:25 specifically states that "Israel dwelt in all the cities of the Amorites"(NKJV). There was no wholesale destruction of cities in Joshua's day and evidently Bethel, Lachish, and Debir were not among them.

Interestingly, the early date of the Exodus easily fits into the flow of Egyptian history. The Amarna Period (C. 1400–1365 B.C.) was a time when the kings of Egypt were much more interested in expending the energies of the nation on gratifying their personal desires or in making religious reforms than they were on maintaining a powerful empire. The royal correspondence found at Amarna demonstrates that Egyptian puppet rulers of Palestine sent the pharaohs frequent calls for help during that half century. Local disturbances and the invasion of the Habiru (possibly related in some way to the Hebrews) were the occasions of such requests. But cushioned amid the luxuries of Egypt and/or wrapped up in religious concerns, the pharaohs chose the path of personal enjoyment rather than royal responsibility. The pleas went unheeded. Egyptian control in Canaan rapidly disintegrated, and the way was open for the Hebrews to move in and conquer.

It should be pointed out that nothing is solved by asserting, as many do, that the Exodus could not have taken place until after 1300 B.C. because the store city or supply city of Rameses was named for the ruling pharaoh. Moses was eighty at the time of the Exodus (Exodus 7:7). If the date of the Exodus is set at about 1275 B.C., Moses would have been born about 1355 B.C. The Hebrews built the store city of Rameses *before* the birth of Moses, long before the reign of the first Rameses. The town of Rameses may not have been named after the ruling king at all.

We need to keep in mind that Exodus 1:11 refers to Hebrew construction of "supply cities" or "store cities," Pithom and Rameses. The Septuagint (Greek) translation adds a third: "On" or Heliopolis. Perhaps there were others that are not mentioned. These are cities that Thutmose III, Amenhotep II, Rameses II, or another pharaoh could have used to meet the needs of the military in preparing for an invasion of Canaan or holding down the countryside. What we are talking about here is not the building of Rameses' great Delta capital called Pi-Rameses (hardly a store city) which Hoffmeier says covered 2,500 acres, compared with Nineveh's 1,800 acres and Babylon's 2,250.[58] We cannot really explain the appearance of "Rameses" in this verse. It is probably a later textual gloss.

Long ago Merrill Unger suggested that the name Rameses is a modernization of the ancient place-name Zoan-Avaris (the old Hyksos capital in the Delta). A similar situation occurs in Genesis 14:14, where *Dan* is substituted for the older city name of *Laish*.[59] But many dismissed this suggestion, asserting that Pi-Rameses was not the same place as Avaris. Now, as a result of Austrian Archaeological Institute excavations at Tell el-Dab'a on the Pelusiac branch of the Nile, that tell has definitely been identified as the site of Avaris. And Pi-Rameses has been located at Qantir just to the north.[60]

Avaris was still in existence when Pi-Rameses was constructed.[61] and, in fact, as Rohl notes, Avaris was the "southern quarter/district" of Pi-Rameses. The two were

The Ramesseum or mortuary temple of Ramses II at Luxor
Lehnert & Landrock

actually connected.[62] Rohl also notes that excavations at Avaris show that the site was abandoned around 1447 B.C. (the time he gives for the Israelite Exodus). And between about 1583 and 1447 B.C. (the period of the bondage) 65 percent of all burials there were those of children under the age of eighteen months, and more adult women were buried in the settlement than men, which might reflect the killing off of male infants. Moreover, the majority of the population of Avaris at the time was Asiatic.[63] Rohl considers the Exodus 1:11 reference to the city of Rameses to be an anachronism or a later gloss. And the real Israelite city of the bondage was Avaris.[64]

From the foregoing discussion, it appears that all the evidence, factual or circumstantial, supports the early date of the Exodus. Depending on how we work out Egyptian chronology, Thutmose III or Amenhotep II would have been ruling at the time. Amenhotep II may fit better. After extensive military campaigns in Palestine during the first few years of his rule, "peace reigned." Possibly his great loss of men and chariots in the Red Sea had something to do with later suspension of military activity: "Then the waters returned and covered the chariots, the horsemen, and

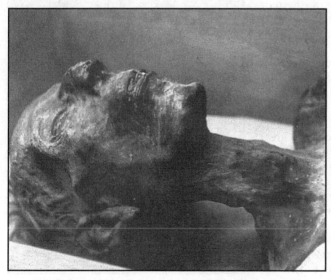

The mummy of Ramses II in the Cairo Museum.
Lehnert & Landrock

The Temple of Medinet Habu with its inscription of the victory of Ramses II over the Sea Peoples.

all the army of Pharaoh that came into the sea after them" (Exodus 14:28 NKJV, cf. Exodus 14: 23).

The Later Ramessides

Merneptah (1237–1227 or 1232–1222 B.C.), the thirteenth son of Rameses II, ruled during changing times. This was the period of the Trojan War (see chapter 9 on Greece) and the collapse of the Bronze Age in the eastern Mediterranean. In his fifth year he met an attack from Libya, apparently from the region of Cyrenaica, whose people were allied with some peoples of the northern or western Delta. Merneptah crushed this invasion and killed over six thousand, producing their phalli as proof. This detail reflects that Assyrians were only one of the warlike people of the ancient Near East that mutilated their enemies. Almost immediately thereafter Merneptah had to put down a revolt in Nubia.

Of special interest is Merneptah's great Victory Stele, now in the Cairo Museum, which tells of the successes of his seventh year. Near the end of it appears the claim "Israel is laid waste, his seed is not." This is the only reference to the Hebrews in ancient Egyptian literature. A common view among Egyptologists is that the Victory Stele represents standard royal braggadocio. That is, the king is depicted as victorious over his enemies, even if he never meets them in battle. As a matter of fact, they believe Merneptah

never waged war in Palestine. There is a minority view based on new information that gives Merneptah credit for a victory there, however. But it does not matter whether he actually went to Palestine; his inscription indicates that the Hebrews were settled there at least by about 1230–25 B.C.

Ramses III.
University of Pennsylvania.

The next ruler of any significance was Rameses III (1198–1167 B.C.). He also fought off Libyan invasions of the Delta in his fifth and eleventh years, and in his eighth year repulsed an invasion of "Sea Peoples," among whom were Philistines. The graphically illustrated account of this battle is recorded on the wall of his great and well-preserved temple at Medinet Habu (in the Thebes area).

The old and rather standard view is that these peoples came by sea, invaded Egypt, were repulsed, and then settled in Palestine, to which they gave their name. Hence biblical critics have said that Genesis references to Abraham's dealings with Philistines (e.g., Genesis 21: 32-34) are incorrect because the Philistines weren't there before the twelfth century B.C. Drews has argued that the Philistines and other invaders came from Canaan by land and sea, were repulsed, and returned to Canaan. So our whole view of the Philistine problem is changed.[65]

Rameses III was the last ruler of the empire period to maintain outposts in Palestine and Syria. In his later years the Egyptian economy deteriorated and inflation and breakdown of the government's ability to meet the public payroll brought great suffering. Hunger marches resulted.

During the reigns of Rameses IV–XI (1167–1085 B.C.) the state steadily declined. Graft and inflation increased. During the reign of Rameses IX (1138–1119 B.C.) unpaid mercenary troops seem to have roamed as marauders in the Delta and tomb robbery reached epidemic proportions. Finally Herihor, viceroy of Nubia and commander of military forces in the south, seized control of Upper Egypt and made himself high priest of Amon in Thebes. The empire had come to an end.

The Post-Empire Period

In the post-empire period, Egypt was commonly acted upon instead of playing the aggressor. She came under the rule of Libyan kings (945–712 B.C.), Nubian kings from the once despised lands of the south (712–670 B.C.), Assyrians, Persians, and Alexander the Great. Much of the time her weakness arose from internal disunity as the north and south broke apart or as rulers of major cities or regions tried to assert their independence or to control their neighbors. As a result of continued archaeological and historical research it is now possible to tell the story of this extended period of time in some detail. But since it is confusing and rather irrelevant to the average student even of Egyptian history, we shall look only at those events that have specific connection with Scripture or are important for the general historical flow.

The first contact with Scripture came during the Twenty-First Dynasty (1067–945 B.C.) which ruled from Tanis in the Delta. These kings engaged in diplomatic marriages to enhance their power. One of them, probably Siamun (978–959 B.C.), married his daughter to Solomon. For a dowry the Egyptian captured Gezer from the weakened Philistines and presented it to Solomon (1 Kings 9:16). Thus the Egyptians focused on Palestine once more.

When the next king's daughter, Maatkare, married Sheshonq I (a Libyan who launched the Libyan dynasty—the twenty-second) he apparently had stars in his eyes as he thought about the glories of Solomon. Sheshonq (Shishak of Scripture, 945–924 B.C.) sought to take advantage of the new weakness in Israel that resulted from the division of the kingdom in the days of Rehoboam. He invaded Judah in the fifth year of Rehoboam's reign (925 B.C.) and administered a crushing defeat, carrying off the treasures of the temple and palace (1 Kings 14:25; 2 Chronicles 12:2). While that is all we read about in Scripture, Egyptian records point to a more far-reaching disaster.

On a wall in the Temple of Karnak, Shishak inscribed a relief depicting 156 captives taken in this campaign. They are led by cords clasped in the hand of the god Amon, and on the body of each captive appears a Palestinian place name. So we have there a listing of the towns the Egyptian king took during his Judean conquests. At present about 120 of the names are legible, but by no means can all of them be identified geographically. Some of the more important that can be recognized are

Shishak's relief on a wall in the Temple of Karnak in which he described a great victory over king Rehoboam of Judah. The relief pictures the god Amon holding cords tied to figures bearing Palestinian place names

Megiddo, Gibeon, Taanach, Beth-shean, and Ajalon.[66] Evidently Shishak sacked scores of towns in both the northern and southern kingdoms.

Struggles with Assyria

Later in the dynasty the Assyrian threat began to loom on the horizon. Tiglath-Pileser III (744–727 B.C.) of Assyria gained control of the Palestinian coast as far south as Gaza and interfered with Egyptian trade by putting an embargo on Lebanese exports of timber to Egypt. About this time the Nubian or Kushite Dynasty (the twenty-fifth) had gained control of Egypt. In 701 B.C. while Sennacherib was campaigning in Judah and threatening the very existence of Hezekiah's state, the Egyptian king Shebitku called on his brother Tirhaka (Egyptian Taharqa) to lead an army into Judah against the Assyrians (2 Kings 19:9). At the time Tirhaka was about twenty and was crown prince. Scripture calls him "king of Ethiopia," but that can be explained— ancient Oriental writers, as well as modern writers, often referred to persons by titles acquired after the period being described. And the reference to Ethiopia is under-

The pillar of Tirhaka which he erected in the Temple of Karnak at Luxor

standable because Tirhaka's dynasty was Nubian, black rulers from the lands south of Egypt. In his inscriptions Sennacherib tells of defeating the Egyptian/Ethiopian army and capturing alive many of the Egyptian charioteers.[67]

But this was only the beginning of Assyrian involvement with Egypt. The next Assyrian king, Esarhaddon (680–669 B.C.), invaded Egypt, defeated Taharqa (690–664 B.C.) and took Memphis in 671 B.C. Then he appointed officials over the native princedoms in the Delta and proclaimed himself king of Lower and Upper Egypt. But hardly had the Assyrian army left the country when Taharqa returned to recapture Memphis.

Esarhaddon took the road to Egypt again in 669 but died on the way. His successor Ashurbanipal (668–663 B.C.) sent a strong Assyrian army to Egypt in 667 and again took Memphis. But Egyptians did not give up easily. Taharqa's successor, Tanutamun (664–656 B.C.), besieged the Assyrian garrison in Memphis in 664. The Assyrians sent

another army into Egypt and drove the Egyptian defenders all the way to Thebes, which they captured and looted, taking its treasures and its people off to Assyria. Nahum 3:8–10 refers to its fate under the Hebrew name of No-Amon. But the Egyptians were resilient, and Assyria under Ashurbanipal no longer had the strength for prolonged warfare. By 651 Psamtik I (664–610 B.C.) had chased the Assyrians out of Egypt.

A New Native Dynasty

With Psamtik a new native dynasty (the twenty-sixth) had risen in Egypt. During the more than half century of Psamtik's reign, a restored stability and prosperity came to Egypt. Trade improved as Egypt moved more fully into the economy of the Mediterranean. But the gradual Assyrian collapse brought to the fore vultures such as Babylonians and Medes who sought to devour the prey. The Babylonians especially posed a danger for the Egyptians. Therefore, as the Assyrian Empire was convulsed in her death throes, the Egyptians came to her aid as a defensive measure.

Egyptian aid for Assyria became even more pronounced during the reign of Psamtik's son and successor Necho or Neku (610–595B.C.). Necho sent an army north to help the Assyrians against the advancing Babylonians (609 B.C.). King Josiah of Judah, delighted that his great enemy of Assyria was about to fall, tried to stop Necho. For his efforts Josiah lost his life (2 Kings 23:28–30).

Now Necho changed his focus and decided to carve out an empire for himself, taking control of Syria and Palestine. He deposed the Judean King Jehoahaz and installed a puppet, Jehoiakim, in his place. Necho's success was short-lived, however. He lost his Syrian empire to the Babylonians when Nebuchadnezzar defeated him at the battle of Carchemish in 605 B.C. Evidently Nebuchadnezzar did not have to fight much to extend his control over Syria and Palestine all the way to the border of Egypt. The Judean king submitted to him voluntarily.

For his part Nebuchadnezzar was encouraged to believe that he could march south into Egypt and conquer there too. When he attacked in 601, he incurred such heavy losses that his imperialistic designs received a severe setback. Jehoiakim seems to have interpreted the situation as an opportunity to strike for independence, for he "rebelled" against Nebuchadnezzar (2 Kings 24:1). Again Judah entertained the elusive hope that it could count on Egyptian help against a powerful force from the north. Nebuchadnezzar did not attack immediately; he took a couple of years to rebuild his army. When he did field his army in 598, Necho did not march against him; evidently the Egyptians had not been able to recoup their losses. Jerusalem surrendered on January 15/16 597 B.C., after a siege of little over two months.

Before we leave Necho, we should note that he did more than fight Babylonians. He expanded Egypt's commercial contacts and built an Egyptian navy with the help of displaced Ionian Greeks. He also began to dig a navigable canal through the Wadi Tumilat between the Pelusiac branch of the Nile and the Red Sea. Thus he anticipated the Suez Canal by some 2,500 years. Darius I of Persia would complete what he began.

The advance of Egyptian power continued in the reign of Necho's son Psamtik II (595–589 B.C.), who campaigned in Nubia as far south as the third cataract. And Egyptian opposition to the Babylonians continued into the reign of Necho's grandson Haibre (589–570 B.C.), whom the Greeks called Apries and the Hebrews Hophra. Hophra marched to the assistance of Zedekiah of Judah, last king of the southern kingdom, causing the Babylonians to temporarily lift the siege of Jerusalem (January 15, 588–July 18, 586 B.C.) at about the halfway point (Jeremiah 37:5–11; 44:30).

After the fall of Jerusalem a number of Jews fled to Egypt, forcing Jeremiah to go with them against his will (Jeremiah 42:7–43:7). Jewish settlements were established especially at Tahpanhes in the Delta and at Memphis (Jeremiah 44:1). In the later years of the Babylonian Empire the Babylonians simply did not have the strength to continue to pursue conquest of Egypt. For her part Egypt enjoyed commercial benefits from the creation of a kind of commercial free zone in the Delta during the last decades of the dynasty.

Persian Control

Important to the Persian conquest of Egypt is the fact that the Egyptian King Amasis (570–526 B.C.) had quarreled with the Greek mercenaries in the Egyptian army, and some of them defected to invading Persian forces under Cambyses with valuable strategic information. To make matters worse, as the Persians were about to enter Egypt, King Amasis died and his inexperienced son Psamtik III took the throne. A well-fought battle at Pelusium in the Delta—there were Greek mercenaries on both sides—ended with a Persian victory. Psamtik fled across the river to Memphis, which the Persians then besieged and captured. At first, Psamtik was well treated but later was executed for plotting against the Persians. Thus ended the native Egyptian dynasty. Cambyses marched up the Nile and took Thebes and the rest of the valley all the way to the second cataract. Egypt was organized into the satrapy of Mudraya with Memphis as its capital. Thereafter the Persians ruled Egypt like absentee landlords, leaving a satrap or governor in control.

Cambyses got bad press from the native Egyptians for his supposed irreverent acts toward the gods of Egypt and various acts of savagery and destruction. It is understandable that the priests would set up a howl because he was upset over the incredibly high offerings they received and cut them considerably. The slander he endured was terrible then, and the accusations are sometimes still repeated by native guides. But all this must be greatly discounted and generally is by modern Egyptians. In fact, officials of that period seem to have been fairly well disposed toward Cambyses. He did show respect in general for the customs and religious practices of Egypt.

At the death of Cambyses in 522 B.C. there was political unrest and revolution in Persia, from which Darius I (521–486 B.C.) emerged victorious. The story is told in the chapter on Iran. As far as Egypt was concerned, Darius was important for his administration and conquests. He tried to establish a standard coinage and standard weights and measures for the entire empire. Especially he tried to improve communications. This resulted in completion of the canal across the Isthmus of Suez that Necho had begun. When completed it was 150 feet wide and deep enough for merchant vessels to move through it. Thus it was now possible to sail from the Mediterranean to the Red Sea, the Persian Gulf, and the Indian Ocean. Put another way, the river valleys of the Nile, the Tigris-Euphrates, and the Indus were linked by water routes. Darius' conquests were also important for Egypt because he invaded Greece and brought the Persian Empire to its greatest extent. Greeks in Egypt and Egypt as a whole would get involved in imperial politics.

As a matter of fact, when the Greeks defeated the Persians at Marathon in 490 B.C. and Darius was thus distracted, the Egyptians struck for independence. The next Persian king, Xerxes (485–465 B.C.), put down the revolt with great severity, and the Persian satrap ruled with such cruelty thereafter that the Egyptians revolted again when Xerxes was assassinated and Artaxerxes I (464–424 B.C.) assumed the throne. Though the Egyptians had initial successes, aided as they were by Greek allies, they were eventually brought to heel. For the rest of the reign of Artaxerxes there was relative quiet. With the next change of administrations, when Darius II (422–405 B.C.) came to the throne, Egyptians again tried to break free. Darius put down the revolt and tried to woo nationalistic elements with a program of public works. Thereafter, for the rest of the Persian period, the Egyptians were able to take advantage of the weakness of the Persian administration and family problems of the Persian royal house to maintain a quasi-independence. Though the Persians were able to reassert fairly strong control in 343, they were swept away forever by the invasion of Alexander the Great.

As noted earlier, some Jews migrated to Egypt after the Babylonian destruction of Jerusalem. One of the most interesting Jewish colonies, a military garrison, settled on the island of Elephantine at Aswan under the Persian Empire. We are left with most of the basic questions of how and why they settled there and what happened to them. Of special interest are the Elephantine papyri, that came to light in 1903. Written in Aramaic, they tell of a Jewish temple there that was sacked around 411 B.C. and show Jewish appreciation of their Persian masters, in contrast to their resentment against all their other conquerors. For more information about Elephantine, an especially useful book about Elephantine is Bezalel Porten's *Archives from Elephantine* (1968). Porten and others have produced a massive new work, *The Elephantine Papyri in English* (1996).

JEWS IN EGYPT

Of course there were many Jews in Egypt during the Middle Kingdom and the Empire. Presumably they all left at the time of the Exodus. But a reverse flow began when the Babylonians destroyed the kingdom of Judah in 586 B.C. Then a group of Jews, fearing for their lives, fled to Egypt and carried Jeremiah with them, against his will (Jeremiah 40:7–43:7). Subsequently, during the Persian period, a group of them were active on the island of Elephantine in the Nile at Aswan.

When the Ptolemies took control of Palestine in 319 B.C. (and then held it for over a century), many Jews moved to Egypt. They were especially welcomed in the city of Alexandria. With the passing of time they forgot their Hebrew and needed a Bible in Greek. The translation that gradually was produced (over the years from about 250 to 150 B.C.) is known as the Septuagint. Along with Jewish acceptance of the Greek language came adoption of some non-supernaturalistic aspects of Hellenistic culture. Some scholars would put the Jewish population of Egypt as high as a million during the New Testament period, with the largest concentration of them living in Alexandria.

The Conquest of Alexander the Great

It is probably inaccurate to speak of Alexander's "conquest" of Egypt, for he really faced no opposition as he moved from Gaza along the coast into Egypt in 332 B.C. We may question the claim that crowds turned out to hail him as liberator. Egyptians would not have rejoiced to substitute one bondage for another. But some of the many Greeks then living in the land may have staged one or more demonstrations of welcome.

While in Egypt Alexander made the exhausting trip out to the oasis of Siwa, considerably west of Memphis. Why he went is a subject of much debate—engaged in by ancient Greek historians and modern historians as well. At the minimum he needed to be recognized as the authentic ruler of Egypt. And it was important to keep his army supplied with Egyptian grain. So he took a month off from campaigning and went to the oracle of Zeus-Amon at Siwa to get himself declared Pharaoh. This carried with it a recognition of his divinity, for all pharaohs were considered to be divine. And perhaps in Alexander's mind what the priests said to him involved divine approval on his expedition. Perhaps now he could believe that destiny was on his side. What they said to him at Siwa was probably never reported and we shall not know what it was. Whether he was crowned as Pharaoh by the priests at Memphis later on we do not certainly know either.

Alexander went out of his way to conciliate the Egyptians, and there seems to have been no real resistance to him. He left only four thousand men as a garrison at Memphis. Whether he went to Thebes we do not know, but he is pictured on a wall in the great Temple of Luxor. After his return from Siwa he formally marked out the foundations of Alexandria on the coast of Egypt—the first of over thirty cities that would bear his name. The traditional date is probably to be equated to January 20, 331 B.C. The city was destined to be the crossroads of the world.

The Ptolemaic Kingdom

When Alexander died in Babylon in 323 B.C., his able generals and associates, like vultures, descended on the empire he had created, trying to get all of it, or as much of it as they could, for themselves. Because no one of them was strong enough to be Alexander's successor, they at first agreed on a regency and arranged a division of old Persian satrapies for administrative purposes. In the decades that followed, Alexander's mentally deficient half-brother and his posthumous son were liquidated. And after numerous wars and reshufflings of power, by 275 the new Hellenistic East had taken shape and Macedonian kings ruled in the lands of the old Persian Empire. There were a few smaller states, but three major ones emerged: Macedonia; Seleucid holdings, extending from Asia Minor to the borders of India; and Egypt.

From about 275, for most of a century, relative peace permitted rapid economic and cultural development of a new Hellenistic world. After Alexander's conquests, most of the Greek and Macedonian soldiers settled in veterans' colonies in the new Greek monarchies of the East. There they furnished forces for the king's army and formed a privileged element in the population. Many other individual Greeks joined them as settlers, seeking to benefit from economic, and thus political and social, opportunities to be gained. Greeks and Macedonians everywhere formed a governing class and furnished the bureaucrats, technicians, architects, and craftsmen that the new societies required. Greek culture modified by local oriental elements became a new Hellenistic way of life.

Of all Alexander's generals, Ptolemy (in Egypt) was in an especially strong position. In part this came from a clever piece of body snatching. When the corpse of Alexander made its way from Babylon back to Macedonia, Ptolemy managed to persuade the officer in charge to take it to Egypt, claiming that Alexander had wished to be buried in the Oasis of Siwa. But then Ptolemy kept the body in Memphis until a proper tomb could be prepared in Alexandria. Hence Ptolemy could appear in the light of a successor to Alexander, looking after his burial. Ptolemy extended his control into Palestine and the Aegean and proclaimed himself king in 306 B.C. Thus he established a Greek line that was to rule Egypt until the suicide of Cleopatra in 30 B.C.

Ptolemy I (306–282 B.C.), apparently an extremely able man, laid the foundation of all that was to follow, both in foreign and domestic affairs. Seeking to get the jump on his competitors and also to protect Egypt, he launched an aggressive foreign policy. This had already begun in 322 when he took control of Cyrenaica (in modern Libya) to protect approaches from the west. Then he proceeded to build up the Egyptian navy, which became so powerful as to control the eastern Mediterranean and the Aegean Sea. The larger islands of the Aegean became Egyptian allies. Small ports along the Greek coast were garrisoned and used as bases. Lycia and Cyprus were vassal kingdoms. Naval activity in the Greek theater enabled Ptolemy I to recruit desirable Greek soldiers and settlers.

On land Ptolemy I took Phoenicia, Palestine, and southern Syria in 319 B.C., leading to conflict with the Seleucids in a series of five wars during the third century and finally to a loss of Palestine to the Seleucids in 198. But during the century that the Ptolemies held the region, they enjoyed control of the western terminus of trade routes from Arabia and Mesopotamia. And Hellenization of Palestine proceeded as the Jewish upper classes fell under the spell of Greek culture.

As the Ptolemies governed, they ruled the native Egyptians as pharaohs and gradually developed the ruler cult for the Greek community. Ptolemy I established the cult of the deified Alexander in 311. When he died, his son introduced worship of the dead king. And in 271 living members of the royal family were included with the dead in the ruler cult. During the third century the Macedonian kings worked hard and lived in comparative simplicity. But during the following century they began to lapse into a more luxurious and indolent Oriental lifestyle. And increasingly they tended to neglect their foreign possessions. Also the Greek ruling class gradually intermarried with the native population, and the old elaborate governmental organization began to break down. In its later stages the Ptolemaic line could not get adequate recruits of Greek soldiers, so the military efficiency declined.

The economy under the Ptolemies had no place for private enterprise as the Greek city-states had. Like the pharaohs before them, the Ptolemies were the owners of Egypt and managed the country as a great private estate. There was also the estate of the gods worked by temple tenants. Most of the land was worked directly for the king under contract in which the rent was set. But there was also *cleruch* land assigned to the Greek soldiers for their use and support. Most of these lots were on newly reclaimed land.

In the planned community a system of state monopolies controlled production and sale of vegetable oils, textiles, papyrus, beer, and numerous other products. Of course the government also controlled the grain trade which was especially exported through Alexandria.

ALEXANDRIA

Alexandria in Egypt, named for Alexander the Great, was founded by the conqueror himself. Ptolemy I and II were responsible for much of the significant construction around 300 B.C. They laid out the city on a grid, with the two major streets (each about 100 feet wide) intersecting at right angles, and other streets dividing the city into blocks.

In the palace sector they built royal palaces that were groups of Greek pavilions, with halls and living rooms clustered around elegant parks. The tomb of Alexander stood nearby. Also in the palace sector the Ptolemies built the museum—a large dining room with a colonnaded, tree-lined garden designed to house a group of scholars (a kind of university). Nearby they constructed the famous library with a half million volumes or more, the largest library in the ancient world.

Other famous structures included the gymnasium and the Serapeum.

The circuit of the walls measured a good nine miles, and the population in New Testament times must have been at least a half million. The Pharos Lighthouse, one of the seven wonders of the ancient world, stood at the entrance to the two great artificial harbors.

Several excavations have taken place on land in the environs of ancient Alexandria during the 1990s, and Jean-Yves Empereur has carried on considerable underwater excavation in the Alexandria harbor. A significant publication is his *Alexandria Rediscovered* (George Braziller, 1998).

The Construction of Alexandria

The tremendous energy of Ptolemy I expended in empire building is also reflected in construction of the great city of Alexandria. This city was to dominate the eastern Mediterranean politically, culturally, and economically for 6.5 centuries and to rival the new foundation of Constantinople thereafter for another three. Ptolemy I moved his capital from Memphis to Alexandria and began the construction of the royal palaces, the museum, the library, the tomb of Alexander, and the lighthouse (the Pharos), one of the seven wonders of the ancient world.

Actually Ptolemy II (285–246 B.C.) finished much of what his father began. The lighthouse stood some 400 feet in the air and was built in three stories: the first square, the second octagonal, and the third round. The fire that burned in it was reflected in a metal mirror and could be seen many miles at sea. The palaces consisted of a cluster of Greek pavilions and living rooms arranged around elegant parks. The museum, a kind of university, had a large dining room and a colonnaded, tree-lined garden and was designed to house a group of scholars. The great library, that eventually contained as many as a half million volumes, was located nearby.

The city grew rapidly and had an estimated half million people by the first century

B.C. If it grew to a million in the first century A.D., as some claim, it rivaled Rome in size. In any case, it was the second city in the Roman Empire. The population was basically Greek, but a considerable variety of people from all over the Mediterranean came to do business and to live there. Apparently about two-fifths of the Alexandrians were Jews, with a total of one million Jews in the country by about the time of Christ.[68]

These Jews gradually forgot their Hebrew, and a demand for a Bible in Greek resulted in the translation of the Septuagint. This was produced gradually between about 250 and 150 B.C. Alexandria became a great center of Jewish and later of Christian scholarship. Philo was the great Jewish scholar of the time of Christ. Outstanding Christian scholars of the third century A.D. were Clement and Origen.

Philo, or Philo Judaeus as he is known, lived in Alexandria from around 25 B.C. to A.D. 50. Thus he was contemporary with Jesus and the apostles. He and Josephus are the only Jewish authors of the Dispersion whose works have been preserved in considerable quantity.[69] So his writings are a primary source of information for the Judaism of the Dispersion and an understanding of how Jews responded to the Hellenistic culture of the times. We need to be careful here, however, because we have no way of knowing how representative he is of the thought processes of the time. But we do know that he was important and influential.

He sought to harmonize the philosophy of Plato, Aristotle, and other Greek philosophers with the doctrines of the Pentateuch. In doing so, he took over the allegorical method from the Stoics, which enabled him to read his philosophy into the Scripture. He came to the conclusion that the Greeks borrowed all they knew about religious thought from Moses. He is characterized by a firm and steadfast loyalty to Judaism. His allegorical approach greatly influenced Clement of Alexandria and Origen and the approach of the Alexandrian school in general in its interpretation of Scripture. On the political level, Philo was important as the leader of an embassy of five that went to

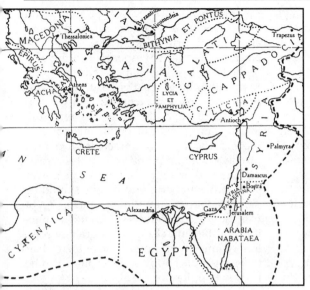

The Roman provincial arrangement in the southeastern Mediterranean during the early second century A.D.

More direct involvement came in 80 B.C. when the Roman General Sulla was campaigning in the East. Ptolemy IX died in that year without a legitimate male heir, and Sulla filled the void by placing on the throne a Ptolemaic prince of his choice. Then when that Ptolemy XII died in 51 B.C., his will named his eldest daughter Cleopatra (age 17 or 18) and his eldest son Ptolemy (age 9–10) as successors; Rome was named as their guardians.

During the Roman civil wars after Caesar defeated Pompey (48 B.C.), Pompey fled to Egypt where he was killed. When Caesar followed him there, he fell under the spell of Cleopatra VII—and she became his mistress, bearing him a son—Caesarion. After the assassination of Caesar (44 B.C.), Cleopatra went to Tarsus to meet Mark Antony (42 B.C.), and later married him and bore him twin sons and a daughter. When Octavian (Augustus) defeated Antony and Cleopatra at Actium in Greece in 31 B.C., they both fled to Egypt where they committed suicide (30 B.C.) rather than grace the triumph (a kind of ticker tape parade) of Augustus through the streets of Rome. Cleopatra was not yet forty; the line of the Ptolemies had come to an end.

Rome in the winter of A.D. 39–40 to plead with Caligula not to set up his images in the synagogues of Alexandria and thus to demand divine honors from the Jews.

Roman Involvement with Egypt

A discussion of the individual reigns and later history of the Ptolemies is tedious and unnecessary for present purposes. Before we look at Cleopatra VII and the end of the line of the Ptolemies, it is useful to become aware of Roman involvement with Egypt.

Actually that began in around 273–72 B.C., in the days of Ptolemy II. In the wake of the Roman victory over King Pyrrhus of Epirus he sent an embassy to Rome to exchange assurances of friendship. This act was extremely important for Egypt, for it won a hands-off policy of Rome as she expanded eastward and dealt severely with the other Hellenistic monarchies. Around 200 B.C. Rome intervened in the East, ordering Antiochus III of Syria to cancel plans to invade Egypt. A generation later Antiochus IV did invade Egypt and threatened to take over the entire country. Ptolemy VI sent an urgent request to Rome for help in 169 B.C. As a result Roman officials hurried to Egypt and ordered Antiochus out of the country. In subsequent decades numerous Roman merchants and shippers settled in Egypt.

Roman Rule in Egypt

Of course Egypt had to have a government. Octavian installed a Roman governor, appointed an administrative staff, and left a Roman army of occupation. Henceforth Egypt was his personal estate, ruled by a prefect, answerable to the emperor and appointed by him. The term of office was at the pleasure of the emperor, but it turned out to last one-to-three years on average, rarely more than four or five. Augustus continued the pre-existing division of the province into thirty administrative districts or nomes, each governed by a strategos. But unlike under the Ptolemaic arrangement, they had only civil power.

Military power was in the hands of the armed forces. Soldiers did not live with their families on their lands, however, as in the Ptolemaic period, but in fortified camps and outposts. One legion was stationed at Alexandria, a second at Egyptian Babylon near Memphis across the Nile, and additional garrisons at mines, grain supply depots, and elsewhere.

Top posts in the government were staffed by Romans from Italy, but the rest were drawn from the local population. Government business was conducted in Greek but some clerks were bilingual in Latin and Greek. The Roman emperors continued the pharaonic fiction, appearing in Egyptian dress on reliefs or statues, participating in the old religious rituals, and having their names inscribed in cartouches here and there. But Roman period monuments are few in Egypt. Pharaonic Egypt had effectively died with the last native pharaoh in the fourth century B.C.

For the mass of the peasants, probably about seven million in number, life in the villages continued essentially unchanged from what it had been from time immemorial. Egyptian craftsmen and the bureaucracy had been trained by centuries of hereditary skill. Egypt was tremendously prosperous in the New Testament period. Agricultural production increased with added acreage brought under cultivation. Manufacturing was extensive, especially in the production of fabrics, papyrus, and glass. Unlike the Ptolemies, the Romans encouraged private industry. Many new cities were founded, especially in the area of the Fayum. In them appeared the typical Roman buildings of baths, basilicas, agoras, or forums, and some temples.

Augustus and the emperors who followed him would not permit members of the imperial family or the senate to visit the province without permission of the emperor. This was an important economic power base of the emperor and no one should be permitted to stir up trouble there. Egypt was assigned the duty of producing one-third of the annual supply of grain needed to feed the city of Rome. The emperor had to keep people happy in the capital. And he needed supplies for the army.

But large numbers of other people—businessmen, tourists, government officials, and others—constantly traveled into or through the province. When Joseph brought Mary and Jesus (Matthew 2:13–15) they would hardly have been noticed among the substantial numbers of foreigners that constantly moved through the land. And of course they would have been safe there. The long arm of Herod could not reach across the borders of his client kingdom to interfere in the emperor's domain on the Nile.

NOTES

1. The cultivated part of Egypt in modern times is less than 14,000 square miles, roughly equal to that of Maryland and Connecticut combined. Those two states with a combined population of about 8.4 million, compare with the current Egyptian population of about 67 million. Greater Cairo alone has about 13 million people.

2. Joyce Filer, *Egyptian Bookshelf: Disease* (Austin: University of Texas Press, 1995), 25.

3. The climate of Egypt is subtropical. Blue skies, strong sunlight, and dry atmosphere are characteristic of the Nile valley. Mean temperatures for January and July, the coldest and hottest months, range as follows:

	January		July	
	Max.	Min.	Max.	Min.
Alexandria	65°	50°	86°	71°
Cairo	65°	42°	100°	71°
Aswan	74°	48°	107°	79

In Cairo the thermometer may go up to 113° in the summer, and in the valley it sometimes reaches 122°.

4. It is interesting to note that the Egyptian hieroglyphic for "to go north" was a boat with no sail and "to go south" or "go upstream" was a boat with a sail.

5. Efraim Orni and Elisha Efrat, *Geography of Israel*, 3rd ed., rev. (Jerusalem: Israel University, 1971), 359.

6. Arie Issar, "Fossil Water under the Sinai-Negev Peninsula," *Scientific American*, July 1985, 110.

7. Ibid., 104; an interesting popular article on the Sinai is Harvey Arden, "Eternal Sinai," *National Geographic*, April 1982, 420–461.

8. See Gerald P. Verbrugghe and John M. Wickersham, *Berossus and Manetho* (Ann Arbor: University of Michigan Press, 1996).

9. See James B. Pritchard, ed., *The Ancient Near East*, vol. 1 of *An Anthology of Texts and Pictures* (Princeton: Princeton University Press, 1958), illus. 84.

10. See Hosea 9:6; Isaiah 19:13; Jeremiah 2:16; 44:1; 46:14, 19; Ezekiel 30:13, 16.

11. Cyril Aldred, *The Egyptians*, rev. ed. (London: Thames & Hudson, 1984), 97.

12. John Taylor in 1859 set forth the view that the Great Pyramid had been built by a divinely chosen race acting under God's guidance. In 1864 Charles Piazzi Smith, Astronomer Royal of Scotland, more fully developed the mathematics of the pyramid theory and the concept that the pyramid was a revelation of God, intended to portray the plan of the ages. Thus there was an entrance passage supposedly representing mankind on a descending path until the crossing of the Red Sea, then a low incline passage (the age of Law) leading to an intersection representing the birth and crucifix-

ion of Christ, next a grand gallery standing for the age of grace, and finally the burial chamber representing the Millennium. The pyramid theory has become intertwined with the cult of British Israelism but is not necessarily linked with it. The idea that the Great Pyramid was designed at one time as a special revelation suffers greatly when we discover that it went through several changes of design as the pharaoh enjoyed increasing longevity of life. Moreover, the pyramids were built by native Egyptians, not a "divinely chosen race." We may also assert that God has revealed His plan for and observations about the human race in inspired Scripture and we should not look in human constructions for specific revelations about God's communication to humanity.

13. Rosalie David, *The Pyramid Builders of Ancient Egypt* (New York: Routledge, 1986), 58–59.

14. I. E. S. Edwards, *The Pyramids of Egypt*, rev. ed. (New York: Penguin, 1985), 276.

15. Ibid., 277.

16. For a description, see this book chapter 4 on Phoenicia, "Early Relations with Egypt."

17. For an up-to-date discussion of papyrus growth and manufacture, see Richard Parkinson and Stephen Quirke, *Papyrus* (London: British Museum, 1995); and Paul T. Nicholson and Ian Shaw, eds. *Ancient Egyptian Materials and Technology* (Cambridge: Cambridge University Press, 2000), pp. 227–253.

18. Aldred, *Eygptians.*, 120.

19. For a long and definitive discussion see Mary Lefkowitz, *Not Out of Africa* (New York: Harper, 1996), 34–52

20. John A. Wilson, *The Burden of Egypt* (Chicago: University of Chicago Press, 1951), 36–41.

21. For additional dimensions of the Joseph story, see James K. Hoffmeier, *Israel in Egypt* (New York: Oxford University Press, 1997), 83–106.

22. Pritchard, *Ancient Near East*, 1, illus. 2.

23. Wilson, *Burden at Egypt.*, 133.

24. Ibid., 137.

25. Loc. cit.

26. James B. Pritchard, *Ancient Near Eastern Texts* (Princeton: Princeton University Press, 2nd ed., 1955), 230.

27. One of the most valuable studies on mummification is by A. Lucas, former director of the Chemical Department of Egypt and Honorary Consulting Chemist of the Department of Antiquities of Egypt. See A. Lucas, "Mummification," *Ancient Egyptian Materials and Industries*, 3rd ed. (London: Edward Arnold, 1948), 307–390. See also James E. Harris and Kent R. Weeks, *X-Raying the Pharaohs* (New York: Scribner's, 1973); Christine El Mahdy, *Mummies, Myth and Magic in Ancient Egypt* (London:

Thames & Hudson, 1989); and Nicholson and Shaw, *Ancient Egyptian Materials*, 372–389.

28. Philip K. Hitti, *History of Syria* (New York: Macmillan, 1951), 146.

29. Incidentally, it is for this same reason that we cannot expect to find archaeological remains of Hebrew life in Egypt; they lived in Goshen in the eastern delta. Hebrews also, as slaves, would have had little knowledge of writing and would have left few records. Moreover, just as the Egyptians sought to erase any memory of the Hyksos, they may have sought to do the same for the Hebrews after the humiliation of the plagues.

30. Her recent biography is Joyce Tyldesley, *Hatchepsut* (New York: Viking, 1996).

31. Charles F. Aling, *Egypt and Bible History* (Grand Rapids: Baker, 1981), 74.

32. See Pritchard, *Ancient Near East*, 1, illus. 18.

33. Wilson, *Burden of Egypt*, 201.

34. Some object that it was not fair for God to harden Pharaoh's heart and then to punish him for having a hard heart. A study of Exodus 4–14 will show that Pharaoh, as a wicked man, hardened his own heart seven times before God is said to have hardened it once and then ultimately Pharaoh hardened his own heart a total of ten times, and God hardened it ten times. Perhaps this illustrates the truth that when people willfully turn their backs on God, ultimately He may in judgment confirm them in their wayward state (see Romans 1:24, 26–28, "God gave them up"). Moreover, this hardening of heart had to do with an issue of public policy—whether or not the Hebrews could go free. It should not be confused with the issue of salvation as such, as if God hardens the hearts of people and then sends them to perdition. Salvation is not in view here.

35. Joseph P. Free, *Archaeology and Bible History*, rev. and exp. by Howard F. Vos (Grand Rapids: Zondervan, 1992), 84.

36. Some of this information appears in John D. Currid, *Ancient Egypt and the Old Testament* (Grand Rapids: Baker, 1997), 117–123.

37. Ibid., 131.

38. James K. Hoffmeier, *Israel in Egypt* (New York: Oxford University Press, 1997), 172, 175.

39. Bernard F. Batto, "Red Sea or Reed Sea?" *Biblical Archaeology Review,* (July/August 1984) 59.

40. Currid, *Ancient East.*, 135.

41. Batto, "Red Sea"59–60.

42. See John N. Wilford, "Oceanographers Say Winds May Have Parted the Waters," *New York Times*, 15 March 1992, Doron Nof and Nathan Paldor, "Are There Oceanographic

Explanations for the Israelites' Crossing of the Red Sea?" *Bulletin of the American Meteorological Society* (March 1992): 305–314.

43. Itzhaq Beit-Arieh, "Fifteen Years in Sinai," *Biblical Archaeology Review,* (July/August 1984) 52.

44. Actually the tomb was opened twice shortly after the king's death. The first time precious oils, glass, and fabrics were taken. The second time the robbers got into the inner chamber and took a considerable amount of jewelry and other valuable objects. This time they were caught.

45. See *U.S. News & World Report,* 21 March 1988, 10.

46. Three books on Tutankhamon that are especially useful are Howard Carter, *The Tomb of Tutankhamen* (London: Sphere Books, 1972); Thomas Hoving, *Tutankhamun, The Untold Story* (New York: Simon & Schuster, 1978); Nicholas Reeves, *The Complete Tutankhamun* (London: Thames & Hudson, 1990).

47. See RSV and argumentation in Gleason Archer, *A Survey of Old Testament Introduction,* rev. ed. (Chicago: Moody Press, 1994), 239.

48. John Garstang, *Joshua and Judges* (New York: Harper, 1931), 147.

49. John and J. B. E. Garstang, *The Story of Jericho* (London: Marshall, Morgan & Scott, 1948), xiv.

50. Kathleen Kenyon, *Digging Up Jericho* (New York: Praeger, 1957), 262.

51. Bryant G. Wood, "Did the Israelites Conquer Jericho?" *Biblical Archaeology Review* (March/April 1990): 50.

52. William F. Albright, *From the Stone Age to Christianity,* 2nd ed. (Baltimore: Johns Hopkins, 1957), 195.

53. Archer, *Old Testament Introduction,* 242.

54. Yigael Yadin, "Hazor," *Encyclopedia of Archaeological Excavations in the Holy Land,* vol. 2, ed. Michael Avi-Yonah (Englewood Cliffs: Prentice-Hall, 1976), 494.

55. Ibid., 481–2.

56. Beno Rothenberg, *Were These King Solomon's Mines?* (New York: Stein & Day, 1972), 184.

57. J. L. Kelso, "Bethel," *Encyclopedia of Archaeological Excavations in the Holy Land,* vol. 1, ed. Michael Avi-Yonah, v 192; Y. Aharoni, "Lachish," Ibid., vol. 3, ed. Michael Avi-Yonah and Ephraim Stern, 743; W. F. Albright, "Tell Beit Mirsim," Ibid., vol. 1, 177.

58. Hoffmeier, *Israel in Egypt,* 119.

59. Merrill F. Unger, *Archaeology and the Old Testament* (Grand Rapids: Zondervan, 1954), 149.

60. Manfred Bietak, *Avaris* (London: British Museum Press, 1996), 1.

61. Ibid., 82.

62. David M. Rohl, *Pharaohs and Kings* (New York: Crown, 1995), 268.

63. Ibid., 270–71.

64. Ibid., 275.

65. Robert Drews, *The End of the Bronze Age* (Princeton: Princeton University Press, 1993), Chap. 4.

66. Finegan, *Light from the Ancient Past*, Princeton: Princeton University Press 1959, 113.

67. Pritchard, *Ancient Near Eastern Texts*, 287.

68. Abba Eban, *My People* (New York: Random House, 1968), 104.

69. His complete and unabridged works have been translated by C. D. Yonge and published, by Hendrickson (Peabody, Mass: Hendrickson, 1993).

BIBLIOGRPAHY

Aldred, Cyril. *Akhenaten Pharaoh of Egypt.* New York: McGraw Hill, 1968.

Aldred, Cyril. *Egyptian Art.* London: Thames & Hudson, 1980.

Aldred, Cyril. The Egyptians. London: Thames & Hudson, 3rd ed., 1998.

Aling, Charles F. *Egypt and Bible History.* Grand Rapids: Baker, 1981.

Allen, James P. and others. *Religion and Philosophy in Ancient Egypt.* New Haven,: Yale University Press, 1989.

Alston, Richard. *Soldier and Society in Roman Egypt.* New York: Routledge, 1995.

Amati, Emmanuel. *The Mountain of God.* New York: Rizzoli, 1986.

Andrews, Carol. *The Rosetta Stone.* London: British Museum Press, 1981.

Arnold, Dieter. *Building in Egypt.* Oxford: Oxford University Press, 1991.

Barocas, Claudio. *Monuments of Civilization: Egypt.* New York: Grosset and Dunlap, 1972.

Baines, John, and Jaromir Malek. *Atlas of Ancient Egypt.* New York: Facts on File, 1980.

Bierbrier, Morris. T*he Tomb-Builders of the Pharaohs.* New York: Charles Scribner's, 1984.

Bietak, Manfred. *Avaris, The Capital of the Hyksos.* London: British Museum Press, 1996.

Bowman, Alan K. *Egypt After the Pharaohs.* Berkeley: University of California Press, 1986.

Breasted, James H. *Ancient Records of Egypt.* 5 vols. New York: Russell & Russell, 1962.

Breasted, James H. *The Dawn of Conscience.* New York: Charles Scribner's, 1933.

Breasted, James H. *Development of Religion and Thought in Ancient Egypt.* Philadelphia: University of Pennsylvania Press, 1986.

Breasted, James H. *A History of Egypt.* New York: Charles Scribner's, 1946.

Brewer, Douglas J., and Emily Teeter. *Egypt and the Egyptians.* Cambridge: Cambridge University Press, 1999.

Brier, Bob. *The Murder of Tutankhamen.* New York: G. P. Putnam, 1998.

Bunson, Margaret, *The Encyclopedia of Ancient Egypt.* New York: Facts on File, 1991.

Carter, Howard. *The Tomb of Tutankhamen.* London: Sphere Books, 1972.

Casson, Lionel. *Everyday Life in Ancient Egpyt.* Rev. Ed. Baltimore: Johns Hopkins, 2001.

Clayton, Peter A. *Chronicle of the Pharaohs.* New York: Thames & Hudson, 1994.

Collier, Joy. *The Heretic Pharaoh.* New York: Dorset Press, 1970.

Coogan, Michael D., ed. *The Oxford History of the Biblical World.* New York: Oxford University Press, 1998.

Currid, John D. *Ancient Egypt and the Old Testament.* Grand Rapids: Baker, 1997.

David, Rosalie. *The Pyramid Builders of Ancient Egypt.* London: Routledge, 1986.

Davis, John J. *Moses and the Gods of Egypt.* Grand Rapids: Baker, 1971.

Delia, Robert D. *A Study of the Reign of Senwosret III.* Ann Arbor: University of Michigan Microfilms, 1990.

Desroches-Noblecourt, Christiane. *Tutankhamen.* New York: New York Graphic Society, 1963.

Dodson, Aidan. *Monarchs of the Nile.* London: Rubicon, 1995.

Edwards, I. E. S. *The Pyramids of Egypt.* Rev. ed. New York: Viking Penguin, 1985.

El-Din, Morsi Saad and others. *Sinai.* New York: New York University Press, 1998.

El Mahdy, Christine. *Mummies, Myth and Magic*. New York: Thames & Hudson, 1989.

Emery, Walter B. *Egypt in Nubia*. London: Hutchinson & Co., 1965.

Empereur, Jean-Yves. *Alexandria Rediscovered*. New York: George Braziller, 1998.

Erman, Adolf. *Life in Ancient Egypt*. Trans. H. M. Tirard. New York: Dover Publications, 1971.

Fairservis, Walter A. *The Ancient Kingdoms of the Nile*. New York: New American Library, 1962.

Fakhry, Ahmed. *The Pyramids*. Chicago: University of Chicago Press, 1961.

Faulkner, Raymond O. *The Ancient Egyptian Book of the Dead*. Rev. ed., Austin, TX: University of Texas Press, 1985.

Feiler, Bruce. *Walking the Bible*. New York: HarperCollins, 2001.

Filer, Joyce. *Egyptian Bookshelf: Disease*. Austin, TX: University of Texas Press, 1995.

Frankfort, Henri. *Ancient Egyptian Religion*. New York: Columbia University Press, 1948.

Frankfurter, David. *Religion in Roman Egypt*. Princeton: Princeton University Press, 1998.

Freeman, Charles. Egypt, *Greece and Rome*. Oxford: Oxford University Press, 1996.

Gardiner, Alan. *Egypt of the Pharaohs*. London: Oxford University Press, 1961.

Grimal, Nicolas. *A History of Ancient Egypt*. New York: Barnes & Noble, 1997.

Harris, James E., and Kent R. Weeks. *X-Raying the Pharaohs*. New York: Charles Scribner's, 1984.

Hart, George. A Dictionary of Egyptian Gods and Goddesses. London: Routledge & Kegan Paul, 1986.

Hart, George. *Pharaohs and Pyramids*. London: Herbert Press, 1991.

Hobbs, Joseph J. *Mount Sinai*. Austin: University of Texas Press, 1995.

Hobson, Christina. *The World of the Pharaohs*. London: Thames & Hudson, 1987.

Hoffmeier, James K. *Israel in Egypt*. New York: Oxford University Press, 1997.

Hülbl, Günther. *A History of the Ptolemic Empire*. New York: Routledge, 2001.

Hoving, Thomas. *Tutankhamun, The Untold Story*. New York: Simon & Schuster, 1978.

Hughes-Hallett, Lucy. *Cleopatra*. New York: Harper & Row, 1990.

Ikram, Salima, and Aidan Dodson. *The Mummy in Ancient Egypt*. New York: Thames & Hudson, 1998.

Jack, J. W. *The Date of the Exodus*. Edinburgh: T. & T. Clark, 1925.

James, T. G. H. *Ancient Egypt, The Land and Its Legacy*. Austin: University of Texas Press, 1988.

James, T. G. H. *An Introduction to Ancient Egypt*. London: British Museum Press, 1979.

James, T. G. H. *Pharaoh's People*. London: Bodley Head, 1984.

Janssen, Rosaline and Jac. *Growing up in Ancient Egypt*. London: Rubicon Press, 1990.

Johnson, Janet H., ed. *Life in a Multi-Cultural Society, Egypt from Cambyses to Constantine*. Chicago: Oriental Institute, 1992.

Jordan, Paul. *Egypt the Black Land*. New York: E. P. Dutton, 1976.

Kamil, Jill. *Luxor. 2nd ed.*, New York: Longmans, 1976.

Kamil, Jill. *Sakkara*. New York: Longmans, 1978.

Kaster, Joseph, ed. *Wings of the Falcon*. New York: Holt, Rinehart, and Winston, 1968.

Kees, Hermann. *Ancient Egypt*. Chicago: University of Chicago Press, 1961.

Kemp, Barry. *Ancient Egypt*. New York: Routledge, 1989.

Lefkowitz, Mary. *Not Out of Africa.* New York: Basic Books, 1996.

Lehner, Mark. *The Complete Pyramids.* New York: Thames & Hudson, 1997.

Lewis, Naphtali. *Greeks in Ptolemaic Egypt.* Oxford: Clarendon Press, 1986.

Lichtheim, Miriam. *Ancient Egyptian Literature.* 3 vols. Los Angeles: University of California Press, 1973.

Lucas, A. *Ancient Egyptian Materials and Industries. 3rd ed.* London: Edward Arnold, 1948.

Lurker, Manfred. *The Gods and Symbols of Ancient Egypt.* London: Thames & Hudson, 1980.

McDonald, John K. *House of Eternity; The Tomb of Nefertari.* Los Angeles: J. Paul Getty Museum, 1996.

Manniche, Lise. *City of the Dead; Thebes in Egypt.* Chicago: University of Chicago Press, 1987.

Manniche, Lise. *Music and Musicians in Ancient Egypt.* London: British Museum Press, 1991.

Martin, Geoffrey T. *The Hidden Tombs of Memphis.* New York: Thames & Hudson, 1991.

Meskell, Lynn. *Private Life in New Kingdom Egypt.* Princeton: Princeton University Press, 2002.

Michalowski, Kazimierz. *Art of Ancient Egypt.* New York: Henry N. Abrams, n.d.

Michalowski, Kazimierz. *Karnak.* New York: Praeger, 1969.

Modrzejewski, Joseph M. *The Jews of Egypt From Rameses II to Emperor Hadrian.* Princeton: Princeton University Press, 1995.

Mommsen, Theodor. *The Provinces of the Roman Empire.* reprint, 2 vols. New York: Barnes & Noble 1996.

Montet, Pierre. *Eternal Egypt.* New York: New American Library, 1964.

Montet, Pierre. *Everyday Life in Egypt.* London: Edward Arnold, 1958

Moran, William L., ed. *The Amarna Letters.* Baltimore: John Hopkins, 1992.

Morenz, Siegfried. *Egyptian Religion.* Ithaca: Cornell University Press, 1973.

Murnane, William J. *The Penguin Guide to Ancient Egypt.* New York: Penguin Books, 1983.

Murray, Margaret A. *The Splendor That Was Egypt.* New York: Frederick A. Praeger, 1969.

Nibbi, Alessandra. *The Sea Peoples and Egypt.* Park Ridge, NJ: Noyes Press, 1975.

Nicholson, Paul T., and Ian Shaw. *Ancient Egyptian Materials and Technology.* Cambridge: Cambridge University Press, 2000.

Nims, Charles F. *Thebes of the Pharaohs.* London: Elek Books, 1965.

Nunn, John F. *Ancient Egyptian Medicine.* Norman, OK: University of Oklahoma Press, 1996.

O'Conner, David, *Ancient Nubia.* Philadelphia: University of Pennsylvania, 1993.

Oren, Eliezer D., ed. *The Hyksos: New Historical and Archaeological Perspectives.* Philadelphia: The University Museum, 1997.

Parkinson, Richard, and Stephen Quirke. *Papyrus.* London: British Museum Press, 1995.

Partridge, Robert B. *Faces of the Pharaohs.* London: The Rubicon Press, 1994.

Pearlman, Moshe. *In the Footsteps of Moses.* Jerusalem: Steimatzky Agency, 1973.

Pfeiffer, Charles F. *Tell El-Amarna and the Bible.* Grand Rapids: Baker, 1963.

Quirke. Stephen. *The Cult of Ra: Sun-Worship in Ancient Egypt.* London: Thames & Hudson, 2001.

Rainey, Anson F., ed. *Egypt, Israel, Sinai.* Tel Aviv:Tel Aviv University, 1987.

Redford, Donald B. *Akhenaten the Heretic King.* Princeton: Princeton University Press, 1984.

Redford, Donald B. *Egypt, Canaan, and Israel in Ancient Times*. Princeton: Princeton University Press, 1992.

Redford, Donald B., ed. Oxford *Encyclopedia of Ancient Egypt*. 3 vols. New York: Oxford University Press, 2001.

Reeves, Nicholas. *The Complete Tutankhamun*. London: Thames & Hudson, 1990.

Reeves, Nicholas, and Richard H. Wilkinson. *The Complete Valley of the Kings*. London: Thames & Hudson, 1996.

Rice, Michael. *Egypt's Making*. New York: Routledge, 1990.

Robins, Gay. *The Art of Ancient Egypt*. Cambridge: Harvard University Press, 1997.

Robins, Gay. *Women in Ancient Egypt*. Cambridge: Harvard University Press, 1993.

Robins, Gay, and Charles Shute. *The Rhind Mathematical Papyrus*. London: British Museum Press, 1987.

Rohl, David M. *Pharaohs and Kings, a Biblical Quest*. New York: Crown Publishers, 1995.

Romer, John. *Ancient Lives*. New York: Holt, Rinehart & Winston, 1984.

Romer, John. *People of the Nile*. New York: Crown Publishers, 1982.

Romer, John. *Valley of the Kings*. New York: William Morrow, 1981.

Romer, John, and Elizabeth. *The Rape of Tutankhamun*. New York: Barnes & Noble, 1994.

Sandars, Nancy K. *The Sea Peoples*. London: Thames & Hudson, 1978.

Sauneron, Serge. *The Priests of Ancient Egypt*. New York: Grove Press, 1969.

Save-Soderbergh, Torgny. *Pharaohs and Mortals*. New York: Barnes & Noble, 1996.

Schulz, Regine, and Matthias Seidel. *Egypt the World of the Pharaohs*. Cologne: Könemann, 1998.

Shafer, Byron E., ed. *Religion in Ancient Egypt*. Ithaca: Cornell University Press, 1991.

Shafer, Byron E., ed. *Temples of Ancient Egypt*. London: I. B. Tauris, 1997.

Shaw, Ian, and Paul Nicholson. *The Dictionary of Ancient Egypt*. New York: Henry N. Abrams, 1995.

Shorter, Alan W. *The Egyptian Gods*. London: Kegan Paul, 1937.

Siliotti, Alberto. *Guide to the Valley of the Kings*. New York: Barnes & Noble, 1997.

Silverman, David P., ed. *Ancient Egypt*. New York: Oxford University Press, 1997.

Smith, Wilbur M. *Egypt in Biblical Prophecy*. Grand Rapids: Baker, 1957.

Spalinger, Anthony J. *Aspects of the Military Documents of the Ancient Egyptians*. New Haven: Yale University Press, 1982.

Spencer, Alan J. *Death in Ancient Egypt*. New York: Penguin, 1982.

Stead, Miriam. *Egyptian Life*. London: British Museum Press, 1986.

Steindorff, G., and Keith C. Seele. *When Egypt Ruled the East*. Rev ed. Chicago: University of Chicago Press, 1957.

Strouhal, Eugen. *Life of the Ancient Egyptians*. Norman: University of Oklahoma Press, 1992.

Strudwick, Nigel, and Helen. *Thebes in Egypt*. Ithaca, New York: Cornell University Press, 1999.

Tiradritti, Francesco, ed. *Egyptian Treasures from the Egyptian Museum in Cairo*. New York: Harry N. Abrams, 1999.

Trigger, B. G., and others. *Ancient Egypt, a Social History*. Cambridge: Cambridge University Press, 1983.

Time-Life. *What Life was Like on the Banks of the Nile*. Alexandria, VA: Time-Life, 1994.

Tyldesley, Joyce. *Hatchepsut*. New York: Viking, 1996.

Tyldesley, Joyce. *Judgment of the Pharaoh: Crime and Punishment in Ancient Egypt.* London: Weidenfeld & Nicolson, 2000.

Van Seters, John. *The Hyksos.* New Haven: Yale University Press, 1996.

Verbrugghe, Gerald P., and John M. Wickersham. *Berossos and Manetho.* Ann Arbor: University of Michigan Press, 1996.

Watterson, Barbara. *The Egyptians.* Oxford: Blackwell, 1997.

Weeks, Kent. *The Lost Tomb.* London: Weidenfeld & Nicolson, 1998.

Welsby, Derek A. *The Kingdom of Kush.* London: British Museum Press, 1996.

Wilkinson, J. Gardiner. *The Ancient Egyptians.* New York: Crown Publishers, 1989.

Wilkinson, Richard H. *The Complete Gods and Goddesses of Ancient Egypt.* London: Thames & Hudson, 2003.

Wilkinson, Richard H. *The Complete Temples of Ancient Egypt.* New York: Thames & Hudson, 2000.

Wilson, Hilary. *Egyptian Food and Drink.* Aylesbury, Bucks, UK: Shire Publications, 1988.

Wilson, Hilary. *People of the Pharaohs: From Peasant to Courtier.* London: Brockhampton Press, 1999.

Wilson, Ian. *Exodus.* San Francisco: Harper & Row, 1985.

Wilson, John A. *The Burden of Egypt.* Chicago: University

The Mosque of Hebron is the perfectly-preserved wall (now roofed) that Herod the Great built around the traditional Cave of Machpelah, burial place of Abraham, Sarah, Isaac, Rebekah, and Jacob and Leah.

3

PALESTINE

Palestine is preeminently the land of the Bible. Here Abraham, Isaac, and Jacob lived for 215 years during the patriarchal period before the entire clan of the Hebrews moved to Egypt. Most of the book of Genesis concerns these 215 years in Palestine. Then later Abraham's descendants returned to live here during the days of the conquest; the judges; the united kingdom under Saul, David, and Solomon; and the divided kingdom of Israel and Judah. The account of all these events appears in Joshua, Judges, Ruth, 1 and 2 Samuel, 1 and 2 Kings, and 1 and 2 Chronicles. Although the Assyrians and the Babylonians deported many Hebrews, some continued to live in Palestine during the captivity. Hebrews occupied the land in force once more in the days of restoration under Persian auspices (see Ezra, Nehemiah, Esther). And the Gospels and Acts record that this is the land where the Lord Jesus and early disciples lived and worked.

The land has been called by various names, according to the people who occupied it. The older name of the land, Canaan, appears in Scripture as early as Genesis 11:11. Sometimes it has been known as the land of the Amorites or the land of Israel; but today it is commonly known as Palestine. The name is derived from the Philistines, who settled on the coastal plain. Their land, Philistia, the Romans called *Palestina*, hence the English *Palestine*. Actually "Palestine" is not a biblical term. Though the King James Version uses it in Exodus 15:14; Isaiah 14:29, 31; and Joel 3:4, the newer versions properly read "Philistia" in these references. Use of the name Palestine for the region west of the Jordan became popular during the time of the British Mandate, 1918–48.

Palestine is a land bridge between the two oldest civilizations in the world—Mesopotamia and Egypt. But its civilization was immensely different from these two. Mesopotamia and Egypt were made possible by irrigation of river systems. Palestine, on the other hand, could engage in dry farming because there was adequate rainfall in much of the area. Rainfall varies, however: 25 inches per year in Nazareth in Galilee, 16 inches at Tiberias on the Sea of Galilee, 22 inches in the Valley of Jezreel, 32–36 inches on Mount Carmel, 22 inches at Jerusalem, 8 inches at Beersheba, and 6 inches at Jericho.[1] Though the scenery of Mesopotamia and Egypt is rather monotonous; Palestine has much variety. In fact, it is probably true that no other place in the world offers such diversity of scenery and climate in such a small area. As a land bridge, Palestine has been so frequently invaded and so often dominated by foreign

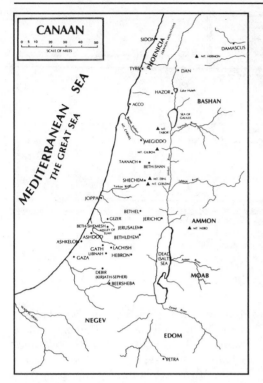

powers that it could never develop the high degree of cultural homogeneity found in Egypt or even the lesser degree in Mesopotamia.

Geographical Features

Borders

It is difficult to be specific about the borders of Palestine. From the Old Testament perspective, the boundaries of Canaan were the Jordan River and the Mediterranean on the east and west, and Dan and Beersheba on the north and south (Judges 20:1; 1 Samuel 3:20). The distance from Dan to Beersheba is just under 150 miles. The width of the country at the Sea of Galilee is 25–30 miles; at the northern end of the Dead Sea, about 55 miles; and at the southern end of the Dead Sea, about 85 miles. This area totals some 6,000 to 7,000 square miles, about the size of Connecticut and Delaware combined. But the Hebrews sometimes controlled additional territory west of the Jordan, as well as the highlands east of the Jordan (about 4,000 square miles). At the outside, then, they normally controlled no more than 10,000 to 12,000 square miles—

about the size of Maryland or a little less than that of Belgium. Of course the Hebrew Empire at its height under David and Solomon was larger than that.

We should not confuse the land of Canaan with the promised land, however. The latter as spelled out to Abraham extended "from the river of Egypt unto . . . the river Euphrates" (Genesis 15:18). The Hebrew word translated "river" in Genesis 15:18 refers to an ever-flowing river and apparently must be applied to the Nile; other streams of southern Palestine and the Sinai flow only during the rainy season. The easternmost branch of the Nile—the Pelusiac—flows out near modern Port Said and hence near the ancient line of fortifications that protected Egypt from marauding Asiatics. Thus the Pelusiac branch could properly be thought of as the border of Egypt. The distance from Port Said to the Euphrates may be variously measured—in a straight line or in an arc. The former would measure between 600 and 700 miles. Of course the Israelites have never enjoyed possession of all this land; fulfillment of the prophesy must be reserved for the millennial era at the end times.

Climate

Palestine enjoys a moderate climate. January is the coldest month with average temperatures as follows: 46°–50° at Jerusalem, 53° in the coastal plain, and 53°–55° in the Jordan Valley. August is the warmest month and has mean temperatures of 71°–79° F at Jerusalem, 75°–79° in the coastal plain, and 82°–93° in the Jordan Valley. The highest known temperature to date in the Jordan Valley was registered at 129° F in June 1941; at that same time the highest known temperature in Jerusalem stood at 111°. The lowest temperature ever recorded at Jerusalem is 24° F and in Lower Galilee 8.6° (both in February 1950).

Divisions of the Land

As noted above, Palestine has a varied topography and climate. The land divides into five longitudinal divisions and two lateral regions. Along the Mediterranean extends the coastal plain, east of which rises the foothills, also known as the piedmont or

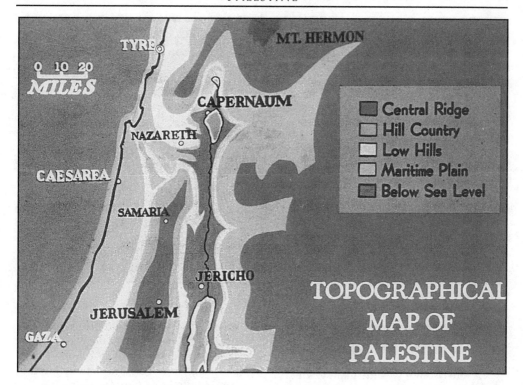

TYRE

MT. HERMON

0 10 20
MILES

CAPERNAUM

NAZARETH

CAESAREA

SAMARIA

JERICHO

JERUSALEM

GAZA

Central Ridge
Hill Country
Low Hills
Maritime Plain
Below Sea Level

TOPOGRAPHICAL
MAP OF
PALESTINE

Shephelah. Farther east stands the (Western Plateau or Western Mountain Ridge or Central Mountain Ridge). Then comes the Great rift of the Jordan Valley, east of which rises the Eastern Plateau, or Eastern Mountain Ridge. The northern lateral region is the Plain of Esdraelon, which extends from Mount Carmel to the Jordan Valley. And the southern lateral zone, which cuts across southern Palestine from the Mediterranean to the southern end of the Dead Sea, is the Negev.

The Coastal Plain

The coastal plain extends from the Wadi el-Arish to Rosh ha-Niqra or the Ladder of Tyre at the present Lebanese-Israeli border—a distance of some 150 miles. In the north the plain measures less than three miles wide, but it gradually increases to about twenty-five miles near Gaza. The altitude gently rises from sea level to about 500 feet. Along most of the coast, which is very straight and poor in promontories and bays, is a belt of arid sand dunes. These block the outflow of the small rivers and create marshes. The

coastline itself may consist of either a gently inclined shore with a beach or precipitous cliffs 30 to 120 feet in height. The nature of the coastline tended to force the building of towns of any size and importance a short distance inland. The same was true of the main coastal road. Both because of occupational preferences of the Hebrews (farmers, herders, vine dressers, etc.) and the lack of good harbors, the Hebrews did not build any Mediterranean ports worthy of the name in Old Testament times. Not until just before the birth of Christ did Herod the Great construct the magnificent port of Caesarea (about 25 miles south of Haifa), naming it after Augustus Caesar. The city was a typical Greco-Roman center with its hippodrome (seating 20,000), amphitheater, theater, aqueducts, temples, and colonnaded street. The port was protected by a massive breakwater. Caesarea was the capital of Palestine during Paul's ministry, and there he was imprisoned for two years (Acts 23–27). There too began the bloody struggle that ended with the destruction of Jerusalem and the Temple in A.D. 70.

A Crusader bastion at Acre.

ACRE

Acre (Accho) was the main town of the Plain of Acre, also known as the Plain of Asher because it was assigned to the tribe of Asher in the division of Canaan after the Conquest. But the men of Asher were unable to occupy the city (Judges 1:31), and it remained in Phoenician hands throughout Old Testament times.

In Hellenistic times the name of Accho was changed to Ptolemais, probably in honor of Ptolemy Philadelphus (who reigned 285–246 B.C.), and it bore that name during the Maccabean period (cf. 1 Maccabees 5:15; 12:45–48) and in the New Testament period (Acts 21:7). Toward the end of his third missionary journey, Paul stopped briefly en route from Tyre to Caesarea and spent a day in fellowship with a group of Christians at Ptolemais. At that time Ptolemais was a Roman colony with a population that included war veterans who had received grants of land from the emperor Claudius.

The name was changed back to Accho in early Arabic times. The Crusaders conquered the city and made it one of their strongholds under the name of "Acre," but the Israeli city is known as "Accho."

At first archaeological activity there concentrated on Crusader structures under the present city. In 1955 the Israel Department of Antiquities cleared the refectory of the Knights of St. John, and in 1956 and from 1959 to 1962 the Department of Antiquities and the National Parks Authority cleared a hospital and chapel of the order. Zeev Goldmann and Zeev Yeivin directed some of the work. Here, then, was a magnificent complex of twelfth-century buildings with some fine Gothic elements where pilgrims and knights commonly made their first stay on arrival in Palestine.

The original site of the town, Tell Acco, is located one mile east of the present city. From 1973 to 1989 several Israeli agencies and the University of Marburg in Germany excavated on the Tell under the leadership of Moshe Dothan and others. Finds dated from the Early Bronze Age to Roman and Byzantine times. Additional exploratory excavations were conducted in 1995 and 1996.

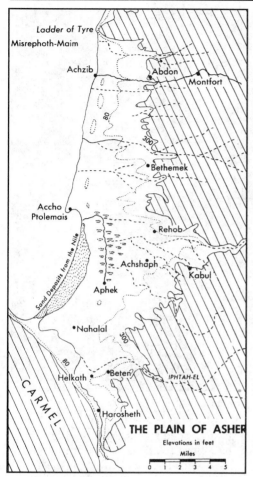

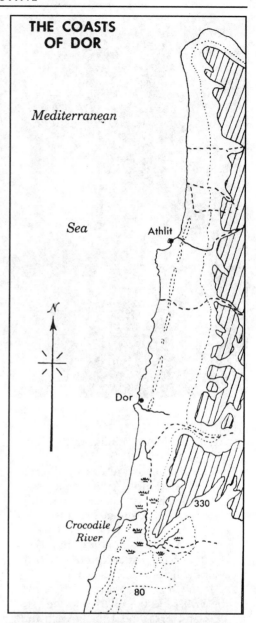

The coastal plain subdivides into four regions. On the north lies the Plain of Acre (Accho), which is about twenty miles long between Rosh ha-Niqra and Mount Carmel. Its width increases from around three miles in the north to ten miles in the south. Acre is the main town of the plain, and a river that flows through the plain into Haifa Bay is the Kishon—of some interest because Elijah slew the prophets of Baal by its banks (1 Kings 18:40), and along which King Jabin II was defeated in the battle with Deborah and Barak (Judges 4:7, 13; 5:21; Psalms 83:4).

The narrow coastal plain extending about twenty miles south of Mount Carmel was known in ancient times as "the coasts of Dor." Its natural boundary on the south was the marshes of the Crocodile River (Nahal Tannanim). The main center of the plain was the town of Dor, the only town in the region mentioned in the Bible.

DOR

Dor (Khirbet el-Burj), eight miles north of Caesarea, was an important Canaanite city-state in the league of Jabin, king of Hazor (Joshua 11:1–12). Not conquered during the Conquest or the subsequent period of the judges (Judges 1:27), it became part of David's empire and was in

Recent excavations at Dor.

Solomon's fourth administrative district (1 Kings 4:11).

The Sidonians ruled Dor during the Persian period. In the Hellenistic period it was a particularly powerful fortress. The Hasmoneans ruled the city until Pompey took it in 63 B.C. and granted it autonomy. But Dor began to decline after Herod the Great built the harbor at Caesarea.

John Garstang excavated there for the British School of Archaeology in 1923 and 1924 and J. Leibovitch for the Israel Department of Antiquities in 1950 and 1952. New large scale excavations resumed in 1980 under the auspices of the Hebrew University of Jerusalem and the Israel Exploration Society and under the leadership of Ephraim Stern.

The site was first inhabited in about the nineteenth century B.C. and continued to exist almost without interruption until the Roman period.

It developed an important harbor and had close relations with Cyprus and the Aegean world. A Roman theater dated probably to the second or third century A.D. and a large Byzantine church to the fifth–seventh centuries A.D. (rebuilt during the period). Crusaders established a stronghold on the summit of the mound.

The central part of the coastal plain is called Sharon and extends about fifty miles from the Crocodile River to the Yarkon River near Tel Aviv-Joppa, though the southern boundary of the plain is not clearly distinguished. It varies from six to twelve miles in breadth. Joppa, at its southern end, served as the main port of Jerusalem, even though it was poorly protected from the sea. In ancient times Sharon was heavily forested and had luxuriant vegetation and extensive pasture lands (cf., 1 Chronicles 5:16; 27:29).

western sector of the Carmel Range, was sparsely occupied in ancient times. The lower western slope, however, contains caves in which remains of a Stone Age culture were discovered by Dorothy Garrod of the British School of Archaeology in Jerusalem and Theodore McCown, representing the American School of Prehistoric Research.

Elijah gave Mount Carmel its grandest moment when he challenged the prophets of Baal to a showdown encounter. Ahab and Jezebel had encouraged the cult of the Canaanite fertility god Baal, with the result that Israel's God was largely forgotten. Elijah, however, proved the futility of Baal worship (1 Kings 18:19–40) and demonstrated the fact that Yahweh, the God of Israel, was the living God who answered by fire.

The plain of Philistia in the south is about seventy miles long and reaches a width of twenty-five miles opposite Beersheba. Although rainfall decreases in the south, there is enough moisture for growing crops as far south as Gaza. Gaza was the most southerly and the main city of the plain. Farther north stand Ashkelon and Ashdod. These three joined with Gath and Ekron in the Shephelah to form the Philistine pentapolis (league of five cities). This combination of power posed a threat to the freedom and independence of the Hebrews for two centuries.

The statue of Elijah that stands on Mount Carmel today commemorates his victory over the prophets of Baal.

MOUNT CARMEL

Mount Carmel, jutting out into the Mediterranean, splits the Palestinian coastal plain into two sectors and forms a barrier to communication between the two. Commercial and military traffic usually crossed the Carmel Range through passes leading to such points as Taanach, Megiddo, and Ibleam. The range extends southeast from the Mediterranean (at modern Haifa) for approximately thirteen miles, with a maximum height of 1,742 feet. In ancient times, as at present, Carmel was covered with luxuriant foliage.

Somewhat isolated from the normal flow of traffic, Mount Carmel, the

JOPPA, ANCIENT SEAPORT OF ISRAEL

Joppa, in the Plain of Sharon, served as the seaport for Jerusalem, thirty-five miles distant. It was a walled town as early as the reign of Pharaoh Thutmose III (1482–1450 B.C.), who mentions Joppa in his town lists.

At the division of the land of Canaan to the Hebrew tribes, Joppa was assigned to Dan (Joshua 19:46), but it did not come under Israelite

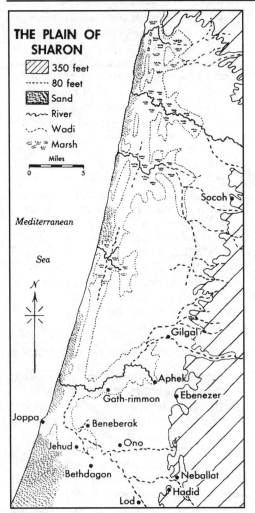

THE PLAIN OF SHARON

- ▨ 350 feet
- ----- 80 feet
- ▨ Sand
- ∿∿ River
- ⌇⌁ Wadi
- ⱳⱳ Marsh

Miles
0   5

Mediterranean

Sea

N

Socoh

Gilgal

Aphek

Gath-rimmon   Ebenezer

Joppa

Beneberak

Jehud   Ono

Bethdagon   Neballat

Lod   Hadid

times during the Crusades. Jaffa, or Yafa, now forms the southern part of the combined Israeli metropolis Tel Aviv-Jaffa.

The Shephelah

The Shephelah,[2] (or piedmont or foothills) rises east of the coastal plain to an average altitude of five hundred to a thousand feet, though some points are as much as fifteen hundred feet high. It is a well-defined transitional section almost forty miles long from north to south and eight miles east and west. Apparently plentiful forests blanketed the hills of the Shephelah in Old Testament times (1 Kings 10:27). Three important valleys cross this hilly region. At the northern limits is the Valley of Ajalon, beginning five miles northwest of Jerusalem, where Joshua decisively defeated the Canaanites (Joshua 10:12). It is the gate to Jerusalem from the Plain of Sharon. Some ten miles to the south and immediately west of Jerusalem is the Valley of Sorek, scene of numerous exploits of Samson (Judges 16:4). Another seven to eight miles farther south is the Valley of Elah, where David killed Goliath (1 Samuel 17:2). Since these valleys led into the heart of Judah, it is understandable that their control would be disputed between Philistines and Hebrews. Important towns of the Shephelah include Beth-Shemesh, Libnah, Azekah, Mareshah, and Lachish.

The Western Plateau

Interests of many Bible students center on the Western Plateau or the Western Mountain Ridge sector of Palestine because among those hills and valleys of Galilee, Samaria, and Judea took place a great many Old and New Testament events. Here lived a wide variety of individuals, from faithful Abraham to faithless Judas, from godly Hezekiah to reprobate Ahab, from devout Hannah to scheming Jezebel. And, of course, special significance attaches to Christ's earthly ministry in all three parts of this region.

Although many for convenience look at the western ridge as something of a unit, each of the three parts has its own characteristics. Judea has more compact hills, while in Samaria they are more scattered, and in

control until David gained effective control of the coast. Hiram of Tyre had timber floated from Lebanon to the seaport of Joppa for Solomon's Temple (2 Chronicles 2:16). In the time of Cyrus, cedars were again transported by water to Joppa for building the second temple (Ezra 3:7).

When Jonah embarked for Tarshish in order to avoid going to Nineveh, he boarded a ship at Joppa (Jonah 1:3). Here Peter spent some time in the house of a tanner named Simon (Acts 9:43) and received the vision that told him he should not term unclean that which God had cleansed (Acts 10:5–16).

Joppa was twice destroyed by the Romans and changed hands several

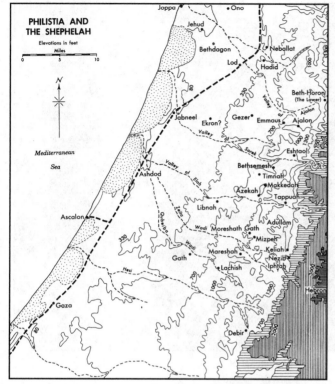

PHILISTIA AND
THE SHEPHELAH

Elevations in feet

Miles

thus has attractive agricultural and pastoral possibilities. In ancient times it had a considerable forest cover. Its numerous roads leading to all parts of Canaan and adjacent lands contributed to a greater cosmopolitanism than was true of other parts of Palestine. Important towns of Galilee that receive attention later include Nazareth, Sepphoris, Cana, Hazor, Tiberias, Capernaum, Chorazin, and Bethsaida.

Samaria. Samaria is separated from Galilee by the Valley of Jezreel on the north. From Judah on the south it is separated by a less pronounced division along the line of the Valley of the Craftsmen (Nehemiah 11:35) and the Valley of Ajalon to Bethel and thence by other valleys to Jericho. On the east lies the Jordan Valley; and on the west,

Galilee the low hills of the south gradually ascend as one goes northward. The altitude of the whole ridge ranges from approximately two thousand to four thousand feet.

Galilee. The hill regions of Galilee are clearly defined. On the west they touch the coastal plain, in the north they stop at the gorge of the Litani River, in the east they border on the Jordan Valley, and in the south they rise above the Valley of Jezreel. It is customary to make a distinction between Lower and Upper Galilee. The hills of southern or Lower Galilee reach a maximum of two thousand feet. Upper Galilee has heights ranging from two thousand to four thousand feet. Between the two parts of Galilee the fault of Esh-Shaghur cuts across the country at about the latitude of the north end of the Sea of Galilee. Galilee has adequate rainfall and fertile soil and

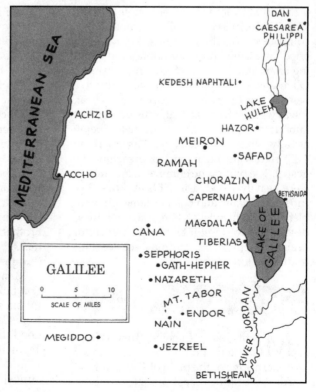

GALILEE

0   5   10

SCALE OF MILES

Mount Tabor

the Plain of Sharon. As already noted, in the region of Samaria the hills are not closely compacted together, leaving stretches of good land with abundant rainfall for growing crops and foothills for grazing purposes. Olive and grape production was extensive here, as was the raising of barley and wheat. It was while in Samaria that Jesus uttered His famous observation about the fields being already white and ready for harvest (John 4:35), signifying the urgency of preaching the gospel. The hills of the entire area apparently were heavily wooded in biblical times. The tribes of Ephraim and half of Manasseh occupied the highlands of Samaria, and these descendants of Joseph buried their ancestor near Shechem; there one may see Joseph's traditional tomb today.

MOUNT TABOR

Mount Tabor (Jebel et-Tur) is a limestone mound on the northeastern edge of the plain of Esdraelon. About 6 miles east of Nazareth,

twelve miles north of Mount Gilboa, and twelve miles southwest of the Sea of Galilee, it rises to a height of 1,350 feet above the plain and 1,929 feet above the Mediterranean. The more or less flat top measures about a half mile by a quarter mile.

Tabor served as a boundary between the territories of Issachar and Zebulun. During the period of the judges Barak gathered his forces on Tabor and then descended with ten thousand men into the plain, conquering Sisera on the bank of the Kishon (Judges 4:6–15). Here the brothers of Gideon met death at the hands of Zebah and Zalmunna (Judges 8:18–19).

Many locate Christ's transfiguration on Mount Tabor, but that is open to question because of its distance from Caesarea-Philippi and the likelihood that a town occupied the top of Tabor in New Testament times. That would have made the secluded atmosphere of the Transfiguration

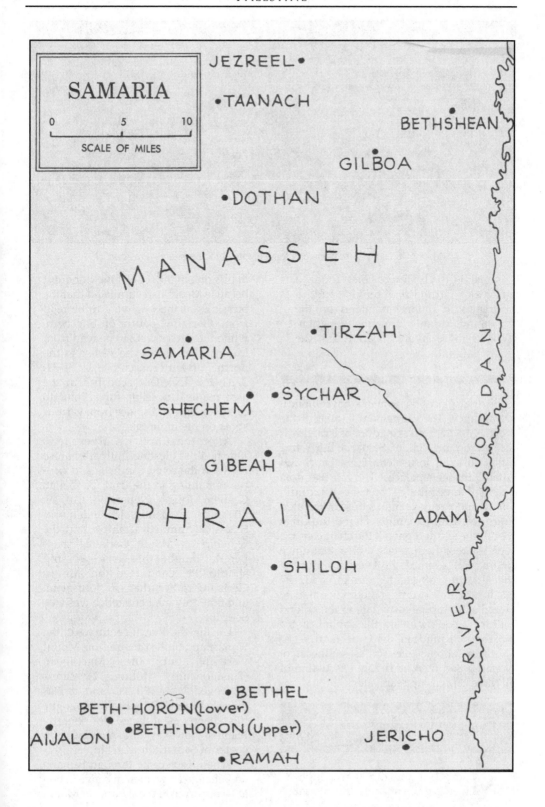

SAMARIA

0   5   10
SCALE OF MILES

JEZREEL •

• TAANACH

BETHSHEAN

GILBOA

• DOTHAN

MANASSEH

• TIRZAH

SAMARIA

SHECHEM • • SYCHAR

GIBEAH

EPHRAIM

ADAM

SHILOH

JORDAN

RIVER

• BETHEL

BETH-HORON (Lower)

AIJALON • BETH-HORON (Upper)

JERICHO

• RAMAH

Mount Gerizim with remains of a temple, thought to be a temple to Zeus.

scene virtually impossible. Today a Greek Orthodox church and a Franciscan monastery stand on the summit. Mount Hermon is thought to be a more likely location for the Transfiguration.

Several places in Samaria have biblical significance. The permanent capital of the Northern Kingdom (kingdom of Israel) was located on the hill of Samaria thirty-five miles north of Jerusalem. Here Omri and Ahab built their palaces. The hill rises to a height of three hundred feet above a fruitful valley, and ravines on all sides contributed to its defensive capability. Herod the Great rebuilt the site and gave it the character of a typical Greco-Roman city with a stadium, a forum, and a temple to Augustus. But the theater, the colonnaded street, and the basilica of the forum, sometimes dated to Herod's day, apparently date to the second century A.D. Previously the capital of the Northern Kingdom had been first at Shechem (about seven miles southeast of Samaria) and then at Tirzah. Discussion of all three capitals appears later.

MOUNT GERIZIM AND THE QUESTION OF WHERE TO WORSHIP

Mount Gerizim (2,850 feet high) won significance as the mount

of blessing at the time of the Conquest because Moses had stipulated that the blessings of the law were to be read from Gerizim, south of Shechem, while the curses were to be read from Mount Ebal across the valley to the north (Deuteronomy 11:29–31; 27:11–26). Excellent acoustics in the area made it possible for a voice to carry for a great distance from various spots on the mountain.

After the Captivity, when Jews returned to Palestine, antipathy arose between the returning Jews and people remaining in the land (Sanballat, Geshem, Tobiah, Nehemiah 2:10, 19; 4:11; 6:1). Evidently descendants of Sanballat founded a temple and the worship on Mount Gerizim. These people taught that true worship should be conducted on Mount Gerizim, rather than in Jerusalem, and that only the Pentateuch was true Scripture.

During the fourth century B.C. the Samaritans built a temple on Mount Gerizim but the Maccabean (Hasmonean) John Hyrcanus destroyed it in 128 B.C. and it was never rebuilt. A Samaritan synagogue has been established in nearby Nablus, however, and remains as a center of Samaritan worship.

When Jesus came through Samaria and engaged a woman in conversation at Jacob's Well in the shadow of Mount

Gerizim (John 4), she raised a question about whether the place of true worship was Mount Gerizim or Jerusalem. In response, Jesus changed the focus of the question from place to attitude: "God is Spirit, and those who worship Him must worship in spirit and truth" (John 4:24, NKJV).

In 1964, 1966, and 1968 Robert J. Bull of Drew University excavated at Tell Er-Ras, one of the northernmost peaks of Mount Gerizim and uncovered there a temple that turned out to be a Roman period temple to Zeus, dating to the second century A.D. Under its foundations lay another building which some believe was the Samaritan temple that John Hyrcanus destroyed.

Yitzhak Magen of the Israel Department of Antiquities has been excavating on the main peak of Mount Gerizim since 1984 and has uncovered there a fortified city built in about 200 B.C. and covering a hundred acres. This, too, was destroyed by John Hyrcanus between 114 and 111 B.C.

A Samaritan priest with the Samaritan Pentateuch

At Shechem the patriarchs stayed (Genesis 12:6; 5:4), Joshua delivered his farewell address (Joshua 24:1), and later the kingdom was divided (1 Kings 12:1). Shechem stood in a valley between the famous mountains Ebal on the north (3,100 feet high) and Gerizim on the south (2,900 feet high). On the former, six tribes stood to hear the curses for disobeying the law, and on the latter, six tribes stood to bless the people for obedience (Deutoronomy 27–28). The town of Dothan figures in the Joseph narrative and later in the activities of Elisha.

DOTHAN AND JOSEPH

Dothan enters the biblical narrative in connection with the story of Joseph. Here he was thrown into a dry well, or cistern, and later pulled out and sold to a merchant caravan on the way to Egypt (Genesis 37). The town is twelve miles north of Samaria and just east of the modern road from Samaria to Jenin. The area was prized for its excellent pastorage that had attracted Joseph's brothers.

Later, during the ninth century B.C., Elisha the prophet was staying at Dothan when the Syrian army came to capture him because he had been an effective military informant to king Jehoram of Israel (2 Kings 6).

Joseph P. Free of Wheaton College (Illinois) excavated the ten-acre site for nine seasons (1953–64). Excavations revealed, among other things, evidence of a thriving city in the general period of Elisha (c. 850 B.C.), with house walls still standing along one street to a height of seven feet in places.

Judea. The highlands of Judea extend about sixty miles from Bethel to Beersheba and have an average elevation range of two

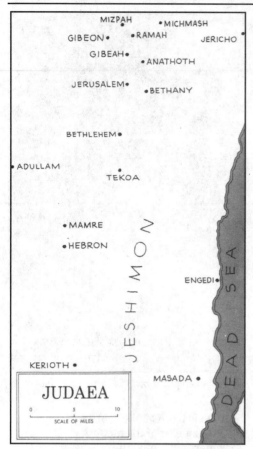

MIZPAH • • MICHMASH
GIBEON • • RAMAH   JERICHO •
GIBEAH •
• ANATHOTH
JERUSALEM •
• BETHANY

BETHLEHEM •

• ADULLAM
•
TEKOA

• MAMRE
• HEBRON

ENGEDI •

KERIOTH •
MASADA •

JUDAEA
0   5   10
SCALE OF MILES

JESHIMON

DEAD SEA

the Judean Desert. Groundwaters drain to the east and provide springs in that desert. What little rainfall there is descends the steep slopes rapidly to the west and cuts deep wadis (stream beds that are dry during the summer, similar to arroyos in the American southwest). Although rainfall in the highest hills of Judea may be as much as twenty-eight inches a year, about six miles east of Jerusalem it dwindles to twelve inches, and around the Dead Sea between to two to four inches. The wilderness of Judea on various occasions in history has given refuge to separatists from society, whether by choice (as in the case of the Qumran community) or pursuit (as in the case of David—Ziph is about three miles southeast of Hebron).

Jerusalem is, of course, the most famous of all Judean cities and assumed importance for the Hebrews after David captured it and made it his capital. At that time the fortified area covered about eleven acres, as excavations have shown.[3] It stood where the valleys of the Kidron, Hinnom, and Tyropoeon come together. Actually, however, Jerusalem came to occupy five hills in ancient times (Ophel, Moriah, Bezetha, Acra, Zion), the highest of which is about 2,550 feet above sea level. To the east of the Kidron Valley stands the Mount of Olives (2,680 feet above sea level), part of a ridge that divides Jerusalem from the wilderness of Judea.

thousand to three thousand feet. On the west they are bounded by the Shephelah, and on the east by the Jordan Valley. Access from the latter into the Judean highlands is difficult. A good north-south road ran near the eastern edge of the highlands, and along it stood such important cities as Jerusalem and Hebron. Judea has good soil, especially for fruit trees and vines, but it must be retained by terraces on the hillsides.

Just west of Jerusalem is the watershed and east of the watershed line spreads

Mount of Olives, with the Church of All Nations (center), to the left of which is the Garden of Gethsemane.

Modern Hebron

MOUNT OF OLIVES

The Mount of Olives refers broadly to the four hills east of Jerusalem, rising from the Kidron Valley and running in a north-south direction. More specifically, the northernmost hill is called Mount Scopas and the southernmost the Mount of Offense, the place of pagan temples of Solomon's foreign wives (2 Kings 23:13).

The two central hills, then, opposite the Temple area, are especially known as the Mount of Olives. These rise to a height of just over 2,700 feet; the highest point in Jerusalem is 2,550 feet. A shallow saddle lies between the summits of the two central hills. The southern of these two hills is especially revered today. At its western foot lies the Garden of Gethsemane and the adjacent Church of All Nations, which covers the traditional Rock of Agony, where Jesus agonized in prayer during the Passion week. On its crest is the Mosque, or Chapel of the Ascension (the traditional spot where Jesus rose to heaven), and around its foot to the east a road winds to Bethany, where Jesus stayed during the Passion week.

At several points on the crest of the hill a marvelous panorama of Jerusalem unrolls before the spectator. A spectacular view of the Temple would have been visible to the disciples as they and Jesus sat there together during the Olivet Discourse (Matthew 24–25), when Jesus predicted the destruction of the Temple.

The Mount of Olives is also mentioned in connection with David's flight from Absalom (2 Samuel 15:30); the departure of God's presence from Jerusalem in Ezekiel's day (Ezekiel 11:23); and the Lord's Second Coming, when the mountain will split in two from east to west (Zechariah 14:4).

Bethlehem, six miles to the south of Jerusalem is slightly higher in altitude, and Hebron, twenty-three miles south of Jerusalem, is 3,300 feet in altitude, the highest town in Judah. Although Hebron was important for its connection with numerous events in Scripture, it is especially known for the Cave of Machpelah, where Abraham and various other members of the patriarchal family were buried. Today the cave is generally considered to be under the city mosque at Hebron. At the southern edge of Judea, about fifty miles from Jerusalem,

Hazor was the important bastion of northern Canaan

stands Beersheba at an altitude of one thousand feet. Jerusalem, Hebron, and Beersheba all gain significance from the fact that they are at crossroads, located on important routes north and south, and east and west.

THE JORDAN RIFT

The fourth longitudinal division of Palestine is the Jordan Rift, which extends some three hundred miles from Mount Hermon to the Red Sea.[4] This deep depression has an average width of ten miles and descends to a depth of approximately thirteen hundred feet below sea level at the shore of the Dead Sea, the lowest spot on earth. More importantly, however, the mountains generally rise steeply and abruptly to a height of two thousand feet or more above the valley floor. There are few places where the topography moderates and the Jordan may be crossed easily. Thus, the rift is an effective dividing line between Palestine west of Jordan and Transjordan. It does not matter, then, that the Jordan River itself

The Hasbani, one of the tributaries of the Jordon River in northern Israel.

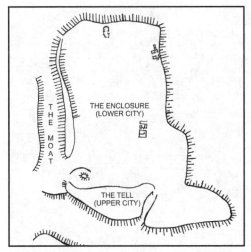

Hazor consisted of a bottle-shaped mound of about 25 acres and a lower city of about 180 acres

gular 175-acre enclosure to the north, some one thousand yards long by seven hundred yards wide. This was the largest city of Palestine in Canaanite times, with a population of roughly forty thousand.[6] Joshua defeated Jabin I of Hazor, who headed a northern confederacy at the time of the conquest (Joshua 11:10–14). Later a second Jabin of Hazor met defeat at the hands of judges Deborah and Barak (Judges 4).

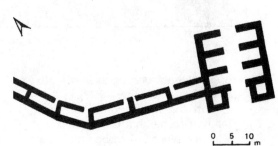

Plan of the six-chambered Solomonic gate at Hazor, attached to a casemate city well.

is not especially wide or deep, for the real barrier is not the river but the rift.

Towering over the northern end of the Jordan Valley is Mount Hermon at 9,232 feet above sea level. From the slopes of Hermon comes most of the water for the Jordan,[5] which has four sources. The Hasbani flows from the western slope of Hermon; the Baniyas from the southwestern slope of Hermon; the Liddani (Leddan) originates at Dan; from the northwest comes the Bareighit. These four join about five miles south of Dan and flow as a single stream another ten miles into Lake Huleh at 220 feet above sea level. The Huleh region used to be a swampy area surrounding a lake measuring about four by three miles. Israeli engineers have drained the area and reclaimed fifteen thousand acres of excellent farmland and improved the condition of another fifteen thousand acres that were often too muddy when rains were heavy.

Dominating the Huleh valley at the southwest was Hazor, standing at the junction of the north-south road and the route to Damascus—which crossed the Jordan just below the lake. Hazor consisted of two parts: a 25-acre mound and a roughly rectan-

HAZOR—BASTION OF THE NORTH

Strategically located in northern Palestine, Hazor was an important bastion, both for the Canaanites and then for the Hebrews who displaced them. Located nine miles north of the Sea of Galilee at Tell el-Qedah, it stood at the junction of the north-south road and the east-west route to Damascus and dominated the Huleh valley.

The site was significant in the Old Testament, first in connection with Joshua's conquest when King Jabin of Hazor led a Canaanite confederation against Joshua and was defeated, suffering the destruction of his city (Joshua 11). Later, another Jabin met defeat at the hands of judges Deborah and Barak (Judges 4). Solomon fortified the city (1 Kings 9:15), and Tiglath-pileser III of Assyria carried

Entrance to the underground water system at Hazor

off its Hebrew occupants into captivity in 732 B.C. (2 Kings 15:29).

With the destruction of the second Jabin, it seems that Canaanite Hazor was permanently crushed and incorporated into the tribe of Naphtali. The unfortified Israelite settlement of the eleventh century was followed by a return to former splendor during the days of Solomon's tenth century B.C. constructions. The casemate wall and large gate flanked by two towers, and backed up by three guardrooms on either side, were identical with the fortifications he constructed at Gezer and Megiddo.

Later Ahab rebuilt the site in the ninth century, erecting a strong citadel and a number of public buildings. A large underground water system, roughly on the same plan and larger than the one at Megiddo, also seems to date to Ahab's day. To create this system, a vertical shaft with a rock-cut staircase was dug one hundred feet into the tell where it entered an eighty-two-foot tunnel that led to water. Ahab's citadel continued in use

Remains of one of Ahab's stables or storage buildings at Hazor.

The Sea of Galilee, seen through palm trees at Capernaum. At this point the Sea is only three or four miles wide.

until the conquest and destruction by Tiglath-Pileser III of Assyria in 732 B.C. Subsequent levels of occupation included Assyrian, Persian, and Hellenistic forts, but the city remained largely uninhabited.

Hazor consists of two parts: a tell, or mound, and a lower city. The tell is about 130 feet high and covers 25–30 acres. Adjacent to it on the north was a lower city of 175–200 acres within a large rectangle about 2,300 feet wide and 3,300 feet long. After defeat of the second Jabin the lower city was abandoned, and later construction (noted above) centered on the mound.

Archaeological work at the site began with John Garstang, who excavated there briefly in 1928. Yigael Yadin led a Hebrew University dig there for five seasons during 1955 to 1958 and in 1968. Excavation was renewed in 1990 as a cooperative venture of several institutions under the leadership of Amnon Ben-Tor of the Hebrew University.

Some ten miles south of Huleh the Jordan flows into the Sea of Galilee. This pear-shaped lake (also called, Lake Kinneret, Sea of Chinnereth, Lake of Gennesaret, and Sea of Tiberias) is thirteen miles long and 7 miles wide at its greatest extent and covers sixty-four square miles. Its surface varies between 684 and 710 feet below sea level, depending on amounts of rainfall. Its deepest point is 833 feet below the Mediterranean, or about 150 feet below the surface of the lake. Northwest of the lake lies the plain of Gennasaret,and around the northern and western sides once stood

The Jordan where it flows out of the Sea of Galilee

The Dead Sea at a point where tourists often swim.

Chorazin, Capernaum, and Tiberias. Bethsaida was on its northeastern shore. The idyllic beauty and quiet of the Sea of Galilee today are a sharp contrast to conditions during New Testament times. Then bustling towns stood at or near the shore. Fishing boats dotted the surface, and grain boats often crossed over from the east.

As the Jordan continues its southerly course, it descends until at the surface of the Dead Sea it drops to 1,308 feet below sea level.[7] The distance between the Sea of Galilee and the Dead Sea measures sixty-five miles in a straight line, but because the river often flows as the snake slithers, its bed measures some two hundred miles. The Jordan's average width is 90–100 feet during much of the year but is considerably wider at flood stage. Important tributaries flow into the Jordan south of the Sea of Galilee; chief of

At the southern end of the Dead Sea massive salt deposits collect.

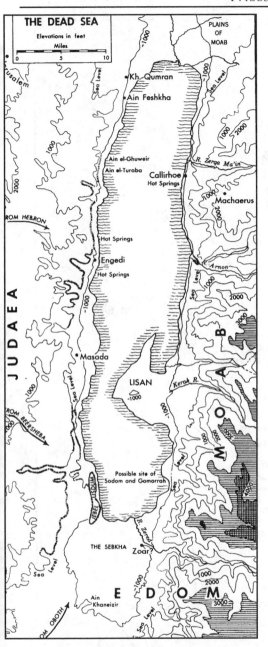

THE DEAD SEA

Elevations in feet

Miles

PLAINS OF MOAB

Kh. Qumran

Ain Feshkha

Ain el-Ghuweir
Ain el-Turaba

Callirhoe
Hot Springs

R. Zerqa Ma'in

Machaerus

Hot Springs

Engedi

Hot Springs

Arnon

JUDAEA

Masada

LISAN

Kerak R.

M O A B

Possible site of
Sodom and Gomorrah

JEBEL USDUM

THE SEBKHA Zoar?

Sea

Ain
Khaneizir

E   D   O   M

measures thirteen hundred feet deep in spots. Its southern basin averages only about twenty feet in depth (maximum of 30–35 feet),[8] however, and is commonly thought to cover Sodom and the other cities of the plain. The southern basin of the Dead Sea (south of el Lisan, or the "tongue," which juts into it from the east) is now increasingly dried up. Massive beds of salt crystals spread along the southern shore. The northern basin is shrinking too and those who wish to bathe in the Dead Sea often take motor vehicles down to the shore. It used to be possible to walk right into the water. Shrinkage of the Dead Sea is a result of increased water use from the Jordan River system on the part of Syria, Jordan, and Israel. Israel has periodically considered digging a canal from the Mediterranean to the Dead Sea to replenish its waters, but nothing has yet come of the proposal.

Since the Dead Sea has no outlet and is subject to high evaporation by the heat of the area (plus inflow of water from mineral springs), its saline content regularly increases. It now contains over 30 percent salts in solution at the surface of the southern basin and 33 percent at depth, the highest salt content of any lake in the world and several times that of the great oceans or seas. Numerous chemicals exist in the Dead Sea, and some are now being extracted by Israeli firms. About seven miles northwest of the Dead Sea stood Old Testament Jericho, gateway to central Palestine. A mile or two from Old Testament Jericho the Herodian family later built up New Testament Jericho.

South of the Dead Sea is the Arabah, 115 miles in length. This narrow valley rises at its floor to about 725 feet above sea level. Though a desert region, it was valuable for its copper resources in ancient times, and at its southern end Solomon built an important seaport near where modern Israelis maintain the port of Eilat.

EZION-GEBER: SOLOMON'S SOUTHERN SEAPORT

Ezion-geber (or Elath, Eloth; 1 Kings 9:26; 2 Chronicles 8:17) was Solomon's seaport on the Gulf of

these are the Yarmuk and the Jabbok, both of which flow down from the eastern highlands. The bed of the river and its immediate vicinity is called the Zor. Varying from a few hundred feet to a mile in width, it is for much of its distance an impenetrable jungle that still harbors wild beasts, though the lion is no longer numbered among them.

The Dead Sea is about fifty miles long and eleven miles wide, and in its northern basin

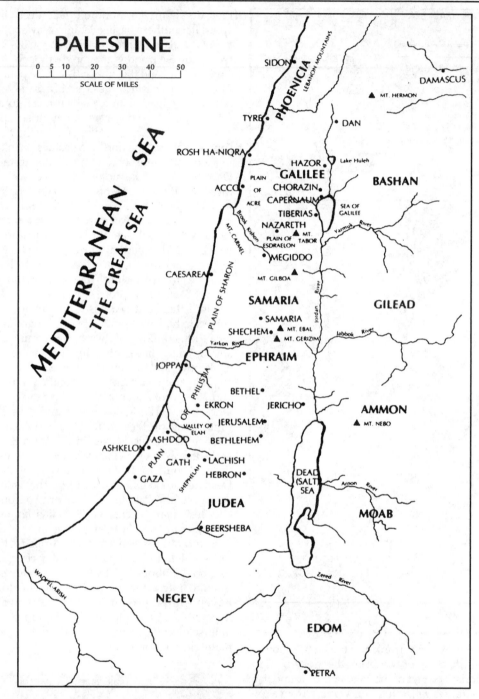

PALESTINE

SCALE OF MILES
0 5 10 20 30 40 50

MEDITERRANEAN SEA
THE GREAT SEA

SIDON
PHOENICIA
LEBANON MOUNTAINS
DAMASCUS
MT. HERMON

TYRE
DAN

ROSH HA-NIQRA
HAZOR
Lake Huleh
GALILEE
PLAIN OF ACRE
ACCO
CHORAZIN
CAPERNAUM
BASHAN
SEA OF GALILEE
TIBERIAS
Yarmuk River
NAZARETH
MT. CARMEL
Brook Kishon
PLAIN OF ESDRAELON
MT. TABOR
MEGIDDO
CAESAREA
MT. GILBOA

PLAIN OF SHARON
SAMARIA
GILEAD
SAMARIA
Jordan River
SHECHEM
MT. EBAL
Jabbok River
MT. GERIZIM
Yarkon River

EPHRAIM

JOPPA
PHILISTIA
BETHEL
EKRON
JERICHO
AMMON
MT. NEBO
VALLEY OF ELAH
JERUSALEM
ASHDOD
BETHLEHEM
ASHKELON
PLAIN
GATH
LACHISH
SHEPHELAH
HEBRON
DEAD (SALT) SEA
Arnon River
GAZA

JUDEA
MOAB
BEERSHEBA

WADI EL-ARISH
NEGEV
Zered River

EDOM

PETRA

Aqaba. For many years it was identified with Tell el-Kheleifeh, midway between Jordanian Aqabah and Israeli Eilat in no-man's-land about five hundred yards from the shore of the Gulf of Aqaba.

Nelson Glueck led a Smithsonian-American Schools of Oriental Research dig there from 1938 to 40 and found what he identified as a smelting and refining plant used for finishing copper ore partially smelted in the Arabah to

Megiddo dominated the Plain of Esdraelon. The cut visible in the far center of the picture is where archaeologists have cut down through layers of occupation to bedrock.

the north. Supposedly this was another feature of the port facility. Then over the years Glueck modified his conclusions and finally suggested that what he found may have been a satellite of Ezion-geber instead of the port itself. It should be noted that there is no evidence of port facilities at the tell nor is it now on the seacoast.

Then about 1970 the suggestion arose that the island of Jezira Fara'un, about three hundred yards from the shore at Eilat, may have been the site of Ezion-Geber. This comes with the observation that no great fortress and port installation would have been necessary for the occasional use that Solomon or other subsequent kings may have made of it. As things now stand, we do not have a viable candidate for the site of Ezion-Geber, but in Solomon's day it was somewhere in the vicinity of modern Eilat at the head of the Gulf of Aqaba.

Transjordan

Transjordan includes the area between the Jordan Rift and the Syrian Desert. This consists of Bashan in the north, from Mount Hermon and the Hauran Mountains to the Yarmuk (thirty-five miles); Gilead, between the Yarmuk and the Jabbok River (thirty-five miles); Ammon and Moab, between the Jabbok and Zered Rivers (eighty miles); and Edom, from the Zered to the Gulf of Aqabah (one hundred miles).

Bashan. Bashan has more rainfall than the rest of Transjordan, and its seventy-mile-wide belt of fertile basalt soil made it the granary of the Levant in ancient times. Its elevation ranges from seven hundred to a thousand feet in the plateau region. At the northern rim of the plateau, peaks rise to more than four thousand feet and one reaches fifty-nine hundred feet. In Jesus' day this was the Tetrarchy of Philip, and included Ituraea, Gaulanitis, Auranitis, and Batanea. The contested Golan Heights, overlooking the Sea of Galilee on the east, are located on the western edge of Bashan.

Gilead. Gilead is similar in terrain to the Western Mountain Ridge with an altitude of three thousand to four thousand feet. It has a plateau in the north and a mountainous region in the south where rainfall measures approximately thirty inches per year. The region of settlement is 30–40 miles wide.

Moab and Ammon. The Moab plateau is about 20–30 miles wide east of the Dead Sea and has an altitude of about 4,000 feet. Its

The University of Chicago excavations identified Stratum IV at Megiddo as Solomonic. As seen in the Megiddo Museum plan, the fortress had north and south stable compounds housing 450 horses and 150 chariots, and a governor's palace. There was also a great water system that rivaled the one at Hazor. More recently scholars have tended to assign the stables to the time of Ahab and the wall and gate to Solomon's time. Possibly the controversy may be solved by crediting Solomon with the design of the stable compounds and rebuilding to the days of Ahab.

rainfall is reasonably reliable and adequate for grain production, as the book of Ruth attests. Mount Nebo, a promontory from which Moses saw the Promised Land, juts westward from the Moab plateau and reaches an altitude of 2,630 feet. Thus, it towers over the Dead Sea and the Jordan Valley. As far as Ammon and the Ammonites are concerned, at an early date these people occupied the land between the Arnon and Jabbok rivers. Later the Amorites took part of this territory from them and the Ammonites were confined to a strip of land along the upper reaches of the Jabbok, extending north from Rabbath-Ammon or Amman. Their holdings continued eastward to the desert. In New Testament times, Gilead and the northern part of Ammon were known as Perea, part of the kingdom of Herod Antipas.

Edom. Edom is more mountainous than Gilead, Moab, and Bashan to the north, with heights often exceeding five thousand feet. The southern part of the area gets little rainfall, but in the north the annual average is 16–20 inches. During the period of the Hebrew monarchy, the capital was Sela ("rock"), built on a flat-topped crag at the southern end of a mountain-ringed valley. Sela presumably became Petra. The kingdom derived its economic strength from agriculture, mineral resources, and tolls levied on caravans crossing its territory. In the third century B.C., the Nabateans occupied Edom and drove the Edomites into southern Judah. The family of Herod the Great was of Idumean (Edomite) stock. Apparently Petra enjoyed its most prosperous period under Nabatean control.

MEGIDDO AND THE WAR OF ARMAGEDDON

Megiddo is an imposing seventy-foot mound overlooking Israel's

Reconstruction of Solomon's (Ahab's) stables at Megiddo. *Courtesy Oriental Institute*

fertile Jezreel Valley, about twenty-two miles southeast of Haifa and seventy miles northwest of Jerusalem. At its feet sprawls a plain that has run red with the blood of soldiers who have fought for nations and empires over the millennia, from ancient Egypt in the days of Thutmose III (c. 1480 B.C.) to Great Britain during World War I. Hebrew kings Saul (1 Samuel 31) and Josiah (2 Kings 23) and the Canaanite general Sisera (Judges 4) were among those who met their ends nearby. As a matter of fact, Megiddo has been occupied almost continuously from about 6000 B.C. to A.D. 500. Solomon fortified it to help maintain his empire and Ahab improved on Solomon's earlier efforts.

So significant has Megiddo been in history that the Oriental Institute of the University of Chicago chose the site for a study of archaeological history and method. Their goal was to cut down the mound layer by layer to bedrock and to make a complete archaeological record. Beginning in 1925, they continued for fourteen seasons until the outbreak of World War II in 1939. When the project was interrupted by the war, it never revived—though others have worked there since.

In a strategic location at the edge of empires, Megiddo will be the scene of the last great struggle at the end times,

according to the book of Revelation. That book describes a great war of Armageddon that will center on the valley (Revelation 16:14–16). Armageddon comes from the Greek *Harmagedon* and presumably is derived from the Hebrew "Har Megiddon," meaning "Mount of Megiddo." Many Bible versions speak of the "battle" of Armageddon in the Revelation passage, but the Greek there refers to a "war" of Armageddon—evidently a series of battles. Several versions correctly refer to a "war" (e.g., New American Standard Bible, New Jerusalem Bible, Contemporary English Version, and Berkeley Version).

The Lateral Regions

Esdraelon. The northern lateral region of Palestine is the Plain of Esdraelon, which extends northwest and southeast and is about twenty-four miles in length from Mount Carmel to Mount Gilboa. The region varies in altitude from 60 to 160 feet, and the soil is dark, heavy, and rich in organic matter. Its fertility compares favorably with that of the Nile delta. Esdraelon lies astride all important lines of communication in northern Palestine and was the scene of many struggles reported in and outside of Scripture. Dominating the southern flank of

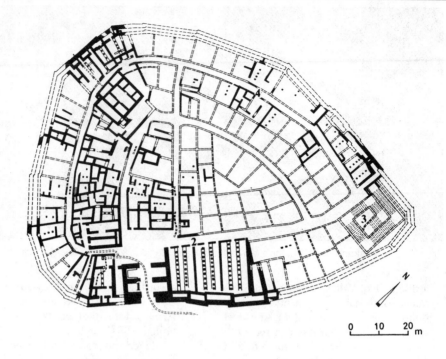

The city plan of the Iron Age city of Beersheba—*Z. Herzog*

the valley is the city mound of Megiddo, which was one of the most important towns of ancient Palestinian history. Solomon fortified it to help maintain his empire, and Ahab improved on Solomon's earlier efforts. In the last times the great War of Armageddon will center on the valley (also called Valley of Jezreel and Armageddon, according to Revelation 16:14–16).[9] Mount Carmel overshadows Esdraelon on the west. Twenty miles long at its base, Carmel reaches nine miles at its greatest width. Its greatest height is 1,792 feet, but the traditional site of the struggle between Elijah and the prophets of Baal is below the peak at Qeren ha-Karmel at 1,581 feet in altitude.

BEERSHEBA—AT THE SOUTHERN BORDER OF ISRAEL

Beersheba (twenty-eight miles southwest of Hebron and forty-five miles southwest of Jerusalem) stood at the southern extremity of Palestine, as did Dan in the north (Judges 20:1; 1 Samuel 3:20; 2 Sam. 3:10; 17:11). The distance between Dan and Beersheba was just under one hundred and fifty miles. Beersheba stood at an altitude of about eight hundred feet, midway between the Mediterranean and the southern end of the Dead Sea. It was an important Negev site in ancient times and today serves as the cultural and administrative center for the Negev, with an approximate population of 140,000. The main road from the Judean highlands to Egypt, passing through Beersheba, was known as "the way to Shur."

Beersheba means "well of the oath," so designated because of the digging of a well and the making of a covenant between Abraham and Abimlech (Genesis 21:31). The place was significant in the lives of the Patriarchs. It was a favorite residence of Abraham and Isaac, and from there Jacob started on his journey to Mesopotamia. Samuel's sons were appointed deputy judges for the

The traditional well of Abraham at Beersheba.

southernmost districts in Beersheba, and Elijah fled there during the ninth century B.C.

The biblical town of Beersheba has been located at Tell es-Seba, or Tell Beersheba, two miles northeast of the modern city. Yohanan Aharoni directed a Tel Aviv University excavation there from 1969 to 1975. He discovered that the city had a Hebrew foundation, built in the twelfth and eleventh centuries B.C., and was probably the city where the sons of Samuel judged the people (1 Samuel 8:2). This city was fortified in the tenth century B.C., with an artificial rampart about twenty feet high with a sloping front and surrounded by a moat twelve to fifteen feet deep. In the ninth century a casemate wall was built on the foundation of this earlier wall.

This Iron Age city was only about 2H acres in size. A circular street started from the gate and encircled the city. Rows of buildings stood on either side of this street, and the houses on one side backed up against the wall. Adjacent to the gate were three storehouses, each about fifty feet long. These were found by contents to have held cereals, wine, and oil.

Aharoni concluded that Tell Beersheba was a well-planned royal city of the United Monarchy period (destroyed probably by Sennacherib in 701 B.C.) and that patriarchal Beersheba was located near the valley and the wells, probably at Bir es-Saba, within the area of modern Beersheba. He believed, however, that an ancient well near the city gate was the one attributed to the patriarch (Genesis 21:19; 26:25).

It is unwarranted to claim, as some do, that the patriarchal activity as it relates to Beersheba did not exist because occupation on the mound began only in the twelfth century B.C. The earlier patriarchal activity may have taken place within the area of modern Beersheba, as Aharoni suggested. Remains from the earlier period would have been sparse because of the migratory nature of the patriarchs, who lived in tents, and it is now impossible to excavate widely in the vicinity because of the extensive modern population.

Earliest evidences of human habitation in Palestine come from the Mount Carmel caves, near Haifa

The Negev. The great southern lateral region of Palestine is the Negev. It is roughly a triangle, with its base at the southern edge of the Judean hills and its apex on the Gulf of Aqaba. At its base it measures roughly seventy miles wide, and its total area is about forty-six hundred square miles, the size of Connecticut. The altitude of the Eilat hills in the south reaches three thousand feet. The central Negev hills, which occupy more than half of the region, are slightly higher. In the Beersheba region, altitude ranges from about one hundred and fifty feet to about 1,650 feet and is eight hundred feet at Beersheba itself. Rainfall in the north measures approximately fourteen inches per year and is considerably less in the south. Although it is debated whether there has been a great change in the climate of the Negev since biblical times, it is certain that ancients knew better than more recent inhabitants how to utilize water resources. In Abraham's day and subsequently (especially in the Nabatean period), there was a considerable number of settlements in this now virtually desert and uninhabited region. Although important trade and communication lines crossed the Negev, not the least of which was Solomon's route to his port at Ezion-Geber, the region was an important buffer against Israel's enemies, who would find it hard to attack across such an inhospitable region. Israeli engineers have piped water from the Galilee region into the Negev, and numerous settlers are once again

causing the desert to blossom as a rose (Isaiah 37:1, NKJV).

History of Palestine

The Earliest Days

The Hebrews were not of course the earliest inhabitants of Palestine. Anthropologists and archaeologists have continued to push back the horizons of human habitation there into Paleolithic (Old Stone Age) times, to a half million or more years ago. Though we may debate the conclusions of these scholars, it is beyond the purpose of the book to do so. Some of these discoveries were the product of Dorothy Garrod's work in the caves of the lower western slope of Mount Carmel on behalf of the British School of Archaeology in Jerusalem (1929–1934). Since then numerous other scholars have worked at Mount Carmel, in the central Jordan Valley, on the coastal plain, in the Negev, the Sinai and elsewhere, recovering evidences of Old Stone Age culture.

Neolithic Developments

I have chosen to begin the chronicle of Palestinian history between about 8500 and 8000 B.C., as Palestine emerged into the Neolithic period, when people began to cultivate crops, domesticate animals, and live in village sites. The earliest cultural development is usually divided into Pre-Pottery Neolithic A (PPNA, c. 8500–7500 B.C.) and

A great stone tower, twenty-five feet high, dates to the Neolithic level at Old Testament Jericho

Pre-Pottery Neolithic B (PPNB, c. 7500–6000 B.C.). PPNA appeared especially in the Jordan Valley, at sites such as Jericho and Gilgal to the north of it and at the southern end of the Sea of Galilee; but also on Mount Carmel; in the northern Shephelah; and in the southern Sinai.

The especially important place was Jericho, which Mazar believes may have had a population of about a thousand in the 6.5 acre site.[10] A massive protection wall (partially of stone) stood to a height of about eighteen feet at the western edge of the mound. Inside the wall rose a great stone round tower over twenty-five feet in diameter and about twenty-five feet high, with an interior stairway leading to the top. This is one of the main tourist attractions at the site today. Scholars debate its function, but at least the tower and wall reflect sufficient social and political organization to coordinate manpower for such building

operations. Houses of this early period were round or oval; and the people of the community cultivated barley, wheat, lentils, and legumes and irrigated their crops with water from the nearby spring. Commerce existed between the communities of Palestine and Syria and Anatolia, probably involving exchange of salt and bitumen of the Dead Sea area for the obsidian (a volcanic glass) of Asia Minor,[11] which was used as a cutting tool and for mirrors.

The PPNB period represents an increase of population and expansion of settlement. Presumably this culture evolved out of its predecessor with some cultural innovations from the north. PPNB sites appear not only all over Palestine (along the Mediterranean, in the Jordan Valley, the Judean Desert, in the Negev, and in Transjordan) but also in Syria and adjacent areas of Mesopotamia. The culture of this whole area was largely homogeneous. Along with the increase in population came the rise of some significant towns: Ain Ghazal, a 30-acre site north of Amman, Beisamoun (a 10-acre site) north of the Sea of Galilee, and Jericho (a 6.5-acre).[12]

Agriculture progressed significantly with the development of new varieties of wheat and barley. So did animal husbandry, as goats were widely raised and sheep and cattle seem to have been introduced. By that time houses were now standardly rectangular in design. Finds demonstrate notable

Neolithic houses at Jericho

advances in making a variety of tools from flint and bone, and textiles made of wool and flax. Small clay and stone statuettes of animals and human figures reveal artistic advancement and cultic development; many of these figurines were used in religious expression.

Pottery Neolithic (PN) developments occurred between about 6000 and 4300 B.C. Unfortunately this period is poorly known; few excavations date from this time. Of course the most important invention was pottery production: cooking pots, storage jars, dishes for eating, and more. Probably pottery manufacture resulted from either a chance or intended fire that unexpectedly changed clay into a hard and durable material. From that time onward pottery styles have served archaeologists with means of dating and discovery of diffusion of culture and interrelationships of peoples.

There is a debate over whether a time gap existed between the Pre-Pottery and Pottery Neolithic periods. If there was a gap, it more likely occurred in Palestine than in Syria, where continuity with the earlier period is more evident. The subsistence economy of this period was based on the cultivation of grains and legumes, goat and sheep herding, and some raising of pigs. Pastoral nomadism, a seasonal mobility, seems to have been common and may reflect more unstable climatic conditions than during PPN times. The Yarmukian or northern Palestinian culture of the period is known especially for its fertility goddesses, but temples or shrines are as yet unknown from the sedentary sites. Since the flint tools known to us were made for agricultural purposes and arrowheads were rare, the conclusion seems to be that there was a decline in hunting with a greater emphasis on food production during this era.

The Chalcolithic Age[13]

Chalcolithic means copper and stone. Copper and stone weapons and implements were used side by side, and the period is dated about 4300 to 3300 B.C. The main

David's refuge at En Gedi

site for the study of the period is Teleilat Ghassul, a fifty-acre mound just northeast of the Dead Sea. But Chalcolithic sites have been discovered in the northern Negev, in the Judean Desert, on the Golan Heights, in the Beth-Shan valley, and elsewhere. During this period herding greatly increased and agriculture advanced, including cultivation of the olive, which has played an important part in the lives of Palestinians ever since.

The only public buildings that have been found so far are temples at Teleilat Ghassul and En Gedi, on the western shore of the Dead Sea. At En Gedi, where David was later to take refuge (1 Samuel 24: 1–4), stood a temple in a stone-fenced enclosure. The structure itself measured roughly sixteen by sixty-five feet and its entrance was in the long side facing the courtyard. Houses of the period were rectangular, commonly of stone on stone-paved floors, and often strung together in a chain. That is, they might be joined at their narrow sides to create a chain of houses—perhaps for extended families.

Pottery was better made than in the previous period and was plentiful. Though all large vessels were handmade, many of the smaller ones were produced on a potter's wheel. Churns for making butter made their appearance during this time, as did various forms of decorations. The flint

A Canaanite altar at Megiddo, twenty-five feet in diameter, dates to about 2700 B.C.

industry of the period produced axes and adzes for working wood; hoes for working the soil; awls and scrapers for leather work; and sickles (made by inserting a series of flints along the curve of a stick) for use in harvesting. Axe heads and mace-heads predominated among copper weapons. Pieces of linen and woolen cloth and fragments of wooden looms and loom weights of the period have also survived. The art of the millennium, including numerous figurines, represents a considerable faith in fertility deities, thought to ensure fertility of human beings, animals, and crops.

Why the Chalcolithic Age came to an end about 3300 B.C. is speculative. Whether new migrants, an Egyptian invasion, drought or other climatic changes, epidemics or other natural catastrophes may have been the cause is unknown. But many important centers were abandoned.

The Bronze Age

The Bronze Age (c. 3000–1200 B.C.) marks an industrial advance over the Chalcolithic Age. Now copper, normally mixed with tin, was fired at a greater heat to produce a wide variety of commodities. The Bronze Age began a little before 3000 B.C. (perhaps as early as 3300) and lasted until about 1200 B.C. It is standardly divided into Early (c.

3300–2200 B.C.), Middle (c. 2200–1500 B.C.) and Late Bronze Ages (c. 1500–1200 B.C.). And each of these three major division is commonly subdivided into smaller units, varying with the preferences of numerous scholars. The dating of the Early, Middle, and Late Bronze ages also varies slightly in the hands of various scholars.

Just as scholars differ on dating aspects of the Bronze Age, so also they do not agree on what initiated the age. In earlier decades there was a tendency to give credit for beginnings of the Bronze Age in Palestine to immigration from the north or east. But the inclination today is to see Bronze Age culture as a development from the earlier Chalcolithic Age, with perhaps some migrants and influences of trade relations. But we really do not know who or what is responsible for the changes.

We do know, however, that there was a radical shift in occupational patterns. Most of the towns coming into being in the early centuries of the Bronze Age were on new foundations. Not over a third of them were built on old Chalcolithic sites, which tended to go unoccupied. The new towns grew up in fertile regions—the Jordan Valley, the coastal plain, the central hill country—near water resources, trade routes, and good soil. Agriculture rather than herding seems

An Early Bronze cultic shrine from Arad

to have been the main occupation, and grapes and figs may have been produced during the first centuries of the Early Bronze Age for the first time.

Around 3000 B.C., when Egypt was becoming a united nation, Egyptian involvement in southern Palestine was considerable, including at the minimum some military action and trade relations, but possibly a certain amount of colonization. Egyptians seem to have been interested in copper resources of the Arabah and possibly bitumen from the Dead Sea area.

As the Bronze Age wore on, there was considerable urbanization throughout Palestine. This occurred because of progress in trade and agriculture, and an increase in population. The estimated population of the towns of Palestine during the Early Bronze period is 150,000.[14] In fact, an urban culture held sway from about 3000 to 2300 B.C. Over three dozen fortified cities dominated the countryside, and public architecture became prominent: fortifications (walls, gates, tower systems), temples (circular altars and rectangular buildings), palaces, public granaries, and water systems. The list of fortified places is impressive and includes Dan, Beth-Yerah, Hazor, Beth Shean, Megiddo, Dothan, Yarmuth, Jericho, Lachish, Tell el-Hesi, Ai (Et-Tell), and Arad, to name a few.

Large cities were surrounded by smaller settlements. And a prosperous agriculture provided a surplus that made possible the advance of urbanization. Crops included cereals, peas, lentils, chick-peas, flax, olives, figs, grapes (for wine and raisins), pomegranates, and dates. The animal-propelled plow now enabled easier cultivation of the land and the cultivation of many more acres, and thus the support of more city dwellers.

The bronze industry provided weapons (including axes, spearheads, daggers and/or short swords,), tools for forestry and woodworking (such as adzes, and chisels), and a variety of farm implements.

The entire Early Bronze Age urban culture in western Palestine collapsed within a short time around 2300–2200 B.C., to be replaced by a non-urban pattern that lasted for more than three hundred years. The downfall of cities was fairly abrupt and was once attributed to invasion of Semitic speakers from the north. Now it appears that the abandonment of towns resulted primarily from a significant weather shift to drier conditions, combined with a greatly weakened economy and the disruption of trade systems.[15]

Several other factors were responsible for the end of the Early Bronze Age, however. There were a few Egyptian military operations in southern Palestine during the

Fifth and Sixth Dynasties, perhaps to head off Asiatic invasions. Then, perhaps internal warfare hastened urban decline, especially if there was a struggle to control dwindling natural resources. And Amorite tribes from Syria may have contributed to the demise of urban civilization, especially in the north.

Deurbanization explains why Abraham could so readily roam about without seeming to conflict with local peoples when he came to Palestine from Ur by way of Haran. Almost no significant cities or organized city-state would have confronted him and his large retinue.

New cities were gradually built up in Palestine during the period 2000–1900 B.C. and reurbanization was completed during the following century. This means that towns and cities began to reappear during the days of Isaac and Jacob. Cities and towns could well have caused problems for these Hebrew families if the Hebrews had remained in the land after about 1875 B.C. Instead Jacob and his extended family went to Egypt at the invitation of Joseph. It is noteworthy, however, that the central and southern hill country of Palestine, where many of the patriarchal activities occurred, continued to be rather thinly settled even after the land reurbanized.

The Middle Bronze Age and the Patriarchs

To understand the age of Abraham in particular and the patriarchs in general, it is necessary to explore what contemporary scholarship has to say about conditions in Palestine during the late third and early second millennia B.C. And Palestinian developments should be placed in the larger context of the Middle East. Before about 2200 B.C. the whole area had entered into an "intermediate period." The Old Akkadian period had ended in Mesopotamia and the hated Guti were in that land. The Old Kingdom had collapsed in Egypt and local governors, or nomarchs, had asserted themselves in the confused times of the First Intermediate Period. In Palestine and much of Syria deurbanization had set in as early as the twenty-fourth century B.C. and

certainly characterized the land during the period 2200–2000 B.C.

It used to be claimed that the last centuries of the third millennium B.C. in Palestine represented a major cultural break perpetrated by an invasion of Amorites who wrought great destruction everywhere, bringing urban life to an end. The degree of break in civilization was thought to justify the view that the Early Bronze Age had come to an end and the Middle Bronze Age had begun. Now, however, that view is greatly modified. Evidently there was no major cultural break in Palestine during the latter part of the third millennium B.C., and the last quarter of the millennium should be designated as Early Bronze IV. Moreover, apparently there was no invasion of Amorites with consequent destruction at the various sites. Such cultural intrusions as occurred evidently resulted from an entrance of outside influences rather than a migration of peoples. To be sure, as noted earlier, there was general deurbanization throughout Palestine by the end of the twenty-third century B.C., but it is argued that this did not occur as a result of invasion, with the possible exception of a few sites in the south, which suffered Egyptian attack before the fall of the Old Kingdom. Rather, the abandonment of towns resulted from a significant shift to drier conditions combined with a greatly weakened economy and the disruption of trade systems.

Then, gradually at first and later more rapidly, reurbanization of Palestine began during the twentieth century B.C. and was completed during the nineteenth century. As late as about 2050 B.C. Egyptian rulers showed disdain for the weak Asiatics of Palestine, but shortly after 2000 B.C. Pharaoh Amenemhet I built a line of forts along the eastern frontier to keep check on their movements. Subsequently Egyptian execration texts (curses inscribed against enemies of Egypt) reveal something of the rise of urbanization in Palestine. These curses pronounced against towns and districts of Palestine date to two periods: the end of the twentieth and beginning of the nineteenth centuries B.C., and the end of nineteenth century B.C. A large number of

Canaanite towns (including some mentioned in the Old Testament; e.g., Ashkelon, and Jerusalem) and their rulers were cursed.

It is interesting to note that the central and southern hill country of Palestine continued to be rather thinly settled even after the rapid growth of urbanization elsewhere. The new developments that occurred in Palestine after 2000 B.C. represented a real cultural break and ushered in the Middle Bronze Age. It is generally believed that an Amorite intrusion had much to do with the political and cultural changes.[16] Apparently those people had greater affinities with the population of the Orontes Valley in Syria than with peoples of northern Mesopotamia farther east. As the newcomers established a new urban culture in Palestine, evidently they absorbed the semi-nomadic population of the earlier period to some extent. The rest of the existent population was pushed to the periphery, where it became the nucleus of a new semi-nomadic group.[17]

In the eighteenth century B.C. or earlier a people known to the Egyptians as Hyksos (meaning "rulers of foreign lands") came to dominate Palestine and much of Syria. Evidence points to the conclusion that these people were essentially Semitic but were somewhat infused with Hurrian and Indo-Aryan elements. The Hyksos infiltrated Egypt during the eighteenth century or earlier and were sufficiently numerous there that they were able to take the reins of government in the Nile delta and Lower Egypt from weak native dynasts around 1730 and hold them until the middle of the sixteenth century. Their domination of Upper Egypt lasted for about a hundred years. It is now generally believed that the Hyksos did not have to fight much to topple native Egyptian rulers.

The patriarchal period in Palestine fits admirably into the historical context just sketched. If we follow the chronology of the Hebrew text (see chapter on Mesopotamia), Abraham would have entered the land just after 2100 B.C., when urban life had virtually ceased and when seminomadism would have been possible. No great cities or city-states would have confronted the patriarch.

And, as noted, when reurbanization occurred, it was less pronounced in the central and southern hill country, where the patriarchs spent most of their time. Moreover, the Hebrew chronology would put the Israelite entrance into Egypt about 1875, when Asiatic migration into Egypt was getting under way and when Palestine was becoming sufficiently built up into powerful city-states as to make seminomadism more difficult there. Utilization of later chronologies for the patriarchal period would place the patriarchs in adverse to impossible circumstances, as far as pastoral seminomadism is concerned.

As Abraham and his entourage moved around in Palestine, they came in contact with a number of other groups that had also entered the area. Actually, Scripture views nearly all these peoples as Canaanites, as Genesis 10:15–19 indicates. But with the passage of time they had become separate groups and had staked out territories for themselves (Genesis 15: 19–21; Exodus 23:23; Deuteronomy 7:1). The mere listing of these groups seems to demonstrate how politically or ethnically fragmentized Palestine was in Abraham's day and how it was therefore possible for him to maintain himself under somewhat hostile circumstances. Brief comments on some of these groups follow.

Canaanites. Canaan, ancestor of the Canaanites, was a son of Ham and brother of Mizraim, ancestor of the Egyptians (Genesis 10:6).[18] Ethnically, as noted, Canaan is viewed as the ancestor of all the peoples Abraham met in Palestine. Geographically, the term applied to the area from Phoenicia south to Gaza and inland to the Dead Sea (Genesis 10:19). Culturally, Canaanite referred to developments in Egyptian Asia, which were influenced by Egypt but modified by Hyksos, Indo-Iranian, and others. Excavations reveal that Canaanite achievements in architecture, metal and wood working, needlecraft, and commerce, and in many other ways were very advanced. But the Canaanites were also a morally debased people, engaging in sex worship and infant sacrifice.[19] This moral degradation became more evident around the middle of the second millennium B.C. than it had been around 2000 B.C.

The term *Canaanite* came to be used in two senses in the Old Testament—referring either to the people who lived west of the Jordan or to a tribe inhabiting a particular locality. When used in the latter sense it denoted a people settled by the Mediterranean and alongside the Jordan—in the lowlands of Palestine (Numbers 13:29). The Canaanites spoke a Semitic language and developed the alphabetic writing (which the Greeks later adopted), as discovered at Ugarit. Hebrew of the Old Testament is called the "language of Canaan" (Isaiah 19:18).

Amorites. Genesis 10:16 indicates that the Amorites were descended from Canaan, but they must have intermarried with Semites very early because they appear as a Semitic people in Near Eastern references to them. Their origin is something of a mystery, but they probably arose not too far from the Syro-Palestine region, perhaps in the northern Euphrates area. Their language was one of the Northwest Semitic dialects and thus closely related to Canaanite and biblical Hebrew.

The Amorites began to appear in southern Mesopotamia before 2500 B.C. By 2000 B.C. they had mingled with the native Mesopotamians and founded or controlled several city-states. Mari was one of the most powerful of these. Amorites also became the ruling dynasty of the Old Babylonian Kingdom; Hammurabi was of Amorite stock. In Syria they established or controlled kingdoms at Aleppo, Alalakh, and elsewhere. After 2000 B.C. they appeared in force in Palestine, and from certain artistic representations we may conclude that they were entering Egypt as traders by 1900 B.C. Presumably they formed an important element in the Hyksos development.

In the Old Testament the term sometimes refers to the inhabitants of Palestine in general (Genesis 15:16; Judges 6:10). Similarly the Amarna tablets (Egyptian, fourteenth century B.C.) refer to the entire area of Palestine and Syria as *Amurru* (land of the Amorites). Sometimes in the Old Testament the Amorites are said to occupy the hill country,

while the Canaanites lived in the lowlands of Palestine. Occasionally Amorites are spoken of as a specific people under a king of their own. For example, during the patriarchal period they appeared as a power on the western shore of the Dead Sea (Genesis 14:7), at Hebron (Genesis 14:13), and at Shechem (Genesis 48:22). Later the Amorites occupied an area in Transjordan as well as in Canaan. Numbers 21:21 speaks of Sihon, king of the Amorites, and Joshua 10:5 lists the towns of the Amorite league: Jerusalem, Hebron, Jarmuth, Lachish, and Eglon. Liverani argues that the "Amorites and Canaanites should not be separated into two peoples" and that "'Canaanite' came into use at least from the middle of the second millennium B.C., to indicate, at least in part, those populations which had before been referred to by the term 'Amorite.'"[20] The Amorites developed a fairly advanced culture, especially demonstrating craftsmanship in gold, silver, bronze, and leather; and they were very successful in commercial activities and administrative efficiency.

Philistines. Both Abraham (Genesis 21:22–32) and Isaac (Genesis 26:15) had dealings with the Philistines. But such an assertion creates problems for the Bible student because biblical critics commonly have thought the Scripture to be in error at this point. They commonly point to a Philistine sea borne attack on Egypt shortly after 1200 B.C., which Raamses III repulsed, and conclude that then the Philistines settled near the sea, in the Plain of Philistia, in Palestine. But scholars have not generally accepted the idea that Philistines may have occupied the area as early as 1900 or 2000 B.C.

To deal with this problem, we need to note that the Old Testament says the Philistines came from the island of Caphtor (Jeremiah 47:4; Amos 9:7), commonly identified as Crete. Moreover, the term *Cherethites* (Cretans) is used to designate the Philistines in Ezekiel 25:12, Zephaniah 2:5, and 1 Samuel 30:14.

If the Philistines of about 1200 B.C. came from Crete, they would have been part of the warlike maritime culture known as Mycenean or else of the Sea Peoples whom the Mycenean Greeks pushed out of the

The cenotaph over Sarah's traditional tomb in the Mosque at Hebron

Aegean. And in Palestine the Philistines were warlike and a constant threat to the Israelites during the days of the Judges and early monarchy. This later development is extensively documented by archaeological discovery. No earlier stage of Philistine presence has turned up in Palestinian excavation, however, and therein lies the problem.

By way of solution we should note, first, that Minoan Cretans were establishing trading colonies around the Mediterranean by about 2000 B.C., and evidence of their contact with Palestine and Egypt during this early period is substantial. Moreover, the Philistines of Abraham's day were peace-loving agricultural people, as were the Minoans.

Second, G. Ernest Wright has pointed out that the Hebrew word translated "Philistine" was used for all "Sea Peoples," of whom the Philistines were the most important for the inhabitants of Palestine.[21] Possibly the reference in Genesis should be translated by some other term. And possibly the Hebrew term translated "Philistine" included more groups from overseas than the Peleset of the Egyptian inscriptions— conceivably even Canaanite groups.[22] And certainly the people of Gerar were Canaanites.

It is interesting to note that the Gerar of Abimelech (Genesis 21 and 26) has now been identified with Tell Abu Hureireh or Tel Haror, about eleven miles southeast of Gaza and twelve miles west of Beersheba. In 1956, D. Alon excavated there and found that it was inhabited continually through every period from Chalcolithic times to the Iron Age and was very prosperous during the Middle Bronze (the patriarchal) Age. He also found several smelting furnaces, giving evidence of Philistine iron working.[23]

Then E. D. Oren, under the auspices of Ben-Gurion University, excavated at the site from 1982 to 1990. Since the Middle Bronze Age settlement extended over an area of about forty acres, the excavators focused their work on a large temple, a building identified as a palace, and the massive defense system of the site. Surrounding the wall was a ditch approximately fifty feet across and twenty feet deep. The rampart itself was about sixty-five feet wide at the base and some 25–30 feet high. Because of surface erosion it was impossible to tell whether there had been a wall on top of the ramparts.[24] So some evidence of the context of which the Abimelech of Abraham's day was a part has been found, but the name "Philistine" has not been connected with it.

Robert Drews in his incisive study on the end of the Bronze Age concludes that the Philistines and other troublesome "Sea Peoples" who invaded Egypt in the days of Raamses III came "from" Palestine and returned there after defeat. He does not believe they came from somewhere else and settled in Palestine after the Egyptians repulsed them from their shores.[25]

Hittites. According to the patriarchal narrative, when Sarah died, Abraham bought from a Hittite a field in which was located a cave suitable for burial purposes (Genesis 23:7; 25:9–10). Critics commonly treat this reference to Hittites as an anachronism later inserted by an editor or by a historian who made a mistake. It is thought not to reflect historical conditions during Abraham's lifetime. The problem is that the Old Hittite Kingdom in Asia Minor (modern Turkey) did not exist until about 1650 B.C., and Hittite remains in Syria and Palestine (even those recovered in recent excavations) do not date before the thirteenth century B.C.. When the Hittite kingdom did exist, it did not extend its authority into southern Palestine. So it would seem to be in error to conclude that Abraham may have met them there about 2000 B.C.

A possible solution to the problem may be found in a better understanding of Hittite history. When scholars began to excavate Hittite towns and to recreate history, they found themselves working with a language and culture that was Indo-European in character. Of course this was dubbed "Hittite." Then it was discovered that long before the Indo-European developments a non-Indo-European culture had existed in Hittite land. But since the term *Hittite* had been specifically assigned, those people could not be called Hittites. Actually, discoveries reveal that several rather prosperous non-Indo-European states had come into existence in Asia Minor during the third millennium B.C. or at least early in the second millennium. Then Indo-European peoples came into Asia Minor either from the northwest or the northeast around 2000 B.C. and gradually made their way across the peninsula. Apparently they reached the Hittite heart-land and subdued its inhabitants about the middle of the nineteenth century B.C. And it took another two centuries before the invaders established the Old Hittite Kingdom. The "Proto-Hittite" element remained as a sub-stratum in the society.

The suggested solution to the problem is that some of the "Proto-Hittite" non-Indo-European sons of Heth (Genesis 10:5) may have found their way to Palestine and settled in the Hebron area as part of the larger Canaanite culture. As noted, the Proto-Hittites of the third millennium B.C. had developed rather prosperous states in Asia Minor and some of them were involved in rather extensive and far-flung commercial activities. It is not out of line to speculate that citizens of these states may have found their way into Palestine and had dealings with Abraham and it is not necessary to conclude that the Bible is in error in alluding to Hittites in Palestine in Abraham's day. As a matter of fact, Khirbet Kerak (at the southwestern end of the Sea of Galilee) ware in Palestine is virtually identical with pottery in central Anatolia in the third millennium B.C. This may suggest an incursion or migration of Hattians into Palestine in the twenty-third century B.C.

Harry Hoffner, professor of Hittite studies at the University of Chicago and editor of the Hittite Dictionary there, does not believe that the Hittites of the patriarchal period had any connection with the Proto-Hittites, but he does not deny the historical validity of the Genesis references. He observes that the Hittites of the patriarchal period had good Semitic names (rather than the Indo-European of the northern Hittites) and concludes that their customs did not diverge greatly from those of their Palestinian neighbors. He simply classifies them as another group that could validly be called Hittites in ancient times.[26]

A Summary Statement on the Middle Bronze Age, c. 2000–1500 B.C.

Reurbanization spread rapidly in the twentieth century B.C. and following—especially on a Syrian model. There was a migration of Semitic-speaking and Hurrian groups from north to south, and the ruling elites in

The mound of Gibeon

rising towns sought to follow foreign practices. Towns located on the trade routes leading from Syria to Egypt grew especially rapidly and were also the first to fortify. Pottery styles also tended to follow Syrian examples; and pottery, now made on a fast wheel, was thinner and finer. Bronze (an alloy of copper and tin) was used exclusively for weapons and tools. The tin, which formed about ten percent of the alloy with copper, came especially through Mari on the Euphrates to centers in the north of Palestine. And the chariot with its spoked wheels came into use in Syria and Palestine during the early centuries of the millennium. Through the Hyksos the chariot made its entrance into Egypt.

Migrant Amorite groups moved south along the coast from Lebanon and from the Orontes Valley of Syria. The cultural influences coming from the north merged with the Egyptian influences coming from the south to produce the Canaanite culture that we discover in the Late Bronze Age. Actually it appears that the earlier Amorites were later called Canaanites. And the Hyksos appear to have been Canaanites who infiltrated Egypt and established their capital at Avaris (Tell el-Dab 'a) in the eastern Delta.

As the cities grew they were fortified—with walls and glacis. Earthen ramparts were common, especially in reasonably level topography, e.g., Hazor (lower city), Shechem, and Ashkelon. Earth was scooped from the center and used for a

defense bastion, creating a crater in which the city itself developed. Or material for the rampart might come from a moat surrounding the rampart. Then sometimes a stone revetment wall held the rampart in place, and a wall might be built on the rampart. The practice of creating such ramparts apparently originated in northern Syria.

On the other hand, the glacis was an artificial slope created by dumping earth on an existing defense mound to create a steeper slope and thicker embankment; often it was piled against an existing wall, preventing tunneling under or through a wall. The outer embankment was commonly covered with lime to create a smooth, steep surface. The glacis was thought to be a Hyksos kind of defense bastion, found in Palestine south of the Valley of Jezreel.

The type of city gate commonly constructed during the last half of the Middle Bronze Age consisted of two large towers flanking an elongated passage. The passage was divided into two guard chambers by three pairs of pilasters (square pillars that protruded from the passage), as at Hazor, Megiddo, Gezer, Beth-shemesh, and Shechem.

There is some evidence of urban planning in a number of cities: paved streets laid at right angles to one another, wide plazas, and a palace with a temple nearby. Parallel streets might enclose rectangular blocks of dwellings. Larger houses, of the

The pool of Gibeon

wealthy, had many rooms grouped around a small central courtyard, introducing the Mediterranean style house for the first time during this period. Temples of Syria, Phoenicia, Palestine, and Avaris in the Egyptian Delta "had similarities in planning and design."[27] They were large rectangular or square buildings with thick walls. Normally they had an entrance chamber that gave access to a holy of holies. The main gods worshiped were Hadad, Ishtar, Shamash, Dagan, and Reshef.

There were dozens of fortified Canaanite cities in Palestine during the Middle Bronze Age. Among the names familiar to most Bible students were Dan, Acre, Hazor, Beth-Shean, Aphek, Ashdod, Lachish, Shiloh, Shechem, Bethel, Gibeon, Jerusalem, and Beth-Shemesh.

GIBEON'S ROLE IN HEBREW HISTORY

Among the Canaanite cities, Gibeon's role in Hebrew history was especially significant, or at least dramatic. First, following the fall of Jericho and Ai, a Gibeonite delegation persuaded Joshua to make a treaty with them on the pretense that they had come from a great distance and were not inhabitants of a nearby Canaanite city (Joshua 9). When the deception was found out, Joshua honored the treaty but reduced the Gibeonites to the status of servants. Then when the Israelites came to the rescue of the Gibeonites as they were attacked by other Canaanites, the "sun stood still" (Joshua 10:12–14). What happened on that occasion has given rise to extensive scientific debate in modern times.

Later, in David's day, during the conflict between the partisans of Ishbosheth, Saul's son, and the partisans of David, representatives met at the pool of Gibeon and settled the issue by armed conflict (2 Samuel 2:12–17). Then at the beginning of Solomon's reign, when the king made a great sacrifice at Gibeon, God dramatically broke into his consciousness with a promise of the gift of wisdom and of riches (1 Kings 3:4–15). A later conflict that terminated at Gibeon was the rebellion of Absalom. Amasa, commander of Absalom's rebel army, met his death at the hands of Joab there (2 Samuel 20:8). After the Babylonian destruction of Jerusalem, the assassins of Gedaliah were overtaken by the "great pool which is in Gibeon," and their prisoners were set free (Jeremiah 41:11–14). Finally, Gibeonites helped Nehemiah in the work of rebuilding the walls of Jerusalem (Nehemiah 3:7). In all, Gibeon is mentioned forty-five times in Scripture.

Gibeon, identified with el-Jib, sits atop a limestone hill at the eastern end of the Valley of Aijalon, six miles northwest of Jerusalem. James B. Pritchard excavated there on behalf of the University of Pennsylvania Museum from 1956 to 1962. Confirmation of the fact that el-Jib is Gibeon came in the form of thirty-one jar handles found in the excavation with the name "Gibeon" on them.

The most dramatic find was the "pool" of Gibeon. Measuring thirty-seven feet in diameter and thirty-five feet in depth, this cylindrical cutting had a circular staircase. At the bottom of the cylindrical cutting a stepped tunnel led downward another forty-five feet to a water chamber. An alternate water system involved a stepped tunnel of ninety-three steps that led from inside the city wall into a kidney-shaped water chamber about twenty-three by eleven feet. A 112-foot-long "feeder" tunnel had been cut from the city's main spring to this cistern. Completion of the pool arrangement was dated by the excavator to the tenth century B.C., and the alternate system to a somewhat later time.

Gibeon was founded about 3000 B.C., as confirmed by a collection of pottery dating to the period, and magnificent tomb discoveries abundantly documented the Middle Bronze and Late Bronze periods. Iron Age I (1200–900 B.C.) apparently was the city's golden age. Near the beginning of the period, a wall about twelve feet thick enclosed the sixteen-acre town. Within the northeast corner of this wall was the pool of Gibeon and access to the alternate water system.

In the area of the pool a winery was found, in use in the eighth and seventh centuries B.C. Here were simple winepresses, each with a treading floor, fermentation tanks, and jar-shaped cisterns cut into the rock to serve as storage cellars for filler jars. It is estimated that the total storage capacity of these wine cellars was over twenty-five thousand gallons.

The most important urban centers of Palestine during the Middle Bronze Age were Hazor, Shechem, and Megiddo. Hazor outstripped the others. Located nine miles north of the Sea of Galilee on a bottle-shaped mound of over twenty-five acres, with a large rectangular enclosure of some two hundred acres sprawled at its feet, it boasted an approximate population of some forty thousand. Founded around 1800 B.C., or earlier, Hazor reached its zenith in the fifteenth century B.C. and continued to be the largest city of Palestine until the thirteenth century B.C.

Megiddo stood sentinel at the southern edge of the Plain of Jezreel. The area of the summit of the tell consisted of about fifteen acres and the slopes composed thirty-five more. Massive fortifications dated to the Middle Bronze Period.

Shechem stood astride the road that led through the valley between Ebal and Gerizim, thirty-one miles north of Jerusalem. At Shechem, during the first half of the second millennium B.C. the Hyksos surrounded the city with an immense glacis about eighty feet wide and twenty feet high, upon which they built a brick wall. Two gate complexes (on the northwest and east) date to the Hykos period. Egyptians destroyed the city in about 1550. Subsequently it was rebuilt on a smaller scale. Interestingly the Bible makes no reference to any battle between Joshua and Shechem, and this fact has led many Bible students to surmise that the Shechemites came to a friendly agreement with the Israelites.

SHECHEM IN THE HISTORY OF ISRAEL

Shechem (identified with the six-acre Tell Balatah) was located in the valley between Mounts Ebal and Gerizim, thirty-one miles north of Jerusalem and six miles southeast of Samaria. The site figures prominently in the Old Testament. It was the place of Abraham's first altar in Canaan (Genesis 12:6–7), a rallying point at the time of the Conquest (Joshua 8:33–35; 24:25), the burial place of Joseph (Joshua 24:32), the capital of Abimelech (Judges 9), and later the capital of the Northern Kingdom under Jeroboam I (1 Kings 12:25).

The site was excavated by Ernst Sellin, C. Watzinger, and others on behalf of the German Society for Scientific Research from 1913 to 1914, 1926 to 1928, 1932, and in 1934; and by the Drew-McCormick-Harvard Expedition from 1956 to 1973 under the leadership of G. Ernest Wright, Lawrence E. Toombs, and Edward F. Campbell Jr.

The earliest settlement at Shechem occurred in the fourth millennium B.C., but the first permanent settlement dates to the Hyksos period during the first half of the second millennium. The Hyksos surrounded the city with an immense glacis or sloping embarkment about eighty feet wide and twenty feet high, upon which they built a brick wall. On the acropolis they erected what has been interpreted as a shrine—a courtyard with several adjoining rooms. This fortress temple was rebuilt several times and finally destroyed by the Egyptians around 1550 B.C. Two gate complexes (on the northwest and the east) date to the Hyksos period.

After the Egyptian conquest, Shechem was rebuilt on a smaller scale. The east gate was reconstructed on the same plan. And a new temple-fortress was built above the first one. This structure was fifty-three feet wide and forty-one feet long and had three sacred standing stones adjacent to an altar in the open court. This is identified as the house of Baal-berith destroyed by Abimelech (c. 1150 B.C.; Judges 9:3–4, 46). There is no archaeological evidence that the Hebrews destroyed the city at the time of the Conquest, however; thus the discoveries tally with biblical indications.

The Fortress Temple, Shechem

Joseph's tomb near Shechem

Solomon apparently rebuilt Shechem as a provincial capital, but it was violently destroyed when Shishak of Egypt invaded in 926 B.C. (1 Kings 14:25). Jeroboam I fortified it and made it his first capital (1 Kings 12:25). Above the temple he built a structure that has been identified as a royal granary. Israelite Shechem met its end at the hands of Shalmaneser V in 724 and the town was abandoned until the fourth century B.C.

Then Alexander the Great turned it into a rest camp for his soldiers, and the Samaritans subsequently occupied it. Many think Shechem is the Sychar of John 4:5–7 (Sychem in the Syriac Version), near which was Jacob's well. But others opt for Tell 'Askar northeast of Tell Balatah on the eastern slope of Mount Ebal, about a half mile north of Jacob's Well. The Jewish king John Hyrcanus was responsible for the last destruction of the Samaritan town of Shechem in 128 B.C. and thereafter it ceased to be occupied.

Three factors led to the end of the Middle Bronze Age during the first half of the sixteenth century B.C. (1) Hittite raids on northern Syria, (2) an influx of Hurrian peoples

from northern Mesopotamia into Syria and to a lesser degree into Palestine, and (3) an expulsion of the Hyksos from Egypt and some Egyptian attacks on Hyksos centers in southern Palestine and destruction there. But Canaanite civilization remained essentially intact, and many of the great urban centers continued to exist into the Late Bronze Age. Probably the damage inflicted on some of them was repaired by the time Joshua and the other spies reported back to the tribes gathered at Kadesh Barnea that the cities of Canaan were "walled to heaven" (Deuteronomy 1:28). Indeed it must have appeared to them that such was the case. Cities perched on hills, effectively walled, could appear to be walled to heaven on a day when clouds hung low over them. Though we now know from archaeological and historical studies that many of the great urban centers of the Middle Bronze Age lay in ruins and were deserted by that time, some did remain. And we need not take the report of the spies at face value, i.e., implying that powerful cities stood everywhere. They were looking for excuses not to invade, and there were examples of fortified towns to which they could point.

The Late Bronze Age (c. 1550–1200 B.C.)

The Late Bronze Age was a momentous era. Those were the days when the

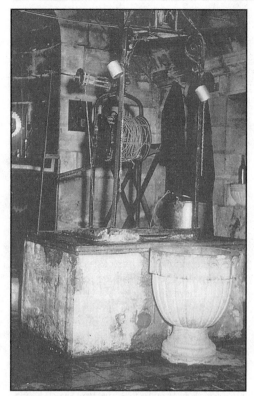
Jacob's well near Shechem. John 4:5–7

1570–1530) and then marched north to besiege Sharuhen (Tell el-'Ajjul, some four miles southeast of Gaza), where Hyksos troops had holed up. He established the Eighteenth Dynasty and inaugurated the Empire period. Subsequent Pharaohs made only sporadic invasions of Canaan, leaving it to Thutmose III (c. 1482–1450), often called the "Napoleon of Ancient Egypt," to establish Egyptian control over Canaan.

At the beginning of his reign he marched north to meet a coalition of 330 native princes[28] under the leadership of the king of Kadesh on the Orontes. They chose to make their stand at Megiddo. The story is often told of how Thutmose, in an act of bravery, decided to take the direct route to the city through a narrow valley where the army could have been mowed down. He volunteered to lead the march in person. As it turned out, the defenders of Megiddo, like Thutmose's generals, did not think the Egyptians should or would take the dangerous route. So the Egyptians surprised the Canaanites and took their camp. While the Egyptians engaged in a massive plunder, the defenders escaped into the city of Megiddo, where they held out through a seven month siege.

When Megiddo capitulated, the back of Palestinian opposition to Egypt was broken. But the Palestinians didn't give up. Thutmose had to make sixteen more campaigns into the northland to establish Egyptian sovereignty there. These campaigns were sometimes a show of force, but they did not always involve severe fighting. Egypt had in fact established her control over all Palestine and Syria as far north as Kadesh on the Orontes. But Thutmose was not merely involved in taking control of Canaan; he was fighting the Hurrian kingdom of Mitanni that ruled in northern Syria and northern Mesopotamia. This he defeated in his eighth campaign. For all his efforts he came to be known as a great warrior king. Interestingly, Thutmose's victory obelisks have been carted off to Istanbul, Rome, London, and Central Park in New York City.

Thutmose's son Amenhotep II was forced to fight in north Syria and Palestine, where he carried off enormous quantities of booty and some ninety thousand prisoners.

Egyptians broke the back of Hyksos power in Egypt and pursued them up into Palestine, creating an empire in the process. But the Hittites had imperial ideas of their own and advanced south into Syria, where they engaged in a titanic struggle with the Egyptians. The age ended with both powers exhausted and unable to pursue imperial designs in Palestine.

In the midst of this contest, the Hebrews managed to move into Palestine, launch an incomplete conquest, and settle down for an extended period of time under the leadership of the Judges and in a loose confederation. Of course the Hebrews did not completely dispossess the previous occupants of the land, and in some places and at some times conditions seemed a bit crowded.

Egyptian Presence in Canaan. Egyptians fought a furious contest to destroy Hyksos enclaves and to re-establish native Egyptian control over all the land of the Nile. Ahomse I conquered the Hyksos capital of Avaris (c. 1550 B.C., variously dated

Thutmose III, the builder of Egyptian empire in Palestine

religious revolution—a form of monotheism, Aton worship, and building a new capital at Amarna. The reigns of these two rulers are called the Amarna period, and it roughly extended from 1400 to 1350 B.C., depending on whose chronology we follow. The empire slipped through the fingers of the Pharaohs. Interestingly, if we follow the biblical chronology adopted in this book, the Hebrew conquest of Canaan and the elders who outlived Joshua took place about 1400–1375, the very time when Egyptian power waned. And we must remember that the Hebrews took only Transjordan, where there was little Egyptian involvement, and the highlands of Galilee, Samaria, and Judea. They did not take the coastline, where Egyptians continued to make their influence felt.

The disintegration of the Egyptian empire during the Amarna Period is reflected in the Amarna Letters. These 380 tablets, most of which were written in Akkadian and addressed to Amenhotep III and IV, largely deal with a constant state of conflict and requests to the Pharaoh to intervene. The local princes of Palestine and Syria, loyal to the Pharaoh, pled for troops to help maintain the Egyptian Empire against other disloyal Canaanite princes, the unidentified 'Apiru or Habiru, the rising state of Amurru (which had shifted its allegiance from Egypt to the Hittites), and against the Hittites themselves. As far as we know the Egyptian kings did not respond.

Soon after 1300 B.C. Seti I decided to rehabilitate the empire in Canaan that Amenhotep IV had lost. He enjoyed some success against the Canaanites around Beth-Shean and in the Jordan Valley, as well as in Syria against the kingdom of Amruru and Kadesh on the Orontes. Meanwhile, the Hittites had moved south into northern Syria and eastward into northern Mesopotamia. Though Seti had a partial victory against the Hittites, the Hittites regrouped after Seti died and while Egypt went through a change of administrations. They amassed an army of some 25,000–30,000 to reassert their power in Syria and northern Canaan.

Raamses II (1299–1232, or 1290–1224, or 1279–1213) decided to contest Hittite

After that, Egyptian forays into Canaan seem to have largely ceased for a long time. One reason seems to have been the policy of Thutmose III in taking hostages to Egypt where they were fully Egyptianized and then returned to Canaan to assume positions of leadership.

In time Egyptian rulers grew soft, not concerned with maintenance of empire as Thutmose III and Amenhotep II had been, Amenhotep III enjoyed a life of luxury and his son Amenhotep IV concentrated on a

Amenhotep II may have been the Pharaoh of the Exodus. Here he is seated in the Temple of Karnak at Luxor

The Hittites were to control northern Syria and the empire of Amurru, while the Egyptians held southern Syria and the whole of Palestine. Marriage of a daughter of Raamses to the Hittite king confirmed the treaty, which remained in force until the fall of the Hittite Empire. This pact is a remarkable document. Ancient empires of the Middle East were not typically given to mutual agreements; normally they just clobbered their foes if they could. Otherwise they capitulated to their enemies.

When Raamses died, his thirteenth son Merneptah took the throne. There was a minor revolt in Canaan which he subdued with little difficulty. His victory stele (now in the Cairo Museum) tells of conquest of Ashkelon, Gezer, and "Israel," the only time Egyptian records mention the Hebrews.[29]

The question is often asked as to how the Israelites could have entered Palestine in the first place when the Egyptians were building an empire there. Moreover, where were they when the Egyptians rebuilt empire in the days of Raamses II and Merneptah? We have already noted that the empire that Thutmose III launched was on the decline about 1400 when the Hebrews probably conquered the land. When they did enter, they settled in Transjordan and the hills of Galilee, Samaria, and Jordan. The Egyptians continued to dominate the coastal plain and parts of the Negev. When Raamses II and Merneptah tried to rebuild the empire they again did not need to cross paths with the Hebrews. Egyptian armies marched along the coast on their way north. Merneptah fought battles at Ashkelon in the Philistine plain and Gezer in the Shephelah. He could have encountered some Hebrews in the Shephelah or the nearby hills of Judea, but there is no indication of massive conflict between the Egyptians and Hebrews in Merneptah's day. As to subsequent developments, the Egyptian Empire disintegrated by about 1100 B.C., during the days of the Judges. And the Hittite Empire came to an end just after 1200 B.C. So they both passed off the scene by around the end of the Late Bronze Age.

advance and pulled together an army that must have been roughly the Hittite equal. In his fifth year he met the Hittites at Kadesh on the Orontes. Unknowingly he marched into a Hittite ambush and faced utter destruction. But a combination of Raamses' personal bravery and the timely arrival of additional detachments of troops saved the day. Raamses went home to record accounts of great victory on Egyptian temple walls, and there was plenty of Hittite braggadocio as well, but in reality the outcome of the battle must have been a draw.

Subsequent contests in Palestine and Syria led in Raamses' twenty-first year to a treaty of friendship with Hattushili III. It provided for specifically defined spheres of interest.

Canaan During the Late Bronze Age

The population and density of settlement during the Late Bronze Age declined

Ramses II is one of Egypt's best known pharaohs. His reputation derives from his restoration of the Egyptian empire, his extensive construction all over Egypt, and the fact that many believe he was the pharaoh of the Exodus. *British Museum*

from the Middle Bronze period. This involved a general decline in urbanization, as well as in rural settlement, especially in the hill country. A survey of 270 Middle Bronze sites revealed that only about a hundred of them were inhabited in the Late Bronze Age.[30] The central hills were almost devoid of settlement, except by a non-sedentary population. This fact "had a decisive significance for Israelite settlement."[31] There was a relative vacuum that Israelites could fill. Most excavated Late Bronze sites revealed no evidence of fortification walls. Presumably the situation resulted from Egyptian prohibition against erection of such defenses.[32] Also, Egyptian financial exactions on Canaanite towns in order to maintain their imperial program were so great that towns probably could not afford to build elaborate defenses. Probably, too, the financial burden on the towns was so significant that many people simply left the

towns to avoid the Egyptian demand for supplies and manpower.[33]

Canaan benefited to some degree from her position within the Egyptian Empire. Trade with Egypt resulted in importation of goods from the South and the shipment of Canaan's goods to Egypt. Importation of pottery from Cyprus and the Myceneans of Greece and the Aegean islands demonstrates the vitality of Mycenean mercantile enterprise during the Late Bronze Age. Cyprus was the main source of copper throughout the Mediterranean during the Late Bronze Age. And after the thirteenth century B.C. copper was mined in the Arabah, where Egypt established mines at Timna (15 miles miles north of the Gulf of Akaba). Turquoise was also mined in the Sinai.

Carved ivories were perhaps the best representation of the artistic world of the Late Bronze Age. Some three hundred pieces were excavated in the palace at Megiddo, but carved ivory also surfaced at Lachish and Tell el-Far 'ah (south). These pieces consisted of cosmetic boxes and especially of furniture inlay with scenes of palace life. These ivories show Canaanite, Egyptian, and Mycenean influences. Excavations also demonstrate that figurines and decorated pendants of bronze, silver, and gold were popular in the Late Bronze Age. Though Canaan was part of the Egyptian Empire for some four hundred years, it maintained a degree of independence in areas of religion, literature, and art.[34]

The Hebrew Conquest

As far as the Bible is concerned, the most important event of the Palestinian Late Bronze Age was the Hebrew conquest. First came the defeat of the people east of the Jordan, then the crossing of the Jordan River, followed by the fall of Jericho and Ai. Next came the defeat of the Amorite League as it mustered against Gibeon. Then Joshua destroyed the towns or the populations of Makkedah, Libnah, Lachish, Gezer, Eglon, Hebron, and Debir. Israelite success in the south stimulated a northern confederacy under the leadership of Hazor to mount an attack. Again God gave the victory and

A Megiddo ivory of a sphinx, showing Egyptian influence. *Courtesy of the Oriental Institute*

Hazor was destroyed, (cf. Deuteronomy 2:24–3:20; Joshua 2–12). The point needs to be made that destruction of Hebrew opponents refers primarily to military forces and population, not necessarily to all of the physical remains of the cities, thus limiting the information archaeology can provide concerning the Conquest. Moreover, the Hebrews failed to take whole sections of western Palestine (cf. Joshua 13–15). The struggle to complete the conquest extended on into the period of the Judges, that is into the Early Iron Age.

As is true with other parts of the Bible, the Conquest narrative has suffered greatly at the hands of twentieth century critical scholars. Today they reject the Israelite conquest as described in the Bible. Some of the reasons they give for doing so, especially in connection with the fall of Jericho and Ai appear later. At this point it is enough to note the alternate schools or theories of interpretation.

First, some scholars argue for peaceful infiltration, that generally the Hebrews came in search of new pastures in areas not heavily populated or land not controlled by city-states of the time. Conquest narratives were invented to explain why places like Jericho or Ai were in ruins.

Second, the Joshua story is a peasants' revolt, a conflict between seminomadic herdsmen and settled farmers, a revolt against Canaanites stimulated by a group of prisoners from Egypt who arrived with a belief in a new God, Yahweh.

Third, some groups who settled in the hills of Canaan during Iron I came from the Canaanite society of the lowlands. As the population increased, a conflict arose that resulted in the destruction of several towns, e.g., Bethel. Walter C. Kaiser provides a brief survey of these three schools of interpretation.[35]

The position taken in this book is that the Conquest occurred just as the book of Joshua reports. Some answers to scholarly attacks and denials appear in following discussions.

Crossing the Jordan. Of course Israelite crossing of the Jordan is not subject to archaeological verification, but it can be discussed in terms of plausibility. And it must be understood geographically. According to the Joshua account, the waters of the Jordan stopped flowing just as the priests who bore the ark stepped into the water. And the waters rose in a heap at the towns of Adam and Zaretan (Joshua 3:15–16). The location of Adam is marked by the present site of Damieh, some sixteen miles north of Jericho. Inasmuch as Jericho is a few miles north of the Dead Sea, this would give a stretch of at least twenty miles of dry river bed over which Israel could cross. They would not have been restricted to a narrow passageway but could have crossed several hundred or even several thousand abreast.

Where the Israelites crossed, the Jordan ordinarily was about a hundred feet wide, although at harvest time (cf. Joshua 3:15) it was wider and measured about ten or twelve feet in depth. It is difficult today to visualize what the Jordan was like in Joshua's day because Syrian, Jordanian, and Israeli use of water from the Jordan River system for irrigation and other purposes has reduced the

The mound of Old Testament Jericho and the Jericho Oasis

river to an insignificant stream. This water use has also resulted in a continued shrinkage of the Dead Sea.

It has been suggested that God may have used an earthquake to cause a landslide to stop the Jordan River. Scripture gives possible evidence of an earthquake at the time of Israel's entrance into Canaan. Referring to that time, Judges 5:4, says, "the earth trembled," and Psalm 114:3–4 reads, "Jordan turned back; the mountains skipped like rams," which seems to be a poetic description of an earthquake.

At Damieh, the site of modern Adam, there are high banks that, when broken loose in a landslide, block the water. Such a blocking of the Jordan occurred in the year A.D. 1267, when a lofty mound overlooking the river on the west fell into the river and dammed it up for sixteen hours.[36] There was a similar occurrence in 1927, when a section of the cliff 150 feet high fell into the Jordan and blocked the water for twenty-one and a half hours.[37] Whether God used an earthquake to produce a landslide to block the Jordan cannot be proved. But at precisely the right time He caused the Jordan to cease flowing so that Israel could cross the river. The miracle would then be in the timing and in the very rapid drying of the muddy river bed rather than in the means of accomplishing God's purposes. Damming up of the Jordan for extended periods in modern times at exactly the same spot as mentioned in the Joshua narrative shows that such a thing did happen and that a similar occurrence in Joshua's day is plausible.

JERICHO AND ITS OASIS

Anyone who stands on the mound of Old Testament Jericho today and looks out over the Jericho oasis must be impressed with this spot of

A cut through the mound of Old Testament Jericho to bedrock, with the traditional Mount of Temptation in the distance

The palace of Herod the Great at New Testament Jericho: the cold bath and the reception area beyond in the north wing

greenery in an otherwise arid region. At the foot of the mound gushes the 'Ain-es Sultan, one of the largest freshwater springs in all of Palestine. About a mile away in the Wadi Qelt, where New Testament Jericho was located, are additional springs. Old Testament Jericho was known as the "city of palm trees" (Deuteronomy 34:3; 2 Chronicles 28:15). How extensive its cultivated area was we do not know. But Herod the Great turned Jericho into a garden city that covered hundreds of acres and was inhabited by tens of thousands of Jews.

Jericho was important as more than a garden spot, however. Its strategic importance may be traced to its location near a ford of the Jordan. The ancient trade routes from the East crossed the Jordan near Jericho and then branched out in three directions: the northern route in the direction of Bethel and Shechem, the westward road toward Jerusalem, and the southern route to Hebron. Jericho controlled all these access routes to the hill country of Palestine. Jericho (Tell es-Sultan) lay in the Jordan Valley eight hundred feet below sea level, eight miles

northwest of the junction of the Jordan River with the Dead Sea, and five miles west of the Jordan itself.

Jericho's strategic position plays an important part in the record of the Israelite conquest. By taking Jericho (Joshua 6), Joshua drove a wedge into

Statuary niches in the south wing of Herod's palace at Jericho

the land of Canaan and struck terror into the hearts of its inhabitants. Canaanite Jericho was completely destroyed, and for centuries no attempt was made to rebuild the town (cf. Joshua 6:26), although the spring and the oasis located there were frequented.

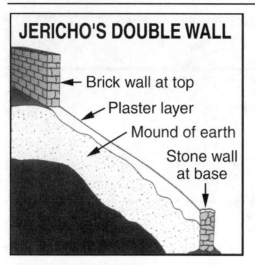

JERICHO'S DOUBLE WALL

← Brick wall at top

↙ Plaster layer

↙ Mound of earth

Stone wall
at base

A stone wall surrounded the mound on which Jericho was built. This held in place a flat rampart, above which (higher up the slope) stood a second (mudbrick) wall that constituted Jericho's city wall proper. So there were two concentric walls. When the walls fell, the mudbrick wall collapsed and slid down the slope, creating a pile of rubble over which the attackers could climb.

In the days of the Judges, Eglon of Moab temporarily occupied the oasis (Judges 3:12–13). It was not until Ahab's reign that the city proper was rebuilt (1 Kings 16:34), only to be destroyed again by the Babylonians in 587/586 B.C. After the exile, Jericho was inhabited by Israelites again (Ezra 2:34; Nehemiah 3:2; 7:36), and by New Testament times it had become a thriving town. New Testament Jericho was built during the Maccabean (Hasmonean) period, possibly as early as 134 B.C. by Simon Maccabeus, and was expanded in the days of Herod the Great. This Jericho lies on the two banks of the Wadi Qelt about a mile west of modern Jericho and seventeen miles east-northeast of Jerusalem. Modern Jericho was founded in the time of the Crusades and lies to the east of New Testament Jericho and southeast of Old Testament Jericho.

The Fall of Jericho. The fall of the walls of Jericho is one of the most familiar stories of the Bible. Even those who have not read the

book of Joshua or may not even own a Bible have probably heard the words of the spiritual, "Joshua fit the battle of Jericho, and the walls come tumbling down." As Joshua 6 tells it, the Hebrews were to march around the city once a day for six days and seven times on the seventh day, at which time they were to shout and the walls would fall down. Then they were to destroy everything in the city except Rahab and her family and metal objects that were to be dedicated to the tabernacle worship. The Hebrews obeyed and the city was destroyed as predicted.

Is the Joshua narrative just so much folklore and religious rhetoric or did the destruction of Jericho happen that way? In order to find an answer, we must turn to archaeology.

Although Charles Warren excavated briefly at Jericho (1868) and Ernst Sellin and Carl Watzinger did so later (1907–1909, 1911), a more serious expedition conducted excavations there from 1930 to 1936 under the direction of John Garstang. It is useful to note that Sellin and Watzinger showed that the city mound covered only about eight and one-half acres, about two city blocks. Thus, it was possible for the Israelites to have marched around it once a day, or even seven times a day. Some, equating the amount of attention that is given to Jericho in the Old Testament with a great city like Babylon or Nineveh, previously believed that Jericho could not have been encircled as the biblical narrative indicates. But excavation at the site eliminated that argument.

Garstang's work at Jericho led to great excitement, at least in the Western world. He identified the wall of Joshua's day as a double wall on top of the mound on which the city was built—the outer one six feet thick and the inner twelve feet thick—separated by a fifteen-foot space. Garstang stated further that when the city fell to the Hebrews, the walls collapsed outward and slid down the slope on which the town was built. So completely were they destroyed that it would have been possible for attackers to climb over the rubble and into the city.

In additional confirmation of Scripture, he found that the site was burned at the time of conquest. Moreover, as a result of

The Et Tell High Place with altars for sacrifice

Israelite obedience to God's prohibition against plundering the city, foodstuffs were found in abundance in the remains—a remarkable discovery when we consider that the Israelites had not yet had the opportunity to raise crops since coming in from the desert. The walls originally may have been as high as thirty feet, and Garstang concluded that they fell about 1400 B.C. [38] We should note that Garstang was no wild-eyed biblicist who set out to prove the accuracy of Scripture. He was so startled by what he found that he asked the eminent Clarence S. Fisher (associated with Harvard, University of Chicago, and University of Pennsylvania excavations) and Roland de Vaux (director of Ecole Biblique in Jerusalem) to join him in issuing a statement about his discoveries.

Though critics attacked Garstang's work and his conclusions, he steadfastly insisted on their accuracy. And when World War II was over and he could gain access to his stored records, he and his son published an affirmation volume: *The Story of Jericho*, by John and J. B. E. Garstang.

Controversy over Garstang's claims as to what he had found led to a new Jericho expedition, a joint enterprise of the British school of Archaeology in Jerusalem and the American Schools of Oriental Research, under the leadership of Kathleen Kenyon

(1952–58), director of the British School. She concluded that Garstang had erroneously dated Early Bronze Age walls (3000–2000 B.C.) to the time of Joshua and that the mud-brick walls of Joshua's day had eroded away during the many centuries when the site was unoccupied. Thus there was very little left from Joshua's day and almost nothing left from the days of reoccupation in the ninth century B.C. by Hiel the Bethelite (1 Kings 16:34). When pressed about Joshua's conquest, Kenyon did, however, state that she had found some artifacts that she dated to the time of Joshua's conquest and concluded that she would probably not satisfy either the late or early date exponents of the fall of the city by saying that it probably fell between about 1350 and 1325 B.C. [39]

Critics pounced on Kenyon's statements about Garstang's assessment of the walls as evidence that the biblical account was unhistorical, and some used them as support for denying the historicity of the Conquest. They tended to ignore Kenyon's suggestion that the city did fall to the Israelites around 1350 B.C. or later and Garstang's other evidence, especially from tombs, that pointed to a 1400 B.C. date for the fall of the city. There the matter lay until after Kenyon's death in 1978.

Her excavation reports, published posthumously at the end of the 1980's, received careful analysis by Bryant Wood, at that time an archaeologist at the University of Toronto and a specialist on Jericho. Based on Kenyon's reports, Wood observed that there stood a stone revetment surrounding the mound on which the town was built, and on this revetment was a mudbrick wall. The revetment held in place a flat rampart, above which (higher up the slope) stood a second mudbrick wall that constituted Jericho's city wall proper. So, there were two concentric walls with houses in between, one of which may have been Rahab's. Kenyon herself had discovered piles of bricks that had fallen down from the revetment wall surrounding the city and that would have enabled attackers to climb up into the city.[40] Moreover, in line with God's command not to take the city's goods, abundant and valuable supplies of grain turned up in the excavation.[41] Evidently the city did not fall as a result of a starvation siege, as was common in the ancient Near East. Stones, bricks, and timbers were found, blackened from a citywide fire, tallying with the biblical indication that the Israelites burned the city. On the basis of Kenyon's excavation reports, Wood also argued that all evidence pointed to an approximate 1400 B.C. date for the fall of the city, including a Carbon-14 analysis that yielded a date of 1410, plus or minus forty years.

To summarize, Wood concluded that the walls of Jericho did indeed fall so attackers could climb up over the debris to burn the city but not plunder it. He, like many others, believed it was an earthquake that triggered the destruction. Interestingly, the headline of the *New York Times* article reporting on the posthumous analysis of Kenyon's works; reads, "Believers Score in Battle Over the Battle of Jericho."[42]

Ai. Just as critics have used discoveries at Jericho to disprove the accuracy of Scripture and even the very existence of the Conquest, in like manner they have pounced on finds at Ai. As the account goes, Israel suffered defeat at Ai initially because a certain Achan had taken some plunder from Jericho at the time of its capture, contrary to God's command (Joshua 7–8). But ultimately, after Achan's judgment, Israel went on to victory.

During much of the twentieth century Ai has been identified with Et-Tell, a site about three miles northeast of El Bireh. Judith Marquet-Krause excavated there in 1934 and 1935, discovering that the mound had not been inhabited between 2400 and 1200 B.C.[43] So whenever we date the Conquest, Ai would have been uninhabited at the time, and the Bible would appear to be in error. Many critics have assumed this to be the case.

J. Simons, however, has offered four objections to the identification of Et-Tell with Ai: (1) Et-Tell is not particularly near Beitin (Bethel), whereas Joshua 12:9 indicates that Ai is "beside Bethel"; (2) Et-Tell is a large site, whereas Joshua 7:3 describes the people as "few"; (3) Et-Tell was not a ruin in the postconquest period, whereas Joshua 8:28 indicates that it was destroyed; and (4) There is no broad valley to the north of Et-Tell, whereas Joshua 8:11 indicates the existence of a valley near Ai.[44]

And when Professor Joseph A. Callaway of Southern Baptist Theological Seminary led a new expedition to Et-Tell in 1964, he concluded, "Nothing in the present evidence warrants an identification of the village with the city of Ai captured by Joshua as described in Joshua 8:1–29."[45] Apparently Callaway never quite dismissed the idea that Et-Tell was Ai, however. In a 1975 publication (after seven seasons of excavation at Et-Tell, 1964–1972) he seemed to accept the identification.[46] Presumably his chief problem was that no other more likely candidate for the site of Ai had yet turned up.

On the basis of Simons' arguments and Callaway's hesitancy in accepting Et-Tell as Ai (in his 1964 article and my conversation with him), I question that biblical Ai is to be located at Et-Tell. Many others have questioned the identification also. John Bimson and David Livingston believed that the true site might be Khirbet Nisya, eleven miles north of Jerusalem, and they excavated there for six seasons (1979–1986).[47] But there is little convincing evidence to support this claim either. Bryant G. Wood of Associates for Biblical Research has been leading a consortium of institutions in excavations at Khirbet El-Maqatir, a site ten

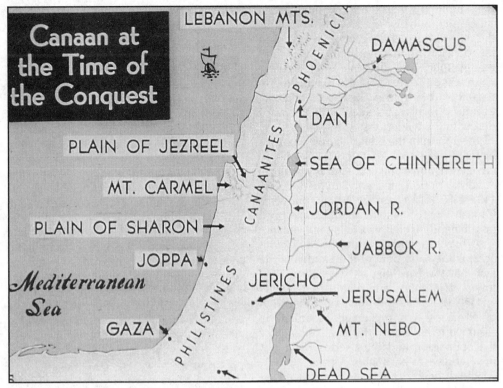

Canaan at the time of Conquest

miles north of Jerusalem and a half mile west of Et-Tell, since 1995. A new season of excavation took place at the site during May and June of 2000. Discoveries there are promising, but the jury is still out on this identification. Until the site of Ai is firmly established, it is unwarranted to draw any conclusions about the supposed inaccuracy of the Joshua narrative.

Hazor. A third major site connected with the Hebrew conquest is Hazor, leader of Canaanite opposition to the Hebrews in the north. There the eminent Yigael Yadin concluded that destruction late in the thirteenth century B.C., which brought an end to occupation in the lower city, was probably "caused by the Israelites."[48] Thus destruction at Jericho and Hazor may be attributed to the Hebrew conquest. And based on discoveries there, as well as other indications, it is unwarranted to dismiss the Conquest narrative from Scripture.

Moreover, we need to keep in mind that there was to be no general destruction of Palestinian cities when the Hebrews entered. God had told them that they were to occupy cities and houses that they had not built, wells that they had not dug, and vineyards and olive groves that they had not planted (Deuteronomy 6:10–11). As they took over existing facilities they would not have left much archaeological evidence of conquest.

The Date of the Exodus and Conquest

The tendency of a great many Bible students has been to assume that the Exodus took place during the thirteenth century B.C., (perhaps around 1290 B.C.)and the Conquest around 1250 B.C. This assumption is especially related to the belief that Raamses II (c. 1299–1232 or 1279–1212) was the Pharaoh of the Exodus. This late date of the Exodus is at variance with the indications of biblical chronology, however. First Kings 6:1 says that the Exodus took place 480 years before the fourth year of Solomon's reign, when he began to build the temple. If we base out computation on Thiele's chronology (he assigns 931 B.C. as the date of the end of Solomon's reign and the division of the monarchy),[49] we find that the fourth year of Solomon's forty-year reign was 967/6 B.C. and the Exodus therefore took place in 1447/6 B.C. and the Conquest forty years later, after the wandering in the wilderness.

In support of the biblical chronology, we have already seen that Jericho seems to have fallen about 1400 B.C. And this was the Amarna period in Egyptian history (c. 1400–1350 B.C.) when Egyptian control of Canaan slipped, and it would have been possible for the Hebrews to enter Canaan.

A major problem confronting one who accepts the early date of the Exodus is the fact that the Israelites, as slaves, built the towns of Pithom and Raamses (Exodus 1:11). And Raamses II (for whom the town of Raamses was presumably named) is assumed to have been the great pharaoh of the oppression and the Exodus, who put the Hebrews to hard labor. Unger suggested the difficulty here may be removed by concluding that Raamses is a modernization of the ancient place-name *Zoan-Avaris,* the name by which it was known when the Hebrews built it. A similar situation occurred in Genesis 14:14, where *Dan* is substituted for the older city name of *Laish.*[50] It should be added that Avaris served as the old Hyskos capital in the Delta, and we now know as a result of recent excavations that the town of Raamses adjoined it on the north. That is, Raamses-Avaris had become almost a double city, with Raamses on the north and Avaris on the south. [51]

Then, too, the claim of Yadin that Hazor fell to Joshua in the thirteenth century B.C. has to be faced. Scripture indicates that Hazor fell to the Israelites twice: in the days of Joshua (Joshua 11:10–11), when Jabin I ruled, and in the days of the judges Deborah and Barak (Judges 4:2, 23–24), when another Jabin ruled. Yadin assumed that Joshua's conquest was to be related to thirteenth-century B.C. destruction in the lower city of Hazor. There was, however, some evidence of destruction at the site around 1400 B.C. or a little later during the

Amarna period.[52] It seems likely that the 1400 B.C. destruction dates to Joshua's day and the thirteenth-century destruction dates to the period of the judges. We await a more definitive word on the subject from Amnon Ben-Tor's excavations at Hazor now in progress.

Further it is argued that the palace's accessibility to Moses militates against the early date of the Exodus. The reasoning is that such accessibility indicates the palace was in the delta region, where the Israelites lived, and the periods when the palace was located in the delta were the days of Joseph during the thirteenth century B.C. But the pharaoh of the Exodus could have met Moses at a secondary palace or administrative center. The argument fails to provide convincing support for the late date of the Exodus. Moreover, both Thutmose III and Amenhotep II, who ruled 1482-1425 B.C., were active in building projects in the delta. And both of them were present there a great deal as they launched military campaigns up into Palestine and Syria.

PI–RAMESSE–AVARIS

Raamses II's great capital of Pi-Ramesse and the Hyksos capital of Avaris are now known to form a great two-part complex at Qantir-Tell el-Dab'a in the eastern Delta. Pi-Ramesse is to be identified with Qantir in the north (about 6.5 square miles) and Avaris with Tell el-Dab'a in the south (about 1.5 square miles, and three times the size of Hazor, the largest contemporary site in Palestine).

Because the new Libyan dynasty (after c. 1045 B.C.) transported many remains from Pi-Ramesse to Tanis, their new capital in the Delta, it is not now possible to view Pi-Ramesse as it was. But we know that an extensive royal palace stood in the center of the city, flanked by temples of Amon, Re, Ptah, and Seth at the four principal compass points. In the square before the palace stood four colossal statues of Raamses, each over sixty-eight feet tall—the largest free-standing statues in Egypt. All over the city there were obelisks and statues of gods, kings, priests, and high-ranking officials. About fifty such statues now may be seen elsewhere in Egypt or in museums around the world.[51]

Archaeologists also claim that the destruction of Bethel, Lachish, and Debir, presumably by the Israelites, occurred around 1230 B.C.[53] and therefore supports a late date for the Exodus and the Conquest. But while the Bible reports that Joshua captured Bethel, Lachish, and Debir, it says nothing about his men destroying them; they burned only Ai, Jericho, and Hazor (Joshua 6:24; 8:19; 11:13). In fact, Joshua 11:13 specifically states Joshua burned none of the other cities that he conquered. Some of Joshua's conquests were not permanent either. We know that Debir had to be recaptured later (Joshua 15:13-17), and possibly the others did also. If the 1230 B.C. date of destuction of Bethel, Lachish, and Debir is correct, it may well refer to attacks during the days of the Judges instead of to Joshua's conquests.

The date of the Exodus must also be related to the biography of Moses. Moses was eighty at the time of the Exodus (Ex. 7:7). If the Exodus took place around 1275 B.C., the birth of Moses would have occurred about 1355. And before that the Hebrews had built the store cities of Pithom and Raamses (Exodus 1:11), long *before* the reign of the first Raamses and long before a thirteenth century date for the Exodus.

Finally, Benno Rothenberg explored and excavated in the Timna' valley (fifteen miles north of the Gulf of Akaba) between 1964 and 1960 and concluded that the Egyptian working of the copper mines in the area was especially extensive in the days of Raamses II. Therefore, hordes of Egyptian soldiers and workers would have been moving around the Sinai and the Arabah at the time when many scholars, including Israelis generally, believed the Exodus and wilderness wandering took place. No way could the Hebrews have been moving through the area then. So he believed his discoveries would require a "reconsideration" of the thirteenth-century B.C. date of the Exodus.[54]

Iron Age Palestine

The Iron Age in Palestine is usually divided into three periods: Early Iron, 1200–900 B.C.; Middle Iron, 900–600 B.C.; Late Iron, 600–300 B.C. The first concerns the days of the Judges, the contest between the Philistines and Hebrews, and the establishment of the Hebrew monarchy; the second, the divided monarchy, the fall of the Northern Kingdom to Assyria, and the fall of the Southern Kingdom to Babylon; the third, the restoration of the Hebrews to their homeland and the rule of the Persians. Of course the use of iron for tools and weapons had now become dominant.

To properly introduce the Iron Age, a word about the transition between the Bronze and Iron Ages is in order. Around 1200 B.C. the props on the world stage changed drastically. The Hittite Empire in Asia Minor came crashing down soon thereafter. So did the Mycenean kingdoms over in the Greek world. And within a hundred years the Egyptian Empire was gone too. In Mesopotamia an Assyrian dynasty rose to power about 1100 and after one administration ran out of steam. So the whole Early Iron Age was a time of small states and migrating peoples in the eastern Mediterranean.

Why this massive shift occurred used to be attributed largely to the Dorian invasion of Greece and the migration of Sea Peoples. But more recently drought and economic difficulties have been given more credit. And Robert Drews has argued that transition from chariot to infantry warfare was especially responsible. For four hundred years chariot armies had been supreme, but now the infantry took back the field. His book, *The End of the Bronze Age,* is especially instructive.

Within Palestine foreign empires no longer exercised the power and influence they had previously enjoyed. At least that was true after 1100 B.C., when the Egyptian Empire disintegrated. Nor did Canaanite city-states control large chunks of territory. In western Palestine Israelites, Philistines, and remnants of the old Canaanite population vied for the mastery. In Transjordan Israelites sought to dominate Edomites, Moabites, Amorites, and Aramaeans. Of course the reason why the Israelites did not quickly overwhelm the other ethnic elements was that they constituted a loose federation of tribes during the period of the judges, when everyone did that which was right in his own eyes (Judges 17:6). After the monarchy galvanized the nation to united action, the loose federation became an effective empire.

Early Iron Age

Philistines. During the Early Iron Age the Philistines and Hebrews primarily contested for the mastery in western Palestine. Philistine power centered around five main cities: Gaza, Ashkelon, and Ashdod in the coastal plain, and Gath and Ekron in the Shephelah. To date Philistine remains have been excavated at Ashdod (approx. 100 acres), Ekron (approx. 50 acres), and Ashkelon. But the Philistines occupied other sites on or near the coast and in the Shephelah (including Tell Qasile, on the Yarkon Rover at the northern city limits of Tel Aviv), Aphek, Beth-Shemesh, Gezer, and Tel Batash. Tel Batash, about five miles south of Gezer is presumably the Timnah that figured in the Samson narrative (Judges 14–15). The Philistines were responsible for maintenance of city life in western Palestine while major Canaanite cities such as Hazor and Lachish were abandoned. Apparently the Philistine immigrants did not replace the local population but became the military and civil aristocracy in the cities that they dominated.[55]

THE CITIES OF PHILISTIA

Gaza. Gaza (about 5 miles inland from the Mediterranean) was the southernmost of the cities of the Philistine pentapolis (the five cities of Joshua 13:1–3) and marked the southern limit of Canaan on the Mediterranean coast (Genesis 10:19). It was the center of busy caravan routes that led southwest into Egypt, south to Arabia by way of Beersheba, southeast into Edom, and north along the Mediterranean, and then overland to Damascus and beyond. In the days of the Egyptian Empire (c. 1550–1200 B.C.), Gaza served as an administrative center for protecting Egyptian interests in Canaan.

During the period of the Judges, Gaza was a Philistine stronghold. There blinded Samson worked in the prison mill (Judges 16:21); and when his strength was revived, he caused the death of the assembled multitude (Judges 16:28–30).

Although Gaza was nominally a part of the kingdoms of David and Solomon (cf. 1 Kings 4:24), Israelite control of the city was tenuous. The Assyrian annals record a series of battles for Gaza. At the time of Sennacherib's campaign against Judah (701 B.C.), Gaza was evidently loyal to Assyria, for Sennacherib gave to the king of Gaza territory taken from Judah. By the time of Jeremiah, Gaza had fallen into Egyptian control (Jeremiah 47:1). It was nominally a part of the Persian Empire until it fell to Alexander the Great after a five-month siege (332 B.C.). Alexander colonized Gaza as a Hellenistic city, but sovereignty was disputed by the Egyptian Ptolemies and the Syrian Seleucids after his death. In 198 B.C. The city was annexed by Antiochus III of Syria. Under the Maccabean ruler Alexander Jannaeus, Gaza was destroyed along with other coastal cities (93 B.C.). Pompey, however, declared Gaza a free city in 61 B.C.

Gaza became an important trading city in the days of the Nabataean Arabs. In 57 B.C. Pompey's general, Aulus Gabinius, rebuilt the city at a new site south of the old location and nearer the ocean. It was on the road to the old, or "desert," Gaza that Philip met an Ethiopian (i.e., Nubian) eunuch and led him to Christ (Acts 8:26–40). Gaza is now the principal city of the Gaza Strip and populated

The goddess of Victory standing on the globe supported by Atlas, in the antiquities park, Ashkelon

the exile, Nehemiah was shocked to learn that Jews had married women of Ashdod and that their children spoke the language of Ashdod rather than the language of Judah (Nehemiah 13:23–24).

According to Herodotus, Ashdod was besieged for twenty-nine years by Psamtik (Psammetichos) of Egypt. The city was conquered and partially destroyed by the Maccabees (1 Maccabees 5:68; 10:84). It flourished, however, following Herod's reconstruction. The Roman governor Gabinius beautified Ashdod's inner city which Augustus presented to Salome, Herod's sister. In New Testament times, the city was known as Azotus. Following the conversion of the Ethiopian eunuch, Philip preached in the communities between Azotus and Caesarea (Acts 8:40).

largely by Arab refugees. Though excavations at Gaza have uncovered remains from the Roman, Byzantine, and subsequent periods, they have yet to reveal anything of the Philistine period.

Ashdod. Eighteen miles northeast of Gaza lay Ashdod, the Philistine city with the famed temple of Dagon (Dagan) to which the ark was taken following the Israelite debacle at Aphek (1 Samuel 5:1–5). The history of Ashdod was largely parallel to that of other Philistine city-states. Its governor rebelled against Sargon II (711 B.C.), after which the Assyrians sacked the city (Isaiah 20:1). Jeremiah spoke of "the remnant of Ashdod" (Jeremiah 25:20), implying that the city was weak in his day. Following

A Roman milestone from the Via Maris, dating to the reign of the emperor Hadrian (117-138 A.D.)

The mound frequently identified as the site of Gath

The site of ancient Ashdod (Tel Ashdod) is about 3.5 miles south of modern Ashdod and consists of a mound of about twenty acres and a lower city of some seventy acres. The mound is roughly 165 feet above sea level and some 50 feet above the surrounding area. It was a major city in the Late Bronze and Early Iron ages.

Nine seasons of excavation were conducted at Tel Ashdod between 1962 and 1972 with the cooperation of several institutions and especially under the leadership of David N. Freedman and Moshe Dothan, and a new dig was conducted in 1995 under the leadership of Y. Baumgarten. Clearly the Philistines controlled the town during the twelfth and eleventh centuries B.C., when Tel Ashdod was protected by a wall and fortifications; during the eleventh century B.C. occupation spread to the lower city.

Ashkelon. Ashkelon (about thirty-two miles south of Joppa, twelve miles north of Gaza, ten miles south of Ashdod) was one of the five principal cities of the Philistines (Joshua 13:3; 1 Samuel 6:17). A large site, ancient Ashkelon at times covered about 160 acres, with perhaps fifteen thousand inhabitants. The oldest part lies in the center of the ruins at Tell el-Hader. It was an important way sta-

tion on the coastal route, known to the Egyptians as the Way of Horus, later as the Way of the Philistines, and during the Roman period as the Via Maris (Way of the Sea).

Though an archaeological expedition went to Ashkelon as early as 1815 and again in 1921–22, the first large scale excavation began in 1985 under the leadership of L. E. Stager and sponsored by the Harvard Semitic Museum. Excavations show that the site was occupied throughout the Early Bronze Age (3000–2000 B.C.). Its king is mentioned in Egyptian execration texts (c. 1850 B.C.) and the Amarna letters (c. 1400 B.C.). In about 1280 B.C. Ramses II of Egypt sacked Ashkelon. During the time of the Judges it was temporarily occupied by Judah (Judges 1:18) but had reverted to Philistine rule by the time of Samson (Judges 14:19). Ashkelon contributed one of the golden tumors (emerods) sent to Israel when the Philistines returned the ark, which they had taken in battle (1 Samuel 6:17).

Under Tiglath-Pileser III, Ashkelon became a vassal to Assyria (734 B.C.), but it later rebelled and, after a brief period of freedom, was sacked by Sennacherib. By 630 B.C. Ashkelon regained its independence from the disintegrating Assyrian Empire. Babylonia, however, attempted to regain in her own name the lands that had once paid tribute to Assyria, and Ashkelon was again sacked in 604 B.C. This time it was the army of Nebuchadnezzar that destroyed Ashkelon, slew its king, and took prisoners to Babylon (cf. Jeremiah 47:5–7).

According to tradition, Ashkelon was the birthplace of Herod the Great and the residence of his sister Salome. Herod embellished the city with ornate buildings and colonnaded courts. It is Herodian and Roman Ashkelon that has yielded the most impressive ruins.

Gath. The Philistine city of Gath ("wine press") is best known as the home of Goliath, the giant who was felled by a stone from David's sling (1 Samuel 17). Later in fleeing from Saul, David came to Gath and feigned madness before Achish, the king of the city (1 Samuel 21:10–15). David, with a company of six hundred men, spent over a year in Gath, where they were safe from Saul's murderous intent (1 Samuel 27). After the death of Saul, David was able to add Gath to his own territory (1 Chronicles 18:1). Throughout the rest of his life David seems to have maintained friendly relations with the people of Gath, who are known in Scripture as Gittites. At the time of Absalom's rebellion, David had six hundred Gittites among his mercenaries (2 Samuel 15:18).

Rehoboam fortified Gath (2 Chronicles 11:8), but the city fell to Hazael of Damascus in the ninth century B.C. (2 Kings 12:17). It was evidently in Philistine hands again when Uzziah broke down its walls (2 Chronicles 26:6). Sargon II of Assyria besieged and conquered Gath in the eighth century B.C., and subsequently it dropped out of history (cf. Amos 6:2).

The exact location of Gath remains unknown. Gath means "wine press,"

and there are numerous references to Palestinian Gaths in both biblical and secular sources. Sometimes an additional element was added to the name to distinguish it from other Gaths (e.g., Gath-Hepher, Gath-Rimmon), but in numerous instances the name Gath stands alone. Some have identified Tel 'Erani, twenty miles northeast of Gaza, as the Gath of the Philistines. It is a significant site of some sixty acres divided into three parts: a nearly flat acropolis of about four acres and rising about seventy feet above the surrounding plain, a high terrace stretching around the acropolis hill over an area of about forty acres, and a lower terrace around much of the bottom part of the hill. S. Yeivin excavated at the site on behalf of the Israel Department of Antiquities and Museums for six seasons (1956–61) and A. Kempinski of Tel Aviv University worked there in 1985, 1987, and 1988. Unfortunately the excavators are not yet prepared to offer an acceptable identification of the site.

Ekron. During the period of the Judges, Ekron, the northernmost city of the Philistine pentapolis, was occupied by the men of Judah (Judges 1:18), but it did not remain in Israelite control. It was close to Israelite territory but remained essentially Philistine. When the ark was removed from Gath, it was taken to Ekron, the last of the Philistine cities, and then sent on to Beth-shemesh in Israel (1 Samuel 5:10–6:12).

The fortunes of Ekron, like the other Philistine cities, varied through its long history. Padi, its king in the days of Sennacherib, remained loyal to the Assyrians, but a group of rebels seized the throne and turned Padi over to Hezekiah, who was evidently a leader in the opposition to Sennacherib. The *Annals* of Sennacherib tell how the Assyrians took Ekron and restored Padi to his throne as a loyal vassal. The Assyrian king Esarhaddon also mentioned

Ekron as a Philistine city, loyal to its Assyrian overlord. In fact, Ekron prospered greatly during the *Pax Assyriaca* (Assyrian Peace), as did the Phoenician city-states.

The god of Ekron was Baal-zebub (Beel-zebub). Ahaziah of Israel was on his way to consult the shrine of Baal-zebub when he was intercepted by Elijah who demanded to know if Israel was without a god and why the god of Ekron must be consulted (2 Kings 1:1–6, 16). *Baal-zebub* ("lord of flies") may be an intentional Hebrew alteration of the Canaanite *Baal-zebul* ("Lord of the High Place," or "Exalted Baal"). Baal-zebub (or Baal-zebul) is used in the New Testament as a synonym for Satan, and is rendered "the prince of the devils" (Matthew 12:24–29).

In 147 B.C., Alexander Balas, king of Syria, transferred Ekron to the Maccabean ruler Jonathan (1 Maccabees 10:89). According to Eusebius, it had a large Jewish population in the third century A.D.

The site of Ekron is to be identified with Tel Miqne, twenty-two miles southwest of Jerusalem, overlooking the ancient network of roads leading northwest from Ashdod to Beth-Shemesh. It is one of the largest Iron Age sites in Israel, composed of a forty-acre lower tell and a ten-acre upper tell. The tell rises only about twenty-three feet above the surrounding plain.

In 1981 a long term excavation project was instituted by the Albright Institute and the Hebrew University of Jerusalem under the direction of Trude Dothan and Seymour Gitin. The work at Miqne was significant, especially in discoveries connected with the olive oil industry; here was the largest olive oil industrial center in the ancient Near East. Ekron was also an important center of textile production. Beyond what these excavations contributed to the knowledge of a single Philistine town, they made a significant contribution to the research of Trude and Moshe Dothan concerning the culture of the ancient Philistines.

Archaeologists Trude and Moshe Dothan are primarily responsible for rediscovery of the Philistines and the rehabilitation of their reputation. Now the Philistines emerge as civilized people, advanced artisans and craftsmen, and town planners. The Dothans found among them a flourishing olive oil industry, cast bronze and iron industries, ivory artifacts, weaving looms, wine presses, and distinctive pottery, among other things. (Especially the record appears in Trude and Moshe Dothan, *People of the Sea* (1992) and Trude Dothan, *The Philistines and Their Material Culture* (1982)). Amihar Mazar is credited with excavation of the only Philistine temple unearthed to date—at Tell Qasile.[56] While it may throw some light on the sanctuaries connected with the travels of the Ark (cf. 1 Samuel 5), it hardly helps us picture the huge temple in which three thousand gathered to make sport of Samson (Judges 16:27).

The Hebrews—the Days of the Judges. The judges were divinely enlisted leaders who ruled over Israel when the nation was a loose confederacy. They served as judges, civil functionaries, and military leaders.

The chronology of the judges presents some very real problems. Adding up all the years of oppression and rest recorded in the book yields a total of 410 years. But the book of Acts gives a total of 450 years from the days of Joshua to Samuel (Acts 13:20). Apparently the difference is to be accounted for by the forty years of Eli's ministry (1 Samuel 4:18). Even if one dates the Exodus at about 1440 B.C. there is not room in the chronology for a 410-year period of the Judges. The period is more than a hundred years too long. This conclusion is arrived at as follows.

Saul apparently began to rule about 1050 B.C. To that date must be added forty years for Eli's judgeship, the 410 years of history recorded in the book of Judges, thirty years of Joshua's leadership, and forty years of wandering in the wilderness, plus an

Canaan in the time of the Judges

Involving especially the eastern frontier of Canaan, they could have been roughly contemporary with Jabin's attack in the west.

By the time Joshua and the elders who outlived him passed off the scene, the Israelites apparently had occupied the hill country of Galilee, Samaria, and Judea west of the Jordan River (from Dan to Beersheba) and the hill country east of the Jordan (from about the south end of the Sea of Galilee to about the middle of the Dead Sea). Surveys have now identified hundreds of new small settlement sites dating back to the Early Iron Period: for example, about twenty-five in the hills of western Galilee (tribe of Naphtali), fifteen in lower Galilee (territory of Zebulun), about a hundred in the territory of Manasseh, about a hundred in the land of Ephraim, twelve in the land of Banjamin, and dozens of small Iron Age sites in Gilead north of the Jabbok River.[58]

The book of Judges is a sad book chronicalling the human tendency to wander from God and the results of spiritual decline. Actually it pictures a series of recurring cycles: apostasy from God, punishment in the form of oppression by neighboring tribes, cries to God for relief, redemption or release from bondage, and a period of rest from oppression. We must not conclude that the book depicts only gloom, however. Of the 410 years referred to in the book, during only some one hundred years of that time are the people said to have been in sin. So it can also be described as a book of faithfulness to God, and of God's grace in watchcare and restoration.

The book of Judges provides an important historical link between the conquest of Palestine and the beginnings of the monarchy. Without it, our understanding of later Hebrew developments would be much less clear. The book demonstrates by means of numerous examples the principle laid down in the earlier Old Testament books that obedience to the law meant life and peace, while disobedience resulted in oppression and death. Further, the book shows that God was always ready to forgive His penitent people, and it indicates the degree to which the Hebrews had already departed from the high moral and

unknown number of years for Samuel's leadership. The total would push the date back to before 1570 B.C.—much earlier than an Exodus of 1440 B.C. The usual conclusion, then, is that some of the judges ruled at the same time, which was possible because they did not always govern the entire land. For instance, Deborah and Barak exercised power in northern Palestine; Samson, in southwest Palestine; and Jephthah, on the eastern frontier.[57] Thus many scholars suggest that the period of the Judges lasted a little over three hundred years.

It is also presumed too that the book is roughly chronological. At least struggles with the Philistines must have come last (involving Samuel and Eli 13:1–16:31) and have continued on into the days of Samuel, Saul, and David. And the conflict with the second Jabin king of Hazor (Judges 4:1–5:31) may have come fairly early and ended with the destruction layer that Yadin found, dating to the thirteenth century B.C. Struggles with the Ammonites, Amalekites, Midianites, and Moabites round out the list.

At the Springs of Harod (Judges 7) Gideon made his
famous test to reduce the size of his army. The springs still send their waters into extensive channels
where the test could have taken place. The area is now a public park.

ethical demands of the law. For example, following Gideon's great victory over the Midianites and Amalekites and the period of rest that God gave Israel, the Hebrew people turned openly to Baal worship (Judges 8:33–35). And this was centuries before the reign of Ahab and Jezebel. In its vivid portrayal of the weakness and confusion of a period when every man did that which was right in his own eyes, the book prepares the way for the single superior authority of kingship.

As noted, the last great foreign oppression of the Israelites was by the Philistines, who Scripture says oppressed the Israelites for forty years before Samson began to deliver them from bondage. Actually the bondage would not cease until David's conquests established the Hebrew kingdom or empire. Though it is common to picture Samson as a huge man with great muscles, there is no hint in Scripture of anything unusual about his physique. In fact, his strength was such a puzzle to the Philistines that they tried every ruse to learn his secret. If he had been an unusual physical phenomenon, they would not have had any question

about the matter. The truth is, Samson was a rather normal human being who was an example to both Israelites and Philistines of God's ability to empower an individual. Probably the stories of Samson's feats of strength are only selected accounts of his many acts of physical prowess.

For twenty years he judged Israel, perhaps at Hebron; and during those years his life apparently was generally exemplary. Presumably, however, he became involved with the harlot at Gaza and with Delilah near the end of his ministry. He was to pay dearly for his sin—first with the loss of his eyesight and later with his life. The Philistines were able to catch him and blind him. Then they sought to make sport of him at the temple of their god Dagon. But Samson's dying moment was destined to be his greatest triumph. God answered his prayer for the restoration of divine power, and he pulled down the temple of Dagon upon himself, with tremendous loss of Philistine life—of the thousands gathered there, Judges 16;25–31) as well as his own. Though he had failed to deliver Israel from the Philistines, he had restrained them temporarily and kept his people from being

Excavations at the Philistine site of Tel Qasile at the northern edge of Tel Aviv help to illuminate the Samson narrative. There, in the temple, stone bases would have supported pillars that held up the roof. Samson could have pushed similar pillars off their bases, bringing down the roof. This is the only Philistine temple excavated to date.

completely uprooted or enslaved. In spite of his moral compromise, he won a place among the heroes of faith (Hebrews 11:32). The grace of God appeared in the life of Samson as in that of David later on. After a fall came restoration to divine favor, although the sin itself was not without consequence.

Eli. Evidently the life and ministry of Samson overlapped that of Eli and Samuel; and all three of them were concerned with the Philistine threat. Eli was the high priest who presided at the tabernacle at Shiloh. In this capacity he led and ruled the Hebrews for forty years. Scripture also calls him a judge (1 Sam. 4:18), thus his listing here. He was not really a warrior and deliverer as the other judges were. Eli was pious and patriotic, but his great fault lay in his indulgent treatment of his sons. They were so evil that they brought reproach upon God, upon their father, and upon themselves. Ultimately they died under the judgment of God.

SHILOH, RELIGIOUS CAPITAL

OF THE TRIBES

Shiloh is identified with Seilun, nineteen miles north of Jerusalem. Under Joshua the tabernacle was erected there (Joshua 18:1), and at Shiloh the accounts of Eli's and Samuel's early life occurred. Evidently the Philistines destroyed the site after defeating the Israelites and capturing the Ark. The Israelites did not return the Ark to Shiloh when the Philistines brought it back.

The National Museum of Denmark conducted excavations at Shiloh in 1922 and 1926 to 1932. And Bar-Ilan University resumed them from 1981 to 1984.

In general, excavation results confirm biblical indications. They show that the place was settled in the nine-

The ruins of an Ottoman fortress now stand on the summit of the mound of Aphek

teenth and eighteenth centuries B.C., that it was abandoned and resettled at the beginning of the Israelite period, and that it was destroyed around 1050 B.C. by a violent fire and largely abandoned from then until about 300 B.C. in the sixth century B.C. Jeremiah. compared the fate of Shiloh with that foreseen for the Temple (Jeremiah 26:6–9); apparently the place was still in ruins in his day. Excavations further show that the town revived during the Hellenistic period and reached a high point of development in Roman and Byzantine Times.

Conditions were destined to get worse for Israel before they got better. During Eli's later years the Philistines continued to encroach on Hebrew territory. Expanding from their base along the Mediterranean in Southwestern Palestine, the Philistines gradually moved up the valleys into the highlands. The Hebrews finally decided to challenge the Philistines near Aphek (New Testament Antipatris, Acts 23:31), a strategically located site at the headwaters of the Yarkon River, about ten miles northeast of modern Tel Aviv. While the Philistines camped at Aphek, the Hebrews camped at Ebenezer, now identified with Izbet Sartah, about two miles east of Aphek. The initial encounter was costly for the Hebrews; they suffered almost four thousand casualties, who perhaps were mowed down by Philistine chariotry.

APHEK AND THE LOSS OF THE ARK

Aphek is identified with Tell Ras el-Ain, about twenty-six miles south of Caesarea and ten miles from the Mediterranean at the headwaters of the Yarkon River, which flows into the sea at Tel Aviv. Aphek appears in the Bible first as one of the Canaanite cities conquered by Joshua (Joshua 13:4) and emerges later as the principal city on the northern border of Philistia in the wars between the Philistines and the Israelites. Here the Philistines rallied their armies prior to a crucial battles against the Hebrews and captured the ark (1 Samuel 4, 29). Herod rebuilt the town about 9 B.C. and named it after his father, Antipatris. Here Paul stopped overnight when he was taken from Jerusalem to the Roman governor Felix in Caesarea (Acts 23:31).

With an area of over twenty-five acres, Aphek is one of the largest mounds in Palestine. It was an important stop on the international highway known as the Via Maris. Though brief excavations were conducted at Aphek earlier, the main work there took place between 1972 and 1985, when thirteen seasons of excavation were conducted by Tel Aviv University and cooperating institutions, under the leadership of Moshe Kochavi and P. Beck.

A Philistine stronghold evidently occupied the site early in the Iron Age (1200–1000 B.C.), and resettlement in the tenth century B.C. probably involved Israelites who came in after David's victories over the Philistines. During the Herodian period a fortress stood on the acropolis (possibly the facility where Paul stayed), along with shops on both sides of the main street. The town was destroyed by fire, probably connected with Roman efforts to stamp out the Jewish rebellion that led to the destruction of Jerusalem in A.D. 70.

Today ruins of an Ottoman fortress (built 1572–74), extending over about five acres, stand on the summit of the mound of Aphek. Its walls encompass the ancient acropolis of Aphek. The fortress was the main Ottoman base for overseeing the coastal road between the Carmel Range and Gaza.

On the face of it there is no reason why the Hebrews should have won. The Philistines held superiority in metallurgy, and their effort to deprive the Hebrews of iron (1 Samuel 13:19) gave them an overwhelming military advantage. But the Hebrews were accustomed to having God fight battles for them; and when they lost on this occasion, they anguished, "Why did the Lord defeat us?" (1 Samuel 4:3).

EBENEZER, "STONE OF HELP"

Ebenezer, meaning "stone of help," was the name of a stone that Samuel set up to commemorate God's assistance given to Israel in battle, whereby they were victorious over the Philistines (1 Samuel 7;12). Its position was carefully defined as a place between Mizpah and Shen, near Aphek. The site is currently identified with Izbet Sartah, about two miles east of Aphek (which see).

Moshe Kochavi of Tel Aviv University directed a dig there for four seasons during the years 1976 to 1978. He found three occupational layers covering the period of about 1200–1000 B.C. From the lowest level came an ostracon bearing the earliest proto-Canaanite alphabet that has yet come to light. Level II evidently was abandoned around 1050 B.C., about the time of the battle that resulted in the Israelite loss of the Ark of the Covenant. About 1000 B.C. the site was reoccupied briefly and then abandoned to the present.

Izbet Sartah, about two miles east of Aphek, has been identified with Ebenezer

Shiloh

Apparently they failed to keep in mind that God would not bless people who turned from Him and entered into idolatrous practices (1 Samuel 7:3). Probably they would not have appealed to aged Eli, then ninety-eight (1 Samuel 4:15), to intercede with God on their behalf, for he was no longer able to be very active in the work of God. And certainly the conduct of Hophni and Phinehas would not have inspired them to soul-searching or a higher plane of devotion.

If God had not been present with them in battle, then one way to guarantee His presence, they thought, might be to bring His ark into the camp. For many, confidence in the presence of the ark was a form of fetishism—the ultimate good luck charm. Magical potency was believed to dwell in the object itself. "The people sent to Shiloh" for the ark (1 Samuel 4:4). There is no hint that they inquired whether it was proper for the ark to be carried into battle or whether God had any instructions for them as they faced this unequal struggle. In their superstitious fear they simply demanded the ark, and evidently Eli was powerless to block its departure from the sanctuary. Of course the priests had to accompany the ark, just as they did during the period of desert wandering. Thus wicked and condemned Hophni and Phinehas went with the ark to the battlefront.

What a perfect setup for catastrophe! An idolatrous people who had largely turned

their backs on Yahweh deserved His punishment. The army of the people of God was going into battle with no particular instruction from God and with greater trust in a piece of religious furniture than in the God whose presence it symbolized. The priests who accompanied the ark had been repudiated by God and marked for judgment.

When the ark arrived in the camp, the Hebrews shouted so vociferously that the earth itself reverberated (1 Samuel 4:5). Their clamor probably was both a shout for joy and a battle cry. Some of them no doubt conjured up visions of the kind of victories Israel had enjoyed in the days of Moses and Joshua.

The commotion was so great in the Hebrew camp that at least Philistine scouting parties or advance guards could hear it. When they learned what had happened, panic seized the Philistine camp. Even if the Hebrews were not superstitious about the ark, the Philistines were; to them the presence of the ark symbolized God's physical presence. Then, with their backs to the wall, so to speak, and facing probable enslavement, the Philistines fought with the courage of despair. The outcome was resounding defeat for the Hebrews, with a reported casualty figure of thirty thousand, the loss of the ark, and the deaths of Hophni and Phinehas. Some doubt the large numbers given for the armies and casualties in the historical books of the Old Testament, but there is no need to be particularly skeptical when we understand the nature of the warfare described. It was common that when a town or an area was threatened during the days of the conquest of Canaan, the period of the Judges, or the monarchy, all the able-bodied men turned out—including the older teenagers. Thus the numbers involved were considerably swollen. Then, precisely because most of those engaged in conflict were not disciplined soldiers, casualties frequently were excessive; and if an enemy was put to flight, the confusion or the rout often was total.

When a runner reported news of the defeat at Shiloh, the whole town erupted in an uproar. And when the blind Eli learned what had happened, the shock was too much. Perhaps due to fainting or suffering a stroke, he fell over backward; the weight of his body broke his neck and he died. The sacred historian added that Eli had judged Israel forty years (1 Samuel 4:18). Fully twenty years passed before the curtain rose again on the biblical narrative (1 Samuel 7:2). And during that time Samuel had risen to a position of commanding leadership in Israel.

Samuel and the Transition to Kingship. Even before the catastrophe at Aphek, Samuel's reputation had been firmly established in all Israel from Dan to Beersheba (1 Samuel 3:20). Actually Samuel is called a prophet (1 Samuel 3:20) and a judge (1 Samuel 7:15–17), and acted as priest (1 Samuel 9:12–13; 13:8–13). He took over at a very difficult time in Israelite history. After Aphek, the Philistines had moved into Israelite territory, destroying Shiloh itself (Jeremiah 7:12, 14; 26:6, 9; Psalms 78:60) and eliminating what little Hebrew metal industry still existed. Their goal was to make the Hebrews completely dependent upon them.

As noted, after about a twenty-year silence in the biblical narrative, the curtain went up again (perhaps around 1060 B.C.). Samuel was at Mizpah, calling the people to repentance and revival. Evidently he had doggedly persevered all during those "silent years," trying to get his people to turn to God. Finally "there was a movement throughout Israel to follow the Lord" (1 Samuel 7:2 NEB). This movement presumably came about not so much by a pricking of their consciences as by Philistine oppression.

MIZPAH

Though Mizpah, meaning "watchtower," was a common biblical name, the significant Mizpah of Old Testament times was located in the territory of Benjamin near Gibeon and Ramah (Joshua 18:25–26; 1 Kings 5:22). It seems to have been a place of assembly for Israel.

In the days of Samuel, Israel gathered at Mizpah for prayers twenty years after the Philistines had returned the ark (1 Samuel 7:5–6). The Philistines attacked the assembled Israelites, but they were repulsed and Samuel was able to erect a stone commemorating divine aid at nearby Ebenezer ("Stone of Help"). Saul, a native of Gibeah, was presented to Israel at Mizpah (1 Samuel 10:17) and there acclaimed king.

In his controversies with Baasha of Israel, Asa of Judah fortified Mizpah as an important border town (1 Kings 15:22). Following Nebuchadnezzar's destruction of Jerusalem, Mizpah had a brief period of importance when it served as the capital ruled by Gedaliah (2 Kings 25:23, 25). Jeremiah and other refugees migrated to Mizpah, but a group of Zealots killed Gedaliah and thereby brought an end to the last vestige of Israelite independence (Jeremiah 41). Mizpah's history continued into Maccabean times, when Judas the Maccabee assembled his partisans there for prayer (1 Maccabees 3:46).

Though there is still some debate over the location of Mizpah, contemporary scholarship has fairly well settled on the site of Tell en-Nasbeh, eight miles north of Jerusalem (about twenty-six hundred feet above sea level), beside the main north-south road running from Jerusalem to Shechem and Samaria.

W. F. Bade of the Pacific School of Religion excavated at Tell en-Nasbeh for five seasons between 1926 and 1935. Excavations indicate that a small town, probably founded by Israelites, existed there during the twelfth century B.C. It was defended by a wall about three feet thick, built of rubble. Much stronger walls, between fifteen and twenty feet thick, were built about 900 B.C., enclosing an area of eight acres. At important salients, nine or ten rectangular stone towers projected as much as seven feet beyond the wall. At the northeast

Mizpah is now generally identified with Tell en-Nasbeh

side of the city stood a large city gate. Inside the gate were guardrooms; on the outside, benches lined a court. The gate of an oriental city was the place where business and legal transactions were conducted, and the Tell en-Nasbeh gate offers an excellent illustration of that practice (cf. Deuteronomy 22:24; Ruth 4:11; 2 Samuel 19:8). Tell en-Nasbeh was occupied to Hellenistic times, although the population was greatly reduced after the fifth century B.C.

As this seeking after God began to manifest itself, Samuel urged the people to demonstrate the sincerity of their repentance by forsaking their idol worship and committing themselves unreservedly to God. He accompanied his exhortation with a promise that after personal and national reformation God "will deliver you out of the hand of the Philistines" (1 Samuel 7:3). The Hebrews responded positively to Samuel's call to turn from their apostasy. Then Samuel summoned them for a public confession and reaffirmation of faith at Mizpah, identified by most scholars with Tell en-Nasbeh, eight miles north of Jerusalem. "All Israel" (I Samuel 7:5) evidently does not mean literally that all Israelites were to gather at that small town—an impossible feat—but that at

least their official representatives were to convene.

Apparently the Philistines sought to take advantage of Israel's preoccupation with a religious observance (as Arabs did in the Yom Kippur War of 1973), and possibly resolved to launch a preemptive strike because they interpreted the Hebrew gathering as preparation for war. Whether or not the Philistines believed that the Hebrews were getting ready to rebel against them, spiritual revival among the Hebrews would put them in a better position to throw off the Philistine yoke. After all, oppression had plagued the Hebrews because of their waywardness. Fear gripped the Hebrews as reports of a Philistine advance reached the holy convocation. Unprepared for war, they begged Samuel not to stop crying out to God on their behalf. Though not an ordained priest, Samuel offered a lamb as a whole burnt offering, thus representing the total consecration of the people to their God.

God's response was dramatic and vivid. While Samuel was offering the sacrifice and as the Philistines were advancing against the Hebrews, God split the heavens with a terrorizing thunderstorm that threw the Philistine army into complete panic. Perhaps He struck down many of them with bolts of lightning. God defeated the Philistines before the Hebrews had a chance to strike a blow. All the Hebrews had to do was launch a mopping-up exercise. Emboldened by the turn of events, they rushed against the confused and fleeing foe with such success that the Philistines "no longer encroached on the territory of Israel" (1 Samuel 7:13 NEB). Evidently this does not mean the Philistines made no effort to recover lost territory or supremacy, but such attacks were doomed to failure because of divine intervention. Moreover, resurgent Israelite power was so impressive that the Amorites, the most powerful of the Canaanite tribes, did not greatly trouble the Hebrews either during the rest of the days of Samuel's leadership.

From the time that Samuel's ministry was so dramatically vindicated at Mizpah, he evidently exercised the judgeship, or rule, over the nation. This leadership function was to continue along with his prophetic office the rest of his life. To make it possible for more of the people to have direct access to his ministry, he established a judicial circuit, including Bethel, Gilgal, Mizpah, and Ramah. While problems attend locating these towns, the generalization can be made that they were only a few miles apart in the hills of Ephraim in central Palestine. Therefore, even though Samuel may have been respected at a greater distance, his itinerant ministry did not take him to Galilee, Trans-Jordan, or farther afield than the northern edge of Judah. That his authority was accepted widely, however, is clear from 1 Samuel 8, in which his sons acted as his deputies at Beersheba in the south and "all the elders of Israel" (I Samuel 8:4) came to him with the request for a king.

As Samuel grew older, he no longer had the vigor to shoulder the entire load of ruling Israel. But sharing responsibility with his sons proved to be no solution, for evidently they never fully subscribed to the spiritual and ethical ideals of their father. When they assumed judicial responsibilities at Beersheba, some fifty miles southwest of Jerusalem, the strictures of their father's watchful eye no longer controlled them. They took bribes and perverted justice and thus provided the Hebrews with an excuse for requesting a change in government.

Using Samuel's advancing age and his sons' degenerate behavior as the basis for their request, the elders of Israel came as representatives of the people to plead for the institution of a monarchy. Of course, Samuel was upset over the elders' vote of no confidence in his administration, but he did not answer their charges. His concern centered rather on their desire for a king and the implications of that request for the divine order of things in Israel. God (or Yahweh) had originally established Israel as a theocratic nation (or kingdom) with himself as their king. Not knowing how to respond, Samuel sought God's face for wisdom and comfort. God's reply was that Israel was not really rejecting Samuel. Instead, lack of confidence in God Himself had led them to reject an invisible God-king and ask for a visible king. Their impatience with their powerlessness as a nation had goaded them to want a king like those of other peoples—one who could lead them into war and make something of them as a people. They failed to realize that their weakness resulted from disobedience to God. Had they been faithful to God, an earthly visible king would have been unnecessary.

It should be clear, however, that Israel was only demanding a change in executive headship; they were not repudiating God's moral code. Moreover, they wanted a king whom God would sanction and whom Samuel would anoint. Furthermore, the promise of an earthly king (Genesis 49:10; Numbers 24:17; 1 Samuel 2:10) and the request for a king had been predicted hundreds of years before and actually had been sanctioned in the law. In fact, some commentators argue that their request so closely resembles the original Hebrew of Deuteronomy 17:14 that the elders had Moses' provisions in mind. Presumably this was the time for the kingship to be instituted because God acceded to their request. A further indication of the degree of Hebrew obedience to God is seen in the willingness of the people to go home and await God's time and method of choosing their king (1 Samuel 8:22).

God granted the demand for a king but instructed Samuel to warn the people about what sort of person he would be. In a word he would be an absolute monarch of Oriental style who would exercise the right to use persons and property for his own purposes as he saw fit. He would be guilty of personal aggrandizement and rapaciousness. And since ostentations royal courts and military establishments do not come cheaply, he would exact heavy taxes.

Specifically, 1 Samuel 8:11–17 warns of at least five actions to be expected of the king: (1) conscription for military service (vv. 11–12); (2) the exercise of eminent domain: sovereign power over all property within the state, by which the state or the king can appropriate private property for public use (vv. 14–15); (3) corvée or conscript labor—obligation imposed on inhabitants of a district to perform services during part of the year (vv. 12, 16); sometimes a tax in the form of labor; (4) impressment of persons—to force them into permanent/full-time public service, to seize or take for public use (vv. 13, 16, 17b); and (5) heavy taxation (vv. 15, 17).

The elders or representatives of Israel repudiated the warnings about the monarchy. They insisted on a visible "king" (8:19) in a permanent institution of monarchy as opposed to a temporary magistracy directed by an unseen governor. Moreover, they wanted a standing army under his command to deal with the threats of neighboring states. It was convenient to forget how often God had fought their battles for them when they were unable to fight their own. Though they had insisted on a king "like all the other nations" (8:5), God would not grant them that wish. He would insist on a king who was different: reverent toward God and just toward His people. Failure in either respect would bring removal from office, termination of his dynasty, or other forms of judgment.

THE UNITED MONARCHY

Israel asked for a king and got one. The first king was Saul, who ruled for forty years (Acts 13:21); the second was David, who likewise ruled for forty years (2 Samuel 5:5); and the third was Solomon, who also ruled

for forty years (1 Kings 11:42). This span of about 120 years is commonly called the united monarchy because these men ruled over all Israel. It was followed by the period of divided monarchy, when there were two kingdoms, Israel and Judah. An exact chronology is hard to set, but one of the finest chronological studies ever done on a segment of Scripture is E. R. Thiele's *The Mysterious Numbers of the Hebrew Kings.* Thiele put the division of the kingdom at 931 B.C. Working backward, then, the dates of Solomon would be 970–931 B.C.; David, 1010–970 B.C.; and Saul, 1050–1010 B.C. This is the chronology followed here.

The people asked for a king like those of other nations and God in fact granted them a king, but not one like those of the surrounding nations. The Hebrew king was to be a man of God's own choice. In his public and private life he should follow God's dictates, and he was not to intrude into the affairs of the priesthood, for God had His own appointed leaders there. Above all, this king must not slip into the ways of idolatry but rather was to exert all the influence of his office to keep his people on God-honoring paths. If a Hebrew king failed in one or more of these respects, he ran the risk of being deposed by God, of having his line brought to an end, or even of bringing his people into captivity to a foreign power. All this must be kept in mind when studying the reigns of Saul, David, Solomon, or the kings of the divided monarchy.

Saul. Saul's reign began well. He was endowed with a kingly appearance and was head and shoulders taller than almost any other Israelite (1 Samuel 10:23). He came from the small tribe of Benjamin and so was not a party to tribal jealousy, as would have been the case if he were from the leading tribes of Ephraim or Judah. He was *God's* choice and enjoyed confirming signs, among which was the

The mound of Gibeah

Spirit of God coming upon him when he joined the company of prophets (1 Samuel 10:1–10). When Samuel presented him to the people at Mizpah, they received him, and a kind of "palace guard" joined him (1 Samuel 10:26). But Saul was still unknown to the people; there was no capital city; and strongly separatist tendencies existed among the tribes.

SAUL'S CAPITAL AT GIBEAH

When Saul became the first king of Israel, there was no national capital. Evidently he simply chose to locate the seat of government at his home town of Gibeah (1 Samuel 10:26; 11:4; 13:2; 15:34). After some eighty years of debate about the location of Gibeah, W. F. Albright was especially responsible for fixing its location of the town at Tell el-Ful, three miles north of the Damascus Gate in Jerusalem. The mound rises about 100 feet above the surrounding plain to a height of some thirty-five hundred feet. Not all scholars have yet accepted Albright's conclusions about identification of the site.

Albright excavated at Tell el-Ful (1922–1923, 1933), uncovering what

he interpreted to be the palace fortress of Saul, built just before 1000 B.C. The stone structure measured 169 by 114 feet with towers extending from each of the four corners. This would have been the place where David played his lyre before Saul.

Presumably the Philistines destroyed Gibeah after the Battle of Gilboa. Josiah probably rebuilt it late in the seventh century B.C. The Babylonians destroyed it again before taking Jerusalem in 586 B.C. and Titus administered the final blow just before the siege of Jerusalem (A.D. 70). By the time Eusebius wrote in the fourth century A.D., the site was forgotten.

An opportunity soon presented itself for Saul to win general public approval, however. The Ammonites advanced on the eastern frontier and threatened the town of Jabesh-Gilead, which sent to Saul for help. Saul answered their call by sending a general appeal to the tribes. A total of thirty thousand came from Judah and three hundred thousand from other tribes. From the many who appeared, Saul selected a fighting force and won a crushing victory. The Israelites now accepted him as king, and

Samuel crowned him at Gilgal. Subsequently, he had the good sense to avoid heavy tax burdens or radical changes in the Hebrew pattern of life. He established his capital at his home town of Gibeah, three miles north of Jerusalem, and built a fortress-palace there. William F. Albright of Johns Hopkins University excavated Saul's administrative center there in 1922–23. Dating the structure to about 1020–1000 B.C., he believed that Saul probably built it and David possibly repaired it. The structure measured roughly 169 feet long by 114 feet wide, with towers extending from each of the four corners (see Albright's reconstructed floor plan accompanying.).[59]

But Saul had ruled for only about two years when he began to show signs of slipping from God's way. At Gilgal he grew impatient waiting for Samuel to come to offer a sacrifice, and he did it himself. Soon afterward, Samuel appeared and rebuked Saul, declaring that God would ultimately rend the kingdom from him for his sin of intruding into the priestly office (1 Samuel 13:13–14).

However, God was not through with Saul's administration. Soon thereafter, he gave Saul a great victory over the Philistines and, subsequently, over the Moabites, Ammonites, and Edomites east of the Jordan and Zobah to the north of Damascus. These successes show Saul to have been a much more effective military leader than is commonly recognized; and they were no doubt foundational to the later establishment of David's empire.

Presumably for some twenty years Saul was on reasonably good behavior. Then Samuel commissioned him to fulfill God's curse against the Amalekites (Exodus 17:14; Deuteronomy 25:17–19) and destroy them utterly. When Saul only partially obeyed, Samuel broke with him and never saw him again as long as he lived. Soon afterward, God commanded Samuel secretly to anoint David to be king. Bereft of Samuel, Saul began to show signs of depression. In an effort to lift him from these moods, his advisors sought a court musician and settled on David, son of Jesse, who had only recently killed Goliath.

David's lyre was effective at times in restoring Saul to a better frame of mind, but the king passed increasingly through alternating moods of depression, rage, and normalcy. Seemingly this mental condition was brought on by a frustration derangement: God was against him; David's star constantly rose as Saul's set; Saul's son Jonathan had placed himself on David's side; Saul lived under the realization that his days were numbered; and Samuel's counsel was no longer available.

David's rise to prominence was significantly spurred by his victory over Goliath and the accompanying defeat of the Philistines. The king made David commander of the army, and with his continuing successes David built a great reputation throughout the land and was more highly thought of than Saul himself. Soon the king in fits of rage began to make attempts on David's life. David ducked the spears Saul hurled at him in the palace. Then he experienced deliverance at Gibeah by the help of his

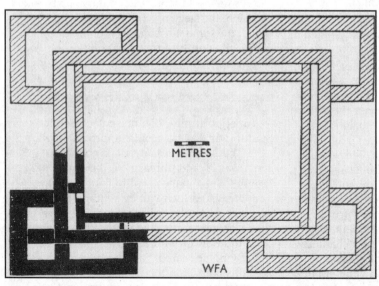

The Citadel of Saul, restored. After William F. Albright

WFA

METRES

David's lyre probably did not look much different from the lyre played by a Semitic visitor to Egypt about the time of Joseph. From the tomb of Khnumhotep at Beni Hassan in Egypt.

Egyptian lyres from the Empire period were somewhat more sophisticated. They could be played with or without the plectrum. From a tomb painting at Thebes

wife (Saul's daughter) Michal (1 Samuel 19:1–17); at Ramah by the help of the Spirit (1 Samuel 19:18–24); at Gibeah by the help of Jonathan (1 Samuel 20:1–42); at Keilah by the help of Abiathar (1 Samuel 23:7–13); at Maon by the help of the Philistines (1 Samuel 23:15–29); at Engedi (1 Samuel 24:1–22); at Hachilah (1 Samuel 26:1–25); and finally, by the death of Saul at the hand of the Philistines.

The Philistines had been a threat to the Hebrews throughout Saul's reign. Declining in ability to manage the kingdom and unable to locate an equally capable replacement for David as commander of the forces, the king found it impossible to prevent Philistine inroads into Hebrew territory. At length they moved in force through the Valley of Esdraelon and camped at Shunem (on the southwest slope of the Hill of Moreh, Judges 7:1), a few miles south of which, at Mount Gilboa, the Israelites took up battle stations.

Terrified at the outcome and unable to get counsel from God (1 Samuel 26:6), Saul searched out a spiritistic medium in an effort to communicate with the dead Samuel (1 Samuel 28:7–25). This act not only violated a Mosaic prohibition, but also Saul's own earlier command (Leviticus 20:27; 1 Samuel 28:9). Instead of some sort of contact with an impersonating demon, the medium experienced a supernatural appearance of the prophet Samuel himself, who bypassed her and spoke directly to Saul, predicting utter defeat for Israel and the death of Saul and his sons. The prediction came true the following day. Utterly crushed, the Israelites fled from many of their towns to escape the victorious Philistines, who now moved into Israelite territory in force.

VICTORY AND DEFEAT ON MOUNT GILBOA

Mount Gilboa stands sentinel at the southeast edge of the plain of Jezreel, to a height of almost seventeen hundred feet above sea level. Modern Fuqu 'ah, it is located seven miles west

The valley of Elah, where David and the Israelites fought Goliath and the Philistines. The Philistines camped on the right, the Israelites on the left

of Beth-Shean and three miles south-east of Jezreel. From Gilboa's northern slopes drain the waters that feed the springs of Harod, where Gideon had encamped and where he made his famous test to reduce the size of his army (Judges 7:1–7). His Midianite opponents lay just north of the Hebrews near the hill of Moreh, four miles away across the valley (Judges 7:1). From the height of Gilboa, Gideon and his men rushed down to rout the Midianites and their allies.

Later (c. 1010 B.C.), King Saul camped on this mountain during his war with the Philistines. From that vantage point, a thousand feet above the plain, he could watch every movement of the enemy. The Philistines assembled their forces at Shunem at the southwestern foot of the hill of Moreh. On the north shoulder of the hill of Moreh, barely four miles from the Philistine camp, stood the town of Endor, where Saul went by night to inquire of a witch concerning the outcome of the battle. The following morning during the battle on the northernmost slopes of Gilboa, the Philistines defeated the Hebrews and Saul died with three of his sons, including Jonathan (1 Samuel 28:4; 31:1–8; 2 Samuel 1:21).

Thus, he who began well ended disastrously. Saul left his land in worse condition than he had found it—at least as far as the Philistine threat was concerned. Probably the effects of his earlier victories east of the Jordan were largely dissipated. The country was as disunited as it had been forty years earlier. The people who wanted a king like other nations had gotten one too much like the others. God wanted the king to be different. Because he was not, God deposed him and sought another king, one "after His own heart."

David. That man was David, anointed by Samuel, but on the run to escape Saul's designs on his life. More than once David's cause seemed lost, but he continued doggedly on; more than once he had opportunity to take Saul's life, but he determined not to do so. On two occasions, however, David's difficulties proved too much for him, and in frustration he sought refuge among the enemies of Israel. The first of these occurrences took place soon after his flight from Saul's court. At that time it seemed that the place of refuge he could reach most quickly was the court of Achish, king of Gath. When he arrived there, the king called attention to the Hebrew warrior's victories over the Philistines, and David in fear feigned madness (1 Samuel 21).

David took flight to Gath a second time after Saul had been pursuing him for an extended period of time, and his will to resist

Mount Gilboa stands sentinel at the southeast edge of the plain of Jezreel. On its slopes Saul and his sons died in battle

was worn down. This time his circumstances were different. He had several hundred men with their families under his leadership, and provision for them was difficult indeed. Apparently he and his men accepted mercenary status in the Philistine armed forces, a fact that obligated them to participate in the great battle that destroyed Saul and his sons. On that occasion, David's contingent was saved from fighting the Israelites for fear on the part of some Philistines that he might defect. While David lived at Ziklag in southern Philistine territory (for about eighteen months), he carried on military action against tribes that were traditionally enemies of Israel. He shared his spoils of war with Judean towns, thus keeping his political fences mended in preparation for the day when he should be king.

ZIKLAG—DAVID'S HOME IN PHILISTIA

When David fled to Gath and apparently took mercenary status with the Philistines, King Achish assigned him and his warriors residency in the town of Ziklag (1 Samuel 27:6), which functioned as a military and administrative outpost at the southern edge of his kingdom and which bordered on territories occupied by nomadic tribes. Here David lived for a year and four months and here he received word of Saul's death. In later years Ziklag was known as crown property, belonging to the "kings of Judah to this day" (1 Samuel 27:6).

Ziklag has been variously located but many scholars currently identify it with Tell Sera', some twelve miles northwest of Beersheba on the main road from Gaza to Beersheba. The mound of 4–5 acres rises about 45 feet above the surrounding land, to a height of some 550 feet above sea level. Eliezer Oren of Ben Gurion University conducted excavations there from 1972 to 1979. Discoveries indicate Canaanite occupation, superceded by Philistine and then Israelite occupation.

That day was not long in coming. When David and his men returned to Ziklag from the conclave that prepared for the battle of Mount Gilboa, they discovered their homes burned and their families gone. A punitive expedition against the Amalekites, who

The mound of Beth Shan, atop which stood the ancient town, on the walls of which the bodies of Saul and his sons were hanged (1 Samuel 31:10,12)

were responsible, recovered everything, with much booty besides. Soon after David and his men returned to Ziklag, word came of the Israelite defeat and the death of Saul and his son Jonathan (David's friend). Following a period of mourning, David by divine guidance took his entire company to Hebron, where he was declared king over Judah (2 Samuel 2:1–4). It was natural that the tribe of Judah should take such a step because David's home was Bethlehem of Judah; his campaigning as captain of Saul's army had been largely on the edge of Judah, so he was better known there than in the north; and he had been sending gifts to Judean cities for some time.

HEBRON, HOME OF THE PATRIARCHS AND A CAPITAL OF DAVID

Hebron, nineteen miles southwest of Jerusalem, is 3,040 feet above sea level, the highest town in Palestine. It was known to the biblical Patriarchs as "Kirjath-Arba" ("tetrapolis"). Abraham spent much of his time in the vicinity of Hebron and purchased his family burial plot from a Hittite chieftain named Ephron who lived nearby (Genesis 23:8; 25:9). Twenty-five springs in the

area provided an adequate water supply in antiquity for the inhabitants and their flocks.

At the time of Joshua's invasion, Hebron was allied with Adonizedek of Jerusalem in an attempt to halt the Israelite advance (Joshua 10:1–27). After Joshua's death, Caleb succeeded in conquering the Hebron region from the Anakim (Joshua 14:6–15; cf. Numbers 13:22, 28, 33).

David ruled as king of Judah from Hebron for seven and one-half years before moving his capital to Jerusalem farther north. Absalom was born in Hebron; and when he revolted against his father, David, he attempted to establish headquarters there (2 Samuel 15:7–10).

Hebron did not occupy an important place in later Old Testament history, and it is not mentioned in the New Testament. Following the exile, Jews resettled in Hebron (Nehemiah 11:25) but in subsequent years the Idumaeans pushed northward as far as Hebron when their homeland south of the Dead Sea was taken by the Nabataean Arabs. During the Maccabean wars the Jews conquered Hebron (164 B.C.). And in subsequent years, Herod the Great erected an imposing structure at the traditional site of the Cave of

Abraham's well at Mamre, with part of the enclosure wall built by the emperor Hadrian. Note the cups for watering sheep.

Machpelah, now the Mosque of Hebron, (Genesis 23:19) and another at Mamre (Genesis 13:18).

Philip C. Hammond of Princeton Theological Seminary, in cooperation with several other institutions, launched an excavation on Jebel er-Rumeideh, the hill directly west of the mosque of Hebron, from 1964 to 1966. There Hammond found evidence of occupation going back to before 3000 B.C., a city wall of the entire Middle Bronze period (2000–1500 B.C.) and other remains from the Early and Late Bronze periods, the Iron Age, as well as Hellenistic, Byzantine, and Arabic periods. Evidence of Israelite occupation was extremely limited. The effort was too brief to be definitive, and Hammond's finds have not been fully published. From 1983 to 1986 the Judean Hills Survey Expedition under the leadership of Avi Ofer excavated at Hebron, but that work is not fully published either.

At Mamre, two miles north of Hebron, Herod the Great built a wall around the well of Abraham, enclosing an area 150 by 200 feet. Destroyed by Vespasian in A.D. 68, this enclosure was rebuilt by Hadrian in the second century A.D. and made the center of a pagan cult dedicated to Hermes-Mercury. Constantine removed Hadrian's pagan altar from the supposed site of Abraham's altar and erected a church on the spot.

Within the enclosure, one may today see ruins of a church that were excavated by Father A. E. Mader (1926–32, with a further excavation in 1964) and are thought to represent the site and plan of the Constantinian basilica, repaired during the Byzantine period. Excavations reveal that there was a sanctuary at Mamre during the entire Israelite royal period. David probably used it during his seven years of rule there; rebuildings occurred during the days of Rehoboam and John Hyrcanus.

The other tribes elevated a son of Saul, Ishbosheth, to the throne at the new capital of Mahanaim. This town, east of the Jordan, was safe from the Philistines, who then controlled much of the West Bank of Jordan. As time passed, periodic armed clashes occurred between Israel and Judah. Ishbosheth's cause gradually weakened, and ultimately both the Israelite commander-in-chief Abner and the king were assassinated. Then armed contingents, or their representatives, from all over Israel came to Hebron to beg David to become their king (cf. 1 Chronicles 12:23–40). Apparently some hard bargaining occurred, and understandings were reached that led to the establishment of a more fully-integrated state than Saul had ruled. So "David made a league with them" and "they anointed David king over Israel" (2 Samuel 5:3). He had begun to reign in Hebron seven and one-half years earlier at the age of thirty, and was destined to reign another thirty-three years over all Israel from Jerusalem (2 Samuel 5:4–5).

Apparently the Philistines did not interfere with David's rule in Judah; they may even have considered him a vassal. The rest of Israel west of the Jordan was largely under their control. But when David became king of all Israel, they clearly recognized his rising threat and mounted an attack. While it is difficult to sort out from Scripture the exact order of events, the Philistines probably attacked before he captured Jerusalem. At any rate, near the beginning of his reign David fought two major contests with the Philistines and so completely defeated them that they never again posed a major threat to Israel (2 Samuel 5:17–25).

Also, near the beginning of his reign, David sought a new, more centrally located capital. He chose Jerusalem, which was in many ways ideal. Its location was fairly central, its water supply adequate, and its defense capability excellent. Moreover, it did not belong to any tribe and so was not involved in jealousies between them. Finally, it stood on the north-south and east-west trade routes.

Much of the town had fallen to the Israelites during the period of the judges (Judges 1:8), but the stronghold remained in alien hands. To the cocky Jebusite defenders that stronghold seemed almost impregnable, surrounded as it was by ravines on three sides. They believed that even the "blind and lame" could ward off attackers (2 Samuel 5:6). But David was determined to take it, and he did, making it his capital. And as it belonged to none of the tribes, it became known as the "City of David." David offered the captaincy of the armed forces to the one who would lead the successful attack against the Jebusite defenders.

David said the conqueror should go up by means of the *tsinnor* (2 Samuel 5:8). Scholars have translated the word as either some sort of grappling hook used in scaling a wall, or a water course. In the last few years the preponderance of opinion has gravitated to the latter, and many translations of the Bible have fallen in line; e.g., "water shaft,"(NKJV); "water-shaft"(REB); "water shaft"(NIV); "water tunnel" (NASB); "water shaft."(NRSV).

In this view, the Israelites had discovered the main water system of the city and scaled that to come up inside the walls and surprise the defenders. The means they used to enter the city has frequently been identified with "Warren's Shaft," named for Charles Warren, who discovered it in 1867 while exploring underground Jerusalem. That ancient water channel consists of two parts: a tunnel (about 147 feet long) cut diagonally from inside the city wall, and a 52-foot vertical shaft down which a bucket or jar could be lowered to obtain water from the gushing Gihon spring below.

A. Rendle Short observed that some British army officers scaled Warren's Shaft in 1910.[60] The water system was finally cleared in 1980, and two young Americans subsequently did manage to ascend the shaft.

Recent discoveries, however, have cast new light on this entire discussion. It now appears that Warren's Shaft actually dated after David's day.[61] Also, the Israel Antiquities Authority launched new excavations in the City of David in 1995. In the last couple of years archaeologists have discovered a large and complex water system

The Roman theater at Amman, New Testament Philadelphia

that involved a combination of underground tunnels and large above-ground towers, dating to long before David's conquest, perhaps to the eighteenth or seventeenth century B.C.[62] They conclude that Warren's Shaft was never used as a water shaft.[63] But of course the newly-discovered water system would have permitted Hebrew access to the city. Whatever the case, Joab was awarded command of the armed forces for his success in taking Jerusalem from the Jebusites.

Then David sought to make Jerusalem the religious as well as the political capital of Israel. For several decades the ark had been separated from the tabernacle. So David made arrangements to bring the ark to Jerusalem, and installed it there in a tabernacle (or tent, 2 Samuel 6:17 NASB; also Psalms 27:5), amid great rejoicing and offering of sacrifices. Though he planned to build a proper house for God in the capital later in his reign, God made it clear that David's son, who would be a man of peace, should build it instead (1 Chronicles 29:2–6).

Though David spoke about building a house for God, God declared that He would establish David's house. In fact, He unconditionally promised David a house or royal dynasty line forever, a throne forever, and a kingdom forever (2 Samuel 7; 1 Chronicles 17). This prediction could be fulfilled only in the person of David's greater Son, the Lord Jesus Christ, who will reign on Mount Zion during the millennial kingdom and forever in the new Jerusalem. David submitted in humble gratitude to the wishes of God and collected large quantities of material for future construction of the temple.

Though David could not build the temple, he did give careful attention to organization of the priesthood, liturgy, and music of the tabernacle, and thus of temple worship (1 Chronicles 24–25). The titles of the Psalms ascribe seventy-three of them to David. From his youth he had been both a musician and a devout person. David was a poet of the heart, a universal poet. His hymns of praise and confession run the whole gamut of human experience and are loved and sung in palaces and hovels all over the earth. For God's believing people down through the centuries, these were perhaps David's greatest contribution. Scripture calls him the "sweet psalmist of Israel" (2 Samuel 23:1).

References to the numerous wars of David and his building of an empire appear in 2 Samuel 5, 8, 10–12, and 1 Chronicles 18–20. There is no evidence that he was a conscious imperialist, but apparently he responded to military situations as they arose. First he fought the Philistines, breaking the back of Philistine power and incorporating Gath and its dependencies into his kingdom. Evidently he brought the Philistines within the Israelite sphere of influence. But he merely contained the Philistines within their borders; he did not occupy their land nor utterly crush them the way he did other peoples surrounding Israel. David later employed a bodyguard of Philistine mercenaries. These Cherethites, Pelethites, Gittites, and Carites proved to be so loyal to him that when Absalom revolted against him, they stuck with him.

After David neutralized the Philistines, it would have been logical for him to gain firm control of lands west of the Jordan before embarking on Trans-Jordanian conquests. Herzog and Gichon claim that he did just that. He conquered the Sharon Plain, the Valley of Jezreel, and remaining Canaanite holdouts, as is clear from numerous archaeological excavations.[64] The Old Testament does not spell out these military ventures.

Now free to move east of the Jordan, David first turned his attention to Moab. Whatever friendly relations had existed between David and the Moabites, they had evaporated. Ancient Jewish commentators state that David's actions toward the Moabites reflect their massacre of his parents and family.

Next came the conquest of the Ammonites. In good faith David sent a delegation to their capital Rabbah (modern Amman), to express his sympathy for the death of their king and to extend good wishes to the new one (2 Samuel 10:1–5). But the Ammonites deliberately humiliated the delegation. Then the Ammonites realized that in effect they had made a declaration of war. So they hired a substantial number of mercenary troops from Aramean states in the north, which is how those far northern principalities became involved in hostilities with the Israelite state.

When the Israelite army under the command of Joab faced the Ammonites in Rabbah and the mercenary army in the field, they attacked first the mercenaries and thoroughly destroyed them. At this point they were not prepared for a long siege of the city and so went home. After their defeat the Arameans also went back home. Realizing that they would be forced to fight on alone, they immediately pulled together all the troops they could muster from the small states of northern Syria. When David learned of this threatened invasion, he mobilized the armies of Israel and apparently moved with great energy against the Arameans under the leadership of Hadadezer of Zobah and routed them completely. David so decisively squashed the Arameans that the vassals broke away from Hadadezer and became subject to Israel. Evidently Hadadezer also became tributary to Israel. David then stationed troops in Damascus.

After this autumn engagement in the north, the rainy season set in and warfare ceased. The end of the rains in the spring signaled the beginning of the campaign season once more, and David sent the armies against the Ammonites under the leadership of Joab (2 Samuel 11:1). After initial victories in the countryside, Joab began the long siege of the capital city, Rabbah. It was during this siege that David's adultery, the murder of Uriah the Hittite, and the birth and death of Bathsheba's son took place. Joab finally succeeded in taking the lower city. And as a loyal subordinate, he wanted David to have the honor of taking the citadel, so he urged the king to come with some reinforcements and complete the conquest. David complied and conquered the city, bringing Ammonite resistance to an end.

David subsequently engaged in a campaign against the Edomites. Once Edom had been vanquished, he stationed occupation forces in the key centers of the country.

Now Israel had achieved reasonably secure borders. David had subdued the Edomites, Moabites, and Ammonites on the east of the Jordan. Thus the foes of Hebrew tribes settled there were dislodged and the tribes were secure. Likewise, the southern frontier was pacified with the defeat of the Amalekites, the western frontier with the subjugation of the Philistines, and the northern frontier with the vanquishing of Zobah and Damascus. The repetition of the statement, "The Lord gave David victory wherever he went" (2 Samuel 8:6, 14) helps to underscore divine involvement in the cause of Israel.

David may well have been the strongest ruler in the contemporary world. By this

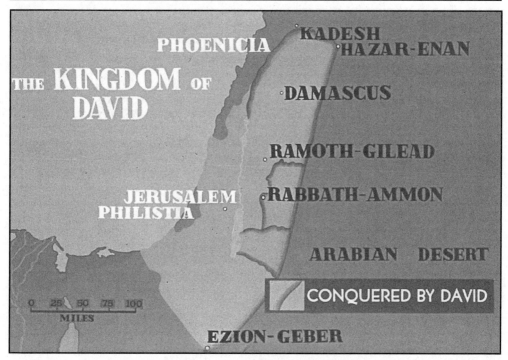

PHOENICIA

KADESH
HAZAR-ENAN

THE KINGDOM OF
DAVID

DAMASCUS

RAMOTH-GILEAD

JERUSALEM
PHILISTIA

RABBATH-AMMON

ARABIAN DESERT

CONQUERED BY DAVID

0 25 50 75 100
MILES

EZION-GEBER

The Kingdom of David or Palestine under David and Solomon

time the Minoan, Mycenaean, Hittite, Old Babylonian, Assyrian, and Egyptian powers were either down or utterly destroyed. A power vacuum in the Middle East would have permitted an even greater empire if David had wanted to build it. The only places to rival David's power were India and China. The former, in its Vedic Age, was not united and had a multiplicity of states ruled by relatively independent princes. The latter was in the Chou period, when emperors were increasingly weak and checkmated by numerous feudal lords, much the same as kings of Western Europe were during the Middle Ages.

During all of David's foreign wars, he maintained an excellent system of government at home. In saying David ruled over "all Israel" (2 Samuel 8:15), the historian put emphasis on the United Kingdom. As an ideal king David maintained "law and justice" (v. 15). It appears that, with the naming of heads of departments of government, the conclusion must be reached that David himself acted as chief justice of the court system and was relatively accessible to the people. Joab was commander of the army, having

gained his position by heroism in the conquest of Jerusalem. He maintained his role throughout David's reign until he supported Solomon's rival for the throne (1 Kings 1—2).

Jehoshaphat acted as "remembrancer" (2 Samuel 8:16); as recorder or historian he would have kept the annals or registered the current events. Zadok and Ahimelech, the son of Abiathar, are listed as priests (8:17). Zadok had been priest under Saul and Abiathar under David; now both retained their dignity. Seraiah as scribe or secretary of state kept the records and carried out royal instructions. Benaiah commanded the royal bodyguard of Cherethites and Pelethites, mercenaries from Philistia. David followed the practice of many rulers to secure a bodyguard of mercenaries rather than home guards because they were more dependent on the ruler alone.

The bureaucracy also included David's sons, who in the Hebrew are called "priests" (2 Samuel 8:18). But evidently they did not perform a priestly function. In the parallel passage in 1 Chronicles 18:17, David's sons are called "the first at the hand of the king," which the NIV translates

The rock under the "Dome of the Rock" in Jerusalem, the presumed site of Mount Moriah and the threshing floor of Araunah

as "chief officials at the king's side." And in 1 Kings 4:5 the priest is called "the king's friend," or adviser. Justifiably the NIV translates 2 Samuel 8:18, "David's sons were royal advisers."

But unfortunately David's reign was not one grand success story. Scripture records two major sins of David. The first was committing adultery with Bathsheba and the subsequent murder of Uriah her husband (2

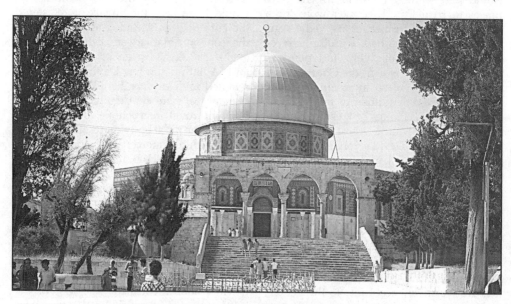

The Dome of the Rock that stands over the traditional site of the Rock Moriah

The traditional tomb of Absalom in the Kidron Valley, Jerusalem

Samuel 11–12). God severely reprimanded David through Nathan the prophet, who predicted that the child of the adultery would die and that the sword would never depart from his house. The child died soon after birth. Fulfillment of the prophecy of strife in David's household is abundantly evident in the troubles of the last years of his life. Parenthetically, we may wonder about Bathsheba's personal conduct. She must have known that her bathing would be visible from the roof of the palace or some other house. Also, a word about the size of Jerusalem is in order. It was only about eleven acres at the time and houses were packed tightly together. The question of whether Bathsheba had ambitions of her own must be left open.

David's second great sin involved a census-taking (2 Samuel 24; 1 Chronicles 21). The occasion for this sin is that "Again the anger of the Lord burned against Israel" (1 Samuel 24:1), for what reason is unknown. In His anger God "moved" (24:1 KJV) or "incited" David to take a census. But God cannot tempt anyone to sin (James 1:13), and the parallel passage in 1 Chronicles 21:1 says that God permitted David to fall into temptation by failing to provide restraining grace. In what sense David's taking of a census was sinful has to be deduced from the context in 1 Chronicles and 2 Samuel and especially from Joab's response. That David's attitude was sinful certainly is evident in his pride, or self-exaltation, as he sought to revel in the number of his fighting men and the strength of his military establishment. And perhaps, worse, he fell to the temptation of measuring his real strength in terms of human and material resources instead of the "Rock" and "Shield" 2 Samuel 22. Joab responded, in effect, that if David had such great delight in numbers, he wished that God would greatly multiply the troops and that the king would live to see it.

Evidently, soon after the census was completed, David realized he had done a very foolish thing. Conscience-smitten, he prayed to God for forgiveness. During the night God responded by delivering a message to the prophet Gad who was directed to communicate it to David. As a punishment the king was given a choice of seven years of famine, three months of pursuit before his enemies, or three days of pestilence. All would humble the pride and diminish the resources of the king. Knowing that God was merciful, David chose the last of three alternatives.

So the virulent plague descended: "From the morning until the time designated" (2 Samuel 24:15), commonly taken to mean until the time of evening sacrifice (about 3:00 PM.), seventy thousand "men" (presumably of combat age) died. At that point, on the first day instead of the third, God "relented," (NASB). God changed His attitude toward the people because of their changed attitude toward Him. The plague must have been terrible to kill so many in such a short time; that very fact helped to establish it as a supernatural act.

Moreover, the angel that evidently brought the plague was clearly visible to

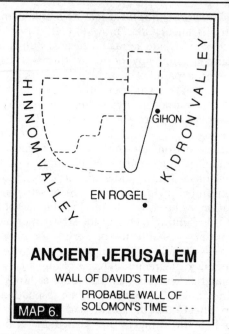

ANCIENT JERUSALEM

WALL OF DAVID'S TIME ———

PROBABLE WALL OF
SOLOMON'S TIME - - - -

MAP 6.

The anointing ceremony of Adonijah took place at En Rogel, and that of Solomon at Gihon, about two-fifths of a mile away. A rise in the ground level kept the two groups from seeing each other, but close proximity permitted them to hear the cheering of the alternate camps.

some at least. David saw him by the threshing floor of Araunah the Jebusite, just north of the walled city of Jerusalem. As David saw the terrifying specter of the angel of death, he offered a substitutionary sacrifice—himself and his house: "Let your hand fall upon me and my family" (2 Samuel 24:17 NIV). God responded with a command through the prophet Gad to build an altar on the threshing floor of Araunah, a descendant of one of the original Jebusite inhabitants of the city. David acted promptly and bought the property, making burnt offerings (expiatory) and peace offerings (in thanksgiving for the end of the plague) at the newly established holy place. Second Chronicles 3:1 makes it clear that the threshing floor of Araunah was on the northeast hill of Jerusalem, which was also Mount Moriah, the place where Abraham had offered Isaac (Genesis 22:2). So this sin and its result were important in bringing under royal control the area where the temple was later to be built.

The Succession Problem. Like other oriental monarchs, David fell into the practice of keeping a harem. Scripture names eight wives and twenty-one children and refers to other wives and concubines. Such a situation opened the door to all sorts of evils, not the least of which were the inability of a king to exercise proper parental supervision, the rise of harem squabbles, and the question of succession to the throne.

At the time of Solomon's birth, Bathsheba, the child's mother, was David's favorite; and Solomon was, at least privately, designated as heir to the throne; but he was far down in the list of heirs. While David was king in Hebron, six sons were born to him. The first was Amnon, later killed by Absalom; the second was Chileab, unheard of in later life, who presumably died young; the third was Absalom, and the fourth Adonijah (cf. 2 Samuel 3:2–5). It is the third and fourth sons who particularly figured in the succession squabble.

Abslom, a very handsome and clever young man with a considerable amount of leadership ability and a flair for public relations, decided to campaign for the throne (2 Samuel 15–18). Making a special effort to win the hearts of the people and laying his plans well, he pulled together a force at Hebron and had himself anointed king. Then he marched on Jerusalem. David had no choice but to flee. He went to Mahanaim, which had served as the capital of Israel while David ruled at Hebron. In a hard-fought battle, David's men won a decisive victory, and Joab himself killed Absalom, contrary to orders, bringing the rebellion to an end. On the heels of Absalom's revolt, Sheba, a Benjamite, led a secession movement of the northern tribes. It was quickly stamped out (2 Samuel 19–20).

Probably two or three years later, David's fourth son, Adonijah, made an attempt to seize the throne. If the law of the firstborn had been strictly followed, he would have been heir to the throne. Adonijah's support was formidable, and included Joab and the high priest Abiathar. Plans were made for an anointing ceremony at the spring En-rogel southeast of Jerusalem. When news of the affair leaked out, Nathan the prophet and Bathsheba took the lead in reporting the situation and persuading David to announce for Solomon. This he did, and plans proceeded immediately for the anointing of Solomon at the spring Gihon below the east wall of Jerusalem. The cheering at Solomon's ceremony could be heard at Adonijah's gathering just over a little ridge and around a bend in the Kidron Valley about two-fifths of a mile away. Adonijah's following melted away, and Adonijah submitted to Solomon, averting civil war (1 Kings 1:1–2:9; 1 Chronicles 22:6–23:1; 28–29).

David in Retrospect. Without question, David was Israel's greatest king. Jerusalem came to be known as the city of David. Christ was to be born in the line of David and will some day rule on David's throne. In fact, David is called a "man after God's own heart" (1 Samuel 13:14; Acts 13:22; 2 Chronicles 8:14). Exactly what this means is open to interpretation, But certainly it does not mean that he was perfect, nor even that he never committed a major sin. In fact, he broke many of the commandments, being guilty among other things of adultery and murder. The answer comes first from the context in which God initially used the descriptive. Saul had been disobedient; in his public policies he had failed God and later had even sought to kill God's anointed (David). Therefore God had rejected Saul, and now sought out a "man after His own heart" to lead His people.

David was always faithful to God in his public pronouncements and actions. He respected God's anointed—Saul—and refused to kill him even under great duress. In his early warfare, which is all that is described in any detail, he sought God's instruction about going into battle. He made the sanctuary of God prominent in Jerusalem at the center of the affairs of state and sought to build a house for God. When denied the privilege, he amassed quantities of precious metals for that purpose instead of collecting them for himself as other Oriental potentates did. He organized the worship of Israel and honored God in prayer in the presence of the whole assembly (1 Chronicles 29:10–13). Moreover, he wrote many psalms, some of which were adapted for the ritual of public worship. In general, the principles by which David lived ring clear from his charge to Solomon before his death: to walk in God's ways, to keep God's commandments, and to serve God with a perfect heart and a willing mind (1 Kings 2:3–4; 1 Chronicles 28:9).

Second, David was a man after God's own heart in his private or inner life. He meditated on the Word of God and generally had a beautiful devotional life, as the psalms he wrote indicate. To be sure he sinned and sinned grievously, and he paid dearly for his failures. But what matters especially is what he did about his sins. He had a heart tender toward God. When he realized his sins or was confronted with them, he demonstrated a broken and a contrite heart and sought God's forgiveness. It must be remembered that he lived before the cross, before there was a canon of Scripture, and before the permanent indwelling of the Holy Spirit in the believer. His was the faithful struggle of an earnest human soul to know God. Even though he suffered shipwreck as he sailed the seas of life, by the grace of God he never went down for the third time. Modern believers may identify with him as they struggle against heavy seas, and by grace they may experience the same rescuing and sustaining hand of God.

Solomon. While David was a man of war and a builder of empire, Solomon was a man of peace and builder of palaces, cities, fortifications, and the temple. But before he could start his building activities, Solomon had to consolidate his power. How much real opposition he had is questionable, but there were problems left from the latter days of David's reign. Adonijah apparently was still a threat to the crown and was liquidated, along with the somewhat unscrupulous Joab and David's opponent Shimei. Abiathar the high priest suffered expulsion from office for his complicity in the Adonijah coronation. After this minimal action, Solomon seems to have been firmly entrenched as head of state.

Apparently much impressed by the spiritual testimony left by David and greatly desiring God's blessing on his rule, Solomon, near the beginning of his reign, made a great sacrifice to God at Gibeon. God met him there and in effect said, "Make a wish, and I will grant it." Instead of asking for the things sovereigns usually would (wealth, power, fame, etc.), Solomon asked for wisdom. God was so pleased with this request that He granted it and promised riches and honor as well. Since the wisdom of Solomon is so proverbial, it may be useful to note what it was. Solomon requested, "Give to Your servant an understanding heart to judge Your people" (1 Kings 3:9, NKJV), and the writer of 1 Kings relates a test case of two women who were arguing over which of them was the real mother of an infant (3:16–28). The point seems to be that the wisdom sought and granted primarily concerned administrative or judicial decisions, and did not necessarily extend to all areas of life.

However, 1 Kings 4:29–34 indicates that Solomon's wisdom was more general than the judicial wisdom of 1 Kings 3:28. God's threefold endowment of "wisdom," "discernment" or "insight," and "understanding" or "largeness of mind" was to be immeasurable "as sands on the seashore." The word "wisdom" (hokmah, v. 29) involves an understanding of the basic issues of life, a proper discernment between good and evil, and a skill in performing business affairs and the handling of people.[65] "Discernment" or "insight" (binah) concerns the ability to distinguish between truth and error, between the valid and invalid.[66] "Largeness of mind" probably refers to breadth of interests. Solomon's wisdom exceeded that of the "people" or "sons of the east" (usually a reference to the Arab tribes east of Israel and extending to the Euphrates) and of "Egypt" (known for its wisdom literature, e.g., of Ptah-hotep, c. 2450 B.C.; and Amenemope, c. 1000 B.C.).

Next, Solomon's wisdom is declared to be superior to that of several specific individuals who must have been highly regarded in Solomon's day, though they are almost completely unknown now. Then the biblical record credits Solomon with three thousand proverbs (short, pithy saying setting forth truth in the form of simile or metaphor) and "a thousand and five" songs. Since canonical Proverbs contain only eight hundred verses and the Song of Solomon a limited number of songs (in addition to Psalms 72 and 127), the great king must have been responsible for much that has not been preserved. The subsequent allusion to his knowledge of botany and zoology may refer only to his insights in those fields as revealed in his proverbs, or to more scientific studies such as botanical or zoological classification.

The fame of Solomon's wisdom attracted people who wanted to "hear" it from his own lips. But the coming of the queen of Sheba (1 Kings 10), is the only biblical example of such a visit. "All the kings of the earth" is hyperbole designed to describe a widespread practice.

But evidently Solomon's wisdom did not necessarily extend to all things. Or he, like us, may have had greater wisdom than he sometimes displayed. For instance we may seriously question whether a truly wise man would have tried to maintain a harem of seven hundred wives and three hundred concubines (1 Kings 11:3), for it would have been impossible physically and financially. And the many foreign deities these women brought into the very center of Israelite affairs threatened to undermine the true faith. Moreover, his numerous children would not have enjoyed proper parental attention. Perhaps his wisdom did not include a very complete understanding of fiscal matters either, because he tried to do more than the economy would allow and left the state in serious financial straits.

Solomon's administration involved, first of all, appointment of eleven men as a kind of cabinet for leadership in the government. Though delegation of authority is a mark of wisdom, he was not the first ruler in Israel to do so. In fact, his father had appointed men with similar functions, and even some of the names are the same (1 Kings 4:1–6; cf. 2 Samuel 8:16–18; 20:23–26). We cannot give Solomon credit for something David inaugurated. We have to assume that these eleven functioned as only a small part of the official family. Jones estimates that in the days of David and Solomon the public payroll in the Jerusalem area probably stood at upwards of fifty-six hundred court officials and their dependents.[67]

As the bureaucracy grew, Solomon found it necessary to make provision for it. He divided the land into twelve districts, each under the supervision of a district governor. He ordered each district to provide food for the royal household for one month of the year—but there was a fatal flaw in the divisions. He exempted Judah. The twelve districts in number equaled the twelve tribes of Israel, but they were not coextensive with the old tribal regions. Since he exempted Judah from the obligation, the term "Israel" does not refer to all of Israel in this passage. Judah's favored status accentuated tribal rivalries and contributed to the split that occurred in Rehoboam's day.

The districts were as follows: (1) the hill country of Ephraim (including Samaria, Shiloh, Bethel, etc.); (2) a section of the Shephelah or foothills southeast of modern Tel Aviv; (3) the central Sharon plain and Mount Carmel; (4) the coastal region north of the third district; (5) the northern hill country, including Megiddo, Taanach, and Dothan; (6) the old territory of Bashan, northeast of the Sea of Galilee; (7) Gilead and western Ammon; (8) the land of Naphtali, west of the Sea of Galilee and north to Dan; (9) the land of Asher, to the west of Naphtali; (10) land southwest of the Sea of Galilee, including Jezreel; (11) Benjamin, a narrow swath extending west from Jericho about two-thirds of the way across western Palestine; (12) the land of Gad, much of old Moab.

Solomon enjoyed a general prosperity. First Kings 4:20–28 portrays Solomon's kingdom as secure and prosperous. Prosperity is defined first in terms of a large population: "as numerous as the sand by the sea" (v. 20), and secondly by the fact that these people generally enjoyed the basic comforts of life: "They ate, and drank, and lived happily" (v. 20):

Israel experienced a wonderful security, a kind of *Pax Hebraica*, or Hebrew peace. Solomon's rule extended to all the lands from Tipsah (Greek, *Thapsacus*) at the bend of the Euphrates in the north to the land of Philistia in the west and the "border of

Egypt" (the Wadi el-Arish at the northern edge of the Sinai) in the south. The various subject peoples of these lands brought tribute, and Solomon generally enjoyed peace. Presumably the unrest in Edom and Syria that arose at the beginning of his reign (1 Kings 11:14–25) was not a serious threat to the well-being of the empire. At least from Dan to Beersheba, the traditional borders of Hebrew Palestine, Judah and Israel "dwelt in safety" (I Kings 4:25).

This security pervaded not only because of the blessing of God but also because of Solomon's fortifications and military preparedness. He kept forty thousand horses (I Kings 4:26; cf. 2 Chronicles 1:14) and 1,400 chariots in several locations called "chariot cities" (I Kings 10:26; 2 Chronicles 9:25).

Solomon's system of fortresses created a formidable barrier for would-be invaders. Hazor guarded a strategic point north of the Sea of Galilee; Megiddo stood at the base of the Plain of Esdraelon; Bethhoron blocked the pass to Jerusalem by way of Aijalon; Baalath stood on the highway from Jerusalem to the port of Joppa; Gezer protected the main road and entrance to the valley of Sorek; and Tamar on the southern border could defend caravans from Ezion-geber. No fortress stood east of Jerusalem, the valley of the Jordan being considered a sufficient barrier. Excavations at Hazor, Megiddo, and Gezer reveal significant Solomonic construction at each place.

GEZER, SENTINEL IN THE WEST

Gezer (Tell Jezer, twenty miles southeast of Tel Aviv) guards one of the most important crossroads in Palestine. It stands near the junction of the Via Maris or coastal road with the main highway going laterally into the hill country up the valley of Ajalon toward Jerusalem. It is perched on the last of the foothills in the Judean Range, where it slopes down to meet the Shephelah. Though the mound is only about 825 feet above sea level, it is nearly cut off from the surrounding terrain and is therefore effectively defensible. The

Reconstruction of the Solomonic gate at Megiddo. Courtesy Oriental Institute

city covered thirty-three acres and was one of the largest in pre-Roman Palestine.

Gezer entered the pages of history during the days of the great Thutmose III of Egypt, who defeated its forces around 1468 B.C. Later, the Hebrews under Joshua defeated its armies (Joshua 10:33), but did not take the city (Joshua 16:10; Judges 1:29). During the Amarna Age (c. 1400 B.C.) Gezer was under nominal Egyptian rule and three of its kings authored Amarna letters. Then just before 1200 B.C. Pharaoh Merneptah on a campaign into Canaan claimed to have destroyed the Israelites and to have taken Gezer.

A later Egyptian Pharaoh captured the city and then presented it to Solomon as a dowry for his daughter on her marriage to Solomon (1 Kings 9:15–17). Solomon then fortified it

along with Jerusalem, Megiddo, and Hazor. After the division of the Hebrew kingdom, Pharaoh Shishak in 925 B.C. conquered Gezer when he attacked Jerusalem (1 Kings 14:25; 2 Chronicles 12:2–4). And Tiglath-pileser III of Assyria (probably in 734/733 B.C.) conquered the city.

Later, during the Maccabean wars, Simon Maccabaeus in 142 B.C. besieged and took Gezer and reforti-fied it (1 Maccabees 13:43–48). And Simon's son John Hyrcanus made his headquarters there (1 Maccabees 13:53).

The first excavations at Gezer occurred 1902–1909 under the aus-pices of the Palestine Exploration Fund and the leadership of R. A. S. Macalister. Then in 1964 a ten-year project was launched there by Hebrew Union College's Jerusalem School. G. Ernest Wright, J. D. Seger,

Limestone altar of incense from Megiddo

About the same time dates the so-called Gezer Calendar, which lists or outlines the main agricultural activities over a twelve-month period. The underground water system at Gezer cannot now be dated precisely, but it may have been dug about the tenth century B.C., when those of Hazor, Megiddo, and Gibeon were created.

Though Joppa provided a port of sorts on the Mediterranean, Solomon established a much more effective port at Ezion-geber, near modern Eilat on the Red Sea. Hiram of Tyre was happy to help build harbor facilities there, to help the Hebrews construct a merchant marine, and then to provide sailors to operate the fleet.

Solomon's construction projects are almost too numerous to itemize. In addition to those mentioned above, they include a palace complex, the temple, supporting terraces on which buildings could be erected in Jerusalem, and the extension of the wall of Jerusalem northward to enclose the palace complex and the temple (more than doubling the enclosed area of the city).

Solomon's Palace Complex. Solomon spent thirteen years building his palace complex, which functioned as the administrative hub of his kingdom (cf. 1 Kings 7: 1–12; 10:18–20). The buildings or functional structures in the royal complex are five in number, apparently introduced from south to north as one moves from the City of David toward the temple. They are: the House of the Forest of Lebanon, the hall of pillars, the throne room, a palace for Pharaoh's daughter, and a palace for Solomon. A courtyard enclosed by a stone wall surrounded the area. Unfortunately sketchy detail prevents a clear picture of size, nature, and function of the structures.

The House of the Forest of Lebanon is so called because of the extensive use of cedar of Lebanon in the building. The exterior was built of stone, as was true of the rest of the constructions in the complex, and measured roughly 150 feet long, 75 feet wide,

and William G. Dever directed the excavations. Dever directed two final seasons of work in 1984 and 1990.

Excavations revealed that the Canaanite city experienced its greatest prosperity and expansion between about 1650 and 1450 B.C. A fortification wall, dating to the beginning of this period, encircled the entire site, for perhaps thirteen hundred yards. It averaged about twelve feet in width and still stands in places to as much as fourteen feet. Also dating around that same time is the great high place or worship center, with its row of monoliths, some about ten feet high, and erected on a north-south line. Then around 1400 B.C. the defenders of Gezer built an outer wall, about fifteen feet wide and in some places still measuring 12–14 feet tall.

After Solomon got control of the city he built a four-entryway city gate and a stretch of casemate wall, like those of Hazor and Megiddo.

The Solomonic gate at Gezer

and 45 feet high. It functioned primarily as a storehouse, though Solomon also used it as an armory (1 Kings 10:17; Isaiah 22:8). Four rows of cedar pillars supported the upper part of the structure (so Hebrew text, preferable to the three rows of the Septuagint). Then, presumably two rows stood against the side walls and two rows stood opposite them to form side aisles.

The four rows supported cedar beams that, in turn, supported chambers above them. It may be inferred from the Hebrew that I Kings 7:3 refers not to forty-five pillars but to forty-five chambers in three stories, fifteen to a story on each side of the building. Thus the rooms could be about ten feet wide and useful for storage of armaments.

Visualization of the interior of the building based on this interpretation is as follows. Two rows of pillars supported three stories of rooms on either of the long sides of the building. A large assembly hall with a high ceiling occupied the middle section, with the central aisle open to the roof beams. At either end of the hall were three rows of windows (v. 4) with latticework (cf. Heb.; cf. 1 Kings 6:4). Three doors faced each other at either end of the structure (v. 5).

The hall of pillars (v. 6) may have been freestanding, though it was probably attached to one end of the House of the Forest of Lebanon. It measured fifty cubits (seventy-five feet) long, as long as the House of the Forest of Lebanon was wide. Apparently it was an open portico. The last part of verse 6 is difficult to translate, but very possibly it refers to a columned porch placed in the middle of the portico, much as a propylaeum or vestibule to some Greek temple or complex, such as the Acropolis at Athens.

Next, the writer mentions the throne hall or hall of judgment (v. 7), probably a separate freestanding structure and may have been connected with the hall of pillars. The hall of pillars could provide plenty of space for persons to wait to see the king or to socialize after an audience with him. The building was paneled with cedar from floor to ceiling.

Solomon's throne was made of wood and inlaid with ivory. Apparently the wooden parts not inlaid were covered with gold. Though there is some controversy over the nature of the back of it, the Hebrew text indicates it was "rounded" (I Kings 10:19), and there were arm rests. Six steps approached the throne, which apparently stood on a seventh level, or dais. At either end of each of the six steps stood a lion, perhaps representing the twelve tribes of Israel. The lion seems to have been the symbol of the tribe of Judah and symbolized royal strength. We know nothing about the composition of the lions.

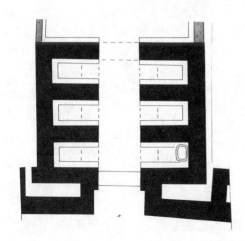

Plan of the six-chambered Solomic gate at Gezer

the quarry and carefully dressed, "trimmed with a saw" on both the inside and outside. This was true of the foundations and the upper courses of the buildings all the way to the eaves, and of the wall surrounding the courtyard. Foundation stones were sometimes eight or ten cubits (twelve or fifteen feet) long.

Carefully dressed cedar beams supported the roofs. The wall surrounding the royal complex was constructed like the temple courtyard wall with three courses of cut stone and one of cedar beams to give greater ability to absorb the shock of an earthquake. Perhaps it would be useful to note that Palestinian limestone is quite soft when first quarried and hardens with exposure to the elements.

"Set farther back" (v. 8 NIV), or "in a court set back from the colonnade" (NEB), that is, in an inner courtyard, separated from the outer courtyard where the previously mentioned structures stood, Solomon had his private apartments and a house for Pharaoh's daughter (cf. 3:1; 9:24). It is unclear what the chronicler means by the observation that these private dwellings were "similar in design." But they were both built of limestone and paneled with cedar, as the following summary indicates.

"All these structures," (I Kings 7:9) all the ones described in verses 2–8, were made of "choice" or "costly" stone "cut to size" in

The Temple. Evidently construction of the temple was going on while Solomon was building his administrative complex. He began the temple project after he had established himself on his throne and had developed a certain amount of governmental machinery. Furthermore, he had arranged a treaty with Hiram of Tyre that would assure him of the supplies and expertise required to build the temple. He began the temple in the second month of his fourth year (967 or 966 B.C.) and completed it in the eighth month of his eleventh year (1 Kings 6:1, 38).

First Kings 6:2–10 describes the general plan. The temple measured sixty cubits

The great high place or worship center at Gezer, with its row of monoliths

Philistine pottery from Gezer

long, twenty cubits wide, and thirty cubits high, twice the size of the tabernacle (Exodus 16:16, 18). If the cubit is computed at its usual length of about eighteen inches, the measurements were ninety feet long, thirty feet wide, and forty-five feet high. Thus it was not a large structure; its expense in time and materials resulted not from size but from care and exquisiteness of ornamentation.

The "portico" or "porch" in front of the temple extended across the entire structure (twenty-cubits, or thirty feet) and was ten cubits (fifteen feet) deep. We do not know for sure what the windows were like (I Kings 6:4). The NIV considers them to be "clerestory windows," and they probably were, but that does not really describe them. The Jewish Publication Society version and the New Jerusalem Bible identify them as "latticed." Perhaps they were framed with immovable latticework that would permit circulation of air but would cut down the glare of bright light; small latticework would prevent the entrance of birds. "Windows of narrow lights" (KJV) may indicate windows of close or small latticework.

According to verses 5, 6, 8, and 10, rooms were built around three sides of the temple (excluding the entrance side). Constructed in three stories, these rooms were entered from the "right" side of the temple (v. 8). Rooms on the lower floor were five cubits broad on the inside; those on the middle level, six cubits; and those on the upper level, seven cubits.

Thus the builders made the walls successively thinner on the two upper levels, creating ledges ("narrow ledges," NKJV) on which ceiling beams of cedar could be placed. This avoided cutting holes in the temple wall for ceiling beams (v. 6).

"Winding stairs provided access to the upper floors," (according to KJV, NASB, and JPS), but the nature of the stairs is unclear in the Hebrew. Evidently each of the three floors was five cubits high, equalling a total of fifteen cubits. So the height of the roof of the temple proper was thirty cubits and the height of this service area fifteen cubits plus (if one adds ceilings), and windows on the side of the temple above the addition thus would be "clerestory" windows (I Kings 6:4 NIV).

There is a question whether the "covering" with beams and planks of cedar (v. 9) refers to roofing (so NIV) or paneling on the inside of the stone work (so JPS). It seems that roofing (beams and planks) is in view in this general descriptive; paneling of the interior is mentioned later (I Kings 6:16–18). To maintain the dignity and sanctity of this holy place during construction, stone was so carefully prepared in the quarries that it was not necessary to use heavy tools to dress it on location (v. 7).

When Solomon had completed the exterior stone work, he turned his attention to the interior of the temple (1 Kings 6:14–38). He lined the entire interior with boards of cedar from floor to ceiling, and covered the

A reproduction of Solomon's Temple at the Lebanorama, a theme park in Lebanon. It is patterned on Phoenician architecture, presumably influenced by the fact that Phoenicians helped to build the Temple. The two great bronze pillars, the "sea" or laver, and the great altar are clearly visible.

floor with planks of cypress. He left no stone exposed. To form the Most Holy Place, Solomon instructed that a wooden screen be erected from floor to ceiling to partition off the rear twenty cubits of the interior. That left a Holy Place forty cubits long as a main hall.

He decorated the interior surface with "gourds" (oval ornaments) and "open flowers" (v. 18), and with cherubim and palm trees (v. 29) carved into the wall. We do not know where all of this decoration was placed, but on the basis of Ezekiel 41:17–18 and other Near Eastern decorative motifs, Keil suggests the alternation of cherubim and palm trees, with garlands of flowers above and a border of gourds below. A single band, or row, could have run around the wall, but

he thinks a double or even triple band, located one above the other, was more likely.[68]

Then Solomon ordered preparation of an "inner sanctuary," or Most Holy Place. This was to be a cube: twenty cubits long, twenty cubits wide, and twenty cubits high and placed behind the screen. That left ten cubits between it and the ceiling. Some suggest that it was elevated on a platform, but there is no evidence of that fact or of any steps needed to ascend to it. Probably there was simply a loft above it.

Within the Most Holy Place stood two immense cherubim (winged creatures with human faces), carved from olive wood and covered with gold. These were ten cubits high (half the height of the room) and each had a wingspan of ten cubits. When they were put in place against the west (back) wall, their combined wingspan extended across the entire wall, the wing of the one touching the north wall and the wing of the other touching the south wall. Their wings met in the center above the ark of the covenant. In front of the inner sanctuary stood the altar of incense made of cedar wood and covered with gold. In fact, the entire inner surface of the temple is said to have been covered with gold (I King 6:20–22, 30).

Verses 31–35 describe the doors, but the Hebrew is extremely difficult and unclear. At the entrance to the Most Holy Place were doors of olive wood carved with cherubim, palm trees, and flowers to match the inner walls. They were overlaid with gold, but the nature of the doors is uncertain. It seems that there was also a curtain (2 Chronicles 3:14) and a gold chain (1 Kings 6:21) across this doorway. The doors of the Holy Place are likewise hard to visualize. But they were made of cypress wood and matched the doors of the Most Holy Place in carving and gold overlay.

The inner courtyard of the temple is described only in the most general terms (v. 36) as constructed of three rows of cut stone and a row of cedar beams. This would then be timbered masonry, timber alternating with every three rows of masonry to provide wall flexibility in the event of an earthquake, as found in the excavations of Megiddo. We do not have the size of the courtyard, but if it was proportionate to the dimensions of the tabernacle courtyard, it must have been about 150 feet wide by about 400 feet long.

The furniture of the temple is described in 1 Kings 7:13–51. At Solomon's request (2 Chronicles 2:7), Hiram, king of Tyre, sent a craftsman to Solomon to direct the work of furnishing the temple. (Though the craftsman and the king had the same name, they were unrelated.) The craftsman the king sent was half Israelite. His mother evidently was a Danite (2 Chronicles 2:13) who had married into the tribe of Naphtali. When her husband died, she married again as a widow of a Naphtalite, a Tyrian, and bore him Hiram. He was "endowed with wisdom, understanding, and, knowledge" (2 Chronicles 2:14) in craftsmanship in bronze; but according to the same reference, he could work effectively in gold, silver, iron, and other mediums as well. No doubt he brought with him additional skilled craftsmen.

Hiram's first task was to cast two great bronze pillars to flank the entrance to the temple. These freestanding columns rose twenty-seven feet into the air, and with their capitals reached to a total height of over thirty-four feet. They were eighteen feet in circumference and about six feet in diameter with a hollow center, the metal itself being three inches thick.

Freestanding pillars stood in front of some Phoenician temples and held a fire that glowed at night, but what function these pillars were supposed to serve is unclear. The pillar on the south (left) was called Jachin—"He [Yahweh] establishes"—and the one on the north (right) Boaz—"In Him [Yahweh] is strength." At the minimum they were a witness to God's security and strength available to the Hebrews.

The next item the text describes is the "sea of cast metal" (I Kings 7:23 NIV). According to 2 Chronicles 4:6 the sea was for priests to wash in. In view of the fact that it was 7½ feet high, either there had to be some means of siphoning off water or there was a means of ascent. Possibly this was also a source of water for lavers described later. This great bronze basin was fifteen feet from rim to rim. It rested on twelve bulls, their hindquarters toward the center and three of them facing each point of the compass. They may have represented the twelve tribes of Israel. The sea could hold two thousand baths. Computed at the usual rate of just under five gallons per bath, its capacity would have been a little less than ten thousand gallons.

Hiram also cast ten lavers for distribution of water for purification as well as cleansing the altar and the court (1 Kings 7:27–29; 2 Chronicles 4:6). These consisted of two parts: the basins and the stands to put them on. The stands were about six feet square and 4½ feet high and mounted on four wheels like chariot wheels. The stands consisted of four panels attached to uprights, and the whole of the exterior was decorated with lions, bulls, cherubim, and wreaths. In the top of the stand was a circular band on which the laver itself could rest. The bronze lavers measured six feet across and each held forty baths, or just over 190 gallons. Hiram put five of these stands on the south side of the temple and five on the north.

The list of furniture also included the "golden altar" (table of incense made of cedar and overlaid with gold), the "table of the bread of the Presence" (likewise of cedar and overlaid with gold; there were ten of these), the "ten lampstands of pure gold," an assortment of gold dishes, and wick trimmers and the like for use in the Holy Place (1 Kings 7:48–50).

Nearly all of the huge front pillars, basins/lavers and their stands, and utensils that Hiram made were cast from burnished bronze (polished to make it shine), and he cast his productions in clay molds in the "plains of the Jordan between Succoth and Zarethan" (I Kings 7:46). Succoth is usually identified with Deir Alla, on the east side of the Jordan Valley just north of the river Jabbok. Excavations there demonstrate that it was a center of metallurgy during the Hebrew monarchy. Deposits of metal slag and furnaces have been found. The clay in the region was of a superior kind for making molds, and a supply of charcoal was available nearby, from the Forest of Ephraim where Absalom died (2 Samuel 18:6–17).

When the day to dedicate the temple arrived (cf. 1 Kings 8:1–66), the completed work was a magnificent sight: the exterior white limestone reflected the brilliant rays of the sun and the interior gold surfaces displayed their richness in the muted light that shone through the latticed windows. The marvelous burnished bronze creations of Hiram of Tyre and his crew stood in place, as brightly polished as devoted priests could make them. The gold furniture reposed in all its pristine glory in the appropriate places. The treasury was filled with the precious service utensils that David and Solomon had collected. Only the Ark of the covenant was lacking, and the Shekinah glory of God had not yet filled the place. Nor had the prayers and sacrifices of dedication been offered.

To proceed to the dedication, Solomon called together the "elders of Israel" (the community chiefs), the "heads of the tribes," and the "princes of the father's houses" as representatives of all Israel to bring up the ark from the "City of David," where it was located in a tent only a few hundred yards to the south (2 Chronicles 5:2–5; 1 Kings 8:1–4). The time of this gala occasion was the month Ethanim (the earlier name for Tishri), the seventh month of the year (September–October), when the "Feast" (2 Chronicles 5;3) of Tabernacles was celebrated.

When the company arrived in the temple courtyard, they stopped and offered numerous sacrifices, no doubt as acts of thanksgiving and rejoicing—on this occasion the focus was not on penitence. After the sacrifices the priests carried the Ark into the Most Holy Place and set it beneath the protective wings of the cherubim. "When the priests came out of the Most Holy Place, the cloud filled the temple" (I Kings 8:10), visible evidence that God Himself had taken up residence in the house. A similar phenomenon had occurred when the tabernacle was completed (Exodus 40:34–35). The Shekinah glory was not removed until just before the Babylonians destroyed the temple (Ezekiel 9:3; 10:4; 11:23).

While still facing the Most Holy Place, Solomon responded to God who had come to take up His abode: "I have built for you a stately house, a place for you to dwell forever" (1 Kings 8:13).

Then the king, who had been facing the Most Holy Place, turned around and addressed the assembled crowd in the court. First he praised God who had fulfilled His promise to his father David. Then he introduced a historical summary. God, who in the earlier centuries of Hebrew history had not chosen a place for His abode, had ultimately chosen Jerusalem (cf. 2 Chronicles 6:6) and David to rule there. David had had it in his heart to build the temple, and God had complimented him for it but had denied him the privilege, saying that David's son would do it instead. God has kept His word. Solomon now sits on the throne of Israel and has built the temple "for the name of Yahweh."

Next Solomon then made a prayer for the people, at first standing before the altar and then kneeling. Apparently he prayed from a bronze platform or pulpit that he ascended in the outer court (2 Chronicles 6:13).

As the king finished speaking, "fire came down from heaven and consumed the burnt offering, and the sacrifices and the glory of the Lord filled the temple" (2 Chronicles 7:1 NIV). Thus, God demonstrated His acceptance of the proceedings up to that point. Naturally, all the assembled throng were awestruck and they worshiped God. Yahweh's march from Sinai to the place of His earthly enthronement had reached a culmination. Then began a round of sacrificial offerings in dedication of the temple.

But construction of the temple was only one aspect of the glory of Solomon's reign. Scripture is replete with references to his wealth and ostentation. Some of this was made possible by saddling the Hebrews with a heavy burden of taxation, in part by gifts and tribute from foreign peoples (1 Kings 10:24–25), and in part by trading activities. Solomon had an alliance with Hiram, king of Tyre, that involved much more than a supply of cedar from the forests of Lebanon. Phoenician sailors served regularly in Solomon's fleet, which ranged the Red Sea and probably the Indian Ocean. Luxury goods were no doubt brought north from Eziongeber to Phoenician ports and from the East through Damascus to Phoenician ports, as well as south to Israel. The Phoenicians transshipped many of these commodities all over the Mediterranean world. It has been suggested that the Queen of Sheba (Sabeans in South Arabia, area of modern Yemen) would not have come twelve hundred miles on camelback through dangerous territory with rich gifts for Solomon merely to bask in his wisdom; perhaps he was too effectively moving in on her sphere of economic influence (1 Kings 10:1–13; 2 Chronicles 9:1–12). Or possibly she sought a commercial alliance with him. It is even possible that there was a three-way economic agreement between Solomon, Hiram, and the Queen.

There are evidences of decline in Solomon's latter days. His foreign wives began to turn his heart away from God, and he even built places of worship for many foreign deities (1 Kings 11:7–8), thus incurring the wrath of God. Jeroboam, the son of Nebat, later to become Jeroboam I of the Northern Kingdom, began to entertain ideas of revolt and fled to Egypt to escape Solomon's wrath (1 Kings 11:26–40). Meanwhile, Hadad of Edom (1 Kings 11:14–22) and Rezon of Damascus (1 Kings 11:23–25) were apparently loosening the apron strings of the empire and achieving a considerable amount of independence for their areas. Solomon began well and sought mightily to honor God, especially in building the magnificent temple. But foreign wives and their idolatry proved to be his downfall. Before Solomon died God informed him that for this reason He would rend the kingdom at his death and give most of it to someone other than Solomon's son. But for David's sake, God would keep Judah and Jerusalem in the hands of the Davidic line (1 Kings 11:9–13).

Middle Iron Age

After the death of Solomon, during the Middle Iron Age (900–600 B.C.), Palestine, Western Asia, and the Mediterranean were destined to be very different from what they had been in the earlier period. During the days of Saul, David, and Solomon, there had been a political vacuum in the area into which the Hebrews and Phoenicians could move. Now Egypt was aggressive again and under a Libyan dynasty invaded Palestine under the leadership of Shishak (or Sheshonk). The Assyrians sought to build an empire in the Westland and gobbled up the Northern Kingdom (or Kingdom of Israel) and seriously threatened the Kingdom of Judah. By the end of the Middle Iron Age, Babylonia extended her empire all the way to Egypt, absorbing the Kingdom of Judah in the process. That God was responsible for this new ordering of affairs in punishment for Hebrew apostasy is clear from Scripture. Assyria served as the "rod of God's anger" (Isaiah 10:5–6), and Nebuchadnezzar became "my servant" in executing judgment (Jeremiah 25:9). Meanwhile, in the West, a new arrangement of city-states would rise in Greece, political stirrings would occur in Rome, and Phoenicians would plant numerous colonies along the Mediterranean coastlands of Europe and North Africa.

In Palestine by 900 B.C. the Hebrew kingdom was divided into two warring segments. The twenty rulers in Israel and the twenty in Judah presented in the books of Kings and 2 Chronicles involve a welter of detail that is extremely hard to keep straight.

Perhaps the best way to handle the material is first to present a chart of the rulers and then to discuss developments in the kingdoms of Israel and Judah by looking briefly at the individual royal administrations. The following chart of rulers is adapted from E. R. Thiele, *The Mysterious Numbers of the Hebrew Kings*. Occasionally dates overlap; in such cases there were periods of co-regency.

The Northern Kingdom (1 Kings 12–22; 2 Kings 1–17)

The separate existence of Israel or the Northern Kingdom was not a new development. After Saul's death the north had gone its own way while David ruled in Hebron, and David had subsequently extended his rule over the northern tribes only after

RULERS OF THE DIVIDED KINGDOM

NORTHERN KINGDOM		SOUTHERN KINGDOM	
Jeroboam I	930–909	Rehobaom	931–913
Nadab	909–908	Abijam	913–910
Baasha	908–886	Asa	910–869
Elah	886–885		
Zimri	885		
Tibni	885–880		
Omri	885–874	Jehoshaphat	873–848
Ahab	874–853		
Ahaziah	853–852	Jehoram	853–841
Jehoram	852–841	Ahazian	841
Jehu	841–814	Athaliah	841–835
Jehoahaz	814–798	Joash	835–796
Jehoash	798–782	Amaziah	796–767
Jeroboam II	793–753	Azariah (Uzziah)	792–740
Zachariah	753–752	Jotham	750–732
Shallum	752		
Menahem	752–74		
Pekahiah	742–740		
Pekah	752–732	Ahaz	735–715
Hoshea	732–723/22	Hezekiah	715–686
		Manasseh	696–642
		Amon	642–640
		Josiah	640–609
		Jehoahaz	609
		Jehoiakim	609–597
		Jenoiachin	597
		Zedekiah	597–586

James Kelso excavating a worship center at Bethel,
It proved to be Canaanite rather than Israelite

tough negotiations (2 Samuel 5:1–3). Some thirty years later, Israel had briefly supported Sheba in a revolt against David. But now, under the leadership of Jeroboam, the division was to become permanent. Ahijah had predicted it, and God had informed Solomon that it would occur because of Solomon's idolatry. With the death of Solomon, Jeroboam had returned to Israel from exile in Egypt; and when Rehoboam went to Shechem to be crowned by all the tribes, Jeroboam led the opposition forces in demanding a reduction of taxes. Upon Rehoboam's refusal to exercise leniency, the northern tribes split off and crowned Jeroboam king. When Rehoboam gathered an army of 180,000 to force reunification, a prophet of God stopped him and the rupture became final.

RELIGIOUS CENTERS OF THE
NORTHERN KINGDOM

Dan and Bethel

When Jeroboam became king of the Northern Kingdom, he set up worship centers with calves of gold at Dan and Bethel. Bethel is usually identified with Beitin, ten miles north of Jerusalem. But some who debate the location of nearby Ai, question the identification.

Bethel was a religious center as early as the days of Abraham, when the patriarch built an altar nearby (Genesis 12:6–8). He later returned there after a stay in Egypt. Bethel is particularly associated with Jacob, who spent the night there during his journey from Beersheba to Padan-Aram and dreamed of a ladder that reached from earth to heaven and where he met God (Genesis 28:11–12). Later God appeared to him again at the site (Genesis 35). During the time of the Judges, the sacred Ark was located at Bethel (Judges 20:18–28). Bethel was regarded as a holy place (1 Samuel 10:3) and was one of the three cities in which Samuel sat to judge Israel (1 Samuel 7:16). So when Jeroboam set up a cult center for the Northern Kingdom, it was a religious center with a long heritage. Bethel was formerly called Luz, but Jacob renamed it Bethel, meaning *house of God* (Genesis 28:19).

Excavations were conducted at Beitin in 1934, 1954, 1957, and 1960 by the American Schools of Oriental Research and Pittsburgh-Xenia Theological Seminary, the first season led by W. F. Albright, and the other three by James L. Kelso.

Although there was a village at Beitin as early as 3200 B.C., continuous occupation of the site apparently began just before 2000 B.C. During the sixteenth century B.C. the settlement was enlarged and surrounded with an eleven-foot-thick stone wall and possessed some of the best-laid masonry of that period yet discovered in Palestine. During the thirteenth century the city was destroyed in a great fire that left debris five feet thick in places. Presumably this conflagration is to be attributed to the Israelite conquest of Judges 1:22–25.

The mound of Dan

The subsequent Israelite level of occupation has construction strikingly inferior to Canaanite levels, but the period of David and Solomon shows noticeable recovery. No sanctuary dating to the days when Jeroboam I instituted calf worship there has yet been uncovered, but Kelso did in 1960 discover a Canaanite holy place stained with sacrificial blood and sacred to the god El. Although Bethel was only a small village during Nehemiah's day (fifth century B.C.), it became an important place during the Hellenistic period and grew even larger in Roman and Byzantine days. Remains in the area show that the city continued to exist throughout the Byzantine era but apparently disap-

peared when the Muslims took over Palestine.

Dan. Different from Bethel, Dan was a center of idolatry from the time the Hebrews conquered it during the period of the Judges (Judges 18). When the Danites conquered the place they gave their name Dan to the town that was previously called Laish (Judges 18:29) and at a worship center there set up a carved image with an illegitimate priesthood (Judges 18:30).

The Dan gate, showing a place for a throne of a god or a king and a bench where the city officials could sit.

Dan is located at Tell el-Qadi (identification confirmed by an inscription found there) at the foot of Mount Hermon and at the junction of the country's ancient north-south and east-west caravan routes. Springs flowing around the mound provide one of the three sources of the Jordan River. Dan was considered to be the northernmost point in Israel: "from Dan to Beersheba" (Judges 20:1). The sixty-five-foot-high mound covers about fifty acres. Avraham Biran began an Israel Department of Antiquities dig there in 1966. Since 1974 the annual excavations have continued under the auspices of the Nelson Glueck School of Biblical Archaeology.

Excavations have demonstrated that the city was founded about 2500 B.C. Middle Bronze Age ramparts of

The Dan High Place

After the death of Ahab Moab rebelled against Israel (2 Kings 3:4-27). An interesting confirmation of the revolt appears on the Moabite Stone, now in the Louvre in Paris.

the typical Hyksos variety were about twenty-two feet thick and enclosed an important city. Biran concluded that the Danites moved to Dan during the twelfth century B.C., and he found evidence of a violent (possibly Philistine) destruction around 1050 B.C.

Of special interest was the discovery of a high place at Dan, dating to the Israelite period and evidently passing through two stages of construction. The lower, apparently built by Jeroboam I in the tenth century B.C., was about twenty by sixty-one feet in size; the upper, of Ahab's day, measured sixty by sixty-two feet and had walls of limestone five to seven feet thick and was approached by a monumental flight of steps twenty-seven feet wide.

A great double gateway, the largest ever discovered in Palestine, was uncovered on the east side of the Israelite city. This was probably built by Jeroboam I and destroyed by Benhadad of Damascus around the middle of the ninth century B.C. (1 Kings 15:20). Between the inner and outer gates was a paved square roughly sixty by thirty feet that served as a gathering place and may throw some light on business done at the gate (see 2 Chronicles 32:6; Ruth 4:1–11). A stone bench about fifteen feet long may have been used by the city fathers, and an adjacent structure may have served as a canopy for the king's throne or a cult statue.

Jeroboam and Nadab (1 Kings 12:25–14:20). Jeroboam had the responsibility of setting up the government of the Northern Kingdom. He established his capital first at Shechem (thirty-one miles north of Jerusalem on the eastern outskirts of modern Nablus) and later at Tirzah (six miles northeast of Nablus). In order to prevent continuing contacts with Judah and ultimate reunification of the two states, he felt he had to set up a new worship; so he built shrines at Dan in the north and at Bethel in the south for the new calf worship. Presumably he knew he could not succeed in persuading the people to worship calves as gods and may have intended that God be

In the Near East gods were often thought of as enthroned on or riding on the backs of lions or bulls. Here at the Hittite sanctuary in central Turkey two gods stand on the backs of lions. The Israelites at Sinai may have thought of Yahweh as enthroned invisibly on the golden calf. And at Dan and Bethel they may have had the same idea.

A statue of Baal in the Beirut Museum

Baal, the god of fertility, was also portrayed as the storm god. Here he brandishes a club and wields a stylized thunderbolt. From Ras Shamra in Syria *C. F. A. Schaeffer*

thought of as invisibly riding on the calves. Several peoples of Western Asia represented their deities as standing or sitting on the backs of animals. At any rate, God condemned the false worship and informed Jeroboam that his son would be assassinated in office and his line wiped out. Jeroboam suffered loss of territory too; Damascus and Moab became independent. His son, Nadab (1 Kings 15:25–31), ruled for only two years before Baasha killed him and the other members of Jeroboam's household. Nadab is said to have continued in the sin of his father (in maintaining the calf worship), as did all the other rulers of Israel who followed.

Baasha and Elah (1 Kings 15:32–16:20; 2 Chronicles 16:1–6). Baasha succeeded Nadab. Baasha's twenty-four-year administration was characterized by warfare against Judah. When he began to enjoy some degree of success in ventures against the Southern Kingdom, Asa of Judah persuaded Syria to invade Israel. Because

Baasha continued in the way of Jeroboam religiously, his line was also condemned, and his son Elah ruled only two years before being assassinated.

Zimri and Tibni, Omri (1 Kings 16:11–38). Zimri assassinated Elah, and during his seven days of rule managed to wipe out the house of Baasha. Omri, commander of the armed forces under Elah, then declared himself king and killed Zimri, but had to compete with another contender, Tibni, who managed to rule over a part of the Northern Kingdom for four years.

Omri established a dynasty that was to last through three additional kings (Ahab, Ahaziah, and Jehoram). He was a powerful ruler, and for some time to come Assyrian rulers called Israel "the land of Omri." He built the permanent capital of the Northern Kingdom on the excellent site of Samaria (thirty-five miles north of Jerusalem), an

Some have identified this construction at Tirzah as part of the unfinished place of Omri

easily defended hill three to four hundred feet high, surrounded by a prosperous agricultural region. After he achieved internal stability, Omri began to look outward, conquering Moab and possibly making an alliance with King Ethbaal of Tyre. At the least, he married his son Ahab to Jezebel, daughter of Ethbaal.

King Ahab (1 Kings 16:28–22:40) is one of the best-known figures of the Old Testament. This is true in part because his wife was Jezebel and in part because the prophet Elijah so dramatically opposed him. Since Scripture is always primarily interested in moral and spiritual affairs, attention during Ahab's reign focuses on the reintroduction of Baal worship. Baal worship was not new to Israel. It had crept in from the north during the latter days of the judges, and Samuel had fought it then; but under David and Solomon it had apparently almost disappeared. Now, however, Ahab and Jezebel promoted worship of this idol and even persecuted followers of God. Worse than Jeroboam's calf worship, this was open, blatant polytheism with its

accompanying licentious worship, including religious prostitution. Thus, Ahab earned the reputation of being the most sinful of Israel's kings.

THE THREE CAPITALS OF THE NORTHERN KINGDOM: SHECHEM, TIRZAH, SAMARIA

As Jeroboam launched his separate kingdom, he could not count on having a well established capital, as Rehoboam could in Jerusalem. Probably as a path of least resistance he first ruled from Shechem. This site, thirty-one miles north of Jerusalem and about a mile east of modern Nablus, had enjoyed a significant place in the affairs of the Hebrews ever since the days of Joshua. And there Jeroboam had won out in his contest with Rehoboam, pulling the ten tribes out of the Hebrew confederation. How long Jeroboam ruled from

The mound of Samaria

Shechem is not clear, but it was only for a few years.

Jeroboam then moved the capital to Tirzah, a royal city of the Canaanites that Joshua had subdued (Joshua 12:24). Tirzah is now generally identified with Tell el-Far'ah north, seven miles northeast of Shechem. Here the capital remained for some forty years, until Omri transferred it to Samaria about 885–880 B.C. Tirzah must have been a place noted for its beauty because Solomon compared his beautiful Shulamite woman to the beauty of Tirzah (Song of Solomon 6:4). Tirzah perched on a high bluff overlooking a valley with abundant perennial

Ruins of the palace of Ahab at Samaria

springs, at the western end of the Wadi Far 'ah, a major east-west avenue from the hill country to the Jordan Valley. The mound of twenty-five acres is located six miles northeast of Nablus.

Roland de Vaux excavated for nine seasons at Tirzah, from 1946 to 1960. Unfortunately he died before writing his final reports. While there is debate over whether an unfinished building of the ninth century B.C. was Omri's palace that he abandoned when he moved the capital to Samaria, there is no debate about Assyrian destruction of the site about 723 B.C., when Shalmaneser V of Assyria invaded the land.

Finally Omri moved the capital of the Northern Kingdom from Tirzah to Samaria, around 880 B.C. The hill of Samaria is over three hundred feet high and located seven miles northwest of Shechem and thirty-five miles north of Jerusalem in a fruitful plain surrounded by a rich hinterland. The hill stands in a wide basin formed by a valley that runs from Shechem to the coast and commands the main trade route to Esdraelon. The hill was easily defensible, being surrounded by valleys on all sides. From the summit there is a clear view to the Mediterranean. The work of Omri was continued by his son Ahab who

The general area on Mount Carmel where the contest between the prophets of Baal and Elijah is thought to have taken place

the course of the excavations, revealing the source of water for the long sieges the city experienced.

Light is shed on the economic and religious situation in the Northern Kingdom by the Samaria ostraca, about seventy in number. These are inscribed pieces of pottery dated largely to the reign of Jeroboam II during the first half of the eighth century B.C. or the reign of Menahem later in the century. Since these are primarily tax and revenue receipts, they tell something of the economic situation of their time; their handwriting provides information as to the science of Hebrew paleography of the eighth century B.C. And the fact that many of the names found on them are compounds of Baal reveals the influence of Phoenician religion in Israel as a result of Jezebel's efforts in that connection. But some are compounds of Ya and show that the true faith was not entirely snuffed out.

The abundance of ivory was another interesting discovery of the excavators. Probably the "ivory house" (the palace) was so-called because the walls were thickly inlaid with carved ivory. In addition, the excavators found many pieces of ivory inlay that once had been part of

is known for the ivory palace that he built at Samaria (1 Kings 22:39).

The first period of excavations at Samaria was carried on from 1908 to 1910 under the direction of G. A. Reisner, C. S. Fisher, and D. G. Lyon. Harvard University was the sponsoring institution. J. W. Crowfoot led a second expedition from 1931 to 1933, in which Harvard and several other institutions cooperated. Three of these organizations excavated at the site again in 1935. And an excavation under the sponsorship of the Jordanian Department of Antiquities took place in 1965–67.

Work at Samaria proved to be particularly fruitful in illuminating and confirming the biblical record. Omri and Ahab apparently leveled the top of the hill, which was previously almost uninhabited, as Scripture attests (1 Kings 16:24), surrounded the summit with a wall thirty-three feet thick in places, and began the palace compound. Originally the palace measured 160 feet square and was composed of a number of rooms arranged around open courts. Later kings enlarged the palace area greatly and built a second wall on the slope of the hill and a third at the base of it. Numerous large cisterns turned up in

The brook Kishon near the foot of Mount Carmel, where Elijah killed the prophets of Baal (1 Kings 18:40). The brook was wider then.

Scripture mentions several Assyrian kings who crossed the paths of Israelite kings. But it does not allude to Ashurnasirpal II (883-859 B.C.), the real founder of the Neo-Assyrian Empire, that so terrorized Israel. Here he is shown being ritually anointed on a relief from his palace at Nimrud.
British Museum

The great opponent of Ahab and Jezebel was the prophet Elijah, who appeared suddenly from Gilead and predicted a drought, which lasted over three years. After that, he arranged the famous contest with the prophets of Baal on Mount Carmel (1 Kings 18), which brought acknowledgment of God by the people and death to many prophets of Baal. Subsequently, Elijah predicted the destruction of Ahab's line for his murder of Naboth and seizure of Naboth's vineyard (1 Kings 21:1–29).

Scripture presents Ahab as more than merely an ungodly king; he was a powerful military man. In two major campaigns he worsted the Syrians, showing them leniency because of the threat of rising Assyrian power. However, Scripture does not allude to Ahab's biggest battle of all—participation in a coalition that sought to stop Shalmaneser III of Assyria (at Qarqar) from expanding his empire into Syria and Palestine. For the great battle of Qarqar in 853 B.C. Ahab furnished two thousand chariots and ten thousand soldiers, according to Assyrian records. Apparently the coalition stopped the Assyrians for the moment. Ahab's ability to field two thousand chariots shows something of the wealth and power of the Northern Kingdom. It should be remembered that Solomon kept only fourteen hundred chariots. Ahab's building activity is also ignored in Scripture. How widespread it was we cannot say, but excavations show that it extended at least to Samaria, Hazor, and Megiddo.

furniture. By these we are reminded of Amos's denunciation of the beds of ivory (Amos 6;4).

While the excavations show that a high point in the development of Old Testament Samaria occurred in the days of Jeroboam II, they point to another great period of glory during the reign of Herod the Great. Herod renamed the city Sebaste, the Greek form of Augustus, in honor of the emperor, and beautified it greatly. He built a temple to Augustus on top of the ruins of the ancient Israelite palaces, a forum flanked by a basilica, a stadium, and an aqueduct.

Ahaziah (2 Kings 1:2–18). Ahab's son Ahaziah succeeded to the throne when his father was killed in a third war against the Syrians. During his short reign of a year or two, Ahaziah was unable to resubjugate the Moabites, saw his joint naval expedition with Judah down on the Gulf of Aqaba end in failure (2 Chronicles 20:35–37), suffered the condemnation of Elijah, and finally died of a fall. About this time, the ministry of Elijah came to an end, and God swept him to heaven in a whirlwind. Subsequently Elisha continued the ministry of his spiritual father.

Jehoram (2 Kings 3:1–9:26). A second son of Ahab and Jezebel, Jehoram, now took the

On the Black Obelisk of Shalmaneser III Jehu is
shown paying tribute to Shalmaneser

Jehu (2 Kings 9:11–10:36). Jehu became
God's agent for punishing the house of
Omri and destroying Baal worship in Israel.
Actually, Jehu was no friend of God and
seems to have exterminated Baalism to a
large degree because of the strong link
between religion and state. That is, if he
would eliminate the Omri dynasty, he must
destroy the religious system that formed
one of its important bases of support. The
blood purge of the outgoing dynasty was
swift and complete. It began with Jezebel
and extended to the seventy "sons" or male
"descendants" of the house of Ahab, as well
as forty-two relatives of Ahaziah, all the
court officials of Jezreel and Samaria, and
the prophets and priests of Baal. Jehu was
doomed to a very troubled reign.
Apparently he did not enjoy full support of
the populace and no doubt suffered
because he killed too many individuals
who knew how to make the machinery of
government work.

JEZREEL AND THE DEMISE OF JEZEBEL

throne for twelve years. At the beginning of
his reign he fought a major war with Moab;
but in spite of initial successes, he ultimately failed to resubjugate the Moabites.
Jehoram's reign was marked by frequent
relations (mostly unfriendly) with the
Aramean kingdom of Damascus. Elisha
was at the height of his ministry during the
reign of Jehoram and performed numerous
miracles. For instance, he provided water
when the combined armies of Israel, Judah,
and Edom were about to die of thirst during the attack on Moab; he healed Naaman,
captain of the forces of Syria, of his leprosy;
and he temporarily blinded the Syrian soldiers who came to capture him.

Jehoram faced several fierce Syrian
attacks, one of which was successful in laying siege to Samaria itself, and a second
which resulted in the wounding of
Jehoram. While Jehoram lay recuperating at
Jezreel, the usurper Jehu (anointed at the
command of Elisha) attacked, killing not
only the king of Israel but the visiting king
of Judah (Ahaziah) as well.

If we remember the town of Jezreel
at all, it is usually in connection
with the death of Jezebel. Scripture
tells us that Jehu, the next king, after
Ahab, commanded that servants
throw Jezebel from an upper window
in the town and she met a grisly fate
(2 Kings 9:30–37). Jezreel's function is
uncertain. It may have been a secondary political capital, a winter capital, a
religious capital, or a military base for
the kingdom.

Jezreel was located fifty-five miles
north of Jerusalem, about eight miles
east-southeast of Megiddo in the eastern part of the Jezreel Valley on a
ridge extending along its southern
side. The breathtaking view of the
Valley of Jezreel from the mound
helps us understand why Ahab and
Jezebel built a palace there and why
they so heavily fortified the site.

Excavations on the fifteen acre
mound were conducted between
1990 and 1995 by David Ussishkin of

Tel Aviv University and John Woodhead of the British School of Archaeology in Jerusalem. Discoveries show that the royal enclosure, heavily fortified and surrounded by a moat, occupied about eleven acres. The site was occupied virtually uninterrupted from the days of Ahab and Jezebel (ninth century B.C.) to the twentieth century A.D.

According to an Assyrian inscription, Shalmaneser III of Assyria forced Jehu to pay tribute. Hazael of Damascus defeated him and took Bashan and Gilead. He got no help from Phoenicia or Judah because of his attacks on Ahab's house and Baalism. The Phoenicians were, of course, devotees of Baal; and Jezebel, whom Jehu killed, had been a Tyrian princess. Moreover, Athaliah, a daughter of Ahab and Jezebel, had become queen of Judah and continued to rule there after the death of her husband. She was a sworn enemy of Jehu because he had killed her mother.

Jehoahaz and Jehoash (2 Kings 13:1–14:14). Jehu's son Jehoahaz, capitulated to the armed might of Hazael of Syria, and ultimately found his armed forces reduced to ten thousand foot soldiers, ten chariots, and fifty in the cavalry corps. Finally, in desperation, Jehoahaz turned to God for help and in his last days enjoyed some relief because of the death of Hazael and Assyrian pressure on the Syrians. His son Jehoash began the restoration of Israel's power. Receiving Elisha's deathbed promise of victory over the Syrians, Jehoash went on to recover all the territory lost to Hazael earlier and also to enjoy a decisive victory over Judah, even breaking down part of the wall of Jerusalem.

Jeroboam II (2 Kings 14:23–29). Jeroboam II (son of Jehoash) was the outstanding king of the Northern Kingdom. Scripture focuses on Jeroboam's evil ways but observes that in spite of them God brought relief to Israel and expanded her borders in his days. In fact, Israel under Jeroboam II's leadership

was able to expand her borders northward approximately as far as David and Solomon had done and to enjoy an accompanying economic prosperity. All this was possible in part because the Assyrians greatly weakened Syria and then became so preoccupied with their own internal affairs for some decades that they were no threat to the Westland. Jeroboam's son, Zachariah (2 Kings 15:8–12), proved to be either incompetent or to have too many enemies. At any rate, he was assassinated after only six months. But Shallum (2 Kings 15:13–15), his assassin, lasted only one month and was in turn killed by Menahem.

Menahem and Pekahiah (2 Kings 15:16–26). Menahem was more successful, but by now the Assyrian Empire was expanding again. Pul (2 Kings 15:19), otherwise known as Tiglath-Pileser III (744–727 B.C.), campaigned in Syria and Palestine in the last days of Menahem and put Israel to tribute. By laying a heavy tax on his people in order to pay the sum Pul exacted, Menahem retained his throne, and the Assyrians let Israel alone. Menahem's son Pekahiah (2 Kings 15:23–26) continued the policies of his father but apparently was opposed by those who favored revolt against Assyria. After two years of rule, Pekah assassinated Pekahiah and began to rule.

On another panel on the Black Obelisk Israelite porters bear tribute for Shalmaneser III

Tiglath-Pileser III put Israel to tribute
during the reign of Menahem

Pekah (2 Kings 15:27–31). Pekah presumably ruled for several years over a portion of Transjordan before the coup that gave him control over the entire state. During the eight years when he ruled all Israel, he cooperated with Syria in an effort to establish an alliance against Assyria. Ahaz of Judah refused to go along with that. Of course, there was no sufficient power in the West to stand against Assyria, which advanced and brought an end to the kingdom of Damascus in 732 B.C., as well as taking the northern part of Israel (2 Kings 15:29). A revolt placed Hoshea on the throne in the same year.

Hoshea (2 Kings 17:1–6). Evidently coming to the throne with the approval of Tiglath-Pileser III of Assyria, Hoshea was powerless to change Israel's tributary status. When Tiglath-Pileser died in 727 B.C., Hoshea entertained heady ideas of revolt, hoping the new king, Shalmaneser V, would not be able to maintain the power of his predecessor. He was wrong. Shalmaneser began a three-year siege of Samaria in 725 B.C., and the Assyrian army took the city either in the last days of Shalmaneser V or the early days of his successor, Sargon II. Probably the city fell before Shalmaneser died. But Sargon (722–705 B.C.) claimed the victory and certainly did the mopping up after the battle. His cuneiform records state that he carried off 27,290 captives into Assyria. Numerous non-Jews were resettled in the Northern Kingdom, leading to the half-breed population and mixed religious situation that existed there in post-exilic and New Testament times. For two centuries God's faithful prophets had been warning the kings and the people of Israel that their idolatry and other sins would bring judgment at the hand of God, and they had refused to listen.

The Southern Kingdom (1 Kings 14:21–15:24; 22:41–50; 2 Kings 8:16–29; 11–25; 2 Chronicles 10–36)

The history of the Southern Kingdom, or Judah, was destined to be quite different from that of the Northern Kingdom. The temple was there, and so were many Levites. Soon after the division of the kingdom, numerous Levites and others who refused to compromise with the paganism of the north came south, strengthening the

Sargon II of Assyria claimed to have destroyed the Northern Kingdom. Here is a 30-ton bull from his palace at Khorsabad. *The Louvre*

Some of the personified towns of Palestine that Shishak claimed to have conquered. From his inscription at the Temple of Karnak

the god Amon, and on the body of each captive appears a Palestinian place name; so we have there a listing of the towns the Egyptian king took during his Judean conquests. At present about 120 of the names are legible, but by no means can all of them be identified geographically. Some of the more important that can be recognized are Megiddo, Gibeon, Taanach, Beth-Shean, and Ajalon.[69] Evidently Shishak sacked scores of towns in both the Northern and Southern Kingdoms. Interestingly, Egyptologist Kenneth A. Kitchen of the University of Liverpool, recently made claim that this inscription in row eight also mentions what he translates as "The Heights of David." If we accept this translation, it provides us with the third reference to David to appear in recent archaeological discoveries.[70]

When God made it clear to Rehoboam that this invasion had come as punishment for idolatry (2 Chronicles 12:5), the king and many of the leaders of the state confessed their sins and God moderated the attack. Subsequently, Rehoboam fortified at least fifteen cities to the south and west of Jerusalem to prevent a recurrence of Egyptian inroads. Rehoboam was also involved in warfare with Jeroboam I of Israel all during his reign, but the struggle must have consisted of border skirmishes rather than major pitched battles because at the beginning of the kingdom God forbade a major effort to resubjugate Israel (2 Chronicles 11:1–4), and Rehoboam had obeyed.

spiritual element in the state. Of course it is also true that Levites would have experienced increasing difficulty finding financial support in the north as apostasy gained ground.

Since only Judah and Benjamin made up the Southern Kingdom, it enjoyed greater political unity than did the north. All the kings were of the Davidic dynasty instead of being from several dynasties. Eight of her kings were good to excellent, whereas none of the northern kings were classified as good. Because of this better record, God permitted Judah to survive about one hundred years longer than the northern kingdom. But in spite of its advantages, Judah also slipped into idolatry and ultimately went into captivity for her sins.

Rehoboam (1 Kings 14:21–31; 2 Chronicles 10–12). Rehoboam started well. During the first three years of his rule, he led the kingdom in the ways of righteousness. But then a rapid decline set in, and pagan high places and groves began to appear everywhere. In punishment, God sent against the land a massive Egyptian invasion under the leadership of Shishak (Sheshonk I, 945–924 B.C.), probably in 925.

Shishak inscribed a relief on a wall in the Temple of Karnak at Luxor, Egypt, depicting 156 captives taken in this campaign. They are led by cords clasped in the hand of

Abijam (1 Kings 15:1–8; 2 Chronicles 13). During his brief three-year reign, Abijam (or Abijah) continued the warlike policies of his father and enjoyed considerable success in taking Israelite border towns. Also, as his father had done, he fell into idolatry. In fact, conditions got so bad that God would have brought an end to Abijam's line if it had not been for His covenant with David.

Asa (1 Kings 15:9–24; 2 Chronicles 14–16). Abijam's son, Asa, began his forty-one-year reign well. He launched a reform program and destroyed many of the foreign altars and idols that had infested the land during the days of his father. Moreover, Asa built up his army and defenses. All his efforts were not enough, however, to meet the mighty Egyptian onslaught that came during his fourteenth or fifteenth year (c. 896 B.C.). When the Ethiopian Zerah, apparently commander under Osorkon I (924–889 B.C.), invaded the land, his force was so overwhelming that Asa ran to God for help. Winning a great victory, he listened to the appeals of the prophet Azariah and launched a major religious reform throughout Judah.

But strangely, soon afterward Asa suffered a spiritual relapse. In the face of an attack by Baasha of the Northern Kingdom, he robbed the temple treasury and sent a gift to Benhadad in Syria, with a plea for an attack on the Northern Kingdom. Though this move was very successful, the prophet Hanani criticized Asa for failure to depend on God and for making an unholy alliance. Angered, the king threw Hanani into prison, and from then on Asa does not appear to have been faithful to God. When seized with illness near the end of his life, he put his trust in physicians and sought no help from God.

Jehoshaphat (1 Kings 22:41–50; 2 Chronicles 17–20). Apparently Asa's disease was so crippling that he made his son Jehoshaphat coregent during his last three years ,and Jehoshaphat went on to rule another twenty-two years on his own after his father died. A good king, he instituted reforms near the beginning of his reign and gave orders to the Levites to teach the law, an indication that they had become lax in their duties. When Jehoshaphat was faced with a combined attack of Moab, Ammon, and Edom (2 Chronicles 20:1–30), he called for a time of fasting and prayer and was rewarded with a great victory. He also improved and expanded legal services in the kingdom. In spite of his good points, Jehoshaphat failed miserably by making an alliance with the house of Omri. This involved marriage of the crown prince, Jehoram, to Ahab's daughter Athaliah, and subsequently introduced Baal worship in Judah. Moreover, it linked Jehoshaphat in joint ventures with three Israelite kings.

When he joined Ahab in war against Syria, Ahab lost his life in the venture, and Jehoshaphat nearly did. Jehoshaphat built a commercial fleet in Judah's port of Ezion-geber with the help of Ahaziah of Israel, and the fleet was wrecked. Then Jehoshaphat allied himself with another son of Ahab, Jehoram, in a war against Moab, and nearly perished for lack of water during the struggle, which ultimately turned out to be a defeat for Israel.

Jehoram (2 Kings 8:15–24; 2 Chronicles 21). Jehoram ruled for four years as coregent with his father, and then went on to rule alone for eight years. His reign contrasted markedly to his father's. No doubt under the influence of his wife Athaliah, daughter of Ahab and Jezebel, he restored the idolatry that Jehoshaphat had destroyed. He also murdered his six brothers, endured two successful revolts by Edom and Libnah, and experienced a humiliating invasion by Philistines and Arabians, who even carried off Jehoram's wives and all his sons except Ahaziah (2 Chronicles 21:14). Either Athaliah was not among the wives carried off or she was ransomed, because she served as advisor to her son Ahaziah and ruled subsequently in her own right. When Jehoram died of a terrible intestinal disease, he was so disliked that no one regretted his passing.

Ahaziah (2 Kings 8:25–29; 9:27–29; 2 Chronicles 22:1–9). The only remaining son of Jehoram, Ahaziah, ruled Judah for less than a year. Under the domination of his mother (Athaliah) and influenced by the example of his father, he promoted Baal worship and allied himself with his mother's brother Jehoram of Israel in war against Syria. Jehoram was wounded in the struggle; and when Ahaziah went to visit his uncle Jehoram at Jezreel, Jehu usurped the throne and killed both Jehoram and Ahaziah.

Athaliah (2 Kings 11:1–16; 2 Chronicles 22:10–23:15). Athaliah was cruel and ambitious like Jezebel, her mother. After the death of her son, Ahaziah, she decided to seize the throne for herself, and killed her grandchildren so there would be no other claimants to the throne. But she was unsuccessful. One of Ahaziah's sons, the infant Joash, was rescued and hidden for six years. Then Jehoiada, the high priest, laid careful plans to crown Joash. When he did so, Athaliah fled and was caught and executed.

Joash (2 Kings 12; 2 Chronicles 23:16–24:27). Joash had a good record in his early years, due largely to the counsel of Jehoiada, the high priest. He destroyed the temple of Baal in Jerusalem and fully reinstituted Mosaic offerings in the temple. A religious revival broke out in the land, and needed repairs were made on the temple. But after the death of Jehoiada, Joash lapsed into idolatry. So far did he slip that he even had Jehoiada's own son, Zechariah, stoned to death for rebuking his sinful actions (2 Chronicles 24:20–22). But God does not condone sin in high or low places; later that same year Hazael of Damascus marched through the country on a devastating campaign and spared Jerusalem only after Joash paid in tribute every bit of treasure he could find. Finally, Joash became so unpopular that he was assassinated.

Amaziah (2 Kings 14:1–20; 2 Chronicles 25). Amaziah, the son of Joash, ruled for twenty-nine years, only about five as sole ruler and the rest as coregent with his son Uzziah. Like his father, Joash, Amaziah started well and enjoyed the blessing of God. Greatly interested in regaining use of the port of Ezion-geber, he launched a very successful war against Edom. But he made the great mistake of bringing back Edom's false gods and worshiping them. For this a prophet of God forecast the king's destruction. Defeat came to him at the hands of Israel, and apparently Amaziah was taken as a prisoner of war and remained in captivity until the death of the Israelite king Jehoash (2 Kings 14:13, 17). Finally he was released and ultimately died at the hands of an assassin. This action did not affect the continuity of the Davidic line because Uzziah (Azariah) had already been ruler of Judah in fact for many years.

Uzziah (2 Kings 14:21–22; 15:1–7; 2 Chronicles 26). Uzziah, also known as Azariah, was a very good king whose success related directly to his dependence on God (2 Chronicles 26:5, 7). He ruled for a total of fifty-two years and thus was second only to Manasseh in length of reign among the kings of Israel and Judah. He was sole ruler for only seventeen years, however, serving as co-regent with Amaziah at the beginning and with Jotham at the end of his reign.

When Uzziah came to the throne, Judah lay almost flattened by the power of Israel. But gradually Uzziah asserted independent power and built up the walls of Jerusalem, improved the fortifications of the city, regrouped the army, and equipped it with superior weapons. As he became strong at home, he was soon in a position to expand. He subdued the Philistines to the west, strengthened his hold on Edom to the south, and extended his rule over the Ammonites. Good relations apparently existed with Jeroboam II in Israel, who was also powerful, wealthy, and expansionistic. Between them, the two Hebrew kings controlled approximately the equivalent of David's empire. This was possible because Assyria was somewhat in decline at the time. Unfortunately, at the height of his power, Uzziah forgot the real source of his strength, and in the face of opposition by eighty priests insisted on going into the holy place and burning incense. For this act of sacrilege, God smote Uzziah with leprosy, and he could no longer go into the temple at all and could not even enjoy ordinary social privileges. His son Jotham became co-regent during the years 750–740 B.C.

Jotham (2 Kings 15:32–38; 2 Chronicles 27). During much of his reign, Jotham merely carried out the policies of Uzziah, including the building of fortifications. He is classed as a good king, and enjoyed the favor of God. He put down an Ammonite revolt, the only serious internal threat to the realm. The power of Assyria was rising again, but Jotham refused to join Rezin of Damascus and Pekah of Israel in an alliance to oppose the great Tiglath-Pileser III of Assyria. Isaiah and Micah prophesied in Judah during this time, and as is evident by their words, continuing prosperity had made its inroads. Judah had settled into a compla-

The mound of Lachish

cent type of secularism; sacrifices continued at the temple, but there was no real religious vitality.

Ahaz (2 Kings 16; 2 Chronicles 28). Ahaz endured the combined wrath of Rezin and Pekah, who tried to force him to abandon his pro-Assyrian policy and join them against Tiglath-Pileser III. Unable to withstand the combined attack, he sent a gift to the Assyrian ruler and begged his help. Tiglath-Pileser was only too glad to respond. But before Rezin and Pekah were forced to go back home, they inflicted great destruction on Judah and killed some 120,000 people (2 Chronicles 28:6). Their 200,000 captives were soon released, however (28:8–15). Shortly thereafter, Ahaz drifted into religious apostasy: he made images to Baal and worshiped in high places. For his sins he began to experience military reverses at the hands of the Edomites and Philistines. Meanwhile, Tiglath-Pileser was successful against Judah's enemies; he destroyed the kingdom of Syria and annexed it along with part of the kingdom of Israel (732 B.C.).

LACHISH, SECOND CITY OF JUDAH

Lashish (Tell ed-Duwer) was the most important city of the Shephelah, the low rolling foothills between Philistia and the highlands of Judah. One of the chief fortresses of

Judah, second to Jerusalem, its summit covered eighteen acres, larger than Old Testament Jerusalem or Megiddo. Located thirty miles southwest of Jerusalem and fifteen miles west of Hebron, it had immense strategic importance, dominating the old road from the Palestinian highlands to the Nile valley.

Lachish was an important city when the Israelites invaded Palestine. Its king, Japhia, joined a confederacy against Joshua (Joshua 10:3, 5) but was captured by the Israelites (10:31–35; 12:11). Later Rehoboam rebuilt or fortified Lachish (2 Chronicles 11:9). Amaziah fled there and was slain (2 Kings 14:19; 2 Chronicles 25:27). Lachish fiercely resisted the siege of Sennacherib of Assyria when on his way to Egypt (2 Kings 18:13–17; 2 Chronicles 32:9; Isaiah 36:2; 37:8) but ultimately capitulated in 701 B.C. Sennacherib portrayed the event on the walls of his palace at Nineveh (now removed to the British Museum in London, with a cast in the Oriental Institute Museum of the University of Chicago). The city experienced two destructions at the hands of Nebuchadnezzar, one in 598 B.C., when Jehoiachin and the Jerusalem citizens were carried into captivity (2 Kings 24) and another 589/88, when the city was reduced to

After Sennacherib captured Lachish, he carried off large numbers of captives. Here are some of the Hebrew captives as pictured on Sennaceriib's palace reliefs in the British Museum

ome of the Israelite leaders Sennacherib flayed alive, as pictured in his palace reliefs

A temple to the sun at Lachish, from the Persian period

ashes. After the Exile it was reoccupied (Nehemiah 11:30).

J. L. Starkey began excavations at the site (1933–38). After his murder, Charles H. Inge and Lankester Harding continued his work. Yohanan Aharoni led Israeli digs there in 1966 and 1968, and David Ussishkin of Tel Aviv University excavated there 1973–1987.

Most dramatic of the Lachish discoveries are the so-called Lachish Letters. These priceless documents, of epigraphic importance, illustrate the Hebrew language current in the time of Jeremiah. They are to be dated to the time of the Babylonian siege of 589/88 B.C. Eighteen of these pieces of ancient

inscribed pottery were found in 1935 and three more in 1938. Practically all of these ostraca were written by a Hoshaiah, who was thought to be stationed at a military outpost near Lachish, to a man named Jaosh, believed to be the high commanding officer at Lachish. This traditional interpretation has been disputed by Yigael Yadin, who concluded that the letters were first drafts of letters sent by Hoshaiah, the commander at Lachish, to Jaosh, his superior in Jerusalem. In any event, they give a sense of "you are there" at Nebuchadnezzar's destruction of Judah.

Other significant finds at the site include the 105-foot-square platform

he platform on top of the mound of Lachish where David built a government house

The room at the Lachish gate where the Lachish Letters were found

During Sennacherib's invasion of Judah, an Egyptian army under the leadership of Tirhaka attacked the Assyrians (2 Kings 19:9). Here Tirhaka is pictured as a sphinx. *British Museum*

On the Taylor Prism in the British Museum Sennacherib boasted of having shut up Hezekiah "like a bird in a cage"

on which David built a government house, a Late Bronze temple, the walls of Rehoboam, a mass grave of fifteen hundred bodies probably dating to the Assyrian attack, the gate complex, and an Assyrian siege ramp and a Judean counter-ramp.

Hezekiah (2 Kings 18–20; 2 Chronicles 29–32; Isa. 36–39). Hezekiah was one of Judah's very best kings. He worked hard to destroy idols, high places, altars, and other trappings of idolatry, and is said to have conducted himself as had David his father (2 Chronicles 29:2). There was plenty of need for reform after the evil influence of Ahaz. Hezekiah was anti-Assyrian in his foreign policy, but that did not become evident as long as the powerful Sargon II lived. When Sargon died in 705 B.C., Hezekiah apparently decided that Sargon's son Sennacherib would be an easier target so Hezekiah joined a coalition of western Asiatic powers against Assyria.

Busy elsewhere for about four years, Sennacherib did not mount a major western offensive until 701 B.C. At that time he crushed the power of Tyre, moved south against the Philistines and defeated them, and then invaded Judah. About this time,

an Egyptian army came north against Assyria, and Sennacherib had to dispose of that before he could proceed with his Judean campaign. Also about this time, or possibly a little earlier, Hezekiah was afflicted with a severe illness which appeared terminal. Concerned not only for himself but also for his people who might be leaderless at such a crucial time, Hezekiah prayed for healing and received a grant of fifteen years of additional life. Sennacherib marched almost irresistibly into Judah and took Lachish after a siege.

The fight was fierce, as excavations at the site reveal. When the Assyrians built a ramp against the wall to give them the advantage of height for throwing missiles into the city, the defenders raised a counter-ramp to position themselves above the Assyrian soldiers on the ramp. When the battle was over, Sennacherib commissioned a whole wall of pictorial inscription for his palace at Nineveh to describe the event.

Hezekiah's "Broad Wall." It stood twenty-three feet wide and probably twenty-seven feet high

Archaeologists have removed that to the British Museum in London. A cast of part of the scene stands in the Oriental Institute of the University of Chicago.

After conquering forty-six towns of Judah according to his own cuneiform account, Sennacherib encamped around Jerusalem. God gave assurance of His help through Isaiah, the court prophet, and brought an end to Sennacherib's invasion by destroying most of his army with some sort of plague. Predictably Sennacherib did not mention the defeat in his records; the best he could do was claim to have shut up Hezekiah "like a bird in a cage" in his capital city, Jerusalem. Since Jerusalem was a major objective, he would have made much of its conquest if he had achieved it. After Sennacherib returned to Assyria, Hezekiah evidently was very prosperous and very successful in his administration (2 Chronicles 32:27–29), no doubt doing much to rehabilitate the state.

It should be noted that in preparation for Sennacherib's invasion Hezekiah had repaired the walls of Jerusalem and had built "another wall outside" (2 Chronicles 32:5). This involved enclosing a good part of the western hill with what is now known as "the Broad Wall," a massive wall twenty-three feet thick, which Nahman Avigad discovered in the Jewish Quarter (cf. Nehemiah 3:8).

Hezekiah had also constructed what is known as "Hezekiah's Tunnel," a remark-able tunnel 1,750 feet long underneath the City of David. This cut, dug from both ends, permitted water from the Gihon Spring on the east to flow into the Pool of Siloam at the southwestern corner of the city. Thus, during the Assyrian siege and the later Babylonian siege, for that matter, residents of Jerusalem had a supply of water that besiegers could not cut off.

SENNACHERIB'S ATTACK ON JUDAH

King Hezekiah was desperate. Assyrian hosts had invaded the land and sacked city after city. Then they besieged Jerusalem and threatened to extinguish the Kingdom of Judah. Hezekiah himself went to the temple to pray to God for relief and then sent an official delegation to Isaiah the prophet begging for divine intervention. God responded with a plague on the Assyrian army that decimated the attackers and sent Sennacherib packing (Isaiah 36–37). Lord Byron eloquently described the scene.

THE DESTRUCTION OF SENNACHERIB

The Assyrian came down like the
   wolf on the fold,
And his cohorts were gleaming in
   purple and gold;
And the sheen of their spears was like
   stars on the sea,
When the blue wave rolls nightly on
   deep Galilee.

Like the leaves of the forest when
   Summer is green,
That host with their banners at sunset
   were seen:
Like the leaves of the forest when
   Autumn hath blown,
That host on the morrow lay withered
   and strown.

For the Angel of Death spread his
   wings on the blast,
And breathed in the face of the foe as
   he passed;

And the eyes of the sleepers waxed
deadly and chill,
And their hearts but once heaved—
and forever grew still!

And there lay the steed with his nos-
tril all wide,
But through it there rolled not the
breath of his pride;
And the foam of his gasping lay white
on the turf,
And cold as the spray of the rock-
beating surf.

And there lay the rider distorted and
pale,
With the dew on his brow, and the
rust on his mail:
And the tents were all silent—the
banners alone—
The lances unlifted—the trumpet
unblown.

And the widows of Ashur are loud in
their wail,
And the idols are broke in the temple
of Baal;
And the might of the Gentile,
unsmote by the sword,
Hath melted like snow in the glance
of the Lord!

Manasseh (2 Kings 21:1–18; 2 Chronicles
33:1–20). Manasseh did not follow in the steps
of his father, Hezekiah, but became one of the
very worst kings of Judah. During the first
eleven of his fifty-five years of reign (longest
of any king of Israel or Judah), he was co-
regent with Hezekiah and must have been
kept on a tight leash. But after Hezekiah's
death, Manasseh established altars of Baal
throughout the land and even set up an
image of a Canaanite deity in the temple. He
killed many who opposed his idolatry, perhaps even the prophet Isaiah, as tradition
indicates. The prophets warned Manasseh
about his evil ways, but he paid no attention.

Finally, the Assyrians invaded Judah and
carried Manasseh captive to Babylon. There
the Judean had a real change of heart and
subsequently was allowed to return to

Jerusalem. But the Assyrians never permitted him to rebuild his fortifications to protect
the realm against Egypt. On return home,
Manasseh sought to abolish the idolatry for
which he had earlier been responsible, but
evidently he was not very successful.

Amon (2 Kings 21:19–26; 2 Chronicles
33:21–25). Manasseh's son Amon ruled only
two years and reverted to the idolatry of his
father's earlier years. Some of his servants
banded together and assassinated him.

Josiah (2 Kings 22:1–23:30; 2 Chronicles
34–35). Josiah, the eight-year-old son of
Amon, became the next king. He must have
had excellent advisors from the onset, for by
the time of his sixteenth year, he began of his
own accord "to seek after the God of David"
(2 Chronicles 34:3). Subsequently, he
launched a major program to cleanse the
entire kingdom of idolatry and even extended his efforts to the Northern Kingdom, now
only loosely under Assyrian control. Assyria
was rapidly declining and about to fall, so
Judah had nothing further to fear from that
quarter. Babylon was on the rise. Finally, in
609 B.C., after the fall of Nineveh (612),
Pharaoh Necho of Egypt marched north
through Palestine to aid remaining Assyrian
forces. Anti-Assyrian Josiah tried to stop
Necho at Megiddo and lost his life in the
process. During Josiah's reign, Jeremiah
began his ministry. Zephaniah, certainly, and
Nahum and Habakkuk, probably, also
prophesied during his reign.

Jehoahaz (2 Kings 23:31–33; 2 Chronicles
36:1–3), the first of Josiah's three sons to
rule, lasted for only three months, apparently because Necho (who then dominated
Palestine) did not think him to be sufficiently cooperative.

Jehoiakim. Necho appointed as king
Jehoiakim, a second son of Josiah (2 Kings
23:34–24:7; 2 Chronicles 36:4–8), later in 609
B.C., but he was unable to control the situation for long. In 605 Nebuchadnezzar sent
Necho fleeing back to Egypt and moved
into Syria and Palestine, where he demanded numerous hostages—including Daniel
and his friends—to guarantee Hebrew submission. In the midst of this campaign, on

Assyrian and Babylonian sieges were terrifying experiences. Among other things, they built siege ramps on which they deployed battering rams for breaching the walls. Here Sennacherib sends a battering ram up a ramp at Lachish

August 15/16, 605 B.C., Nebuchadnezzar's father, Nabopolassar, died in Babylon and Nebuchadnezzar made a speedy return to the capital to assume the throne.

After some successful campaigns in Syria and Palestine in subsequent years, in 601 Nebuchadnezzar attacked Egypt and sustained such heavy losses that his imperialistic designs received a severe setback. Jehoiakim seems to have interpreted the situation as an opportunity to strike for independence, for he "rebelled" against Nebuchadnezzar (2 Kings 24:1). Again Judah entertained the elusive hope that it could count on Egyptian help against a powerful force from the north. Unable to come in person with a Babylonian army, Nebuchadnezzar evidently sent "raiding bands," lightly armed mercenaries, from east of the Jordan (Syrians, Moabites, and Ammonites) to engage in guerrilla activities and weaken the state (2 Kings 24:2). Jehoiakim ruled for eleven years (609–598) and apparently died in December 598, about the time Nebuchadnezzar finally sent an army to deal with rebellious Judah.

Jehoiachin (2 Chronicles 36:8–10). When Jehoiakim died, his eighteen-year-old son Jehoiachin came to the throne and continued the evil policies of his father. While Jehoiachin was trying to consolidate his power in Jerusalem, Babylonian forces were on the way. They must have begun the siege of the city in January of 597, and apparently it did not last much over two months. Jerusalem fell to the Babylonians on the second of Adar (March 15/16) 597 B.C.[71] Evidently the siege began at the hands of the advance guard and concluded after Nebuchadnezzar himself arrived.

Then the Babylonians helped themselves to the spoils of war, thoroughly looting the treasures of temple and palace in fulfillment of the prophecy of 2 Kings 20:16. Probably not everything was taken, because Nebuchadnezzar provided for continuation of the religious, economic, and political life of Judah after this first deportation. Therefore Jeremiah 27:19–22 need not be thought of as contradictory when it speaks of furnishings still remaining in the temple during the reign of Zedekiah. Of course, what Jeremiah

Azekah

referred to was largely made of bronze rather than of gold or silver.

The captives deported included the king, his mother, wives, officials, the notables of the land, craftsmen and metal workers, the seven thousand in the standing army left within the city, and Ezekiel (Ezekiel 1:1–3). Some have found a disagreement between the ten thousand of 2 Kings 24:14 and the seven thousand fighting men plus a thousand craftsmen mentioned in 2 Kings 24:16, but it is not necessary to reach such a conclusion. Probably the total was ten thousand and that included seven thousand in the army, a thousand craftsmen, and two thousand others (officials, notables, etc.). The total of 3,023 taken in the first captivity as listed in Jeremiah 52:28 might refer to the civilian population of Jerusalem; the army of seven thousand would have come from all Judah and would have been only temporarily in the city. In any case, only the poorest of the land were left (v. 14); all those capable of mounting an effective rebellion and running a viable war effort were carried off.

Zedekiah (2 Chronicles 36:11–21). Nebuchadnezzar replaced Jehoiachim with Mattaniah (subsequently known as Zedekiah), the full brother of Jehoahaz, a third son of Josiah, and uncle of Jehoiachin His kingship was conditional, hinging on his loyalty to Nebuchadnezzar to serve him and make no alliance with the Egyptians. Zedekiah, the last king of Judah, reigned for eleven years (597–586) and was classified as

an evil king, like Jehoiakim, probably denoting he also refused to heed the prophetic word. In his ninth year of reign Zedekiah rebelled against Nebuchadnezzar. All during his reign the pro-Egyptian faction pressured him to rebel against Babylon, while Jeremiah repeatedly urged him to knuckle under to Babylon (Jeremiah 21:1–10; 34:1–3; 37:6–10; 38:17–23).

Finally, in his ninth year, Zedekiah decided to rebel, and the inevitable happened. Nebuchadnezzar prepared to attack. The assertion that "Nebuchadnezzar . . . advanced against Jerusalem" (2 Kings 25:1) when he remained at his headquarters at Riblah (2 Kings 25:6), and his officers conducted the siege (Jeremiah 38:17), is not a mistake. He masterminded the campaign and his army represented his power and will, and he was therefore present in a very real sense in the persons of his deputies. The beginning of the siege in the ninth year and tenth day of the tenth month of Zedekiah's reign is to be equated with January 15, 588 B.C., according to E. R. Thiele.[72] The seige continued until the eleventh year, the fourth month, and the ninth day, or July 18, 586.[73] The destruction of the city began a month later, on August 14 (the seventh day of the fifth month, 2 Kings 25:8). There was a temporary lifting of the siege, probably at about the halfway point, when Pharaoh Hophra of Egypt (588–570) invaded Palestine with his army and sent his fleet against Phoenicia (cf. Jeremiah 37:5–11; Ezekiel 17:15–17).

Assyrian and Babylonian sieges of ancient cities were terrifying experiences.[74] They did not merely surround a city and cut off its supplies, but they built siege ramps around it (2 Kings 25:1). On these they deployed battering rams for breaching the walls and constructed platforms higher than the city walls in order to rain down arrows and other missiles on the defenders. In the case of Judah they were also busy reducing all the fortified towns (e.g., Lachish and Azekah), as archaeological discoveries indicate, and engaging in psychological warfare to encourage defections. That the latter effort was successful is clear from Jeremiah 38:19, where Zedekiah expressed a fear to surrender because he

Judah went into captivity. Hebrew captives probably were marched down Procession Way through the Ishtar Gate into Babylon, as in this picture. *Courtesy the Oriental Institute*

thought the Babylonians might turn him over to these defectors to make sport of him as they wished. Of course the real horror of the siege was the famine (2 Kings 25:3) and the lengths to which people went to get food. As a result of Hezekiah's efforts, the city did have an adequate supply of water.

AZEKAH IN THE HISTORY OF ISRAEL

Azekah was a city located on a high hill northeast of Lachish and southwest of Jerusalem. Her king

joined the enemies of Israel in Joshua's day and suffered defeat at the hands of the Hebrews (Joshua 10:10–11). Near this city the Philistines later encamped when David killed Goliath (1 Samuel 17:1). Then, during the divided monarchy Rehoboam fortified Azekah (2 Chronicles 11:9) and it remained an important fort when Nebuchadnezzar attacked Jerusalem in 588 B.C. On that occasion it was one of the last remaining strongholds of Judah (Jeremiah 34:7). One of the Lachish Letters (Number IV), written at that time by an officer in charge of an outpost near Azekah, mentions that he could not see fire signals from Azekah. It is uncertain whether this implies Azekah had already fallen to the Babylonians. The city again figured in Hebrew history after the return from Babylonian captivity (Nehemiah 11:30).

Azekah is identified with Tell Zakariyeh in the Shephelah or foothills region of Judah (Joshua 15:35), guarding the lower end of the valley of Elah (Wadi es-Sant), c. sixteen miles west of Bethlehem. F. J. Bliss and R. A. S. Macalister in 1898–99 uncovered there an inner citadel fortified with six large towers, and part of the city wall with three towers. They thought Rehoboam was responsible for the fortifications. Now it is thought that the fortress was built during the period of the Judges and the wall with its towers in the time of Rehoboam. But Rehoboam also repaired the fortress.

Finally on July 18, 586 B.C. the food supplies gave out completely and about the same time the Babylonians breached the wall (2 Kings 25:3–4). Probably they broke through the wall on the north of the city where access was easiest. The king and a body of troops fled at night through a narrow passage at the southeast end of the city into the Hinnom Valley and out to Jericho. Presumably this was possible because the Babylonians were concentrated at the north and west of the city; the precipitous slopes on the east and south would have been hard to attack and scaling the walls there would have resulted in unnecessary loss of life. Perhaps the Judeans hoped to get across the Jordan to Moab and Ammon, who had also been involved in the revolt against Babylon (Jeremiah 27:4). The Babylonians caught up with the refugees on the "plains of Jericho," probably the next day. This area, east of Jericho, offered little or no cover to troops trying to cross it. The Judeans deserted their king in panic and scattered to the winds. Nothing is said about whether the Babylonians tried to round up the Judeans.

The Babylonians were after Zedekiah, and they hauled him off to Riblah in northern Syria to face Nebuchadnezzar. The Babylonian king "passed sentence on him" (2 Kings 25:6), presumably for breaking his covenant of vassalage or treaty obligations and meted out harsh punishment. Nebuchadnezzar's men "slaughtered" Zedekiah's sons before his eyes and then blinded him to render him powerless and sent him off to Babylon in chains (2 Kings 25:7). At the age of thirty-two he had nothing to look forward to but a dark and lonely life in exile.

About a month after the fall of Jerusalem, on August 14, 586, "Nebuzaradan, commander of the guard" (2 Kings 25:8), came to take charge of liquidating the Judean state and reorganizing government there. The Babylonians destroyed every important structure in the city: the temple, palace, and houses of the well-to-do after thoroughly looting them (2 Kings 25:9, 13–17).

Then they pulled down the protective walls so the inhabitants could not again stage an effective rebellion against Babylon (2 Kings 25:10). Apparently the destruction was most complete on the east where stones could be thrown down the slope toward the Kidron Valley. When Nehemiah rebuilt the walls in 444 B.C., he constructed a whole new section on the east but had only to repair the walls elsewhere. Nebuchadnezzar also depopulated the city and deported its inhabitants. But some of the lower classes, including farmers and vinedressers, were to remain behind in the countryside to continue some form of agricultural life in the land.

Finally Nebuzaradan dealt with a group of people who did not fit into any of his other categories of deportees or people to be left behind: leaders of state and ringleaders of the rebellion against Babylon (2 Kings 25:18–21). These were all believed to be expendable; and after they were paraded before Nebuchadnezzar at Riblah, they were executed.

Though "Judah went into captivity" (2 Kings 25:21), it is clear that some form of life and administration continued after the fall of Jerusalem. The new masters attempted to set up a government of sorts and appointed

An ancient wine press near Shechem

honey" (Exodus 3:8, 17; 13:5; 33:3; Leviticus 20:24, *et al.*). And Moses portrayed the land as a "good land" (Deuteronomy 8:7). Then he proceeded to list seven crops, fruit trees, and products most abundant in the land of Canaan: wheat, barley, vines (grapes), figs, pomegranates, olives, and honey (Deuteronomy 8:7–8). When we combine this passage with 1 Samuel 25:18, where Abigail sent a generous present to David's men— two hundred loaves of bread, two skins of wine, five dressed sheep, five measures of roasted grain, one hundred clusters of raisins, and two hundred fig cakes—we have a fairly good idea of what was grown in Palestine and therefore what provided a typical menu for the Hebrews during the days of the monarchy and subsequently.

Gedaliah governor over the remaining populace, but the physical boundaries of his province aren't clear. Gedaliah came from a noble family, and his father Ahikan (2 Kings 22:12) had supported Jeremiah's policy (Jeremiah 26:24). He was associated with the Jerusalem establishment and the pro-Babylonian group in Jerusalem.

Gedaliah set up his administration at Mizpah, about nine miles north of Jerusalem and not far from Bethel. But Ishmael, son of Nethaniah and of royal blood, was perhaps personally ambitious and also anti-Babylonian. Sometime in October, hardly two months after Gedaliah's appointment, Ishmael and his band killed Gedaliah, his Judean administrative assistants, and his Babylonian attachés. Johanan, son of Kareah, defeated Ishmael soon thereafter and rescued the large number of captives or hostages he had taken. Subsequently, a band of Judeans, fearful of Babylonian reprisal against them because of Gedaliah's murder, determined to flee to Egypt, in spite of Jeremiah's assurances that they would come to no harm if they remained in the land. These emigrants took Jeremiah with them (cf. Jeremiah 40:7–43:7).

Agriculture in Iron Age Palestine

We have looked at the political history of Palestine during the Iron Age and previously surveyed its geographical features. But God often described Palestine as a very special place—a "land flowing with milk and

Palestinian Crops.

Wheat was a winter crop sown between the end of October and mid-December and harvested between the end of April and the end of May. In Canaan it grew best in the coastal valleys, the Valley of Jezreel, the upper Jordan Valley, the Beth-Shean Valley, and in the northern Negev during the more rainy seasons. The Hebrews ground wheat into flour for use in bread, but also ate it parched and raw.

Barley is a winter cereal sown about the same time as wheat but harvested between the end of March and the end of April. It tolerates saline and alkaline conditions and grows well on soils derived from limestone and located in high altitude and low rainfall regions. Popular in Canaan, barley was used in bread and other baked goods and eaten parched (2 Samuel 17:28) and raw (2 Kings 4:42).

Grapes. Red grapes seem to have been the dominant if not the exclusive variety grown in Canaan. Vineyards could be used for grapes alone or they could be grown among olive trees. The Hebrews had to protect their grapes from animals and people, so they erected walls, thorn hedges, and watch towers. Grapevines might be allowed to spread on the ground or grow on trees, or they might be trained to grow on poles or trellises. There was an official arrangement for harvesting grapes from newly planted

Ripe figs ready for harvest

An olive tree, probably over 1000 years old, in the Garden of Gethsemane

vines. The fourth year the produce of the vines was brought to Yahweh. In the fifth and subsequent years the farmer could consume the crop himself (Leviticus 19:24–25).

The Hebrews used grapes to make wine or eat as fresh fruit. They also used them to produce vinegar (a popular condiment) and raisins. They soaked grapes in oil and water or in a solution of potash and then spread them in the sun to dry as raisins. Persons on a journey took raisin cakes along as a favorite food. The time for grape harvesting varied from region to region.

Figs. Fig trees produce two crops a year, the first ripening in June (Song of Solomon 2:13; Isaiah 28:4) and the second in August and September (Numbers 13:23; Nehemiah 13:15). The Hebrews ate the first fresh and dried the second for use as a food during the winter or on trips (cf. 1 Samuel 25:18). They also used them in making wine.

Pomegranates. The pomegranate ripens in the summer (Numbers 13:23) and its fruit

contains compartments filled with juicy seeds, which can be eaten fresh or dried and stored. The juice of these seeds was consumed fresh or fermented as wine.

Olives. The olive tree sometimes can reach a height of twenty-five feet. It grows best in well-drained or rocky soils. Leaves stay on the tree all year round. It flowers at the beginning of summer and ripe olives are ready for picking in September and October. At harvest the branches were beaten with sticks (Deuteronomy 24:20). The fallen olives were then gathered into baskets and taken off to the press. Evidently the Hebrews did not eat olives in Old Testament times but used the oil in food preparation, for burning in lamps for illumination, for anointing the body, for treating wounds, and for official anointing of kings, prophets, and priests.

Dates—Honey. Oded Borowski believes that the honey of Palestine (Exodus 3:8; Deuteronomy 8:8) was especially a product

A threshing scene at the threshing floor of Samaria. Animals drag a heavy sledge over the stalks of wheat to separate the grain from the stalks

After the threshing was complete at the threshing floor of Samaria, the winnowing process took place

of the date palm tree.[75] The juice extracted from the trunk could also be served as a drink, either fresh or fermented. The fronds of the date palm were woven into mats and baskets and its fibrous sheath used for making ropes, pillows, and mattresses. But Scripture clearly states that bee-produced honey was also commonly consumed in ancient Palestine (cf. Judges 14:8–18; 1 Samuel 14:25–29; Psalm 19:10; Proverbs 24:13; Song of Solomon 4:11; 5:1).

Other produce of the land. In addition to the seven major commodities of Canaan noted above, numerous other products provided variety in the diet of the Israelites. Other fruit trees included the sycamore, which produced figs in the summer, eaten mostly by the poor; the black mulberry, and a tree hard to identify but possibly the apricot. They also had nut trees—almond, pistachio, and the common walnut. Known legumes included broad beans, lentils, chick-peas, and peas. Though difficult to identify, vegetables or fruits are referred to in the Bible by a whole collection of Hebrew words, which seem to indicate cucumbers, watermelons, leeks, onions, and garlic.[76]

Agricultural Techniques

Hebrews made their plows entirely of wood, except for the plow point, the part that penetrated the soil, which was made of iron during the Iron Age. Normally a team of oxen pulled the plow with a wooden yoke that rested on the back of their necks. Young cows were also used (Judges 14:18). An ox and a donkey were not supposed to be yoked together because of the inequity to the smaller animal (Deuteronomy 22:1). Normally a farmer broadcast seed over the field first and then plowed the field to cover the seeds and protect them from birds and animals.

Reaping of a small area could be done without tools; the farmer simply pulled up the whole plant. In a larger operation, foremen led reapers as they held a sickle in one hand while grabbing a bunch of stalks with the other. Sickles had flint, bronze, or iron blades, depending on the economic status of the farmer or the date of the activity. That is, during the Early Iron Age bronze blades were still common; iron became more common during the Middle Iron Age. Sometimes reapers cut off only the top of the stalk, reducing the amount of straw to contend with on the threshing floor. Harvested bundles of stalks were bound into sheaves and carted off to the threshing floor.

The Hebrews transported grain to the threshing floor by wagon, mule back, or people carrying large baskets. The threshing floor could be a private or a community facility that was located outside of town, often near the city gate. Threshing might be

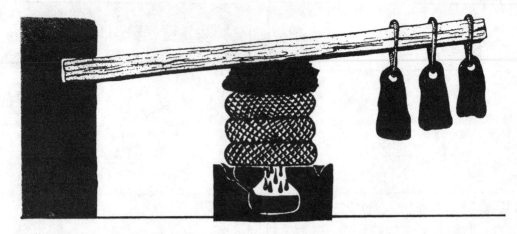

The beam-press for extracting olive oil. Baskets of olives were piled on a collection basin and then a large stone was placed on top of them. On top of the pile was a beam with one end inserted in a large stone and the other end free. On the free end were hung stones that would continue to exert a crushing pressure.

done with a stick (beating out the grain), by means of animals treading over the stalks while they were tied next to each other to form a row, or with a wooden sledge dragged across the grain by oxen or donkeys. The sledge was a wooden platform with stones on the underside to break the grain from the stalks.

During winnowing the farmer threw the grain into the air with a winnowing fork of five or seven tines on a windy day, so the wind could blow away the chaff (cf. Psalm 1:4), while the heavier kernels fell at his feet. After that he used a wooden shovel to winnow the grain further and collect it into a heap. Finally, he took a sieve to sift out stones, small pieces of straw, and other undesirable matter.

Of course grain also had to be properly stored. It might be put in containers (usually large pottery jars) in a private or public storeroom, in a public building, or stored in bulk in a granary. Below ground it might be put in a cellar in containers or stored in bulk in a stone-lined or plastered pit.

For the processing of grapes, the winepress consisted of a flat surface for treading the grapes and a receptacle for the juice, located in or next to the vineyard. Sometimes a press might be built of stones and mortar inside a city. Workers collected the grape juice into large jars holding about ten gallons each. They then sealed the

mouths with clay, leaving a small hole to permit the escape of gases produced through fermentation. The jars were then put in rock-cut cellars to ferment and were sealed completely when the fermentation process was complete. Smaller jars were used for transportation of the wine.

Olive processing required a different technique. In this case slow pressing of the olives was required to squeeze out the oil. The common press in use during the period was the beam-press. This process involved piling baskets of olives on a collection basin. On top of these was placed a large stone and on top of that a beam with one end inserted in a large stone and the other end free. On the free end stones were hung to exert a crushing pressure. Alternatively, if one wanted a small amount of olive oil for immediate use, a few olives could be pounded in a stone mortar. Olives were too bitter for eating without pickling or salting, which came in the Hellenistic period. Evidently they were not eaten in Old Testament times.[77]

Animal husbandry was also an important aspect of Iron Age agriculture. In fact, the Hebrews raised sheep in substantial numbers throughout Israel's life in Palestine. They sheared the sheep twice a year: in the spring, after lambing time, and in the fall. Before shearing, sheep; fleece was washed in a pool and then dried out.

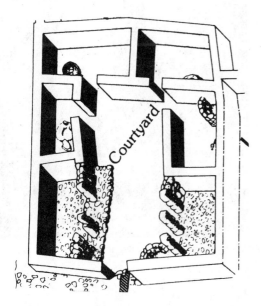

A four room house at Tirzah, first capital of Omri before he built Samaria. The four-room house was the typical Israelite house for centuries. This was not literally four rooms but a fourfold division of space with three parallel units closed on the end by a perpendicular unit. The middle unit was an open court, with storage on the right, often animal pens on the left, and living quarters on the end. There could be a second story.

After shearing the women washed the bulk wool again and combed it. So sheep produced wool for clothing, as a cash crop, as well as milk and thus butter and cheese. When killed, sheep provided meat, and their skins were made into bags and coverings. The Hebrews used the male sheep, the ram, as the sacrificial animal at the central sanctuary.

Goats and sheep got along well and were raised together, with goats usually leading the way when on trek. Thus in Scripture they are sometimes compared to political leaders (cf., Ezekiel 34:17; Daniel 8:5). A nanny goat provided a substantial supply of milk (up to three quarts a day). Leben, a favorite dish resembling yogurt, came from sour goat's milk. A young roasted kid was considered to be something of a delicacy. The goat also was a sacrificial animal and it produced hair from which tent and garment cloth, tent curtains, and pillows could be made. And

whole goatskins could be cleaned and turned into water or wine "bottles."

The four-room house that farmers and almost everyone else lived in during the Iron Age persisted as the basic plan of most Israelite houses. This house plan seems to have originated before 1200 B.C. and continued through the united monarchy and the northern and southern kingdoms down to the destruction of Jerusalem at the hands of the Babylonians in 586 B.C. After that it passed out of fashion. How the Israelites came to adopt this house plan is unknown, but it seems that they developed it. In excavations it appeared everywhere—in towns, on the farms, and in isolated houses.

These houses were comprised of a fourfold division of space (not necessarily four rooms), with three parallel units closed on the end by a perpendicular unit. Normally the outside "house" door led into an open court where cooking and other kinds of work took place, such as grinding of grain or weaving of cloth. On the right a storage area might be separated from the courtyard by a solid wall or square stone pillars. And of course it might be divided into two or more rooms. On the left were usually animal pens. The perpendicular area in the rear served as living quarters and also could be subdivided. Often external stone stairways led to an upper floor or roof where additional living space was available. No doubt in some cases wooden stairs or ladders to a second floor have disappeared. The Israelites usually constructed the flat roofs of houses with wooden

The Cyrus Cylinder in the British Museum records Cyrus' decree to let captive peoples return to their ancestral homes

Nehemiah rebuilt the walls of Jerusalem. Sections of his wall have been excavated in Jerusalem and are shown here.

beams covered with brush and finished off with tamped clay.

The residents of these houses used little furniture. People normally sat on the ground. Bedrolls might be laid on the ground or on a stone or brick bench which could serve as a place to sit during the day. While King Saul, King David, or King Solomon may have sat at a low table to eat, probably most poor people spread their food on skins or some other covering on the ground.

Light reached the other rooms of the house from the central courtyard. But additional illumination came from small oil lamps. These changed style frequently, but during the united and divided monarchies were open clay saucers that would fit in an adult hand when held open. Part of the lamp rim was pinched to hold a wick of flax; the fuel was olive oil. Normally there were no toilets in the houses; human excrement was disposed of in nearby waste ground. Sewage and animal manure commonly littered the streets of towns. Conditions in houses or in town usually were anything but sanitary.

Not only did houses not have sewage disposal, they also didn't have a water supply piped in. From time immemorial and on down into New Testament times women went with their water jars to the village well in the evening to get water for the next day.

Late Iron Age

The Late Iron Age (c. 600–300 B.C.) was essentially a time of Persian control in Palestine. Cyrus the Great of Persia marched into the city of Babylon on October 29, 539 B.C. and took control of it for Persia. During the first year of his rule over the Babylonian Empire, Cyrus issued a decree to permit the Jews to return to Palestine and rebuild Jerusalem and the temple (Ezra 1:1; cf. Isaiah 45:13). Since Cyrus did not enter Babylon until near the end of 539, he must have issued the decree in 538. And it must have taken another year or two for the thousands of repatriates (42,360 Israelites plus 7,337 servants, Ezra 1:64; Nehemiah 7:66) to get their wagons and gear together for the journey.

Cyrus' action is detailed on the Cyrus Cylinder now in the British Museum; it permitted all captive minorities who had been deported from their homeland within the Babylonian Empire to return to their former homes and reestablish their sanctuaries. He concluded by asking their gods to intercede with Marduk on his behalf so he might enjoy long life and other blessings.[78]

Cyrus' motivation for issuing such a decree may easily be inferred. In the first place, he could by this means remove a sore spot among captive or deported peoples. They were no longer forced to remain in captivity but were free to go home. If most of them chose not to do so, at least they need not blame his government for forcing them to live where they were against their will. In fact, they could hail Cyrus as a great liberator and would tend to support his government. Second, though it is not known how religious a man Cyrus was personally, his decree publicly sought to win the support and blessing of all the gods of the captive peoples. He may be viewed as either religious or superstitious or the diplomat *par excellence.* Finally, the historical sources portray Cyrus as a humane, generous, and tolerant man; a decree of this sort is in keeping with his character. Although Cyrus benefited the Jews by helping them return home and although Isaiah called him God's anointed (evidently to accomplish divine purposes, Isaiah 45:1), he was no worshiper of the true God of heaven.

Cyrus apparently chose to rule the provinces of the empire through his own appointees instead of vassal kings, but he did not insist that they all be Persians. A case in point is the Jewish Sheshbazzar (Ezra 1:8, 11), whom he sent as a governor to Jerusalem. Likewise, Cyrus and his son Cambyses appointed non-Persians as army commanders. Of the three known generals of Cyrus, two were Medes and one a former Babylonian governor. He seems to have been generous toward his nobles and apparently had a certain charisma, or at least an effective propaganda machine, that led Medes, Babylonians, Elamites, Jews, and others to accept him as their legitimate ruler.

The territory of Judah in the days of the Restoration, as indicated in the books of Ezra and Nehemiah, extended from just north of Bethel almost to Hebron in the south, and from the Jordan River to Gezer in the west. This was an area about twenty-five miles north and south and slightly more than that east and west. In size the district was about eight hundred square miles, or four-fifths as large as Rhode Island.

The Jews tried to "do it right" as they returned to Palestine. In the first place, those who went back were the ones God had "stirred up" (Ezra 1:5) to do so. Second, those

who remained in Babylonia generously helped finance the venture (Ezra 1:6). King Cyrus for his part sent along 5,400 gold and silver articles that Nebuchadnezzar had confiscated from the temple of Solomon (Ezra 1:11). Third, when the exiles reached Jerusalem, they gathered with great unity (as "one man," Ezra 3:1) to rebuild the altar of sacrifice and correctly offer on it the sacrifices prescribed in the Law and to keep the Feast of Tabernacles. Then they laid the foundation for the rebuilt temple (Ezra 3:6–13).

When people of the land (Samaritans and others) desired to join with the Jews in rebuilding the temple, the Jews refused the offer, not wishing to get mixed up with any false religion. After this the Samaritans became openly hostile, first engaging in guerrilla tactics and then hiring lobbyists at the Persian court to work against Jewish interests. Presumably this was possible because Daniel was no longer living. These men were able to frustrate progress of rebuilding the city of Jerusalem and the temple for some fifteen years. The opposition of those in the land is understandable because their control of the land and their economic position were threatened by the newcomers. Incidentally, the people of the land may have offered to join with the Jews in rebuilding the temple so they could frustrate or upset the effort, and the Jews may have suspected ulterior motives. In any case, the opposition became so intense that what had begun with great fanfare came to an abrupt halt.

Following Cyrus, his son Cambyses ruled from 530 to 522 B.C., conquering Egypt for the empire. Then, after a period of unrest, Darius I established himself on the throne. He launched conquests that brought the empire to its greatest extent. Under him it extended from the Indus River in the East to the Aegean Sea and on into Greece in the West, and through Syria, Palestine, and Egypt to Libya in the southwest. From east to west, it was as wide as the continental United States, and was the largest empire of western Asia in ancient times. After he took this vast territory, Darius proceeded to organize his empire as Cyrus had never done—and became a key figure in the rebuilding of Jerusalem.

Darius evidently divided his empire into twenty provinces, or satrapies, ruled by governors, or satraps. Many of these satrapies encompassed several peoples, with one of them serving as a nucleus. He initiated land surveys and assessed annual taxes or tribute. He placed Palestine in the fifth satrapy, along with Phoenicia, Syria, and Cyprus and he installed strong garrisons, partly Persian in composition, in great cities and at important frontier posts. Satraps normally shouldered both civil and military responsibilities. They collected tribute, raised military levies, and provided for justice and security, modeling their courts and their protocol after that of the king.

For purposes of commerce and communication, Darius reopened the canal between the Pelusiac branch of the Nile near Bubastis and the Red Sea near Suez. About eighty feet wide, it was broad enough for two ships to pass. The last Egyptian pharaoh to concern himself with this canal had been Necho (c. 600 B.C.). Thus Darius united by water the three heavily populated river valleys of the ancient world (Indus, Tigris-Euphrates, Nile). On land, he built some important roads, queen of which was the great royal road extending sixteen hundred miles from Susa to Sardis.

Darius also sought to provide a standard currency and a system of weights and measures. He tried to ensure that the laws of the land were known to those who administered them, but he does not seem to deserve his reputation as a lawgiver, claimed for him in modern times.

Darius transformed a feudal kingship into an oriental despotism with an elaborate court ceremony, and thus he greatly increased the distance between himself and his subjects. He enjoyed building palaces and constructed several, but the two greatest were at Susa and Persepolis. A faithful Zoroastrian, Darius viewed himself as the representative on earth of Ahuramazda.

During his reign the second stage of the Jewish restoration in Palestine took place: the completion of the temple. Though the foundation of the second temple had been laid in the second year after the return from Babylon, fierce opposition to the work had forced it to cease. Finally during the second year of Darius (520 B.C.), the preaching of the prophets Haggai and Zechariah stirred up the people to resume construction (cf. Haggai 1:1; Zechariah 1:1; Ezra 5:1–2).

When the local enemies of the Jews tried to stop the work again, the leaders of the Jews asked that a check of the archives be made to see if Cyrus' decree permitting reconstruction of the temple could be found. When it did not turn up in Babylon, where Jewish leaders thought it would be, the search moved to Ecbatana in Media, where it did appear. Hence the decree must have been issued when the court was there during the summer of the year 539–538. Darius fully honored the decree and ordered that the costs of construction be paid out of the royal treasury (Ezra 6:1–15). The temple was completed in the sixth year of Darius (Ezra 6:15), on the third day of the month Adar, which would have been March 12, 515 B.C.

The governmental procedures and practices that Darius I initiated continued more or less intact through the two centuries of Persian history down to the days of Alexander the Great. But of course there were variations. For one thing, the number of provinces apparently varied slightly from time to time. And within the provinces there were dozens of ethnic groups or "nations," frequently mentioned in Greek or Persian sources. The 127 provinces of Esther 1:1 and the 120 of Daniel 6:1 are to be understood as groups of peoples or ethnic districts within the satrapies, and should not be thought to conflict with the official numbers of twenty or twenty-three satrapies. Though the Hebrews spoke of provinces of Judah and Samaria, they were only subdistricts in the fifth Persian satrapy.

Darius died near the end of November 486 B.C. and his son Xerxes, who reigned 485–465, ascended the throne. Xerxes was the king's Greek name; in the Old Testament he is known as Ahasuerus (Ezra 4:6; Est. 1:1; etc.), a rough equivalent of his Persian name. As Ahasuerus he appears as the husband of Esther. When Darius died Xerxes inherited his two major tasks. First he had to suppress a revolt in Egypt, which had flared up just before his father's death, and then he had to deal with the Greek problem. Within about a year he thoroughly squelched the Egyptian rebellion. The Greek challenge was quite another matter.

Darius had fought major contests with the Greeks and had suffered a great defeat at their hands at Marathon in 490. He died while preparing for a return contest with the Greeks. The banquet referred to in the book of Esther, when Xerxes deposed Queen Vashti, sought to entertain the notables he had gathered for the strategy session preparatory to the invasion of Greece. Subsequently the Persians suffered major defeats at Salamis and Plataea in Greece and at Mount Mycale on the Ionian shore. After these fiascos of 480 and 479, Xerxes sought to bury his sorrows in attention to his harem. He brought Esther into the palace in the seventh year of his reign, 479 (Esther 2:16).

After Xerxes, Artaxerxes I ruled Persia, from 464 to 424. Records of his reign are sparse, so it is not as well documented as other Persian administrations. We do know that during the first twenty years of his reign he was involved in considerable warfare, but a treaty with Athens in 445 brought an end to that. Thereafter the reign of Artaxerxes seems to have been peaceful, and the king enjoyed a reputation for mildness and magnanimity.

Evidently Artaxerxes I, rather than Artaxerxes II (404–359 B.C.) figures in the narrative of Ezra and Nehemiah. This is the general, though not universal, conclusion of scholarship today. Ezra led a second contingent of Jews to Jerusalem in the seventh year of Artaxerxes I, 458 B.C. (Ezra 7:1, 8). It is clear, then, that the narrative of Ezra has a gap of over fifty-seven years between chapters 6 and 7. Chapter 6 ends with the dedication of the temple in 515, in the sixth year of Darius. Chapter 7 picks up the account in the seventh year of Artaxerxes (458).

Between the two chapters occurred the reign of Xerxes. Since Esther was married to Xerxes, the story of Esther must be placed between Ezra 6 and 7. The events of the book of Nehemiah occurred later in the reign of Artaxerxes. Nehemiah returned to Jerusalem in the twentieth year of Artaxerxes, 444 B.C., to rebuild the walls (Nehemiah 2:1) and made a second visit to Jerusalem in the thirty-second year of Artaxerxes, 443 B.C. (Nehemiah 13:6).

During the fourth century B.C. the Persian Empire gradually declined. In the earlier history of the Empire, the Persian royal family had generally pulled together and maintained effective control of the empire. The fourth century saw an increasing amount of squabbling in the extended ruling family. The young king Darius III had taken the throne only two years before Alexander the Great attacked. And he did so after a series of murders that left bitter competing factions among the high nobles of the court. While the royal family was at odds with itself, powerful satraps shook the control of the central authority during the century in a series of revolts. Some ruled their provinces almost as private kingdoms.

Further, in an effort to bring tighter integration of the populace, Darius III's predecessors had discarded the traditional policy of religious tolerance for subject peoples and began to put pressure on all to become Zoroastrians. The resulting revolts illustrated the declining loyalty to the Persian government. Jews, Egyptians, and Babylonians especially objected to this loss of religious freedom and welcomed Alexander as liberator.

Finally, the Persian monarchy of the fourth century did not pay the kind of attention to the economic health of the empire that Darius I and his immediate successors had. So inflation, depressed wages, and a heavy tax burden made the populace increasingly less enthusiastic about the maintenance of the empire.

The Hellenistic Period— Alexander and His Successors

When Alexander the Great invaded the Persian Empire, he had to fight only two major battles before taking Palestine (the story of his conquests appears in the chapter on Greece). The Battle of the Granicus River (334 B.C.) opened to him all of Asia

Coins of the cities of Antioch (left, the capital) and Seleucia (right, its port) of the Seleucid Kingdom

Minor and the Battle of Issus (333) permitted him to move south into Syria and Palestine almost without opposition.

During 332 Alexander proceeded down the Mediterranean coast. As along the Aegean, here one of his goals was to take the ports of the Persian navy and so to neutralize the fleet without having to build one of his own. Most towns capitulated but Tyre did not and suffered through a seven-month siege. When Alexander finally took the city he destroyed it, executed many of the inhabitants, and sold the rest into slavery. Gaza also resisted and held out against him for two months. When it fell, he killed all the males and sold the women and children into slavery. Jerusalem surrendered to him without a struggle, and the outlying towns apparently also received him with kindness. Josephus tells a dramatic account of how the high priest, Jaddua, went out in procession with the priests and many of the populace to welcome Alexander. The conqueror then reportedly offered sacrifice in the temple and promised to permit the Jews in Judah and the eastern provinces to practice their religion without interference.[79] Though this account is frequently considered to be unhistorical in many of its details, it at least reflects the generally good relations between Alexander and the Jews.

Alexander did not live long after taking Palestine. When he died in Babylon in 323 B.C., members of his inner circle began a struggle to take over his empire. Soon it became clear that no one of them could succeed in doing so. Details of the contest are not important for this account, but a general statement is useful.

Ptolemy became satrap of Egypt in 323 B.C. and sought in addition to control Cyprus, Cyrenaica (modern Libya), and Palestine. In fact, he invaded Palestine four times between 318 and 301, holding it briefly during the first three occupations. His dynasty then controlled it for the next hundred years, from 301 until 198. The victory of the Seleucids at the battle of Panium (198) resulted in the transfer of Palestine to the Seleucids.

The hundred years of Ptolemaic control of Palestine are important to the history of Judaism. Jews were at first forcibly taken to Egypt, to Alexandria especially, and later were welcomed there. Many settled in Alexandria. Gradually they forgot their Hebrew and between 250 and 150 B.C. they translated their Bible (our Old Testament) into Greek (the Septuagint). In time some Jews of Palestine and Egypt also modified their thought patterns, accepting aspects of non-supernaturalistic Hellenism and the pagan lifestyle that went with it. Hellenistic ways caught on more readily under the Ptolemies and the early Seleucids because at that time they were not forced on the populace, and Jews were generally well treated.

Seleucus received the Babylonian satrapy in the second partition of Alexander's empire (321). A successful warrior, he eventually managed to bring almost the whole of Alexander's empire except Egypt under his control. After he took Syria, he founded his new capital there at Antioch-on-the-Orontes. The fortunes of the Seleucid dynasty fluctuated greatly over the years but reached a high point during the reign of Antiochus III, the Great (223–187). He conquered Palestine in 198, taking advantage of the weakness of Egypt while the infant Ptolemy V had come to the throne there. When Antiochus came to Jerusalem, the inhabitants reportedly gave him a cordial welcome, apparently hoping to exploit this new relationship to their advantage.

But near the end of his reign Antiochus suffered a disastrous defeat at the hands of the Romans. This cost him much territory in Asia Minor, the surrender of his navy, and a huge indemnity. Collection of funds to pay off the indemnity to Rome rested heavily on the Jews, along with other peoples of the Seleucid kingdom. And, as sovereigns, the Seleucid kings now reserved the right to appoint the high priests of the Jews and through them to maintain Seleucid sovereignty over their people. Both actions were destined to create serious friction between the Jews and the Syrian monarchy. Moreover, in the background was a Seleucid effort to force the Jews to accept Hellenistic religious practices (including the ruler cult) in an effort to unify their people for the defense of their realm against the Romans.

Parenthetically, the impact of Hellenism in Palestine during the Ptolemaic and Seleucid periods resulted in part from the founding of Greek colonies there since Alexander's conquests—of Sebaste (Samaria), Philadelphia (Amman), Ptolemais (Acre), Philoteria (south of the Sea of Galilee), Scythopolis (Beth-Shean), and Marisa (Mareshah) in the Judean foothills.

Friction between Seleucids and Jews need not have brought on a Jewish revolt, however, if the Jews had remained united. As a matter of fact they did not, and the divisions not only provided opportunity for the Seleucids to exploit the differences but also seemed to require that they take action to maintain order. When the Seleucids occupied Palestine, they initially upheld Jewish customs and exempted the temple in Jerusalem from taxes. Onias III, an orthodox Jew, served as high priest. By the time Antiochus IV (175–163 B.C.) came to the Seleucid throne, however, many Jews had become so hellenized that they wanted change in the religious system.

At that point apparently some accused Onias of pro-Ptolemaic leanings, and his brother Joshua paid a huge bribe for appointment as high priest and the right to build a gymnasium in Jerusalem (2 Maccabees 4:8–10). Taking the Greek name Jason, Joshua proceeded to build the gymnasium, to introduce athletic competition in the nude, and to encourage other actions totally repugnant to orthodox Jews. The orthodox organized under the name *Hasidim* (the pious ones), a movement from which the Pharisees eventually arose.

After three years in office (175–172 B.C.) Jason was deposed by a close associate, Menelaus, who outbid him in the bribery game (2 Maccabees 4:23–26), and Jason fled to Transjordan. Menelaus proved to be an even more thoroughgoing Hellenist than Jason, and more unscrupulous as well. He helped himself to temple assets to pay off his debt to Antiochus. Jason waited impatiently in Transjordan for a chance to regain his lost position. Finally, in 168 B.C., when Antiochus was busy with a military campaign in Egypt, Jason raised a force and attacked Jerusalem. The disorders that followed evidently were clashes primarily between those loyal to Jason and Menelaus and those of the pro-Egyptian and pro-Syrian factions, but Antiochus chose to regard them as open rebellion against his rule. He sent a force to Jerusalem that broke down the walls, destroyed many houses, slaughtered countless inhabitants, and built a fortified citadel for a Syrian garrison.

Then in 167 B.C., realizing that Jewish opposition against him rose ultimately from their religion, Antiochus decided to destroy Judaism. He made religious observances such as circumcision and Sabbath keeping and the possession of a copy of the Law punishable by death. The temple was dedicated to the Olympian Zeus, and it was desecrated with a sacrifice of swine on the altar. Worship of heathen gods became compulsory.

Maccabean Revolt and Jewish Statehood

Response to these severe measures was predictable. Some capitulated, some offered passive resistance, and some decided to fight for their faith. The spark that touched off open revolt was struck at the mountain village of Modin, west of Jerusalem. There a priest named Mattathias lived with his five sons. When a royal officer came to town to enforce the decree requiring the Jews to perform pagan sacrifice, Mattathias killed a Jew who was about to offer sacrifice, as well as the officer. Then he fled to the hills with his sons, there to conduct guerrilla warfare. The insurgents raided towns and villages, killing Syrian officers and Hellenized Jews who supported them. A few months after the beginning of the struggle Mattathias died, but before he did he saw to it that the mantle of leadership fell on his third son, Judas, "the Maccabee" (interpreted to mean "the hammer").

Judas received increasing numbers of recruits from the towns and villages. Both because the Syrians underestimated the valor of Judas and the power of the Maccabees and because they had to deal with a revolt in Parthia to the east, they sent fairly small and inferior armies against the Jews. When Judas defeated them, the Syrians sent stronger forces. A particularly important victory at Emmaus permitted Judas to march on Jerusalem. As he entered the city, Menelaus and his supporters fled and Judas took everything but the fortified citadel. He was able to cleanse the temple, where for three years sacrifices had been offered to the Olympian Zeus, on the twenty-fifth of Chislev (December) 165 B.C. The day has been celebrated ever since as the Feast of Hanukkah (or Rededication or Lights).[80]

All did not go well for the Jews, however. Lysias, commander of the Syrian forces, now descended on Judah, defeated Judas near Jerusalem, and then besieged the capital. But in the Maccabees' blackest hour a sudden reversal occurred. With news of an enemy force marching on the Syrian capital of Antioch, Lysias now offered peace, repeal of the laws proscribing Judaism, removal of Menelaus from the high priesthood, and amnesty for Judas and his followers. The Hasidim accepted the terms because their goal of religious liberty had been achieved. Judas, not satisfied with anything less than full political liberty as well, left the city with a small force. Soon the new high priest, Alcimus, seized and executed a number of Hasidim, and Judas renewed the war. With greatly reduced forces, Judas was defeated and killed on the battlefield in 161 B.C.

To put the Maccabean conflict in proper perspective, it is necessary to recognize that the Jews were not united. The Maccabees drew much of their support from the rural peasants and faced the animosity of the well-to-do Hellenizing priests of Jerusalem and many of the upper classes of the city. The priests won over many of the followers of Judas so he faced the Syrians in a very weakened position and suffered defeat at their hands.

Jonathan, Judas' younger brother, now became leader of the band of Maccabees, who maintained themselves virtually as freebooters in the Wilderness of Tekoa, as David had, and in Transjordan. Jonathan constantly augmented his forces. Ultimately, the Syrian general, Bacchides, found it impossible to destroy Jonathan and made peace with him in 158 B.C. Thus, during the following five years Jonathan was able to consolidate his power. Meanwhile, the Seleucids, through their dynastic quarrels, proceeded to commit national suicide and gave Jonathan a chance to gain by diplomacy what Judas had not been able to accomplish by force of arms.

In the Seleucid struggle between the pretender Balas Alexander and Demetrius I (after 153 B.C.), Jonathan received generous offers from both sides. The latter withdrew almost all Syrian garrisons from Judea, and the former appointed him military and civil governor of Judea. Jonathan threw in his lot with Balas, who killed Demetrius I in 150 B.C. When Balas was assassinated five years later, Jonathan was strong enough to stand up to the Syrian Demetrius II. His brother Simon became military governor of coastal Palestine from Tyre to the Egyptian border. Although one of Balas' generals killed Jonathan in 143 B.C., the Maccabean cause was too well established to be snuffed out. Simon rushed to Jerusalem and took over leadership of the nationalist movement and gained independence of the Jews from Syria the following year.

With *Simon*, the Hasmonean line took over rule of the Jews and held sway until the Roman conquest in 63 B.C. The name *Hasmonean* is thought to be derived from an ancestor of the Maccabeans named Asmoneus. In 141 B.C. the Jews conferred on

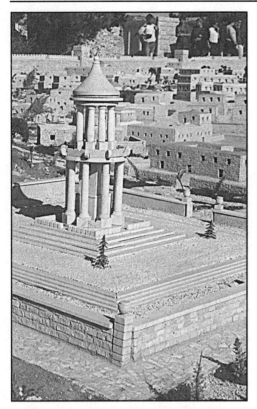

The Alexander Jannaeus monument in the Jerusalem model at the Holyland Hotel in West Jerusalem

Simon (142–135 B.C.), as noted, won for himself and his posterity permanent authority as ruling high priests and the recognition of Rome. Moreover, he secured Joppa as a Jewish harbor and conquered Gazara (Gezer), Beth-zur, and the Acra (or citadel) in Jerusalem where Seleucids had continued to hold out. When in 138 B.C. Simon rejected the demands of Antiochus VII for return of these conquests, the Syrian Antiochus attacked the Jewish state. Simon's sons repulsed Antiochus, and he did not renew the attack during Simon's lifetime. As with other sons of Mattathias, however, Simon also met a violent death. The governor of Jericho assassinated him and two of his sons in 135 B.C. But John Hyrcanus, a third son, was in Gezer at the time and escaped to become the next high priest (1 Maccabees 16:18).

John Hyrcanus (135–104 B.C.) began his reign fighting for his life and his kingdom but ended it with the Jewish state at the height of its power. Antiochus VII of Syria attacked Hyrcanus at the beginning of his reign, devastated Judea, forced the surrender of Jerusalem and the payment of a huge indemnity, and then compelled Hyrcanus and a Jewish army to accompany Antiochus in a renewed war against the Parthians on his eastern front. But there Antiochus met more than his match and committed suicide to avoid capture (129 B.C.). The lifting of the strong hand of Antiochus from Syrian affairs was very beneficial to Hyrcanus; for the next several decades Syria was convulsed by dynastic struggles.

Hyrcanus was avowedly expansionistic. First he reestablished control of the coastal cities of Palestine and promoted the development of Jewish commerce. Then he conquered east of the Jordan and followed that with the capture of Shechem and the destruction of the Samaritan temple on Mount Gerizim. Next he subjugated the Idumeans (Edomites) in the south and forced them to accept Judaism and be circumcised.

Internally the Jewish state changed significantly too. It transformed itself from a religious community into a secular state. Though the Hellenistic party as a separate group disappeared with Syrian interference

Simon and his descendants permanent authority as ruling high priests (1 Maccabees 14:25–49), and the Roman senate recognized him as a friendly independent ruler (1 Maccabees 14:16–19, 24; 15:15–24). In international affairs, for the next eighty years the Romans valued the Hasmonean dynasty as a counterbalance to the Seleucid state. Thus for a relatively short time the Jews did have national independence subsequent to the Babylonian captivity.

Domestically, the Hasmoneans depended on the aristocratic Sadducean party with its power base in the Temple. Partially Hellenized, this sect usually contested with the Pharisees—with their power base especially in the synagogue—for control of the public at large. The Hasmoneans gradually increased their military strength, expanded their borders in all directions, and transformed their body politic from a religious community into a secular state on Greek lines.

in Jewish affairs, its views were perpetuated by the Sadducees, as the views of the Hasidim were perpetuated by the Pharisees. These two parties, so prominent in the New Testament, first surfaced during Hyrcanus' reign. Hyrcanus publicly aligned himself with the Sadducees, but he was safely Jewish (reflective of his Hasidic background), having brought both the Samaritans and Edomites to heel. Thus he did not unduly upset the more conservative elements of the realm. But his sons received an education in Greek culture and tended to repudiate the Pharisees.

Aristobulus (104–103 B.C.), the eldest of those sons, emerged as victor in the dynastic struggle that erupted after the death of Hyrcanus. Then he proceeded to imprison his brothers and his mother to guarantee his position as chief of state. It is said that his mother starved to death in prison, and he unjustly executed his brother Antigonus for his alleged involvement in a plot against him. Aside from these family tragedies, he apparently ruled well. He continued the expansionist policies of his father and extended Jewish rule into Galilee. He also continued the Hasmonean tendency to transform the religious community into a secular state, adopting the title *Philhellene* ("love of things Greek") and taking the title of king.

When Aristobulus died from drink and disease, his widow, Salome Alexandra, released his brothers from prison and married the eldest, *Alexander Jannaeus* (103–76 B.C.). Jannaeus continued the expansionistic policies of his predecessors, and by the time he died he had extended the borders of the Jewish state to include almost all the territory that Solomon had ruled. Jannaeus was almost constantly at war, however, and more than once suffered almost total disaster. Defeated by Ptolemy Lathyrus of Egypt, he was saved by the forces of Cleopatra III, who headed another faction in the Egyptian government (100 B.C.). Suffering complete destruction of his army at the hands of Obadas, the Nabatean king (94 B.C.), he faced a violent rebellion when he returned to Jerusalem without his army. This rebellion had also been occasioned by Jannaeus' violation of temple ritual at the Feast of Tabernacles. At that time the crowd had assaulted him for his impiety and he had called in troops to restore order, resulting in the death of a large number of defenseless people (Josephus said 6,000). The rebels then called on Demetrius III of Syria to champion their cause.

It is sometimes stated categorically that the Pharisees, usually pacifistic, were responsible for the rebellion and the Syrian alliance, but it is not certain that the Pharisees had instigated the violence. At any rate, a rebellion did take place and the Syrian king did decisively defeat Jannaeus, forcing him to flee to the Judean hills. At that point, apparently many Jews began to fear Syrian annexation of Palestine, and six thousand Jews transferred their loyalty to Jannaeus, enabling him to regain the throne. After he had reestablished his control, Jannaeus hunted down his enemies and crucified about eight hundred of them.[81] Subsequently Jannaeus suffered defeat at the hands of the Nabatean king Aretas, but again managed to restore his personal and national power.

When Jannaeus died, his widow *Salome Alexandra* (76–67 B.C.) succeeded him on the throne, as she had when Aristobulus, her first husband, died. Because she was a woman she could not exercise the high priesthood, so her eldest son, Hyrcanus II, filled that position. Her more able second son, Aristobulus II, received command of the army. The Pharisees, who had enjoyed little influence under earlier Hasmonean rulers, now played an important role in the government and for the first time were admitted to the Sanhedrin. This change in their fortunes seems due in part to the fact that Alexandra's brother was the famous Pharisee, Simon ben Shetach. As a whole, Alexandra's reign was peaceful and prosperous. The only military action of her reign, taken against Damascus, was unsuccessful. She was saved from a potentially disastrous invasion by the king of Armenia by bribing him and especially by Roman attack on his domain. When she died at the age of seventy-three, the days of Jewish independence were nearing an end. Though Jannaeus had established control over an extended territory, his hold upon it was somewhat tenous (as implied above), and Roman power loomed on the horizon.

As a matter of fact, it was sparring between Alexandra's two sons that gave the Romans a chance to add Palestine to their empire. Hyrcanus II, the elder son and legitimate successor, was weak and incompetent. Aristobulus II, the younger son, was more aggressive and had control of his father's veteran troops. Three months after the death of Alexandra, Aristobulus managed to defeat the forces of Hyrcanus II at Jericho, and the latter gave up all rights to the high priesthood and the crown and retired to private life.

All might have gone well for Aristobulus had it not been for the ambition of Antipater, military governor of Idumea and father of Herod the Great. Antipater saw that he could manipulate the weak Hyrcanus II but had no future under a strong leader like Aristobulus. So he arranged with Aretas, king of the Nabateans (with their capital at Petra), to put Hyrcanus on the throne in exchange for some towns on the Nabatean frontier. Meanwhile the Roman general Pompey had become involved in conquests in the East, in Pontus and Armenia. In 66 B.C. one of his lieutenants visited Judea, where he heard appeals from representatives of both brothers and made some tentative decisions, pending the later actions of Pompey. When Pompey came to Damascus in 63 B.C., he heard appeals from Hyrcanus and Aristobulus and the Jewish people, who wanted abolition of the monarchy and return to priestly government. He promised a decision after a campaign against the Nabateans.

When Pompey's general, Gabinius, returned, he found that Aristobulus had locked the gates of Jerusalem against him. Gabinius then issued an arrest warrant for Aristobulus. Presently the followers of Hyrcanus opened the city gates, and Pompey launched a siege of Aristobulus' forces holding out on the Temple hill. When the battle was over Palestine passed under Roman rule. All non-Jewish areas (the Mediterranean coastlands, Transjordan, and Samaria) were detached from the Jewish state, and what was left was placed under the rule of Hyrcanus II as high priest. Thus the kingship was abolished, as the representatives of the Jews had asked, and Hyrcanus II (with Antipater at his elbow) controlled the Jewish state, at the pleasure of the Romans. Aristobulus was then taken to Rome, where he marched in Pompey's triumph, along with many Jews who were sold into slavery in the capital. In later years, as they won their freedom, they became the nucleus of the Jewish community there.

During the whole Maccabean/Hasmonean period the government could not operate effectively and efficiently. At first the Jews fought to establish their independence. Having done so, they still faced occasional intrusions of either Syrian or Egyptian forces—sometimes invited in by a faction in Israel. Then they experienced the occasional revolution, as in the days of Alexander Jannaeus. And strife persisted between Pharisees and Sadducees. Under these chaotic circumstances, it became difficult to establish government agencies and make them operate efficiently. It also proved difficult to put in place a workable taxing system for the support of the government.

Roman Rule in Palestine

The Confusing Period of the Roman Civil Wars

After Palestine passed under Roman rule in 63 B.C., it became embroiled in Roman politics. So over the following decades there were factions loyal to Hyrcanus II, Aristobulus II, Pompey, Julius Caesar, Mark Antony, Augustus, Herod the Great, and others. It is very difficult for even the best informed scholar to follow accurately the history of the period.

Some details are clear, however. First, Hyrcanus II continued as high priest and ruler of the Jews during the confused period from 63 to 40 B.C. For almost all those years, Antipater was the real power in the state and faithfully carried out Roman policies. Second, the Aristobulus faction did not easily give up trying to regain power. Aristobulus II's son Alexander stirred up rebellions in 57, 56 and 55 B.C. and both Aristobulus II and Alexander were assassinated by Pompey or his supporters when

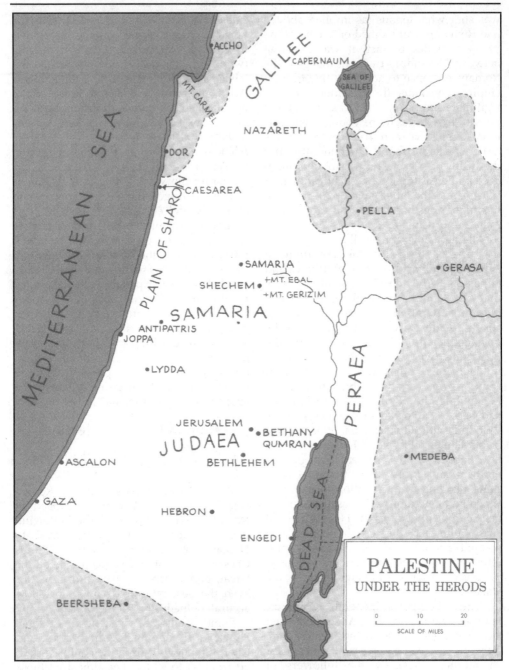

PALESTINE
UNDER THE HERODS

SCALE OF MILES
0   10   20

they tried to help Julius Caesar in 49 B.C. Third, after Pompey's defeat at the hands of Julius Caesar in 48 B.C., Hyrcanus II and Antipater became loyal supporters of Caesar. In appreciation, Caesar confirmed their political position in Judah, added some of the Mediterranean coastland in Palestine to the Jewish province, and

showed numerous favors to Jews of the Dispersion, many of which continued under subsequent rulers. Fourth, after the assassination of Julius Caesar (44 B.C.), Hyrcanus II and now Herod gave their loyalty to Mark Antony, who appointed Herod and his brother Phasael tetrarchs of Judea (41 B.C.), with the approval of Hyrcanus II.

Fifth, at that point the Parthians on Rome's eastern frontier took advantage of her political and military weakness and invaded Syria and Palestine. They made Antigonus, son of Aristobulus II, king and high priest of the Jews (40–37 B.C.). The Jews hailed the Parthians as deliverers from the Romans, and all classes supported the rule of Aristobulus II. When Hyrcanus and Phasael went to negotiate with the Parthian king, he threw them in prison, where Phasael committed suicide; Hyrcanus was carried off to Babylonia. Herod put his family in the fortress of Masada for protection and went to Rome to get help from Antony. He was appointed king of the Jews in 40 B.C. Of course the Romans counterattacked. Herod managed to rescue his family and with Roman help eventually took much of Palestine. After the fall of Jerusalem to the Romans in (37 B.C.), Antony ordered the execution of Antigonus.

Roman arrangements under Pompey. With Pompey's conquest (63 B.C.), completed by Gabinius, who was proconsul of Syria 57–55 B.C., Rome divided Palestine into numerous units. Pompey freed the Greek cities (e.g., Gaza, Joppa) that the Jews had controlled since the days of John Hyrcanus (135–104) and made them autonomous enclaves under the supervision of the Roman proconsul in Syria. He joined most of those east of the Jordan in a new League of Ten Cities or the Decapolis (Matthew 4:25; Mark 5:20; 7:31). Some of the better known cities of this group were Philadelphia (Amman), Gerasa (Jerash), Pella, Scythopolis (Beth Shan), and Gadara. Samaria became independent, while Judea, Perea, and Galilee were ruled by the Jews (also under the supervision of the Roman proconsul in Syria).

Roman arrangements under Herod. Herod the Great persuaded the Roman Senate to appoint him king of the Jews, giving him Judea, Idumea, Perea, and Samaria. But when Herod returned to Palestine, he had to fight to take the granted territory. By 37 B.C. he was successful in conquering Judea, Idumea, Perea, Samaria, Galilee, and the port of Joppa.

After Augustus became master of the Roman world in 31 B.C., he confirmed Herod in his rule of the territories he now controlled and gave him several cities in the coastal plain. Later he added the Golan Heights (Gaulanitis) and Panias (the area of Caesarea Philippi) and gave him the task of pacifying the region to the east of Gaulanitis. So, Herod's kingdom at its height included almost all the territory between the Dead Sea and the Jordan rift and the Mediterranean, and nearly all the east bank of the Jordan as well.

Herod held the position of an allied king, with local autonomy but subject to Rome in foreign affairs. Rome used him like other allied kings to pacify a recalcitrant frontier province and prepare it for a stage when Rome could directly appoint governors. Those direct appointees ruled Judea in the days of Jesus and Paul, when such governors as Pilate, Felix, and Festus held the reins of government. Herod's pacification of territory east of the Jordan also made possible organization of the Roman province of Arabia.

Herod also served the Romans as an agent for the spread of Hellenism, which he greatly admired. Rome sought to bring unity to the empire through the inculcation of a single Greco-Roman culture and through establishment of the emperor cult.

Roman arrangements under Herod's sons and the procurators. After Herod died in 4 B.C (our Julian calendar is slightly in error, placing Jesus' birth about 6 B.C.), Augustus divided his kingdom among his three living sons, as the dead king had wished. Archelaus received Judea, Idumea, and Samaria; Herod Antipas got Galilee and Perea; and Philip was awarded the area east and northeast of the Sea of Galilee. Herod's sister, Salome, won the cities of Azotus and Jamnia on the Mediterranean and Phasaelis in the Jordan Valley.

Archelaus proved to be a dismal failure in his rule. The Romans banished him in A.D. 6 and handed his lands over to a Roman procurator. Herod Antipas continued to rule until A.D. 39, when he fell out of favor with the emperor Caligula. And Philip died a natural death in A.D. 34.

Caligula granted the lands of Philip to Agrippa I in A.D. 37, and lands of Herod Antipas to Agrippa in A.D. 39. Then in A.D. 41 the emperor Claudius gave Agrippa the territory that Archelaus had ruled. Thus, from A.D. 41 to 44 he controlled almost all of the kingdom of Herod the Great. When Agrippa I died in A.D. 44 (Acts 12), the Romans decided to return to the procurators lands they had controlled earlier (Idumea, Judea, Perea, Samaria), plus Galilee. Agrippa II ruled the tetrarchy of Philip, A.D. 50 to about 100 (cf. Acts 25–26).

The Herods and Their Construction Projects

The Herods, and especially Herod the Great, literally changed the landscape of Palestine with their building projects. Peter Richardson in his 1996 biography of Herod lists eighteen building projects in Jerusalem and twenty-seven outside Jerusalem but within his territories.[82] He did some of this to placate the Jews (e.g., the temple in Jerusalem); some to provide his defense needs (e.g., Herodium and Masada); and some to indulge his own vanity and to impress observers with the splendor of his kingdom (e.g., his palace in Jerusalem).

But in addition he built all over the eastern part of the Roman Empire: ten projects in Phoenicia and Syria and fifteen in Asia Minor and Greece.[83] Herod's goal was to improve his standing with the governments and peoples of the East, in part so they would not hinder Jews from sending the annual temple tax to Jerusalem, and in part to improve the lot of the Jews in the East and so to curry favor with the Palestinian populace.

Herod the Great—in Jerusalem

Of course pride of place among all Herod's projects was the rebuilding of the temple—of the second temple, that had stood in its then present condition since the sixth year of Darius I of Persia (515 B.C., Ezra 6:15). Herod doubled the temple area with the construction of great supporting walls and the leveling of the surface inside. The western wall is the longest (1,590 feet) and the eastern wall somewhat shorter (1,536 feet). The southern wall is the shortest (912 feet) and the northern wall a little longer than that (1,035 feet). So the trapezoidal area was almost a mile in circumference.

The retaining walls of the Temple Mount rose ninety-eight feet above the paved area at the foot of the mount. And in some places the lower courses of these walls, always planted on bedrock, go as far down as sixty-five feet below the street, making walls at such a point more than 165 feet high. Most of the stones in these walls weighed two to five tons. But in the southwest corner of the Temple Mount are stones that weigh about fifty tons apiece. And in the western wall may be seen larger stones yet. One of these is forty feet long, ten feet high, and thirteen feet thick and weighs some four hundred tons.[84] Stupendous as these stones are, they are still not the largest in the ancient world. A few decades later, at Baalbek in Lebanon, engineers put in place numerous large stones, the three largest measuring about sixty-four feet long, fourteen feet high, and eleven feet thick and each weighing some one thousand tons.

JERUSALEM DURING THE DAYS OF THE APOSTLES

Jerusalem round A.D. 50, when the church was getting established, had a circumference of about 3.5 miles. Though scholars debate the population figure, probably it was about a hundred thousand.

The Temple area, in the center of the eastern side of the city, comprised about a tenth of the total area of the city. At the northwest corner of the Temple stood the Antonia Fortress, which not only protected the Temple and its treasures but also protected the city and helped to keep order when the droves of pilgrims descended on Jerusalem during the pilgrimage feasts (Passover, etc.). North of the Temple area lay the sheep pool and market. Just to the west, inside the second wall were the markets of Jerusalem and the living quarters of those who worked there. Outside the

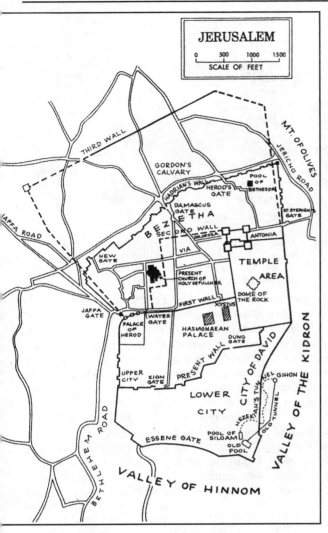

JERUSALEM

SCALE OF FEET
0 500 1000 1500

Caiaphas' palace stood there. And there was a market, the upper market, surrounded with colonnades and shops. The streets of the Upper city were laid out at right angles in a checkerboard fashion. Perched on the eastern edge of the hill, overlooking the Tyropoeon Valley, stood Herod's theater.

Below in the Tyropoeon, in the Lower City, crowded small houses of the poor. And farther east, where the Tyropoeon and the Hinnom join, was an industrial quarter, where there were weaveries, potteries, and tanneries. Nearby lay the Pool of Siloam. And up the Tyropoeon Valley a short distance sprawled Herod's hippodrome. On the east side of Jerusalem, south of the Temple mount, still part of the Lower City, crowded houses for the poor, and an area where the Zealots had their headquarters.

A chiseled frame around the edge of each stone characterizes Herodian stone masonry, with each course of masonry set an inch or so further in than the one below it, for aesthetic reasons. That way the wall would not appear to lean but to stand up straight.

Herod began construction of the temple in his eighteenth year (20–19 B.C.). His men built the temple building in a year and a half, while the courts and porticoes required eight years. Josephus said that construction and repairs continued into the reign of Nero (A.D. 54–68; *Antiquities*, XX.9.7). Moreover, John 2:20 says that it took forty-six years to build the temple. Scholars argue over whether the Greek indicates that it was complete then (when Jesus was about thirty) or was still in the process of construction. Probably the latter is true.

second wall, was the wood market and then south of that the place of execution (Calvary).

On the west side of the city there was a gate in the wall where the present Jaffa Gate stands. South of it rose the three towers connected with Herod's palace, the soldiers' barracks, and Herod's palace itself. East of that complex lay the area of the Upper City, the southwest hill. This was the elegant section of Jerusalem. Houses of the elite stood there—structures of a Hellenistic sort with rooms grouped around courtyards open to the sky and equipped with gardens and pools. A Hasmonean palace and

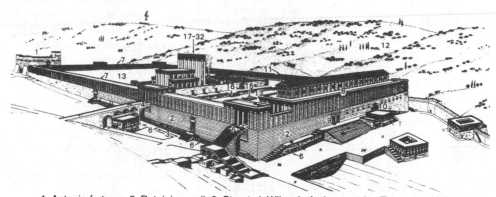

1. Antonia fortress 2. Retaining wall 3. Street 4. Wilson's Arch, spanning Tyropeoen Valley 5. Robinson's Arch, leading to street below 6. Shops 7. Porticoes/stoa 9. Exit gate 10. Entrance gate 11. Solomon's Portico (pre-Herodian) 12. Mount of Olives 13. Court of Gentiles 14. Entrance to platform 15. Exit from platform 16. Steps and railing prohibiting Gentiles

Along the southern side of the temple area broad stairways led through a triple gate at the southeast and a double gate at the southwest. These steps, as excavated, have special significance for modern Bible students. Jesus must have walked there, and the apostles must have preached on these stairways on the Day of Pentecost and subsequently.

Along the southern edge of the Temple Mount extended the Royal Stoa—a Roman basilica with a higher central aisle (nave) and two lower side aisles. Four rows of forty Corinthian columns each supported the roof.

At the eastern end of the nave the Sanhedrin (the supreme Jewish legislative, religious, and judicial body) met in a semi-circular apse. The northern colonnade was open and provided access to the temple court—the Court of the Gentiles. Business could be conducted in the Stoa and the adjacent court. Pilgrims from abroad could change money into the sacred shekels there so they could pay their temple tax and buy sacrificial animals.

A tunnel ran under the Royal Stoa and led to the Court of the Gentiles, where anyone could go. This court was separated from the area reserved for Jews by a railing about 4.5 feet high. On this railing warning notices forbade Gentiles further access. Excavators found one of these inscriptions in 1871 and it may now be seen in the Archaeological Museum in Istanbul. Translated from the Greek it reads, "Let no foreigner enter within the screen and enclosure surrounding the sanctuary. Whosoever is taken so doing will be the cause that death overtaketh him."[85] That this prohibition had real force is clear from Acts 21:28, where a mob scene erupted when a rumor spread

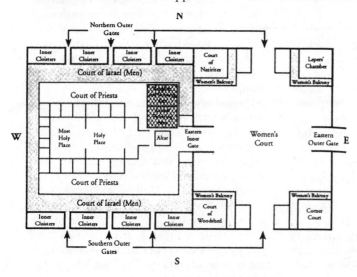

Plan of the interior of or Jewish section of Herod's temple

Part of the inscription forbidding Gentiles from entering the Temple area, from the Archaeological Museum, Istanbul

that the apostle Paul had taken Trophimus, a Gentile, into the inner precincts. This fracas led to Paul's arrest and ultimately to his trial before Nero's court in Rome.

When Jewish worshipers moved on to the temple itself, they had to walk to the center of the temple area and turn left because the temple proper faced east. They passed the railing with its warning notices, climbed fourteen steps, crossed a terrace fif-

teen feet wide, and went up another five steps to the inner wall with its ten gates. Inside this wall lay first the Court of the Women. Apparently a gallery enabled the women to see over the heads of the men into the Court of the Priests.

Men climbed fifteen more steps and went through a gate into the Court of the Israelites—for Jewish males who were not priests or Levites. There they could watch the priests at work from behind a low stone fence some eighteen inches high. In the court of the priests they saw the altar, the laver where priests washed their hands and feet, and the place where priests butchered animals.

From the Court of the Priests twelve steps led up to the temple, the front part of which (the Holy Place) contained a lampstand, a table for the showbread or the Bread of the presence, and an altar for burning incense. A curtain separated the Holy Place from the Most Holy Place, which in Herod's day stood completely empty. It was appropriate that it should be, for God was invisible. Even the ark had become something of a fetish in Old Testament times and had been treated almost as the God who could help them in their war

The Temple building itself, from the Jerusalem Model at the Holyland Hotel in West Jerusalem

The Western Wall or the Wailing Wall of the Temple

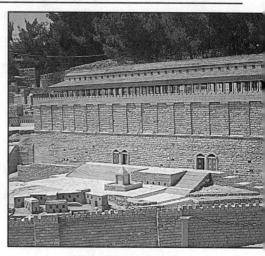

The south side of the Temple

against the Philistines (1 Samuel 4:3). Apparently the Babylonians destroyed the original Ark when they demolished Jerusalem and the temple in 586 B.C. (2 Kings 25:8–10), and it had not been replaced in the second temple. Only the high priest could enter the Most Holy Place—and that only on the Day of Atonement.

The façade of the temple was 150 feet across and 150 feet high. But behind this the building narrowed to 90 feet in width,

One of some thirty mikves or ritual immersion baths (pools or plastered cisterns hewn out of bedrock) near the Temple steps, where worshipers purified themselves before entering the sanctuary (steps for descent on the left). These answer the question of where the large numbers converted on the day of Pentecost might have been baptized (Acts 2:41).

though the ceiling was almost as high as the top of the façade. Entrance to the Holy Place was through two doors covered with gold, and on either side of the Holy Place were three stories containing rooms.

Herod's masons were busy elsewhere in Jerusalem too. At the northwest corner of the temple enclosure they built the Antonia Fortress. This was a logical move because much wealth needed to be protected in the form of expensive decoration and utensils for the temple rituals. And the temple and state treasuries were kept there, as was true of temples elsewhere in Mediterranean lands (for example, the Parthenon in Athens or the Temple of Saturn in the Forum at Rome).

Elsewhere in Jerusalem. To assure Herod's hold on the city of Jerusalem and to provide for his creature comforts, he built a palace and barracks on the west side of the city, just south of where the Jaffa Gate now stands. He enclosed this complex within its own separate wall. At the north of the compound he built three great towers to protect the palace. The biggest of the three was called Phasael, after his brother. Its base still stands inside the Old City and is commonly called "David's Tower." The lower part of it was a fortification, and the upper part was outfitted like a palace. It was 148 feet high. The second tower, named Hippicus for a friend of the king, stood 132 feet high. The third was called Mariamne after his

Herod's Palace, from the Jerusalem model at the Holyland Hotel in West Jerusalem

queen. A total of 74 feet high, it had luxurious residential quarters.

Between these towers and the palace stood barracks for Herod's soldiers. The palace itself consisted of two great buildings, each with banquet halls, baths, and bedrooms for hundreds of guests. Around the palace were groves of trees and ponds and bronze figures discharging water.

Herod's theater lay on the eastern edge of the hill of the upper city on what is now Mount Zion. Like all ancient Greco-Roman theaters, it was open to the sky and had seats arranged in step-like fashion in a semicircle and facing the stage. Players performed Greek and Roman plays there.

South of the Temple Mount in the Tyropoeon Valley, Herod built a hippodrome or stadium. This served primarily as a place for chariot races. Shaped like a giant hairpin, it had a rounded end and a straight end. Spectators sat on stair-like seats, and chariots raced around a spina (or divider) that ran down the middle of the structure.

Caesarea. Outside Jerusalem, Caesarea ranks as Herod's most spectacular building project. He constructed it on the site of Straton's Tower, a small town twenty-five miles north of Tel Aviv during the years 22–9 B.C. and named it for Augustus Caesar. When the Romans removed Herod Archelaus from the kingship in A.D. 6 and appointed procurators to rule Palestine, they made Caesarea the capital of the province. Caesarea became a prosperous city, half the size of Manhattan Island, with a population estimated at fifty thousand.

HEROD'S SHOWPIECE
ON THE MEDITERRANEAN

Outside Jerusalem, Caesarea ranks as Herod's most spectacular building project. On the site of Straton's Tower, twenty-five miles north of Tel Aviv, he built a city of

Herod's hippodrome, from the Jerusalem model at the Holyland Hotel in West Jerusalem

which he could be proud during the years 22–9 B.C. It enhanced his own reputation, strengthened his position with the emperor Augustus, for which it was named, and contributed to the prosperity of his realm through its commercial activities.

Its size was substantial—half the size of Manhattan Island in New York. Its design was exemplary—following the usual plan of a proper Hellenistic city. Laid out on a grid pattern, it had streets that intersected at right angles. A Greek-style theater that could seat 4,000 stood at the south end of the main street. To the northeast of town sprawled a spacious amphitheater.

The city's harbor was the first all-weather harbor on the Palestinian coast. The outer breakwater enclosed an area of about twenty-five acres. The body of the breakwater was built of conglomerate blocks that were composed of rubble and mortar poured into great wooden forms. The

concrete the Romans used was approximately equivalent to what we use today. They had available in unlimited quantities a volcanic sand, *pozzolana*, containing silica in suitable form for making mortar and concrete that would harden under water. Without knowing the chemical properties involved, they learned by a happy accident how to make concrete about as good as we can mix today.

Remains in the great barrel-vaulted warehouses of Caesarea's port revealed evidence of trade with North Africa, Spain, Italy, Syria, and the Aegean. Towering over the port rose a great platform on which Herod built a temple to the goddess Roma and the divine Augustus. Engineering along the waterfront made possible the regular flushing or scouring of the sewers with sea water—the only city on the Mediterranean with such amenities. Adjacent to the port stood a sumptuous palace, believed to belong to Herod. To provide plenty of good,

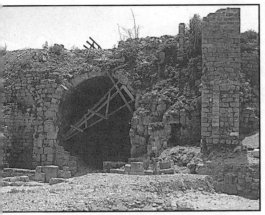

One of several warehouses excavated at Caesarea

safe drinking water, Herod built an aqueduct that tapped the springs on Mount Carmel, over six miles to the north.

Herod laid out the streets of his city in a checkerboard pattern. At least the main north-south street was paved with limestone blocks. He had the sewer system constructed in such a way that it would be constantly flushed by action of the sea—unique for a Mediterranean city. At the south end of the main street stood a theater that could probably hold about four thousand spectators. In the theater, excavators found a block with an inscription mentioning Pontius Pilate as the prefect of Judea in the reign of Tiberius, providing extra-biblical evidence of Pilate's existence. Just west of the theater on a little promontory stood a sumptuous building that excavators believe was Herod's palace. Fine mosaic floors are still visable there.

Herod provided an adequate water supply for Caesarea by means of a high-level aqueduct that brought good fresh water from springs on Mount Carmel, some six miles to the north. There was also a low-level aqueduct that brought water from the Zarqa River, about three miles away. Its date is uncertain, but it may have functioned as early as Herod's day to provide water for irrigation.

For his port Herod constructed a breakwater made of huge blocks of concrete that created the first protected harbor along the Palestinian coast. Overlooking the harbor to the east he erected a huge platform on which he built a temple to Augustus and the goddess Roma. South of the temple stood warehouses. Judging from objects found in them, trade was carried on with North Africa, Spain, Italy, and the Aegean. Herod also built an amphitheater northeast of the city. Its arena measured some 290 by 190 feet and compared favorably with the arena of the Colosseum in Rome (281 by 177 feet).

Masada. Of Herod's fortifications, Masada is the most impressive. An almost impregnable bastion, it rose some fifteen hundred feet above the Dead sea on an isolated mesa about two-thirds of the way down the western shore of that Sea. Its summit of twenty-three acres gave space for palaces, barracks for soldiers, and storerooms for military equipment and supplies of food.

Yigael Yadin of the Hebrew University in Jerusalem led an excavation team of professionals and thousands of volunteers there for two years, from 1963 to 1965. They accomplished an almost total excavation of the site. The exciting account appears in Yadin's *Masada* (1966).

Though the Hasmoneans had built some fortifications at Masada, and Herod had left his future wife Mariamne and members of her family there when he fled to Rome, Herod must have dismantled the earlier construction. Yadin found that almost everything on the site dated to Herod's day or later.

The temple to Augustus at Caesarea

A casemate wall (a double wall with the area between divided into rooms or compartments) about 4,250 feet in perimeter surrounded the boat-shaped rock, and had an abundance of defense towers. The excavators found about 110 rooms (or casemates) inside the wall and towers. The enclosed area provided space for four palaces—three small ones and a large one next to the western gate. The large western palace had four blocks of rooms: royal apartments, workshops, storerooms, and an administrative section with what the excavators identified as a throne room with a colored mosaic.

The theater of Caesarea

HEROD'S GREAT FORTRESS AT MASADA

As a famous royal citadel of Herod the Great and an emporium of ancient biblical manuscripts, Masada has tangential significance for biblical study. It was the last outpost of the Zealots during the Jewish War against Rome (A.D. 66–70/73) when 960 Jews fought to the death there. The account of its fall to the Romans has always been known from Josephus' *Wars of the Jews*.

Located about fifteen miles south of En-gedi on the western side of the Dead Sea, Masada is an isolated and largely inaccessible rock, narrow in the north and broad in the center. It measures about two thousand feet from north to south, a thousand feet from east to west, and has a sharp drop of thirteen hundred feet on the Dead Sea side. The Americans Edward Robinson and E. Smith first correctly identified the site in 1838. Though others worked there, Yigael Yadin led the major excavation from

The fortress of Masada

The aqueduct of Caesarea

The lower aqueduct of Caesarea

A Roman columbarium on Masada. Jars containing ashes of cremated individuals were put in the niches

1963 to 1965, which was an international undertaking in which thousands of volunteers from all over the world participated.

While there was some slight evidence of earlier occupation, the days of Herod the Great mark the real beginnings at Masada. Herod apparently launched construction by providing an adequate water supply through a system of dams and an aqueduct and cisterns. Twelve large cisterns with a capacity of 1,400,000 cubic feet were found on the slope, and additional cisterns were cut into the summit. Then Herod built a wall around the summit, about 1,530 yards long. About seventy rooms, thirty towers, and four gates were found in the wall.

At the northern tip of the rock, Herod built a three-tiered private villa and in the western part of the summit an official palace covering an area of nearly thirty-six thousand square feet and having three wings: royal apartments, servants' quarters/service wing, and storerooms; and there was an adjacent administrative building. Also on the summit were three small palaces, presumably for members of the royal family, as well as a swimming pool, a bathhouse, and storerooms.

Finds in the ruins included personal effects and skeletons of the defenders at the time of the first Jewish revolt against Rome, large collections of coins

dated from the individual years of the Jewish War (A.D. 66–70), more than seven hundred ostraca written in Hebrew or Aramaic and parts of fourteen biblical, as well as apocryphal and sectarian scrolls. The biblical scrolls include parts of Psalms, Genesis, Leviticus, Deuteronomy, and Ezekiel.

The Roman siege wall fortified with towers and the remains of eight Roman camps around the base of Masada are still clearly visible. After capturing the site, the Romans stationed a garrison there for forty years. A group of monks settled at Masada during the fifth and sixth centuries and built a small church there.

Roman catapult stones found at Masada

The three-tiered private villa of Herod at the northern tip of Masada

At the northernmost point of Masada, at the cliff's edge, stood a palace-villa built in three tiers. On the top level Herod built living quarters with a semicircular porch. The middle terrace, about sixty-five feet below the upper terrace, contained a circular building and was connected with the upper terrace by a staircase. The lower terrace lies some fifty feet below the middle terrace and contains a small bathhouse with a mosaic floor and plastered walls.

Machaerus. Another of Herod's forts was located at Machaerus (about thirty-eight miles south of Amman). It figured in the New Testament narrative in connection with the execution of John the Baptist on the demands of Herodias (Matthew 14:3–10; cf. Josephus, *Antiquities* XVIII.5.2). Initially the Hasmoneans had erected the fortress there on the southern border of Perea to defend against the Nabateans. Alexander Jannaeus (103–76 B.C.) built the fortress, and the Roman Gabinius destroyed it in 57 B.C. Herod the Great rebuilt it after he consolidated his hold on Palestine (37 B.C. ff.), and it served the Jewish rebels as an important bastion dur-

ing the war that resulted in the destruction of Jerusalem in A.D. 70.

The most important excavations at the site took place from 1978 to 1981 under the direction of Virgilio Corbo of the Franciscan order. The Herodian palace-fortress measured about 360 feet east to west and 195 feet north to south. A north-south corridor divided the palace into two blocks. The eastern section had a paved courtyard in the center flanked by baths on the south. The western part had a small court surrounded by columns. Several of the rooms showed traces of mosaic floors. The lower city, that provided housing for the palace personnel, has yet to be excavated.[86]

The Herodium. Among palaces outside Jerusalem Herod built one at the Herodium and another near Jericho. He constructed the Herodium on a spot (7.5 miles south of Jerusalem) where he enjoyed one of his most important victories over the Parthians and Hasmoneans in 40 B.C. Near the end of his life he gave orders that he be buried there.

The Herodium was a hill some two hundred feet high, on which a round building was erected. This consisted of two parallel

The mound of Machaerus

circular walls (diameter of the outer one was two hundred feet) with four towers extending from the outer wall at the points of the compass. Herod built three of them semicircular and the fourth round. Then he surrounded the walls with earth and stone, so the completed structure looks like a truncated cone.

He divided the inside of the palace-fortress into two parts, the eastern half occupied by a garden surrounded by columns and the western half by a bathhouse and various rooms. The eastern sector may have had three upper stories. The bath was a typical Roman bath with a dressing room and warm, hot, and cold rooms. It had mosaic floors and wall frescoes similar to some of those found in Pompeii. The hot bath had the usual form, with hot air passing under the floor and through pipes in the walls. A network of huge cisterns provided water for the site. A rectangular room about 35 by 50 feet was slightly remodeled for use as a synagogue during the first or second Jewish revolt (A.D. 67–70 or A.D. 132–135). Thus it ranks with the synagogue at Masada as among the earliest known.

The Lower Herodium sprawled at the foot of, and to the north of, the palace-fortress and contained a large pool—a kind of artificial lake, possibly for swimming or sailing small boats. Adjacent to the pool lay an ornamental garden, and several buildings stood nearby. One of these was a bathhouse, but the use of most of them has yet to be decided. To date Herod's tomb has not been found, though archaeologists continue to look for it and to speculate about its location.

Jericho and Samaria. Early in his reign during the years 35–30 B.C. Herod built a rectangular winter palace near the Hasmonean palace at the Wadi Qelt, over a mile southwest of Old Testament Jericho. This had a central peristyle or colonnaded court, a bathhouse, and a pair of small pools. Later Herod created an enlarged winter palace on both sides of the Wadi Qelt, and connected the two units with a bridge. On the north side of the wadi stood a five-room bathhouse, two peristyle courts, and several other rooms.

On the south side lay a sunken garden with an impressive façade holding statuary niches. At the end of the façade he had built a pool for swimming and water games. And behind the façade stood an artificial mound with a building on it. Herod also built a hippodrome and a theater south of ancient Jericho.

Among Herod's other projects, he renamed Samaria (thirty-five miles north of Jerusalem) Sebaste, the Greek equivalent of the Latin Augustus (meaning "the revered one") and built extensively there. But we need to be careful not to give him credit for the work of others during the Roman period. The provincial governor Gabinius seems to have rebuilt the walls (57–55 B.C.),

The Herodium, general view

Air view of the Herodium, showing the tower arrangements

almost two miles long, which surrounded an irregular area of some 160 acres. Gabinius also appears to have been largely responsible for the Roman Forum and the adjacent basilica. However Josephus gives Herod credit for the city wall (*Wars,* I.21–2). Perhaps those projects were too ambitious for Gabinius' brief tenure and Herod finished what Gabinius had started.

But Herod does deserve credit for the round towers of the west gate of the city and the stadium (approximately 750 by 195 feet), and he also built the great temple to Augustus on a height overlooking the city and over part of the ruins of Ahab's palace. The complex included the temple building proper (114 by 78 feet) and a large forecourt on a platform (270 by 234 feet). A

The peristyle garden in the Herodium

The heating arrangement in the hot bath at the Herodium

wide staircase led from the forecourt to the temple. The emperor Septimius Severus, who reigned from 193 to 211 A.D. rebuilt the temple complex, according to its original plan, and the stairs connecting the upper and lower city. Various other remains that can be seen there today date from this later period.

Remains of the theater (on the hill of Samaria) to be seen there today date to about A.D. 225. And the colonnaded covered bazaar street (of the lower Roman city), which seems to have run the length of the city, evidently dates to about the same time.

So the New Testament student should not include either in a recreation of the city in the days of the apostles.[87]

Mamre and Hebron. The walled enclosure at Mamre (2 miles north of Hebron), sacred to the memory of Abraham (cf. Genesis 13:18; 23:19; 35:27), seems to date to the reign of Herod the Great.

The monumental structure at Hebron (now a mosque), covering what is commonly identified as the Cave of Machpelah (where some of the Patriarchs were buried, beginning with Abraham's wife Sarah, Genesis 23:19), is attributed to Herod the

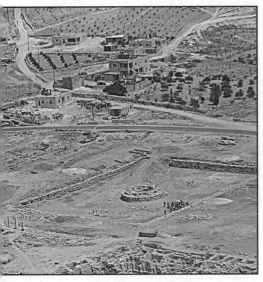

The lower Herodium

The synagogue (left) at the Herodium

The Jericho Oasis

Great. It was built with the typical Herodian masonry having the chiseled frame.

Herod Antipas' Two Capitals

Sepphoris became the capital of Galilee in 63 B.C., after Pompey's conquest. But the Romans destroyed it after Herod the Great died in 4 B.C., in the process of squelching a revolt. When Herod's son, Herod Antipas, became tetrarch of Galilee and Perea (A.D. 6–39), he rebuilt the city and used it as his capital. Sepphoris stood about 3.5 miles northwest of Nazareth and could be seen from Nazareth. Jesus could have walked there in about an hour. This city of perhaps 30,000 people, with its palace, forum, Greco-Roman theater, villas, and more provided a stark contrast to the sleepy village of Nazareth with its some four hundred inhabitants. Possibly Sepphoris was Jesus' "city set on a hill" (Matthew 5:14).[88]

In A.D. 18 or 19 Herod Antipas built Tiberias on the Sea of Galilee to serve as his new capital. He named it in honor of Tiberius, who reigned from A.D. 14 to 37, and peopled it primarily with non-Jews or Jews who were unconcerned with laws of purity. There he built his palace on a hill, a stadium, a synagogue, a fortress, a town center, and hot baths. In the early days it was another of the Hellenistic-type cities of Palestine that helped to dilute the Jewish nature of the land. But during the second century A.D. it became the seat of the Sanhedrin.[89]

In recent years it has been popular to suggest that Jesus knew the pagan culture of both Sepphoris and Tiberias, and especially to conclude that His references to hypocrites may have been influenced by the theater in Sepphoris. The point is this. An *hypocrites* was a play actor or stage actor who wore a mask and practiced deceit. In a

The reception hall in Herod's palace at Jericho

The round towers at the west gate of Samaria

in Jerusalem—a creation of Herod the Great, as noted above. And most of Jesus' references to hypocrites took place in Jerusalem.

Though there was a considerable amount of Greco-Roman influence in Palestine in Jesus' day, the world with which He interacted was especially that of the small towns and villages of Galilee. And new information leads to the conclusion that the population of Sepphoris during the first century A.D. was largely Jewish. If Joseph was employed in the rebuilding of Sepphoris, and if he took young Jesus along, as some suggest, the experience need not have been as non-Jewish as has been guessed.

proper Greek play there were only three actors; when an actor had to play another part, he simply clapped on another mask. In his performance he pretended to be something he was not. Jesus condemned those whose religion was an external form rather than an inner reality. Interestingly, nearly all occurrences of the word *hypocrites* in the New Testament appear in Jesus' sayings in the Synoptic Gospels.

Now most scholars conclude that the theater in Sepphoris does not date earlier than the end of the first century A.D. Moreover, it appears that though Jesus entered the territory of Gentile cities, he did not go into the cities themselves (e.g., Mark 7:24). And there is no record of his visiting any Jewish cities other than Jerusalem. But there was a theater

HEROD PHILIP'S CONSTRUCTIONS: CAESAREA PHILIPPI AND BETHSAIDA

Herod Philip, who reigned from 4 B.C.to A.D. 34, the best of all the sons of Herod the Great, had a peaceful rule for 37 years. Among his constructions were his new capital, Caesarea Philippi, and Bethsaida on the Sea of Galilee.

At Caesarea Philippi V. Tzaferis for the Israel Department of Antiquities

Steps to Herod's temple to Augustus at Samaria

Herod Anipas established his second capital at Tiberias on the Sea of Galilee

continues to excavate with the cooperation of several American colleges and universities and has discovered what may have been the palace of King Herod Agrippa II, who reigned from A.D. 50 to 70. A bathhouse was later built over the floor of the palace and we await a clarification of the finds. At this point in the excavation process it is impossible to know what the city was like in New Testament times.

Herod Philip's other construction, Bethsaida Julias, was named for the mother of the emperor Tiberius and wife of Augustus. Excavations and explorations have been conducted at the site since 1988 under the leadership of Rami Arav and Fred Strichert. Among other things they have shown that Bethsaida in Jesus' day stood on the northeast shore of the Sea of Galilee, whereas today the townsite is located over a mile from the shore. The topography of the area has changed since New Testament times. Land routes being somewhat difficult, communication with Capernaum and other points west and south was normally by water rather than by land. So Jesus and the disciples took a boat "for the other side."

The shrine to Pan at Caesarea Philippi

Herod Philip—Caesarea Philippi and Bethsaida

Caesarea Philippi, a city at the southwest base of Mount Hermon, had strategic value because it guarded the fertile plain to the west. One of the springs that feeds the Jordan emerges from a nearby cave that housed a shrine dedicated to Baal in Old Testament times (Joshua 11:17; Judges 3:3). The Greeks made it a shrine to Pan and the place became known as Paneas, now called Banias. Augustus gave the region to Herod the Great in

20 B.C., who then built a white marble temple there to the emperor.

When Herod died the area became part of the tetrarchy of Philip, who rebuilt the town, making it his capital, and named it Caesarea in honor of the emperor, adding his own name to distinguish it from Caesarea on the Mediterranean. Since 1985 V. Tzaferis, has been conducting excavations at the site for the Israel Department of Antiquities.[90] To date most of the discoveries have dated to late Roman, Crusader, or Arabic times and do not throw much light on the town in New Testament times. First century remains have been unearthed in the cemeteries, however. The modern visitor to the site may see some ruins of Herod's temple to Augustus and twelve parallel vaults (each c. 25 feet deep, 21 feet high, and 16 feet wide), within the Medieval fortifications. These have been identified as warehouses associated with the market of the first century town.

Bethsaida, on the northeast shore of the Sea of Galilee, was another of Philip's constructions. But he did not found the town. Excavations at the twenty-acre site reveal that settlement there goes all the way back to the Early Bronze Age (c. 3000–2700 B.C.). During the days of the Israelite monarchy (1000–586 B.C.) it was a substantial town surrounded by an impressive wall. A Hellenistic settlement had also stood there.[91]

Philip brought a large number of settlers to the town and launched extensive building projects there. The refounding took place between the years 8 and 13 A.D.,[92] when it was named Bethsaida Julia, after the mother of the emperor Tiberius and wife of Augustus. A Roman temple has been excavated at Bethsaida which has been connected with the cult of Livia.[93]

Excavations at Bethsaida began in 1988 and have continued to the present under the direction of Rami Arav and Fred Strickert. In addition to the Roman temple just noted, numerous houses of fishermen have also been excavated, along with fishing gear. The excavation has yielded the best selection of fishing equipment from any one site around the Sea of Galilee: stone anchors, stone and lead net weights, fish hooks, and needles.[94]

A typical house in Bethsaida was basically square and measured roughly twenty-one feet by twenty-one feet. It consisted of two rooms, the first a family room where family members socialized and where they ate their meals. At a meal they usually sat on the floor around a small raised platform. There might be a mat on the floor. A doorway led into a bedroom where the family slept side by side on straw mattresses unrolled on the floor. The stone walls were strong enough to support a second floor, but not all houses had them. Cooking was done in an adjacent courtyard that might be shared with other families.

A second style house was a courtyard house. These varied in size but averaged about three thousand square feet, the courtyard comprising about one-third of the space and providing room for business activities, such as repairing fishing nets. A kitchen, a common room (for dining and sitting), and bedrooms opened off the courtyard. There might be a stairway to a second floor.

Agrippa I

Agrippa I, who reigned from 41 to 44, enlarged the city of Jerusalem and began the north wall (the third wall), which was hastily completed during the First Revolt (A.D. 66–70). The circumference of walls one and two had been 2.67 miles. Wall three brought the total circumference to 3.4 miles by the time Titus besieged the city in A.D. 70.[95]

The Decapolis

In addition to towns the Herods built, there were in non-Jewish Roman Palestine the cities of the Decapolis. Decapolis means "ten cities" and refers to the league of cities or the region where they were located— generally east and south of the Sea of Galilee. Only one of them, Scythopolis (Old Testament Beth Shean) was located west of the Jordan, twenty-five miles south of the Sea of Galilee.

As early as the third century B.C., when the Ptolemies controlled Palestine, and increasingly during the following Seleucid occupation, Greeks migrated to Palestine. There they either established new cities or came to dominate older ones. During the

Maccabean (or Hasmonean) period, fighting sometimes broke out between the Jews and those cities. When Pompey conquered Palestine (63 B.C.) he freed some of those cities from Jewish control and attached them to the province of Syria.

The Roman Pliny, who wrote during the generation after Christ, was the first to list the Decapolis: Scythopolis, Pella, Hippos, Gadara, Rephana, Dion, Gerasa, Canatha, Damascus, Philadelphia. Later, as many as eighteen cities were part of the league. The Decapolis served Rome as a barrier against marauders from the eastern desert and as a counterbalance against Jewish nationalism. It served its members as a communal league and as a means of mutual defense. Jesus did go there (Mark 7:31) but apparently only briefly.

To date only two of the Decapolis cities have been extensively excavated: Scythopolis and Jerash. Though Scythopolis is effectively emerging from the soil of Israel, what is visible today dates long after the New Testament period—the great theater to the end of the second century A.D. and the remains of the city later than that.

Only Jerash, twenty miles east of the Jordan River and twenty-one miles north of Amman, the capital of Jordan, gives some idea of what these Greco-Roman cities were like. An Anglo-American team began to dig there in 1925 and numerous agencies continued there sporadically down through the 1970s and 1980s.

The south gate of Jerash leads into the circular or elliptical forum (measuring about 280 by 245 feet), unique in the Greco-Roman world. Though the Ionic colonnade of the forum, comprised of 160 pillars, dates to the second century, the forum itself (the business center of town) evidently dates from early in the first century. From the forum on the left (at the southwest of town) a great flight of steps leads up to the temple of Zeus, built about 200 B.C. but renovated A.D. 22–24. The temple has eight columns along its façade and twelve along its sides. Nestled in the hillside next to the temple of Zeus stands the late first century south theater with its thirty-two tiers of seats that could accommodate four to five thousand people.

The first-century main street of the city, just over a half mile long, was flanked by 260 Ionic and Corinthian columns on either side and ran north from the forum. All the principal buildings had their entrance from it, and the best shops were located there. This north-south street (about thirty-seven feet wide) was intersected at right angles by two east-west streets (about twenty-seven feet wide). An underground sewage system lay under the main street.

Six gates pierced the city wall and 101 towers, spaced at 50–70 foot intervals, guarded the wall. As the city prospered during the second century, a north theater, baths, and a great temple to Artemis were added within the city, and a hippodrome and arch of Hadrian at the south gate. Dating to a later time, remains of thirteen churches turned up in the excavations. Jerash illustrates for us the type of city to which the prodigal son may have gone (Luke 15:12–32).

Essene Communities

Towns of the Herods and of the Decapolis were not the only communities dotting the landscape of Palestine in New Testament times. Some monastic groups

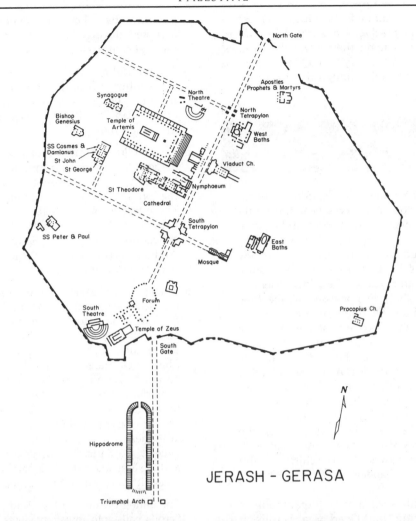

North Gate

Apostles
Prophets & Martyrs

Synagogue

North
Theatre

Bishop
Genesius

North
Tetrapylon

Temple of
Artemis

West
Baths

SS Cosmes &
Damianus

St John

Viaduct Ch.

St George

St Theodore

Nymphaeum

Cathedral

South
Tetrapylon

SS Peter & Paul

East
Baths

Mosque

Forum

Procopius Ch.

South
Theatre

Temple of Zeus

South
Gate

N

Hippodrome

JERASH – GERASA

Triumphal Arch

The circular forum at Jerash

generally shunned the cities and established themselves in rural areas. Most important among them were the Essenes, which many identify with Qumran and the Dead Sea Scrolls, though this is not a universal position.

THE IMPACT OF THE DEAD SEA SCROLLS

When the Dead Sea Scrolls (scrolls found in caves near the northwest shore of the Dead Sea) began to appear in 1948 and following, they pushed back the history of the Hebrew text of the Old Testament by about a thousand years. The oldest Hebrew Bible that we possessed at the time dated to the ninth century A.D. But upon the discovery of the Dead Sea Scrolls, we suddenly had texts dating before 100 B.C. The literature on the Dead Sea Scrolls is now vast and full of technical discussion. Many of the better books on the subject are listed in the General Bibliography at the end of this volume. Especially helpful is the *Encyclopedia of the Dead Sea Scrolls*, edited by Lawrence H. Schiffman and James C. VanderKam (2 vols., Oxford, 2000).

With such a vast literary output covering the Dead Sea Scrolls it would be impossible to do more than to summarize here with a few personal observations.

1. The Dead Sea Scrolls push back the history of the Hebrew text by about a thousand years.

2. In the transmission of the Hebrew text the integrity of the text has been marvelously preserved. Apparently only eight valid changes were made in the Revised Standard Version of Isaiah, based on the complete Isaiah manuscript from the Scrolls collection.

3. The standardized or Masoretic textual tradition (the traditional text

we now use) became generally accepted during the latter part of the first century A.D.

4. The biblical materials dating to the first century A.D. at Qumran and to the first century A.D. and later at other Dead Sea sites are Masoretic in textual tradition.

5. All the Old Testament books except Esther have turned up in Qumran literature, but this has no real bearing on the subject of canonicity. These works are nowhere declared to be books belonging to the sacred collection or canon of Scripture. And apocryphal literature is found in abundance at Qumran.

6. Scholars have decided on the basis of the Dead Sea Scrolls that more than the Masoretic textual tradition existed in antiquity. There was also a textual tradition behind the Septuagint (the Greek translation of the Old Testament) and one behind the Samaritan Pentateuch. Presumably the Septuagint textual tradition existed in Egypt (where the Old Testament was translated into Greek), the Samaritan in Palestine, and the Masoretic in Babylonia, from where it was brought to Palestine.

7. The dating of some of the Dead Sea Scrolls calls into question views of some textual critics. For instance, Ecclesiastes, sometimes believed to have been composed in the second or first century B.C., appears in a manuscript from Cave 4 dating from 175 to 150 B.C. A manuscript of Daniel dating about 120 B.C. calls into question the alleged Maccabean date of its composition. Moreover, the Dead Sea Scrolls do not support the existence of a deutero- or trito-Isaiah, at least during the second century B.C. The complete Isaiah and the long fragment of Isaiah from Cave 1 (second century B.C.) treat the book as a unit.

8. The Dead Sea Scrolls have contributed much to the study of the

Cave 4 is the large cave that appears in the left center of the picture. In it fragments of all Old Testament books except Esther were found

Testament that they did during and after the days of the Masoretes (fifth to ninth centuries A.D.). Probably it is reasonably correct to say that there is at least 95 percent agreement between the various biblical texts found near the Dead Sea and the Old Testament we've had all along. Most of the variations are minor, and none of the doctrines have been put in jeopardy.

Hebrew language. They give new information on the history of the Hebrew language, trends in spelling, formation of words, and pronunciation. They also prove that Hebrew was not a completely dead language in New Testament times because a fair amount of various kinds of literature was being written in Hebrew: religious, commercial, contractual, and military documents. This body of formal and informal literature throws much light on the meanings of individual words often not clearly understood from their Old Testament usage. And, interestingly, the Aramaic manuscripts of Qumran provide the first literary documents in the form of Aramaic used in Palestine in the time of Christ. Previously only brief inscriptions in Aramaic were known from this period.

9. Finally, the content of the Bible is not "changed" by the discoveries of the Dead Sea Scrolls. Nothing in those discoveries endangers the essential reliability of our standard Hebrew Bible text. All the evidence attests to the fact that Jewish scribes of the early Christian centuries exercised the same care in copying the Old

After the discovery and excavation of Dead Sea Scrolls in Cave 1 (in 1947), some eight miles south of Jericho and a mile west of the Dead Sea, attention turned to Khirbet Qumran, a ruin on a plateau between Cave 1 and the Dead Sea. Excavation there between 1949 and 1956 uncovered a complex that had one main structure approximately 100 by 122 feet with additional buildings on the northeast, west, and south. A tower at the northwest corner was used for defense. East of that lay a kitchen area. South of the tower stood assembly or dining rooms for the community. Above them on the second floor was a writing room where at least some of the Dead Sea Scrolls were produced. An intricate system of cisterns and pools provided water storage and for the many ritual washings performed there.

Evidently Khirbet Qumran was the center of a religious community, presumably

A view out of Cave 4

The Dead Sea from Qumran

largely celibate. Between two hundred and four hundred people are thought to have lived there at one time. Their living quarters were probably comprised of tents, huts, or some of the caves of the region. Most have concluded that the occupants were Essenes, but some scholars are still reluctant to make this identification. It is now generally agreed that the scrolls found in Caves 1–11 constituted the library of the Qumran community and that some of them were no doubt produced in their scriptorium, or writing room.

Less than two miles south of Qumran, Pere R. de Vaux excavated a major ruin at Ain Feshka in 1958. The structure measured 78 by 59 feet and had an inner courtyard with rooms on all sides. He interpreted his discoveries as directly related to the Qumran site, serving as an agricultural and tanning center for the Qumran community.

Air view of Qumran. *Courtesy Rockefeller Museum, Jerusalem*

Tables on which the Dead Sea scrolls were written.
They are made of plaster on wood frames.
Courtesy Rockefeller Museum, Jerusalem

Roads of Palestine

Some knowledge of Palestinian roads is crucial to understanding Palestine's geopolitical history. Towns developed along roads and they dictated the movements of armies, merchants, and ordinary people. Major roads crisscrossed Palestine in New Testament times. The Romans built a coastal road from Pelusium in Egypt through Gaza, Ascalon, Caesarea and Tyre. Then it continued north to the Syrian capital of Antioch and east to the Tigris. This route had been used from antiquity.

Other ancient roads were busy with commerce. One led from Babylon across the central Euphrates and the desert to the Jordan River, crossed it north of the Sea of Galilee, descended into the Jordan Valley to Beth Shean, where it turned into the Jezreel Valley and finally joined the coastal road at Mount Carmel.

After the Six-Day War in 1967 an Israeli team under the leadership of P. Bar-Adon excavated a building complex and adjoining cemetery at Ras Feshka, ten miles south of Qumran. The excavator dated his finds to the last century B.C. and the first century A.D. and linked them to Qumran and Ein Feshka structures, as belonging to the Essene community. Ras Feshka was a center for meeting and work, not living quarters. It is interesting to note that the cemetery at Ras Feshka was not celibate, and new work at the Qumran cemetery indicates it wasn't either. A few of the skeletons exhumed were identified as those of females.

In the past it was debated whether the Essenes avoided Jerusalem, but new excavations on Mount Zion in the area of the Jerusalem University College (formerly American Institute of Holy Land Studies) have found Josephus' "Gate of the Essenes" as well as remains of the Essene quarter. Roughly fifty Essenes are belived to have lived in the Essene quarter in Jesus' day.[96]

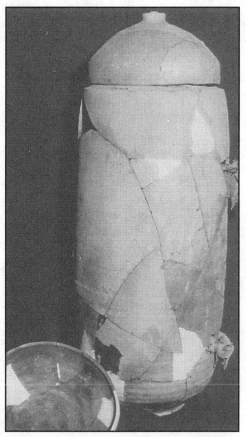

A jar in which one of the Dead Sea Scrolls was stored

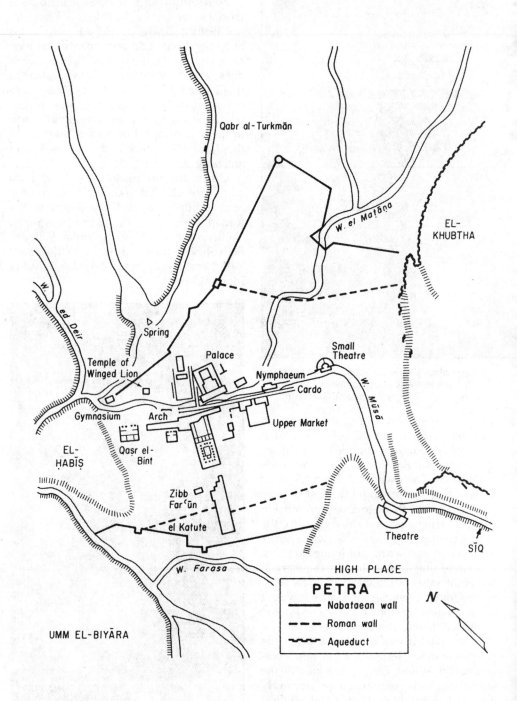

Qabr al-Turkmān

W. el Maṭāḥa

EL-
KHUBTHA

W. ed Deir

Spring

Temple of
Winged Lion

Palace

Nymphaeum

Small
Theatre

Cardo

W. Mūsā

Gymnasium

Arch

Upper Market

EL-
ḤABĪṢ

Qaṣr el-
Bint

Zibb
Farʿūn

el Katute

Theatre

SĪQ

W. Farasa

HIGH PLACE

PETRA

—— Nabataean wall

- - - Roman wall

〜〜〜 Aqueduct

N

UMM EL-BIYĀRA

The Isaiah Manuscript from Cave 1 at Qumran, second century B.C., written on leather

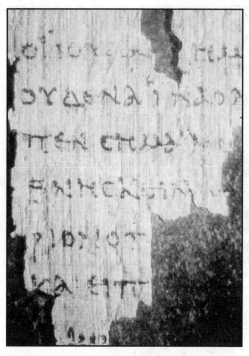

A fragment of Deuteronomy (32:41–43) from Cave 4 at Qumran

Another ran from southwest Arabia north, parallel to the Red Sea, carrying luxury goods of Arabia and Africa. At Petra (about fifty miles south of the Dead Sea) it branched to Egypt, Gaza, and Damascus. A road also ran north-south along the watershed, through Hebron, Jerusalem, Samaria, and points north.

THE ROSE RED CITY OF PETRA

Petra is a striking place, even in ruins. Access to the site is through a narrow twisting Siq between cliffs towering 500 feet high. Suddenly the Siq opens upon the magnificent rose-red "treasury."

Some of Petra's structures are rose red and others a dark red ochre shade of sandstone with bands of yellow, gray, and white. These buildings and tombs are almost all cut into the rock cliffs of the area. Among the most exciting remains are the Khazneh (often called "the treasury," with a

The Siq, the entrance to Petra

The Khazneh or Treasury of Petra

façade 92 feet wide and 130 feet high), probably a tomb of a Nabataean king, carved into the rose red cliff; a wide colonnaded street laid out in Roman style; a Roman theater carved from the solid rock and capable of seating four thousand; the Palace Tomb; Ed Deir, a temple with a façade 165 feet wide, 148 feet high, and a door 23½ feet high; the great high place, an ancient Nabataean worship center of the god Dushara; and the natural fortress of Umm el-Biyara.

Petra was located about fifty miles south of the Dead Sea in the highlands of Transjordan at an altitude of twenty-seven hundred feet. The town lay in a basin surrounded by mountains, and its principal entrance was through the narrow, twisting Siq. The site is about a mile long and a mile and a half wide.

Many identify Petra with Old Testament Sela (meaning "rock"; cf. 2 Kings 14:7–10; 2 Chronicles 25:11–12; Isaiah 16:1; Jeremiah 49:16–17; Obadiah 3–4). Petra apparently was not Old Testament Sela, however, because excavations on the acropolis or fortress of Umm el-Biyara did not reveal evidence of occupation before about 700 B.C.,

The main theater of Petra

The high place of Petra

century B.C. They derived much of their income from fees levied on trade along caravan routes between Arabia and Mesopotamia. During the second century B.C. they extended their power over all Transjordan, and as far north as Damascus. In the following century they defeated the Maccabean king Alexander Jannaeus. When the Romans moved into the area, the Nabataeans often assisted them. Aretas IV supported the Romans, and eventually Rome annexed their kingdom during the reign of the emperor Trajan in the second century A.D.

after the days of Amaziah of Judah (cf. 2 Kings 14:7–10). Whether or not the Old Testament refers to Petra, the New Testament does indirectly refer to it. Aretas IV, king of Petra from 9 B.C. to A.D. 40, ruled Damascus during the days of Paul's conversion and sought to capture the apostle there (2 Corinthians 11:32–33).

Though numerous explorations took place at the site during the nineteenth century, systematic excavation began there in 1929. Excavations have been numerous and have continued almost to the present.

When Petra's king Aretas IV tried to get his hands on the apostle Paul, the Nabataeans controlled the region. They were a Semitic people from northwest Arabia who began to settle the area between the Dead Sea and the Gulf of Aqaba during the sixth

As to width, a Roman road through the Judean wilderness measured about ten to forty feet in width. A road through the Beth Shean Valley measured rather consistently about thirty feet in width. The Romans installed mile markers along their roads.

Sites Sacred to the Beginnings of Christianity

Nazareth—Houses of Mary and Joseph

Nazareth lies in a basin some twenty miles east of the Mediterranean and fifteen miles southwest of the Sea of Galilee. In Jesus' day it was entirely Jewish in character and had a synagogue (Mark 6:2; Luke 4:16). In fact, the Jewish nature of the region was largely a result of the efforts of the Maccabean (Hasmonean) King Alexander Jannaeus (103–76 B.C.), who conquered Galilee and did his best to make it Jewish. Those who migrated there from Judea under his prompting were

Um el-Biyara

Mediterranean, in the hill country north of the Plain of Esdraelon stands Nazareth, the boyhood home of Jesus. Nazareth is situated in a basin enclosed by hills, except on the south where a narrow rocky gorge leads to the plain. The town itself is on a hillside facing east and southeast. It was separated from, but near, the important trade centers of that day.

From the hills surrounding Nazareth, the view to the north included rich plains and snowcapped Mount Hermon. Majestic Mount Carmel was visible to the west and Tabor's wooded heights to the east. To the south lay the Plain of Esdraelon.

Although in no sense isolated from the world, the Nazareth where Jesus grew up was a small village with only one spring from which Mary certainly drew water for her household. Today it is appropriately named "Mary's Well." The spring rises in the

zealous Jews who desired to bring their religion to the pagan Galileans. Possibly the families of Joseph and Mary were part of that migration.

Though the Jewish element was then strong, the region was still a mosaic of pagan and Jewish elements. For example, the Hellenistic city of Sepphoris (approximately 3.5 miles to the northwest, discussed earlier) was the capital of Herod Antipas until he moved it to Tiberias. The descriptive "Galilee of the Gentiles" (Matthew 4:15) reflects the diverse character of the region. The district of Galilee under Roman administration extended about thirty-five by twenty-five miles.

NAZARETH—JESUS' BOYHOOD HOME

About midway between the south end of the Sea of Galilee and the

The Church of the Annunciation, Nazareth

Modern Nazareth with the Church of the Annunciation in the center

hill behind the Greek Orthodox Church of St. Gabriel. The water is then piped into the church and flows five hundred feet down the hill to an outlet adjacent to the modern main road through town. The population of the city is now about fifty thousand.

About two miles southeast of Nazareth is Jebel Kafsy, the traditional "Mount of Precipitation" from which the people of Nazareth tried to cast Jesus when they rejected Him (Luke 4:29). But as with so many other so-called holy places, the tradition that identifies the place cannot be either confirmed or denied.

The house where the angel met Mary of Nazareth is today, on the basis of tradition, marked by the Church of the Annunciation. A series of structures on the site goes all the way back to at least the fourth century A.D. The Franciscans built the present church between 1955 and 1959, where they had previously built one in 1730. The 1730 church stood on the spot where the Crusaders had erected their sanctuary in the twelfth century (destroyed by the

Mamelukes in 1263). For their part, the Crusaders had put up a cathedral over the spot where the Persian conquest of 614 had destroyed a Byzantine church, built around A.D. 427. An earlier structure at the site (dating before the time of Constantine) may have been a church. The cave house under the present church may be the one that the pilgrim Egeria visited in 384 and identified as the house of Mary. Beyond this we cannot go in locating the traditional house of Mary.[97]

Next to the Church of the Annunciation stands the Church of St. Joseph (completed in 1914), which according to tradition was built over the cave where the Holy Family lived and where Joseph had his carpentry shop. In its crypt are remnants of Byzantine and Crusader churches and below them a cave where Joseph supposedly worked. This has been identified as Joseph's workshop only since the seventeenth century, and there is no real basis for the tradition.

Bethlehem—the Place of Jesus' Birth

Bethlehem was indeed a "little town" on the caravan route between Jerusalem and Egypt by way of Hebron in New Testament times. That fact would later facilitate Joseph

Modern Bethlehem

and Mary's flight with the infant Jesus. The place, some five miles south of Jerusalem, gained new importance when Herod build fortresses at Herodium and Masada because Bethlehem overlooked the roads to those fortresses.

In the second century A.D. a tradition existed that Jesus' birth had occurred in a certain cave that had been behind the inn. Apparently many people lived in caves in the area or used them for stables. If Mary had lived in a cave in Nazareth, it would not have been extremely unusual for Mary and Joseph to stay in a cave while in Bethlehem. The argument that the traditional cave was too small to be used as a stable lacks strength because its present division into sections is misleading. This cave is presumably the same one that the emperor Hadrian (A.D. 117–138) desecrated by including it in a grove dedicated to Tammuz-Adonis. At that time both

Bethlehem and Jerusalem were declared off limits to Jews.

Bethlehem's status changed dramatically, however, under Constantine. After a pilgrimage to Palestine by his mother, Queen Helena, he ordered construction (in A.D. 326) of a church over the revered cave. This structure was roughly square, with an octagonal apse over the traditional grotto. The church was about eighty-six feet on a side and was divided internally by four rows of nine columns into a nave and four aisles, two on each side. The entire floor was paved with mosaics, some of which can now be seen under the floor of the present church. At the end of the fourth century A.D. Jerome lived in the cave and translated the Hebrew Bible into Latin (called the Vulgate) there.

After this church was destroyed by a Samaritan revolt in 529, the emperor Justinian (527–565) rebuilt the church, essentially in its present form. The side

The Church of the Nativity, Bethlehem

A mosaic in the floor of Constantine's church, under the present Church of the Nativity

walls of the church were reconstructed on Constantinian foundations, but the structure was lengthened to about 107 feet, so it was now a rectangle instead of a square. The nave was widened and the side aisles narrowed. Only minor changes have been made in the church since Justinian's day.

The church escaped destruction during the Persian conquest in 614 because, according to the oft-repeated tradition, the Magi portrayed in the scene of the birth of Christ on the façade were shown in Persian dress. The church also escaped destruction during the Muslim conquest and subsequent occupation, but it fell into a condition of decay from neglect. When the Crusaders took the area, they launched a program of restoration. The first two kings of Crusader Jerusalem were crowned there: Baldwin I (in 1101) and Baldwin II (in 1109). Not only did the Crusaders repair the structure, but they also covered much of the interior with paintings and mosaics, very little of which survives to the present. Over the years the main door has been gradually reduced in size to its present small opening. Archaeological work at the site of the church was conducted in 1934 under the leadership of W. Harvey for the Department of Antiquities of the British Mandate and by the Franciscans from 1948 to 1951.[98]

Cana—Site of Jesus' First Miracle

In the search for the location of biblical Cana, two sites surface as possibilities:

Khirbet Qana and Kefar Kenna. They are only six miles apart. The former is six miles north of Sepphoris and nine miles north of Nazareth, Khirbet Qana is currently unoccupied. Kefar Kenna lies four miles northeast of Nazareth on the road to Tiberias and is still inhabited. Finegan argues persuasively and in some detail that Kefar Kenna is in fact the site where Jesus turned water into wine. A Franciscan church marks the location of an early synagogue-church where the miracle is thought to have occurred.[99] Others prefer Khirbet Qana.

Towns Around the Sea of Galilee

The Sea of Galilee and its surrounding towns figured significantly in the ministry of Jesus and the disciples. Fishing was extremely profitable on the lake and formed the basis of the economy of towns such as Capernaum, Bethsaida, and Magdala (or Taricheae).

But the fishing business there was different from what most modern Bible students imagine. Individuals didn't just go out fishing and sell their catch to a processor. Rather, the local ruler (during Jesus' ministry, Herod Antipas) controlled the sea, the harbors, fishing rights, and roads and bridges over which the catch traveled. They

A first century anchor raised from the Sea of Galilee

fathers seem to have formed such a cooperative (Matthew 4:21; Luke 5:10).

The common mode of fishing appears to have been with nets made of flax. The fishermen made them, as well as mended, washed, and dried them. The casting net was cast from a boat or along the shoreline (Matthew 4:18). The larger dragnet was also cast from a boat (Matthew 13:47).[100]

Bethsaida-Julias was a place where Jesus evidently performed many miracles. For example, there He healed a blind man (Mark 8:22) as well as many who were sick (Luke 9:10), and it was in the vicinity that He fed the five thousand (Luke 9:13–17). In spite of His miraculous works in the town, the inhabitants failed to believe in Him, and He leveled a curse against the town, as He did against Capernaum and Chorazin (Matthew 11:21; Luke 10:13). But the emphasis here is not on Jesus' works, which He performed in many places, but on the fact that this was the original home of Philip, Andrew, and Peter, who later moved to Capernaum (John 1:44). There is also a tradition that James and John came from here.

Bethsaida was located on the northeast shore of the Sea of Galilee, just above where the Jordan River entered the Sea of Galilee.

sold those rights to brokers, the New Testament "tax collectors" or "publicans," who contracted with the fishermen. Matthew (Levi) evidently was one of those publicans or contractors, and Zebedee was a fisher with two working sons (James and John) and hired laborers. Fishing families sometimes formed collectives or cooperatives to bid for fishing contracts or leases. Peter, Andrew, James, and John with their

An early synagogue at Chorazin

A reconstruction of the synagogue at Capernaum, perhaps third or fourth century

Department of Antiquities. The town stood on a flat plateau in the middle of a hill and covered some fifteen acres.

Dominating the site is the synagogue, of a basilical plan as at Capernaum. The main hall is sixty-five feet long and forty-five feet wide. Three rows of columns outline a central nave and three aisles—one on each side and one in the back. There is some difference of opinion on the date of the synagogue, but it appears to have been constructed in the third or fourth century A.D. Other remains there also date especially to the third or fourth century or later and include a civic center consisting of seven large buildings, an industrial quarter with two olive presses, and five large buildings adjacent to the synagogue. All are built of squared blocks of black basalt, the stone of the surrounding countryside. To date we do not really have information on how the site looked in New Testament times.

Capernaum holds a special place in the hearts of Christians as the center of Jesus' ministry during a good part of His earthly life. In a sense it was Jesus' "own city" (Matthew 9:1). Here He preached and performed many miracles. Here He called five of his disciples to full-time service: Peter,

Bethsaida was not in Galilee but in Gaulanitis (modern Golan), under the rule of Herod Philip during Jesus' ministry. A Roman road connected Bethsaida, Chorazin, and Acco on the coast and a bridge crossed the Jordan River just north of Bethsaida. Though Bethsaida is today located over a mile from the shore of the Sea of Galilee, in New Testament times the Sea came up to the base of the hill on which the town was located.[101]

Bethsaida is the largest mound on the northern shore of the Sea of Galilee. It measures 1360 by 600 feet and rises 80 feet above the surrounding terrain. Excavations have been conducted there since 1988 and reveal settlement going back to about 3000 B.C. The site was resettled around 300 B.C. and became one of the largest towns on the Sea of Galilee. The Romans destroyed it during the First Jewish War, A.D. 66–70. As noted, Jesus spent some time there, and perhaps from there went to Decapolis, only six miles away.

Chorazin was located about two miles up in the hills northwest of Capernaum and nine hundred feet above the Sea of Galilee. Though explorations took place there earlier, excavations were conducted at the site 1962–1965 and 1980–1986 under the leadership of Ze'ev Yeivin on behalf of the Israel

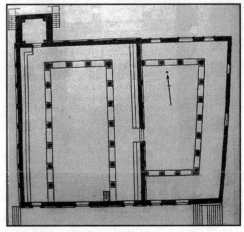

Floor plan of the Capernaum synagogue

Remains of houses of fishermen at Capernaum

Andrew, James, John, and Matthew (Mark 1:16–19; Matthew 9:9). And here He often stayed in the home of Simon Peter and taught in the town's synagogue, built by a Roman centurion who was possibly a Jewish proselyte (Luke 7:50).

The town was located on the northern shore of the Sea of Galilee, about 2.5 miles west of where the Jordan River flows into the sea. The unfortified village was small,

The modern chapel built over what is believed to be Peter's house. *Courtesy Frederick C. Veit*

extending some 300–400 yards along the shore and covering a little over ten acres. Its occupants made their living by fishing, farming, and trade. In his day, Herod Antipas apparently levied customs duties on goods that came across the Sea of Galilee from the direction of Damascus on goods and that moved along the imperial road that skirted the western shore of the Sea of Galilee. Levi (Matthew) must have been in his employ (Matthew 9:9). As Jesus' headquarters, Capernaum, on the sea and near a main highway, provided opportunities for reaching more than just the local population with the Gospel.

The Franciscans acquired the ruins of Capernaum (Tell Hum) in 1894 and of course were especially interested in uncovering the synagogue where Jesus had taught and the home where Peter had lived. But the archaeological history of the site did not begin until 1905. In that year H. Kohl and C. Watzinger, working for the German Oriental Society, uncovered part of the ruins of the synagogue. From 1905 to 1914 W. von Menden worked in the area of the synagogue and the octagonal church (possibly the location of Peter's house) which stood to the south of it. Gaudentius Orfali restored part of the synagogue and worked on the octagonal church from 1921 to 1926.

And since 1968 Virgilio Corbo and Stanislao Loffreda have been excavating inside and around the synagogue, on the site of the octagonal church, and on adjacent parts of the town. On the adjacent Greek orthodox property V. Tzaferis directed an Israel Department of Antiquities dig from 1978 to 1987.

The synagogue at Capernaum is an imposing structure of white limestone, which was imported into this region where black basalt is native. Naturally the quality stone attracted pilferers who carried off a good part of the superstructure over time, making a full reconstruction impossible. Though there is some debate over the date of construction, probably the synagogue was built in the fourth century A.D. Adjoining the synagogue on the east was an open court surrounded on the other three sides by a covered colonnade. This could have been used as a social hall or a school.

The synagogue itself is a basilica in form, with one large and two small entrances leading into a hall that consists of a nave and two side aisles created by a colonnade of sixteen Corinthian columns. Interior dimensions are approximately seventy feet long by fifty feet wide. Stone benches along the sides provided seating. Earlier the excavators believed that there was a gallery for the women, but they have now abandoned that view. The structure was richly decorated with animals, birds, floral motifs, grapes, pomegranates, and an ark to hold Torah scrolls.

Excavations in the 1970s revealed that under the floor of the nave was a floor of a building dating back to the first century. In view of the Eastern practice of rebuilding synagogues, churches, and temples on identical sites, it is likely that this earlier floor belonged to the synagogue of Jesus' day.

South of the synagogue and near the water's edge is an octagonal structure, which on excavation proved to be a fifth century A.D. church built over a first century A.D. house that was converted into a church in the fourth century A.D. Inscriptions and graffiti at the site (in Aramaic, Greek, Hebrew, Latin, and Syriac) and accounts of early pilgrims identify this

as the house of St. Peter. Artifacts unearthed there demonstrate that the people who lived in and around this house were involved in the fishing business. Streets and houses dating back to the first century A.D. have been excavated around the octagonal church and the synagogue and in the area between them. Now a modern sanctuary (built in 1987–88), shaped like a flying saucer, hovers a few feet over the octagonal church.[102]

Magdala (Arabic *Migdal Nuna*, "Tower of Fish"; Greek *Taricheae*, "place of smoked fish") was the main center of fish processing on the Sea of Galilee. It is identified with the present day village of Migdal on the western shore of the Sea of Galilee, three miles north of Tiberias. This was the home of Mary Magdalene (Mary of Magdala).

Virgilio Corbo and Stanislao Loffreda excavated there 1971–74 on behalf of the Franciscan Custody of the Holy Land. They found what was first identified as a paved street but turned out to be a quay, about 300 feet long, north-to-south, built of limestone blocks with basalt edges and basalt mooring stones for boats. Its southern end connected with a breakwater that extended eastward into the Sea of Galilee. At the other end of the quay a second breakwater extended about 230 feet into the sea. This was a wall of basalt paved with flat limestone slabs.[103] Corbo and Loffreda also found a structure they identified as a small synagogue that was later turned into a city fountain house, but probably it was a fountain house all along.[104]

Tiberias was a leading city on the western shore of the Sea of Galilee, less than ten miles south of Capernaum. Herod Antipas, ruler of Galilee and Perea, moved his capital there from Sepphoris in A.D. 18 or 19 to provide a more central location for his headquarters. He named it after the ruling emperor Tiberius. As Antipas began construction of the town, his workmen came upon a cemetery. Thus Jews tended to avoid the place because of ceremonial uncleanness, and Herod had a hard time populating his capital. At the end of the first century A.D. Herod Agrippa II moved the capital back to Sepphoris. And ironical-

The Garden Tomb

ly during the second century the Sanhedrin moved to Tiberias, and it became the place of important schools of rabbinic study. Here the Mishnah was compiled and the Massoretes added vowels to the Hebrew text. It was an important center of Judaism during the Middle Ages.

Antipas erected numerous important buildings at Tiberias: his palace, a stadium, a synagogue, an agora, hot baths, and a fortress. In A.D. 61 Nero detached Tiberias, Magdala, and Bethsaida Julius from Galilee and gave them to Agrippa II. During the First Jewish Revolt, Tiberias remained loyal to Agrippa and surrendered to Vespasian, thus avoiding destruction. So far only the southern city gate and a paved street of Herod Antipas' day have been excavated. There is no indication Jesus ever went to Tiberias, perhaps because of the tradition of Jewish uncleanness and because it was the capital of Herod Antipas, "that fox" (Luke 13:32).

Jerusalem Sites

Pilate's Judgment Hall—the Pavement

Christians have been eager to locate the Pavement (John 19:13), made sacred by the sufferings of Christ. No doubt it would have been connected with the palace that Pilate used in Jerusalem, which stood in the Upper City, just inside the present Jaffa Gate—not in the Antonia Fortress, just to the north of the temple area, as is often assumed.

During much of this century the Pavement has been identified with a wonderful Roman pavement (believed to have been part of the Antonia Fortress) in the basement of the Sisters of Zion Convent, located at the second Station of the Cross on the Via Dolorosa. Outside the convent an arch crosses the Via Dolorosa and was presumed to be the arch under which Pilate proclaimed, "Behold the Man" (John 19:5). Hence the name the *Ecce Homo* Arch, Latin for "Behold the Man." Part of the triple arch may still be seen inside the convent.

The pavement under the Sisters of Zion Convent is now known to date to the second century A.D. The emperor Hadrian laid

Inside the Garden Tomb, the place where the body of Jesus is said to have been laid

Gordon's Calvary

it as part of the city forum after putting down the second Jewish revolt in A.D. 135. And the arch was a triple victory arch celebrating Hadrian's victory over the Jews. Neither that pavement, nor the arch, nor the Via Dolorosa existed in Jesus' day.

The Church of the Holy Sepulcher

The real Pavement of John 19:13 should be located in the area of Herod's palace in the Upper City. But though the foundations of that palace have been excavated, the Pavement has not yet been found.[105]

Calvary and the Tomb

Some have believed that Gordon's Calvary and the nearby Garden Tomb were the place of the crucifixion and burial of Jesus. Though with a degree of imagination the cliff face of Gordon's Calvary may look a little like the eye sockets of a skull today, it has assumed its present form since New Testament times as a result of quarrying or soil use over the centuries.

As for the Garden Tomb, there always remained some doubt as to whether the site had any validity. A few years ago, Gabriel Barkay, who teaches at Tel Aviv University and the Jerusalem University College (formerly American Institute of Holy Land Studies), made a new study of the case for the Garden Tomb. He concluded that it was first hewn in the Iron Age II period, during the eighth to the sixth centuries B.C., and was not used again for burial purposes until the Byzantine period. So it could not have been the tomb in which Jesus was buried.[106]

The traditional site of Calvary and the tomb of Jesus is in the Church of the Holy

The traditional tomb of Jesus in the Church of the Holy Sepulcher

site requires a considerable amount of space to describe in full,[108] but the main outline is as follows. When Hadrian rebuilt Jerusalem early in the second century A.D., he desecrated the site of Jesus' burial by constructing a temple to Venus (Aphrodite) upon it.

Later, when Constantine prepared to build his memorial there, he totally destroyed Hadrian's temple and then constructed a complex adjacent to the north-south main street of Jerusalem (dedicated A.D. 335). Laid out in an east-west direction, the complex involved first (on the east and next to the street) an atrium open to the sky, then a basilica type church with a nave and a double colonnade on each side. Next came a holy garden open to the sky and surrounded on three sides by columns—at the southeast of which rose the rock of Calvary. Finally (on the other side of a wall with eight gates) there was a rotunda covering the tomb of Jesus (which had been under Hadrian's temple).

Fire damaged this complex by the time of the Persian invasion of A.D. 614 and it was repaired. Then El Khakin, Caliph of Cairo, almost completely destroyed the entire church complex in 1009. The basilica was never rebuilt, but the Byzantine emperor Constantine IX restored the rotunda and

Sepulcher, now located deep inside the old city of Jerusalem. But was it outside the city in New Testament times? As a result of various discoveries in recent decades, the line of the wall has now been established. There was a jog in the wall in Jesus' day, and Calvary was located just outside that jog. The wall lay about 500 feet to the south and 350 feet to the east of where the church now stands.[107] If the church was outside the wall, the next issue is the legitimacy of the claim that Jesus was buried there.

The Church of the Holy Sepulcher as it now stands is essentially a Crusader structure, begun after the Crusaders captured Jerusalem in 1099. The prior history of the

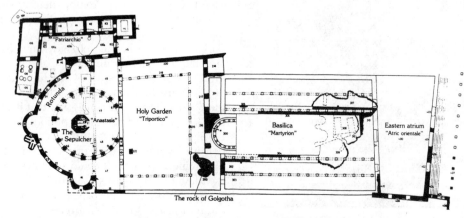

Plan of Constatine's Church, after Corbo

the holy garden fairly successfully between 1042 and 1048. Finally the Crusaders rebuilt the church essentially in the form we know it today. The entrance is now on the south side of the church. Inside and to the right rises the rock of Calvary. Straight ahead is the nave, which lies across the old holy garden. At the western end of the nave (to the left) is the rotunda with the tomb of Jesus. Thus both Calvary and the tomb are now within the church and thus under cover.

Over the centuries the Crusader church became quite decrepit. The religious bodies having access to the church finally agreed on a restoration plan in 1959. The following year Virgilio Corbo of the Franciscan School in Jerusalem was appointed archaeologist for the project. The restoration involved a considerable amount of excavation under the church. The Franciscan Printing Press published the three-volume report, *The Holy Sepulcher of Jerusalem,* in 1981–1982.

After completing his study on the Church of the Holy Sepulcher, Finegan concluded, "We may with confidence seek beneath the roof of this structure the true place of Golgotha and the sepulcher of Christ."[109] More specifically, in response to the question of whether the Constantinian rotunda was built over the true site of Jesus' burial, Bahat responds, "It seems very likely that it was,"[110] "and we really have no reason to reject the authenticity of the site."[111]

The Upper Room

On the southwestern hill of Jerusalem, now called Mount Zion, next to the Dormition Abbey, stand the remains of the first century Church of the Apostles. This church was built to mark the place where the apostles prayed after they returned from witnessing the Ascension. All that remains of that church is a small chamber now venerated as the tomb of King David. Of course it is impossible that David was buried here because the early kings of Israel were entombed at the southeast edge of the city of David, which lay south of the Temple Mount.

In the twelfth century the Crusaders incorporated the remains of the first century church into the Church of St. Mary.

The Upper Room on Mount Zion

Above it they built a room to commemorate the spot where Jesus and the disciples celebrated the Last Supper and where the Spirit descended on the day of Pentecost (Matthew 26:17–30; Acts 1:12–14; 2:1–3).

In the sixteenth century Muslims turned the Upper Room into a mosque by adding a prayer niche in its southern wall. An Arabic inscription on the wall dating to 1524 commemorates this event. The Upper Room was restored in the mid-1980s and is obviously not the Upper Room of New Testament times. About the best that can be said for this traditional Upper Room is that somewhere near here the Last Supper and the Pentecostal drama took place.

An alternate view of the place of the descent of the Spirit on the Day of Pentecost observes that the apostolic group was "continually in the temple" (Luke 24:53) after the Ascension and that the events of the Day of Pentecost (Acts 2) demanded a larger place than a single room, such as the Temple courtyard, where a large crowd could assemble. But Acts 2:2 does mention the "house" where the Spirit descended. And being "continually in the temple" does not mean they were there "continuously" and that there was no opportunity for a secluded experience of the apostolic group. The subsequent involvement of Jews and proselytes must have taken place in the Temple (Acts 2:5–47). Certainly apostolic ministry did occur in "Solomon's portico" of the Temple thereafter (Acts 3:11; 5:12).

Site of the Ascension

As to the Ascension, the New Jerusalem Bible translates, "Then he took them out as far as the outskirts of Bethany, and raising his hands he blessed them. Now as he blessed them, he withdrew from them and was carried up into heaven" (Luke 24:50).

In an alternative translation, Jesus led the disciples "to the vicinity of Bethany" (NIV). There He ascended to heaven. Bethany remains a small village about a mile and a half east of Jerusalem on the eastern slope of the Mount of Olives. On the face it, Jesus seems to have ascended to heaven near the spot where He began the Triumphal Entry into Jerusalem, the place where He raised Lazarus from the dead, and the home of Mary, Martha, and Lazarus.

The Acts account of the Ascension (1:12) indicates that the apostles returned to Jerusalem from the Mount of Olives after Jesus' departure. And it says that the Mount of Olives lay a "Sabbath day's journey" from Jerusalem. As a matter of fact, the distance from the top of the Mount of Olives to the wall of the city is about three thousand feet—the extent of a Sabbath day's journey. The common assumption is that Jesus ascended from the top of the Mount of Olives. But the Luke reference seems to locate the event on the east slope of the mountain near Bethany. Scripture does not say He ascended from the highest point. It is possible that reference to the Sabbath day's journey indicates only the last and more organized part of their walk—the descent after they had wandered up from Bethany.

At least by the late fourth century A.D. the site of the Ascension had been localized on the summit of the Mount of Olives, and about 378 A.D. the faithful built the Church of the Holy Ascension there.[112] This seems to have consisted of an inner circular colonnade of sixteen columns that supported a dome. Surrounding this they built an octagonal outer wall. When the Persians destroyed this building in A.D. 614, the patriarch of Jerusalem rebuilt it. In their turn the Crusaders rebuilt that decaying structure early in the twelfth century.

When the great Muslim conqueror Saladin took Palestine in 1187, he converted the Church of the Ascension into a mosque, which it remains to the present. It consists of an octagonal wall enclosing a courtyard about a hundred feet in diameter. Near the

The Chapel of the Ascension

center of this stands an octagonal building (the old Crusader chapel), twenty-one feet in diameter topped by a dome. The arches on the eight sides have now been walled in. It is appropriate for Muslims to use this as a place of prayer because Sura IV of the Koran says of Jesus (a great prophet) that "God raised him up unto himself." In this chapel a modern tourist may see what is supposed to be the footprint of Jesus as He ascended. But this print likely marks the extent of the Sabbath day's journey from Jerusalem (Acts 1:12), as noted above.

From my perspective, it seems unnecessary to conclude that Jesus rose up to heaven from the top of the Mount of Olives. It is enough to say that He ascended from somewhere on the Mount. Luke 24:50 specifically indicates it was from the vicinity of Bethany. And what would have been more beautiful than His Ascension from near Bethany, where the resurrection of Lazarus anticipated His own resurrection, and a household of faith (especially Mary) symbolized complete faith in Him?

NOTES

1. As a supplement to the rain, dew falls in the coastal plain about 250 nights of the year and in the hills between 100 and 180 nights per year. It varies, as does the rainfall. The dew is, of course, very beneficial to summer vegetation. God observed that the Hebrews would have this agricultural benefit, even before they conquered Palestine (Deuteronomy 33:28).

2. This Hebrew term, meaning "to be low," is variously translated in the Old Testament: "vale" (Deuteronomy 1:7; Joshua 10:40); "valley" (Joshua 11:2); "low plains" (1 Chronicles 27:28). See also Joshua 9:1; 11:16, 12:8; 15:8; Judges 1:9; 1 Kings 10:27; 2 Chronicles 1:15; 9:27; 26:10; 28:18; Jeremiah 17:26; 32:44; 33:13; Obadiah 19; Zechariah 7:7.

3. Kathleen Kenyon, *Royal Cities of the Old Testament* (New York: Schocken, 1971) 32.

4. Actually this rift is part of a geological fault that extends more than four thousand miles from northern Syria through the Red Sea and down into the great lakes of East Africa.

5. Mount Hermon has an average annual rainfall of sixty inches.

6. Yigael Yadin, "Excavations at Hazor," *The Biblical Archaeologist*, February 1956, 11.

7. This figure varies from year to year, depending on amounts of rainfall and use of water from the Jordan system.

8. See note 7 above.

9. Esdraelon may refer to the western part of this plain and Jezreel its eastern part. The western part is also called the Valley of Har Megiddo (or "mound of Megiddo"), or Armageddon. Unfortunately, Bible commentators and even the basic reference works do not standardly distinguish the use of those terms.

10. Amihai Mazar, *Archaeology of the Land of the Bible* (New York: Doubleday, 1990), 40.

11. Ibid., 43.

12. Ibid., 44.

13. An excellent brief summary of the Chalcolithic age in Palestine appears in Mazar, *Archaeology*, chap. 3. See also W. F. Albright, *Archaeology of Palestine*, rev. ed., (Baltimore: Penguin Books, 1960), chap. 4.

14. Mazar, *Archaeology*, 112.

15. See Suzanne Richard, "Toward a Consensus of Opinion on the End of the Early Bronze Age in Palestine-Transjordan," *Bulletin of the American Schools of Oriental Research* (Winter 1980), 5–34.

16. See Yohanan Aharoni, *The Archaeology of the Land of Israel*, Anson F. Rainey, trans. (Philadelphia: Westminster Press, 1982), 81–97; John Bright, *A History of Israel*, 3rd ed. (Philadelphia: Westminster Press, 1981), 54–55.

17. Aharon Kempinski, "The Middle Bronze Age," *The Archaeology of Ancient Israel*, ed. by Amnon Ben-Tor (New Haven: Yale, 1992), 167.

18. In connection with the continuing race question, it is important to observe that the curse of Genesis 9:25 was leveled against Canaan, not Ham. As those who have studied Palestinian archaeology know, the Canaanites were not Negroid and they were a morally debased people. We may suggest with good reason that now that the Canaanites have passed off the world stage the curse against them has been completely fulfilled and we need not look for contemporary fulfillment.

19. See William F. Albright, *Yahweh and the Gods of Canaan* (Garden City, NY: Doubleday, 1968); and John Gray, *The Canaanites* (New York: Frederick A. Praeger, 1964).

20. M. Liverani, "The Amorites," *Peoples of Old Testament Times,* ed. D. J. Wiseman (Oxford: Clarendon Press, 1973), 102.

21. G. Ernest Wright, "Philistine Coffins and Mercenaries," *Biblical Archaeologist* (September 1959), 61.

22. David M. Howard, "Philistines," *Peoples of the Old Testament World,* ed. Alfred J. Hoerth, et al., (Grand Rapids: Baker, 1994), 237.

23. Edward E. Hindson, *The Philistines and the Old Testament* (Grand Rapids: Baker, 1971), 72. See also Trude Dothan, *The Philistines and Their Material Culture* (New Haven: Yale University Press, 1982); Eliezer D. Oren, ed., *The Sea Peoples and Their World: A Reassessment,* (Philadelphia: The University Museum, 2000., N. K. Sandars, *The Sea Peoples* (London: Thames and Hudson, 1978); and D. J. Wiseman, ed., *Peoples of the Old Testament Times* (Oxford: Clarendon Press, 1973).

24. Eliezer D. Oren, "Tel Haror," *The New Encyclopedia of Archaeological Excavations in the Holy Land,* ed., Ephraim Stern, (New York: Simon & Schuster, 1993), 2, 580–84.

25. Robert Drews, *The End of the Bronze Age* (Princeton: Princeton University Press, 1993), 52–53.

26. H. A. Hoffner, "The Hittites and Hurrians," *Peoples of Old Testament Times,* ed., D. J. Wiseman, (Oxford: Clarendon Press, 1973), 213–14. For reference on Khirbet Kerak ware, see *Bulletin of the American Schools of Oriental Research* #189 (1968), 28f.

27. Mazar, *Archaeology,* 211.

28. George Steindorff and Keith C. Seele, *When Egypt Ruled the East,* rev. ed. (Chicago: University of Chicago Press, 1957), 53.

29. For the text of the inscription see James B. Pritchard, ed., *Ancient Near Eastern Texts* 2nd ed., (Princeton: Princeton University Press, 1955), 376–78.

30. Rivka Gonen, "The Late Bronze Age," *The Archaeology of Ancient Israel,* Amnon Ben-Tor, ed. (New Haven: Yale, 1992), 217.

31. Ibid.

32. Gonen, "Bronze Age," 218; *Archaeology,* Mazar, 243.

33. Gonen, "Bronze Age," 218.

34. For discussion of aspects of Canaanite culture, see Gonen, "Bronze Age," 218–257.

35. Walter C. Kaiser, *A History of Israel* (Nashville: Broadman & Holman, 1998), 144–150.

36. John Garstang, *Joshua and Judges* (London: Constable, 1931), 136–37.

37. Ibid., 137.

38. Ibid., 145–47.

39. Kathleen Kenyon, *Digging Up Jericho* (New York: Praeger, 1957), 261–63.

40. Bryant G. Wood, "Did the Israelites Conquer Jericho? *Biblical Archaeology Review* (March/April 1990), 54.

41. Ibid., 56.

42. John Noble Wilford, *New York Times,* 22 February 1990, A8.

43. *Encyclopedia of Archaeological Excavations in the Holy Land,* 1,49, 1975 edition.

44. Summarized in "Archaeological Digest" *American Journal of Archaeology* (July-September 1947), 311.

45. Joseph A. Callaway, "The 1964 Ai (et Tell) Excavations," *Bulletin of the American Schools of Oriental Research* (April 1965), 27–28.

46. *Encyclopedia of Archaeological Excavations in the Holy Land*, 1, 36.

47. John J. Bimson and David Livingston, "Redating the Exodus," *Biblical Archaeology Review* (September/October 1987), 48.

48. *Encyclopedia of Archaeological Excavations in the Holy Land*, II, 477.

49. E. R. Thiele, *The Mysterious Numbers of the Hebrew Kings*, new rev. ed. (Grand Rapids: Zondervan, 1982), 55.

50. Merrill F. Unger, *Archaeology and the Old Testament* (Grand Rapids: Zondervan, 1954), 149.

51. Manfred Bietak, *Avaris* (London: British Museum Press, 1996). See also, Regina Schulz and Matthias Seidel, ed., *Egypt: The World of the Pharaohs* (Cologne: Könemann, 1998), 207.

52. *Encyclopedia of Archaeological Excavations*, 2, 481–2.

53. J. L. Kelso, "Bethel," *encyclopedia of Archaeological Excavations in the Holy Land*, 1, 192; Y. Aharoni, "Lachish," in ibid., 3, 743; W. F. Albright, "Tell Beit Mirsim," in ibid., 1, 177.

54. Benno Rothenberg, *Were These King Solomon's Mines?* (New York: Stein & Day, 1972), 184.

55. Mazar, *Archaeology*, 327.

56. Ibid., 319–323.

57. Several Old Testament scholars have worked out chronologies for the Judges. For Unger's chronology see Unger, *Archaeology*, 182–87.

58. Mazar, *Archaeology*, 334–337.

59. William F. Albright, *Archaeology of Palestine*, rev. ed., (Baltimore: Penguin Books, 1960), 120–21.

60. A. Rendle Short, *Modern Discovery and the Bible*, 3rd ed. (London: InterVarsity, 1952), 182.

61. See, Mazar, *Archaeology*, 480–81.

62. See Ronny Reich and Eli Shukron, "Light at the End of the Tunnel," *Biblical Archaeological Review*, January/February 1999.

63. Reich and Shukron, "Light", 24.

64. Chaim Herzog and Mordechai Gichon, *Battles of the Bible* (Jerusalem: Steimatzky's Agency, 1978), 81–82.

65. Gleason L. Archer, *A Survey of Old Testament Introduction*, rev. ed. (Chicago: Moody, 1974), 467.

66. Ibid.

67. Gwilym H. Jones, "1 and 2 Kings" *New Century Bible Commentary* (Grand Rapids: Eerdmans, 1984), 1:133.

68. C. F. Keil, "The Books of the Kings" in *Biblical Commentary on the Old Testament*, 2nd ed., ed. C. F. Keil and F. Delitzsch, (Edinburgh: T. & T. Clark, n.d.), 80.

69. Jack Finegan, *Light from the Ancient Past*, 2nd ed. (Princeton: Princeton University Press, 1959), 113.

70. See "Has David Been Found in Egypt?" *Biblical Archaeology Review,* January/February 1999, 34–35.

71. Donald J. Wiseman, *Chronicles of the Chaldaean Kings* (London: British Museum, 1961, 33.

72. Thiele, *Mysterious Numbers,* 190.

73. Ibid.

74. See Paul B. Kern, *Ancient Siege Warfare* (Bloomington: Indiana University Press, 1999).

75. Oded Borowski, *Agriculture in Iron Age Israel* (Winona Lake, IN: Eisenbrauns, 1987), 127.

76. Ibid., 137–39.

77. Ibid., 25.

78. Pritchard, *Ancient,* 315–16.

79. Josephus, *Antiquities,* XI.8.4–6.

80. 1 Maccabees 4:52–59; John 10:22; Josephus, *Antiquities,* XII.7.7.

81. Josephus, *Antiquities,* VIII.13.5–14.2.

82. Peter Richardson, *Herod* (Columbia: University of South Carolina Press, 1996), 197–201.

83. Ibid., 201–02.

84. Meier Ben-Tov, "Herod's Mighty Temple Mount," *Archaeology and the Bible,* ed. by Hershel Shanks (Washington, DC: Biblical Archaeology Society, 1990), 22–23.

85. Adolf Deismann, *Light from the Ancient East,* 4th ed. (New York: Harper & Brothers, 1922), 80.

86. *Oxford Encyclopedia of Archaeology in the Near East* (Oxford: Oxford University Press, 1997), 3, 391–92.

87. For dating of the various structures at Samaria, see *New Encyclopedia of Archaeological Excavations in the Holy Land,* 4, 1307–08.

88. Excavations at Sepphoris have been conducted during the 1980s to the present. For a popular discussion, see Richard A. Batey, *Jesus and the Forgotten City* (Grand Rapids: Baker, 1991). Later Rebecca Nagy and others edited a more definitive work on the city: *Sepphoris in Galilee* (Raleigh: North Carolina Museum of Art, 1996); distributed by Eisenbrauns, Winona Lake, IN. See also *Biblical Archaeology Review* July/August 2000.

89. For a discussion of excavations, see Gideon Foerster, "Tiberias," *New Encyclopedia of Archaeological Excavations,* 4, 1464–73.

90. See *New Encyclopedia of Archaeological Excavations in the Holy Land,* 1, 136–143; and *Excavations and Surveys in Israel,* published annually by the Israel Antiquities Authority.

91. Fred Strickert, *Bethsaida, Home of the Apostles* (Collegeville, MN: Liturgical Press, 1998), pp. 13–17.

92. Ibid., 91, 95.

93. Ibid., 103.

94. Ibid., 49.

95. E. P. Sanders, *Judaism Practice and Belief 63 BCE-66 CE* (London: SCM Press, 1991), 125.

96. Bargil Pixner, "Jerusalem's Essene Gateway," *Biblical Archaeology Review* (May/June 1997), 22–31, 64–66.

97. See Vassilios Tzaferis, "Nazareth," *New Encyclopedia of Archaeological Excavations in the Holy Land*, 3, 1103–1105.

98. See Michael Avi-Yonah and Vassilios Tzaferis, "Bethlehem," *New Encyclopedia of Archaeological Excavations in the Holy Land*, 1, 204–209.

99. Jack Finegan, *The Archeology of the New Testament*, rev. ed. (Princeton: Princeton University Press, 1992), 62–65.

100. K. C. Hanson and Douglas E. Okaman, *Palestine in the Time of Jesus* (Minneapolis: Fortress Press, 1998), 106–10.

101. Strickert, *Bethsaida*, 41.

102. See Stanislao Loffreda, "Capernaum," *New Encyclopedia of Archaeological Excavations*, 1, 291–296; Virgilio Corbo, *The House of St. Peter at Capharnaum* (Jerusalem: Franciscan Printing Press, 1972); John J. Rousseau and Rami Arav, *Jesus and His World* (Minneapolis: Fortress Press, 1995), 39–47.

103. *New Encyclopedia of Archaeological Excavations*, 3, 965.

104. Rousseau and Arav, *Jesus and His World*, 189.

105. For discussion, see Hershel Shanks, *Jerusalem, An Archaeological Biography* (New York: Random House, 1995), 189–196.

106. Gabriel Barkay, "The Garden Tomb—Was Jesus Buried Here?" *Biblical Archaeology Review* (March/April 1986), 57.

107. Dan Bahat, "Does the Holy Sepulcher Church Mark the Burial of Jesus?" *Biblical Archaeology Review* (May/June 1986), 38.

108. Jack Finegan, *Light from the Ancient Past*, 2nd ed. (Princeton: Princeton University Press, 1959), 527–32; Bahat, "Holy Sepulcher Church," 26–45.

109. Finegan, *Light*, 531–32.

110. Bahat, "Holy Sepulcher Church," 37.

111. Ibid., 38.

112. Jack Finegan, *The Archaeology of the New Testament*, rev. ed. (Princeton: Princeton University Press, 1992), 167–70.

BIBLIOGRPAHY

Atlases, encyclopedias, dictionaries, and various background books, including references on the Dead Sea Scrolls, appear in the General Bibliography.

Aharoni, Yohanan. *The Archaeology of the Land of Israel*. Philadelphia: Westminster, 1978.

Aharoni, Yohanan. *The Land of the Bible*. London: Burns & Oates, 1967.

Albright, William F. *Archaeology and the Religion of Israel*. Baltimore: Johns Hopkins Press, 1942.

Albright, William F. *The Archaeology of Palestine*. rev. ed., Baltimore: Penguin Books, 1954.

Albright, William F. *Yahweh and the Gods of Canaan*. Garden City, NY: Doubleday, 1968.

Applebaum, Shimon. *Judea in Hellenistic and Roman Times*. Leiden: E. J. Brill, 1989.

Archaeological Institute of America. *Archaeological Discoveries in the Holy Land*. New York: Bonanza Books, 1967.

Avigad, Nahman. *Discovering Jerusalem*. Nashville: Thomas Nelson, 1980.

Avi-Yonah, Michael, ed. *The World History of the Jewish People: The Herodian Period*. New Brunswick, NJ: Rutgers University Press, 1975.

Baly, Denis. *The Geography of the Bible*. New York: Harper & Brothers, 1957.

Barclay, John M. G. *Jews in the Mediterranean Diaspora*. Edinburgh: T & T Clark, 1996.

Batey, Richard A. *Jesus and the Forgotten City*. Grand Rapids: Baker, 1991.

Bell, Albert A. Jr. *Exploring the New Testament World*. Nashville: Thomas Nelson, 1998.

Ben-Tor, Ammon, ed. *The Archaeology of Ancient Israel*. New Haven: Yale University Press, 1992.

Bierling, Neal. *Giving Goliath His Due*. Grand Rapids: Baker, 1992.

Borowski, Oded. *Agriculture in Iron Age Israel*. Winona Lake, IN: Eisenbrauns, 1987.

Bouquet, A. D. *Everyday Life in New Testament Times*. London: B. T. Batsford, 1953.

Bright, John. *A History of Israel*. 3rd ed., Philadelphia: Westminster Press, 1981.

Browning, Ian. *Petra*. Rev.ed. London: Chatto & Windus, 1982.

Browning, Ian. *Palmyra*. Park Ridge, NJ: Noyes Press, 1979.

Bruce, F. F. *Jesus and Paul, Places They Knew*. Nashville: Thomas Nelson, 1983.

Cohen, Shaye. *From the Maccabees to the Mishnah*. Philadelphia: Westminster Press, 1987.

Connolly, Peter. *The Jews in the Time of Jesus*. Oxford: Oxford University Press, 1994.

Couasnon, Charles. *The Church of the Holy Sepulchre, Jerusalem*. London: Oxford University Press, 1974.

Cross, Frank M. *Canaanite Myth and Hebrew Epic*. Cambridge, MA: Harvard University Press, 1973.

Dalman, Gustaf. *Sacred Sites and Ways*. London: SPCK, 1935.

Davis, John J., and John C. Whitcomb. *A History of Israel*. Grand Rapids: Baker Book House, 1980.

Dorsey, David A. *The Roads and Highways of Ancient Israel*. Baltimore: Johns Hopkins University Press, 1991.

Dothan Trude. *The Philistines and Their Material Culture*. New Haven: Yale University Press, 1982.

Dothan, Trude, and Moshe Dothan. *People of the Sea: The Search for the Philistines*. New York: Macmillan, 1992.

Fairweather, W. *The Background of the Epistles*. Edinburgh: T. & T. Clark, 1935.

Fairweather, William. *The Background of the Gospels*. 4th ed., Edinburgh: T. & T. Clark, 1926.

Feldman, Louis H., and Gohei Hata. *Josephus, the Bible and History*. Detroit: Wayne State University Press, 1989.

Finegan, Jack. *The Archeology of the New Testament*. Rev. ed., Princeton: Princeton University Press, 1992.

Finegan, Jack. *Handbook of Biblical Chronology*. 2nd ed., Peabody, MA: Hendrickson, 1998.

Finegan, Jack. *Light From the Ancient Past*. 2nd ed., Princeton: Princeton University Press, 1959.

Fleming, Wallace B. *The History of Tyre*. New York: AMS Press, reprint, 1966.

Fleming, Wallace B. *Sidon, A Study in Oriental History*. New York: AMS Press, reprint, 1966.

Free, Joseph P. *Archaeology and Bible History*. Revised by Howard F. Vos. Grand Rapids: Zondervan, 1992.

Freyne, Sean. *Galilee from Alexander the Great to Hadrian, 323 B.C.E. to 135 C.E.* Notre Dame: Notre Dame Press, 1980.

Garstang, John. *Joshua and Judges*. London: Constable & Co., 1931.

Garstang, John, and J. B. E. Garstang. *The Story of Jericho*. Rev. ed. London: Marshall, Morgan and Scott, 1948.

Glueck, Nelson. *The Other Side of the Jordan*. Rev. ed., Cambridge: American Schools of Oriental Research, 1970.

Gonen, Rivka. *Biblical Holy Places*. London: A. & C. Black, 1987.

Goodman, Martin. *The Ruling Class of Judaea*. Cambridge: Cambridge University Press, 1987.

Gordon, Cyrus H. and Gary A. Rendsburg. *The Bible and the Ancient Near East*. 4th ed., New York: W. W. Norton, 1997.

Grant, Michael. *The Army of the Caesars*. New York: M. Evans & Company, 1974.

Grant, Michael. *The History of Ancient Israel*. New York: Charles Scribner's Sons, 1984.

Hanson, K. C., and Douglas E. Oakman. *Palestine in the Time of Jesus*. Minneapolis: Fortress Press, 1988.

Herzog, Chaim, and Mordechai Gichon. *Battles of the Bible*. London: Greenhill Books, 1997.

Hindson, Edward E. *The Philistines and the Old Testament*. Grand Rapids: Baker, 1971.

Hitti, Philip K. *History of Syria*. New York: Macmillan, 1951.

Hoehner, Harold W. *Chronological Aspects of the Life of Christ*. Grand Rapids: Zondervan, 1977.

Hoehner, Harold. *Herod Antipas*. Grand Rapids: Zondervan, 1972.

Hoerth, Alfred J. *Archaeology and the Old Testament*. Grand Rapids: Baker, 1998.

Hoerth, Alfred J., and others, ed. *Peoples of the Old Testament World*. Grand Rapids: Baker, 1994.

Holum, Kenneth G., and others. *King Herod's Dream: Caesarea on the Sea*. New York: W. W. Norton, 1988.

Horsley, Richard A. *Archaeology, History and Society in Galilee*. Valley Forge, PA: Trinity Press, International, 1996.

Isserlin, B. S. J. *The Israelites*. London: Thames & Hudson, 1998.

Jeremiah, Joachim. *Jerusalem in the Time of Jesus*. London: SCM Press, 1967.

Johnson, Sherman. *Jesus and His Towns*. Wilmington: Michael Glazier, 1989.

Jones, A. H. M. *The Herods of Judaea*. Oxford: Oxford University Press, 1967.

Kaiser, Walter C. *A History of Israel*. Nashville: Broadman & Holman, 1998.

Kee, Howard C., and Lynn H. Cohick. *Evolution of the Synagogue*. Harrisburg, PA: Trinity Press International, 1999.

Kenyon, Kathleen M. *Digging Up Jericho.* New York: Praeger, 1957.

Kenyon, Kathleen M. *Digging Up Jerusalem.* New York: Praeger, 1974.

Kenyon, Kathleen M. *Jerusalem, Excavating 3000 Years of History.* New York: McGraw Hill, 1967.

Kenyon Kathleen. *Royal Cities of the Old Testament.* New York: Shocken, 1971.

Kern, Paul B. *Ancient Siege Warfare.* Bloomington: Indiana University Press, 1999.

Kraeling, E. G. H. *Aram and Israel.* New York: Columbia University Press, 1918.

Levine, Lee I., *The Ancient Synagogue.* New Haven: Yale University Press, 2000.

Levy, Thomas E. ed. *The Archaeology of Society in the Holy Land.* New York: Facts on File, 1995.

Maccabees, First and Second. Contemporary English translations are available in the New Revised Standard Version and the Revised English Bible.

Matthews, Victor H., and Don C. Benjamin. *Social World of Ancient Israel.* Peabody, MA: Hendrickson, 1993.

Mazar, Amihai. *Archaeology of the Land of the Bible.* New York: Doubleday, 1990.

Mazar, Benjamin. *The Mountain of the Lord.* Garden City, NY: Doubleday, 1975.

McNamara, Martin. *Palestinian Judaism and the New Testament.* Wilmington: Michael Glazier, 1983.

McRay, John. *Archaeology and the New Testament.* Grand Rapids: Baker, 1991.

Merrill, Eugene H. *Kingdom of Priests: A History of Old Testament Israel.* Grand Rapids: Baker, 1987.

Millard, Alan. *Discoveries from the Time of Jesus.* Oxford: Lion, 1990.

Miller, J. Maxwell and John H. Hayes. *A History of Ancient Israel and Judah.* Philadelphia: Westminster Press, 1986.

Moore, George F. *Judaism in the First Centuries of the Christian Era.* 3 vols. Peabody, MA: Hendrickson, 1960,

Morton, H. V. *In the Steps of the Master.* New York: Dodd, Mead & Co., 1934.

Murphy-O'Connor, Jerome. *The Holy Land.* 4th ed. New York: Oxford University Press, 1998.

Nagy, Rebecca M. ed. *Sepphoris in Galilee.* Winona Lake, IN: Eisenbrauns, distributor, 1996.

Orni, Efraim, and Elisha Efrat. *Geography of Israel.* 3rd ed., Jerusalem: Israel Universities Press, 1971.

Parrot, André. *Land of Christ.* Philadelphia: Fortress Press, 1968.

Patai, Raphael. *The Children of Noah: Jewish Seafaring in Ancient Times.* Princeton: Princeton University Press, 1998.

Pax, W. E. *In the Footsteps of Jesus.* Jerusalem: Steimatzky's Agency, 1970.

Perowne, Stewart. *The Life and Times of Herod the Great.* London: Arrow Books, 1960.

Pfeiffer, Robert H. *History of New Testament Times, with an Introduction to the Apocrypha.* New York: Harper & Brothers, 1949.

Pitard, Wayne T. *Ancient Damascus.* Winona Lake, IN: Eisenbrauns, 1987.

Pritchard, James B. *Gibeon.* Princeton: Princeton University Press, 1962.

Redford, Donald B. *Egypt, Canaan and Israel in Ancient Times.* Princeton: Princeton University Press, 1992.

Richardson, Peter. *Herod.* Columbia, SC: University of South Carolina Press, 1996.

Rogerson, John. *Chronicle of the Old Testament Kings.* London: Thames & Hudson, 1999.

Rothenberg, Benno. *Were These King Solomon's Mines?* New York: Stein & Day, 1972.

Rousseau, John J., and Rami Arav. *Jesus and His World.* Minneapolis: Fortress, 1995.

Sandars, N. K. *The Sea Peoples.* London: Thames & Hudson, 1978.

Sanders, E. P. *Jesus and Judaism.* Philadelphia: Fortress, 1985.

Sanders, E.P. *Judaism, Practice and Belief 63 BCE–66 CE*. Philadelphia: Trinity Press International, 1992.

Shanks, Hershel, ed. *Archaeology and the Bible*. Washington, DC: Biblical Archaeology Society, 1990.

Shanks, Hershel. *Jerusalem, an Archaeological Biography*. New York: Random House, 1995.

Sherwin-White, Susan, and Amelie Kuhrt. *From Samarkhand to Sardis: A New Approach to the Seleucid Empire*. Berkeley: University of California Press, 1993.

Smick, Elmer B. *Archaeology of the Jordan Valley*. Grand Rapisd: Baker, 1973.

Sperber, Daniel. *The City in Roman Palestine*. New York: Oxford University Press, 1998.

Strickert, Fred. *Bethsaida, Home of the Apostles*. Collegeville, MN: Liturgical Press, 1998.

Tenney, Merrill C. *New Testament Times*. London: Inter-Varsity Press, 1965.

Thiele, E. R. *The Mysterious Numbers of the Hebrew Kings*. Rev. ed. Grand Rapids: Zondervan, 1983.

Thompson, J. A. *The Bible and Archaeology*. Grand Rapids: Eerdmans, 1962.

Tubb, Jonathan N. *Canaanites*. Norman, OK: University of Oklahoma Press, 1998.

Unger, Merrill F. *Israel and the Aramaeans of Damascus*. Grand Rapids: Zondervan, 1957.

Vos, Howard F. *Bible Study Commentary: 1, 2 Kings*. Grand Rapids: Zondervan, 1989.

Vos, Howard F. *Nelson's New Illustrated Bible Manners & Customs*. Nashville: Thomas Nelson, 1999.

Wilkinson, John. *Jerusalem As Jesus Knew It*. Jerusalem: Steimatzky's Agency, 1978.

Wiseman, D. J. *Chronicles of the Chaldaean Kings*. London: British Museum, 1961.

Wood, Leon J. *A Survey of Israel's History*. Revised by David O'Brien. Grand Rapids: Zondervan, 1986.

Wood, Leon J. *Israel's United Monarchy*. Grand Rapids: Baker, 1979.

Yadin, Yigael. *Hazor*. Jerusalem: Weidenfeld & Nicolson, 1975.

Yadin, Yigael. *Masada*. New York: Random House, 1966.

Cedars of Lebanon. The trees in this grove are over 200 years old.

4

PHOENICIA

Phoenicia has a special appeal to some Bible students because of her role in furnishing Solomon with cedars and other materials for his magnificent temple and palace. To others it is significant as a source of Baal worship, that flooded the kingdom of Israel in the days when Jezebel ruled as Ahab's queen. It serves yet others as a good example of the fulfillment of God's prophetic judgment on a pagan society. Though small, Phoenicia played an important part in the biblical narrative—much greater than any or all of these three functions suggest. It also played a significant role in the affairs of the ancient world in general.

Geographers have commonly classified Phoenicia, along with Palestine, as a part of Syria. However, in many periods of history it has been politically separated from them. For purposes of organization and simplification of treatment, Phoenicia, Palestine, and Syria receive separate consideration in this volume.

Geographical Features

During most of her history, Phoenicia occupied a strip of the Syrian coastal plain roughly contained within the present north and south boundaries of Lebanon. But at her height she extended her control south to Mount Carmel and north to Arvad—a dis-

tance of some two hundred miles. Nowhere is this coastal plain—opposite the Lebanon Mountains—more than four miles wide, and it averages little over a mile. We know that the Phoenicians controlled part of the Lebanon Range because they possessed substantial timber resources in the cedar forests. How far inland their boundaries extended is not clear; certainly they were largely shut up to the coastal plain. Ancient Phoenicia probably never exceeded in area more than half of modern Lebanon and therefore would have approximated the size of the state of Delaware or the country of Luxembourg.

The Coastal Plain

It is somewhat misleading to refer to a Phoenician "coastal plain" because it is far from being one continuous stretch of plain. Rather, it is a series of pockets of plains surrounding the lower basins of rivers or rivulets, their existence being made possible by the mountains' slight withdrawal to the east. These plains came to be known for the principal cities located in them. For instance, on the south lay the Plain of Accho (modern Acre), then the Plain of Tyre, followed by the Plain of Sidon and the Plain of Beirut, and so on up the coast. None of these plains was very extensive. Sidon's was about ten miles in length, Tyre's about fifteen; neither was more than about two miles in width.

The Dog River and the Dog River pass.

Rivers

Fortunately for the inhabitants, the coastal plain was extremely fertile and well watered. Average annual rainfall at Beirut is about thirty-eight inches. The rivers that cross the plain on their way to the sea are no more than mountain torrents. Fall rains and melting snows of spring render them unfordable near their mouths, and no boat can survive in them. But the rivers did bring down new deposits of rich soil and plenty of water for irrigation. Most important of the rivers of Lebanon are the Nahr el Litani (ancient Leontes), which enters the sea about five miles south of Sidon; and Nahr el Kelb (Dog River, ancient Lycus), which flows into the Mediterranean about seven miles north of Beirut.

Barriers to Communication

Not only did these mountain streams prove to be a hindrance to communication, at least at certain seasons of the year, but rocky spurs posed more effective barriers. In fact, during the centuries before man learned to modify the configuration of the land, it was difficult—in some places impossible—to follow the coast by land. At Nahr el Kelb, for instance, the mountains wash their feet in the ocean, forming a virtually impassable promontory. Although the natives were thus inconvenienced, they had a strategic position for intercepting invaders. And conquerors made it a practice of carving inscriptions on the cliffs at the Dog River Pass after signal victories. A total of twelve inscriptions may be seen there—ranging in date from the time of the Egyptian, Assyrian, and Babylonian empires to the A.D. 1946 Lebanese inscription commemorating the evacuation of all foreign troops from the country. The Romans were the first to overcome the dangers of the precarious path of ancient times at Nahr el Kelb by building a road along the coast. The new Lebanese highway, completed in A.D. 1960, made possible by the blasting away of cliffs there, leaves the visitor entirely unappreciative of the difficulty of moving through this area when Phoenicians ruled the coast.

Inscriptions on the cliffs at the Dog River Pass

(Greek Byblos, modern Jubayl), Tripoli, and Arvad (ancient Aradus, modern Arwad).

The Lebanon Mountains

To the east of the coastal plain stand the virtually impassable Lebanon Mountains. If the Phoenicians wanted to penetrate the interior, they usually had to wait until summer, then make their way along the beds of dried-up mountain streams. There were two places, however, that gave easy access to the interior: at Accho in the south along the Nahr al Muqatta (biblical Kishon) and at Tripoli in the north along the Nahr al Kabir. Understandably these became important trade routes in antiquity. Even today, with the aid of modern engineering, there are few roads that cross the Lebanons.

The Lebanon Mountains are part of the western ranges of Syria, which consist of a number of separate groups divided by river valleys. The northernmost are the Amanus Mountains (modern Alma Dag), which begin in the Anti-Taurus system and extend south to the Orontes River. The second are the Nusairiyah Mountains, extending from the Orontes to Nahr al Kabir. Next come the Lebanons proper, bounded by the Nahr al Kabir (near modern Tripoli) on the north and the Nahr al Litani (near Tyre) on the south, a distance of 105 miles. South of the Litani rise the mountains of Galilee.

The Lebanon Mountains are the highest, steepest, and largest of the western Syrian ranges. As already indicated, they are over a hundred miles in length. Their width varies from about thirty-five miles in the north to six in the south. They have many peaks as high as seven-to-eight thousand feet, and in the north a few peaks ten thousand feet or more. Geologically, the Lebanons are composed of upper and lower strata of limestone, with an intermediate layer of sandstone.

The name Lebanon is derived from a Semitic word meaning "to be white." This whiteness refers to the snow-capped peaks of these mountains, which hold their blanket of snow for several months of the year. Melting snows, augmented by spring rains, send scores of rivulets, some of considerable size, tumbling down the Lebanons toward the Mediterranean. Some of these rivers contin-

A terraced slope of the Lebanon Mountains. All agricultural land there is gained and maintained with great effort

Unpromising Shoreline

Since the Phoenicians were the finest sailors of antiquity, it is surprising that they had almost no natural harbors to use as maritime bases. The coast is one of the straightest on the map. The man-made harbors that played so important a part in antiquity are nearly all silted up. Only Beirut offers safe anchorage for large modern vessels.

IMPORTANT PHOENICIAN CITIES

Tyre
Sidon
Accho (modern Acre)
Berytus (modern Beirut)
Gebal or Byblos (modern Jubayl)
Tripoli
Arvad or Aradus (modern Arwad)

Phoenician Cities

Silting and the activities of conquerors, such as Alexander the Great, have also joined to the mainland islands on which Sidon and Tyre were originally built. Phoenicians preferred such sites because they were convenient for shipping and easily defensible against attack by land. Other important cities of ancient Phoenicia included Accho, or Akko (modern Acre, Roman Ptolemais), Berytus (Biruta in Egyptian, now Beirut, or Bayrut), Gebal

El Beqa and the Lebanon Mountains

ue to flow throughout the year, and many of them have cut substantial gorges in the mountain chain.

While the western side of the Lebanons is well watered and descends in a series of ledges to the Mediterranean, the eastern side is without substantial water supply. Its steep slopes rise almost vertically from El Beqa, or the valley, between the Lebanon and Anti-Liban Mountains.

Cedars of Lebanon

The Phoenicians, confined to a narrow plain by such formidable mountains, had to trade or die. They traded, becoming the finest mariners of antiquity. They were helped in their conquest of the sea by having some of the finest timber of the Near East at hand. The timber was not only of value to them for shipbuilding but also neighboring monarchs sought after it for shipbuilding and construction of important buildings.

Lebanon for their palaces and their construction projects. David and Solomon used it extensively in their palaces, in the temple, in the construction of the Hebrew navy, and in such fortress cities as Megiddo. Persian kings hauled quantities of cedar to faraway Susa (biblical Shushan) for use in their palaces. Cedars of Lebanon supported the roof of the palace at Susa in which Queen Esther lived. A little earlier, exiles returning to Jerusalem had obtained cedar of Lebanon for the rebuilding of the temple in Jerusalem. Egyptian kings had been purchasing cedars of Lebanon as early as 3000 B.C. for use in a variety of projects. Khufu, builder of the great pyramid (c. 2600 B.C.), used cedar of Lebanon in his solar boat, and it proudly stands in its own museum at the Giza pyramid field today.

CEDARS OF LEBANON AND THE KINGS OF THE EAST

Monarchs of a timber-starved Near East highly valued cedars of

Egyptians, Assyrians, Hebrews, and others desired this valuable wood. Darius I, from far away Persia, secured cedars of Lebanon for his winter palace at Susa (biblical Shushan). Bible readers are naturally

This cedar of Lebanon is pictured on the Lebanese flag

just a few miles west of the Besharreh stand. The Hadet group is more numerous than those of Besharreh but not as beautiful. Cedars of Lebanon (*Cedrus Libani*) are also found in the Taurus and Amanus Mountains in Turkey.

Cedars of Lebanon may live to be 1,500 years old, and about a dozen of those at Besharreh are over 1,000 years old. The youngest at Besharreh are said to be 200 years old. These cedars can reach a height of over 100 feet and a girth at the base of 40-to-45 feet. They may have a branch circumference of 200 or 300 feet. Their trunks are unusually straight, and their branches are horizontal and shaped like fans. Cedarwood is hard, smooth, and reddish and finds its chief protection in its bitter taste which repels worms and other insects.

The cedar forest of ancient Phoenicia must have been extensive indeed because extremely slow growth would have prevented substantial replacement of depleted stands of timber. In recent years reforestation efforts have resulted in the planting of cedar seeds all over the Lebanon Mountains. A grove of tiny trees may be seen near the Besharreh group. But they are still very small, illustrating the slow growth of these majestic trees.

Cedar was not the only timber available in ancient Phoenicia. Aleppo pine and cypress still grow widely on the slopes of the Lebanons.

most familiar with the Hebrews' use of cedar during the days of their greatest kings—a use made possible by David and Solomon's alliances with Tyrian kings. David built a palace in Jerusalem in which he used quantities of cedar after he captured the city from the Jebusites (2 Samuel 5:11; 7:2). Solomon built a palace largely of cedar, which must have been very beautiful indeed (see 1 Kings 7). It is interesting to note that it was called "the house of the forest of Lebanon." Best known of Hebrew structures employing quantities of cedar was Solomon's Temple, which was at least faced on the interior entirely with cedar (1 Kings 6:18). In the days of Solomon or soon thereafter, cedar was extensively used in construction at Megiddo—one of the cities Solomon rebuilt and fortified. In the second temple, Zerubbabel employed cedars of Lebanon (Ezra 3:7).

Best known of the remaining cedars is the stand near Besharreh (Bsherri), almost one hundred miles northeast of Beirut by road. This grove of four hundred trees is the most beautiful, the most ancient, and the most accessible to the modern tourist. It is located at an altitude of 6,300 feet. Another grove of several hundred trees may be seen near Barook (Baruk), southeast of Beirut, at an altitude of about 5,900 feet. The wind has twisted and stunted these. A third group of cedars is located near Hadet at 5,000 feet,

Historical Developments

Beginnings

The stream of Phoenician history, flowing so close to the stream of Hebrew development, could hardly avoid overflowing its banks on occasion and spilling over on the Hebrews. This contact is intimated in numerous biblical passages. The town name of Sidon appears as early as the Table of Nations in Genesis 10, and Tyre figures in the biblical narrative as late as the end of Paul's third missionary journey (Acts 21:2–4). Along the way came the Phoenician alliances with David and Solomon, the marriage of the Phoenician Jezebel to Ahab of Israel, and prophecies of Isaiah and Ezekiel against the cities of Tyre and Sidon.

Third millennium B.C. temples at Byblos. The so-called Temple of the Obelisks is in the distance.

The name Phoenician, according to some, is traceable to the ancient Egyptians, who called the people of the Syrian coast "Fenkhu," meaning "shipbuilders." This name the Greeks rendered as "Phoinikes" (Plural of *Phoinix*), from which comes the English name for the people and area. Others do not find any connection between the Egyptian and Greek names. But they do find the origin of the English name for the inhabitants of the area in the Greek name. The singular form of the word *phoinix* may mean "dark red" or "purple" and may refer to the extensive production and export of reddish-purple dye obtained from Tyrian sea snails (murex).

In any case, the terms Phoenicia and Phoenicians are of Greek origin. And Greeks and Romans standardly used these designations both for the people of Lebanon and the Carthaginians in the West (Poeni=Punic). What the Phoenicians called themselves in the earliest days we do not know. But by the last half of the second millennium B.C., at least, they called themselves Canaanites. Phoenicians, even in the West, so designated themselves. The Bible follows that terminology. Genesis 10:15 says that Canaan had two sons, Sidon and Heth. Though Mark, writing for Gentile readers, speaks of a Syrophoenician woman (Mark 7:26), Matthew, writing for Jews, calls her a woman of Canaan (Matthew 15:22). But reflecting the disunity of the land, the Canaanites of the Phoenician area also called themselves by other terms, such as Sidonians or Tyrians.

While Paleolithic remains have been found in Lebanon. It seems that the earliest and basic ethnic element in the eastern Mediterranean area was of Mediterranean stock. They were white men and of the Caucasian race, of short to medium height, of slight or moderate build. Their heads were long with black or dark brown hair. They appeared in Lebanon by 4000 B.C. or shortly thereafter. Byblos seems to have achieved a fair degree of importance during the fourth millennium; the necropolis there goes back to the first half of that millennium.[1]

Historians argue over origins of the Phoenicians, some insisting that they arose and developed in their homeland from that original Mediterranean stock as a result of historical evolution, and others as a result of several waves of migrating Semites. We cannot come down definitively on one side or the other. Suffice it to say that there is no evidence of a Semitic conquest during the early centuries of the third millennium B.C. Therefore we are forced to believe that Semites were there at least by 3000 B.C. Jidejian asserts that a new folk settled at Byblos around 3500 to 3450 B.C.[2] Often it is concluded that Sargon of Akkad, brought the first Semitic migration to the area around 2350 B.C.

Ancient port of Byblos

Phoenicia did not begin to assume a position of any importance in international affairs until the third millennium B.C. Its rise occurred under the Canaanites, who occupied the Lebanese littoral by at least 3000 B.C. According to the Table of Nations, Sidon was the "firstborn" of Canaan (Genesis 10:15). And the city he founded gradually assumed domination of the Phoenician coast and maintained it for several centuries, finally losing it to Tyre. So marked was this ascendancy that Sidonian and Phoenician largely became interchangeable terms. This was true during the early period when Sidon was predominant in Phoenicia (Deuteronomy 3:9; Joshua 13:4, 6; 19:28) as well as long after Tyre attained the hegemony. Thus Ethbaal, king of Tyre, is called "king of the Sidonians" in 1 Kings 16:31 (NKJV). Phoenicia never attained full political unity. Its city-states maintained a

considerable degree of independence, with Byblos, Sidon, and Tyre, in that order, achieving partial or total ascendancy over the others. Phoenician society was therefore urban and its economy industrial and commercial. Jealousy and competition between the coastal cities contributed to military weakness and political instability.

The Phoenician Canaanites are often called Semites, even though they were descendants of Ham. The explanation for this switch is that at an early date an admixture of Semites and Hamites occurred in Phoenicia, with the result that the Semites became predominant. Semitic supremacy especially occurred as a result of a great Amorite invasion of Phoenicia, Syria, and Palestine a century or two before 2000 B.C. Maurice Dunand put the Amorite invasion in the period 2300–1900 B.C., and deemed it responsible for much chaos and disorder, including the destruction of Byblos.[3]

A sacrificial altar at Byblos

Early Relations with Egypt

Earliest known contacts between Phoenicia and a foreign power occurred with Egypt. Even before Upper and Lower Egypt combined to form a united nation (c. 3000 B.C.), the people of the Delta area had trading relationships with Phoenicia.[4] The Phoenician trading capital of those early days was Gebal (Greek Byblos), twenty-five miles north of Beirut. It sent wine, oils used in the mummification process, and cedarwood for ships, coffins, and choice furniture. In exchange, the Egyptians sent gold,

Phoenician walls at Byblos

Phoenician sarcophagi at Byblos

by Mesopotamian culture, and that even Aegean metalwork may have been derived from this industry.[5] Steindorff and Seele suggest that possibly Byblos was an Egyptian colony during the Old Kingdom period. Its prince was proud to refer to himself in Egyptian as "the Son of Re [chief solar deity of Egypt], beloved of the gods of his land."[6]

HOW THE EGYPTIANS BUILT SHIPS THAT SAILED TO LEBANON

fine metalwork, and especially papyrus. In fact, so large was the volume of papyrus that flowed into Gebal that its Greek name *Byblos* came to be synonymous with papyrus, or book; our word *Bible* ("the book") perpetuates the name of the ancient port.

ORIGIN OF THE WORD "BIBLE"

Egypt sent such a large volume of its writing material—papyrus—to the Phoenician port of Gebal that its Greek name *Byblos* came to be synonymous with papyrus, or book. Our word *Bible* ("the book") perpetuates the name of the ancient port and its chief import.

Throughout the Old Kingdom of Egypt (2700–2200 B.C.), extensive trade relations with Byblos continued to such a degree that Egyptian long-distance sailing vessels came to be named "Byblos travelers." Naturally such extensive commercial relations brought cultural interchange. In religion, in writing, and in decorative motif, the Phoenicians borrowed heavily from the Egyptians, whereas the Egyptians learned certain techniques of metalworking from the Phoenicians. V. Gordon Childe held that this highly advanced metal industry was an independent development, not influenced

The Egyptians, unlike other ancient shipbuilders, did not use a keel and ribs as a framework for their ships. Quiet waters of the Nile had not required such quality construction. They built their ships by fastening planks together, without keel and with few ribs, furnishing added stiffening by means of beams that supported the deck. As a substitute for keel and ribs, they looped an enormous hawser around one end of the ship, carried it along the center of the deck and looped it around the other end of the ship. When tightened by means of a pole thrust through the strands of the hawser, the hawser acted as an enormous tourniquet. Moreover a netting ran horizontally around the upper part of the hold, either as chafing protection or as an aid in holding the ship together. Because there was no keel, there was nothing in which to set a single mast. Therefore a double mast was used and held in place by lines fore and aft. On it was hung a square sail with yards on poles at the head and foot to ensure the spread of the sail. The ship was also propelled by rowers when sailing became difficult. Ships could be as much as 180 feet in length and 60 in beam.

Mention of Byblos travelers excites some curiosity as to the nature of early Egyptian

A model of Sahure's ship. *Department of Classics, New York University*

Plenty of tangible evidence of contacts between Egypt and Phoenicia in these early days is available. For example, Pharaohs began to send offerings to the temple of Baalat (Baalath) at Gebal as early as the Second Dynasty (shortly after 3000 B.C.).[8] Pharaoh Snefru, founder of the Fourth Dynasty, in the second year of his reign around 2650 B.C., brought from Lebanon forty ships filled with cedarwood. In the third year of his reign, he built a ship of cedar; in the fourth year of his reign he mentions making doors of cedar for his palace.[9] A visitor to Egypt can see cedar beam supports still in use in Snefru's burial chamber in his pyramid at Dahshur, a few miles southwest of Cairo. About fifty years later Khufu (Cheops), builder of the great pyramid, also imported cedars from Lebanon. This is known from the discovery in 1954 of his sixty-foot funerary boat of cedar, which had been housed for 4.5 millennia in its limestone vault adjacent to the great pyramid. This boat is now on display in its own museum at Giza.

Although Sargon of Akkad carved out an empire (c. 2360 B.C.) stretching from the Persian Gulf to the Mediterranean, and although he claimed control of "the forests of cedar," Egyptian influence in Phoenicia reigned supreme during the Old Kingdom and for some time thereafter. The Phoenician city-states were protected from Mesopotamian encroachment by the lofty Lebanons. Moreover, the forests of cedar that Sargon valued may have been located on the slopes of the Amanus Mountains in Asia Minor. After Sargon passed from the scene, Ur developed her empire in the twenty-first century B.C. Jidejian notes some support for a belief that Byblos was part of that empire.[10]

freighters. From an inscription and a pictorial representation left in Pharaoh Sahure's pyramid (c. 2500 B.C.), taken in conjunction with other information on Egyptian shipping, the following facts appear. The Egyptians, unlike other ancient shipbuilders, did not use a keel and ribs as a framework for their ships. Quiet waters of the Nile had not required such quality of construction. They built their ships by fastening planks together, without keel and with few ribs, furnishing added stiffening by means of beams that supported the deck.

As a substitute for keel and ribs, Sahure's men had looped an enormous hawser around one end of the ship, carried it along the center of the deck and looped it around the other end of the ship. When tightened by means of a pole thrust through the strands of the hawser, the hawser acted as an enormous tourniquet. Moreover a netting ran horizontally around the upper part of the hold, either as chafing protection or as an aid in holding the ship together. Because there was no keel, there was nothing in which to set a single mast. Therefore a double mast was used and held in place by lines fore and aft. On it was hung a square sail with yards at head and foot. The ship was also propelled by rowers when sailing became difficult. How large these ships were is unknown; but "The Story of the Shipwrecked Sailor," dating to the Old Kingdom period, shows that ships could be as much as 180 feet in length and 60 feet in beam.[7]

The Egyptian Middle Kingdom

Having declined somewhat during Egypt's First Intermediate period (2200–2050 B.C.), Egyptian commerce with and interest in Phoenicia were thoroughly rehabilitated during the Middle Kingdom years (2050–1800 B.C.). Egyptian Pharaohs now exercised stronger overlordship in Phoenicia as well as in Syria and Palestine, but it can hardly be said that they brought these areas within the bounds of their empire. Rather, they brought them within the Egyptian sphere of political and cultural influence—to the extent that natives of those areas were willing to send gifts and/or tribute to Egypt and were careful not to offend the Egyptians.

Around 1800 B.C. the Egyptian Middle Kingdom began to disintegrate. Egypt was beset with enemies on every side—and within—as the execration texts show. These texts ceremonially and magically cursed all royal enemies, including those apparently involved in palace intrigues. It is interesting to observe that Byblos is among the places cursed.[11]

The Hyksos

Peacefully infiltrating Egypt much earlier, the Hyksos overwhelmed at least the Delta of Egypt by military force around 1720 B.C. Becoming a ruling caste that controlled the Delta, they largely utilized the bureaucratic machinery of their Egyptian predecessors to rule the kingdom on the Nile. While never successful in thoroughly conquering southern Egypt, the Hyksos ruled Palestine, Phoenicia, and much of Syria, as well as achieving some control on Cyprus.

THE HYKSOS

"An unclassified goulash of humanity"

Who the Hyksos were is unknown. Though they were a mixture of humanity, they were predominantly Semitic. They trickled into Egypt from Palestine in small bands during the 1800s B.C. and by about 1720 B.C. were numerous enough and strong enough to take over northern Egypt and to dominate Egyptian affairs farther south. When they became the controlling force in Syria and Palestine is also unknown. The Egyptians learned from them how to make the composite bow and superior swords, and to employ the horse and chariot. All these they turned against their conquerors. And after tossing the Hyksos out of Egypt about 1550 B.C. they pursued the native Egyptians up into Palestine and Syria and built the Egyptian Empire there. Unfortunately historical records do not shed much light on their activities in Lebanon.

The last word is still to be written as to exactly who the Hyksos were. Whether they were originally a homogeneous people is not at all certain. At any rate, their movement into Greater Syria and Egypt was part of a series of migrations in the eastern Mediterranean world during the eighteenth century B.C. And on the way they became "an unclassified goulash of humanity," as Hitti says,[12] with a preponderant Semitic racial strain. Hitti observes that as far as Lebanon is concerned, the Hyksos seem to have been responsible for the injection of a large Armenoid element into the area.[13]

The Egyptians hated the Hyksos. Naturally no people likes to have its soil occupied by foreigners. But the Hyksos made themselves additionally obnoxious by remaining a caste largely aloof from the native Egyptians in a feudal type of society and by largely ignoring the worship of the Egyptian gods. To be defeated by foreigners, which had not occurred during Egypt's more than 1,200 years of national life, to have her culture ignored, and to find her weapons ineffective against the superior arms of the Hyksos was almost too much for the Egyptians.

The war of revenge began around 1600 B.C., spearheaded by Theban rulers, who had never been more than nominally under the control of the Hyksos. The Egyptians were successful because they effectively turned against their overlords the weapons they had introduced to Egypt. These included the horse and war chariot, the composite bow, and better swords. Though we know that the Hyksos controlled northern Egypt and Palestine and Syria for a while, we do not know much about them as a people. And we know even less about their rule in Lebanon.

The Egyptian Empire Period

We do know, however, that once the Egyptians had defeated and/or ejected the Hyksos, they continued advancing into Palestine and Syria. A case may be made for the idea that the Egyptian Empire was a natural result of the pursuit and defeat of the Hyksos, whose fortresses dotted the landscape of Palestine and Syria. But the Egyptians also may have desired a more extensive buffer area to forestall a future invasion. And they may have been interested in controlling more firmly some of the resources they knew existed in such places as Lebanon.

Conquest of Phoenicia. At any rate, the Pharaohs of the Eighteenth Dynasty kept moving farther and farther north. The military expeditions of Ahmose I, Amenhotep I, and Thutmose I and II into Palestine and Syria were in the nature of punitive raids. Thutmose I, shortly after 1525 B.C., penetrated as far as the Euphrates River. But it was Thutmose III (1490–1439 B.C. alternatively 1482–1450 B.C.) who, conducting almost annual campaigns into Syria (for a total of seventeen), broke the last remnants of Hyksos power and established the Egyptian Empire there. His annals mention successful campaigns against several Phoenician towns, including Byblos, Tyre, Aradus (modern Arwad, biblical Arvad), and Simyra. The last two are the Arvadite and Zemarite of Genesis 10:18. During his eighth and ninth campaigns we see him giving orders to have cedar trees cut in the vicinity of Byblos.[14]

The spoils Thutmose III records show something of the cosmopolitan elegance of Phoenicia at that time. Her princes had chairs of ivory and ebony decorated with gold and accompanied by footstools, tables of ivory and carob wood decorated with gold, and many other objects of great value.

In order to insure the maintenance of his empire, Thutmose III,—"Napoleon of ancient Egypt"— gave much attention to the Phoenician ports. In each he stored adequate food supplies, outfitted harbors, and commandeered ships to maintain communications with Egypt. Gradually, in Lebanon as well as throughout the rest of Greater Syria, Thutmose was able to keep the area in subjection by means of small contingents of soldiers stationed in each town. Behind these stood all the military power of Egypt, which could rapidly be brought into action.

And with his sixth campaign, Thutmose inaugurated the practice of carrying sons of the kings of the northern city-states to Egypt as hostages. There he educated them and thoroughly indoctrinated them with the Egyptian viewpoint. When the fathers of these princes died, he sent the sons home to rule as loyal subjects of Egypt. The system worked quite effectively, as future events would demonstrate. Meanwhile, large quantities of agricultural commodities, metal goods, cedar logs, and other Lebanese products found their way to Egypt annually, as spoils of war tribute, or in exchange for Egyptian goods.

Despite Thutmose's prodigious and effective show of might in Phoenicia, his son Amenhotep II (1439–1406 B.C., alternatively 1450–1425 B.C.) also found it necessary to rattle the sword under the noses of the Phoenicians. The area was probably rather docile during his reign, but his eulogist tried to show him as a fierce conqueror. The eulogies of the Pharaohs are quite misleading because they overplay the power that Egyptian kings demonstrated, and they do not give a true picture of conditions in lands they invaded. We need to keep in mind that the Pharaohs were considered to be divine and that gods are not supposed to be defeated in battle or to appear to be weak.

Decline of Egyptian Control. But liberty like truth when crushed to earth will rise again. During the Amarna Age (c. 1400–1350 B.C.), luxury-loving Amenhotep III and IV were more engrossed in religious reform, building a new capital, or sailing around on a private yacht on an artificial lake, than they were in maintaining their empire. Subject peoples would naturally become restive.

The rise of new forces further complicated the situation in Lebanon during the first half of the fourteenth century B.C. To the north the Hittites attained their height of

Ramses II, as conqueror and builder, erected large statues of himself all over Egypt. Here he stands tall in the Temple of Karnak at Luxor

power. Suppliluliuma strode out of his Asia Minor homeland, toppled the Mitanni Kingdom to the east, and marched south to face the Egyptians. Nomads and refugees (the Habiru) moved in from the desert to the east.

Caught in the power struggle between the Hittites and Egyptians and seized with a desire to obtain their freedom, the Phoenicians were tempted to play off one major power against the other—to their own advantage. Some of the city-states openly revolted. The documents that tell

the most about developments during the period are the Amarna Letters (about three hundred in number), found by an Egyptian peasant woman in the ruins of Amarna in A.D. 1887. These letters were written by petty rulers of Palestine and Syria to Amenhotep III and IV pleading for help against insurrectionists and invaders. Written in cuneiform, they demonstrate the extent of Mesopotamian influence on Greater Syria at that time.

The story told in the Amarna Tablets runs something like this. A certain Abdi-Ashirta, an Amorite with headquarters on the upper Orontes River in Syria, attempted to extend his domain by employing Machiavellian tactics. Professing allegiance to Egypt or to the Hittites, whichever best suited his purposes at the moment, he managed to enlarge his territory until it included such important Syrian cities as Qatna and Damascus.[15] He also had significant successes along the Phoenician coast. Whether the coastal cities made league with him because he pressured them militarily or whether they felt he supported their cause of independence from Egypt is not certain.

At any rate, biblical Arvad (Aradus) and Sidon early threw off the Egyptian yoke and became active foes of the Pharaohs. Perhaps their anti-Egyptian sentiment was related to their trade rivalry with Gebal (Byblos). Soon they made common cause with Abdi-Ashirta, who proceeded to conquer the coastal towns of Lebanon.

The center of pro-Egyptian power was at Byblos, and for good reason. Her economy was tied to trade with Egypt and her culture was strongly influenced by Egypt. Rib-Addi of Byblos was chief spokesman for the Egyptian faction. As pressure against his city and opposition to his cause mounted, he sent appeals to Egypt for help—some fifty in all—almost without response. After a courageous stand, Rib-Addi was forced to flee when Byblos was isolated from her hinterland. The southward march of the Abdi-Ashirta forces (now headed by his sons who took over after the death of their father) sent Rib-Addi fleeing from his refuge in Beirut. Ultimately, at Sidon, his enemies sealed his fate. Subsequently the

Sidonians and the Amorites besieged Tyre. During the protracted siege Abi-Milki, the king of Tyre, sent repeated pleas to Egypt, without response. Finally Tyre, the last great Egyptian stronghold on the Lebanese littoral, fell. Soon Egyptian power in all of Greater Syria had ended. Aziru, son of Abdi-Ashirta, had established a hegemony over Phoenicia; but he himself was a vassal of the Hittites.

Resurgence of Egyptian Power. About a half century later (c. 1300 B.C.), Seti I of Egypt again subdued the coastal cities of Phoenicia and had some success in reestablishing the Egyptian empire in Asia. His son and successor, Ramses II, ran into trouble. After making his power known in Phoenicia, where he carved his inscription beside the Dog River, (Nahr el Kelb), he determined to halt the Hittite advance into Syria.

Marching east from Lebanon, Ramses II was ambushed by the Hittites at Kadesh on the Orontes in 1286 B.C. Exercising unusual courage, he was able to save himself from annihilation and went home to chisel into the temple walls a claim of great victory in classic Egyptian braggadocio. The Hittites also went home claiming a victory. The truth is that the outcome of the battle was something of a draw. Intermittent fighting between Egyptians and Hittites continued for a few more years, and the two powers signed a nonaggression pact about fifteen years later. By the terms of the pact Egypt retained control of Palestine and Syria. Obviously neither power could topple the other.

During the remainder of Ramses II's reign, the pact with the Hittites stood. His successor, Merneptah, concerned himself with a brief struggle with enemies in southern Palestine and claimed a devastating defeat of the Hebrews. At the beginning of the twelfth century, Ramses III with great effort turned back an invasion of his northern coasts by the Sea Peoples (Libyans, Philistines, and others).

After the days of Ramses II, the Phoenicians were no longer disturbed by either Egyptians or Hittites. By shortly after 1200 B.C. the Hittite Empire was convulsed

in dying gasps; the Egyptian Empire was declining. Around 1100 B.C., when the Pharaonic envoy Wen-Amon came to Byblos to obtain cedar, he was at first told to go home and then was made to wait for days before having his request granted. Ultimately he seems to have paid a handsome price for the Pharaoh's cedar logs. By then the Aramaens had occupied Syria, the Hebrews the highlands of Palestine, and the Philistines the southwest coast of Palestine. The Egyptian Empire in Asia had come to an end.

The Sea Peoples who splashed ashore in Phoenicia around 1200 B.C. do not seem to have been as destructive as they were farther north in Ugarit. And some believe that the Phoenicians were not victims but rather allies of these sea raiders.[16] Though the ethnic composition of the area may have been somewhat changed, the culture remained Canaanite. Modest economic prosperity existed at Sidon, Byblos, and Aradus, at least. Then, gradually establishing control over the Mediterranean, the Phoenicians launched their golden age.

Phoenician Independence

The period of Phoenician independence (c. 1200–800 B.C.) is probably the era of Phoenician history most appealing to the Bible student. During these centuries David and Solomon, Israel's greatest monarchs, allied themselves with Tyre and used Phoenician knowledge and cedars to construct buildings on land and ships at sea.

The international conditions that permitted both the Phoenician and Hebrew developments at that time are worth reviewing. These conditions allowed the expansion of the Hebrew kingdom to the Euphrates on the north and the border of Egypt on the south and permitted the Phoenicians under the leadership of Tyre to achieve a maritime supremacy of the Mediterranean that was not to be broken completely until the days of Alexander the Great.

Imperial Weakness. There was a power vacuum in the Mediterranean world during these centuries of Phoenician independence. Around 1200 B.C. the Hittite Empire collapsed. The traditional date for the fall of

Troy, on the Hittites' western border, is 1184 B.C. though it must have occurred much earlier. Troy's supposed destroyers, the Mycenaeans, passed off the scene about 1100 B.C., and Greece went through a period of readjustment until 800 or after—often called the Greek Middle Age. Also around 1100 B.C. the Egyptian Empire disintegrated. Babylonian power (of the dynasty of Hamurabi) had disappeared centuries earlier and would remain ineffective until shortly before 600 B.C. Assyria, after a brief spurt of activity under Tiglath-Pileser I around 1100 B.C., went into eclipse for more than two hundred years. In the West there was nothing of significance. While the traditional date of the founding of Rome is 753 B.C., we now know there were some insignificant villages on the hills of Rome as early as 1000. Elsewhere in the western basin of the Mediterranean there were a few tribes scattered around. Even Phoenician colonies like Carthage were not founded until around 800 B.C. or possibly later. So it is quite obvious that there was little in the Mediterranean world to stop Phoenician or Hebrew expansion at the beginning of the first millennium B.C.

Dearth of Information. Unfortunately our sources of knowledge for the period of Phoenician independence are quite sketchy, as is true of many other periods of Phoenician history. Little has been done in the way of archaeological investigation. One of the most extensive excavations has been conducted at Byblos intermittently by the French since 1924. Among the directors of this work have been Pierre Montet and Maurice Dunand. Digging at the site has uncovered layers of occupation dating from the second millennium to the Roman period. At Tyre since 1947 the Lebanese Department of Antiquities has uncovered ruins of the Byzantine and Greek periods. Excavation of the Phoenician levels below them would require destruction of Greco-Roman materials. James B. Pritchard of the University of Pennsylvania directed archaeological work at Sarepta (modern Sarafand) from 1969 to 1974, uncovering the port area, pottery production and purple dye production facilities, and shrines dating to the

Phoenician period. During the last few years archaeologists have had a chance to conduct rush digs in Beirut while contractors were waiting to rebuild the center of the city destroyed in the civil war of recent years. Not much excavation has been done elsewhere.

For information on Phoenician history prior to the Assyrian period, the greatest help comes from Josephus (who alludes to some historical works extant in his day) in both his *Antiquities* (VIII.5) and *Against Apion* (I.14–18); Justin, a Roman historian of the third century A.D., who wrote *Historiarum Philippicarum* (see XLIV); and the Bible. From the available materials it is possible to sketch an outline history of the period of independence.

As has been noted, the indication in Genesis 10:15 of the priority of Sidon (or Zidon) seems supported by the common equation of "Phoenician" and "Sidonian"—in Scripture, in Homer, and in other ancient sources. While the Phoenicians called their land Canaan, their name for themselves was Sidonians.[17] Moreover, Isaiah speaks of Tyre as "daughter of Sidon" (Isaiah 23:12 NKJV).

In connection with this latter assertion, it should be noted that Josephus claimed that Tyre was founded 240 years before the building of the temple at Jerusalem (*Antiquities*, VIII, 3). And Justin asserted that Tyre was founded one year before the destruction of Troy (XVIII, 3). Both of these notations would put the founding of Tyre around 1200 B.C., at the beginning of the period of independence. However, we have noted that Sidon besieged Tyre during the Amarna Age. And Herodotus, in his history of the Greco-Persian wars, supports an approximate date of around 2750 B.C. for the founding of Tyre (II, 44).

The truth of the matter seems to be that both Tyre and Sidon were founded very early, Sidon achieving an ascendancy much earlier than Tyre. During the Amarna Age, Sidon was successful in a siege of Tyre. How much destruction occurred at Tyre then is not known. At any rate, Sidon continued in a predominant position. At the end of the thirteenth century the Sea Peoples began to make raids on Egypt and the Syrian coast. One of these peoples, the Philistines, had a league of five cities in southern Palestine. The king of one of these cities, Ascalon (biblical Ashkelon), sacked Sidon and left it very largely in ruins around 1200 B.C. Around that same time Greek expansion in the Aegean and the fierce rivalry of the mariners of Crete and Cyprus drastically cut the prosperity of the beleaguered city-state.

At the time of her military defeat, many Sidonians migrated to Tyre. In this sense Tyre could be called the "daughter of Sidon." And in this sense the city could be said to have a founding around 1200 B.C., as Josephus and Justin indicate. In this way all of the historical indications are cared for, and it is explained how Sidon lost her ascendancy to Tyre early in the period of independence.

As an added note, Ugarit and Alalakh had controlled most of the Syrian trade with the Aegean during the second millennium B.C. Elimination of both these centers of commerce by the beginning of the period of Phoenician independence opened the way for the increase of Phoenician trade with Greece. To claim, however, that Tyre or Sidon had something to do with establishing a Phoenician colony under the leadership of Cadmus at Thebes, about thirty-three miles northwest of Athens, during the period of Phoenician independence or earlier seems quite unlikely, if not mythological.[18]

Spotlignt on Tyre. The story of the period of Phoenician independence is largely the story of the expansion of Tyre. Perhaps this is true to some extent because the available sources do not permit a well-rounded history of the Lebanese littoral. At Byblos, for instance, there is a lack of stratified materials for the period 1200–600 B.C. This may be the result of later use of those remains (e.g., by the Crusaders). Or, as some believe, Byblos of the Iron Age may have been located outside the earlier area of occupation, perhaps under the modern town.[19] From what we can learn, however, it is apparent that Byblos had kings of her own. Other city-states in the area probably did also.

But certainly a greater knowledge of the times would not rob Tyre of her place of preeminence. She was clearly ascendant over Sidon. Byblos, tied largely to Egyptian trade, apparently decayed with the decline of the colossus to the south. Moreover, Tyre was largely responsible for the extensive Phoenician colonization and maritime activity that occurred soon after the end of the period. Says Warmington, "It is probable that Tyre exercised some sort of control over almost all the cities of Phoenicia from the time of Hiram to the seventh century; there was a common system of weights and measures, and it is impossible as yet to distinguish between the products of the different cities."[20]

Phoenician sea power rapidly expanded from 1100 to 1000 B.C. This may have occurred because of land need or the pressure of the Aramaeans in the hinterland. Or possibly, as Arthur Evans and Hogarth suggest, this advance came as a result of immigration of peoples from Aegean lands.[21]

Phoenician Ships. What sort of ships the Phoenicians sailed is a matter of some interest, since they dominated the Mediterranean for several centuries. Phoenician ships of about 1350 B.C. are pictured on an Egyptian inscription. These were deep-bellied freighters with curved ends that terminated in straight stem and sternposts. Their substantial holds were covered with flush decks and surrounded with a high railing that permitted a large deck load. Along the top and foot they carried broad square sails bent to two yards,.[22] A clay model of a boat uncovered at Byblos shows an undecked merchantman with high sides, giving the appearance of an elongated bowl.[23] The latter was probably used for short coastal hauls as it would easily have swamped on the open sea. Presumably Phoenician ships of the period of independence were similar to those pictured earlier on the Egyptian tomb wall, though Aegean influence may have modified them somewhat.

While the Greeks used galleys powered by rowers for warships (and perhaps the Phoenicians did also before the days of Hiram and Solomon), merchantmen of the pre-Christian era do not seem to have changed much from the slow sail-powered vessels of the late second millennium B.C.

Hiram the Great. The best days of Tyre probably began during the reign of Hiram I.[24] When he took the reins of government, Tyre consisted of a small island about a half mile from the Phoenician coast, with a yet smaller island lying to the southwest. (Whether there was a Tyre on the mainland at the time is uncertain; at least it is commonly agreed that the island Tyre was founded earlier than the town on the mainland.) Hiram I joined these two islands and then claimed from the sea an area on the east of the larger island. The total circumference of the island was now about 2.5 miles. He then proceeded to rebuild and beautify the temples, the most famous being to the god Melkart; this latter temple had long stood on the smaller island. Subsequently he gave attention to the harbors and fortifications of the city, constructing by means of piers the Sidonian harbor on the north and the Egyptian harbor on the south. Father Poidebard confirmed the existence of these harbors in three aerial and underwater expeditions in 1934–36. He found that in some places the well-built breakwater extended to a depth fifty feet below the surface of the water.[25] A wall eventually rose to a height of 150 feet on the mainland side of the island. This was surmounted by battlements. Exactly when the breakwaters and fortifications were constructed is unknown, though Hiram I is given credit for enlarging earlier harbors and is sometimes credited with constructing the wall.

HIRAM THE GREAT AND THE REAL BEGINNINGS OF TYRE

Hiram the Great (c. 1000 B.C.) also known as Hiram I gets credit for the real beginnings of Tyre. He joined together two small islands about a half mile off the Lebanese coast, constructed its northern and southern harbors, rebuilt and beautified its temples, and perhaps was responsible for the 150-foot-high defense wall on the mainland side of the island.

When Hiram I ruled is somewhat problematical. Josephus says that Hiram ruled for thirty-four years and that he was in his twelfth year when Solomon began the Temple. According to 1 Kings 6:1 Solomon began the Temple in his fourth year. This would mean that Hiram began his reign eight years before Solomon began his and therefore overlapped David's reign by that much. It would seem, however, that David enjoyed the assistance of Hiram for longer than eight years. Indications in 2 Samuel 5:11–12 (in context) and 1 Chronicles 14:1–2 (in context) imply that Hiram furnished David with cedar and artisans for the construction of his palace soon after David's conquest of Jerusalem, in about the eighth year of his forty-year reign. We might suggest that Hiram rendered this assistance while he was still crown prince and perhaps coregent with his father Abi-Baal. But Hiram was only about twenty when his father died and he assumed full control of the government. Perhaps it is assumed incorrectly that Hiram I had associations with David before the middle of David's reign. Possibly Josephus is in error in stating that the Temple was begun during the twelfth year of Hiram's reign.

At any rate, Josephus supports the Scripture in asserting the overlap of the reign of Hiram I with both David and Solomon. That is really all the situation absolutely demands. When Hiram I is dated will depend on what biblical chronology we adopt. If we follow E. R. Thiele, who would begin Solomon's reign in 970 B.C., Hiram began his reign about 978 B.C. If we follow W. F. Albright, Hiram's reign began around 970 B.C.

Hiram's Successors. Hiram's successors were not able to retain the purple as long as he (thirty-four years). Either they were not such hardy souls, or they were not so adept in squelching revolution. After Hiram died, his son Beleazarus (Baalusur) ruled for seven years. Beleazarus' son Abd-Astartus ruled nine years and was assassinated by four of his sons. The eldest of these, Deleastartus, ruled twelve years and was succeeded by his son Astartus, who likewise ruled twelve years. Astartus' brother Aserymus then ruled nine years and was murdered by his brother Pheles, who lasted only eight months and was in turn assassinated by Ithobalus (Ethbaal), priest of Astarte, who ruled thirty-two years. Ethbaal's son Badezorus ruled six years and Badezorus' son Matgenus nine years. It was Ethbaal's infamous daughter Jezebel who married Ahab of Israel (1 Kings 6:31).

Relations Between Phoenicians and Hebrews. Having noted the dynastic development at Tyre during the period of independence, we return to a consideration of relations between the Phoenicians and Hebrews during the days of Hiram I and to the success of the Phoenicians in industrial and commercial activity during the period.

After David had become king over all Israel and while he was enjoying evident success in warfare against his neighbors, Hiram of Tyre sent a friendly embassy to David to open negotiations with him. The result was a supply of cedar trees and Tyrian carpenters and masons to David for the construction of his royal palace (2 Samuel 5:11–12; 1 Chronicles 14:1–2).

Some have suggested that the close relations between the Tyrians and Hebrews during the reigns of David and Solomon involved an alliance against the Philistines, their common enemy. While this is plausible, there is no indication that this pact ever issued in anything but peaceful pursuits. Initially Hiram may have wanted to gain favor with a rising potential enemy by sending an embassy to David. But soon it must have become evident that both powers would benefit economically from such an alliance. Of course the biblical account is extremely abbreviated. We need not assume that David got his new palace as a gift from Hiram; he probably had to pay dearly for it.

In David's later years he made preparation for construction of the Temple in Jerusalem. His collection of materials included a large amount of cedarwood furnished by Tyre and Sidon (1 Chronicles 22:4). When God prevented David from building the Temple because he was a warlike man, David under divine orders passed the task on to his son Solomon (1 Chronicles 22:5–12).

Solomon accepted the charge and shortly after the beginning of his reign sent correspondence to Hiram to make specific arrangements for actual construction. The exchange between the two kings appears in 2 Chronicles 2 and 1 Kings 5:1–12. Solomon needed wood, gold, and artisans in various trades. In exchange for the wood and skilled labor Solomon furnished agricultural products, and for the gold a section of land.

The wood desired included cedar, fir (or perhaps cypress), and algum (or almug, probably red sandalwood, 2 Chronicles 2:8). Solomon was to send woodcutters to Phoenicia to help fell the timber, which was then to be floated to Joppa (modern Jaffa). Stonecutters and other workers were to be sent from Phoenicia. Solomon especially wanted a master workman to direct all the artistic work in gold, silver, brass, iron, stone, wood, and cloth. The man chosen for this task was another Hiram (not the king; see 1 Kings 7:13–14), whose specialty seems to have been "brass" (copper) casting. Solomon also needed a considerable amount of gold for decoration of the Temple and his palace. King Hiram also agreed to furnish this.

The total amount of what Solomon agreed to pay annually for the wood and laborers was 20,000 measures (Hebrew *kor*, 10–11 bushels each) of wheat, 20,000 measures of barley, 20,000 measures (Hebrew *bath*, 4.5 gallons each) of wine, and 20,000 measures of oil (thought to be a textual corruption; the amount is seemingly too much; see 2 Chronicles 2:10).

HIRAM THE GREAT AND THE HEBREWS

Hiram helped David build his palace and helped Solomon build his palace, the Temple, and Solomon's fleet and its port. Then he apparently engaged in maritime ventures with Solomon. The Hebrew kings paid handsomely for the Tyrian products and expertise, as Scripture makes clear.

The fact that this payment differs from that mentioned in 1 Kings 5:11 is easily explained. The latter reference speaks of a payment of 20,000 measures of wheat and 20 measures of pure oil and says this was for "his [Hiram's] household." The 2 Chronicles statistics probably include receipts for public expenditures as well. For gold Solomon gave a tract of land in Galilee to Hiram; encompassing twenty towns. Upon seeing this district, Hiram was quite unhappy and called it *cabul*. According to Josephus this word is a Phoenician term meaning "that which does not please" (1 Kings 9:10–14; Josephus, *Antiquities*, VIII, 5).

It's apparent that the Temple was a remarkable structure indeed and that the craftsmanship of the Phoenicians greatly impressed the Hebrews. Every indication points to the influence or adoption of Phoenician architectural and artistic design. (Description of the Temple appears in Chapter 3).

Having established an agreement for building purposes, Solomon and Hiram also seem to have drawn up a pact for joint commercial endeavor. Solomon's conquest of the Edomites gave him access to the Red Sea. There he constructed the port of Ezion-Geber and built a fleet of ships for trade in eastern and southern waters (1 Kings 9:26–28). Up to this point, the Hebrews had never possessed good port facilities and had never engaged extensively in travel by sea.[26]

When constructing a port and fleet, the most natural place for the Hebrews to turn for skilled technicians was to the Phoenicians, acknowledged leaders in the field. And the Phoenicians were glad to cooperate in construction of a southern fleet because, on the one hand, such a fleet would not contest their mastery of the Mediterranean, since there was no Suez Canal in those days. On the other hand, the Phoenicians would in this way have access to goods of Arabia and Africa for their Mediterranean trade; these products they previously had had to do without. The land of Ophir mentioned in 1 Kings 9:28 as a source of gold was located in southwest Arabia (modern Yemen) and perhaps included the adjacent coast of Africa.

On the eve of World War II, Nelson Glueck excavated at Tell el-Kheleifeh near the modern Israeli port of Eilat on the Gulf of Aqaba and identified it as Solomon's seaport of Ezion-Geber. Initially he made somewhat sensational claims for the site (e.g., that it was a copper smelting site, a sort of Pittsburgh of the ancient Near East). Later Glueck modified his views and Beno Rothenberg, Glueck's assistant at Tell el-Kheleifeh, believes the tell is not to be identified with Ezion-geber. Rothenberg and others have suggested the possibility that the island of Jezirat Fara' un, about three hundred yards from the shore at Eilat, may have been the site of Ezion-geber. Rothenberg has observed further that no great fortress and port installation would have been necessary for the occasional use that Egyptian miners, Solomon, and Jehoshaphat of Judah required in the area.[27]

Some have thought, on the basis of 2 Chronicles 9:21, that Solomon had a fleet in the Mediterranean that accompanied Tyrian fleets to Tarshish. Many identify Tarshish with Tartessus, not far west of Gibraltar in southern Spain. If we compare 2 Chronicles 9:21 with a parallel passage in 1 Kings 10:22, we seem to arrive at a different opinion. The latter reference alludes to a navy or ships *of* Tarshish rather than to ships *to* Tarshish. Ships of Tarshish seem to have been a special kind of ship for long hauls,[28] just as "Byblos travelers," alluded to earlier in this chapter, referred to a kind of ship (see 1 Kings 22:48). Our conclusion is, then, that the ships of Tarshish actually sailed in the Red Sea and probably even out into the Indian Ocean. Certainly the products brought back were not for the most part of Mediterranean origin (ivory, apes, and peacocks—native to India and Ceylon) but freight that would more likely dock at Ezion-Geber.

Not only did Hiram, and Solomon have a public commercial alliance, they seem to have had a private tilt of shrewdness over solving riddles. Josephus records that the two monarchs exchanged riddles or enigmatic sayings, with the understanding that the one who could not solve those submitted to him had to forfeit a money payment. At first Hiram seems to have been the substantial

A Phoenician warship pictured in a relief in the palace of Sennacherib at Nineveh. *British Museum*

loser; but later, with the help of a certain Abdemon of Tyre, he managed to solve the riddles. Later Hiram proposed a number of riddles that even wise Solomon could not unravel, and Solomon paid considerable sums of money to Hiram (Josephus, *Antiquities*, VIII, 5 *Against Apion*, I, 17).

As indicated in Scripture, Solomon reaped substantial wealth from his joint maritime exploits with the Phoenicians (see 1 Kings 9:28). And we may be sure that the Phoenicians were reaping much more wealth from their commercial endeavors than was previously the case. Not only were they middlemen for a large percentage of the commerce of the Near East, but they also dominated the trade of the entire Mediterranean world.

PHOENICIAN OVERSEAS EXPLOITS

The Phoenicians were intrepid seafarers. They traded all across the Mediterranean, establishing trade depots on Sicily, Malta; in Carthage, Spain; and elsewhere. They sailed through the Straits of Gibraltar (2,300 miles from home) and evidently eventually tapped the British tin trade in Cornwall. There is even support for their circumnavigation of Africa around 600 B.C. Reportedly they

sailed up the Nile, took Pharaoh Necho's canal to the Red Sea, and then went south along the east coast of Africa, returning to Egypt in the third year after their departure.

Phoenician Commerce. The Phoenicians were intrepid seafarers. After the fall of Cretan and Mycenaean sea power, they became predominant in the Mediterranean world and the Near East. Goods which they secured from Egyptian or Mesopotamian sources or produced in their own shops, they carried into the Aegean Sea and throughout the Mediterranean and even beyond the Pillars of Hercules at Gibraltar. They sailed in ships with Solomon's men down the coasts of Africa and Arabia and perhaps as far as India and Ceylon. How early and how close they got to tin-producing Cornwall in England is a matter of some controversy.

Their crowning achievement (if indeed they accomplished it) was the circumnavigation of Africa during the reign of Pharaoh-Necho of Egypt (609–593 B.C.). Necho, who reopened the ancient canal between the Nile and the Red Sea, suggested the project to the Phoenicians. Reportedly, they took the canal route and then went south along the east coast of

Africa, returning to Egypt in the third year after departure. The trip took so long because they stopped to plant wheat on the way and wait for a harvest. Herodotus, who reported the event, commented, "There [Egypt] they said (what some may believe, though I do not) that in sailing round Libya [Africa] they had the sun on their right hand" (IV, 42). But Hitti observes, "This last detail which made Herodotus suspect the veracity of the story is precisely what confirms its authenticity. As ships sail west around the Cape of Good Hope, the sun of the southern hemisphere would be on their right."[29]

Whatever we may think about Phoenician circumnavigation of Africa, evidently they did not discover the New World, reaching Brazil in the sixth or fifth century B.C. Lipinski reports that the inscription on which the claim of discovery is based is evidently a forgery, judged by the "contents and language of the text.[30]

The important discovery that made possible greater maritime success for the Phoenicians was that one could lay a course by the polestar (i.e., Polaris, the North Star) especially in conjunction with other heavenly bodies. The Greeks named the polestar the Phoenician Star. Prior to this discovery, it was common to sail by day along the shore or within sight of land, to beach or anchor a boat at night, or to engage in island hopping (in places such as the Aegean).

As Phoenician commercial contacts became more frequent in various areas, they tended to plant trading stations which in many instances grew into full-fledged colonies. This subject is explored subsequently.

The Phoenicians were the great middlemen of culture and commerce. Their civilization was blended under Egyptian, Babylonian, and Greek influence; and what they learned from the older peoples they put to good use in the development of their culture and in the products they produced for export throughout the Mediterranean. As the middlemen of commerce, they carried the goods of the Nile and Tigris-Euphrates valleys, of Syria, of the Red Sea area (transported overland through Solomon's domain), of the Aegean, and of the lands around the Mediterranean.

While the Phoenicians were more skillful as traders than as manufacturers, they were skillful at making a number of commodities. In metallurgy, especially in connection with copper and bronze, the Canaanites were probably unequalled from about 2100 to 1200 B.C. They were very skilled in the casting and engraving of metals and in the making of jewelry. They learned from Egypt the manufacture of glass and glazed ware, perfected the art, and marketed the product. They also excelled in needlework and the production of linen and woolen cloth.

Perhaps the Phoenicians' most famous product was purple dye. The Minoans and Greeks utilized the mollusk in making purple dye before them; but the Phoenicians, especially of Tyre and Sidon, had a superior grade of the shellfish with which to work. So much work was involved in dyeing a single piece of cloth, because only a few drops of dye could be obtained from one mollusk, that only the wealthy, and especially kings could afford such material.

Phoenician imports were mainly comprised of raw materials, metals (e.g. silver, iron, tin, and lead from Tartessus in Spain), and slaves. They seem to have organized the first widespread trade in slaves.[31] Of course, slaves, like all other imports, were geared to the export market. The most important exports were timber, metal goods, glass products, jewelry, and purple textiles.

Though Ezekiel 27 refers to a time some three centuries later than the period now under discussion, it is a remarkable description of the cosmopolitan character and extent of the trade of Tyre (and, by extension, all of Phoenicia). There was little difference between the nature of Phoenician trade in 900 and in 600 B.C.; the former date preceded the greatest days of Phoenician prosperity, the latter followed it. There was one difference in shipping, however, as intimated in the Ezekiel passage. In 1000 B.C., Phoenician merchantmen depended almost exclusively on sail; by 600 B.C., galleys powered by oars were in common use.

The Assyrian Period

To a large degree, the development of Greater Syria was made possible by the fact that Assyria was quiescent. Although

Ashurnasirpal II built the terrifying might of
Assyria's military system. Here is one of his larger
than life statues from his capital at Calah.
British Museum

with a little cash was better than destruction; the Assyrians never dealt lightly with
those who dared to oppose them. Then, too,
by paying tribute, they purchased immunity from undue interference. Moreover, a
strong power controlling western Asia
meant more stable conditions, which were
favorable for commercial relations. Besides,
when powerful rulers died, there was
always the hope that their successors
would be weak and incapable of controlling
subject powers.

Shalmaneser III (858–824 B.C.) continued
the expansionist policies of his father,
Ashurnasirpal. Shalmaneser was apparently more of a threat to Syrian independence
than his father had been; for when he
marched west, a coalition of twelve kings
met him at Karkar (Qarqar) in 853 B.C.
Leading the forces was Benhadad II of
Damascus with 20,000 infantry and 1,200
chariots. Ahab of Israel provided the next
largest force: 10,000 infantry and 2,000 chariots. Several Phoenician city-states sent contingents to the 60,000-man army. The battle
seems to have ended in something of a
draw. While the Assyrian king claimed a
total victory, he found it necessary to make
repeated expeditions into Syria. Around
842 B.C. he recorded having received tribute
from Tyrians, Sidonians, and Jehu of Israel.
In the twenty-first year of his reign, he
records having crossed the Euphrates for
the twenty-first time and having received
tribute from Tyrians, Sidonians, and
Byblians.

It is quite possible that at least during the
early part of the Assyrian period Phoenicia
had a considerable amount of local autonomy. And it is quite probable that the sway of
Assyria was favorable to the land commerce of Tyre by making caravan routes
more safe. Phoenicia attained the height of
her prosperity during the eighth century—
under Assyrian suzerainty. Near the end of
the eighth century, Isaiah wrote of Tyre,
"The harvest of the River, is her revenue;
and she is a marketplace for the nations . . .
the crowning city, Whose merchants are
princes, Whose traders are the honorable of
the earth" (Isaiah 23:3–8 NJKV). Modern
Bible translations identify the "river" of
Isaiah 23:3 as the Nile.

Tiglath-Pileser I (c. 1114–1076 B.C.) gave
promise of building a formidable empire,
his successors for some two hundred years
were not at all of his mettle and posed little
threat to surrounding lands. Everything
changed, however, with Ashurnasirpal II
(883–859 B.C.). Having developed a powerful army, he proceeded to use it, especially
against the westland. Around 868 he
"washed his weapons in the great sea"[32]
and received tribute from Arvad, Byblos,
Tyre, Sidon, and other nearby towns.

While the Phoenicians could fight if they
had to, as history well demonstrates, they
were a commercial rather than a warlike
people. They apparently felt that parting

Tiglath-Pileser III restored Assyrian power over Phoenicia after Assyrian decline early in the eighth century B.C. *British Museum*

Perhaps another reason for the general prosperity and peace in Phoenicia during the first half of the eighth century B.C. is that Assyria was moribund during the reigns of the three kings who ruled from 782 to 745 B.C. But with Tiglath-Pileser III (745–727 B.C.) the empire came to life once more. Around 740 B.C. (scholars vary on the date between 743 and 738 B.C.), he had a successful western campaign during which he received tribute from, among others, Rezin of Damascus, Menahem of Samaria, and Hiram II of Tyre. In 732 B.C. he destroyed the kingdom of Syria and he annexed northern Israel. It was only a matter of time until Assyria effectively controlled Phoenicia. During his Philistine campaign in 734 B.C., Tiglath-Pileser had received tribute from Arvad, Byblos, and Tyre. The fact that Sidon is missing from the tribute lists of Tiglath-Pileser has led some to believe that Tyre controlled Sidon at the time.

During the reign of Shalmaneser V (727–722 B.C.) Phoenicia again felt the heavy hand of Assyria. According to Josephus (*Antiquities*, IX, 14, 2), whom some scholars doubt at this point, Shalmaneser overran all Phoenicia. Sidon, Palaetyrus (mainland Tyre), and other nearby towns under Tyre's control capitulated to Assyria. Island Tyre refused to surrender. Subsequently Shalmaneser gathered a fleet to attack the island. Repulsed, the Assyrian settled down to an unsuccessful five-year siege of the island. It is not unreasonable to accept Josephus' account of this struggle. Shalmaneser was active in the West during his reign. It was he who initiated the three-year siege of Samaria.

Subsequently Phoenicia seems to have been unmolested for some twenty years, while Eluleus (Luli), king of Tyre (725–690 B.C.), regained control over much of the adjacent mainland. Sargon II (722–705 B.C.), king of Assyria, devoted his energies to the conquest of Cyprus, or at least the southern part of the island, which was in Phoenician hands, and accomplished his aim in 709 B.C.

Sennacherib (705–681 B.C.) had to face one of those ever-recurring rebellions in the West. Eluleus of Tyre, supported by other Phoenician city-states, was one of the leaders of the defection. The Philistines, the Egyptians, Hezekiah of Judah, and others cooperated in the venture. As Lord Byron put it, in his poem "Destruction of Sennacherib," "The Assyrian came down like the wolf on the fold," defeated the Egyptians before Ekron in 701 B.C., ravaged Judea and shut up Hezekiah "like a bird in a cage" (Sennacherib's claim) in Jerusalem, and completely subdued Phoenicia. Eluleus fled to Cyprus, or possibly just to island Tyre—the situation is not clear. Sennacherib destroyed the powerful combination of Tyre and Sidon and placed a pro-Assyrian king on the throne of Sidon.

But Phoenician efforts to retain liberty would not forever be blocked. With a change of rulers in Assyria, the caldron of liberty boiled over again along the Lebanese littoral. Sidon led the revolt (c. 678 B.C.) against Esarhaddon, king of Assyria (681–668 B.C.). In his fury Esarhaddon absolutely obliterated the city. Most of the inhabitants were killed or sold into slavery; some escaped to nearby cities. Such barbarity had an immediate, though temporary, effect. The other towns of Phoenicia submitted to Esarhaddon, only to rebel again in 672 under the leadership of King Baal of Tyre and in alliance with Taharka (biblical Tirhakah, 2 Kings 19:9; Isaiah 37:9) of Egypt. Though he claimed to have done so, Esarhaddon probably did not defeat either Baal or Taharka at the time.

But Ashurbanipal (668–663 B.C.) finally conquered Egypt and the indomitable Tyrians. The princes of Gebal and Arvad and other Canaanite chiefs, as well as Manasseh of Judah, capitulated. The return of peace brought a return of commercial prosperity and a reduction of military expenditure at Tyre. And after the middle of the seventh century the power of Assyria declined; Tyre certainly obtained her independence by about 625 B.C. and held it for most of the following forty years. Her greatness, while tarnished, still remained. Ezekiel, who lived during these decades of independence, penned a remarkable description of her attainments (Ezekiel 27).

Any discussion of the Assyrian period of Phoenician history would be quite incomplete without a brief treatment of three topics: 1) Phoenicia's export of people to establish colonies, which would affect the subsequent history of the Mediterranean world; 2) her export of the alphabet, which would affect cultural developments throughout the world; 3) and her export of Baal worship, which would affect religious developments in Israel.

Phoenician Colonies. The when and why of Phoenician colonial expansion have been the subject of much study in recent decades. Traditionally it has been the practice to accept the date of 814 B.C. for the founding of Carthage and a date of about 1100 B.C. for the founding of Gadir (modern Cadiz in Spain) and Utica (on North African coast, west of Carthage). These dates were based on the writings of Timaeus, a Sicilian Greek of the third century B.C. But archaeological investigation has raised numerous questions about the traditional picture.

PHOENICIAN COLONIES

Phoenician colonies grew up at stopping points or supply stations on their trade routes and at places where they could exploit metals. Then other Phoenicians migrated to such places because of economic opportunity. Or they went because of scarcity of land at home or because of Assyrian or Babylonian pressure on the homeland. It appears that Carthage was one of the first colonies to be settled, around the beginning of the eighth century B.C., to be followed by most of the rest during that century or later. The rough order is Carthage (and nearby Utica), Sicily, Sardinia, Malta, Balaeric Islands, and Spain. There is still a question, however, whether the colony at Cadiz (thirty-eight miles northwest of Gibralter) in Spain was founded before Carthage.

Warmington observes, "the cumulative effect of the archaeological evidence that there were no Phoenician settlements in the west before the middle of the eighth century is impressive."[33] Carpenter asserts that Utica and Carthage were not settled before the latter part of the eighth century B.C.; from Carthage, western Sicily was settled in the seventh century B.C., Sardinia late in the seventh or early in the sixth century B.C., and the Balaeric Islands and southern Spain still later in the sixth century B.C.[34] Carpenter tends toward a very compressed chronology in all of his writing, and his reckonings are probably too late. The tendency today is to put the founding of Carthage about the beginning of the eighth century B.C. and the rest of the Phoenician colonies in the western Mediterranean also in the eighth century B.C., during the time of the Neo-Assyrian Empire.

Many reasons have been given as to why the Phoenicians settled their many colonies. Some have emphasized population surplus and social discord at home. Others have urged that Assyrian pressure was largely the reason. But the key reasons seem to have been economic and commercial: the exploitation of metals of a given region and the provision of supply stations or stopping points on their trade routes. In other words, colonists were "pulled rather than pushed." They had considerable economic opportunity in supplying goods and services that resulted from the rapid expansion of Assyria and Phoenicia's place in that empire.

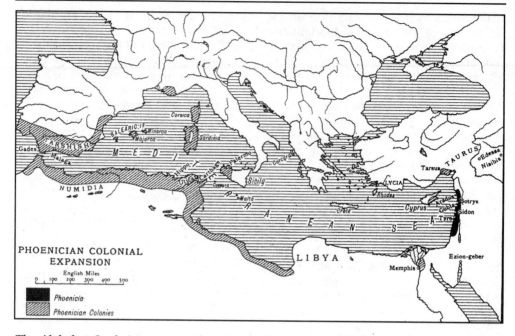

PHOENICIAN COLONIAL
EXPANSION

English Miles

0   100   200   300   400   500

■ Phoenicia

▨ Phoenician Colonies

The Alphabet. In their commercial contacts with the Greeks, the Phoenicians passed on to them their consonantal alphabet, to which the Greeks added vowels and which they spread farther afield. There has been some controversy as to just when the Greeks borrowed the alphabet. Some have placed the date as early as 1100 or 1000 B.C. It seems best, however, to hold with Albright to a date in the late ninth or early eighth century.[35] And that appears to be the general view today. Some put it about 750 B.C.

A few have claimed that the Phoenicians invented the alphabet and have considered it their great contribution to culture. But that is open to question. The famous Ahiram sarcophagus inscription (from Byblos, now in the Beirut Museum) is commonly dated about 1000 B.C. (though some would put it in the thirteenth century); none of the other Byblos alphabetic inscriptions date before the thirteenth century B.C. Alphabetic materials at Ugarit (Ras Shamra) in Syria were penned during the fifteenth century B.C. The Sinai inscriptions are commonly dated around 1500 B.C. (but a recent study dates them to about 1900 B.C., which was the date originally assigned to them).

Three other alphabetic inscriptions, dating between 1800 and 1500 B.C., have been found at Gezer, Shechem (modern Nablus), and Lachish in Palestine.[36] New alphabetic inscriptions found in Egypt may date to 1800 B.C. or earlier.[37] Clearly, then, the earliest alphabetic inscriptions do not come from Phoenicia proper. When and where the alphabet was invented is unknown— possibly in Egypt during the Hyksos period, possibly in Palestine or Phoenicia during the Hyksos era, or slightly earlier.

In passing, it is of some interest to note that alphabetic Hebrew is called in Scripture the "language of Canaan" (Isaiah 19:18). Apparently the Patriarchs (with an Akkadian or Sumerian background) found it there and carried it with them to Egypt. That would explain how Moses could write Scripture in alphabetic Hebrew/Canaanite without its having to be translated from Akkadian or Egyptian. While we cannot claim that the Phoenicians invented the alphabet, we do know that at the minimum they fulfilled the very important function of transmitting the Semitic alphabet to the Greeks, who added vowels and in turn introduced it to many other peoples.

Phoenician Religion. Because Jezebel, daughter of Ethbaal of Tyre, married Ahab and imposed Baal worship on Israel (where it had existed minimally since the days of

The Ahiram sarcophagus with its alphabetic inscription. *Beirut Museum*

and the tree or pole symbolized the Baalath. But commonly the Phoenicians, an urban people, worshiped in temples consisting of a court or enclosure and a roofed shrine, at the entrance of which was a porch or pillared hall. The altar, a conical stone pillar, and a pole or tree stood in the court. A statue of the deity was housed in the shrine. In one of the temples excavated at Gebal, about twenty stone pillars came to light. Cut in the general form of obelisks, the highest was ten feet high. (See page 338).

As to the worship connected with Baalism, clearly one important feature was sacrifice of animals, food, and drink. Human sacrifices were offered too, though very rarely and only in time of greatest calamity. Human sacrifice almost always involved offering infants in situations of emergency, war, or epidemic to restore the

the judges), and because Ahab and Jezebel's daughter Athaliah married Jehoram of Judah and strengthened Baal worship there, Phoenician religion holds considerable interest for most Bible students.

Father of the gods and head of the Phoenician pantheon was El. Baal, his son, was one of the chief male deities and served as god of agriculture and of storms. As such he was responsible for fertility of the field and was associated with human and animal reproduction. Baalath, who seems to have been the consort of Baal, represented the principle of fertility and generation. Actually, Baal simply means "lord" and Baalath, "lady."

Every community had its own Baal and Baalath. Melkart (Melqarth) was the supreme deity, or Baal of Tyre, and was styled "Lord of the sun, supreme ruler, giver of life, embodiment of the male principle, god of productivity." The Greeks identified him with Heracles or Hercules. Eshmun, god of vital force and healing, was worshiped at Sidon; the Greeks identified him with Asclepius. Reshef, the lightning god, was especially popular in Cyprus, where the Greeks identified him with Apollo. The Baalath of Gebal, Ashtaroth (or Astarte), a fertility goddess, was the most popular Baalath of Phoenicia.

The places for worship of Baal were often merely high places in the hills, consisting of an altar, a sacred tree or pole, and a sacred stone pillar. The pillar represented the Baal,

A Baal from Ras Shamra. *Louvre Museum*

A gold Baal in the collection of the Oriental Institute, *University of Chicago*

23:37) and at least two kings sacrificed their sons in the valley of Hinnom (Ahaz, 2 Kings 16:3; and his grandson Manasseh, 2 Kings 21:6; cf. Jeremiah 32:31–35). Josiah in his reform destroyed the *tophet* in the valley of the Hinnon (2 Kings 23:10).

Religious festivals, associated with the rhythm of the seasons, were also connected with Baal worship. That is to say, the god presumably died in the fall and arose in the spring. (Perhaps Elijah was referring to these festivals in 1 Kings 18:27.) The fall festival was accompanied by great mourning, funeral rites, and perhaps self-torture or mutilation. Sacramental sex indulgence characterized the spring festival. Temple prostitutes, both men and women, were attached to all of the temples, where chambers for sexual intercourse were available.

Women commonly sacrificed their virginity at the shrines of Astarte in the hope of winning the favor of the goddess. Says Lucian of the festival at Byblos: "But when they have bewailed and lamented, first they perform funeral rites for Adonis as if he were dead, but afterward upon another day they say he lives . . . and they shave their heads as the Egyptians do when Apis dies. But such women as do not wish to be shaven pay the following penalty: on a certain day they stand for prostitution at the proper time and the market is open for strangers only, and the pay goes as a sacrifice to Aphrodite."[39] The festival of Adonis was regularly held at Byblos or Gebal, and the festival of Melkart at Tyre. The debased and debasing worship of Phoenicia deserved the total condemnation meted out to it in the Old Testament.

The Neo-Babylonian Period

After the fall of Nineveh (612 B.C.) the Neo-Babylonian Empire replaced the Assyrian Empire. But remnants of the Assyrian army held out in the upper Euphrates region until 609/608 B.C. In the confusion of that three-year period, the Egyptians under Necho (609–594 B.C.) tried to reestablish their power in Palestine and Syria. During the first year or two of his reign, Necho penetrated to the Euphrates River. Seemingly several of the Phoenician cities came under his sway but retained

forces of nature or the power of the state. For Phoenicia proper or for Israel infected with Baal worship, all we have to support existence of this practice is written references. In the Phoenician west there are excavated sanctuaries where victims were sacrificed to the deity by fire. These places of sacrifice, or *tophets,* were open-air enclosures surrounded by walls, inside of which were cinerary urns, sealed at the top and accompanied by inscriptions dedicated to Baal or Tanit. The *tophets* at Carthage, Motya, Sardinia, and at Limassol on Cyprus, are especially significant or extensive. At Carthage it appears that kings, military personnel, and dignitaries—the ruling class—carried on this practice, evidently in the interests of the state or the community.[38]

As far as Israel is concerned, we note that the prophets scored the practice (Jeremiah 7:31ff.; 19:5ff.; Ezekiel 16:20–21;

their autonomy and secured conditions favorable to trade.

The Babylonians were not long in meeting the threat. Nebuchadnezzar, son of the ruling monarch Nabopolassar, advanced to wrest from the Egyptians the area once controlled by the Assyrians. He defeated Necho at the famous Battle of Carchemish in 605 B.C. and in short order marched to the very borders of Egypt. The city-states of Phoenicia capitulated and paid tribute, retaining a semi-independent status under their own rulers.

Just as Nebuchadnezzar reached the borders of Egypt, he received news of his father's death and had to hurry home to forestall any moves against his kingly rights. In the process of subduing the Westland in 605 B.C., he apparently besieged Jerusalem and deported many of her best citizens (e.g., Daniel, Daniel 1:1–3). Subsequent disorders in the West resulted in Nebuchadnezzar's again besieging Jerusalem and carrying off a large number of hostages (including Ezekiel) in 597 B.C. The Egyptians were not yet over their expansionist dreams, and Hophra (Apries, 588–569) in 588 B.C. successfully attacked Tyre and Sidon and managed to intimidate most of the Phoenician coast. But Nebuchadnezzar responded promptly to this threat, as well as to the revolt of the Judeans, who had allied themselves with Hophra. He destroyed Jerusalem, her walls, and the Temple in 586 B.C. Phoenicia fell next.

A few years before this Babylonian attack, Ezekiel had prophesied the ultimate ruin of Tyre and Sidon (Ezekiel 26:3–12, 14, 19; 28:21–23). Sifted and itemized, these verses present several predictions. The first group is against Tyre: (1) her strongholds will be destroyed; (2) many nations will come up against her; (3) dust will be scraped from her until she is as bare as the top of a rock; (4) her ruins will provide a place for spreading of nets; (5) Nebuchadnezzar will descend and cast battlements against her; (6) Nebuchadnezzar will break through the walls, tread the streets, and kill the garrisons, taking much spoil; (7) ruins of the city will be dumped in the water; (8) Tyre will be desolated and uninhabited. Other prophecies are against

Sidon: (1) judgments will be executed in her; and (2) pestilence and slaughter will descend upon her.

Sweeping into Phoenicia, Nebuchadnezzar took Sidon and then settled down to a thirteen-year siege of Tyre (585–572 B.C.). It seems that ultimately Nebuchadnezzar was successful in taking the mainland part of Tyre. But without a fleet he could not conquer the island city, which surrendered on conditions favorable to the citizens of the island. Mainland Tyre remained in ruins until the days of Alexander the Great.[40] In this way the first stage of Ezekiel's prophecy against Tyre was fulfilled. Nebuchadnezzar had besieged the city, broken through the walls, killed the defenders, and taken much spoil.

Tyre's greatest days were gone. Her commerce was ruined by the siege as well as by Greek capture of Phoenician trade in the northeastern Mediterranean and to some extent elsewhere. Tyre's role in international trade was further usurped on land by Aramaean merchants and on the sea by the Carthaginians. Temporarily Sidon assumed Phoenician leadership. Although the Assyrians had destroyed Sidon and built a small post on the site populated by foreigners, it had again gradually become a relatively prosperous Phoenician city.

The Persian Period

Transition from Babylonian to Persian rule in Phoenicia seems to have been peaceful. Cyrus' policy of leniency toward all his foreign subjects produced favorable conditions for Phoenicia, whose cities seem to have enjoyed a practical independence and were ruled by their own kings. Treated more like allies than subjects, they furnished the Persians with a fleet on numerous occasions, especially during Persian attacks on Greece. On the other hand they received the protection of a strong empire. During this entire period, Sidon was the predominant city. It even served as a royal residence when Persian kings carried out duties in the West. Of the twenty satrapies (administrative areas) into which Darius divided the empire, Phoenicia was in the fifth, which also included Palestine, Syria, and Cyprus.

The Phoenician harbor at Sidon

During the fourth century B.C., the Phoenicians grew increasingly restless under Persian rule. Perhaps this was due in part to increasing relations with the Greeks. Phoenicians began to settle in large numbers in Attica.[40] At least Tyre (how voluntarily we do not know) participated in the unsuccessful revolt of Evagoras in Cyprus in 392, which was also supported by the Greeks and Egyptians. The Phoenicians participated in the War of the Satraps in 362—a rebellion which the Persians also effectively subdued. Then in 352 B.C., after suffering extremely insolent treatment at the hands of the Persians, the Phoenicians determined to revolt. They got help from Egypt. When the Persian army stood before the city of Sidon, the leaders defected to save their own lives. Robbed of all protection, the people determined to set fire to their own homes and perish with them. It is said that over 40,000 died in the horrible conflagration.[42] Certainly this was sufficient fulfillment of Ezekiel's prophecy against the city. After this terrible catastrophe, the other Phoenician cities had no heart to continue the rebellion against Persia.

The Greek Period

In 334 B.C. Alexander the Great crossed the Hellespont (Dardanelles) to begin his conquest of the Persian Empire. His victory at the Granicus River opened Asia Minor to him. Near the end of the following year, his victory at Issus gained Syria for him. Seeking to neutralize or control the Persian fleet, Alexander chose to continue south around the coast of the Mediterranean. Since he had no fleet, the only way Alexander could conquer the Persian fleet was to conquer its bases. For this reason

The castle offshore at Sidon

The castle at Sidon reconstructed in the Lebanorama

Alexander moved south into Syria and Egypt before pursuing the Persians eastward.

Sidon, now largely rebuilt, was still bitter over the destruction in the days of Artaxerxes Ochus and welcomed the conqueror. Byblos and other cities of the coast offered no opposition. Tyre alone opposed Alexander. The Tyrians initially offered submission and tribute to him, thinking they would thereby gain substantial freedom, as they had before. But when they saw that Alexander intended to occupy the city personally, they determined to resist.

Hope of Tyrian success in withstanding the siege was not unfounded. Their city was located on an island a half mile from shore; the current in the channel that separated it from land was fairly swift. Their fleet controlled the sea. The city wall on the landside rose to 150 feet. There were assurances of help from Carthage and elsewhere. But Alexander devised unexpected tactics. He resolved to construct a roadway 200 feet wide out to the island, on which he could plant his siege engines. Ruins of mainland Tyre furnished material for the road. The Tyrians fought heroically. They destroyed the engines of war by fireships and damaged the mole, or roadway. They hurled pots of burning naphtha, sulfur, and red-hot sand from catapults. Seeing that the battle could not be won without the use of a fleet, Alexander obtained contingents from Sidon, and Cyprus, and from his Greek allies. After a

siege of seven months, he breached the wall and took the city after savage fighting. It is reported that eight thousand were killed in the fighting, two thousand were later executed, thirty thousand were sold into slavery, and fifteen thousand were secretly smuggled away by attacking Sidonian ships whose sailors were sympathetic with the defenders.[43] Previously thousands of women, children, and older people had been evacuated to Carthage.

For all practical purposes it can be said that the prophecies of Ezekiel had been fulfilled. The mainland city had been scraped bare as the top of a rock in building the causeway to the island city. The island city had been destroyed. And though the city was rebuilt once more and was fairly prosperous by 315 B.C., the colonists were largely Carian (Greek) rather than Phoenician. Therefore it can be said that little ethnic connection existed between the old and new cities and that although the city was rebuilt, it was not to be another Phoenician city—mart of nations.[44] In fact, Phoenicians tended to lose their racial characteristics altogether during the Greek period, when the area was merged with Syria. Continued invasions had even before that time considerably diluted the racial stock. With Alexander's conquest, the Greeks were definitely supreme in the Mediterranean; the old Phoenician mercantile and maritime supremacy was forever broken. Rhodes

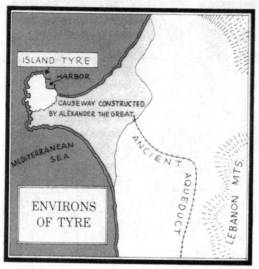

ISLAND TYRE

HARBOR

CAUSEWAY CONSTRUCTED
BY ALEXANDER THE GREAT

MEDITERRANEAN
SEA

ANCIENT AQUEDUCT

LEBANON MTS.

ENVIRONS
OF TYRE

Because Tyre was one-half mile off shore and Alexander was without a navy, he decided to build a road out to the island. In time sand drifted against the road, and both the island and the road became encased in a peninsula. The approximate shoreline is indicated above, adjacent to the peninsula.

later attained the position proud Tyre had enjoyed.

With the death of Alexander in 323 B.C., Phoenicia once again became an international football, passed from one to another of Alexander's generals. The military activities of those years were hard on the prosperity of the area. Finally in 286 B.C. the Ptolemies of Egypt gained firm control, and Sidon again achieved supremacy among the Phoenician city-states. With Ptolemaic decline, the Seleucids of Syria became masters of Phoenicia in 198 B.C. Under the Seleucids the Phoenician city-states one by one obtained autonomous status. But while they attained a degree of prosperity, the old glory was gone. With the demise of the Seleucids, Pompey occupied Phoenicia for Rome in 64 B.C.

The Roman Period

Officially Phoenicia ceased to exist, being incorporated with Palestine and Syria proper into the Roman province of Syria. Although Phoenicia suffered during the Roman civil wars, a new era of prosperity dawned with the victory of Augustus, the

Roman peace or *Pax Romona,* and imperial reorganization. Four legions stationed in Syria kept the peace. Aradus, Sidon, Tyre, and Tripolis won rights of self-government. A new road system facilitated commerce. Phoenician industrial and commercial activity again became widespread. Mommsen observes that Tyrians had factories (trade depots) in the two great import harbors of Italy: Ostia and Puteoli. Berytus (Beirut) had similar factories in Italian ports.[45] The wine of Byblos and Tyre was especially valued by the Romans; Byblos, Tyre, and Berytus sent their linen all over the world. Tyrian purple was still much in demand and continued to be the city's most significant export. At Tyre and Aradus, both of which were located on islands, houses and other buildings rose skyscraperlike in several stories.

Some idea of prosperity during the Roman period comes from excavations at Tyre, which the Lebanese department of Antiquities began in 1947. On the island city, perpendicular to the main road, lay a great hippodrome or racetrack for horses and chariots. One of the largest in the Roman world, it could seat some sixty thousand spectators. There was also a huge Roman bath. Shops lined the roadway, and the main street and side streets were colonnaded. As was true of other Roman cities, tombs lined the main roads beyond the city limits. For a considerable distance along the east-west road, the excavators found scores of sarcophagi dating to the Roman and Byzantine periods. Most of these marble sarcophagi were decorated around the sides with figures sculptured in low relief. Many were beautifully executed, some with mythological scenes. These sarcophagi alone say much about the wealth of the community; families with modest means could not have afforded most of them.

The literary activity in Phoenician cities during the early Roman period surpassed that of any earlier period. Strabo (died A.D. 24) eulogized the Sidonian philosophers in the sciences of astronomy and arithmetic. Other classical writers referred to celebrated Phoenician poets whose names are not known. Sidon, Byblos, Berytus, and Tyre

A street in Roman Tyre

seem to have contributed most to the intellectual production of the age.[46] Sidon had a law school that was famed throughout the classical East. Two early Stoic philosophers of Tyre are known: Antipater, an intimate of Cato; and Apollonius, who wrote a work about Zeno and compiled a bibliography of Stoic philosophy.

During the Roman period the whole character of Phoenicia changed. Hellenization went on apace. The native language fell into disuse and was replaced by Aramaic, Greek, and Latin for official documents. Roman rule tended to obliterate the characteristic features of national life. Roman colonies were established at Berytus, Accho (Ptolemais), Tyre, and Sidon.

Phoenicia figures inconspicuously in the New Testament narrative. Jesus went to the region of Tyre and Sidon (Matthew 15:21; Mark 7:24, 31), where he healed a Syro-Phoenician woman's daughter. Whether he actually went into Phoenicia or just to the borders of it is an open question. Numbered among the followers of the Master were inhabitants of Phoenicia (Mark 3:8).

Christianity came to Phoenicia shortly after Pentecost. The persecution accompanying the stoning of Stephen scattered believers to Phoenicia, among other places (Acts 11:19). Barnabas and Saul preached there briefly on their return to Jerusalem from their period of ministry in Antioch (Acts 15:3). At the close of Paul's third missionary journey, he stopped at Tyre for a week while his ship unloaded her cargo. There he seems to have contacted a considerable number of believers (Acts 21:2–7). The apostle stopped briefly at Sidon on his way to Rome and met some friends there (Acts 27:3).

Tyre was the early center of Christianity in Phoenicia, and she became the seat of a Christian bishop late in the second century. Sidon also became an important center of Christianity, as is demonstrated by the fact that she had a bishop present at the Council of Nicaea in A.D. 325.

While people tend to judge the importance of a country by its size or its ability to control its neighbors, Phoenicia cannot be so judged. If she did not invent the alphabet, she at least developed it and passed it on to the Greeks. She made significant achievements in production of both molded and blown glass; some would credit her with having invented at least the latter process.[47] Having learned from Babylonian astronomers to use the stars as a guide to

The great racetrack at Roman Tyre

navigation, she passed this knowledge on to the Greeks and Romans and thereby revolutionized navigation. Phoenician ships controlled the Mediterranean for almost half a millennium and then the Aegean for some three centuries. Phoenician colonies made their impact too. The Phoenician colony of Carthage was so powerful that it came close to toppling Rome in the third century B.C.

In her merchant role she bartered ideas as well as goods, bringing ideas of the East to the West and vice versa. In this way she sped the progress of culture in the ancient world. The Bible student is also alert to Phoenician impact on Hebrew cultural and religious development. So notorious is the latter involvement that the name Jezebel has become a byword in western Christian culture—both as the wife of wicked Ahab and as a synonym for a shameless woman (e.g., Revelation 2:20). And of course we cannot forget the influence of Phoenician architecture on the building of the temple and other structures in Israel.

NOTES

1. Philip K. Hitti, *Lebanon in History* (London: Macmillan, 1957), 60.

2. Nina Jidejian, *Byblos Through the Ages* (Beirut: Dar El Machreq, 1971), 11.

3. Ibid., 21.

4. S. R. K. Glanville, ed., *The Legacy of Egypt* (Oxford: Clarendon Press, 1942), 6.

5. V. Gordon Childe, *New Light on the Most Ancient East* (London: Routledge and Kegan Paul, rewritten, 1952), 224.

6. George Steindorff and Keith C. Seele, *When Egypt Ruled the East*, 2nd ed. (Chicago: University of Chicago Press, 1957), 21.

7. Lionel Casson, *The Ancient Mariners*, 2nd ed. (Princeton: Princeton University Press, 1991), 11.

8. Hitti, *Lebanon*, 72.

9. James H. Breasted, *Ancient Records of Egypt* (Chicago: University of Chicago Press, 1906), vol. I, 66.

10. Jidejian, *Byblos*, 23.

11. John A. Wilson, *The Burden of Egypt* (Chicago: University of Chicago Press, 1951), 156; James B. Pritchard, ed., *Ancient Near Eastern Texts*, 2nd ed. (Princeton: Princeton University Press, 1955), 329.

12. Hitti, *Lebanon*, 77.

13. Ibid.

14. Pritchard, *Ancient Near Eastern Texts*, 240–41.

15. Hitti, *Lebanon*, 83.

16. Glenn Markoe, "Phoenicians," *Oxford Encyclopedia of Archaeology in the Near East* (1997), 4, 326.

17. B. H. Warmington, *Carthage* (London: Robert Hale, 1960), 16.

18. This question has been rather exhaustively investigated. Summary statements with bibliographical references appear in Sarantis Symeonoglou, *The Topography of Thebes from the Bronze Age to Modern Times* (Princeton: Princeton University Press, 1985), Chapter 2. This issue also relates to the origin of the alphabet in Greece and is referred to in subsequent discussion.

19. Jidejian, *Byblos*, 57–58.

20. Ibid., 19.

21. As cited by Albert A. Trever, *History of Ancient Civilization* (New York: Harcourt, Brace, 1936), vol 2, 80.

22. Casson, *Ancient Mariners*, 16.

23. Ibid.

24. For documentation on the ruling dynasty and the development of the city of Tyre, see especially Josephus (who quotes ancient authorities), *Antiquities* VIII, 2, 5, 7 and *Against Apion*, I, 17–18; see also Wallace B. Fleming, *The History of Tyre* (New York: Columbia University Press, 1915), 4, 16.

25. Emily D. Wright, "News About Old Tyre," *Biblical Archaeologist*, May 1939, 20–22.

26. An interesting book on Jewish seafaring is Raphael Patai, *The Children of Noah: Jewish Seafaring in Ancient Times* (Princeton: Princeton University Press, 1998).

27. Beno Rothenberg, *Were These King Solomon's Mines?* (New York: Stein & Day, 1972), 206–7.

28. Unger points out that *Tarshish* is a Phoenician word from the Akkadian meaning "smelting plant" or "refinery" and that Tarshish fleets were originally large ships constructed for the purpose of bringing smelted ore to Phoenicia from the mining towns of Sardinia and Spain. "Smeltery fleets" would be a good synonym for "Tarshish ships." Eventually all large ships were referred to as "Tarshish ships," regardless of the nature of their cargo or destination. Merrill F. Unger, *The New Unger's Bible Dictionary*, ed. R.K. Harrison and others (Chicago: Moody Press, 1985) 1252.

29. Hitti, 114.

30. Edward Lipinski, "The Phoenicians," *Civilizations of the Ancient Near East.* Jack M. Sasson (New York: Scribner's, 1995), vol. II, 1331.

31. Ralph Turner, *The Great Cultural Traditions* (New York: McGraw-Hill 1941), vol. I, 238. For some idea of the cargo of a Canaanite ship (or possibly a Mycenaean ship), see Cemal Pulak, "Shipwreck! Recovering 3,000-Year-Old Cargo," *Odyssey,* September/October 1999, 18–29.

32. For inscriptions of the kings of Assyria see Pritchard, *Ancient Near Eastern Texts,* 329; and Daniel D. Luckenbill, *Ancient Records of Assyria and Babylonia.* 2 vols. (Chicago: University of Chicago Press, 1926).

33. Warmington, *Carthage,* 29.

34. Rhys Carpenter, "Phoenicians in the West," *American Journal of Archaeology,* 62 (January, 1958): 53. Excavations at Kerkouane, Tunisia, seventy-five miles from Carthage, show that it was founded circa 550 B.C. See *Odyssey,* September/October 1999, 60–63.

35. W. F. Albright, *Archaeology of Palestine*, Rev. ed. (Harmondsworth, England: Penguin Books, 1960), 196. Martin Barnal in his *Cadmean Letters* (Winona Lake, IN: Eisenbrauns, 1990) tries to make a case for the transmission of the alphabet to Greece as early as 1400 B.C., but he has not yet gained much of a following.

36. Albright, *Archaeology,* 188–91, and correspondence with Dr. Albright addressed to me.

37. *Biblical Archaeology Review,* January/February 2000, 12.

38. For an especially detailed treatment of the subject, see Maria Eugenia Aubet, *The Phoenicians and the West* (Cambridge: Cambridge University Press, 1993), 207–217.

39. W. B. Fleming, *History of Tyre* (New York: Columbia University Press, 1915), 151.

40. Ibid., 56.

41. Frederick C. Eiselen, *Sidon a Study in Oriental History* (New York: Columbua University Press, 1907), 64.

42. Ibid., 66.

43. Fleming, *History of Tyre,* 64.

44. Tyre suffered several attacks and partial destructions in subsequent centuries, suffering almost complete destruction at the hands of the Muslims in 1291 A.D., after which it lay in ruins for centuries. Today Tyre has a population of some 30,000 and occupies the site of the ancient island city and Alexander's mole—now consider-

ably widened by sands that have drifted against it. The site of the mainland city is largely unoccupied; the island site has been partially excavated.

45. Theodor Mommsen, *The Provinces of the Roman Empire from Caesar to Diocletian*, trans. William P. Dickson (New York: Charles Scribner's Sons, 1906), vol. I, 151–152.

46. Hitti, *Lebanon*, 201.

47. Dimitri Baramki, *Phoenicia and the Phoenicians* (Beirut: Khayats, 1961), 112.

BIBLIOGRPAHY

Albright, William F. *Archaeology of Palestine*. Rev. ed. Baltimore: Penguin Books,1960.

Aubet, Maria E. *The Phoenicians and the West*. Cambridge: Cambridge University Press, 1993.

Baramki, Dimitri. *Phoenicia and the Phoenicians*. Beirut: Khayats, 1961.

Bouchier, E. S. *Syria as a Roman Province*. Oxford: Blackwell, 1916.

Boutros, Labib. *Phoenician Sport*. Amsterdam: Gieben, 1981.

Breasted, James H. *Ancient Records of Egypt*. Vols. 1–2. Chicago: University of Chicago Press, 1906.

Carpenter, Rhys. "Phoenicians in the West," *American Journal of Archaeology*, 62 (January 1958).

Casson, Lionel. *The Ancient Mariners*. 2nd ed. Princeton: Princeton University Press, 1991.

Childe, V. Gordon. *New Light on the Most Ancient East*. Rewritten, London: Routledge and Kegan Paul, 1952.

Contenau, Georges. *La Civilisation Phénicienne*. Paris: Payot, 1926.

Dussaud, Rene. *Topographie historique de la Syrie antique et médiévale*. Paris: P. Geuthner, 1927.

Eiselen, Frederick C. *Sidon a Study in Oriental History*. New York: Columbia University Press, 1907. Reissued: New York, A. M. S. Press, 1966.

Fleming, W. B. *History of Tyre*. 1915. Reissued, New York: A. M. S. Press, 1966.

Harden, Donald. *The Phoenicians*. New York: Frederick A. Praeger, 1962.

Herm, Gerhard. *The Phoenicians*. New York: William Morrow, 1975.

Hitti, Philip K. *History of Syria*. London: Macmillan, 1951.

Hitti, Philip K. *Lebanon in History*. London: Macmillan, 1957.

Hitti, Philip K. *The Near East in History*. Princeton: D. Van Nostrand, 1961.

Jidejian, Nina. *Byblos Through the Ages*. Beirut: Dar El Machreq, 1972.

Jidejian, Nina. *Sidon Through the Ages*. Beirut: Dar El Machreq, 1971.

Jidejian, Nina. *Tyre Through the Ages*. Beirut: Dar El Machreq, 1969.

Markoe, Glenn E. *Phoenicians*. Berkeley: University of California, 2000.

Mommsen, Theodor. *The Provinces of the Roman Empire from Caesar to Diocletian*. Vol 1, Trans. William P. Dickson. New York: Charles Scribner's Sons, 1906.

Montet, Pierre. *Byblos et l'Egypte*. 2 vols. Paris: P. Geuthner, 1928, 1929.

Moscati, Sabatino. *The World of the Phoenicians*. New York: Frederick A. Praeger, 1968.

Perrot, Georges, and Charles Chipiez,. *History of Art in Phoenicia and Its Dependencies*. 2 vols. London: Chapman and Hall, 1885.

Pritchard, James B. *Recovering Sarepta, A Phoenician City*. Princeton: Princeton University Press, 1978.

Warmington, B. H. *Carthage*. Rev. ed. New York: Barnes & Noble, 1969.

Six columns of the Temple of Jupiter still stand magestically, to a height of 65 feet, among the ruins of Baalbek

5

SYRIA

Some have called Syria an international football kicked around by the major powers surrounding her. Others have described Syria as a crossroads of civilization. However one looks at her, Greater Syria has commonly been acted upon in history rather than acting upon her neighbors. The existence of a strong power in Asia Minor, Mesopotamia, or Egypt meant aggressive action against Syria. With a strong power on both the northern and southern borders, Syria became a battleground. Sargon of Akkad (or Accad), Hammurabi of Babylon, the Egyptians, Hittites, Assyrians, Chaldeans, Persians, Greeks, and Romans—all in their turn conducted military campaigns there, sent in their cultural influences, or politically dominated the area. Syria also tried to advance her own position by playing off one major power against another. This was true even as recently as during the Cold War, when Syria exploited animosity between Russia and the United States, receiving Russian armaments. And just as she is now in a weakened position with the end of the Cold War, so in ancient times she lost her bargaining power when confronted by a single major nation.

Strategic Position. Syria has held too good a position for neighboring countries to ignore her. A land bridge between Asia and Africa, she naturally provided a route for conquering armies. Arteries of trade extending from Mesopotamia, Asia Minor, and Egypt converged on such cities as Damascus, Palmyra, and Ugairt. Although the Syrian coast is not hospitable, throughout Syrian history, people have been coming to it and from it; and almost every town on the coast has had its heyday of maritime activity.

Wealth. Moreover, Syria had too many riches to be ignored. Many countries sought after the wealth of her forests, especially of the Lebanon region and north Syria, but also of the area near Damascus. The cedars and cypresses of Lebanon, the wood and resin of the Syrian terebinth and sumac, and the laurel wood of Daphne were all famous. Of the fruits, Syrian figs were renowned and olive culture widespread, as was the culture of the vine. Plums, pears, apples, and dates produced in the region were much in demand, especially in the Roman period. Syrian wines were the only ones imported by all countries or provinces of the Mediterranean world. Papyrus grown in Syrian fens, here as in Egypt, provided writing material. We must not neglect to mention the products of medicinal and aromatic plants that were an important source of revenue for the country. Note especially the Syrian styrax (storax), nard, silphion (silphium), and magydaris. The

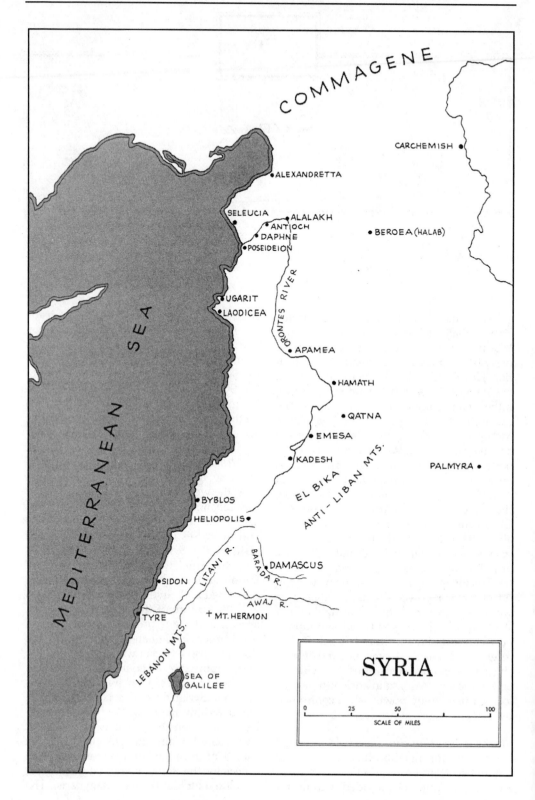

COMMAGENE

CARCHEMISH •

• ALEXANDRETTA

SELEUCIA • • ALALAKH
• ANTIOCH
• DAPHNE
• POSEIDEION

• BEROEA (HALAB)

ORONTES RIVER

• UGARIT
• LAODICEA

• APAMEA

• HAMATH

MEDITERRANEAN SEA

• QATNA

• EMESA

• KADESH

PALMYRA •

EL BIKA

ANTI - LIBAN MTS.

• BYBLOS

HELIOPOLIS •

LITANI R.

BARADA R.

• DAMASCUS

• SIDON

AWAJ R.

• TYRE

+ MT. HERMON

LEBANON MTS.

SEA OF
GALILEE

SYRIA

0   25   50   100

SCALE OF MILES

The Syrian Gates

vegetables of the area apparently were superior to those of Egypt. Well-known Syrian centers of cattle breeding were Damascus and Apamea. The exploitation of the mineral wealth of the region in ancient times is not so widely known, but cinnabar, alabaster, amber, and gypsum were extensively produced in Syria.[1]

Geographical Features

The Boundaries of Syria. The boundaries of Syria have fluctuated over the centuries according to political arrangements. When the power of the central government was strong, it exerted its control over the nomadic peoples of the desert; so the boundary line moved east. When the central government weakened, the nomads pushed the boundary line westward. During the days of David and Solomon, the Hebrew kingdom virtually engulfed Syria. At the height of the Assyrian Empire, Assyrians pushed the northern boundary of Syria southward. In days of Israelite weakness, Syrian kings moved their southern boundary southward. When Seleucid kings ruled from Antioch (modern Antakya), they managed, at least temporarily, to control most of the old Persian Empire (including Phoenicia and Palestine). Roman provincial organization also gave Syria a rather large territory.

Originally "Syria" was a term that applied only to a powerful state centered in the Lebanon district with its capital at Damascus. The Assyrians called this country west of the Euphrates "the Land of Amurrû." But geographers, following such ancient authorities as Strabo (who wrote during the lifetime of Jesus Christ) and the Arab geographers, commonly considered the limits of Syria to be the Taurus Mountains and the Euphrates River on the north, the Sinai Desert on the south, and the Mediterranean Sea and the Syrian Desert on the west and east. Strabo divided Syria into four regions: Commagene (a district between the Taurus and the Euphrates), Seleucid Syria (the central section around Antioch and Latakia), Coele-Syria (including the valley between the Lebanon and Anti-Lebanon [Anti-Liban] Mountains and much of southern Syria), and Phoenicia-Palestine.[2]

But biblical students generally—and many others as well—make a distinction between Syria and Palestine. Syria is restricted to the territory at the arch of the Fertile Crescent, bounded on the west by the Mediterranean, on the south by what became known as Galilee and Bashan, on the east by the Syrian Desert, and on the north by the Euphrates River and the Amanus Mountains. Sometimes it is considered to include Phoenicia. In this book Syria does not generally include either Palestine or Phoenicia; separate chapters describe those areas. The southwest boundary is set at the Lebanon Mountains, which effectively shut off Syria from the coast.

The Regions of Syria. Syria consists of a series of strongly marked zones from west to east—coastal plain, mountain ranges, valleys with luxuriant vegetation, and stony tracts in the east which are either desert or largely unproductive.

El Bika (El Beqa') and the Anti-Liban Mountains

The coast of the eastern Mediterranean, some 440 miles from Alexandretta to the Egyptian border, is one of the straightest in the world, with no deep estuary or gulf and no protecting island of any size. However, at Carmel and northward, where hills approach the coast, short capes jut out and there are a few bays and inlets that formed harbors sufficient for ships of antiquity. In Syria proper there were small harbors at such places as Latakia (ancient Laodicea) and Ras Shamra (ancient Ugarit). Seleucia (the port for Antioch) was hardly more than a roadstead or anchorage. The coastal plain, never more than a few miles wide, was largely inconsequential in Syrian history. Much of it is merely a broad strip of sand dunes covered by short grass and low bushes.

Overlooking the coastal plain is a line of mountains that begins with the Amanus Mountains in the north and extends all the way to the towering massif of Sinai in the south. The Amanus (rising to a height of some 5,000 feet) are a southward offshoot of the Tauric system. Separating Syria from Asia Minor, the Amanus is cut on its southern fringe by the Orontes gorge and is crossed by roads to Antioch and Aleppo. The chief pass over the mountains is at Beilan, the Syrian Gates, at an altitude of

2,400 feet. South of the Orontes the range is continued by Jebel Akra ("the bald," classical Casius), which rises to a height of 5,750 feet and extends to Latakia, south of which it bears the name of Nusayriyah (Bargylus). The Nusayriyah chain is broken on the south by the Nahr el Kebeer (the Kebeer River), which today forms the border between Syria and Lebanon and to the south of which extend for 105 miles the Lebanon Mountains (with peaks over 10,000 feet).

Behind the western mountain range is a deep valley, a great fault extending from Armenia to the Gulf of 'Aqaba on the Red Sea and containing the deepest ditch on the earth's surface. We may start along this third topographical region of Syria in the neighborhood of Antioch, where the Orontes River turns westward to cut through the mountains to the sea. Here the plain is broad and extremely rich, none of it more than 600 feet above sea level. From Antioch the valley of the Orontes ascends slowly between the western range and the high plateau of north Syria. At Hama (Hamath) the altitude is 1,015 feet, and at Homs (ancient Emesa) it rises to 1,660 feet.

After Homs the valley becomes El Bika (El Beqa', "the cleft") between the Lebanon and Anti-Liban Mountains. Varying in breadth from six to ten miles, El Bika rises around Baalbek (ancient Heliopolis) to over 3,770 feet. Here is the watershed; to the north flows the Orontes (246 miles long and largely unnavigable), to the south flows the Litani (90 miles long). Both rivers eventually turn westward and flow into the Mediterranean. El Bika is some seventy-five miles long and has always been a rich agricultural and pastoral region. Its grazing land supports large flocks of sheep and goats. Its vines and other fruits flourish, and there is good wheatland. Here, as well as along the lower course of the Orontes, there are abundant ruins of ancient towns, testifying to the fact that this whole area was prosperous in ancient times—much more so than at present.

The eastern mountain range (Anti-Liban) constitutes the fourth topographical region of Syria. But it has no counterpart to the northernmost sections of the western

Damascus

mountain range. Rising from the Syrian plateau south of Homs, it opposes the Lebanons in almost equal length and height. This mountain complex is divided into two parts by the broad plateau and gorge of the Barada (biblical Abana) River. To the north stands the Jebel esh Sherqi ("Eastern Mountain"), the uppermost ledge of which is a high plateau some twenty miles broad and about 7,500 feet high. It is a stony desert resting on a foundation of chalky limestone. Its western flank falls steeply to El Bika and is virtually uninhabited; the eastern side is more accessible.

The southern part of the eastern range, Jebel esh Sheikh, or Mount Hermon, rises to a height of 9,232 feet and is one of the highest and most majestic peaks of Syria. Here snow settles deep in winter and hardly disappears from the summit in summer. In contrast with the northern part of the Anti-Libans, Mount Hermon has more villages on its western slopes and fewer on its eastern.

On the south and east, the slopes of Hermon fall swiftly to the vast plateau of Hauran, the treeless surface of which is volcanic and its soil a rich, red loam. The lava field covers an area almost sixty miles long by as many wide. On the east the Hauran is bounded by the mountain of Hauran, or the "Mountain of the Druzes." This bulwark is about thirty-five miles north and south and twenty east and west, with a summit that rises to 6,000 feet. In the north the Hauran is

two to three thousand feet above sea level, but on the south it shelves off to its limit in the deep valley of the Yarmuk. Known in classical times as "Auranitis" and in Old Testament times as "Bashan," the Hauran has some of the best wheatland in the Near East. It was one of the granaries of the empire during the Roman period.

The Anti-Libans collect their waters and send them southward into the Jordan system and eastward far into the desert (Damascus is about thirty miles east of Hermon) in the channel of the Barada River. On a lofty and drainable plateau some 2,200 feet in altitude, the Barada has created 150 square miles of fertility, the Ghutah, from which rises the city of Damascus, civilization's outpost in the desert. Though defenseless and on no natural line of commerce, Damascus has learned to exploit the fertility of her hinterland and to bend to herself much of the traffic between Egypt and Mesopotamia, as well as points west. In this way she has retained her prosperity over the centuries and today has a population well in excess of a million and a half.

The Barada River (c. 45 miles long) divides into five branches in the Damascus oasis and finally loses itself in the desert. Another river that rises in the Anti-Libans is the biblical Pharpar, identified with the Awaj, which flows some distance south of Damascus and disappears in swamps east of the city. Naaman was immensely proud

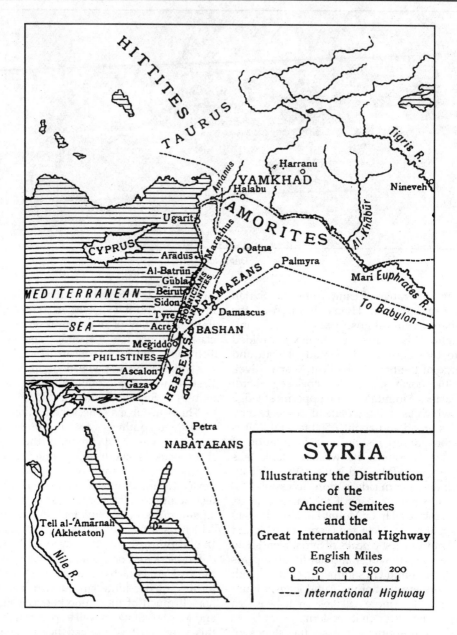

SYRIA

Illustrating the Distribution
of the
Ancient Semites
and the
Great International Highway

English Miles

0   50   100   150   200

---- International Highway

of both of these life-giving rivers of his homeland (2 Kings 5:12).

East of the Hauran Plateau and its boundary of Jebel ed Druz (Jebel Druze) lies the Syrian Desert, which is a continuation of the great Arabian Desert. The Syro-Iraqi Desert forms a huge triangle whose base rests on the Gulf of Aqaba on the southwest and the Gulf of Kuwait on the east and whose apex reaches toward Aleppo on the

north. At its widest this desert stretches about 800 miles.

Trade Routes. Numerous trade routes crossed the sands of Syria. A Transjordanic route led from the Gulf of Aqaba to Petra and from there to Damascus. A coastal route ran from Gaza to Carmel, across Esdraelon, and in Galilee divided into two branches, one eastward to Damascus and the other more directly north along the Orontes. The northern road to Mesopotamia led from Damascus north and passed through Homs (ancient Emesa), Arabian Haleb (Aleppo, ancient Beroea) and then east down the Euphrates River. Another link between Syria and Mesopotamia by a more southerly track took off from Damascus or Homs and proceeded by way of Palmyra to ancient Dura-Europos. In the days of the Sino-Roman world peace (1st and 2nd centuries A.D.), the Aleppo Road formed the last stage of the "silk route" from the Yellow Sea to the Mediterranean.

Climate. The climate of Syria has changed over the centuries. For instance, a dry cycle hit Palestine and Syria about 2000 B.C., and a shift toward increased precipitation occurred during the following couple of centuries. Then beginning around 300 B.C. and continuing into the New Testament period, the climate of the whole Mediterranean basin turned colder and more humid than today. If we can document two climate changes, possibly there were others.[3]

Large sections of areas which are now mere desert were formerly cultivated. East of Homs, where there is now not a green leaf nor a drop of water, heavy basalt slabs of former oil presses appear in quantity.[4] But it is not clear how much of the change is related to shifts in rainfall and to what extent the change is due to lack of water regulation resulting from erratic political conditions. The Syrian summer is hot and long (May to September), its winter short and mild. But there is considerable regional variation. Rainfall on the western mountain slopes and in the north of Syria is adequate. The eastern slopes have less precipitation. While Latakia on the coast enjoys over thirty inches of rainfall per year, the average at Damascus is about nine inches and at Aleppo approximately eighteen inches. Most of the population of the country lives in areas where the average winter temperature is 42 to 43 degrees, the average summer temperature 83 degrees, and the average annual temperature 61 to 63 degrees. These figures apply to both Aleppo and Damascus and include many of the towns of interior Syria.

Historical Developments

The Beginnings

The origins of life in Syria are lost in the mists of prehistory. Nor is it important for us to unravel the details of those early years. They have nothing specifically to do with the biblical narrative. The onward march of civilization began in some sense with the domestication of such basic crops as wheat, barley, lentils, and peas in the Damascus basin by about 7500–7000 B.C. and the development of village life at Abu Hureyra (Hureira) on the Euphrates in north Syria about 9500 B.C. At that village site (c 40 acres in size) inhabitants not only built mudbrick houses of several rooms but also cultivated a variety of crops by 7700 B.C., and before 6000 B.C. domesticated sheep, goats, cattle, and pigs.[5]

By approximately 5,000 B.C. other villages had begun to develop at such places as Hama and Ras Shamra (Ugarit) and the making of pottery was widespread. Of course Syria was now in the Neolithic or New Stone Age, characterized by domestication of plants and animals, village life, the manufacture of pottery, polished stone tools, and some fairly long-distance trade.

As noted in the chapter on Asia Minor, before 5,000 B.C., workers in northern Mesopotamia (and adjacent areas of Syria) had learned to smelt copper. Thus the Chalcolithic (copper-stone) Age had begun, and it continued through the next two millennia. Between about 4000 and 3500 B.C., lands from the "Mediterranean to the Persian Gulf were united in one cultural province"[6] and the main characteristic of this area was its fairly standardized pottery. Long distance trade increased.

The Early Bronze Age

Between about 3000 and 2500 B.C. urban culture came to Syria. Several cities and towns of all sizes began to arise everywhere on the Syrian plateau. A city of great importance was Ebla (Tell Mardikh), about forty miles south of Aleppo. For some two centuries, from about 2550 to 2350 it controlled north Syria and the transit trade through Syria. Excavations there began in 1964 under the direction of Paolo Matthiae of the University of Rome. A 1968 discovery identified the 140-acre site as ancient Ebla, and the location of the city archives (some 20,000) in 1975 and 1976 opened a whole chapter in Syrian history. About eighty percent of the texts were written in Sumerian and the rest in "Eblaite," an unknown Semitic language. Fortunately the ancient scribes produced bilingual texts in Sumerian and "Eblaite," so decipherment could proceed with a degree of ease. Some of the tablets are economic in character, others literary, and yet others legal and political. In the early days of translation sensational claims identified the names of several biblical cities with which Ebla had connections. More recently scholars have repudiated those early claims and deny that the Ebla tablets, as least as far as is now known, make any reference to Jerusalem, Megiddo, Lachish, Shechem, Sodom, and other cities of the plain, or Palestine or Egypt in general. Ebla was a Syrian site and the texts focus on inner Syria. Those claims had arisen as a result of inadequate understanding of the language.

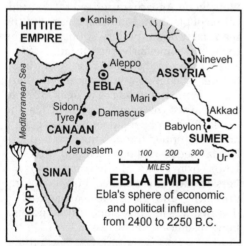

EBLA EMPIRE
Ebla's sphere of economic and political influence from 2400 to 2250 B.C.

Ebla's glorious days came to an end with a massive destruction about 2350 B.C., presumably at the hands of Sargon of Akkad. Rebuilt, the city was a flourishing metropolis once more by 2000 B.C., only to meet its end as an important center with a Hittite attack about 1600 B.C. Thereafter it survived only as an insignificant village.

An important chapter in the history of the Near East during the Early Bronze Age concerns Sargon of Agade (Akkade). This Semite burst on the scene about 2350 B.C., subdued the Sumerian city-states and created an empire that extended from Elam in the East to the Mediterranean. In the process he of course took control of Syria and apparently burned the important Syrian city of Ebla to the ground. Sargon's capital of Agade, not found as yet, was located somewhere in northern Babylonia, where the Tigris and Euphrates flow close together. The Sargonid empire continued for about 150 years, through the reign of his powerful grandson Naram-Sin and beyond. During this period Semitic Akkadian became the language of Mesopotamia and Syria, though Sumerian culture continued to dominate the region. It is important to note that Semitic groups ("pre-Akkadian" had already appeared in Babylonia during the Early Dynastic period (c. 2800–2360 B.C.).[7]

The Amorites

Late in the Early Bronze Age Amorites gradually began to make their appearance in central Syria, perhaps as early as the days of Sargon of Akkad. Some scholars put their origin in the Syrian Steppe and find them to be a nomadic population interacting with the urban centers of Syria and Mesopotamia. Others see them as peasants originally living in the valley of the Middle Euphrates River, with a link to an urban setting. Presumably they moved from there to the steppe in order to find more rangeland for their flocks. Actually their society combined elements of nomadism and agriculture into one ethnic unit. In either case they do not seem to have come into the region in a massive migration, as formerly believed, but to have infiltrated from the periphery of the settled area of Syria.

Amorites pressed against the boundaries of empire all during the Ur III period in Mesopotamia and finally did much to destroy that empire about 2000 B.C. During the next 400 years they occupied the thrones in Aleppo, Mari, Babylon, and other capital cities of Syria and Mesopotamia. They dominated the region politically and Akkadian served as the international language of the period. The culture remained basically

Sumerian. So in spite of the political division and periodic warfare, there was a linguistic and cultural cohesion.

The Amorite language belonged to the west Semitic group and was therefore related to Phoenician, Canaanite, and the later Hebrew and Aramaic. "Amorite" is a non-Semitic word meaning "Westerner." This is what the Sumerians of Mesopotamia called them; what the Semitic group called themselves is not known. The name of their country came to be known as "Amurru" or "Martu" ("westland").

The Amorites' chief deity was Amor, or Amurru, a god of war and hunting (behind whom stood a host of ill-defined gods). His consort was Ashirat, goddess of the waste places and lusty energy, of the common Ishtar type. Her name corresponds to the asherah, the sacred pole or tree trunk, a well-known cult object condemned in the Old Testament. The Amorites introduced into southern Syria the cult of the sacred pillar or monolith, apparently representing the tribal deity, which was erected with altars in caves and other worship centers. Another important deity of their pantheon was the rain god Hadad or Adad, also known as Rimmon. Grain was personified in Dagon.

The Middle Bronze Age

Just as Ebla had dominated north Syria for centuries during the Early Bronze Age, so the state of Yamkhad (capital at Aleppo) controlled the region for much of the Middle Bronze Age, from about 1800 to 1600 B.C. Reportedly twenty kings of the region were its vassals about 1800.[8] Its territory extended from near the Mediterranean to the Euphrates; thus its kings had a grip on the trade routes of Syria. Finally the Hittites destroyed the capital about 1600.

But Yamkhad did not rule over all of Syria. Qatna, Mari, and Carchemish were prominent independent powers in the interior and Alalakh, Ugarit, and Byblos in the west.

Qatna (Tell Mishrifeh), eleven miles northeast of Homs, came under control of an Amorite dynasty during the first half of the second millennium B.C. Its kings surrounded its 247 acres with a square earthen wall 2.5 miles long and about 50 feet high. Mesopotamian influences dominated at

Qatna during the Ur III Period; it had good relations with Mari and Egypt during the first two centuries of the second millennium B.C. At the end of the sixteenth century the Mitanni spread their control over both Aleppo and Qatna, and later the Egyptians and Mitanni struggled to control the state.

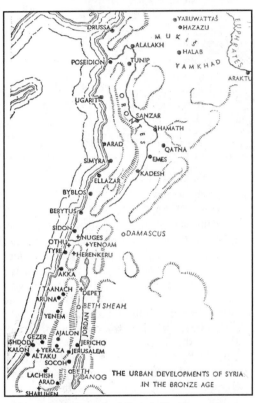

Urban developments of Syria in the Bronze Age

It met destruction about 1350, perhaps at the hands of the Hittites.

Qatna is one of the best-known sites of Syria in this period. As usual, the most thoroughly explored part of the ruins is the palace complex. The palace and temple formed one great center and sat on a raised clay platform 400 feet east and west and about 230 feet north and south. The main entrance on the south gave access to a court about 66 by 33 feet, on the east side of which two large doors led to the royal apartments. To the west of the court a passageway led to the throne room, from the anteroom of which access was gained to the temple court. At the northeast corner of the temple court lay a holy place separated by a curtain from the holy of holies where stood a small golden statue of the goddess Ninegal, "Lady of Qatna."

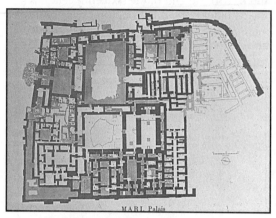

Floor plan of the Mari palace, where the royal archives were housed

Mari[9] (Tell Hariri) was located in the Middle Euphrates region about fifteen miles north of the present Syria-Iraq border near the town of Abu Kemal. In ancient times the river flowed past the edge of the city, but the mound is now over a mile west of the Euphrates. The mounds of the site cover an area about a half mile long by a mile wide. Mari was the only major city of the middle Euphrates and as such controlled the trade routes by land and river from southern Mesopotamia to northern Syria and Anatolia and across the desert via Damascus to Palestine and the Mediterranean. Here lack of rainfall required irrigation, and several canals supported agriculture; the longest of these was about 75 miles long and 35 feet wide and thus navigable.

THE MARI TABLETS

Mari, located in the middle Euphrates region, is only one of several ancient cities to surrender large collections of ancient clay tablets that have value for biblical studies. The almost 25,000 tablets found in the palace of Mari help to establish the chronology of the second millennium

B.C., and the historicity of some Old Testament names. They also mention customs reflected in the patriarchal narratives and provide materials useful in achieving greater understanding of the Akkadian language.

The history of Mari goes back to near the beginning of the third millennium B.C. Then it fell under the control of the Akkadian kings Sargon and Naram-Sin in the twenty-fourth and twenty-third centuries. Those kings undertook major construction projects, especially a new royal palace and a temple. The city continued to be prosperous during the twenty-second century, when Ur made it part of her empire. Then the Amorites dominated the region during the nineteenth and early eighteenth centuries B.C. This was a time when the palace came to the height of its glory. The six-acre structure had nearly 300 rooms on the ground floor, with an undetermined number on the second floor. It included a house for the king and administrative quarters, a house for the women, a temple area, and storerooms. The earthen walls were sometimes 14 feet thick and still stand to a height of 12-25 feet in places. Lime plaster coated the interior and exterior of the walls and sometimes they were decorated with wall paintings. The courtyards were not open to the sky but had clerestory roofs. This extensive structure is a unique example of a Bronze Age palace.[10]

The royal archives (close to 25,000 texts) were mostly in Akkadian, but some of the texts were in Hurrian. Many of the documents represent diplomatic correspondence

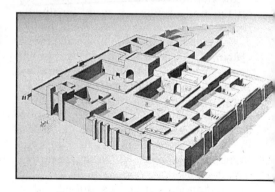

Reconstruction of the Mari palace

between King Zimri-Lim of Mari and Hammurabi of Babylon and thus help to establish the chronology of Mesopotamia during the second millennium B.C. They also contain names equivalent to those mentioned in Genesis 11:16, 23, 24, 27 (e.g., Peleg, Serug, Nahor), showing that they were good historical names. Moreover, they mention customs reflected in the patriarchal narrative and throw light on the tribal organization and traditions of Syria in patriarchal times.

What led Hammurabi to destroy the city in about 1760 B.C. we do not know. But he looted and burned the palace, leaving behind enough objects to give some idea of its former glory. The city continued on in a modest condition for another millennium but has been deserted since the Roman Era. André Parrot of the Louvre conducted several seasons of excavation at the site before and after World War II (beginning in 1933) and Jean Claude Margueron has led more than ten campaigns there since 1979.

Carchemish, located on the west bank of the Euphrates River near its great bend at the Syria-Turkey border, is in such a strategically sensitive location that excavation cannot now be conducted there. Work done at the site before World War I threw light especially on the city's history as a Neo-Hittite state during the early first millennium B.C. We shall return to that development later.

During Ebla's golden age Carchemish was part of the commercial network of the period. The Mari texts picture Carchemish as an independent kingdom during the early second millennium B.C. By the middle of that millennium Carchemish had been absorbed into the kingdom of Mitanni. Subsequently the Hittites captured the city and it became an important outpost of that empire. The Hittite king Suppiluliuma installed his son as a king there, and his descendants ruled at Carchemish for several generations.

As to what was going on in the West during the Middle Bronze Age, comments on Byblos appear in the chapter on Phoenicia. Alalakh (Tell 'Atchana), located near the mouth of the Orontes River and about forty miles west of Aleppo, com-

King Idrimi of Alalakh. This statue is in the British Museum

manded the area's main trade routes. The town stood in the Amq plain, a wide flat alluvial area, about 30 by 30 miles, in northwest Syria—occupying the greater part of the Turkish province of Hatay. That the Amq plain was prosperous in antiquity is indicated by the fact that some 200 mounds containing ancient cities dot its landscape.

Sir C. Leonard Woolley excavated at Alalakh for eight seasons (1937–39, 1946–49) and had considerable success in discovering the early history of the site. The mound of Alalakh is an oval measuring about 3000 by 1000 feet. The city was a vassal of the kingdom of Aleppo or Yamkhad in the eighteenth-sixteenth centuries B.C. and of Mitanni in the fifteenth–fourteenth centuries B.C. In all there were seventeen levels of occupation dating from 2400 to about 1195 B.C. Excavations yielded 515 texts, almost all written in Akkadian, and dating to the Aleppo and Mitanni periods. These help to establish the chronology of the second millennium B.C.[11]

Ras Shamra and environs

The buildings that Woolley excavated at Alalakh were the royal palace, the city temple, and the city gate. The palace was quite sumptuous, measuring 320 by 50 feet, and was divided into two parts, official and private quarters, separated by a courtyard. Most, if not all, of the better rooms of the palace were decorated with frescoes painted with an architectural design like some of those in the royal palace of Minos in Crete.[12] Moreover, the methods of construction employed are the same as those of Knossos. In fact, the similarities between the palaces of Alalakh and Knossos were so evident that Woolley suggested that trained experts from the former actually may have been involved in construction of the latter.[13]

Adjacent to the palace was a temple courtyard which gave entrance to the almost square single-room sanctuary about sixty feet on a side. This was equipped with raised benches along its sides and a stepped altar of basalt stones on the side opposite the entrance.

Alalakh's wealth was based largely on international trade, which was considerable because the city stood astride both the north-south and east-west routes. But its prosperity was short-lived. About 1700 a great catastrophe overtook the city. Its temple and palace were thoroughly plundered and burned. Whether the Babylonians, the Hyksos, or an internal revolution was responsible is not known, but Woolley argued cogently for the third possibility. He pointed out that the ruling caste was from Aleppo and was not native, that pottery styles revert mostly to local styles after the destruction, and that the palace and temple areas were unoccupied for long thereafter as if cursed.[14] Aleppo itself shows no sign of violence at this period.

Ugarit (modern Ras Shamra) is located on a sixty-five foot hill a half mile from the Mediterranean, just across from the eastern tip of Cyprus. The city derived its wealth largely from the trade that flowed through its port, Minet el-Beida. Today Minet el-Beida ("the white harbor") is neither a large or safe harbor. The white chalk cliffs from which it received its name have become eroded and have tumbled into the sea. Also the shoreline has advanced some 400 feet since the town ceased to exist.

Almost ever since a Syrian peasant accidentally broke into an ancient tomb with his plow at the site in 1928, excavations have been going on there. In 1929, Claude F. A. Schaeffer of the Strasbourg Museum initiated the excavations, which continued until the outbreak of World War II and resumed again in 1950. Henri de Contenson subsequently assumed leadership of the excavation (1971–1974), to be followed by Jean Margueron (1975–1977) and Marguerite Yon (since 1978).

Occupation of the site goes back to the seventh millennium B.C., but our interest centers on the Middle and Late Bronze Ages. In about 2000 B.C. Amorites occupied Ugarit and introduced a new urban civilization there. The town covered the entire mound and was surrounded by a strong wall. Some inhabitants seemed to be expert in metallurgy, and molds for weapons and jewelry have been recovered. Egyptians dominated the site for a time, probably during the Twelfth

Dynasty (c. 2000–1780 B.C.). Mari texts mention diplomatic and trade contacts with Ugarit. Comments on the significant Late Bronze Age, when Ugarit was at its height, appear later.

Canaanites. Any discussion of the Middle Bronze Age in Syria must deal with the Canaanites. And immediately we are confronted with the problem of meaning or identification of the term. The *territory* of Canaan is fairly easily identifiable from Genesis 10:15–19: the land of Sidon, Heth, the Jebusites, and others. It stretched south from Sidon to Gaza along the coast and inland to the cities at the south end of the Dead Sea. In Exodus 13:5 several tribal groups appear as inhabitants of the Promised Land. Although their holdings are differentiated in Numbers 12:29, in Numbers 35:10 Canaan was a name applied to the whole territory west of the Jordan and extending up the coast almost to Latakia and inland to Hamath on the upper Orontes River (cf. Numbers 34:2–12).

The *meaning* of Canaanite is another matter. An older view, held until World War II, is that their name is related to the Hebrew *kanan* ("to be made low") and that Canaanites therefore were "lowlanders," as opposed to the Amorites, who lived in the higher regions. A newer view, proposed about the time of World War II, is that Canaan should be related to the Hebrew *Kena'an*, which came from a Hurrian and Akkadian word for the purple dye for which Phoenician city-states became famous. But more recently that connection has been repudiated, and a satisfactory explanation of the name currently remains to be found.

Early in the second millennium B.C., the Canaanites established themselves in Palestine and Syria. Perhaps they had arrived at an earlier time (see Genesis 12:6). At least in Palestine they seem to have preceded the Amorites. Where they came from is a question not answered with certainty, but some scholars suggest that they originated in Arabia. Historical and archaeological sources portray the Canaanites as Semites. The Old Testament points to Hamitic rather than Semitic extraction for Canaan (Genesis 10:6). There is no necessary contradiction here because whatever their origin may have been, the Canaanites did not long remain in their early "pure" state but soon were racially and culturally mixed with other tribes of Palestine and Syria.

The Canaanites were not greatly different from the Amorites. Linguistically they were both from the northwest Semitic family and differed only dialectically. Ethnically they were not very dissimilar either. But gradually the Amorites assimilated Sumerian and Hurrian elements, and the Canaanites absorbed other local elements. Culturally the difference between them arose from the fact that the Amorites came more under the influence of the Sumerians and Babylonians while the Canaanites were influenced by Egyptian culture.

But the latter generalization is not completely accurate, for the Canaanites of Palestine and Syria did not have a homogeneous culture. Egyptian culture had more influence in Palestine, Mesopotamian in Syria. The regional differences in Canaanite culture may be readily seen by a study of excavations at two typical towns: Beth-Shean (modern Beisan) in the south and Ugarit (modern Ras Shamra) in the north. The former, located just south of the Sea of Galilee, was under Egyptian political domination c. 1450 to 1200 B.C. While the five temples of the town were patterned after Egyptian models, they were built of brick with wood pillars rather than stone. Within the temples Canaanite deities were worshiped, but they were modeled in the Egyptian style. The chief Canaanite deities were Reshef, a war and storm god; Astarte, the fertility goddess; and Mekal, possibly the Semitic Hercules.

Excavations at Ugarit have demonstrated how Canaanite culture in the north differed from that in the south. Farther away from Egyptian influence than the southern Canaanites, and farther from the Mesopotamians than the southern Canaanites were from Egypt, the northern Canaanites had sufficient independence to create a complex and influential civilization. This was true in spite of the fact that Ras Shamra was a vassal of Egypt from 1500 to 1350 B.C.

The city traded extensively with Cyprus and other Mediterranean islands and Egypt. Copper from Cyprus made possible a sizable copper-smelting industry. Other metal goods, cosmetics, and purple dye were also among the town's industries. Her commercial and industrial activities were similar to those of the Canaanite towns of Phoenicia. At the head of the Ugaritic pantheon was El, and his consort was Athirat, or Ashera, equitable with Aphrodite. There was also the grain god Dagon and his son Baal, or Adonis. The latter's consort was Anat, identifiable with Artemis. How much of the religion of Ugarit was Canaanite and how much Hurrian is yet to be determined. Ugarit is later discussed at more length.

The Canaanites never succeeded in establishing a strong unified state. Their political fragmentation in city-states may be explained variously, but more important is the fact that this division left the country at the mercy of neighboring powers, whether conquerors like the Egyptians or Mesopotamians or new settlers like the Hebrews. Sometimes, however, leagues of Canaanite cities were formed under the leadership of a strong center (such as Ugarit, Byblos, Tyre, or Hazor) which established a political hegemony. Sometimes these leagues were organized under the stress of mutual danger, as was the case when Kadesh (Qadesh) on the Orontes River led a coalition against Thutmose III early in the fifteenth century.

Basically an agricultural people, the Canaanites also developed various crafts to a very high degree of perfection. Their pottery was made by a wheel early in the second millennium, and styles and decoration were influenced by Egyptian, Minoan, Mycenean, and Cypriot ware. Their metallurgy was probably unexcelled during most of the second millennium B.C. They were excellent goldsmiths and silversmiths. Copper and bronze working was common among them, and they knew how to use tin for hardening iron.[15] The Canaanites excelled in the manufacture of glass too, as well as in the production of woolen cloth and dyestuffs.

One of the most important cultural contributions of the Canaanites to the Hebrews was their language. The Akkadian-speaking Patriarchs apparently borrowed the alphabetic "language of Canaan" (Isaiah 19:18) and carried it with them into Egypt, retained it during their long sojourn there, and then brought it back to Palestine at the time of the Conquest.[16]

Egyptian Control. Egyptians had come to dominate the Phoenician coast and were to do so, with interruptions, from about 2400 B.C. to 1200 B.C. Twelfth Dynasty Pharaohs (c. 2000–1780 B.C.) claimed and probably exercised loose control over Palestine and a large part of Syria as well. According to the place-names on Egyptian lists of about 1800 B.C., the Egyptian Empire included Damascus and most of El Bika.

The Hyksos. Egyptian conquest of Canaan and part of Syria during the Late Bronze Age (see below) was especially connected with the Hyksos conquest of Egypt. The Egyptian name for the Hyksos means "rulers of foreign lands." And evidently these people began migrating from Canaan into Egypt in small groups, beginning soon after 2000 B.C. Present indications lead to the conclusion that their land of origin was Palestine, rather than Syria (though some still point to a Syrian origin), and that they seem to have been primarily Amorite. While they became more numerous in the Delta region, the power of the Egyptian central government weakened. In a few localities the Hyksos seem to have been able to establish small independent principalities. And finally, about 1730 B.C., they launched military action that won for them control of the Delta region and some territory south of that.

Although the Hyksos do not appear to have been a tightly-knit political entity, their center of power (capital) was Avaris in the Delta. This is modern Tell el-Dab 'a, which has been extensively excavated. During the Middle Bronze Age there was a lively traffic in goods between the Delta and Palestine-Syria. And though the contact between the Delta and points north does not seem to prove the existence of an Amorite empire, when the Pharaohs of the Egyptian Empire period (after c. 1500 B.C.)

tossed off Hyksos control they went on to occupy the homeland of the Hyksos as well and thus built an empire that extended all the way to the Euphrates. We need to keep in mind that the Hebrew entrance into and residence in Egypt took place alongside the Hyksos activity in the Delta, but should not be confused with it. Moreover, when the Egyptians overcame the Hyksos in the sixteenth century and expelled many of them from the land, the Hebrews remained.

To be sure, Hittites and Hurrians were active in Syria during the late Middle Bronze Age, but they figure more prominently during the Late Bronze Age, and we return to them subsequently.

The Late Bronze Age

During the Late Bronze Age (c. 1500–1200) Syria fell under foreign rule: the Egyptians in the south, the Hittites in the north, and the Mitanni in the east. And it was a battleground between these warring powers.

The Egyptians

The expansion of the Egyptian Empire up into Palestine and Syria was almost a natural outcome of Egyptian expulsion of the Hyksos from the land of the Nile. Having defeated the Hyksos in Egypt, the Egyptians proceeded to attack them in their northern strongholds. About the middle of the sixteenth century B.C., Ahmose began the subjection of the Asiatic provinces for Egypt. Thutmose I marched as far as the Euphrates in 1520. But the restless inhabitants of the area did not long remain subdued.

Thutmose III found himself making seventeen sorties into Palestine and Syria in almost as many years. He fought one of his greatest battles at Megiddo in 1479, when he met a confederation of some 300 princes of Palestine and Syria and vanquished them. In subsequent campaigns he took Aradus (biblical Arvad, modern Arwad) on the Mediterranean and Qadesh on the Orontes, the prince of which had been the leader of the confederation that had met Thutmose at Megiddo. In fact, Thutmose III traversed Syria all the way to the Euphrates River.

Syrians could be momentarily impressed with Egyptian might. But when Egyptian Pharaohs left the country and/or when there was a change of rulers in Egypt, Syrians commonly entertained ideas of revolt. This tendency is well illustrated in the Amarna Letters, which address frantic pleas for help to Amenhotep III and Amenhotep IV. But these luxury-loving kings who ruled during the first half of the fourteenth century B.C. had no interest in helping their loyal vassals in Palestine and Syria in maintaining the empire. By the middle of the century, Syria had passed completely out of Egyptian control. Later kings, such as Seti I and Ramses II, tried to restore Egyptian power there, but their success was restricted very largely to the Phoenician coast.

The Mitanni

Decline of Egyptian strength in Syria on any occasion provided opportunity for other powers to take over there or for native dynasts to assert themselves. One of the people who came in from the outside were the Hurrians. By the beginning of the Middle Bronze Age Hurrian tribesmen from the mountain ranges in eastern Anatolia and the Zagros mountains east of Mesopotamia had infiltrated the Syrian plateau and northern Mesopotamia. These people, with linguistic affinities to ancient India, gradually established small Hurrian kingdoms and developed one major power, the kingdom of Mitanni. A dynasty of Mitannian kings ruled continuously at their capital of Wasshukkani in upper Mesopotamia (currently not positively located) from about 1500 B.C. until about 1370. At its height the Mitanni Kingdom stretched from the Mediterranean to the highlands of Media and included Assyria. About 1450 B.C. Thutmose III of Egypt bested the Mitanni and took much of their territory west of the Euphrates. Thereafter Egypt and the Mitanni made a treaty of alliance, apparently in the face of the rising threat of the Hittites. Successive Mitanni kings gave daughters in marriage to Thutmose IV, and Amenhotep III and IV of Egypt.

But in about 1370 the Hittite king Suppululiuma I destroyed the Mitanni Kingdom and installed his own choice as

puppet ruler. Then in 1346 the Assyrian king Ashur-uballit I overcame Mitanni and incorporated its territory into his kingdom. That did not mark the end of Hurrian influence or presence in the region, however. Suppiluliuma I and his dynasty were Hurrians, and Hurrians made up a large percentage of the population of Syria and northern Mesopotamia. As for connections with the Old Testament, perhaps Hivites and Jebusites were Hurrians, but not the Horites, who were inhabitants of Edom or Mount Seir and descendants of Esau.

The Hittites

When Egyptian power in Syria declined during the Amarna Age (c. 1400–1360 B.C.), the Hittites moved into northern Syria and warred effectively against the Mitanni. Frantic appeals from the latter to Amenhotep III and Amenhotep IV (in the Amarna Letters) brought no help from the colossus on the Nile. Advancing from their Asia Minor strongholds, the Hittites were successful under Suppiluliuma about 1370 B.C. in carving out a Syrian empire, which by the end of the Hittite kings' reign stretched south of Byblos. The Hittites were able to control most of this area unhindered by outside interference for about a century. Then in the thir-

teenth century Ramses II attempted to restore Egyptian authority in Syria. Meeting the Hittite Mutalli at Kadesh on the Orontes River in 1286, Ramses claimed an important victory—which was more nearly a draw. From this battle a nonaggression pact eventually ensued, according to the provisions of which the Hittites retained nearly all of Syria north of Palestine as their sphere of influence and the Egyptians roughly the area of Palestine as theirs.

Ugarit

We have already thought briefly about Ugarit; now we return to the site during the Late Bronze Age, its golden era. During the Middle Kingdom period of Egypt (c. 2000–1775 B.C.) Ugarit had attained great prosperity as a crossroads of trade flowing between Mesopotamia and Egypt. Contacts with the Minoan civilization on Crete also proved to be lucrative. Suffering a commercial eclipse during Hyksos domination, Ugarit revived when Egypt gained effective control of the Syrian coast during the Empire period. Allied with Egypt, Ugarit benefited greatly from Egyptian alliance with the Mitanni (c. 1440–1380). And fortunately for the city she remained unmolested by the Hittites for several decades after the Hittite

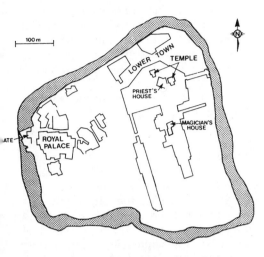

Ras Shamra: Buildings on the tell

Tablets dealing with fiscal affairs of the provinces were stored by the main western entrance, records concerning financial matters of the city in the eastern archive by the entrance to the palace from the city, legal records (deeds, etc.) in the central archive, and foreign correspondence in the south archive. Near the palace stood the royal stables and a building identified as the town arsenal. South of the palace was another building called the little palace.

Between the palace and temple complexes along the north side of the tell sprawled a residential district with rather comfortable homes. On a slope of the hill another residential area was investigated. Off the tell, a harbor residential area appeared on excavation to have been occupied mostly by Aegean and Cypriot immigrants.

Even apart from numerous tablet finds at Ras Shamra, the site would have been important archaeologically because of its strategic position in the ancient world and its widespread contact with the Aegean world, the Hittites, Cyprus, Phoenicia, Palestine, Egypt, North Syria, and Mesopotamia. But the texts are of special importance.

The total collection is in no less than seven languages written in five scripts, mostly during the fifteenth through the thirteenth centuries B.C. Egyptian, Sumerian, Akkadian, Hurrian, and Hittite texts are very useful for understanding the history of the Near East and firming up the area's chronology. Thus they provide excellent contextual information for Old Testament studies. But of special interest and most numerous in the archives were materials written in a new Canaanite script of thirty letters. This body of literature, now called Ugaritic, became available through the pioneer decipherment work of C. Virolleaud, E. Dhorme, and R. Dussaud. Cyrus H. Gordon, in his *Ugaritic Manual* and other writing, has helped to bring our knowledge of the language to its present development.

defeat of the Mitanni (1370 ff.). During the fifteenth and fourteenth centuries, then, Ugarit enjoyed a golden age, with Syrians, Cypriots, Cretans, Greeks, Hurrians, and Egyptians living together amicably there.

As Egyptian power in Syria declined during the Amarna age, the Hittites took over at Ugarit (c. 1360 B.C.). As a tribute-paying vassal of the Hittites, Ugarit was unmolested and she prospered. After Ramses II engaged the Hittites at the battle of Kadesh in 1286 B.C., Ugarit found herself in the delicate position of having to maintain good relations with both Egyptians and Hittites. This she seems to have managed fairly successfully. But around 1200 B.C. Aegean peoples destroyed Ugarit, and she never recovered her earlier prosperity.

Now we look more specifically at the discoveries at the site. During his first season of excavation in 1929 Claude Schaeffer found two temples on the northeast corner of the tell—to Baal and Dagon. Near the temple of Dagon was a temple library with a large tablet collection, a school for scribes with exercises for schoolboys, and a residence of the high priest of Ugarit.

At the northwest corner of the tell, French teams subsequently excavated the palace of Ugarit. This great stone structure, covering some three acres, was the administrative center as well as the residence of the royal family. Here were housed the archives of the realm in systematic fashion.

DISCOVERIES AT UGARIT (RAS SHAMRA)

Excavations at ancient Ugarit (modern Ras Shamra, about twenty-five miles south of the mouth of the Orontes River) have ranked high in biblical significance. A library of religious texts found near temples to Baal and Dagon, palace archives dealing with financial, legal, and diplomatic affairs, and records from homes of leading citizens have opened new vistas on Old Testament study. These thousands of texts in seven languages written in five scripts date mostly to the fifteenth through the thirteenth centuries B.C.

Of special interest and most numerous in the archives were materials written in an alphabetic script of thirty letters now known as Ugaritic. Closely related to biblical Hebrew, Ugaritic provides knowledge of the latter at the time of Moses, when Evangelicals claim the Pentateuch was composed. Ugaritic studies have enabled some previously misunderstood words in the Old Testament to be defined and the meaning of others made clearer.

A study of similarities between Pentateuchal ritual and that of the inhabitants of ancient Ugarit is especially interesting and may be pursued in Charles Pfeiffer's *Ras Shamra and the Bible*. Especially, the Ugaritic material hits on the head the critical assertion that the Pentateuch could not have been written in the days of Moses because law and ritual were not so highly developed then. As a matter of fact, there are parallels between Ugaritic and biblical sacrificial systems.

Ugaritic is closely related to biblical Hebrew and provides knowledge of the language at the time of Moses. It has enabled many previously unknown words in the Old Testament to be identified and the meaning of others made clear. Some Old Testament words or phrases formerly regarded as suspect have been confirmed by Ugaritic readings, and thus the Masoretic text often has been supported.

The Ugaritic Texts serve along with the Dead Sea Scrolls to provide a means of arriving at an understanding of what Old Testament words meant to the people to whom the Old Testament was addressed. These texts help in understanding Hebrew grammar too, as well as the poetic structure of vast portions of the Old Testament.[17]

Now scholars could know the Canaanite religion through its own literature, although it had long been known through such things as temples and cult objects. Ugaritic literature strengthened archaeological evidence to the effect that the Canaanites had perhaps the most depraved of all Near Eastern religions. The chief emphasis in Canaanite religion centered on fertility and sex. Sacred prostitution—both male and female—was common and practiced at numerous centers of worship. (By contrast, note the prohibition against sacred prostitution in Deuteronomy 23:17–18.) By means of these texts we are better able to appreciate some of the bristling condemnation that Old Testament prophets hurled against the Canaanites and things Canaanite.

There are, however, similarities between the Hebrew and Canaanite religions. For instance, both made "peace offerings" and "burnt offerings" and used comparable sacrificial animals in the process. But we must be careful not to conclude that the Hebrews merely borrowed from the Canaanites and purified their religious institutions. As Charles Pfeiffer observed, "There is no evidence of borrowing on the part of Israel or the Canaanites of Ugarit. Similarities are doubtless the result of common Semitic background of both peoples."[18] While technical terms used by the two systems of worship may have been similar, meanings poured into those terms stood in striking contrast. The Ras Shamra texts demonstrate that Canaanite mythology and Israelite theology were poles apart.

Further, Pfeiffer argues, "Elements which Israelites and Canaanites held in common may be traced to the common traditions possessed by the two peoples concerning worship. The New Testament insists that there was a genuine revelation of God to the pre-Abrahamic peoples which was never completely forgotten (Romans 1:21–32)."[19]

In conclusion, it is interesting to note that critics used to insist that the Mosaic institutions described in the Pentateuch came late in Israel, during the Persian period, at the end of a process of religious evolution. They believed no such highly developed legal institutions could have arisen in the eastern Mediterranean world at such an early time. Of course the Code of Hammurabi and other ancient legal codes helped to answer such an assertion. But the Ugaritic texts came from the same Semitic context as the Hebrew religious system and dated to the very time of Moses! It is no longer tenable to hold that Hebrew religious institutions had to come late and that Moses could not have been involved with their establishment.

The Iron Age

The eastern Mediterranean world came apart at the seams about 1200 B.C. or a little later. Walled Mycenaean palace centers at Pylos, Mycenae, Tiryns and elsewhere, that had seemed so impregnable, now stood silent and alone. The mighty Hittite Empire came crashing down before the onslaughts of enemies that probably descended from the north. Troy suffered the destruction that may be commemorated in Homer's *Iliad*. Sea Peoples attacked numerous centers, in Asia Minor, Egypt, and Ugarit, and destroyed them. With the Iron Age new peoples strode across the Syrian landscape: Aramaeans, Hebrews, and Assyrians. Some Hittite states still maintained themselves. And Damascus achieved a significance that other Syrian cities had previously enjoyed. Over on the Mediterranean coast Tyre rose to greatness as an emporium of trade. The account of Tyre appears in the chapter on Phoenicia.

The Aramaeans

The Aramaeans (whose ancestry is traced to Shem, Genesis: 22–23) were Bedouins who probably spread from the fringe areas north of the Syro-Arabian desert into the more settled region of the Fertile Crescent. They were established in upper Mesopotamia from early Patriarchal times, as the accounts of Isaac and Jacob and a Naram-Sin inscription indicate.[20] There Aram Naharaim (Nahor, Genesis 24:10), or Padan-Aram (Genesis 25:20; 28:2), had as its center the biblical Haran (ancient Carrhae). Evidently the Aramaeans moved into north and central Syria earlier, but events of the twelfth century offered them an unparalleled opportunity to dominate the area. As noted, Hittite power had collapsed and the Egyptian Empire in Western Asia was gone. The Hebrews were a politically ineffective collection of tribes living under the leadership of the Judges.

The tendency currently is not to see the Aramaeans as newcomers to Syria and northern Mesopotamia in the second-first millennium B.C. but to conclude that they lived in the area much earlier as pastoralists and village occupants. They now surfaced in places where the Amorites had been active earlier and established themselves politically with the lifting of hindrances to city-state formation.

As is commonly noted, the earliest certain secular reference to the Aramaeans occurs in the records of the Assyrian king Tiglath-pileser I, dating to about 1000 B.C. He tells about crossing the Euphrates twenty-eight times, twice in one year, to attack the Aramaeans.[21] His purpose in doing so evidently was to protect the trade routes against these pastoralist nomads who were raiding caravans to supplement their incomes.

Most powerful of the Aramaean kingdoms of Syria in the late eleventh century was Zobah, located in northern Lebanon and extending into the Plain of Homs in central Syria. Damascus must at that time have been part of the kingdom of Zobah; later it became one of the most important of the Aramaean states. Other Aramaean states included Hama, Bit-Adini, Bit-Agusi, Beth-rehob, Maachah, Tob, and Gesher. It would be tedious to discuss these and others here.

The small Aramaean states of Syria never did achieve a political unity and therefore could not stand against the Assyrians or Hebrews or even against the kingdom of Damascus. For some two hundred years Assyrian kings fought the

The Storm god. Late Hittite. *Istanbul Museum*

Hittite City-Sates

The spotlight now shifts for a moment from the Aramaeans to the Hittite states of north Syria. The fall of the Hittite Empire shortly after 1200 B.C. did not spell the end of the Hittites. Indeed, they appear in various places for almost 500 years more. This "Indian summer" of Hittite power has bequeathed more monuments than did the empire. Assyrian records continue to refer to Syria and Asia Minor just east of the Taurus as the "Land of Hatti" and mention rulers with names identical to those of the Imperial period. The list of Hittite city-states is long, but a few examples will suffice. On the fringe of Cappadocia a Hittite state was established at the classical Tyana. At the eastern edge of the Taurus, Hittite cities stood at Adana (or Seyhan) and Zinjirli. In north Syria proper, important Hittite settlements appeared at Carchemish and Tell Ahmar on the Euphrates and at Aleppo to the southwest. Most southerly of all was the important kingdom of Hamath (modern Hama, classical Epiphania).

Some of these city-states were large; others were unpretentious. Never achieving any political unity, they managed in spite of that fact to resist the Assyrians with a determined opposition that kept them independent of Assyria until about 876 B.C. Even after that time, they were in almost continuous revolt for a half century or more and enjoyed a degree of freedom again during the middle of the eighth century when the Urartaeans invaded Assyria. But finally Sargon II of Assyria (722–705) effectively annexed these city-states one by one. Zinjirli probably fell in 724 B.C., Hamath in 720, Carchemish in 717. All of the rest probably capitulated by 709 B.C.

In passing, it should be noted that the Aramaeans clashed with the newly established Hittite principalities and overthrew the ruling houses of some of them in the eleventh or tenth century B.C. Other Hittite territories maintained themselves until the Assyrians toppled them.

When the Hebrews controlled Syria, they came in contact with the Hittites, conducting business with them (2 Chronicles 1:17) and using such Hittite mercenaries as Uriah (2 Samuel 11:3 ff.) and Ahimelech (1

Aramaeans, defeated them, deported their peoples to Assyria, and ultimately converted their lands into Assyrian provinces.

Aramaean art and architecture and other cultural aspects had little influence in the ancient world, but their language had a wide-ranging impact. As Assyrians deported large numbers of Aramaeans into Assyria, Aramaic gained importance there and was used in official communications between Assyria and the West. Later it became the most common spoken language in Babylonia. By the time the Medo-Persians built their empire, Aramaic had become the most widespread language in the Near East and was used for official Persian communiqués. Thus it appears in sections of Ezra and Daniel. Later it became the primary language of Judea and thus of Jesus and the disciples and served as the common language of Western Asia until the Arab conquest in the seventh century A.D., when Arabic superceded it.

Samuel 26:6) in their military forces. Solomon introduced Hittite women into his harem (1 Kings 11:1).

Al Mina.[22] An infrequently-told chapter in Syrian history concerns the port of Al Mina on the south bank of the Orontes at its mouth. The site was located about four miles south of the later Seleucia, destined to be the harbor for Antioch during the Seleucid and Roman periods. Actually the port was a double town: the harbor itself which lay on very low ground at the mouth of the Orontes, where the warehouses were located, and the residential area on an easily defensible and healthful height three miles inland. The double town served as the port for the old town of Alalakh which has been noted above and which was destroyed about 1200 B.C.

Presumably Al Mina was also destroyed about the same time, but it was rebuilt again and had a continuous history until its abandonment about 300 B.C. During its later years the town was known by the Greek name of Poseideion. One of its most prosperous periods came during the first half of the eighth century B.C., when the Assyrian grip on Syria relaxed because of the rise of the kingdom of Urartu (Hebrew Ararat) and its incursions on Assyrian territory. At that time Syria was in a sense split in two. South Syria was controlled by Aramaeans. North Syria was still largely Hittite and seemingly confederate with Urartu. The trade of north Syria moved through Poseideion.

This prosperity was seriously affected when Tiglath-pileser III about 742 B.C. marched into the westland in the third year of his reign to subdue Syria once for all. Sarduris (Sardur) of Urartu came in person to defend his vassals there, but he was ignominiously defeated. By 740 all Syria was effectively under the heel of Assyria once more.

Poseideion continued to be a fairly busy port under Assyrian rule and became the emporium for the manufactures of eastern Greece. The wares of Rhodes were especially prominent in the ruins of the town. And, unbelievable as it may seem, it was a thriving port under Persian control, even during the period when the Greeks and Persians were at war. Apparently both powers needed or at least wanted the goods that could be obtained through the commerce of Poseideion enough to permit this trade to continue. The town finally withered and died in 301 B.C. when Seleucus Nicator built his new port at Seleucia. Probably he even forcibly deported the population from the old town to his new site to serve as a nucleus of population for Seleucia.

A column base with double sphinx, late Hittite, eighth century B.C. From the palace of the Aramaen king Barrekup. *Istanbul Museum*

Hebrew Advance into Syria

After a seven-year reign over Judah at Hebron, David became king over all Israel about 1000 B.C. Taking Jerusalem from the Jebusites and making it his capital, he proceeded to subdue the peoples surrounding the Hebrew kingdom. As internal strength of Israel grew and as one after the other of David's adversaries fell before him in battle, other nations became fearful. Consequently, when David sent an embassy with condolences to King Hanun of Ammon upon the death of his father, Hanun treated the Hebrew king's representative in a manner calculated to instigate war (2 Samuel 10:1–7).

Then Hanun quickly made an alliance with the Aramaean kingdoms of Zobah, Rehob, Tob, and Maacah (2 Samuel 10:8), which no doubt also feared increasing Israelite power. David thoroughly defeated the Aramaeans, with Zobah and Damascus suffering heavy casualties; and the Hebrew king stationed occupation troops in the latter city (2 Samuel 8:3–6). After David worsted Zobah (which lay to the north of Damascus), King Toi of the Hittite kingdom of Hamath apparently acknowledged Hebrew suzerainty (2 Samuel 8:9–11). It would seem that the districts under Israelite rule in the days of David can be divided into two categories: those in which occupation troops were stationed (e.g., Damascus) and those that were satellites (e.g., Zobah).

Apparently Solomon (970–931 B.C.) expanded the kingdom bequeathed to him and ruled the entire area from the border of Egypt to the Euphrates River, including Transjordan (2 Chronicles 9:26). He even brought the Phoenicians within his sphere of influence. His geographical position gave him a good opportunity to make his state the chief middleman for overland trade among Arabia, Egypt, Phoenicia, and the Hittite and Aramaean states of Syria and Asia Minor. Under the Pax Hebraica the whole area enjoyed a remarkable prosperity.

However, this is not to imply that all peoples of Palestine and Syria were docile followers of the great king in the Holy City. Apparently Zobah rebelled against Solomon and had to be subdued (2 Chronicles 8:3). As the state disintegrated late in Solomon's reign, Rezon[23] of Zobah headed a rebel movement that captured Damascus (1 Kings 11:23–25). There Rezon established a new dynasty. With the death of Solomon the subject states all seem to have reestablished their independence.

Israel and the Kingdom of Damascus

After Rezon's revolt against Solomon, his son Tabrimon and grandson Benhadad I ruled after him (1 Kings 15:18). Apparently Rezon set a pattern of Syrian animosity to the Hebrews from the beginning (1 Kings 11:23–25). Although the kingdom of Damascus gradually increased in power, its big chance came as a result of the hostility between Israel and Judah. As war progressed between the northern and southern kingdoms, Judah found herself in trying circumstances. Baasha of Israel advanced to

within five miles of Jerusalem and proceeded to fortify Ramah as a border fortress. In desperation, Asa of Judah sent a large gift to Benhadad of Syria and asked him to break his alliance with Israel and establish a compact with Judah instead.

Benhadad did this with eagerness. He advanced into Israel and took several cities in the north with their rich farmlands and at the same time secured the important trade route to Acre on the Phoenician coast (1 Kings 15:16–20). This occurred in the thirty-sixth year of Asa's reign or about 885 B.C. (2 Chronicles 16:1).

DAMASCUS AS A COMMERCIAL HUB

Damascus sat astride several caravan routes over which people moved to all areas of the ancient Near East. From Mari on the middle Euphrates came a route over which traveled products from the entire Mesopotamian valley. To the west, goods from all over the Mediterranean world landed at ports in Beirut, Tyre, Sidon, and Accho. Especially from Accho they came across northern Galilee to Damascus.

From this north Galilee road merchants also could journey south through the plain of Esdraelon and along the coastal road to Egypt. Or they could take another branch of that road through the hills of Samaria to Jerusalem or the Jordan Valley.

And it was possible to go south from Damascus through the highlands east of the Jordan on the King's Highway to the Gulf of Aqaba and Arabia.

Within a decade or so Omri established a new dynasty in Israel and launched his kingdom on an imperialist road once more. He made an alliance with Ethbaal of Tyre, thereby seeking to counteract Syrian trade with southern Phoenicia; he gained control of northern Moab and relocated the capital of the realm on the impressive hill of

Samaria. The kingdom of Damascus, alarmed by the advance of Assyria, did not try to curb the Israelites during the reign of Omri or in the early days of his son Ahab. But finally, near the end of Ahab's reign (c. 855 B.C.), Benhadad moved against Ahab but met defeat. Seeking revenge in the following year, the Syrians attacked again and suffered even worse defeat.

Ahab was now in a position to humiliate his northern rival, but he chose not to do so because it was quite clear that all possible aid would be needed to meet the imminent Assyrian invasion of the westlands (1 Kings 20). So in 853 the inveterate enemies marched side by side in the coalition that met Shalmaneser III at Qarqar north of Hamath (modern Hama). The Assyrian apparently won a victory on that occasion, but it was not sufficiently overwhelming to assure him control of Syria. Benhadad had supplied 1,200 chariots and 20,000 men for the battle, Ahab 2,000 chariots and 10,000 infantry. Irhulenu (Irhuleni) of Hamath contributed 700 chariots and 10,000 men.

Five years later, Shalmaneser met another Syrian confederacy of twelve kings, again under the leadership of Benhadad. Three years after that (845 B.C.) Shalmaneser found it necessary to engage in yet another major campaign against Syria. Again he met and defeated a coalition of a dozen kings under the leadership of Benhadad of Damascus and Irhulenu of Hamath. Apparently the Assyrian's victories were not sufficiently decisive to give him assured possession of Syria.

Finally, about 843, Benhadad of Damascus met his end at the hands of the usurper Hazael, and a new dynasty came to power in Syria. Within a couple of years Jehu had dispatched the house of Ahab and initiated a new dynasty in Israel. At this juncture, with new dynasties trying to establish themselves in Syria and Israel and with the populace of both countries shaken by revolution, Shalmaneser elected to come against Damascus. Hazael tried, like his predecessor, to pull together an alliance. But the other kings of the area would not stand with him. Fighting alone, he suffered a costly defeat at the hands of the Assyrians.

On his monolith inscription, Shalmaneser III of Assyria tells of meeting Ahab of Israel, Benhadad of Damascus, and Irhuleni of Hamath at the Battle of QarQar in 853 B.C., and he lists the number of men and chariots each furnished for the battle. Because cuneiform is written all across the monument, pictures of it are somewhat indistinct.
British Museum

But the Assyrians, either because they could not or did not have the will to destroy Damascus, circled westward and received the tribute of the Phoenician towns and Jehu of Israel. In 837, the twenty-first year of his reign, Shalmaneser made one last move against Hazael; again Hazael stood alone, again Shalmaneser defeated but did not destroy him.

Revolts within Assyria and other bothersome problems occupied the attention of Assyria until about the end of the ninth century; so there were no more thrusts into Syria for the moment. Hazael determined to settle a score with Jehu for refusing to aid him against Shalmaneser. He took all of Israel's holdings east of the Jordan in Gilead and Bashan (2 Kings 10:32–33). Hazael continued to attack Israel in the days of Jehu's son Jehoahaz (814–798). As indicated in 2 Kings 13:1–9, 22, Hazael brought Israel very low indeed, apparently reducing her to a puppet status. With Israel on her knees, Hazael was free to move southward. Taking the Philistine stronghold of Gath, he turned upon Judah and exacted tribute from King Jehoash (Joash; 2 Kings 12:17–18). Hazael was now master of south Syria and Palestine.

But the fortunes of Syria took a downturn once more. The vigorous Hazael finally died about 800 B.C. after a long reign. Moreover, Adad-nirari III of Assyria, during the last years of Hazael, campaigned against Syria and sufficiently weakened Israel's northern adversary to enable a Hebrew comeback.

Joash, or Jehoash, of Israel (798–782 B.C.) faced Benhadad II, a son of Hazael, in three battles and overcame the Syrian in all three. The result was considerable expansion of the Israelite state, as they retrieved territory lost previously to the Damascenes (2 Kings 13:24–25). Joash built a substantial military capability, as evidenced by the fact that he hired out 100,000 men to Amaziah of Judah, who wanted them for his campaign against Edom. When a prophet of God warned him not to use these men in the war, the Judean king sent the Israelite mercenaries home again (2 Chronicles 25:5–10).

This insult resulted in bitter Israelite animosity against Judah. And after the Judean victory over the Edomites, the Israelites turned upon the Judeans, worsted them, and made the Southern Kingdom a virtual vassal of Israel (2 Kings 14:8–14). Thus Joash defeated both Syria and Judah.

However, the kingdom of Damascus was by no means on her knees. The Old Testament itself indicates that Israelite victory over Benhadad was partial (2 Kings 13:19). Moreover, Adad-nirari III of Assyria had not effectively cowed Syria. The Damascenes soon managed to slip out from under the burden of tribute to Assyria. Benhadad appeared at the head of a Syrian coalition preying on a principality southwest of Aleppo.[24] Apparently the Damascene was worried about the expansion of the kingdom of Hamath, which threatened to upset the balance of power in Syria. Benhadad lost. He may have died in this battle or soon thereafter.

Weakened as it was by Adad-nirari III, Joash, and the kingdom of Hamath, the kingdom of Damascus was easy prey for Jeroboam II (793–753 B.C.), successor of Joash of Israel and for some years coregent with him. Jeroboam continued to chip away at the southern boundaries of Damascus. Assyria was in no position to prevent the rise of the Hebrews because of the inroads of the kingdom of Urartu, or Ararat. Established on the shore of Lake Van (ancient Thospitis) about 840 B.C., the Urartian Kingdom invaded Assyria and some areas of north Syria in 772 B.C. Under Jeroboam II of Israel and his contemporary Uzziah in Judah, the two prosperous Hebrew kingdoms controlled approximately the same territory over which David and Solomon had ruled. Details are wanting, but Damascus and Hamath apparently became tributary to Jeroboam II for a time (2 Kings 14:28).

Probably about 750 B.C. Damascus, with Rezin as king, became independent of Israel. Soon thereafter, Tiglath-pileser III (745–727) determined to bring the moribund Assyrian empire back to vigorous life. The westland was hardly ready for him. Hamath and Damascus were just emerging from subject status; Israel was harassed by internal strife. When Tiglath-pileser advanced into north Syria in his third year, Rezin of Damascus and Menahem of Israel (2 Kings 15:19; "Pul" is the name by which Tiglath-pileser was known in Babylon) were among those forced to pay tribute to him.

Then Tiglath-pileser turned his attention to the destruction of the kingdom of Urartu

Tiglath-Pileser III of Assyria. *British Museum*

and crushingly defeated it around 740 B.C. or a little later.[25] During this respite Rezin and Pekah of Israel moved to punish Ahaz of Judah for refusing to support them in the struggle against Assyria. The allies besieged Jerusalem and pushed past the capital to take Judah's Red Sea port, Ezion-geber (Elath, 2 Kings 16:5–6). The slaughter and pillage in Judah were great (2 Chronicles 28:5–15). Desperate, Ahaz sent an embassy to Tiglath-pileser, professing to be a vassal of Assyria and bearing tribute (2 Kings 16:7–8).

The Assyrian gladly intervened. He descended on the foes of Judah, destroying the rich gardens of the Ghûtah (Damascus oasis), slaying Rezin, and bringing the king-dom of Damascus to an end in 732 B.C. (2 Kings 16:9). He annexed the whole north-ern part of Israel and carried off thousands of captives and resettled them in Assyria (2 Kings 15:29).

The Last Days of Assyria

Syrian history now became identified with that of Assyria. The kingdom of Damascus was carved into four Assyrian provinces. The Assyrians had already formed six provinces out of the northern part of Syria. However, Syrian freedom died hard. In 727 B.C. there was a revolt in Damascus that was quickly put down. A rev-olution in Israel terminated with Assyrian

destruction of Samaria, no later than 722 B.C. In 720 Hamath led an insurrection against Assyria in which Damascus and Samaria were involved, along with others. In a battle at Qarqar the allies were completely routed and the survivors cruelly treated. Sargon II of Assyria, who was then on the throne, marched to the southwest and defeated Gaza and her confederates.

For about another seventy years Assyria more or less effectively controlled Syria. The major excitement in the area involved the humiliation of Judah (Sennacherib in 701 B.C.), which the Babylonians would later destroy.

Then about 650 B.C. the Scythians, proto-Russians or proto-Turks from behind the Caucasus Mountains, rushed down on the seats of luxury in the most fruitful parts of the Assyrian Empire. The invasion itself probably occurred about 635 to 625 in the form of a series of inroads. The whole of Syria came under Scythian rule for about twenty-eight years, and this Scythian dominion extended south to the Egyptian border. Babylon asserted her independence under Nabopolassar in 626. And in 612 B.C. the Scythians joined the Babylonians and Medes under Cyaxares in the destruction of the Assyrian capital. The terrifying might of the hordes of Ashur and Nineveh had come to an end.

The Neo-Babylonian Period

When Nineveh fell, the Medes occupied the northern and eastern parts of the Assyrian Empire, leaving the task of wiping out remaining Assyrian resistance to the Babylonians. Ashur-uballit II, the last king of Assyria, set up his capital at Haran in western Assyria. There a coalition of Babylonians and Scythians defeated him in 609 B.C., and then returned home while the Assyrians retreated westward.

At this juncture Pharaoh-Necho of Egypt rushed to the assistance of Ashur-uballit. Marching up the Palestinian coast with a large army and his flank covered by a well-equipped fleet, he pushed across Mt. Carmel. On the plain of Megiddo, Josiah of Judah met Pharaoh-Necho with an army in an effort to prevent aid from reaching the Assyrian enemy (see 2 Kings 23:29ff.; 2 Chronicles

35:20–24). Josiah's efforts cost him his life, and Necho brushed past his attackers. The Egyptians then moved up the Beqa' (El Bika) and advanced through Riblah (on the present northern border of Lebanon) and Hamath to the Euphrates River at Carchemish. The combined Egyptian and Assyrian forces were unsuccessful in recapturing Haran.[26]

But the Egyptians did not return home. As a by-product of their northward march, they carved out for themselves a Syrian empire that included Phoenicia, most of Palestine, and the kingdom of Damascus. Riblah was probably the administrative capital of this territory and Carchemish the military headquarters. This empire was destined to be short-lived, however, enjoying an existence of only some three years, 608–605 B.C. Its story is one of the most obscure chapters in the history of the Mediterranean world. Nebuchadnezzar II, crown prince of Babylon, crushed Necho's forces in a strategic battle at Carchemish (605) and chased him back to Egypt (cf. 2 Kings 24:7; Jeremiah 46:2).

While Nebuchadnezzar was campaigning in the westland, he received news of his father's death (605) and hurried home to establish his claim to the throne. Hope of a war of liberation rose in the breasts of Syrians. Tyre and Judah were among the rebels, and they counted on Egypt as a source of aid. Ultimately Babylon destroyed Jerusalem in 587/586 B.C. Mainland Tyre suffered the same fate in 572 B.C. Syria seems to have been generally quiet during the next two decades of Babylonian rule. But Nabonidus, last king of Babylon, was forced to quell a revolt there in 553.

The Persian Empire

About 700 B.C. Achaemenes came to the throne of Anshan in Persia and established the Achaemenid line. Long a tributary to the Medes, the Persians broke with their servile past under Cyrus the Great. Cyrus became king in Anshan about 559 B.C. When the Median king Astyages realized that Cyrus intended revolt, he decided to attack first. Unfortunately, however, his army mutinied, and Cyrus became master of the Median Empire about 550. In 547/546

he toppled Croesus of Lydia from his throne. Next on Cyrus' conquest timetable was Babylon. There the incompetent Belshazzar (Bel-shar-usur) ruled while his father pursued his antiquarian and religious interests at various spots in the empire.

Cyrus took the capital in 539 B.C., and with it went the empire. Cyrus now ruled a vast region extending almost from the borders of India to the Aegean Sea and from the Caspian Sea to the border of Sinai. The small states of Syria became part of a mighty empire, one of the largest of antiquity.

In contrast with the fearsome rule that Syria endured under the Assyrians and Babylonians, Persian rule was the most enlightened that the area was to enjoy for many years. Cyrus tried to conciliate subject peoples, permitting those that the Assyrians and Babylonians had deported to return to their former homes, and even aiding them (as in the case of the Jews) to restore the old sanctuaries. Imperial unity was augmented by an improved road system and postal system (the work of Darius I), a uniform coinage, and an official language—Aramaic. Long the speech of commerce, Aramaic now became the official language of the western provinces. The Pax Persica (the Persian Peace) enhanced prosperity.

Cyrus joined Syria, Phoenicia, and Palestine to Babylonia in one huge satrapy. The satrap Gobryas (or Gubaru, probably the Darius of Dan. 6) officially called the province "Babirush." Over this whole vast stretch of fertile country, Gobryas ruled almost as an independent monarch. But under Darius I (522–486 B.C.), the great organizer of the Persian Empire, "Ebirnari" (Assyrian for "across the river"), or most of Syria-Palestine, was linked with Cyprus to form the Fifth Satrapy.

In all there were twenty-three satrapies or provinces in the Persian Empire in Darius' day, each ruled by a governor called a satrap, who was a civil, not a military, official. Each satrapy also had a general and a secretary, and all three were authorized to communicate directly with the capital. Within the satrapies, subject nationalities enjoyed a relatively independent position, e.g., the Jews and the Phoenician cities. Thus was created a recipe for empire that included proper amounts of the ingredients of local autonomy, centralized responsibility, and overall control.

Damascus was the capital of the Fifth Satrapy, but unfortunately little is known of the city during either the Babylonian or Persian periods. In fact, Damascus played a remarkably small part in the political history of the Levant through the ages. "There is not the dramatic rhythm of greatness and desolation alternating as at Jerusalem and Tyre, but merely a hoary and generally prosperous antiquity, like the steady prosperity of Egypt."[27]

In spite of the generally humane treatment accorded subject peoples under Persian rule, those people were still subjects and could be expected to make a bid for freedom when the opportunity presented itself. Egypt raised the standard of revolt in 358 B.C., as did Tripoli in Lebanon in 351. Soon the rest of the Phoenician city-states and Cyprus threw off the Persian yoke. But the uprising was premature, and the flames of freedom were quickly extinguished in Syria. Sidon was destroyed.

However, Persia was about to flounder, and ominous clouds were blowing in from the Greek quarter. Philip of Macedon had been busily subjugating the city-states there and was making preparations to "liberate" the Greek cities in Asia Minor held by Persia. When an assassin's dagger terminated those plans, his eighteen-year-old son Alexander took up the battle-ax.

In 334 B.C. Alexander crossed the Hellespont (Dardanelles) at the head of about 35,000 men and with an empty treasury. Victory over the Persians at the Granicus River won him control of Asia Minor. The following year he again faced the Persians in eastern Asia Minor, on the borders of the Fifth Satrapy. On the shores of the gulf now called Iskenderun, or Alexandretta, he won the Battle of Issus. Alexander's generalship was never better. The victory restored the morale of his troops and the booty captured enabled him to pay his men for the first time in months.

Alexander was now faced with the choice of pursuing Darius III or marching southward into Syria. He chose the latter in order to cut off the Persian navy from its bases and destroy it. He dispatched a battalion to Damascus while he drove southward along the coast. Damascus, manned by a treacherous governor, yielded up the rich treasures Darius had deposited there. Thereafter it became the seat of authority for occupying forces. Except for Tyre, which required a siege of seven months, the Phoenicians threw in their lot with Alexander. The Fifth Satrapy had become a Greek province. The rest of the story of Alexander's conquests appears in other chapters of this book.

Seleucid Control of Syria

Brought down by a fever at Babylon in 323 B.C., Alexander never had a chance to develop an imperial administration. When he died, he left behind a group of ambitious generals, each of whom sought mastery of the empire Alexander had carved out. From the anarchy that followed, a workable arrangement finally emerged with Ptolemy controlling Egypt, Cyrene, Cyprus, and Palestine; Antigonus ruling Macedonia; and Seleucus founding a dynasty at Babylon in 312. At their height the Seleucids ruled over most of the old Persian Empire except Egypt. Because the Ptolemies needed a fleet to hold their territories, it was necessary for them to have the naval supplies of the Lebanons and Asia Minor. In seeking to control those areas the Ptolemies clashed constantly with the Seleucids.

Historical Review. Before turning to the cultural affairs and the city building activities of the Seleucids, a brief historical statement should prove useful. Seleucus I Nicator (312–280) not only established himself at Babylon but also conquered eastern Asia Minor and extended his frontier in the east to the Indus River. But his ambition proved to be his undoing. When he invaded Macedonia, he was assassinated. Seleucus II (246–226) lost almost everything his grandfather had gained. Ptolemy Euergetes I invaded Syria and advanced all the way to the Euphrates and then withdrew because of difficulties at home.

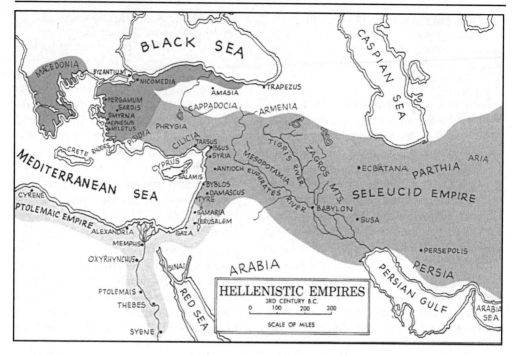

Meanwhile, the Parthians successfully revolted a little after 240 and removed Iran from the Seleucid orbit. The Pergamenes were also busy chipping away at Seleucid lands in Asia Minor.

Antiochus III (223–187 B.C.) managed to reconquer Iranian territory and extend Seleucid borders to the Indus once more. In 198 B.C. he defeated Ptolemy and won Palestine. For all his successes he secured the epithet of "Great." But now Antiochus over-reached himself. The famous Carthaginian, Hannibal, had come to Syria at the end of the Second Punic War and urged Antiochus to war on the Romans. When Antiochus interfered in Greece to save it from Rome, he met defeat at the hands of the new colossus of the West and in 188 was forced to cede all Seleucid lands west of the Taurus Mountains and pay a huge indemnity. The wealth of Asia Minor was forever lost.

By the time of Antiochus IV Epiphanes (175–163 B.C.), Syria was strong enough once more to take the offensive. Learning that Egypt was preparing for war, Antiochus beat Ptolemy Philometor to the draw and took nearly all of the Delta region except Alexandria. When Rome made Antiochus return home, he turned his attention to more effective Hellenization of his subjects and ignited the Maccabean or Jewish revolt in 168. This eventuated in Jewish independence and further truncation of Seleucid domains.

Meanwhile the Nabataeans were pressing on the southern fringe of the empire. In the east Parthia, Bactria (Bactriana), and adjoining lands were asserting their independence. In Syria itself Arab dynasties set themselves up at Edessa and Emesa (modern Homs). And another native state, Ituraea, established itself in Coele-Syria (El Bika). About 85 B.C. the Nabataeans took Coele-Syria and Damascus. Several of the Phoenician cities were gaining their independence. By 130 the Parthians had expanded their empire to include all the territory from the Euphrates to the Indus. Early in the first Century B.C. the ambitious Tigranes of Armenia overran Mesopotamia and by 83 moved into north Syria and Cilicia and in 69 occupied Acre. At this point Rome went into action against the Armenians, chased Tigranes out of Syria, and acknowledged the right of Antiochus XIII to rule at Antioch-on-the-Orontes. Pompey occupied Syria for Rome in 64 B.C., and an era had come to an end.

COMMAGENE

Samosat

Doliche

'Ayntāb

CYRRHESTICE

Cyrrhus

Hierapolis

Euphrates R.

Antioch

Beroea

Seleucia

Daphne

Mt. Casius

Orontes R.

Laodicea

Apamea

PIERIA SEA

Aradus

Emesa

Tripoli

Arka

Palmyra

MEDITERRANEAN SEA

Byblus

Berytus

PHOENICIA

Mt. Lebanon

COELE-SYRIA

Heliopolis

Chalcis

Al-Līṭāni R. (Leontes R.)

Sidon

Damascus

Tyre

Mt. Hermon

Caesarea Philippi

TRACHONITIS

Acre (Ptolemais)

GALILEE

BATANAEA

Raphana?

Philippopolis

Hippos

AURANITIS

Kanatha

Dion

Dora

Gadara

Bostra

Caesarea

Scythopolis

SAMARIA

Pella

DECAPOLIS

Sebaste

Gerasa

Neapolis

Jordan R.

Jaffa

Emmaus ('Amwās)

Emmaus

Philadelphia

Ascalon

Jerusalem

Gaza

JUDAEA

SYRIA
AS A
ROMAN PROVINCE

English Miles

0   20   40   60   80   100

A coin of Antiochus IV (king 175–163), once worshiped as a divine king of Syria

When Syria became a Roman province in that year, it was only a fragment of the great Seleucid Empire. Roughly, its boundaries ran from the Mediterranean on a line a few miles south of Damascus to the edge of the Syrian desert, then arched east of Palmyra to the Euphrates River, then followed the Euphrates to a point east of the Gulf of Iskenderum (or Gulf of Alexandretta or Issus), and finally extended to the Mediterranean at the Gulf. For purposes of present comparison, it approximately included the land of modern Lebanon and Syria, plus the Hatay region of contemporary Turkey, in which stood the capital, the great city of Antioch.

Cultural Affairs. At the head of the Seleucid state reigned the absolute monarch whose bases of power were at least threefold: religious, military, and bureaucratic-ethnic. During the third century B.C., the ruler cult was gradually established as a result of efforts of successive kings. Worshiped first as founders or benefactors of individual cities, the Seleucid kings eventually managed to establish temples for royal worship at the provincial centers and to develop a statewide cult. Ultimately Antiochus IV (175–164) took the epithet "Epiphanes," which means "God manifest." He was probably not a megalomaniac, as some writers of religious literature assert, but had a political purpose in mind—to strengthen the religious foundations of the kingship at a time when royal power was slipping.

Moreover, Antiochus sought to create an integrated state and to bring the native population into the ruler cult. Up to that time only the Macedonian element and some others in the cities had participated in worship of the royal family. This development explains the unrest in Palestine and the Maccabean revolt that occurred during his reign.

The king had at his disposal a formidable military establishment. The army, at full strength perhaps 70,000 cavalry and foot soldiers, had as its nucleus the phalanx, recruited from Greek and Macedonian settlers. The infantrymen were armed with swords, huge spears, shields, and helmets. Supporting contingents were obtained from non-Greek elements of the population and from mercenaries. These formed the cavalry (to a large extent), missile (archers, slingers, javelin throwers), and artillery (siege engines) units. Camel and elephant corps also made an effective contribution. Headquarters of the army, the military training schools, and the elephant training depot were located at Apamea. But the camp of the royal guard was located in Antioch. The fleet apparently served primarily the function of troop transport, but the ships were equipped with a metal projection on the prow for ramming the enemy and could effectively destroy opposition in that way. No doubt Phoenicians manned the fleet.

The king was also supported by a numerous bureaucracy that owed its appointment and livelihood to him and by the considerable Macedonian or Greek population in the cities of the realm. The cities were essentially city-states in which the urban center controlled the surrounding rural area and the serfs on its farms. Imperial taxes seem to have been levied on the community as a whole instead of on the individual. The native population seems rather apathetically to have supported the Seleucid regime.

Greek and Oriental elements intermingled in the Seleucid state. The king ruled as an Oriental potentate in Oriental splendor, but he and his court spoke Greek. At the center of his army stood the Greek phalanx and Greek soldiers. But the military power was rendered effective by native auxiliary units in the infantry, by Phoenician naval squadrons, by Indian elephants and Syrian and Median cavalry. Eating habits, dress, and intellectual diet also mirrored this synthesis of East and West.

Seleucid Cities. In an effort to lay solid foundations for their empire, the Seleucid kings built numerous cities throughout the realm. These they planted with care at strategic spots, where they could control river valleys, caravan routes, rich agricultural districts, and other centers of importance. Ethnically they were colonies of Greek and Macedonian soldiers and mercenaries who could dominate the native population. Their wives were supplied partly from native stock, and to these new foundations would gravitate natives who had put on or were willing to put on the externals of Hellenism, as well as traders, artists, scholars, and slaves. Partly out of a desire to build a cultural foundation for the state and partly out of a desire to spread a "superior" culture throughout the realm, the Seleucids established cities as effective missionary centers for the preaching of Hellenism.

They built these cities according to a prepared plan in which streets were laid out in grid or checkerboard fashion, with proper allowance for political, market, and social and recreational centers. Of course they provided these towns with theaters, baths, gymnasia, and other institutions where individuals could express themselves as members of society.

According to Appianus, Seleucus Nicator was responsible for founding at least thirty-three cities: sixteen Antiochs (in different provinces, of course), nine Seleucias, five Laodiceas, and three Apameas.[28] But many of these were not new foundations; they merely represented a re-colonization and renaming of older Semitic towns. Some were probably not genuine cities, i.e., not established with full municipal organization. Four important new foundations in western Syria included Antioch-on-the-Orontes, named for his wife; and Laodicea on the Sea, named after

his mother.[29] These constituted two pairs of cities with their seaports. Comment on each of these is in order.

Apamea dominated the middle Orontes where the valley widens into a swampy basin, into which continual streams flow and produce luxuriant vegetation. It stood on the lower slopes of the eastern hills that open out south of the city, providing easy communication between the Orontes Valley and the East. As has been noted, here was the central office for the Seleucid army, the location of the military schools, the training center for some 500 Indian elephants, and stables for tens of thousands of horses. All around Apamea were settlements of soldiers dependent on this vital city.

The lower harbor area of Seleucia was hardly more than a roadstead, but it handled a huge amount of trade. And Paul and his companions were among the large numbers of people who took passage or landed there. The present deserted beach area, with no remains of warehouses, gives no hint of the ancient bustling port

Opposite Apamea on one of the few safe anchorages along the rocky Syrian coast stood the port of Laodicea. Communication between the inland city and its port was by road over the intervening mountain ridge. Since passage was difficult at certain times during the year and since Laodicea did not enjoy the advantage of standing on a major commercial route, the city did not enjoy the prosperity of Seleucia, farther north. Laodicea had a rich wine-producing hinterland, however, and enjoyed a brisk trade, especially with Egypt.

The springs of Daphne send their waters down the hillside as they did in ancient times.

Seleucia was built about five miles north of the Orontes River and guarded its mouth. Above this principal harbor of the coast Mount Pieria rises from the sea in a series of ledges. The lower city with the harbor and warehouses stood on a level about twenty feet above the quay. Above the lower city on a much higher shelf perched the upper city. The elevation displayed to best advantage the magnificence of the public buildings and temples of the city and made it a worthy gateway to an affluent kingdom. The sight must have been an impressive one to the Apostle Paul as he sailed toward this port of Antioch at the end of his first missionary journey. However, it was not necessary to disembark at Seleucia. The Orontes was navigable as far as Antioch up to the time of the Crusades in the eleventh century.

Greatest of all the Seleucid foundations was Antioch-on-the-Orontes, destined to become the third city of the Roman Empire,

after Rome and Alexandria. And it was destined to become a great center of Christianity. Antioch was the birthplace of foreign missions; Paul launched all three of his missionary journeys from there (Acts 13:1–4; 15:35–36; 18:23). Disciples of Jesus were first called "Christians" there (Acts 11:26); and among the Antiochians the question of Gentile relation to the Mosaic law first arose, with the resultant decision at the Jerusalem council that Gentiles were not under the law (Acts 15).

If Paul and Barnabas chose to sail up the Orontes as they returned from their first missionary journey, they would have had on their left the plain of Seleucia and on their right the base of the sacred Mount Casius (Jebel Akra). As they continued to ascend the river (which fell 300 feet in the some twenty miles between Antioch and its mouth), they would have found themselves in a beautiful gorge, about six miles long, where the Orontes cut through the coastal range to the sea. Coming out of the gorge, they would have emerged on the plains of Syria; but on their right a spur of Casius still would have hovered, resplendent in its cloak of timber and flowering shrubs, and sending its numerous torrents into the river. At last the mountain chain ends in Mount Silpius, around which the Orontes makes a westward bend coming from the south; now the two missionaries would have been in the middle of the city. (The Orontes is approximately 125 feet wide at this point.)

A Hellenistic foundation, Antioch enjoyed all the advantages of scientific city planning that men of that age desired. The area had a healthful climate, an adequate water supply, good drainage, fertile land, and good opportunity for commercial advantage. Moreover, a city located at this spot would be far enough from the sea for protection and close enough for easy communication.

In this part of Syria the limestone is fissured, containing underground caverns and reservoirs in which collects the water that falls during the winter rainy season. Faults in the limestone produce springs that flow all year. Thus numerous springs were available for a new city foundation. Especially was this true of the plateau of

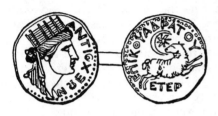

A coin of ancient Antioch

Daphne, some five miles southwest of Antioch. This plateau, roughly square in shape and measuring about 2,000 yards on a side, averaged about 300 feet above the level of the city. As a result water from its springs could easily be carried by gravity through aqueducts to the city. In ancient times, five springs served the double function of watering the surface of the Daphne Plateau and supplying water for Antioch.

Antioch enjoyed a benign climate. A regular breeze blew daily from the sea up the Orontes River. This steady stream of fresh cool air was especially welcome during the summer months, when it brought relief from high temperatures. The streets of the city were carefully oriented so the main thoroughfares caught the breeze as it blew up the valley. So pleasant were summers at Antioch that it became a popular vacation spot for people from Egypt and Palestine, as well as for native Syrians.

The neighborhood was rich. A vast open, fertile plain spread to the north of the city, and an abundance of grain, fruits, and vegetables grew there. Good stands of timber grew in nearby forests. The quarries in the adjoining mountains provided excellent building stone. Plenty of fish could be caught in the Lake of Antioch, which lay about twelve miles northeast of the city, and in the Mediterranean Sea.

As to commercial advantage, the Orontes Valley at Antioch opened into the plains of north Syria, across which passed the regular land routes from Iran and Mesopotamia to the Mediterranean. So it became a terminus of the caravan route from the East. And as has been said, the Orontes was navigable as far as Antioch. Moreover, the city controlled the north-south road that joined Palestine, Syria, and Asia Minor.

With all of these advantages, the site of Antioch appealed greatly to Hellenistic city planners. Seleucus I founded the city under the northern slopes of Mount Silpius (which rose some 1500 feet above the plain) in May of 300 B.C. The first settlers were Macedonian soldiers and Athenian colonists. The people of Antioch traced the greatness of their city to their Attic origin.[30]

As the city expanded, other Greeks came—Aetolians, Cretans, Euboeans. There was a large and flourishing Jewish community too, to whom Seleucus showed great favor. To the original quarter Seleucus later added a second quarter with its own separate wall. Seleucus II and Antiochus III built a third quarter on an island in the Orontes, which no longer appears to be an island because the channel on one side of it has silted up. Apparently the palace was located there. The fourth and last great section of the city was a creation of Antiochus IV Epiphanes on the slopes of Mount Silpius. The fully developed city as Paul would have known it is described in connection with the period of Roman rule.

The Orontes River flows through Antioch (modern Antakya). The river was a greater stream in New Testament times, when less of its waters were used for irrigation.

Seleucus Nicator is also credited with establishing a settlement at Daphne, and Antiochus Epiphanes further developed it. The Seleucids erected the famous Temple of Apollo there, as well as many other temples, baths, public buildings, the Olympic stadium, and villas of the wealthy.

The Roman Peace

When Pompey took over Syria in 64 B.C., Seleucid administration had broken down and the area was in a state of chaos. Northern Syria was almost entirely in the hands of Arab chiefs. Damascus had placed itself under the protection of the Nabataean king of Petra. Several princelings had established native principalities of their own. Judea was torn by civil war. Agriculture and commerce, both by land and sea, were languishing.

The modern Kurtulus Caddesi follows the line of the main thoroughfare of New Testament Antioch

Now that the Seleucid kingdom had become the province of Syria, the Romans at once set about restoring order. Damascus became the capital of an administrative unit within which Pompey allowed many free cities and kings to manage their own affairs. This concession resulted from sheer necessity, for Rome could not have governed such a large and heterogeneous region at that time. Therefore the original area of the province of Syria was small. The towns were held responsible for control of their surrounding districts. And the native princes were held responsible for the more remote districts. As the Roman grip tightened, independent or semiautonomous areas were gradually absorbed, and Provincial Syria stretched ever farther to the north, east, and south.

And so the Romans had introduced to Syria the most prosperous era it had ever known—the Roman Peace—and with it some 200 years of almost unbroken quiet. Unruly tribes were pushed back, roads built, trade fostered, and civil government established. Four legions were stationed there to keep order and to protect the frontier. Never was Syria so effectively ruled, and never was she so populous.

But peace and order did not come immediately. The Romans' descent into Syria had brought them face to face with the Parthians, a formidable power that represented Persia under a new guise. Rome took the offensive against the Parthians in 53 B.C. but met humiliating defeat and the loss of 10,000 soldiers who were carried away into slavery. In 44 B.C. Rome moved the capital of Syria (which from 44 B.C. to A.D. 72 probably included Cilicia) from Damascus to Antioch. Four years later a Parthian force poured across the Euphrates River, defeated the Romans, took Apamea and then Antioch itself, and marched south into Phoenicia, conquering all the towns there except Tyre. The Jews welcomed the Parthians as deliverers, and for three years 40–37 B.C.) the entire area between the Taurus and Sinai was lost to Rome.

In 37 B.C. Roman power surged back, drove the Parthians across the Euphrates, forced the Nabataeans to pay an indemnity, and established Herod the Great on the throne of Judea (and Samaria). Rome had lost out temporarily in Syria because of the civil wars that brought the end of the Republic. After Augustus' victory at Actium in 31 B.C., he effected a reorganization that brought Syria as well as the rest of the Empire to peace and affluence once more.

Since the frontier province of Syria bordered on the territory of a powerful rival (Parthia), Rome constituted Syria an imperial province. As such it was directly under the control of the emperor, who appointed as governors legates of consular rank for terms of three to five years. A variety of governments presided in local communities. In the Greco-Macedonian colonies the old magistrates continued to rule, associated with a senate and popular assembly. The Greek city-state remained the organization type. In the Phoenician towns the old oligarchic systems continued, as did the tribal and patriarchal administrations in less urbanized areas. Urbanization was an important aspect of Roman policy. The Romans planted only a few colonies, the most important being at Beirut and Baalbek (ancient Heliopolis). Aramaic had by this time become the language of society generally, and Greek the trade language.

Rome built a chain of garrison posts along the fringe of the desert to protect the more settled areas. They enhanced communication with a good road system. The great east-west road led from the Mediterranean through Palmyra to the Euphrates River,, while the north-south road ran from Damascus through Hauran, Gilead, Moab, and southward to join the Arabian caravan route. This north-south road followed the King's Highway of the Old Testament (Genesis 14:1–5; Numbers 20:17; 21:22). As noted, four legions were regularly stationed in Syria and could pose as a political as well as a military force. In A.D. 69 these legions made Vespasian emperor. A detachment of the Misenum fleet from Italy was stationed at Seleucia, and the sailors had barracks in the town. This flotilla presumably had the task of searching out pirates in eastern waters.

It is of interest to the Bible student that Quirinius (Cyrenius, Luke 2:2), one of the Roman governors, conducted an accurate census for Syria which became the basis for future taxation. This count came on orders of Augustus and is related to the question of when Christ was born. Historians used to claim that Quirinius was governor of Syria A.D. 6–7 but not when Christ was born. But Ramsay has tried to show that Quirinius was also governor of Syria about 8 B.C. and conceivably a little later than that.[31] We know that the Gregorian calendar (ours) is several years in error—perhaps as much as six or seven. It is off at least four years because Herod the Great died in the spring of 4 B.C., and Christ was born before that.

The general curve of prosperity continued to rise in Syria during the period of the Roman Peace. Heichelheim estimates that the population may have risen to 7,000,000 early in the second century.[32] Areas of the country which now present a barren appearance were then covered with thriving towns. Fruits, vegetables, and cereals grew in abundance. Advanced methods of fertilization and irrigation were employed. Among chief industries were leather, linen, and wine production. And, as noted elsewhere in this chapter, a chief source of Syrian wealth was the trade that flowed along her busy caravan routes and through her ports.

Thousands of villages studded the Syrian countryside, and the free peasants who inhabited them lived mostly on the produce of their farms and vineyards. Probably these villagers did not make much provision for education or public health. Little Hellenizing or Romanizing influence was brought to bear upon these Semitic people.

But the case was very different with the cities of Syria, which were large and populous and centers of Hellenistic culture. In the sophisticated cities Greek was commonly spoken, at least in public and commercial activities. And, as in other cities of the Roman world, amphitheaters, theaters, baths, and marketplaces attracted the multitudes.

So great was the interest in entertainment in the metropolitan centers of Syria that the province became known throughout the Roman world for its professional performers who organized in regular troupes and hired out for programs at banquets, circuses, and other events. Comments on several of the Syrian cities should prove useful in helping to set the stage for the drama of New Testament history enacted in Syria.

THE CITY OF ANTIOCH

Seleucus I founded the city of Antioch in May of 300 B.C. in the valley of the Orontes River, about sixteen miles from the Mediterranean. He brought in retired Macedonian soldiers, Athenian colonists, and Jews. And he laid out the city on a grid plan with streets intersecting at right angles. City planners also sought to make the best use of the sun in both summer and winter and to take advantage of the sea breezes that blew up the Orontes Valley. To the original quarter Seleucus later added a second quarter with its own separate wall. Seleucus II (247–226 B.C.) and Antiochus III (223–187 B.C.) built a third quarter on an island in the Orontes, with its palace and circus or hippodrome—with an area over 1600 feet long. Antiochus IV Epiphanes (175–163 B.C.) added a fourth and final quarter.

Antioch. The most prominent of all Syrian cities during the Roman period was Antioch, the capital. Third city of the Empire after Rome and Alexandria, it has frequently been estimated to have sported a population of about a half million during the first century A.D. Though the Jewish community at Antioch was smaller in number than those of Rome and Alexandria, it was large. Metzger estimates that the Jews comprised one-seventh of the population and that during the first Christian century three Jewish settlements existed in Antioch. One was west of the city near Daphne, a second east of the city in the plain of Antioch, and a third in the city proper.[33] Jews enjoyed considerable wealth and prestige there and apparently influenced their pagan neighbors with their monotheistic beliefs to the point that through them many turned from paganism.

The prosperity of Antioch came in part from its political position, in part from the arteries of commerce that flowed through her, and in part from the commodities produced there. Among the luxury goods for sale in the city were fine leather shoes, perfume, spices, textiles, jewelry, books, and products of goldsmiths and silversmiths, who had held first place among the city's craftsmen ever since its founding.

The ancient critics emphasized the Oriental sensuality of Antioch's citizens wholly devoted to luxury, ease, and licentious pleasure. The pleasure garden of Daphne became the hotbed of every kind of

vice and depravity. Juvenal, a Roman satirical poet writing in the second century A.D., scored his society for its decadent morals and complained:

> Obscene Orontes, diving
>   underground,
> Conveys his wealth to Tiber's
>   hungry shores
> And fattens Italy with foreign
>   whores.

But Muller makes something of an apology for the Antiochenes:

> In fairness to Antioch, it was born too late. It never knew independence, never was a genuine Greek *polis*. It was just Greek enough to be sophisticated, satirical in its wit, notoriously critical in spirit, often hostile to its rulers, always turbulent. Having been denied real freedom, its citizens took to license. They exercised their lively wit in ridiculing the traditional virtues of manliness and womanliness, honoring the arts and the vices of luxury. They expressed their civic pride in the magnificence of their games, festivals, and spectacles.[33]

Antioch had schools of rhetoric and eminent sophists who attracted disciples from all over the Mediterranean world, but it had no creative writers or singers of note. In the artistic sphere the city enjoyed a leading position only in regard to the theater, and performances there were less strictly dramatic productions than noisy musicals and ballets. The populace had a fondness for animal hunts and gladiatorial games.

Antiochus IV celebrated games at Daphne in 195 B.C. before he became king. On Augustus' second visit to the city in 20 B.C., he founded local games which in time became the Olympic Games of Antioch, one of the most famous festivals of the Roman world. In July and August of every leap year of the Julian calendar, visitors journeyed to Antioch from all over the Greco-Roman world for these quadrennial games. Lasting for thirty days during the first century A.D. (apparently for forty-five days in

Antioch and Mount Stauris

later centuries), they offered competition and/or entertainment for everyone: boxing, wrestling, chariot racing, musical competitions, and recitation of tragic passages. Presented regularly at first, the games ceased altogether by the time of Claudius (A.D. 41–54) because embezzlement of funds from the treasury of the games on occasion brought them into disrepute. Claudius refounded the games in 43/44 and called them "Olympic."[35]

Into this milieu of sensuality and frivolity came Christianity not long after the death of Christ. In Antioch Christian missionaries apparently had little to fear from the attacks of fanatical Jews; the same could not be said of Jerusalem. In the cosmopolitan society of Antioch both classical and oriental cults were familiar, and new religious ideas were not a novelty. Many, dissatisfied with the traditional pagan cults, were attracted to the Jewish synagogue with its monotheistic and ethical teachings.

At Antioch believers in Jesus were first called "Christians," and here Christians were more well-to-do than those at Jerusalem and were therefore able to provide financial resources important for the growth of Christianity. From Antioch all three of Paul's missionary journeys were launched.

The fact that believers at Antioch had a fair amount of wealth is further indicated by their sending an offering for relief of the poor in Jerusalem at the time of the severe famine (Acts 11:27–30). Moreover, Antioch's geographical position as the hub of a network of well-established communications fitted it to serve efficiently and fruitfully as a focal point for expansion.

The finding of a chalice at Antioch (now in the Metropolitan Museum of Art in New York City) has been connected with early Christianity there. The chalice is of two parts: a plain inner cup of silver about seven and one-half inches high and an outer gilded silver holder with twelve figures displayed on the outside. Much has been written about the date and interpretation of this piece. The outer cup has been said to represent Christ and His disciples, and the inner cup has even been identified as the Holy Grail, used by Christ at the Last Supper. Dates as early as the first century have been assigned.[36] But probably the best that can be said about this chalice is that it is an early piece of Christian art of some century later that the first and that Christ or some of the disciples may be intended by the artistic representations. The historian of Antioch, Glanville Downey, dates it to the fourth or fifth century.[37]

ANTIOCH IN PAUL'S DAY

A ntioch, as Paul and Barnabas and other New Testament Christians would have known it, was magnificent indeed. Towering above it on the southeast stood fifteen-hundred-foot-high Mount Silpius. To the northwest of the city walls flowed the Orontes. In the northeast wall stood a heavily fortified gate on top of which the emperor Tiberius had placed a stone statue of the she-wolf nursing Romulus and Remus.

Inside the gate lay an open roadway thirty feet wide paved with Egyptian granite. All along both sides of this four and one-half-mile long thoroughfare (running northeast-southwest) stood covered colonnades, each thirty feet wide. As a result of this construction, a pedestrian could walk the entire length of the city protected from sun and rain. Houses and public buildings could be entered between the columns of the walkway. Augustus and Tiberius, with the assistance of Herod the Great of Judea, built this street with its walks in the period from 23 B.C. to A.D. 37.

Side streets intersected the main street and the more important were colonnaded. Public fountains stood at the corners of the streets, where women and children could get the family water supply. There were numerous squares where children played, shopkeepers sold their wares, philosophers taught, and entertainers performed. In the middle of the city the main thoroughfare opened into a plaza where a striking bronze statue of Tiberius stood, erected by the grateful city for all the emperor's benefactions.

In the river to the north of the city lay an island some two miles long by two miles wide. There had stood the palaces of the Seleucids, and Roman royal residences had succeeded them. On the island was also a hippodrome with an arena over 1,600 feet long, built in the first century.

Along the southeast bank of the river and south of the island was located the city's original quarter as established by Seleucus Nicator in 300 B.C. Here barges discharged cargoes at stone quays. Nearby stood an agora (covering four city blocks) and a temple of Zeus.

In the southeastern part of the city, against the western slopes of Silpius, was the quarter built by Antiochus IV Epiphanes. Facing his new agora stood his famous council chamber resembling the one at Miletus, as well as the great temple of Jupiter Capitolinus, the leading Roman deity. During the reign of Tiberius (A.D. 14–37) a great fire destroyed part of this agora, and Tiberius engaged in a sizable rebuilding program, including the redecoration of the temple of Jupiter. In this quarter were located temples of Dionysus and Pan as well. A theater stood on the slope of Mount Silpius.

At the southern edge of Antiochus's quarter and just inside the city's southwest gate was the Jewish section which was established when the city was founded.

St. Peter's Church in Antioch is a cave where early Christians were supposed to have met in secret. The Crusaders faced it with a stone facade.

The Mosque of Hebron stands over the traditional site of the Cave of Machpelah, which Abraham bought as a burial place for Sarah (Genesis 23). The Mosque as it now stands was originally built by Herod the Great. Inside stand cenotaphs marking the traditional tombs of Sarah, Abraham, Isaac, Rebekah, Jacob, and Leah

The second pyramid as viewed from the gardens of Mena House Hotel near Cairo. Built about 2550 B.C. by Khafre (Chephren), the pyramid still has some of its original facing stone at the top

Springs of Banias, one of the tributaries of the Jordan River

The Jordan River as it flows out of the Sea of Galilee

Cedars of Lebanon, somewhat similar to the Redwoods of California. Some of these are over 1000 years old.

The springs of Harod, where Gideon made the famous test of his prospective soldiers (Judges 7). Today the springs (located at the foot of Mount Gilboa, east of Jezreel) are in a public park, and children play there peacefully

The Jericho Oasis viewed from the mound of Jericho

Obelisks at Luxor, one of Thutmose I on the left and of Hatshepsut on the right

The tomb of Tutankhamon (foreground) in the floor of the Valley of the Kings at Luxor. The tomb of Rameses VI was cut from the cliff above it; tons of chipped stone from that tomb covered the entrance to Tut's tomb and kept it from discovery until 1922

Remains of the palace of Ahab at Samaria. At the far end of the picture stands part of the substructure of the temple to Augustus Caesar, which Herod the Great built there

The actual facade of Nebuchadnezzar's throne room as it is preserved in the Staatliche Museen, Berlin. Not having stone, the Babylonians made enameled colored brick for decoration

A lion from Procession Way in Babylon. The lion was the animal holy to Ishtar, goddess of love, fertility, and war (Archaeological Museum, Istanbul)

Enameled, colored bricks used as tapestries on the palace walls at Shushan (Susa) in the days when Esther and Nehemiah were active there. Left an archer from the royal guard; right, winged sphinxes (Louvre museum Paris)

The Pnyx at Athens. An open place on a hill west of the Agora where the assembly met in the days of the Athenian democracy. The podium for a speaker appears in the center of the picture

A bust of Pericles, who led Athens during her Golden Age in the mid-fifth century B.C. (British Museum)

Original coloring of some elements of the Parthenon at Athens as reproduced in the British Museum in London. The faded block that provided clues to the restoration stands below. Greek temples and statues were commonly painted

The Parthenon at Athens, home of the goddess Athena

The Theater of Dionysus at Athens where drama was born

The temple to Vulcan or Haphaestus, Athens

The Pangaeus hills near Philippi, site of gold mines that helped to finance the war effort of Philip and Alexander the Great of Macedon

The Hellespont or Dardanelles at the approximate spot where Xerxes and Alexander the Great crossed with their armies between Europe and Asia to pursue their conquests

In caves around Qumran ancient biblical scrolls were found. In the center of this picture is Cave 4, where fragments of nearly all Old Testament books were discovered

Orpheus charming the wild beasts, a mosaic from Tarsus, third century A.D. (Antakya [Antioch] Museum)

The narrow, winding passage leading into Petra

The Church of the Annunciation in Nazareth, covering the traditional site of the house of the Virgin Mary

Bethany was the home of Mary, Martha, and Lazarus. The Church of St: Lazarus dominates the sky-line of the small town

The Garden of Gethsemane at the foot of the Mount of Olives

The falls on the Cydnus River just north of Tarsus

Reconstructed facade of the Roman gymnasium at Sardis

Lime flowing from the hot springs of Hierapolis creates the effect of a frozen waterfall on the cliff sides of the city.

The Appian Way, the first of Rome's great highways (built in the third century B.C.) is now black-topped and used by modern vehicular traffic. Here is a stretch of the road south of Rome

The traditional burial place of the apostle John is located under the altar of the church of St. John (foreground) in Ephesus

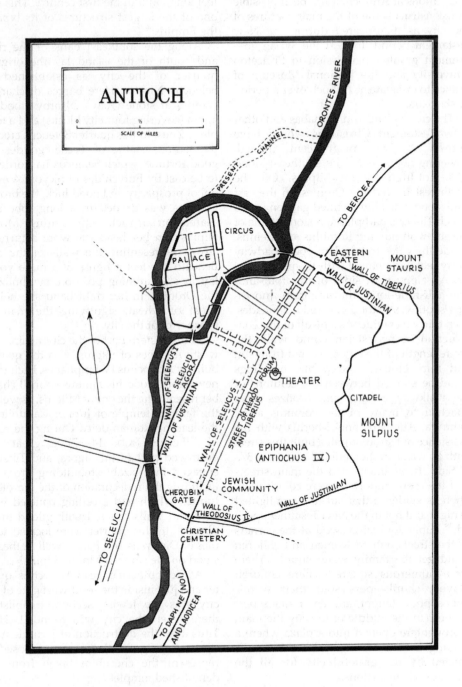

ANTIOCH

0   ½   1
SCALE OF MILES

ORONTES RIVER

PRESENT CHANNEL

CIRCUS

PALACE

TO BEROEA

EASTERN GATE

WALL OF TIBERIUS

MOUNT STAURIS

WALL OF JUSTINIAN

WALL OF SELEUCUS I

SELEUCID AGORA

WALL OF JUSTINIAN

WALL OF SELEUCUS I

STREET OF HEROD AND TIBERIUS

FORUM

THEATER

CITADEL

MOUNT SILPIUS

EPIPHANIA
(ANTIOCHUS IV)

JEWISH COMMUNITY

CHERUBIM GATE

WALL OF JUSTINIAN

WALL OF THEODOSIUS II

CHRISTIAN CEMETERY

TO SELEUCIA

TO DAPHNE (NOW)
AND LAODICEA

By means of historical references and excavations at Antioch, it has been possible to reconstruct some of the main features of the city as it appeared during the New Testament period. In 1931 the Syrian government granted permission to Princeton University and the National Museum of France to excavate at Antioch over a period of six years.

The city, as Paul and Barnabas and other New Testament Christians would have known it, was magnificent indeed. Towering above it on the southeast stood 1500-foot-high Mount Silpius. On the northwest flowed the Orontes. In the east wall stood a heavily fortified gate on top of which Tiberius had placed a stone statue of the she-wolf nursing Romulus and Remus. Inside the gate stretched an open roadway thirty feet wide paved with Egyptian granite. All along both sides of this four-and-one-half-mile-long thoroughfare (northeast-southwest) stood covered colonnades, each thirty feet wide. As a result of this construction, a pedestrian could walk the entire length of the city protected from sun and rain. Houses and public buildings could be entered between the columns of the walkway. Statues and bronzes were attached to many of the columns as at Palmyra. Augustus and Tiberius with the assistance of Herod of Judea built this street with its walks in the period 23 B.C.–A.D. 37.

Side streets intersected the main streets and the more important were colonnaded. There is evidence that streets were lighted at night, but not in the New Testament period.[38] Public fountains stood at the corners of the streets, where women and children could get the family water supply. There were numerous squares where children played, shopkeepers sold their wares, philosophers taught, and entertainers performed. In the middle of the city the main thoroughfare opened into a plaza where a striking bronze statue of Tiberius stood, erected by the grateful city for all the emperor's benefactions.

In the river in the northern part of the city lay an island some two miles long by as many wide. There had stood the palaces of the Seleucids, and Roman royal residences had succeeded them. On the island was also a hippodrome with an arena over 1600 feet long, built in the first century. This was one of the largest structures of its type in the Empire.[39]

Along the southeast bank of the river and south of the island lay the original quarter of the city, as established by Seleucus Nicator. Here barges discharged cargoes at stone Quays. Nearby stood an agora (covering four city blocks) and a temple of Zeus. In this quarter Seleucus erected the famous statue of Tyche, goddess of good fortune, which Seleucus had ordered to be cast by Eutychides of Sicyon. A symbol of prosperity and good luck, the bronze goddess was draped in a long robe and seated on a rock representing Mount Silpius. On her head she wore a turreted crown representing the walls of the city. Beneath her feet a figure of a nude youth lay in a swimming position, symbolizing the Orontes. In her right hand she held a sheaf of wheat, signifying the material prosperity of the city.

In the eastern part of the city, against the western slopes of Silpius, was the quarter built by Antiochus IV Epiphanes. Facing his new agora stood his famous council chamber resembling the one at Miletus, as well as the famous temple of Jupiter Capitolinus, the leading Roman deity. During the reign of Tiberius (A.D. 14–37) a great fire destroyed part of this agora, and Tiberius engaged in a sizable rebuilding program, including the redecoration of the temple of Jupiter, which had a ceiling paneled with gold and walls covered with gilded metal plates.[40] In this quarter were located temples of Dionysus and Pan as well. A theater stood on the slope of Mount Silpius.

At the southern edge of Antiochus' quarter and just inside the southwest gate of the city was the Jewish section, established there when the city was founded. Here Titus after the destruction of Jerusalem set up bronze figures that were supposed to represent the cherubim taken from the demolished temple.

From the southwest gate the road ascended to Daphne, five miles away to the southwest. The walk was a beautiful one. A constant succession of orchards and gardens filled with roses and other flowers

The Tyche of Antioch. Early in the history of Antioch, Seleucus Nicator erected the famous statue of Tyche, goddess of good fortune, cast by Eutychides of Sicyon. A symbol of prosperity and good luck, the bronze goddess was draped in a long robe and was seated on a rock representing Mount Silpius. On her head she wore a turreted crown representing the walls of the city. Beneath her feet a figure of a nude youth lay in a swimming position, symbolizing the Orontes. In her right hand she held a sheaf of wheat, signifying the material prosperity of the city.

temple of Apollo (built by Seleucus Nicator) stood at the foot of the springs. Nearby lay the Olympic stadium. Daphne was dedicated to Apollo as Antioch was to Zeus.

The proud city of Antioch was destined to have her share of woes. She suffered from numerous earthquakes. The one of A.D. 115, when Trajan was present in the city, was bad enough; but the worst came in the sixth century A.D. when a reported quarter million are said to have perished.[41] Most of the city was burned by the Persian emperor Chosroes I in A.D. 540. Justinian rebuilt it, but it never fully regained its greatness. Arabs conquered it in 638, and Crusaders held it for about 200 years during the later Middle Ages. Under Ottoman administration it dwindled to an insignificant town.

Today Antakya has a population of some 125,000 but almost nothing is left to remind the visitor that this was once the center of

scented the air. Here grew the roses used in making the perfume for which Antioch was famous. Beautiful country houses and villas stood among these gardens. Travelers could pause at inns along the way where, in the shade of vine-covered arbors, they could sip the wine or fruit juices cooled in underground cellars.

The pleasure garden of Daphne was ten miles in circumference. It was famous for its laurel trees, old cypresses, flowing and gushing waters, its shining temple of Apollo, and its magnificent festival of the tenth of August. At the center of Daphne was an agora with baths and temples. The streets were laid out on a regular grid plan and lined with spacious houses. At the south edge of the suburb gushed ever-flowing springs; the

Antioch floor mosaic from a second-century house at Antioch. The various rooms of the upper classes also often had busts or full-sized statues.
Antakya Museum.

A street scene in modern Antakya with Mount Stauris in the background

Christian missionary activity or that it was a great metropolis of the Roman Empire. A cave, St. Peter's Cave, is a traditional spot in which Christians of Antioch were supposed to have met in secret. The Crusaders faced it with a stone façade. Local inhabitants have carted off all the stones of the great theater. The Roman bridge that crossed the Orontes until a few years ago has now been demolished. A main street of the city, Kurtulus Caddesi, follows the line of the main thoroughfare of New Testament Antioch. The citadel, much of which dates to the reign of Theodosius about A.D. 400 or later, survives in a badly ruined state. More satisfying is the magnificent collection of floor mosaics from the houses of Antioch that are displayed in the local museum. But unfortunately, for our purposes, these date to centuries later than the first.

Beroea (modern Aleppo or Haleb). Some fifty miles east of Antioch, between the valley of the Orontes and the Euphrates, lay Beroea at an altitude of 1220 feet above sea level in a basin surrounded by low, rocky hills. Called "Haleb" in ancient times, the city was the center of a kingdom in the early sixteenth century B.C. when the Hittite Mursili I swept down through the Taurus passes and took the city. The scene of conflict between the Hittites and Egyptians during the fifteenth century, Haleb fell to Thutmose III of Egypt about 1480 B.C. Later

in the fifteenth century the city capitulated to the Hittites, and at the battle of Kadesh a king of Haleb fought on the Hittite side against Ramses II. Haleb was an independent Hittite principality when Shalmaneser III of Assyria conquered it in 853.

Seleucus Nicator (312–280 B.C.) enlarged the city and named it Beroea after the Macedonian city of the same name. It became the chief commercial center of north Syria and during the days of the Sino-Roman world peace (first-second centuries A.D.), Beroea served as an important terminus of the silk route from the Yellow Sea to the Mediterranean and she knew considerable prosperity. It is still an important Syrian city with a population of about 1,500,000.

Laodicea and Apamea. About fifty miles southwest of Antioch stands Laodicea (modern Latakia), a favorite pleasure resort for dignitaries. During the New Testament period it conducted from its excellent harbor a brisk export trade in wines. Exported chiefly to Alexandria, these wines came from the vineyards that stretched inland almost to Apamea. Herod the Great, in an effort to win imperial favor, built an aqueduct for Laodicea and some other cities.

Apamea, Laodicea's sister city inland, had been a considerable city since Seleucid days. Its hinterland was rich in pasturage, and its temple was an important religious center that housed a famous oracle.

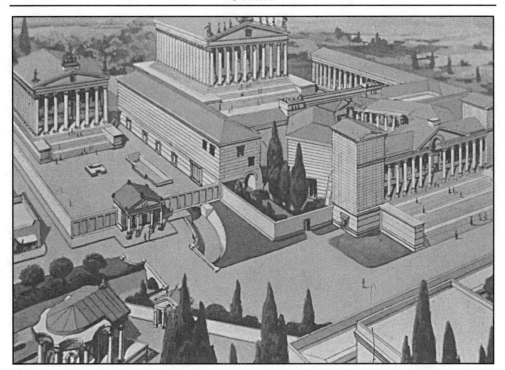

Reconstruction of the temple complex at Baalbek. The Temple of Jupiter towers above the rest and is entered through a magnificent gateway and a courtyard. To the left, foreground, is the round Temple of Venus. Behind that, below the Temple of Jupiter, stands the Temple of Bacchus.

Dedications to the Baal of Apamea have been found as far west as southern France.[42] Beloch estimated the population of Apamea to have been as high as 400,000 to 500,000 early in the first century A.D.[43]

Epiphania. Up the Orontes River some twenty-five miles southeast of Apamea stood Epiphania (modern Hama). An early Hittite settlement, Hama became the seat of a local dynasty after the fall of the Hittite Empire and eventually capitulated to the Assyrians (2 Kings 18:34). The biblical Hamath (Isaiah 11:11), the city in the Seleucid period received the name "Epiphania" in honor of Antiochus Epiphanes. In the center of a rich agricultural region, the town was dominated by a citadel hill about 130 feet high. Down through the centuries Epiphania-Hama has been an important site and today has a population of about 230,000.

Emesa. Farther up the Orontes about twenty-five miles south of Epiphania and

eighty-five miles north of Damascus, stood Emesa (modern Homs), which retained its native priest-kings (of the cult of the sun god) throughout the Roman period. The town gained notoriety in the third century A.D. when one of these, Heliogabulus (Elagabalus), became Roman emperor for a brief time. At Emesa the Orontes is some 100 feet broad, and the area has always been fertile, boasting fine gardens and orchards and a good climate. The plain of Emesa was a battleground of warring kings, and about fifteen miles to the southwest was Kadesh, where the Hittites and Egyptians met in the days of Ramses II. This city has maintained a degree of prosperity through the centuries and today has a population of about 350,000.

Heliopolis/Baalbek. Modern Christians are probably much more impressed with the greatness of Baalbek than first century Christians would have been, for the magnificent complex of temples there was not

The Temple of Bacchus

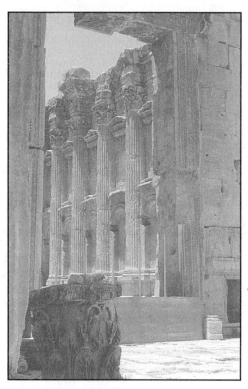

Interior of the Temple of Bacchus

completed until sometime during the third century.

Baalbek is located on a superb site fifty-one miles east of Beirut at an altitude of 3,850 feet above sea level. On the caravan route linking Damascus, Emesa, and Tyre, it had a fertile hinterland as well as commercial advantages. The site is beautiful too, nestled as it is between the Lebanon and Anti-Liban ranges.

The origins of Baalbek are lost in antiquity. Alouf thinks it probable that Baalbek is to be identified with the Baalath that Solomon built up as a store city and a relay station for his caravans (1 Kings 9:17–19). He also thinks that Solomon built there near the end of his reign a temple to Baal to please his concubines.[44] After Solomon's death the Phoenicians beautified the Baalbek temple of Hadad-Baal, and thousands from many directions made pilgrimages to the site.

BAALBEK

Probably as early as the reign of Augustus, the massive temple complex at Baalbek was begun. Inscriptions show that the work on the temple of Jupiter was well under way during Nero's reign. And the temple of Bacchus apparently was begun about the middle of the first century A.D. For over two centuries construction went on at the site to produce a magnificent complex exhaling a sense of power, size, and glorious magnificence.

A huge substructure (24 to 42 feet above the ground) was built for the temples to fulfill a psychological function—to render them more imposing by lifting them high above the neighboring landscape.

Worshipers would enter the temple complex through a tower-flanked propylaea 165 feet wide and 38 feet deep with columns brought from far-away Aswan in Egypt. They would then pass through a hexagonal court into a great altar court 350 feet square. On either side of the altar were large stone basins (actually tanks) 68 feet long by 23 feet broad and 2 feet 7 inches high for ritual washing.

From this court a magnificent stairway led to the temple of Jupiter. Surrounded by a colonnade of fifty-four columns, the cella, or holy of holies, was 290 by 160 feet, over five times as large as that of the Parthenon. Six of the great 100-ton Corinthian columns of the peristyle remain standing. Sixty-five feet high, they are the tallest in the Greco-Roman world. Atop the columns is a 16-foot entablature ornately decorated with lions' and bulls' heads, showing Oriental influence.

Adjacent to the temple of Jupiter on the south and at a lower level stands the temple of Bacchus with a cella eighty-seven by seventy-five feet, originally surrounded by a peristyle of forty-six columns fifty-seven feet high. Beautifully preserved, no better example of a Roman temple interior survives. East of the acropolis was a round temple, rare in Syria, that was probably a temple of Venus, constructed about A.D. 250.

Huge stones appear in the temple complex substructure, the three largest being about 64 feet long, 14 feet high and 11 feet thick and each weighing over a thousand tons. The largest stone of all never made it out of the quarry and may be seen about a mile south of the modern town. It measures 70 by 14 by 13 feet.

Baalbek means "Baal" or "lord of the Bekaa (Biqa')" and seems to have been of Phoenician origin. Because it was considered to be the birthplace of Baal,[45] the site was held in special veneration. The Ptolemies called the city "Heliopolis" ("the city of the Sun"). They must have equated the Baal of the Bekaa with the Egyptian God Re and the Greek Helios; and the Romans identified the Baal of this city with Jupiter and called him "Jupiter Heliopolitanus." When the Romans took over, Augustus planted a Roman colony there and named it "Colonia Julia Augusta Felix Heliopolitana" (c. A.D. 10).

Probably as early as the reign of Augustus, construction of the massive temple complex at Heliopolis began. Inscriptions show that the work on the temple of Jupiter was well under way during Nero's reign. And the temple of Bacchus apparently was begun about the middle of the first century A.D. For three centuries construction went on at the site to produce a magnificent complex exhaling a sense of power, size, and glorious magnificence.

The huge substructure (24–42 feet above the ground) of the temples fulfilled a psychological function—rendering them more imposing by lifting them high above the neighboring landscape. Worshipers entered the temple complex through a tower-flanked propylaea 165 feet wide and 38 feet deep. They would then pass through a hexagonal court into a great altar court about 350 feet square. On either side of the altar were large stone basins (actually tanks) 68 feet long by 23 feet broad and 2 feet 7 inches high for ritual washing.

The Roman Jupiter Heliopolitanus of Baalbek

87 by 75 feet, originally surrounded by a peristyle of 46 columns 57 feet high. Beautifully preserved, no better example of a Roman temple interior survives. East of the acropolis stood a round temple, rare in Syria, that was probably a temple of Venus, constructed about A.D. 250.

The walls of the temple complex were two miles in circumference. Huge stones appear in this wall, the three largest being about 64 feet long, 14 feet high, and 11 feet thick and each weighing some 1,000 tons. The largest stone of all never made it out of the quarry and may be seen about a mile south of the modern town. It measures 70 by 14 by 13 feet. The busy town that once surrounded the temples at Baalbek has vanished. No attempt to excavate its remains has yet been made. Alouf believes the population of Baalbek must have totaled at least 200,000.[46]

The Temple of Venus at Baalbek reconstructed

From this court a magnificent stairway led to the temple of Jupiter. Surrounded by a colonnade of fifty-four columns, the cella, or holy of holies, measured 290 by 160 feet, over five times as large as that of the Parthenon. Six of the great 100-ton Corinthian columns of the peristyle (colonnade) remain standing. Sixty-five feet high, they are the tallest in the Greco-Roman world. Atop the columns is a sixteen-foot entablature ornately decorated with lions' and bulls' heads, showing oriental influence.

Adjoining the temple of Jupiter on the south is the temple of Bacchus with a cella

Damascus. Not long after Pentecost, Christianity spread to Damascus, and Saul of Tarsus went there to stamp out the new faith. What the city was like then no one will probably ever know. Damascus is the oldest continuously inhabited large city in the world. It has never lapsed into ruin or been reduced to small town or village status. Because of this, remains of earlier civilizations there cannot be unearthed while the city's life still throbs above them. Large

The cornice of the Temple of Jupiter at Baalbek

in the New Testament period, Damascus is even bigger today with a population over 1,500,000.

Damascus figures prominently in the New Testament in connection with the conversion of Saul of Tarsus. It will be remembered that Saul met God on the Damascus Road on his way to persecute Jews who had turned to Christianity (Acts 9:1–8) and that he entered the city through the East Gate and stayed for a while on the street called "Straight." Apparently almost immediately after his conversion Saul went out into Arabia for the better part of three years, subsequently returning to Damascus to preach (Gal. 1:17–18). The object of a plot against his life instigated by Jews who opposed his ministry, Paul escaped over the

The largest stone never made it out of the quarry at Baalbek. It measures 70 by 14 by 13 feet

city wall, being lowered in a basket. According to 2 Corinthians 11:32, a governor appointed by King Aretas of the Nabataeans ruled Damascus when Paul escaped.

The East Gate, which any visitor to Damascus may see today, probably dates to Roman times, and the "street called Straight" still follows the course it did in Paul's day. A few stones in the lower courses of the present wall of Damascus date to the Roman period, and houses perch on the walls now as then. No doubt Paul would have been lowered from a window of one of the houses on the wall. A traditional window is revered.

As to where Paul went when he entered Arabia and for exactly what reason he went is not certain. Some have claimed he traveled as far away as Petra, and others have said that he settled in or at some oasis near to Damascus. It seems most reasonable to believe that Paul did not go far from Damascus; at least the biblical narrative does not require that he did. Near Damascus the Syrian Desert runs off to meet the northern section of the Arabian Peninsula. Paul may have gone into seclusion in some sparsely populated place; but there were cities in Arabia, and there is no reason to suppose he did not visit one of them. He may have gone to "begin a tremendous inner reconstruction of his religious thinking," as someone has suggested. Presumably he received the revelation of the gospel at this time (see Gal. 1:11–17). But there is no light on exactly where Paul went during this silent period in his life.

As to the Aretas who ruled Damascus at the time of Paul's conversion (2 Cor. 11:32), it is known that Aretas III took control of Damascus after defeating Antiochus II of Seleucia in 85 B.C. and lost it again to the Romans in 64 B.C. Aretas IV (3 B.C.–A.D. 40) would have been the Aretas of Paul's day. It is interesting to note that while Roman coins of Tiberius appear at Damascus until A.D. 34, imperial coins are absent until coins with Nero's image appear again in A.D. 62. Damascus may have been under Nabataean control in the meantime.[47] But the argument from silence is not conclusive.[48]

Apparently Damascus enjoyed increasing prosperity and improved status in the second century. This may have had some-thing to do with Trajan's reduction of Petra and the breaking of Nabataean commercial power in A.D. 105. Damascus depended on its trade and its gardens for its prosperity. But whether or not Damascene prosperity had anything to do with the decline of Petra, the development of Palmyra did.

The Barada River in downtown Damascus

Palmyra. The oasis of Palmyra is located halfway between the Mediterranean Sea and the Euphrates River at an altitude of 1300 feet. Through it passed the great trade routes to Persia from Phoenicia and from Egypt, Petra, and Arabia. Whether one trav-eled from Emesa or Damascus to the Euphrates, he would find Palmyra a con-venient halfway point on his journey. A clearer idea of Palmyra's position on the caravan routes, from which it derived its very life, is gained from the realization that the city was located 150 miles northeast of Damascus and 190 miles west of the Euphrates. The city lies in the middle of the great Arabian Desert with its mantle of arid sands, from which emerge the unclothed ribs of bare low mountains and projecting scarps. To the west still stand the remains of numerous tower tombs of rich Palmyrene families; some of these towers are seventy feet high. To the east toward the Euphrates stretches a flat waste as far as eye can see.

Presumably the Palmyrene trade route began to be regularly utilized not long after 2000 B.C. Assyrian documents speak of Palmyra under its Semitic name of Tadmor

before the first millennium B.C. At the beginning of the first millennium B.C., Solomon fortified Tadmor (2 Chronicles 8:4) and made it a secure outpost through which the wealth of India could be brought to his kingdom. Throughout the classical and Hellenistic periods it must have been a flourishing trading post. However, nothing further is heard about it until Mark Antony tried unsuccessfully to capture it in 38 B.C.

At that time Palmyra was no more than a prosperous oasis village. But Roman com-mercial policy created the greatness of the site. When Trajan broke the power of Petra and incorporated it into Provincia Arabia in A.D. 106, Palmyra rose to new heights because of its new commercial opportunity. In the stalemate between Parthia and Rome, Palmyra had its chance, serving as a go-between state with its liberty guaran-teed by both her neighbors and reaping rich rewards from that position. There the goods of China, India, and Parthia were changed for the goods of Rome. Of special interest is the fact that just before World War II beau-tiful Chinese silks of the first and second centuries A.D. were excavated there—the first evidence in the West for importation from China during the Han Dynasty.[49]

In the third century Palmyra took the opportunity provided by the weakness of its Roman protector to build up its own power. Queen Zenobia after A.D. 266 made

The East Gate and the Street Called Straight, Damascus

The Street Called Straight, Damascus

courtyard over 200 yards square, the whole raised on a masonry base and approached by a splendid staircase that led through a formal entrance complex. The court was surrounded on the inside by covered porticoes and within the court was a cella, or holy of holies, an altar, and a libation tank. A discussion of the temple of Bel-shamin, the theater, the great agora (c. 90 by 75 yards), and other great ruins of the city would be of much interest to the classical student but is not within the province of the present study.

While Palmyra was adorned with some of its greatest architectural glories during the second century A.D. after it became the financial capital of the Eastern world, it was already a prosperous site in the first century. And some of the greatest structures, such as the temples of Bel and Bel-shamin, were built by the time followers of Christ were first called "Christians" at Antioch.

Modern visitors to such dead cities of Syria as Palmyra may sit in solitude among the ruins and ponder the greatness of these cities and the reasons for their demise. They will be struck by their elegance and evidences of a departed prosperity. But the student of Christianity will be overwhelmed even more by the fact that all across Syria stand ruins of great old Christian churches. Unfortunately today, in this land where believers were first called "Christians" and where the early church first launched its missionary enterprise, very few professing Christians may be found. Worse, in this land in many places even the ruins are gone as Islam has sought to obliterate even the memory of a vibrant Christianity.

THE SYRIAC BIBLE

The Peshitta is the most important ancient Syriac translation of the Bible. Peshitta means "simple" and may signify either a straight translation without interpretive expansion or one unencumbered by critical apparatus.

We do not know whether the Old Testament translation was the work of

Palmyra ("city of palms") the capital of a caravan empire. In its heyday the city probably had a population over 30,000 and set up commercial agents in Mesopotamia, Egypt, Spain, Gaul, Italy, and on the Danube.[50]

Palmyra was laid out on a grid plan with the main streets intersecting at right angles. Arches marked the junction of the main with the principal cross streets. Along the ancient caravan route where it passed through the middle of the city stood one of the grandest avenues in all Syria. Sixty feet wide, it was once bordered by 375 Corinthian columns of rose-white limestone, each fifty-five feet high. Of these about 150 still stand. On these columns were projecting brackets on which statues were placed.

North of the colonnade lay the chief residential area of the city. Some of the houses were veritable palaces with splendid colonnades around their central courtyards. The great temple of Bel stood in the eastern section of the city. It consisted of an open

Jews or Jewish Christians, but it seems to have been based on a text similar to the Hebrew Masoretic text and to have come into existence in the first or second century. All the canonical books, as well as the apocrypha, were included.

Apparently the New Testament came into existence more gradually. Part of that process involved the work of Tatian, who produced the *Diatessaron*, a harmony of the four gospels, about 170. Tatian was born into a pagan family in east Syria, traveled to the West, and may have become a Christian in Rome. Later he founded a school in Mesopotamia and was influential in Syria and Cilicia. The *Diatessaron* may have been created for use in his school. It became the text of the Syriac-speaking churches into the fifth century, when a new version of the "separated" gospels appeared. We do not know whether the *Diatessaron* was originally produced in Greek or Syriac. When the Peshitta New Testament finally came into being it included only twenty-two books, omitting 2 Peter, 2 and 3 John, Jude, Revelation.

NOTES

1. For documentation and summary on the wealth of Syria, see especially F. M. Heichelheim, "Roman Syria," *An Economic Survey of Ancient Rome*, ed. Tenney Frank (Baltimore: Johns Hopkins Press, 1938), IV, 127–40, 152, 156, and the whole section 123–257.

2. René Dussaud, *Topographie Historique de la Syrie Antique et Médiévale* (Paris: Paul Geuthner, 1927), pp. 1–2.

3. See Suzanne Richard, "Toward a Consensus of Opinion on the End of the Early Bronze Age in Palestine-Transjordan," *Bulletin of the American Schools of Oriental Research* (Winter 1980), 5–34; Arie S. Issar and Dan Yakir, "The Roman Period's Colder climate," *Biblical Archaeologist*, June 1997, 101–06.

4. Theodor Mommsen, *The Provinces of the Roman Empire from Caesar to Diocletian*, trans. William P. Dickson (New York: Charles Scribner's, 1906), II, 148.

5. "Syria," *Oxford Encyclopedia of Archaeology in the Near East*, 1997), 5, 125; See also A. M. T. Moore and others. *Village on the Euphrates.* (Oxford: Oxford University Press, 2000), pp. 518–9.

6. *Ibid.*, p. 126.

7. Jack M. Sasson, ed., *Civilizations of the Ancient Near East* (New York: Charles Scribner's Sons, 1995), 2, 805.

8. Sasson, 2, 1201.

9. See Gordon Young, ed., *Mari in Retrospect* (Winona Lake, IN: Eisenbrauns, 1992); Stephanie Dalley, *Mari and Karana* (London: Longmans, 1984); Abraham Malamat, *Mari and the Early Israelite Experience* (Oxford: Oxford University Press, 1989).

10. For a detailed description of the palace by the excavator, see Jean-Claude Margueron, "Mari: A Portrait in Art of a Mesopotamian City-State," in Sasson, *Op. Cit.*, 2, 885–899.

11. For discussion of Alalakh and the Alalakh texts, see Diana L. Stein, "Alalakh," and Edward L. Greenstein, "Alalakh Texts," in *The Oxford Encyclopedia of Archaeology in the Near East*, 1, 55–61.

12. C. Leonard Woolley, *A Forgotten Kingdom* (Harmondsworth, England: Penguin Books Ltd., 1953), p. 73.

13. *Ibid.*, p. 74.

14. *Ibid.*, p. 81–82.

15. Philip K. Hitti, *History of Syria*. New York: Macmillan, 1951, p. 87.

16. For a discussion of the origins of the alphabet, see section on Phoenicia, pp. 00.

17. For translations of Ugaritic literature see especially H. L. Ginsberg, "Ugaritic Myths and Legends," *Ancient Near Eastern Texts*, ed. J. B. Pritchard (Princeton: Princeton University Press, 1953); Theodor Gaster, *The Oldest Stories in the World* (New York: Viking Press, 1952). For other information on Ugarit see Peter C. Craigie, *Ugarit and the Old Testament* (Grand Rapids: Eerdmans, 1983); Adrian Curtis, *Ugarit* (Grand Rapids: Eerdmans, 1985); Gordon D. Young, ed., *Ugarit in Retrospect* (Winona Lake, IN: Eisenbrauns, 1981).

18. Charles F. Pfeiffer, *Ras Shamra and the Bible* (Grand Rapids: Baker, 1962), p. 39.

19. *Ibid.*, p. 58.

20. Merrill F. Unger, *Israel and the Aramaeans of Damascus* (Grand Rapids: Zondervan, 1957), p. 39.

21. James B. Pritchard, ed., *Ancient Near Eastern Texts*, 2nd ed., *Ancient Near Eastern Texts*, 2nd ed. (Princeton: Princeton University Press, 1955), p. 275.

22. For further information on Al Mina, see Leonard Woolley, *A Forgotten Kingdom* (Baltimore: Penguin Books, 1953), pp. 165-81. Woolley excavated the site.

23. In 1 Kings 15:8 the descent of the royal line in Damascus is from Hezion to Tabrimon to Benhadad. No mention is made of Rezon as founder of the dynasty. Mazar was of the opinion that Hezion is the founder's proper name and Rezon his royal title (Benjamin Mazar, "The Aramaean Empire and Its Relations with Israel," *Biblical Archaeologist*, Dec., 1962, p. 104). Some assume that after Rezon, Hezion was the founder of a new dynasty. The problem is as yet unsolved. The votive stele of Benhadad I confirms the 1 Kings 15:18 account (Unger, pp. 56–57).

24. Unger, p. 85.

25. For a history of Urartu, see Boris B. Piotrovsky, *The Ancient Civilization of Urartu* (New York: Cowles Book Co., 1969).

26. Jack Finegan, *Light from the Ancient Past*, 2nd. Ed. (Princeton: Princeton University Press, 1959), pp. 129–30.

27. Wilfrid Castle, *Syrian Pageant* (London: Hutchinson & Co., 1946), p. 38.

28. A. .H. M. Jones, *The Cities of the Eastern Roman Provinces* (Oxford: At the Clarendon Press, 1937), p. 245.

29. Dussaud, p. 1.

30. Glanville Downey, *Antioch in the Age of Theodosius the Great* (Norman: University of Oklahoma Press, 1962), p. 12.

31. William M. Ramsay, *The Bearing of Recent Discovery on the Trustworthiness of the New Testament* (2nd ed; Grand Rapids: Baker Book House reprint, 1979), pp. 278–99.

32. Heichelheim, p. 158.

33. Bruce M. Metzger, "Antioch-on-the Orontes," *The Biblical Archaeologist*, XI (Dec., 1948), 81.

34. Herbert J. Muller, *The Loom of History* (New York: Harper & Brothers, 1958), p. 402.

35. Glanville Downey, *A History of Antioch in Syria* (Princeton: Princeton University Press, 1961), p. 168.

36. For discussion see H. Harvard Arnason, "The History of the Chalice of Antioch," *The Biblical Archaeologist*, IV (1941), 49–64; V (1942), 10–16; Floyd V. Filson, "Who Are the Figures on the Chalice of Antioch?" *The Biblical Archaeologist*, V (1942), 1–10.

37. Glanville Downey, *Ancient Antioch* (Princeton: Princeton University Press, 1963), p. 215.

38. Downey, *History*, p. 363.

39. Downey, *History*, p. 647.

40. *Ibid.*, p. 179.

41. Muller, p. 403.

42. Hitti, p. 307.

43. Heichelheim, p. 158.

44. Michel M. Alouf, *History of Baalbek,* 20th ed. (Beirut: American Press, 1959), pp. 42–43.

45. *Ibid.*, p. 50.

46. *Ibic.*, p. 4.

47. Finegan, pp. 336–37.

48. See Jean Starcky, "The Nabataeans: A Historical Sketch," *The Biblical Archaeologist,* XVIII (Dec., 1995), 97–100.

49. David M. Robinson, *Baalbek, Palmyra* (New York: J. J. Augustin Publishers, 1946), p. 64.

50. Julian Huxley, *From an Antique Land* (New York: Crown Publishers, Inc., 1954), p. 151.

BIBLIOGRAPHY

Albright, William F. *Archaeology and the Religion of Israel.* Baltimore: The Johns Hopkins Press, 1946.

Alouf, Michel M. *History of Baalbek.* Beirut: American Press, 20th ed., 1951.

Bevan, Edwyn R. *The House of Seleucus.* 2 vols. London: Edward Arnold, 1902.

Bickerman, E. *Institutions Des Séleucides.* Paris: Paul Geuthner, 1938.

Binst, Olivier, ed. *The Levant.* Cologne: Konemann,, 1999.

Bouchier, E. S. *A Short History of Syria.* Oxford: Basil Blackwell, 1921.

Bouchier, E. S. *Syria as a Roman Province.* Oxford: Basil Blackwell, 1916.

Cary, M. *The Geographic Background of Greek and Roman History.* Oxford: At the Clarendon Press, 1949.

Castle, Wilfrid. *Syrian Pageant.* London: Hutchinson & Co., 1946.

Craigie, Peter C. *Ugarit and the Old Testament.* Grand Rapids: Eerdmans, 1983.

Curtis, Adrian. *Ugarit.* Grand Rapids: Eerdmans, 1985.

Dalley, Stephanie. *Mari and Karana.* London: Longmans, 1984.

Downey, Glanville, *Ancient Antioch.* Princeton: Princeton University Press, 1963.

Downey, Glanville. *Antioch in the Age of Theodosius the Great.* Norman: University of Oklahoma Press, 1962.

Downey, Glanville, *A History of Antioch in Syria from Seleucus to the Arab Conquest.* Princeton: Princeton University Press, 1961.

Dussaud, René. *Topographie Historique de la Syrie Antique et Médiévale.* Paris: Paul Geuthner, 1927.

Fedden, Robin. *Syria.* London: Robert Hale, 1946.

Finegan, Jack. *The Archeology of the New Testament: The Mediterranean World of the Early Christian Apostles.* Boulder, CO: Westview Press, 1981.

Gaster, Theodor. *The Oldest Stories in the World.* New York: Viking Press, 1952.

Ginsberg, H. L., "Ugaritic Myths and Legends," *Ancient Near Eastern Texts,* ed. By J. B. Pritchard. Princeton: Princeton University Press, 1952.

Goodspeed, Edgar J. *Paul.* Philadelphia: The John C. Winston Co., 1947.

Gurney, O. R. *The Hittites.* Baltimore: Penguin Books, rev. ed., 1961.

Hallo, William W. "From Qarqar to Carchemish: Assyria and Israel in the Light of New Discoveries," *Biblical Archaeologist,* XXIII (1960), 34–61.

Heichelheim, F. M., "Roman Syria," *An Economic Survey of Ancient Rome,* ed. Tenney Frank. Blatimore: Johns Hopkins Press, 1938. Vol. IV.

Hitti, Philip K. *History of Syria.* New York: Macmillan, 1951.

Hopkins, Clark. *The Discovery of Dura-Europos.* New Haven: Yale University Press, 1979.

Huxley, Julian. *From an Antique Land.* New York: Crown Publishers, 1954.

Jones, A. H. M. *The Cities of the Eastern Roman Provinces.* Oxford: At the Clarendon Press, 1937.

Kondoleon, Christine. *Antioch.* Princeton: Princeton University Press, 2001.

Malamat, Abraham. *Mari and the Early Israelite Experience.* Oxford: Oxford University Press, 1989.

Mazar, Benjamin. "The Aramean Empire and Its Relations with Israel," *Biblical Archaeologist,* XXV (1962), 98–120.

McRay, John. *Archaeology and the New Testament*. Grand Rapids: Baker, 1991.

Metzger, Bruce M. "Antioch-on-the-Orontes," *Biblical Archaeologist*, XI (1948), 69–88.

Mommsen, Theodor. *The Provinces of the Roman Empire from Caesar to Diocletian*, trans. William P. Dickson. New York: Scribner's, 1906, II.

Olmstead, A. T. *History of Palestine and Syria*. New York: Charles Scribner's Sons, 1931.

Olmstead, A. T. *History of the Persian Empire*. Chicago: University of Chicago Press, 1948.

Paton, Lewis B. *The Early History of Syria and Palestine*. New York: Charles Scribner's Sons, 1901.

Pfeiffer, Charles F. *Ras Shamra and the Bible*. Grand Rapids: Baker, 1962.

Pitard, Wayne T. *Ancient Damascus*. Winona Lake, IN: Eisenbrauns, 1987.

Pollard, Nigel. *Soldiers, Cities, & Civilians in Roman Syria*. Ann Arbor: University of Michian Press, 2000.

Ragette, Friedrich. *Baalbek*. Park Ridge, NJ: Noyes Press, 1980.

Rainey, A. F., "The Kingdom of Ugarit," *Biblical Archaeologist*, XXVIII (1965), 102–25.

Ramsay, William M. *The Bearing of Recent Discovery on the Trustworthiness of the New Testament*. Grand Rapids: Baker Book House reprint, 1979.

Robinson, David M. *Baalbek; Palmyra*. New York: J. J. Augustin Publishers, 1946.

Rostovtzeff, Mikhail. *Social and Economic History of the Hellenistic World*. Oxford: Clarendon Press, Vol. 2, 1953.

Sherwin-White, Susan, and Amelie Kuhrt. *From Samarkhand to Sardis*. Berkeley: University of California Press, 1993.

Smith, George Adam. *Syria and the Holy Land*. New York: George H. Doran Co., 1918.

Starcky, Jean, "The Nabataeans: A Historical Sketch," *Biblical Archaeologist*, XVIII (1955), 84–106.

Stevenson, G. H. *Roman Provincial Administration*. New York: G. E. Stechert & Co., 1939.

Stillwell, Richard, ed. *Antioch On-the-Orontes*. Princeton: Princeton University Press, 1938.

Stoneman, Richard. *Palmyra and Its Empire*. Ann Arbor: University of Michigan, 1994.

"Syria," *Oxford Encyclopedia of Archaeology in the Near East*, 1997, Vol. 5.

Unger, Merrill F. *Israel and the Aramaeans of Damascus*. Grand Rapids: Zondervan, 1957.

Wiegand, Theodor. *Baalbek*. Berlin: W. de Gruyter & Co., 1921–25 (in German).

Woolley, C. Leonard. *A Forgotten Kingdom*. Baltimore: Penguin Books, 1953.

Young, Gordon, ed. *Mari in Retrospect*. Winona Lake, IN: Eisenbrauns, 1992.

Young, Gordon, ed. *Ugarit in Retrospect*. Winona Lake, IN: Eisenbrauns, 1981.

A bull capital from one of the columns of the palace at Susa (biblical Shushan).
Courtesy of the Lourvre, Paris

6

BIBLICAL IRAN

Iran as a Bible Land

When Nebuchadnezzar's armies destroyed the city of Jerusalem in 586 B.C., the Neo-Babylonian Empire stood at its zenith. But within a scant half century its very existence was challenged by the ruler of an obscure Persian province who had forged an empire from the states of Media and Persia, conquered Lydia in Asia Minor, and triumphantly entered Babylon itself.

Isaiah had prophesied of this ruler, Cyrus, as the Lord's anointed (Isaiah 44:28; 45:1); it was Cyrus' decree of 538 B.C. that made possible the return of the exiled Judeans to their homeland (2 Chronicles 36:22–23). Under Darius, the second temple in Jerusalem was dedicated in 515 B.C. (Ezra 6:13–18). While Artaxerxes was on the Persian throne (444 B.C.), Ezra the scribe and Nehemiah the statesman brought revival and reform to the life of the Palestinian Jews and rebuilt the walls of Jerusalem.

PERSIANS OFTEN CROSSED PATHS WITH THE HEBREWS

The Persians cross the pages of Hebrew history and even give order to Hebrew chronology more than most of us realize. Back in Isaiah's day (c. 700 B.C.) the prophet had predicted that the Persian king Cyrus would serve as God's anointed to accomplish His purposes (Isaiah 44:28; 45:1). Then in 539–38 B.C., in fulfillment, during his first year of rule over Babylon, Cyrus issued the decree that permitted the Hebrews to return from Babylonian exile (2 Chronicles 36:22–23; Ezra 1:1–4). And Daniel, who had served God faithfully in his youth in the court of Nebuchadnezzar of Babylon, was permitted to live to see the repatriation; he continued to the first year of Cyrus (Daniel 1:21). And he even had a vision in the third year of Cyrus (Daniel 10:1).

But as the Jews returned, they failed to complete reconstruction of the Temple. Then the prophets Haggai (1:1) and Zechariah (1:1) stirred up the people in the second year of King Darius of Persia (520 B.C.) to spring to action. Finally the Jews completed the temple in the sixth year of Darius (515 B.C.) (Ezra 6:15).

The walls of Jerusalem still lay in ruins, however, and Nehemiah rebuilt them in the twentieth year of

Artaxerxes of Persia (444 B.C.; Nehemiah 2:1). Nehemiah's first governorship in Judea lasted from the twentieth to the thirty-second year of Artaxerxes (445–433 B.C., Nehemiah 5:14).

Then the story of Esther took place during the reign of Ahasuerus, whom the Greeks called Xerxes, which lasted from 485 to 465 B.C. In his third year, 483/2, occurred the feast recorded in Esther, chapter 1 (Esther 1:3). In Xerxes' seventh year (Esther 2:16, 479 B.C.) Esther became his queen.

The story of Esther is concerned with events during the reign of Ahasuerus (Xerxes) which took place at the Persian capital of Susa (biblical Shushan) when the very life of the Jewish people was threatened. Thus, under Medo-Persian rulers the damage wrought by the Neo-Babylonians was to be at least partially undone. In addition to these involvements of Persia, Haggai, Zechariah, and Malachi report events that took place during the Persian period. Moreover, Isaiah and Daniel prophesied concerning Persian affairs. Thus, Iran was indeed a Bible land.

Geographical Features

Persia is the anglicized form of *Persis* (modern Fars), the section of Iran adjacent to the Persian Gulf. Native Persians have always used the term *Iran* to designate their indefinitely bounded country. And this has been the official name of the country since 1935. The modern name *Iran* is derived from the ancient *Ariana,* meaning "the country of the Aryans." The Aryans were various Indo-European peoples who settled during prehistoric times in areas north and east of the Persian Gulf.

Geographically *Iran* is an inclusive term referring to the large plateau between the plain of the Tigris on the west and the Indus River valley to the east. On the south it is bounded by the Persian Gulf and the Indian Ocean and on the north by the Caspian Sea and chains of mountains that extend eastward and westward from the south end of the Caspian Sea.

Geographical Areas

In the days of the Persian Empire, Iran was divided into geographical and political areas as follows. At the north end of the Persian Gulf was Susiana, with its main center at Susa (biblical Shushan). North of Susiana in the interior was Media, the chief city of which was Ecbatana (modern Hamadan). Hyrcania (Asterabad) occupied a narrow strip of land south of the Caspian Sea. East of Susiana along the Persian Gulf lay Persis with its leading royal cities of Persepolis and Pasargadae. North of Persis in the interior was Parthia. Gedrosia stretched along the Indian Ocean east of Persis. It was bounded on the northwest by Drangiana and on the northeast by Arachosia. North of these two regions stretched Aria, and north of that, Bactria.

The Plateau

The plateau of Iran averages three thousand to five thousand feet in altitude. Over half of the drainage of the plateau flows inward to form inland lakes and sterile swamps. In its central region lie the great sand and salt deserts of Dasht-i-Lut and Dasht-i-Kavir. This continuous desert region stretches northwest to southeast about 800 miles in length and varies from 100 to 200 miles in width.

At the western edge of the plateau rise the Zagros Mountains with several peaks above ten thousand feet. This range is over 600 miles in length and 120 miles in width. It consists of numerous parallel folds enclosing fruitful valleys where wheat, barley, and other grains and fruits grow. South

of the Caspian stand the Elburz Mountains, the highest peak of which is Mount Damavand, about sixty miles northeast of Tehran. It is a conical peak 18,934 feet high, which was once volcanic. Damavand is thought to be the Mount Bikni, rich in lapis lazuli, mentioned in Assyrian documents dating before 800 B.C. and considered the farthest point to which Aryans were chased by the Assyrian kings.

To the northwest, the Iranian Plateau is united by the highlands of Armenia with the mountains of Asia Minor. To the northeast, the plateau is linked by the mountains of Khurasan (or Khorasan) and the Hindu Kush Range to the Himalayas. The total area of the plateau is over one million square miles, more then one-third the size of the forty-eight contiguous United States.

Rainfall

Iran is a country singularly lacking in rainfall. Only on the plain south of the Caspian and on the Elburz Mountains and Zagros Mountains is rainfall abundant. At Resht (in the Elburz), precipitation measures over fifty-six inches per year. But south of the Elburz at the national capital of Tehran, the figure drops to nine inches. Farther south in the interior rainfall is about two inches per year and at the head of the Persian Gulf it annually measures about ten inches. Only about 5–10 percent of the land surface of Iran is arable and about half of that must be irrigated.

Resources

Iran is primarily an agricultural and stockbreeding country. The northwestern part of the country, Azerbaijan, has fertile valleys with sufficient rainfall for growing various kinds of grains and fruits and vegetables. Agriculture prospers on the plain between the Caspian Sea and the Elburz Mountains, as it does in the fertile valleys of the mountains of Khurasan. The latter constitute the granary of Iran.

But Iran also possessed rich mineral resources in ancient times. Its quarries provided marble, lapis lazuli, and turquoise; and its mountain slopes yielded building woods for the Sumerian princes as early as the third millennium B.C. Gold, iron, copper, tin, and lead were exploited early and especially attracted the attention of the Assyrians in the first millennium B.C. Sargon of Akkad (c. 2350 B.C.) was interested in the wealth of the region fifteen hundred years earlier, however. The oil deposits, so critical to Iran's economy today, did not of course have any importance for ancient peoples.

Historical Developments

The earliest villages of ancient Iran date back to about 7000 B.C. Most of them were not larger than a couple of acres. Food producing villages were numerous during the seventh millennium B.C. and occurred first in the valleys of the Zagros Mountains and after that across the region later known as Susiana. There is now a rapidly increasing body of information about early Iran. But it involves dozens of towns with names strange to us, and it holds slight interest for few except advanced students of anthropology. Moreover, there is no evident connection between these discoveries and the biblical narrative. Therefore we shall begin our discussion with one of the important biblical peoples of the region—the Elamites.

The Elamites

The Elamites, one of the important biblical peoples of the region, first appear in the Table of Nations. There it is recorded that Elam was a son of Shem (Genesis 10:22). Then Abraham had to fight a king of Elam when he set out to rescue Lot (Genesis 14). And later Jeremiah pronounced a judgment against the Elamites (Jereremiah 49:34–39). Numerous other references to them appear in Scripture.

The Elamites were one of the major peoples in the ancient Near East from the third through the first millennia B.C. They occupied parts of southern and western Iran and ruled both in the lowland area, Khuzistan, with its center of Susa (biblical Shushan), and in the Zagros Mountain region, from the center at Anshan (300 miles southeast of Susa). They established a dynasty at Susa during the first quarter of the third millennium and constructed a fairly large kingdom. With the rise of Sargon of Akkad during the twenty-fourth

century B.C., a conflict broke out between the Semites of southern Mesopotamia and the Elamites. Ultimately Sargon seems to have absorbed Elam into his empire. Under Sargon's grandson, Naram-Sin, an Elamite revolt erupted, but it was repressed. The Elamites won their independence, however, after the death of Naram-Sin, c. 2200 B.C.

About a century after the collapse of the Sargonid state, Ur under the Ur III dynasty reunified southern Mesopotamia and moved against Elam. The area of Khuzistan was incorporated into the Ur III provincial system, but the Elamites in the highland region maintained their autonomy. Moreover they established defensive alliances. From this activity arose the Shimaski dynasty, which took the lead in the destruction of the Ur III empire around 1900 B.C.

During the second millennium B.C., as Iran passed into the Bronze Age, there was considerable military and political activity in the area. A new dynasty rose to power in Elam (the Sukkalmah, which ruled c. 1900–1600 B.C.) and invaded Babylonia. Elamites established themselves at Larsa and became masters of Isin, Uruk (biblical Erech), and Babylon. By the early eighteenth century Elam was one of the largest states in the region. It extended southward along the Persian Gulf and influenced or perhaps controlled the city-states of eastern Mesopotamia. Its diplomatic and economic contacts stretched across Mesopotamia and Syria to the Mediterranean. Susa (covering over two hundred acres) was the main city of Khuzistan during the Sukkalmah period. After considerable warfare Hammurabi finally checked this Elamite expansion. Elam then seems to have spent several centuries in decline.

During this period the Elamites fell under Kassite control. The Kassites consisted mainly of an Asiatic element that had been invaded around 2000 B.C. by Indo-Europeans, who formed a military aristocracy among them. The Kassites became a powerful people, dominating the Zagros region and Mesopotamia for about a half millennium and finally disappearing from history around 1175 B.C.

Although the Kassites continued to dominate Mesopotamia, Elam gained independence during the thirteenth century and attained the height of its power around 1200 B.C. Ousting the Kassites from Babylonia, Elam won control of the whole Tigris Valley, most of the shore of the Persian Gulf, and the Zagros Range. In fact, all of western Iran fell under Elamite control. However, her power was destined to be short-lived. Nebuchadnezzar I of Babylon (1125–1104 B.C.) soundly defeated Elam, which virtually disappeared from the pages of history for about three centuries. Later it served as a political refuge for Babylonian opponents of Assyria.

By around 700 B.C. Elam found herself in a changing world. Assyrians and Babylonians pressured her in the west, Medes and Assyrians in the northern highlands, and Persians in the southeast. Finally in 646 B.C. the Assyrian Ashurbanipal conquered Khuzistan, destroyed Susa, and depopulated the region. By 550 B.C. former Elamite territory had fallen under Persian control and Elam ceased to exist as an independent entity.

Coming of the Aryans/Indo-Europeans

Aryans, or Indo-Europeans, moved onto the Iranian plateau around 1000 B.C. and absorbed the aboriginal Caspians already living there. They came in successive waves, some from the northwest via the Caucasus Mountains, and others from the northeast via Khurasan. These Aryans were blocked from an eastward movement by more powerful Aryans already established in the Indus Valley. They were blocked from a westward movement by the developing kingdom of Urartu in the northwest, by Assyrians in the center, and Elamites in the southwest.

The Iron Age came to Iran about the same time as the Aryans did. But in addition to the exploitation of metals, the economy was based on agriculture, spoils of war, and commerce. Since Assyria had no iron mines, she turned to Iran in part for a supply of this metal that was so necessary to her war machine. The Assyrians were also interested in the Iranians as a source of horses and because the Aryans posed a threat to Assyria's eastern borders.

Not all Aryan tribes penetrated the Iranian Plateau gradually. From the end of the eighth century B.C., the Cimmerians and Scythians caused serious trouble in northwest Iran. Pouring down over the Caucasus Mountains, these hordes plundered wherever they went. The Cimmerians established themselves on the southern shore of the Black Sea near the mouth of the Halys River (modern Kizil Irmak), from where they attacked the Phrygian kingdom of Asia Minor and brought it to an end. And the Scythians established a kingdom in the area of modern Azerbaijan.

The two tribes that rose to prominence among the Aryans were the Medes and Persians. Beginning as nomads, these two peoples gradually settled down, the Medes to the southeast of Lake Urmia and the Persians to the west and southwest of Lake Urmia, if one can believe the Assyrian scribes, who first mentioned them in the last half of the ninth century B.C. As the ninth century wore on, these two tribes continued to move south and were forced to pay tribute to the Assyrians. During the first half of the eighth century, when Assyria declined, Medes and Persians came under control of Urartu. And with the resurgence of Assyria during the last half of the century, they again came under Assyrian control.

Rise of the Medes

The Medes were an important people who were spread across the central western Zagros from the mid-ninth to the mid-seventh century B.C. Their heartland seems to have been the region around ancient Ecbatana or modern Hamadan (180 miles west-southwest of Tehran; see Ezra 6:2), along the so-called High Road. Ruled by numerous kings in small regional states in the earlier period, they presumably achieved a centralized state during the reign of Cyaxeres, who rose to the throne in 625 B.C. Perhaps this centralization took place to meet the need of defense against Assyria.

Cyaxares (625–585) united with the Babylonians to attack Nineveh in 612 B.C. and to obliterate the Assyrian Empire. Subsequently the two powers divided the Assyrian Empire, Babylon taking the area to the west and south of the Tigris and the

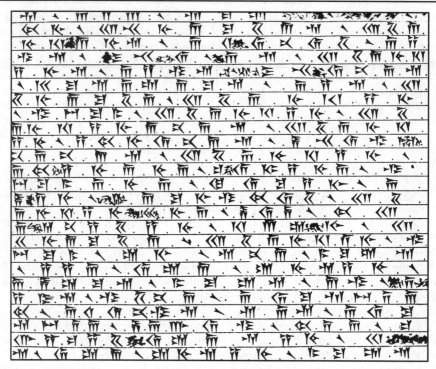

Examples of Persian writing from the fifth century B.C. Copied by Carsten Niebuhr at Persepolis in 1765.

Medes taking lands to the north and east of the Tigris. Cyaxares then went on to campaign successfully in Iranian lands to the east. Apparently his father, Phraortes, had conquered the Persians earlier. And the Persians had been allowed to expand into an area once held by Elam along the Persian Gulf, then possible because the Assyrians had destroyed Elam and depopulated it (646). This area then became the Persian homeland (Persis or Parsa, modern Fars, in the district of Anshan). Thus the Median Empire had come to extend east from the Tigris and north from the Persian Gulf all the way to the Oxus River in Bactria. So when Cyrus the Great revolted against the Medes and conquered them and began to build his empire, he did not have to start from scratch. He could take over an empire ready made from his Median overlords.

READING ANCIENT PERSIAN

Ultimately what we can really know about an ancient people is available only when we can translate the written records they have left behind. The story of our knowledge of Achaemenid Persian and the translation of it in a sense began in the early seventeenth century A.D. Then an Italian nobleman, Pietro della Valle, brought back to Europe some of the Persian inscriptions from Persepolis, the great Persian capital. Thomas Hyde of Oxford in 1700 coined the term *cuneiform* to apply to the wedge-shaped writing of those inscriptions. (Cuneiform was written in wet clay with a stylus having a triangular-shaped point and a sharp side. A combination of triangles and lines could then be written. With a hammer and chisel it could also be cut in stone.) Carsten Niebuhr, a German explorer, in 1765 made additional copies of Persepolis inscriptions.

Several individuals were to have a part in translating cuneiform. Between 1789 and 1791, a French scholar, Sylvestre de Sacy, deciphered some late Persian inscriptions, written at a time when cuneiform had given way to the Phoenician alphabet. In those materials he kept coming across a formula: "X, the great king, king of kings, son of Y."

In 1802 Georg Grotefend, a German scholar, read a paper before the Learned Society of Göttingen claiming to have worked out the value of thirteen cuneiform signs and to have identified the names Hystaspis, Darius, and Xerxes and the words *king* and *son.* He had used Niebuhr's texts, which had appeared over the heads of Persian kings at Persepolis and had guessed that de Sacy's formula was represented in them. But he could go no further.

Paralleling the work of Grotefend was that of Henry C. Rawlinson, an officer of the British army in India, who was later stationed in Persia (1833). Rawlinson was very much intrigued by the trilingual inscriptions on the cliffs of Bisitun, sixty-five miles west of Hamadan and not far from his camp. In 1835 he began copying these texts, which Darius the Great (521–486 B.C.) had carved in the side of the cliff. (See sidebar "Darius' Great Propaganda Piece at Bisitun" later in this chapter.). The boastful king had engraved a record of his exploits about 500 feet above the plain and 100 feet above the highest point to which a man can climb. Then he had cut away most of the ledge on which his men had worked so no defacing of his inscription would occur.

Rawlinson continued the hazardous work of copying the inscription until 1847. To copy the top lines he had to stand on the top step of a ladder, on a narrow ledge with a 350-foot drop, steadying his body with his left arm and holding his notebook in his left hand while writing with his right hand.

Darius' inscription at Bisitun. It appears high on the mountain in right center of the picture.
Oriental Institute of the University of Chicago.

As Rawlinson analyzed Darius' three-part inscription, he decided that it had been produced in three languages (These he called Classes I, II, and III). Further, he guessed that Class I was Old Persian and that it would be the key to the decipherment of Classes II and III (Babylonian and Elamite). He realized that in order to identify all forty-three signs in Class I he would have to work through a large number of proper names. Fortunately, he had already learned late Persian in India so he had the benefit of that background.

Rawlinson guessed that words occurring many times would be common nouns like "king." Using a combination of shrewd guesses, clues from late Persian (such as the formula de Sacy had discovered) and other helps, he made amazing progress. Actually Rawlinson began his work as Grotefend had; but instead of brief inscriptions accompanying statues, he had two trilingual inscriptions engraved by Darius and his son Xerxes. By 1839, through a variety of tactics, he had worked out the values of all forty-three signs and translated two hundred lines of the text. But when he read a survey paper before the Royal Asiatic Society of London in that year, he realized that many imperfections still existed. However, he was finally able to publish a full interpretation of the Persian column in 1846. Then he went to work on Class II (Assyro-Babylonian, or Akkadian) and was able to publish 112 lines in 1851. Edwin Norris cracked Elamite (Class III) in 1853.

Rawlinson's work was imperfect for a variety of reasons. Among them were the conditions under which he worked, partially defaced signs, and his imperfect understanding of the signs. In 1904 the British Museum sent L. W. King and R. Campbell Thomson to Bisitun to check Rawlinson's readings by making fresh copies of the inscription. Then in 1948 George C. Cameron of the University of Michigan was able to suspend scaffolding from above the inscription and make latex copies of it. As a result, scholars were able to base their work on a more definitive text.

Rule of the Persians

About seven hundred B.C. Achaemenes established the Persian royal line. His successors were Teispes, Cyrus I, Cambyses I, and Cyrus II the Great. Forced to pay tribute to Assyria in 640 B.C., the Persians next were then absorbed by the Medes as Assyrian power declined. But the Achaemenids managed to continue to rule as tributary kings in Anshan. When Cyrus came to the throne of Anshan in 560/559 B.C., Astyages, the Median king, recognized that Cyrus intended to rebel and take Persia out of the Median Empire. Astyages struck first, but his efforts proved to be a fiasco. In the struggle, which lasted about four years (554–550), Cyrus not only established Persian independence from the

Median Empire, but also so thoroughly defeated Astyages that he was able to establish his own control over the Median Empire. The Median Empire had become the empire of the Medes and Persians or the Persians and Medes (Esther 1:19; Daniel 5:28). Though Medes still held many positions of leadership, Achaemenid Persians were the top brass. The empire stretched from the Halys River in Asia Minor (modern Turkey) through Armenia and Media to Bactria in northeast Iran.

Hardly had Cyrus consolidated his hold over the Median Empire when he became involved in expansionist activities. Whether Croesus of Lydia (west of the Halys) or Cyrus started the conflict on the western front is immaterial. Cyrus defeated Croesus in 547/546 and extended his empire all the way to the Aegean.

He then turned his attention to the Neo-Babylonian Empire. There Nabunaid (555–539) increasingly antagonized his subjects. For starters, he was not of the Chaldean dynasty and had no special love for Babylon. Then, soon after becoming king, Nabunaid marched off to Harran in the North to restore the temple of the moon god Sin, whom he seems to have worshiped more than Marduk, god of Babylon. Subsequently he took his army into western Arabia to conquer a string of oases and establish his power there; in the process he ignored problems in Babylon. Before leaving the capital, Nabunaid appointed his son Belshazzar as co-regent and as actual ruler while he was away. Therefore Daniel was not wrong in referring to Belshazzar as the last king of Babylon (Daniel 5:30), as critics often have alleged. For several years thereafter, Nabunaid remained in Tema in Arabia, perhaps because it also (in addition to Haran) was a center for the worship of Sin.

CYRUS AT THE GATES OF BABYLON

Cyrus II the Great of Persia marched victoriously against the forces of Babylon. The inept crown prince Belshazzar, instead of straining every nerve to meet the onslaught, threw a party. And he dared to use gold and silver vessels that Nebuchadnezzar had taken from the Temple in Jerusalem as table service. Suddenly the famous handwriting appeared on the wall that told of Persian conquest of the empire and the city. Daniel 5 tells the story and Lord Byron dramatically recounts the event as follows.

Vision of Belshazzar

The king was on his throne,
The satraps thronged the hall:
A thousand bright lamps shone
O'er that high festival.
A thousand cups of gold,
In Judah deemed divine—
Jehovah's vessels hold
The godless Heathen's wine!

In that same hour and hall,
The fingers of a hand
Came forth against the wall,
And wrote as if on sand:
The fingers of a man:—
A solitary hand
Along the letters ran,
And traced them like a wand.

The monarch saw and shook,
And bade no more rejoice;
All bloodless waxed his look,
And tremulous his voice.
'Let the men of lore appear,
The wisest of the earth,
And expound the words of fear,
Which mar our royal mirth.'

Chaldea's seers are good,
But here they have no skill;
And the unknown letters stood
Untold and awful still.
And Babel's men of age
Are wise and deep in lore;
But now they were not sage,
They saw—but knew no more.

A captive in the land,
A stranger and a youth,
He heard the king's command,

He saw that writing's truth.
The lamps around were bright,
The prophecy in view;
He read it on that night—
The morrow proved it true.
'Belshazzar's grave is made,
His kingdom passed away,
He, in the balance weighed,
Is light and worthless clay;
The shroud his robe of state,
His canopy the stone;
The Mede is at his gate!
The Persian on his throne!'

The date was October 12, 539 B.C.

As he absented himself from Babylon, Nabunaid failed to conduct the New Year festival in honor of Marduk and thus antagonized the priesthood and populace alike. While the economy sagged, Nabunaid was not in the capital to exert a firm hand. Defenses of the realm against the Persian threat on the East were in the hands of his inept son Belshazzar. Finally in 539 B.C., Nabunaid returned from Arabia, but there was little heart in his subjects to resist Persian advance. Probably about the end of September, Cyrus took Opis (43 miles north

Nabonidus, last king of the Neo-Babylonian Empire, and father of the crown prince Belshazzar. He stands before the symbols of the moon god, the sun god, and the goddess of love and war.
British Museum

The tomb of Cyrus at Pasargadae. Believed to be the actual tomb of the founder of the Persian Empire. *The Oriental Institute of the University of Chicago*

Massagetai, who lived in northeastern Iran. The struggle was fierce, but finally the Massagetai prevailed and killed Cyrus and the greater part of his army. But there is no evidence that Cyrus' enemies or restless subjects in the northeast took advantage of his death, for the Persian Empire did not suffer any loss of territory.

At his death Cyrus controlled Asia Minor and Western Asia from the border of Egypt eastward across Syria and Mesopotamia almost to the Indus River. Cyrus had been successful in building his empire so rapidly because of the aggressive nationalism of the Persians and the exhaustion of the peoples of the Near East. Centuries of imperialism had broken the independent spirit of the Near East. The Assyrians and Babylonians especially had uprooted masses of people from their homelands and settled them elsewhere, destroying their nationalistic entities. The Persians had only to defeat ruling minorities and their mercenary armies—and then to hire the mercenaries for their own purposes.

It is now in order to look at Cyrus' administration. Apparently he chose to rule the provinces of the empire through his own appointees instead of vassal kings, but he did not insist that they all be Persians. For example, he sent the Jewish Sheshbazzar, as governor to Jerusalem (Ezra 1:8). Moreover, Cyrus and his son Cambyses appointed non-Persians as army commanders. Of the three known generals of Cyrus, two were Medes and one a former Babylonian governor. Cyrus seems to have been generous toward his nobles and apparently had a certain charisma or at least an effective propaganda machine that led Medes, Babylonians, Elamites, Jews, and others to accept him as their legitimate ruler. Generally he seems to have been humane. For example, when he took over the Babylonian Empire, Nabunaid was permitted to live in peace. When Nabunaid died a year later, Cyrus ordered a period of national mourning for him. Though Cyrus may have been a worshiper of Ahuramazda, he followed a policy of religious tolerance that portrayed himself as a ruler chosen by Marduk among the

of Baghdad) after a pitched battle, devastating the city and annihilating most of its population. It was not necessary to terrorize the Babylonians further. On October 10, Sippar in the north fell without a struggle and Nabunaid fled. Two days later Cyrus' general Ugbaru took Babylon virtually without resistance. Cyrus himself entered the city on October 29 and prevented it from being sacked or looted. He presented himself not as conqueror but liberator. His propaganda that portrayed him as the elect of Marduk apparently had been effective, and the priesthood and bureaucracy received him well. The Jews hailed him as a deliverer; it has been suggested that he used them as a fifth column.

Parenthetically, it should be noted that the Darius the Mede, with whom Daniel was involved, was a governor of Babylon. He was already sixty-two in 539 and should not be confused with Darius the Persian, who became king over the entire Persian Empire in 521 (Daniel 5:31). Darius the Mede's appointment of 120 administrators (satraps over regions of the old Babylonian Empire; cf. Daniel 6:1) should not be confused with Darius the Great's organization of the whole Persian Empire into twenty satrapies.

Cyrus had conquered another empire. But he was still not content; he wanted more. In 530 B.C. he set off to subdue the

The Cyrus Cylinder, which records King Cyrus' decree permitting captive peoples to return to their ancestral homes.
British Museum

Babylonians, Yahweh among the Jews, and by other deities as it served his purpose.

According to the Cyrus Cylinder (a cuneiform inscription found by H. Rassam at Babylon late in the nineteenth century and now in the British Museum), dating to 538 B.C., Cyrus reversed the deportation policies of the Assyrians and Babylonians and permitted deported peoples to return to their ancestral lands to rebuild their homes and the sanctuaries of their deities.[1] Presumably, this general policy was made specific in individual decrees to subject peoples. Ezra 1 and 1 Chronicles 36 detail this pronouncement given to the Jews. By this means Cyrus could have expected to win the favor of the many gods involved and the support of their devotees, and to have removed sources of irritation among captive peoples.

RETURN OF THE HEBREW EXILES

What a procession it was. Imagine a total of 42,360 Israelites, 7,337 slaves, and 200 singing men and women (secular musicians that could provide entertainment) making their way from the province of Babylonia, through western Assyria, and down through Syria and northern Palestine into Judah (Ezra 2:64; Neh. 7:16; 1 Esdras 5:41). Most walked, but some women and children rode in the great train of wagons and carts or on the

backs of animals that carried the clothing and household gear.

And there was a great herd of livestock (736 horses, 245 mules, 435 camels, and 6,720 donkeys, Ezra 2:66–67). We have no way of knowing how many cows, sheep, and goats they may have herded along by their sides.

Scripture leaves to our imagination the cloud of dust, the noise of animal drivers as they coaxed and prodded their beasts, the cacophony of sound as the beasts responded or balked, and the crying of babies or the yelling of children at play. Nor do we know how long it took the Jews to make the journey, how they met their needs on the way, or what kinds of conflicts they may have had with local residents as they passed through their territories.

This move may be taken as an indication of Cyrus' humaneness or his astuteness or his religious superstition, or possibly all three. His astuteness would of course recognize that peoples permitted to return to the land of their ancestry or remain where they were would no longer constitute pockets of disaffection. Especially they would think kindly of him if he gave some recognition to their gods. And perhaps the gods themselves would smile on him. It must not be concluded that Cyrus had suddenly become a worshiper of the God of the Hebrews, however. What Cyrus did for the Jews he also did for other captive peoples.

In his first year as a ruler of Babylon, Cyrus issued the decree that permitted the Jews to return to their homeland and to rebuild their temple (Ezra 1:1). Since Cyrus did not enter Babylon until the end of October, 539 B.C., the decree must have been issued in 538. Later, when there was some question about the legality of Jewish action in building the temple, search was made in the royal archives for a copy of the decree. It was assumed that the order had been given in Babylon, but the record of it was actually found in Ecbatana (Agbatana, or Achmatha), the old Median capital (Ezra

A drawing of Darius' relief at Bisitun, depicting his victory over contenders for the throne of Persia, roped together by their necks. The king's left foot rests on the prostrate form of Gaumata, the leading rebel. In his left hand the king grasps a bow, while he lifts his right hand toward the winged disk, the symbol of the god Ahuramazda.

6:2). Ecbatana was located at the foot of Mount Alwand, 180 miles west-southwest of Tehran. Evidently Cyrus had not downgraded that city but was still using it as an administrative center after the conquest of Babylon and the decision to build his capital at Pasargadae.

More specifically, the decree must have been issued during the summer of 538 B.C. when the court had moved to the mountains. Persian kings enjoyed the winter months in the warmer lowlands of Susa (biblical Shushan), not unlike traveling to Florida for the winter. Apparently the events of Esther and Nehemiah, which occurred at Shushan, took place during the winter.

The next ruler, Cyrus' son, Cambyses II, held the throne 529–522. Co-regent with his father and "king of Babylon" during the last eight years of Cyrus' reign, Cambyses also had been in charge of preparations for a campaign against Egypt. It is only natural then that as king he should seek to add Egypt to his dominions. By the middle of 525 he had become master of Lower and Upper Egypt and of Egypt's dependency on Cyprus. Libya also submitted to the Persians. Egyptians circulated stories of Cambyses' atrocities in Egypt and of his having gone mad, but J.M. Cook concludes

that those accounts were concocted by the Egyptian priesthood as a result of Cambyses' drive to reduce what he considered to be exorbitant exactions of the temples of Egypt, and he largely discounts them.[2]

Actually Cyrus had left behind two sons: Cambyses, and Bardiya, or Smerdis. While Cambyses was off in Egypt, Smerdis was consolidating his power in Persia. But Darius, an Achaemenid prince of a collateral line, was rising to power in the military and got control of the disciplined Persian infantry and cavalry.

When Cambyses heard of Smerdis' revolt, according to one commonly-held account, he committed suicide. But the ancient Greek historian Herodotus said that when Cambyses received word of Smerdis' revolt in Persis, he leapt on his horse in a hurry and accidentally stabbed himself in the thigh with his sword when the metal tip of his sheath came off. He died some weeks later from the wound. Cook stands by Herodotus' account[3], which seems the more likely of the two. In any case, Cambyses was dead and Darius managed to take over the empire. After he had done so, he put forth the story that Cambyses had murdered Smerdis earlier in his reign to eliminate a threat to his rule and that a certain

Gaumata had impersonated Smerdis and seized the throne in 522. Darius then declared that he and six other cohorts slew Gaumata on September 29, 522 and took the throne. But A.T. Olmstead and others contest the story and are convinced that Darius slew the true Smerdis, not an impostor.[4]

DARIUS' GREAT PROPAGANDA PIECE AT BISITUN

Along the main caravan route from Ecbatana to Babylon stands the famous Bisitun mountain to a height of thirty-eight hundred feet. Here on the rock, known in the Achaemenid period as *bagastana* ("place of the gods") Darius I carved an indestructible propaganda piece. Then after the inscription was completed, about five hundred feet above the plain, he had the face of the cliff cut away to prevent the inscription from being defaced or erased.

What Darius sought to represent here was his victory over the various rebel uprisings during the first year of his reign. He carved a large relief panel representing the king accompanied by two of his officers. His left foot rests on the prostrate form of Gaumata, the leading rebel. Behind Gaumata is a procession of eight rival contenders, their necks roped together and their hands tied behind their backs.

Then in many columns of text he told the story in the three main languages of the empire: Old Persian, the language of king and court; Babylonian; and Elamite.

By this means Darius advertised the legitimacy of his reign and presented his regime as a remedy against disorder and insecurity. Of course Darius did not intend for his inscription to remain inaccessible. He sent copies of it all over the empire.

At the foot of Bisitun springs bubble up into a pool of crystal clear water. Here every army that has marched from Iran into Iraq (or in the reverse direction) has camped. And so have caravans of merchants and shepherds with their sheep. All could look up and see the record of the great king and his military exploits. (For more on Bisitun, see the sidebar on Bisitun and the Decipherment of Persian.)

Darius. In any event, Darius did take the throne and spent all of 521 putting down revolts and consolidating his hold on the empire. One significant factor that gave Darius the edge was his control of the disciplined Persian standing army while his opponents normally fielded less experienced and less equipped recruits. Darius then campaigned in the East and established the borders of his empire at the Indus River. Next he turned his attention to Europe. Crossing the Bosporus, he sought to reduce the Scythians north of the Danube. But they simply moved farther north and Darius never seems to have been able to engage them in battle. Darius himself crossed back into Asia, but he had something to show for his efforts because his men reduced Thrace up to the borders of Macedonia (512 B.C.), and Macedonia itself accepted Persian suzerainty.

Thus the Persian Empire had reached its greatest extent and constituted the largest empire of Western Asia in ancient times. It extended from the Jaxartes River in the north to the Persian Gulf and the Indian Ocean in the south, from the Indus River in the east to the Aegean Sea and on into Thrace in the west, and through Syria, Palestine, and Egypt to Libya in the southwest. From east to west, it was as wide as the continental United States.

Though Darius had a firm hold on the Greeks of Ionia (eastern coast of the Aegean) and had moved effectively across the Hellespont, the Greeks were restless under Persian control. In 499 Aristagoras of Miletus in Ionia led a revolt against the Persians; Athens and Eretria from the Greek mainland joined in. Athens had good reason to get involved because the Persians

Sculptured head of Darius I, from the rock relief of Bisitun

had engaged in an act of war by taking some Athenian dependencies along the Bosphorus. Flames of rebellion engulfed the whole western part of Asia Minor. So fierce was the struggle that it took the Persians six years to bring the Greeks back into full subjugation. When they did, they destroyed the proud old city of Miletus.

Next they determined to punish Athens and Eretria. In 492 they collected a vast armada of ships for the attack, but some three hundred of them were lost in a storm in the northern Aegean. Two years later the Persians tried again, but this time were worsted by the Athenians at Marathon (490 B.C.). Failed by his generals and admirals, Darius made preparations to lead a major expedition himself to deal with the Greeks. He spent the next three years preparing for the event but died before he was able to launch the attack. He left the task to Xerxes, his son and successor.

Before looking at Xerxes' rule, it is important to consider the administration of Darius. The refounder of the Persian Empire, Darius was also its real organizer. To begin with, Darius divided the empire into twenty provinces or satrapies, each under a satrap or governor chosen from the Persian nobility or the royal family. Many of these satrapies encompassed several peoples, with one of them serving as a nucleus. Land surveys were made and annual taxes/tribute assessed. Palestine was part of the fifth satrapy, along with Phoenicia, Syria, and Cyprus. Great cities and important frontier posts had strong garrisons, partly Iranian in composition. Satraps normally shouldered both civil and military responsibilities. They collected tribute, raised military levies, and provided for justice and security. Their courts and their protocol were modeled on that of the king.

Next to each satrap Darius placed a commander-in-chief of the forces in the province, a collector of the imperial taxes, and a secretary to maintain liaison between the satrap and the central government. Inspectors traveled all over the empire and made unexpected visits to the administrators and examined their conduct.

For purposes of commerce and communication, Darius reopened the canal between the Pelusiac branch of the Nile near Bubastis and the Red Sea near Suez. About eighty feet wide, it was broad enough for two ships to pass. The last Egyptian Pharaoh to concern himself with this canal had been Necho (c. 600 B.C.). Thus Darius was able to unite by water the three heavily populated river valleys of the ancient world (Indus, Tigris-Euphrates, Nile).

On land he built a network of roads, queen of which was the great royal road, extending over sixteen hundred miles from Susa to Sardis. Ancient historians reported that royal messengers could travel this distance in a week, a feat achieved by frequent changes of fast horses.

Darius is also credited with a standard currency and a system of weights and measures. He tried to ensure that the laws of the land were known to those who administered them, but he does not seem to deserve his reputation as a lawgiver, promulgated in modern times.

PERSIAN ZOROASTRIANISM

Any discussion of Persian religion during the period of the Jewish

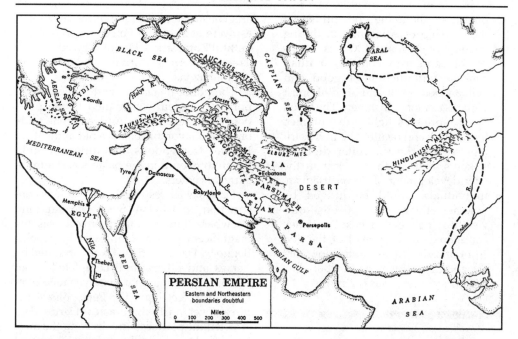

PERSIAN EMPIRE
Eastern and Northeastern
boundaries doubtful
Miles
0   100   200   300   400   500

restoration to Palestine must center on the development of Zoroastrianism. The evolution of Zoroastrianism and the degree to which Persian kings or others in Persian society subscribed to its beliefs in the days of Zerubbabel, Ezra, and Nehemiah are very controversial and involved subjects. Certainly we should not base our conclusions about this religion on its later fully-developed stage or on current practices. Some popular books simply assert that the Persian kings of the Restoration period were Zoroastrians and then proceed to discuss some of the beliefs of that faith. But the matter is not that simple.

First, scholars do not agree on when the prophet Zoroaster lived (the Greek spelling of his name is *Zoroaster*, the Avestan, *Zarathushtra*). Some place him as late as Cyrus or Darius I in the fifth century B.C., others place him centuries earlier. Second, there is no agreement as to the location of Zoroaster's home. Some put it in the east near the Indus valley, others in northwest Iran. Third, scholars debate whether Zoroaster preached monotheism, a

dualism, or the superiority of one god over others. Fourth, scholars disagree over whether the Persian kings (of the Achaemenid line) embraced Zoroastrianism.

To be sure, Darius and Xerxes exalted Ahuramazda, the god Zoroaster preached, but they do not mention Zoroaster. Cyrus comes across as very tolerant of various religions, making him simply an Iranian polytheist. Though some argue that he embraced Zoroastrianism, we really cannot be certain of his religious belief.

In his inscriptions Darius mentions Ahuramazda dozens of times and claims to be under that god's protection. Though Darius calls Ahuramazda the "greatest of gods," he does not describe him as the only god. In Darius' tomb the king is pictured as facing a fire altar—a Zoroastrian symbol. It appears, then, that Darius may have been a Zoroastrian, but he was not an intolerant worshiper of the god. Likewise Xerxes in his inscriptions claimed to be under the favor of Ahuramazda and in opposition to the demons. Presumably Zoroaster's preaching about the god influenced the worship of Ahuramazda during the days of Darius and Xerxes.

Zoroastrianism contains a dualism—a contradiction of good and evil, a Good Spirit and an Evil Spirit with his demon henchmen. The Good Spirit represents light, fire, summer, fertile land, and health. The Evil Spirit represents darkness, winter, drought, sickness, and death. At least in the later development of Zoroastrianism, individuals would be judged by whether their good deeds outweighed their evil deeds. And they considered fire a symbol of the god Ahuramazda, as an indication that the god himself was there when they performed a religious ceremony.

A fire-altar with the relief of a Magus, a member of the Zoroastrian priestly tribe—the Magi (from Kayseri, Turkey)

Darius transformed a feudal kingship into an oriental despotism with an elaborate court ceremony, and thus he greatly increased the distance between himself and his subjects. He enjoyed building palaces and constructed several, but the two greatest were at Susa and Persepolis. Possibly a faithful Zoroastrian, Darius viewed himself as the representative on earth of Ahuramazda.

The political stability and a good transportation system contributed to the prosperity of the empire. And external trade brought a favorable balance of payments to Persia. Tremendous quantities of gold began to pile up in the palaces and administrative centers.

Darius was responsible for much construction at Babylon, Susa, Ecbatana and elsewhere; but his major project was the magnificent palace complex at Persepolis. Begun by Darius in 520, it was continued by Xerxes and others until completed about 450 B.C. Standing on a massive stone platform forty feet high, the Persepolis structures cover thirty-three acres. Darius constructed the platform and drew up the master plan. Then he built a brick wall around the platform, massive stairways carved with bas relief leading up to it, his private palace, the treasury, and began the Apadana or audience hall. Xerxes completed the Apadana, his own palace and began the throne hall. Artaxerxes I later completed the throne hall and may have constructed a private palace.

During the reign of Darius I, the second stage of the Jewish restoration in Palestine took place: the completion of the temple. Though the foundations of the second temple had been laid in the second year after the return from Babylon, fierce opposition to the work had forced its cessation. Finally during the second year of Darius (520), the preaching of the prophets Haggai and Zechariah stirred up the people to resume construction (cf. Haggai 1:1; Zechariah 1:1; Ezra 5:1–2). When the local enemies of the Jews tried to stop the work again, the leaders of the Jews asked that a check of the archives be made to see if Cyrus' decree permitting reconstruction of the temple could be found. As previously mentioned, the decree was located. But the decree was not in Babylon where Jewish leaders thought it would be; it was found at Ecbatana in Media. And Darius fully honored the decree and ordered that the costs

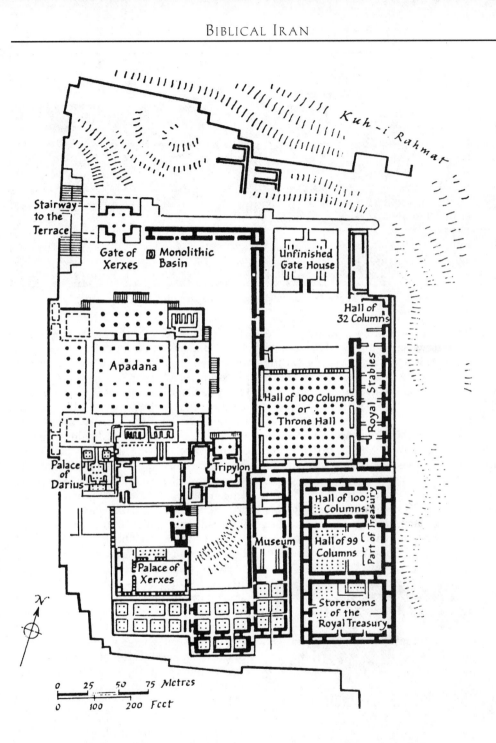

Plan of the terrace at Persepolis *After Houser, Courtesy of Chicago Press*

Palace of Darius and Xerxes at Persepolis and reliefs on the side of the platform. *Slideco, Tehran*

of construction should be paid out of the royal treasury (Ezra 6:1–15). The temple was completed in the sixth year of Darius (Ezra 6:15), on the third day of the month Adar, which would have been March 12, 515 B.C.

Xerxes. Darius died near the end of November 486 B.C. and his son Xerxes ascended the throne. Xerxes had already ruled for twelve years as viceroy at Babylon. At the beginning of his reign in 485 he was faced with a revolt in Egypt, which he put down with great severity. He exercised the same brutality in suppressing a revolt in Babylon, where he destroyed the walls, fortifications, and temples of the city.

The Greek challenge against Persia was destined to have a far different outcome. For their part, the Greeks had been feverishly preparing for a Persian onslaught. Especially, the Athenians had been building up their navy as fast as possible. On the Persian side Xerxes laid extensive plans with the military and political leaders of his realm, which is chronicled in Esther 1. (Though the Greeks called him Xerxes, the Hebrews called him Ahasuerus, the rough equivalent of his Persian name.) And after that planning session Xerxes staged a banquet for the top brass—all this in his third year, 483 B.C. (Esther 1:1, 3). And in the midst of the festivities Xerxes deposed his queen.

The picture that is usually painted of the Greco-Persian war is that a handful of Greek patriots held at bay the great king of Persia who had half the east at his back. But that is not a very realistic portrayal. Though the Persians had a large empire from which to draw resources for the invasion of Greece, they were fighting at a great distance from home in a difficult and unfamiliar terrain. Moreover, the Persians suffered numerical inferiority in a subject population of mixed character. As pointed out in the chapter on Greece, they may have constituted only about one-sixtieth of the population of their empire. And as pointed out there, the old figure of a Persian invasion army of 3,000,000 must be abandoned in favor of a total of 360,000 or less.

Tomb of Darius I at Naksh-i-Rustam, near Persepolis. *Slideco, Tehran*

One of the Ten Thousand Immortals, as portrayed in glazed brick relief on the palace wall at Susa, the biblical Shushan.
Louvre Museum

THE PERSIAN ARMY ON THE MARCH

When the Persian army marched by on its way to war, local civilians experienced it as high entertainment. First came the empty chariot of the invisible god Ahuramazda drawn by eight white horses, with the charioteer trotting alongside on foot. He could not ride in the chariot with the god. Then the king himself rode in a chariot. But he also had a covered carriage in which he could relax when he grew tired.

Next came the carriages containing his wives, concubines, and children and their governesses. Some of the ladies-in-waiting were mounted. The size and nature of this group varied from king to king and battle to battle.

Mess tents and luxurious furnishings—gilded and silver tables and chairs carried on camels—accompanied the king and army. Valets came along to see to the king's wardrobe. Dozens of cooks and bakers also rode by. And though they requisitioned foodstuffs from subject peoples en route, they herded flocks of animals along to provide the king and the top brass with fresh meat. Because the king could not drink ordinary local water, mule-drawn four-wheeled carts carried silver urns filled with boiled water from the Choaspes River, near Susa. The king also traveled with a war chest of gold and silver, both in coin and bullion so large it had to be carried by hundreds of mules and camels. It does not take much imagination to see how the troops of Alexander the Great, who carried much of their supply on their backs and rarely used supply wagons, could out-maneuver the lumbering Persian armies.

The procession of soldiers was also significant. First came the Ten Thousand Immortals—the elite corps. A thousand of them served as the king's bodyguard. Each of them carried a spear with a glittering silver blade. A bow and quiver of arrows hung from every man's left shoulder. And they were decked out in brightly-colored robes that extended to their wrists and ankles, and in earrings and bracelets. Their full beards were curled, as were the buns of long hair wound up at the neck. This pampered unit also had concubines and attendants who traveled in carriages, their food transported on camels and other baggage animals. Apparently this unit came from the Persian nobility and other regiments from Persian commoners.

A reconstruction of the complex at Persepolis. At the left is the Apadana, a great reception hall. At the left front corner of the Apadana stands the gate of Xerxes.
After J. A. Gobineau, Geneva

Behind the Immortals came the crack cavalry units. And after them came Persian infantrymen with loose felt caps and various-colored sleeved tunics over iron-scaled armor and trousers. They carried wicker shields, long bows with quivers filled with reed arrows, short spears, and a short sword hung from a belt on the right hip. Military service was compulsory for all Persians.

Finally the masses of mercenaries marched by in their national dress, a sort of "walking encyclopedia of the empire." It would not have been possible to outfit all of them in standard uniforms, and it was probably unwise to try to do so. Since they fought in units with national dress they reflected a certain pride and camaraderie.

The story of what happened in the Greco-Persian conflict is often recounted and is told in some detail in chapter 9 on Greece. Suffice it to say here that in the spring of 480 B.C. Xerxes crossed the Hellespont and moved across Macedonia and down into Greece. The Greeks decided to stand at Thermopylae in central Greece; both the Persians and the Greeks had a land force covered by a navy offshore. The Persians lost several hundred ships in storms along the shore of Magnesia, but they were still able to inflict heavy damage on the Athenian fleet near Thermopylae. The betrayal of the Spartan position at Thermopylae and the Persian victory there is well known. The Persians then poured into central Greece and occupied Athens.

Soon thereafter the allied forces enjoyed a signal naval victory at Salamis, a few miles from Athens. Persian losses were heavy and included the admiral, a brother of the king. The morale of the fleet snapped and the armada sailed for the Hellespont. Without a fleet to cover and supply his

Guardsmen in Median (left) and Persian (right) dress from Persepolis, with spears and bows

A drawing of a gold armband of the type that Xerxes would have worn. The two carefully detailed creatures represent griffons, mythological beasts that were part eagle and part lion. Persian artists often pictured griffons with rams' horns. Both men and women wore a profusion of jewelry, especially earrings, bracelets, and armbands. This armband is 4 ¾ inches in diameter.

Xerxes passed his later years in constructing a new palace at Persepolis and in dissolute living at Susa and other Persian capitals. Finally he was murdered by Artabanus, captain of the guards, who was in turn killed in 464 by Xerxes' son Artaxerxes I.

Artaxerxes I. Records of the reign of Artaxerxes I (464–424) are sparse, so his reign is not as well documented as other Persian administrations. At the outset he faced a rebellion in Bactria from which he emerged victorious. Later he put down a revolt in Egypt, fomented by Athens; this ended in a disaster for Athens and her allies. Finally, about 445, the Athenians negotiated the Peace of Kallias with the Persians, according to which the Persians apparently agreed not to conduct warlike activity in the Greek sphere along the coast of Asia Minor and the Athenians agreed not to interfere in Persian territory. Thereafter the reign of Artaxerxes seems to have been peaceful, and the king enjoyed a reputation for mildness and magnanimity.

These were the days of the golden age of Athens. Greek historians and men of science such as Herodotus and Democritus traveled in Egypt, Babylonia, and Persia and profited from the cultural cross-fertilization. These were the days too when the great dramatists Aeschylus, Sophocles, and Euripides were producing their tragedies. Pindar and others were composing their poetry. Architects and sculptors were crafting buildings such as the Parthenon and statues and busts of outstanding figures and mythological heroes. The democracy was at its peak.

Evidently Artaxerxes I is the ruler who figures in the narratives of Ezra and Nehemiah, rather than Artaxerxes II (404–359 B.C.). This is the general (but not universal) conclusion of scholarship today.[5] Ezra led a second contingent of Jews to Jerusalem in the seventh year of Artaxerxes I, i.e. 458 (Ezra 7:1, 8). It is clear, then, that the narrative of Ezra has a gap of over fifty-seven years between chapters 6 and 7. Chapter 6 ends with the dedication of the temple in 515 B.C., in the sixth year of Darius. Chapter 7 picks up the account in the seventh year of Artaxerxes (458).

forces, Xerxes had to leave for Asia Minor. Mardonius, the Persian commander, was left to winter in central Greece with perhaps a hundred thousand men. In the spring of 479 Mardonius' army was cut to pieces at Plataea; shortly thereafter at Mount Mycale on the Ionian shore the Greeks enjoyed another overwhelming victory, with much of the Ionian coastal region rising in revolt. Thus, the myth of Persian invincibility had been shattered. The flower of the Persian army had been wiped out. The famous ten thousand Immortals and the crack-line infantry were among them. Many members of the royal family had lost their lives. Casualties probably included about twenty-five thousand Persians, plus thousands of auxiliaries.

As noted, Xerxes had deposed Queen Vashti during preparations for the invasion of Greece in 483/2 B.C. The process of preparing candidates from whom might be selected a new queen must have gone forward during the invasion of Greece. Then after the fiasco in the west in 479, Xerxes returned to the interests of his harem, bringing Esther into the palace in the seventh year of his reign, 479 (Esther 2:16).

Tomb of Artaxerxes in the hillside at Naksh-i-Rustam, near Persepolis. *Slideco, Tehran*

Between the two chapters occurred the reign of Xerxes. Since Esther was married to Xerxes, the story of Esther must be placed between Ezra 6 and 7. The events of the book of Nehemiah occurred later in the reign of Artaxerxes I. Nehemiah returned to Jerusalem in the twentieth year of Artaxerxes or 444 B.C. to rebuild the walls (Nehemiah 2:1) and made a second visit to Jerusalem in the thirty-second year of Artaxerxes or 433/32 B.C. (Nehemiah 13:6).

So, restoration of Judah occurred under Persian auspices. When placed against a backdrop of Persian royal administrations, the historical development becomes clear and chronologically understandable. Cyrus the Great issued the decree permitting the return of the Jews to Palestine in 538 B.C. Pursuant to that, the first contingent of exiles returned and established themselves and laid the foundation of the second temple. In the days of Darius I, under the urging of Haggai and Zechariah, the temple was completed between 520 and 515. Xerxes brought Esther into his harem as queen in 479 B.C., and twenty years later

Ezra led the second contingent of exiles back to Jerusalem and ministered there fairly early in the reign of Artaxerxes I. Then in 444 B.C., in the twentieth year of Artaxerxes I, Nehemiah rebuilt the walls of Jerusalem. With that event a Jewish social and political entity had been reestablished. Malachi, the last writing prophet of the Old Testament period, evidently was contemporary with Nehemiah's second visit to Jerusalem and hence may be dated about 435 B.C.[6] With the book of Malachi the Old Testament canon closed and the prophetic voice was stilled for some four hundred years.

Later Persian rulers. After Artaxerxes I, the reigns of the succeeding rulers of the Persian Empire present a dreary chronicle of decadence. Frequently they bribed external states such as Sparta and Athens to remove a threat to their borders and bought loyalty or bought off revolutionaries within the Persian Empire to maintain the power of the central government.

The administration of Darius II (423–405) was riddled by intrigue and corruption. He

Persians decorated their palace walls with enameled colored bricks as "tapestries." Subjects included unicorns, sphinxes, and more. The following wall decorations were excavated at Susa (biblical Shushan) and are in the Louvre

A unicorn

Human headed sphinxes

A spearman of the guard.

A gold drinking horn of the kind that Esther might have used at her dinner parties with Xerxes

was especially involved in Greek affairs, enabling Sparta to defeat Athens during the Peloponnesian War. Artaxerxes II (404–359) suffered first a rebellion of Egypt, then of a Cyrus the Younger, and later a rebellion of the satraps; the empire seemed to be coming apart at the seams. But a series of circumstances fortunate for Persia gave victory to the central government, the power of which was largely restored by the time of Artaxerxes II's death.

With the reign of Artaxerxes III (358–338) Persia seemed to have a last chance to survive. A cruel and brutal man, he possessed a will of iron and statesmanlike qualities. He engaged in major and successful campaigns in Phoenicia and Egypt and completely restored the empire. But in 338 an assassin destroyed this powerful Persian, striking a mortal blow at the empire from within during the same year as the victory of Philip of Macedon over the Greeks. Philip's victory was to make possible a pan-Hellenic war against the colossus of the east. The son of Artaxerxes III, Arses, reigned for about two years and then was poisoned and replaced by Darius III (335–331). Philip was likewise assassinated and replaced by his son Alexander, to be called Alexander the Great. Darius III did not take Alexander's invasion of his empire in 334 sufficiently seriously and sent an inadequate force to stop him. In 330 the Persian Empire lay at Alexander's feet and Darius III was dead.

How did the fall come so suddenly and apparently so easily? In the first place, the empire was too huge and the Persians too few to maintain it. But in spite of these difficulties, the Persians did maintain their empire for over two hundred years.

Second, in the later years of the empire rivalries and intrigues surrounded the throne and murder and assassination killed off some of the best members of the royal family. Yet the institutions were still "perfectly adequate to the needs of the empire."[7]

Third, with the passage of time some of the satraps appear to have found the temptation of power stronger than patriotism, and the apron strings of the empire were somewhat loosened. But even though the satraps of Asia Minor tended to be less than loyal in the latter days, there was no general disaffection among the satraps.

Fourth, a few of the last kings lacked the good qualities of Cyrus the Great and Darius I and proved incapable of the tasks of administration required of them.

Fifth, apparently the reason for the collapse of the Persian Empire was primarily military. As Fine has said, "The empire did not decay or break up: it was assassinated."[8] What, then, were the military reasons for Persia's demise?

1. Darius III was an incompetent soldier, a "military nincompoop," according to Fine,[9] who was pitted against Alexander, one of the greatest generals of all time.

2. The battle strategy of the Persians centered too much on the king, both on his conduct and his instructions. Thus, when Darius III fled the field at Issus and Gaugamela, battles whose outcome had until then been uncertain became a rout.

3. The military techniques of the Persians were "obsolete."[10] They continued with the same battle tactics in 331 that they had used a century or two earlier. Usually the Persians began a battle by having bowmen and slingers discharge their deadly missiles, with the aim of throwing the enemy into disarray. Then the Persians sought to crush their opponents through a flank attack of heavily armed men and cavalry. But such a tactic did not work against the infantry units of the fifth and fourth centuries B.C.

This was true because though the Persians used their bows to good advantage, they had inadequate small arms with which to fight in close combat. Moreover, the infantry units now had heavier body armor and helmets and suffered less either from missile attacks or fighting in close combat. Helmets were an exception among the Persians; they wore felt hoods. Finally, though the Persians used cavalry as mobile infantry, they did not have enough of them to protect their infantry against the enemy infantry charges in close formation. In the last battles of the war between the Persians and the Macedonians, the Persian army failed to adjust to the newer battle tactics used by the Greeks and thus were more easily defeated.

What had happened in the military history of the Eastern Mediterranean world was this. The Greek hoplite or infantry tactics became the standard for conducting warfare. Greek mercenaries were employed everywhere as recognized masters of the battlefield—by the Egyptians around 650 B.C., by the Lydians in the sixth century,[11] by the Babylonians in the sixth century,[12] and even by the Persians. The core of the Persian army consisted of 50,000 Greek mercenaries.[13] But these were used against Alexander mostly in the west. The tens of thousands of men massed against Alexander at the battle of Gaugamela were essentially Persian regulars and eastern auxiliaries. Especially, after the end of the Peloponnesian Wars in 404 B.C. a host of unemployed Greek infantrymen were available for hire.

THE CAPITALS AND PALACES OF PERSIA

Susa

Darius I made Susa the administrative capital of the Persian Empire. There, north of the acropolis of Susa, he built a great terrace almost fifty feet high and covering about thirty-five acres. He surrounded the entire city of some 175 acres with a defensive wall and perhaps a moat. North of the palace he erected a great audience hall with columns presumably about sixty-five feet high and topped with capitals in the form of bulls' heads. The palace (arranged around three courts) and the audience hall were decorated with glazed brick panels of lions, winged bulls and griffions, and the famous spearmen of the guard. Many of these the French excavators carted off to the Louvre in Paris, where they are now on display. There we can look at the very scenes

Esther saw when she walked the palace in 479 B.C.

A monumental gatehouse stood to the east of the palace. This measured 131 by 92 feet and had a central room 69 feet square. It was in this area that Mordecai sat (cf., Esther 2:19, 21; 5:9, 13). The Persians commonly used Susa as a capital during the winter months from October to May, and Xerxes held court there. In the summer temperatures grew intolerable—as high as 140° in August—and the king and his court moved to the mountains. Susa (biblical Shushan) was located about 150 miles from the head of the Persian Gulf.

Ecbatana (Achmetha)

Ecbatana, where in the summer of 538 B.C. Cyrus issued the decree permitting the Jews to return to Palestine and rebuild the temple (cf. Ezra 6:2), was located at an altitude of 5,500 feet, about 230 miles southwest of Tehran. This former Median capital often served as the summer residence of the Persian kings. The palace there had been built of cedar and cypress, its exposed parts plated with silver or gold.

Ecbatana (modern Hamadan) enjoyed strategic control over the major east-west route, the High Road, through the central Zagros Mountains. A fertile plain lies to the east of the city, and in ancient times the area was famous for its raising of horses and wheat production. The city served as the satrapal seat of the province of Media during the Achaemenid, Parthian, and Sassanian periods. The tomb of Esther and Mordechai, that may be seen there, probably belong to Jewish figures of about A.D. 400. To date there has been little excavation in the area.

Pasargadae

Cyrus the Great (II) chose Pasargadae (about fifty miles

Palace of Darius at Persepolis, with Egyptian style doors and windows. *Slideco, Tehran*

north of Persepolis) as his capital in 550, and most of the buildings there date from 546 to 530. In later years it served as a religious center and a place for the coronation of Persian kings. The site today consists of four areas: at the north, a sacred precinct; south of that, the citadel; farther south, the palace complex; and southwest of the palace, the tomb of Cyrus II.

In the sacred precinct are two blocks of limestone. One consists of an eight-step staircase and a white limestone block seven feet high and eight feet square. The other may have had a black limestone cap and was almost seven feet high and nine feet square. Some scholars believe that the two blocks of limestone were twin altars to Ahuramazda and Anahita.

The citadel stood on a hill that rose over 160 feet above the plain. A terrace constructed on the hill was 48 feet high and consisted of well-formed limestone blocks fitted together with metal clamps. On this stood a columned hall 82 by 23 feet. Many believe the citadel to have been one of the Persian treasuries.

The palace complex had, first, the residential palace, measuring 250 by 138 feet. This had a brilliantly decorated central hall with five rows of six columns. Side rooms probably served domestic purposes. South of the residential palace stood the audience palace with its central columned hall measuring 106 by 72 feet. One of these columns still stands to a height of 43 feet. The gatehouse was a monumental entrance to the palace area measuring 93 by 83 feet. Between the audience palace and the residential palace stood two pavilions in a park-like setting.

About a mile southwest of the palace area Cyrus II erected his tomb, where his gold coffin was originally placed. Built of white limestone, it consists of a base of six steps, eighteen feet high, on which stands a rectangular gabled mausoleum (now empty) also eighteen feet high.

Persepolis

Persepolis (meaning Persian city) is forty-eight miles south of

Monumental entrance at Persepolis and columns of the Apadana or audience hall, begun by Darius I and completed by Xerxes.

Pasargadae and thirty-five miles northeast of modern Shiraz. The altitude of almost six thousand feet gives it a comfortable climate in the summer months. Darius I began construction there shortly after 520, and for all practical purposes Artaxerxes I completed it about sixty years later. Because Persepolis is so far off the beaten track, it did not serve very well as an administrative center, so many scholars earlier in the twentieth century thought of it primarily as a religious shrine—for the celebration of the new year. But there is currently a tendency to back off that view and simply to treat this great center as a pompous statement of Persian power and wealth.

Darius I designed the structures of Persepolis to stand on a great terrace. Not quite rectangular, this terrace was over 1,400 feet long, about 1,000 feet wide, and 40 feet high, and built of stone blocks bound together by iron bands. A double stairway 24 feet wide with steps only four inches high and easily ascended by mounted horse-men gave access to the platform. At the top of the stairs Xerxes built the Gate of All Nations, 118 feet square, which housed a throne room. At the eastern and western entrances stood pairs of guardian bulls, winged and human-headed.

The audience hall of Apadana was the largest building on the terrace, almost 400 feet square. It consisted of a main hall almost 200 feet on a side, surrounded on three sides by porticoes. A total of 72 columns 62 feet high supported the roof of the structure. The columns were capped by the heads and shoulders of bulls and the walls were made of sundried bricks.

At the southwest corner of the audience hall Darius I built a palace measuring 95 by 131 feet. South of that Xerxes outdid Darius by constructing a palace twice that in size (135 by 187 feet). At the southern edge of the terrace stood the harem and next to it at the southeast corner, the treasury. Three other palaces and the throne hall completed the group of structures at the site.

The approximate spot where Alexander crossed the Dardanelles and invaded the Persian Empire

Three and a half miles north of Persepolis rises a rock cliff (Naqsh-i Rustam). Four tombs of Persian kings were cut into the side of the cliff. Inscriptions identify one of them as the tomb of Darius I. The others are thought to belong to Xerxes, Artaxerxes I, and Darius II.

Alexander the Great and the Persians[14]

It was a May morning in 334 B.C. Alexander's army crossed the narrows of the Dardanelles from Sestos to Abydos with 160 ships. The Persians failed to stop the disembarkation. What would come next?

It is necessary to tell the story of the struggle between Alexander and the Persians in some detail in order to appreciate the generalship of Alexander. An account of what happened during the next four years is significant in the flow of history. If Alexander had lost, Oriental culture would have engulfed the West and the whole history of the world would have been fundamentally different. The Hellenistic culture, which is at the basis of modern Western culture, never would have developed.

As Alexander's forces advanced on that spring morning in 334, the Persian high command held a war council. One urged a scorched earth policy to deny the invaders needed supplies, but the majority decided to fight. They drew up their cavalry units on the banks of the Granicus River (modern Koçabas Çay) that flows north into the Sea of Marmara. Behind the cavalry stood Greek mercenaries from towns opposed to Macedonia. Alexander's men would have to ford the river (possible in the spring when the water level was down) and ascend the slippery bank to attack the enemy. How many the Persians commanded differs from source to source—but not over 20,000 cavalry and a like number of infantry. Though the day was growing late, Alexander decided to attack without delay.

With a blare of trumpets and a fierce battle cry Alexander launched a feint attack at the Persian center, drawing some of the Persian cavalry down into the water. Then he sent his elite cavalry units out to the right to outflank the Persians and attack them from the side. At one point a group of Persian officers tried to close in on Alexander, and one of them used his scimitar to split Alexander's helmet and penetrated to his scalp. Eight of the Persian commanders were cut down, including Darius' son, brother-in-law, and son-in-law. The Persian cavalry retreated and left their infantry standing there in astonishment. In the bitter conflict that followed, losses among the Persian infantry were heavy, and the survivors were captured and sent off to Thrace to work in the mines. Persian losses were comparatively heavy but figures vary in the sources.

The victory opened up the Ionian coast to Alexander. Here at the battle site of the ancient road along the Sea of Marmara joins the route that runs south to Sardis. As Alexander took that road, Sardis surrendered and welcomed him. This was the main center of the Persian Empire in the west—the terminus of the Royal Road from Susa in Iran. But not all cities along the route welcomed the Macedonian. He had to fight to bring Miletus in line. And at Halicarnassus (Bodrum), the Persians' main base in southwest Anatolia, he had to fight Memnon, the commander of Persian western operations and his mercenary forces. It was touch and go for a few days, but finally Memnon evacuated his force and supplies by sea in the middle of the night. When Alexander awoke in the morning he was greeted by the smoke of burning supplies that Memnon had been unable to move. Alexander now continued on his way, marching along the southwest coast, through Caria and Lycia.

In the spring of 333, after over thirty cities had surrendered to Alexander in Lycia, he ascended the Anatolian plateau and made his way toward Ankara. En route he passed through Gordion and cut the Gordion knot (See chapter on Asia Minor). Finally he came down from the plateau of central Anatolia through the Cilician Gates, thirty-eight miles north of modern Adana, into Tarsus. The gates (the pass) are about a hundred yards in length, and the rocks rise sharply on both sides to a maximum height of six hundred feet. At Tarsus Alexander fell ill, perhaps with malaria, and some around him despaired of his life. But he recovered and in late October moved into the narrow plain between the Amanus Mountains and the sea—into the plain of Issus. During that year the Macedonian had marched through an area equivalent in size to the northeastern United States, from Maine south to Virginia.

At Tarsus Alexander learned that his intelligence corps had failed him and that Darius had come around behind him and cut off his line of retreat. That was not all bad, however, because now Darius would have to fight him on a narrow front where Persian cavalry could not be deployed to very great advantage. In the plains of Issus the river Pinarus cuts across the plain to the sea. Darius deployed his forces along the northern side of the river. In the center he stationed his Greek mercenary infantry; on his left, light armed troops; on his right, along the shore, the Persian cavalry. Alexander placed his heavy infantry in the center; the Macedonian and Thessalian cavalry on the right under his command; on the left, some allied cavalry. Later he moved the Thessalian cavalry to his left.

As the battle began, Alexander made a sudden charge through the stream against the Persian left, which collapsed. Then Alexander made a dash straight for Darius and came close to him. Several of the Persian commanders near the king were killed in defending him. At that point Alexander's center experienced difficulty, so he left off fighting Darius and attacked the enemy in the flank. In the process Alexander saved the day. Meanwhile Darius, whose chariot horses had been wounded and were starting to panic, mounted a fresh horse and fled the field. With the king gone there was pandemonium on the battlefield. Casualty figures among the Persians ran high. including about sixty thousand infantry and ten thousand horses; some forty thousand were captured. Alexander's army lost only a few hundred.

But that doesn't tell the real story of what happened. First, though there may be a debate over casualty figures, the Persians had in effect lost an entire army. Second, the Persian royal family fell into Alexander's hands. Two efforts of Darius III to ransom them drew no response from Alexander. Neither did Darius' offer to give Alexander the whole western part of the empire. Third, and closely related, it now became clear that Alexander could take the entire

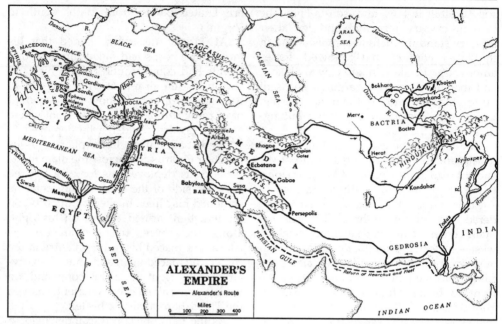

Alexander the Great built on the earlier Greek foundation when he conquered the whole area from the Mediterranean to the Indus. He and his successors strengthened the widespread hold of Greek culture.

empire. Fourth, Alexander had been in serious financial straits before the battle. Now, with the capture of untold wealth in the Persian camp, he could pay his men and finance the war effort. As an aside, a mosaic representation of the Battle of Issus turned up in the excavations of Pompeii. It is thought to be a faithful representation of a fourth century B.C. painting. Darius would have about two years to build a new army and prepare to meet Alexander one more time.

Meanwhile, Alexander marched south to take Phoenicia, Syria, Palestine, and Egypt. He experienced no serious opposition except at Tyre, where the Tyrians held him at bay for seven months, during 332 B.C., until he destroyed the proud city. Of special importance among his activities in Egypt was his founding of the city of Alexandria—destined to be the greatest city of the eastern Mediterranean for many centuries.

Finally, in the spring of 331 B.C., Alexander was ready to advance against Darius III himself. The route took him through Damascus, Aleppo, Thapsacus

(modern Dibse, biblical Tiphsah, 1 Kings 4:24—border of Solomon's empire, on the Euphrates), Nisibis or Nusaybin (now in southeastern Turkey); and he forded the Tigris northwest of Mosul just after the middle of September.

Darius prepared to meet Alexander near the small town of Gaugamela, east of the Tigris. The number of men Alexander had under his command apparently was about forty thousand infantry and seven thousand cavalry.[15] Darius presumably had a cavalry force of some thirty-four thousand, five times as many as Alexander.[16] It is impossible to determine the size of his infantry units, however. The lowest estimate in the sources is 200,000, but that appears to be much too high. Marsden observes that it doesn't matter how many there were because Darius determined to pin all his hopes on the cavalry, to put all his eggs in one basket, and did not try to use the infantry, even in the most critical stages of the battle.[17]

Darius had not only been gathering men from the whole eastern part of the empire, all the way to the Indus Valley and beyond, but he also had been introducing innovations. These included, especially, longer spears and one hundred scythed chariots (chariots that had scythes attached to their wheels so as to terrify and cut down the infantry of the opposition). Before the battle Darius practiced a scorched-earth policy to deny the Greeks supplies or even housing. He worked at preparing the battleground—leveling it to give his chariots maximum advantage against the Macedonian infantry units.

As the battle was about to begin on October 1, the Persian cavalry line extended well beyond the Macedonian line on both wings. To counter this, Alexander stationed his infantry in the middle and his cavalry on both wings in an echelon or steplike fashion; that is, with units arranged to appear like steps leading away from the Persian line. Then he placed a reserve of infantry in the rear with instructions to face about to meet any threat from behind in the event of encirclement.

Early in the battle the Persian cavalry launched an attack on Alexander's right and subsequently a gap opened in Alexander's advancing infantry line. Persian cavalry broke through to the Macedonian baggage train. Then the Persian cavalry swept around Alexander's left. It sounds as if the Persians were having it all their way. But when Alexander's situation looked particularly black, a gap opened in the Persian line and Alexander launched a fierce attack of cavalry and infantry through it. Darius himself was suddenly exposed and his center gave way. The commander on the Persian left sounded the retreat. Darius fled the field as he had at Issus. Persian troops who in their overconfidence had been attacking the Macedonian baggage train found that they were wasting precious energy. Though the battle was essentially over when Darius left, fierce fighting continued for several hours. And while Macedonian casualties numbered only a few hundred, the Persians lost thousands. The actual number of casualties is unknown.

The scythed chariots had proved to be a non-weapon. When they attacked the Macedonian line at full speed, the Macedonians simply let them through and closed ranks behind them once more. Of course the Greeks were able to kill many of the drivers, but then the horses careened about—a danger to both Greeks and Persians.

Darius III for his part managed to collect numerous survivors and flee eastward through the Armenian Mountains to Ecbatana (Hamadan) in Media. In the process he abandoned Babylon and the rest of Mesopotamia and Susa, the winter capital by the Persian Gulf. Reports tended to exaggerate Persian losses and underestimated Macedonian casualties at Gaugamela. With Darius fled the nucleus of his royal guard and what was left of his mercenary army. Subsequently the commander Bessus and his cavalry, more or less intact, joined the king. Many other survivors simply dispersed—probably finding their way home. Alexander's victory at Gaugamela ended the threat of Persian domination of the civilized world. Gaugamela was certainly one of the most important battles of all time, for it determined whether Oriental or Hellenistic culture was to dominate Western civilization.

A couple of days after Gaugamela, Alexander left for the march to Babylon. During the more than three weeks he was on the way, negotiations were in process for its peaceful surrender, along with the treasury. He left the Persian satrap, Mazaeus, in control in Babylon when he continued on his way after a month of rest.

Near the end of November 331, Alexander began his march to Susa, the occupancy of which was assured through negotiations. Again the treasury was impounded and held for him. Meanwhile fifteen thousand fresh troops had arrived from Macedonia and Thrace.

Alexander now fought his way into Persis with its great center of Persepolis. Again he got hold of the treasury with its incredible hoard of gold and silver. But this time he let his men loot and sack the homes of the Persian nobility. Evidently he sought to placate the army, who up to this point had had to look on helplessly while he impounded the treasures of the empire. They justified the looting as an act of revenge, presumably as a reprisal for Xerxes' destruction at Athens. At nearby Pasargadae (forty-eight miles northeast of Persepolis) Alexander showed respect for the monuments, especially for the tomb of Cyrus there. But there was no mercy shown to Persepolis, where the magnificent palace was torched in the spring of 330 B.C.

Meanwhile Darius waited at the old Median capital of Ecbatana. He had a plan to stage one last defense but he had too few forces with him. So he withdrew to the eastern satrapies. Alexander now abandoned his plan to take Ecbatana and pursued Darius before he could muster a fighting force. At this point internal dissension arose in the Persian camp, accompanied by increasing demoralization. Finally word came that Bessus had arrested Darius and he was being transported as a prisoner in chains. As the Macedonians closed in, the royal captors stabbed the king and went their separate ways to their satrapies. The murder took place near Hecatompylus, in northeast Iran at the foot of the south slope of the Elburz Mountains. Alexander took the body of Darius to Persepolis for burial. The last Achaemenid king was dead.

After that various groups capitulated to Alexander. But the peace was temporary. Not only was there a conspiracy within his own camp but also a decision on the part of Bessus, the satrap of Bactria, to take the kingship for himself. After Alexander put down the conspiracy, he took out after Bessus, who had proclaimed himself Artaxerxes V. Alexander put forth the propaganda that his quarrel was with Bessus alone and managed to persuade Bessus' supporters to surrender him. Alexander brought the Persian back to Ecbatana and had him executed there.

Alexander campaigned in Central Asia from 329 to 327 and in the Indus Valley in 326 and 325. Returning to Mesopotamia in 324, he addressed the various administrative challenges before him. As a means of placating his men, he arranged a great wedding ceremony at Susa in which ten thousand Macedonian soldiers formalized their unions with native women and the senior officers took noble Persian brides. Alexander himself had married a daughter

of Darius III. Then in 324 he faced a great personnel need and organized an ethnically mixed military system, incorporating Macedonians and Iranians. The Macedonians mutinied, and he faced them down at Opis on the Tigris in 324. Finally in 323, in the midst of plans for conquests in Arabia, he fell ill and died at Babylon on June 10, 323 B.C. Why he died continues to be debated—whether it was from malaria or another tropical disease, perhaps complicated by too much drink, or from the continued effects of a recently sustained chest wound, or from poison. Evidence of foul play is usually thought to be negligible.

The Seleucids

In any event, Alexander was gone. He had not had time to build an imperial organization, and the extent of his administrative capabilities if he had lived is unknown. Presumably they were considerable, if his military logistical system is any indication. With Alexander out of the way, his generals and other members of his entourage began jockeying for power.

For about fifty years after the death of Alexander, his empire was torn by the efforts of his ambitious generals to become supreme. At first they united under the titular headship of Alexander's half-witted brother Philip and Alexander's posthumous son, both of whom were killed by 310 B.C. Eventually the empire was divided into three large states and a number of smaller ones. The larger ones were Macedonia, Egypt (the Ptolemaic Empire), and the Seleucid territories (Syria, Mesopotamia, and Iran).

Seleucus, one of Alexander's generals, after numerous difficulties managed to conquer the whole of Iran as far as the Indus River (311–302) and to extend his domains to include most of the old Persian Empire. He founded a new capital, Seleucia-on-the-Tigris, as well as numerous other Greek towns. These cities became outposts of Hellenic life in Oriental territory, as they were populated by a ruling clique of Greeks and a Hellenized native element. Greek towns in Iran included Susa and Hamadan. As they built the Greek towns, Seleucus and his son, Antiochus I (281–261 B.C.),

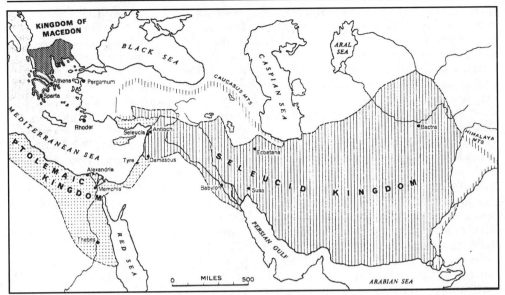

The partitioning of Alexander's Empire

tried to foster an image of tolerance and support for local beliefs and traditions, but also a dynastic link with the god Apollo. Antiochus also moved the capital to Antioch-on-the-Orontes, destined to become the birthplace of Christian missions in the days of the apostle Paul. The shift of the capital was designed to facilitate the struggle with the Ptolemies in the west.

The Seleucid dynasty produced over two dozen kings and many usurpers. Under Seleucus I (312–281) their empire stretched from Anatolia to Afghanistan. Thereafter occurred a slow dissolution of their vast state with the rise of many local dynasties in areas such as Bactria and Parthia in the east and Pergamon in the west.

During the third century B.C., while Seleucid attention was especially diverted to the struggle with the Ptolemies, trouble was brewing in the east. Andragora, the Greek satrap of Parthia, declared his independence from the Seleucids in 245. For the rest of the century Seleucids and Parthians fought, with the Seleucids generally gaining the upper hand. But probably the Parthians enjoyed local autonomy under Seleucid rule.

Then, after Antiochus III (223–187 B.C.) met his great defeat at the hands of the Romans at the Battle of Magnesia (in Asia Minor) in 190 B.C., Seleucia was weakened and the rise and expansion of the Parthian Empire began. But Parthian expansion was slow in the west and the struggle with the Seleucids did not give the upper hand to the Parthians until 141 B.C. Thereafter the Seleucids also continued to suffer internal dissension. Not the least of their problems had been the Maccabean War, that resulted in the independence of Palestine in 142 B.C. (See the chapter on Palestine.) Finally the Roman general Pompey took what was left of the Seleucid kingdom in 64 B.C. and annexed it to the Roman Empire.

The Parthians and Rome

Meanwhile the Parthians continued to gain power in the East. Mithridates I (171–137 B.C.) gradually conquered Media and Mesopotamia. And by the time of his death he had established an empire that extended from eastern Bactria to Mesopotamia. Though his successors had difficulty keeping hold of all that territory, Mithridates II (124–87) saved the empire. He also moved north into Armenia and there came into conflict with Rome. Moreover, Mithridates enjoyed control of the Silk Road, which passed through his lands, connecting Rome with China. Thus the Parthians profited from the overland trade and the growing demand of Rome for luxury goods from the Orient. Mithridates' successor, Orodes II, faced a major conflict with Rome and in 53 B.C. wiped out a Roman army under the command of Crassus at Carrhae (biblical Harran) in southeastern Turkey. The Romans were no match for the Parthian cavalry. The Euphrates came to be recognized as the frontier between the two powers.

In succeeding decades the internal politics of Parthia were complicated by numerous contenders for the throne and rebellions of sorts. Yet externally Parthia was still able to stand up to Rome. And they occupied Palestine briefly from 40 to 37 B.C. during the Roman civil wars (At this stage the struggle was between Mark Antony and Octavian and Herod the Great was rising to power). A conflict between Rome and Parthia over Armenia terminated with a peace treaty in A.D. 63. In A.D. 114 Trajan invaded Armenia and Mesopotamia, but his successor Hadrian concluded a peace treaty with Parthia. There were subsequent minor struggles between the two powers, but major conflicts erupted again during the reign of Septimius Severus (A.D. 193–211) and Caracalla in 216–218. The treaty arranged in A.D. 218 ended the last brush that Rome had with the Parthians.

The Sassanids

The Parthian dynasty came to an end in 224, to be succeeded by over 400 years of Sassanid rule in Iran (A.D. 226–651). During the Sassanid period there was a continual struggle between the Byzantine Empire (the continuing Roman Empire) and the Persians.

But we should not discuss this era, with its interminable warfare, as boring and unimportant. It holds great significance for us today. The constant struggle, especially in the seventh century during the reign of the Byzantine emperor Heraclius (A.D. 610–641), exhausted both the Byzantines (Christians) and the Persians (Zorastrians) and created a power vacuum in the Near East. Those were the days of Mohammed (died A.D. 632). Muslim Arabs charged into this power vacuum, conquering in the name of Allah. They took Damascus in 635, Palestine in 638, Mesopotamia and Egypt in 635–641. And they kept on going across North Africa and into Europe. There was really no stopping them. Though they have suffered setbacks, they have continued to increase in numbers until there are now over one billion, two hundred million of them worldwide—one-fifth of the world's population and growing. Politically they dominate about forty countries. Think of how different the religious and political history of the world might be if there had been no weak spot where the Muslims could drive a wedge and establish themselves!

NOTES

1. James B. Pritchard, ed. *Ancient Near Eastern Texts Relating to the Old Testament*, 2nd ed. (Princeton: Princeton University Press, 1955), 316.

2. J. M. Cook, *The Persian Empire* (New York: Schocken, 1983), 49.

3. Cook, *The Persian Empire*, 49–50.

4. A. T. Olmstead, *History of the Persian Empire* (Chicago: University of Chicago Press, 1948), 108–9.

5. See Olmstead, *Persian Empire*, 304–7, 313–17; Gleason Archer Jr., *A Survey of Old Testament Introduction*, rev. ed. (Chicago: Moody, 1994), 457; Jack Finegan, *Light from the Ancient Past*, 2nd ed. (Princeton: Princeton University Press, 1959), 238.

6. Archer, *Old Testament*, 479.

7. S. E. Finer, *The History of Government* (Oxford: Oxford University Press, 1997), I, 310.

8. Ibid., 311.

9. Ibid., 313.

10. Ibid., 311.

11 King Croesus of Lydia might have defeated Cyrus in 547 B.C. if he had not sent his Greek mercenaries away for the winter, Finer, *History of Government*, 311.

12. Critics sometimes claim that Greek words appearing in Daniel 3:5 are an argument for a late date of the prophecy, after the days of Alexander the Great. But Greek mercenaries and musical instruments were current in the Semitic Near East long before the time of Daniel. See Archer, *Old Testament*, 431.

13. Cook, *The Persian Empire*, 226.

14. Further discussion of Alexander's invasion of Asia appears in the chapter on Greece.

15. E. W. Marsden, *The Campaign of Gaugamela* (Liverpool: Liverpool University Press, 1964, 24.

16. Ibid., 37.

17. Ibid., 34.

BIBLIOGRPAHY

Barthold, W. *An Historical Geography of Iran.* Princeton: Princeton University Press, 1984.

Boardman, John. *Persia and the West,* London: Thames and Hudson, 2000.

Bosworth, A. B. *Conquest and Empire: The Reign of Alexander the Great.* Cambridge: Cambridge University Press, 1988.

Briant, Pierre. *From Cyrus to Alexander.* Winona Lake, IN: Eisenbrauns, 2002.

Brinkman, J. A. *Materials and Studies for Kassite History,* Vol. I. Chicago: the Oriental Institute.

Cameron, George G. "Darius Carved History on Ageless Rock," *National Geographic,* December 1950.

Cameron, George G. *History of Early Iran.* New York: Greenwood Press, 1968.

Collins, Robert. *The Medes and Persians.* New York: McGraw-Hill., n.d.

Coogan, Michael D., ed. *The Oxford History of the Biblical World.* Oxford: Oxford University Press, 1998.

Cook, John M. *The Persian Empire.* New York: Schocken Books, 1983.

Culican, William. *The Medes and Persians.* New York: Frederick A. Praeger, 1965.

Curtis, John, ed. *Later Mesopotamia and Iran.* London: British Museum Press, 1995.

Curtis, John, ed. *Mesopotamia and Iran in the Parthian and Sasanian Periods.* London: British Museum Press, 2000.

De Gobineau, J. A. *The World of the Persians.* Geneva: Minerva, 1971.

Finer, S. E. *The History of Government.* Oxford: Oxford University Press, Vol. I, 1997.

Fraser, P. M. *Cities of Alexander the Great.* Oxford: Clarendon Press, 1996.

Frye, Richard N. *The Heritage of Persia.* New York: New American Library, 1963.

Ghirsham, R. *Iran.* Baltimore: Penguin Books, 1954.

Green, Peter. *The Greco-Persian Wars.* Berkeley: University of California Press, 1996.

Harper, Prudence O., and others, eds. *The Royal City of Susa.* New York: Metropolitan Museum of Art, 1992.

Head, Duncan. *The Achaemenid Persian Army.* Stockport, SK, England: Montvert Publications, 1992.

Hole, Frank, ed. *The Archaeology of Western Iran.* Washington, DC: Smithsonian Institution Press, 1987.

Marsden, E. W. *The Campaign of Gaugamela.* Liverpool: Liverpool University Press, 1964.

Matheson, Sylvia. *Persia: An Archeological Guide.* London: Faber and Faber, 1972.

Montagu, John D. *Battles of the Greek and Roman Worlds.* Mechanicsburg, PA: Stackpole Books, 2000.

Olmstead, A. T. *History of the Persian Empire.* Chicago: University of Chicago Press, 1948.

Potts, Daniel T. *The Archaeology of Elam.* Cambridge: Cambridge University Press, 1999.

Rolle, Renate. *The World of the Scythians.* London: B. T. Batsford, 1989.

Sekunda, Nick and Simon Chew. *The Persian Army 560–330 B.C.* London: Osprey Publishing, 1992.

Stronach, David. *Pasargadae.* Oxford: Clarendon Press, 1978.

Suse Derneres Decouvertes in Dossiers Histoire et Archeologie, No. 138, May 1989.

Vos, Howard F. *Ezra, Nehemiah, and Esther.* Grand Rapids: Zondervan, 1987.

Whitcomb, John C. *Darius the Mede.* Philadelphia: Presbyterian and Reformed, 1963.

Wiesehöfer, Josef. *Ancient Persia.* London: I. B. Tauris, 1996.

Wilber, Donald N. *Persepolis.* New York: Thomas Y. Crowell, 1969.

Wood, Michael. *In the Footsteps of Alexander the Great.* Berkeley: University of California Press, 1997.

Yamauchi, Edwin M. *Persia and the Bible.* Grand Rapids: Baker, 1990.

The gymnasium at Salamis

7

CYPRUS

A Missionary Journey to Cyprus

The year was probably A.D. 45. The Church at Antioch of Syria was now thriving. A year of concentrated effort there on the part of Barnabas and Saul had been most fruitful (Acts 11:26). Spiritually responsive, the Christian community at Antioch felt an obligation to share the gospel with others who had not been so fortunate as they. And under the direction of the Holy Spirit, this church sent off the apostles on the first of the most remarkable series of missionary journeys on record. John Mark was their companion (Acts 13:5).[1]

Whether the trio took the road to Seleucia, the port of Antioch sixteen miles away, or a small skiff down the Orontes River and then north five miles along the coast to Seleucia, is unknown. At any rate, they reached the port and took passage on a ship bound for Cyprus.

Though there were a few ships in the Mediterranean with a regular schedule or prescribed routes, such scheduled ships seem to have been rare. Generally eastern merchants "tramped" from port to port with whatever cargo seemed to promise the best profits. Probably the ship on which Barnabas and Saul sailed was the common "tramp" vessel.

More than likely the time was late spring or early summer when the missionaries set sail for Cyprus. The sailing season in the Mediterranean ran from April to November. And it is reasonable to believe that Barnabas, Saul, and John Mark, who had recently returned from delivering a collection for the poor at Jerusalem (Acts 12:25), would have remained in the holy city until after Passover. Allowing time for the church at Antioch to receive the report from Jerusalem and prepare to send off the trio, late spring would seem to be the earliest that the group could depart. A sailing date of late summer or fall would have necessitated beginning a trip just before the inclement winter weather; therefore it is highly unlikely that they would have started so late.

Roman Ships

The kind of ship on which the missionary party sailed is unknown. The freighters that carried official government cargoes during the first century A.D. were commonly 340 tons. Those of Rome's grain fleet ran to 1,200 tons and were sometimes almost 200 feet long. Since there is no indication that this ship carried government cargo, it may well have been smaller than 340 tons. Generally ships of the period carried a square sail, above which was a topsail, and at least a few oars for emergency or auxiliary work. Some freighters were designed to be driven by sail and rowers together.

A typical Roman merchant vessel with foresail and topsail, a goose-headed sternpost ornament, and steering oar.

Merchantmen were fairly beamy: a length to beam ratio of four to one was common. Freighters generally had a cabin aft and above deck—big enough for the captain and his mates. Passengers lived and slept on deck. They brought their own food, and their servants might use the galley to prepare it. If they wanted some privacy or protection from the elements, they could have erected a tentlike shelter. Behind the cabin rose the sternpost, which was generally carried high and finished off in the shape of a goose head.

As to building materials, the planks of the hull were constructed of pine, fir, or cedar, depending on what was available. Inside the ship any kind of wood might have been used; fir was preferred for oars because of its light weight. Sails were chiefly made of linen, and ropes of flax, hemp, papyrus, or sometimes leather. Often the underwater surface of the hull was sheathed with sheet lead; in such cases it was the practice to put a layer of tarred fabric between the hull and the lead. Ships were brightly painted in purple, blue, white, yellow, green, or red—unless they were pirate or reconnaissance vessels, in which case they would be painted with a shade that matched sea water and served as a camouflage. As to speed, merchantmen averaged four-to-six knots.[2] So the journey between Seleucia and Salamis on Cyprus

would have taken about twenty-four hours, with a favorable wind. The distance from Seleucia to the eastern tip of Cyprus is about eighty miles and it is another fifty along the southern shore of the Karpas Peninsula to Salamis.[3]

Reason for Missionary Work

Why Barnabas, Saul, and John Mark went to Cyprus is not hard to discern. Barnabas himself was a native of Cyprus (Acts 4:36) and could be expected to have an interest in the evangelization of his Jewish kinsmen there. Moreover, Jews of Cyprus had been partially responsible for sparking a revival at Antioch (Acts 11:20–21). No doubt the Antiochian church, which had now become quite large, felt an obligation to send Christian workers to Cyprus. Since Barnabas and Saul had accomplished such a remarkable ministry in Antioch (where Barnabas had been sent by the Jerusalem church), it seemed only logical that these men would be entrusted with further evangelistic and supervisory work. Who better could be sent to Cyprus than these experienced leaders—one of whom was a native of the island?

That the gospel message preceded Barnabas and Saul to Cyprus by some years is evident from passages such as Acts 11:19, which declares that the persecution arising at the time of the martyrdom of Stephen scattered a number of converts to Cyprus. Stephen's martyrdom occurred shortly after the Pentecost of Acts 2. Perhaps these early Christians on Cyprus appealed to Antioch for help—with the result that Barnabas and Saul went to them.

NOT MANY NOBLE?

Saul is first called Paul in connection with the interview with the governor of Cyprus (Acts 13:6-12). This was his first significant Gentile contact and the first use of his Greek name. It is also noteworthy that Sergius Paulus, the governor, believed in Christ. Later the ruler of the synagogue in Corinth did also (Acts 18:8), as did a member of the

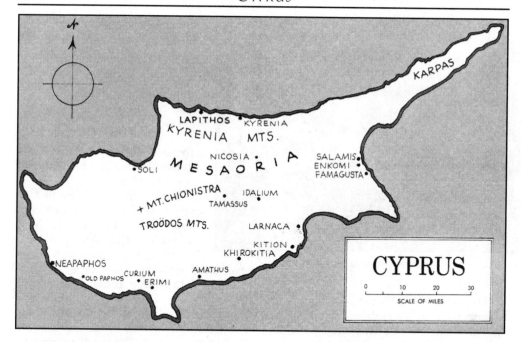

prestigious Areopagus Council in Athens (Acts 17:34). Other examples of outstanding, or upper-class, individuals coming to faith in Christ could be given.

We should not fall into the mistaken view of some that only the poorest or most insignificant members of society constituted the church in the early days. Christians often quote 1 Corinthians 1:26 to prove that not many wise, mighty, or noble are called to faith, and that the church therefore consisted mostly or almost exclusively of the poor, slaves, and others of the lower classes of society.

Magnitude of Task

The task of evangelizing the Jews on Cyprus was a substantial one, as is shown by evidence of large numbers of Jews on the island. Apparently the first Jews were brought to Cyprus by Ptolemy Soter, who is reported after the capture of Jerusalem in 320 B.C. to have transported large numbers of them to Egypt and other parts of his dominions.[4] Many more came to the island just before the birth of Christ with the hope

of employment in the copper mines, which at one time were assigned to Herod the Great.[5] That the number of Jews on Cyprus was large in the middle of the first century A.D. is indicated by events of the early second century. In A.D. 116 a Jewish revolt spread over the eastern Mediterranean world; and according to Dio Cassius, Jews killed 240,000 of their fellow citizens on Cyprus alone.[6] Even if this figure is exaggerated, as is very likely, atrocities of such approximate magnitude would require a considerable Jewish population. In retaliation, imperial forces killed thousands of Jews, and the rest were banished from the island. For centuries thereafter no Jew was allowed on Cyprus.

Geographical Features

Location and Size

Cyprus is the third largest island of the Mediterranean Sea. Exceeded in size only by Sicily and Sardinia, it has an area of 3,572 square miles—a little less than that of Delaware and Rhode Island combined. Located in the extreme northeast corner of the Mediterranean, Cyprus can be seen from both Asia Minor and Syria on a clear day. The former distance is about 43 miles

The Kyrenia Mountains

and the latter about 75. Between Egypt and Cyprus the distance is about 265 miles. It is therefore easy to see why cultural influences from Asia Minor and Syria were felt on Cyprus long before those of Egypt.

As to shape, Cyprus is sometimes likened to a silhouetted wheelbarrow being pushed along. The long Karpas Peninsula represents the handles, and the Akrotiri Peninsula to the south, the wheels. In ancient times it was compared to a deerskin or bullock's hide spread out on the ground. The tail is represented by the Karpas Peninsula and the legs by four large promontories. The greatest length of the island is 138 miles and the greatest width 60 miles. Subtracting the approximately 40-mile-long Karpas Peninsula, Cyprus averages some 90–100 miles in length. The total coastline is 486 miles.

Mountains

The surface of Cyprus is almost evenly divided between mountain and plain. The mountains divide into two ranges: the Kyrenia, or Northern, Range and the Troodos Range in the southwest. The gray-pink limestone Kyrenia Range extends along the whole of the northern coast some three miles from the coast and rises to a height of two-to-three thousand feet. Highest of the several peaks of this range is Akromandra, 3,433 feet in altitude. Conveniently, three gaps pierce this range:

Panagra in the west, Kyrenia in the center, and Akanthou in the east. The Kyrenia Range tends to force the moisture from the vapor-laden winds from the north, providing sufficient moisture for the fertile coastal plain. The seaward slopes of the Kyrenia Mountains are profusely covered with trees (especially olive in modern times), shrubs, and flowers; the southern slopes are often bare.

Most of the southern half of Cyprus consists of a confusion of steep-sided mountain ridges, arrayed in such tangled profusion that it is almost impossible to discover any backbone or watershed. Several of the peaks of these Troodos Mountains rise more than 4,500 feet. The highest is Chionistra, or Olympus (6,404 feet). White limestone plateaus occupy the area south of the Troodos massif. These fall in steplike fashion as they approach the southern coast. In places they become sea cliffs, but occasionally they recede to allow small coastal plains with rich alluvial soil.

The Central Plain

Between the two mountain ranges lies a broad plain, almost sixty miles long and twelve-to-twenty-five miles broad. This divides into two parts: Mesaoria on the east and Morphou on the west. The granary of the island, this plain also produces substantial quantities of vegetables and fruit. Though now nearly treeless except for the few trees recently planted, it was in ancient times heavily forested. Through this plain flow the two chief rivers of Cyprus—the Pedias (ancient Pediaeus) and Yalias (ancient Idalia), which used to dump their waters into the Mediterranean near ancient Salamis on the east coast. Now reservoirs tap most of their water before it reaches the Mediterranean. During the rainy season these are fairly substantial streams, but they are dry during the summer season.

Rainfall and Climate

Rainfall occurs mainly from December to February, but the amount is not large. The main agricultural areas receive only

A copper mine in the Troodos Mountains.

twelve-to-sixteen inches per year. Even this amount comes irregularly, and serious droughts occur on the average of every ten years. And since high evaporation involves considerable loss, the supply of water presents a serious problem. Visitors to Cyprus become aware of how acute the problem is when they read a sign in their hotel room urging them to inform the management at once of any leaky or defective plumbing for the purpose of conserving water.

It is easy to guess from what has been said about rainfall that prolonged drizzling from gray skies is rare in Cyprus even during the rainy season—when the sun usually shines for at least some part of every day. The climate is very healthy, and the death rate is one of the lowest in the world. The growing season roughly corresponds with the rainy season, and crops are harvested by March or April. During the summer and early fall, when there is rarely any rainfall, the fields give an appearance of aridity.

Forests

Forests were once one of the main resources of Cyprus; and her timber, so important for shipbuilding, was much sought after by the ancient imperial powers of the Mediterranean area. Actually, however, more trees were felled for copper and silver smelting than for shipbuilding. Eratosthenes, Greek astronomer and geographer of the third century B.C., talks of the plains as being "formerly full of wood run to riot, choked in fact with undergrowth and uncultivated."[7] The famous cedars have almost disappeared, but there are considerable stands of Aleppo and black pine. The main forests today occupy a good part of the Kyrenia Range, the Karpas Peninsula, and the Troodos mass. These forests occupy some nineteen percent of the total land area.

Mineral Deposits

More important than timber to the economy of Cyprus in antiquity was her production of copper. In fact, so extensive was the island's export of this mineral that copper obtained its name from the name of Cyprus. The English word *copper* is derived from the Greek name of the island, Kypros, through the Latin *cuprum*. Produced as early as the third millennium B.C.,[8] copper has continued to be mined extensively into modern times.

The Asy from which Thutmose III obtained his copper shortly after 1500 B.C. is often identified with Cyprus.[9] The island's copper, which was shipped all over the Mediterranean world in ancient times in the form of both ore and ingots, came from the foothills of the Troodos, especially along the southern coast and at Tamassus, southwest of Nicosia. To gain some understanding of the extent of the copper deposits on Cyprus and the extent of trade in the commodity over the millennia, it is helpful to note that Cypriot copper exports during the fiscal year ending in A.D. 1960 totaled 430,000 long tons.[10] But in 2001 copper mining is virtually non-existent, and all Cypriots working in all types of mining total less than 600.

Though iron was mined on Cyprus in antiquity, the extent is in question. In modern times iron production has sometimes outstripped copper production. Gold and silver were also mined on the island in ancient times. The mining of silver there is thought to account for the large issues of silver coinage in the Ptolemaic Age.[11]

An important source of income that is rarely mentioned, and one that must have flourished in ancient times, is the salt industry. There are two main natural salt lakes in Cyprus: Larnaca Salt Lake (1.5 miles southwest of Larnaca) and Akrotiri Salt Lake (10 miles southwest of Limassol on the Akrotiri peninsula). The former covers about 2.4 square miles and the latter 4.4 square miles. The Larnaca salt is of higher quality. Salt can be "mined" or "harvested" in July when the lakes dry up and a compact crust forms over the dry beds.

Historical Development

Early Biblical Connections

While it would be easy to assume that Cyprus appears in the biblical drama only briefly in connection with the first and second missionary journeys of Paul, deeper probing indicates that such is not the case. In the Old Testament there are several references to biblical Kittim, or Chittim (anc. Citium e.g., Genesis 10:4; Numbers 24:24; Isaiah 23:1, 12; Jeremiah 2:10; Ezekiel 27:6; Daniel 11:30). Admittedly this is a word with somewhat general significance, referring to various islands and coasts of the Mediterranean. But the term did have some specific application to Cyprus. The city of Kition (Citium), on the southeast coast of Cyprus, and a center of Phoenician influence, gradually gave its name to the whole of the island. The Phoenicians referred to Cyprians as "Kitti."

The first biblical reference to Kittim occurs in Genesis 10:4, where its association with Javan (Ionia), Elishah (Alashiya), and Dodanim (or Rodanim, Rhodes, 1 Chronicles 1:7) seems to point to a Greek connection. It is not necessary to conclude, however, that therefore it could have no connection with Cyprus. The influence on Cyprus has always been largely Greek, and the earliest foreign migration there seems to have come from Asia Minor, where Greek culture appeared very early. Josephus, the famous first century Jewish historian, definitely identified the "Kittim" of Genesis 10:4 as Cyprus.[12]

Neolithic Beginnings

The earliest known inhabitants of Cyprus (pre-Neolithic) are now dated to about 10,000 B.C. and are thought to have come from Asia Minor. This stone-age culture has appeared at only one site, Aetokremnos on the Akrotiri peninsula at the southern tip of the island.[13]

But remains of the pre-pottery Neolithic stage (c. 7000–5500 B.C.) are considerable, having been found at over twenty-five sites on Cyprus. This stage was first discovered at Khirokitia, about thirty miles south of Nicosia and four miles from the sea, and is still the most representative settlement of the group. At nearly all of these sites there was adequate water supply and arable land in the area. And they were easily accessible from the coast. At Khirokitia the circular, domed huts were built on foundations of river stones with a superstructure of unbaked mudbrick. Though pottery was not yet used, bowls, trays, and figurines of gray-green stone demonstrate a high degree of technical skill.

These huts have diameters ranging from ten-to-twenty feet, beaten earth floors, platforms built against the walls for sleeping, and a central post to support the domed roof. At nearby Kalavassos-Tenta the circular or elliptical huts had inner walls that were plastered and one of which seems to have had a scene painted on it. These huts had piers to support an upper story.[14]

The pre-pottery Neolithic people cut their wheat and barley with flint sickle blades and ground it into flour with querns and grinders. They also raised lentils, beans, peas, and must have harvested wild olives. They domesticated sheep, goats, and pigs, and they supplemented their diet with fish and shellfish and hunted deer. They used bone for needles and awls, and their possession of spindle whorls shows that weaving, perhaps of wool, was practiced.

The ceramic Neolithic, or Neolithic II, dates about 5000–3700 B.C. It is often called the Sotira culture, after Sotira in the southwest, where it was initially found. Again, this culture has been found at fully twenty-five sites. The period is marked by the introduction of pottery, a significant growth in population, and a new wave of settlers to the island. At Sotira itself forty-seven houses have been excavated, and they vary considerably in shape: circular, oval, irregular, etc. They were built with stone bases and mudbrick superstructures. They had central poles to support the roof, and a hearth and mudbrick benches as sleeping places. In some houses there were partitions to fence off work areas. These farmers left remains of wheat, barley, lentils, grapes, and olives, as well as evidence of the domestication of pigs.

The Chalcolithic Age

The Chalcolithic or copper-stone period on Cyprus was, of course, a time when copper implements were used alongside those made of stone. Dating of the period varies slightly in the studies of scholars working in the field, but 3700 and 2500 B.C. would probably receive reasonably wide acceptance as beginning and ending dates. It is easy to assume that during this period Cypriots learned to exploit native copper resources and to manufacture a variety of copper objects. But N. H. Gale's definitive study, based on chemical analysis of copper objects, asserts that we do not know whether the copper objects so far excavated "represent any use of Cypriot copper ores at all."[15] In fact, they support the existence of copper trade apparently with Asia Minor. Known Chalcolithic objects recovered include hooks, pins, daggers, chisels, knives, an awl, and an axe.

Erimi, near the south coast of Cyprus, was the first Chalcolithic site excavated and thus has given its name to the culture of the period. Now more than 125 Chalcolithic sites are known across the island. The western part of Cyprus, essentially uninhabited during the Neolithic period, was now well populated, as was the central plain. Typical houses were round huts with stone foundations and superstructures of wattle and daub and conical roofs, probably of mud and reeds. In some sites the dead were buried inside or outside the houses. And in others there were separate cemeteries with a large number of gifts buried with the dead.

The Bronze Age

Scholars debate when and how the Bronze[16] Age came to Cyprus. The tendency now is to conclude that it was an evolutionary process, rather than coming about as a result of the migration of a new people from Asia Minor. And the tendency is to date the period about 2500 B.C. to 1100 B.C. It was subdivided into Early Bronze (2500–1900 B.C.) or Early Cypriot, Middle Bronze (1900–1650 B.C.) or Middle Cypriot, and Late Bronze (c. 1650–1000 B.C.) or Late Cypriot periods.

The Bronze Age dawned in Cyprus during the Early Minoan period on Crete, the Early Helladic period on the Greek mainland, the Old Kingdom or pyramid age of Egypt, and the Early Dynastic period in Mesopotamia, when Ur was beginning to develop its remarkable culture.

During the Early and Middle Bronze periods, Cyprus became part of the international world of the eastern Mediterranean and the Near East. And it began to be enfolded by the movements and crosscurrents of that world. But in spite of that, she managed to preserve a high degree of individuality. Probably this was true because Cyprus did not lie astride any of the main lines of communication between east and west or north and south. Nor was Cyprus a route to supremacy or a necessary outpost of defense for one of the great empires or an obstacle to the maintenance of empire. Therefore it did not suffer the same bloody conquests as peoples who lived in strategically important locations. But Cyprus was not immune from conquest or domination. From the Bronze Age on, she became the prey of more powerful neighbors as they attempted to control her valuable resources of copper and timber.

Early Bronze Age. As a witness to the fact that Cyprus had become part of the international world, discoveries dating to the period reveal imported commodities from Minoan Crete, Egypt, Syria, and Anatolia. What Cypriots sent in exchange is uncertain.

Cypriot developments include the introduction of the ox-drawn plow, asses or horses (probably from Anatolia) for use in overland transport, and apparently cattle to replace or at least supplement the pig. Bronze Age culture spread throughout the island, and a flourishing economy gave rise to a population increase. Pottery-making was a major activity, and tomb excavations evidence a considerable amount of clothes production. Spindle whorls were plentiful and some remains of woven cloth have survived.

Though we don't know where copper was mined or smelted during the period, it must have occurred because of the degree of sophistication in the industry during the Middle Bronze period and the number of bronze objects appearing in the tombs— including daggers, knives, axes, chisels, and razors.[17]

We have specific information about the religion of the period as revealed in three models of clay sanctuaries found in tombs. The worship of the bull-god (showing adoption of the fertility cult) with animal sacrifices and libations is prominent. The snake as the symbol of death and the divinity of death is also prominent.

Though there is not a lot of information about house design, what we have indicates a change from a circular to a rectangular form, with rubble foundations, a superstructure of mudbrick, and a flat roof. The dead were now buried not in or near their houses but in cemeteries where they were provided with a number of objects for use in the afterlife.

Iron was also smelted on Cyprus by the end of the Early Bronze Age, as excavations at Lapithos, on the northwest coast, show.[18]

Middle Bronze Age. During the Middle Bronze period the copper industry on Cyprus greatly expanded. This led to population increase, the rise of important towns, and the expansion of trade. Lapithos became the most important settlement of northern Cyprus and probably was the port through which the copper trade passed. Kalopsidha was the leading town of eastern Cyprus. During the period there were numerous references in Near Eastern texts to copper from Alashiya, which now is generally agreed to have been the name for Cyprus at that time. Though copper was the chief export, Cypriot pottery has been found all along the Palestinian and Syrian coast, in Egypt, and even in Cilicia (the region around Tarsus in eastern Asia Minor).

Reflecting the greater prosperity of the period, houses at Kalopsidha and Alambra, for example, have been found with several large rooms. Rooms were as large as twenty by twenty feet and houses fifty by twenty feet. Animal bones found in the excavations come from sheep, goats, donkeys, cows, and horses. In religion, worship of the bull god and snakes occurred and the prominence of the fertility cult continued.

The existence of several forts on Cyprus during the Middle Bronze period has led Karageorghis to conclude that they were not designed as defense against an external enemy but reflected tensions between the regions of the island.[19] But Alastos has argued that the Hyksos were responsible for construction of at least three of these forts.[20] After taking Syria, Palestine, and northern Egypt, they spilled over onto Cyprus, probably in the seventeenth century B.C. And then, at last the one at Enkomi fell to local inhabitants shortly after the Egyptians expelled the Hyksos about 1580 B.C. The Swedish scholar Paul Aström has made a tabulation of finds of the Egyptian-style Tell-Yahudiyeh ware (Hyksos pottery) excavated on Cyprus, showing again the influence of the Hyksos on the island.[21] But how much of this pottery found its way to Cyprus by trade rather than occupation should remain an open question. The definitive story of Hyksos involvement on Cyprus is yet to be written. Karageorghis himself raises the question whether strife at the beginning of the Late Bronze Age is connected with Hyksos activity.[22]

The Late Bronze Age. During the Late Bronze Age (1600–1000 B.C.), Cyprus became very prosperous as a center of cultural and commercial interchange between East and West. Enkomi, near Salamis, was founded near the beginning of the period and quickly became an important town. It evidently served as the capital of the Cyprus kingdom of Alashiya (hence the use of the name "Elishah" in Genesis 10:4) and dominated the Cypriot copper industry from about 1600 to 1300 B.C. Then in the thirteenth century several other towns on the south of the island rose to compete in copper production. Kition, Hala Sultan Tekke, and Kalavasos were among the other rising centers.

Both the Egyptians and Hittites claimed control of Cyprus from time to time in the fourteenth and thirteenth centuries. But the language of conquest appearing in Near Eastern literature is so grossly exaggerated that a claim to control of Cyprus by either Hittites or Egyptians may mean little more than Cyprus' sending royal presents and engaging in increasing trade relations. And it would appear from some of the literature that Cyprus was for a while an ally of Egypt, not a subject people.

There is plenty of evidence that Egyptian and Hittite contacts with Cyprus were extensive, however. Numerous objects from both countries appear especially in Cypriot tombs. On the other hand, Cypriot commodities, including copper and especially pottery, were shipped across the Mediterranean—to Syria, Palestine, Egypt, the Hittite Empire, and as far west as Sicily and Sardinia. Cypriot "White-Slip" and "Base-Ring" pottery gained considerable popularity outside Cyprus during the Late Bronze Period, as discoveries ranging from Syria to Sardinia help to demonstrate.

The greater prosperity of the Late Bronze Age is reflected in the houses of cities such as Enkomi and Kition, where rooms faced three sides of a rectangular courtyard. And bathrooms had cemented floors with clay bathtubs and lavatories with well-constructed drainage systems.[23] The city wall of Enkomi measured some 1,300 feet north and south by about 1,200 feet east and west. Straight streets intersected at right angles, forming a grid.[24] Among the known sanctuaries of the period was the sanctuary of the horned god at Enkomi, in which was found a bronze statue about nineteen inches high of a god wearing a helmet with two horns springing from the sides.

Of course international developments significantly affected Cyprus. When Myceneans succeeded Minoans in the Aegean theater after the fall of Knossos (c. 1380 B.C.), Myceneans became involved on Cyprus, as their pottery and other remains found in Cypriot excavations have shown. The international character of the Late Bronze Age seems to have come to an end in the twelfth century B.C. The Hittite Empire passed from history about 1200 B.C. and the Egyptian Empire by about 1100. Around the same time, the Mycenean kingdoms disintegrated, finding it impossible to maintain themselves. Commerce declined and prosperity with it. (That story is told in the chapter 9 on Greece.) Muhly observes that Cyprus seems to have suffered less destruction than other areas at the time because there a highly centralized palace economy did not run affairs as fully as was true elsewhere in the Mycenean and Near Eastern communities. So there was more flexibility in dealing with conditions in Cyprus.[25]

The Iron Age

Our understanding of the past is constantly changing. This is abundantly true of the so-called "Dark Ages" of early Greece and Cyprus. The view that the period from about 1100 to 800 B.C. was a time when writing ceased, culture declined, poverty was general, and trade virtually ended has been radically altered. Writing did not cease; there was considerable contact between Cyprus, the Aegean, and the Levant. Technological skills are in evidence in the archaeological discoveries. Three inscriptions, dating to just before 1000 B.C. have been excavated at ancient Paphos (Palaepaphos) alone, and one of them is in the Arcadian dialect.[26] (Arcadia in the Peloponnesus is the traditional homeland of the Greeks who colonized Cyprus after the Trojan War.) Interestingly, James Roy of the University of Nottingham observes that the Arcadian dialect, which differs considerably from other Peloponnesian dialects, resembled *Cypriot*.[27] The so-called "Dark Ages" on Cyprus was actually a time of prosperity.[28]

During the eleventh century B.C., when Dorians moved into Crete, Cretans migrated to Cyprus and settled in such places as Enkomi and Kition, as the discovery of numerous pottery items indicates.[29] And around 1050 Salamis took the place of Enkomi as the chief site in eastern Cyprus, while Phoenicians settled in Kition in the south. The rise of Salamis seems to have been related to a catastrophe, such as an earthquake, that brought an end to the Bronze Age on Cyprus. Enkomi was abandoned, and Salamis was built closer to the sea. While during the Bronze Age Cyprus was known as Alashiya, during the Iron Age and later, with the predominance of Greek, it was called Kypros.

Soon a new culture emerged on Cyprus—an Iron Age culture, with a metal for making tools and weapons that was superior to bronze. The Cypriots emerged as shipbuilders and a sea power of some consequence. They transported their copper and especially their Cypro-geometric pottery (bearing stiff geometric designs representing a fusion of old Cypriot and Mycenean types) to many eastern Mediterranean lands. Salamis and Paphos were the most important cities during this period (c. 1050–700 B.C.).

About the middle of the tenth century Phoenician commercial activity became pronounced on Cyprus and contributed greatly to the prosperity of the island. The main Phoenician centers of power were at Kition (Citium) near modern Larnaca on the southern coast and at Idalium (Dali), a few miles inland. Phoenician merchant communities grew up in many other Cypriot towns, but they always remained a foreign element. Whatever is said in general about the identity of Chittim in the Old Testament, it seems that Isaiah (Isaiah 23:1–12) had Cyprus in mind. He refers to a seaport where merchantmen put in on their homeward voyage to Tyre, and where Tyrian refugees found a place of safety. Moreover, in 741 B.C. Hiram II of Tyre had some sort of governor on the island,[30] pre-cisely at the time of the great prophet, who ministered about 740–700 B.C.

How much actual Phoenician migration there was to Cyprus is open to question. But it is clear that from about 925 to 600 B.C. Cyprus must have been part of a Cypro-Phoenician cultural province. Also, during the same period, trade among Cyprus, Greece, Sardinia, and Etruscan Italy was extensive. Cypriot development was scarcely affected by Assyrian conquests on the mainland.[31]

Hardly had the Phoenician city-states reached their height of prosperity when the Assyrians swooped down on the westlands, reducing them to dependencies. Not long after the fall of the Northern Kingdom of Israel to Sargon II (722 B.C.), in 707, Cyprus capitulated to the Assyrians. Probably the kings of seven Cypriot city-states surrendered and paid homage without an attack, though Sargon claimed a victory over them and erected a monument (now in Berlin) in Kition (Citium) to commemorate the victory. According to the inscription, they paid tribute in gold, silver, utensils, and valuable furniture. Assyrian rule does not seem to have been oppressive, and the Cypriot kings apparently were free to exercise local authority. The prosperity of the period is reflected in the nine so-called royal tombs at Salamis with their rich collections of burial goods, as well as comparable tombs at places like Idalion and Tamassos. These date to the period 800–600 B.C. Salamis was probably one of the largest and most prosperous cities of the eastern Mediterranean during the seventh century B.C.[32]

By 650 native Egyptians had chased the Assyrians out of Egypt. And Assyrian domination of Cyprus had ended before that. The island's great period came during the subsequent century of independence.[33] But Cyprus was not destined to enjoy independence for long. In the future her fortunes would be linked with those of the powerful empires surrounding her.

About 570 B.C. the Egyptian king Amasis took control of Cyprus. And though Egyptian rule was more severe than that of the Assyrians, Cypriots did much as they wished as long as they paid their tribute.

A tomb of one of the kings of Cyprus, eighth century B.C. The throne was found in the right corner where there is a pile of dirt.

Commercial and cultural relations with the Aegean progressed undisturbed.

With regard to religion, the rural sanctuaries of Cyprus continued to be devoted to worship of the deity of fertility, as symbolized by the bull. But the god sometimes also took on the function of healing or war or weather. The sanctuaries often consisted of a small holy place with an altar and a large courtyard. However, the Greek population in the towns gradually introduced the gods of Olympus: Zeus at Salamis and elsewhere; Hera at Palaepaphos, Amathus, and Idalion; Artemis at Paphos and Idalion; Apollo at Kourion; Athena at Vouni, Soloi, and Idalion; and Aphrodite at Paphos, to name some of the most outstanding sanctuaries. The Phoenician population especially worshiped Astarte, but Phoenician inscriptions also mention Eshmoun, Melqart, and Reshef.

Persian Control

In 545 B.C. the kingdoms of Cyprus submitted voluntarily to Cyrus of Persia and began two hundred years of subjection to the colossus of the East. Soon the Cypriots became as restless as the Greeks of Ionia under Persian domination. Especially under the rule of Darius the Great (521–486 B.C.) Persian rule became ruthless. And when the Greeks of Ionia revolted against Persia in 499/8, the Cypriots joined them. Greek and Cypriot naval forces were at first victorious. But when the Persians started to have victories on land, the naval forces had to withdraw. The Persians besieged the rebellious cities of Cyprus one by one—some for as long as four or five months.

After the victory, the Persians enthroned pro-Persian kings in all of the ten major kingdoms of Cyprus: Salamis, Marion, Lapithos, Tamassos, Idalion, Paphos, Kourion, Kyrenia, Amathus, and Kition. And they subsequently ruled by playing off the kingdoms against each other. Defeat was not enough. The Cypriots were forced

A limestone head of a bearded worshiper.

to contribute to the Persian invasion of Greece, and they provided Xerxes with a fleet of 150 ships for the important Battle of Salamis in 480 B.C.

The Greeks believed it their duty to liberate Cyprus from the Persian yoke. During succeeding decades Cyprus, with its predominantly Greek population, was frequently involved in Greek intrigues against Persia and local efforts to obtain independence from their Persian overlords. One of the most successful of the Cypriot rebellions was engineered by Evagoras, who maintained himself as king of Salamis for thirty-six years (410–374 B.C.).

Alexander and the Ptolemies

However, the revolutionaries never achieved their aim of freedom from Persia until 333 B.C., when Alexander the Great defeated Darius III at the Battle of Issus. Rejoicing in this, the Cypriots sent Alexander 120 ships to help him in the siege of Tyre (332). Alexander granted the island independence, but clearly he considered it part of his empire and issued coins for the whole of Cyprus—abolishing the coinage of the city-states.

Cyprus had little cause for happiness over the successes of Alexander. With his death in 323, conflict over control of his empire arose among his generals. Cyprus was especially desirable to Ptolemy of Egypt for its supply of copper and timber, neither of which Egypt possessed. After almost thirty years of struggle with the Antigonids of Syria, the Ptolemies won undisputed control of Cyprus in 295 B.C. and maintained that control for some 250 years. It is interesting that in spite of Egyptian and Persian rule over Cyprus, Greek influence dominated on the island during the last half of the first millennium B.C. But there was still a strong Phoenician presence on Cyprus as late as Alexander's day.

While the Ptolemies could be cruel despots, they were energetic rulers who displayed a high degree of administrative ability and interest in scholarly pursuits. Under them Alexandria became the leading intellectual and commercial center of the Mediterranean. Study and experimentation in many branches of science prospered there.

Knowledge became a direct concern of the state, as did economic life, which was scientifically arranged down to minute details. All land was cultivated under a far-reaching supervisory system. The type of plant, quality of seed, agricultural implements, and irrigation machinery were all carefully superintended with a view to increased productivity and prosperity. An efficient bureaucracy made all the decisions.

In Cyprus, administrative control was not quite the same as in Egypt. In Egypt a Greek ruling class subjected a native population; in Cyprus the vast majority of the people were Greek. And in Cyprus the lack of water supply prevented the degree of intense cultivation of land that was possible in Egypt. There was, nevertheless, detailed bureaucratic control of the island under a strategos, or general, who acted as governor. A secretary supervised the administrative machine. Certain local institutions possessed some power, however, and authoritarian tyranny did not exist on the island until the latter part of the period.

One of the most beneficial moves of the first years of Ptolemaic rule on Cyprus (or perhaps a little earlier) was a decree to abolish the petty kingships which had for more than 1,200 years dissected the island and hindered its prosperity. The years of peace and affluence of the Ptolemaic era were the greatest the island had ever known. Heightened prosperity brought increased population and the establishment of new cities. And existing cities were beautified with baths, schools, gymnasia, and theaters. The population of the capital, Salamis, has been estimated at 120,000.[34]

Eighteen important cities existed at the end of the Ptolemaic era. Greek art flourished, and beautiful sculptures dating to the Ptolemaic period have been found on the island. Main sources of wealth were the shipbuilding industry and the export of timber, grain, wine, and copper. One of the most famous Cypriots of the period was Zeno of Kition (Citium), founder of the Stoic school at Athens. Another was Pyrgoteles, a naval architect.

After the middle of the second century B.C., the Ptolemies made it a practice to call on Rome for arbitration of their dynastic squabbles—driving a wedge for Roman imperial expansion in the eastern Mediterranean. These dynastic troubles, accompanied by Roman conquests in the North, increasing piracy on the high seas, and military ambitions of the Ptolemies in the East, brought about financial difficulties on Cyprus during the first century B.C. Cyprus became a separate Ptolemaic kingdom in 80 B.C.

Roman Control

The Romans took over Cyprus in 58 B.C. But their reason for doing so is not clear. Evidently they wanted the island and manufactured claims for the right to take it. For example, they asserted a right to the island as heirs named in the last legitimate Ptolemy's will (Ptolemy Alexander II). Moreover, they held that the king of Cyprus had given aid to pirates in their raids along the Cilician coast and that the annexation of Cyprus was necessary to future security of the seas. Marcus Cato was in charge of the operation. The island was looted on a grand scale. The king's treasures were auctioned off and the money sent to Rome. A brilliant chapter in Cypriot history had come to an end.

Initially Cyprus was made part of the province of Cilicia and was ruled from Tarsus. Rapacity of the early governors was indescribable; and when Cicero, an honest man, became governor in 51 B.C., he could hardly find words strong enough to portray the injustices of his predecessor. Near the beginning of his administration, Cicero received an appeal from Salamis. In 56 B.C. Brutus had made a loan to Salamis, through agents, at 48 percent interest; and when the Salaminians refused to pay, his agents' troops besieged the city councilors in their own senate chamber until five died of hunger. Cicero withdrew troops from the island and reduced the interest to 12 percent, but the matter was never solved during his term of office.

In 47 B.C. Julius Caesar restored Cyprus to the Ptolemies. With the victory of Augustus over the forces of Antony at Actium in 31 and the subsequent suicide of Antony and Cleopatra, the Romans took command once more. Now Cyprus became a province separate from Cilicia. From 27 to 22 B.C. it was administered as an imperial province and ruled by a personal appointee of Augustus. In 22 Augustus turned it over to the Senate; thereafter it was governed by an ex-praetor with the title of proconsul. Luke refers to him accurately in the Greek of Acts 13:7 ("proconsul" in NKJV and RSV).

Not much is known of affairs on Cyprus during the civil wars. But Crassus, Pompey, and Caesar drew heavily on the financial and naval resources of the island. The victory of Augustus led to administrative reorganization and the reintroduction of stable conditions in the eastern Mediterranean. Economic prosperity resulted and continued on Cyprus for a couple of centuries.

Apparently Rome did not markedly disturb the pattern of social and political life as it had existed under the Ptolemies. Municipalities possessed self-government in varying degrees, as was true of cities elsewhere in the Empire. For instance, Salamis had a popular assembly, a senate, and a council of elders. Probably officials of many of the cities were appointed by the Romans.

The *Koinon Ton Kyprion*, a sort of representative body acting on behalf of the Greek inhabitants of the island, a carry-over from Ptolemaic days, exercised a degree of power. It was responsible for religious matters throughout the island, including maintenance of the imperial cult, and organized festivals and games. The most important annual festival was held in honor of Aphrodite. The *Koinon* also issued coins.

The Romans transferred the capital of Cyprus from Salamis to Paphos, perhaps because it was the port closest to Rome, or because they wished to honor Aphrodite, whose temple was located at Paphos, or because the port at Salamis was beginning to silt up.

Cyprus and the New Testament

When Barnabas and Saul landed on Cyprus in A.D. 45 or 46, it had regained much of the prosperity it had lost a century earlier. Strabo, who completed his geography in A.D. 23, says of Cyprus in his day that it was rich

The harbor at Salamis, where Paul and Barnabas landed.

in wine and oil, used homegrown wheat, had plenty of copper, and engaged in extensive shipbuilding.[35] The main cities were Salamis, its greatest port and commercial center, and Paphos, its capital.

Salamis

As has been noted, the missionaries landed at Salamis, commonly assumed to be the home of Barnabas, a native of Cyprus. Ancient writers were unanimous in asserting that the city was founded by Teucer, son of Telamon, king of the island of Salamis in Greece. These early accounts state that this founding took place after Teucer was shipwrecked on his way home from the Trojan War. And excavations have shown that a Mycenean town was built at Enkomi, three miles inland from Salamis, around 1230 B.C. This was destroyed by the Sea Peoples around 1200 B.C. and rebuilt. An earthquake leveled that town around 1150 B.C. Enkomi was again rebuilt but was abandoned around 1100 B.C., after which the inhabitants founded Salamis on the coast. Salamis seems always to have been a characteristically Hellenic town with a predominately Greek population.[36]

Both because of several destructions and rebuildings of Salamis and because of the partial excavation of the site, it is difficult to picture what it looked like in Paul's day. The great limestone forum belongs to the early years of the Roman province (and therefore to Paul's day). The forum covered with its surrounding shops an area of more than 3.5 acres. The open area of the forum, or agora, was some 750 by 180 feet and was surrounded by columns of the Corinthian order approximately twenty-seven feet high. On a platform at the south end stood a temple dedicated to the Olympian Zeus, which was constructed during the lifetime of Augustus. This was probably the largest agora in the Roman colonial empire.[37]

Some eight hundred yards north of the forum are the remains of a complex of baths and a gymnasium (commonly known as "the marble forum"). While most of the construction to be seen there today dates to the second century A.D. or later, there are some remains of earlier Hellenistic baths among the ruins of the later Roman baths.

The theater at Salamis, south of the baths, is the largest yet found on Cyprus and one of the largest ever discovered in the eastern Mediterranean area. The diameter of the orchestra is approximately eighty-eight feet, and it could hold roughly fifteen thousand spectators. This compares favorably with the well-known theater at Epidaurus in southern Greece, which could hold a maximum of about fourteen thousand in its best days, or the famous theater of Dionysus at Athens, where drama was born, which could seat about the same number or perhaps one or two thousand more. Since the Salamis theater was built in the days of Augustus Caesar, it stood there when Barnabas and Paul arrived.

Between the gymnasium/baths and the theater are remains of a stadium and an amphitheater (for gladiatorial games), and a large water reservoir. Of course the harbor of Salamis holds interest for us because Barnabas and Paul landed there. Now largely silted in, in New Testament times it was a bustling port where most of the products of Cyprus, especially copper, timber, and grain, were exported. An inland road connected the port with the important port of Soli (Soloi) in the west.

Salamis suffered a disastrous earthquake in A.D. 76 or 77. In 116 during the Jewish uprising, the city was largely destroyed. After the earthquakes of A.D. 332 and 342

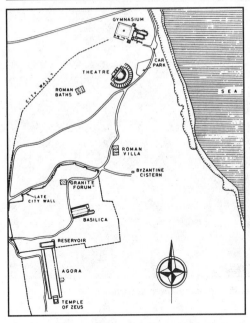

Plan of Salamis

(accompanied by a tidal wave) which virtually demolished the city, it was rebuilt on a smaller scale by Constantius II and renamed "Constantia."

Since the Turkish occupation of northern Cyprus in 1974, they have carried off all movable objects from Salamis to Istanbul, where they may be seen in the Archaeological Museum.

Population of Cyprus

The potential audience to whom Barnabas and Paul might have ministered on the whole island is frequently estimated at about 500,000. But that figure is probably quite low—especially if we accept Karageorghis' first century estimate of 350,000 for Salamis alone.[38] Judging from the usual practice of Paul to preach in the synagogues of the Jews and from the specific reference in Acts 13:5, it seems that the aim of the missionaries was only to reach the Jewish element of the population. Of course there would be God-fearers (sympathetic Gentiles) who could form part of the

The forum at Salamis

Ruins of the temple of Zeus at the south end of the forum at Salamis.

Seats of the stadium at Salamis, with the water reservoir behind them.

audience. Since Christian witnesses preceded Barnabas and Paul to Cyprus, it may be assumed that there was a small audience ready to listen to them (Acts 11:19).

The Apostolic Journey

After ministry in Salamis, Barnabas and Paul went through the island to Paphos (Acts 13:6). The passage is better rendered "through the whole island." Probably this means a relatively complete tour of the Jewish communities on Cyprus, involving preaching in the synagogues. How long this mission took is open to conjecture. William Ramsay thought at least two months would

have been required.[39] Others have estimated that the journey took as much as four months.

The route of the apostolic itinerary is also a matter of speculation. The Romans built a road around the main part of the island; that road ran from Salamis diagonally to Kyrenia in the north, and from there it roughly followed the west and south coasts and then back to Salamis. Other roads were constructed in the interior, but their exact routes are not known. Probably the missionary pair took the southern road through Kition (Citium) and Kourion (Curium). The non-canonical Acts of Barnabas, chapter 44, has them passing through Kourion. At the time the population of Kourion was perhaps

The theater at Salamis.

Temple of Apollo, west of Kourion.
Courtesy Richard Weir.

20,000. Outstanding sights would have been the temple of Apollo and the beautifully-positioned theater (which seated some 3,500).[40] The temple of Apollo stood about a mile west of Kourion. Worshipers approached it by a paved street that led into a walled enclosure. The temple itself was a small structure with a four-columned porch in front that could be reached by a broad flight of steps. The enclosure included dormitories for pilgrims, store-rooms for their offerings, a treasury, baths, and a priest's house.

Paphos

Whatever route the missionaries took, they finally reached Paphos. The Paphos to which they went was Nea Paphos, or "New Paphos," supposed to have been founded by Agapenor, who was wrecked there late in the thirteenth century B.C. when returning from the Trojan War. Gradually New Paphos superseded Old Paphos (modern Kouklia), some ten miles to the southeast. Old Paphos was long famous for the worship of Aphrodite (Agapenor found a temple to her located there when he arrived), who legend declares landed here after her birth among the waves near Cythera.

Nea Paphos, capital of the island during Roman times, was largely destroyed by an earthquake in 15 B.C., after which it was rebuilt with funds received from Augustus and renamed "Augusta" in his honor.

During the Roman era the city was adorned with magnificent temples and public buildings and was important not only as the capital but as the port for Kouklia and the shrine of Venus, or Aphrodite. Here countless pilgrims landed to visit and worship. Paphos became a great center for the worship of Aphrodite, just as Ephesus was for the worship of Diana.

All the Greek Gods were worshiped on Cyprus. But Aphrodite was most widely worshiped—and Apollo second. Because Cyprus was the meeting place of so many peoples, there occurred a fusion of the worship of Aphrodite as practiced among various peoples. The rites included Oriental, Greek, and Roman practices. Aphrodite was the Greek goddess of love, beauty, and fertility and was akin to the Phoenician Astarte, the Babylonian Ishtar, the Anatolian Cybele, and the Roman Venus. Religious prostitution accompanied her rites at Paphos.

Although many legends were told concerning the birth of Aphrodite, the most commonly accepted was that she was born of the foam of the sea, floated in a shell on the waves, and later landed on Cyprus near Paphos. The greatest festival in Cyprus in honor of Aphrodite was the Aphrodisia, held for three days each spring. It was attended by great crowds not only from all

Traditional spot of landing of Aphrodite (Venus) near Paphos.

"The Birth of Venus" by Botticelli. *Uffizi Gallery, Florence.*

parts of Cyprus but also from surrounding countries. During the Aphrodisia a religious procession started at New Paphos and wound its way to Old Paphos, passing through the gardens and sanctuaries of the goddess there.

THE LEGENDS ABOUT THE GODDESS APHRODITE

The most commonly accepted legend concerning the birth of Aphrodite indicated that she was born of the foam of the sea, floated in a shell on the waves, and later landed on Cyprus near Paphos. The shrine to Aphrodite at Paphos was located close to the spot on the coast where she was believed to have risen from the sea. The sanctuary there had a small covered hall that probably housed the idol of the goddess. Adjacent to the hall was a large open

sacred precinct filled with altars and votive gifts.

The greatest festival in Cyprus in honor of Aphrodite was the Aphrodisia, held for three days each spring. Each year great crowds attended it, not only from all parts of Cyprus but also from surrounding countries. During the Aphrodisia a religious procession started at New Paphos and wound its way to Old Paphos, some ten miles away, passing through the gardens and sanctuaries of the goddess there.

Temple of Aphrodite

What was believed to be the great Temple of Aphrodite at Old Paphos was investigated by De Cesnola during the last century. He was able to trace the wall of the sanctuary itself and found that it measured 221 feet on the east and west sides and 167 feet on the north and south sides. It was

There was an element of modernity in the houses and public facilities of Cyprus during the Roman period. Here in a public latrine is a spigot in the wall that could be turned on to flush the facility.

surrounded by an outer wall, which he was not able to trace completely. But on the basis of his discoveries, he concluded that the east and west sides of this enclosure measured 690 feet and the north and south sides 539 feet. The entire structure was built of a kind of blue granite which must have come from Cilicia or Egypt. Between this large structure on the heights (probably visible for many miles at sea) and the shoreline was a smaller temple. De Cesnola thought this was the temple built to commemorate the spot on which the goddess is said to have appeared to the Cypriots for the first time. Here the annual procession stopped to sacrifice before ascending the hill to the sanctuary.[41]

Combining evidence from archaeological investigation on the site, coins, a reference to the temple in Tacitus, and a comparison of this temple with what is known of Phoenician temples, Perrot and Chipiez have put together a description of the worship center.[42] Surrounding the complex was a wall, against the inside of which abutted a covered colonnade designed to protect worshipers or pilgrims from the heat. Within this was an inner court, to which the faithful gained entrance after accomplishing certain rites and paying certain fees. This "holy of holies" was roofless and the deity stood in the center of it, perhaps raised on a pedestal and covered with some

sort of canopy. The goddess herself was represented by a conical stone, a symbol of fertility, to which a head and arms may have been attached. In its entirety the structure reflects Phoenician influence.

A local fertility cult existed at Paphos as early as the third millennium B.C. Apparently Greek settlers converted it into the worship of Aphrodite. Later the cult incorporated elements of the Syrian Astarte. The earliest large sanctuary buildings date to about 1200 B.C. and show Near Eastern influence.

Like Salamis, Paphos suffered greatly from the earthquake of A.D. 76 or 77. It was virtually destroyed by an earthquake in the fourth century A.D. and lay for a long time in ruins.

Remains at Paphos

In addition to ruins of the Temple of Aphrodite at Old Paphos, the early city defenses have been cleared on a hill three thousand feet above sea level. Excavations of siege and counter-siege works point to heavy fighting at the time of the Ionian revolt against the Persians in 499/98.

At New Paphos (founded c. 312 B.C.) breakwaters of the ancient harbor are still to be seen and the outline of the city wall is traceable. A large theater and a small theater (odeon) have been located. An agora sprawled in front of the odeon, and next to the odeon stood what may have been a temple to Asklepios, the god of healing. Outside the city walls was a sanctuary of Apollo, dating to the fourth century B.C., and a necropolis in which were buried the Ptolemaic princes of the island. Excavations have especially centered on several Roman villas dating to the third century A.D. These have wonderful mosaics. The House of Dionysus had twenty spacious rooms arranged around two open peristyle courts. The House of Theseus, which depicts the story of Theseus and the Minotaur in mosaic, has been identified as the palace of the Roman governor.

Challenge of Aphrodite Worship

At Old Paphos there was from ancient times a priestly family—the Cinyradae—the senior member of which was the chief priest of the Temple of Aphrodite. The authority of the chief priest at Old Paphos extended to all Aphrodite temples in Cyprus. Before the rule of the Ptolemies he had political and religious authority, but they took his political power away. This family retained its religious authority in Roman times.

Aphrodite worship along with Judaism would have been the chief contender with Christianity for the religious affections of Cypriots. Certainly Barnabas and Paul repeatedly would have had to meet the opposition of vested interests of Aphrodite, just as Paul later experienced the antagonism of the vested interests of Diana at Ephesus.

Elymas the Sorcerer

The two missionaries met another form of spiritual blight at Paphos in the person of Elymas the sorcerer or magician. Possibly the proconsul Sergius Paulus, who apparently was a man of high caliber, became disgusted with the immoral excesses of Aphrodite worship and desired some other religious expression. At any rate, Elymas seems to have gained some sort of hearing with or power over the governor. When Sergius Paulus became interested in learning what Paul had to say, Elymas became afraid of losing his prey and attempted to prevent the proconsul's conversion. When the apostle smote the magician with temporary blindness, he performed a miracle that was perhaps the crowning evidence for the governor of the truth of the Christian message. Sergius Paulus believed, and a great victory was won for Christianity (Acts 13:6–12). In passing, it is interesting to observe that Saul is first called Paul in connection with the interview with the governor. This was his first significant Gentile contact and the first use of his Greek name.

Sergius Paulus

Sergius Paulus was proconsul of Cyprus from approximately A.D. 46 to 48. The fact that he held this position is confirmed by an inscription from Paphos, dating to the middle of the first century, which mentions the proconsul Paulus.[43] Other inscriptions have been found that mention "Lucius Sergius Paullus the Younger" and "Sergia Paulla, the daughter of Lucius Sergius Paullus." William Ramsay thought these individuals were the son and daughter of the proconsul. Ramsay also advanced an argument to demonstrate that Sergius Paulus and his family became Christians.[44] In passing, it should be noted that the Latin spelling of the governor's name would have been rendered with one *l* while the Greek rendering would have required two.

The early history of Christianity on Cyprus is virtually without records, but its growth is evident. Three bishops (of Paphos, Salamis, and Trimythus) represented Cyprus at the great Council of Nicea in A.D. 325.

Of course there have been efforts to fill the literary gap in early Cyprus church history. One of these efforts was the *Acts of Barnabas,* a fifth century A.D. work that recounts especially the activities of Barnabas and Mark on their subsequent trip to the island (Acts 15:39). Most of the account is probably unreliable, but possibly its mention of Barnabas's martyrdom and burial at Salamis is factual. Early legend also has it that Paul received thirty-nine strokes of the lash at Paphos, and a column there is pointed out as the place where he was tied to be scourged; but there is no historical evidence for this persecution.

Cyprus in the Postbiblical Period

After the first few centuries of the Roman era, Cyprus slipped into economic decline. Natural phenomena were very much to blame. A devastating earthquake hit the island on July 21, A.D. 365. And drought and famine in the fourth century are said to have lasted thirty-six years and to have largely depopulated the island.

The great earthquake of A.D. 365 brought to an end the pagan era of Cyprus. The rebuilding produced a Christian culture. From 395 to 1191 Cyprus was under the control of Byzantine emperors; but from the middle of the seventh century and for three hundred years, the Arabs attacked intermittently, causing terrible suffering. For instance, Salamis was sacked and the population massacred by the Arabs in A.D. 647. Islamic forces destroyed Paphos in 960.

In 1191 Richard the Lion-Hearted took the island, and a Crusader dynasty known as the Lusignans held it until 1489. Subsequently the Venetians controlled Cyprus. Then the Turks conquered it in 1571 and held it until 1878, when British administration began. The British lease from Turkey turned to outright annexation in 1915 when she found herself at war with Turkey. Britain held the island until August 16, 1960, when Cyprus became an independent republic. Tensions between the Greek and Turkish elements in the population led to a Turkish invasion and occupation of the northern third of the island in 1974. Since 1983 Turkish and Greek Cypriot republics have existed side by side, with the border quite successfully monitored by UN peace-keeping troops. As a result, Nicosia and the Greek-speaking southern part of Cyprus have tended to replace Beirut and Lebanon as a modern financial and diplomatic center for the near East because of Beirut's terrible ordeals since 1974. Since 2002 negotiations have been in progress for reunification of Cyprus.

NOTES

1. Acts does not say that John Mark was "separated unto" the missionary endeavor by the church, as were Barnabas and Saul. John Mark merely accompanied them and apparently was not necessary to the work. His return home from Asia Minor does not seem to have impeded the program of the other two (Acts 13:13).

2. A knot is a unit of speed equivalent to one nautical mile, or about 6,080 feet per hour.

3. One of the finest introductions to a study of seafaring in the Mediterranean in ancient times is Lionel Casson, *The Ancient Mariners*, 2nd ed. (Princeton: Princeton University Press, 1991). See especially pages 191–197 for documentation on the preceding two paragraphs. Perhaps it would be helpful to add that ships of the early Roman Empire were well built and equipped with charts to plot courses, a lead line to test depths, semaphore flags to send messages, a ship's boat (usually pulled behind) for emergencies, an anchor, but not a compass. It was the lack of a compass that dictated a sailing season of March to November in the Mediterranean—along with the fear of winter storms. The point is that in the Mediterranean the skies are clear enough in the summer to permit mariners to sail by sun, stars, and landmarks; these are obscured by overcast winter skies. Other very helpful books on shipping of the period include Lionel Casson's *Ships and Seamanship in the Ancient World* (Princeton: Princeton University Press, 1971) and his *Travel in the Ancient World* (Toronto: Hakkert, 1974); Fik Meijer, *A History of Seafaring in the Classical World* (New York: St. Martin's, 1986); Cecil Torr, *Ancient Ships* (Chicago: Argonaut, 1964); and Chester G. Starr, *The Roman Imperial Navy*, 2nd ed. (Westport, CT: Greenwood, 1979).

4. J. Hackett, *A History of the Orthodox Church of Cyprus* (London: Methuen & Co., 1901), p. 3.

5. Josephus, *Antiquities of the Jews*, XVI.IV.5.

6. Hackett, *Orthodox Church.*

7. Claude D. Cobbam trans., Eratosthenes, *Excerpta Cypria* (Cambridge: Cambridge University Press, 1908), 3.

8. N. G. L. Hammond, *A History of Greece to 322 B.C.* (Oxford: Clarendon Press, 1959), 25.

9. George Hill, *A History of Cyprus* (Cambridge: Cambridge University Press, 1940), I, 9.

10. Vernon J. Parry, "Cyprus," *Britannica Book of the Year, 1961,* 202.

11. Hill, *History of Cyprus.*, I, 10.

12. Josephus, *Antiquities of the Jews*, I.VI.1. Alashiya appears as an early name for Cyprus in records from Mari, Alalakh, Ugarit, the Amarna Letters, and Hattusas.

13. J. E. Muhly, "Cyprus," *Oxford Encyclopedia of Archaeology in the Near East*, 2, 90.

14. Vassos Karageorghis, *Cyprus, From the Stone Age to the Romans* (London: Thames & Hudson, 1982), 21.

15. N. H. Gale, "Metals and Metallurgy in the Chalcolithic Period," *Bulletin of the American Schools of Oriental Research*, May/August 1991, 57.

16. Bronze is an alloy of copper and tin, and a Bronze Age culture is one characterized by the use of bronze implements, utensils, and weapons at least among the upper classes.

17. Karageorghis, *Cyprus*, 48.

18. Paul Aström, *The Middle Cypriote Bronze Age* (Lund: Hakan Ohlssons Boktryckeri, 1957), 240.

19. Karageorghis, *Cyprus*, 53.

20. Doros Alastos, *Cyprus in History* (London: Zeno Publishers, 1955), 23–24.

21. Aström, *Bronze Age*, 233.

22.. Karageorghis, *Cyprus*, 62.

23. Ibid., 70.

24. Ibid., 90.

25. Muhly, *Cyprus*, 93–94.

26. Ibid., 94.

27. *Oxford Classical Dictionary*, 3rd ed. (Oxford: Oxford University Press, 1996), p. 138. Note also, Martin Bernal, *Cadmean Letters* (Winona Lake, IN: Eisenbrauns, 1990), for a discussion of the transmission of the alphabet.

28. Karageorghis, *Cyprus*, 94.

29. Ibid., 110.

30. Gordon Home, *Cyprus Then and Now* (London: J. M. Dent & Sons, 1960), 22.

31. Judy Birmingham, "The Chronology of Some Early and Middle Iron Age Cypriot Sites:" *American Journal of Archaeology*, 67 (January 1963) 42.

32. Karageorghis, *Cyprus*, 136.

33. Carl Roebuck, *Ionian Trade and Colonization* (New York: Archaeological Institute of America, 1959), 65.

34. Alastos, *Cyprus in History*, 89.

35. Cobbam, *Excerpta Cypria*, p. 3.

36. Discussed by Porphyrios Dikaios, former director of the Department of Antiquities, Cyprus, at the Oriental Institute of the University of Chicago, 18 March 1964.

37. Rupert Guiness, *Historic Cyprus* (London: Methuen & Col., 1936), 420.

38. Karageorghis, *Cyprus*, 181.

39. William M. Ramsay, *The Church in the Roman Empire Before A.D. 170* (Grand Rapids: Baker Book House reprint, 1979), 61.

40. See especially David Soren and Jamie James, *Kourion, The Search for a Lost Roman City* (New York: Doubleday, 1988).

41. Louis P. De Cesnola, *Cyprus: Its Ancient Cities, Tombs, and Temples* (London: John Murray, 1877), 210–13.

42. Georges Perrot and Charles Chipiez, *History of Art in Phoenicia and Its Dependencies* (London: Chapman and Hall, 1885), I, 274–80.

43. Camden M. Cobern, *New Archaeological Discoveries*, 9th ed. (New York: Funk & Wagnalls, 1929), 552.

44. William M. Ramsay, *The Bearing of Recent Discoveries on the Trustworthiness of the New Testament* (Grand Rapids: Baker Book House reprint, 1979), 150–72.

BIBLIOGRPAHY

Alastos, Doros. *Cyprus in History.* London: Zeno Publishers, 1955.

Astrom, Paul. *The Middle Cypriote Bronze Age.* Lund: Hakan Ohlssons Boktryckeri, 1957.

A Brief History and Description of Salamis. 3rd ed. Nicosia: Antiquities Department of the Government of Cyprus, 1959.

Casson, Lionel. *The Ancient Mariners.* Princeton, 2nd ed.: Princeton University Press, 1991.

Casson, Lionel. *Ships and Seamanship in the Ancient World.* Princeton: Princeton University Press, 1971.

Cobern, Camden M. *New Archaeological Discoveries.* 9th ed., New York: Funk & Wagnalls, 1929.

De Cesnola, Louis P. *Cyprus: Its Ancient Cities, Tombs and Temples.* London: John Murray, 1877.

Excerpta Cypria. Trans. Claude D. Cobbam. Cambridge: Cambridge University Press, 1908.

Gjerstad, Einar, et al. *The Swedish Cyprus Expedition.* 3 vols. Stockholm: Swedish Cyprus Expedition, 1934.

Guiness, Rupert. *Historic Cyprus.* London: Methuen, 1936.

Hackett, J. *A History of the Orthodox Church of Cyprus.* London: Methuen, 1901.

Hammond, N. G. L. *A History of Greece.* 3rd ed., Oxford: Oxford University Press, 1986.

Herscher, Ellen. "Archaeology in Cyprus." *American Journal of Archaeology* (April 1998): 309–54.

Hill, George. *A History of Cyprus.* 4 vols. Cambridge: Cambridge University Press, 1940–52.

Home, Gordon. *Cyprus Then and Now.* London: J. M. Dent & Sons, 1960.

Karageorgis, Vassos. *The Ancient Civilization of Cyprus.* New York: Cowles Education Corporation, 1969.

Karageorghis, Vassos. *Cyprus: From the Stone Age to the Romans.* London: Thames & Hudson, 1982.

Karageorghis, Vassos. *Salamis in Cyprus.* London: Thames & Hudson, 1969.

Keshishian, Kevork K. *Everybody's Guide to Romantic Cyprus.* Nicosia: Government Tourist Office, 1966.

Mangoian, L., and H. A. Mangoian. *The Island of Cyprus.* Nicosia: Mangoian Bros., 1947.

Mitford, T. B. *The Inscriptions of Kourion.* Philadelphia: American Philosophical Society, 1971.

Peltenburg, Edgar, ed. *Early Society in Cyprus.* Edinburgh: Edinburgh University Press, 1989.

Perrot, Georges, and Charles Chipiez. *History of Art in Phoenicia and Its Dependencies.* 2 vols. London: Chapman and Hall, 1885.

Ramsay, William M. *The Bearing of Recent Discoveries on the Trustworthiness of the New Testament.* Grand Rapids: Baker Book House reprint, 1979.

Ramsay, William M. *The Church in the Roman Empire Before A.D. 170.* Grand Rapids: Baker Book House reprint, 1979.

Robertson, Noel, ed. *The Archaeology of Cyprus.* Park Ridge, NJ: Noyes Press, 1975.

Roebuck, Carl. *Ionian Trade and Colonization.* New York: Archaeological Institute of America, 1959.

Soren, David, and Jamie James. *Kourion: The Search for a Lost Roman City.* New York: Doubleday, 1988.

Starr, Chester G. *The Roman Imperial Navy 31 B.C.–A.D. 324.* Ithaca,: Cornell University Press, 1941.

The restored main gate leading into the Hellenistic Agora at Ephesus. Paul often would have walked through this gate during his some three years in the city. Several shops of silversmiths were located inside the Agora to the left.

The lintel over the main gate of the Hellenistic Agora as it used to lie among the ruins. The inscription indicates the gate was erected during the reign of Augustus Caesar, about 7 B.C.

8

ASIA MINOR

Crossroads of civilization converged on this important peninsula of the eastern Mediterranean world. At an early time peoples and ideas moved in from the Mesopotamian valley. From this center some migrated to Crete, the Aegean islands, and even the Greek mainland. Waves of Greeks washed onto her shores during the first millennium B.C.

During the same millennium Persians swept across her plateaus from the east into Greece; Alexander's hosts, advancing from the west, conquered her on the way to deal with the Persian king, and his successors established flourishing centers there. Those cities enjoyed new heights of prosperity under the Roman peace (the Pax Romana) during the first and second centuries A.D. And Asia Minor contributed much to the development of Greco-Roman civilization.

Not only was this peninsula important for the flow of population and culture in ancient times, it was also important to the advance of Christianity. Paul, the great apostle of Christianity, was born at Tarsus in the East and in his missionary activities ranged over the entire length of Asia Minor. Subsequently Peter seems to have preached in the northern and central parts of the peninsula (1 Peter 1:1). And the apostle John spent the last decades of his life ministering in the populous cities of the province of Asia (cf. Revelation 1:4; 2–3). Altogether at least thirty-five towns and provinces of Asia Minor and islands adjacent to it figure in the New Testament narrative.

During the Middle Ages a flourishing Byzantine Empire was based on the prosperity of Asia Minor. But when the Seljuk Turks cut up the Byzantine armies at Manzikert in A.D. 1071 and occupied the peninsula, they deprived the Byzantines of their granary, their tax base, and the recruiting base for the army. Subsequently the Ottoman Turks worsted the Seljuks and went on to take Constantinople in A.D. 1453, establishing their control over not only Asia Minor but also a considerable part of the rest of the Near East.

Reaching its height in the sixteenth century A.D., the Ottoman Empire declined in subsequent centuries and in the nineteenth century became the "Sick Man of Europe." With the dissolution of the Ottoman Empire after World War I, the history of modern Turkey began. While the present cultural level and economic development of the area may not measure up to what they were during the first two centuries of the Christian Era, the landscape is still beautiful, the soil is still productive, and signs and sounds of progress stir the air.

Study of this crossroads of civilization is significant for contemporary Christians, first, because it gives a sense of reality to the biblical narrative. The events recorded in the New Testament actually happened to real people confronted with most of the same kinds of issues facing people today. And as we learn the history and geography of Asia Minor, we gain greater understanding of the biblical text and its message.

Second, we discover how ruler or emperor worship arose there and spread throughout the Roman Empire, becoming a major obstacle to the Christian church and a cause of Christian persecution.

Third, by studying our Greco-Roman heritage we gain some understanding of the rise of mother goddess worship with its contemporary implications. Though people worshiped the mother goddess in various places in the Mediterranean world, the practice was especially strong in Asia Minor and went all the way back to 6000 B.C. Veneration of *Magna Mater* (the great mother), Cybele, and Diana of the Ephesians involved aspects of the practice. Some scholars point to this development as contributing to the veneration of the Virgin Mary in Asia Minor during the early Christian centuries and later in the Eastern Orthodox and Roman Catholic churches. In non-Christian contexts in New Age teachings—*Gaia* (the earth goddess of the Greeks), also known as Mother Earth, is seen to be alive and functioning as an organism in which living things interact with geophysical and chemical processes to maintain conditions suitable for life.[1]

ASIA MINOR AND THE DOCTRINE OF THE PERSON OF CHRIST

The orthodox statement concerning the person of Christ was worked out during the first several ecumenical or churchwide councils—all held in Asia Minor. It taught

- that Christ was truly divine and truly human
- that the human and divine natures were truly united in one person

- and that the two natures were not fused or changed by that union.

Thus the human sufferings of Christ had value for the redemption of all humanity because His human nature was truly linked to His infinite divine nature. But the linkage of the two natures does not mean that either nature changes the other. So now, as a result of the Ascension, Christ in His humanity is locally present in heaven and will return to earth some day. But in His deity He is spiritually everywhere present.

Fourth, the study of Asia Minor is significant because it provides the stage for the Galatian heresy. There in Galatia Judaizers taught that those who placed their faith in Christ had also to keep the law to obtain or maintain salvation. The apostle Paul responded with his blistering counterattack recorded in the book of Galatians, "The Charter of Christian Liberty." At its core it teaches that salvation comes by faith alone through Christ alone. This teaching became the hallmark of the Reformation, and Martin Luther's commentary on Galatians serves as one of the great texts of that movement.

Fifth, and preeminently, in Asia Minor the first four ecumenical or churchwide councils hammered out the doctrine of the person of Christ. The first council, at Nicaea (modern Iznik), southeast of Constantinople or Istanbul, in A.D. 325 established the true and full deity of Christ. Richard Rubenstein developed the story of the debates and decisions of this council in his 1999 study *When Jesus Became God*. The second council, at Constantinople in 381, declared for the true and full humanity of Christ. The third council, at Ephesus in 431, asserted the linkage of the divine and human natures of Christ in one person. Finally, at Chalcedon (modern Kadiköy), a suburb of Constantinople, in 451, a council declared that Christ was truly God and truly man, that the two natures were truly united in one person, without confusion, change, division, or separation. Out of

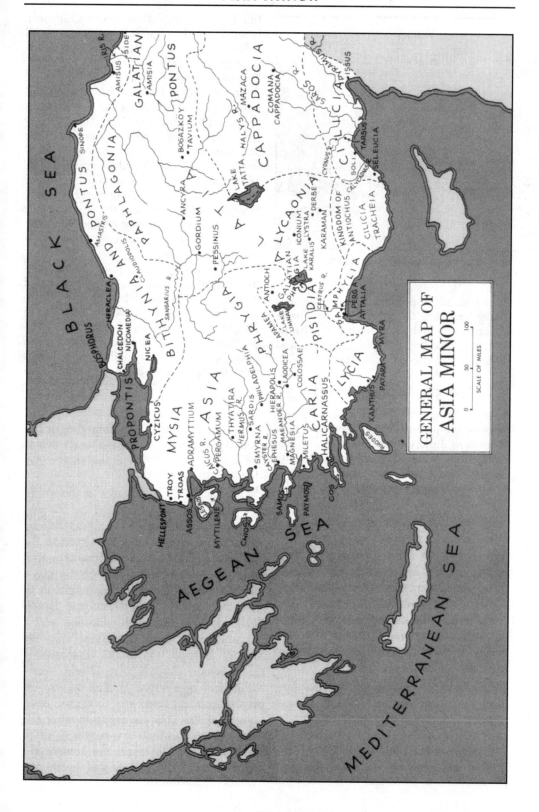

GENERAL MAP OF
ASIA MINOR

SCALE OF MILES

0   50   100

The Taurus Mountains north of Tarsus

these councils (especially from Nicaea and Chalcedon) came the great orthodox creeds of Christianity that have been adopted by the Eastern Orthodox, Roman Catholic, and Protestant churches of the world.

Geographical Features

Asia Minor is the general geographical term for the peninsula that forms the bulk of modern Turkey. Not in use in classical times, it seems to have arisen in the fifth century A.D. Anatolia commonly applies to that part of the peninsula west of the Halys River but is frequently used as a virtual synonym for Asia Minor.

Asia Minor is bounded on the north by the Black Sea, on the west by the Aegean and the straits of the Bosporus and Dardanelles (ancient Hellespont), on the south by the Mediterranean, and on the east by a line running northeastward from below the Gulf of Iskenderun to the Euphrates and up that stream to the Coruh (Chorokh) River and then to the Black Sea. The total area of the peninsula approximates 200,000 square miles, equal to that of New England, New York, New Jersey, Pennsylvania, Delaware, Maryland, and West Virginia.

The Central Plateau

The mass of Asia Minor consists of a plateau 3,000 to 5,000 feet above sea level,

tilted down toward the north and west. Extensive and irregular, it is fringed on all sides by higher mountain ranges, but on the west the hills are fewer and less imposing. Though the plateau consists largely of rolling upland, it is diversified by highland massifs and numerous sunken basins occupied by lakes and marshes. Although the rivers entering the interior plains from the adjoining mountains now are largely swallowed up in salt lakes and swamps, in New Testament times their waters provided for irrigation and helped to support numerous large cities. The surface of the northern part of the plateau is deeply eroded; in many places there are precipitous valley walls and rugged hillsides.

As a whole the central plateau has slender resources. Because of its enclosed nature, much of the plateau is arid. It supports little plant or animal life and is used for grazing sheep. Town life did not develop there until the Hellenistic and Roman periods, and even then the larger towns were strung out along the edge rather than across the heart of the tableland.

The Mountain Ranges

As already noted, mountain ranges surround the central plateau. The Armenian mountains extend westward and fork near the eastern boundary of the peninsula into two ranges—the Taurus on the south and the mountains of Pontus on the north. The northern rim of Mountains rises to about nine thousand feet and the southern to ten thousand feet. Both consist of a series of overlapping ridges which permit only a few narrow and tortuous passages between the coast and the interior. East and northeast of the main Taurus system and parallel to it lies the Anti-Taurus Range.

Along the southeast edge of the plateau for a distance of about 150 miles rise groups of volcanic peaks. At the northeast end of this range stands Mount Erciyas Dagi (ancient Argaeus) at a height of 13,100 feet, the highest point in Asia Minor. Here in western Cappadocia, fertilized by lava dust and supplied with snow waters in summer, were fine orchards and the best horse pastures of the Near East. On these a strain of racers for the Roman circus was bred.

From the Phrygian mountains on the west of the central plateau extend mountain spurs: the Temnos, Boz Dag (ancient Tmolus), and Messogis—which delimit respectively the valleys of the Caicus, Gediz (ancient Hermus), and Menderes (ancient Maeander). Since these valleys run east and west, they naturally conduct traffic in those directions. Thus the only open face of Asia Minor is toward the west and northwest, where the plateau ends in a staircase down to a piedmont or foothills region. Since the western shore is easily accessible, most invasions of Asia Minor that have had lasting results have been launched from Europe (e.g., Phrygians, Greeks, and Galatians or Celts).

As intimated, the mountains of Asia Minor constitute formidable barriers, but there are strategic passes. The most important was the Cilician Gates north of Tarsus. Two passes made possible routes from Antalya (biblical Attalia) on the Mediterranean to Laodicea and to Pisidian Antioch or Apamea. Another gave passage between Seleucia in western Cilicia to Karaman (ancient Laranda) in the interior. One other gave access between central Cappadocia and eastern Cilicia.

While the mountains might and did constitute hindrances to communication and transportation, they provided sources of mineral wealth. Since Asia Minor was significant in the biblical narrative during Roman times, only a statement of minerals known and mined then is provided here. The gold of Asia Minor was depleted by Roman times. A little silver was still mined in Pontus and some in central Cappadocia. Some copper was produced at Chalcedon and in Pontus and Cilicia. How many of the abandoned copper pits all over the country were productive in Roman times is unknown. Iron came chiefly from Pontus, Cappadocia, Bithynia, and some from the Troad (south of the Hellespont) and possibly Caria. Lead was mined in western Mysia. Zinc seems to have been extracted in the Troad and on Mount Tmolus. While various marbles of local importance were quarried, the variegated marble of Docimium was widely exported, as was the white marble of the territory of Cyzicus (modern Kapidagi). The mountains were also important for their timber resources. Forests of pine, oak, and fir abounded in the mountains of both the north and the south.

The Black Sea Coastlands

The Black Sea coast is generally steep and rocky; an irregular line of highlands rises 6,000 to 7,000 feet within fifteen to twenty miles from the sea, leaving almost no intervening coastal plain. Rivers of the region generally are short torrents that do not provide access to the interior. Moreover, there are few acceptable harbors. All of these drawbacks, plus the liability to earthquakes, tended to hold back the progress of the area.

The northern seaboard of Asia Minor divides into two sections. The eastern section consists of the biblical Pontus and Paphlagonia. A persistent northerly wind keeps the area cool and moderately rainy throughout the entire year. But Trapezus (modern Trabzon, or Trebizond), the capital of ancient Pontus, enjoys the weather of a Mediterranean Riviera, screened as it is by the Caucasus Range. The mountains are well clad with ship and carpenter's timber and are provided with deposits of silver and iron, which probably gave rise in Hittite days to the earliest iron industry of Nearer Asia. The inner side of the mountains opened to fertile valleys, and the broad valley of the Lycus River served as a main artery for the Pontic area. Poor harbors were always a drawback. But Sinope (modern Sinop), at the most northerly point on the Black Sea coastline, did become a great maritime center.

The western section of the northern seaboard of Asia Minor consists of ancient Bithynia and Mysia. Here the climate is similar to that of the eastern region. There isn't so much mineral wealth as in the eastern section, but the mountains stand farther back from the coast, leaving room for good grain and orchard country. And there are better harbors, an especially good one being located at Kapidagi (ancient Cyzicus).

Western Asia Minor

The western fringe of Asia Minor contributed most to the country's history in

The Bosphorus near Istanbul.

Greek and Roman days. Its weather is milder than the Greek homeland, and the soil is more fertile. The coastline is highly intricate and broken, with many good harbors and irregularly shaped islands.

Beginning in the north, the Bosporus is sixteen miles long and on the average one mile wide, though it narrows in places to less than seven hundred yards. Both banks rise steeply from the waters. The Sea of Marmara is a natural creel for trapping shoals of fish on their annual migration from the Mediterranean to the Black Sea. The Dardanelles (ancient Hellespont) is twenty-five miles long and increases in width toward the south, from about a half mile in the north to four miles in the south. Because of evaporation in the Mediterranean, a continuous flow of water south from the Black Sea produces a strong current in the Bosporus and Dardanelles. The current is three miles an hour at Istanbul, six in the Bosporus, and five in the Dardanelles.

To report statistics on the Hellespont is rather matter-of-fact. To stand at the narrowest spot in the channel and reminisce about the flow of history is not. Here at this divide between Europe and Asia occurred some of the most important and dramatic events of all time. To look out over the scene on a peaceful summer afternoon when the sun is dancing on the waters betrays nothing of the pivotal and Herculean events that took place there.

For example, in the spring of 480 B.C. the Persian king Xerxes crossed the Hellespont

with as many as 300,000 men on bridges prepared for the invasion of Europe. Reportedly the crossing took seven days and nights.[2] Think of the titanic effort involved in moving such a large army, cavalry, and baggage. Xerxes sought to crush the Greeks utterly. After initial victories in Greece, the Persians suffered a terrible naval defeat at Salamis, near Attica. Without a fleet to service the troops, Xerxes was forced to beat a hasty retreat back across the Hellespont. After the further destruction of his forces at Plataea, Xerxes (Ahasuerus) buried his sorrows in his harem. The story of Esther picked up in 479 or early 478 B.C. (cf. Esther 2:16). Xerxes' defeat is important to all of us. If Greek civilization had been wiped out in 480 B.C. and following, no Greco-Roman civilization would have developed, and the current basis of Western civilization would not have come into being.

A second important crossing of the Hellespont occurred in 334 B.C. when Alexander the Great launched his famous attack on the Persian Empire and destroyed it. We don't know much about the crossing, but it probably took place in late April or early May and Alexander probably used boats or possibly pontoon bridges to transport his army to Asia. Again the task was monumental. Depending on which authorities we follow, we conclude that he had to move some fifty thousand men plus cavalry horses. This event too was not merely a military venture. Alexander's victory

The Hellespont; Alexander crossed from the far side.

resulted in the firm entrenchment of Greek culture all over the eastern Mediterranean. And it effectively contributed to the later development of Greco-Roman culture throughout the Mediterranean world, so that Western European and American culture are now basically Greco-Roman.

South of the Dardanelles along the Aegean coast lie a series of east-west valleys, which, generally speaking, are broad and flat-bottomed and well furnished with rich alluvial deposits laid by the rivers. But while this deposit makes for very productive valleys when drained and cultivated, it also contributed to the silting up of river mouths and harbors. For instance, the mouth of the Menderes is now several miles west of where it was in Roman times. The site of Miletus, once a focus of naval communication, is entirely cut off from the sea. The harbor of Ephesus is completely filled in. A further disadvantage of this silting is the creation of marshes with their malarial threat.

In biblical times there were four broad river valleys in western Asia Minor: Caicus, Hermus, Cayster, and Maeander. Each provided access to an important hinterland. Pergamum was located in the Caicus. Smyrna, Sardis, and Philadelphia had access to the Hermus. The Cayster flowed north of Ephesus, and that great city of Diana also tapped the trade of the Maeander, as did Laodicea. In Roman times Miletus also lay on the Maeander.

The accidents of geography led to the development of two largely distinct cultures in Asia Minor. The culture of the plateau in the interior was essentially oriental, that of the coastal cities largely Greek or Greco-Roman.

The Mediterranean Coastlands

Along the entire length of the southern seaboard of Asia Minor, the mountains descend steeply to the sea, except in the regions of Pamphylia and eastern Cilicia. Thus the Mediterranean coastlands entered little into ancient history. The southerly winds of the winter season brought sufficient rainfall for a rich forest growth, which the Egyptians and many after them coveted for timber resources. Western Cilicia was the most trackless part of the coast and served as a pirate hideout.

The mountains of southern Asia Minor are fold ranges, not rift valleys. In the north the western Taurus folds are so closely packed against the plateau of Anatolia that hardly any streams cut their way through the mountains to the sea. Here the mountains are a serious barrier to contact with the interior and roads are few. The main Taurus, reaching twelve thousand feet, are much higher than the western Taurus. However, they are not as wide as the western Taurus, and erosion is more active. So a number of narrow and steep river valleys have been cut through the mountain chain at several points. One of these gorges was cut by the Yeziloluk, a tributary of the Cydnus, and formed the famous Cilician Gates.

Eastern Asia Minor

Eastern Asia Minor consists of a series of mountain ranges in the north, falling away into broken plateaus and finally into an undulating plain that continues into north Syria and Iraq.

Climate

The climate of Asia Minor is one of extremes. Parts of the Aegean coastlands never experience frost. In the east snow lies even in the valleys for a third of the year. The Black Sea coastlands have an annual rainfall that ranges from twenty-five inches in the west to one hundred inches in the east and a mean temperature of 45° F for January and 70° F for August. The Aegean coastlands have a rainfall of twenty-five to thirty inches and a mean temperature of 45° F for January and 75° F in July and August. The Mediterranean coastlands have a rainfall of about thirty inches and a mean temperature of 50° F in January and 83° F in the summer. The central plateau has about ten to seventeen inches of rainfall; all districts have more than a hundred days of frost during the year. The January temperature mean is 30° F and the summer mean about 70° F. In the east the climate is one of the most difficult and inhospitable in the world with hot and dry summers and bitterly cold winters. Rainfall averages seventeen to

The Halys River

twenty-four inches, and temperatures of forty degrees below zero have been recorded in January.

Rivers and Lakes

Several rivers have already been mentioned. Among others, the most important river of the peninsula is the Kizil Irmak (ancient Halys), six hundred miles long, which originates in eastern Asia Minor and flows in a great bend to the southwest and finally into the Black Sea through what was Pontus. Unfortunately its gorge is often too narrow to permit it to be an important means of communication into the interior. The Sakarya (ancient Sangarius), three hundred miles long, originates in what was ancient Phrygia and makes a great bend to the east and flows into the Black Sea through biblical Bithynia. The Cestrus (c. 80 miles long) was the chief river of Pamphylia. The Calycadnus (c. 150 miles long) drained western Cilicia. And the

The Cydnus River at Tarsus.

Cydnus (c. 40 miles long), the Sarus (748 miles long), and the Pyramus (230 miles long) flowed through eastern Cilicia, the latter two originating in the mountains of Cappadocia.

Of the lakes, the greatest is Tatta, a salt lake in the central plain, some sixty by ten to thirty miles in winter and a mere marsh in the summer drought. Karalis, a freshwater lake southeast of Pisidian Antioch on the road to Lystra, is about thirty-five miles long and lies at 3,770 feet in altitude. Southwest of Pisidian Antioch is Limnai, thirty miles long, at 2,850 feet in altitude.

Roads

Numerous roads spanned Asia Minor by the days of Paul and John. The great eastern trade route to the Euphrates began at Ephesus and traveled the Maeander Valley, passing through Laodicea, Colossae, Apamea, and then arching north of Pisidian Antioch, and dropping south to Galatian Laodicea and cutting east through Cappadocia.

The trade route from Ephesus to Syria would have been the same as the former to Apamea and then would have passed through Pisidian Antioch and Iconium and then south through Laranda or southeast through Hyde and then through the Cilician Gates to Tarsus. A western road led north from Ephesus through Smyrna, Pergamum, and Adramyttium to Cyzicus. A northern road led east from Byzantium through Nicomedia and Claudiopolis in Bithynia and then arched northward through Pompeiopolis and dipped south to Amisia. Other lesser north-south and east-west routes also existed.

Historical Developments

Beginnings

On the basis of numerous investigations and excavations in Turkey, Seton Lloyd concluded that human habitation in Anatolia goes back to the beginnings of the Paleolithic period. Four Paleolithic cultures have been reported in stratification in a cave near Antalya in south central Turkey.[3] Signs of habitation of Asia Minor during the Neolithic period are sparse but growing. They have

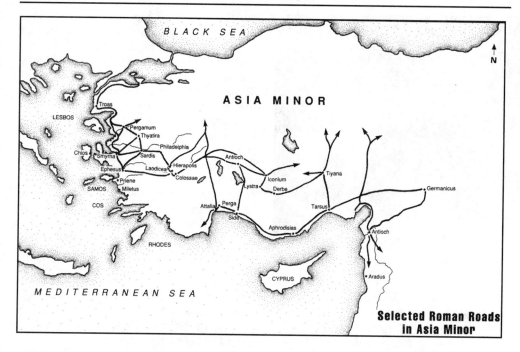

Selected Roman Roads in Asia Minor

appeared at Mersin (southwest of Tarsus), Sakjegözü (a considerable distance northeast of Tarsus), Hacilar (west of Konya), Beldibi (near Antalya), and Çatal Hüyük (southeast of Konya). At the latter site James Mellaart unearthed a well-developed civilization dating to the seventh millennium B.C. The thirty-two-acre site there is the largest known Neolithic site in the Near East. The buildings were constructed of sundried, mold-made mud bricks, with plastered floors and walls. Several of the buildings, which Mellaart classified as shrines, were elaborately decorated with wall paintings.

The Chalcolithic Age

The invention of the smelting process to extract copper dates back to at least 5500 B.C., as finds at Çatal Hüyük indicate. About the same time workers at Yarim Tepe, over the border in northern Mesopotamia, were smelting copper. [4] The Chalcolithic (copperstone) age in Asia Minor lasted for a very long time, probably during most of the fifth and fourth millennia B.C. During this period the great plateau of Anatolia seems to have remained unoccupied, the Chalcolithic peoples becoming aware of it only during the last years of their existence. Near the close of

the fourth millennium, the lands of Anatolia proper were at last "discovered" and the first farming settlements appeared on the plateau itself and in the Aegean province to the west. But there is no degree of certainty as to the origin of these settlers. Chalcolithic cultures have not yet come to light in Pontic and eastern Anatolia. In the late Chalcolithic period Anatolia fell far behind Mesopotamia in cultural and political development.

The Early Bronze Age

Probably about 3500 B.C. the Bronze (alloy of copper and tin) age came to Asia Minor.[5] Only in the Cilician Plain did newcomers introduce it; elsewhere it developed out of the late Chalcolithic culture. Northwestern and central Anatolia became conspicuous for the first time in Anatolian prehistory. While northwestern, central, and southwestern Anatolia possessed considerable mineral resources, the Cilicia and Konya (ancient Iconium) plains contained some of the richest alluvial soil in the country; and Cilicia controlled an important trade route as well. Metallurgy was so highly developed in Anatolia by the end of the Early Bronze age that this region was the

A ramp of the propylon and a fortification wall at Troy, third millenium B.C.

market from which Assyria and Syria obtained much of their metalwork.[6]

Seemingly the great prosperity of Anatolia during the period 3500–2300 B.C. rested largely on the systematic exploitation of its metal wealth and the ability to market it in many areas of the Middle East. Fully urbanized communities now arose, probably organized under kings, with a considerable percentage of the population engaged in the metal industry and trade by land and sea. Though its people were illiterate and the cities smaller than those of Egypt and Sumer, Anatolian culture displayed at some of the royal courts there was second to none.[7] Troy, Thermi on the island of Lesbos, Tarsus, Alishar (Alaja) Hüyük, Kültepe, and Poliochni on the island of Lemnos are among the important sites from which our information comes for this period.

Houses of the Early Bronze I period (3500–2800 B.C.), at least in the West, were generally rectangular, of a hall-and-porch or megaron type, with several raised platforms that may have been used for sleeping. A hearth stood in the middle of the floor and food was stored in large pots or clay-lined bins sunk in the floor. In some towns, houses were grouped in blocks separated by streets and alleys. Most houses seem to have been of one story and were almost certainly flat-roofed.

Finds of metal objects are comparatively few. All pottery was still handmade, with-

out the benefit of a pottery wheel; and it was superior to contemporary pottery of Mesopotamia, Egypt, and Syria.

Though the transition from the Early Bronze I period to Early Bronze II (2800–2300 B.C.) was generally peaceful, in the northwest there was considerable destruction which Mellaart feels most likely was produced by an enemy who came from the Thracian coast.[8] During Early Bronze II the main schools of Anatolian metalwork (the northwestern and central) were of local origin, owing little if anything to influences from Mesopotamia, Syria, or Cyprus.[9] Trade was widespread.

Excavations seem to indicate that several kingdoms, large and small, existed in Asia Minor at that time. The rich burials of some of the kings and queens demonstrate their wealth and power, as well as a high level of craftsmanship. Alishar Hüyük, east of modern Ankara, was especially productive of richly buried persons.

There is evidence of city planning during this period. A good example is Poliochni on the island of Lemnos, where a main street ran in a north-south direction through the town. Along this street lay a number of blocks or squares, some containing one large house, some containing several houses. A moderate-sized house consisted of a hall and porch with a courtyard and a row of smaller rooms along one of the long sides of the hall. Larger houses simply elaborated on this plan with additional rooms around the hall and court, sometimes with a second courtyard. Typical public buildings included an assembly hall and a huge granary.

Houses in Cilicia differed from those of the West. At Tarsus they were oblong and were entered directly from the street. In the main room stood a built-up hearth, and at the rear of it a door led into one or two other rooms. Probably these houses had two stories. The hall-and-porch type of house did not become common in the East until after 2300 B.C., when cultural influences from the northwest became strong.

Two Early Bronze Age temples have surfaced at Beycesultan in west central Turkey. Measuring forty-five to fifty feet in length, they are of the hall-and-porch plan, with a back room added. Constructed of mudbrick and plastered over, these temples were painted blue. Inside of each stood an altar behind which a screen sheltered the inner sanctum from the view of worshipers. Numerous storage vessels and bins were found in the sanctuary.

As noted above, the metal industry was well developed during Early Bronze II. Casting in closed molds, *repoussé* work, metal inlay, sweating and soldering, and techniques of hammering were all known. Considerable use was made of copper, bronze, iron, gold, silver, electrum (an alloy of gold and silver), and lead—all native to Anatolia except the tin used to produce bronze. The large number of weapons and armor found in tombs has led to the belief that the population was warlike. Pottery at Troy and Tarsus was made on a pottery wheel during Early Bronze II. Elsewhere in Anatolia it was handmade.

A particularly destructive invasion brought to an end Early Bronze II in western and southern Anatolia about 2300–2200 B.C. There the number of settlements during Early Bronze III (2300–1900 B.C.) stood at only about a quarter of the number in the previous period.[10] Town after town (e.g., Troy, Tarsus, Poliochni, Beycesultan) met its end by burning. Every townsite on the Konya plain shows evidence of conflagration dating to the end of the Early Bronze II period. Subsequently nearly every village there was deserted and never again occupied.

James Mellaart has suggested that Luwians from the Balkans moved in at the end of Early Bronze I and effected destruction in western Anatolia, became "Anatolianized" during Early Bronze II, and were joined by fresh groups of destructive Luwians (and probably others) at the end of Early Bronze II.[11] The invaders who came around 2300 B.C. brought to Anatolia a taste for exotic painted pottery (Gay colors on light clay). This was quite revolutionary for the region, accustomed to plain and burnished ware with decoration that was almost completely limited to simple lines or white paint on a dark background. Seton Lloyd hints that this remarkable change in pottery styles may have something to do with the arrival of Indo-Europeans in Asia Minor,[12] and Mellaart notes the possibility

that Indo-Europeans came to the peninsula in the wake of Luwian invasion about 2300–2200 B.C. But he observes that most Greek scholars feel that the Indo-Europeans did not come so early and that much work still needs to be done on the problem.[13]

Middle and Late Bronze Ages

At any rate, Indo-Europeans did certainly make their appearance in Asia Minor by the beginning of the Middle Bronze Age (c. 1900 B.C.). For purposes of organization the Middle and Late Bronze Ages (covering the period 1900–1200 B.C.) are discussed as a unit here. Troy and the Hittites were the chief powers during the period. But Assyrian influence in the east was important, and the Mitanni were a power to be reckoned with.

At around 2000 B.C. Anatolia was divided into a large number of tiny political units, each centered on a fortified settlement only a few acres in extent and controlling a small amount of surrounding territory. After that time truly urban centers began to develop—many of them covering fifty to seventy acres. In the east at least this development resulted from the ability of local rulers to exploit the natural resources of the region.

Assyrian Merchant Colonies in the East

Stimulus to the central Anatolian economy rose from the presence of merchants from Asshur in northern Mesopotamia. And the independent urban communities of eastern Asia Minor were drawn into cooperative trade relations with Assyria sometime after 1900 B.C. A total of twenty-one of these settlements can be attested from the written sources.[14] But only three have been located: at Kanesh (thirteen miles northeast of Kayseri); at Alishar (forty-five miles north of Kanesh) and at Hittite Hattusa (the capital, seventy-seven miles northeast of Kanesh). By about 1750, this whole system had collapsed, perhaps as a result of local interstate rivalry, which coincided with Hurrian (Mitanni) and Amorite pressure on Assyria itself and on the trade routes.

As early as 1871 Assyrian commercial tablets began to appear in eastern Turkey, and archaeologists eagerly sought their source. The Czechoslovakian Bedrich Hrozny in 1925 was finally successful in this quest at Kültepe (ancient Kanesh). He was rewarded with about one thousand tablets for his efforts. Since 1948 the Turkish archaeologist Tashin Özgüc has expended considerable effort at the site. More than fifteen thousand merchants' tablets have now come to light. Excavations there continue on behalf of the Turkish Historical Foundation and the General Directorate of Monuments and Museums.

Regulating the trading community was the *karum*, a kind of chamber of commerce. It controlled trade with Assyria and served as a tribunal for fixing prices and settling disputes. The colony seems to have been an integral part of the Assyrian state economy, and official messengers maintained regular and effective communications with the homeland.[15] The caravans of donkeys which these traders employed seem to have been extremely free from robbery. Their main cargo imported from Assyria was lead and woven materials; the main export to Assyria was copper. The local princes levied taxes upon the Assyrians and reserved the right to purchase any of their goods.

The Assyrian merchants seem to have been on good terms with the native Anatolians and to have intermarried freely with them. They lived in houses which seem generally to have been of two stories with rooms grouped around an open court or along a corridor. These houses were built of sundried brick on foundations of uncut stone and were plastered without and within. Family rooms usually were on the second floor. Burials were commonly made beneath the floor of the houses, and the deceased provided with numerous funerary gifts. Occupants arranged their business records on shelves or placed them in large jars in a main floor room. They painted their pottery, called "Cappadocian ware," with intricate designs, and sometimes they shaped their cups in the form of a bull's or lion's head.

Apparently this interesting chapter in Anatolian history came to an end with little warning. The town of Kanesh was destroyed by fire; and the inhabitants departed hastily, leaving the contents of their houses in their proper places—where they remained until the archaeologists uncovered them.

When these merchant colonies came to an end, the towns with which they were associated declined. Some of them simply passed out of existence. But one of them, Hattusa, later rose to control a Hittite kingdom and then empire.

Hittites

The Bible effectively attests that the Hittites were an ancient people. The Table of Nations lists Heth as one of the sons of Canaan (Genesis 10:15). Hittites were involved in the founding of Jerusalem (Ezekiel 16:3), Abraham bought the cave of Machpelah from the sons of Heth (Genesis 23), and Esau married Hittite wives (Genesis 26:34; 36:1–3). Tribal lists include them among the peoples living in Palestine when Abraham arrived and at the time of the conquest (Genesis 15:18–21; Numbers 13:29). Two passages refer to "kings of the Hittites" (2 Chronicles 1:17; 2 Kings 7:6–7) and about a dozen other Old Testament books mention the Hittites in numerous passages.

Although higher critics used to doubt the existence of the Hittites because secular history had failed to verify their existence, evidence of their historicity gradually accumulated. For example, Thutmose III of Egypt in the fifteenth century B.C. and Ramses II of Egypt in the thirteenth century B.C. had fought against a people called "Kheta" in Syria, according to Egyptian records. Some scholars identified these with the Hittites of the Old Testament. Assyrian records referred to Syria as the "Land of Hatti" after about 1100 B.C.

PLACE OF THE HITTITES

IN SCRIPTURE

The Bible presents the Hittites as an important people. The term

Remains of the building at Bogazkoy where the Hittite archives were found.

"Hittite" or "Hittites" appears forty-seven times in fifteen biblical books. In addition, there are fourteen mentions of Heth, the ancestor of the Hittites. Probably the best-known reference to the Hittites is to Uriah the Hittite, husband of Bathsheba (2 Samuel 11). He was a soldier in David's army who had evidently been recruited from one of the Hittite city-states of Syria that David had conquered. These states continued to exist after the fall of the Hittite Empire after 1200 B.C. The Assyrians absorbed the last of those states around 700 B.C.

But long before the Hittite Old Kingdom came into existence around 1600 B.C., Abraham had bought the cave of Machpelah from the sons of Heth as a burial place for Sarah (Genesis 23) and Hittites had been involved in the founding of Jerusalem (Ezekiel 16:3).

During the long centuries of the Hittite Old Kingdom and the Empire (c. 1600–1175 B.C.) the Hittites and Hebrews did not make contact. For the Hebrews were in bondage in Egypt, wandering in the wilderness, and establishing themselves in Palestine during the days of Joshua and the Judges. For their part the Hittites were active in Asia Minor, Syria, and Mesopotamia.

Only after the breakup of the Hittite Empire and the creation of Hittite city-states (after 1175 B.C.) did the Hebrews and Hittites cross paths—when David's forces moved north to conquer some of the later small Hittite states of north Syria.

Over a period of decades travelers and scholars identified some archaeological remains in Syria as Hittite. Then similar objects and construction began to turn up in Asia Minor. Finally in 1880 A. H. Sayce read a paper to the Society for Biblical Archaeology in London in which he declared that the Hittites must have occupied much of Asia Minor in ancient times. Subsequently numerous archaeologists made extended surveys in Turkey which tended to confirm Sayce's thesis.

Exploration led to excavation. The British Museum conducted an excavation at Carchemish in northwestern Syria in 1879, locating numerous monuments and inscriptions in a Hittite hieroglyphic script. A German team worked at Zinjirli (in Turkey, northeast of ancient Antioch-on-the-Orontes) from 1888 to 92, finding additional relevant monuments and inscriptions. Meanwhile the Amarna Letters, discovered in 1887 in Egypt,

A Hittite hieroglyphic inscription in the Hittite Museum in Ankara.

threw new light on Egypto-Hittite relations. These letters served to indicate the importance of excavations in Anatolia proper.

Finally, in 1906 Hugo Winckler on behalf of the German Oriental Society began to excavate at what proved to be the Hittite capital at Bogazköy (ancient Hattusa), one hundred miles east of Ankara. In addition to monumental remains, he discovered royal and temple archives there with some ten thousand tablets written in cuneiform. Excavations at Bogazköy, interrupted by World War I, were resumed by the Germans under the leadership of K. Bittel in 1931. Interrupted again by war, the excavations at the Hittite capital were reopened by Bittel in 1952. More recently Peter Neve has led the German dig.

But others were busy with pick and spade in Hittite land. Among the long list of excavations must be included the work of University of Chicago teams at Alishar and Tell Tainat, a Danish team at Hama (ancient Hamath), Sir Leonard Woolley at Tell Atchana, and Hetty Goldman of Bryn Mawr at Tarsus. And under the leadership of Professors Hans Gütterbock of the University of Ankara (later of Chicago) and H. T. Bossert of the University of Istanbul, the Turks themselves began to do effective work in Hittite archaeology.

Before a definitive story of the Hittites could be told, their written records had to be translated. Bedrich Hrozny made a

beginning in 1915 when he published a sketch of Hittite grammar and showed that its structure was Indo-European. Ferdinand Sommer, Johannes Friedrich, H. Eheolf, and Albrecht Götze were some of the more important pioneers of decipherment in Germany. By 1933 they had translated most of the better-preserved Hittite cuneiform historical texts into German. The American E. H. Sturtevant and the Frenchman Louis Delaporte also contributed to the linguistic developments.

Hittite hieroglyphic was much harder to decipher. The important names here were the German H. T. Bossert, the American I.J. Gelb, the Czech B. Hrozny, the Swiss Emil Forrer, and the Italian P. Meriggi. Actually a total of eight languages were written in these two scripts, five of which were spoken by peoples of Asia Minor. Currently the University of Chicago is producing a Hittite dictionary, of which Harry Hoffner and Theo Van den Hout are co-editors.

Now it remains to sketch the history that the Hittite texts and artifacts can be made to surrender. Something should be said first about the peoples of Asia Minor and their languages. Three of the languages and/or ethnic groups were related to the Indo-European family. The Luwian-speaking peoples probably arrived in Asia Minor at the end of the Early Bronze Age (about 2300 B.C.) and by 1750, controlled much of the southern and western parts of the peninsula. As time passed, they played an increasing role in the Hittite kingdom. Palaic was the language of Pala, commonly placed in Paphlagonia in north central Asia Minor.

The official Hittite language itself, in which most of the Hittite texts were written, was referred to in the Bogazköy texts as the "language of Nesha," the Hittite form of Kanesh. These people probably entered the area around Kanesh (Kültepe in east central Asia Minor) during the latter part of the Early Bronze Age and were present in the country during the most flourishing period of the Assyrian merchant colony.

These Indo-European "Kaneshites" mingled freely with the non-Indo-European Hatti (Khatti) of the northeastern part of Asia Minor, and their language gradually replaced that of their predecessors. As can

The Lion Gate at Bogazkoy.

readily be seen, Hatti is linguistically equitable with the English "Hittite." Since the archaeologists had already assigned the name Hittite to the Kaneshites, they had to find another term for the "true Hittites." Khattian, Khattic, and Proto-Hittite have been used to designate this non-Indo-European substratum of the population.

Hittite History

There is some justification for beginning Hittite history earlier (perhaps 1750 B.C. or a little before), but the tendency today is to launch the story of the Hittite kingdom with King Labarnas, about 1600. Says O.R. Gurney, "The later Hittite kings liked to trace their descent back to the ancient King Labarnas, and with him therefore Hittite history may be said to begin."[16]

At any rate, Hittite history is commonly divided into two distinct periods: the Old Kingdom and the New Kingdom or Empire, the latter beginning about 1420 B.C. and ending about 1180. Actually Hittite power was fairly weak between roughly 1500 and 1380, when the Mitanni (Hurrians) controlled much of the upper Tigris-Euphrates Valley, as well as Syria and a portion of Asia Minor.

Labarnas' immediate successor decided to build a new fortress on the deserted site of Hattusa (alternately Hattusa or Khattusha) and adopted the throne name Hattusili or Khattushili, meaning "man of Hattusa." Then he proceeded to expand his borders to the south in order to reach the Mediterranean and gain access to the Near Eastern trade routes. In order to control those trade routes, he especially locked horns with the king of Halab (Aleppo) in Syria. But before he could complete that conquest he had to deal with the state of Arzawa in western Asia Minor. Apparently victorious there, he returned to his struggle with Halab but never did conquer it.

Hattusili's grandson and successor, Mursili I, was victorious in Syria, conquering the king of Halab. Then he kept going along the Euphrates until he took Babylon and brought an end to Hammurabi's dynasty, about 1595 B.C. But it soon became evident that the Hittites had overreached themselves and their administrative machinery was not strong enough to maintain the power of state. Away from his capital, Mursili no longer exerted a strong hold of governance, and factions arose. His brother-in-law assassinated him when he returned home. During the following years a succession of dynastic coups followed, and the foreign conquests were lost.

Around 1500 B.C. Telepinu sparked something of a revival of Hittite fortunes. But his efforts were largely in vain. And when he died without sons, his reign was followed by about another fifty years of

The King Gate at Bogazkoy. Some believe that the figure at the left should be identified as a god.

weakness and dynastic strife. The whole period is obscure. In fact, Hittite records cease for about half a century.

When the curtain rises again, a shadowy figure, Tudhaliya II, is busy founding a new dynasty approximately 1420 B.C. But during the silent period of Hittite records, some decades earlier, Thutmose III of Egypt had been victorious in Palestine and Syria and established Egyptian power there, posing a future threat to the Hittites.

To Suppiluliuma I (1344–1322) goes the credit for real establishment of the Hittite Empire. Securing a firm hold on the throne, he proceeded to build the fortifications of Bogazköy. Then he marched off to settle accounts with the Mitanni. Initially repulsed, he was later successful in defeating the Mitanni and taking all of Syria. The great Hittite king also reconquered lands in the south and west that had gained independence during the Hittite period of weakness. The widow of Tutankhamon in Egypt even sent an appeal for one of Suppululiuma's sons to marry her and become king of Egypt. When the young man arrived in Egypt, he died under mysterious circumstances, probably murdered by local leaders opposed to the marriage. Suppiluliuma also set up a vassal kingdom in Mitanni as protection against the rising power of Assyria, but this proved to be no deterrent to military advance from the east, and before long Assyrians and Hittites were glaring at each other across the Euphrates.

It soon became evident, however, that the real enemy of the Hittites lay in the south. After a period of preoccupation with internal affairs, the Egyptians under Seti I moved up into Canaan around 1300 B.C. When Ramses II came to the throne approximately a decade later, it became clear that the two powers would soon clash. The Hittite Muwatallis II and Ramses met at Kadesh on the Orontes River during 1286/1285. Though the Egyptian carved accounts of a great victory there on the temple walls of his homeland it is quite clear that only by a stroke of good fortune was he kept from annihilation. The Hittites had won at least a partial victory; the result can fairly be classified as a draw. About fifteen years later, in 1269, during the reign of Hattusili III, the two powers concluded a peace pact. Hattusili visited Egypt, and his daughter was married to Ramses II.

Probably this treaty was a sign of weakness rather than strength. Egyptian power gradually waned during the thirteenth century. And although Hattusili (1275–1250) seems in general to have enjoyed peace and prosperity, there is evidence that he had to march against his enemies to the west and that relations with Babylonia were deteriorating. For him to have allowed a worsening of relations with Egypt as well might have been suicidal.

During the reign of his son and successor Tudhaliya IV (c. 1250–1220 B.C.) the Hittites managed to launch a successful attack on Cyprus; his successors held at least part of the island for some years. Tudhaliya also finished construction of Yazilikaya, the great sanctuary of the gods about a mile from Hattusa, and of the capital itself. But by the end of his reign, clouds began to gather on the horizon. Assyria was a threat in the east, the Kashka peoples in the north, and the Ahhiyawa in the west.

Actually the campaign against Cyprus may well have been an effort to prevent encirclement. And some believe it was designed to protect the trade routes over which food supplies to Hittite lands had to travel. It also seems that a gradual climate change was occurring, with decreasing rainfall and rising temperatures and a failure of harvests, requiring the importation of

Ramses II of Egypt met Hittite forces at the Battle of Kadesh in 1286/85 B.C. Here Ramses' statue stands among the ruins of the Temple of Luxor at Karnak, Egypt.

Entrance to the Hittite worship center at Yazilikaya, with foundations of buildings that stood there during the Hittite Empire.

grain from Egypt and elsewhere. Some also believe that completion of the great sanctuary of Yazilikaya at this time was an effort to placate the gods, when the state was faced by natural and military adversity.

Finally in about 1180 attackers reduced the capital city to ashes and the Hittite Empire ceased to exist. Apparently the Assyrians proved to be no real threat at the end; they were having internal problems. With factional infighting of their own, the Hittites did not have the strength to stand up to external attack. Presumably the Kashka peoples, an almost annual menace to the Hittites, put Hattusa to the torch. But we should not dismiss the part that the marauding Sea Peoples may have played in destroying the Hittite Empire, as Itamar Singer of Tel Aviv University has claimed.[16a]

The Ahhiyawans to the west present a problem of identification. Whether or not the name of this enemy principality is to be equated with "Achaean" and to imply that the Greeks were active in the East at this time is uncertain. The balance of probability at present seems to favor the equation with Mycenean Greeks. Circumstantial evidence for doing so is strong. At any rate, the Ahhiyawans appeared on the Anatolian mainland at least by the fifteenth century B.C. and their involvement reached its peak during the thirteenth century. Apparently they did not seek permanent occupation of Western Anatolian territory but rather influence in vassal states to gain access to resources in demand in the Greek mainland. It was to their advantage to keep the Hittites weak, to prevent them from effective control of those resources.

A procession of gods carved into a wall in the Hittite worship center at Yazilikaya.

A king of the late Hittite city state of Carchemish.
Ankara Museum

But not all the great urban centers disappeared when Hattusa did. Many inhabitants of the Hittite central region were squeezed in a southeasterly direction and populated several Neo-Hittite kingdoms grouped around such cities as Carchemish and Melid (Malatya) on the Euphrates or Tarhuntassa north of the Taurus Mountains in southeast Asia Minor. David of Israel conquered some of these city-states early in the tenth century, when he pushed his borders up to the region of the Euphrates. Men from some of these states took service in the Israelite army. A well-known example is Uriah the Hittite, first husband of Bathsheba (2 Samuel 11:3 ff.). Actually these Neo-Hittite kingdoms managed to survive for some five hundred years, the last of them falling to the Assyrians in 709 B.C.

But these Syrian city-states should be called Hittite only with numerous qualifications. Their script is hieroglyphic rather than cuneiform. Their language is not that of the official records of Bogazköy but is similar to that of the Luwians. Their culture is strongly permeated with Phoenician and Aramaic elements.

If the Hittites' homeland was Asia Minor and if they are not known to have established effective city-states in Syria until the latter part of the second millennium B.C., then it must be asked how this historical evidence may be squared with biblical claims of Hittites in Palestine as early as the days of Abraham. Numerous critics have been quick to assign biblical references to late and inaccurate sources. It does not seem at all necessary to concede to such an allegation, however. And the problems are not all solved even in that fashion.

Remember that the non-Indo-European peoples who lived in north central Asia Minor before the "Hittites" came were called "Hatti" and spoke a language referred to in the texts as "Hattili." Remember, too, that after historians had used up the term Hittite on the later Indo-European invaders of the area, the "true Hittites" had to be addressed by other terminology. There is nothing to prove that these earlier non-Indo-European Hatti did not live in considerable numbers in Palestine as well as in Asia Minor. The Bible could very easily have reference to these earlier peoples. After all, Heth is classified as a son of Canaan (Genesis 10:15), who was not an Indo-European.

Layout of the great Valley Temple at Bogazkoy.

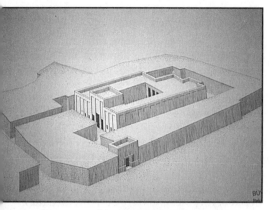

Reconstruction of the great valley temple at Bogazkoy.

It is interesting to observe that the red and black highly burnished Khirbet Kerah pottery in Palestine is virtually identical with pottery in central Anatolia and the Kurgan homeland in Transcaucasia in the third millennium B.C. This may suggest an incursion or migration of Hattians into Palestine in the twenty-third century B.C.[17]

Hittite Culture

At the head of the Hittite state stood the king, who controlled all areas of life. He was commander-in-chief of the army, supreme judge, and chief priest. Though he might delegate his judicial responsibilities, he was expected to perform his other duties in person. There are instances when the king had to leave the front during an important campaign to return home to conduct religious ceremonies. The king was never deified during his lifetime, but there was a cult of the spirits of former kings. It was said that at his death "he became a god."

While Hittite laws distinguish two social classes—free and slave—there were in fact three social classes: the high-ranking nobles; a middle class of warriors, farmers, and artisans; and a lower class of serfs and slaves.

THE SIZE OF ANCIENT CITIES

Comments on the Hittite capital, Hattusa, as a "huge" city make us wonder about the size of ancient Near Eastern cities. For example, Hattusa

during the Hittite Empire covered 400 acres. By comparison, contemporary Troy on the Hellespont, far more famous, was only about 4 acres. The Jericho that Joshua's armies surrounded was 8.5 acres in extent and therefore covered about two Chicago—or New York-sized city blocks. That is how the Israelite army could march around Jericho seven times on the seventh day (Joshua 6:15).

The Hazor that with its King Jabin confronted Joshua at the time of the Conquest (Joshua 11:1–13) measured 30 acres on the mound and 175–200 acres in the lower city. This was the largest city in ancient Palestine. The Jerusalem of David covered about 11 acres and the Beersheba of the United Kingdom period, 2.5 acres. Nineveh at its height was 1,800 acres, and Lachish in Judah when Sennacherib of Assyria destroyed it, about 18 acres.

The base of the economy was agricultural. Farmers plowed with oxen; horses were reserved for drawing chariots. Mules served as pack animals, especially because of their sure-footedness in the mountainous terrain. Sheep provided wool, milk, and meat; goats provided hair, milk, and cheese. Grains included wheat, emmer wheat, barley, and probably oats. Chief among the

The Holy of Holies in the valley temple at Bogazkoy. The statue stood in the alcove at the far end and openings on either side of it permitted light to flood the statue.

fruits were apples, pears, plums, figs, and grapes, which were processed as raisins and for wine. The sweetener in the diet came from honey, commercially produced, and the names of numerous vegetables appear in the texts.

Metal production and processing were very important to the Hittites, however. Copper, lead, silver, and especially iron were among the chief metals worked. A list of the Hittite craftsmen includes potters, leather workers, weavers, blacksmiths, bakers, carpenters, and beekeepers.

The Hittite law code bears striking similarities to Hammurabi's code, even being set up on a case system (i.e., "If a man committed a certain crime, then such a penalty would be his punishment"). But while the Babylonian code stressed retaliation by way of punishment, the Hittite code stressed compensation for the one wronged.

Hittite cities were stone-walled. The most imposing, Hattusa (Bogazköy), the capital, covered four hundred acres at its greatest extent. The principal subjects of their stone sculpture, both in the round and in bas-relief (low relief), were kings, gods, and other religious representations and warriors. Religious and magical rather than artistic considerations seem to have prompted the sculpture of their massive monuments. Chief among the deities were the sun goddess and the weather god and his consort. Cultural indebtedness of the Hittites to the Hurrians and Babylonians was great. From the former they borrowed most of their myths, for instance. From the latter came such contributions as legal influences and their script.

Troy

While the Hittites were building their kingdom and empire in most of Asia Minor, Troy dominated the northwestern part of Asia Minor. Strategically located, it occupied a low ridge some four miles from the Aegean to the west and an equal distance from the Dardanelles to the north. From its vantage point the city controlled traffic through the straits as well as an important land route.

Although as early as 1822 Charles Maclaren identified Turkish Hissarlik as the site of Troy, it was Heinrich Schliemann who fixed the identification and excavated there for seven seasons between 1870 and 1890. Wilhelm Dörpfeld dug there in 1893 and 1894. From 1932 to 1938 a University of Cincinnati team worked there for seven seasons under the leadership of Carl Blegen. Since 1988 an international team under the direction of Manfred Korfmann of Tübingen University in Germany has been conducting excavations on the mound. The University of Cincinnati is a participating member. Occupational debris covered the hill to a depth of fifty feet and have been divided into forty-six strata. Archaeologists describe nine main occupational levels at the site.

Troy was first occupied during the Early Bronze Age, about 3000 B.C. The earliest settlement was a small fortress some 270 feet across, within which stood a few large houses—homes of the ruler and his followers—built of crude brick on stone foundations. Frequently rebuilt, the remains of this complex yielded to the archaeologists copper implements, much pottery (with highly polished surfaces in black, brownish, grayish, or greenish black, and some lighter colors), and many other artifacts. The culture of Troy I influenced or was closely related to that of the eastern shore of the Aegean and the Gallipoli Peninsula across the Dardanelles. By the end of the period, contacts with Greece were considerable; but little evidence of contacts with central Anatolia is yet available.

Troy II dates to the period 2500–2300 B.C. The new citadel, increased in diameter to four hundred feet, was completely gutted by fire during the invasion at the end of Troy II. The fire must have completely surprised the inhabitants and must have spread very rapidly because, without exception, the floors were covered with household gear, a considerable quantity of gold ornaments and jewelry, and vessels of gold, copper, and bronze weapons.[18] These objects demonstrated a great advance in the arts and crafts over Troy I. Also the pottery wheel had been introduced and made possible a greater variety of shapes. Colors of pottery tended to be lighter. Commercial contacts with the Aegean world were more numerous than during Troy I.

The considerable fortification of Troy VI.

Troy III, IV, and V occurred during the Early Bronze III period, between 2300 and 1700 B.C. There was no discernible cultural break between those cities or between them and Troy II. Troy III covered more ground than Troy II and had a town plan with blocks of houses separated by narrow streets. Exterior house walls were now of stone instead of brick. The fourth settlement at Troy was larger than Troy III, but there was a reversion to building house walls of crude brick. House plans became more complex in Troy V, quality of construction improved, and pottery was of better quality too. Throughout the period extensive relations with the West continued. The degree of contact that existed between Troy and central Asia Minor is problematic.

How Troy V met its end is uncertain. But Troy VI marked a considerable break with the past, no doubt resulting from a movement of Indo-European peoples that flooded the Aegean world. The citadel, now greatly expanded, had a wall some two thousand feet in circumference around the base of the hill, which was terraced and covered with freestanding houses. The wall originally stood to a height of more than twenty-three feet. Presumably these houses were occupied by the king's courtiers and favorites, and presumably the palace stood on the summit of the hill. The masonry of many of these structures was carefully dressed and fitted and in some instances almost attained classical Greek excellence. Wooden columns set on shaped stone bases were used in several of these buildings. A settlement for the common people lay adjacent to the citadel.

Finds of metal objects and pottery at Troy VI indicate extensive external relations with the Aegean world, though some of the commodities may have been produced locally. To date nothing has been found either at Troy or at Hittite sites to indicate that those powers had any contact with each other. But this is merely an argument from silence and is not therefore conclusive.

Blegen concluded that Troy VI was destroyed by a great upheaval around 1300 B.C.—an upheaval that knocked down the fortification walls and ruined most of the large houses within the citadel. He believed that an earthquake must have been responsible; there was no evidence of fire. Troy VIIa continued directly upon the cultural foundations of Troy VI. Instead of a smaller number of large freestanding houses within the citadel, there were now more numerous smaller houses packed so close together that many of them had common walls. Each house had several large storage jars sunk deep beneath the floors with the mouths projecting only slightly above the ground.

Blegen identified Troy VIIa as the Troy destroyed by the Achaeans. This city was

A worship center at Troy, used during the period 700 B.C. to A.D. 300.

the *Iliad* itself tells a glorious tale of how Bronze Age Greeks (Myceneans) under the command of Agamemnon launched a vast Greek armada against Troy because of the abduction of Helen of Sparta by the Trojan prince Paris, and after ten years of warfare subdued the Trojans and destroyed the city. Schliemann believed the essential truthfulness of the account as he began excavations there. So did Blegen as he concluded his work at the site.[21] Many others, including recent excavators, consider the *Iliad* to be based on myth.

There is something of a middle way. Homer was a poet who knew how to tell a powerfully good story and we do not expect poets or writers of historical novels to stick closely to historical details. The size, duration, or reason for the Trojan War may not be strictly factual. But the actuality of the conflict, parties involved, and outcome may be.

From Hittite sources we discover that Mycenean involvement in affairs along the western shores of Asia Minor continued over a period of some two hundred years, from about 1425 to 1225 B.C., and Miletus was the most important base of operations.[22] As Michael Wood observes, Mycenean rulers had to "reward and equip their war host with loot" and support their highly organized "state industries" with booty, slaves, and treasure. Thus, predatory

completely reduced to ruins by fire that seems to have been of human origin. The crowding of houses within the citadel and the large number of storage jars in private houses indicated preparation for siege.

Blegen suggested that Troy fell about 1250.[19] At that time the Greeks might still have mustered enough strength to defeat Troy. Troy VIIb was built on the ruins of VIIa without a break in continuity of culture and it lasted only a generation or two. Then came a definite break in culture (possibly c. 1200). The closest analogy for the pottery introduced at that time was pottery found in Late Bronze Age sites in Hungary,[20] tying the destruction of Troy VIIb closely to the Phrygian invasion (from southeastern Europe).

The new excavations at Troy indicate that it might have been occupied continuously during the following millennium. Whether or not that is the case, successors of Alexander the Great conducted a major rebuilding campaign there. That city suffered destruction in 85 B.C., during the First Mithridatic war. But Augustus, who claimed descent from the Trojan Aeneas, considerably rebuilt the town, which continued to exist until the fourth century A.D.

In evaluating Homer, the *Iliad*, and the Trojan War, we should note that

Remains of the Athena Temple at Troy, built during Troy IX, about the time of Christ.

forays were common. In fact, he observes that the greatest praise in Homer is heaped upon a "sacker of cities."[23]

After Miletus fell to the Hittites, Myceneans moved farther north in their raids, sacking such places as Lemnos and Lesbos, not far from Troy, and carrying off cattle and women, according to the *Iliad*. The destruction of Thermi on Lesbos during the thirteenth century B.C. is confirmed by archaeological evidence.[24] And Wood concludes, "Seen in this light, an attack on Troy, among other places, seems so obvious that if we had no tale of Troy we would have to postulate it."[25]

The reason for the attack on Troy may have been simply to secure plunder and slaves, but there may also have been a squabble over the use of the Hellespont by Greek merchant ships or the control of the excellent fishing ground provided by the Hellespont.

If the Mycenean attack on Troy really did occur, where does it fit into the historical and archaeological framework? As noted, Blegen believed that Troy VIIa was the town destroyed in the Trojan War around 1250 B.C., but scholars now believe that that level was destroyed about 1200 at the earliest—too late to be the brunt of a major Mycenean assault from the Greek mainland. Mycenean power would have been too weak by then. Troy VIb is thought to be a more likely candidate, destroyed perhaps around 1250. As to Blegen's argument that Troy VI was destroyed by earthquake and not by fire kindled by attackers, both Bryce[26] and Wood[27] suggest that the town might have been so damaged by earthquake that conquest and looting were fairly easy. The feeling is that Troy VI as revealed by excavations is closer to the *Iliad*'s description of Troy than the village of VIIa.

Thus, we conclude that there may indeed have been some sort of Mycenean attack on Troy around 1250 B.C. or a little later that resulted in a destruction of the city. But the reason for the attack, the duration of it, and the details of the struggle must be left to conjecture.

Phrygians and Lydians

With the collapse of the Hittite Empire around 1180 B.C., Asia Minor entered a dark age about which little is known. This was a period of unsettled conditions and migrations. Eventually, by about 1000 B.C., the Phrygians, who apparently came from Thrace, seem to have extended their power over nearly all of Asia Minor, refortifying many old Hittite sites.

The Phrygians established their capital at Gordium (Gordion), fifty-five miles southwest of Ankara. The main excavation there has been the University of Pennsylvania Museum's Gordion Project, under the direction of Rodney S. Young 1950–1972. In 1988 Mary N. Voigt began a new cycle of excavation at the site. The occupation of Gordion dates back to the mid-third millennium B.C.; it became in the second millennium a Hittite stronghold; and the Phrygians settled there shortly after 1000 B.C. The city suffered some destruction when Alexander the Great passed through in 333 B.C., but presumably Gallic hordes were responsible for ruining the city in the third century B.C. so that it was only a small village in Roman times.

Scattered around the site are about one hundred burial mounds, dating from the eighth to the first century B.C.; archaeologists have investigated about forty of them. The largest (called the tomb of Midas) rises about 165 feet in height, with a diameter of almost a thousand feet.

On the mound of Gordium itself stood the capital of the king, whom the Greeks called Midas and the Assyrians Mita or Mushki. Around 700 B.C. the town was divided into two zones, the walled aristocratic quarter on the east and an unwalled residential area on the west, presumably occupied by the lower classes. In the walled quarter stood a palace complex divided into two courts, two long service buildings, and a building that may have been a temple. Evidently the Phrygians took over the site shortly after the Hittites left around 1000 B.C., and early in the sixth century it was incorporated into the kingdom of Lydia.

The most enduring impact of the Phrygians was their worship of the mother goddess, Cybele, a national deity that they borrowed from the earlier inhabitants of Asia Minor. The chief male deity was her lover-son Attis. Although the Greeks and Romans looked upon her as the mother of the gods, Cybele was for the Phrygians an earth mother, a symbol of the union of humankind, nature, and deity in a single divine life that triumphed over death. Cybele offered no moral teaching to her devotees, but she did extend to them the hope of joining her after death. Her cult spread among the Greek cities because of its affinities with other mystery religions, and Cybele worship had something to do with the rise of Orphism, which spread the idea of immortality among the Greeks.

The mother goddess Cybele.

Shortly before 700 B.C. the Cimmerians poured in from the north and east, especially from the Caucasus and the region of Pontus. A barbarous people whom even the cruel Assyrians called "Creatures of hell," the Cimmerians inflicted terrible suffering on the Urartians (northeast of Asia Minor) and then turned on the Phrygians, depriving them of their possessions in eastern Asia Minor. The contemporary King Midas committed suicide. Sargon II of Assyria lost his life fighting the Cimmerians in 705 B.C. Early in the seventh century (c. 680) a second Cimmerian invasion finished off the Phrygian kingdom and did away with the last King Midas, the man famous in Greek legend for turning all that he touched into gold.

Lydia, previously a Phrygian dependency, now successfully bore the brunt of the Cimmerian attack and in so doing gained national strength and unity and replaced the weakened Phrygians as the dominant political power in western Asia Minor. For a while, however, there continued to be Phrygian princes at Gordium, and Phrygian culture survived side by side with that of Lydia. But the race of great warriors had become docile subjects and were known to later Greeks as flute players, authors of elegy, and a source of slaves. Aesop was one of these Phrygian slaves. After the fall of Phrygia, the history of central and eastern Asia Minor was always overshadowed or determined by history being made in the west.

Before looking briefly at the history of Lydia, it is important to note the entrance of the Greeks into Asia Minor. Migrating Greeks not only affected the history of the area but also impacted on the development of civilization and indirectly contributed to the character of Western civilization. During the Greek Middle Age (c. 1100–800 B.C.), a considerable number of Greeks sailed across the Aegean to the Asia Minor coast and adjacent islands. Greek settlement on Lesbos took place no later than 1000 B.C. Aeolic settlement at Smyrna goes back to about the same time, and Aeolians settled in the Troad at least as early as the eighth century. Ionian migration to the east central coast of the Aegean and adjacent islands to form ultimately the twelve cities of the Panionic League (including Samos, Chios, Miletus, Ephesus, Colophon, etc.) must also go back to 1000 B.C. Rhodes and Cos were, of course, occupied by Myceneans but Dorian occupation there dates at least as early as 900 B.C. Dorian settlements on the Carian coast at such places as Cnidus and Halicarnassus can be traced at least to the eighth century. Subsequently Greeks planted colonies along the south coast of the Black Sea and at a few places along the Mediterranean coast.

Gyges (known to the Assyrians as Gugu, "Gog" in Ezekiel 38–39) was the first Lydian king to fight the Cimmerians, this time apparently invading from Thrace, but he died in the struggle. Chronological synchronisms indicate that his reign dated between about 680 and 645. He started the

The Pactolus River, where ancient Lydians panned gold. The river is much shrunken today because its waters are used for a variety of purposes.

panning of gold from the Pactolus River and began to move against Greek cities on the Asia Minor coast.

His successors (Ardys, Sadyattes, Alyattes) managed to overcome many of the Greek city-states along the Asia Minor coast and to expand eastward. The Medes stopped the Lydians at the Halys River in 585 B.C., however. Subsequently a daughter of Alyattes was married to Astyages, heir to the Median throne. Under Alyattes' son Croesus, who ascended the throne around 560 B.C., the Lydian kingdom reached its height. Croesus possessed fabulous wealth, the source of which came partly because of the gold washed down by the Pactolus River (a tributary of the Hermus), but especially because of the skill of Lydian artisans and traders and because the great trade route from Assyria to the Aegean crossed his territory. The Lydians are given credit for originating the coinage of money.

"RICH AS CROESUS"

"Rich as Croesus" is a saying that became legendary in Greek tradition and has lasted through modern history to the present. The wealth of King Croesus' Lydia came from the fertility of her river valleys and the good grazing land of the mountain plateaus. But its most famous resource was precious metal. Lydians especially panned placer gold in the Pactolus River, but there were gold deposits elsewhere in the country.

Archaeologists have found a substantial Lydian gold refinery along the Pactolus River in the capital of Sardis. It contained furnaces, cupels, slag, and small pieces of gold, including foil and droplets, and an altar, probably associated with the goddess Cybele. Lydians get credit for originating the coinage of money—either during the reign of Croesus (560–546 B.C.) or the reign of his father Alyattes (c. 580). See Andrew Ramage and Paul Craddock, *King Croesus' Gold* (Harvard University Press, 2000).

The Lydian kings became rather enamored with Greek culture. Alyattes took an Ionian wife, presented two temples to Miletus, and gave gifts to the Delphic oracle. Croesus made rich gifts to all the well-known Greek oracles, contributed heavily to the rebuilding of the temple of Artemis (Diana) at Ephesus, which the Cimmerians had destroyed, and at his capital, Sardis, maintained a brilliant and cosmopolitan court where he welcomed Greeks.

The Lydian gold refinery along the Pactolus River at Sardis. An altar is prominent in the ruins.

When Cyrus the Persian began his revolt against his Median overlords, Croesus was duty bound to come to the aid of his Median brother-in-law. In the ensuing struggle, Croesus lost his throne, and the Lydian kingdom came to an end in 547/546 B.C. But Sardis survived its royal master and remained a great city during the Persian, Hellenistic, and Roman periods.

CROESUS AND THE ORACLE OF DELPHI

Greeks did not undertake an important enterprise, whether national, civic, or personal, without first consulting the oracle at Delphi. And the reputation of the oracle was so great that people in nearby lands also sought its wisdom for a course of action. Usually the answer was given in somewhat vague phraseology, capable of various interpretations.

When Croesus of Lydia was threatened by conflict with Cyrus of Persia, he inquired of the oracle of Delphi as to whether he should undertake a military expedition against the Persians. The oracle declared that in doing so he would destroy a mighty empire. Croesus chose this to be a prediction of the defeat of the Persians

when it could just as well apply to his own destruction. And it did.

The Persian Period

Two events occurred during the Persian period that were especially significant for Asia Minor. The first was the Ionian revolt and its aftermath. One of the causes of this struggle was that the Greeks in Asia Minor discovered the Persians to be much less lovers of things Greek than the Lydians had been and much more exacting taskmasters. Moreover, Persian advance in Thrace had not only resulted in Persian conquest of Athenian holdings in the area of the Dardanelles but it also had led them to fear Persian conquest of Greece.

The uprising began about 499 B.C. at Miletus, and soon spread to the other Greek towns of the Asia Minor coast, winning the support of Athens and Eretria. Initially the revolutionaries had success and attacked the Persian administrative center of Sardis, sacking and burning it. But ultimately they lost. The Persians leveled Miletus for her part in the fiasco.

Now the Persians became more severe than ever with the Greek cities and determined to punish Athens and Eretria. A Persian force sent in 490 B.C. met defeat at Marathon. But before Darius the Great could mount another attack, he died; and it was ten years before Xerxes could try again

Xerxes made Sardis his headquarters and, after collecting a huge army and fleet, attacked through northern Greece, carrying the pass at Thermopylae and marching into central Greece. Athens was evacuated.

The Greeks won a signal naval victory at Salamis, however, and in the spring of 479 B.C. they were victorious in a land battle at Plataea. Traditionally, on the same day, the Greeks won another great naval victory off Mycale on the Asia Minor coast. Greek states along the eastern shore of the Aegean were freed from Persia. The Delian League of Greek states, that had been organized for war against Persia, was gradually transformed into an Athenian empire. Virtually the whole eastern coast of Asia Minor, as well as adjacent islands, became part of that empire.

The second event of significance for Asia Minor history to occur during the Persian period was the revolt of Cyrus the Younger. After the Peloponnesian War was over in 404 B.C., Cyrus planned a revolt against his brother Artaxerxes II. At his provincial capital, Sardis, Cyrus collected troops, supposedly to put down tribes in Asia Minor not loyal to Persia. He recruited more than ten thousand Greek mercenaries for his army. In 401 they marched across Asia Minor, through the Cilician Gates, and across northern Syria to the Euphrates and then south toward Babylon. At Cunaxa they defeated Artaxerxes; but Cyrus was killed and the revolt collapsed. After the Greek generals were killed by treachery, Xenophon was chosen to lead the force, which fought its way north to Trapezus (Trabzon) on the Black Sea coast.

During the Peloponnesian War (between Athens and Sparta, 431–404 B.C.) Persia had frequently interfered in Greek affairs. Thus she regained control of the Greek cities of the Asia Minor coast in 386, as a result of the selfish diplomacy of Sparta. But this Persian interference merely kindled greater hatred of the Persians among the Greeks and prepared the way for the Panhellenic war of revenge that Alexander the Great was to initiate in 334 B.C.

Alexander and His Successors

In the spring of that year, Alexander crossed the Hellespont with a force of some thirty-two thousand infantry and five thousand cavalry, plus specialists. Alexander himself first disembarked near Troy at a spot where tradition said Achilles had landed many centuries earlier. Throwing a spear from his boat to the shore as a token that the land was his by right of conquest, he reportedly declared, "I accept from the gods Asia won by the spear." Subsequently he made offerings to the great Homeric dead and then joined the main army and advanced against the Persians. The defenders prepared to meet Alexander at the Granicus River in Mysia. Largely a cavalry melee, the battle ended that May sunset with the highways of Asia Minor clear for the invader.

Alexander now marched south to Sardis, the Persian headquarters west of the Taurus; and that strong city surrendered without a blow. Presently in all the Greek cities of the northwestern and central western Asia Minor coast the oligarchies or tyrants friendly to Persia fell and democracies were established in their place. At Ephesus there was an unsavory massacre of the oligarchs. Miletus required a siege. Alexander then ordered the rebuilding of Smyrna, which the Persians had destroyed more than 150 years earlier. At Halicarnassus the Persians offered determined resistance; the citadel did not fall until the spring of 333 B.C.

Meanwhile Alexander's forces occupied the ports of Lycia and Pamphylia and moved into central Asia Minor to establish winter quarters. At Gordium, the old Phrygian capital, he cut the Gordian knot (see sidebar). By the time he left Gordium for the campaign of 333, he had determined to destroy the Persian navy—by occupying the Syrian and Egyptian coasts and depriving the navy of its bases. Alexander made it through the Cilician Gates before the Persians could organize an adequate defense.

ALEXANDER THE GREAT AND THE GORDIAN KNOT

The story is told that during the winter of 333 B.C. Alexander went to Gordium to try to untie the Gordian knot, which fastened the yoke to the chariot of Gordius. An oracle had said that the one who loosened it would rule Asia. Unsuccessful in untying the knot, Alexander pulled out his sword and cut the knot and went on to conquer western Asia. The story is often told to illustrate the cleverness and/or vigorous purpose of Alexander.

Yet one observer has concluded that his action did not indicate either manual skill or cleverness but only impetuosity.

Then while Alexander lay violently ill of fever at Tarsus, the Persian army waited for him not far away under the command of Darius himself. In October Alexander met Darius on the Plain of Issus at the head of the gulf of the same name. After his defeat, Darius fled eastward, leaving the door to Syria and Egypt ajar. Alexander elected to follow his previously worked-out plan rather than pursue the enemy. Many of Darius' troops retreated northward to Cappadocia where they posed a continuing threat to Alexander's supply lines.

The rest of the story of Alexander's victories and problems appears in the chapter on Greece and Iran. Suffice it to say here that Alexander died in Babylon on June 13, 323 B.C. The contest among his generals for his legacy, however, is very much a concern of Asia Minor history. Unfortunately the story of Alexander's successors (the Diadochi) is a very confusing one to follow.

Alexander gave his seal to Perdiccas, who assigned a number of Greek satraps to the old Persian provinces: Antigonus to Phrygia (where he had ruled since Issus); Ptolemy to Egypt; Eumenes to Cappadocia, Pontus, and Paphlagonia; Lysimachus to Thrace (he later acquired much of Asia Minor); and Seleucus to Babylonia (he eventually ruled nearly all Asiatic provinces). When in 306 B.C. Antigonus took the title of king, the others quickly did likewise.

At Ipsus in west central Asia Minor in 301, Antigonus was killed by his rivals and Alexander's empire divided four ways. Cassander got Macedonia and Greece;

Lysimachus, was awarded Thrace and much of Asia Minor; Ptolemy received Egypt, Cyrenaica, and Palestine; and Seleucus got the rest. However, this arrangement did not stick. In 281 Seleucus defeated Lysimachus and took most of Asia Minor. And in 276 B.C. Antigonus' grandson, Antigonus Gonatas, became king of Macedon, and his line retained control there for over a century.

Finding themselves in possession of a vast and heterogeneous empire, the Seleucids usually followed the old Persian practices of government. They preserved the old division into more than thirty satrapies, and the satraps enjoyed considerable independence. Moreover, many Persian nobles retained their old estates, and huge temple estates remained intact. In Asia Minor the latter were almost independent countries ruled by Oriental priests.

The Seleucids, especially Seleucus I and his son Antiochus I, were active in founding cities. Some were military outposts, and others were designed to act as missionary centers for the spread of the gospel of Hellenism and to act as bonds for cementing the vast heterogeneous empire. In this founding or refounding of cities, Greeks and Jews were usually imported. Many of the cities so established were later centers of Christian missionary activity.

The Seleucids never did control all of Asia Minor, and they had a remarkable facility for losing what they did have. Seleucus I did not make good his claim to Bithynia, Pontus, and Cappadocia, most of which Alexander had not conquered. Then, soon after the death of Seleucus, the Gauls or Celts invaded Asia Minor from Thrace (278–277 B.C.). Antiochus I (280–261) defeated them near Sardis two years later, and they subsequently located in Phrygia, which was renamed Galatia. In the midst of the confusion brought on by the Celtic invasion and the struggle between Lysimachus and Seleucus I (306–280), Philetaeros set himself up as an independent ruler at Pergamum and founded the Attalid dynasty there. The Pergamenes controlled much of northwest Asia Minor during the third century B.C. and after 190 much of the southwestern part as well. Antiochus I also lost parts of southern and western Asia

Minor to Ptolemy II. Although the Seleucids asserted control over parts of Cappadocia and Pontus under Antiochus III (223–187), that recovery was ephemeral.

It is easy to get lost in historical detail when looking at Alexander's conquest of Asia Minor and the aftermath. But the cultural impact of all that activity is fundamentally simple and very significant for that day and for ours. After that conquest Greek culture and institutions became dominant in Asia Minor. The Greek language and culture supplanted local styles and dialects. Greek-style cities were founded all over the peninsula, and Greek political institutions governed those cities: council, popular assembly, college of magistrates. The gymnasium was their chief cultural and educational institution. In terms of physical characteristics, the grid pattern (laying out of streets crossing at right angles, with business areas or agoras—shopping malls, parks or public places, theaters, and stadiums) became dominant. Many of the cities, on the Aegean coast at least, became or remained nominally free. And a degree of freedom continued into the New Testament period, when, for example, Ephesian officials were worried about loss of that freedom if the furor that Demetrius the silversmith created should get out of hand (Acts 19:35–41).

Alongside those cities rose the Hellenistic monarchies with all their trappings, especially the ruler cult. And from that context developed emperor worship and the cult of Roma, that would create a great problem for Christians later and would lead to severe persecution. We need to remind ourselves periodically that the Hellenistic culture as it evolved in such places as Asia Minor, Alexandria, and Greece itself proved to be very attractive to the Romans. In fact, the Romans adopted much of the Hellenistic culture as their own, so that a Greco-Roman culture developed (rather than a strictly Roman culture), and this was passed on through the Middle Ages to the West, becoming to a large degree our own culture today.

Moreover, we need to remind ourselves that the urbanization advocated by Alexander and implemented by his successors caught on with the Romans. Each city,

with its surrounding territory (including farms, towns, and sanctuaries and their estates) became the political, military, economic, cultural, and religious center for a whole region so it could hold down the countryside and influence it in a multitude of ways. As the Hellenistic leaders and the Romans sought to use the urban center to reach and control its hinterland, so Paul as a Roman citizen followed an urban strategy for reaching the Roman world with the gospel. For example, from Ephesus he sought to impact the province of Asia, from Antioch of Pisidia perhaps much of the province of Galatia, from Thessalonica the province of Macedonia, from Corinth the province of Achaia, and so on.

Roman Interference and Control

As early as 200 B.C. the expanding power of Rome could be felt in Asia Minor. During the second century B.C. Rome began to annex territory—the province of Asia in 133 B.C. and Cilicia in 103 B.C., and the remaining Hellenistic kingdoms gradually fell under her sway. By the end of the first century B.C., almost all the rest of the peninsula had been organized as Roman provinces: Bithynia in 74 B.C. and Galatia and Pamphylia in 25 B.C. Cappadocia did not become a Roman province until A.D. 17.

ROMAN PROVINCES IN ASIA MINOR

At the time Paul and his associates traveled across Asia Minor there were six Roman provinces on the peninsula. Actually the number and composition varied from time to time.

Provinces	Date of Roman Acquisition or Organization
Asia	129 B.C.
Cilicia	103 B.C.
Pamphylia	103 B.C.
Bithynia	74 B.C.
Galatia	25 B.C.
Cappadocia	17 A.D.

Mithridates, king of Pontus.

Though Latin was the language of the Empire, Greek remained the language of the educated classes and of official notices in Asia Minor. The Romans continued the urbanization process, and by the end of Paul's life a network of cities was established in central Anatolia for the first time. And there was a road system to link those cities with the coast. In the cities bath-gymnasium complexes gradually became the symbol of imperial culture, and the populace took public entertainment for granted, especially at theaters and amphitheaters. As the first century A.D. wore on, the tentacles of the imperial cult reached into almost all aspects of public life, as the cult sponsored public sacrifices, festivals, games, wild animal fights, and more.

In general, the peninsula was prosperous during the first Christian century. Though in A.D. 17 a terrible earthquake leveled twelve of the great cities in the west, imperial and local rebuilding efforts quickly restored normal life. Timber, marble, silver, iron, mica, and semiprecious stones were among mineral resources extensively exported. Salted fish, olives, grapes, wine, grain, wool, skins, flax, and woven linen were important non-mineral exports.

Now we return to political and military developments in Asia Minor. Antiochus III, still dreaming of reviving Alexander's world empire, had regained lost Seleucid ground in the east, virtually annexed Egypt by marrying his daughter to the king of Egypt, and now turned his attention to Asia Minor. Soon after Philip V of Macedon met defeat at the hands of the Romans in 197 B.C. (and was therefore no threat to Syria in the west), Antiochus began to occupy Asia Minor cities held by Egypt. He established his headquarters at Ephesus and laid plans for an attack on Pergamum. Eumenes II of Pergamum decided to seek aid from Rome and never let Rome forget the East.

A further complication arose from the arrival of Hannibal, the famous Carthaginian general, at Ephesus in 195 B.C. He had escaped from Carthage when his political opponents stirred up Roman suspicion against him there, and he now began to urge Antiochus to take action against Rome. Antiochus was further encouraged to aggression against Rome by the Aetolian League in Greece which urged him to free Greece from Roman oppression.

In 192 Antiochus invaded Thrace and the following year attempted an invasion of Greece. Defeated at Thermopylae, he fled to Ephesus, leaving his army to take care of itself. During 190 the Romans destroyed the Seleucid fleet which Hannibal, a great general but no admiral, had been given to command. Early in January of 189 the Romans and Pergamenes advanced upon Antiochus at Ephesus and defeated him in a fierce battle at Magnesia, southeast of Ephesus on the Maeander River. The Romans spent the summer in a campaign against the Galatians during which they extended their power over most of Asia Minor west of the Taurus Mountains.

According to the peace made in 188 B.C., Antiochus surrendered all Asia Minor west of the Taurus Mountains and Halys River to the Romans; but he kept Cilicia, which he had recently taken from the Ptolemies. He also agreed to pay an indemnity. Rome then handed over much of Asia Minor to Pergamum.

Eumenes II of Pergamum (197–160 B.C.) was an intelligent and forceful leader who brought his kingdom to the height of her glory. He chose to follow a program of Greek solidarity, according to which he married Stratonice, daughter of Ariarathes IV of Cappadocia (partly oriental), whom he regarded as a Greek ruling over Asiatics. Another partly oriental Greek, the king of Bithynia, joined an alliance with Pergamum and Cappadicia. Eumenes also curried favor with the Achaean League in Greece.

During the latter stages of the Third Macedonian War (172–168 B.C.) Pergamum and Rhodes aroused Roman suspicion by their intrigues with Macedon. Rome transferred the Galatian territories of Eumenes to a native king and punished Rhodes by taking away Caria and Lycia and by giving Delos to Athens. Rhodian greatness soon declined and was forever gone; and the island kingdom lost the power to suppress piracy in the eastern Mediterranean, something Rome would later regret. Roman friendship with Pergamum was not permanently destroyed; it was renewed in the days of Attalus II (160–138).

In 133 B.C. Attalus III of Pergamum died, leaving no direct heir and having willed his kingdom to the Romans. At this point there was a change in the Roman policy of creating in Asia Minor numerous weak and autonomous states dependent on Rome. Rome turned to annexation, constituting newly-acquired territories as Roman provinces. Asia, the first of these provinces, was the old kingdom of Pergamum, virtually as it had come to hand. The prosperity of Asia was greatly affected by Roman unwillingness to continue the commercial and industrial enterprises of the Pergamene kings and the decision to contract the collection of taxes in Asia to the Roman business class on five-year terms.

The next significant series of events in Asia Minor history were the Mithridatic wars. Mithridates IV Philopater Philadelphus of Pontus (170–150 B.C.) had formed an alliance with Rome. This pact was renewed under his successor Mithridates V Euergetes (150–121). Soon after Mithridates V ascended the throne, he sent warships and a force of soldiers to aid Rome in the Third Carthaginian War. In 133 he responded quickly to the Senate's request for help in putting down a rebellion in Pergamum and was rewarded by a gift of a district of Phrygia. But later some in Rome had second thoughts about the loss of Phrygian revenue, and Mithridates V lost favor in Rome over an alleged attempt to purchase support among the voters for some favor he wished to obtain.

When Mithridates V was assassinated and left his kingdom to his wife and two young sons, the elder of whom, Mithridates VI, was about eleven, some in Rome thought this was a good time to take back Phrygia. This act aroused the resentment of the young king toward Rome. When Mithridates VI was about twenty, he began to form a plan for building an empire that would include all of Asia Minor. At this point Greeks of the Crimea sought his help against the Scythians, and within a few years the Crimea had become part of Mithridates' realm. Soon he took Greek cities on the western shore of the Black Sea as well. Then he expanded eastward, taking lesser Armenia. From the latter he obtained iron and silver, from the former large supplies of grain and army recruits.

In order to enter the province of Asia, it was necessary for Mithridates to extend his kingdom westward. Therefore, he allied himself with Nicomedes of Bithynia, and the two of them conquered and divided Paphlagonia. Next Mithridates took the part of Galatia that lay between his kingdom and the border of the province of Asia. Rome was wary of all this advance but was busy with Germanic invaders and only remonstrated with Pontus.

Nicomedes was a remarkable man. He was so huge that men marveled at the size of his armor. He was reputed to be able to ride 120 miles in a day and to drive a chariot drawn by sixteen horses. While he could be ruthless and cruel, his tastes were those of an educated Greek rather than a barbarian. He loved music and art, had power as an orator, and his interest in letters and philosophy led him to invite poets and scholars to his court.[28] Unfortunately he knew no way to govern except through terror and violence and therefore failed to win the support of those whom he professed to rescue from tyranny.

A little before 100 B.C. Mithridates attempted to control Cappadocia and in the process crossed swords with Nicomedes of Bithynia, who had been his ally. Both kings made representation to Rome as supporting the proper ruler for the contested throne of Cappadocia, which was virtually a client kingdom of Rome. Rome disallowed the claims of both, approving Ariobarzanes, a Cappadocian noble, as the new king. Mithridates sought a new alliance, which he found in the person of Tigranes, king of Greater Armenia, who was pursuing the same course of self-aggrandizement as Mithridates. The Pontic king gave his daughter in marriage to Tigranes.

Mithridates tried to bring Cappadocia under his control no less than five times between 112 and 92 B.C., but each time Roman interference forced him to withdraw. Then in 91 B.C. he occupied Bithynia and again yielded to Roman demands to withdraw. However, when Roman commissioners encouraged the king of Bithynia to raid Pontic territory and refused Mithridates any satisfaction, he decided to challenge Rome by force of arms. He reached this decision in part because Rome was involved in civil war in Italy.

Mithridates began the struggle late in 89 B.C. Well prepared, he had a highly trained army and a fleet of three hundred ships. Speedily he overran Bithynia and most of Asia. There, at his orders, the provincials massacred eighty thousand Roman tax gatherers, moneylenders, and others who had been oppressing them. In 88 Athens joined his cause, and most of southern Greece followed suit. But Roman armies under the leadership of Sulla ultimately reversed the tide. The peace of 85 B.C. required that Mithridates surrender Cappadocia, Bithynia, and Asia and pay an indemnity. His kingdom was left intact. Sulla required such a huge indemnity from the rebellious communities that they were saddled with a crushing burden of debt. So extensive was the devastation in Greece that she never fully recovered from it.

Meanwhile piracy had been growing steadily as Rhodes, Syria, and Egypt grew weaker. Moreover, the severity of the Mithridatic wars had driven masses of men of Syrian, Cyprian, and Asia Minor origin into piratical activities. Furthermore, the financial exactions of Sulla greatly aggravated the situation. The pirates made common cause with Mithridates VI, under whose patronage their operations expanded enormously. Their power eventually made the Mediterranean unnavigable. Rome's efforts to destroy them were ineffectual until Pompey's complete victory.

The Second Mithridatic War (88–81 B.C.) really consisted of a series of raids. Murena, a Roman general left in Asia with two legions, made three sorties into Pontus. During the first two he carried off great plunder but was unopposed by Mithridates who made representations to Rome. When the third raid occurred, Mithridates lost his patience and soundly defeated Murena, devastating much of Cappadocia in the process. Rome now agreed to abide by the peace treaty. Meanwhile, by 83, Tigranes had occupied Syria (putting an end to the Seleucid house) and Cilicia and deported hundreds of thousands of people from Cappadocia (which he annexed) to Armenia.

When Nicomedes III of Bithynia died in 74 B.C., he bequeathed his kingdom to Rome. But Mithridates championed the claims of a son of Nicomedes and invaded Bithynia, occupying nearly the entire province. In 73 the Roman Lucullus defeated Mithridates' Aegean fleet and the following year routed his land forces and chased him into exile in Armenia. When Tigranes refused to surrender his father-in-law, Lucullus invaded Armenia. But his troops mutinied because of his strict discipline and because the terms of enlistment of many had expired. At this point Mithridates returned to his kingdom and raised another force while Tigranes made a recovery.

Meanwhile Pompey had been given an extraordinary command to destroy the pirate scourge (67 B.C.), which he succeeded in doing in three months. His victory was more sure because of the mildness he showed to those who submitted, many of whom he used as colonists to revive Mediterranean towns with a declining population. The following year the provinces of Bithynia and Cilicia (which Pompey organized after the victory over the pirates) were transferred to Pompey, along with the conduct of the war against Mithridates and Tigranes. Pompey soon defeated Mithridates who, failing to find refuge with Tigranes this time, sailed for his dependencies north of the Black Sea where his war-weary people revolted and he committed suicide. Tigranes came to terms with Pompey.

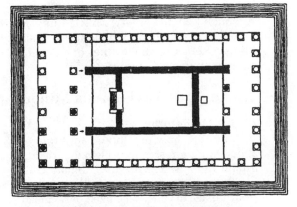

Floor plan of the temple to Rome and Augustus at the Galatian city of Ancyra (modern Ankara). On its wall was inscribed Augustus' Res Gestae, a sort of record of his accomplishments

Thus the Mithridatic wars came to a close, with Pontus annexed as a Roman province. It is estimated that human casualties during the first war totaled 300,000 and during the third war 120,000 on the Pontic side alone.[29] While destruction during the first war occurred over a large area, such damage was restricted during the third war to Bithynia and Pontus.

Pompey's settlement, then, included the annexation of Cilicia and Pontus, which became linked with Bithynia for administrative purposes. Settlement involved as well the confirmation of Tigranes on his throne and the restoration of Ariobarzanes to his throne in Cappadocia (along with a considerable loan for the restoration of his kingdom) and the confirmation of Deiotarus of Galatia in his ancestral kingdom. In addition, several petty dynasts were given or permitted to hold slices of real estate in central Asia Minor. Pompey also endeavored to revive the cities of Asia Minor, drawing up municipal charters that were still operative in the early second century A.D.

Few changes occurred in Asia Minor between 63 B.C. and the outbreak of civil war in 49. The most important was the annexation in 58 of Cyprus, which was joined to the province of Cilicia.

Asia Minor suffered much at the hands of Rome during the late Republic. The publicans (tax collectors) exacted all they could, not so much through graft connected with tax collecting as through interest collections on unpaid debts. The requisitions and fines that Pompey and Caesar levied were heavy, but not nearly so devastating as those exacted by Brutus and Cassius who, armed with senatorial authority to collect the regular revenues, ordered (as a loan) anything else they needed.

Subsequently Antony's exactions must have reduced most of Asia Minor to the last extremity, but at least he did reward those that had resisted Brutus and Cassius: Rhodes, Lycia, and Tarsus. All these burdens left the client kingdoms and the provinces of the East bare of capital. Octavian found it necessary to cancel all public debt in the provinces of Asia Minor. Under the long period of peace during the first and second centuries A.D., Asia Minor regained her prosperity, some areas enjoying the greatest prosperity they had ever known.

The first major political change in Asia Minor under the Empire came in 25 B.C. when King Amyntas of Galatia died and willed his kingdom to Rome. Augustus decided to annex the territory as the province of Galatia. At that time it included Galatia proper, Pisidia, Isauria, Pamphylia, and parts of Phrygia, Lycaonia, and Cilicia. Under Tiberius in A.D. 17 Rome annexed Cappadocia when its king Archelaus died. This left the kingdom of Polemon in eastern Pontus, which was added to Galatia under Nero in A.D. 64. The Lycian League, which Augustus had permitted to remain independent, was annexed by Claudius in A.D. 43 and united to Pamphylia, which was separated from the province of Galatia. Although Caligula (37–41) reverted in part to reliance on client kingdoms in Asia Minor, Rome resumed the practice of annexation under Claudius (41–54).

The Apostle Paul in Asia Minor

Paul's Hometown

After the howling mob had brought about Paul's arrest in Jerusalem, he tried to establish himself with the Roman chiliarch[30] with the proud boast, "I am a Jew from Tarsus, in Cilicia, a citizen of no mean city" (Acts 21:39 NKJV). The allegation won him the respect of the chiliarch and the right to address his attackers, for Tarsus in Cilicia was one of the great cities of Asia Minor during the first century A.D. In order to gain proper understanding of the city, it is necessary first to consider its environs.

Cilicia. Geographically Cilicia referred to the area of southeastern Asia Minor between Pamphylia on the west, the Amanus Mountains on the east, Lycaonia and Cappadocia on the north, and the Mediterranean on the south. It had a coastline of about 430 miles, extending from the eastern boundary of Pamphylia to the southern end of the Gulf of Issus. It was roughly coextensive with the modern Turkish vilayet of Adana. Politically (in Paul's day at least) Cilicia designated the Roman province that encompassed the eastern part of the geographical area. When Luke spoke of the "sea which is off Cilicia" (Acts 27:5), he probably had in mind the Mediterranean opposite the entire geographical region. Since Paul used Roman political terminology, he must have applied Cilicia to the Roman province only (c.f., Acts 21:39; 22:3).

Cilicia Tracheia. Cilicia was commonly divided into two territories almost as dissimilar in their physical characteristics as they could be. The western part, Cilicia Tracheia, was a tangled mass of mountains descending abruptly to the sea, with a narrow tract of land along the coast and little or no plain country. The shoreline presented to the sea a convex outline. The moun-

tains of Tracheia were valuable only for their timber (chiefly cedar), and this rugged terrain succeeded effectively in cutting off the inhabitants from much peaceful contact with the rest of the world. The main line of communication skirted the northern edge of the mountains of Tracheia.

In this area primitive tribal life characterized the interior, while a few small towns existed along the coast as ports of call for coastal trade and depots from which timber could be exported. Other than for its timber resources, Tracheia was of little consequence from prehistoric to Roman times except as a haven for pirates. When the depredations of the eastern Mediterranean pirates became intolerable to the Romans, they assigned to Pompey the task of wiping them out in 67 B.C. That he was successful in Cilicia Tracheia, as elsewhere, is certain; but we do not know what internal arrangements Pompey made in the area.

Tracheia again appears on the stage of history in Mark Antony's days. Part of this territory he granted to Cleopatra as a source of ship timber; members of the Teucrid family continued to rule the rest as client kings. When, after the Battle of Actium, Cleopatra lost control of her lands there, Octavian granted part of Tracheia to Amyntas of Galatia and confirmed the Teucrid house in the rest of it. When Amyntas died, the western part of his Cilician domain became part of the province of Galatia. Rome gave the rest to Archelaus of Cappadocia; it subsequently passed to Archelaus' son and in A.D. 38 was granted to Antiochus IV of Commagene who ruled until A.D. 72. Thus, when Paul went north from Tarsus, through the Cilician Gates, and struck out west for Derbe on his second and third missionary journeys, he passed through the northern part of the domains of this client king.

Cilicia Pedias. The eastern part of Cilicia was known as Cilicia Pedias. Roughly speaking this area was triangular in shape, its apex at the northeast formed by the Amanus and Taurus Mountains. The Amanus Mountains ran due south and separated Cilicia from Syria; the Taurus Mountains ran southwest to the sea, cutting off the region from Cappadocia and

The Cilician Gates.

Lycaonia. The third side of the triangle was the Mediterranean. Three rivers watered Pedias and flowed in a southwesterly direction. On each river a city developed. In the east Mallus rose on the Pyramus (modern Ceyhan), in the center Adana on the Sarus (Seyhan), and in the west Tarsus on the Cydnus. These rivers have changed their courses several times over the years. During the first century A.D. they followed much different routes than they now do. In Paul's day the Sarus apparently did not flow into the sea but into a large lagoon. The mouth of the Pyramus was about fifteen miles east of the Sarus, and the Cydnus about nine miles west of the Sarus.[31]

While Cilicia Pedias is often called one plain, in fact, it is not. In the east the Plain of Issus, where Alexander fought his great battle in 333 B.C., is only a narrow strip around the Gulf of Issus, except at the head of the gulf where it extends eight to ten miles inland. There was also a plain which was coextensive with the upper valley of the Pyramus. But the main plain was the lower valley of the three rivers. This region now contains about eight hundred square miles of arable land with a strip of dunes and lagoons some two to three miles wide along the coast.

Cilicia Pedias had much in its favor from a geographical standpoint. Its land was fertile and grew cereals of all kinds, and its flax made possible a thriving linen industry. Timber from the nearby mountains moved through Cilician ports. Goats living on the slopes of the Taurus, where snow lies until May, grew magnificent coats used in the famous tentmaking industry of the area. Paul followed this trade (Acts 18:3). The fact that Pedias was located on one of the great trade routes of the ancient world, the most frequented land route from the East to the Aegean, promoted commerce and industry and contributed to the growth of towns. The trade route coming from the Euphrates over the Amanus Pass and another trade route coming from Antioch in Syria via the Syrian Gates met about fifty miles east of Tarsus, entered the city as a

Falls on the Cydnus River, north of Tarsus.
Kemal Tongue, Tarsus.

single road, swung north through the Cilician Gates, and led across south central Asia Minor to Ephesus.

About thirty miles north of Tarsus stood the Cilician Gates, a narrow gorge that originally was just wide enough to allow passage of the small stream that ran through it. With much effort the Tarsians in early times widened the gorge and built a wagon road up to its approaches and through it. When this occurred is uncertain. The route was well known when Xenophon came through in 401 B.C., and the work must actually have been done centuries earlier, perhaps as early as 1000 B.C. At any rate, their industry had put the Tarsians in possession of the one wagon road across the Taurus Mountains. At the Gates (which are about one hundred yards in length) the rocks rise steeply on both sides to a height of 500 to 600 feet and the roadbed itself ascends directly to the broad, bare summit of the Taurus Range, here 4,300 feet in altitude. With their engineering skill the Romans in imperial times improved on the work that the men of Tarsus had done earlier.

According to tradition the earliest Cilicians were of the same stock as the Phoenicians. Later Egyptians and then Hittites dominated them, and probably Aegean peoples invaded during the disturbed period of the twelfth and eleventh centuries B.C. Seemingly other Greeks reinforced these people in later centuries. During the period of Assyrian control, while Sargon II was on the throne (721–705 B.C.), the area suffered from Phrygian ravages. With the demise of the Assyrian Empire, Cilicia won her independence and maintained a considerable degree of autonomy under the early Persians. Apparently they gained their freedom once more during the latter days of the Persian Empire.

Alexander controlled the area, and after his death the region became debatable ground between the Ptolemies and the Seleucids. Although the Seleucids won out, they did not maintain effective control for long. By the middle of the second century B.C. most of the important towns of Cilicia Pedias had gained local autonomy and issued municipal coinages. During the latter part of the second century B.C. the

Seleucid kingdom was reduced to anarchy. And with the subsequent breakdown of Rhodian Sea power, the Cilician cities suffered greatly at the hands of their piratical neighbors.

At last the pirate menace became so serious that in 102 B.C. Rome organized the province of Cilicia to deal with it. This was merely a chain of coast guard stations along the mountain rim of Asia Minor, and Jones does not think it actually included Cilicia itself.[32] But after Pompey crushed the pirate scourge in 67 B.C., he did organize Cilicia Pedias as a Roman province. At the time he showed great statesmanship, recognizing that much of the piracy of the area was caused by serious economic disorder. Therefore he sought to bring about improved conditions and refounded many towns, in which he settled some of the more respectable of the pirate captives. He organized coastal Cilicia as a group of city-states and recognized a client king in the interior.

Several of the cities of the plain won status as free cities during the civil wars. For instance, Antony freed Tarsus and Julius Caesar Aegae. Though exactions of the period of the civil wars were crippling, the cities of Cilicia regained prosperity under the early Roman Empire. But unfortunately they, like so many other cities of the East, dissipated their wealth and energy in feuds and rivalries with each other.

Tarsus. Tarsus was located about ten miles from the Mediterranean at eighty feet above sea level. Normally the oppressive atmosphere of such a place would have been destructive of vigorous municipal or commercial life. But about two miles north of the city the hills begin to rise gently and extend in undulating ridges until they meet the Taurus. And about ten miles north of the lowland city a second Tarsus rose. Partly a summer residence, it served a considerable population as a year-round home. The more bracing climate of the upland town provided a means of offsetting the enervating climate of the lower region.

In New Testament times Tarsus lay astride the Cydnus River, then navigable by light vessels right up into the middle of the city. However, most ships docked at the

Cleopatra's Gate in the center of modern Tarsus at least preserves the tradition that the queen met Antony there

who claimed to have captured the city. Assyrians do not seem to have remained in power in Cilicia long, however. During the sixth century B.C. a line of native kings arose with the name Syennesis prominent among them. These kings were powerful enough to take part in arranging a peace treaty between the Medes and the Lydians.

Under the Persian Empire, the kings of Tarsus seem to have maintained a degree of autonomy for more than a century. But after the city supported the revolt of Cyrus the Younger in 401 B.C. (whether by choice or by force is unclear), the Persians took away what freedom Tarsus had enjoyed. Some of the Greek mercenaries on that occasion plundered the city which Xenophon, leader of the Greek armies in the revolt, described as a "great and prosperous city, a joy of heart."[34] When Alexander the Great came thundering through the Cilician Gates less than a century later, the retreating Persians set fire to the city. But Alexander's advance guard saved it from destruction.

The coming of Alexander did not accomplish much toward the Hellenization of Tarsus. Soon he died. In the struggle for power that ensued among Alexander's generals, Seleucus ultimately won out in Cilicia. For all the Hellenization the Seleucids generally achieved, they were not successful in that respect in Tarsus, where they ruled very much according to the old Persian methods. Free city life on the Greek pattern did not develop under the early Seleucids. But conditions changed after 190 B.C. when Rome won the Battle of Magnesia and took away from Antiochus III of Seleucia most of his Asia Minor domains.

Tarsus and other cities of Cilicia now became frontier towns. And the Seleucid kings were forced to pay more attention to their defenses and to give these subjects greater freedom in order to win their loyalty. During the reign of Antiochus IV Epiphanes (175–164), almost all of the towns of Cilicia began to produce coins as self-governing municipalities. They were also more thoroughly Grecized. Tarsus was

harbor, five to six miles south of the city. At that point lay a spring-fed lake, Rhegma, around all but the south sides of which extended the harbor town and the wharf installations. Great skill and diligence must have been expended on maintaining the channel of the Cydnus and the harbor. In later centuries slackness required an auxiliary channel to reduce flooding. The cut to the east of town (made by Justinian, 527–563) in time became the main bed of the river and remains so today.

Tarsians were proud of the Cydnus, which was normally clear as it flowed through the city because its bed to the north was gravel. But south of the city, where the soil was deeper, the water became muddy and took on a yellowish hue. Ramsay thinks the population of the three parts of Tarsus (city proper, hill town, and harbor) reached a half million.[33]

The origins of Tarsus are shrouded in antiquity, but its history goes back at least to Hittite times when the city was a Hittite stronghold. Around 1200 B.C., during the general upheaval in the eastern Mediterranean world, Tarsus suffered considerable destruction, as a burned layer in excavations there demonstrates. Subsequently Greeks settled among the older inhabitants. The first historical reference to Tarsus appears on the Black Obelisk of Shalmaneser III of Assyria (c. 850 B.C.), given the name Antioch-on-the-Cydnus. Ramsay well summarizes the situation:

> Cilicia was then recast, and its cities were reinvigorated. New life was breathed into a country which for centuries had been plunged in Orientalism and ruled by despotism. But, of all the cities, Tarsus was treated most honourably . . . It now stands forth as the principal city of the whole country, with the fullest rights of self-government and coinage permitted to any town in the Seleucid Empire. The Tarsus of St. Paul dates in a very real sense from the refoundation by Antiochus Epiphanes.
>
> Now at last Tarsus had the status of an autonomous city, choosing its own magistrates and making its own laws, though doubtless subject in all foreign relations to the king.[35]

The Seleucids relied mostly on Greeks and Jews to manage the Oriental peasantry and to lead in the urbanization of their realm. The Greek colonists brought to Tarsus in 171 B.C. seem to have come largely from Argos. A considerable number of Jews probably came about the same time. Ramsay argues that the Jews were at settlement granted citizenship with full burgess rights and that the Jews had a tribe set apart for them as at Alexandria, where the Jews were all enrolled in one tribe.[36] In a tribe of their own, Jews could control their religious rites and relate them to the service of the synagogue. Concludes Ramsay: "No Jew could possibly become a member of an ordinary tribe in a Greek city, because he would have been obliged to participate frequently in a pagan ritual, which even the most degraded of Jews would hardly have faced."[37]

As noted above, when the Romans set up the province of Cilicia just before 100 B.C., this section of the Roman Empire apparently did not include Cilicia Pedias—only Tracheia. Tigranes, king of Armenia, held Tarsus from about 83 until Pompey chased him out and reorganized the East in 65–64, making Tarsus the capital of the newly constructed Cilicia in 64. Not much

is known of Tarsus during the Republican period except that it was the scene of Cicero's activities as governor in 51 B.C. Julius Caesar paid a brief visit to the city in 47, and from then on its inhabitants were enthusiastically for the Empire. Cassius forced them in 43 to take his and Brutus' side, but the Tarsians returned to their former loyalty at the first opportunity.

Antony rewarded the city by granting it the status of a free city, permitting Tarsus the right to duty-free import and export trade. Here Antony lived for some time; and here he met Cleopatra (38 B.C.), who sailed up the Cydnus in her luxurious galley right into the middle of the city. Augustus renewed Antony's grants to Tarsus after the Battle of Actium (31 B.C.), when he became master of the Roman world. It seems evident that many citizens of Tarsus received Roman citizenship at the hands of Pompey, Julius Caesar, Antony, and Augustus. Paul's ancestors may have been among them.

PAUL'S ROMAN CITIZENSHIP

When Paul was imprisoned in Jerusalem he had an exchange with the captain of the guard concerning Roman citizenship. Paul asserted, "I was born a citizen" (Acts 22:28), but the captain of the guard observed that he had paid a large sum to get his.

The customary way to gain Roman citizenship was to be born to a Roman father, as was Paul. One might also be a retired auxiliary soldier who had earned citizenship for his years of military service. Slaves also sometimes accumulated enough funds to buy their freedom, or they were granted it by their owners, or individuals bought citizenship by a bribe.

Then, too, Rome sometimes honored a whole group with citizenship in various places in the empire. For example, in the case of Tarsus, Antiochus Epiphanes of the Seleucid Kingdom had brought a substantial number of Jews to Tarsus in 171 B.C. A group of these received citizenship at the hands of the Romans, presumably during Pompey's grant of citizenship before the middle of the first century B.C. Paul's ancestor (grandfather?) may have been one of them. If his ancestors did not gain citizenship then, they may have done so in the block grants of citizenship to inhabitants of Tarsus in the days of Julius Caesar, Antony, and Augustus.

Roman citizenship guaranteed numerous rights and the protection of the law. On this occasion Paul was protected from physical abuse and later had the right of appeal to Caesar, the equivalent of appeal to the Supreme Court of the United States.

Remains of a Roman city gate at Tarsus, known as St. Paul's Gate.

A tutor of Augustus in his youth was Athenodorus of the Stoic school at Tarsus. The great philosopher followed his former pupil to Rome in 44 B.C. and remained his adviser there until 15 B.C. In that year he returned to Tarsus invested with extraordinary authority to reform the government. Finding the city seriously misgoverned, he sent the ruling clique into exile and revised the constitution. His successor in A.D. 7 was another philosopher, Nestor, who had risen to a position of imperial trust and who had tutored Augustus' nephew Marcellus from 26 to 23 B.C. Nestor must have held the reins of authority in Tarsus for at least another decade.

The reforms that Athenodorus carried out at Tarsus have significant connection with the Pauline narrative. An oligarchic arrangement was instituted in which the power of the people was curtailed and certain property qualifications required for the exercise of voting rights. Thus, the burgesses of the city, who enjoyed the franchise and held the right of election, were men of some means. Within this oligarchic body was an inner aristocracy consisting of Roman citizens. So then Paul, in claiming to be a citizen of Tarsus and as well a Roman citizen,

was proclaiming to the world that he was a member of the upper aristocracy of the city.

It is significant that after Paul was beaten in Jerusalem, his first words were that he was a Jew, a citizen of Tarsus, which was "no mean city" (Acts 21:39). He did not claim at that point to be a Roman citizen. As noted earlier, Xenophon, four centuries before Christ, was impressed with the greatness of the city. Its coins called it "Loveliest Greatest Metropolis."

During the first century A.D. Tarsus was the one great city of Cilicia (which until A.D. 72 was joined to Syria for administrative purposes). It was a free city with a fine harbor, and it controlled an important trade route and a rich hinterland. The metropolis had been a self-governing city since about 170 B.C. and was one of the three great eastern university cities, ranking with Alexandria and Athens. But in contrast to its two eastern rivals, Tarsus had the great distinction that its students were largely natives; it did not have to draw extensively from the outside for intellectual greatness. The city's fine scholars were numerous. Athenodorus the Stoic was the companion of Cato the Younger; Athenodorus Cananites was tutor and adviser of Augustus; Nestor taught Marcellus and, reportedly, Tiberius; and Antipater was head of a school in Athens. Thus, Tarsus was a city with great economic and cultural attainments.

Here met East and West, Semite and Hellene. Here was born Saul of Tarsus, probably within ten years of the birth of Christ. It is significant that the Jew who was destined to become the apostle to the Gentiles was born here. And it is questionable whether a Palestinian Jew could so effectively have met the Greek on his own level, quoting his own philosophers, and alluding on occasion to his athletic contests. Certainly Paul was influenced by his early environment, but there is no proof that he ever attended the University of Tarsus. He always emphasized his Jewish background without mentioning Greco-Roman influences upon him.

It is important to be careful in our assumptions about Paul. Evidently he went to Jerusalem at a fairly early age and studied there at the feet of Gamaliel (Acts 22:3). How much he may have imbibed of Hellenistic literature or culture in general at a young age before going to Jerusalem is questionable. But he did return to the place of his birth in his mature years and may have studied some of that literature then (Acts 9:30; 11:25). Moreover, we don't know about his knowledge of or ability at tentmaking. Did he serve as an apprentice while a young boy? Did he pick up the trade in his mature years after returning to Tarsus? And are we to translate the Greek as "Tentmaker" or to understand the term to mean "Leather-worker," as some Greek scholars claim? At least we know he could support himself when necessary (cf. Acts 20:34; 1 Corinthians 4:12; 1 Thessalonians. 2:9; 2 Thessalonians 3:8). And he had an unusual combination of qualifications for ministry. He was a Roman citizen, a Jewish citizen of Tarsus, a highly trained and faithful Hebrew (apparently with an impeccable lifestyle—blameless before the law, Philippians 3:6), and a familiarity with Hellenistic culture.

While the glory of ancient Tarsus has departed, its remains do not lie far below the surface. Roman baths were discovered in the middle of the city in 1960. Tarsus has not experienced any extensive excavations, however. Even the location of the university is unknown. Hetty Goldman's excavations (1934–39, 1947–48) do not seem to have found anything dating closer than a hundred years to Paul. Her finds especially related to the Hittite period. Works of that period are on display at the Adana Museum. One structure unearthed was a Hittite temple or administration building. But a Roman arch that stands in the middle of town does seem to have been contemporary with the apostle. The beautiful Cydnus no longer flows through the center of the city (population now c. 190,000). The harbor of Rhegma has silted up. And miles away in open country, bits of the city wall stand in the cotton fields like old teeth.

Pamphylia. The region of Pamphylia (to the west of Cilicia) consisted of a plain eighty miles long and twenty miles broad at its widest, lying on the southern coast of Asia Minor between the Taurus Mountains and the Mediterranean. Cilicia bordered it on the east and Lycia on the west. The plain was shut in from northern winds but was well watered by springs from the Taurus ranges.

Very likely Dorians came to Pamphylia at the time of the Dorian migrations early in the first millennium B.C. and mingled with the aborigines. The region was subject successively to Lydia, Persia, Alexander the Great, the Seleucids, Pergamum, and Rome. Pamphylia does not seem to have benefited greatly from civilizing influences and long remained a rough and rather dangerous area. The port of Side is said to have earned its prosperity as the market of Cilician pirates.

About 102 B.C. Rome established the province of Cilicia (merely a series of posts along the Pamphylian coast) to deal with the Mediterranean pirates. When Pompey took Cilicia after his tilt with the pirates (67 B.C.), Pamphylia became part of that province and remained such until 36 B.C., when Antony gave it to Amyntas of Galatia. It was probably not detached from Galatia until A.D. 43 when Claudius took away the freedom of the Lycians and added them to the province of Pamphylia. Nero again freed the Lycians, and in A.D. 69 Pamphylia and Galatia were put under one governor. Vespasian rescinded Lycian freedom and reunited Lycia and Pamphilia. In A.D. 74 he

PAUL'S FIRST AND SECOND MISSIONARY JOURNEYS
·····▷····▷ Paul's first journey
–·▷–·▷ Paul's second journey
0   50   100   200
SCALE OF MILES

extended the province of Pamphylia to include the mountainous area to the north, properly known as Pisidia. Therefore it is evident that when Paul traveled through Pamphylia, it was part of the combined province Lycia-Pamphylia. Besides Perga, the chief cities of Pamphylia were Attalia (c. twelve miles southwest of the metropolis) and Side (more than thirty miles southeast of Perga).

According to his custom, Paul must have been concerned for the Jews of Pamphylia. That some Jews lived there is clear from the fact that representatives from the province were present in Jerusalem on the day of Pentecost (Acts 2:10). Although Paul and Barnabas introduced Christianity there, its progress was slow.

The First Missionary Journey

Perga. After Paul and his party embarked at Paphos on Cyprus, they headed for the Asia Minor coast, 180 miles away (Acts 13:13). Sailing up the Cestrus River, they docked at Perga (Perge), or rather its port, five miles from the city. Perga itself lay eight miles inland at a junction of a small stream with the Cestrus and was a very ancient place when the apostolic company arrived.

The founding of the city evidently dates to before 1000 B.C., though the story of its establishment is unknown. The earliest city was built on the 160-foot-high acropolis and seems to have been a Hittite settlement. As Perga grew during the Persian period, it expanded to the south of the acropolis and was a considerable town when Alexander the Great arrived. Alexander used Perga as a base for conquest of the interior of Asia Minor. After death and the dismemberment of his empire, the Seleucids took over the area. Set free from the Seleucids in 188 B.C., the city became part of the Pergamene kingdom and passed to Rome in 133 B.C.

Perga was an important place during imperial times. Inscriptions on contemporary coins reveal that it was called the metropolis of Pamphylia. The city minted its own coins over a very long period of time—from the second century B.C. to A.D. 276. It was a great center for the worship of Artemis, which like the Ephesian Artemis (or Diana) was more Asiatic than Greek. In her honor an annual festival was held, and vast crowds assembled. Pergan coins commonly represented her in the Asiatic way, as a pillar of stone with the top rounded or carved to represent a head. Likely this was originally a meteorite. Where the great temple to Artemis was

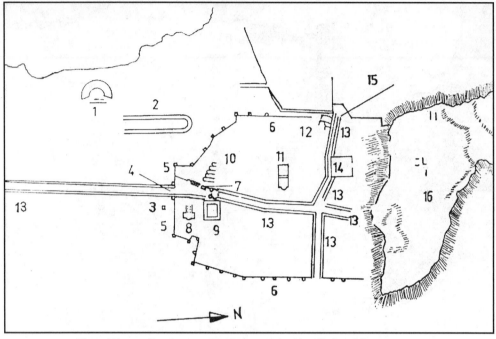

Plan of Perga. Numbers on the plan are to be identified as follows:

1.	theater	9.	agora
2.	stadium	10.	roman baths
3.	a tomb	11.	a bishopric basilica
4.	later city gate	12.	baths
5.	later southern city wall	13.	colonnaded street
6.	hellenistic city wall	14.	a palestra dedicated to Claudius (A.D. 41-54)
7.	city gate complex	15.	streets lined with tombs
8.	a church	16.	acropolis

located is not yet known. But it stood on high ground outside the city and was Ionic in style.

Considerable ruins can still be seen at Perga, where Turkish archaeologists have been working for decades. Arif Mansel of the University of Istanbul led Turkish Historical Society digs there in 1946, 1953–57, and since 1967. In recent years, to the present, other Turkish archaeologists have directed the work. Much of this effort has centered on late Roman and Byzantine remains. Some idea of the size and prosperity of the place may be gained from the fact that a second century A.D. theater could accommodate fifteen thousand spectators; and a stadium, also second century A.D., could hold twelve thousand spectators.

As to what the city was like in Paul's day, archaeological research has not yet told

us as much as we would like to know. But we do have some basic information. The city extended south from its acropolis and roughly formed a rectangle, surrounded by walls built during the Hellenistic period, probably the third century B.C. Those walls still stand in places to a height of about forty feet and are reinforced with square towers. A colonnaded street ran north and south directly to the foot of the acropolis. Another colonnaded street crossed it running east and west, dividing the city into four unequal parts. A water channel ran along the middle of each street. During recent years a restoration project has been raising some of these columns to their original position. A Hellenistic gate, flanked by two round towers, led into the main street of Perga. After a Roman extension of the wall southward in the fourth century A.D. a

The colonnaded streets of Perga. The main street is in the foreground and the columns of the cross street can be seen in the background on the right

Roman gate was erected farther south along the main street. In the northwest quarter of the city not far from the foot of the acropolis stood a palestra, a place for athletic exercise. Built during the reign of the emperor Claudius (A.D. 41–54) and thus dating to the time of Paul, it measured about 235 feet on a side.

Pisidia. From Perga Paul wanted to go inland to Antioch. In order to do so, he had to pass through Pisidia. This district was about 120 miles long (east to west) and fifty miles wide and was entirely filled by ranges of the Taurus. It had always been a wild country infested by brigands. Alexander the Great had had to fight his way through them as he tried to conquer the interior of Asia Minor. About 25 B.C., Augustus determined to reduce these bandits by establishing a chain of posts that included Antioch and Lystra on the northern side. Apparently the Romans felt they had achieved their goal by A.D. 74, when they linked Pisidia to the Pamphylian plain in the province of Pamphylia. Formerly they had treated Pisidia as part of Galatia.

But the area of Pisidia was still very dangerous when Paul came

through on his first missionary journey. Some believe that Paul had travel through Pisidia in mind when he made his autobiographical comment about "perils of robbers" in 2 Corinthians 11:26. Commentators often suggest too that the dangers in further missionary activity to the north of Perga caused John Mark to turn back, and for this reason Paul refused to take the young man with him on his second missionary journey (Acts 13:13; 15:37–39). Of course there is no way of knowing whether either supposition is correct.

Antioch. At any rate, Paul and Barnabas made the hundred-mile trek north to Antioch. Very likely they took the route that followed one of the tributaries of Cestrus to Adada and thence went north. Perhaps the altitude of some 3,600 feet at Antioch was welcome to Paul, if indeed he had contracted malaria in the fever-infested plain of Pamphylia, as has been suggested. It seems that Paul was ill when he reached the interior (Galatians 4:13–14).

Antioch was not a city of Pisidia but lay on the north side of that district in Phrygia when Paul came through on his first missionary journey. Ramsay observed that the accurate and full geographical description of Antioch at that time would have been "a Phrygian city on the side of Pisidia." But the convenient way of alluding to it came to be "Pisidian Antioch" to distinguish it from the Antioch on the Orontes River. Only as

The gate of Perga

The great aqueduct at Antioch of Pisidia.

the term Pisidia became widened in inclusiveness did Antioch of Pisidia receive universal acceptance. The title Antioch of Pisidia found its way into some of the later, inferior biblical manuscripts and appears in the King James Version. But the better manuscripts read correctly "Pisidian Antioch."[38] Thus Luke's language is seen again to correlate minutely with contemporary conditions.

The reason why Paul went to Antioch at all seems fairly obvious when we consider Paul's strategy of missions and the nature of Antioch. Paul worked longest in fairly large and strategic centers where there was a mobile population, centers that could act as springboards for the rapid spread of the gospel. Corinth and Ephesus illustrate this procedure. Antioch was a main stop on the great eastern trade route from Ephesus to the Euphrates. It was a city that the Seleucids had established for Hellenization of the district and Romans used as a chief center for the pacification of southern Galatia. Moreover, it was situated in a fertile valley at the natural center of its district.

But there may also have been a personal urging for Paul to go there. The Sergii Paulli were substantial landowners and a senatorial family of Pisidian Antioch.[39] Sergius Paulus, the proconsul of Cyprus and a convert to Christianity through Paul's ministry (Acts 12:12), may have urged the apostle to go to Antioch to evangelize his relatives there.

Antioch stood just to the west of the Anthios River (which flowed southwest into Lake Limnai), on a roughly rectangular plateau some two miles in circumference. The plateau sloped upward to the east, where there was a sharp drop to the Anthios, about two hundred feet below. At the western end the plateau is only about fifty feet above the plain. The natural configuration of the site made it a strong fortress, a great asset in so unruly a region. The ordinary water supply came by means of an aqueduct that brought water from a spring in the mountains six or seven miles to the north of the city. During most of its course the aqueduct lay underground, but for the last mile it marched across the landscape on great arches, twenty of which still remain. Though this source might easily have been cut, water in sufficient amounts was also available from the Anthios. Just to the east of the Anthios rose a range of hills, on one of which stood the great sanctuary of the god Men.

Whether or not there was a Phrygian fortress at or near Antioch is uncertain. Probably the town was originally a temple village on the vast estates of the god Men located in the area. About 280 B.C. or a little earlier, Seleucus Nicator founded the city, and named it after his father, Antiochus, using as the main population element Greeks from Magnesia on the Maeander River. This Antioch, one of the more than sixteen Seleucus founded, was designed to strengthen his hold on native tribes and to spread Hellenistic culture in this Phrygian area.

When defeat of Antiochus III of Syria at Magnesia in 189 B.C. resulted in his expulsion from Asia Minor, Antioch became an independent city. And it seems to have remained such until Mark Antony gave it to Amyntas, last king of Galatia. When on his death in 25 B.C. Amyntas willed his kingdom to Rome, the city passed with the rest of the province into Roman hands. Soon after the province of Galatia was organized, the Romans constituted Antioch a Roman colony and settled it with veterans of the Fifth Legion (the Gallic) and apparently of the Seventh also.[40]

The new colony was officially called Colonia Caesarea, but the old name had such a strong hold that by the end of the first century B.C. "Antiocheia" began to appear with the official name. Apparently Amyntas had confiscated much of the land used by the Roman colony from the temple of Men. Thus the temple lost its political significance but continued to be religiously important.[41]

Colonia Caesarea was the most important of a chain of military colonies that Augustus founded to control the wild tribes of Pisidia and Pamphylia. It was the administrative center of the southern half of the province of Galatia. By now it had become quite cosmopolitan. There were some Phrygians. To these Seleucus had added Greeks. He and his successors had settled thousands of Jews in the cities of Phrygia,[42] and no doubt many of these found their way into Antioch because the Jewish element there was strong when Paul arrived (Acts 13:50).

Finally, Romans had come in to dominate the social and political structure. They exerted every effort to make the new colony as Roman as possible. When Paul went to bed in Pisidian Antioch, he heard the night watch give their commands in Latin. The appearance of the city itself also made the impression that a little bit of Rome had been flung down on this hillside in Asia Minor. The city was prosperous during the Roman and Byzantine periods but apparently was completely destroyed by the Arabs around A.D. 713.

As the 1924 University of Michigan excavations have shown, life at Antioch in Paul's day centered around two paved squares, the Square of Tiberius and the Square of Augustus.[43] The former lay at a lower level, and scattered around on its three thousand square feet of paving stones were many incised circles or rectangles on which the Romans in their idle hours could play all kinds of games. From the lower square, twelve steps some seventy feet long led into the Square of Augustus through a magnificent triple-arched gateway. The façade of this gate was faced with two pairs of Corinthian columns that flanked two enormous reliefs of

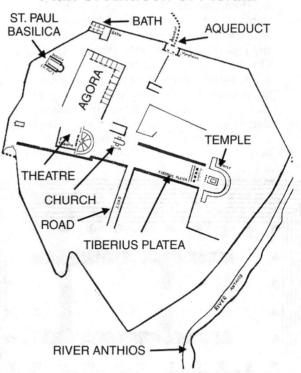

Plan of Antioch of Pisidia

Pisidian captives (representing Augustus' victories on land) and had a frieze with tritons, Neptune, dolphins, and other marine symbols (commemorating Augustus' victories on the sea, especially at Actium).

At the east end of the Square of Augustus a semicircle was cut out of the native rock, before which rose a two-story colonnade with Doric columns below and Ionic above. In front of the center of the semicircle stood a Roman temple, the base of which was cut out of native rock and the superstructure built of white marble. It had a portico of four Corinthian columns across the front. The frieze of this temple, apparently dedicated to the god Men and to Augustus, consisted of beautifully executed bulls' heads (the symbol of Men) bound together with garlands of all sorts of leaves and fruits.

A main street about twenty feet wide led up from the city gate on the west side of town to the Square of Tiberius and another street, also about twenty feet wide, extended from the square of Tiberius to the north gate.

What the rest of the city was like in New Testament times the excavators were not able to determine. The squares were at least partly faced with shops and houses. The water system was superb. Everywhere in the excavations terra-cotta pipes surfaced. On the northern, western, and southern sides of the town substantial fortifications were built. On the east side, where the plateau dropped sharply to the Anthios, defenses do not seem to have been so necessary. The walled town covered about 115 acres.

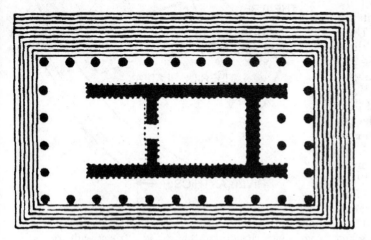

Plan of the temple to Men at Antioch

Much of what archaeologists have uncovered at Antioch dates after the days of Paul's visit there. The city gate on the west side, which took the form of a triumphal arch with three entrances, was dedicated to the emperor Hadrian in A.D. 129. The theater apparently was constructed around A.D. 311–313. Three churches, two of basilica style (with a central aisle and two side aisles) and one in the shape of a Latin cross, were built several hundred years later. And a stadium, outside the west wall, has not yet been dated.

Some two miles southeast of the city on a mountain spur about 5,500 feet in altitude stood the great sanctuary of Men. Actually there were two temples, built in the second century B.C., the larger to Men and the smaller unidentified. The larger temple was set in a sacred precinct, measuring about 137 by 230 feet, and surrounded by a 5.5 -

foot wall. The temple itself (about 66 by 41 feet) was Ionic in style. It had six columns on the short sides and eleven on the long sides. Inscriptions by devotees covered the inside and outside of the wall, which had porticoes along two sides. And around the sanctuary there were about twenty buildings designed to accommodate worshipers' banquets. Here, as in so many other places in the eastern Mediterranean world, individuals could participate in social events and eat food offered to idols (cf. 1 Corinthians 8:10).

To the north of the sacred enclosure in a hollow on the mountaintop stood a semicircular structure, thought to be a theater or possibly a stadium with only one end constructed. It measures 113 feet wide and 130 feet deep. Statue bases lined the sacred way adjacent to it. Apparently this was the stadium where the annual gymnastic contests in honor of the god Men were held.[44]

Men was the chief god of Antioch. He commonly appears on the city's coins as a standing, fully draped figure with a Phrygian high-pointed cap on his head. In his outstretched left hand he holds a figure representing victory, and he rests his left arm on a column to help bear the weight. In his right hand he holds a long scepter, and behind his shoulders appear the horns of a crescent moon. Variously called "Dionysius," "Apollo," and "Asklepios" by the ancients, he must have been thought of as the giver of wine, the giver of prophecy, (or as the sun god), and the great physician. In short, he was the Anatolian supreme god.[45]

One of the more interesting of the inscriptions found at Antioch was one discovered and interpreted by Sir William Ramsay. Dedicated to Lucius Sergius Paullus the Younger, it was studied by Ramsay in conjunction with another published earlier that mentioned Sergia Paulla. He tried to show that Sergia Paulla and Lucius Sergius Paullus were daughter and son of the Proconsul Sergius Paulus of

Cyprus (Acts 13:7). Ramsay thought further that the inscription about the daughter suggested she may have been a Christian and trained her children in the Christian faith.[46] Ramsay has had numerous followers who have accepted his conclusions. He explained the difference in spelling by saying that the spelling of the Latin name is always *Paullus* but the Greek *Paulos*.

As was their custom, Paul and Barnabas preached first to the Jews in Antioch. By the second Sabbath the Gentiles of the community readily heard the missionaries. Apparently the evangelization was rapid and effective, because Acts 13:49 states that the whole area had heard the Christian gospel. At this juncture the Jews of the city determined to expel the apostle. Since they were living in a Roman colony, his opponents did not try riot tactics. Nor did they try to arraign him before Roman courts on a fraudulent charge. Rather they decided to take the indirect approach, to enlist the "devout and honourable women," no doubt the proselytes of the synagogue in a campaign to persuade their Roman husbands to get rid of the "blasphemous visitors."

JEWS IN ASIA MINOR

Apparently as early as the third century B.C. Seleucids permitted the Jews to "follow their own laws." In the days of Augustus Caesar the Roman government granted the Jews of the empire the right to live as they had been accustomed, which meant the confirmation of numerous special rights (e.g., to hold Jewish festivals, feasts, and gatherings; to send the annual temple tax to Jerusalem; exemption from enrollment in the legions and participation in public events on the Sabbath).

Jews were so numerous that their special privileges created considerable problems for society at large. There is support for the conclusion that they totaled over a million of the some thirteen million living in the peninsula.

Cities or provincial governments periodically attempted to abridge Jewish rights. As a result, friction developed. Difficulties occurred especially when Jewish citizens demanded exemption from civic religious practices (e.g., emperor worship or worship of local deities). They wounded civic pride by abstention from idolatry and limited participation in the main currents of civic life.

Evidently Jews generally kept the Sabbath, sent the annual temple tax to Jerusalem, practiced circumcision as sons of the covenant, went to synagogue to worship, and kept the Mosaic Law. Many traveled to Jerusalem for Passover. Jews from five of the six provinces of Asia Minor were present in Jerusalem on the day of Pentecost (Acts 2:9–10).

It seems that Jews developed a sense of belonging in their communities and made significant social contributions without compromising their Jewish identity.

Iconium. Paul and Barnabas were expelled from Antioch and traveled southeastward to Iconium at the western edge of the vast central plains of Asia Minor. Almost certainly the missionary pair took the Royal Road about eighteen miles south to Neapolis. After about another eighteen miles, at the north end of Lake Karalis, they left the Royal Road and traveled almost due east to Iconium (modern Konya with a population of over 500,000). The total distance was about eighty miles.[47]

Iconium stood on a level plateau about 3,400 feet above sea level. Approximately six miles west of the city, mountains rose to a height of 5000 to 6000 feet. From them a stream flowed down into the city, and other smaller streams flowed into the surrounding region, making the land around into a great garden. On the north and south, hills rose at a distance of ten to twelve miles from the city. To the east lay the plains of Lycaonia.

Although Iconium was unsuited for defense, a site such as this with an ever-flowing natural supply of water and fertile soil was a center of human life among arid plateaus. Unfortunately the supply of water pouring into the plains is not so well regulated and properly distributed now as in ancient times, and much of it is at present left to stagnate in marshes.

During the first century A.D., Iconium controlled the fertile district around it for some two hundred square miles.[48] The population was, of course, scattered in numerous villages, the ruins of which have never been carefully or exhaustively studied by modern explorers. These villages were just fragments of the central city, each having its chief officer or "first man." The free inhabitants were not villagers but citizens of the chief city where they enjoyed political rights.

The origins of Iconium are hidden in the immemorial recesses of antiquity. A local Phrygian tradition pushes the beginnings of the city to "before the flood." What that means is unclear. Iconium was, of course, part of the Persian Empire. Later, perhaps during the third century B.C. under Seleucid control, it came to be recognized as the chief city of Lycaonia. After the Roman victory at Magnesia in 190 B.C., when most of Asia Minor was taken from the Seleucids, Iconium was assigned to Pergamum. But the Pergamenes never seem to have actually controlled it, and the city probably soon passed under the power of the Galatians. The Pontic kings took over from about 130 to 125 B.C., and the city was set free after the Roman defeat of Mithridates.

Possibly it was in 63 B.C. that a tetrarchy of Lycaonia was formed, containing fourteen cities; Iconium was the capital. In 39 B.C. Mark Antony gave this city to King Polemon but three years later transferred it to King Amyntas of Galatia. When Amyntas died in 25 B.C., Iconium was incorporated in the Roman Empire as part of the province of Galatia. The Seleucids settled Jews in Iconium during the third century B.C., but they apparently did not become influential until the Roman period.

How and when Iconium was transformed from an Oriental town to a Hellenic self-governing city is unknown. But transformed it was. And when Paul and Barnabas came through on their first missionary journey, it was still a Greek city, in which the powers of the state were exercised by the demos, the Greek assembly of all citizens. It was not yet a Roman colony, in which the body of colonists in assembly would have ruled. That would come during Hadrian's reign (A.D. 117–138). Thus, as H.V. Morton observes, the approach of the Jews in discrediting the effective ministry of Paul in this town was not to try to influence the leading citizens indirectly as at Antioch. "The most effective way to expel the apostles was obviously to create a public argument, to rouse the whole city against them, and then sit back and allow democracy to do its worst."[49] When a plot against the lives of the missionaries was discovered, they left for Lystra. This action should not be construed as cowardice. Events at Lystra would demonstrate the real stuff of which Paul and Barnabas were made.

Luke observed that when the missionaries left Iconium for Lystra and Derbe they crossed over the line from Phrygia into Lycaonia (Acts 14:6). This long created a problem for Bible students because many ancient authorities who wrote from the Roman provincial point of view assigned Iconium to Lycaonia. William Ramsay has demonstrated, however, that many of these ancient authorities had not been carefully read and that the most authoritative of them called it a city of Phrygia. Ramsay has shown further from inscriptions he found at Iconium that the city was so completely Phrygian that even leading citizens were using the Phrygian language on inscriptions as late as A.D. 150 to 250.[50] Perhaps, as Ramsay has suggested, Luke mentioned this particular frontier because when Paul and Barnabas crossed it they were safe for the moment. They were now under a new jurisdiction.

Lystra. The hurried flight of Paul and Barnabas brought them in one day to Lystra, about eighteen miles southwest of Iconium. American Professor J. R. Sitlington Sterret in 1885 identified the site as lying a mile northwest of Khatyn Serai, at Zoldera. He achieved positive identification by means of an inscribed altar still

The mound of Lystra.

standing, on which appeared the name of the city and the indication that it had been a Roman colony. Support of the testimony of the altar stone came from coins found at the site.

Augustus founded Lystra as a Roman colony, probably in 6 B.C., for the purpose of restraining and regulating the mountain tribes on the southern frontier of the province of Galatia. It seems to have been a place of some importance under the early emperors, but during the last quarter of the first century it sank back into the insignificance of a small provincial town. It was not on a main commercial route, and its purpose as a military outpost had been achieved. The area had been subdued.

The city stood on a small, elongated hill in the center of a valley abundantly supplied with water by two streams. Lystra possessed a considerable territory of fertile soil in the valley, as well as a tract of low hilly ground. The site was off the main roads, and its seclusion marked it out as a small rustic town, where the people and customs would be quite provincial. Note that the inhabitants addressed Paul not in Greek but in the "Lycaonia" language (Acts 14:11). Moreover, there do not even seem to have been enough Jews in the place to build a synagogue. The relative seclusion of Lystra has been compared with that of Berea; at both towns Paul sought to wait out a storm of opposition.

Initially the missionaries were very well received. Luke reported that Paul's healing of a lame man led the native population to hail the pair as gods, identifying Barnabas as Zeus (Jupiter) and Paul as Hermes (Mercury) (Acts 14:8–12). The implication seems to be that Barnabas was the older of the two and had a dignified bearing. They addressed Paul as Hermes, the messenger of the gods, because he did most of the speaking. It has also been suggested that Paul's being addressed as Hermes indicates he must have been a virile-looking, gracious, and attractive younger man. Inscriptions show that Zeus and Hermes were especially coupled in the worship of the Lycaonians. Apparently the worship of these two deities represented an essentially native cult under a thin Greek disguise.

In spite of their protestation against being considered as gods, Paul and Barnabas were still hailed as such by the natives. They seem to have had considerable success in preaching the Christian gospel, however. At length Jews came down from Iconium and caused trouble for the evangelists. Ramsay suggests that the Jews who came to Lystra were middle men who were speculating in the approaching harvest and that the time of the stoning of Paul was August.[51]

At any rate, the Jews came and stirred up the fickle multitude to turn against Paul and to stone him and leave him for dead. But his followers cared for him, and he left with Barnabas for a second refuge, Derbe. This time the pair seem to have been unmolested in their religious endeavors.

The mound of Derbe.

Derbe. After William Ramsay identified Derbe with Gudelisin (c. 1890), some forty miles southeast of Lystra, this view became traditional. But in 1956 an inscription was found at Kerti Hüyük, which seemed to fix that site definitely as ancient Derbe.[52] In 1961 a second inscription was found nearby Kerti Hüyük and helped to demonstrate almost beyond doubt that the mound was ancient Derbe.[53] In terms of location, Gudelisin is about thirty miles west of the modern Turkish town of Karaman (sixty-six miles by road southeast of Konya), Kerti Hüyük is some fifteen miles north-north-east of Karaman (ancient Laranda), and Karaman is about sixty miles southeast of Konya (ancient Iconium).

Since the journey from Lystra to Derbe would have taken more than a day, the reading in Acts 14:20 should be construed to mean that "the next day he departed with Barnabus to Derbe."

Historically, Derbe had been the capital of Antipater, the son of Perilaus and the only survivor of a number of insignificant Macedonian chiefdoms established around the edges of the central Anatolian plateau. The dates of his rule were about 63 to 35 B.C. and his kingdom included the towns of Derbe, Lystra, and Laranda. When Rome took over, they integrated the whole of south Galatia into a single administrative system that held the province together and consolidated their grip on the Taurus. To do this they founded a number of new cities

and refounded others—all of them taking the names of members of the ruling dynasty. Derbe, already existing as a Macedonian colony, became Claudioderbe. The impact of the emperor Claudius appears all over south Galatia.[54]

Paul and Barnabas apparently had a fruitful ministry at Derbe, where they must have remained for some time. Since Derbe was near the Galatian frontier, it seemed appropriate for them to refrain from going farther east. At length they retraced their steps and passed once more through Lystra, Iconium, and Antioch, establishing churches among the converts made earlier. Ramsay suggests that this return route was possible because by this time new magistrates had been installed in office in the three cities.[55] Also, trouble was not so likely to occur from a quiet organization of churches as from extensive evangelistic outreach.

Perga and Attalia. Paul had not preached at Perga before he headed for the interior of Asia Minor. Now he determined to do so, apparently without effect. So he headed for the seacoast town of Attalia (modern Antalya) about twelve miles southwest of Perga.

Attalia had the most important harbor of the coastal belt of old Pamphylia, which was largely a steep cliff on the seashore. Along the coast on both sides of the town the mountains soar up in tier after amber-colored tier, woods-green and olive-green, clothed in a forest of leaves, the sea sweeping their feet. The city itself rests on a flat limestone terrace 120 feet above the seashore. To the north of the city is a fertile plain. Attalians shipped timber from the Taurus to Egypt and Phoenicia, and Attalia had developed into a big and rich commercial city in Paul's day.

Although there certainly must have been inhabitants of the place much earlier, Attalus III of Pergamum (159–138 B.C.) receives credit for having founded Attalia. But evidently the Pergamenes did not effectively control the place. Apparently the port was not involved to any considerable extent with the pirate activity of the first century B.C. But it was a base for

The port of Attalia (modern Antalya).

Pompey in assembling his fleet in 67 B.C. Though Attalia suffered during the Roman civil wars, it grew rich again by the time Paul and Barnabas arrived. It was the richest town of the area during Byzantine times, and during the Seljuk period (after A.D. 1100) it was the headquarters of the Seljuk Mediterranean fleet.

The chief god of Attalia was Zeus, as at Pergamum. But Athena and Apollo were also worshiped. Since the modern town covers the ancient site, almost nothing of the Roman period can be detected; so little is known concerning what the place was like in the middle of the first century A.D. Researchers have not been able to locate a theater, a stadium, a temple, or any public building. The wall circuit remains virtually whole, but only a few sections in the north may possibly date back to the time of the city's founding. The most prominent monument surviving from classical times is Hadrian's gate, erected on the occasion of the emperor's visit to the city in A.D. 130.

Paul and Barnabas apparently did not try to preach in this port but merely sought passage for Antioch. Back in Syria, they faced a controversy over whether or not their numerous Gentile converts should be forced to keep the Mosaic law. The Council of Jerusalem was called to settle the matter.

Paul's Second Missionary Journey

The Council of Jerusalem was over (Acts 15:1–35). The mother church had taken its stand. Gentile Christians were not to be required to keep the law of Moses, and they sent a record of the decision to Antioch in the hands of Barnabas and Paul, Judas Barsabas, and Silas. Having delivered their message, Paul and Barnabas stayed in Antioch for a while preaching and teaching. Then they decided to embark on another missionary journey to "visit our brethren in every city where we have preached the word of the Lord, and see how they are doing" (Acts 15:36). Barnabas wanted to take John Mark along, but Paul was opposed; so the two parted company, Barnabas taking Mark to Cyprus, and Paul choosing Silas and setting out for Asia Minor.

The Arch of Hadrian in Attalia

This time Paul went through Syria and Cilicia and then came to Derbe and Lystra (Acts 15:41–16:1). Obviously this means that he went by land from Antioch into the province of Cilicia. The road led north out of Antioch and crossed the Amanus Mountains (modern Alma Dag) at the Syrian Gates. The Amanus, a short offshoot sent southward by the Tauric system, separated the provinces of Syria and Cilicia at an altitude of five thousand feet. The Syrian Gates (Beilan Pass) at an altitude of twenty-four hundred feet was the practicable route through the Amanus. About thirty-eight miles north of Antioch lay Alexandretta (modern Iskenderun). From there the road curved around the Bay of Issus to the town of Issus twenty miles away. Here Alexander the Great won a great battle against Persian forces in October 333 B.C.

From Issus the road led inland, crossed the Pyramus and Sarus rivers, and passed through Adana (c. 125 miles from Antioch) and Tarsus (c. 150 miles away). The Acts narrative does not record that Paul visited his hometown on this occasion, but it is almost certain that he did go there because the main road led past Tarsus and to the Cilician Gates. Going north from Tarsus Paul passed through the Cilician Gates about thirty miles away. The road then ran in a northwesterly direction and about 170 miles farther ran down the main street of Iconium.

But Paul and Silas made stops south of Iconium at Derbe and Lystra. At the latter Paul met Timothy and made him a part of the apostolic company. The young man already had a good testimony in his own and nearby communities, and he was to serve Paul faithfully until the end of his days (cf. 2 Timothy).

At this point a geographic problem arises that has given rise to considerable discussion. In Acts 16:6 the statement appears in the King James Version that the apostolic company went "throughout Phrygia and the region of Galatia." In trying to discover the meaning, it should be useful first to comment on Phrygia, then on Galatia, and then to draw some conclusions.

Phrygia. The Phrygians apparently moved across the Hellespont from what is now European Turkey around 1200 B.C. and gradually spread over Asia Minor, destroying Hittite rule in many areas. They established a kingdom with considerable power and governed from Gordium, about fifty miles west southwest of modern Ankara. Gradually other powers encroached upon their territory in Asia Minor—Greeks in the west, Bithynians in the northwest, Assyrians in the east. Around 700 B.C. the Cimmerians, a Thracian people, destroyed the Phrygian kingdom but later passed out of existence. During the Lydian period there was a Phrygian revival, but these people experienced decline under Persian rule.

In 278 B.C. the eastern part of Phrygia came under the control of Celtic invaders (or Gauls) from the Danubian area and was renamed Galatia. At approximately the same time the Pergamene kingdom took over western Phrygia, which was their undisputed possession after the Roman victory at Magnesia in 190 B.C. expelled the Seleucid kings from Asia Minor and forced the Celts to settle in Galatia. When the Pergamene kingdom became the province of Asia in 133 B.C., most of Phrygia came under control of Rome.

By that time Phrygia in a narrower sense was considered to be that interior tableland of Asia Minor (c. 3,000–5,000 feet) roughly bordered by the Sangarius River (modern Sakarya) on the north and northeast, the upper Hermus River on the west, the upper Maeander River on the south and southwest, and Galatia on the east. It was a region best suited for grazing. Most of the area of Phrygia in Paul's day was part of the province of Asia, but a small portion of it lay in the province of Galatia. Iconium and Antioch (of Pisidia) were cities of Galatian Phrygia.

Galatia. "Galatia," derived from "Galatai," was the Greek name for the Gauls, or Celts, who invaded Asia Minor in 278–277 B.C. at the invitation of Nicomedes of Bithynia. After much raiding and plundering, the Gauls were finally penned in an area between the Sangarius and Halys rivers in north central Asia Minor by Attalus I of Pergamum about 230 B.C. For the next forty years they continued

The harbor at Troas, now silted in.

to harass their neighbors. After the battle of Magnesia in 190, Rome sent forces to subdue them. They then remained loyal to Rome during the Mithridatic wars, and after 64 B.C. they were a client state of Rome.

At that time the territory was organized on the Celtic tribal basis; and three tribes occupied separate areas with their respective capitals at Pessinus, Ancyra (modern Ankara), and Tavium. From 44 B.C. one ruler held sway in Galatia. Four years later Mark Antony conferred Galatian domains on Castor and gave Amyntas a kingdom comprising Pisidic Phrygia and Pisidia generally. In 36 B.C. Castor's kingdom was given to Amyntas, along with additional territory in subsequent years. His government was so effective in pacifying the area that when he died in 25 B.C. and bequeathed his kingdom to Rome, he left it in such an orderly state that Rome incorporated it into the Empire as the province of Galatia.

The province of Galatia then included, besides Galatia proper, parts of Phrygia, Lycaonia, Pisidia, and Pamphylia. It remained in this form until about A.D. 72, when additional increases in its territory were made. The two principal cities of the province of Galatia were Ancyra (the metropolis) and Pisidian Antioch. Actually the history of Galatia is extremely complicated, both before and after Roman control. A good source of information on the subject is William M. Ramsay's *A Historical Commentary on St. Paul's Epistle to the Galatians.* In width the Galatian province varied from 100 to 175 miles; it measured some 250 miles north and south.

Remains of Roman baths at Troas.

Since "Galatia" could refer either in an ethnic sense to a territory in north central Asia Minor or in a political sense to the province of Galatia, questions often arise as to the sense in which Luke and Paul used the term and to whom Paul wrote when he penned the epistle to the Galatians. Paul, proud of his Roman citizenship, always used the provincial names of the areas under Roman control, never the territorial, except as the two were identical in significance. Paul used the term "Galatia" only three times: in 1 Corinthians 16:1, Galatians 1:2, and 2 Timothy 4:10, all of which certainly must refer to the Roman province. Peter must have used the term in the same sense in 1 Peter 1:1, because the other four areas he addressed in the same verse were adjacent Roman provinces.

Luke does not use either "Galatia" or "Galatians" but only the adjective "Galatic" or "Galatian." Following Ramsay, Souter argues that Acts 16:6 should be translated "the Phrygo-Galatic region," which no doubt referred to that section of the province of Galatia known as Phrygia Galatica, containing Pisidian Antioch and Iconium. He further argues that in Acts 18:23 the Greek may be translated either

"the Galatico-Phrygian region" or "the Galatian region and Phrygia" (preferably the latter), the Galatian region including Derbe and Lystra, and the Phrygian, Iconium, and Pisidian Antioch.[56]

Ramsay also notes that Acts 16:6 must be looked upon as connected with Acts 15:36 and 16:1, verses 2 to 5 being considered somewhat parenthetical.[57] The apostle purposed to visit churches he had previously founded in Derbe, Lystra, Iconium, and Antioch. After he had visited these towns Luke said, "When they had gone through Phrygia and the region of Galatia . . ." (Acts 16:6). Obviously there is no room here for the idea that Paul on this journey circled far north through the old ethnic area of Galatia. The north Galatian theory lacks substantial support in regard to Paul's either having visited the area or writing his epistle to the people of it.[58]

Where Paul and Silas went from Pisidian Antioch is uncertain. They may have taken the main east-west trade route through Colossae and Laodicea, out the Maeander Valley to Ephesus and north along the coast to Mysia. Or they may have gone northwest on the main road through Phrygia (via Philadelphia, Sardis, and Thyatira) to

Pergamum and from there to Mysia. At any rate, the Holy Spirit made it clear to them that they should not preach in Asia and Bithynia (Acts 16:6). So they passed through Mysia and came to the port town of Troas.

Mysia was a district of northwest Asia Minor south of the Propontis (modern Marmara) and Hellespont. Its boundaries were never carefully defined. After being part of the dominions of Persia and Alexander, it came under the control of Pergamum and thus of Rome, forming part of the province of Asia in 133 B.C. Mysia is mentioned only in Acts 16:7 in the Bible. Assos and Troas, both of which Paul visited, lay within its bounds. The greater part of Mysia is mountainous, being traversed by northwest branches of the Taurus range; the main branches were Mount Ida and Mount Temnus. Most of its rivers were small and not navigable.

When Paul arrived at Troas, he received the vision of the man from Macedonia (Acts 16:9–11) and decided to heed the call to do missionary work in Greece. The rest of the second missionary journey, took the apostolic company to Greek shores.

Troas. A visit to Troas today reveals nothing of the city's golden past. Weeds and brush choke everything, including the colossal Roman baths of Herodes Atticus that dominate the ruins. But with effort it is possible to wade through weeds to find remains of the theater, the stadium, city walls, and the harbor. The walls are six miles in circumference, showing something of the size and prosperity of the place in ancient times. The harbor from which Paul sailed for Europe is silted in and a sandbar blocks the entrance. The scene gives the impression of a salt pan.

Antigonus, king of Thrace, founded Troas (ten miles south of Troy) in 310 B.C. at the invitation of Alexander the Great. He called the place Antigonia Troas. Later Lysimachus, king of Macedonia after Alexander's death, killed Antigonus, took possession of the Troad, and renamed the city Alexandria Troas. During Hellenistic times Troas grew rich and powerful as it controlled the passing sea trade through the Hellespont. Augustus made it a Roman

colony, and its port became important for travel between the northwest part of the Roman province of Asia and Macedonia and the West.

Troas especially prospered in the second century A.D., when the famous Herodes Atticus sponsored construction of several public structures there. His great baths there ranked with building programs at Athens, Corinth, Delphi, and elsewhere. The importance of Troas waned in the fourth century when Constantinople became the capital of the Roman Empire. Later the town passed out of existence, and in the seventeenth century A.D. the Ottomans plundered its ruins to obtain building stone for construction in Istanbul, including the famous Blue Mosque.

Paul returned to Troas later. And while he was preaching there a young man fell out of a window and apparently was killed. Paul evidently performed a miracle and restored him (Acts 20:10). Presumably at a later time, perhaps on a fourth missionary journey after his Roman imprisonment, he left his cloak, books, and parchments there and called for them to be brought to him (2 Timothy 4:13).

Research at Troas is now beginning. Cokun Özgünel began a first season of exploration (not excavation) at the site in 1992. During his third season in 1995 E. Schwertheim joined him. We await more definitive studies.

Paul's Third Missionary Journey

Luke does not tell us how long Paul remained at Antioch in Syria at the end of his second missionary journey. At length Paul decided to make a third visit to the cities of the Galatic region and Phrygia (Acts 18:23). No doubt he took the same route he followed at the beginning of the second journey—through the Syrian Gates, Tarsus, and the Cilician Gates. The "Galatic region" is a general term that could cover the portion of Galatia where Derbe, Lystra, Iconium, and Pisidian Antioch were located. The region also included Galatian Phrygia, adjacent to which was Asian Phrygia. So it would be a simple matter for him to move from one area of Phrygia to the other and to pass "through the upper regions" (better, "the higher districts") to Ephesus (Acts 19:1).

William Ramsay observes that during the first century the terms "High Phrygia" and "Low Phrygia" (referring to the elevation of land) had specific distinction, the former designating the mountain country just west of Pisidian Antioch and equitable here with "the higher districts." The main trade route to Ephesus traversed Low Phrygia and the Lycus and Maeander valleys. The shorter hill road, practicable for foot passengers but not for wheeled vehicles, ran more or less due west from Pisidian Antioch and came into Ephesus north of the Messogis Range.[59]

Ephesus. Paul's real destination on the third missionary journey was Ephesus, and he apparently wished to arrive there with all reasonable speed. This was not his first contact with the city. On his return trip to Jerusalem at the end of the second missionary journey, he had stopped at Ephesus briefly and had even ministered in the synagogue there (Acts 18:19). Perhaps on that occasion he had recognized the strategic value of evangelistic endeavors in this important city and had made plans to return at an early date. Ephesus was at that time one of the greatest cities of the Roman world.

Broughton estimates the population conservatively at more then 200,000,[60] while Paul MacKendrick reports that the excavators calculate its peak population to have been 500,000.[61] The importance of the city was at least threefold when Paul arrived: political, economic, and religious. Politically, it had become the *de facto* capital of the province, and the Roman governor resided there. Its economic prowess lay in the fact that Ephesus stood astride the great route to the interior up the Maeander and Lycus valleys and the great north-south road through Smyrna, Pergamum, Adramyttium, and Cyzicus on the Propontis Sea. And it had access to the Aegean by way of the Cayster River. At its port docked cedar of Lebanon, copper of Cyprus, silver of Spain, tin of Britain, marble from the Greek islands, cloth and spices from Syria and Palestine, and more.

Religiously, Ephesus was a leading center for the worship of Diana or Artemis.

A CIRCUIT OF GAMES AND FESTIVALS

A circuit of games or festivals annually entertained worshipers at Ephesus, Smyrna, Pergamum, and a few other places. These were associated with the celebration of both Artemis (Diana) and emperor cults. A time of carnival included athletic games at the stadium, plays at the theater, and concerts at the Odeum (Odeion). Of course enterprising individuals have always taken advantage of an opportunity to make a buck or a drachma or a sesterce from the milling crowds. Demetrius of Ephesus was one of the silversmiths who crafted small silver models of the temple of Diana or statues of the goddess as souvenirs for sale to the crowds who came to the festivals (Acts 19:24–29). The inroads of the gospel endangered their business.

The importance of Ephesus as a crossroads of civilization held the apostle there for two years and three months according to Acts 19:8 and 10, and three years according to Acts 20:31. This discrepancy is easily explained by reference to the Roman method of computing time. Any part of a year was reckoned as a year. Thus, considering two years and three months to be the correct figure, Paul could have spent four months there the first year, twelve the second, and eleven the third; and according to the prevailing method of computation, he would have been there three years.

Ephesus also attracted the ministry of other New Testament figures: Tychicus (Ephesians 6:21), Timothy (1 Timothy 1:3), John Mark (1 Peter 5:13), and John the apostle (Revelation 1:11; 2:1).

Ephesus was already an ancient city when the apostle arrived. Though a Mycenean building level has been found in the area of the temple of Diana, the real

After the apostle John was exiled to the Isle of Patmos, he evidently returned to Ephesus, where he died a natural death. His traditional burial spot is under the altar of the Church of St. John, shown here.

beginnings of Ephesus should be dated to the eleventh century B.C., when Athenians arrived and founded the most important metropolis in Ionian Asia Minor. The city of this period occupied an area along the lower slopes of Mount Coressus at the southwest of the later city complex. The temple of Diana lay about a mile to the north. During this period Ephesus maintained itself against the Cimmerians and Lydians.

About 560 B.C., however, Croesus of Lydia finally managed to conquer Ephesus and forced the inhabitants to take up their abode on the plain near the temple of Diana, with whom the old mother goddess of the Asians had been identified. Soon thereafter Cyrus the Great took over. Ephesus was involved in the abortive Ionian revolt against Darius I in 499 B.C. but was ultimately freed from Persia and joined the Delian League in 479 B.C. Ephesus revolted against Athenian control in 415 B.C. and presently sided with Sparta. For about a century the history of the city is quite complicated and need not detain us here.

After brief control by Alexander the Great, Ephesus passed under the suzerainty of Lysimachus, one of his generals, who about 286 B.C. refounded the city once more in the valley between Mounts Pion and Coressus. Shaped like a bent bow, with Mount Pion at its eastern end and the Hill of Astyages at the western end, the lower town and its port were surrounded by a wall some five miles long. The town was called Arsinoe after its builder's wife.

Ephesus was involved in the power struggle between Macedonia, Seleucia, and Egypt. In 196 B.C. Antiochus of Syria landed at Ephesus and controlled the city briefly, but his defeat at Magnesia in 190 freed the city from Syria. Then the Roman conquerors gave it to Pergamum. When Attalus III of Pergamum willed his kingdom to Rome in 133, Ephesus became part of the province of Asia.

During the Republic rapacious tax collectors and money lenders descended like vultures on the rich province of Asia and especially on Ephesus, which had become the leading port. Therefore, when

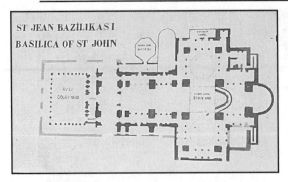

Floor plan of the Church of St. John.

Mithridates invaded Ionia in 88 B.C., Ephesus and other towns gladly received him, participated in the massacre of Romans living there, and threw down the statues and monuments they had erected. Later the Ephesians changed sides and murdered Mithridates' general. Rome punished the province with heavy fines. After the murder of Julius Caesar, Brutus and Cassius exacted tremendous tribute from Ephesus to aid their cause. Mark Antony did likewise. Thus the Ephesian economy was ruined.

Under the Empire, Ephesus enjoyed a long period of peace and prosperity. Augustus saw to it that the extreme exactions of Republican days ceased, and he began a number of structures in the city. Tiberius continued his predecessor's policy, and when the destructive earthquake of A.D. 17 occurred, he helped to restore Ephesus. About the same time Strabo wrote that the prosperity of the city was increasing daily. Early in the second century A.D.,

Hadrian did considerable building there, as did Antoninus Pius (138–161).

However, by the middle of the third century, signs of decay had appeared. In A.D. 263 Goths raided the city and caused great destruction at the temple of Diana. By the fourth century the port was silting up fast. Since Christianity was now the official religion, the great temples were dismantled, and their marble used for other buildings. During the first half of the sixth century, when the great Justinian was emperor, the town of Ephesus was moved once more, this time to the area around the Church of St. John to the north of the famous temple of Artemis. The site was heavily fortified and the population of the area gradually moved behind the city walls. By the tenth century the prosperous city of Roman times was completely deserted and invaded by marshes. The Ottoman Turks took Justinian's city late in the Middle Ages.

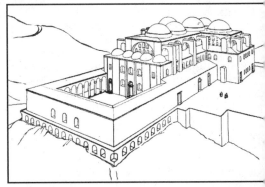

The Church of St. John reconstructed. It was originall built by the Emperor Justinian (527-565).

Understanding the geography and archaeology of Ephesus aids us in picturing the city as Paul and John would have known it. Ephesus stood at the entrance to one of the four clefts in the hills of west central Asia Minor. It was along these valleys that the roads across the central plateau of Asia Minor passed. (Other great cities standing at the entrance of clefts into the interior were Pergamum, Smyrna, and Miletus.) Chief of these four routes ran up the Maeander and Lycus valleys to Apamea and eastward. Miletus and Ephesus both contested for mastery of the trade flowing over this route. Ephesus won out because

The baptistry in the Church of St. John, a typical baptistry in one of the Eastern churches.

A model of the Church of St. John, as it stands in Ephesus today. *Judy Barringer*

the track across the hills from the main road to Ephesus was shorter than the road to Miletus. As already noted, Ephesus was also on the great north-south road of western Asia Minor and was on the main sea route from Rome to the east.

In his researches J. T. Wood demonstrated that Ephesus was approximately four miles from the sea and that the shoreline was therefore about the same in apostolic times as it is today.[62] Its inland harbor was connected with the Cayster River, which wound through the plain to the north of the city. The harbor was kept large enough and deep enough only by constant dredging; and when the empire declined and efforts to maintain the harbor slackened, it silted up entirely.

As to the configuration of the land, the hill of Astyages stood directly west of the

The house of Mary at Ephesus. Tradition has it that the apostle John took Mary to Ephesus after the fall of Jerusalem and that she lived in this house. She must have been at least 85 at the time.

harbor and Mount Coressus to the south of it. Mount Pion towered over the harbor at its eastern end, and to the northeast, across the fertile plain, stood the little hill of Ayassoluk, which has always been a religious center. Below its southwest slope was the magnificent temple to Diana, or Artemis. In later centuries on the hill itself stood the great Church of St. John (supposedly built over the apostle's tomb) which has been partially restored.

The archaeological history of Ephesus began on May 2, 1863, when the British architect, John Turtle Wood, started his search for the Temple of Diana. He dug seventy-five trial pits the first year, without success. Year after year Wood continued his excavations at the site. Finally, while clearing the theater, he came upon an inscription which indicated that when the images of the goddess were carried from the temple to the theater, the procession was to enter the city by the Magnesian Gate. Wood found the magnificent triple-arched gateway and the thirty-five-foot wide road paved with marble that led from it. Following this sacred road for more than a mile northeast of the city, he came to the boundary wall of the sacred precincts on May 2, six years to the day after beginning his quest. But he did not actually discover the ruins of the temple itself until December 31, 1869. These he found at a depth of over twenty feet. He worked five more years at the temple site.

The work at the temple proceeded under the leadership of D. G. Hogarth (1904–5), who found a magnificent foundation deposit of hundreds of objects—jewelry,

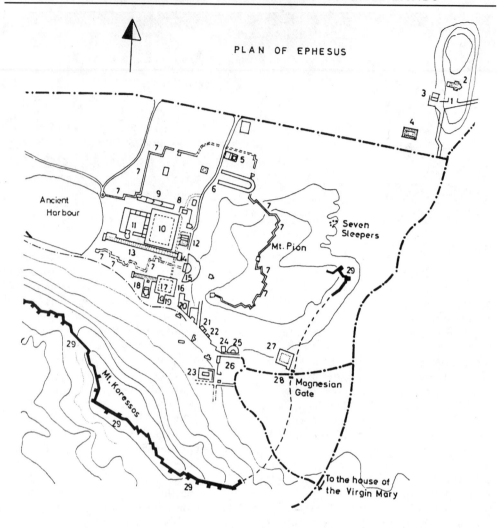

PLAN OF EPHESUS

Plan of Ephesus with identification of numbers

1.	Gate to Church of St. John	15.	Theater
2.	St. John's Church	16.	Marble street
3.	Isa Bey Mosque, A.D 1375	17.	Hellenistic agora, shops of silversmiths
4.	Temple of Diana or Artemis	18.	Temple of Serapis
5.	Vedius Gymasium	19.	Library of Celsus
6.	Stadium	20.	Baths of Scholastikia
7.	City wall of Byzantine period	21.	Fountain of Trajan
8.	Byzantine baths, sixth century	22.	Memmius monument
9.	Church of the Virgin Mary, a building used for commercial purposes in John's day	23.	Temple of Domitian
		24.	Town Hall
10.	Harbor gymnasium and baths	25.	Odeion or music hall
11.	Baths	26.	Roman agora
12.	Theater gymnasium	27.	East Gymnasium
13.	Arkadiane or harbor street	28.	Magnesian Gate
14.	Hellenistic fountain	29.	City wall, built by Lysimachus, founder of the Hellenistic city

figurines of the goddess, and the like. In the meantime the Austrian Archaeological Institute began work there in November 1897 and excavated continuously for sixteen years. The Austrians, in part subsidized by Rockefeller money, worked there again (1926–35) under the direction of Josef Keil. Keil resumed excavation at Ephesus in 1954 and continued until his death in 1959. Then F. Miltner took over the directorship, which Stefan Karwiese has more recently assumed. The Austrians celebrated their centenary at Ephesus in 1995 (their forty-second continuous season). The excavation team that year numbered almost a hundred. The Austrians have shouldered the task of uncovering the city proper, and they have done a magnificent job on the Roman period. Ephesus now very definitely has that edited look which archaeology brings to ruins.

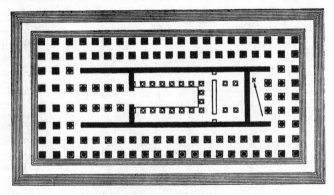

Plan of the Temple of Diana, Ephesus, one of the seven wonders of the ancient world. From I. H. Grinnell, Greek Temples, Metropolitan.

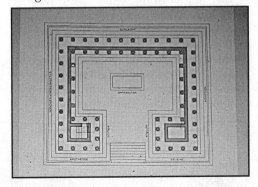

The floor plan of the altar that stood in front of the temple of Diana, below; jewelry found in the foundation deposit of the altar. *Courtesy of Ephesus Museum, Vienna*

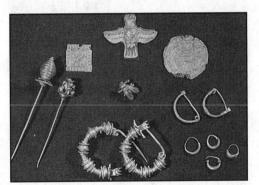

A great many of the structures that the archaeologists have uncovered at Ephesus date to the prosperous days of the second century A.D. or to some other period with no biblical relevance and therefore generally are not mentioned here. Several, however, hold special interest for the New Testament student.

Since the devotees of Artemis (Diana) came into such violent conflict with Christianity at Ephesus and since the goddess' temple there was one of the wonders of the ancient world, it seems logical to begin our study of the archaeological remains of Ephesus with this structure. Hogarth in his work at the site was able to distinguish five phases of temple construction. The earliest of these, dated by coins from the foundation deposit, was not erected earlier than 600 B.C.[63] Construction of the latest, now known as the Hellenistic temple, was begun probably before 350 B.C. and continued until 334 B.C. when Alexander the Great arrived. The conqueror offered to pay the costs of completion if his name were inscribed upon it, but he was refused. This was the temple Paul and John saw, which was destroyed by the Goths in A.D. 262.

The temple platform was 239 feet wide by 418 feet long. A flight of ten steps led up to the pavement of the platform and three more to the pavement of the peristyle (colonnade around the temple). The temple itself was 180 feet wide and 377 feet long, and the roof was supported by 117 sixty-foot columns. These columns measured six

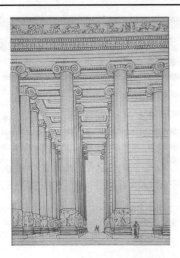

A partial reconstruction of the temple of Diana.

her position as "temple guardian" of Diana (or "worshiper" Acts 19:35), a boast that has been found on inscriptions excavated there. The temple treasury acted as a bank in which cities, kings, and private persons made deposits.

THE THEATERS OF ASIA MINOR

The mob scene in the great theater of Ephesus (Acts 19:29–41) throws the spotlight on one of the great recreational structures of Asia Minor. Originating in Greece, the theater was common wherever Greeks settled in the Mediterranean world. Almost every self-respecting city of Asia Minor had at least one. There were great theaters in cities like Ephesus, Pergamum, Miletus, Sardis, and Hierapolis. But Laodicea, Assos, Myra, Patara, and Perga were among the many other cities with New Testament connections where Greco-Roman theaters stood. They could have lasted to the present virtually intact, but the good stone with which they were seated proved to be tempting stone quarries for local inhabitants down through the centuries.

feet in diameter, and thirty-six of them were sculptured at the base with life-size figures. Praxiteles and Scopas are believed to have done some of the sculpture of the temple. White, blue, red, and yellow marble, as well as gold, were used to decorate the structure. The cella or holy of holies was seventy feet wide and apparently open to the sky. In it stood the statue of Artemis, which many believe was carved from a large meteorite. This they deduce in part from the reference that the "image which fell down from Zeus" (Acts 19:35).

Artemis is the Greek name for the Roman goddess Diana, who had been equated with the Asia Minor Cybele, the mother goddess. As worshiped in Ephesus, the goddess was a considerably Orientalized deity, adored as the mother of life and the nourisher of all creatures of the earth, air, and sea. Her statue was a many-breasted figure, rather than the gracefully draped Greek or Roman goddess. One suggestion is that the many breasts are ostrich eggs, also a symbol of fertility. Hundreds, if not thousands, of priests were connected with her ritual in Ephesus. Many of these had cells within the temple area. Numerous priestesses were also dedicated to prostitution in the temple service. The Artemision (March–April) was the sacred month especially devoted to the worship of the goddess. The religious festivals held during this month included athletic, dramatic, and musical contests. Ephesus was proud of

One of the column bases of the temple of Diana, sculpted with life-sized figures. *British Museum*

Two concepts of Diana. On the left is the Greco-Roman Diana the Huntress (Louvre Museum).
On the right is the Oriental goddess of fertility, Diana of the Ephesians, excavated at Ephesus.
Ephesus Museum

Theaters were originally designed primarily for acting out tragedies and comedies, but they proved useful for all sorts of public gatherings. Note, for example, the great mob meeting that Demetrius the silversmith was able to instigate in Ephesus.

As to structure, the theater consisted of the orchestra, the flat semi-circular place where the choral and dramatic events were originally performed; the auditorium or cavea, where the audience sat or stood; and the skene or stage building, which could serve as a background for plays, a stage on which they were acted, or a storage facility.

The auditorium or cavea normally was a hillside slope on which spectators could sit or stand (theaters were rarely free-standing structures). In time, wooden seats and later stone seats were installed. In some cases awnings could be drawn on ropes over the auditorium as necessary. Normally, but not always, a small altar stood in the orchestra, where sacrifices to the god Dionysus could be offered.

A structure mentioned specifically in connection with Paul's ministry in Ephesus is the great theater (Acts 19:29). It was situated on the western slopes of Mount Pion

The great theater of Ephesus that held the howling mob of about 25,000 (Acts 19).

square ones. Though construction antedated Paul's time, the theater was remodeled during the reign of Claudius (A.D. 41–54) and again in the days of Trajan (98–117).

With the recent restoration of the seating in the theater, the structure has served as an auditorium for concerts and other entertainments. Unfortunately however, damage to the structure from recent use has forced cancellation of further concerts there. As was true of other Greek theaters, the acoustics of this one are remarkable. Audiences could hear someone standing on the stage and speaking in a normal tone of voice. Imagine the din of twenty-five thousand citizens yelling "Great is Diana of the Ephesians" for two solid hours (Acts 19:34–35)!

and looked west toward the harbor. Measuring some 495 feet in diameter, the theater held almost 25,000 persons. The cavea of the theater was divided into three bands of twenty-two rows of seats each, and twelve stairways divided the cavea into huge wedge-shaped sections. The orchestra measured eighty by thirty-seven feet. Behind the orchestra stood a stage eighty feet long and twenty feet deep, supported by twenty-six round pillars and ten

If we walk through the Magnesian Gate into Ephesus in a westerly direction, on our right are the east baths (second century A.D.). A short distance farther on the right stands an odeion, or covered concert hall (A.D. 150), which often served as the meeting place of the town council, along with its

A view of central Ephesus. In the foreground is the great Hellenistic agora. In the center the great theater nestles in the hillside, and Harbor Street leads from the theater to the harbor.
Courtesy Keskin Color, Ephesus

Curetes Street, that led from the city gate of Ephesus to the Hellenistic Agora.

Here at the beginning of Curetes Street is a gateway formed by two pillars adorned with reliefs of Hermes or Mercury. Descending the street, we soon see on the right a fountain of Trajan followed by the temple of Hadrian (both from the early second century A.D.). Behind the temple of Hadrian stand the baths of Scholastikia (built c. A.D. 100 or earlier). Across the street from the temple of Hadrian on a hillside rises a complex of houses on three successive terraces. Luxurious houses, they are built around peristyles open to the sky, and have mosaic floors, painted walls, and running water. In use during the first century A.D., these houses were remodeled and occupied until the seventh century.

Beyond other minor structures, is the junction of Curetes and Marble Streets. On the right is a large forty-eight-room brothel dating to the early second century A.D. Across from it stood the library of Celsus (now restored), built at the same time.

To the right of the library plaza stands a monumental gate, now restored. The lintel above the gate has an inscription in Latin that dates its construction to 4/3 B.C. Thus it stood there when Paul came to town. The gate gives access to the Hellenistic agora, or marketplace, of the New Testament city. It measured 360 feet square and was surrounded by shops, some of which were shops of the silversmiths.

Along the east wall of the agora runs Marble Street, which shortly gives access to

provision for entertainments (capacity about 1,400). Next to it is the town hall, built about the time of Christ's birth. Facing these two civic structures, on the left is a long basilica (built about the beginning of the first century A.D.) which served as a court building. This was the northernmost structure of the Roman state agora, which is not yet fully excavated and which sprawls out to our left.

When we come to the end of the basilica, we enter the open roadway of Curetes Street (which runs northwest). This is lined on both sides with inscribed statue bases and excavated structures. Immediately on the left is a plaza with an altar to the goddess Roma at its entrance. At the other end of it stands a temple of Domitian, built during his reign when the apostle John was living there. On the right of Curetes Street is the Memmius monument (erected at the end of the first century B.C.) in honor of a grandson of the dictator Sulla (82–79 B.C.).

The altar to the emperor cult, that stood before the temple to Domitian.

Finally Curetes street led to the gate of the Hellenistic agora, that stood there when Paul was in Ephesus. He would have passed through its arches many times.

the theater. From the theater the Arcadian Way, 1,735 feet long, led to the harbor. This marble-paved street 36 feet in width was lined on both sides by a colonnade behind which were shops. At both ends of the street stood monumental gateways. While this street, in the form the excavators found it, dates long after the days of Paul and John, there was a fairly sumptuous street on the site in their time. A late first-century gymnasium and bath stands between the theater and the harbor.

If we return to the theater and walk on an extension of Marble Street, we soon pass on our left the Church of St. Mary. This great structure (about 900 feet long and 100 feet wide) was built for secular purposes during the second century A.D. and later converted into a church. Here the early Church Council of Ephesus was held in A.D. 431. Soon, on our right, we come upon the city stadium, where excavators have been working in recent years. Nero built this stadium, probably while Paul was there, on the site where a small stadium had stood in the third century B.C.

As was his custom in the towns where he went to preach, Paul went first to the synagogue at Ephesus, where he presented the Christian message (Acts 19:8). When he got nowhere with the Jews, he turned to the Gentiles. According to Josephus, the Syrian ruler

Antiochus II (261–247 B.C.) granted citizenship to the Jews of Ionia (including Ephesus). When the Ionians tried to deprive them of citizenship rights in the first century B.C., Rome protected them, as did the Ephesian officials.[64] It is thought that the Jewish quarter at Ephesus was at the northern outskirts of the city, but this has not been proved. Their synagogue has not been found.[65]

As Christianity spread in the city, its converts determined to make public demonstration of the fact that they had forsaken their old ways. To do so they consigned books (scrolls) of magical formulas and incantation to a huge bonfire. The heap of

Arcadian Way or Harbor Street, that led from the theater to the Ephesus harbor. After Niemann's reconstruction.

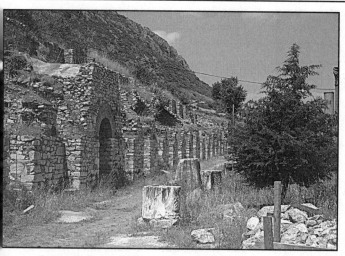
Shops of silversmiths in the Hellenistic agora.

Demetrius is said to have been the leader of a guild of silversmiths that made shrines for Diana. No doubt what is meant is miniature replicas of the temple of Diana for the pilgrims who came to Ephesus. Numerous replicas in terra cotta and marble have been found but none of silver. This has led some to doubt the accuracy of the New Testament narrative. But as Ramsay has pointed out, these shrines were probably presented as votive offerings at the temple, rather than carried away from the city. Therefore one should not expect to find them at widely scattered places. Moreover, the number of votive offerings in various materials must have grown so great at the temple that the priests had to clean house from time to time. Silver shrines they would have melted down; less expensive ones they would have destroyed. Not only would priests have destroyed them, less reverent hands would readily have made off with them for their intrinsic value.[68] An argument from silence in this instance is not proof of error. Most of the great villas of Ephesus remain unexcavated.

The "Chiefs of Asia" (Greek, "Asiarchs," Acts 19:31) are well known from the inscriptions. These men (whose existence used to be doubted) were chosen from the chief families of Asia and were provincial rather than municipal officers. They led the rites of the emperor cult observed by the league of cities in the province and were expected to give handsomely from their own estates to put on games and celebrations in connection with the emperor worship. Since these "high priests of Asia" held office for only one year, there would have been several in Ephesus at the time of the riot who deserved the honorific title, just as our ex-governors are called "governor" out of courtesy.

books was valued at fifty thousand pieces of silver (Acts 19:19). This biblical allusion is quite in keeping with what is known of life at Ephesus, where such literature was so common that it came to be known in the Roman world as Ephesian Writings. Even some of the Jews became involved in exorcism at Ephesus. A formula similar to the one mentioned in Acts—"We adjure you by Jesus" (Acts 19:13)—has been found in Egyptian papyri: "I adjure you . . . by this god."[66]

The expenditure of fifty thousand pieces of silver for magical books indicates that Ephesus was a place of great wealth. Literary sources attest to the fact. Her commercial and political position further support it. Likewise, Ephesian possession of surrounding towns and farmlands would have greatly bolstered her economy, as would the stature of her Artemis cult in the Roman world.

Luke alluded to the craft of Demetrius the silversmith who made silver shrines for Diana and stirred up his compatriots when their business was in danger (Acts 19:23–27). An inscription has been found at Ephesus that mentions a Demetrius and indicates that he was a very influential citizen of the community. Hicks dates the inscription A.D. 50–60 and thinks it may have reference to Paul's great opponent. Ramsay prefers to date the inscription slightly later.[67]

Presiding at the assembly in the theater was the town clerk (Acts 19:35), who we know from the inscriptions was the dominant figure in the political life of the city. He chaired meetings of the assembly, helped

The mention of Asiarchs (Acts 19:31) as officials of Asia used to be thought to be erroneous. Now numerous inscriptions have been found referring to them. Here is an inscription from Izmir. "Asiarch" appears in line four.

After the riot caused by the silversmiths at Ephesus had subsided, Paul decided to leave the city. No doubt it was in the fall of that year.[69] Traveling across Macedonia, he settled down in Achaia (probably Corinth) for three months (Acts 20:3) and then determined to return to Syria. When a plot against his life was discovered, Paul thought it wiser to take a less direct route eastward. Journeying through Macedonia once more, he sailed from Phillipi to Troas.

Troas again. There the apostolic company spent a week. There too occurred the somewhat amusing incident of a young man falling asleep as the long-winded apostle spoke. Falling out of a third floor window, the young fellow was taken up for dead but Paul restored him—seemingly by a miracle of healing (Acts 20:6–12). Windows as the chief source of light and ventilation commonly were large and open. When covered by shutters or cloths or skins the light could not come in. If this window had been shuttered, perhaps the shutters were open for ventilation. In any case Eutychus fell out. After being up all night and subjected to the strain and confusion of the evening hours, Paul set out on foot in the morning for Assos, about thirty miles away. What stamina he must have had! He could have sailed south with the rest of his party but for some reason decided not to do so.

Assos. Assos stood on a volcanic hill some seven hundred feet in altitude. Since it was located on the Gulf of Adramyttium and faced south toward Lesbos (about six miles distant), it is not at all surprising that Aeolians of Lesbos (Mytilene) founded it about 700 B.C. This virtually impregnable site rose in steep cliffs sheer from the sea. Its sides were covered with both natural and artificial terraces.

Assos was successively a part of the Lydian Kingdom, the Persian Empire, Alexander's empire, the kingdom of Pergamum, and the Roman Empire. Aristotle taught there for three years (348–345 B.C.), and Cleanthes the Stoic philosopher was born there.

An American Archaeological Institute team under the leadership of J. T. Clarke

draft decrees to be submitted to it, sealed such decrees with the public seal, and had charge of money bequeathed to the people. The office was held in rotation by the city's leading citizens. The clerk's social prestige plus his political power insured ready attention on the part of the crowd, especially since he had let them yell themselves hoarse for two hours and came to the rostrum at a point when they were ready to listen to responsible leadership. The crowd was especially ready to listen when he reminded them that this irresponsible action put the city in jeopardy of losing its privileges of local autonomy. Rome took freedom from towns whose native officials could not maintain order.

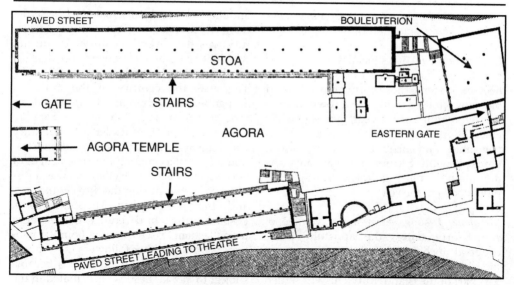

Plan of the agora area at Assos.

and F. H. Bacon explored and excavated at Assos from 1881 to 1883. The Turkish archaeologist Ümit Serdaroglu has now been working at the site for over fifteen years, restoring the fortifications and the theater, and excavating in the necropolis outside the main gate and in the residential district on the terrace overlooking the gymnasium.

Around the base of the hill stood a Hellenistic wall dating back to the fourth century B.C. About two miles in length, it still stands to a height of thirty feet. Remains of the eastern tower at the main entrance gate stand forty-five feet tall. These carefully-worked stone fortifications are the most complete in the Greek world.

The agora stands on the south slope of the acropolis. It consists of a north stoa (third–second century B.C.), a south stoa with a "covered bazaar" (dating to about the same time), a Hellenistic town council building (a Bouleuterion), a temple (second century B.C.), and other shops.

On the slope west of the agora lie remains of a second century B.C. gymnasium, with a paved courtyard measuring about 100 by 125 feet. South of the agora lower on the slope stands the theater, built in the third century B.C. and remodeled in the Roman period. Now badly ruined, it was completely preserved a century ago. On the crest of the acropolis lie remains of a temple to Athena, dating back to the sixth century B.C. It is worth noting that the classical structures of Asia Minor used such beautifully worked stone that they provide tempting stone quarries for the surrounding population. Current efforts of the Turkish government to protect the antiquities of the country are somewhat successful, but there are so many wonderful ruins all over the country that a watchful eye cannot protect everything.

The harbor from which Paul sailed to Mitylene (Mytilene) has since silted up and is covered with

Part of the Hellenistic fortifications of Assos.

gardens. Modern inhabitants have constructed an artificial harbor at its side.

Island journey. Paul's journey through the coastal islands off Asia Minor must have been most scenic those spring days. Instead of being clothed with the brown mantle they wore much of the year, they shone like emeralds, green with growing wheat, fruits, vegetables, and shrubs and trees of various kinds. Benefiting from seasonal rains, the mountain torrents coursed through the pine woods to the sea.

Mitylene, Lesbos. After a sea voyage of some forty miles, the apostolic party dropped anchor at Mitylene, chief city of the island of Lesbos. Located on the southeast part of the island, Mitylene was settled by Aeolians who claimed to have migrated from Boeotia before 1000 B.C. and whose nobles traced their descent from Agamemnon, who reportedly captured the place during the Trojan War. These early Greeks settled down on a small offshore island. With growth in population, the town spread to include a portion of Lesbos proper. Bridges connected the two parts of the city. Harbors were constructed on the north and south of the city, and it was possible to pass from one to the other via the channel between the smaller island and Lesbos. Although the two islands are now linked by the silting up of the channel between them, they were still separate in Paul's day, as is clear from references in Strabo (contemporary with Christ) and Pausanias (second century A.D.).

Located some six or seven miles from the Asia Minor coast, Lesbos is about forty-three miles long and twenty-eight miles wide. Roughly triangular, it is indented by two bays in the south and has an area of 623 square miles. Its surface is rugged, the highest mountain being Olympus, about 3,100 feet high. Despite the nature of the terrain, the country is fertile in olives, grapes, and grain. Its position near the old trade route between the Hellespont and points south and east made Lesbos and her capital an important center at all times.

As Lesbos expanded her commercial activity, she established colonies in Thrace and the Troad and participated in the settlement of Naucratis in Egypt. Her great century was the seventh century B.C., during which her commercial power was extensive and her cultural development considerable. This was the century of the musician Terpander, the dithyrambist Arion, and the lyric poet Alcaeus and the poetess Sappho. The greatest political leader of the century was Pittacus, who for his wise administration won a place among the Seven Sages of Greece. The historian Hellanicus was a resident of Lesbos during the fifth century B.C. and the philosopher Theophrastus a Lesbian of the third century. Our modern term "lesbian" rises from the homosexuality of Sappho and her followers in Lesbos.

After the fall of Lydia, Lesbos became subject to Persia. Lesbos participated in the ill-fated Ionian revolt of 499–493 B.C. Later freed from Persia she became a member of the Delian League (Athenian Empire). In spite of the fact that she enjoyed a privileged status in the league, Mitylene, her chief city, led a revolt against Athens in 428 B.C. Defeated, Mitylene lost her fleet, fortifications, and much of her land and was brought to the verge of destruction. Released from the Athenian Empire at the end of the Peloponnesian War (404), she oscillated between Athenian, Spartan, and Persian rule until Alexander the Great took over. Mitylene supported Athens in her struggle with Macedonia.

Lesbos and her capital fell under the sway of Alexander the Great and successively under Antigonus, Lysimachus, and the rule of the Ptolemies. When Rome took over, the island became a favorite resort area for Roman aristocrats. Tacitus described it as a "noble and pleasant island." Though Mithridates occupied it from 88 to 79 B.C., Pompey restored Mitylene to Rome and granted it the status of a free city within the province of Asia. Mitylene enjoyed this privilege when Paul arrived, though it was later suspended by Vespasian and then restored by Hadrian.

Reportedly Pompey was so impressed with the beauty of the Greek theater of Lesbos that he copied the plan when he built the first great stone theater in Rome. Excavation of the theater began in 1958. Its orchestra, almost perfectly circular, measures about 82 feet.

Chios (modern Khios). The next stop on the apostolic itinerary, was near the island of Chios. Luke says, "We came the following day over against Chios" (Acts 20:15). Some interpret this statement to mean that the ship was becalmed there. Others feel that because of a dark moon, the ship lay at anchor on the Asian coast opposite the island until daybreak would facilitate further sailing.

As Paul approached from the northeast, the bold yellow mountains of Chios formed a striking outline against the blue sky. Straight ahead the channel between the island and the mainland narrowed to 4.5 miles, and this was blocked by a group of small islands.

Chios itself, shaped like a bow aimed at the Asia Minor coast, stretched thirty miles along the starboard side of the ship. Its width varies from eight to fifteen miles. Some 110 miles in circumference, Chios has a surface of about 325 square miles. While the north end of the island is mountainous (its highest altitude is 4,255 feet) with steep coasts, there are four plains (mostly in the south) with very fertile soil. In spite of the fact that there is no real watercourse on the island, luxuriant vegetation is made possible by numerous springs. The place was renowned in antiquity for its wine, figs, wheat, and gum mastic. The last was obtained from the lentiscus tree by making incisions in the branches, from which a sort of resin would flow and form a gum. This still constitutes an important element of the economy of the island.

The chief city, located in the southeastern part of the island and bearing the same name as the island, was founded on the finest harbor of the eastern seaboard of the Aegean. Eighty ships could anchor in her roadstead.

Colonized by Ionians from Euboea in the ninth century B.C., Chios early became highly prosperous. Schools of artists working in metal and stone flourished there, and the island had a distinguished literary tradition. It was perhaps the leading contender for the honor of being the birthplace of Homer.

Incorporated into the Persian Empire under Cyrus, Chios fought heroically against her overlord during the Ionian revolt of about 500 B.C. Crushing the revolt, the Persians burned the cities and temples of the island and carried off her most beautiful girls. During the fifth century B.C. Chios joined the Delian League (Athenian Alliance) and remained loyal until 413. For her insurrection she suffered terribly at the hands of the Athenians who ultimately recaptured the entire island. During the fourth century Chios joined the Second Athenian Alliance and revolted successfully only a few years before conquest by Alexander the Great. Independent during the early Hellenistic era, she allied with Rome during the second century and was virtually depopulated by the sack of 86 B.C., carried out by Mithridates in his temporarily successful contest with Rome.

The Roman general Sulla restored the Chians to their homes and bestowed on them the rights of a free city, which implied that there was local autonomy and in certain respects the privilege of being governed according to native law, while many of their neighboring cities in the province of Asia were governed according to Roman law. Chian efforts to regain prosperity were interrupted by a violent earthquake during the reign of Tiberius. The Roman emperor helped in the rehabilitation, and the island attained a reasonable degree of prosperity by the time Paul sailed by.

Samos. Sailing in a southeasterly direction from Chios, the apostolic company on the next day headed for the northern shore of the island of Samos. The coast was rocky, precipitous, and thickly wooded. The ship veered east and sailed through the channel between Samos and the mainland, here only about a mile wide. Rising above them on the left was Mount Mycale. They dropped anchor in the harbor of the town of Samos at the southeastern edge of the island.

Apparently the ship stopped every evening. The reason seems to lay in the action of the wind, which at that time of the year generally blows from the north, beginning at an early hour in the morning and dying away in the afternoon. At sunset there is a dead calm; a gentle southerly wind blows during the night.

Samos is twenty-seven miles long and fourteen miles at its greatest width. A little over a hundred miles in circumference, the island has an area of about 184 square miles. A continuation of the Mycale Ridge cuts across Samos and gives it a rugged, picturesque appearance. The highest elevation occurs in the west, where Mount Kerkis stands at an altitude of 4,725 feet. The several small plains on the southern part of the island are remarkably fertile and largely covered with vineyards.

Ionians colonized Samos during the century before 1000 B.C., and the settlers became distinguished mariners and merchants. Samos established colonies of her own in numerous places, including Thrace, Egypt, Libya, Cilicia, Sicily, and perhaps southern Italy. Her sailors were probably the first Greeks to reach the Strait of Gibraltar. Important Samian industries in classical times were metalwork and woolen production.

Samos became an important center of Ionian luxury, art, and science. The sixth century B.C. was her greatest. Samos was the home of notable architects, sculptors, gem engravers, moralists, and poets (including Aesop). The greatest of all Samians, Pythagoras, migrated to southern Italy. The tyrant Polycrates (c. 535–522) was her great political leader. A friend and contemporary of Pisistratus of Athens, Polycrates cut a subterranean aqueduct a mile long right through the mountain on which the citadel of the town stood, built the great temple of Hera, a large harbor mole, and fortification walls (4.5 miles long with 35 towers), and in other ways made the city significant. The Samian navy ruled the waves around her island from her new deep-sea harbor and blockaded mainland subjects of Persia.

After the death of Polycrates by treachery, the Persians conquered Samos and partly depopulated it. The Samians had largely recovered by 499 B.C. when they joined the general Ionian revolt. At a critical moment during the sea battle off Lade in 494, the Samians deserted the Greek side, probably because of jealousy of Miletus, dooming the Ionian cause. They redeemed themselves, however, at the Greek victory off Mycale in 479.

Samos held a privileged status in the first Athenian confederacy until 441, when revolt brought them degradation to tributary rank. Thereafter Samos was one of the most loyal dependencies of Athens, serving for a time as the home of the democracy (411 and winning the Athenian franchise during the last stages of the Peloponnesian War. Thereafter it was occupied by Sparta, then Persia, and later recovered by Athens (365). After the death of Alexander, Samos was for a time controlled in turn by Egypt and Syria. During the Hellenistic age it was eclipsed by Rhodian sea power and wealth.

Made a part of the Roman province of Asia in 129 B.C., Samos entertained Augustus during the winter after the Battle of Actium (31 B.C.), and in 17 B.C. he made it a free city, a position that it retained until the days of Vespasian. There were many Jewish residents on the island; Herod visited there and bestowed numerous benefits on the Samians. Samos seems to have enjoyed a fairly high degree of prosperity during the entire New Testament period.

If Paul had had a little longer to spend on Samos, he might have walked the three-mile sacred way westward from the city to the great temple of Hera (Juno), reputed spot of her birth and marriage to Zeus. Though the early temple had been destroyed around 517 B.C., it was rebuilt shortly thereafter. However, the edifice was never completely finished (i.e., some of the columns were not fluted, etc.). Cicero and Strabo recorded their visits to this religious center during the first century B.C. German excavations[70] at the site reveal that the temple measured 368 by 179 feet, that it was of the Ionic order, and that it had 132 columns in all—a triple row of eight at each end and a double row of twenty-four on each long side, together with ten in the front chamber of the temple. Herodotus called this "the greatest temple of all those we know." When this temple is compared with the Parthenon at Athens (228 by 101 feet) and the Temple of Zeus at Olympia (slightly smaller than the Parthenon), one may be inclined to think Herodotus was right. The agora lay near the port.

Considerable remains of the ancient wall of Samos may also still be seen. Some of these ruins stand to a height of eighteen feet and are ten to twelve feet thick. In the higher part of town, portions of the theater survive. Little remains of the ancient city itself, which Herodotus says was the greatest of cities, Hellenic or barbarian, while under Polycrates.

Trogyllium. After leaving Samos, Paul "tarried at Trogyllium" (Acts 20:15), according to the Authorized Version. The principal manuscripts (Aleph, A, B, C) omit these words but D included them. Possibly the latter rested on a tradition that survived in the church of Asia and gives a detail that is highly probable. The NRSV, the REB, and the NIV all omit the reference. The promontory of Trogyllium juts out from the mainland opposite Samos, and it is entirely possible that Paul's ship lay becalmed in the lee of the promontory. Close by was an island bearing the same name, and at the end of the promontory lies an anchorage still called St. Paul's Bay.

Miletus. At any rate, the apostle sailed on to Miletus (twenty-three miles from Trogyllium), which he reached the following day. On the way he passed the site of the battle of Mycale (479 B.C.) and moved through waters where the great battle of Lade had been fought in 494. In fact, the island of Lade protected the main harbor of Miletus.

Miletus lay on the southern shore of the Latonian Gulf, which penetrated Caria south of Mycale. Paul stopped there and sent a messenger to Ephesus to summon the elders to Miletus. No doubt the messenger sailed the twelve miles north across the gulf to Priene and traveled another twenty-five miles by land to Ephesus. This sending of a messenger, waiting for the Ephesian elders, and the subsequent conference must have taken several days (Acts 20:15–38). Meanwhile Paul had a chance to look around Miletus. When the apostle arrived at Miletus, it was an important city with a population of something like one hundred

thousand.[71] But its most illustrious days had occurred several centuries earlier.

Tradition has it that Ionians from Athens founded Miletus, perhaps as early as the tenth or eleventh century B.C. But excavations reveal that Myceneans had settled there by around 1500 B.C. In any case, Miletus was a Greek city during all her centuries of greatness. A great commercial center, she sent her ships to every part of the Mediterranean and even the Atlantic. She is said to have founded some ninety colonies in the eighth, seventh, and sixth centuries B.C. on the Black Sea and its approaches and in Egypt. In the context of economic prosperity developed a significant cultural advancement. Among her greatest sons were the philosophers Thales, Anaximander, and Anaximines; the chronicler and cartographer Hecataeus; and the town-planning architect Hippodamus. By the end of the fifth century B.C. the Athenians officially adopted the Milesian alphabet, which then became the standard writing system of the Greeks.

Maintaining a running contest with Lydia for some time, Miletus finally fell to her neighbor in the days of Croesus (who took all Ionia) but apparently maintained a privileged status. This position she seems to have held in 547/6 B.C. when Lydia fell to Cyrus' and when the Greek cities of the coast came under Cyrus' control. In 499 Miletus led the Ionain revolt against Persia. After the naval disaster at Lade, Miletus was destroyed, her inhabitants killed or sent into slavery, and the temple at Didyma burned.

During the fifth century B.C. Miletus rose from the ashes and became a member of the Delian League (Athenian Empire). Fifth century greats were Hippodamus, the city planner who laid out the new city of Miletus on the grid pattern and the Piraeus at Athens on the same plan, and the poet Timotheus. Revolting against Athens in 412 B.C. the city fell under the control of Persia and subsequently Alexander the Great. Hellenistic monarchs—the Seleucids, Antigonids, Ptolemies, and Pergamenes— successively held the city and erected impressive buildings there. Miletus became a part of the Roman province of Asia in 129 B.C. and thereafter tended to live on past

The harbor monument at Miletus.

glories. During Paul's day she was unimportant by comparison but still quite prosperous. The trade of the Maeander River

MILETUS

valley now flowed through Ephesus, and Ephesus shared with Smyrna the trade that moved along the great road from interior Asia Minor.

The Miletus Paul saw was not the city that once had been the intellectual center of Ionian Asia Minor; the Persians had destroyed that. Rather, he experienced the metropolis that Hippodamus had designed in the fifth century B.C. and had since enjoyed the benefactions of Hellenistic and Roman rulers.

Presumably Paul sailed to Miletus on a small freighter that docked at the Lion's Port, the commercial port of Miletus on the north side of town. Flanked by two huge stone lions, this port could be protected by closing off the mouth with chains. As the apostle disembarked on a marble-paved quayside, before him sprawled the horseshoe-shaped stoa that curved around the end of the harbor. Some five hundred feet long, it was faced with sixty-four Doric style columns. Next to it on the apostle's left was the harbor gate with its sixteen columns, giving access to the city center. As Paul went through the gate, to his left stood one of the largest temples of the city, the Delphinion, dedicated to Apollo. Built during Hellenistic times, this consisted of an enclosure surrounded by porticoes. In part this structure served as a public archive.

THE GYMNASIUMS OF ASIA MINOR

The Greco-Roman peoples of Asia Minor emphasized education. They maintained scores of gymnasiums in the larger cities and in the small urban centers as well. The gymnasiums consisted of rectangular open spaces, exercise grounds, surrounded by colonnaded porticos, off which opened instructional rooms. Here boys fifteen to seventeen learned physical training, music, some mathematics and science, but especially literature, speech, and social behavior. Thus what they got there became a sort of preparation for citizenship. Sometimes cities maintained gymnasiums, but frequently wealthy private citizens endowed them or otherwise provided financial backing.

Of course the youth could not enroll in what amounted to high school without preparation. Lower schools for children seven to fourteen were private and were maintained by tuition fees. There a child learned reading, writing, gymnastics, music, and sometimes painting. The degree of opportunity that girls enjoyed in attending lower school is unknown, but supervisors of girls' education existed in several places.

Education beyond the gymnasium was available for the *neoi*, aged eighteen to twenty. Coming only from the most wealthy families, they studied athletics, music, literature, philosophy, and civic affairs. For more serious study they could go on to one of the universities—Pergamum or Rhodes for philosophy and rhetoric, Cos or Pergamum or Ephesus for medicine, Tarsus for philosophy.

The road on which the apostle now walked was over a hundred yards long and about thirty yards wide, with about eighteen-foot-wide pedestrian walks on either side. On the left stood baths constructed during the reign of the emperor Claudius, next to which was a second century B.C. gymnasium with an exercise ground and five rooms for study.

On the right lay a market or agora surrounded by shops, next to which stood a small shrine of the emperor cult, and next to that the bouleuterion (hall of assembly of the city council). This structure, apparently built in the days of Antiochus IV Epiphanes (c. 170 B.C.) was rectangular on the outside and fitted inside with a semicircle of seats rising in tiers, with seating for fifteen hundred.

The street now opened into the great south agora of the city. Occupying an area roughly equal to sixteen city blocks (some

thirty-three thousand square yards), it was surrounded by a Doric colonnade, behind which shops were located.

The theater of Miletus.

If Paul had walked around to the right end of the harbor stoa, he would have found there a Jewish synagogue (about which we know little). And if he had left the south agora in a northwesterly direction, he would have passed, first, the stadium with seating for fifteen thousand and then the theater, also with seating for fifteen thousand. If he had continued to walk south from the south agora, through a residential district, he would have come to the south gate of Miletus. Outside the gate, along the road, lay the necropolis or cemetery.

And ten miles down the road stood Didyma, with its great temple of Apollo. The Persians had destroyed this ancient temple in 494 B.C., but it was subsequently

The Maeander River near Miletus.

The temple of Apollo at Didyma.

rebuilt. The new builders planned too big, however, and the structure never was completely finished. Measuring 163 by 341 feet on the ground plan (and thus third in size in the Greek world behind Ephesus and Samos), the temple had 120 sixty-foot columns.

After his conference with the Ephesian elders, Paul sailed away from Miletus. Much later, he returned again briefly, probably after release from his first Roman imprisonment, and was forced to leave Trophimus there ill (2 Timothy 4:20).

Gradually during succeeding centuries the waters of the Maeander River silted up the Latonian Gulf, and Miletus is now five miles from the sea, while the former island of Lade, which helped to make the largest harbor of the town, is a hill rising in the alluvial plain. The area has become in large part a malarial swamp, and much of the ancient city is now under water.

In spite of these difficulties, Theodor Wiegand led a German team to the site in 1899 and continued season after season to lay bare the city which fifth century B.C. leaders had planned and which Paul saw. German excavators also worked at Didyma, beginning in 1906. Wiegand continued to excavate at Miletus until 1914. Carl Weickert took over when the work resumed in 1938. He returned from 1955 to 1957. In more recent years Professor G. Kleiner, then Professor Wolfgang Müller-Wiener, and now Professor Volkmar von Graeve have led the excavations at Miletus. They are making progress on resolving the problem of the annual winter flooding of the site, and soon excavating and visiting there may be a much more pleasant experience. For the last several years Klaus Tuchelt has been directing the work at Didyma and on the sacred road leading from Miletus to Didyma. Up-to-date annual surveys of work at Miletus or other sites in Asia Minor appear in the April issue of the *American Journal of Archaeology.*

Cos. The next stop on the apostolic itinerary, probably about a day out of Miletus, was Cos, on an island of the same name (Acts 21:1). Cos was a long, narrow island oriented east and west. About twenty-three miles long, it had a circumference of sixty-five miles and consisted of an area of

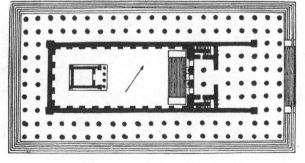

Plan of the temple of Apollo at Didyma.

111 square miles. It was divided into three parts or regions: an abrupt limestone ridge along the eastern half of the southern coast, a rugged peninsula at the west end, and along the northern coast a central lowland of fertile soil that produced an excellent quality of grapes. The harbor lay at the eastern end of the island. Mount Oromedon, a landmark for navigators, rose in the middle of the island.

Greeks settled on Cos as early as the fifteenth century B.C. During the sixth century B.C. it fell under Persian domination and in the following century joined the Delian League (Athenian alliance), suffering considerable destruction during the Peloponnesian War (431–404). A member of the second Athenian Alliance, it revolted successfully against Athens in 354. Coming under the control of Alexander, Cos subsequently oscillated between Macedon, Syria, and Egypt, to find its greatest glory as a literary center under the Ptolemies, when it was the home of such greats as the poets Philetas, Theocritus, and Herodas. In the second century Cos was loyal to Rome even before it became a part of the province of Asia. Claudius, influenced by his Coan physician, Xenophon, made Cos a free city and conferred immunity from taxation upon it in A.D. 53.

Cos was one of the most beautiful ports of the ancient world and no doubt was most famous as a health resort and as the site of the first school of scientific medicine

Ruins of Hippocrates' hospital at Cos.

and the sanctuary of Asclepius. The island had a healthy climate and hot ferrous- and sulphur-bearing springs which the great Hippocrates (c. 460–377 B.C.), the father of medicine, first used to cure his patients.

IS THERE A DOCTOR IN THE HOUSE?

Often we get the impression that all there was to medicine in New Testament times was prayer to the gods, the wearing of amulets, magical incantations, the taking of various herbs and drugs, and rest and relaxation. But there was much that sounded quite modern.

Doctors performed surgery of various sorts with surgical instruments found widely throughout the Roman Empire. Surgeons' equipment included scalpels, forceps, hooks, and probes. Precision tools were sometimes made of iron, but more commonly of bronze and brass. Roman blacksmiths could produce steeled tools.

Doctors apparently did quite well in treating fractures. They also achieved considerable success in dentistry—in extracting teeth, in capping teeth, and doing bridgework. Eye operations, especially for the removal of cataracts, were carried out quite routinely. They treated urinary disorders and patched mutilations of ears, lips, noses, and more, and they practiced brain surgery. The treating and removal of hemorrhoids, a common ailment, was also quite routine.

We need to be careful, however, not to become too enthusiastic. Doctors had an imperfect knowledge of anatomy and were hindered by a lack of anesthetics. Primarily extracts obtained from the opium poppy and henbane were used as sedatives and painkillers. Doctors had to work fast and to have a steady hand. Good antiseptics were also not available; wine, vinegar, pitch, and turpentine were used instead. Blood poisoning often occurred with surgery and necessitated amputation of limbs.

Army doctors, especially, developed skill in treating wounds, even abdominal wounds, with abdominal surgery, which civilian doctors avoided whenever possible. Beginning with Augustus, medical provision was made for every branch of the armed forces, and every legion had a hospital. We have information about numerous army hospitals. Because army doctors traveled and worked on the frontiers, they came in contact with drugs and practices of other peoples. Thus they became the most important means for the improvement of Roman medicine.

Though several military hospitals are known, civilians were apparently normally treated at home or at the home of the doctor, or in rooms he had rented. Without doubt the masses had little opportunity to benefit from what medical expertise the doctors did possess. We need to keep in mind that the well-appointed doctor's office in Pompeii was located in an affluent community. The tenement dwellers of Rome or the larger cities of Asia Minor must have had little access to doctors. There was little medical care available in rural areas. Midwives often provided help in dealing with women's diseases and disorders, and some of them must have become quite proficient. A useful survey on the practice of medicine in New Testament times is Ralph Jackson's *Doctors and Diseases in the Roman Empire* (London: The British Museum, 1988).

Rudolf Herzog of Tübingen University excavated the sanctuary of Asclepius (the god of healing) from 1898 to 1907. He uncovered a center on three terraces set in a sacred grove of cypresses about two miles southwest of town. The topmost terrace had a Doric temple built of white island marble surrounded on three sides by a U-shaped portico with its open side facing the lower terraces and dating about 160 B.C. The middle terrace dated about 280 B.C and supported a great altar faced by a small temple and other structures. The lowest terrace had a U-shaped portico with its open side facing the one on the top level. Dating from 350 to 250 B.C., the stoa contained rooms where the patients slept.[72]

When an earthquake nearly devastated the city of Cos in 1933, the Italians, who then controlled the island, took the opportunity to excavate the ancient city. They found a planned Hellenistic town dating back to 366 B.C with main cross streets, a stadium, gymnasium, theater, baths, an agora (about 350 feet wide), and a surrounding wall about two miles in circumference. And they found evidence of occupation at the site as early as Mycenaean times. The Italians also excavated at the sanctuary and did a great deal of restoration there. At the lower level there they uncovered Roman baths which utilized the healing waters of the island's springs and which (by inscriptions) dated to Nero's reign (and thus to the time of Paul's ministry).

Rhodes. A regular port of call for the small ships coasting the Aegean, Rhodes was the next stop of Paul and his associates. As they sailed up to the double harbor, they probably were struck with wonder at the sight of the great colossus which guarded the entrance. This great statue of the sun god stood to a height of approximately 105 feet and was recognized as one of the seven wonders of the ancient world.[73] A hollow casting of bronze on an iron armature, the colossus was filled with blocks of stone.[74] In his left hand the image held a javelin with the blunt end resting on the ground. In his right hand he held a torch aloft, and on his head he wore a crown adorned with sunrays protruding somewhat in the fashion of the American Statue of Liberty. Dedicated around 290 B.C., the statue was broken off at the knees by an earthquake around 225 B.C., restored by the Romans, and demolished by the Arabs during the seventh century A.D.

Rising from the harbor, the city lay in the form of a theater against the surrounding hillsides, and it was protected by strong walls and towers. The acropolis stood at the southwest extremity of the city. And the ancient buildings most worth seeing perched on the east brow of the acropolis. There were two temples (one dedicated to Zeus and Athena and the other to Apollo), a stadium over six hundred feet long, a small adjacent theater, a gymnasium, and other structures. In the lower city, laid out on the grid plan, the agora extended west from the great harbor. And in the vicinity stood a temple to Aphrodite and a shrine of Dionysus.

The temple to Apollo on the acropolis of Rhodes.

Perhaps Paul could have said with the Roman geographer Strabo, who was there not long before him, that Rhodes was the most splendid city known to him in respect to harbors, streets, walls, and public buildings, all of which were adorned with a profusion of works of art, both painting and sculpture. In spite of the fact that under Roman rule Rhodes kept a modicum of prosperity and boasted no small distinction as a beautiful city and center of higher education, it was no longer at its height when Paul came.

Largest of the Dodecanese Islands (about 45 miles long by 22 wide and covering an area of 540 square miles), Rhodes had a long history. Many believe that the "Dodanim" of Genesis 10:4 and 1 Chronicles 1:7 should read "Rodanim" instead and that the reference is to Rhodes. Minoan culture maintained itself there, as archaeological remains indicate. The "Dorian invasion" resulted on Rhodes in the establishment of three towns: Lindus (modern Lindos), Ialysus, and Camirus. In subsequent centuries Rhodians founded colonies in Spain, Italy, Sicily, and Asia Minor.

Under Persian control in the sixth century, during the fifth century Rhodes was a member of the Athenian Empire but revolted against Athens in 412 B.C. The war with Athens led to union of the three cities as a single federated city (at the northern tip of the island) in 408. Early in the fourth century, Rhodes fell into the hands of the Athenians again and subsequently was controlled by Alexander the Great. After Alexander's death, Rhodes won her freedom again, and her really great period of history began.

Rhodian prosperity always came mainly from the carrying trade. Her commercial activities received great impetus from the conquests of Alexander the Great, which gave unrestricted access to Egypt, Cyprus, and Phoenicia; and in the third century B.C. she became the richest of the Greek city-states. Rhodian wine jars have been found in excavations and on sunken ships all over the Mediterranean world. A center of exchange and capital, Rhodes was naturally the enemy of piracy and for a long time effectively checked it on the high seas.

St. Paul's Harbor, Rhodes.

The Mediterranean near Patara.

By her appeal to Rome (along with Pergamum) for help against Syria and Macedonia (201 B.C.), Rhodes was largely responsible for the first major intervention of Rome in eastern affairs. She cooperated with Rome in subsequent wars against Syria and Macedonia and was rewarded with territory in Caria and Lycia. Rhodes achieved her height of prosperity during the first part of the second century B.C. When Rome thought Rhodian actions too equivocal during the Third Macedonian War, she took away the Carian and Lycian territory and made Delos a free port (167 B.C.). This competition plus a probable increase in piracy ruined Rhodes. She later became an ally of Rome on unfavorable terms. However, she remained a free city even down to the apostle Paul's time and retained her fine harbors, public buildings, and other indications of a past glory.

Patara. In Paul's desire to reach Jerusalem by Pentecost, he next sailed to Patara. Since the prevailing winds in this part of the Mediterranean are from the west, ships sailing from the Aegean or Italy to Phoenicia or Egypt would often risk the voyage straight across the sea from Patara, rather than taking the slow coastal route along the southern shores of Asia Minor. Apparently the apostle embarked on the more daring course at this time (Acts 21:2). It was her position on the maritime routes rather than the value of her hinterland that gave wealth and prominence to Patara during the first

century A.D. Though the city lay on the coast of Lycia only seven or eight miles southeast of the mouth of the Xanthus (modern Koca) River and though the valley of this river is the best part of Lycia, Patara's location in relation to the Xanthus was of relative unimportance compared with her relation to international trade and passenger routes.

Lycia was not definitely colonized by Greeks in early times, and not until the third century B.C., under Ptolemaic rule, did the natives of the area abandon their native tongue for Greek. Thought to be of Phoenician origin with a later infusion of Dorians, Patara was enlarged by Ptolemy Philadelphus of Egypt. The chief Lycian god was identified with Apollo, who had a celebrated oracle at Patara—second only in renown to that of Delphi. Since the oracle spoke only during the six winter months, Paul would not have known of any revelations given during his visit there.

Patara is only now being explored and excavated, so the ancient city is not well known. A walk around the site will allow us to identify a few remains, however. As we approach (on the north) there is a well-preserved gateway, erected about A.D. 100, according to its inscriptions. Remains of walls appear here and there. At the south wall near the harbor stands a fairly intact theater; its stage building dates to the second century A.D. Within the walls we can see a well-preserved temple of the Corinthian order, scanty remains of two other temples, Roman baths of uncertain date, a Christian basilica, and baths dating to the reign of Vespasian (A.D. 69–79). At the western edge of the harbor stands a well-preserved granary of Hadrian (A.D. 117–138), identified by its Latin inscription. The location of the harbor is still apparent, but the area is at present a swamp, choked with sand and bushes.

Fahri Isik and his associates began annual research and restoration efforts at Patara in 1992. They have done some work on restoration of the Roman baths, plotting the city's main colonnaded street, and exploring the fortifications enclosing the classical and later city, a large basilica, two Hellenistic temples, and more. Soundings

A gateway at Patara, a triple arch erected about A.D. 100 by Mettius Modestus, governor of Lycia/Pamphylia

have produced Iron Age pottery in the lowest levels. Havva Yilmaz and her team have investigated five intact tombs of the Early Roman Empire. Of special interest is discovery at the site of an inscription dating from the reign of Claudius (contemporary with Paul's ministry) that lists all roads connecting Patara and other Roman towns.

To Palestine and Back to Myra. The apostolic company reached Jerusalem safely, but the success of the trip was quite in contrast with the treatment Paul was to suffer at the hands of Jews and Romans in the center of Judaism (cf. Acts 21:10–26:32) More than two years after Paul left the coast of Asia Minor, he was back again (Acts 27:5), but this time he was in the custody of a Roman centurion who had the responsibility of bringing him to Rome for trial before Caesar.

The westerly winds that favored the voyage from Patara or Myra to Tyre made the return voyage from Tyre to Myra an impossibility. The regular course for ships from Palestine or Phoenicia was northward past the east end of Cyprus and thence along the Asia Minor coast. Then, by means of ocean currents and land winds that blew off the coast, they made

their way westward toward Myra. The voyage from Caesarea to Myra might be done in as short a time as ten days, but recorded trips over that route took as long as twenty days. Ships of the Roman grain fleet (on one of which Paul probably sailed) might take the same route if the winds required, but normally they sailed directly from Alexandria to Myra on the Lycian coast, from there westward across the Aegean north of Crete, through the Ionian Sea, and then up the western coast of Italy.

In Greek times Patara surpassed Myra, but when Rome ruled the area, Myra, forty miles east of Patara, became the chief seaport of Lycia. It grew especially as a result

The theater at Myra.

Church of St. Nicholas at Demre, near Myra. St. Nicholas was born in Patara around A.D. 300. He was buried in the crypt (now badly broken) but in 1087 his body was stolen by sailors from Bari in southern Italy, where it now lies.

of the Alexandrian grain trade with Italy. Though Myra was located 2.5 miles up the Andracus river from the coast, the same name was often applied to its harbor Andriace (Andriake).

There is no indication in the Acts narrative whether Paul stayed on board ship in the Myra harbor until the centurion found a ship sailing for Rome or whether the prisoner and his guard went into Myra briefly. No archaeological work has taken place either at Andriake or Myra that would give us a clue as to what either was like in Paul's day. A ten-minute walk from the shore would bring us to a well-preserved granary of Hadrian's day (A.D. 117–138), but of course that was built long after Paul disembarked.

At Myra itself stands a theater (355 feet in diameter) in a reasonably good state of preservation. We know that this was restored or remodeled in the second century A.D., but we do not know if a theater existed there during the first century. In the cliffs behind the theater there are magnificent tombs cut in the rock cliff face. These Lycian tombs date to the fourth century B.C. Of some interest to Westerners is the Byzantine Church of St. Nicholas in the nearby village of Demre. A sarcophagus, believed to be the tomb of St. Nicholas, is shown there.

Other Pauline Cities

Three additional cities of Asia Minor figure in the Pauline narrative: Colossae, Hierapolis, and Laodicea (Colossians 2:1; 4:13–16). Laodicea is more important as one of the seven cities that John addressed in Revelation, but we may more conveniently discuss it here along with its sister cities of the Lycus Valley. Of the three sites, Colossae figures more prominently in the New Testament narrative because Paul addressed an entire epistle to the church there. But apparently Paul considered the Colossian epistle was pertinent to the Laodiceans as well because he urged that it be read in their church (Colossians 4:16).

It is commonly assumed that Paul never visited these Lycus cities, and such references as Colossians 1:4, 7–8; 2:1 are cited to prove it. But I think that the apostle more than likely did visit one or more of these Phrygian cities. He might possibly have done so on his second missionary journey (Acts 16:6). The natural route for him to have taken then was from Syria, through the Cilician Gates, then to Derbe, Lystra, Iconium, Antioch of Pisidia, Apamea, Colossae, Laodicea, and down the Maeander River to Ephesus. The statement of Colossians 2:1 need not force us to believe that Paul knew none of the Christians at Colossae personally, though nearly all of them may have been converts made later by someone else. At any rate, he could have visited the Lycus cities on one of his journeys.

The best way to introduce these Lycus cities to modern students is to take them on a journey up the Maeander River (modern Menderes) from its mouth near Miletus. (The Maeander Valley was the eastern trade route between Ephesus and the Euphrates in Roman times.) As we travel inland, the broad and fertile Maeander Valley narrows; and about seventy-five miles from its mouth, the foothills compress the valley to a width of about a mile. Approximately twenty-five miles farther on, the Maeander makes a sharp turn northward. At the bend it is joined by the Lycus, one of its principal tributaries, and leads to the open Lycus Valley.

Roughly triangular in form, the plain of the Lycus (which runs from southeast to northwest) is about twenty-four miles long. At its widest the plain spans six miles. It is hemmed in on all sides by highlands which on the south ascend to Mount Cadmus (8,250 feet) and the Salbacus Mountains (7,590 feet) and which on the west form part of the Messogis Range that stretches from interior Anatolia out to Mycale. The Lycus Valley is on the edge of the steppe-land; to the east is lonely sheep country.

Laodicea. About twelve miles southeast of the junction of the Lycus with the Maeander stood ancient Laodicea. This city was situated on the long spur of a hill between the narrow valleys of the small rivers Asopus (on the west) and Cadmus (on the east), which emptied their waters into the Lycus. Laodicea stood at an altitude of about 850 feet approximately three miles south of the Lycus. By Roman road the distance from Ephesus was some hundred miles.[75] The great road[76] from the coast to the interior of Asia Minor passed right

through the middle of the city, making it an important center of trade and communication.

Exactly when the first settlers came to Laodicea is unknown, but it was called successively in ancient times "Diospolis" and "Rhoas." Antiochus II, who ruled Seleucia from 261 to 246 B.C., refounded the city and named it after his wife, Laodice. When the Romans defeated the Seleucids in 190 B.C., they assigned Laodicea to their ally Eumenes of Pergamum. Thus when the Pergamene king willed his state to Rome in 133 B.C., Laodicea became Roman territory and part of the province of Asia. Mithridates, king of Pontus, besieged the city in 88 B.C. and held it until 84, when the Romans returned. Thereafter Roman rule was on the whole favorable to Laodicean prosperity.

The city's wealth came from its favorable location on the great east-west commercial route across Asia Minor and especially from its production of a very fine quality of world-famous black, glossy wool. The city was also a center of banking; Cicero was one of the more famous men of the Roman world to cash drafts there. Furthermore, the establishment of a celebrated school of medicine in connection with the temple of the Phrygian god Men Karou, thirteen miles west of Laodicea, contributed to the importance of the area. Actually the school of medicine was located in Laodicea itself. Ramsay notes that a market was held under the auspices of the god somewhere near the temple and that people of the valley met and traded there with strangers from a distance.[77] The prosperity of Laodicea is well attested by the fact that the rebuilding of the city after devastating earthquakes in the reigns of Tiberius and Nero was accomplished without proffered imperial or provincial aid.

Almost every phase of John's condemnation of the Laodiceans in Revelation 3:14–19 has been related by commentators to some phase of the city's character or activity. The apostle condemns them for being neither cold nor hot but lukewarm. Ramsay described the people there as follows: "There are no extremes, and hardly any very strongly marked features . . . ever pliable and accommodating, full of the spirit of compromise."[78] Others have seen in this mention of lukewarmness an allusion to the condition of the water supply, carried by a six-mile aqueduct from the south. The water either came from hot springs and was cooled to lukewarm or came from a cooler source and warmed up in the aqueduct on the way.

The aqueduct of Laodicea.

Revelation 3:17 scored the Laodiceans for trust in their riches. The following verse tells those who were noted for their beautiful black cloth to seek white raiment (symbolic of spiritual cleansing). Likewise they were told to anoint themselves with (spiritual) eye salve that they might really see. No doubt this is an allusion to the "Phrygian powder" used as a medicine for the eyes—a treatment that seems to have come through Laodicea into general use among the Greeks. This was mentioned with respect as early as Aristotle's day. Laodicean ointment for treating the ears also became renowned.

There were many Jewish inhabitants of Laodicea, and this may well explain the early spread of Christianity in the area.[79] Apparently Paul did not found the church there but Epaphras may have established it (Colossians 4:12–13). Laodicea early became the chief bishopric of Phrygia.

The identification of the "epistle from Laodicea" (Colossians 4:16) which the Colossians were encouraged to read has given rise to much discussion. Some have held that it was written by Laodiceans, others that it was written by Paul from Laodicea, yet others that it was an epistle written by Paul to the Laodiceans and subsequently lost. An additional view which many accept is that the reference here is to the canonical Ephesians. The words "at Ephesus" in Ephesians 1:1 do not appear in the best manuscripts, and many have held that this epistle was a circular letter or perhaps designed originally for instruction of the Laodiceans.[80]

Laodicea continued prosperous during Roman and Byzantine times, but it was badly damaged by the Seljuk Turks who captured it in A.D. 1094. The Byzantines recaptured it three years later and held it until the end of the thirteenth century. After that it continued to decline and finally became uninhabited. In recent centuries the ruins have served as a stone quarry for surrounding villages. This practice has continued until the present so that some ruins which were fairly extensive a century ago have now largely disappeared.

In spite of this it is possible to make some general comments on the nature of the site during the first century A.D. The city was approximately square with the corners oriented toward the points of the compass. Covering about a square mile, the city was surrounded by walls dating to Hellenistic times. The great aqueduct came into Laodicea at about the middle of the southwest wall. The Ephesus gate pierced the northwest wall, and a road led from it across a bridge over the Asopus River. At the north corner of the city stood the acropolis and at its feet the gate which led to Hierapolis.

Against the southwest wall stood an amphitheatric stadium, so-called because both ends were semicircular and because rows of seats ran continuously around the whole circumference. The proper Greek stadium had only one or neither end rounded. Buildings of this type are sometimes found in Asia Minor and are indiscriminately called "stadiums" and "amphitheaters." This structure was nine hundred feet long in the arena, had an axis line approximately northwest to southeast, and was dedicated in the latter part of A.D. 79 after news of the

The north gate of Laodicea framing the white cliffs of Hierapolis, six miles away.

death of Vespasian had been received (according to the dedicatory inscription). Next to the stadium on the east lay a gymnasium, probably constructed A.D. 123–24. Just east of the stadium stood an odeion or covered hall, in the form of a theater.

There were two theaters inside the walls of Laodicea: a small one near the Hierapolis gate in the north, and a larger one along the northeast wall. The dates of these are unknown. Few temples have yet been found; possibly they were purposely destroyed by Christians as paganism declined. A small Ionic temple has been found some 230 yards southwest of the small theater. Remains of other buildings dot the site, but they have not yet been positively identified.

Exploration and excavation at Laodicea occurred during the years 1961–63 under the direction of Professor Jean des Gagniers of Laval University, Quebec. The team made a survey of the site, cleared some buildings, found a number of inscriptions, and paid special attention to a nymphaion or monumental fountain that dated to the early third century A.D.

Hierapolis. The white cliffs of Hierapolis are visible from the north gate of ancient Laodicea,

six miles away, gleaming in the sunshine. The water from the hot springs of the place have tumbled over the cliffs from earliest times, depositing its heavy content of carbonates, sodium, and chlorides of calcium in its wake. Though from a distance the cliff is blinding white, we can see on closer inspection that it is streaked with yellow and black and gives the appearance of a frozen waterfall.

Hierapolis perched on a shelf or terrace about 1,100 feet above sea level and 150 to 300 feet above the plain. This shelf is some three hundred yards wide and a couple of

Waters from the hot springs of Hierapolis have tumbled over the cliffs from earliest times, depositing their heavy content of salts and creating the appearance of a frozen waterfall.

Baths of Hierapolis converted to a church, probably in the fifth century.

the large number of Jews in the place, settled there by one of the Hellenistic kings. The inscriptions attest to their power in the city. They were organized in trade guilds: the purple-dyers, the carpet-makers, and possibly others.[82] The hot springs of Hierapolis, rich in alum, were especially useful in the dyeing process.

But Judaism and Christianity were minority religions at Hierapolis, probably until Byzantine times. No doubt the hot springs of the area were sacred to nature divinities, as was a cave filled with deadly fumes. This cave was called the "Plutonium" or "Charonion." It has been thought that a priest or priestess sat upon a stool deep in the Plutonium and when under the influence of the vapors uttered prophecies of value to those who sought them. One of the temples of the town was dedicated to Apollo (prophecy was one of his functions), as was a temple near the Plutonium. Cybele, the mother goddess, was especially worshiped, along with Pluto, Men, Isis, and the imperial cult.

Evidence in the ruins of Hierapolis, suggests that, like other Hellenistic cities, it had been laid out all at one time. One main street ran the length of the city (southeast to northwest). On either side were covered sidewalks, and cross streets intersected it at right angles. As we go up on the plateau, the first structure we meet is the city baths, evidently built in the second century A.D. In a good state of preservation, this provided baths, a large hall for athletics and gymnastic exercises, and a courtyard or exercise ground. In front of the city baths stands a Christian basilica that dates to the sixth century A.D.

To the right of the main road through town the beautifully preserved Roman theater of the second century A.D. rises in the distance. But close at hand on the right stands a monumental fountain of the fourth century A.D., next to which is the temple of Apollo, the principal deity of the city. The structure dates to the third century A.D., but the lower

miles long. It stands on the north side of the Lycus while Laodicea is on the south.

King Eumenes II of Pergamum is thought to have founded the city early in the second century B.C. and to have colonized it with settlers from Macedonia and Pergamum. Though the name means "holy city," it was probably named for Hiera, wife of Telephos, the legendary founder of Pergamum. When the kingdom of Pergamum came into the Roman Empire in 133 B.C., Hierapolis took her place as one of the towns of the province of Asia. The terrible earthquake of A.D. 17 destroyed the city but it was rebuilt, only to suffer another severe earthquake in 60 during the reign of Nero. Again rebuilt, it experienced considerable prosperity during the second and third centuries A.D.

Who brought Christianity to Hierapolis is not exactly clear—perhaps Paul or Timothy, or according to a later tradition, Philip the Evangelist. Eusebius the historian said Philip spent his latter days there and two of his daughters were buried in the city.[81] In any case, it seems evident that a church existed at Hierpolis by the time Paul wrote Colossians (4:13), about 60. During the Byzantine period it became the seat of a bishopric, and it possessed a large church erected to St. Philip.

The acceptance of Christianity in Hierapolis may have some connection with parts of the building go back to the early days of the city. Next comes the agora, which is reappearing from the soil. Far off to the right and out of sight stands the Martyrium of St. Philip, an imposing octagonal building dating to the fifth century A.D. Next a Byzantine gateway gives entrance to the best-preserved section of the colonnaded roadway. At the other end of this stretch of the road stands the Arch of Domitian, erected A.D. 82–83. Beyond that are third century A.D. baths, converted to a church in the fifth century.

The theater of Hierapolis.

A little farther along is the necropolis that stretches for more than a mile on both sides of the road. The tombs here span the centuries from the late Hellenistic age to early Christian times. One of the best preserved of the ancient cemeteries of Turkey, it has three types of tombs: house-shaped tombs, tumulus tombs, and a large number of sarcophagi. As is clear from the dates given above, not much of this has any connection with the New Testament period.

Investigations of the remains at Hierapolis began with Karl Humann, who in 1887 led an exploratory team to the site. Beginning in 1957, Italian archaeologists under the direction of Paolo Verzone engaged in fruitful excavation and restoration. During the last decade the Italian professor Daria de Barnardi Ferrero has succeeded him and has led annual expeditions to the site. She has excavated in the agora and on the main street, re-erected columned porticoes along the street, restored the Apollo temple and the theater, and continued the inventory of tombs in the necropolis.

Colossae. The third of the Lycus Valley cities, Colossae, lay near the upper end of the valley about eleven miles east and a little south of Laodicea. At Colossae the valley narrowed to approximately two miles, and the city was overshadowed by great mountain heights. Colossae itself stood at an altitude of 1,150 feet. Mount Cadmus towered above it some three miles to the south at an altitude of 8,013 feet. The streams that watered the Colossae area coursed down the sides of Cadmus. The fortified acropolis of the city lay on the south bank of the Lycus, but buildings and tombs stretched out on the north bank.

Colossae was once a great city of Phrygia. According to Herodotus it was an important city when Xerxes came through it in 481 B.C. According to Xenophon it was still important in 401 B.C. when Cyrus the Younger marched through. The rise of Hierapolis and especially Laodicea brought crippling competition to the older town, and it gradually dwindled, occupying a comparatively insignificant status by New Testament times. In its better days it had been an important center for the wool and dye industries. Its specialty was woolen

The Byzantine gate of Hierapolis.

House and tumulus graves in the cemetery of Hierapolis.

goods of Colossene red. The surrounding countryside produced sheep that were known for the softness of their wool.

Epaphras, a member of Paul's missionary team, seems to have been chiefly responsible for the evangelization of Colossae as well as Laodicea and Hierapolis (Colossians 4:12–13). But it is clear from the epistle which Paul wrote to the Colossian church that Christianity there had a severe contest with aspects of paganism, Judaism, and asceticism. Among the deities worshiped there during the Roman Period were Isis and Serapis, Helios, Demeter, and Artemis, in addition to the native Phrygian god Men.

Though Colossae later achieved the status of a bishopric, the city was deserted sometime between A.D. 600 and 700. Large blocks of stone, foundations of buildings, column fragments and remains of a theater may still be seen, though inhabitants of nearby villages have extensively rifled the site. It is still possible, however, that a systematic excavation there would be productive.

The Apostle Peter and Asia Minor

The apostle Peter wrote to "sojourners of the dispersion in [preferred reading]

Pontus, Galatia, Cappadocia, Asia, and Bithynia" (1 Peter 1:1). Note that the provinces named include all of Asia Minor north of the Taurus Range and that the persons addressed were not Jews only nor even Christian Jews but Christians in general, as the contents of the epistle bear out. Thus the NIV chooses to translate the address "strangers in the world, scattered . . ." and the REB "the scattered people of God now living as aliens in . . ."

We do not certainly know that Peter preached in the areas he addressed. Since the New Testament is almost completely silent about him after Herod's imprisonment of him, we are left to guess at what he may have done or where he may have gone. Possibly he simply wrote to Christians in Asia Minor to encourage them, but it seems more likely that some ministry there established a contact and concern that led Peter to write to his children in the faith.

Where Peter was when he wrote has also led to considerable discussion. He said he was in Babylon (1 Peter 5:13). Some have argued that he meant literally the famous Babylon on the Euphrates (so Erasmus, Calvin, Alford, and others). But a much larger number of scholars have considered Babylon to be used here symbolically of Rome. John followed this practice in the

Revelation, and writers of the second century and following did also. Whether or not Peter did as early as about A.D. 65 is open to question.

The peculiar order in which the provinces appear in Peter's address also has received scholarly attention. An explanation that many have followed was advanced by F. J. A. Hort. He says the reason for the order lies in the route followed by the messenger who brought the letter (perhaps in so many distinct copies) to the central cities of the various provinces.[83] Some have suggested that the order in which the provinces are named favors the Babylonian origin of the epistle. Others suggest that the bearer of the letter sailed from Rome, landed at some port on the Black Sea, possibly Sinope (modern Sinop) in Pontus, traveled through the provinces named, took ship again at some Bithynian port, and sailed back to Rome.

If the latter is true, the apostolic messenger may have landed at Sinope or Amisus (modern Samsun) in Pontus, dropped south to Ancyra (Ankara) in Galatia, traveled southeast to such a place as Archelais (modern Akserai) in western Cappadocia, moved westward from there on the east-west trade route to Ephesus, journeyed by road north to Cyzicus, taken ship to Nicomedia (modern Izmit) in Bithynia, and then sailed to Rome. All this is of course hypothetical, but it is a reasonable reconstruction. At any rate discussion of the provinces follows the order in which Peter introduced them.

Pontus. Pontus was originally an area along the southern shore of the Black Sea bordered on the west by the Halys River (modern Kizil Irmak), on the east and southeast by Armenia, on the south by Cappadocia, and on the southwest by Galatia. The area varied according to the political fortunes of its rulers. Along the Black Sea is a beautiful and well-watered but narrow coastland, with wider plains at the mouths of the Halys and the Iris Rivers, which provided the main lines of drainage and communication. Backing the coastal plain is a noble series of mountain ranges running parallel to the coast. The mountain valleys, containing good pasture land, were fertile, producing olives and other fruits, nuts, and grains. The mountains themselves were clad with forests of beech, pine, oak, and fir, which were exported to the forestless countries of the Mediterranean and used for local construction of ships. But the greatest wealth of the mountains lay in the mineral deposits of iron, copper, silver, and alum.

Under the Mithridatic line Amasia (modern Amasya) on the Iris River was the capital (and was later important as the birthplace of Strabo). Amisus, west of the Iris on the coast, possessed a large part of the coastal plain and controlled the easiest road to the plateau. Sinope to the west, the most northerly point in Asia Minor, had the best harbor on the Black Sea and was beautifully walled and adorned with public buildings in Peter's day. Amastris in western Pontus also had a good harbor, a good supply of timber, and numerous ships. Trapezus (Trabzon, or Trebizond), in the east gained immensely in importance during Nero's Armenian campaigns and maintained that position as the nearest port of supply for armies on the frontier. Nicopolis, Neocaesarea, and Sebastea are among other important towns of the region.

No doubt the Hittites occupied towns in the region of Pontus, but they held only uneasy control over the area at best. During the first half of the first millennium B.C. Greek colonists established themselves all along the southern shore of the Black Sea and in Pontus settled at such places as Sinope, Amisus, and Trapezus. (It was near Trapezus that Xenophon and his famous ten thousand reached the sea in 400 B.C.)

When the Persians took control of Asia Minor in 546 B.C., they joined Pontus to the empire and it was ruled by a dynasty of satraps, who managed to gain their independence a little before 350 B.C. and to maintain it during the Macedonian Period. As a result of the confusion following the death of Alexander the Great, Mithridates II was able to carve out for himself a fair-sized kingdom east of the Halys river (c. 300–280). In concert with Nicomedes of Bithynia, he succeeded in quieting the Galatians (Gauls, i.e., Celts) in Phrygia. The

Mithridatic dynasty lasted until 63 B.C., when for all practical purposes Pompey brought it to an end.

The greatest of the Mithridatic line was Mithridates VI. He made an alliance with his son-in-law Tigranes of Armenia and then attacked Roman forces in Asia Minor. The first war (89–85 B.C.) began with striking Pontic successes but ended with Mithridates contained once more within the original bounds of his kingdom. The second war (83–81) was little more than a series of three raids. The third war began in 74; and after initial Pontic advances, the Roman Lucullus took Mithridates' capital by siege, scattered his army and drove him from the country. Finally Pompey, appointed to command Roman forces in 66 B.C., utterly destroyed Mithridates' power, and the aged king died by suicide in the Crimea in 63 B.C.

Mithridates' kingdom was incorporated into the Roman Empire under the name Pontus and constituted half of the combined province Bithynia-Pontus. During the civil wars of Rome, Pharnaces II, a son of Mithridates VI, was able to establish himself as ruler over his father's kingdom. But his success was short-lived; Caesar defeated him in 47 B.C. While Mark Antony was ruling in the East, he reestablished a narrowed kingdom of Pontus alongside the Roman province and gave it in 36 B.C. to Polemon, who founded a dynasty that ruled the kingdom until A.D. 63. This was a client kingdom on the order of that of Herod the Great in Judea. When in 63 Polemon's kingdom (Pontus Polemoniacus) was brought to an end, part of it was added to the province of Cappadocia (and remained so until Diocletian) and part to Galatia (Pontus Galaticus).

In early Pontus, society was essentially feudal, some of the villages and territorial units being ruled by the nobility and some by the priests as part of large temple estates. Some of the mountainous regions were for a long time uncivilized tribal territories. The kings apparently brought priests and nobility under effective control but did little to develop cities. To the end of the Roman Empire, Pontus kept much of its native character. The cities were artificial construc-tions; the feudal aristocracy remained important. In the eastern part the natives were only slightly touched by Hellenistic civilization.

During the first century A.D. the name Pontus had at least two significations: client kingdom and Roman province. No doubt the Roman province is in view in 1 Peter 1:1 and Acts 18:2, where Aquila is said to have been a native of the place. It is interesting to note that an inscription has been found which refers to an Aquila at Sinope. Perhaps the Pontic Jews who were present in Jerusalem on the Day of Pentecost (Acts 2:9) were likewise from the province, though they might have been from the kingdom (Pontus Polemoniacus).

How Christianity came to Pontus is unknown. Possibly some natives of the place were converted on the Day of Pentecost. Perhaps some Christians from the western Asian coast settled at Sinope or Amastris. At any rate by the beginning of the second century A.D., Christianity was widespread there. Pliny the Younger, who governed the province A.D. 111–13, inquired of the emperor Trajan how to treat Christians there (in respect to persecution) and indicated that they were to be found among men and women of all ages and rank and in town and country. However, the Christianization of the inland districts of Pontus did not begin until about the middle of the third century.

Galatia. Galatia has already been discussed in connection with Paul's ministry in Asia Minor.

Cappadocia. In early classical times Cappadocia was thought of as the whole inland district of eastern Asia Minor extending from the Taurus Mountains to the Black Sea. But during the latter days of the Persian Empire, the area was divided into two administrative districts called Cappadocia and Pontus. So Cappadocia has come to be defined as that area of east central Asia Minor bounded by the Euphrates River on the east, the Taurus Mountains on the south, Pontus and Galatia on the north and northwest, and Lake Tatta on the west.

Cappadocia covered some 250 miles east and west and 150 miles north and south. The Anti-Taurus Mountains cross the eastern part. The rest of the region consists of a great rolling plateau about 3,000 feet in altitude. Almost treeless in the west, the plains provide pasture for flocks of sheep. Rising from the plains in the central and western parts of the area are detached groups or masses of volcanic mountains, the highest of which is Argaeus (Erciyas Dagi, over 13,000 feet). The ranges of the Taurus and Anti-Taurus are for the most part well watered and well timbered. The severe winter climate limits agricultural production to hardy cereals and sheep. The Roman emperors kept studs of racehorses there. Quartz, salt, and silver mines were found in the province.

The chief rivers of Cappadocia were the Halys, which flowed north, and the Sarus (Seyhan) and Pyramus (Ceyhan), which flowed south through Cilicia. The chief cities, according to Strabo, were Caesarea Mazaca (modern Kayseri), the capital of the Roman province in central Cappadocia, and Tyana in the southwest. Archelais, a Roman colony in the western part of the province on the vital east-west trade road, was also a place of some importance during the Empire period.

Cappadocia seems first to have had some historical significance early in the second millennium B.C. when the Assyrian merchant colonies were established there. Later in the millennium the Hittites controlled the area. It next figured in international affairs during the Persian Period, when an Iranian nobility with feudal dominion over considerable districts established itself. Besides these estates of the nobles, the temples owned large areas that were ruled by priests. The ordinary people lived in villages on land owned by nobles or temples. This socioeconomic structure lasted many centuries.

For a while Cappadocians ruled there more or less independently as tributary to Persia. Later this freedom was destroyed, to be regained once more under Ariarathes I, a contemporary of Alexander the Great. Alexander was content to accept tributary acknowledgment of the Cappadocian without entering his territory.

Eumenes I of Pergamum interrupted Ariarathes' line, but it later returned to power. Under the fourth Ariarathes, Cappadocia came into relations with Rome. After the battle of Magnesia in 190 B.C. he and his successors adopted a pro-Roman policy. During the Mithridatic wars, Tigranes the Great of Armenia devastated Cappadocia, but Pompey restored it, giving the king large loans for reconstruction. During the civil wars Cappadocia sided first with Pompey, then with Caesar, then with Antony and later against him. Antony replaced the Ariobarzanes dynasty, which by that time controlled the throne, with Archelaus Sisines.

When the latter lost the favor of Rome, Tiberius annexed Cappadocia in A.D. 17; and it remained a procuratorial province until A.D. 70. In that year Vespasian united to it Armenia Minor and formed a large and important frontier province, governed by an ex-consul. Afterward the province received various accessions of territory.

Efforts of the later kings and of the Roman rulers of Cappadocia to achieve Hellenization and urbanization in the area were not greatly successful. Urbanization was never fully developed in Cappadocia, and with the economic decline in the Empire during the later second and third centuries A.D., large imperial estates grew up there. The area subsequently became part of the Byzantine Empire and suffered greatly from Arab encroachment, passing into Muslim hands in the eleventh century.

As to religion, Cappadocia boasted several famous pagan temples. The most celebrated was at Comana, where the goddess Ma was served by six thousand priestesses. At Venasa over three thousand devotees served a male god equitable with Zeus. Jews were settled in the kingdom by the middle of the second century B.C., as is implied in 1 Maccabees 15:22, where a letter on their behalf is addressed by the Roman Senate to King Ariarathes. Jews from Cappadocia were present at Jerusalem on the Day of Pentecost (Acts 2:9). The address of 1 Peter 1:1 demonstrates that Christianity had taken root there by shortly after the middle of the first century. During the fourth century the Christian church there was especially served by the three great Cappadocians: Basil the Great, Gregory of Nyssa, and Gregory of Nazianzus.

Asia. Asia, the finest jewel in the imperial crown, came to the Empire without the expenditure of blood. Attalus III of Pergamum had willed his kingdom to the Senate and the Roman people; and on his death in 133 B.C., his legacy was constituted, virtually as it came, into the province of Asia. Including Ionia, Mysia, Lydia, Caria, and western Phrygia (approximately the western third of Asia Minor), the province remained geographically intact until Diocletian broke it up in the fourth century A.D. Sulla did reorganize it in 84 B.C., however.

When Asia came into the Roman Empire, it was the most highly urbanized of all the provinces. Mommsen gives five hundred as the total number of urban communities existing there at the time.[84] But none of these completely dominated the others as Antioch in Syria and Alexandria in Egypt dominated the other towns in their provinces. Pergamum was the residence of the Attalids and seat of the diet and therefore the proper metropolis. Ephesus was the *de facto* capital and location of the governor's residence and the public records. Smyrna was in constant rivalry with Ephesus, calling itself on coins "the first in greatness and beauty." Sardis strove after the same honorary right. Many other important cities could be noted, and great rivalry existed among a number of them. This competition may ultimately have had much to do with the decline of Asian municipalities because it caused them to over extend themselves financially.

The traditional forms of political organization were in general retained in the Hellenistic cities of Asia. Magistrates continued to be chosen by the burgesses; but everywhere the determining influence was placed in the hands of the wealthy, and no free play was allowed to the pleasure of the multitude. Having established oligarchic systems of government in the municipalities, Rome left them very largely to manage their own affairs. She was content to extract from them certain taxes and to exercise a limited degree of jurisdiction, principally in foreign affairs and in cases affecting Roman citizenship.

Asia suffered terribly under its "tax farmers" during the period of the Republic, under Mithridates, under Sulla's indemnity and the rapacious moneylenders who helped the provincials raise the sum, and under Pompey as a result of his levy of ship money to support the fleet designed to destroy the pirates. Whatever degree of prosperity was left was almost obliterated during the civil wars.

Under the Principate and settled conditions, prosperity returned. The finances of the province had been so disordered by the civil wars that Augustus resorted to the extreme expedient of striking off all claims to debt. Other evidence of a new imperial attitude came in A.D. 17. When an earthquake in that year destroyed twelve cities of Asia, the emperor sent immediate aid. For instance, Sardis received ten million sesterces and remission of all contributions to the public or imperial treasury for five years. Apparently by the time of Titus (79–81) the province had regained a prosperity surpassing her condition in pre-Roman times.[85] Her highest prosperity came under the Antonine emperors in the following century. T.R.S. Broughton estimates that the population of Asia reached 4,600,000 during the second century.[86]

POPULATION ESTIMATES FOR SOME ASIA MINOR CITIES IN NEW TESTAMENT TIMES	
Ephesus	225,000
Pergamum	200,000
Smyrna	200,000
Miletus	100,000
Sardis	100,000
Thyatira	25,000

A steady growth in urbanization, promoted by the emperors, accompanied rising prosperity. Most of the remaining tribal communities were urbanized during the Principate, and by the end of the second century A.D., tribal organization seems to have been almost eliminated. But because of the haphazard way in which they had grown, cities (really city-states) varied greatly in size. Ephesus and Rhodes acquired enormous territories. In some areas cities were sparse and ruled large territories; in others they were thickly clustered, each ruling a tiny territory. Pliny gave the number of communities in the province in this day (first century A.D.) as 282.[87] Evidently this figure is to be squared with Mommsen's total, given above, by an understanding that some of the smaller communities of the earlier day had been combined. The Romans on the whole left unchanged the kaleidoscopic variety of the old city constitutions. The Greek city with its characteristic institutions and its ideal of life flowered a second time.

Although the imperial government was more beneficent in its attitude toward Asia under the Empire than under the Republic, the prosperity of the province was not primarily the work of a government of superior insight and energetic activity. Asia was basically rich. Cereals were cultivated to some extent almost everywhere. The wines of the off-shore islands and a number of Lydian and Carian wines were favored. Fruits and nuts were produced in most regions. Timber was adequate. Pastoral wealth was great and varied. Although the gold and silver deposits were largely exhausted by the Imperial period, lead and other metals were mined. The province was rich in fine marbles and excellent building stone. Her merchants were enterprising, and the larger towns boasted a multitude of artisans and a large manufacturing population. Great cities like Ephesus and Smyrna benefited from their domination of trade that flowed along the Hermus and Maeander River routes into the interior of Asia Minor.

The pre-Roman history of Asia coincides with that of Asia Minor in general. Its history under Rome is to a large degree the history of its individual cities, much of which is detailed in connection with the ministry of the apostles Paul and John in Asia Minor. The wealth and culture of the province did not begin with the Roman period but were already centuries old when Rome came on the scene. Prosperous days also lay ahead under Byzantine leadership.

Jews were numerous in Asia. Some of them were present in Jerusalem on the Day of Pentecost (Acts 2:9). The story of the advance of Christianity among both the Jews and the Gentiles of Asia occupies several chapters in Acts and receives considerable attention in this volume.

Bithynia. The term "Bithynia" originally applied only to the peninsula of Chalcedon, but it gradually extended eastward to Heraclea and south to the Mysian Olympus. It was bordered on the north by the Black Sea and on the west by the Propontis and the Thracian Bosporus. The west coast was indented by two deep inlets, the Gulf of Astacus (modern Izmit) and the Gulf of Cius.

The greater part of the land surface was occupied by mountains, the highest of which was Mount Olympus on the south (7,600 feet). However, Bithynia had districts of great fertility near the seacoast, as well as productive interior valleys. Bithynia produced good timber, excellent pasturage, and a variety of fruits and grain and possessed fine marble quarries. The main river was the Sangarius (modern Sakarya) which bisected the country, flowing from south to north into the Black Sea. The placement of mountains and valleys in the district permitted rather easy communication.

The Bithynians were of Thracian origin and long kept their tribal identity among the people about them. But Croesus incorporated them into the Lydian monarchy; and when Cyrus toppled Lydian power in 547/6, they fell within the Persian Empire. They preserved a measure of autonomy under the Persians, however. Before Alexander launched his successful attack on the Persians, the Bithynians declared their independence from their overlords.

Zipoetus (Zipoetes) founded a dynasty of Thracian stock in 297 B.C. and transmitted his power to his son, who assumed the title of king as Nicomedes I in 278 B.C. The latter founded Nicomedia, which soon became an important city.

Nicomedes I and his successors Prusias I, Prusias II, and Nicomedes II by a combination of aggressive policies and judicious alliances (especially with the Galatians, whom they invited into Asia in 279 B.C.), greatly expanded their domain. They founded cities, fostered trade, and advanced the cause of Hellenism within their realm. They lost some territory to Pergamum during the second century B.C., but they generally maintained their power. The last king, Nicomedes IV, was unable to maintain himself, especially in the face of the Mithridatic disturbances. After being restored to his throne by the Romans, he bequeathed his Kingdom to Rome at his death in 74 B.C.

Bithynia now became a Roman province. Pompey apparently divided the land of the province among the cities for convenience in maintaining order and collecting taxes. For administrative purposes Bithynia was generally united with Pontus under one governor. In the early Empire it was treated as a senatorial province, but in A.D. 165 it was taken over by the emperor.

Paul and Silas wanted to preach in Bithynia, but they were prevented by the Spirit from doing so (Acts 16:7). How Christianity was established there is not known, but apparently believers in considerable numbers were to be found in the province by the time of Peter's later years. As already noted in commenting on Pontus, Christians were numerous in Bithynia-Pontus by A.D. 110. The area played a significant part in the history of the church in later centuries. The first ecumenical council was held at Nicea (modern Nice, 325); another was held at Chalcedon (451).

Diocletian was later to establish his capital at Nicomedia, and Bithynia shared the fortunes and misfortunes of Constantinople for another millennium.

The Apostle John and Asia Minor

Tradition almost universally represents the apostle John as spending his last years at Ephesus. While he was there, he seems to have become a sort of "bishop of the see of Asia." The ring of authority evidenced in 2 and 3 John is certainly apostolic if not Episcopal. He addressed himself to seven churches of Asia in a rather forceful way in the book of Revelation. Whether he wrote Revelation on the Isle of Patmos or subsequently in Ephesus will probably never be determined. At Ephesus the apostle also probably wrote his Gospel. The date of John's move to Ephesus from Jerusalem is a matter of some conjecture. Possibly he went just before the fall of Jerusalem in A.D. 70, or possibly just afterward.

Ephesus, John's headquarters in Asia, has already been discussed in connection with Paul's third missionary journey. Laodicea was treated along with the other Lycus Valley towns. We now turn to the other five.

Why seven cities? Why John should have addressed only seven cities and these particular seven in the Revelation is a question that has led to considerable discussion. Many more cities than these had received the gospel and had established churches by the time John wrote. Perhaps William Ramsay has provided the most useful treatment of the subject.

Ramsey concluded, first of all, that these cities had already achieved preeminence among the churches of Asia. More specifically, he noted that the first three (Ephesus, Smyrna, Pergamum) were the greatest cities of the province, always claiming to be "First of Asia." Of the others, Sardis and Laodicea were each at the head of a conventus (governmental district for legal purposes). But a very real problem occurs in trying to account for Thyatira and Philadelphia, second-rate cities. The former was in the conventus of Pergamum and the latter in the conventus of Sardis. Ramsay finally concluded that these cities rose to prominence because of their location. All seven stood on the important circular road that brought together the most populous and prosperous part of Asia, the west central region.[88] The order in which they lay on the Roman road is precisely the order in which Revelation 2–3 addresses them.

Distances Between the Cities. It should be useful at this point to note the distances of

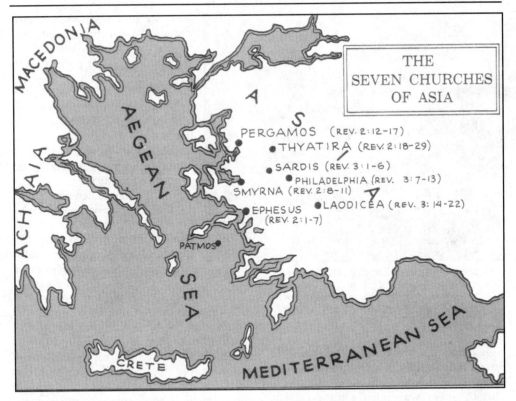

THE
SEVEN CHURCHES
OF ASIA

PERGAMOS (REV. 2:12-17)
THYATIRA (REV. 2:18-29)
SARDIS (REV. 3:1-6)
PHILADELPHIA (REV. 3:7-13)
SMYRNA (REV. 2:8-11)
EPHESUS   LAODICEA (REV. 3:14-22)
(REV. 2:1-7)

PATMOS

AEGEAN SEA

MACEDONIA

ACHAIA

CRETE

MEDITERRANEAN SEA

these cities from each other on the Roman highway system. A few of the figures given here differ considerably from those appearing in other sources. This is true partly because some writers have given distances "as the crow flies," which is an unrealistic approach for a reader who wants to know how long it may have taken these churches to communicate with each other.[89] Others simply were not in possession of the most reliable records.

It seems that William Ramsay is the best authority on this subject. He has critically evaluated the accounts in Roman writers of the road system of Asia and the distances between towns and produced convincing conclusions. Moreover, I have checked the mileage between most of these towns while traveling in the area and found it to tally quite closely with Ramsay's conclusions. In this connection we need to be aware that modern roads do not always follow the route of the ancient roads.

The distances according to Ramsay run as follows (figures are given in Roman miles with approximations of English miles in parentheses): Ephesus to Smyrna, 45 (41.5); Smyrna to Pergamum, 70 (64.5); Pergamum to Thyatira, 48 (44); Thyatira to Sardis, 36 (33); Sardis to Philadelphia, 28 (26); Philadelphia to Laodicea, 51 (47); Laodicea to Ephesus, 107 (98.5).[90]

Smyrna. As we travel north from Ephesus, the first of the seven cities of the Revelation we come to is Smyrna, modern Izmir. The city that John addressed stood in the same spot as the modern city, at the southeast edge of the Gulf of Smyrna (Old Smyrna was located at the northeast end of the gulf). Smyrna was a beautiful city. Located beside the beautiful Aegean Sea, it possessed a good harbor—a double one, in fact. The outer harbor was a part of the gulf that served as a mooring ground; the inner harbor, now silted in and occupied by bazaars, had a narrow entrance that could be blocked by a chain.

The city itself curved around the edge of the bay at the base of 525-foot Mount Pagus, its splendid acropolis. Its streets were excellently paved and were drawn at

Modern Izmir (ancient Smyrna) with the Roman agora in the left center of the picture. The inner Roman harbor is now silted in and covered with buildings. The present harbor was the outer Roman harbor.

was excellently located. Not only did she have a fine harbor but she also had access to the trade of the Hermus Valley (which river flowed into the Gulf of Smyrna) and competed with Miletus and Ephesus for the trade of the Maeander Valley. Throughout the Roman period the city was famous for its wealth and was a center of learning, especially in science and medicine.

The earliest settlement beside the Gulf of Smyrna goes back to the third millennium B.C. At that time Aeolians came in from the islands of the Aegean, especially Lesbos. It is traditionally believed that the town was founded by an Amazon who gave the town her own name. About 700 B.C. Ephesus and Colophon conquered Smyrna, and it became a member of the Ionian Confederacy. Approximately a century later Alyattes of Lydia captured the city and destroyed it. For three to four hundred years Smyrna did not exist as an organized entity. Small villages were scattered around the plain and surrounding hills.

Alexander the Great had planned to restore the city but did not succeed. His successors Antigonus and Lysimachus executed his plan about 290 B.C. The city they founded was located on the southeast shore of the gulf some two to three miles from the earlier site, which had been on the northeast shore. The object of the change was to obtain a good harbor and a convenient location for tapping the trade route to the interior.

right angles. One of them was known as the Street of Gold and ran from west to east along the lower slopes of Pagus. This famous street was lined with especially impressive buildings, and at each end was a temple. Probably the temple of Zeus stood at the western end and the temple of the mother goddess Cybele Sipylene (patroness of the city) at the eastern end. The city had several squares and porticoes, a public library, numerous temples, and other public buildings.

While Smyrna contested with Ephesus and Pergamum for the rank of First of Asia, some of her coins defined her rank as "First of Asia in beauty and size." Her prestige was also enhanced by her claim to have been the birthplace of Homer. About the time of Christ, the theater of the city (located on a slope of Mount Pagus fronting the gulf) could have held twenty thousand spectators, and the total population has been estimated at around one hundred thousand.[91] The population probably reached twice that number in the second century.[92]

Smyrna's wealth was derived from her commerce, for which she

The Hermus River.

Remains of a temple at Old Smyrna.

When the conflict arose between Rome and Seleucia at the beginning of the second century B.C., Smyrna sided with Rome and in 195 B.C. built a temple to the deified Roma. Smyrna also fought on the side of Rome in the war with Mithridates. With the inauguration of the Empire, a new period of prosperity dawned for Smyrna. Tiberius granted the city important privileges, which later emperors confirmed. When the city was virtually destroyed by an earthquake in A.D. 178, Marcus Aurelius rebuilt it at the request of his friend, the orator Aelius Aristides, who then lived there.

Thus the city that John addressed is almost beyond recovery. The excavations conducted at the site have centered on the agora of Marcus Aurelius and Old Smyrna, neither of which tells anything about the first century A.D. Few remains may be seen on the acropolis. Lower courses of walls there date back to Hellenistic times. Since the modern city (now about 2,400,000) covers the ancient city, it is not likely that sufficient work can be done there to recover the plan of New Testament Smyrna.

To be specific about excavation at Smyrna, work at Old Smyrna took place between 1948 and 1951 and since 1966. The earlier work proceeded under the direction of John Cook of the British School of Archaeology at Athens and Ekrem Akurgal of Ankara University. Since 1966 Akurgal has led the dig under the auspices of the Turkish Historical Society and cooperating

institutions. Discoveries include pottery, houses, and a substantial temple to Athena, all of which helped to spell out the history of the site that claimed to Homer's birthplace.

Rudolf Naumann and Salahattin Kantar for the Turkish Historical Society and General Directorate of Museums worked at the state agora of the Hellenistic city 1932–1940. The agora measured some 400 feet along one side and at least 260 feet along the other. Two-story stoas stood around the four sides of the square. To date the north side and parts of the east and west stoas have been excavated. Construction uncovered dates to the rebuilding with the help of the emperor Marcus Aurelius after the great earthquake of A.D. 178. Certainly the agora of New Testament times was located on the same spot, but what it looked like we cannot know.

In spite of the earthquakes and other vicissitudes that Smyrna has suffered through the centuries, the city has continued to prosper and is today at least ten times as large as it was in the apostle John's day. At that time it may have had a population of close to two hundred thousand.

Numerous interesting allusions to Smyrna's history may be discovered in John's message to the church there; his letter was wholly commendatory. Christians there suffered greatly at the hands of the Jews (Revelation 2:9–10). These Christians probably were themselves converted Jews.

The Roman agora at Smyrna, upper level.

It was Jewish Christians rather than pagan converts whom national Jews hated so violently. Ramsay suggests that the word *faithful* (Revelation 2:10) would have a special appeal to people of Smyrna because they had been known for their faithfulness to Rome over a period of three centuries.[93]

Further, Ramsay believed that the promise of a "crown of life" (Revelation 2:10) would also have had meaning for Smyrnean readers. The "crown of Smyrna" was a phrase familiar to the natives of the city, and it probably arose from the appearance of the hill Pagus topped with stately public buildings and covered on its slopes with other structures of the town.[94] The promise was that she would wear not only a mere crown of buildings and towers but a crown of life.

The Roman agora at Smyrna, lower level.

Pergamum. The third church that John addressed stood in the city of Pergamum, capital of Asia. Situated on a hill about a thousand feet high, Pergamum commanded the fertile valley of the Caicus River, in the south of the district of Mysia. The city was located about three miles north of the Caicus and about eighteen miles from the sea opposite the island of Lesbos. Pergamum communicated with the sea via the Caicus, which was navigable for small native craft. From the city a highway ran to the interior of Asia Minor almost to the border of the province of Asia. Pergamum was also located on the important north-south road that ran from Ephesus to Cyzicus on the Propontis or Sea of Marmara.

Although Pergamum was inhabited from early times (at least the eighth century B.C.), extant literature does not mention the city before Xenophon occupied it in 400–399 B.C. Its real history began in the third century B.C. under the Attalid dynasty, when it became the capital of a Hellenistic kingdom of considerable importance. Lysimachus, one of the generals of Alexander the Great, chose this fortress of considerable strength as a depository for his treasure, reputedly totaling nine thousand talents of gold, and selected Philataeros as its keeper. (Evidently by that time Pergamum was effectively walled.) At first loyal, Philataeros revolted and declared himself independent in

A Roman paved street in modern Izmir.

283 B.C. Lysimachus had other troubles and could not give full attention to this insubordination.

Philetaeros was able to transmit control over the principality to his nephew, Eumenes (263–241 B.C.), who was succeeded by his cousin Attalus I (241–197 B.C.). After a victory over the Gauls, Attalus I (Soter) assumed the title of king. Attalus advocated the interests of Rome against Philip of Macedon and in conjunction with the Rhodian fleet rendered important service to Rome. Attalus was succeeded by his son Eumenes II (197–159 B.C.) who, after the defeat of Antiochus (190), received from Rome all of western Asia Minor. Eumenes was followed by his son Attalus II (159–138) and by Attalus III (138–133), who willed his kingdom to Rome. The son of Attalus III, Aristonicus, contested the will but Rome defeated him, and the Attalid kingdom was effectively organized as the province of Asia in 129 B.C. with Pergamum as its capital.

Although Pergamum possessed the constitution of a Greek city-state under the Attalids, the king assumed wide powers of interference. The monarchs directly ruled the native population of the surrounding countryside. And as their domain expanded they controlled it increasingly in the fashion of Hellenistic kings, relying on a Greek bureaucracy and a predominantly Greek semiprofessional army. The Pergamene kings owed their power of expansion to their skillful managing of the country's natural wealth, which included silver mines, a surplus from agriculture (wheat), stock breeding, and the dependent industries of woolen textiles and parchment.[95]

Mainly the first Attalus amassed the wealth for which the dynasty became proverbial. Eumenes II was a liberal patron of the arts and sciences, and Pergamum was especially indebted to him for its embellishment. He built new city walls, decorated the great altar of Zeus with magnificent bas-reliefs, and

The Roman aqueduct at Izmir.

Plan of the Acropolis of Pergamum

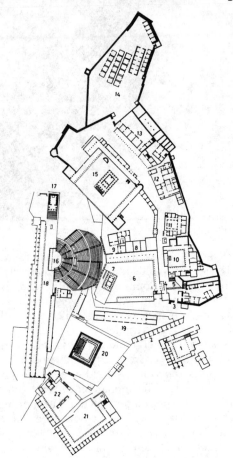

1. A building dedicated to the worship of the Pergamene kings
2. Shops built in the Hellenistic period
3. Main entrance of the Acropolis
4. Foundations of the Propylon
5. Steps leading up to the palaces
6. Sacred precinct of Athena
7. Temple of Athena
8. The library
9. A Hellenistic house complex
10. Palace of Eumenes II
11. Palace of Attalos I
12. Hellenistic houses
13. Barracks
14. Arsenals
15. Temple to Trajan
16. Theater, built in 3rd century B.C.
17. Temple of Dionysus
18. Theater terrace
19. A stoa
20. Altar of Zeus
21. Agora, built in third century B.C.
22. Temple of the agora

constructed a theater on the acropolis, as well as a temple to Athena, a palace, and a library. The library, second only to that of Alexandria, contained some two hundred thousand books and pictures in four halls just northeast of the temple of Athena, goddess of wisdom. The reading room measured about forty-five by fifty feet and had shelves for books written on parchment. A space of almost two feet separated the library shelves from the stone walls of the building, so dampness did not permeate the books. After the destruction of the Alexandria library, Antony later gave the Pergamum library to Cleopatra, and the Romans transferred it to Alexandria.

While the Attalids were not great founders of cities like the other Hellenistic kings, they made Pergamum one of the greatest and most beautiful of all Greek cities. An excellent example of Hellenistic town-planning, Pergamum was laid out in terraces on a hillside, culminating in the palaces and fortifications of the acropolis. The city was renowned for its school of sculpture.

As already noted, Pergamum was the political capital of Asia under the Romans. This fact, coupled with its prestige, its commercial activities, and its religious power, contributed to Pergamene prosperity during the early centuries of the Christian Era. A large new section of the city developed at the foot of the hill during the first and second centuries A.D. The hill on which the old city stood now became the acropolis.

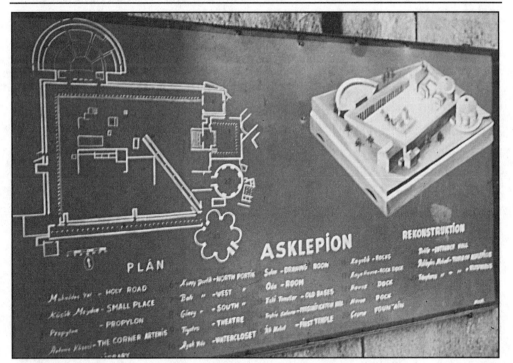

The Asklepion or health center in Pergamum. On the left is the plan and on the right the reconstruction. A theater for group events stood at the top, a round temple to the god in the center right, and a dormitory for patients in the lower right.

One of the most important structures of the lower city was the Asclepion or health resort dedicated to the god Asclepius. Dating back to Hellenistic times, it was at its height during the second century A.D. when the physician Galen practiced there and when the orator and rhetorician Aelius Aristides lectured in its theater. A therapeutic center, here the sick, who often came from great distances, underwent treatment by suggestion, sun and water baths, massage, the use of medicinal herbs, application of ointments, music, prayer, and interpretation of dreams.

At its height in the second century A.D. Pergamum boasted a population of about two hundred thousand, if we can accept Broughton's calculation.[96] Probably it was not much smaller during John's day.

Pergamum is one of the most completely excavated of ancient cities. First visiting the place in 1864, the German architect Karl Humann established his headquarters there in 1868, thus beginning an excavation that was to continue to the present. The first major triumph of the German excavators was the location of the great altar of Zeus with its remarkable sculptures, evidently built by Eumenes about 170 B.C. The rectangular foundations of the altar

e great Altar of Zeus, which German archaeologists carried to Berlin and re-assembled in the Staatliche Museum.

A head of Zeus, from the Ephesus Museum.

Humann and associates excavated at Pergamum from 1878 to 1886, uncovering the upper city. Between 1900 and 1913, W. Dörpfeld and others excavated the middle and lower districts of the acropolis. Theodor Wiegand led the dig from 1927 to 1936, working especially at the Asclepion. Erich Boehringer excavated at Pergamum from 1957 to 1972, and Wolfgang Radt is now in charge. Especially Radt directed the fifteen-year project to restore the Temple of Trajan, high on the acropolis (completed in 1995), and he has worked at the Altar of Zeus and in the residential area on the lower level of the acropolis.

The goal now is to restore at least one major structure at each extended excavation in Turkey. Here it was the Temple of Trajan. At Sardis excavators rebuilt the facade of the Roman gymnasium. And at Ephesus they rebuilt the Library of Celsus and restored the theater and the entrance gate to the Hellenistic agora.

At the foot of the acropolis stood the lower agora dating to the reign of Eumenes II, measuring 210 by 110 feet. Surrounding the paved court were Doric porticoes giving entrance to the shops. Up the hill from this agora lay a gymnasium on three terraces. The gymnasium on the lower terrace was reserved for children. The middle gymnasium was a training place for adolescent boys. The upper gymnasium was reserved for young men. It had an auditorium that could accommodate one thousand people, a temple of Asclepius, and a meeting house connected with the cult of Dionysus.

Continuing up the slope and around in the middle of it, we come to the upper agora. Like the lower one it was surrounded by Doric porticoes, and it had a temple dedicated to Zeus or Hermes. Next to this stood the great Altar of Zeus, above which in turn stood the temple of Athena, built at the very end of the fourth century B.C. and surrounded by stoas of the Doric order. Next we come to the library, which occupied four rooms. Above that on the crest of the hill rose the temple to Trajan, erected by his successor Hadrian (A.D. 117–138); both emperors were worshiped there.

Against the side of the hill adjacent to the temple of Athena lay the theater of the acrop-

measured 125 by 115 feet. The altar rested on a great horseshoe-shaped plinth thirty feet high, approached by twenty-eight sixty-foot steps on the western side. These steps led through an Ionic colonnade into a square court where the altar proper stood.

The three outer sides of the monument were sculptured with scenes of struggle between gods and giants (the former defeating the latter in a struggle symbolic of the conflict between civilization and barbarism), representing Eumenes' defeat of the Gauls. The famous frieze was eight feet high and was placed eight feet above the base of the podium. Another frieze ran around the three inner sides of the altar court on the upper level. This sculpture depicted events from the life of the legendary hero Telephus, son of Hercules, traditional founder of the city. Only the Parthenon frieze exceeds in length that of the altar of Zeus at Pergamum, which was about four hundred feet long. The altar of Zeus was carried off to Berlin and installed in a Pergamum museum there. Hidden during the Second World War, it has since been restored in the Staatliche Museum in Berlin.

The middle gymnasium on the acropolis at Pergamum, a training place for adolescent boys. *Esat Balim*

olis. This was one of the steepest and most spectacular theaters of antiquity, as anyone who has climbed this one and others can testify. Constructed around 170 B.C., the theater contains eighty rows of seats spread out at a height of 165 feet. It could seat about ten thousand. On the level of the stage of the theater, at the bottom of the hill, stretched a theater terrace some eight hundred feet long. Overlooking the Caicus Valley, it was a lovely place for strolling. It led to a Temple of Dionysus perched on a high podium.

On the east slope of the acropolis, about the level of the Altar of Zeus, is a building called the Heroon, apparently dedicated to the worship of the Pergamene kings. Above that is the main entrance to the upper acropolis. Immediately inside stood the palace of Eumenes II and next to it the palace of Attalus I. Behind and above them are remains of Hellenistic houses, probably officers' quarters. Then, at the top of the hill (behind the temple of Trajan) stood an arsenal, probably built about 200 B.C. It was well stocked with catapult balls and had a storage area that could hold enough grain for one thousand men for a year.[97]

Prior to World War II investigation for some years centered on the lower town.

Modern Bergama evidently overlay the Roman city. Its streets and alleys follow the ancient ones, as digging trenches for the modern water system has demonstrated.[98] And since 1951 archaeologists have done much work on the Asklepion, which in part has been reconstructed. This great healing center, as already mentioned, dated back to Hellenistic times and was important in John's day. But its greatest days came during the second century A.D., and some of the buildings there date from that century. Many other structures of Pergamum could be commented on, but they date long after the New Testament era closed and therefore have value for classical rather than biblical studies.

References in John's letter to Pergamum require some attention. He spoke of "Satan's throne" being in Pergamum and of Satan's dwelling there (Revelation 2:13). At least three suggestions have been made as to what John meant. Some have thought that he referred to heathen worship in general. Among the numerous deities worshiped at Pergamum were Zeus, Athena, Asclepius, Dionysus, and Demeter.

Others have thought that the imperial cult was implied. Three temples were dedicated to emperor worship at Pergamum,

It is tempting, however, to suggest that John had specifically in mind the great altar of Zeus, which was one of the wonders of the ancient world and an object of pride to Pergamene citizens.

Parenthetically, it may be useful at this point to note how emperor worship got started in the Roman Empire. Actually it began during the struggle of the Kingdom of Pergamum to standup to the Seleucids of Syria. When Antiochus III of Syria threatened Smyrna, it appealed to

The great theater of the Pergamum acropolis with seating for about 10,000.

Rome, and in the year 195 B.C. Smyrna "formally placed itself under Rome's protection by consecrating a temple to the deified *Urbs Roma* [city of Rome], a *new cult hitherto unknown either in Italy or in Greece*" [italics mine].[99] Soon other principalities followed suit. Alabanda in Caria founded a temple to the Goddess Roma and established a festival in her honor.[100] Magnesia celebrated a festival in honor of the Goddess Roma, with tragedies, comedies, and farces.[101] Pergamum and Ephesus also established temples to Roma early on.

and it would have been easy to think of Satan enthroned there instead of the true Deity. Certainly in the capital of Asia, the state religion would have been more thoroughly promoted than elsewhere. The fact that the martyrdom of Antipas is mentioned in the same verse as "Satan's throne" may give some support to this view. If John was sent to Patmos for refusing to worship the emperor, he may well have chosen such vicious language for a place where the emperor was worshiped.

At this point we need to ask why the cities of Asia could declare for the Goddess Roma as the personification of the Roman state and then accept the divinity of Roman emperors. The answer lies in what was happening in the Kingdom of Pergamum. Just before 200 B.C. Attalus I of Pergamum had been honored with annual sacrifices at Sicyon and a great statue of him was placed beside Apollo's in the agora there. At the same time a priesthood of Attalus was established in Athens. Then shortly after 188 regular deification of the Pergamene kings took place at their death, and at Pergamum they established the worship of the living king.[102]

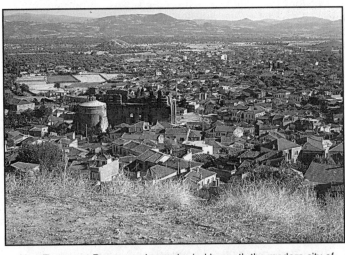

New Testament Pergamum is now buried beneath the modern city of Bergama. The large building in the center of the picture, the Red Basilica, was erected early in the second century A.D. as a pagan temple and later converted to a church, dedicated to John the apostle.

In this context Pergamenes easily switched their allegiance and deified the Roman state. What began there spread elsewhere in the eastern Mediterranean and in Rome itself. Then it was a short step from worshiping the personification or spirit of the Roman state to worshiping her rulers. The cult of Augustus and other emperors spread rapidly, beginning with the establishment of the empire. In 29 B.C. Augustus permitted the inhabitants of Asia and Bithynia to set up sanctuaries in their leading cities, dedicated to the cult of Roma and of Julius Caesar. There resident Roman citizens could worship. At the same time he let the Greeks of Asia set up a worship center for himself at Pergamum.[103] Romans were not yet ready to worship the living emperor, but Greeks of the east were prepared to do so.

Remains of an early church at Thyatira.

John referred to two errors that had crept into the church at Pergamum: the doctrine of Balaam and the doctrine of the Nicolaitans. The former apparently had to do with Christians marrying pagans and thus defiling their separation to God (Numbers 31:15–16; 22:5; 23:8). The latter held that heathen ceremonies meant nothing since pagan deities did not exist anyway and that Christians were therefore at liberty to join in idolatrous feasts in order to maintain their social position and to justify their loyalty in the sight of the law.

Thyatira. Twenty-five miles east of Pergamum up the valley of the Caicus River in ancient times, lay the town of Germa. Nearby the road turned southeast and ran down a long valley that connected the Caicus and the Hermus valleys. Down this main valley flowed a stream that poured its waters into the Hermus River. Thyatira stood on the east bank of this stream (about twenty miles from Germa and forty-five miles from Pergamum) in a fertile plain about 330 feet in altitude. Its citadel or acropolis was built on very slightly rising ground. Since its location was not strong, it was never a fortress—only a military post.

Thyatira's location on a main road meant that it would always be an important trading center. So while it was destroyed several times, it was destined always to be rebuilt. During Roman times, Thyatira was a great trading city, its height of prosperity coming about the end of the first century A.D.

In connection with this commercial activity, there is evidence of more trade guilds there than in any other Asian city. Included among them were wool workers, linen workers, tailors, dyers, leatherworkers, tanners, and bronzesmiths. Lydia, a seller of purple from Thyatira, probably represented her guild at Philippi (Acts 16:14). And the purple that she sold was probably made in the region of Thyatira, which produced the well-known "turkey-red." This came from the madder root, which grows in abundance around Thyatira. The bronze work of the city was also very excellent.

In addition to its commercial importance, Thyatira was also a station on the imperial post road from Brundisium and Dyrrhachium across Macedonia to Thessalonica, Neapolis (port of Philippi), Troas, Adramyttium, Pergamum, Philadelphia, and then across Asia Minor to Tarsus, Syrian Antioch, Caesarea in Palestine, and Alexandria in Egypt.

Old Lydian in origin, Thyatira was refounded by Seleucus Nicator who reportedly named it "Thygatira" or "Thyatira" on being informed that a daughter (Greek, *thygater*) had been born to him. Earlier it had been called "Pelopia," "Euhippa," and "Semiramis." At first a Seleucid outpost against Macedonia, Thyatira became a Pergamene outpost after the defeat of Antiochus at Magnesia in 190 B.C. When the Pergamene kingdom became the Roman province of Asia in 133 B.C., Thyatira passed directly under control of Rome. As already noted, the city enjoyed a considerable amount of prosperity when John addressed the church there.

The apostle condemned "that woman Jezebel" (Revelation 2:20), which some have interpreted to be a literal prophetess living in Thyatira at the end of the first century A.D. But it seems best to treat the name symbolically to refer to the teaching of a lax attitude toward pagan customs and practices and conformity to the pagan social milieu of the day. Pursuit of a trade was almost impossible without belonging to a guild, and no doubt the trade guilds of the city had their patron deities which all members were expected to honor. Christian members of the trade guilds had real problems socially, for when they attended banquets of their associations they were often involved in eating meat that had been offered to idols. And no doubt immorality accompanied some of the Bacchanalian feasts (cf. Revelation 2:20). All phases of contemporary society—music, sports, politics—were so linked to pagan ritual that accommodation to paganism was very tempting to those who wished to remain completely acceptable members of society. But Christianity would have disappeared if it had not stood out in opposition to the popular beliefs and customs of the day.

Christianity must have come to Thyatira early, perhaps from Ephesus. Probably the new faith spread first among the Jews of the community. Seleucus I, founder of the city is known to have shown special favor to Jews and to have made them citizens of cities he founded in Asia; he was likely responsible for bringing Jews to Thyatira. The new faith prospered there. The city sent its Bishop Sozon to the first ecumenical council at Nicea in A.D. 325 and its Bishop

Fuscus to the third ecumenical council at Ephesus in 431.

We know little about the city in ancient or medieval times. At least a couple of dozen inscriptions have come to light in recent years and shed some light on social life of the early Christian centuries. Most of these are housed in the museum in nearby Manisa. Coins supplement these inscriptions. A small excavation in the center of town has uncovered a section of the second century A.D. Roman road and part of a stoa and a sixth century A.D. (Justinian) basilica which was probably a church but may have been an administrative building. Almost no ruins are obvious in the vicinity. The modern town of Akhisar (population over 150,000) which occupies the site makes exploration or excavation there difficult.

Sardis. Sardis is not as much of a historical blank as her northern neighbor. She was more important during several periods of history, and excavation there is gradually expanding our knowledge of the ancient city. Sardis dominated the region of the Hermus River (modern Gediz) and its tributaries, the broadest and most fertile of all the river basins of Asia Minor. She commanded the great trade and military road from the Aegean islands and Ephesus, Smyrna, and Pergamum into the interior of the peninsula.

To the south of the Hermus River rises the Tmolus Range (modern Boz Dag, 6,200 feet), which extends like an arm from the Anatolian Plateau. From the Tmolus stretches a series of hills that form a transition to the valley below. On one of these hills, over a thousand feet above the Hermus and about five miles south of the river, stood early Sardis. Like the other hills of the region, this site forms a small elongated plateau with steep sides and is connected by a narrow ridge with the northern foothills of the Tmolus. In fact, the hill on which Sardis perched had almost perpendicular sides except on the south. Even this approach is none too easy, and the city was virtually impregnable.[104]

As Sardis grew it spread out along the western slopes to the Pactolus River (which flows north into the Hermus), and the hill on which the first city was built became the acropolis. Later Sardis expanded northward into the valley of the Hermus, where ruins of great structures of the Roman period now stand.

Greek legend has it that the fabulous wealth of the Lydians of Sardis came from the gold-bearing sands of the Pactolus River. While some have cast doubt on the gold-producing nature of the river in ancient times, it is quite certain that King Croesus and others found wealth in this way. But all of Lydian wealth did not come in the form of bullion washed down by the river. Sardis stood in a fertile and carefully cultivated area and benefited immensely from her position on the trade and communication routes. Lydian artisans were also highly skilled.

Excavations have shown continuous occupation of the region of Sardis from at least 3000 B.C. Mycenean Greeks founded a dynasty there around 1200 B.C. and the Lydian king Gyges took the place from them around 680 B.C. The city first achieved greatness as the capital of the Lydian Kingdom. With the demise of the Phrygian Kingdom near the beginning of the seventh century B.C., the Lydians conquered Phrygian territory and the Greek cities of Ionia except Miletus. Ultimately they came to rule all of Asia Minor west of the Halys River. The Lydian Kingdom reached her height during the first half of the sixth century B.C. but came to an end with the death of Croesus and the military successes of Cyrus the Persian in 547/546. The population is reported to have been fifty thousand at the time.

Sardis then became the chief town of a Persian satrapy (equivalent to a province) and the western terminus of the great Royal Road, that extended for some sixteen hundred miles from Susa to Sardis. As such it was a prime object of Greek attack during the Ionian revolt. In 499 B.C. the Greeks marched up the Cayster Valley, delivered a surprise attack on Sardis, burned the buildings of the city to the ground, and destroyed the famous temple of the Lydian goddess Cybele.

Quickly rebuilt, Sardis served as headquarters for Xerxes during the winter before his campaign against Greece (481 B.C.). Almost a century later Cyrus the Younger assembled forces there for the revolt against his brother Artaxerxes (401 B.C.). Sardis was an important city when it surrendered to Alexander the Great in 334 B.C. When Alexander died, a struggle ensued among his generals for control of his empire. For a while Antigonus controlled Sardis, then the Seleucids took over and ruled there until 190 B.C. Rome bestowed the city on the king of Pergamum after defeating Antiochus in that year. When the Pergamene kingdom became the province of Asia in 133 B.C. Sardis came under direct control of Rome.

After the terrible earthquake of A.D. 17, the emperor Tiberius rebuilt the city and the Senate remitted the city's taxes for five years. The grateful inhabitants erected a temple to Tiberius. Shortly thereafter Rome made a *conventus juridicus* with Sardis, by which the city became one of the centers of the Roman judicial administration in Asia. Although Sardis never regained the political power it had had in the days of the Lydian kings, the city enjoyed great prosperity during the second and third centuries A.D. It continued to be a wealthy city down to the end of the Byzantine Empire. The Turks took possession in the eleventh century A.D., and in 1402 Tamerlane thoroughly destroyed it, never to be rebuilt.

In an effort to recover a picture of life at ancient Sardis, two major archaeological campaigns have been launched there. In 1910, Howard Crosby Butler of Princeton began to work there on behalf of the American Society for the Excavation of Sardis. His efforts were chiefly centered on the great Temple of Artemis to the west of the acropolis, and he opened more than a thousand graves in the so-called "Cemetery Hill" along the west bank of the Pactolus. World War I halted this dig.

In 1957 the Fogg Art Museum of Harvard, Cornell University, and the American Schools of Oriental Research began a joint excavation at Sardis, made possible in part by a grant from the Bollingen Foundation. George M. A. Hanfmann of Harvard directed the project for many years. In recent years C. H.

The temple of Artemis at Sardis, with a Byzantine chapel built into it on the left, symbolizing the victory of Christianity there

Greenewalt Jr. of the University of California, Berkeley, has conducted excavations there. Periodic reports on progress at the site appear in the *Bulletin* of the American Schools of Oriental Research and the annual survey of "Archaeology in Asia Minor" in the *American Journal of Archaeology.* This expedition has worked at numerous locations in the area—the Temple of Artemis, the necropolis, the acropolis, along the Pactolus, and on Roman and Byzantine ruins in the plain north of the acropolis.

The great Temple of Artemis (that is, the Asiatic Artemis, the mother goddess) was perhaps the most imposing structure of

Sardis in John's day. Located to the west of the acropolis, it measured 160 by 300 feet and covered some five thousand square yards. Though begun in the days of Alexander the Great, it was never finished. Most of its sixty-foot Ionic columns (once seventy-eight in all) are unfluted. Some of the columns rest on rough pedestals; no doubt these were intended to be carved like those of Ephesus. The temple had twenty columns on each of the long sides and eight columns at each of the ends. The cella or main cult chamber on the east end was divided by two rows of six columns. At the west end lay the treasure chamber. The capitals show a variety of form; some of the columns have richly decorated bases. Beneath the cella archaeologists discovered the foundations of the temple that Croesus had built in the sixth century B.C. Symbolic of the victory of Christianity in the city, a Byzantine chapel of the fourth century A.D. stands wedged into the southeast corner of the temple.

On the acropolis most of the structural remains date from the Byzantine period. But there is a castle from the Lydian period, a tower of the Hellenistic age, some parts of

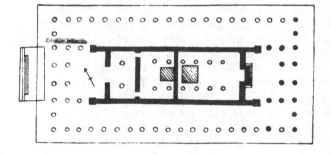

Plan of the temple of Artemis at Sardis

the wall of the Persian period, and a central platform of the Seleucid era.

On the north slope of the acropolis stood a theater with a seating capacity of twenty thousand, erected in the third century B.C. and remodeled in Roman times. The eastern end of a stadium extended west from the stage area of the theater.

Many seasons of excavation along the modern road running through Sardis have produced significant results. North of the road there is a large synagogue dating to the first half of the third century A.D. and now partially restored; a gymnasium with an exercise area, the façade now restored; numerous Byzantine shops; and a late Roman suburb, dating to the fourth to the seventh centuries A.D. East of this large excavated area stand remains of a Byzantine church and Roman and Byzantine baths. South of the modern road opposite the synagogue lie remains of a building called the House of Bronzes because of the large number of bronze works found there (dating to c. A.D. 550). Southwest of the House of Bronzes is the Lydian Trench with remains of the Lydian marketplace and of the Lydian walls of ancient Sardis, dating to the days of the Persian conquest in the sixth century B.C.

Then, along the Pactolus River can be seen remains of Roman and Byzantine houses, a Byzantine church, and Croesus' gold refinery. Between that excavation area and the acropolis stands a stepped structure, a sort of pyramid, which may be the tomb of Abradates, a noble of Susa who died fighting for the Persians.

Excavation at Sardis continues annually with almost annual surprises, but it is clear from what I have reported that we do not yet have any idea of the plan of the city of John's day. And about the only structures known to John's readers of the Revelation would have been the Temple of Artemis, the theater, and the stadium.

Philadelphia. From the Hermus Valley and Sardis a long valley runs up southeast into the flank of the central plateau. Down this

Restored facade of the Roman gymnasium at Sardis.

valley runs the river Cogamus to join the Hermus. And up the valley runs a road, the best means of making the ascent from the Hermus Valley (five hundred feet in altitude) to the main plateau (c. three thousand feet in this area). This was the route by which trade and communication were maintained between Smyrna and northwest Asia Minor and Phrygia and the east. Furthermore, the imperial post road of the first century A.D.—which came from Rome via Troas, Adramyttium (modern Edremit), Pergamum, and Sardis— passed through this valley (and Philadelphia) on its way to the east.

In the Cogamus Valley, some twenty-six miles from Sardis (c. one hundred miles from Smyrna) by Roman road stood Philadelphia. The city was located at around eight hundred feet in altitude on a broad hill that slopes up gently from the valley toward the Tmolus Mountains. The hill is not far south of the Cogamus River and is separated from the Tmolus mass so that it could be made a very strong fortress. The strength of its fortifications was to be proved in several terrible sieges by Muslim forces in later centuries. Northeast of the city lay a great vine-growing district, which contributed substantially to its prosperity.

Its history reached back into the first half of the first millennium B.C., when it was the Lydian town of Callatebus. Cyrus the Great of Persia took control of the place during his advance on Sardis in 547 B.C. and his conquest of the Lydian kingdom.

A section of the Byzantine wall of Philadelphia.

To assist Philadelphia in its plight, the emperor Tiberius gave a large donation for its reconstruction. In gratitude the city voluntarily changed its name to Neocaisarea ("New Caesar"). But later in the century during the reign of Vespasian (A.D. 69–79), it took the name of Flavia, a name that continued to be used along with Philadelphia during the second and third centuries A.D.

During those same centuries Philadelphia continued to increase in prosperity and under Caracalla (A.D. 211–17) was awarded the title Neokoros, or "Temple Warden." This means that it had a provincial temple of the imperial cult at the time. During the Byzantine period the prosperity and importance of Philadelphia increased even more until Islamic attacks destroyed the city.

Subsequently it served as a station on the Persian Royal Road. But the real establishment of the city dates from the Pergamene period. As the kingdom of Pergamum sought to improve its position, it settled a colony of Macedonians on the site during the days of Attalus II Philadelphus (159–138 B.C.), and the new foundation took the name Philadelphia in honor of the king (called Philadelphus—"brother lover"— because of his loyalty to his brother). Ramsay concluded that Philadelphia was established to become a center for consolidating and educating the central regions of the Pergamene Kingdom—a center for the spread of Greco-Asiatic civilization. The city was a successful teacher and was in part responsible for the fact that Lydian ceased to be spoken in Lydia by A.D. 19, and Greek took over.[105]

The same severe earthquake that destroyed Sardis and ten other cities of the western part of Asia Minor in A.D. 17 also destroyed Philadelphia. The earthquake was more demoralizing at Philadelphia than at the other cities hit then because tremors continued over an extended period of time. These shocks produced such a state of panic that many were afraid to return to buildings in the city and lived outside in tents.

The modern Turkish city of Alasehir, with its population of over thirty-seven thousand, reflects almost nothing of its earlier heritage. Of the formidable bastions that stood so long against Turkish attacks, a stretch of some three-fourths of a mile of Byzantine wall remains in a broken condition on the northern and lower side of the city. In the eastern part of town are ruins of the Basilica of St. John (probably the cathedral of Philadelphia) with some poorly-preserved eleventh century frescoes. A second

Ruins of the Basilica of St. John at Philadelphia.

century A.D. city gate still stands. Dr. Recip Meriç began to excavate the theater in 1988, but without extensive excavation of the site it is impossible to view the city as the apostle John knew it.

Commentators have viewed several items in the Revelation passage addressed to Philadelphia as having special significance to residents of the city. The divine challenge was "I have set before you an open door" (Revelation 3:8). Thus came a divine mission to a city that had been a missionary city from the beginning. For some 250 years it had been preaching a gospel of Hellenism and Greek culture to the surrounding area. Now it was encouraged to preach the gospel of Jesus Christ to that same region.

The church there had "a little strength" (Revelation 3:8). Though other suggestions have been made, probably the reference has to do with the church itself, which seems to have been small and struggling and to have remained so for a long time. Philadelphia came to be known as Little Athens because of the considerable attention there to the worship of pagan deities.

God through the apostle also promised these Christians a new name: "I will write upon him the name of My God" (Revelation 3:12). The city had been renamed twice during the first century A.D., and in both instances the imperial cult must have been established. At least this was true in the days of Tiberius. Now a truly divine name was to be bestowed upon all believers in the true God. The promise to keep these believers from the "hour of trial" would, according to some commentators, have had a special appeal to those who lived on the edge of an earthquake belt and stood in dread of terrible suffering at the hands of the forces of nature.

The Isle of Patmos. According to Revelation 1:9 the apostle John received his Revelation on the Isle of Patmos. Whether he wrote the book there or at Ephesus after his release from exile is a matter of conjecture. Tradition has it (Irenaeus, Eusebius, Jerome, and others) that the apostle was exiled there during the fourteenth year of Domitian's reign (A.D. 95) and released during the reign of Nerva (A.D. 96) about eighteen months later.

A map of the Isle of Patmos.

Patmos is one of the Sporades Islands about twenty-eight miles south-southwest of the island of Samos and about the same distance from the coast of Asia Minor. Its length is about eight miles, its greatest width six miles, and it covers an area of approximately twenty-two square miles. The island has been described as a horse's head and neck with the nose pointing eastward, or as similar to a crescent with the horns facing eastward. The harbor of Patmos, which opens eastward, divides the island into two almost equal parts which are connected by a narrow isthmus. The ancient town was at the north of this isthmus; the modern town stands at its southern end. Today the southern half of the island belongs to the monks, and the northern part to the civil community. About a half mile up the hill from the modern town is a cave where John is supposed to have received his visions. About a mile farther is the Monastery of St. John, built in the eleventh century A.D.

The soil of Patmos is volcanic and barren. Red and gray rocks, which frequently break into quaint pinnacles, flank the Patmos coasts. The interior consists of three main masses of volcanic hills, the highest

The Cave of the Apocalypse, where tradition says the Apostle John received the visions recorded in the Revelation.

ror the blue of the heavens, they furnished a not unworthy symbol of "the sea of glass, like unto crystal, which was before the throne." Again he stood upon the cliff, his white hair streaming in the wind, and saw the clouds rolling up on the horizon, the flashes from which lighted up at once the dark heavens above and the angry sea below, and these were images to him of judgments that were coming on earth. And when he speaks of One "whose voice was as the sound of many waters," the very expression is an echo of the deep.[106]

point of which is about nine hundred feet. Patmos depends on a few wells and numerous cisterns for its water supply, which is roughly sufficient.

If John had the freedom of the island, which is likely, he could have seen wonderful panoramas from its heights. The greater part of the irregular island would have lain at his feet. Away to the north would have appeared the peaks of the island of Samos and the promontory of Mycale, and to the south the island of Leros. To the southwest in the open expanse of the Aegean he could have seen Amorgas Island and the distant volcano of Santorini. To the northwest lay Icaria (modern Ikaria) and numerous other islands clustered on the horizon.

There are frequent suggestions concerning the influence of John's surroundings on him as he composed the Revelation (and he probably wrote at least part of it on Patmos). Henry M. Field comments:

And is it too much to say that the Book of Revelation is a different book, written on an island, on the seashore, from what it would have been if written, like the Book of Job, amid Arabian deserts? All its imagery is of the sea. As the Apostle walked along the shore of Patmos when the waters were still reflected as in a mir-

The earliest inhabitants of Patmos seem to have been Dorians. These were probably followed by Ionian immigrants. In the Roman period the island was one of the many places of exile for political prisoners. On the height occupied by the ancient city may be seen the remains of ancient fortifications and walls on both its southern and northern sides. But no one has cared much about the nature of Patmos in classical times; the island is chiefly noted for its ecclesiastical significance.

According to Revelation 1:19 the Voice John heard on Patmos commanded, "Write therefore, what you have seen, what is now and what will take place later" (NIV). While John devoted much of his book to "what will take place later," he had abundant time while on Patmos to think about the past, about his days spent with the Master, about early apostolic efforts at church establishment, and about the present with the church attacked by heresy within and persecuted by civil authorities without.

No doubt he had a sense of satisfaction as he looked back on achievement. No doubt he also had grave apprehensions about the future of the church. He saw numerous danger signs in the churches of Asia and scored them in his letters to the seven churches (Revelation 2–3).

As for Asia Minor itself, it was destined to become home to the Christian Roman Empire (the Byzantine Empire) when Constantine established his New Rome, or Constantinople, on the banks of the Bosphorus (fourth century A.D.). For centuries the peninsula served as the power base of the Byzantine Empire. And near Constantinople at great ecumenical or churchwide councils church leaders hammered out the orthodox creeds of the church that still stand as basic doctrine for all of Christendom.

Later when the Muslims conquered the peninsula (eleventh century A.D.) it became the power base of the Ottoman Turks, who eventually snuffed out almost all vestiges of the Christianity that had once prospered there.

NOTES

1. See Lawrence E. Joseph, *Gaia.*

2. J. M. Cook, *The Persian Empire* (New York: Schocken Books, 1983), 115–117.

3. Seton Lloyd, *Early Anatolia* (Harmondsworth, England: Penguin Books, 1956), 52.

4. H. W. F. Saggs, *Civilization Before Greece and Rome* (New Haven: Yale University Press, 1989), 197.

5. J. Mellaart, *Anatolia c. 4000–2300 B.C.* (Cambridge: Cambridge University Press, 1962), 45. The conventional date for the beginning of the Bronze Age in Asia Minor is 3000 B.C. or a little later.

6. Ibid. 10.

7. Ibid.

8. Ibid., 24.

9. Ibid., 26.

10. Ibid., 46.

11. Ibid., 47–50.

12. Lloyd, *Early Anatolia*, 67.

13. Mellaart, *Anatolia*,50.

14. Trevor Bryce, *The Kingdom of the Hittites* (Oxford: Clarendon Press, 1998), 21.

15. Lloyd, *Early Anatolia*, 117.

16. O. R. Gurney, *The Hittites*, rev. ed (Harmondsworth, England: Penguin, 1961), 21.

16a. Itamar Singer, "New Evidence on the End of the Hittite Empire," *The Sea Peoples and Their World*, edited by Eliezer D. Oren (Philadelphia: University Museum, 2000), 27–28.

17. See *Bulletin of the American Schools of Oriental Research* #89 (1968), 28f.

18. Carl Blegen, *Troy* (Cambridge: Cambridge University Press, 1961), 6.

19. Blegen, 14.

20. Ibid.

21. Ibid.

22. Bryce, *Hittites*, 396.

23. Michael Wood, *In Search of the Trojan War* (London: British Broadcasting Corporation, 1985), 248–49.

24. Wood, 249.

25. Ibid.

26. Bryce, *Hittites*, 398–99.

27. Wood, *Trojan War*, 249.

28. David Magie, *Roman Rule in Asia Minor* (Princeton: Princeton University Press, 1950), I, 199.

29. T. R. S. Broughton, "Roman Asia," *An Economic Survey of Ancient Rome*, ed. Tenney Frank (Baltimore: Johns Hopkins Press, 1938), IV, 516, 529.

30. A chiliarch was an officer in charge of a thousand men, one sixth of a legion at full strength. In actuality, numerical strength of the legion during the first century A.D. stood at about five thousand.

31. William M. Ramsay, *The Cities of St. Paul* (Grand Rapids: Baker Book House reprint, 1979), 100.

32. A. H. M. Jones, *The Cities of the Eastern Roman Provinces* (Oxford: At the Clarendon Press, 1937), 202.

33. Ramsay, *The Cities of St. Paul*, 97.

34. Xenophon, *Anabasis*, Book I, Chap. ii, Section 21ff., 79ff.

35. Ramsay, *The Cities of St. Paul*, 165.

36. Ibid., 174–80. A tribe in a Hellenic or Hellenistic city was commonly a political rather than an ethnic entity. In classical Athens there were ten tribes.

37. Ibid., 176.

38. William M. Ramsay, *The Church in the Roman Empire Before A.D. 170* (Grand Rapids: Baker Book House reprint, 1979), 26.

39. Stephen Mitchell, *Anatolia* (Oxford: Clarendon Press, 1993), I, 151, 154, 157; II, 6–7.

40. Magie, *Roman Rule*, I, 457.

41. Broughton, "Roman Asia," IV, 643.

42. Josephus, *Antiquities of the Jews*, XII.iii.

43. David M. Robinson, "A Preliminary Report on the Excavations at Pisidian Antioch and at Sizma," *American Journal of Archaeology*, XXVIII (October 1924), 435–44.

44. For a discussion of the site see Margaret M. Hardie, "The Shrine of Men Askaenos at Pisidian Antioch," *Journal of Hellenic Studies*, XXIII (1912), 111–50; Broughton, "Roman Asia," 788; Mitchell, II, 24.

45. Ramsay, *Cities of St. Paul*, 285–87.

46. See William M. Ramsay, *The Bearing of Recent Discovery on the Trustworthiness of the New Testament* (Grand Rapids: Baker Book House reprint, 1979), 150–72; Camden M. Cobern, *The New Archaeological Discoveries* 9th ed.; (New York: Funk & Wagnalls, 1929), pp. 538–40; Egbert C. Hudson, "The Principal Family at Pisidian Antioch," *Journal of Near Eastern Studies*, XV (April 1956), 103–7.

47. See Ramsay, *Church in the Roman Empire*, 27–36, for a discussion of the route. The distance he gives is by road over actual terrain, rather than sixty miles in a direct line, as most books give it.

48. Ramsay, *Cities of St. Paul*, 340.

49. H. V. Morton, *In the Steps of Paul* (New York: Dodd, Mead & Co., 1936), 214.

50. Ramsay, *Bearing of Recent Discovery*, 58.

51. Ramsay, *The Church in the Roman Empire*, 69.

52. Jack Finegan, *Light from the Ancient Past* 2nd ed.; (Princeton: Princeton University Press, 1959), 343.

53. Reported on by Prof. Bastiaan Van Elderen at the Wheaton College (IL) Archaeology Conference, October 15, 1962. Van Elderen received permission from Turkish officials to publish the inscription. See also Van Elderen's article, "Derbe," in *International Standard Bible Encyclopedia* (Grand Rapids: Eerdmans, 1979) 1, 924–25.

54. See Mitchell, *Anatolia*, I, 32, 78, 85.

55. William M. Ramsay, *St. Paul the Traveler and the Roman Citizen* (Grand Rapids: Baker Book House reprint, 1979), 120.

56. A. Souter, "Galatia," *Dictionary of the Bible*, ed. James Hastings, rev. ed. F. C. Grand and H. G. Rowley (New York: Charles Scribner's Sons, 1963), 311; Ramsay, *The Church in the Roman Empire*, 75–89.

57. Ramsay, *Church in the Roman Empire*, 77.

58. *Ibid.*; Henry C. Thiessen, *Introduction to the New Testament* (Grand Rapids: Eerdmans, 1943), pp. 214–16; Donald Guthrie, *New Testament Introduction*, 4th ed. (Downers Grove, IL: Intervarsity Press, 1990), 465–72.

59. Ramsay, *St. Paul the Traveler and the Roman Citizen*, 94.

60. Broughton, "Roman Asia," 816.

61. Paul MacKendrick, *The Greek Stones Speak*, 2nd ed. (New York: Norton, 1981), 466.

62. Merrill M. Parvis, "Archaeology and St. Paul's Journeys in Greek Lands, Part IV—Ephesus," *The Biblical Archaeologist*, VIII (September 1945), 62–63.

63. MacKendrick, *Greek Stones*, 351, notes that this correction in chronology was not made until 1951.

64. Josephus, *Antiquities of the Jews*, XII.iii.2; XIV.x.25.

65. Floyd V. Wilson, "Ephesus and the New Testament" *The Biblical Archaeologist*, VIII (September 1945), 78.

66. Ibid., 79.

67. *Cobern, Discoveries*, 482.

68. Ramsay, *Church in the Roman Empire*, 134.

69. He spent three months in Achaia (Achaea) after leaving Ephesus and probably spent a similar amount of time traveling elsewhere. His aim was to reach Jerusalem by Pentecost of the next spring (Acts 20:16).

70. F. H. Marshall, *Discovery in Greek Lands*, (Cambridge: Cambridge University Press, 1920), 84–85.

71. Broughton, "Roman Asia," 813.

72. MacKendrick, *Greek Stones*, 422–24.

73. The Colossus of Rhodes seems somewhat puny compared with the Statue of Liberty, which is 151 feet high and which with its pedestal stands to a height of 305 feet.

74. Shakespeare notwithstanding, there seems to be no basis for concluding that the statue's legs straddled the harbor entrance. In such a case the straddle of the legs would have had to be 400 yards. No doubt it stood on a stone base with the legs together.

75. William M. Ramsay, *The Historical Geography of Asia Minor* (New York: Cooper Square, reprint 1972), 164. Ramsay did a remarkable job of evaluating the ancient sources on Roman roads and distances between towns. His computations for the biblical sites of the province of Asia may be found on pages 164–68 of the above book.

76. This road, extending from Ephesus to Magnesia, Tralleis, Antioch, Laodicea, and Apamea, a distance of about 158 miles, was built by Manius Aquilius, c. 130 B.C. Ramsay, *Historical Geography*, 164.

77. William M. Ramsay, *The Letters to the Seven Churches of Asia* (Grand Rapids: Baker Book House reprint, 1979), 417.

78. Ibid., 422–23.

79. Ramsay notes the evaluation of a tax document for 62 B.C., which seems to give evidence of 7,500 adult Jewish freemen in the district in that year. To this figure must be added women and children. Ibid., 420.

80. For a discussion of this position see John Ruthefurd, "Laodiceans, Epistle to the," *International Standard Bible Encyclopedia*, III, 1837–39, 1943 edition.

81. Eusebius, *Ecclesiastical History*, III,31.3.

82. Ramsay, *Letters to the Seven Churches*, 421.

83. Ibid., 183.

84. Theodor Mommsen, *The History of Rome: The Provinces from Caesar to Diocletian Part I*, trans. William P. Dickson (New York: Charles Scribner's Sons, 1906), 355.

85. J. Keil, *Cambridge Ancient History* (Cambridge: Cambridge University Press, 1936), XI, 583.

86. Broughton, "Roman Asia," IV, 815.

87. Jones, *Cities of the Eastern Roman Provinces*, 95.

88. Ramsay, *The Letters to the Seven Churches*, 178, 181–83.

89. For rates of speed on Roman roads, see William M. Ramsay, "Roads and Travel in the New Testament," in James Hastings, ed., *A Dictionary of the Bible, Supplement* (Peabody, MA: Hendrickson Publishers, reprint 1988), 375–402.

91. Duyuran, *Ancient Cities of Western Anatolia*, 74.

92. Broughton, "Roman Asia," 816.

93. Ramsay, *The Letters to the Seven Churches*, 275.

94. Ibid., 256, 275.

95. Parchment, made from sheepskin or goatskin, gets its name from Pergamum (through the Latin *Pergamenus*, "of or belonging to Pergamum") and was allegedly invented by Eumenes II, founder of the library.

96. Broughton, "Roman Asia," 813.

97. MacKendrick, *Greek Stones*, 396.

98. Ibid., 397.

99. David Magie, *Roman Rule in Asia Minor* (Salem, NH: Ayer Co., reprint 1988), I, 106.

100. Ibid., I, 106.

101. Ibid., I, 167.

102. R. E. Allen, *The Attalid Kingdom* (Oxford: Clarendon Press, 1983), 147–152.

103. Stephen Mitchell, *Anatolia* (Oxford: Clarendon Press, 1993), I, 100.

104. The modern visitor to the acropolis at Sardis finds it hard to visualize what this site was like in the days of the Lydian kings because constant erosion has worn away the plateau at the top so that comparatively little now remains of the upper plateau on which the city stood.

105. Ramsay, *The Letters to the Seven Churches*, 391–92.

106. *The Greek Islands and Turkey After the War* (New York: Charles Scribner's Sons, 1885), 42.

BIBLIOGRPAHY

Akurgal, Ekrem. *Ancient Civilizations and Ruins of Turkey*. 7th ed. Istanbul: Net Turistik Yayinlar, 1990.

Alexander, Robert L. *The Sculpture and Sculptors of Yazilikaya*. Newark, DE: University of Delaware Press, 1986.

Allen, R. E. *The Attalid Kingdom*. Oxford: Clarendon Press, 1983.

Bean, George E. *Aegean Turkey*. New York: Frederick A. Praeger, 1966.

Bean, George E. *Lycian Turkey*. London: John Murray, 1989.

Bean, George E. *Turkey's Southern Shore*. New York: Frederick A. Praeger, 1968.

Bittel, Kurt. *Hattusha: The Capital of the Hittites*. New Nork: Oxford University Press, 1970.

Blake, Everett, and Anna G. Edmonds. *Biblical Sites in Turkey*. Istanbul: Redhouse Press, 1970.

Blegen, Carl W. *Troy*. Cambridge: Cambridge University Press, 1961.

Boardman, John, and others, eds. *Oxford History of the Classical World*. Oxford: Oxford University Press, 1986.

Broughton, T. R. S. "Roman Asia," *An Economic Survey of Ancient Rome*, Ed. Tenney Frank. Baltimore: Johns Hopkins Press, IV, 1938.

Butler, Howard Crosby. *Sardis*. Leyden: E. J. Brill. Vol. I, 1922; Vol. II, 1925.

Bryce, Trevor. *The Kingdom of the Hittites*. Oxford: Clarendon Press, 1998.

Cadoux, Cecil J. *Ancient Smyrna*. Oxford: B. Blackwell, 1938.

Canby, Jeanny V., ed. *Ancient Anatolia*. Madison: University of Wisconsin Press, 1986.

Cary, M. *The Geographic Background of Greek & Roman History*. Oxford: Clarendon Press, 1949.

Cook, J. M. *Greek Settlements in the Eastern Aegean and Asia Minor*. Cambridge: Cambridge University Press, 1961.

Cunliffe, Barry. *The Ancient Celts*. Oxford: Oxford University Press, 1997.

Darke, Diana. *Guide to Aegean and Mediterranean Turkey*. 3rd ed. London: Michael Haag, 1989.

Dreyfus. Renee, and Ellen Schraudolph. *Pergamon: The Telephos Frieze from the Great Alter*. 2 vols. San Francisco: The Fine Arts Museums, 1996.

Dunham, Adelaide G. *The History of Miletus*. London: University of London Press, 1915.

Duyuran, Rustem. *The Ancient Cities of Western Anatolia*. Istanbul: Turkish Press, n.d.

Erdemgil, Selahattin. *Ephesus*. Istanbul: Turistik Yayinlar, 1992.

Filson, Floyd V. "Ephesus and the New Testament," *Biblical Archaeologist*, VIII (Sept. 1945), 73–80.

Finegan, Jack. *Light from the Ancient Past*. 2nd ed. Princeton: Princeton University Press, 1959.

Freely, John, *The Western Shores of Turkey*. London: John Murray, 1988.

Gardner, Ernest A. *Greece and the Aegean*. London: George G. Harap, 1933.

Goetze, Albrecht. "Hittite and Anatolian Studies," *The Bible and the Ancient Near East*. Ed. G. Ernest Wright. Garden City: Doubleday, 1961.

Goodspeed, Edgar J. *Paul*. Philadelphia: The John Winston, 1947.

Gurney, O. R. *Anatolia c. 1750–1600 B.C.* Cambridge: Cambridge University Press, 1962.

Gurney, O. R. *The Hittites*. 4th ed. London: Penguin Books, 1990.

Hanfmann, George M. A. *Sardis from Prehistoric to Roman Times*. Cambridge: Harvard University Press, 1983.

Hanfmann, George M. A. *From Croesus to Constantine*. Ann Arbor: University of Michigan 1975.

Hardie, Margaret M. "The shrine of Men Askaenos at Pisidian Antioch," *Journal of Hellenic Studies*, XXXII (1912), 111–50.

Haspels, Caroline H. W. *The Highlands of Phrygia.* Vol. 1. Princeton: Princeton University Press, 1971.

Hornblower, Simon, and Antony Spawforth, eds. *The Oxford Classical Dictionary.* 3rd ed. Oxford: Oxford University Press, 1996.

Hudson, Egbert C. "The Principal Family at Pisidian Antioch." *Journal of Near Eastern Studies*, XV (April 1957), 103–7.

Johnson, Sherman E. "Laodicea and Its Neighbors," *Biblical Archaeologist*, XIII (February 1950), 1-18.

Jones, A. H. M. *Cities of the Eastern Roman Provinces.* Oxford: Clarendon Press, 1937.

Jones, Charles W. *Saint Nicholas of Myra, Bari, and Manhattan.* Chicago: University of Chicago Press, 1978.

Keil, Josef. *Ephesis: Ein Führer Durch Die Ruinenstätte und ihre Geschichte.* Vienna: Austrian Archaeological Institute, 1957.

Lloyd, Seton. *Early Anatolia.* Baltimore: Penguin Books, 1956.

Lloyd, Seton. *Early Highland Peoples of Anatolia.* London: Thames & Hudson, 1967.

MacMullen, Ramsay. *Paganism in the Roman Empire.* New Haven: Yale University Press, 1981.

Macqueen, J. G. *The Hittites.* Rev. ed. London: Thames & Hudson, 1986.

Magie, David. *Roman Rule in Asia Minor.* 2 vols. Salem, NH: Ayer Company, reprint ed., 1988.

Marrou, H. I. *A History of Education in Antiquity.* New York: New American Library, 1964.

McMahon, Gregory. *The Hittite State Cult of the Tutelary Deities.* Chicago: University of Chicago, 1991.

Meinardus, Otto. *St. Paul in Ephesus.* New Rochelle, NY: Caratzas, 1979.

Mellaart, J. *Anatolia c. 4000–2300 B.C.* Cambridge: Cambridge University Press, 1962.

Millar, Fergus. *The Roman Near East 31 B.C.–A.D. 337.* Cambridge, MA: Harvard University Press, 1993.

Mitchell, Stephen. *Anatolia.* 2 vols. Oxford: Clarendon Press, 1993.

Mitchell, Stephen, and Marc Waelkens. *Pisidian Antioch.* London: Duckworth, 1998.

Onen, U. *Lycia.* Istanbul: Net Turistik Yayinlar, 2nd ed., 1990.

Parvis, Merrill M. "Archaeology and St. Paul's Journeys in Greek Lands, Part IV—Ephesus," *Biblical Archaeologist*, VIII (September 1945), 61–73.

Radt, Wolfgang. *Pergamon.* Istanbul: Turkiye Turing ve Otomibil Kurumu, 1984.

Ramage, Andrew, and Paul Craddock. *King Croesus' Gold.* Cambridge, MA: Harvard University Press, 2000.

Ramsay, William H. *The Bearing of Recent Discovery on the Trustworthiness of the New Testament.* Grand Rapids: Baker Book House reprint, 1979.

Ramsay, William H. *The Church in the Roman Empire Before A.D. 170.* Grand Rapids: Baker Book House reprint, 1979.

Ramsay, William H. *The Cities and Bishoprics of Phrygia.* 2 vols. Oxford: Clarendon Press, 1895.

Ramsay, William H. *The Cities of St. Paul.* Grand Rapids: Baker Book House reprint, 1979.

Ramsay, William H. *The Historical Geography of Asia Minor.* New York: Cooper Square reprint, 1972.

Ramsay, William H. *The Letters to the Seven Churches of Asia.* Grand Rapids: reprint, 1979.

Ramsay, William H. *St. Paul the Traveler and the Roman Citizen.* Grand Rapids: Baker, reprint, 1979.

Ramsay, William H. "Roads and Travel in the New Testament," *A Dictionary of the Bible.* Extra Vol. Ed. James Hastings. 1904.

Robinson, David M. "A Preliminary Report on the Excavations at Pisidian Antioch and at Sizma." *American Journal of Archaeology,* 28 (October 1924), 435–44.

Smith, William, ed. *A Dictionary of Greek and Roman Geography.* New York: AMS Press, reprint, 1966.

Stark, Freya. *The Lycian Shore.* New York: Harcourt Brace, 1956.

Steele, James. *Hellenistic Architecture in Asia Minor.* New York: St. Martin's, 1992.

Stillwell, Richard, ed. *The Princeton Encyclopedia of Classical Sites.* Princeton: Princeton University Press, 1976.

Syme, Ronald. *Anatolica.* Oxford: Clarendon Press, 1995.

Toksoz, Cemil. *Ancient Cities of Western Anatolia.* Istanbul: Zafer Ofset, 1974.

Tolstikov, Vladimir and Mikhail Treister. *The Gold of Troy.* New York: Harry N. Abrams, 1996.

Tozer, Henry F. *The Islands of the Aegean.* Oxford: T Clarendon Press, 1890.

Vos, Howard F. *Archaeology in Bible Lands.* Chicago: Moody, 1977.

Vos, Howard F. *Nelson's New Illustrated Bible Manners & Customs.* Nashville: Thomas Nelson, 1999.

Worth, Roland H. Jr. *The Seven Cities of the Apocalypse & Greco-Asian Culture.* New York: Paulist Press, 1999.

Yamauchi, Edwin. *The Archaeology of New Testament Cities in Western Asia Minor.* Grand Rapids: Baker, 1980.

The Athenian Acropolis in the second century A.D. Roman love for the dramatic or grandiose led them to add the massive entrance stairway. Also, they built a round temple to the goddess Roma at the far end of the Parthenon.

9

GREECE

Greece means many things to many people. To some it is the repository of ancient culture and the birthplace of philosophy, science, classical sculpture, and classical literature. To others it is a place for establishing a nostalgic link with the past as we gaze at the lion gate at Mycenae, walk the battlefield at Marathon, climb the steps to the Acropolis at Athens, or enjoy a dramatic production in the beautiful theater at Epidaurus.

To yet others Greece symbolizes independence or the struggle for independence, whether we think of the titanic conflict of the ancient city-states with Persia or Philip of Macedon, the fight for independence from Turkey in the nineteenth century in which Lord Byron lost his life, the heroic war against Mussolini during World War II, or the bitter post-war struggle against Communists from over the Bulgarian border.

To the Bible student, however, Greece is something more. It is the beachhead where the Gospel invaded fortress Europe and where it began to penetrate Western civilization. It is the scene of some of the most dramatic evangelistic activities of the apostle Paul. In this land the Christian visitor can still stand by the river at Philippi where Paul spoke at the Jewish prayer meeting, on Mars Hill in Athens where he addressed the Areopagus court, by the bema or rostrum at

Corinth where he stood before the governor Gallio, or on an excavated section of the ancient Egnatian Way—the highway across Macedonia which Paul traveled from Neapolis to Thessalonica.

Geographical Features

The Boundaries of Greece

Just as Greece has a variety of appeals, so its geographical bounds have been variously placed. In classical times Greece (or Hellas) was the southern projection of the Balkan Peninsula, stretching south from Thessaly and Epirus, and including the Ionian and Aegean islands. Covering approximately thirty thousand square miles, this Greece was about the size of Scotland or Maine.

Subsequently, as Macedonia was Hellenized, it came to be considered part of the Greek world. Those who include Macedonia as part of Greece have in mind an area of some fifty thousand square miles, comparable to that of England or Alabama. Probably Crete should also be included as part of the Greek world, raising the total by thirty-two hundred square miles, thus constituting an area about the size of Florida or Wisconsin. Modern Greece comprises much of ancient Macedonia and Thrace, the Greek peninsula, Crete, and the islands of the Aegean—about fifty-one thousand square miles.

The Greece of the days of the apostle Paul (when the biblical narrative becomes most involved with the area) was very differently constituted. Crete was a Roman province by itself. The Asia Minor coast and the adjacent islands comprised part of the province of Asia. The province of Thrace occupied eastern Greece. Macedonia and northern Greece were incorporated into the province of Macedonia. The rest of the peninsula and a number of Aegean islands formed the province of Achaea. At one point Luke described Macedonia and Achaea as Macedonia and Greece (Acts 20:1–2), perhaps a carry-over of the old idea that Macedonians were not really Greeks.

In line with the Roman division, the portions of greater Hellas discussed here are Macedonia, Achaea, Crete, and some of the islands of the western Aegean. The Greek communities that were a part of the province of Asia are discussed in the chapter on Asia Minor.

The Mountains

Dominant in the life of any Greek were the mountains and the sea. Mountains covered two-thirds to three-fourths of the land surface, leaving not more than 25 percent of cultivable soil. No other country of the Mediterranean area presents a more tumbled surface than Greece. So resident or visitor is seldom ever out of sight of mountains.

The mountains of Greece are not especially high. Mount Olympus, the highest (located in the northeastern corner of the peninsula), is only about 9,600 feet, and few of the others are over 8,000 feet. Those that are include Mount Pindus (8,500 feet), Mount Ida in Crete (8,200), and Mount Parnassus (8,060 feet). Thus the capacity of Greek mountains for holding snow is limited, and the constancy of water supply is thereby curtailed.

MOUNT OLYMPUS

Olympus is the highest mountain on the Greek peninsula, reaching a height of 9,573 feet. Zeus, king of the Greek gods, was supposed to have his throne on its summit, and the other gods and goddesses were believed to have made their homes somewhere on the mountain. Among the goddesses, the nine muses were especially important to the Greeks because they were thought to impart creative ability to poets, artists, sculptors, philosophers, and intellectuals generally in order to produce their works.

Although the placement of mountains in Greece is chaotic, there is a degree of symmetry. The Magnesian Range extends south from Olympus in eastern Greece the Pindus Range lies between Thessaly and Epirus in central Greece and the Epirus Range stretches along the western coast. These are crossed by other ridges, dividing the country into a vast checkerboard of tiny valleys, few of which are more than a dozen miles long and more than half as wide. Often the mountain passes between these valleys are three thousand feet or more in altitude and some are buried in snow at least part of the winter.

With communications so hampered, a provincialism developed in Greece such as has probably existed in no other historically important area of the world. Moreover, the mountain barriers contributed much to the city-state development of ancient Greece. Though periodic efforts were made to overcome this divisive situation, none was really successful until Macedonia, Rome, and other powers exerted an external pressure for unity.

The top of Mt. Olympus with the supposed throne of Zeus in the center of the picture.

Rivers

Down from the mountainsides coursed the rivers of Greece. They were mostly non-navigable winter and spring torrents whose floods drowned the arable land. In summer their dry beds served as highways for travelers. These raging torrents washed away soil from the hillsides during the rainy season. During the dry season some of them formed stagnant pools, breeding mosquitoes. Therefore, the rivers were a marked hindrance to Greece, eroding the land, forming breeding places for malarial mosquitoes, silting the mouths of rivers so their harbors were virtually useless, and impeding travel. During floods these rivers were difficult to cross for both people and animals. It was almost impossible to build bridges over streams that varied from a few feet in width to more than five hundred feet with the seasons. Moreover, these streams were too muddy to serve as a water supply.

The larger rivers were the Peneus (Salambria) in Thessaly (c. 125 miles long), the Achelous in western Greece (100 miles long), the Arachthus (Arakhthos) in Epirus (80 miles long), and the Alpheus in the western Peloponnesus (75 miles long); but some of the smaller ones were more prominent in song and story.

The Sea

Though the mountains dominated the landscape of Greece and also affected her politics, economy, and climate, the sea was also a major factor in Greek life. Although the mountains almost closed Greece to the European continent, she was accessible on her seafronts. The coast is so deeply indented that Greece has the longest coastline in proportion to enclosed areas of all important historical regions. With a coast of 2,600 miles, it exceeds Italy's (2,150 miles) and the Iberian Peninsula's (2,300 miles), though its land area is only one-third of the former and one-sixth of the latter. As a result, nowhere in central or southern Greece can a person travel more than forty miles from the sea.

The many indentations afforded numerous harbors, and dozens of islands dotted the Aegean. When men sailed the Aegean, they were never out of sight of land on a clear day until they moved south of Crete into the eastern Mediterranean: "An observer on the promontory of Sunium at the tip of Attica may take in at a glance the cluster of the Cyclades as far as Melos, as though he were reading a map . . . Navigation in the Aegean is thus reduced to the simplicity of a ferry service."[1]

So the Greeks, unable to wrest a comfortable (or decent) living from the rocky farms, became a seafaring people. Learning from all the peoples with whom they came in contact, they cross-fertilized the whole Mediterranean area. It is significant for the history of Hellas that her best ports and many of her valleys lay on the east coast. As a result her eastern areas received civilizing influences from the Orient first. In contrast, Italy faced west and was slowed in receiving eastern culture.

It is easy, however, to overemphasize the place of the sea in Greek economic life. The mountains adjacent to many of the city-states did not produce good ship timber and sometimes were literally a barrier between the inhabitants and the sea. Moreover, the Aegean waters are too clear and too devoid of plant life to support large schools of fish and thus a fishing industry. And overseas trade was not vital in the early days when most of the communities of Greece were self-sufficient.

Then, too, the seas around Greece are typically Mediterranean. In winter the Adriatic Sea is a storm center; gusty north winds plague the northern Aegean. The surrounding seas remained closed to all Greeks in winter and to some Greeks most of the time. Sheer cliffs line a good part of the Greek coast. The Thessalians and Boeotians always remained landsmen. The inhabitants of Corinth and Megara were the only people of the Peloponnesus or of the area around the Corinthian Gulf to have much of an overseas trade. Sparta broke out of her landlocked condition for only a brief period during and after her great war with Athens (late fifth century B.C.), when she built a navy with the help of Persia. Even the peoples of the Aegean Islands were not seafarers continually.

The Greeks have always been primarily rural and agricultural. As late as the end of the nineteenth century A.D., 70 percent of them still lived in rural areas. The lack of soil forced them to terrace the hillsides and plant grapevines, olive trees, and whatever else they could produce on some very unpromising land. The stony nature of the soil also often forced them to raise barley and millet rather than wheat; they imported most of their wheat. Pasturelands were more suited to the raising of sheep and goats than cattle.

Climate

The climate of Greece is mild and has not changed appreciably in at least the last two thousand years. Northern Greece has a climate similar to Europe's with a fair amount of snow, while southern Greece has a climate more Mediterranean in nature. However, cold winds bring snow even to Athens in winter. There are two seasons: rainy or winter (October to April) and dry or summer (May to September). The winters are rather boisterous but not devoid of sunshine. Rainfall is fairly heavy, measuring forty inches in the west and slightly less in the east. In the summers there is little precipitation. This period of drought lasts for two months in the North and four months in the Peloponnesus. The hot summer sun is tempered by sea breezes in most places, but some of the cup-shaped valleys are effectively isolated from this relief by the surrounding mountains. In such places summer weather is equal to that of the tropics. For instance, at Larissa in the Thessalian Basin July has a mean temperature of 90° F.

Natural Resources

"To Hellas poverty has always been a foster sister,"[2] the fifth century B.C. Greek historian Herodotus well observed. It is remarkable that this minor poverty-stricken people was able to soar above its environment and produce great cultural achievements. While in very ancient times there was a considerable amount of timber, by the fifth century B.C. Greece was no longer able to supply her needs and had to import.

Not only was Greece's soil of poor quality, neither did she have much in the way of minerals. Silver and lead were mined in Attica, iron and copper in Euboea and Laconia, and some gold near Philippi and on the islands of Siphnos and Thasos. Most of the ancient minefields are now exhausted. Some fields that do exist were never exploited in antiquity. There were considerable supplies of potters' clay, especially at Athens and Corinth. Greece also had plenty of good building stone and was famous for her marble. Modern visitors to Greece are sometimes impressed to find marble used where we might use wood or cheaper materials. But marble is more readily available there than wood.

The finest of the white marbles were quarried in the Cyclades and on Mount Pentelicus in Attica. While Pentelic marble

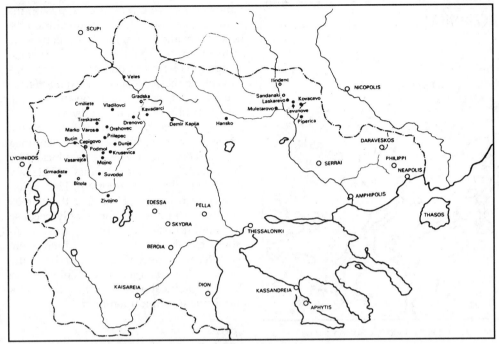

Map of Macedonia

had a smooth grain for sculpture, the ancient Greeks preferred the marble of Paros, which was more translucent, for sculpture. The only colored marbles of Greece quarried extensively in ancient times were the white and green *cipollino* of Euboea, much desired by the Roman emperors, and the *verde antico* (old green) of northern Thessaly.

Significant Areas of Greece

Since the history of ancient Greece was to a large extent the history of its particular districts, some of the chief areas of Greece require further comment. Additional details appear in connection with Paul's ministry in Greece.

Macedonia

At the north of Hellas lay Macedonia. Since its boundaries varied over the centuries and since during much of the country's history the exact boundaries are not known, it is hard indeed to describe its exact size. The kingdom was, however, always located at the northeast corner of the Aegean. Aegae (modern Vergina), about

fifty miles west northwest of Thessalonica, was the early capital, and the tomb of Philip II (359–336 B.C.) has been located there. Archelaus I (413–399 B.C.) moved the capital to Pella (twenty-four miles northwest of Thessalonica), and Alexander the Great was born there. Under Philip II Macedonia came to include Thrace and to dominate all of Greece. Under Alexander it conquered the entire Persian Empire.

When Macedonia became a Roman province in 146 B.C., and throughout most of the first century A.D., the boundaries of the territory were quite well fixed. The Macedonia in which Paul ministered had a borderline that stretched from a point near the Nestos River in eastern Greece to the Adriatic at approximately the latitude of Tirane (Tirana), modern capital of Albania, then south to the northern border of Epirus, which it skirted to its southern end and turned eastward to the Gulf of Volos (ancient Pagasaeus). Therefore it may be seen that the province included not only most of the northern part of modern Greece but also portions of Bulgaria and Yugoslavia and about half of Albania. The

Macedonia during the Roman period.

Romans planted colonies at Pella and Philippi, among other places.

While Macedonia was very mountainous, it also had some fertile plains along the northern rim of the Aegean. Four great rivers (the Haliacmon [Vistritsa], Vardar, Strymon, and Nestos) of the "European" type (which flow all year instead of drying up in the summer) break through the coastal ridges to the sea and deposit around their mouths' rich alluvial plains. In the west, the Haliacmon and Vardar plains have been joined at least since the fifth century B.C. Moving east, we come to the Strymonic Plain which is the most fertile plain of the north Aegean area. Next comes the Philippian Plain and finally the Nestos Plain. The fertility of these plains has enabled the Greeks to export wheat for the last several years—a considerable achievement for such a rocky country.

Thessaly

Moving south from Old Macedonia proper (as distinct from the province of Macedonia), we come next to Thessaly. This region has been likened to a "boxlike compartment with an almost level floor and four upright sides." Hemmed in by the Pindus Range on the west, Mount Olympus on the northeast, and other lesser mountains on the north, east, and south, the Thessalians were virtually cut off from the sea. This situation, compounded by the dangerous wind currents along the coast and a broad and fertile interior plain, contributed toward making the inhabitants of the area landsmen.

The Peneus River drained the basin, which is oppressively hot in the summer, because cooling sea breezes are blocked by the mountains. The inhabitants of Thessaly were not historically important. This region is a good example of the fact that Greek city-states did not develop simply because of geographical barriers. In this basin (about the size of Connecticut) there were no natural barriers to union, and yet the communities of this area achieved no durable political union until Macedonia and Rome forced it upon them.

Epirus

A very mountainous territory in northwestern Greece, Epirus had no important political contacts with the rest of Hellas until the days of King Pyrrhus (died, 272 B.C.), who united the kingdom and aided the southern Italian cities in their war against Rome. The rocky coast has no good harbors, but the interior mountains provided large supplies of timber; and an abundance of rainfall (fifty-two inches a year) contributed to the agricultural productivity of the small valleys, where many cattle were also raised.

Accusing Epirus of supporting Macedonia in her war against Rome (168 B.C.), the Roman Senate decreed that all the towns of Epirus should be destroyed and the inhabitants reduced to slavery. The seventy towns were burned to the ground in one day and 150,000 inhabitants carried away into slavery. Epirus never recovered. As it came under the control of Rome, it was at first part of the province of Macedonia. In 27 B.C. Augustus built the city of Nicopolis as the metropolis of Epirus and separated the region into a province. It was about four-fifths the size of Connecticut. The construction of Nicopolis was to commemorate Augustus' victory over Antony nearby at Actium in 31 B.C.

The Districts of Greece. *From Rostovtzeff, History of the Ancient World.*

Anticipating his release from Roman imprisonment, the apostle Paul instructed Titus to meet him at a Nicopolis (Titus 3:12). Though there were other cities by the same name in the empire, this is usually thought to be Paul's destination. If so, it was apparently his intent to establish a Christian mission on the west coast of Greece.

Boeotia

South of Thessaly lies Boeotia, which reproduces on a smaller scale some of the features of Thessaly. Like Thessaly it is a river basin (the Cephisus) encased in mountains that keep its inhabitants from the sea and which bring to it sultry summers and raw winters. Thebes, its main city,

619

The temple of Apollo and the theater at Delphi.

was in the southern part of Boeotia. Though Thebes figured often in Greek history, it was mostly on the receiving end of blows struck for conquest. It did, however, achieve a brief hegemony in Greece under Epaminondas (371–362 B.C.).

Euboea

Across the Gulf of Euboea from Boeotia lay the island for which the gulf was named. About ninety miles long, it came to within a

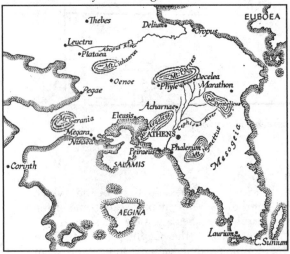

Attica

hundred yards of the mainland at Chalcis. Never politically important, it did have resources of copper and iron that were desired in ancient times but which were exhausted by the Roman period. The Romans, however, appreciated the white and green marble of the southern part of the island.

Phocis

West of Boeotia stretched the territory of Phocis. Dominated by Mount Callidromus on the north and 8,060-foot Paranassus on the south, the area had few resources and little land of value except along the Cephisus River, which flowed between the two mountain ranges. The chief importance of Phocis historically is that Delphi was located within her borders, six miles north of the Corinthian Gulf. Seat of an important oracle and temple of Apollo at least as early as the seventh century B.C., Delphi received pilgrims from all over Greece and from abroad. She was enriched, too, as numerous city-states sent their votive gifts and erected shrines there. The Pythian Games, in honor of Apollo, were held at Delphi every four years.

Aetolia

West of Phocis lay Aetolia, a very mountainous and isolated territory inhabited by a backward group of tribes that did not come to the fore until the formation of the Aetolian League about 275 B.C. At its height this military confederation controlled most of central Greece. The territory became part of the Roman province of Achaea, created in 146 B.C.

Attica

Southeast of Boeotia lies the peninsula of Attica. Though very significant for the history of civilization, this small territory comprises only about a thousand square miles and is approximately the size of Rhode Island. The peninsula is roughly triangular in shape and measures some forty miles east and west and a like distance north and south. No spot in Attica is more than twenty-five miles in a straight line from Athens.

Those who are enamored with the greatness of this area often are unaware of its drawbacks. It is the driest region of Greece with an annual rainfall of only sixteen inches. Only about one-fourth of its soil is arable, and part of that will raise nothing but olives. To its credit are a coast where the mountains leave room for easy landing places, excellent clay beds for pottery manufacture, the famous marble of Mount Pentelicus, and the lead and silver mines of Laurium in the south of the peninsula (virtually exhausted by the time of the Christian Era).

Athens gradually became the true center of all of life in Attica. At the center of Athens stood her citadel on the Acropolis, an isolated hill about five miles from the coast and three to four hundred feet above the town. It has an almost vertical drop on all sides but the west. After about 500 B.C. the great port of Athens was developed at Piraeus. Another important town of Attica was Eleusis, a religious center fourteen miles northwest of Athens.

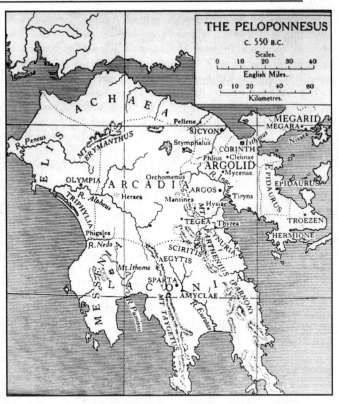

THE PELOPONNESUS
c. 550 B.C.

The Peloponnesus

Moving southwest of Athens, and crossing the Isthmus of Corinth we enter the Peloponnesus. This peninsula, shaped like a mulberry leaf, has actually been an island since the Corinth Canal was finished in A.D. 1893. Slightly smaller than New Hampshire, the Peloponnesus had several important districts, six of which are noted here. The Peloponnesus formed the larger part of the Roman province of Achaea, organized in 146 B.C.

Occupying the northeast corner of the Peloponnesus was the city-state of Corinth, which never did control a large territory (only about 248 square miles, one-quarter the size of Attica or Rhode Island). Blessed with considerable deposits of white and cream-colored clay, Corinth developed the most prolific ceramic industry of early Greece, but after about 550–525 B.C. she lost out to Athenian competition in the field.

More important to the development of Corinth, however, was her geographical position. Located a mile and a half south of the Isthmus of Corinth, she commanded

Remains of the ancient tramway at the Isthmus of Corinth, alongside the modern Corinth canal.

this four-mile-wide neck of land, as well as its eastern port of Cenchreae (Cenchrea, Acts 18:18) and its western port of Lechaeum. In New Testament as well as classical times, a large amount of shipping passed through Greek waters, and the trip around the southern tip of Greece was not only long but extremely dangerous. Therefore it became customary to transport goods across the Isthmus of Corinth, a saving of more than 150 miles. Smaller ships were pulled across the Isthmus on a tramway; larger ones were unloaded and their cargoes reloaded on other ships on the other side. Short stretches of this tramway can still be seen. Corinth served as the capital of the Roman province of Achaea.

South of Corinth lay Argolis, the coasts of which were almost continuously rockbound and the interior of which was a tangled mass of low mountains. While this area was dominated in classical times by Argos, its significance in history lies in the fact that the important site of Mycenae was located there. Standing astride the main road between Corinth and Argos, it not only controlled communications in that area but also came to dominate politically or economically much of the eastern Mediterranean world, or at least to influence it.

Across the northern top of the Peloponnesus stretched Achaea, which occupied a narrow fertile coastland. In this territory twelve cities formed a religious confederacy, meeting in Poseidon's sanctuary at Helice. From this developed the politically important Achaean League of Hellenistic times.

OLYMPIC GAMES

The Olympic Games were held in honor of Zeus near Olympia in Elis every four years. The name of the first victor was recorded in 776 B.C. and by 700 names were being recorded of victors from other parts of Greece. The games were held in midsummer and lasted for five days. They continued to be staged at four-year intervals until the end of the fourth century A.D., when the Christian emperor Theodosius terminated games held in honor of a Greek god. They were revived in A.D. 1896 as a purely athletic event without religious significance.

The Olympic stadium was literally a stade long (about two hundred yards) and was only a straight-away. If a race consisted of two or more stades, the runner caught hold of a pole at the other end of the stadium and swung himself around it, repeating the process as many times as necessary to complete his race.

The Olympic Stadium, literally a stade long, about 600 yards.

Events included running, jumping, wrestling, and javelin and discus throwing. Then there were the Pankration (boxing and wrestling) and Pentathlon (running, jumping, wrestling, and javelin and discus throwing). Boys had their own foot races, wrestling, and boxing events. Horse races took place in another facility.

There were no medals for victors; their crowns were woven of olive branches. Friends gave gifts, and victors received rewards and honors at home after returning from the games.

Starting blocks at the games at Delphi, similar to what they would have been at Olympia. Evident in the picture are grooves where runners could put their toes, holes where iron poles could be inserted, and, at the far end, lane markers. When a race required two or more laps of the track, runners grabbed the pole at the far end, swung themselves around it, and repeated the action as many times as necessary.

To the southwest of Achaea lay Elis, occupying a wide piedmont terrace at the western edge of Arcadia. The area had the best cattle pastures of the Peloponnesus and produced flax as well. Its significance in Greek history arose from the fact that the great Panhellenic sanctuary of Olympia was located there. The local population was entrusted with the stewardship of the Olympic Games.

The two southern districts of the Peloponnesus were Laconia and Messenia. Each consisted of a fertile plain framed in a horseshoe of mountains fronting on a sea gulf. The more significant of these plains historically was the Laconian (on the east),

The two sides of the bay of Fiar Havens, where the ship carrying Paul to Rome briefly took refuge (Acts 27:8).

where Sparta was located. Laconia was watered by an abundance of streams flowing from the Taygetus Range (c. eight thousand feet) on the west. Most important of these was the Eurotas River, along the banks of which Sparta lay.

Since this area could support a considerable population, it was not so necessary for the Spartans, as it was for the Athenians, to engage in commercial and political adventure. In this matter Sparta was fortunate because her natural hindrances to overseas commerce were great. Her ports were not good, and sailing at the southern tip of the Peloponnesus was difficult and dangerous. Although the pass into Messenia was through a difficult gorge which reached a height of forty-five hundred feet and which was impassable in midwinter, the valiant Spartans managed to conquer and control their neighbors.

The Cyclades

A group of about 220 islands, with a total area of only slightly more than a thousand square miles, extends from the tip of Attica in a southeasterly direction. These are known as the Cyclades and were so called by the Greeks because they formed a circle or cluster (*kyklos*) around the sacred Island of Delos, seat of the Delean League (of which Athens was the chief member). Geologically they represent a submerged mountain chain with their tops protruding above water level. While these islands are

mountainous, they are quite productive agriculturally. Their mineral deposits have not as yet been fully exploited. Through the millennia the Cyclades have been subject to the more powerful states in the area. In New Testament times they were part of the Roman province of Achaea.

Crete

Crete is the southernmost and largest of the Greek islands. It is the fourth largest island in the Mediterranean (Sicily, Sardinia, and Cyprus being larger). Located sixty miles south of Cape Malea in the Peloponnesus and 110 miles west of Cape Krio in Asia Minor (with Rhodes and other islands between it and Cape Krio), its location made inevitable its use as a seedbed and distributing center for the cultures of the Near East from the fourth to the first millennia B.C.

Comprising an area of 3,200 square miles (about half the size of New Jersey), Crete is elongated in form—160 miles from east to west but only varying from 6 to 35 miles from north to south. While the northern coast is deeply indented and provides a good natural harbor at least at Suda at the western end of the island, the southern coast is less indented. In the southern part of the island, the mountains often appear to rise from the sea.

In the center of the southern coast is Cape Lithinos, the southernmost point of the island. Immediately to the east of that is

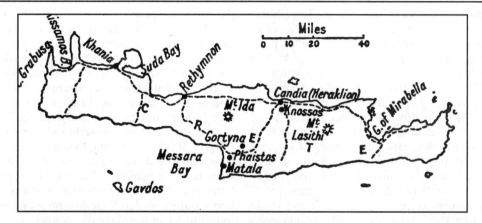

the small bay of Kaloi Limenes, or Fair Havens, where the ship carrying Paul took refuge (Acts 27:8). A little less than twenty-five miles southwest of Cape Lithinos lies the rocky, treeless isle of Cauda or Clauda (modern Gavdos) which Paul's ship passed as it began to fight the storm that eventually blew it to Malta (Acts 27:16). Though the history of Crete is discussed subsequently, it may be useful to mention here that it was a separate Roman province when Paul passed it and when Titus ministered there, having been conquered by Rome 68/67 B.C.

From the coast it looks as though Crete, were a solid mass of mountains. But in fact, mountains divide into four principal groups that between them do cover most of the island. In the West are the White Mountains, which reach an altitude of almost eight thousand feet; in the center is the ancient Mount Ida (modern Psiloriti) eighty-two hundred feet high; in the middle of the eastern half of the island rise the Lasithi to a height of seventy-two hundred feet; and at the east end the Sitia Mountains, reach only forty-eight hundred feet.

Many of these peaks are covered with snow the greater part of the year. Forests which once covered the mountains and which were much valued for ship timber have for the most part disappeared, and the slopes are now desolate wastes. Cypress still grows in some of the higher regions. Numerous caves exist in these mountains, one of the most important to the ancient Greeks being the Dictaean Cave in Lasithi, the legendary birthplace of Zeus. Several

small rivers flow to the north and to the south shores of Crete.

Southeast of Mount Ida lies the Messara Plain, largest on the island, extending about thirty-seven miles in length and ten miles in breadth. One of the richest plains in Greece, it no doubt supplied the wine and olive oil for the huge storage jars found in the palaces at Knossos (Cnossus) and Phaistos (Phaestus), the chief cities in the north and south of Crete, respectively. Probably the Messara furnished the orchard produce which also served as a chief staple in the early trade of Cretan merchants. In several places on Crete there are level upland basins which provide good pasturage for flocks and herds during the summer months.

The rainy season on Crete lasts from October to March and the dry season from April to September, when almost no rain falls. Total rainfall for an average year is about twenty inches. At Candia (Heraklion), near ancient Knossos, mean temperatures vary from 51° F in January to 79 degrees in August.

Peoples of Greece

The Earliest Ages

Though Paleolithic remains have been found in Greece, there is no pattern of human settlement that emerges from those remains. Such a pattern does, however, begin to emerge with the Neolithic period. Neolithic settlements, which then began to appear in various parts of Greece, may be dated to around 6000 B.C. or earlier. One of the richest sites is Nea Nikomedeia (thirty-three miles west of Thessalonica). Neolithic remains also appear in the Thessalian plain (e.g., Argissa, Sesklo, Soufli, Ghediki, and Achilleion), at Nea Makri in Attica, at Corinth, on the island of Melos, at Knossos, as well as in other places.[3]

At these sites cattle, sheep, goats , and pigs were domesticated; the inhabitants raised barley, oats, peas, lentils, olives, and other corps. They built square and rectangular huts (usually of reeds and rushes coated on both sides with mud mixed with straw), in regular village sites and made various styles of pottery with various levels of sophistication. Of course tools and weapons were made largely of stone.

Seafaring developed in the seventh millennium B.C.[4] Apparently cultural influences came primarily from Asia Minor and also apparently primarily as a result of migration of peoples rather than a transmission of ideas. At least this seems to have been the case initially. While the ethnic composition mainly consisted of Mediterranean stock,[5] the skeletal remains in various Neolithic sites show that the people were not entirely Mediterranean but consisted of a variety of human types.[6] The ethnic composition of the Neolithic period does not seem to have changed appreciably during the Early Bronze Age (down to c. 2000 B.C.).

Indo-European Invasion

The whole subject of the Indo-Europeans—their homeland and when and how they came to Greece—is widely debated. Two of the more recent and more credible treatments of the subject are J. P. Mallory's *In Search of the Indo-Europeans* (1989) and Robert Drews' *The Coming of the Greeks* (1988).

The supposition is gaining acceptance that the general area of Armenia and the lake district of Eastern Anatolia was the homeland of the Indo-Europeans. And while Indo-European entrance into Greece may have taken place as early as about 2000 B.C., it is being pushed later, to perhaps 1600 B.C. Moreover, their movement was not a mere migration, but a planned takeover that was achieved by chariotry.[7] And when the Indo-Europeans came, presumably by sea from the coasts of Pontus,[8] they imposed on the earlier population of Greece a minority of Indo-European speakers. Drews hazards a guess that no more than seventy-five thousand Indo-Europeans came in the invasion, to rule over perhaps ten times as many natives.[9]

In thinking about these Indo-European peoples, it is worth noting that they were a conglomeration of humanity who had come to share a common language and certain cultural characteristics. Starr's observation is quite in order: "A man who spoke an Indo-European language did not necessarily share with his comrades one particular structure of body or color of hair and eyes; and his blood stream did not carry any specific outlook on life or aesthetic point of view."[10]

The Minoan peoples of Crete did not suffer greatly from the invasion that upset the mainland but continued to develop to new cultural heights under Near Eastern tutelage and as a result of internal impetus. After around 1600 B.C., when the mainland had achieved an adjustment between the old and new cultures, the Minoans became the educators of Hellas, influencing the culture throughout the Aegean region. About 1400 B.C. these Mycenaean peoples of the mainland established their hegemony in Greece. And a few decades earlier they had conquered the Minoans on Crete.

A Second Indo-European Invasion

Destruction of the Mycenean world began about 1225 B.C. and was accomplished by about 1125–1100 B.C. This occurred in part as a result of struggles between Mycenean states, but especially at the hands of raiders and city-sackers, presumably from northern Greece. These fearsome attacks frightened many of the Mycenean upper classes, who fled to more secure places in Achaea or Argolis or abroad—to Cyprus and elsewhere. The result was that stretches of the countryside were largely depopulated. What was left behind was the rural non-Greek speaking element that the Myceneans had dominated.

Next came a Dorian invasion, beginning after 1000 B.C., not to destroy the old

Mycenean civilization, which was already gone, but to occupy largely vacant lands. These Greeks apparently came from Thessaly or other northern regions and began the process of developing classical Greece. In a couple of generations or so these people managed to assimilate the earlier population linguistically. This statement represents a change in interpretation of Dorian activity. Previously it was thought that the Dorians were responsible for destruction of the Mycenean states. Whether the Dorians brought any very significant cultural developments with them is questionable. Starr feels that their greatest contribution was to free Greece from the Minoan and Mycenean conventions, thereby permitting a new culture to emerge from native roots.[11]

New Cultural Emergence

When the lights came on again at the end of the Dark Ages around 800 B.C., Greeks were speaking three main dialects: Aeolic, Ionic, and Doric. These were spoken in geographical bands which stretched roughly across northern, central, and southern parts of the Greek world, respectively. Aeolic was found in northwestern Asia Minor, Thessaly, and Boeotia; Ionic in west central Asia Minor, the Cyclades, and Attica; and Doric in Rhodes, Crete, and the Peloponnesus. However, the pattern was not so regular as that in other states of the Greek Peninsula.

It must be remembered that these were dialects of one language and that the terms did not necessarily carry with them any greatly differentiated racial or cultural patterns. The peoples of the Aegean Basin were Indo-European by the beginning of the first millennium B.C. and, as sons of Hellas, had one language (with many dialects), a common religion, and a bond in their great athletic events. But they were also sons of their own city-states, to which they pledged fierce loyalty to the point of committing "national" suicide.

The History of Greece

The re-creation of the story of early Greece began with the fabulous Heinrich Schliemann (1822–1890), Homeric fundamentalist, who believed in the literal truth of Homer's *Iliad*. Having dedicated his life to making a fortune and learning several languages in order to prove the accuracy of Homer, he finally began to excavate at the site of Troy in 1870. Successful there, six years later he started to work at Mycenae on mainland Greece. In November 1876, he sent a telegram to the king of Greece announcing that he had discovered the body of Agamemnon.

The romance was continued by Arthur Evans who, as an act of faith, purchased the hillock of Knossos in Crete in the 1890s and, in 1900, when political conditions became more stable, began to excavate. His strong faith was richly rewarded. Others also made their archaeological contributions. In 1953 Michael Ventris and John Chadwick announced the successful decipherment of Linear B (a script found on numerous tablets in Mycenaean sites), which would enable historians to form a clearer picture of early Greek civilization. As a result of the work of these and many others, it is now possible to describe the flowering of early Greek culture and to establish the fact that the greatness of Greece during the Classical Age came late indeed.

The Glory of the Minoans

Historical Developments. The civilization that Evans found at Knossos was called Minoan because this was the capital of the legendary King Minos. But of course the brilliant culture that has been associated with early Crete did not appear full-blown in the same way that Athena was said to have sprung fully armed from the head of Zeus. This culture developed over a period of many centuries. Evans himself found a Neolithic stratum twenty-three to twenty-six feet in depth at the bottom of the Knossos excavation. Crete was first occupied before 6000 B.C. by migrants of Mediterranean stock who presumably came from Asia Minor across the 110 miles of water, aided by intervening islands.

Evans and others following him divided Minoan history into Early, Middle, and Late periods, and each of these periods were subdivided. During the last couple of

MINOAN AND
MYCENAEAN
GREECE

Miles
0   50   100   150

decades, however, a new classification has been developing, roughly as follows. Early Minoan is called the Pre-Palace period; Middle Minoan I and II, the Old Palace period; and Middle Minoan III and Late Minoan I and II, the New Palace period. After that comes the Post-Palace period. Many, however, still stick with the old classification of Early, Middle, and Late periods.

The Early Minoan period may be dated 3000–2100 or 3000–1900 B.C. During this millennium Cretan cultures were not particularly different from or superior to those of the rest of the Aegean. Fairly early in this period bronze came into common use for making tools. And by the middle of the millennium there was a considerable cultural quickening. This apparently occurred as a result of internal development and increased trade with neighboring islands, instead of a new wave of migration, as formerly thought. Fairly early in the period the olive tree and longhorn cattle were introduced. The outdoor hearth and the Cretan house as a collection of rooms around an open court became characteristic. Trade relations with Egypt grew increasingly common. During the last centuries of the millennium Cretan culture began to coalesce.

During the Middle Minoan (2100–1600 or 1900–1600 B.C.) and Late Minoan I (1600–1500/1450 B.C.) periods, Cretan culture attained extraordinary achievements. However, these attainments were not developed in a vacuum. Here was an example of what could happen when early Aegean culture made contact with the highly advanced cultures of the Orient. While some elements came from Egypt and others from Asia, all such cultural borrowings were assimilated by the genius of the Cretan people and transmuted into an individual art.

For instance, the Cretan palace was architecturally unlike the buildings of any other land. The masterpieces of painting on its walls, with all of their evidence of enjoyment of life, contrasted remarkably with contemporary Egyptian preoccupation with another world and the pompous arrogance of later Mesopotamian art.

One of the storage rooms in the palace at Knossos.

The first palaces on a grand scale appeared at the beginning of the Middle Minoan period at Knossos and elsewhere on the island. And during that period came a flowering of Cretan culture. This was the age of the famous eggshell ware with walls as thin as Haviland china. The cartwheel arrived from Asia, and the first stone-paved roads in Europe were constructed on the island, connecting Knossos and Phaistos, and protected by guardposts. The center of power moved from eastern to north-central Crete, which suggests that trade was becoming more oriented to the Greek mainland. Although there were several cities on the island at the time, Knossos and Phaistos seem to have dominated Crete during the period.

After the great earthquake of 1700 B.C., the palaces at Knossos, Phaistos, Mallia and Zakros were rebuilt on a grander scale. From local hieroglyphic scripts developed a linear script—which has become known as Linear A. It was syllabic in nature and written from left to right. Life also became more luxurious on the island as trade developed with Byblos and Ugait in Syria and with the Cyclades, through whose market at Melos goods reached the Greek mainland.

Their chief exports were wine, olive oil, metal products, and their magnificent pottery, which has been found in Egypt, Syria, Greece, and Italy.

The period from about 1700 to 1450 B.C. was the most flourishing of Minoan Crete. The finest surviving creations of Minoan

Plan of the Palace of Minos at Knossos.

The first stone-paved road in Europe (before 1700 B.C.) connected Knossos and Phaistos.

gifts, may have been Minoans. Part of the accompanying inscription reads, "the coming in peace of the Great Ones of Keftiu and of the Isles in the midst of the sea."[12] Keftiu may have been Crete; she was queen among the isles of the sea. Cyprus felt the impact of trade with Crete too.

During the flourishing period of Minoan culture, the volcano on the island of Thera (seventy miles north of Crete) erupted and blew the island apart. Initially it became three small islands and today is five islets. Thera has become the Minoan Pompeii. There excavators found evidence of Minoan life frozen in action. The population seems to have had enough warning to evacuate completely. When the island erupted is a subject of great controversy. Many date the event around 1500 B.C., but some dendrochronologists and carbon 14 specialists assign a date of about 1628. There is at present no resolution to the problem. In any case, the volcanic action does not seem to have had anything to do with the destruction at Knossos in about 1450 B.C., or the end of Minoan civilization, as has often been claimed.

In any event, around 1450 Crete was desolated. The towns and palaces of the island, with the exception of Knossos, where damage was limited, were destroyed and most were never reoccupied. Some still think a natural disaster was the culprit. Most, however, believe the catastrophe resulted from an internal revolution and destruction of the existing social and political order or from a Mycenean invasion.

As has now been confirmed by the decipherment of the Linear B script,[13] Knossos did come under the control of the Mycenean Greeks of the mainland after 1450 B.C. Linear B, which is definitely Greek, replaced the older Minoan Linear A (from which it borrowed heavily) as the script of Knossos. Linear B also became the script of the Mycenean mainland, whereas Crete outside of its chief city retained the use of Linear A.

Many other cultural changes occurred. For instance, mainland themes were introduced into the pottery of Crete. Henceforth far greater attention was paid to warlike representations in the art of the island. The

artists date back to that time. The island was densely inhabited and may have begun to suffer from overpopulation. During the period 1650 to 1500 B.C. Minoans planted colonies on Thera, Melos, and Kea in the Cyclades; on Rhodes; at Miletus in Asia Minor; and elsewhere, possibly even on the Greek mainland. The people of the mainland fell increasingly under the influence of Minoan culture. In fact, the whole Aegean area became something of an economic province of the Minoans.

After about 1600 B.C., Minoan trade with Egypt (then in its Empire period) was extensive, though it seems to have declined somewhat with Ugarit and Byblos in Syria. One of the wall paintings in the tomb of Rekhmire, grand vizier of Thutmose III of Egypt, shows foreigners with gifts who, judged by their dress and the nature of their

Linear A on the Disc of Phaistos.
Herakleion Museum, Crete

Myceneans changed the system of numerical notation and probably of weights and measures. Presumably Mycenean influence also led to introduction of the throne room into the palace at Knossos at this time. Nevertheless it seems quite clear that during her period of Mycenean political and cultural domination Knossos continued to control Crete.

After the take-over of the Myceneans, Knossos passed through an "era of chill military grandeur." Then probably about 1375 B.C. the palace was destroyed again, never to be rebuilt. Destruction was by fire, presumably as a result of an attack by people from the mainland of Greece. The following period down to about 1000 B.C. is not well understood. But it appears to have been more prosperous than previously thought, with the founding of new settlements and the restoration of older ones, and new settlers arriving from the mainland.

Crete has often been considered the home of the Philistines. Scripture itself speaks of Caphtor as the Philistine homeland (Jeremiah 47:4; Amos 9:7).

Caphtor or Caphtorim is also mentioned in Genesis 10:14; Deuteronomy 2:23; and 1 Chronicles 1:12. The question is whether Caphtor and Crete are to be identified. The present knowledge of ancient Near Eastern developments does not permit a final decision, though many scholars are convinced that they should be. In any case, Philistine culture as it appeared in Palestine bore some Mycenean affinities.

Minoan Culture. Before turning to historical developments on the Greek mainland, we should look at non-political aspects of Minoan life. Minoan civilization rested on an agricultural base. Building on that, the populace developed extensive industry and trade during the second millennium.

The finest monument to their prosperity is the great palace at Knossos. (However, the palaces at Phaistos, Mallia, and Zakros should not be ignored.) Covering between five and six acres, this rambling structure consisted of a vast collection of rooms arranged around open courts. Built of stone, brick, and wood, it had fine state entrances with spacious staircases and state halls, in addition to private quarters and extensive storerooms. Pavements, foundations, and some walls were built of stone; upper parts of walls were generally brick; lintels and columns were of wood, and columns tapered downward instead of upward. Parts of the structure were four stories high. More than a mere royal residence, the palace served as an administrative

Linear B tablets in the British Museum.

A fresco depicting flying fish in the queen's bedroom at the palace at Knossos

assumed a permanence. Pigments seem to have been of mineral origin. The natural white often served as a background color, as well as of the exposed parts of the female body. Brown was the standard color of the male body. Blue was used to depict water. Other commonly used colors were yellow, red, and black. Black was used for hair and to provide detail. Some mixing and shading of colors occurred.

headquarters, as well as a storehouse, factory, arsenal, and artistic center.

One of the most impressive features of the palaces was the many wall frescoes, which were quite remarkable for spontaneity, creativity, and sensitivity to natural beauty. Some of the loveliest include a monkey gathering saffron in a meadow filled with crocuses, a bluebird amid rocks and roses, and a cat creeping among the rushes toward an unsuspecting pheasant. These frescoes are even more remarkable when we realize that they were painted while the plaster was still wet and therefore had to be completed within a few hours. The fact that Minoan artists could execute an entire painting in so short a time is a great tribute to their skill.

PRODUCING A MINOAN FRESCO

The wall paintings were among the most magnificent features of the Minoan palaces. By way of preparation, a thin coat of lime plaster was applied to the wall surface. Then, while the plaster was still wet, a taut string or sharp instrument was used to establish a grid or to outline the figures or pattern to be painted.

Also, while the plaster was still wet the artist began painting. His pigments penetrated the wet plaster and

Judging from the themes portrayed in their art, it's reasonable to conclude that the Minoans were a people who loved the beauty of nature and were not warlike. Their subjects were people, social gatherings at court, animals, plants, trees, flying fish, athletic events, and religious motifs. In contrast with contemporary Egypt and Assyria in later centuries, they did not have any interest in pompous military representations.

The importance of religion in the state and in private life is attested to by the position of the pillared shrine in the central court of the palace at Knossos. There were also numerous sanctuaries in mountain caves. Temples are also now known to have existed. The king himself was probably a high priest and was very possibly worshiped as a divine being in a manner similar to the Pharaohs of Egypt. But the Minoan king was not a haughty master like the Egyptian Pharaoh. His throne was a simple chair of gypsum, and a stone bench for his courtiers lined the throne room. Buttressed as it was by religious, economic, and military sanctions, the king's power must have been great, however, and virtually dictatorial during the last century of the Minoan kingdom.

At the center of Minoan religion was the worship of a female deity clothed in Minoan dress, with sacred serpents entwined around her arms. Exactly what this goddess represented is not definitely known. The idea that she was a mother goddess, a fertility deity, is concluded on the basis of comparison with known cults of Asia Minor in later centuries. The characteristic male deity is represented as a young boy.

Minoans were longheaded, narrow-faced, and short, the men averaging five feet two inches and the women four feet eleven inches. Men commonly wore shorts or kilts and sandals, and were beardless, perhaps as a result of Egyptian influence. Women wore more elaborate costumes: low-necked dresses with full skirts, ruffled or flounced. Men and women seem to have mingled rather freely at athletic events and religious festivals, possibly indicating that the Minoans gave their women freedom and dignity above that of any other Near Eastern people.

The common people of Crete lived in one- or two-story houses with no windows on the

The pillared shrine (in the left of the picture) on the west side of the central court at Knossos.

ground floor. Such windows as existed appeared in the second story; houses received their light and ventilation from the open court upon which the rooms faced. There seems to have been a reasonably prosperous middle class of farmers, artisans, and traders, which contrasted with the two-class structure of contemporary Egypt.

The Power of the Myceneans

Historical Developments. While the Minoans were developing their culture on their island of Crete, cultural advancement occurred less rapidly on the Greek mainland. To distinguish it from Minoan culture, that of the mainland is called Helladic (after the ancient name for Greece, Hellas). And it is divided into three periods of historical development: Early Helladic (3000–1900 B.C.), Middle Helladic (1900–1600 B.C.), and Late Helladic (1600–1200 B.C.).

About 3000 B.C. Greece emerged from the Neolithic into the Bronze Age under the impetus of a new wave of settlers. Coming by sea, probably from Asia Minor, they settled in east and central Greece and preferred sites on or near the coast. Meanwhile Macedonia and most of Thessaly retained a Neolithic culture. As noted earlier, the first Greeks, or Indo-Europeans, arrived in the peninsula sometime between 1900 and 1600 B.C., and the Middle Bronze Age is commonly dated 1900–1600 B.C.

The Mycenean Age really began about 1600 B.C. (as did the Late Bronze Age) and

The priest-king, portrayed in the palace at Knossos.

The acropolis of Mycenae

was coextensive with the Late Helladic period. This was a time when kings, who apparently tried to ape the Oriental monarchies, managed to extend their dominions over considerable stretches of countryside. Building their palace complexes at such sites as Mycenae and Tiryns in the northeast Peloponnesus and Pylos in the southwest Peloponnesus, they produced in them masses of pottery, bronze weapons, and other commodities that they marketed extensively in the Mediterranean world. They also exacted taxes from peasants on the surrounding lands as an additional source of wealth.

These palaces, then, were heavily fortified centers in which kings lived with a number of artisans and members of their bureaucracy and in which they kept their accumulated treasure. The palace centers were not true cities, for the bulk of the population seems to have lived in villages nearby. And that population appears to have been non-Greek and non-Greek-speaking.

Mycenaean traders and explorers ranged far and wide with their wares searching for various metals. From Mycenaean objects appearing in excavations elsewhere and foreign objects coming to light at Mycenaean sites, it may be concluded that these intrepid adventurers established contacts in Sicily, southern Italy, Cyprus, the upper Danube region, along the northern shore of the Aegean, the western shores of Asia Minor and the Syrian coast, the Cyclades, and Egypt. Occasionally they went beyond commercial activities and established colonies—in such places as Rhodes, the Asia Minor coast, and perhaps at Tarentum in southern Italy, and elsewhere.

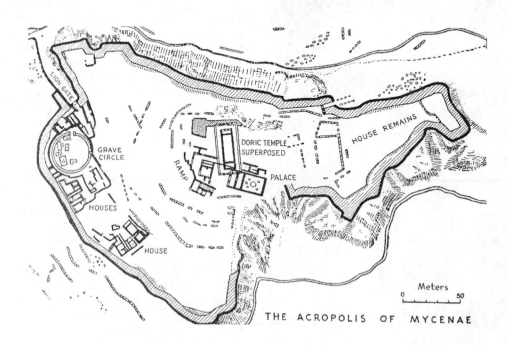

THE ACROPOLIS OF MYCENAE

The Plan of the Mycenae acropolis.

The civilization called "Mycenaean," which developed at the palace centers of the Peloponnesus and Boeotia, was given its name in honor of Mycenae, where Schliemann originally discovered it. By no means all of Hellas participated in the Mycenaean development. Macedonia, Epirus, Thessaly, and other sections of Greece retained much of the earlier culture of the Middle Bronze Age.

The Mycenaean kings especially established and maintained their power by means of chariot corps. Their military establishments paralleled what was happening in other lands of the eastern Mediterranean. In the nineteenth century B.C. came the invention of the spoked wheel and the development of a light, horse-drawn chariot. The earlier solid-wheel carts were cumbersome and too heavy for any animal to draw in battle. Now four-spoke and then six-spoke vehicles came into use. During the eighteenth century B.C. kings used horse-drawn chariots for rapid transportation and display. And during that century they used them in hunting. Small chariot corps appeared in the military establishments of the seventeenth century, and chariot warfare took place in the expansionist activities of the

All Mycenaean palaces were heavily fortified, as this entrance to the palace at Tiryns attests.

Hittites and Hyksos chiefs. After that, Hittites, Egyptians, Mycenaeans, and other rulers of the eastern Mediterranean world standardly maintained themselves or fought their battles with chariot corps.[14]

While a description of any or all of the known centers of Mycenaean culture is tempting to the historian, we focus here only on the best known of them all—Mycenae, the traditional home of Agamemnon, leader of the Greeks in the Trojan War. Actually, however, the palaces are best preserved at Pylos and Tiryns. At the former site is the "Palace of Nestor," named for another participant in the Trojan War. Here it is still possible to see the remains of sixty rooms.

The acropolis of Mycenae enjoyed an enviable location. Situated about ten miles from the sea, it was reasonably safe from pirate attacks. The acropolis stood 912 feet high and was isolated by two steep ravines, on the north and south. The site dominated the main road and thus the trade between Argos and Corinth and central Greece. The wall around the acropolis forms an irregular triangle, measuring 656 feet at the base and 984 feet on the sides. Most of the wall, varying in thickness

The Lion Gate at Mycenae.

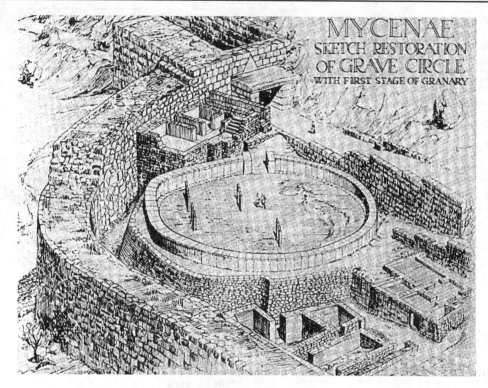

The Grave Circle at Mycenae.

from ten to forty-six feet and standing to a height of fifty-five feet, was built of huge undressed stones. But at the corners and around the gateways, the blocks are squared and arranged in horizontal layers.

The main gate, the famous Gate of the Lions, is in the northwest corner of the wall. Measuring about ten feet in width and slightly over ten feet in height, it is topped by a great lintel over fifteen feet long, which is in turn surmounted by a triangular slab on which is carved two lionesses (protec-

Gold cups found in the grave circle at Mycenae.

tresses of the palace) standing face to face on their hind legs; between them stands a column.

Just inside the Lion Gate on the right is a royal grave circle almost ninety feet in diameter. In this enclosure, ringed by a double row of stone slabs, were found nineteen skeletons. Buried there sometime between 1550 and 1500 B.C., the male skeletons were accompanied by masks and breastplates of gold, swords, daggers, gold and silver drinking cups, gold signet rings, and vessels of metal, stone, and clay. The female skeletons were accompanied by gold frontlets, toilet boxes, and jewelry. The graves were marked by stelae, on some of which horse-drawn chariots were presented. These chariots and scenes of war and hunting portrayed on artifacts within the tombs definitely show a mainland influence rather than Minoan.

This grave area was originally outside the walls but was brought within them during a later expansion about 1400 B.C. In A.D. 1952, a second grave circle (dating before

Entrance to the Treasury of Atreus.

which was twenty-six by thirteen by fifteen feet deep) and by the Perseia spring.

After 1500 B.C. great beehive tombs or tholoi, were built in the surrounding hillsides. The most famous of these is the so-called Treasury of Atreus, or Tomb of Agamemnon, or Tomb of the Lioness, across the road from the Lion Gate. An inclined unroofed passageway led down to the entrance. A doorway about eighteen feet high and nine feet wide opened into a circular chamber, shaped like a beehive, over forty-three feet high and almost forty-seven feet in diameter. The huge lintel over the door is twenty-eight feet long, ten feet thick and four feet high, and is estimated to weigh 120 tons. Above that is a triangular area with sides measuring about ten feet. Probably a carved stone block once filled the gap.

The dome of the tomb was formed of thirty-three rings of stone blocks curved in their inner surface and arranged in corbels, and capped with a round slab that formed the lid. The interior originally was decorated with bronze rosettes at the fourth ring of masonry. On the right of this "beehive" was a chamber about twenty feet wide, twenty-eight feet deep, and twenty feet high. Many of these unusual tombs have been found at Mycenae, Pylos, and elsewhere in Greece.

That Mycenae continued to be inhabited in the classical period is attested both by history and archaeology. For instance,

1600 B.C.) was found outside the walls of Mycenae. It was likewise almost ninety feet in diameter and also contained many rare *objets d'art* but no precious metals.

From the Lion Gate to the palace led the royal way, a ramp for chariots proceeding to the palace. Twenty-two steps ascended from this ramp to an anteroom, which in turn led into the throne room. Adjacent to the throne room was an open courtyard about fifty by forty feet. To the east of this stood the megaron, or great hall, measuring about forty-two by forty feet. The rest of the two-story structure has slid into the ravine.

As to decoration of the palace, the stuccoed floors were laid out in colored checkerboard squares, and the walls were covered with frescoes in the Minoan style. A great painted fireplace stood in the center of the megaron. Water for the acropolis area was supplied by abundant cisterns (the largest of

TREASURY OF ATREUS

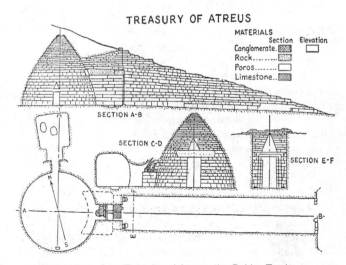

The design of the Treasury of Atreus, the Behive Tomb.

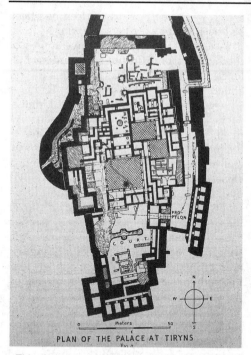

PLAN OF THE PALACE AT TIRYNS

This plan of the palace at Tiryns shows both the heavy fortification and the great hall as the central feature.

Mycenae sent eighty men to the battle of Thermopylae (480 B.C.) and two hundred to the battle of Plataea (479 B.C.) Foundations of a Doric temple were in the seventh century B.C. superimposed on the Mycenaean palace. Hellenistic walls, as well as remains of houses of post-Mycenaean construction may be seen on the acropolis.

Mycenaean Civilization. Mycenaean civilization has been described as basically Minoan with the addition of certain northern or Indo-European elements introduced by the Greeks. The material remains unearthed in such places as the grave circle at Mycenae show a high development in metal working and pottery production, reflecting Minoan influence and perhaps a Minoan hand. But the artistic motifs show northern influence, with a preference for war and hunting scenes and with bearded men, as opposed to the smooth-shaven Minoans with their interest in nature scenes.

Mycenaean houses and palaces had as their chief element the megaron, or great hall, with its fireplace, whereas Minoan structures were generally collections of rooms surrounding open courts. Mycenaean clothes were heavier than those of the Minoans, their body armor more extensive, their weapons more numerous, and their fortifications more formidable. Minoan cities were unwalled.

MYCENAEAN PALACES

Mycenaean palaces functioned as centers of administration, storage, and manufacturing. They ruled over surrounding communities that ranged in size from a few households to hundreds or even a few thousand people. Though on the countryside production was varied, the palaces had specialized economies that concentrated on the cultivation of a few crops, production of perfumed olive oil, textiles, and other craftwork—especially in bronze. A workforce of many hundred was directly under control of the palace, and it was effectively managed by an administrative system.

Palace construction centered around a megaron, a hall containing a hearth and throne approached through an ante-room and porch. Other rooms opened off adjacent corridors. Additional associated structures included storage buildings and workshops. Palace fortification walls consisted of large unworked stone and averaged some twenty-five feet high. Walls were actually double—two faces of massive blocks with a rubble fill and averaging some fifteen to twenty-five feet thick.

Stripped of their poetic additions, the legends of the period reveal a hard, brutal, and violent society in which piracy and murder were not uncommon. In this troubled age the guardian of trade was the sword. While Mycenaean culture developed under the tutelage of the Minoans after 1600 B.C., it was more or less on its own after 1400, when the Cretan palaces were destroyed. During its later stages, art and other aspects of culture showed a noticeable decline.

As to religion of the period, although the tablets mention priests and priestesses, no Mycenaean temples are known. And other than Zeus, Hera, Poseidon, Athena, and Hermes, no deities can be identified with certainty.

Fall of Mycenaean Civilization. The Mycenaean world almost literally came apart at the seams. But as in all periods of stress, outside forces were also tugging at the fabric of civilization and eventually tore it to shreds. There seems to have been serious internal stress among the Mycenaean states. Thebes was destroyed around 1350 B.C. by Mycenae. After about 1250 B.C., Mycenae, Tiryns, Pylos, and Athens were strengthening their defenses, whether against unrest at home or attack from abroad we do not know.

Meanwhile Mycenaean markets must have shriveled with the unrest in the eastern Mediterranean. Philistines, Libyans, and others hit Egyptian defenses around 1230 B.C. and again shortly after 1190. The Egyptian Empire came to an end around 1100. Raiders delivered blows to the Hittites which sent them reeling about 1225 B.C. and destroyed their empire early in the twelfth century. Troy was destroyed around 1250 or a little later, presumably by the Mycenaean chiefs described in Homer's *Iliad*. Between 1200 and 1150 attacks wiped out the Mycenaean political and economic systems built around the kings and their palaces.

Their greatness continued in ancient times only in the shadowy historical memory of Greek legend (later embodied in Homer). Today the memory of Mycenaean greatness is perpetuated in such places as the Mycenaean room in the National Museum, Athens, and the archaeological shrines that dot the landscape of the Peloponnesus.

The old view is that the culprit responsible for the destruction of the Mycenaeans and the subsequent break in civilization was the Dorian invasion. But that is almost completely discounted now. Evidently the Dorians did not even enter the southern part of Greece until long after the death of the old order. They did not have to fight to overcome the earlier lords of the countryside but entered land largely depopulated.

Robert Drews in his *The End of the Bronze Age* (1993) makes a case for the view that about 1200 B.C. barbaric raiders and pirates discovered a way to overcome the military forces on which the Mycenaeans and the eastern kingdoms depended. Infantrymen discovered that javelins and long slashing swords could outmatch chariots. After chariot armies had been supreme for more than four hundred years, the infantry once again took back the field, to hold it for millennia. It was not mass migrations that destroyed the old order but near neighbors and sometimes mercenaries who had served in the Mycenaean military and who as infantrymen helped to defeat Mycenaean chariot armies.

A reconstruction of the megaron at Mycenae.

While Drews has made a contribution, his explanation has not been universally accepted. There are at least two other possible explanations for the massive disruption of the twelfth century B.C. and the decline of population in the Aegean area. One is epidemic or plague. But there is no evidence of mass graves or many simultaneous burials. Another possibility is drought or other weather problems that disrupted the fragile economy and the agriculture of the region and led people to move elsewhere. Especially the climatic changes would have an effect if primitive peoples believed that the weather gods were conspiring against them. Several scholars have found the explanation of weather problems to be appealing, and they have produced some evidence for climatic difficulties at that time. But the truth is that at the present time we do not have an adequate explanation for the systems collapse of the twelfth century B.C.[14a]

The Dark Ages

From about 1150 B.C. to 850 or 800 B.C. Greece passed through what is known as the Dark Ages or the Middle Ages. The period in called a dark era either because so little is known about it or because the light of culture burned very low. Three general observations may be made about the events of these three centuries.

First, the old order died. Probably a sharp decline in population occurred. Economic and social life sank to a primitive level. Craftsmanship became cruder, and sculpture almost disappeared. Commerce passed from the Greeks to the Phoenicians. We need to remember that the tenth century B.C. encompasses the era of Hiram of Tyre and Solomon of Israel, who conducted joint maritime exploits.

Second, this was an age of movement and confusion. Peoples who moved into Greece kept on moving southward into the peninsula and the Peloponnesus, southeastward into the Cyclades, and eastward to the coast of Asia Minor. Also, some of them went to settlements around the Black Sea, as well as in Egypt, Libya, Cyprus, Italy, Sicily, and Spain, among other places.

Third, a new order emerged with an Iron Age culture. In place of the larger Mycenaean kingdoms arose small barbaric states with a local patriotism strong enough to prevent the unity of Greece in the classical period. Greek city-states on the Asia Minor coast developed earlier and prospered more than the communities of the Greek mainland because of trade with the interior and contact with older cultures of the Orient.

The Formative Age (c. 850 or 800–500)[15]

Why these small city-states arose during the Dark Ages, developed more fully during the Formative Age, and came to their zenith during the subsequent Classical Age is a matter of considerable discussion and debate. As previously indicated, the geographical compartmentalization of Greece is given a large share of the credit for the division of Greece into city-states. But that is not the whole story. The Mycenaean kingdoms had managed to slice off larger chunks of real estate than most of the city-states. Moreover, there was between many of the city-states—for example, Corinth and Sicyon—no physical barrier to hinder unification. Some of the most mountainous parts of Greece (Arcadia and Aetolia) did not develop city-states at all, or at least not until very late. They used instead something like the canton system of Switzerland.

There was also something in the unsettled conditions of the times to explain the formation of city-states. Groups of people, related or unrelated, tended to band together for defense, especially around high places, such as the Acropolis of Athens or Corinth. Then, later, geographical conditions, economic self-sufficiency, and especially a fierce local loyalty kept several city-states from uniting.

In his *Republic* Plato expressed the view that an ideal city should have about 5,000 citizens. Actually, many had less than that, and three (Syracuse and Acragas [Agrigentum] in Sicily and Athens) had more than 20,000. At the height of her glory, Athens had a citizen population of some 170,000 to 200,000, including men, women, and children, as well as resident aliens and slaves. As to area, as already noted, Athens controlled about 1,000 square miles in the homeland of Attica, Sparta (including Messenia) controlled 3,200 square miles, and Corinth 248 square miles.

Characteristic of the ninth and eighth centuries B.C. was the Homeric[16] type of kingship. Although the king was com-

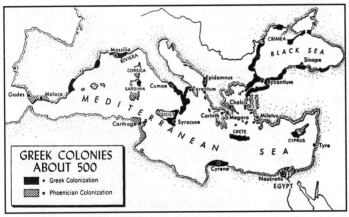

GREEK COLONIES ABOUT 500
- Greek Colonization
- Phoenician Colonization

Greeks settled in many areas around the Mediterranean and Black Sea by 500 B.C., laying down a deposit of Greek culture wherever they went.

mander-in-chief of the army, high priest, arbiter of disputes, and in general the head of state, he was no Oriental autocrat. He enjoyed as much authority as his forcefulness of personality, military prowess, and wealth could gain for him. Moreover, his office seems to have had some religious sanction attached to it, and his subjects were bound to him by an oath of allegiance—at least in wartime. The kingship was not hereditary in one family, though a son might succeed his father in office. Rather, it was bestowed on a candidate possessing the greatest power and prestige on the death of his predecessor. In a very real sense, the king was a noble among peers.

The power of the king was conditioned by the existence of a council and assembly. The council was made up of the nobles or elders or clan heads of the city-state. The council met on the call of the king, whenever some important business arose; it had no formal vote. Seniority determined who should speak first, and in the discussion that followed it would soon be obvious to the king what the consensus of opinion was. He was not obligated to follow the wishes of the council, but he was in no position to ignore their wishes continually.

The assembly probably consisted of men capable of bearing arms in defense of the state. It was normally summoned by the king. Not really a legislative body, the assembly served as a means of sounding public opinion and obtaining approval for a given course of action, and it presumably approved the choice of a new king.

During the eighth century B.C. there was an evolution from monarchy to the age of nobles. This came by gradual limitation of the king's power, while the nobles jealously guarded the traditional rights of their families. The seventh century, then, was the age of nobles—at least the first half of it was.

By the middle of the century a new force arose to challenge the nobles' power. The price of iron, and thus of iron weapons, began to fall, coincidental with a recognition that heavily armed infantry was superior to the old cavalry and chariotry units of the nobility. In addition, a developing commerce made possible new sources of income. Since it was the practice of ancient states to depend on their warriors to provide their own armor, and since it was expected that those who contributed most to the protection of the state should have the most to say about ruling it, this new aristocracy began to demand more voice in government. It is important to observe that with the rise in trade came the urbanization of much of central and eastern Greece.

The sixth century B.C. has often been characterized as the age of tyrants. These men were called tyrants because they won power in defiance of law and ruled without legal restraint. They commonly rose to power because of some social or economic imbalance in the state that produced a crisis.

There is sufficient data to prove that they were not mere cruel despots but often were men of considerably progressive and constructive statesmanship. For instance, Periander of Corinth promoted commerce and letters. Pisistratus of Athens encouraged commerce, manufacturing, art, music, drama, and literature. And often they enforced laws against injustice, stopped oppression of the masses, and confiscated large estates, dividing them among the landless. By bending the upper classes to their iron rule, they helped to establish a reign of law and make future constitutional government possible.

During the classical period of the fifth and fourth centuries B.C. oligarchy and democracy were characteristic. As time went on, the nobles and the wealthy classes tended to merge to form a government in which political rights were determined by property qualifications, regardless of pedigree. In Athens, a democracy of sorts came into being, and that form of government spilled over into some of her imperial possessions. But democracy was never very much at home in the ancient Greek world. It should be observed that while the foregoing description of the pattern of political evolution in the various city-states serves as a useful generalization, the development was not everywhere the same, nor did it come everywhere at the same pace.

Colonization. While there was an evolution in the political and social structure at home, the city-states were expanding abroad. A tremendous colonization movement occurred during the Formative Age. To a degree this was merely a continuation of the earlier migrations, but special forces continued to impel Greeks to settle all along the Asia Minor coast, and also in Cyprus, Egypt, Libya, Sicily and Italy, France, Spain, and along the Black Sea.

The Greeks were a maritime people, and it was natural for them to establish outposts along the sea-lanes. Presumably they realized an economic advantage in the settling of colonies as sources of raw materials and markets for goods. Also, colonization to some extent resulted from social discontent and overpopulation.

Overpopulation may be real or perceived. It is real if there are more people than the slim resources of an area can support. It is thought to be the case when the wealthy and powerful control the best lands, pushing the lower classes out into marginal territory on the hillsides and in other places where agricultural returns are meager. When that happens, a percentage of the population will seek to try their fortunes elsewhere. The amount of good land in Greece was very limited.

This widespread movement of Greeks brought with it a massive dissemination of Greek language and culture. On this early foundation Alexander the Great and his successors were to build effectively in later centuries. So when the Romans later took over the East, they found a Hellenistic culture firmly entrenched. Already highly influenced by Greek culture themselves, the Romans did not try to dislodge the Greek culture where they found it, or to Latinize their empire. As a result a Greco-Roman culture developed throughout the Mediterranean world.

This greatly facilitated the spread of Christianity when it came upon the world scene. Thus Paul could address his message in Greek to the whole Mediterranean world. His letters and other New Testament books could become the common possession of all literate persons of the Empire. And the Old Testament translated into Greek (the Septuagint) served as the Bible of the early church everywhere. Moreover, with a single culture dominating the entire empire, missionaries did not have to learn new languages or cultural ways or suffer culture shock as they went to unevangelized lands.

The Greater Greek States of the Formative Age

The city-states that were most important during the Formative Age were Argos, Aegina, Corinth, Megara, Sicyon, Chalcis, Thebes, Sparta, and Athens. Argos was strong in the eighth and seventh centuries B.C. During the following century, the rise of Sparta and Corinth brought the decline of Argos. Aegina, Corinth, Megara, Sicyon, and Chalcis owed their importance to trade. Thebes was great because she was the chief power of Boeotia and established authority over the other cities of the plain. Sparta and Athens were especially significant to the history of Greece and to the history of civilization.

Sparta. The Spartans occupied one of the richest and most fertile areas of Greece: Laconia in the southeastern part of the Peloponnesus. Before them the Mycenaeans had prospered in that region. Archaeologists have identified over fifty

Mycenaean sites there.[17] How that Mycenaean civilization came to an end around 1200 B.C. we cannot be sure, but it apparently was not at the hands of Dorian invaders. Dorians do not seem to have arrived in the valley before about 1000 B.C. During the next century four adjacent villages slowly developed on the west bank of the Eurotas River. By 800 they had united to form a city-state.[18] And within another fifty years they had become masters of all Laconia. Though popularly the people who settled there are known as Spartans, officially they called their city Lacedaemon and themselves Lacedaemonians.

Until the last few years the picture of Sparta we have almost universally been given is of a kind of military communism, an austere and narrow barrack-room mentality, a city-state in arms. But now that is changing. We have known for some time that in spite of the fact that Sparta had no good natural harbors, she conducted trade abroad. Egyptian and Oriental commerce is implied in certain archaeological finds in the area. In the earlier years of her history Sparta enjoyed the cultural advantages common to much of the rest of Greece. Her sculptors worked in stone and wood, and her builders constructed some fine buildings—notably the council building and the Temple to Athena at Sparta. Such poets as Alcman and Terpander settled in the capital. L. F. Fitzhardinge in *The Spartans* (1980) presents a rather extended summary of Spartan involvements in the arts, metallurgy, and literature.

But he has shown their whole development in a very different light from the usual interpretation. His view is that the traditional account of Spartan history was substantially fictitious. His analysis runs something like this.[19] When the Dorians came down into Laconia they found few inhabitants. The leaders divided the best lands of the valley among themselves. They pushed some lower class persons and later comers out into poorer country. These outdwellers, or *perioeci*, formed their own townships and tended to produce some of the Spartan crafts. They enjoyed a certain amount of autonomy but remained part of the city-state. Between about 736 and 716 B.C. in a

protracted war the Spartans conquered the upper Messenian plain in the west, and the nobles reduced the population to tenants paying a percentage of their produce to their new masters.

Then around 640 the Messenians revolted, supported by inhabitants of the part of Messenia that had not been conquered earlier. The Spartans ultimately won the twenty-year conflict because they adopted the new method of hoplite warfare, which required trained and disciplined armed spearmen. Because there was no class of prosperous farmers from whom such contingents could be drawn, Sparta artificially created a hoplite class. For their support the state granted them the use of tracts of land with a labor force to support them while they were away at war. The land came from public land or land confiscated from the *perioeci*, and later from the lands confiscated from the Messenians, not from the estates of the nobles.

The origin of the labor force, known in history as the helots, is not very clear. Probably they had been landless laborers and poor tenant-farmers. It should be noted, however, that these lands and the helots belonged to the state, not to individual hoplites. And the hoplites could not sell, evict, or maltreat them. Thus a kind of military communism was in the making, with the hoplites eating their meals in a common mess, with food brought from their estates.

After the Second Messenian War the state wanted to disband the system, but the hoplites made such a protest that it was allowed to continue. So from around 620 to around 450 there were two classes of Spartan citizens: the old landed gentry and the hoplites, with very different ways of life. But the hoplite class for a long time was content to follow the gentry in personal tastes and lifestyle. Gradually, however, the hoplite class grew in power and influence and became more, shall we say, "Spartan." And during the Persian wars what had been the propaganda and lifestyle of a party became the ideology of the state. The gentry lost their power in public life and turned to sport, especially horse breeding and racing. Artistic production and construction of public buildings virtually disappeared. In general it may be said that until the fifth century B.C. most Spartans lived much like other Greeks.

Politically, Sparta had four institutions, that were somewhat different during the sixth-fifth centuries from what they had been earlier. A dual kingship was hereditary in two families. Originally enjoying supreme power, they had now lost all political clout, retaining only ceremonial and religious functions. They were supreme commanders of the army in the field, but they could not make war.

The assembly consisted of all citizens. Essentially a hoplite body, it made all major decisions on policy and its decisions were binding on the *perioeci*, though they were not represented.

The council, originally powerful and originally consisting of heads of noble families, now was elective and limited to twenty-eight, together with the two kings, one of whom presided. Members were chosen by the assembly from citizens over sixty. It was still the court for certain crimes.

A board of five ephors was elected annually from the whole citizen body and held office for one year. In particular they were to maintain public order. Its duties were executive, not deliberative. When the assembly had declared war and named the commander, it fell to the ephors to call up the army and decide its strength.

The total result of the political and social system of Sparta was to produce an oligarchy organized in such a way as to prevent change and a state that has often been called a "city-state in arms." At seven boys began rigorous physical training and lived under a harsh discipline; at twenty they became active soldiers and lived in barracks. At thirty, when they were permitted to marry, they joined a military mess of fifteen men, to which they contributed their share of food from their own farms, worked by the helots. Family life was kept to a minimum. At sixty they were freed from their military life and able to live at home with their families. It was not until the middle of the third century B.C. that the helots were freed and a democratic revolution occurred.

The foreign policy of Sparta was effected through the medium of the Peloponnesian League (city-states of the Peloponnesus).

Organized before the end of the sixth century B.C., it was not a federal organization, nor was it in complete subjection to Sparta. Rather, it was a permanent offensive and defensive alliance under Spartan leadership. It had no regular tribute. Decisions of the assembly were binding on all members and none could secede. However, all of the states had local autonomy and could go to war against each other.

Athens. Although Athens was an important center in Greece during the Mycenaean era, she lost much of her early power and prestige during the breakup of Mycenaean power and the Dark Ages. And she was certainly not one of the more progressive Greek states in 750 B.C. For centuries Athens remained a backward little country town with little interest in trade.

During the seventh century B.C. important changes occurred in the legal and political structure of the state. The power of the monarchy was broken and an aristocracy established in its place. The political instrument of the aristocracy was the council of the Areopagus which annually elected an archon, who was the chief executive officer in charge of civic activities and of the chief judicial official. Six thesmothetai presided over the courts and assisted the archon. The old basileus (king) became the priest in charge of religious functions of state. During the latter part of the century, in 621 B.C., Draco codified the laws of Athens and therefore brought more order into the legal processes. However, it was a harsh code and did little to alleviate popular discontent.

This discontent arose largely because of the agrarian problems of the state. The land, which was incapable of supporting the entire population, was concentrated in the hands of a few people, and a large segment of the once free population had been reduced to serfdom. Some had even been sold abroad as slaves. The threat of civil war was averted by giving Solon, an aristocrat trusted by the common people, the authority to make sweeping economic, political, and social changes.

Perhaps such a happy arrangement would not have been effected except for the fact that trouble between clans prevented the upper class from maintaining a solid front against the lower classes. Moreover, Megara was exerting military pressure on Athens at this point, and there was a need for a larger number of free citizens to fill the ranks of the Athenian army.

In order to meet the immediate problem of the early sixth century B.C, Solon put through a reform known as a *seisachtheia,* or "Disburdenment," which freed the peasants who had become slaves because of their debts and forbade debt slavery in the future. Then he proceeded to change the direction of the economy of Attica. Solon encouraged the settlement of foreign artisans at Athens, the teaching of trades by fathers to their sons, and the production of commodities for export. Development of the Athenian olive oil and pottery-making industries dates to this time. (Attica had the finest deposits of ceramic clay in Greece.)

Solon is also credited with having rated the citizen classes according to income to determine their relative participation in government. Of the four classes established at this time, the upper two were eligible for the magistracies, the third could be elected as minor officials, and the fourth—landless men—could not hold office. The citizen assembly was revived and strengthened, and it obtained the right of electing officers and magistrates and became sovereign in the area of legislation. More than likely the Areopagus Court presented the slate of business to the assembly.

Within a generation it became clear that the Solonian program was not an adequate solution for the ills of Attica. Clan groups continued to dominate society; the poor and landless were still in a precarious economic position; and the new group of artisans sought a place in the governmental sun. This fracturing of the socio-political organism made possible the tyranny of the Pisistratid family during the last half of the sixth century B.C. This tyranny may be described as a benevolent despotism designed to solve the economic problems that beset Attica.

Pisistratus and his sons broke the power of the landed aristocracy and confiscated the land of exiled clan chieftains and divided it among the landless or those with insufficient holding to support a family. They also encouraged the industrial and commercial development of the state and broke down the traditional Athenian policy of isolation. They engaged in a deliberate attempt to urbanize Athens and to make it the center of Attica, to establish a state coinage, and to enhance the city with public works. Pisistratus began the construction of the great Temple of Zeus in the southeastern part of the city and a monumental gateway to the acropolis. He also built up the Panathenaic festival in honor of Athena—for commercial as well as religious reasons.

In the struggle that followed the expulsion of the tyranny from Athens, Cleisthenes rose to power and in 508 B.C. was given authority, like Solon, to legally reform the government. He became the real founder of Athenian democracy. First he divided Attica into demes, or townships, of which there were less than two hundred. All residents were enrolled in their local deme, and this enrollment was the basis of citizenship in the state. Adjacent demes were combined into thirty trittyes, and these in turn were organized into ten tribes. In order to destroy the old sectionalism, Cleisthenes formed each tribe by combining an urban, a rural, and a coastal trittyes. Each of the ten tribes furnished a contingent for the army and elected its own general; voting in the assembly was also by tribes.

Then Cleisthenes set up a new council of five hundred—fifty from each tribe; and the representatives of the tribes took turns acting as a committee of the whole for thirty-six-day periods. The council prepared the business for the assembly and developed functions that reduced the power of the magistrates.

The Classical Age of Greece

The Persian Threat. While Athens and Sparta were becoming the leading powers in Hellas, the rest of the world was not standing still. In the West, Rome had established her Republic by about 500 B.C. and was beginning to unify the peninsula of Italy, and Carthage was becoming an increasingly significant power. In the East,

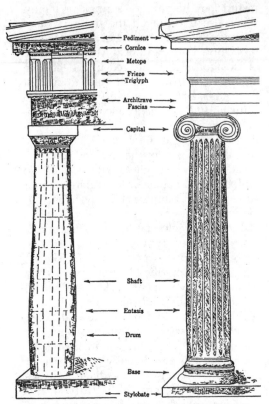

Pediment
Cornice
Metope
Frieze
Triglyph
Architrave
Fascias
Capital
Shaft
Entasis
Drum
Base
Stylobate

DORIC AND IONIC STYLES OF ARCHITECTURE

During the classical age of Greece the Doric style of architecture was common on the Greek mainland and the Ionic among the Greek states in Asia Minor.

Croesus of Lydia had conquered all of the Greek cities in Asia Minor except Miletus by 550 B.C. Four years later Cyrus of Persia toppled the Lydian kingdom and inherited her Greek possessions along the Asia Minor coast. Those Greeks were forced to pay heavier tribute and their freedom-loving inhabitants became cogs in an imperial machine.

After Cyrus destroyed the Babylonian Empire in 539 B.C., his successors began to eye Greek possessions across the Hellespont or Dardanelles, the narrow strait between Europe and Turkey in Asia. In 512 Darius crossed the Hellespont and conquered the Thracian coast, posing a threat to European Greece. For Athens the advance meant loss of colonies, which served as outposts to guard approaches to the Hellespont and the Black Sea trade, as

well as the loss of revenue from mines owned by the Pisistratids in the north Aegean. Persian moves constituted an act of war against Athens. Relations between the Persians and Greeks were strained by two further conditions. The Spartans had been allies of Croesus, king of Lydia, and Hippias, last of the Athenian tyrants, had fled to Persia when the Athenians had expelled him about 510. When the Persians requested that Hippias be restored to power, the delegation had been granted less than diplomatic courtesy.

The immediate cause of the Greco-Persian War was an uprising of the Asiatic Greeks in 499 B.C. Led by Aristagoras of Miletus and supported by Athens and Eretria (in Euboea), the revolt was initially successful. All of Greek Asia Minor burst into flames of rebellion, and the Persian center of Sardis was destroyed. But soon the Persians regained their composure; Athens and Eretria forsook their allies; and the Persians quelled the revolt, destroying Miletus and selling the survivors into slavery. Thus a leading center of the arts and humanities passed temporarily out of existence with a great loss to Hellenic culture.

In 492 B.C., as soon as Asia Minor was secured, the Persians again went into

A Corinthian capital. Corinthian capitals did not become popular until about 350-300 B.C. Later the Romans loved this more decorative style.

action. The purpose of the campaign was twofold: to reconquer Thrace and to punish Athens and Eretria. The first aim they easily accomplished, but the second was thwarted because a storm destroyed the fleet in the north Aegean.

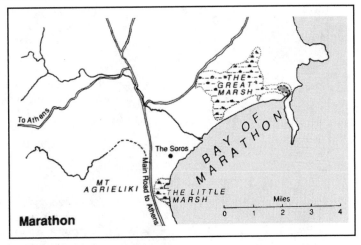

Marathon

Two years later the Persians were ready to go into action once more. This time they determined to attack directly across the Aegean with a force which Herodotus said consisted of six hundred ships. They besieged Eretria and Attica at the same time. With a Persian army occupying the plain of Marathon, the Athenians were not free to go to the aid of their compatriots to the north. After the Persians had destroyed Eretria, they moved southward in force. Hippias, the former tyrant of Athens, guided the Persian troops.[20]

The plain of Marathon is about five miles long and two miles deep. At its northern and southern ends lie marshes, and the plain itself is bisected by the Charadra River. From the plains' northern extremity the Cynosura (Kynosura) promontory extends a mile into the Aegean, forming an anchorage sheltered from the north and east. The battle took place in the southern part of the plain. The Persians were flanked on the right by the river, on the left by the southern marsh; at their backs was the sea. The Greeks had the benefit of descending from a higher position.

Most of the Persians remained on board ship waiting for their troops to destroy the Athenians. Then the victorious Persian army planned to march on Athens by land, while the fleet sailed around Attica to attack the unwalled city by sea. Tradition has it that ten thousand Athenian and Plataean infantrymen defeated a force twice as large, inflicting 6,400 casualties and sustaining 192. Then an Athenian Olympic runner dashed the twenty-six miles to Athens, falling dead from exertion at the outskirts as he gasped, "Rejoice, we conquer!"

Modern historians tend to reduce the numbers of the men involved and of casualties inflicted. The truth is that we do not know exactly how many fought. It is certain, however, that the Athenians won a signal victory, made a forced march during the night (variously thought to be August 10, September 12, or September 21), and appeared at the shore to greet the Persian hosts when they arrived at the port of Phalerum the next morning. Having had enough, the Persians sailed away. Greece enjoyed a ten-year respite from attack.

The conflict with Persia was characterized by disunity of the Greeks, lack of persistence by the Persians, and heroism of the Greek soldiers and sailors. In Greece prior to Marathon, Sparta was perfecting her military machine and achieving greater dominance of the Peloponnesus; she overcame Argos

The burial mound at Marathon that covers the Greek dead.

Monument to the Greek soldiers at Marathon.

Alongside sailed the fleet, which always played an important role in supplying the land forces. Cook estimates that some 750,000 people were on the move with Xerxes—in the land and sea forces.[21]

The next Greek stand was at Thermopylae, on the Malian Gulf just north of Delphi. Here in central Greece the chance of defeating the Persians was good. The pass between the mountains and the Malian Gulf was only about fifty feet wide.[22] Although the army might be out-flanked by naval forces as at Tempe, the Greek navy could and did control the Gulf. Leonidas and his Spartans fought bravely, but a traitor showed the Persians a secret pass through the mountains so they could come in behind Spartan lines. The Greeks were defeated, though they inflicted an esti-mated twenty thousand casualties. And the Persians came pouring into Boeotia and Attica. Athens had no effective defenses and the city was easily taken. The war might have ended quickly, but the entire Athenian populace had been evacuated before the Persians arrived.

The Peloponnesian generals were deter-mined to hold the line at the Isthmus of Corinth, but Themistocles fought against the abandonment of Athens, Aegina, Salamis, and Megara, and even threatened to withdraw and colonize in the West. Reportedly he was able to lure the Persian fleet into the narrow strait between the island of Salamis and the mainland of Attica to attack the Greek fleet anchored there. Xerxes expected a crushing victory and sat enthroned on a slope overlooking the strait in the morning. Clearly he was not prepared for the spectacle that unfolded on that September day.

Though we do not have an exact idea of the formations of the fleets, the Greeks were able somehow to maneuver the Persians into positions where their ships fouled one another or were pinned against the shore. Reportedly some two hundred Persian ships were lost. The loss of personnel included the admiral, who was the king's brother, and other important individuals. Whatever the final statistics, the morale of the Persian fleet snapped and within a day it was on its way back to the Hellespont.

in 494 B.C. At Athens, Themistocles was in control and in 493–492 B.C. began to devel-op port facilities for naval squadrons at Piraeus. The new democracy was creating a small but strong citizen army. After Marathon, Themistocles persuaded the people to invest the proceeds of a rich new vein of silver discovered at Laurium in south Attica in the Athenian navy.

Between 490 and 480 B.C. the Persians did not attack. They were occupied with a revolt in Egypt, and Darius died in 486. Finally, in the spring of 480, Xerxes began his march through Thrace and Macedonia. The Greeks (the Peloponnesian League under the leadership of Sparta) had devised a plan of sorts, but it was by no means an effective united effort. Their first stand was at the vale of Tempe, just south of Olympus on the northern border of Thessaly. There the Greek flank was turned because the Persian fleet was able to sail in behind their position. The Persian army marched south.

Without a fleet to provide supply and cover for the army, Xerxes had no choice but to leave for Sardis, where he could keep the empire under surveillance.

The remaining Persian army of some one hundred thousand wintered in Boeotia. The Athenians returned home. When the Persians under Mardonius started to advance on Athens again in the spring of 479 B.C., the Athenians found it necessary to evacuate their city once more. Finally Sparta grew worried that the Athenians could not stand the strain much longer and gathered a huge allied force, which cut to pieces the Persian army at Plataea, nine miles south of Thebes.

While we cannot be sure of the number of Persian casualties, they were extensive. Among the dead must have been nearly all the ten thousand Immortals, (the crack troops of the army); the Persian line infantry division; and thousands of Persian marines. The Persians could never again regain their former military ascendancy. Apparently Xerxes decided to bury his sorrows in his harem. Interestingly it was at this point, in his seventh year, 479 B.C. or the very beginning of 478, that Esther became his queen (cf. Esther 2:16).

Meanwhile insurrection was brewing in the Greek cities of Asia Minor. A Greek fleet was enticed to come over, and it won a great naval victory at Mycale near Miletus, traditionally on the same day as the battle of Plataea, though it was probably a little later. Within a year most of the Greek cities on the Asia Minor coast were free, and the European side of the Hellespont was recaptured. At the same time the western

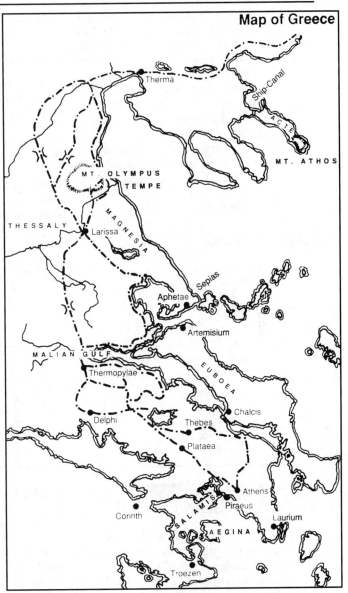

Map of Greece

The route of the Persian army in 480 B.C. After the victory at Thermopylae, they went on to suffer a naval defeat in the Bay of Salamis. Then Xerxes left Greece, but part of his army wintered around Plataea, where they were cut to pieces in 479, probably in mid-August.

Greeks were winning a struggle with the Carthaginians, whose fleet they completely destroyed in 474.

Rise of Athenian Empire. The Greeks were free—but for what? It soon became clear that no continuing cooperation would follow on the heels of the Panhellenic cooperation in the war against Persia. The Hellenic League had been dominated by Sparta during the war. With her military outlook she had been able to provide good leadership. Now Pausanias, Spartan hero of Plataea, began to antagonize some of the Greek states with his overbearing attitude. Moreover, the isolationist home government of Sparta was not in sympathy with the policy of continued aggression against the Persians that Pausanias advocated. At this point, in 478 B.C., under the leadership of Themistocles, Athens proposed a confederacy known as the Delian League.

Thermopylae, 480 B.C.

THE ATHENIAN EMPIRE

The Confederacy of Delos, or the Delian League was formed under Athenian leadership in 478 B.C. for the purpose of protecting the Greeks against the Persians. Initially it aggressively pursued the original goal, and Persian garrisons were driven out of Thrace and Greek communities in western Asia Minor.

But gradually the association fell completely under Athenian control, sometimes as a result of Athenian military subjugation of individual members. And ultimately the two hundred states of the league became an Athenian empire, contributing to Athens' prosperity and cultural

development and the achievement of her golden age.

The Delian League was so-called because its treasury and administrative center were located on the sacred island of Delos (sacred to Apollo) in the Cyclades. Among the stipulations of the league were these important provisions: (1) Each ally was to contribute ships or money for the common cause. (2) Athens was to make the assessments and act as collector. (3) No state might withdraw from the league without the consent of all. (4) There was to be an annual congress of deputies in which each state had an equal vote; this congress was to meet under Athenian leadership.

The league stated well, with just assessments and continued success against the Persians, whom they were able to drive from almost all Ionian cities in Asia Minor by 468 B.C. But gradually the league was turned into an Athenian empire; an increasing number of states were reduced to subject status and forced to enact democratic constitutions.

Meanwhile, politics in Athens turned into a duel between the conservative pro-Spartan faction and the democratic, anti-Spartan faction. Themistocles led the latter, Cimon the former. In 471 Themistocles was exiled and the conservatives ruled for nine years. The democratic element regained power in 462, however, and the following year Pericles gained the reins of government, to hold them until his death in 429. The period is sometimes called the Age of Pericles, and sometimes the Golden Age of Athens.

Pericles was a direct heir of Themistocles—an enemy of Sparta and a democrat. He sought to build up a land empire in central Greece to match the maritime empire Athens already possessed.

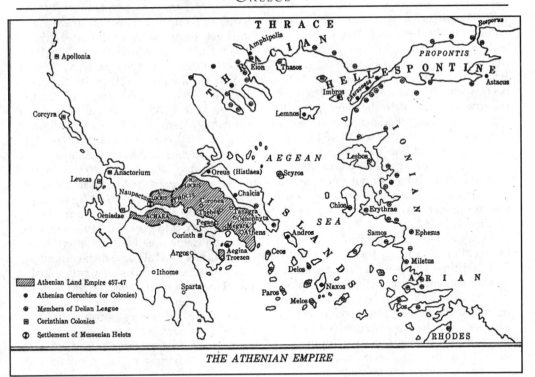

THRACE
Bosporus
Apollonia
Amphipolis
PROPONTIS
Eion
Thasos
Astacus
Imbros
Corcyra
Lemnos
AEGEAN
Lesbos
Oreus (Histiaea)
Scyros
Leucas
Anactorium
IONIAN
Naupactus
Chalcis
Chios
Erythrae
LOCRIS
PHOCIS
Coronea
Oeniadae
ACHAEA
Thebes
Tanagra
SEA
Oenophyta
Samos
Ephesus
Pegae
Megara
Corinth
Athens
Andros
Argos
Aegina
Troezen
Ceos
Miletus
Ithome
Delos
CARIAN
Sparta
Paros
Naxos
Melos
Cos
RHODES

Athenian Land Empire 457-47
Athenian Cleruchies (or Colonies)
Members of Delian League
Corinthian Colonies
Settlement of Messenian Helots

THE ATHENIAN EMPIRE

Temporarily he was successful in attaining his goal, but in the process he incurred the enmity of Sparta and involved himself in warfare with a large number of Greek states. At the same time his interference with Persian affairs in Egypt and Cyprus led to war with the colossus of the East, resulting in a loss of 250 ships and control of the sea as well. In 449 he was forced to make peace with the Persians and five years later arranged a thirty-year truce with Sparta. All he had accomplished was to weaken Athens and arouse the suspicion and enmity of the other Greek states.

Closer to home, Pericles gradually transformed the Delian League into an Athenian Empire. In the face of danger of Persian confiscation, the treasury was moved from Delos to Athens in 454 B.C., and the council of the league ceased to meet in 439. As a further protective measure, the two long walls were built between Athens and Piraeus. Completed in 456, they were 4½ miles long, 12 feet thick, and 30 feet high. And they guaranteed access of Athens to her port and thus to the sea—as long as her fleet kept the sea-lanes open. It should be remembered

Pericles. *The British Museum.*

that Themistocles had previously built walls around Athens and Piraeus.

In political affairs, Pericles succeeded in instituting a fully developed democracy. Before his day the power of the archon had been weakened and the office of strategos, or general, was made the most powerful office in the state; Pericles was elected to this post thirty times. Around 460 B.C. the Areopagus Court was stripped of most of its political power and retained control only over religious matters. About a decade later pay for public office was instituted; so it was no longer necessary for a man to be wealthy to hold office.

In spite of the losses during the early years of Pericles's rule, Athens was wealthy. The maritime empire was intact, and the income was immense. Pericles determined to beautify the city and especially to develop the Acropolis as a fitting symbol of the greatness of Athens and a suitable home for her patron goddess, Athena. Hippodamus of Miletus, the great city planner, was engaged to lay out the port city of Piraeus. Phidias, the master sculptor, was appointed to oversee the construction of the Parthenon and otherwise to beautify the Acropolis.

The Age of Pericles was a time of flowering of culture. Contemporary with Pericles were several of the greatest literary figures of all time, though they produced some of their best work before or after his day. Often called the "Father of history,"[23] Herodotus, of Halicarnassus, an Athenian dependency on the Asia Minor coast, knew Pericles and lived in Athens for a time. Thucydides of Athens, the first scientific historian, was over thirty years old when Pericles died. The great dramatists, Aeschylus, Sophocles, and Euripides all wrote tragedies during his period of rule. And Aristophanes, the great comedy writer, was coming to maturity when Pericles died. A number of the early philosophers were also known to him, including Anaxagoras, who taught for many years at Athens and died one year after Pericles. Greatest of the philosophers of the time, however, was Socrates, whose highest honors were earned during the thirty years after Pericles's death.

Periclean Democracy.[24] Since Athens especially gets credit for the birth of democracy, we are curious as to what it was like. Full-blown direct democracy came to Athens through the efforts of Pericles. At that point all male citizens eighteen and over had the right to vote in the "national" assembly, and male citizens over thirty were allowed to hold office and serve on juries. The assembly met in Athens on the Pnyx, a hill to the west of the Acropolis. There was room for as many as ten thousand to sit on the ground and be addressed by speakers who stood on a low stone platform carved out of the rock. In Pericles' day some forty thousand were qualified to attend. But most citizens lived at some distance and/or could not afford to take off work; usually attendance must have run in the five to six thousand range.

Six thousand jurors were impaneled annually to hear cases in the courts. All jurors, members of the Council of Five Hundred, archons and other public officials, and soldiers and sailors on duty were paid for their services. So citizens were not kept from public service because they could not afford to participate.

COMPARISON OF ATHENIAN AND CONTEMPORARY AMERICAN DEMOCRACY

- Athens had a direct democracy; all citizens had to travel to Athens, where they participated in a kind of "town meeting." Americans have a representative democracy. We elect our representatives who legislate on our behalf, and we can vote for them in convenient polling places.

- Participants in Athenian democracy were free men only, not women or slaves (some one-third of the population). In America both men and women can now vote, and there are no longer any slaves.

- In Athens individuals or groups who were defeated in an election might be exiled for a time or might feel more comfortable temporarily leaving the country. In America those defeated become the loyal opposition and are sometimes designated as sitting "on the other side of the aisle in congress."

- In both Athens and America the voting age was and is 18 and both states pay citizens for service in government, the military, and judicial duties.

The Council of Five Hundred consisted of fifty representatives from each of the ten tribes of the state, chosen by lot. They had the primary responsibility of preparing legislation for the assembly. The ten generals were basically military officials who commanded the army and navy and they were elected annually; this was Pericles's office. The Council of Five Hundred evaluated their qualifications. Market inspectors and commissioners of weights and measures were also chosen by lot.

In the court system on a given day jurors were assigned to specific cases. There was no public prosecutor or state's attorney or any lawyers at all. Plaintiffs and defendants made their own presentations, but they might hire speechwriters to help them present their cases. There was no judge, only a jury. During the trial plaintiffs and defendants presented their cases, rebutted their opponents, quoted the law, called witnesses, and summed up. An official using a water clock limited presentations. Cases were limited to one day and finally went to the jury, which voted by secret ballot, and a majority decided the verdict.[25]

Kagan observes that the democracy ruled Athens in an orderly fashion for 140 years with only two brief interruptions.[26]

We need to observe that the high level of democracy in Athens and the ability of the state to pay for such a large number of services required considerable prosperi-

ty. Athens' ability to pay the bill rested to a large degree on the income from the empire.

All this discussion of the democracy presupposes a fairly high level of education or at least literacy. If individuals were to be chosen by lot for numerous positions, most citizens had to be somewhat literate. How many formal schools there were and how much was communicated by educated slaves is an open question. William V. Harris developed the subject in *Ancient Literacy* (Harvard, 1989).

The Population of Athens. We often wonder how many people lived in the important city-state of Athens during its golden age. Meticulous studies indicate that at the end of the Periclean golden age and on the eve of the great plague that so decimated the population in 431 B.C., there were 43,000 male citizens eighteen to fifty-nine and 9,500 resident aliens in the same age group.[27] One of the outsatnding authorities, A.W. Gomme argues that to arrive at the total population, it is appropriate to multiply the adult citizen males by four to arrive at a figure of 172,000, and resident aliens by three (many without families) to arrive at a total of 28,500.[28] In assessing the strength of the slave labor force, he concludes that at that time there were about 80,000 adult men and 35,000 adult women, for a total of 115,000 between the ages of 18 and 59. When we add 172,000, 28,500, and 115,000, we arrive at a grand total of about 315,500 in the city-state.[29]

A fifth century Athenian trireme cruising. The Ahenian navy ruled the seas.

POPULATION IN ATHENS AT ITS HEIGHT

Citizens	172,000
Resident Aliens	28,500
Slaves	<u>115,000</u>
Total	315,500

The Peloponnesian War. The thirty-year truce that Pericles arranged with Sparta was recognized as just that—a truce. Both sides knew that a showdown could not be postponed forever. Ever since the days immediately after the Battle of Salamis (480 B.C.), fuel had been periodically added to the fire of contention between the two powers that would in a sense turn into a funeral pyre for independence of the city-state. Pericles' efforts to construct a land empire in central Greece had lost friends and had inclined several states to look to Sparta for help. And Athens' high-handedness with many of her dependencies led some of them to intrigue with Sparta. This was especially pronounced after the Peloponnesian War started.

In addition to this basic animosity, there was a specific cause of the war. Corinth was having a tiff with one of her colonies, Corcyra (Corfu), an island in the Adriatic Sea. At the height of the struggle, Corcyra appealed to Athens for help. Although realizing the danger, the Athenians decided to answer the appeal. Corcyra was an important naval power and could be used to outflank the commerce and naval potential of Corinth. The economic struggle between Athens and Corinth had led up to this explosive situation, and now Corinth demanded that the Peloponnesian Congress act. Sparta had tried to remain aloof from the struggle but was no longer able to do so. The Congress sent an ultimatum to Athens, which was not met, and the long-awaited explosion occurred.

The strategy that Pericles adopted was to fight a defensive war, withdrawing the population of Attica, at least the western part of it, within the powerful fortifications around Athens and the Piraeus and depending on the fleet to keep food supplies at an adequate level. Meanwhile, Athenian warships were to make commando raids along Peloponnesian shores and gradually bring the anti-Athenian alliance to its knees. This policy was unpopular with the wealthy, who were unwilling to see their estates in Attica ravaged, and with the military, who wanted action.

During the first year of the war, all went just about as Pericles had planned. But he had reckoned without the effects of population congestion, water pollution, and Leeuwenhoek's "little beasties," germs that cause disease. A plague ravaged the city in 430 and 429 B.C., became virulent again in the winter of 427 and 426, and lasted through 426. It wiped out one-third of Athens' front-line troops and an unnumbered host from the rest of the population, including Pericles himself.[30] Probably something like a third of the total population was lost.[31]

In terms of actual numbers, Gomme in his population studies concluded that between 431 and 425 the male citizen population (age18–59) of Athens was reduced from 172,000 to 116,000, resident aliens from 28,500 to 21,000, and slaves from 115,000 to 81,000.[32] By the end of the Peloponnesian War the adult male citizen register had shrunk to about 90,000,[33] just a little over a half what it had been before the war began.

Of course we would like to know what the plague was that created such havoc. Unfortunately the great physician Hippocrates, known as the Father of Medicine, who lived at the time, left no description. But the great contemporary historian Thucydides did. He describes "a very rapid onset, raging fever, extreme thirst, tongue and throat 'bloody', the skin of the body red and livid, finally breaking out into pustules and ulcers."[34] Medical historian Frederick Cartwright observes, "The majority opinion holds that this was a highly malignant form of scarlet fever, probably the first appearance of the infection in the Mediterranean basin and therefore especially lethal . . . and which later became common and less fatal."[35] But other suggestions include bubonic plague, smallpox, anthrax, typhus, or an unknown disease.

After several more years of inconclusive battle, the Athenian conservative leader Nicias arranged a peace treaty in 421 B.C., which called for a fifty-year truce with Sparta. But Alcibiades, Pericles' nephew, saw no future for himself in this peaceful, conservative arrangement and began to scheme for renewal of the war. He influenced an Athenian alliance with four states of the northern Peloponnesus. These were attacked and defeated by Sparta in 418 B.C., leaving a residue of bitterness both among the Athenian allies (whom Athens failed to support) and the Spartans, who considered the Athenian alliance a warlike act.

Soon thereafter, in 415 B.C., an embassy arrived at Athens from Segesta in Sicily with a request for help against Syracuse. Involvement appealed to the Athenians, and especially Alcibiades, because success would give the Athenians control of the grain supply of Corinth and much of the trade in the West. Therefore an expedition was launched. But hardly had it started on its way when Alcibiades was recalled to stand trial in Athens for impiety. Without an able commander, the whole project became a great fiasco. Athens lost more than two hundred warships and their complement of seamen, some forty thousand recruited from subject states, plus many thousands of cavalrymen and infantry, and an enormous amount of money, weapons, and materials.[36]

Alcibiades escaped to Sparta on the way home for trial and persuaded the Spartans to renew the struggle in 413 B.C. Meanwhile the Athenians were feverishly trying to rebuild the navy and prepare for future attacks. By 411 the Spartans had become disenchanted with Alcibiades, and he went to Asia Minor, where he began to intrigue with the Persians. He persuaded them that it was not in their best interests to have the Spartans achieve a victory in the Greek world; instead they should keep the Greeks fighting among themselves. Thus he won help for Athens, enabling her to win victories for three years. Then Persia switched sides and came to the aid of the Spartans, who with Persian fleets were able to bring

Athens to her knees in 404. As the price of peace, Athens lost her empire, her navy, and her fortifications, and was forced to accept an oligarchic government on the order of Sparta's.

Political and social conditions in Athens were rocky after the war, but Barry S. Strauss in his *Athens After the Peloponnesian War* (Cornell, 1987) argues that political and social conflict might have been greater had it not been for the disproportionately large number of poor Athenians killed in the fighting. There were fewer of them in the assembly to make demands on the middle and upper classes. The democracy was restored in 403 and continued with reasonable stability for some decades.

Continued Persian Interference. Lysander of Sparta was now in control in Greece. States that began to rejoice in freedom from Athens were surprised to discover that they were under a far more exacting master. Soon the Greeks found themselves at war with Persia. Some thirteen thousand mercenaries from various Greek states hired themselves out to Cyrus the Younger, who tried to unseat his brother Artaxerxes II, ruler of the Persian Empire. After Cyrus was killed in battle, the famous retreat of the ten thousand Greeks under Xenophon (401–399 B.C.) occurred, described in his *Anabasis.* Spartan support for the rebellion of Cyrus and later entanglement in a rebellion of Ionian cities in Asia Minor against the Persians involved the Spartans in war against Persia.

Continuing her policy of fomenting strife in Greece, Persia incited Corinth, Athens, Argos, and Thebes to revolt against Sparta. She sent Persian money and ships, and some of these ships under command of the Athenian admiral Conon sailed to Athens in 393 B.C. and rebuilt the walls with Persian money and labor. Five years later Persia and Sparta signed a peace treaty which assigned most of the Greek cities in Asia Minor to Persia and a few to Athens.

The treaty seemed also to herald a new Persian policy. Up to that time Persia had espoused a policy of pitting one Greek state against another. Now she seemed interested in making the strongest Greek state her

Reception area of the palace of Philip of Macedon at Aegae.

executor. Sparta was predominant, then, from 387 to 371 B.C. With a relatively free hand in Greece, Sparta had built up an empire by 379.

Meanwhile, Athens was climbing back to a place of prominence once more. She began forming defensive alliances as early as 384. And in 378 she converted the collection of alliances into a league. This league was fundamentally different from the old Athenian alliance and provided for defense against attack, political autonomy, self government under a constitution of the city-state's preference, no collection of tribute, no imposition of Athenian garrisons or governors, and prohibition of Athenian property ownership in the lands of the member

Unexcavated theater of Aegae, where Philip of Macedon was assasinated.

states. Seventy city-states joined this league, which continued in existence for forty years, until Philip of Macedon disbanded it after the Battle of Chaeronea in 338. On the whole the provisions of membership seem to have been honored. The story of the alliance is told in Jack Cargill's *The Second Athenian League* (University of California Press, 1981).

But Thebes was also pulling herself together and, under Epaminondas, disastrously defeated the Spartans at the battle of Leuctra in (371 B.C.) and was predominant in Greece until 362. The story appears in John Buckle's *The Theban Hegemony, 371–362 B.C.* (Harvard, 1980).

Fourth Century Cultural History. During the fourth century B.C. a number of great figures connected with the cultural history of Greece made their contributions—all of whom were connected with Athens for at least part of their lives. Plato (428–347 B.C.) founded his Academy in Athens about 387. Borrowing the dialogue form of writing from his teacher Socrates, he employed it in his famous *Republic* and his *Laws*, both of which enunciated his conception of the ideal state. Aristotle (384–322 B.C.) was a student in Plato's Academy, tutor of Alexander the Great, and founder of the Lyceum in Athens. His interests were broad, and he wrote on logic, metaphysics, natural history, ethics, rhetoric, aesthetics,

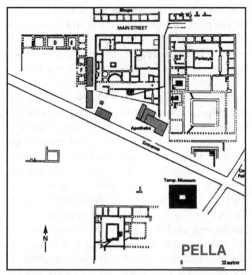

Houses at Pella. Floor plans of the large houses of Pella, birthplace of Alexander the Great, show colonnaded peristyle courtyards surrounded by reception rooms, dining rooms, and family rooms.

and political science. In his *Politics* he, like Plato, saw the city-state as the chief form of government and scored democracy for its inadequacies.

Two great orators are also representative of the century: Isocrates (436–338 B.C.) and Demosthenes (384–322). The former was Panhellenic and favored a confederation of Greek states. He ultimately turned to Philip II of Macedon to unite the Greeks by force. Demosthenes looked backward to the days of the independent city-state and called the Athenians to effective warfare against Philip. Xenophon (430–350) is best remembered for his historical writings, the *Anabasis* and the *Hellenica* (which was intended to be a supplement to Thucydides' *Peloponnesian War*), although Xenophon wrote many other pieces.

Rise of Macedon

During the fourth century it was no longer possible for the petty city-states of Greece to enjoy the luxury of destroying each other without the danger of external conquest. Persian interference during the later fifth and early fourth centuries had demonstrated that fact. Now Macedon loomed on the northern horizon. Soon the colossus of Rome would rise in the West.

The city-states had become second-rate powers with an uncertain future.

Macedonia had had a slow development in the fourth century B.C. from a peasant state to a military state, from a purely rural to a more urbanized state. Philip II (359–336 B.C.) played the most important part in her development.

Apparently the royal family of Macedonia was Dorian from Argos and was related to the royal family of Argos. Thus they were Greek.[37] When they came to Macedonia, they founded their capital at Aegae, today's Vergina. There it remained until Perdiccas II (452–413) and his son Archelaos (413–399) transferred it to Pella. The palace at Aegae covered four acres,[38] and nearby was the theater where Philip II was assassinated. There too Professor Manolis Andronikos found the intact tomb of Philip and his queen with all its wonderful treasures temporarily removed but now returned to the tomb.

Archelaos built Pella, which was laid out in the Hippodamian, or checkerboard, fashion, with streets crossing at right angles. There were straight streets, and pipes of a modern-style system of water supply and drainage turned up in the excavations (ongoing since 1958). The ancient market or agora measured about 800 by 750 feet and was surrounded on all four sides by porticoes, workshops, and trade stores.[39]

Alexander the Great was born at Pella in 356 B.C. and there Aristotle tutored him from 342 to 335. Incidentally, Aristotle was born in Stagira on the Macedonian border, and his Greek father was court physician to Amyntas II of Macedonia, thus evidencing the close connection of Macedonia with Greece. But while their kings were Greek, the Macedonians themselves were not. And the Macedonians were proud to be separate from the Greeks. In the post-Alexandrian period Greeks and Macedonians were merged, in contrast to the separateness of Greeks and native peoples of Egypt and Asia Minor.

Now we return to Philip. He was determined to weld an effective state. Within two years after taking the throne he broke the Illyrian enslavement of Macedonia and began formation of one of the finest armies

The Pangaeus gold fields near Philippi, where Philip of Macedon obtained wealth to help finance his ventures.

destroyed it. That seems like a barbaric act on his part, but the fate of the city was actually in the hands of the Greek Council, and recent Greek history had been full of such atrocities. For example, the Thebans themselves at Orchemenus in 363 B.C. had massacred the adult males and sold the rest of the population into slavery. The Athenians at Sestus in 353 had done the same thing.[41]

By the spring of 334 B.C., Alexander was ready for his invasion of the Persian Empire and the institution of the Panhellenic war of revenge against the colossus of the East. He had put the affairs of Macedonia and Greece in the hands of his senior associate, Antipater, and left him with some twelve thousand crack troops and fifteen hundred cavalry and the right to call up the militia of the cities. He entrusted the religious affairs of the state, including sacrifices of the state cult, and administration of the royal estates, to Olympias, the Queen Mother.

the world had yet known. He drew men into his army from the turbulent vassal states and instilled them with a spirit of nationalism. To help finance his ventures he possessed the gold of the Pangaeus gold fields in the vicinity of Philippi. By the time he died, Philip had built an efficient army of about thirty-five thousand, and the population of his kingdom had risen to over a half million.[40]

In 357 Phillip took the area on his eastern frontier and a year later began the conquest of Greece. Athens, one of Philip's most formidable opponents, was galvanized to action against him by the *Philippics* of Demosthenes, perhaps the greatest orator of all time. Finally Philip crushed a combined Athenian and Theban force at Chaeronea in 338 B.C. and then overran the Peloponnesus. A year later he summoned all the states south of Thermopylae to send delegates to a federal council at Corinth to organize a Hellenic league against Persia. All complied but Sparta. Before Philip could execute his plan of warfare against Persia he was assassinated, and his son Alexander the Great assumed the reins of government at the age of twenty.

Alexander the Great. Alexander promptly set his house in order in Macedonia. When Thebes, led by a false rumor of his death, revolted, he swept down upon that city and

Alexander the Great

He, himself, commanded about 32,000 infantry, 5,000 cavalry, the Macedonian and Greek navies of some 180 ships and crews of 38,000, plus supply ships, and various specialists and servants, for a total of per-

Alexander the god. A generation after his death, Alexander is shown with the ram's horns of the Greek-Egyptian deity Zeus-Ammon, on this silver four drachma coin, minted about 300 B.C. in Thrace, where one of his followers, Lysimachus, ruled.

Third, the Persian rulers were not very effective in Alexander's day and did not firmly control the empire or sufficiently command respect of all the subject peoples. During the fourth century there was an increasing amount of squabbling in the extended ruling family.

Fighting and overcoming the enemy was only part of Alexander's task. An incredible challenge was moving the men, equipment, and supplies. Of course they walked those thousands of miles—all the way to India. At first, when possible, they fought where the navy and supply ships could carry gear and food and water. They could live off the land if they were fortunate enough to arrive in an area soon enough after harvest when the granaries were full. But when a general is responsible for tens of thousands of troops, he cannot leave the question of supply of ordnance and food and water to chance. The army had to carry what it needed.

On the feasibility of such a challenge, Engels has produced numerous computations to show the magnitude or virtual impossibility of the task. For example, he concludes that for an army of 65,000 on foot and 6,100 cavalry horses it would take 1,300 baggage animals to carry tents, blankets, personal possessions, and the like, and 8,400 animals carrying provisions such as grain, forage, and water for just one day.[45] For longer periods the numbers would increase dramatically. Horses, mules, and camels were used, but carts were not until they got to Iran. Philip had forbidden them because in the hilly to mountainous regions of Macedonia they were totally impractical.[46]

What tended to happen, then, is that the infantry carried fairly heavy loads of their own. They were aided by servants and a limited number of pack animals. So they tended to travel fairly light, and the army was characterized by mobility and speed. Certainly it moved much more easily than the Persian armies with their cumbersome baggage trains. It is useful to note parenthetically that in reducing the number of pack animals there was a great decrease in the forage and water that had to be transported for them.

Also, very importantly, Engels argues that Alexander frequently arranged for the

haps 90,000 men.[42] Engels concludes that after he crossed the Hellespont his land forces grew to about 48,000 soldiers, 6,100 horses, and about 16,000 servants and others, for a total of 65,000 personnel.[43]

While it seems foolhardy for Alexander to think that he could take on a colossus like the Persian Empire with such limited resources, on closer examination he had a good chance. In the first place, there is a real question as to what Alexander's objectives were when he began his conquests; possibly they were not too grandiose. But they apparently mushroomed with his phenomenal success. If he merely had in mind to punish the Persians in a Greek war of revenge, he could probably do that; a few western provinces might be lopped off. Though the Persians had great military resources, they stationed their best troops in Iran or at least farther east.[43a]

Second, Alexander had a good chance for success because Persia depended largely on mercenary troops or provincial levies, neither of which were as effective as a citizen army, such as what Alexander commanded. Mercenary troops have a way of switching sides when the opponent seems to be winning or when employers cannot pay their salaries. Significantly, the Persians were a small minority in their empire, perhaps only one-sixtieth.[44]

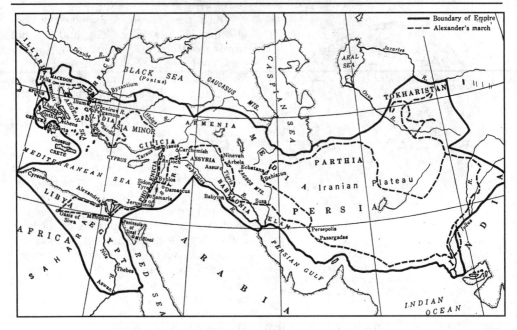

The route of Alexander's conquering march and his empire.

collection of provisions *in advance*. That is, often the local officials surrendered to him before the army marched into their territory.[47] In any case, Alexander's success in provisioning his army contributed almost as much to his ultimate victory as his brilliant strategy on the battlefield.

ALEXANDER'S GREAT VICTORIES

Battle of Granicus River, 334 B.C.
—gave him Asia Minor

Battle of Issus, 333 B.C.
—opened Syria to him

Siege of Tyre and conquest of Egypt, 332 B.C.
—which gave him control of Persian naval bases

Battle of Gaugamela, 331 B.C.
—defeat of Darius III, Darius' assassination in the spring of 330 B.C.

As Alexander marched forward, one victory led to another until he had won the entire Persian Empire. Shortly after he crossed the Hellespont in the spring of 334

B.C., he won the battle of the Granicus River. The destruction of the Persian army there opened to him all of Asia Minor. In 333 B.C. a victory at Issus in Cilicia opened Syria to him. He spent the following year besieging and destroying Tyre, securing the Syrian coast, and occupying Egypt, where he founded the city of Alexandria.

Having protected the rear of his army and having taken control of the Persian fleet by conquering its bases, Alexander marched off in hot pursuit of the hosts of Darius. He caught up with them and defeated them at Gaugamela, southeast of Nineveh, in October of 331. In the next four months Alexander gained possession of Babylon, Susa (biblical Shushan), and Persepolis.

Meanwhile Darius was encamped at Ecbatana in Media. When Alexander set out after him in the spring of 330 B.C., Darius fled northeast toward Bactria. In swift pursuit, Alexander covered four hundred miles in eleven days—only to come upon the corpse of his prey, who had been slain by one of the Persian provincial governors. Alexander was now king of Persia. But rather than consolidating his conquests, he tried to conquer India. After initial successes in the Indus

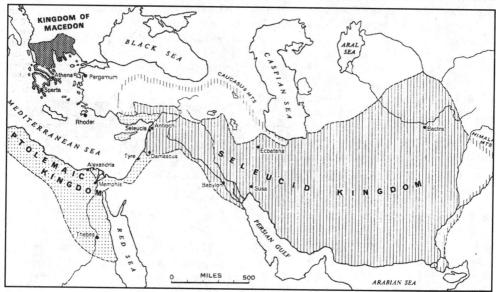

The Partitioning of Alexander's Empire.

Valley, he was unable to persuade his war-weary troops to go farther. While planning further conquests, Alexander fell ill and died at Babylon on June 10, 323.[48]

What killed Alexander is still a matter of debate. Peter Green in his 1991 edition of his biography of Alexander raised the very real possibility of slow strychnine poisoning, as well as advanced alcoholism. But he concluded that if the king was not poisoned, he probably died of malaria.[49] On the other hand, Hammond, in his 1997 biography categorically declared that death came as a result of malaria. He calls allegations of death due to poisoning or alcoholism simply "untrue."[50] Perhaps that is as far as we can go in deciding the debate. Unfortunately, we do not have the body of Alexander or some of his hair to conduct a scientific analysis that would determine, as with Napoleon, that he actually was poisoned.

Exactly what Alexander had in mind as a master plan for his empire—its organization and integration—is unknown. In the 1920s C. A. Robinson and W. W. Tarn spun out a very elevated thesis concerning Alexander's aims. As Tarn put the thesis, it had three closely interconnected facets and aspects:

The first is that God is the common Father of mankind, which may be called the brotherhood of man. The second is Alexander's dream of the various races of mankind, so far as known to him, becoming of one mind together and living in unity and concord, which may be called the unity of mankind. And the third, also part of the dream, is that the various peoples of his Empire might be partners in the realm rather than subjects.[51]

Research on this thesis will show that Tarn's conclusions were based primarily on statements in Plutarch (first century A.D.), the interpretation of which has been somewhat strained. Though the thesis has had little real acceptance among the historians, some embraced it, and it appears occasionally in some of the older books. It seems that the reputedly high-flung ideas and statements of the conqueror did not reflect any emancipated sociological viewpoint on his part.

The reputed Alexandrian statements concerning brotherhood and partnership in the realm were directed only to the Persians—not to Egyptians, Syrians, or anyone else. An appeal to the Persians was particularly timely because Alexander needed Persian troops and Persian loyalty. And while he offered to share the administration with them, he had no intention of relinquishing the top spot, which he himself occupied.

The idealistic interpretation of Alexander seems now to be virtually dead. Peter Green has probably hit it about right when he called Alexander "the League of Nations Alexander." He asserts that Tarn was something of a son of his age when in the heyday of the League of Nations many were swept away on a wave of international idealism.[52] The theological liberalism of the time likely also played a part with its emphasis on the Fatherhood of God and the Brotherhood of man.

But even if Alexander did not have an advanced idealism and in his last years he was an advanced alcoholic who turned many of his most trusted subordinates against him, he was still significant in the flow of history. Politically and militarily, he brought an end to the Persian Empire, the largest that the world had yet known. That in itself was a major historical event.

Culturally, he gave rise to an urbanization movement. Alexander founded the city of Alexandria in Egypt (one of the greatest and most influential in the ancient world) and a limited number of other cities. His initial purpose in founding them was probably military and political. There troops could be stationed to hold down the countryside and there political machinery could be installed for governing the surrounding area.

But in time cities became cultural centers that influenced extensive regions. What Alexander began the Seleucids and later the Romans continued until the whole Mediterranean world and much of the Near East was urbanized. The Ptolemies, the Seleucids, and the Romans sought to use the cities as military, political, and cultural centers for influencing and holding down large stretches of countryside around them. The culture of those cities gradually came to be what we call Hellenistic, Greek modified by the oriental atmosphere in which they arose. And that Hellenistic culture became the culture of the Roman Empire. So when Roman culture was passed on through the Middle Ages and became the basis for much of modern Western Culture, roots of our own culture stretched all the way back to the days of

Alexander. This Greek influence is a pervasive influence. Whether in drama, literature, architecture, sculpture, philosophy, mathematics, political science, natural science, or the language we speak, and more, it continues to make its impact.

THE IMPACT OF ALEXANDER THE GREAT IN HISTORY

- Brought an end to the Persian Empire

- Contributed to the body of military science

- Gave rise to an urbanization movement that influenced Greek and Roman development for centuries to come

- Gave rise to the development of Hellenistic culture, that became the culture of the Roman Empire and formed the basis of much of modern Western culture

- Influenced the development of Judaism with his favor to Jews that continued under the Ptolemies and Romans

While Alexander's greatness especially lies in his influence in history, he deserves to be called great because he was a military genius. Peter Green speaks of his true genius as a field commander, "perhaps . . . the most incomparable general the world has ever seen." And he includes among his attributes a gift for speed, improvisation, variety of strategy, ability to extricate himself from almost impossible situations, mastery of terrain, coolheadedness in crisis, and psychological ability to penetrate the enemy's intentions.[53]

Successors of Alexander the Great

For about fifty years after the death of Alexander, his empire was torn by the efforts of his ambitious generals to become supreme. At first they united under the titular headship of Alexander's half-witted brother Philip and Alexander's posthumous son, both of whom were killed by 310 B.C. Eventually the Empire was divided into three large states and a number of smaller ones.

Ptolemy managed to establish himself in Egypt and in 306 B.C. took the title of king. His kingdom came to include Egypt, Cyrene (modern Libya), Cyprus, and Palestine. His line ruled Egypt until 30 B.C. when the suicide of Cleopatra brought the dynasty to an end; then Rome took over there.

Another of Alexander's generals was Seleucus. After many difficulties he established a dynasty at Babylon in 312 B.C. His descendants were known as Seleucids, and in their days of greatness they controlled almost all of the Persian Empire except Egypt. But dynastic quarrels and external pressures weakened their kingdom and reduced its territory so that by 64 B.C., when Seleucia fell before Rome, it consisted of little more than northern Syria.

Confusion reigned in Macedon after the death of Alexander, as one general after another tried to secure the throne. Finally Antigonus Gonatas, grandson of the great Antigonus of Alexander's entourage, secured control over Macedon and established his dynasty there; it lasted until the Roman conquest. To a large degree Antigonus won the throne of Macedon by defeating in 277 B.C. a horde of Gauls that had moved into Greece. Macedonia was a strong military monarchy in which the rulers were generals who were recognized as kings by consent of the army. Unlike the Ptolemies and Seleucids, the Antigonids made no claim to divinity. The state was financed by income from the royal domains, forests, and mines, and from customs duties.

The great period of these three Hellenistic kingdoms was approximately from 275 to 200 B.C. During those decades large urban centers were developed in the eastern Mediterranean world, and a flourishing culture was disseminated from them.

While most of the great cultural developments of the Hellenistic world occurred outside the boundaries of Greece, Greece maintained its philosophical importance. At Athens, Epicurus set up his school in 306 B.C. This taught a materialistic philosophy that viewed the world as a soulless mechanism. Atoms flying through space met to create life and flying apart caused death. This worldview stated that there was no such thing as existence after death—at least not conscious existence. Therefore one was to live for the present and seek a life of greatest happiness in the present. This life of happiness consisted not of sensual pleasure but of an escape into the gentle, quiet world of the intellect, symbolized by the garden in which Epicurus taught. If there were gods, they lived by themselves and had nothing to do with humanity. Thus fear of divine beings and prayer to them were useless.

Contemporary with Epicureanism was Stoicism. The founder of the movement, Zeno, a Phoenician from Cyprus, began to teach in Athens in 302 B.C. The Stoics believed that a divine fire, a world soul, animated all of matter. This being had established a perfect, unalterable, universal law for the universe. Whatever happened, therefore, had to be endured as part of the divine plan. And the divine spark in the individual—the soul—was constantly engaged in an effort to overcome the flesh. Moreover, since all human beings had this divine spark within, all were brothers and sisters. Therefore they had obligations to their fellow human beings. Upon death the individual would rejoin the world soul in a rather hazy continued existence.

While certain intellectuals were interested in Epicureanism, Stoicism, or other contemporary philosophies, most people still worshiped the old gods, and a large number turned to the Mystery Religions during the Hellenistic Age. In the mysteries, men and women sought a more personal faith that would bring them into immediate contact with deity and a faith that would offer a more emotional experience than the worship of the old gods or involvement in the newer philosophies.

Each of the Mystery Religions was centered about a god whose annual death and resurrection corresponded to the rhythm of the seasons. As plants died in the fall and were reborn in the spring, the vegetation spirits were thought to have gone to the underworld and to have returned from it. Raised from death, they could bestow immortality on humankind. Each of the Mystery Religions had a ritual through which the initiate was made to participate in the experience of the god and rendered a candidate for immortality. Each guaranteed its devotees an ultimate escape from the miserable world about them into an immortal afterlife.

They were called "mysteries" because they aimed by secret and mysterious initiatory ritual (*mysterion* comes from a root meaning "initiate") to achieve the fusion of the worshiper and a divine savior. The chief mysteries were the Eleusinian of Greece, Cybele of Asia Minor, Isis and Osiris of Egypt, and Mithraism of Persia.

Because Christianity bears some similarities to the Mystery Religions, it is often classified as one of them. But obviously that is not the case. The differences greatly exceed the similarities. Christianity is based on an historical rather than mythological person, on a being who died and rose once purposefully in a substitutionary atonement for mankind, rather than repeatedly in some rhythm of the seasons. Normally the Mystery Religions did not put specific demands on an individual to live a new lifestyle. Nor did they offer a supernatural enablement for living, as Christianity did. While the rites of initiation in the Mystery Religions were secret and were never fully revealed even by initiates who defected, the means of becoming a Christian have been almost literally shouted from the housetops and have been published in detail in the Scriptures—now available in part or in whole in about 2,100 languages.

As far as political affairs were concerned, Macedonian control was in no sense complete in Greece. Macedonian garrisons were stationed in Athens, Chalcis, and Corinth; but in central Greece and the Peloponnesus the Achaean and Aetolian leagues exercised considerable power. A backward people during the classical period of Greek history, the Aetolians of central western Greece had joined their villages into a league before 350 B.C. And at its height during the third century, in alliance with Macedon, this league controlled central Greece from sea to sea.

The Achaean League, organized about 275 B.C., was composed of some of the small states along the southern shore of the Gulf of Corinth. It became important after 250 under the leadership of Aratus of Sicyon and expanded to incorporate the whole northern Peloponnesus. During the first part of the third century, the Aetolians were friendly with Macedon and the Achaeans were not.

The picture changed about 230 B.C. when a temporary revival of Spartan power frightened the Achaeans and led them to call for Macedonian help. This alliance outflanked the Aetolians who feared that Macedonian interference would endanger Aetolian independence. This fear led the Aetolians ultimately to link their fortunes with Rome against Macedon. Rome's involvement in Greek and Eastern affairs ultimately resulted in Roman control of the whole area.

Roman Conquest of Greece

Greek interference in Roman affairs began early in the third century B.C. when Pyrrhus of Epirus brought over an army to help the Greek cities of southern Italy in their contest with Rome. Although Pyrrhus lost the flower of his army in conflict with the Romans, he was not destroyed and returned to Greece in 275 B.C. to involve himself in an initially victorious war with Antigonus Gonatas of Macedonia. When Pyrrhus was killed in battle in 272, Epirus entered a cycle of almost continuous decline in prestige and progressive loss of territory; and a Roman punitive expedition to Greece was unnecessary at that time.

Rome did not find it necessary to send troops eastward until after the First Punic War. Greek cities of southern Italy, now allied with Rome, suffered from the depredations of the Illyrians, who lived along the coast of modern Yugoslavia and "elevated piracy to the dignity of a national profession." After a victory over the Illyrians in 229 B.C., the Romans established a certain Demetrius as ruler over the territory. He proved to be a rather intractable puppet and soon outdid the Illyrians in acts of piracy. When Rome defeated him in 219 B.C. he fled to Macedonia where he constantly urged an anti-Roman policy.

This groundwork laid by Demetrius was to bear fruit during the Second Punic War, when in 215 B.C. Philip V of Macedon allied himself with Hannibal of Carthage against the Romans. Hardly had Philip made the alliance when civil war erupted in Greece. At this point Rome entered into an alliance with the Aetolians and their allies, including Sparta and Pergamum, and sought to confine Philip to Macedonia.

After an inconclusive war, both Rome and Macedon were eager for peace—the former to be free for action against Carthage, and the latter to try a hand in the political arena of the Hellenistic monarchies of the East. Philip's activities there brought open conflict with Pergamum and Rhodes. The Aetolians, deciding to renew attacks on Macedonia, sent to Rome in 206 B.C. asking for aid. A few months later Pergamum and Rhodes appealed to Rome for help.

Neither the Roman assembly nor senate wanted war. The long struggle with Hannibal had consumed their energies. But a group of hawkish senators managed to maneuver the Romans into war against Macedon in 200 B.C. Of course Rome was successful, but not without overcoming serious difficulties. At the conclusion of the war in 196, the victorious Flamininus announced the freedom of all Greek cities from Macedonia. He made this proclamation at the Isthmian Games at Corinth. Macedonia was disarmed and forced to pay an indemnity, and Flamininus established pro-Roman and aristocratic governments in several Greek cities.

Romans who thought peace had been achieved were in for a rude awakening. Antiochus III of Syria was nibbling away at Egyptian possessions in Syria and along the Asia Minor coast. Advance around Ephesus alarmed Eumenes of Pergamum, who sought aid from Rome. Meanwhile, Hannibal had escaped from Carthage and was nagging Antiochus into an anti-Roman policy. And the Aetolians, deeply hurt because they had not shared the spoils of war in the victory over Macedon, were stirring up Greeks against Rome and looking to Antiochus for aid. When Antiochus invaded Thrace in 191 B.C. Rome was forced to act.

The success was all with Rome. Antiochus lost all of Asia Minor except Cilicia. Pergamum and Rhodes expanded their influence there. In Greece, Macedon was rewarded for her loyalty and Aetolia punished with the loss of territory and the obligation to pay an indemnity.

This peace of 188 B.C. was not destined to bring settled conditions to the Near East or to Greece. While the Orient was fidgety, Greece had troubles peculiarly Greek. The city-states, "freed" by the Romans, engaged in the liberty of anarchy, as they struggled with one another and as factions within them struggled for supremacy.

Philip V of Macedon sulked in the wings, remaining loyal to Rome until his death but building up his country for his son Perseus, who intrigued with the Achaean League and other states of Greece against Rome in an effort to bring order out of chaos. Rome was not permitted to forget Greek affairs because representatives of one city or another constantly shuttled back and forth to Rome seeking aid against their neighbors. To add to the confusion, Eumenes of Pergamum denounced Perseus to Rome.

A series of these aggravations finally led Rome to send legions against Macedonia once more. The war began in 171 B.C. and ended with the battle of Pydna in 168, after which Rome divided Macedonia into four independent republics and imposed an annual indemnity. The Achaean League was forced to send a thousand hostages to Rome, among whom was the celebrated historian Polybius. And Epirus suffered the destruction of seventy towns and the sale of 150,000 citizens into slavery. It never recovered.

After 168 B.C. Greece slowly declined into economic and spiritual bankruptcy. However, the Greeks were not so completely broken in spirit that they were unable to attempt another bid for independence from Rome. When the three hundred Achaean hostages who were still living returned to Greece in 151, old wounds were reopened. About the same time a pretender named Andriscus appeared in Macedonia, claiming to be the son of Perseus, the last king of the country. After initial difficulties, the

Romans were able to destroy his army of twenty thousand and restore their power in Macedonia.

Fires of insurrection were still smoldering in Greece, and they broke into leaping flames in 147 B.C. when a border dispute between Sparta and the Achaean League ignited a popular uprising. Slaves were freed and armed, aristocrats were murdered, and the poor made a bid for a better life. Roman legions swooped down from Macedonia, destroyed Corinth (chief city of the league), and sold its inhabitants into slavery in 146 B.C. Greece was cowed by this atrocity.

Prior to this conflict, in 148 B.C., Macedonia became a Roman province, in the sense that from this time a Roman governor was regularly in charge. The four republics remained as local organizations and continued to have their assemblies. The status of the rest of Greece is somewhat uncertain. But it appears that Greece was largely under Roman control and that this control was generally exercised through the governor of Macedonia. The Achaean league was apparently broken up, at least temporarily. The Romans probably did not greatly interfere with other loyal leagues and towns.

In succeeding decades, however, Rome gradually established governments of her own choosing in a number of the cities of Greece. Most of Greece was still free, though some cities paid tribute; and the practical value of that freedom had been much reduced. It seems that the rights of free cities depended somewhat upon the good pleasure of the governors and the dictates of the Roman Senate.

GREEK SUFFERINGS DURING THE ROMAN REPUBLIC

During the Mithridatic Wars, beginning in 88 B.C., Mithridates VI of Pontus in Asia Minor, occupied and was responsible for considerable destruction in towns of eastern, central, and southern Greece.

Then the Roman general Sulla defeated Mithridates and punished the towns that had supported him, especially launching an orgy of destruction in Athens.

During the struggles between Pompey and Julius Caesar, the land was racked by those opposing armies, especially in 48 B.C. when Caesar defeated Pompey at Pharsalus.

Then in 42 B.C. Brutus and Cassius collected their forces near Philippi for their last stand against Mark Antony and Octavian. This campaign cost Macedonia and Greece heavily.

The deciding battle between the forces of Octavian and Antony took place at Actium in western Greece in 31 B.C. The stationing of forces of Antony and Cleopatra in Greece for one year bled the area white.

Greece Under the Roman Republic

Greece suffered terribly in the century between 146 and 30 B.C. The hardships brought on by the revolt of Andriscus in Macedonia were compounded during a subsequent revolt of a second pretender and a long series of raids and invasions by neighboring tribes.

In 88 these raids merged with the first of the Mithridatic Wars, which were to plague the Greek area for four years. Mithridates VI of Pontus in Asia Minor occupied several centers in eastern, central, and southern Greece and was responsible for considerable destruction.

Then came Sulla with his Roman legions, thirty thousand strong, subduing Mithridates and punishing the towns that had supported him. His wrath especially centered on Athens. There he systematically destroyed the Piraeus to keep Mithridates from using its magnificent port facilities and where he broke through the walls of the city and looted and killed in an orgy of destruction.

During the Civil Wars the land was racked again by the opposing armies of Pompey and Caesar. The final defeat of Pompey came in Greece at Pharsalus in 48 B.C. Six years later Brutus and Cassius collected their forces near Philippi for a last

Rome's provincial arrangement in Greece during the second century.

stand against Mark Antony and Octavian. This campaign cost Macedonia and eastern Greece heavily.

The deciding battle between the forces of Octavian and Antony took place at Actium in western Greece in 31 B.C. The hardships caused by the stationing of the forces of Antony and Cleopatra in Greece for one year were many. And when Antony's communications began to be cut, he seems to have laid hands on all available supplies and to have impressed Greeks for all kinds of service. Especially burdensome was the galley service. When Octavian became emperor as Augustus, all of Greece was suffering from exhaustion and depopulation.

The Roman Imperial period

Augustus' efforts to bring order out of chaos in the empire involved a provincial reorganization in Greece. In 27 B.C. Achaea and Macedonia became separate provinces under the control of the Senate. Achaea incorporated nearly all of Greece proper, including Thessaly and most of Epirus. Macedonia encompassed Macedonia proper, northern Epirus, and a little of northern Greece.

These provinces fluctuated between senatorial and imperial control. Tiberius brought them under his control. Claudius gave them back to the Senate. Nero declared Achaea free and immune from tribute. A little later, Vespasian revoked the privilege. And under either Hadrian or Antoninus Pius in the early part of the second century, another provincial reorganization took place. In that, Achaea was greatly reduced in size—the western part spun off into a new province of Epirus and Thessaly falling under the control of Macedonia.

In the arrangement that existed in Paul's day (the work of the emperor Claudius) Achaea and Macedonia were senatorial provinces, the former with the capital at Corinth and the latter with the capital at Thessalonica. The eastern part of Macedonia became the province of Thrace. Luke (in Acts 19:21) and Paul (in Romans 15:26 and 1 Timothy 1:7–8) referred to Macedonia and Achaea. But Luke also spoke of Macedonia and Achaea as Macedonia and Greece (Acts 20:1–2), perhaps a carry-over of the old idea that Macedonians were not really Greeks.

In Augustus' organization and throughout the first century A.D., much of the area of Greece was free from the direct domination of the Roman governor of Achaea stationed in Corinth. The towns of Greece most distinguished by material importance and by great memories were set free. Some of the better known were Athens, Sparta, Pharsalus, and Plataea. Several of the old leagues continued too, for example, the Boeotian and Achaean leagues. There were free cities in Macedonia also. Thessalonica and Amphipolis are examples in point. But while the old freedoms were outwardly maintained, they became increasingly meaningless as Rome chipped away at them and found ways to circumvent the forms of Greek independence.

While it is true that Greece suffered greatly during the first century B.C., she experienced a return of a degree of prosperity in the following century. Some of the most pessimistic statements on Greece in the Imperial Period were made by individuals not fully in possession of the facts or by those writing very early in the Empire when conditions were worse. Therefore, such references must be carefully evaluated by those who would construct an accurate picture of Greece during the New Testament period.

What seems to have been the case is that there were fewer flourishing cities than formerly. This may have been due in part to the fact that Rome followed a practice of assigning smaller towns and considerable tracts of land to larger cities for their support. In several areas, such as Boeotia, there seems to have been agricultural prosperity in spite of the decay of cities. This trend of the Roman period is particularly noticeable in the Peloponnesus, where urban life was largely concentrated along the coast, with the interior given over to agriculture and herding. A high point in the economic recovery of Greece appears to have been achieved during the first part of the second century A.D.

Corinth (rebuilt by Julius Caesar) was the great commercial emporium of Greece during the Empire. As such she could easily make her own way. Thessalonica was also a bustling port and governmental center. Athens lived largely on her past. As a center of learning and art and a city with an illustrious history, she attracted many visitors and benefactions from emperors and wealthy patrons. But while the handouts were great and she must be considered something of a parasite, Attica was not without products to export. For instance, her marble and olive oil were widely marketed. Yet, her revenues were insufficient. Hadrian gave the city a large sum of money and arranged that she be provided with annual supplies of grain.

The Apostle Paul in Greece

Although Greece slowly ascended the ladder of prosperity once more during the Roman Imperial Period, she was still quite poor in the middle of the first century A.D. when she entered the biblical narrative. Corinth and Thessalonica were bustling ports, but Greeks in the famous old centers of Athens and Sparta had to look backward to days of greatness. Alexander's capital at Pella was also in a state of decline. While it is possible that the average Greek lived a more secure and prosperous life under the Pax Romana (Roman peace) than during the Hellenistic and Classical times, most of

the chief arteries of commerce now bypassed the country. And her share of the world's economic pie was noticeably smaller. The Greek world of Pericles was considerably different from Paul's.

A Man from Macedonia

During his second missionary journey through Asia Minor, Paul sensed some divine compulsion to refrain from preaching. When he reached the port of Troas, this compulsion was still upon him (Acts 16:6–8). But while there, he received an urgent plea to carry the gospel to Macedonia. According to the Acts narrative, this call came to him in a vision by a man from Macedonia (Acts 16:9) to come over into Macedonia and "help us." The apostle seems to have eagerly embraced this opportunity and apparently left promptly for Europe. Luke joined Paul on the journey to Macedonia.

Identity of the man from Macedonia has raised considerable discussion. Presumably this person was a pagan crying out for some spiritual good news. He is not called a brother, and the Greek word translated "help" is not used anywhere in the New Testament to mean or involve collaboration in God's work.[54] Moreover, it was customary for Paul not to build on another's foundation but to prefer pioneer ministry (Romans 15:20). It is also interesting to note that no Jews or believers from Greece were said to be present in Jerusalem on the Day of Pentecost (Acts 2:9–11). Furthermore, the call for "us" to "preach the gospel to them" fits with the idea that the call for help did not come from a Christian who wanted help. It seems likely, then, that the man from Macedonia was not Luke, as is sometimes suggested, or some other Greek believer seeking help in the ministry.

Troas

Troas lay about ten miles south of the western end of the Dardanelles (ancient Hellespont) and thus about ten miles south of the site of ancient Troy. Troy and Troas are not to be confused, as often happens. Originally called Alexandria Troas, this town, founded at the command of Alexander the Great, came to be referred to as Troas. In

Troas harbor is now silted in and looks like a salt pan.

Paul's day the town had an excellent harbor and was a thriving port. Today the harbor has silted in, and the site is deserted. Ruins of a wall six miles in circumference, a theater, baths, and an aqueduct stand as mute testimony to former prosperity.

Tenedos and Imbros

As the missionaries sailed for Europe, they were never out of sight of land. On the first day they passed the little island of Tenedos (modern Bozcaada), well known from the account of the Trojan War. Then they passed the larger island of Imroz, or Imbros. In keeping with the custom of small Aegean sailing ships of anchoring for the night at a convenient island or port, Paul's ship spent the night at Samothrace, fourteen miles farther on toward the Greek coast (Acts 16:11). From Samothrace Paul could have seen the mainland of Macedonia and Mount Athos at the end of the nearest of the three peninsulas of Chalcidice to the southwest.

Samothrace

Samothrace is a small island of only sixty-eight square miles that had no harbor, only an anchorage, and even this is dangerous in winter because of the north winds and currents from the Dardanelles. The island is crossed from east to west by a chain of bare granite mountains, the highest peak of which is 5,200 feet, the highest point on any of the Aegean islands.

Samothrace owed its importance in ancient times to the existence there of a shrine of the Cabiri, an obscure mystery

cult whose protection people often sought against the perils of the sea. Numerous important persons of antiquity visited the shrine. Philip of Macedon and his wife Olympias were initiated there. Most important structures of the place were built by Arsinoe Philadelphus and her brother during the first half of the third century B.C.

Today the island is best known for the "Victory of Samothrace," now in the Louvre in Paris. Found in 1863, this winged figure was erected at the shrine by Demetrius Poliorcetes of Macedonia to commemorate a naval victory over the Egyptians at Cyprus in 306 B.C. Several archaeological expeditions to the island have systematically studied the very dilapidated antiquities, which include two temples, a theater, a long stoa, and other structures.

On to Neapolis

The next day the apostolic company started for the Macedonian mainland. As they neared shore, on their right the brown, turbid waters of the Nestos River could be seen gushing far out at sea—in marked contrast to the beautiful blue Aegean. On the left were the pyramidal heights of Thasos, an island that protected the bay. On the far side of the bay rose Neapolis, seaport of Philippi.

Neapolis

Neapolis (modern Kavalla, population about sixty thousand) was beautifully situated on a promontory that stretched out into the bay and had a harbor on either side. The harbor on the west was especially suitable for anchorage, and it was there that the galleys of

Neapolis

Brutus and Cassius moored during the battle of Philippi in 42 B.C. In the past there was some question whether the modern city occupies the same site as ancient Neapolis, but it has now been quite conclusively demonstrated that it does. During the early centuries of the Christian Era the town was known as Christopolis (city of Christ), doubtless in commemoration of Paul's visits. More than likely the apostle stopped there during each of his visits to Philippi.

Exactly when Neapolis was founded is not certain, but it is generally thought to have been settled by inhabitants of the nearby island of Thasos. Subsequently it was a member of both the Athenian Empire and the later Athenian Confederacy. Some have thought that the Athenians refounded it. During the fourth century B.C. it passed under the control of Philip of Macedon, and at the time of Paul was part of the Roman province of Macedonia and of the Roman colony at Philippi. Commonly when diggings in the area go very far below the surface, Greek and Roman artifacts are found. And one may see remains of a Roman aqueduct and of the ancient acropolis. Since the town has been continuously occupied, there is little to be seen that dates back to the Roman Imperial period.

To Philippi

Apparently the missionaries had no plan to evangelize at Neapolis, because they turned inland along the much-traveled road to Philippi, some thirteen miles away (Acts 16:12). The road ascended the Symbolon Hills, which reach a height of five hundred feet and descend into the plain of Philippi. This plain is bounded on all sides by mountains or hills. On the west rises Mount Pangaeus and on the east a spur of Mount Orbelos with a conical shape. Philippi was located at the foot of this spur. The plain was bordered along the northern edge by forests and on the south by a marshy area (now drained), formed because the Symbolon Hills created too formidable a barrier for waters from the nearby mountains to make their escape to the sea.

Philippi

Philippi was founded by Philip II of Macedon in 360 B.C., replacing the former Thracian settlement of Crenides. It was significant to the Macedonian as the chief mining center in the Pangaeus gold fields, which provided him with revenue for his gold currency, the support of his army, and the bribery of his enemies. These important mines seem to have been largely exhausted by the time Macedonia passed into Roman hands. Greek efforts to find new veins of gold ore in the area have not been successful.

THE IMPORTANCE OF PHILIPPI

Philippi was important in history out of proportion to its small size. For

The Krenides bubbles over its streambed at the supposed site of the prayer meeting of Acts 16:13.

Philip II (father of Alexander the Great), its founder, it was important economically and politically. With the gold from the mines in the area Philip was able to build his state and his military establishment and bribe his enemies.

The town was important politically because here the forces of Mark Antony and Octavian defeated the Republican forces of Brutus and Cassius; this was a significant step in the death of the Republic and the establishment of the Roman Empire period.

Philippi was important religiously because here the apostle Paul established a beachhead for the Gospel in Europe (Acts 16:12–40).

After the battle of Pydna in 168 B.C., all of Macedonia came under the control of Rome and was divided into four regions. Philippi was in the first of these. The town appears to have declined greatly under Roman occupation, as a result of both the depletion of the mines and the depredations of the civil wars of the first century B.C. She must have suffered especially during the great battle of 42 B.C., fought on the plain of Philippi, in which Octavian and Antony defeated Brutus and Cassius.

After this battle a colony of Roman veterans was settled on the site, which was renamed Colonia Julia Philippensis in honor of the victory of the cause of Julius Caesar (Acts 16:12). After the battle of Actium in 31 B.C., Octavian constituted the city as a colony for defeated partisans of Antony evicted from Italy, and he changed the name to Colonia Augusta Julia Philippensis. The territory of the colony included the port of Neapolis. As a colony Philippi enjoyed many political and economic privileges, including the *Ius Italicum*, which exempted it from imperial taxes. Colonies were a little bit of Italy set down on foreign shores, and their government was closely patterned after that of the municipalities of Italy.

As the Acts narrative suggests, inhabitants of such colonies were very proud of their privileged position. Also, hidden in

The Baptistry of Lydia.

The Philippi Agora

the Greek of Paul's letter to the Philippians are several references that would appeal to Roman veterans. For example, as he dealt with the disunity in the church there, he encouraged them to "walk in step" or "keep rank" (Greek, Philippians 3:17). And he spoke of a superior citizenship, even better than Roman citizenship (Philippians 3:20).

Paul and his associates (including Silas, Timothy, and Luke) probably came to Philippi before the end of A.D. 50. How long they stayed is open to question, but it has been suggested with some basis that they ministered there for as long as two months. Perhaps on the first Sabbath the apostolic company went out by a riverside to attend a prayer meeting held by the Jews of the place

(Acts 16:13). Apparently there were very few Jews living in town because if there had been ten heads of families there, they would have been obligated to build a synagogue. The fact that the group met outside the city probably indicates that they were beyond the pomerium, the sacred area within which foreign deities were not permitted.

A visit to Philippi today makes it easy to accept the spot of the prayer meeting site "outside the gate by the river" (Acts 16:13, NRSV) as a place just outside the west gate of the city. There the Roman road passes through the Krenides Gate, and the Krenides stream flows nearby. As was typical of Roman cities, tomb monuments of Roman officials line the road, and the lovely baptistery of Lydia stands nearby. Here

The podium or bema on the north side of the agora, where Paul and Silas apparently stood before the Philippi magistrates.

The theater of Philippi.

Basilica A at Philippi.

the stream is known locally as the River of Lydia, and the crystal clear waters bubble over the rocks in the streambed. Paving blocks of a Roman road run to the bank of the stream.

This spot seems to be the current choice of Jack Finegan,[55] though earlier he was fairly firm in his choice of a place about a mile and a half farther west. There the Egnatian Way and the Gangites River (the Gangas or Angites), the only real river in the area, intersected. At the junction remains of an archway were found thought to date to the time of Paul. The Gangites is an outlet of the Philippi Lake into Lake Tahinos some thirty miles to the east. Deep

Basilica B at Philippi.

and swift with clear, sweet water, the river is ten to fifteen feet deep and maintains a regular breadth of about forty feet.[56] Finegan now believes that it is unlikely that the women would have gone such a distance outside of town for their place of prayer.

Paul's ministry at Philippi seems to have been almost immediately successful, for a certain businesswoman by the name of Lydia, a seller of purple cloth, was converted along with her whole household (Acts 16:14–15) and immediately opened her guest rooms to the evangelists. Subsequently the apostle restored to normalcy a demented slave girl who served her masters as something of a fortune-teller. Her masters, seeing that their source of gain had vanished, stirred up a riot against Paul, falsely charging that he was spreading social teachings that would destroy the citizens' Roman way of life. They dragged Paul and Silas into the agora or marketplace and accused the missionaries before the magistrates. These magistrates were called *strategoi*, a Greek title to render the untranslatable *duoviri*—the two chief officials of a Roman municipality that corresponded to the consuls of the period of the Republic.

The agora where the judgment scene took place has been completely excavated by the French School at Athens (1914–38) and by Greek archaeologists since World War II. A rectangular area 330 feet long and 165 feet wide, it was bounded by porticoes,

The Egnatian Way near Philippi.

to the days of Philip II and had a capacity of about eight thousand.

Four churches have now been excavated at Philippi. Basilica A (fifth century A.D.) stands to the right (north) of the modern road and measures about 400 feet in length and 160 in breadth. To the south of the agora stand remains of Basilica B (sixth centuryA.D.), 184 feet in length. Because of structural problems, the church was never completed, and within its confines a smaller church was built in the tenth or eleventh century. To the east of the agora an octagonal church was excavated in the early 1970s. Dating perhaps to the fifth century, it measures approximately 108 feet long by 97 feet wide.

As the magistrates rendered their judgment on the north side of the agora, they commanded that Paul and Silas be beaten and cast into prison, ordering the jailer to keep them securely (Acts 16:22–24). The traditional prison stands to the north of the agora next to Basilica A. The story of the subsequent earthquake which opened the prison doors, the conversion of the jailer and his family, and the decision of the magistrates to let Paul and Silas go is familiar to most Sunday school students.

What is probably not so familiar is the distinctly Roman element in the Acts account and in the later epistle to the Philippians. When the magistrates gave the order to release Paul and Silas, Paul decided not to let the officials off so easily. He complained that he and Silas as Roman citizens had the right to be tried properly before the courts and that they should not have been beaten when they had not been sentenced by the court. Then he demanded that the magistrates themselves come and release the missionaries from prison. Greatly disturbed over the whole affair, the officials did so (Acts 16:36–39). Perhaps Paul had tried to make it clear that he was a Roman citizen during the mob scene of the previous day, but no one paid any attention to him or, possibly, did not hear him in the din and confusion.

Elements of interest to Romans are numerous in the epistle to the Philippians, written during Paul's Roman imprisonment to thank them for a gift and to stop

temple facades, and other public buildings. The agora as excavated dates back to the reign of Marcus Aurelius (A.D. 161–180), but the location and basic form are the same as in Paul's day. On the north side stood a rectangular podium with steps leading up to it on either side. This was apparently the place where magistrates dispensed justice and where Paul and Silas appeared (Acts 16:20).

The Egnatian Way, the main Roman road across Macedonia, ran on the north side of the agora and continued about thirteen hundred feet west to the Krenides gate. The total length of the city wall, portions of which may still be seen, was about 12,000 feet. If we enter the Neapolis gate on the east, the theater stands to our right, at the base of the acropolis. The theater dates back some sort of quarrel among them. To those proud of their citizenship, he spoke of a superior citizenship in a spiritual commonwealth (Philippians 3:20). To those accustomed to marching in step he addressed an appeal that they should "walk in step" (literal Greek of Philippians 3:16) and in unity of purpose instead of allowing the ranks of the church to be torn with dissension. Those walking "out of step" (literal Greek of Philippians 3:18) and living in a confused way religiously were compared to enemies of Christ.

To those proud of their military connections, Paul commented that through his imprisonment in Rome, the gospel had been preached to the whole Praetorian Guard, the elite troops of the Empire (literal Greek of Philippians 1:13). Again, he appealed to the military-minded by calling one of the faithful members of their church a "fellow soldier" (Philippians 2:25). To those interested in feats of bodily prowess and success in war, he made a number of appeals in the choice of verbs and figures of speech (e.g., "stand fast" and "striving," Philippians 1:27; the figure of the race in Philippians 3:14).

Soon after Paul's release from prison, he left Philippi, but he left Luke behind, as is clear from the fact that the "we" phraseology, always used when Luke accompanied Paul, abruptly ceased. The narrative is described in the third person until Paul left Philippi on his last journey to Jerusalem, some five years later (Acts 20:6). If Luke remained at Philippi during the entire interim, there would be some explanation for the solid establishment of the church there and its peculiar interest in helping Paul over the years. This church more than any other is singled out for its gifts toward the apostle's support. They sent him at least four gifts (2 Corinthians 8:3–4; 11:8–9; Philippians 4:10–16). It seems that Paul visited the city on his third missionary journey (Acts 19:22; 20:1) and again between his first and second imprisonments in Rome (1 Timothy 1:3).[57]

So then, the town of Philippi was extremely significant for world history. Here Christianity first entered Europe. This faith was to affect the development of the continent from that day to this—whether in connection with the conquests of the "universal church" (Charlemagne, Crusaders, and others) during the Middle Ages, the conflicts of the Reformation Era, or the impetus given to empire building in the nineteenth century as missionaries and others urged assumption of the "white man's burden." On the Plain of Philippi in 42 B.C. the battle was fought that decided to a large degree that the Roman Republic should be an empire. And in this area, Philip of Macedon annually extracted from the earth precious metals valued at 1,000 talents for the construction of a military machine that Alexander the Great used to conquer the East. And of course his conquests were to contribute to a fundamental change in the cultural orientation of much of the world.

The Egnatian Way

When Paul left Philippi, he struck out on the Egnatian Way for Thessalonica. This paved road some fifteen feet wide was the great military highway that connected Illyria, Macedonia, and Thrace. Scholars are almost completely in the dark with regard to its origin, but it must have been built shortly after the formation of the province of Macedonia in 148 B.C. The road started at two points on the Adriatic coast— Dyrrachium (Albanian Durres) and Aulon (modern Vlona). These two branches merged inland and continued as a single road all the way to Byzantium (Istanbul), a distance of 535 Roman miles (a Roman mile is 1,614.6 yards). On such a road one would probably travel about 17 Roman miles per day on foot and would probably ride in a horse-drawn vehicle at the rate of about 4 Roman miles per hour, for an average of 25 Roman miles per day.

As Paul and his associates traveled westward, they passed between mountains most of the way. Near Amphipolis, their next stop (thirty-two Roman miles from Philippi), the foothills dropped away into the Strymonic Plain, the most fertile plain of the north Aegean area. The great Strymon River which flows through it is on an average one hundred feet broad and six to nine feet deep with a current of about four miles per hour. It is fordable at most times of the year except when in strong

The hill on which Amphipolis was built.

flood, and its bottom is mostly firm though sandy.

Amphipolis

A few miles north of the Aegean, the Strymon emerges from Lake Tahinos, through which it flows on its way to the sea. On leaving the lake, the Strymon winds in a horseshoe around the western side of a terraced hill on which Amphipolis was built. Thus the town was protected on three sides by the river. On the east a protecting wall was built. Located three miles from the sea, Amphipolis was served by its seaport Eion.

The position of Amphipolis was one of the most important in this part of Greece. It stood in a pass that cuts through the mountains bordering the Strymonic Gulf and commanded the only easy communication from the coast of that gulf into the great Macedonian plains. In ancient times it was important because it controlled the western approach to the gold and silver mines and timber stands of Mount Pangaeus. Those natural resources meant much to the prosperity of the town, which declined when the veins of ore gave out. Of course, as already implied, Amphipolis was also a significant station on the Egnatian Way, the coastal route between northern Greece and the Hellespont.

Historical developments at Amphipolis began with unsuccessful efforts of Miletus and Athens to establish a colony there early in the fifth century B.C. Athens was finally successful in doing so in 437 B.C. This community fell to Sparta in 425. But after the

Peace of Nicias in 421 Amphipolis became independent and successfully resisted later Athenian attempts to resubjugate her. Philip of Macedon took the town in 358 and annexed it to his domain. Thereafter Amphipolis was part of Macedonia until 168 when the Romans made it the capital of the first of the four districts into which they divided Macedonia (the same district in which Philippi was also located).

Since the extensive ruins of neither the acropolis nor the lower city of Amphipolis have been carefully examined or excavated, it is difficult to picture what the place was like when Paul passed through. So far archaeologists have worked mainly on the acropolis, where they have excavated five churches of the fifth and sixth centuries A.D. They have also uncovered remains of a Roman house, a Hellenistic house, and a Classical gymnasium. But more to our interests, they have traced the wall of the New Testament period and uncovered some of its parts. It had a circuit of about four miles, with an inner acropolis wall of about a mile and a half. It was built of fine masonry, with towers and gates. Archaeologists have also found remains of the Egnation Way and a Roman bridge on the Strymon River. The harbor of Eion is not silted in.

Apparently Paul only passed through Amphipolis—not stopping to evangelize there. Christianity seems to have reached Amphipolis later from Philippi or Thessalonica. One striking landmark along the road in Paul's day has been discovered and properly mounted once more. The

A Hellenistic house at Amphipolis.

"Lion of Amphipolis," erected in the early part of the fourth century B.C. to commemorate some unknown victory, again stands as a silent sentinel along the road.

Apollonia

Continuing westward along the Via Egnatia, the apostolic company found themselves skirting the seacoast for some ten miles. To their right, mountains closely hugged the shore. Then the road struck inland south of Lake Bolbe (Volve) to Apollonia, another of the more important stops on the Egnatian Road, twenty-two Roman miles from Amphipolis (Acts 17:1). The name of the ancient town seems to be preserved in the modern Pollina. Though the town probably existed as early as the fifth century B.C., very little is known of its history or of the nature of the site during the first century A.D. Practically no formal exploration has been conducted there.

Apparently having no intention of ministering extensively at any town short of Thessalonica, Paul led his companions farther westward along the Egnatian Way. As they traveled across the Chalcidice (that land shaped like a bird's foot with three claws extending into the north Aegean), the road continued to follow the southern shore of Lake Bolbe. Leaving that lake behind, the road soon brought the missionary party to the south shore of another lake, the Coronea. As had been true of the route ever since they left Apollonia, mountains hemmed in the Egnatian Way on their left. Nearing Thessalonica (thirty-six Roman miles from Appolonia), the road ascended the foothills of the Cortiates Mountains and dropped down into the city of Thessalonica.

Thessalonica

The city lay on the Gulf of Thessalonica, the largest gulf indenting the Balkan Peninsula, and rose at the end of the bay in amphitheater form, on the slopes of the foothills of the Cortiates Mountains. On the east and west sides of the city, ravines ascend from the shore and converge toward the highest point, on which the citadel stood. The port, which is an open roadstead sheltered by Chalcidice, was and still is convenient for large ships. In the fifth century

The Lion of Amphipolis.

B.C., the Gulf of Thessalonica was perhaps twice as large as it is today. As a result of the silting action of the Vardar (or Axios) River, the western part of the gulf was gradually filled in. By Paul's day silting action had enclosed the western area so that it was a large lake which has since silted up. This silting action created marshy areas that have bred malarial mosquitoes, plaguing the city until recently.

Mount Olympus stands in clear view from the upper streets of the city, rising 9,600 feet above the sea. In ancient times its glittering snow-covered dome was thought to be the throne before which Zeus gathered in council the deities of Greece. Dense forests at the mountain's base concealed the Pierian Spring, beside which the Muses were reputedly born and Orpheus first saw the light.

In early times there were various small villages in the area of Thessalonica. A town

Though medieval, the walls of the acropolis of Thessolonica rest on foundations of the ancient Greek period.

used to be doubted because such a title was unknown from other sources. But numerous inscriptions have turned up in the area, confirming the accuracy of the New Testament.

THE IMPORTANCE OF THESSALONICA

Thessalonica was the largest city in Greece and the capital of the Roman province of Macedonia in Paul's day.

It was the main stop on the Egnatian way, the leading Roman highway across Greece.

It was a naval base and the most important commercial port in the north.

Its large Jewish population gave Paul an especial reason for ministry there.

on the present site was called Therme, from which the Thermaic Gulf received its name. In 315 B.C. Cassander grouped together the villagers of the area (reportedly from twenty-six small villages) and founded the city of Thessalonica, which he named in honor of his wife, the daughter of Philip and stepsister of Alexander the Great. Apparently the town served as a Macedonian naval station. It replaced Pella (where the harbor had silted up) as Macedonia's principal port.

When Macedonia capitulated to Rome in 168 B.C. and the kingdom was divided into four parts, Thessalonica served as the administrative center for the second district. In 148, when the province of Macedonia was formed, Thessalonica became the capital. During the civil wars of the first century B.C., it was the headquarters of the Pompeian party and the Senate and later took the side of Antony and Octavian against Brutus and Cassius. By virtue of the latter action, it was made a free city. It had its own city council and was ruled by politarchs, according to the New Testament narrative (Acts 17:6). This fact

Thessalonica was an important city in Paul's day. The population has been estimated as high as two hundred thousand. Besides serving as the capital of the province of Macedonia, it was the main stop on the Egnatian Way, a naval base, and an important commercial port. With overland caravans thronging its hostelries, with its harbor filled with ships' bottoms from overseas, and with old salts, Roman officials, and thousands of Jewish merchants rubbing shoulders in its streets, Thessalonica became a very cosmopolitan center. It is very appropriate that Paul's Jewish opponents should have called him and his co-workers "world-topplers" (Acts 17:6).

This cosmopolitanism apparently appealed to Paul. Judging from the fact that he spent so long a time at great centers like Corinth and Ephesus and sought to minister at other large centers with great moving populations, it would seem that Paul's strategy was to use these cities as springboards for the propagation of the gospel. Individuals converted in them would move all over the Roman world and would rapidly spread the Christian message.

The fact that he could greet so many persons by name in the Roman church (Romans 16), doubtless acquaintances from other places who had moved to the capital, is proof of the effectiveness of this approach. Probably some of these acquaintances led the group of friends who came to meet the apostle at Appii Forum and Three Taverns when he was on his way to Rome for trial (Acts 28:15). It should be remembered, however, that in general Paul also ministered in cities that had fairly large Jewish populations and that it was his custom to preach first to the Jews wherever he went. When they rejected his message, he then turned to Gentiles.

That there was a fairly large Jewish population in Thessalonica is evident from the fact that a great number of Greeks had become "God seekers" or converts to Judaism. Of these a "great multitude" (Acts 17:4) were won over to Christianity. Moreover, the ease with which the Jews of Thessalonica marshaled the city crowd against Paul and Silas (Acts 17:5) indicates that their numbers were either large or at least influential. Exactly how many Jews were living in the city and their percentage of the population is unknown.

As usual, Paul began his ministry among the Jews of Thessalonica, preaching to them in their synagogue for three Sabbaths (Acts 17:2). It need not be concluded, however, that Paul remained in the city for so short a time. The success of Paul's labor among Gentiles indicates an extended ministry outside the synagogue. A stay of longer than three weeks would certainly have been required for the Philippians to collect and send two gifts to the apostle while he was in Thessalonica (Philippians 4:16).

The success of Paul's ministry in Thessalonica led many Jews who took exception to his message to stir up a riot against him. The mob attacked the house of Jason, Paul's host, but the apostle was away at the time. So they dragged Jason and some fellow Christians to the politarchs, with the accusation of sedition: "These are all acting contrary to the decrees of Caesar, saying that there is another king,—Jesus" (Acts 17:7). The politarchs required the suspects to post bond for good behavior, and

then they freed the Christians. Though greatly disturbed by the tumult, the rulers were apparently bent on justice and the legal protection of Paul and his companions. The inability of free cities to keep order raised a threat of Roman interference.

Paul and Silas now seemed to be a liability to the young church; besides, their lives were in danger. So the Thessalonian believers decided to send the pair to Beroea (modern Veroia) to wait out the storm. The persecution leveled against Paul and Silas continued against the church in the city. Within a few months, while Paul was ministering at Corinth, he found it necessary to write to encourage the Thessalonians to bear up under persecution (1 Thessalonians 2:14; 3:2–4). The Thessalonians had also become involved in erroneous teachings on the Lord's return and were neglecting everyday business. A little later Paul was compelled to send a second epistle to Thessalonica to correct some beliefs concerning the second coming of Christ.

A stone pulpit from Thessalonica (5th century A.D.) in the Archaelogical Museum of Istanbul.

Little detailed information can be produced on the Thessalonica of Paul's day. Excavations are difficult, owing chiefly to the cost of demolishing the overlying buildings of the modern city of Salonika. The main street of the lower city is still called the Egnatian Way, but it is not certain that the ancient Via Egnatia followed exactly the same route. At its western extremity stood

The Arch of Galerius on the Egnatian Way.

an arch until A.D. 1876. Known as the Vardar Gate, it possibly was built long before Paul arrived. It was erected by the people in honor of Octavian and Antony and in memory of the battle of Philippi. Constructed of large blocks of marble, it had on its outside face two bas-reliefs of a Roman wearing the toga and standing before a house. The inscription on this arch, which mentions the politarchs, is now in the British Museum.

The Arch of Galerius, which still stands at the east end of the street, was built about A.D. 305 and therefore has no connection with the New Testament period. The same is true of the several well-preserved Byzantine churches of the town. The wall of the acropolis dates to the Medieval period but it rests on foundations of Greek times and incorporates many ancient blocks bearing inscriptions.

In the 1960s, in the center of the city, part of the Roman forum was excavated with an adjacent odeion or music hall and an underground stoa, all of which may date to the second century A.D.

Because of its location, Thessalonica has remained an important city throughout the Christian Era. It was the second metropolis to Constantinople in the Byzantine Empire, and in spite of all its sufferings it has always arisen from the ashes. Today Thessalonica/Salonika has a population of well over four hundred thousand.

Beroea

Leaving Thessalonica, Paul and Silas traveled westward on the Egnatian Way for about twenty miles. Then, shortly after

Reliefs on the Arch of Galerius.

The Odeion or music hall of Roman Thessalonica.

(youth); this inscription may help to establish the young evangelist's age.[58]

After Macedonia's surrender to Rome, Beroea (modern Veroia, population 37,000) became a part of the third of the four regions into which Macedonia was divided. Pompey spent the winter of 49–48 B.C. there in preparation for the battle of Pharsalus. The Jewish community seems to have been established about the time of Christ.

Paul found the Beroean Jews even more receptive to the Christian message than the Jews of Thessalonica. Many of them were converted, as were numerous Greeks, including some of fairly high social class (Acts 17:12). When word of this success reached the Thessalonian Jews, they sent rabble-rousers to Beroea to stir up trouble. The Beroean church then sent Paul away by sea (by what route is unknown) and conducted him safely to Athens. Paul's stay at Beroea must have been brief but effective. William Ramsay believes Paul spent several months there.[59]

Silas and Timothy remained behind, but Paul sent word with his escorts to request them to come as soon as possible (Acts 17:15). Since Timothy suddenly reappears in the biblical narrative, it seems that he had been left behind at Philippi and now

crossing the bridge over the Axios River, they turned southwest on a side road to Beroea. Thirty miles later they arrived at their destination. On this leg of their journey the terrain had been much different from what they had previously experienced. This time almost their entire journey had been across plains. The town of Beroea itself was located at an altitude of six hundred feet on the tableland of the eastern mountains of the Varmion chain. The area is well supplied with gushing springs and fertile farmland.

The town, though smaller today than in New Testament times, occupies much the same land. Therefore systematic excavation is impossible. But as builders have attempted new construction, they have uncovered remains from Hellenistic and Roman times, especially houses and parts of roads—which generally follow the same routes as modern streets. The local museum has an assortment of ancient materials, including a stele of the second century B.C. inscribed with rules of the local gymnasium. It refers to participating youths by age groups. The 18–22 age bracket are called *neoi*. Paul in 1 Timothy 4:12 refers to Timothy as a *neotes*

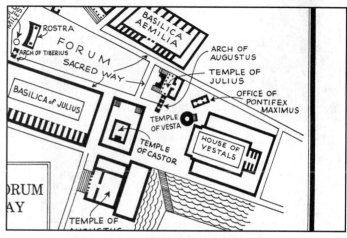

Part of the Roman forum of Thessalonica.

had come directly from that town to Beroea. Apparently too Silas and Timothy came to Athens promptly on receipt of the summons from Paul. But some emergency or concern must have led him to send them away again—Timothy to Thessalonica (1 Thessalonians 3:1–3) and Silas probably to Philippi. Both of them rejoined him at Corinth (Acts 18:5).

The chronicling of these scurryings back and forth should serve to allow the reader to peep behind the curtain to see a little more of the feverish between-acts activity that must have characterized Paul's effort to evangelize, establish churches in, and maintain contact with many of the centers of the eastern Mediterranean. This review also serves to underscore the relative ease and frequency of travel in the Roman world of Nero and Paul.

Athens

As Paul landed at the Piraeus and made his way into Athens (c. five miles away), he must have had much the same feelings as a postwar guest of an impoverished London gentleman. The great house is intact, though there is some destruction around the grounds; the beautiful old furniture is still in place; and the coat of arms still hangs over the mantel. But the rugs are threadbare, few servants circulate about the place, it grows increasingly hard to keep up

A street scene in Beroea.

appearances, and the conversation often turns to a better day long since gone.

The Acropolis with the Parthenon—a temple to Athena, chief deity of the city

The temple to the Olympian Zeus—largest temple in the city

The Athenian Agora—center of life in the city

The Roman Agora—a commercial agora with its beautiful water clock

The Odeion of Pericles—a concert hall at the southeast corner of the Acropolis

The Theater of Dionysus—where drama was born, on the south slope of the Acropolis

The Pnyx—the rustic theater where the assembly had met during the height of the democracy

The Areopagus or Mars Hill—meeting place of the important court of the city

Vestiges of the destruction wrought by Sulla in 86 B.C. still remained. Certainly the effects were still felt. Sulla had burned the arsenals and shipbuilding yards and leveled the city walls. Athens' importance as a commercial and political center was gone. It was now a quiet university town, respected for its learning, its arts, and its past prestige. The young Roman elite were especially impressed by the city's beautiful monuments and the brilliance of her schools of rhetoricians.

Athenian silver resources had been exhausted by the beginning of the Roman imperial period. Athens no longer controlled an empire. And great rival centers such as Corinth, Ephesus, Antioch, and Alexandria had cut into the Athenian share of

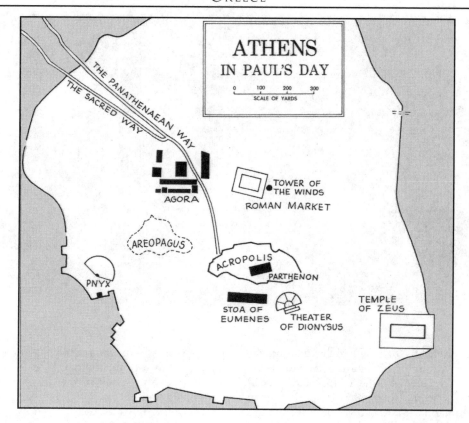

the economic and cultural pie of the eastern Mediterranean world.

In spite of the decline of the imperial city, it remained outwardly beautiful. Her Acropolis, Agora, and other public centers remained intact. And the despoiling of much of her most exquisite statuary did not come until A.D. 64 (after Paul's visit), when Nero sought art pieces to beautify the Rome he was rebuilding.[60] Foreigners expended considerable sums on public buildings there during the first century A.D., some of them having been built before Paul arrived.

For instance, about the time of the birth of Christ, the Temple of Roma and Augustus was erected on the Acropolis, and the Roman agora was constructed near the Athenian Agora. Claudius, not Caligula as some have claimed, built the upper part of the Roman stairway of the Acropolis.[61] Many of the greatest structures erected with funds from abroad were built later, however—in the first half of the second century A.D.—by Trajan, Hadrian, and Herodes Atticus. For all the benefits bestowed, the Athenians became obsequious emperor worshipers.

Not only could the apostle still see the beautiful structures of ancient Athens; he could also enjoy her wonderful climate and her gorgeous scenery. The mean temperature was 63° F, with a high of 99° F in July and a low of 31° F in January. The summer heat was moderated by the sea breezes or the cool northerly winds from the mountains. On the average there were only three days a year that were overcast all day. Observations over a period of 24 years at Athens give on the average 179 clear days when the sun is never hid, 157 bright days when the sun may be hid for a half hour or so, 26 cloudy days, and 3 days when the sun is not seen at all.[62]

If Paul had stood on the 340-foot hill of the Nymphs (where an observatory now stands) at the west wall, he would have been in an excellent position to orient himself to the landscape. Some five hundred yards in front of him to the east and slightly to the left would have been the Agora.

Temple of Olympian Zeus.

Sharply to his right would have stood the Pnyx, a roughly shaped theater where the assembly met. A little to his right would have been the bare-topped rocky Areopagus (Mars Hill), 377 feet high. Towering above the Areopagus would have stood the Acropolis, 512 feet high, capped with its incomparable collection of temples. Behind that and out of sight would have been the great unfinished Temple of Zeus. Far off in the distance to his right would have stretched the Hymettus Range, 3,370 feet high. If it was evening, its barren western flank would have been colored a flaming purple by the reflected rays of the setting sun. Apparently this beautiful sight had led the poet Pindar to describe Athens as the "violet-crowned city."

To Paul's left in the near distance the sharply pointed Lycabettus (1,112 feet high) thrust its top above pine-clad slopes. Almost behind that, ten miles away, arose the conical form of Mount Pentelicus, 3,640 feet high, whose green slopes were dotted with gleaming white mounds from the marble quarries. From the foot of Pentelicus, the Cephisus River flowed to the north of Athens, and coming from the Hymettus, the Ilissus River skirted the city on the southwest. Between Pentelicus and Hymettus was an opening in the mountains leading out toward the Plain of Marathon.

Paul probably walked the five miles from the Piraeus to Athens on the road just north of the long walls and entered by the Dipylon Gate at the northwest corner of the city. Just outside the gate the road passed through a large cemetery that held graves dating from the eleventh century B.C. to Roman times. In this cemetery a number of Jewish gravestones were found. Inside the Dipylon Paul would have found himself on a long avenue leading to the Agora—the political, commercial, and social center of the city. In this northwest section of Athens were the potters' quarters. From the Agora Paul could have gone directly eastward to the Roman marketplace, south to the Areopagus, or southeast to the Acropolis.

Archaeologist Oscar Broneer was quite convinced that Paul spent part of his time sight-seeing in Athens. He felt that the full force of the Greek of Acts 17:23a demanded "going about and examining objects of religious devotion."[63] Ramsay translated the passage, "As I went through the city surveying the monuments of your religion."[64] If Paul went sight-seeing in Athens, a few of the more significant things he saw should be considered.

began the temple in 515 B.C. Antiochus IV Epiphanes of Syria resumed the work during his reign (175–164 B.C.). Hadrian finished it and consecrated it in A.D. 131–32.

The structure had 104 Corinthian columns of Pentelic marble 56 feet high and 5 feet 7 inches in diameter at the base. These were arranged in two rows on the sides and three rows at the ends and rested on a foundation 354 feet long and 135 feet broad. The height was over 90 feet. The image of Zeus was made of gold and ivory. This temple was one of the four largest in the Roman world. Of its three rivals, the best known to Bible students is the Temple of Diana at Ephesus.

The Roman Agora.

Temple of Olympian Zeus. One of the most colossal religious structures of this "city of idol worship" was the Temple of Olympian Zeus, or Jupiter Olympus, located not far to the southeast of the Acropolis. Unfinished and roofless in Paul's day, it was completed by Hadrian. Fifteen of its gigantic columns are still standing. Pisistratus of Athens

The Roman Agora. If Paul carried on his religious disputations daily in the Athenian Agora (Acts 17:17), he certainly must have visited the Roman Agora adjacent to it on the east. This marketplace was a large rectangular area 367 by 315 feet, enclosed by a high wall of stone. It was lined with shops. The interior open courtyard, measuring 269 by 187 feet, was paved with marble and surrounded with an Ionic colonnade, upon which shops opened. The main entrance, on the northwest side, still stands. It consists of four fluted Doric columns 26 feet high and 4 feet in diameter, capped by a gable surmounted by a statue of Lucius Caesar, grandson of Augustus. This entrance also bears an inscription to the effect that the agora was erected with a donation from

The Tower of the Winds.

On the tower of the winds, Caecias, the boisterous northeast wind, is warmly clad and carries a vessel containing what seem to be hailstones.

The assembly in session at the Pnyx.

where the Athenian assembly met during the days of Athens' glory. In this sort of rustic theater, 230 feet deep and 395 feet broad, on the northeast slope of the hill facing the Acropolis, such greats as Aristides, Themistocles, and Pericles had addressed the citizens of the "violet-crowned" city. After the Theater of Dionysus was built in stone during the latter half of the fourth century B.C., the assembly preferred to meet there.

The Acropolis. Greatest of all the tourist attractions in Athens—in Paul's day and ours—is the Acropolis. No effort was spared to make it the crown of Athens and her empire. The southern slope of the Acropolis supported structures that were almost as important as some of those on the sacred hill. At the southeast corner stood the Odeion of Pericles, which was built in 445 B.C. Burned by one of Mithridates' generals in 86 B.C., it was restored some twenty-five years later by the king of Cappadocia and it was considered the most beautiful concert hall of the Greek world. In it were performed the cantatas of the Dionysian festivals, and rehearsals were conducted there for the dramas held in the theater. Its surviving architectural members are so few that reconstruction has been problematic.

Julius Caesar and Augustus. Another inscription on this entrance, by Hadrian, stipulates regulations for the sale of oil. Apparently this was primarily a wine and oil market.

On the southeast side of the Roman Agora stood a most unusual structure, popularly known as the Tower of the Winds. An octagonal structure of Pentelic marble, it stood 42 feet high and 26 feet in diameter. On its roof rose a weather vane in the form of a bronze triton pointing with a wand at the personifications of the prevailing winds as portrayed in the reliefs below the cornice. These eight reliefs bear inscriptions giving their names. For instance, Caecias, the boisterous northeast wind, is bearded and warmly clad and carries a vessel containing what seems to be hailstones; Apeliotes, the mild and rainy east wind, is a youth with a bundle of grain and fruits. This tower was also equipped with a hydraulic clock and sundials so an individual could tell time by it in fair or cloudy weather.

The Pnyx. Over on the other side of town, due west of the Acropolis, was the Pnyx—a place with which many significant memories were already associated in Paul's day. This is

The Acropolis as it appeared in Paul's day.

The Theater of Dionysus.

Walking westward along the south slope of the Acropolis, we come next to the Theater of Dionysus, where a great festival was celebrated every spring (March–April) in honor of the god Dionysus. Out of the dancing and singing of these festivals developed the dramatic forms of tragedy and comedy. Although Dionysiac celebrations were first carried on in the Agora, they were enacted on this site from around 500 B.C. Here the plays of Aeschylus, Sophocles, Euripides, and Aristophanes were acted. Originally in wood, construction of the theater in stone was completed by Lycurgus around 330 B.C. It is estimated that the seats could hold some seventeen thousand spectators, but on occasion many more attended.

In front of the southern slope of the Acropolis, extending westward from the theater, Eumenes II, king of Pergamum (197–159 B.C.), had built a great stoa, or portico, 535 feet long and 58 feet wide. Designed to serve as a shelter for the theater audience, it was faced with a two-story Doric colonnade with sixty-four columns on each story. Behind this, on the slope of the Acropolis, stood several small temples. And at the west end of the stoa the Odeion of Herodes Atticus was to be built during the second century A.D.

The entrance to the Acropolis looked quite different in Paul's day from the way it looked when it was ultimately completed and from the impression that the modern visitor receives. The two pylons flanking

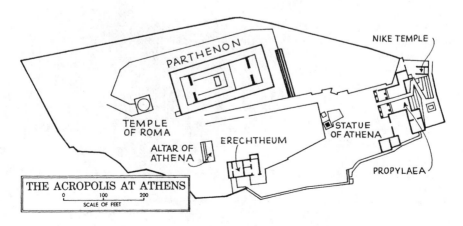

The Erechtheum

the east. Before him, on the west pediment was portrayed in statuary the quarrel between Athena and Poseidon for possession of Attica while the other gods and heroes looked on. On his left stood the Erechtheum, temple of Athena Polias ("of the city") and Poseidon-Erechtheus with its beautiful porch of the maidens (caryatids). The main part of this structure is a rectangle seventy-eight feet long by forty-two feet wide with an Ionic colonnade at either end standing twenty-five feet high. The porch, with its six maidens whose heads support the roof, extends from the southwest corner of the temple.

Next on the left was the great Altar of Athena. Behind that stood the sanctuary of Zeus Polias ("protector of the city"). As the sacred way turned toward the eastern entrance of the Parthenon, the apostle would have seen on his left a circular structure surrounded by nine Ionic columns which housed the altar of Roma and Augustus. This was built between 27 and 14 B.C.

At last the apostle reached the main entrance of the magnificent Parthenon. Begun in 447 B.C., it was dedicated to the goddess Athena in 438, when Athens was at the height of her glory. Pericles was the political chief, and supervision of the work was entrusted to the great sculptor Phidias. What an impressive sight it was for the apostle, who lamented that so much effort

the Roman entrance and jutting out seventeen feet from it were built at a much later date, perhaps in the reign of Septimius Severus, about A.D. 200. In fact the whole monumental stairway, the upper part of which was built by Claudius, was a Roman addition. The Greeks preferred a diagonal pathway that would break the architectural lines.

Entering by a path a little above the lower Roman entrance, Paul would have passed below the exquisite little Ionic Temple of Athena Nike (or victory). The parapet around it had statues representing victories in a variety of poses. And beside the temple was the triple figure of Hekate, awesome queen of the underworld.

In front of the apostle on his left stood the Agrippa monument, a statue mounted on a chariot drawn by four horses atop a thirty-nine-foot rectangular pedestal of marble. There is reason to believe that this was originally erected by Eumenes of Pergamum in the second century B.C.

Passing next through the impressive ornamental gateway or Propylaea, Paul gazed on the colossal bronze figure of Athena Promachos ("the goddess who fights in front"), which Phidias fashioned from spoils taken from the Persians at Marathon. The Parthenon would now have been in full view, its main entrance on

The Erechtheum restored.

The Parthenon from the west.

and expense had been devoted to the worship of a deity that did not exist.

The great marble structure measured at its base 238 feet in length and 111 feet in width. Its encircling row of forty-six fluted Doric columns (seventeen on each side, eight on each end) stood to a height of 34 feet, each column having a diameter of six feet at the base. The top of the pediment rose to a height of 65 feet. And the pediment was filled with sculptures of the important gods of Greece. In the center of the group was Zeus, from whose head Athena sprang fully armed. Encircling the entire structure above the colonnade was the Doric frieze. Divided into ninety-two panels, this frieze consisted of groups of sculptures depicting legendary and mythological stories dear to the hearts of the Greeks. On the east end Paul found himself looking up at scenes from the struggle between the gods and the giants.

Looking between the columns of the peristyle, the apostle saw another frieze near the roof, known as the Ionic frieze. It completely encircled the building with a continuous series of sculptures 524 feet long. The approximately six hundred figures of this frieze included men, women, and animals that participated in the Panathenaic Procession, formed every year to carry a new robe to Athena in proper state.

The Panathenaic Procession occurred during the annual Panathenaic Festival.

This festival originated in 566 B.C. and continued until A.D. 410. While it was held annually, it was celebrated with special pomp every four years, in the third year of each Olympiad. It took place in the first month of the Athenian calendar, which approximated our month of July. Though we do not know the precise length of the festival, it may have lasted for eight days. Events included musical contests; athletic contests for boys, youths, and men; equestrian contests; a torch race preceding an all night revel. This was followed at dawn by the procession to the Acropolis to bring the new garment to Athena and a sacrifice to Athena. The festival concluded with the awarding of prizes to the victors and feasting on the meat distributed after the great sacrifice to Athena.[65]

Peering through the tremendous bronze doors into the sanctuary, Paul would have seen the great gold and ivory image of Athena, one of the greatest works of Phidias. The fleshy parts were carved ivory and the rest consisted of plates of gold suspended on a framework of cedar wood. The room was surrounded by a two-story Doric colonnade and measured 98 feet long, 63 feet wide, and 43 feet high. Paul would not have seen the west room, or treasury, but he was told that in the center of it were four great Ionic columns arranged in a rectangle and extending from the floor to the ceiling. The room was 44 feet long and 63 feet wide.

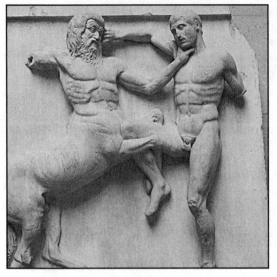

A panel from the Doric frieze.

A panel from the Ionic frieze—the presentation of the new robe for Athena.

Walking around the outside of the temple, the apostle noticed the perfect form of the structure. He was told that there was not a straight line in the building and that the columns bowed slightly inward at the top to avoid optical illusions of sagging lines or leaning columns. Moreover, the upper part of the friezes was cut deeper than the lower to promote optical equalization. His attention was also called to a row of significant statuary along the south wall of the Acropolis adjacent to the Parthenon. These were figures of Gauls and Amazons in defeat, dedicated by King Attalus of Pergamum some two centuries earlier.

As Paul turned to leave the Acropolis, he noticed that the walk was bordered with numerous statues of gods and famous men, many of which were votive offerings to the gods. In fact, all over Athens were altars to the gods, statues of them, and other evidences of the religiosity of the people.

While Paul had come to Athens primarily to wait for conditions to quiet down in Beroea and Thessalonica and had no plans for an extended ministry there, he nevertheless did conduct some evangelistic ministry in the city. As was customary elsewhere, he went first to the Jews, reasoning with them in their synagogue concerning acceptance of the Christian message (Acts 17:17). Where the synagogue was located is unknown. But a stone slab excavated in the eastern section of Athens bearing Psalm 118:20 might have been incorporated in such a building as a synagogue.

The Agora. Not restricting himself to religious discussion with Jews, Paul reasoned daily with chance comers to the Agora (Acts 17:17). Ramsay believes that this "reasoning" was according to the Socratic

A panel from the Ionic frieze showing young men in procession.

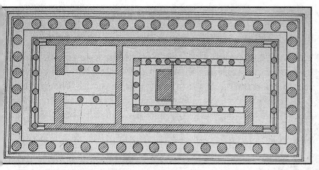

The floor plan of the Parthenon.

and middle stoas facing an open market area. The south stoa consisted of a single wide aisle with Doric columns along its north side. Its back wall acted as a retaining wall against higher ground to the south.

The east stoa connected the south and middle stoas, thus screening the commercial agora from the Panathenaean Way. Facing in two directions, it had

The statue of Athena in the Parthenon.

style of discussion characteristic of the city and cites this as an example of Paul's ability to be "all things to all men."[66] Thanks particularly to the excavations of the American School of Classical Studies at Athens during 1931–40 and since 1946, it is now possible to see quite clearly what the agora was like in Paul's day.

If Paul had entered the area at the southeast corner, on the road leading from the Acropolis (the Panathenaean Way), at the entrance on his left stood the mint of Athens, dating from the second half of the fifth century B.C. Here the famous "owls" of Athens were coined, which provided the standard coinage of the eastern Mediterranean for nearly two centuries. Across the alley from it to the west was a fountain house, the earliest in the Agora. Sprawling out northeast of that lay the commercial Agora. Constructed in the second century B.C., it included south, east,

colonnades on both east and west sides. Since the ground level was so much lower on the west side, the architect divided the stoa down the middle with a solid wall and set the eastern half over a yard higher than the western. Access to the commercial agora was gained by means of a broad stairway leading through this stoa to the lower level. The middle stoa also faced both southward on the commercial Agora and on the larger area to the north. This middle

The east pediment of the Parthenon, portraying the birth of Athena, goddess of wisdom—springing forth from the head of Zeus.

The west pediment of the Parthenon, portraying the struggle of Athena and Poseidon for control of Attica.

stoa was the largest structure in the Agora; it was about 450 feet long and, like the south and east stoas, was faced with unfluted Doric columns. At the end of the south stoa was the Heliaia, largest of the law courts at Athens, dating originally to the sixth century B.C. To the right of its entrance a water clock was erected in the fourth century. Next to the Heliaia was the southwest fountain house.

Having passed through the commercial Agora, the apostle would now have been at the southwest corner of the Agora on the road leading in from the Areopagus. On the west side of the Agora, to his left, would have been the important political center of ancient Athens. First came the circular Tholos, the office and dining room of the prytany, a committee of the city council. Built about 470 B.C., this building was the real headquarters of the Athenian government.

The full Council of Five Hundred met in the Bouleuterion a few feet away off the road. This building, constructed in the form of a theater with raised banks of seats, was set against a steep hillside, called Kolonos Agoraios. Next along the road, was the Metroon, built in the second century B.C. Consisting of four rooms sharing a single colonnade facing the Agora, this structure housed the state archives and the sanctuary of the mother of the gods. Across the road from this, was a fenced enclosure surrounding a long base, on which statues of the tribal heroes of Attica are thought to have stood. The base of these statues served as a public bulletin board.

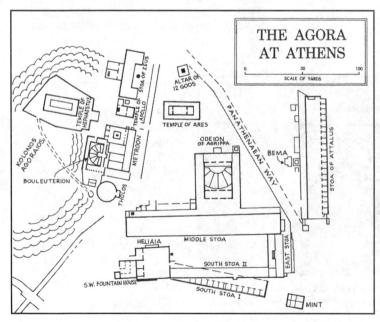

THE AGORA
AT ATHENS

0   50   100
SCALE OF YARDS

The owl of Athens, a four-drachma piece from the Athenian Empire.

Between the Metroon and the Temple of Apollo to the north was a wide passageway that provided access to the Temple of Hephaestus (god of the forge) and Athena on the Kolonos Agoraios. This temple, one of the best preserved of all Greek temples, is entirely constructed of Pentelic marble, except for the lowest of the three steps that lead up to it. It is 104 feet long, 45 feet wide, and 3 feet high. The Doric colonnade consists of six columns at the ends and thirteen on the sides. Within its cella stood cult statues of Athena and Hephaestus. On the east pediment, above the entrance, were sculptures representing the labors of Hercules. A formal garden surrounded the temple (built a few years before the Parthenon), and plants were set out in flower pots which were sunk into the rock and carefully spaced. Just north of the temple on the hill was a Hellenistic building thought by some to have been a state arsenal.

Back on the level of the Agora again, next Paul would have come to the fourth century B.C. Temple of Apollo Patroos, reputed father of the Athenians. Inside the temple Apollo was represented as a musician dressed in long robes and holding a lyre. In a tiny shrine at the side of the Temple of Apollo, Zeus Phratrios and Athena Phratria were worshiped as ancestral gods of Athenian family groups. Across the road to the apostle's right was the Temple of Ares, the god of war whom the Romans called Mars.

North of the Temple of Apollo was the Stoa of Zeus, a large U-shaped structure with wings jutting toward the Agora. In front of the structure stood a colossal statue of Zeus the Deliverer. The walls of this stoa were painted with various religious subjects, including an assembly of the Twelve Gods. Various administrative offices were located here. Socrates is known to have discussed philosophy with his friends in the stoa.

Across the north of the agora stood the Painted Stoa.

The Temple of Hephaestus.

So-called for a series of battle scenes painted on its walls (including Troy, Athenians vs. Amazons, Marathon, etc.). It was a haunt of philosophers in the fourth and third centuries B.C. Here Zeno, founder of the Stoic school, held academic court.

Turning onto the Panathenaean Way, which led diagonally across the Agora to the southeast, Paul would have passed the Altar of the Twelve Gods. This was considered the very center of Athens; from it distances to outside points were measured. After passing the Temple of Ares, he would have stood alongside the Odeion, or music hall, of Agrippa. Built about 15 B.C. it had a seating capacity of approximately a thousand.

The Stoa of Attalos.

All along the east side of the Agora, stretched the magnificent Stoa of Attalus. King Attalus of Pergamum built this stoa for the Athenians around 150 B.C. It was some 385 feet long and 64 feet wide and was faced by a two-story colonnade of forty-five columns, Doric at the base and Ionic at the top. Stairs ascended to the second story at either end. Shops lined the back wall of the structure. This beautiful stoa has been rebuilt by the excavators and serves today as the Agora Museum. In front of it stood the Bema, or public rostrum, where officials could address citizens gathered in the square. Numerous monuments and altars were scattered around the Agora, demonstrating the religiosity of the people.

At length the teachings of Paul began to disturb the philosophers. Perhaps some had heard secondhand and in garbled fashion what he was preaching. No doubt others had caught phrases directly from his mouth as they moved about in the Agora. In this cosmopolitan city of learning they had often come in contact with religious teachings from all over the known world. However, this religion was different; it taught resurrection for the believer and a hope for the life to come.

The Epicureans with their atomistic view believed that the atoms constituting the soul of the individual simply flew apart at death and joined some other form of matter. The Stoics believed that the human soul became part of the universal soul in a very impersonal sense. Both of these views were far from the teachings of Paul.

They called him a "babbler" (NKJV; Greek *spermologos*). Ramsay seeks to give the proper understanding of the Greek term by means of a kind of word study:

. . . a worthless fellow of low class and vulgar habits, with the insinuation that he lives at the expense of others, like those disreputable persons who hang round the markets and the quays in order to pick up anything that falls from the loads that are carried about. Hence, as a term in social slang, it connotes absolute vulgarity and inability to rise above the most contemptible standard of life and conduct; it is often connected with slave life, for the *Spermologos* was near the type of the slave and below the level of the free man; and there clings to it the suggestion of picking up refuse and scraps, and in literature of plagiarism without the capacity to use correctly . . . Probably the nearest and most instructive parallel in modern English life to *Spermologos* is "Bounder," allowing for the difference between England and Athens. In both there lies the idea of one who is "out of the swim," out of the inner circle, one who lacks that thorough knowledge and practice in the rules of the game that mould the whole character and make it one's

Mars Hill

nature to act in the proper way and play the game fair.[67]

Areopagus. Then these philosophers laid hands on Paul—an indication that they (educated men, who are usually more restrained) were greatly disturbed indeed. And they brought him "to the Areopagus" (Acts 17:19). The question immediately arises as to how the word *Areopagus* is to be understood. Some have taken the word merely to signify the Council of the Areopagus. They hold that this meeting could have taken place wherever the Council met. The ancient meeting place was on the Areopagus Hill (Mars Hill, Acts 17:22). By Paul's day they also met on occasion in a stoa at the north end of the Agora. Some scholars feel that the circumstances of Acts 17 seem to fit an agora scene better than the hill.

Others believe, however, myself included, that while this meeting could have taken place in the Agora, it actually did occur on the Areopagus. I hold to that view. Oscar Broneer makes a strong argument for that conclusion in his observation that in Acts 17:19, *epi* with the accusative means "up to" Areopagus.[68] The result is, then, that Areopagus in Acts 17 refers both to the council and its place of meeting. In verse 19 the primary reference seems to be to the hill; in verse 22 it clearly applies to the council. The King James translation "in the midst of Mars' hill" (v. 22) is an impossible rendition of the Greek; the passage must be rendered "in the midst of the Areopagus"—referring to the council. This verse may be coupled with verse 33: "he went forth from the midst of them."

As already indicated, the Areopagus was located just to the west of the Acropolis and in plain view of it. There are at least two interpretations of the word "Areopagus." One says Areopagus derives from *pagos*, "hill," and *Ares*, "god of war," and alludes to the legend that the first case tried on the hill involved a charge of murder against Ares. The other explanation is that the name means "hill of the Arai [curses]," because according to another legend the first trial on the hill was of Orestes who had been hounded by the Furies for the murder of his mother.

The hill itself is 377 feet high. A rocky eminence, it rises gradually to its highest point on the south and east. Sixteen worn steps cut into the rock lead to the summit. Rough rock-hewn benches forming three sides of a square were carved from the rock on top of the hill. There were also two special stones on which the prosecutor and defendant stood. Provided they know Greek, modern visitors to the Areopagus can read Paul's Acts 17 sermon to the Areopagus (from Acts 17) on a bronze plaque attached to the hill to the right of the stairs.

The question next arises as to why Paul should have been taken before the Areopagus council at all. Something has already been said about the place of the Areopagus in Athenian life. It will be remembered that once it held a place of supreme importance in the political and religious affairs of the state. During the period of the democracy in the fifth century, it lost its political power and became largely a criminal court. In Roman times it was charged mainly with religious and educational affairs. Ramsay concludes that the Areopagus had power to appoint or invite lecturers before the council. This authority of appointing lecturers existed at least as early as Cicero's day because he induced the Areopagus to pass a decree inviting Cratippus, a Peripatetic philosopher, to become a lecturer at Athens. What such a privilege entailed is not known.[69] At any rate, the appearance before the Areopagus does not seem to have been a formal trial, because it did not conclude with any sort of verdict. Some mocked him, and others expressed interest in hearing him again (Acts 17:32).

In his appearance on Areopagus, Paul showed an acquaintance with Greco-Roman culture, which he tried to use to make contact with his hearers. It has also been suggested that the speech indicates that he may have addressed the group in the flowery New Alexandrian Rhetoric, which was a favorite among the educated classes of the day. He showed, too, that he had been greatly impressed by the religiosity of the Athenians, as reflected by the multitude of altars and other religious monuments he had seen all over the city. He observed that they even had an altar to an "unknown god," erected just to make sure they had not omitted any possible gods from their worship. This was the god that Paul claimed to be preaching to them. Although remains of no such altar have been found at Athens, Apollonius of Tyana reports having seen one (or more) there later in the century. Pausanias saw one there in the middle of the second century A.D., and one was discovered in 1909 at Pergamum in Asia Minor[70] and is now in the Istanbul Museum.

Paul's ministry at Athens has been declared a failure by some. It may be asked, however, whether one has failed if he did not set out to do anything special in the first place. We need to remember that Paul was very largely marking time while waiting for trouble to die down in Macedonia and while waiting for Silas and Timothy. Moreover, he did have several converts in Athens, including Dionysius, a member of the Council of the Areopagus (Acts 17:34). In commemoration of that fact, the broad street that runs past the entrance to the Acropolis and the Areopagus is still called Dionysius the Areopagite Street. And at one end it joins Apostle Paul Street.

Whether or not Paul was disappointed over the reception of his message in Athens is open to question. Many commentators have felt that he was. Finegan[71] and Broneer[72] have concluded that he learned from his Athenian experience that it was foolishness to try to meet the wisdom of the world with the wisdom of men. Rather he should meet it with the power of God. In support they note such verses as 1 Corinthians 1:1–3, 19, 21, 25, 27. The point is that in Corinth, Paul's tactics changed completely; and he never again sought to impress his hearers with human learning.

But even if Paul did change his whole way of approach at Corinth, this is no indication that thereafter he put a premium on ignorance or believed that ministers of the Christian gospel should be intellectually unprepared for their tasks. He always benefited from his own superior education in the performance of his ministry, and his success was due in part to his education—both Hebrew and Greek.

On to Corinth

At any rate, Paul determined to move from the intellectual center of Greece to Corinth, her commercial center. And if he did change his approach at Corinth it may merely have been a result of the fact that he was going from the intellectual center to the commercial center and that a different public required a different manner of presenting the gospel. And did not Paul in his adaptability say, "I have become all things to all men, that I might by all means save some"? (1 Corinthians 9:22, NKJV).

He probably walked the sixty-mile distance because by this time he was quite low on funds. And by the time he reached Corinth, his resources were so exhausted that he went back to tent-making. When Silas and Timothy arrived at Corinth from Macedonia, however, presumably with an offering from Philippi (or Thessalonica or Berea or all three), Paul was able once more to "hold to the word" (preferred reading for "pressed in the spirit" of Acts 18:5, KJV). He was then able to give up secular employment and to concentrate on preaching the gospel.

As the apostle left Athens, he probably took the Street of the Panathenaea, which led diagonally across the agora toward the Dipylon Gate. As he neared the north end of the agora, he may have paused by the Altar of the Twelve Gods, beyond which rose the colossal statue of Zeus, to pray for the conversion of this pagan center. Possibly Dionysius was at the office of the Areopagus in the Royal Stoa across the street, and there was a chance for a last farewell. As he reached the Dipylon Gate, he almost certainly took the Sacred Way that led to Eleusis, fourteen miles away. If he was disturbed by the extent to which Athens was given to idolatry, he was now in for another shock, for this road was bordered by altars, chapels, and tombs.

In about three miles Paul crossed the bridge over the first branch of the Cephisus River. A couple of blocks down the road on his right stood a temple of Demeter, at which pilgrimages to Eleusis made a stop. About a half mile farther another bridge crossed the second branch of the Cephisus. After about two more miles the road began to ascend the slope of Mount Aegaleos. Much of the way the road had been about fifteen feet wide and was paved. Now it was sometimes as narrow as eight feet and was cut in the rock. At a point about six miles from Athens the Sacred Way reached its greatest altitude, about 625 feet. Here the apostle may have turned around for a last and most impressive glance at the "violet-crowned city." On the height above him

(1,535 feet) Xerxes had sat watching the defeat of his fleet by the Greeks in the Battle of Salamis in 480 B.C. Before the apostle lay the Bay of Eleusis a little over a mile away. At the bay the road turns north. In a plain bordering the sea, it passes two sacred lakes and finally reaches Eleusis. Having now walked fourteen miles, Paul probably decided to spend the night at Eleusis.

Eleusis

Paul might have tried to find out something about the Eleusinian Mysteries, the most famous of the Greek Mysteries. Since he was not an initiate, he would have had a difficult time learning anything. The sanctuary was located on the east slope of the Acropolis of Eleusis, and was surrounded by a wall about twenty-five feet high, over which he cold see only roofs of buildings. A temple of Artemis stood outside the entrance, and on the entrance side was a double wall between which was a long inner courtyard.

The entrance through the second wall into the inner enclosure was an elaborate monumental gateway donated by a friend of Cicero, Appius Claudius Pulcher, about 50 B.C. If Paul could have passed through this monumental gate and ascended the Sacred Way, paved with marble, he would have seen two caves on his right. Before the larger, which represented the entrance into Hades, stood a sanctuary of Pluto. Farther on stood a megaron-type temple of Demeter. Finally the Sacred Way led to the northeast entrance of the Telesterion (sanctuary or initiation room) of the Mysteries. This was a large covered building 168 by 177 feet backed against the rock. There were two doors on each of the three free sides. The timber roof was carried by six rows of six columns, each at a height of twenty feet. These must have greatly impeded the vision of spectators who sat on banks of stone seats around the four sides.

As he stood there on the outside of the wall, Paul could not know that the gospel would not be immediately successful in bringing down this fortress. It was to have a brilliant period of prosperity under Hadrian and Antoninus Pius in the second century A.D. Alaric the Visigoth sacked it in

The Telesterion or place of initiation at Eleusis.

A.D. 395. And finally Theodosius II (401–50) banned the Mysteries.

If the apostle could not have found out much about the sanctuary at Eleusis, he could find out even less about the religious practices connected with it. Initiates would not, of course, divulge the secrets of the cult. Paul knew that the Mysteries involved worship of Demeter and her daughter Kore. According to legend, Hades, god of the underworld, had snatched away Kore (Persephone); and in her great sorrow and searching for her daughter, Demeter had come to Eleusis. After having received hospitality, she had revealed her secret rites to the people of the place. Paul also knew that Demeter was a sister of Zeus and goddess of agriculture.

While in Athens he had learned that on the thirteenth of Boedromion (parts of our September and October) some of the socially elite young men marched out to Eleusis and returned to Athens the next day with some religious objects. On the fifteenth there was a gathering of the catechumens to hear an address by the current cult leader. On the following day the candidates for initiation went to the seashore for ceremonial purification rites and returned to offer sacrifices to the goddess. On the seventeenth of Boedromion there was a great sacrifice with prayers for Athens and the cities of the other delegates participating. The next day was a day of rest for most, and there was opportunity for latecomers to be prepared for initiation.

On the nineteenth of Boedromion a great religious procession started along the sacred way bearing the "fair young god" Iacchus, probably the youthful Dionysus. Arriving at Eleusis, they held a midnight celebration under the stars. The twentieth of the month was spent in resting, fasting, purification, and sacrifice. As to what went on inside of the sanctuary, Paul could not

Demeter was honored in the mysteries at Eleusis.

A ship passing through the Corinth Canal.

perched atop two hills and occupying their slopes as well. The eastern hill is a little under 900 feet in height; the western hill is about 950 feet. Enjoying an illustrious history, Megara retained only a shadow of its former greatness in Paul's day.

With ports on both the Saronic and Corinthian gulfs, the city-state had become an important commercial center as early as the eighth century B.C. Along with its commerce on the Black Sea and in Sicily, Megara had established colonies in those areas. It had also controlled the nearby island of Salamis, which it lost to Athens around 570 B.C. Megara's commerce was ruined during the Peloponnesian War, and it suffered severely during the civil war of 48 B.C. However, it was still a place of importance during the first century A.D. The apostle probably spent the night there.

The Isthmian Journey

West of Megara the road hugged the shore of the Saronic Gulf as it skirted the Geraneia Ridge (c. 4,450 feet high). About six miles from Megara the apostle passed under the dangerous precipices of the famous Scironian rocks. Here travelers had to pick their way on a track along the face of the cliff for six miles at a height of 600 to 700 feet. At points the road perilously poised on the edge of a cliff. Later Hadrian provided a safer road. Gliding along in comfort in a car or bus on the highway between Athens and Corinth, today's tourist little suspects the difficulties of travel experienced by the ancients in this area. After walking for about sixteen miles, Paul came to the town of Crommyon, an ancient possession of Corinth. Perhaps he spent the night there. It was impossible to travel the additional fifteen to twenty miles that day in order to reach Corinth.

The next day the apostle began the last part of his journey to the great commercial emporium of Greece and one of the greatest of the eastern Mediterranean. No doubt excitement rose as he neared his chosen center of ministry. Would there be ready reception for his ministry there? If so, would there be great public opposition stirred up by Jews or others as had been the case at so many other places? He would soon know.

have found out. The whole ceremony lasted for nine days.

From various bits of information, it now appears that initiation included a kind of passion play, probably centering around the sufferings of the goddess. Then there seems to have been a revelation of sacred cult objects and, among other things, the celebration of a sort of holy communion involving a barley drink and certain foods. In this initiation service (little is known of the details), the initiate supposedly established mystic contact with the mother and daughter. And by an act of faith he regarded himself certain of blessing at the hands of Demeter and Kore in the next life because he had established friendship with the pair in this life. Both the sacred pageant and the viewing of sacred objects presumably took place in the Telesterion.[73]

Megara

The next day Paul started out for Corinth once more. The road followed the coast of the Saronic Gulf. For several miles hills crowded close to the shore and then receded to make roof for the Megaran Plain. About fifteen miles from Eleusis the apostle came upon the ancient town of Megara,

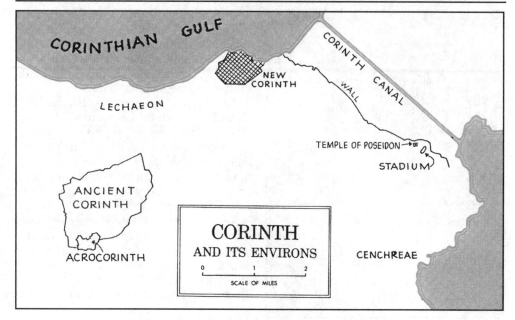

CORINTH
AND ITS ENVIRONS

0   1   2
SCALE OF MILES

About seven miles from Corinth Paul came to the narrowest point of the Isthmus—a section about four miles wide. Here, just southwest of the present Corinth Canal, a tramway was built upon which small ships could be transported between the Saronic and Corinthian gulfs. Larger ships frequently unloaded their cargoes at one of Corinth's ports and arranged for them to be picked up by another freighter at the other port. The geographical situation is this. The voyage around the southern tip of the Peloponnesus was dangerous and some two hundred miles farther than it would have been for a ship crossing the isthmus. So in early times Corinth had built a tramway across the isthmus, between the port of Cenchraea on the Saronic Gulf and the port of Lechaeon on the Corinthian Gulf. It was her geographical position that gave Corinth her reason for existence.

Long before Paul's day, thought had been given to cutting a canal through the isthmus. It is reported that as far back as the days of Periander of Corinth (c. 600 B.C.) the question of the feasibility of a Corinthian canal had been raised. Among the Romans, Julius Caesar considered it and Caligula sent an engineer to work on the project. A few years after Paul arrived, Nero actually began the excavation. But it was not until 1893 that the canal was completed. Its four-mile bed is 75 feet wide and the water 26 feet deep. The cut is 260 feet deep at the highest rise of the terrain of the isthmus.

As Paul crossed over the ship tramway, there loomed before him a wall. This he learned was the Isthmian Wall. Originally constructed in 480 B.C. to repel the Persians, it had subsequently been rebuilt to meet other threats. But now that the Romans had established the Pax Romana, it had fallen into disrepair. Paul noticed that the wall had towers about every three hundred feet and that it rose to a height of about twenty-five feet in places. Passing through the gate in the wall, the apostle probably noticed a lot of activity to his right. Some repairs were being made on the stadium where the Isthmian Games were held in honor of Poseidon. Paul no doubt thought that if he were still there when the games took place,[74] this would be a good place to meet people from all over the Mediterranean world to present the Christian message to them.

Walking southwest, Paul passed stone quarries on his right. After a couple of miles he passed through the great necropolis or cemetery of ancient Corinth. Soon the highway joined the Cenchraea-Corinth Road. Another stone quarry lay at the junction. Paul turned right and after about two miles found himself passing through the Cenchraea gate into the city.

The temple of Apollo and the Acrocorinth.

Corinth

Although the city to which Paul came had been built on a new foundation, the history of Corinth was very ancient indeed. The earliest settlers came in the fifth or sixth millennium B.C., attracted perhaps by the abundance of springwater, nearness to the sea, the easily defensible site, and the fertility of the Corinthian plain. About 3000 B.C. an influx of migrants brought with them the knowledge of the use of metals and introduced the Bronze Age. The site was not heavily occupied until the Iron Age.

The Homeric poems allude to Corinth as a dependency of Mycenae at the time of the Trojan War. If this is an accurate historical reference and not merely a reflection of the times of the writer, there must have been a fair-sized town there in the latter part of the second millennium B.C.

Corinth of the classical period was really established with the Dorian invasion. About 1000 B.C. those Greek people settled at the foot of the Acrocorinth. Occupying a place of safety, they also controlled the main overland trade route between the Peloponnesus and central Greece, as well as the Isthmian route. The city early came to a height of prosperity. This is demonstrated by the fact that in the eighth century B.C. she colonized Syracuse on Sicily and the Island of Corcyra along the

eastern shore of the Adriatic Sea. Under the tyrants Cypselus (655–625 B.C.) and Periander (625–585 B.C.) the town achieved a new peak of prosperity as she expended great energy on commercial and industrial development. Corinthian pottery and bronzes were exported widely over the Mediterranean. About the middle of the fifth century the city's fortunes declined as a result of effective competition of Athenian industrial production. During the days of her independence, Corinth controlled about 248 square miles of territory in the northern part of the Peloponnesus, approximately one-fourth the size of Attica.[75]

During the Persian Wars Corinth served as Greek headquarters. Contingents of her army fought at Thermopylae and Plataea; her navy participated in the Battle of Salamis. In 459 B.C. Corinth made war on Athens and was worsted. The subsequent defection of the Corinthian colony, Corcyra, and its alliance with Athens led Corinth to instigate the Peloponnesian War against Athens (431–404 B.C.). Later Corinth rebelled against the domineering attitude of Sparta and made common cause with Athens, Argos, and Thebes in the Corinthian War (395–387).

Although the city lost her independence with the rise of Macedon, she was the most populous and most prosperous city of mainland Greece during the period 350–240 B.C. Thereafter, as the chief member of the Achaean League, she clashed with Rome. Finally Rome destroyed Corinth in 146 B.C., killed the adult male population, and sent the women and children into slavery. It is generally believed that the city was virtually uninhabited for a century, but there are indications (and excavations may give supporting evidence) that there was at least a small settlement there.

At any rate, Julius Caesar refounded the city in 44 B.C. largely with freedmen, perhaps many of them descended from slaves taken at the second century B.C. destruction. The growth of Corinth was rapid, and by the time Paul arrived it had become the largest and most flourishing center in southern Greece. Perhaps the most definitive assessment of the population at that time is that about eighty thousand lived in the urban area, with another twenty thousand in the countryside nearby.[76]

As to its later history, Corinth was burned by Alaric the Visigoth in A.D. 395. When rebuilt it turned away from its classical, pagan culture toward Christian ways. Destroyed by an earthquake in 521, the city was rebuilt and enjoyed considerable prosperity under Justinian. Its final period of prosperity came to an end with the Norman sacking of 1147. It has suffered various catastrophes since. After the earthquake of 1858 obliterated the old town, the inhabitants moved to a new site on the Corinthian Gulf—a tremendous boon to the excavators. As recently as 1930 this new town was largely destroyed by earthquake.

Of course we are curious to know what sort of place Corinth was when Paul arrived and what sort of ministry he had in it. As to the city's physical situation, we have already noted that Corinth controlled the trade routes between the Peloponnesus and central Greece and across the Isthmus of Corinth. In this connection, she had built a tramway across the Isthmus and was served by ports on the Saronic and Corinthian gulfs. She administered the Isthmian Games, thereby serving as a religious, athletic, and cohesive center in Greece. The city itself lay about a mile and a half south of the Corinthian Gulf on the north side of its acropolis at an altitude of about 400 feet. The acropolis towered about 1,500 feet over the city at an altitude of 1,886 feet. From its peak on a clear day the Acropolis at Athens can be plainly seen.

The city and its acropolis were enclosed by a wall over six miles in circumference, and numerous large towers were spaced along the wall. In the north-central part of town, about equidistant from the east and west walls (about a mile from each) was the Agora, the nerve center of the metropolis. Outside the walls in the surrounding plain stretched grain fields, olive groves, vineyards, and other agricultural holdings of the city.

As to the nonphysical aspects of Corinth, several generalizations can be made. It was a new city—less than a hundred years old when Paul visited it. This means that a social structure with an aristocracy possessing illustrious genealogies had not had time to develop. Probably the social and economic structure was more fluid than at most other centers in Greece. Many of those possessing wealth were the *nouveaux riches*, with all of the attendant inadequacies of that class. Since Corinth had not had time to develop a native culture, the

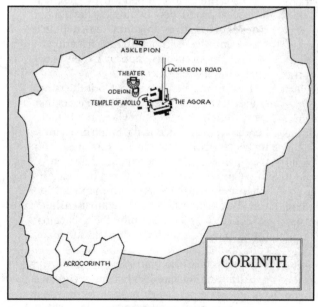

Corinth within the walls.

culture it had was imitative and, as a result of the overweening economic interests of the community, was only a shallow veneer. Much of the population was mobile (sailors, businessmen, government officials, etc.) and was therefore cut off from the inhibitions of a settled society.

But we need to be very careful about claiming that there was extensive religious prostitution in the city, connected with and enjoined by the worship of Aphrodite. Modern books often claim that there were a thousand priestesses connected with the Temple of Aphrodite on the Acropolis and engaged in religious prostitution. By way of response, first, the temple on the Acropolis was small (only about 30 by 50 feet), as were four others in the city and in Lechaion and Cenchreae. And second, while the Phoenician or Near Eastern institution of sacred prostitution dedicated to Aphrodite had existed in the earlier city of Corinth, it "did not survive into Roman times." It "was not practiced in the Roman City."[77]

The cult of Aphrodite was still important in Roman times, however, and Aphrodite was still closely identified with Corinth, as the existence of several temples (at least five) to her indicates. As the goddess of erotic love and goddess of the sea she heavily influenced the mindset and practices of the region and of the mobile population. It is no wonder that Paul had so much to say about the sacredness of the body in his first Corinthian letter.

As was customary in Paul's ministry, he went first to the Jews of Corinth, reasoning "in the synagogue every Sabbath" (Acts 18:4). It is now thought that this synagogue was located east of the Lechaeon Road and just north of the agora. In 1898 a large block of stone bearing the title "Synagogue of the Hebrews" was found on the Lechaeon Road near the foot of the marble steps leading to the marketplace. This has been identified as the lintel of a synagogue, which is believed to have stood nearby. Archaeologists differ as to whether this dates to Paul's time or later. To the present no existing foundation has been convincingly associated with the lintel.

The Jews of Corinth took exception to the Christian message, as they had in such

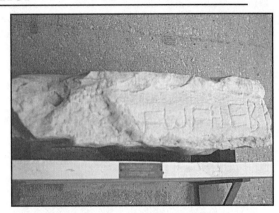

The lintel of the Corinth synagogue.

places as Lystra and Thessalonica, and stirred up some sort of mob action against Paul. They brought him before Gallio with insinuations that he had broken the law (Acts 18:12–23). Gallio is called the "deputy [*anthupatou*, proconsul] of Achaia" quite accurately by Luke the historian. As the governor of a senatorial province, Gallio would correctly have been called "proconsul." The Roman Gallio (like Festus later on in Jerusalem) had no interest in judging questions of Jewish law and dismissed the case brought against Paul (Acts 18:14–17; cf. Acts 25:10–27). Interestingly this Gallio was the elder brother of the philosopher Seneca.

The time of Gallio's rule, and thus of Paul's ministry in Corinth, is fairly well fixed by an inscription discovered at Delphi a few miles to the north of Corinth. This inscription mentions correspondence between the emperor Claudius and Gallio, proconsul of Achaea, and may confidently be dated to the first half of the year A.D. 52. More than likely Gallio took office about the middle of 51. It may be inferred from the Greek of Acts 18:12 that he heard Paul's case shortly after taking office. Also the apostle had been there eighteen months by that time (Acts 18:11). It may therefore be concluded that Paul arrived in Corinth early in A.D. 50.[78] This inscription is the most important single contribution to establishing the Pauline chronology.

The place where Paul was arraigned before Gallio was quite certainly the bema or rostrum in the great agora. This center of Corinthian life measured almost seven

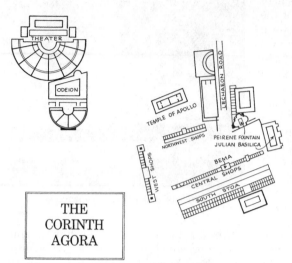

THE
CORINTH
AGORA

for public addresses and a judgment seat for magistrates.

Originally covered with ornately carved marble, the bema is now in a poorly preserved condition. Officials reached the bema from the south, where the ground was nearly level with the floor of the bema. Those who appeared to present their cases or to be judged stood on the lower northern level. While they waited their turn, they might sit on marble benches in waiting rooms on either side of the bema on the lower level.

As Paul waited for his case to be heard, he sat and looked around at the great marble-paved Agora. Towering above the Agora on the northwest, on a rocky terrace of its own, stood the Temple of Apollo. Built during the sixth century B.C., it was not destroyed by the Romans in the terror of 146 B.C. The temple measured 174 feet long by 69 feet wide, and the thirty-eight columns of its peristyle rose almost 24 feet in height. These fluted Doric columns were more impressive than many in Greece because they were made of single blocks of

hundred feet east and west and about three hundred feet north and south. Following the natural configuration of the land, the southern section was about thirteen feet higher than the northern part. At the dividing line of the two levels stood a row of low buildings flanking the rostrum, which served as a speaker's stand

The Bema or judgment seat, where Paul appeared before Gallio.

The Lechaeon Road.

stone instead of being built up with drums of stone.

Lowering his gaze, the apostle let his eye run along a row of shops at the west end of the agora and then along the northwest shops. At the east end of those shops was a beautiful monumental gateway leading to the Lechaeon Road, a limestone-paved thoroughfare forty feet wide and closed to wheeled traffic. East of the Lechaeon Road was the Peirene Fountain, an important source of water for the city. It supplied as much as 3,000 gallons per hour, and its adjacent reservoirs held 100,000 to 120,000 gallons.[79] Along the east side of the Agora

lay a large basilica of the Augustan period. Corinthian columns surrounded a large interior hall and supported a raised clerestory, the side aisles were covered with shed roofs. In this court building many of the cases must have been tried where believers were going to law before unbelievers (1 Corinthians 6:1–8). Alternatively, there was another court building at the south of the Agora, and south of the south stoa.

Stretching across almost the entire south side of the Agora was the south stoa. About five hundred feet long, it was probably the largest secular structure in Greece proper. It consisted of a double colonnade behind which were thirty-three small shops. All of these except two had a well in them, connected with a water channel which in turn was connected to the Peirene Fountain. These were apparently wine shops, each with its private cooler. Other perishables were sold as well. Shops for the sale of meat were also located in the stoa. In one of them archaeologists found an inscription: "Lucius the butcher." In another shop an inscription appeared that called the shop a *macellum*, the Latin equivalent of the

The Peirene Fountain.

The Julian Basilica, a major court building in the city.

Greek *makellon,* used in 1 Corinthians 10:25 and commonly translated "meat market."[80] Paul was dealing with the question of meats offered to idols here and in effect told his readers that they need not be concerned about the source of meats displayed in public markets. If the meats retailed there had been sold by the temples to legitimate business-men, housewives were not responsible for that fact.

Eating meat offered to idols involved more than what one bought in the meat market, however. It was common practice in the Greco-Roman world for people who were or were not devotees of a pagan deity

The South Stoa, with dozens of shops for the sale of wine and meat.

to share in the eating of sacrificial foods in the deity's temple grounds. That such a practice existed in Corinth is evident from the fact that numerous dining rooms were found on a terrace of the acropolis of Corinth in the sacred grounds of Demeter and Kore. Also, near the north wall of Corinth stood the Asklepieion, or hospital, with a temple of Asklepios, god of healing. There were dining rooms where cultic meals could be eaten.[81]

As a matter of fact, Paul specifically referred to eating in a dining room of a tem-ple in Corinth food offered to idols (1 Corinthinas 8:10). He observed that such an act might not negatively affect the one who did so because he had in his own mind dis-missed the reality of the god. But the act of eating might serve as a stumbling block to brothers who were weaker (1 Corinthians 8:11–12) and had not yet fully turned to God from idols (1 Thessalonians 1:9).

This knowing participation in religious feasting is what the Council of Jerusalem must have had primarily in mind when it commanded that Gentiles "abstain from things offered to idols, from blood, from things strangled and from sexual immorality" (Acts 15:29, NKJV). The "sexual immorality" in this context certainly involved abstaining from patronizing the religious prostitutes connected with pagan temples all over the Mediterranean world.

Cut into the hill just to the northwest of the Agora rose the great theater of Corinth.

One of the dining rooms in the sanctuary of Demeter on the terrace of the Acropolis of Corinth.

Its seating capacity was probably about fifteen thousand. Interestingly, near the stage building is an inscription that concerns Erastus, an aedile (a Roman municipal official) of the city who laid a pavement at his own expense. Paul in writing to the Romans from Corinth sent greetings from a "chamberlain" (Greek, *oikonomos*) or steward by this name (Romans 16:23). Erastus is also referred to in 2 Timothy 4:20 and Acts 19:22. A Roman aedile and a Greek *oikonomos* would both have been commissioners of streets and public buildings. Perhaps the Erastus of this inscription is to be equated with the person of the same name mentioned in the New Testament. Some scholars think so.

When Paul had come across the isthmus to Corinth, he had passed the location of the Isthmian Games. The following year, in April or May of A.D. 51, while he was still in Corinth, the biennial games would have been held.[82] Paul probably saw these. And perhaps the opportunity of preaching to the large crowds gathering for the festivities had led Paul to go to Corinth in the first place. Some scholars believe this to have been the case. But we need to remember that Paul always sought to go to the Jew first, and the games were a purely pagan event. In any case, Paul no doubt alluded to this important event in the life of the people in 1 Corinthians 9:24–27.

THE ISTHMIAN GAMES

The Isthmian Games began about 582 B.C. and were held biennially in April or May. Administered by Corinth until Roman destruction of

A head of the god Serapis in the Museum of Corinth.

An inscription mentioning an Erastus, found in the theater of Corinth. Some believe that he is the same Erastus referred to in Romans 16:23.

the city in 146 B.C., they were then transferred to Sicyon. But after Julius Caesar's refounding of Corinth, they were returned there c. 2 B.C.

As to the order of events, musical and literary competitions came first. Next came chariot and horse races. Athletic contests were held last. These included footraces, throwing the javelin and discus, jumping, boxing, and wrestling. There were events for boys, youths, adult men, and during the first century A.D., even a few contests for women and girls.

Though competitors came chiefly from Greece, visitors are known to have come from Sardinia, Syracuse on Sicily, Egypt, Caesarea, Ephesus, and elsewhere in the eastern Mediterranean. In New Testament times the victor's crown was a wreath of celery. It was up to friends and home towns to provide additional honors and gifts.

The competitors came chiefly from Corinth, Aegina, Thebes, Athens, and some of the islands of the Aegean, but there were participants from as far west as Sardinia and Sicily and from all over the eastern Mediterranean.[83] Crowds were probably larger at the Isthmian Games than at the Olympics. Corinth administered the games. Held in honor of Poseidon (god of the sea) and beginning with a sacrifice to the god, the games included athletic, equestrian, musical, and poetic competitions, and perhaps also a regatta. There were separate competitions for men, youths, and boys. And during the first century A.D. there were a few contests for women and girls.[84]

The athletic events included footraces of 200 and 800 yards, races in armor, throwing

The altar to Poseidon at the Isthmia.

The theater of the Isthmus.

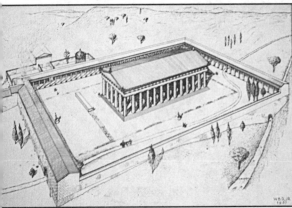

The reconstructed temple of Poseidon at the Isthmia.

Very likely the Isthmian Games occurred prior to Paul's arraignment before Gallio. And after his acquittal he remained in Corinth "a good while" (Acts 18:18). It is not known how long a time is implied, but he may have stayed in Corinth as late as the beginning of A.D. 52, or possibly he left before the sailing season closed in the late fall of 51. Whatever the exact time of his departure, he set out on the road from the southern end of the Agora to Cenchreae (Acts 18:18), taking Aquila and Priscilla with him, and embarked for Antioch. On the way he stopped briefly in Ephesus, where he left his traveling companions and hastened on to Antioch with the fervent hope of reaching Jerusalem in time for Passover (Acts 18:21).

the discus and javelin throwing, two-horse chariot racing, the Pentathlon (running, jumping, discus and javelin throwing, and wrestling), and the Pankration (a combination of boxing and wrestling). Unfortunately, it is difficult to determine exactly what events occurred during the first century A.D. when the games were being re-established at Corinth. The victor's crown seems to have been wild celery during the first century A.D., a "corruptible" or "perishable" crown indeed (1 Corinthians 9:25).

The area given over to the Isthmian Games was about six miles from Corinth, just south of the east end of the present Corinth Canal. In recent years the area has been quite thoroughly investigated and largely excavated. The three main structures at the site were the Temple of Poseidon, the stadium, and the theater. Originally constructed in the seventh century B.C., the temple was ravaged by fire and was rebuilt about 470 B.C. Heavily damaged by fire in 390 B.C., it was restored and stood until the mid-sixth century A.D. Inside were colossal statues of Poseidon, lord of the sea, and the goddess Amphitrite, joint rulers of the sea. Near the temple was an impressive altar to Poseidon.

The stadium was located to the southeast of the sanctuary. From the temple to the stadium stretched an avenue lined with pine trees and statues of victorious athletes. About fifty yards northeast of the sanctuary of Poseidon was the theater, where musical and dramatic events could be staged.[85]

The theater of the Isthmus.

Two or three years later, while Paul was ministering in Ephesus (1 Corinthians 16:8–9), he wrote two epistles to Corinth. The first apparently was occasioned by the coming of Stephanus, Fortunatus, and Achaicus (1 Corinthians 16:17) from the Corinthian church with a letter asking counsel from the apostle. Much of the epistle seems to have been an answer to that letter (cf. "now concerning" in 1 Corinthians 7:25; 8:1; 11:1; 16:1; 16:12). The apostle also received information on problems in the Corinthian church from Apollos (1 Corinthians 16:12) and the household of Chloe (1 Corinthians 1:11).

In 1 Corinthians, Paul dealt with five issues—all involved in the problem of

The starting blocks at the Isthmian Stadium. Holes in the pavement mark places where poles of the lane markers stood.

relating Christianity to Corinthian culture. First, he rebuked the spirit of factionalism, which arose because some of them were impressed with Apollos' rhetorical ability. Others followed the strictly Jewish way. A third group claimed to be followers of Paul. Still others said they were merely followers of Christ (1 Corinthians 1:12).

Second, Paul dealt with problems of sexual morality; third, with the question of eating food offered to idols; fourth, with disorders in public worship; and fifth, with the doctrine of resurrection from the dead, which a Greco-Roman community had great difficulty accepting. While the first letter seems to have made some impact, it did not end the factional strife in Corinth. This was one of the main themes of 2 Corinthians.

Although Christianity had its troubles in first century Greece and was to be persecuted sporadically there until the early fourth century A.D., it ultimately became the official

religion of the area. The many Byzantine churches with their famous old mosaics still to be seen in the country are a testimony to the extent of the official support given to Christianity during later centuries. In spite of the long Muslim occupation of Greece (nearly four centuries), Islam never won over the people there as it did in North Africa and the Near East. Currently the population is only about one percent Muslim. With the establishment of the modern state of Greece, the Orthodox Church has once more assumed the position of guardian over the spiritual affairs of the people.

But over two hundred evangelical congregations exist outside the Orthodox Church (including Free Evangelical Churches, 50 congregations; Greek Evangelical Church, 35 congregations; various Pentecostal churches, about 60 congregations). The Greater Europe Mission and the Assemblies of God maintain training institutes there.

NOTES

1. M. Cary, *The Geographic Background of Greek and Roman History* (Oxford: At the Clarendon Press, 1949), pp. 46–47.

2. Ancient Greece presented a greater impression of prosperity than some of the terrain today. Hillsides terraced and covered with a mantle of trees were less subject to erosion than they have been since. Many rocky slopes in Greece once had a thin topsoil on them.

3. See James Mellaart, *The Neolithic of the Near East* (New York: Charles Scribner's, 1975), pp. 244–54.

4. *Ibid.*, p. 244.

5. A branch of the white race, they were short, slender, dark people of the same physical type as found in North Africa, Spain, and Italy.

6. Chester G. Starr, *The Origins of Greek Civilization 1100–650 B.C.* (New York: Alfred A. Knopf, 1961), p. 18.

7. Robert Drews, *The Coming of the Greeks* (Princeton: Princeton University Press, 1988), p. 198.

8. *Ibid.*, p. 182.

9. *Ibid.*, p. 196.

10. Starr, *Op. Cit.*, p. 34.

11. *Ibid.*, pp. 73–74, 78.

12. N. G. L. Hammond, *A History of Greece to 322 B.C.* (Oxford: At the Clarendon Press, 1959), p. 32.

12a.   For a survey of the problem of dating this volcanic eruption, see Colin F. Macdonald, "Chronologies of the Thera eruption," *American Journal of Archaeology*, 105 (July, 2001), 527–32.

13. Some 4,200 tablets with inscriptions in Linear B now exist, having been excavated in palaces at Knossos and on the Greek mainland at such places as Mycenae, Pylos, and Tiryns. Michael Ventris and John Chadwick were primarily responsible for its decipherment. See M. Ventris and J. Chadwick, *Documents in Mycenaean Greek* (Cambridge: Cambridge University Press, 1956). It appears that this script, found exclusively at palaces, was used only by the ruling class—very largely for keeping palace records and the like. At least no literary compositions written in Linear B have yet com to light. In addition to the tablets there are Linear B inscriptions painted on vases from a number of sites, and more are being found. These indicate ownership or the maker.

14. Drews, *Op. Cit.*, p. 106.

15. In a view of history that looks upon the Classical Era as the zenith of Greek development, the centuries prior to it are commonly considered to be a formative age. Without debating the rightness of such a period name, it is used here as a convenience—with the realization that every age of history is to some extent a formative age.

16. Homer probably lived and wrote about 850 B.C. somewhere along the Asia Minor coast, perhaps at Chios or Smyrna. His great epics, the *Iliad* and *Odyssey*, were composed by weaving together many source materials into effective and enduring dramatic accounts. The historical setting of the poems seems to be that of the Mycenaean

Age (the time of the Trojan War), but the economic, political, and social organization is that of Homer's own day.

17. John V. A. Fine, *The Ancient Greeks* (Cambridge, MA: Harvard University Press, 1983), p. 138.

18. *Loc. Cit.*

19. L. F. Fitzhardinge, *The Spartans* (London: Thames & Hudson, 1980), see especially the last chapter. See also Paul Cartledge's new *Spartan Reflections* (Berkeley: University of California Press, 2001).

20. Herodotus, *History*, Book VI, Section 102.

21. J. M. Cook, *The Persian Empire* New York: Schocken Books, 1983), p. 116.

22. In modern times deposits of the Sphercheus River have spilled out into the Malian Gulf and have widened the pass breadth to 1 1/2–3 miles.

23. R. H. Pfeiffer asserted that the author of the early source of the Old Testament books of Samuel was the father of history "in a much truer sense than Herodotus a half millennium later" (Pfeiffer, *Introduction to the Old Testament* [New York: Harper and Brothers, 1941], p. 357). It should be remembered, however, that Pfeiffer, a liberal scholar, did not accept the Mosaic authorship of the Pentateuch. Accepting the definition that history is an interpreted record of the past, and holding a theologically conservative position, we might claim that Moses was the "father of history" centuries before the writer of Samuel.

24. See *The Athenian Citizen* (Athens: American School of Classical Studies, 1960); Jill N. Claster, ed., *Athenian Democracy: Triumph or Travesty* (New York: Holt, Rinehart & Winston, 1967); Frank J. Frost, ed., *Democracy and the Athenians* (New York: John Wiley & Sons, 1969); A. H. M. Jones, *Athenian Democracy* (Baltimore: Johns Hopkins University Press, 1986); Donald Kagan, *Pericles of Athens and the Birth of Democracy* (New York: Simon & Schuster, 1991); Josiah Ober, *The Athenian Revolution* (Princeton: Princeton University Press, 1996); David Stockton, *The Classical Athenian Democracy* (New York: Oxford University Press, 1990).

25. Kagan, p. 57.

26. Kagan, p. 61.

27. A. W. Gomme, *The Population of Athens in the Fifth and Fourth Centuries B.C.* (Chicago: Argonaut Publishers, 1967), p. 26. On the general subject of Athenian population, see also A. H. M. Jones, *Athenian Democracy*, Appendix.

28. Gomme, p. 75.

29. Gomme, p. 26.

30. Hammond, p. 351.

31. *Ibid.*, p. 369.

32. Gomme, p. 26.

33. *Loc. cit.*

34. Frederick F. Cartwright, *Disease and History* (New York: Dorset, 1991), p. 8.

35. *Loc. cit.*

36. Hammond, p. 400.

37. See Nicolaos K. Martis, *The Falsification of Macedonian History* (Athens: Athanassiades Bros., 1984), pp. 21–28; J. R. Ellis, *Philip II and Macedonian Imperialism* (Princeton: Princeton University Press, 1986), pp. 35ff.

38. Martis, p. 36.

39. *Ibid.*, p. 38.

40. Ellis, p. 34.

41. N. G. L. Hammond, *The Genius of Alexander the Great* (Chapel Hill, NC: University of North Carolina Press, 1997), p. 50.

42. Hammond, pp. 60–61.

43. Donald W. Engels, *Alexander the Great and the Logistics of the Macedonian Army* (Berkeley, CA: University of California Press, 1978), p. 1.

44. Tom B. Jones, *Ancient Civilization*, Rev. ed. (Chicago: Rand McNally, 1964), p. 155.

45. Engels, p. 145.

46. Engels, p. 15.

47. Engels, p. 1.

48. The details of Alexander's battle strategies would require considerable space and are quite beyond the purposes of this book. N. G. L. Hammond provides some good summaries in his *Genius of Alexander the Great*.

49. Peter Green, *Alexander of Macedon, 356–323 B.C.* (Berkeley: University of California Press, 1991), pp. 476–77.

50. N. G. L. Hammond, *The Genius of Alexander the Great* (Chapel Hill, NC: University of North Carolina Press, 1997), p. 198.

51. W. W. Tarn, *Alexander the Great* (Cambridge: Cambridge University Press, 1950), II, 400.

52. Green, p. 484.

53. Green, p. 487.

54. Everett F. Harrison, *Acts: The Expanding Church* (Chicago: Moody, 1975), p. 248.

55. Jack Finegan, *The Archaeology of the New Testament* (Boulder, CO: Westview Press, 1981), p. 103.

56. Jack Finegan, *Light from the Ancient Past*, 2nd ed. (Princeton: Princeton University Press, 1959), p. 351.

57. I hold the view that Paul was released from his first Roman imprisonment and made a fourth missionary journey.

58. John McRay, *Archaeology and the New Testament* (Grand Rapids: Baker Book House, 1991), p. 296.

59. William R. Ramsay, *St. Paul the Traveler and the Roman Citizen* (Grand Rapids: Baker Book House, reprint 1979 from the 1897 edition, p. 234.

60. Paul Graindor, *Athènes De Tibère A Trajan* (Cairo: Imprimerie Misr, Societé Anonyme Egyptienne, 1931), pp. 14–15.

61. *Ibid.*, p. 11.

62. Doremus A. Hayes, *Greek Culture and the Greek Testament* (New York: Abingdon Press, 1925), p. 14.

63. Oscar Broneer, "Athens, 'City of Idol Worship,'" *The Biblical Archaeologist*, XXI (Feb. 1958), 3.

64. Ramsay, p. 237.

65. Jenifer Neils, *Goddess and Polis: The Panathenaic Festival in Ancient Athens* (Princeton: Princeton University Press, 1992), pp. 13–17.

66. Ramsay, p. 237.

67. *Ibid.,* pp. 242–43.

68. Broneer, p. 27.

69. Ramsay, pp. 246–47.

70. Finegan, *Light from the Ancient Past,* pp. 356-57.

71. Finegan, p. 358.

72. Broneer, . 28.

73. Both the ritual and the structures at Eleusis are discussed authoritatively and thoroughly by George E. Mylonas, *Eleusis and the Eleusinian Mysteries* (Princeton: Princeton University Press, 1961).

74. Oscar Broneer, "The Apostle Paul and the Isthmian Games," *The Biblical Archaeologist,* XXV (Feb., 1962), 20. Broneer believes that Paul was there during one of these athletic festivals.

75. J. G. O'Neill, *Ancient Corinth: Part I* (Baltimore: The Johns Hopkins Press, 1930), p. 2.

76. Donald Engels, *Roman Corinth* (Chicago: University of Chicago Press, 1990), p. 33.

77. Donald Engels, *Roman Corinth* (Chicago: University of Chicago Press, 1990), pp. 97, 226. Cf., Oscar Broneer, "Corinth, Center of St. Paul's Missionary Work in Greece," *The Biblical Archaeologist,* XIV (Dec. 1951), 87.

78. Finegan, *Light from the Ancient Past,* pp. 362–63; and Finegan, *Handbook of Biblical Chronology,* Rev. ed. (Peabody, MA: Hendrickson Publishers, 1998), pp. 391–97.

79. Rhys Carpenter, *Ancient Corinth,* rev. by Robert L. Scranton (6th ed.; Athens: American School of Classical Studies, 1960), p. 28.

80. William A. McDonald, "Archaeology and St. Paul's Journeys in Greek Lands, Part III—Corinth," *Biblical Archaeologist,* V (Sept., 1942), 44.

81. Finegan, *Archaeology of the New Testament,* p. 148; Ramsay MacMullen, *Paganism in the Roman Empire* (New Haven: Yale University Press, 1981), pp. 161–2.

82. Broneer, "The Apostle Paul and the Isthmian Games," p. 20.

83. Donald Engels, *Roman Corinth* (Chicago: University of Chicago Press, 1990), p. 20.

84. Engels, p. 52.

85. Elizabeth R. Gebhard, *The Theater at Isthmia* (Chicago: University of Chicago Press, 1973; David G. Romano, *The Origins of the Greek Stadion* (Philadelphia: American Philosophical Society, 1993).

BIBLIOGRPAHY

Adams, W. Lindsay, and Eugene N. Borza, eds. *Philip II, Alexander the Great and the Macedonian Heritage*. Washington, D.C.: University Press of America, 1982.

Adkins, Lesley, and Roy A. *Handbook to Life in Ancient Greece*. New York: Oxford University Press, 1997.

Alexiou, Stylianos. *Minoan Civilization*. Heraklion, Crete: Spyros Alexiou Sons, 1969.

Angus, S. *The Mystery Religions*. New York: Dover Publications, 1975.

Ashley, James R. *The Macedonian Empire*. Jefferson, NC: McFarland, 1998.

Aylen, Leo. *The Greek Theater*. Cranbury, NJ: Associated University Presses, 1985.

Banks, Robert. *Paul's Idea of Community*. Peabody, MA: Hendrickson, 1994.

Bickerman, Elias J. *The Jews In the Greek Age*. Cambridge: Harvard University Press, 1988.

Biers, William R. *The Archaeology of Greece*. Rev. ed., Ithaca, NY: Cornell University Press, 1987.

Boardman, John. *The Greeks Overseas*. 4th ed, London: Thames & Hudson, 1999.

Boardman, John and others. *Oxford History of the Classical World*. Oxford: Oxford University Press, 1986.

Borza, Eugene N. *In the Shadow of Olympus: The Emergence of Macedon*. Princeton: Princeton University Press, 1990.

Bosworth, A. B. *Conquest and Empire: The Reign of Alexander the Great*. Cambridge: Cambridge University Press, 1988.

Branick, Vincent. *The House Church in the Writings of Paul*. Collegeville, MN: The Liturgical Press, 1989.

Broneer, Oscar. "The Apostle Paul and the Isthmian Games." *Biblical Archaeologist*, February, 1962.

Broneer, Oscar. "Athens, 'City of Idol Worship.'" *The Biblical Archaeologist*, Feb. 1958.

Broneer, Oscar. "Corinth, Center of St. Paul's Missionary Work in Greece." *Biblical Archaeologist*, December 1951.

Broneer, Oscar. *Isthmia*, Vol. 1: *Temple of Poseidon*. Princeton: American School of Classical Studies at Athens, 1971.

Buckler, John. *The Theban Hegemony, 371–362 B.C.* Cambridge, MA: Harvard University Press, 1980.

Burkert, Walter. *Ancient Mystery Cults*. Cambridge, MA: Harvard University Press, 1987.

Burkert, Walter. *Greek Religion*. Cambridge, MA: Harvard University Press, 1985.

Camp, John M. *The Athenian Agora*. London: Thames & Hudson, 1986.

Cargill, Jack. *The Second Athenian League*. Berkeley: University of California Press, 1981.

Carpenter, Rhys. *Ancient Corinth*. 6th ed. Revised by Robert L. Scranton and others. Athens: American School of Classical Studies at Athens, 1960.

Carson, D. A. and Others. *An Introduction to the New Testament*. Grand Rapids: Zondervan, 1992.

Cartledge, Paul. *Sparta and Lakonia*. London: Routledge and Kegan Paul, 1979.

Cary, M. *A History of the Greek World from 323 to 146 B.C.*, 2nd ed. London: Methuen, 1951.

Casson, Stanley. *Macedonia, Thrace and Illyria*. London: Oxford University Press, 1926.

Castleden, Rodney. *Minoans*. New York: Routledge, 1990.

Chadwick, John. *The Mycenaean World*. Cambridge: Cambridge University Press, 1976.

Chadwick, John. *The Decipherment of Linear B*. 2nd ed. Cambridge: Cambridge University Press, 1967.

Claster, Jill N., ed. *Athenian Democracy*. New York: Holt, Rinehart, Winston, 1967.

Cohen, Edward E. *Athenian Economy and Society*. Princeton: Princeton University Press, 1992.

Connolly, Peter. *The Ancient City.* Oxford: Oxford University Press, 1998.

Cook, J. M. *The Greeks in Ionia and the East.* New York: Federick A. Praeger, 1963.

Cullen, Tracey, ed. *Aegean Prehistory.* Boston: Archaeological Institute of America, 2001.

Davies, J. K. *Democracy and Classical Greece.* Cambridge, MA: Harvard University Press, 1993.

Day, John. *An Economic History of Athens Under Roman Domination.* New York: Arno Press, 1973.

Del Chiaro, Mario A., ed. *Corinthiaca.* Columbia, MO: University of Missouri Press, 1986.

Dickinson, Oliver. *The Aegean Bronze Age.* Cambridge: Cambridge University Press, 1994.

Dinsmoor, William B. *The Architecture of Ancient Greece.* New York: Norton, 1975.

Doumas, Christos G. *Thera.* London: Thames & Hudson, 1983.

Drees, Ludwig. *Olympia.* New York: Frederick A. Praeger, 1968.

Drews, Robert. *The Coming of the Greeks.* Princeton: Princeton University Press, 1988.

Drews, Robert. *The End of the Bronze Age.* Princeton: Princeton University Press, 1993.

Ducrey, Pierre. *Warfare in Ancient Greece.* New York: Schocken Books, 1986.

Duggan, Alfred. *He Died Old: Mithradates Eupator King of Pontus.* London: Faber & Faber, 1958.

Ehrenberg, Victor. *The Greek State.* New York: Norton, 1964.

Engels, Donald W. *Alexander the Great and the Logistics of the Macedonian Army.* Berkeley: University of California Press, 1978.

Engels, Donald W. *Roman Corinth.* Chicago: University of Chicago Press, 1990.

Errington, R. Malcolm. *A History of Macedonia.* Berkeley: University of California Press, 1990.

Finegan, Jack. *The Archeology of the New Testament: The Mediterranean World of the Early Christian Apostles.* Boulder, CO: Westview Press, 1981.

Finley, M. I. *Economy and Society in Ancient Greece.* New York: Viking Press, 1982.

Finley, M.I. *The World of Odysseus.* New York: Meridian, 1959

Fisher, N. R. E. *Slavery in Classical Greece.* Bristol: Bristol Un., 2000.

Fitzhardinge, L. F. *The Spartans.* London: Thames & Hudson, 1980.

Fox, Robin Lane. *The Search for Alexander.* Boston: Little, Brown, 1980.

Fraser, P. M. *Cities of Alexander the Great.* Oxford: Clarendon Press, 1996.

Freely, John. *Crete.* New York: New Amsterdam, 1988.

Freeman, Charles. *The Greek Achievement.* New York: Viking, 1999

Frost, Frank J., ed. *Democracy and the Athenians.* New York: John Wiley & Sons, 1969.

Fyfe, Theodore. *Hellenistic Architecture.* Chicago: Ares Publishers, 1974.

Gabrielsen, Vincent. *Financing the Athenian Fleet.* Baltimore: Johns Hopkins, 1994.

Gardiner, E. Norman. *Greek Athletic Sports and Festivals.* London: Macmillan & Co., 1910.

Gardner, Ernest A. *Ancient Athens.* New York: Haskell House Publishers, 1968.

Gebhard, Elizabeth R. *The Theater at Isthmia.* Chicago: University of Chicago Press, 1973.

Gill, David, and Conrad Gempf. *The Book of Acts in Its First Century Setting.* Grand Rapids: Eerdmans, 1994.

Ginouvès, René, ed. *Macedonia From Philip II to the Roman Conquest.* Princeton: Princeton University Press, 1994.

Gomme, A. W. *The Population of Athens in the Fifth and Fourth Centuries B.C.* Chicago: Argonaut Publishers, 1967.

Graham, James W. *The Palaces of Crete.* Rev. ed., Princeton: Princeton University Press, 1987.

Graindor, Paul. *Athènes De Tibère A Trajan.* Cairo: Imprimerie Msr, Societe Anonyme, Egyptienne, 1931.

Grant, Michael. *The Classical Greeks.* New York: Scribner's,1989.

Grant, Michael. *From Alexander to Cleopatra: The Hellenistic World.* New York: Scribner's, 1982.

Green, Peter. *Alexander of Macedon, 356–323 B.C.* Berkeley: University of California Press, 1991.

Green, Peter. *Alexander to Actium.* Berkeley: University of California Press, 1990.

Green, Peter. *The Greco-Persian Wars.* Berkeley: University of California Press, 1996.

Grmek, Mirko D. *Diseases in the Ancient Greek World.* Baltimore: Johns Hopkins, 1989.

Gruen, Erich S. *The Hellenistic World and the Coming of Rome.* 2 vols., Berkeley: University of California Press, 1984.

Guthrie, W. K. C. *The Religion and Mythology of the Greeks.* Cambridge: University Press, 1961.

Habicht, Christian. *Athens from Alexander to Antony.* Cambridge: Harvard University Press, 1997.

Hammond, N. G. L. *The Genius of Alexander the Great.* Chapel Hill: University of North Carolina Press, 1997.

Hammond, N. G. L. *A History of Greece to 322 B.C.* 3rd. ed. Oxford: Oxford University Press, 1986.

Hammond, N. G. L. *The Macedonian State.* Oxford: The Clarendon Press, 1989.

Hanson, Victor D. *The Wars of the Ancient Greeks.* London: Cassell, 1999.

Harris, William V. *Ancient Literacy.* Cambridge: Harvard University Press, 1989.

Hayes, Doremus A. *Greek Culture and the Greek Testament.* New York: Abingdon Press, 1925

Hignett, C. *A History of the Athenian Constitution to the End of the Fifth Century B.C.* Oxford: Clarendon Press, 1952.

Holloway, R. Ross. *The Archaeology of Ancient Sicily.* London: Routledge, 1991.

Hood, Sinclair. *The Minoans.* New York: Praeger Publishers, 1971.

Hopper, R. J. *The Early Greeks.* New York: Barnes & Noble, 1976.

Hornblower, Simon, and Antony Spawforth. *The Oxford Classical Dictionary.* 3rd ed., Oxford: Oxford University Press, 1996.

Huxley, G. L. *Early Sparta.* Cambridge: Harvard University Press, 1962.

Isager, Signe and Jens E. Skydsgaard. *Ancient Greek Agriculture.* London: Routledge, 1992.

Jones, A. H. M. *Athenian Democracy.* Baltimore: Johns Hopkins University Press, 1986.

Kagan, Donald. *Pericles of Athens and the Birth of Democracy.* New York: Simon & Schuster, 1991.

Kerenyi, C. *Eleusis.* New York: Pantheon Books, 1967.

Kinsey, Robert S. *With Paul in Greece.* Nashville: Parthenon Press, 1957.

Kitto, H. D. F. *The Greeks.* Baltimore: Penguin Books, 1951.

Kofou, Anna. *Crete.* Athens: Ekdotike Athenon, 1992.

Laistner, M. L. W. *A History of the Greek World from 479 to 323 B.C.* London: Methuen, 1947.

Lang, Magel, and C. W. J. Eliot. *The Athenian Agora.* Athens: American School of Classical Studies, 1954.

Larsen, J. A. O. "Roman Greece," *An Economic Survey of Ancient Rome.* Edited by Tenny Frank. Baltimore: Johns Hopkins Press, 1938.

Lawrence, A. W. *Greek Architecture.* Harmondsworth, England: Penguin Books, 1957.

Leekley, Dorothy, and Nicholas Efstratiou. *Archaeological Excavations in Central and Northern Greece.* Park Ridge, NJ: Noyes Press, 1980.

Lehmann, Karl and Phyllis W, eds. *Samothrace.* Princeton: Princeton University Press, Vol. 5, 1982.

Levi, Peter. *Atlas of the Greek World.* New York: Facts on File, 1980.

MacKendrick, Paul. *The Greek Stones Speak.* 2nd ed., New York: Norton, 1981.

MacMullen, Ramsay. *Paganism in the Roman Empire.* New Haven: Yale University Press, 1981.

Manville, Philip B. *The Origins of Citizenship in Ancient Athens.* Princeton: Princeton University Press, 1997.

Marsden, E. W. *Greek and Roman Artillery.* 2 vols., Oxford: Oxford University Press, 1999.

Martin, Luther H. *Hellenistic Religions.* New York: Oxford University Press, 1987.

Martis, Nicholaos. *The Falsification of Macedonian History.* Athens: Euroekdotiki, 1984.

McDonald, William A. "Archaeology and St. Paul's Journeys in Greek Lands." *Biblical Archaeologist,* February, 1941.

McDonald, William A. *Progress into the Past: The Rediscovery of Mycenaean Civilization.* New York: Macmillan, 1967.

McRay, John. *Archaeology and the New Testament.* Grand Rapids: Baker, 1991.

Mee, Christopher and Antony Spawforth. *Greece: An Oxford Archaeological Guide.* New York: Oxford University Press, 2001.

Meier, Christian. *Athens: Portrait of the City in Its Golden Age.* New York: Henry Holt & Co., 1998.

Meinardus, Otto F. A. *St. Paul in Greece.* New Rochelle, NY: Cartzas Brothers, 1979.

Metzger, Henri. *St. Paul's Journeys in the Greek Orient.* New York: Philosophical Library, 1955.

Mikalson, Jon D. *Athenian Popular Religion.* Chapel Hill: University of North Carolina Press, 1983.

Miller, Stephen G. *Arete: Greek Sports from Ancient Sources.* Berkeley: University of California Press, 1991.

Montagu, John D. *Battles of the Greek and Roman Worlds.* Mechanicsburg, Pennsylvania: Stackpole Books, 2000.

Morris, Ian, ed. *Classical Greece.* Cambridge: Cambridge University Press, 1994.

Murphy-O'Conner, Jerome. *St. Paul's Corinth.* Collegeville, MN: The Liturgical Press, 1983.

Murray, Oswyn, *Early Greece.* Cambridge: Harvard University Press, 1993.

Myers, John L. *Geographical History in Greek Lands.* Oxfrod: Clarendon Press, 1953.

Myers, J. Wilson, and others. *The Aerial Atlas of Ancient Crete.* London: Thames & Hudson, 1992.

Mylonas, George E. *Ancient Mycenae.* Princeton: Princeton University Press, 1957.

Mylonas, George E. *Eleusis and the Eleusinian Mysteries.* Princeton: Princeton University Press, 1961.

Neils, Jenfier. *Goddess and Polis.* Princeton: Princeton University Press, 1992.

Ober, Josiah. *The Athenian Revolution.* Princeton: Princeton University Press, 1996.

O'Brien, John M. *Alexander the Great.* New York: Routledge, 1992.

Oren, Eliezer D., ed. *The Sea Peoples and Their World.* Philadelphia: University Museum, 2000.

Patterson, Cynthia B. *The Family in Greek History.* Cambridge: Harvard University Press, 1998.

Perowne, Stewart. *The Archaeology of Greece and the Aegean.* New York: Viking Press, 1974.

Peters, F. E. *The Harvest of Hellenism.* New York: Barnes & Noble, 1996.

Pomeroy, Sarah B. *Families in Classical and Hellenistic Greece.* Oxford: Clarendon Press, 1997.

Pomeroy, Sarah B. and Others. *Ancient Greece.* New York: Oxford University Press, 1999.

Price, Simon. *Religion of the Ancient Greeks.* Cambridge: Cambridge University Press, 1999.

Ramsay, William M. *St. Paul the Traveler and the Roman Citizen.* Grand Rapids: Baker, reprinted 1979.

Raschke, Wendy J., ed. *The Archaeology of the Olympics: The Olympics and Other Festivals in Antiquity.* Madison: University of Wisconsin Press, 1988.

Robertson, D. S. *A Handbook of Greek and Roman Architecture.* Cambridge: University Press, 1929.

Robertson, Martin, and Alison Frantz. *The Parthenon Frieze*. Oxford: Phaidon, 1975.

Roebuck, Carl. *The World of Ancient Times*. New York: Charles Scribner's Sons, 1966.

Romano, David G. *The Origins of the Greek Stadion*. Philadelphia: American Philosophical Society, 1993.

Rostovtzeff, Mikhail I. *The Social and Economic History of the Hellenistic World*. 3 vols. Oxford: Clarendon Press, 1941.

Sachs, David. *Encyclopedia of the Ancient Greek World*. New York: Facts on File, 1995.

Scranton, Robert L. *Greek Architecture*. New York: George Braziller, 1967.

Sealey, Raphael. *A History of the Greek City States*. Berkeley: University of California Press, 1976.

Sherwin-White, A. N. *Roman Law and Roman Society in the New Testament*. Grand Rapids: Baker, reprinted 1992 by permission of Oxford University Press.

Sherwin-White, Susan, and Amelie Kuhrt. *From Samarkhand to Sardis: A New Approach to the Seleucid Empire*. Berkeley: University of California Press, 1993.

Shipley, Grahm. *The Greek World After Alexander, 323–30 B.C.* New York: Routledge, 2000.

Smith, William. *A Dictionary of Greek and Roman Geography*. 2 vols., New York: AMS Press reprint, 1966

Snodgrass, Anthony M. *An Archaeology of Greece*. Berkeley: University of California Press, 1987.

Snodgrass, Anthony M. *The Dark Age of Greece*. New York: Routledge, 2000.

Starr, Chester G. *The Economic and Social Growth of Early Greece 800–500 B.C.* New York: Oxford University Press, 1977.

Stewart, Andrew. *Greek Sculpture*. 2 vols., New Haven, CT: Yale University Press, 1990.

Stockton, David. *The Classical Athenian Democracy*. New York: Oxford University Press, 1990.

Strauss, Barry S. *Athens After the Peloponnesian War*. Ithaca: Cornell University Press, 1986.

Swaddling, Judith. *The Ancient Olympic Games*. Austin: University of Texas Press, 1984.

Sweet, Waldo E. *Sport and Recreation in Ancient Greece*. New York: Oxford University Press, 1987.

Tarn, William W. *Antigonos Gonatas*. Chicago: Argonaut Publishers, 1969.

Taylour, William. *The Mycenaeans*. Rev. ed., London: Thames & Hudson, 1983.

Tenney, Merrill C. *New Testament Times*. Grand Rapids: Eerdmans, 1965.

Veyne, Paul. *Did the Greeks Believe in Their Myths?* Chicago:University of Chicago Press, 1998.

Vermeule, Emily. *Greece in the Bronze Age*. Chicago, University of Chicago Press, 1964.

Walbank, F. W. *The Hellenistic World*. Rev. ed., Cambridge: Harvard University Press, 1993.

Wardle, K.A. and Diana. *Cities of Legend: The Mycenaean World*. Rev. ed. London: Duckworth, 2000.

Warren, Peter. *The Making of the Past: The Aegean Civilization*. New York: E. P. Dutton, 1975.

Warry, John. *Warfare in the Classical World*. New York: Barnes & Noble, 1980.

Webster, T. B. L. *Athenian Culture and Society*. Berkeley: University of California Press, 1973.

Whitby, Michael, ed. *Sparta*. New York: Routledge, 2002.

Willetts, R. F. *The Civilization of Ancient Crete*. New York: Barnes & Noble, 1976.

Wood, Michael. *In the Footsteps of Alexander the Great*. Berkeley: University of California Press, 1997.

Woudhuizen, Fred. *The Language of the Sea Peoples*. Amsterdam: Najade Press, 1992.

Wycherley, R. E. *How the Greeks Built Cities*. London: Macmillan, 1962.

Wycherley, R. E. *The Stones of Athens*. Princeton: Princeton University Press, 1978.

Zaidman, Louise B. and Pauline S. Pantel. *Religion in the Ancient Greek City*. Cambridge: Cambridge University Press, 1989.

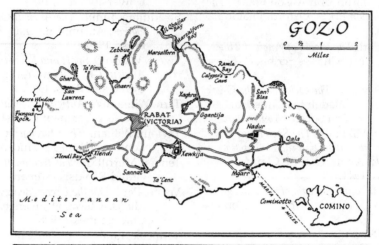

GOZO

Il Qbajjar Bay
Marsalforn Bay
Zebbug   Marsalforn
Ta' Pinu
Gharb   Ghasri   Ramla Bay
San   Xaghra   Calypse's Cave
Lawrenz
Azure Window   San Blas
Fungus   RABAT
Rock   (VICTORIA)   Ggantija
                    Nadur
                         Qala
Xlendi Bay Xlendi   Xewkija
        Sannat   Mgarr
            Ta' Cenc

Mediterranean
Sea

0 ½ 1   2
        Miles

MARFA 4 MILES

Cominotto   COMINO

FERRY
TO
GOZO   Armier Bay
Paradise Bay Marfa
        Mellieha Bay
                St. Paul's Islands
        Selmun Castle
Mellieha   St. Paul's Bay
Golden Bay   Bahar ic-caghak
Ghajn Tuffieha Bay
        Mgarr   Gharghur
                Naxxar   St. Juliens
                    Gzira Sliema
        Mosta Lija Balzan
            San Anton Birkirkara Msida
        Mdina Attard   VALETTA
Imtahlep Rabat   Qormi Hamrun
        Verdala Zebbug   Paola   Marsaskala
        Palace   Tarxien   Marsaskala Bay
Dingli   Siggiewi Luqa   Zejtun   St. Thomas Bay
    Boschetto   Mqabba   Marsaxlokk
        Qrendi   Zurrieq   Ghar Dalam
        Hagar Qim   Peter's Pool
    Mnajdra   St. George's Bay
        Weid iz Zurrieq Blue Grotto

VALETTA (inset)
Ta' Xbiex Marsamxett VALETTA
        Floriana
            Kalkara
        Grand Harbour Vittorosia
                Cospicua
    Marsa   Senglea

Mediterranean
Sea   MALTA

        Fifla Is.

0 1 2 3 4
        Miles

            SICILY   Catania

Tunis   237 MILES   712 MILES
    Pantellaria
TUNISIA
                GOZO
                    MALTA

    Lampedusa   N.S.H.

10

MALTA

Malta is many things to many people. To the World War II buff it is a symbol of the heroism of a whole people. From June 10, 1940, to the end of October 1942, the Maltese stood largely alone to endure the relentless pounding of Italian and German bombers and surface vessels. Initially their three gladiator biplanes—nicknamed Faith, Hope, and Charity—were their only air defense. Often food was almost gone and guns were sometimes without shells. But they fought on. Malta became the "world's most bombed spot" in World War II, suffering more than 1,200 air raids. Over 14,000 tons of bombs fell on the islands, killing 1,468 civilians and wounding thousands more, and wrecking and damaging some 35,000 houses and other buildings. On April 15, 1942, George VI awarded the George Cross "to the Island Fortress of Malta to bear witness to a Heroism and Devotion that will long be famous in History."

To the historian of the later Crusades, the islands are a symbol of military heroism. The Knights of St. John—only 8,000 strong—faced an Ottoman armada on May 18, 1565. The vast Ottoman force consisted of 130 galleys and 50 transports carrying 40,000 troops. Later thirteen more Turkish ships reinforced the original attack group. Fort St. Elmo held out against repeated attacks until June 23. Then, with the fort reduced to a pile of rubble and the grave of 1,300 Christian heroes, St. Elmo fell. The Muslims had lost 8,000. Fort St. Angelo and Senglea continued to hold against fierce attack. Finally on September 7 reinforcements from Sicily arrived to join the knights. The Turks had had enough and retreated. The defenders had lost more than 2,000 and the Ottomans thee-fourths of their forces.

To the student of archaeology Malta is an archaeological paradise. Almost any extensive walk in the country leads to some link with prehistory. Numerous Neolithic, Copper, and Bronze Age temples and other remains dating back to 5000 B.C. dot the landscape. Some of what may be seen is described in the historical development that follows.

To the tourist from America and especially Europe, it is a wonderful mecca—a place to relax and regain one's sanity after the hectic pace that most of us lead. It is easy to write tourist copy for Malta. To breathe the unpolluted air of the countryside, to swim in the unpolluted water of Golden Bay or Ghajn Tuffieha Bay, where the sea temperature averages 74° F from May to October, or take scenic walks on Gozo are all refreshing. The Maltese are renowned for this hospitality, which Paul experienced when he was shipwrecked

The busy Marsaxlokk Bay in the southeast of Malta, where Roman grain ships normally docked. Apparently Paul's ship did not land there but in the northeast part of the island instead. Hence the sailors on the ship did not recognize the place.

ferred reading of Greek, Acts 27: 14, see KJV *Euroclydon*), an "East-Northeaster." They were "exceedingly tempest-tossed" (Acts 27: 18 NKJV). The unabated fury of the gale was strengthened by squalls. Thus the long breaking action of the waves was interrupted by squalls and the ship was turned and plunged heavily into the trough of the sea and took unusually long to recover herself. The hull was strained severely. It was truly a voyage of terror.

Finally the crew sensed they were nearing land and took soundings at twenty fathoms (120 feet) and fifteen fathoms (90 feet). At daybreak they decided to beach the ship to avoid being dashed against rocks somewhere. First they threw out the cargo of wheat to lighten the ship and make it float higher in the water, and then they cut the ropes to the anchors. Hoisting the mainsail they made full tilt for shore. As they ran aground, the ship broke up but the entire crew, the prisoners and other passengers (276 in all, Acts 27:36) made it safely to shore, as God and Paul had promised (Acts 27:24–25). The ship was an Alexandrian ship (Acts 27:6), one of the ships of the fleet that carried wheat from Egypt to Italy (Acts 27:38). Such ships commonly were about 180 feet long, 45 feet wide, and about 40 feet deep, with an estimated cargo of 1,200 tons.

there. Luke, in speaking of the welcome he and Paul received on that occasion, said, "The natives showed us extraordinary kindness" (Acts 28:2, NASB).

But of particular interest to the Bible student, Malta was the site of Paul's shipwreck on his voyage from Palestine to Rome. And even those who are not especially Bible-oriented have heard of Malta in that connection. It was one of the most famous shipwrecks of history. The King James Version calls the place Melita, which is a transliteration of the Greek of Acts 28:1. Though in the past some have identified it with Meleda or Melita on the east coast of the Adriatic Sea off Bosnia, the African Melita (Malta) is almost certainly the correct identification. It was a Roman possession and linked to the province of Sicily. All modern versions of the Bible use the name Malta.

Shipwreck on Malta

Now when neither sun nor stars appeared for many days, and no small tempest beat on us, all hope that we would be saved was finally given up." (Acts 27:20, NKJV)

It was a terrible storm. It blew the ship uncontrollably for fourteen days (Acts 27:27). The sailors had a name for it: *Eurakylon* (pre-

The Place of Landing

The crew did not recognize the land, perhaps partly because of weather conditions and partly because ships putting in at Malta normally docked at the southeast end of the island in Marsascirocco (Marsaxlokk) Bay. Evidently they had landed in the northeast part of the island. Presumably some of the seamen who were active on the grain supply run between Alexandria and Rome had been to Malta before.

The person who, more than any other, described and popularized the apostle Paul's shipwreck on Malta, was James Smith, who wrote *The Voyage and Shipwreck of St. Paul* in 1848. Smith concluded that the shipwreck occurred in what is now called St. Paul's Bay. A town by that name presently stands at the foot of the bay.

At the entrance of the bay are some tiny rocky islands; on the largest, Selmunett, stands a statue of Paul erected in 1845 to mark the spot where Paul and the others supposedly landed. Smith argued, among other things, that the "place where two seas met" (Acts 27:41, KJV) and where the ship broke up, was a beach between two creeks on the west side of the bay.

Nearby the natives of the island built a fire and tried to meet the needs of the ship-wrecked company. In the vicinity was an estate of Publius, the "chief man" or magis-trate of the island, who extended further courtesies (Acts 28:7). He probably did so in part because of his inclination to show kindness, and in part because he was deal-ing with a Roman centurion and his guard (and his prisoners) who were on official business. Today a church, called San Pawl Milqi (meaning "St. Paul Welcomed"), stands on the supposed site of Publius' house.

Before we look further at the church and the supposed authenticity of the site, let's think about the shipwreck site itself. Over time some have questioned Smith's conclu-sions (though they are generally accepted today). The questioning does not concern whether Malta is the place where the ship ran aground but whether Smith had found the exact spot. As a matter of fact, for cen-turies people have associated the shipwreck with the bay that now bears Paul's name, but not the western part of the bay where Smith thought it occurred.

One of those who ques-tioned Smith's conclusions was George H. Musgrave. First Musgrave raised a point about the real meaning of Acts 27:41. He observed that Smith him-self had said the Greek is "gen-erally supposed to mean an

St. Paul's Bay. The beach where the ship ran aground and broke up is supposed to be in the center background.

Isthmus," rather than "a place where two seas met."[1] The new translations take a dif-ferent tack from Smith's translation of Acts 27:41: "striking a reef" (NRSV and NASB); "ran aground on a sandbank" (CEV); "struck a sandbar" (NIV). Second, Musgrave argued that the area around St. Paul's islands in the western part of the bay was not a place to expect exhausted people to get ashore. Third, he said that it was too far for exhausted personnel of the ship to walk from the site on the west of St. Paul's Bay around the end of the bay to the tradi-tional site of Publius' entertainment of them (St. Pawl Milqi), some four or five miles away.

Fourth, Musgrave observed that the sailors "noticed a bay with a beach" (Acts 27:39, NRSV) at fifteen fathoms. They could not have seen a beach in St. Paul's Bay unless they were already in the bay at a

Selmunett island lies at the entrance of St. Paul's Bay. On it stands a statue of the apostle Paul.

Salina Bay with reef at the end of the peninsula in the center background. Presumably Paul's ship broke up on this reef

depth well under fifteen fathoms. Fifth, he noted that the sailors saw no sign of human habitation, but on the eastern side of St. Paul's Bay at that time stood a Neolithic temple that had been there for millennia.

Musgrave argued that the shipwreck actually took place in Salina Bay, just to the east of St. Paul's Bay. There sailors on the ship, while still outside the entrance of the bay, could have looked down the bay to see a sandy shore on which to land. When the ship beached, the passengers could fairly easily have gotten to shore. Further they would not have had to go more than a mile or so to Publius' estate, assuming San Pawl Milqi is built on the site.[2] If we want to stick with the translation of a "place where two seas met" (Acts 27:41 KJV), or even a "reef" or "sandbar," that could be the peninsula or reef that divides St. Paul's Bay and Salina Bay. After walking all over the area on a couple of different trips and looking at all the evidence, I am inclined to agree with Musgrave and to conclude that Paul's ship was perhaps wrecked on the reef separating Salina Bay and St. Paul's Bay and that the men made it ashore in Salina Bay, walking to San Pawl Milqi.

Publius' Estate?

Is there any evidence that San Pawl Milqi had any connection with Paul or the shipwreck or early Christianity? The Italian Archaeological Mission in Malta excavated at the site of the church in the 1960s, finding a villa dating to the New Testament period. The villa involved a substantial residential and agricultural complex laid out around a peristyle courtyard. There were olive oil presses, remains of a flour mill, and possibly some form of a ceramics industry. Living quarters, extending to the west, were decorated with painted wall plaster. One room was fairly elaborately decorated and a series of chapels were later built on the spot. The church that stands there today dates between A.D. 1620 and 1622, and there is a documentary record of a building in A.D. 1488. Excavations turned up evidence of three previous churches at the site. The place was a pilgrimage center at least by the seventh century.

Excavators found numerous indications that the spot was venerated as connected with Paul and Christianity. A block of a wellhead with the name "Paulus" on it dated between the fourth and seventh centuries A.D. A stone with a fish (symbol of

San Pawl Milqi

Excavations in the villa adjacent to San Pawl Milqi with an olive press in the center.

Christ) and a stone with a cross on it dated to the fourth or fifth century A.D. A stone with the figure of Paul went back to the seventh century A.D., a grafitto of a boat to the seventh or eighth century. Then there were bricks with a cross and a fish from the fourth or fifth century A.D.[3]

Evangelization of Malta

Tradition has it that the island was evangelized at the time of Paul's visit, that Publius was one of his converts, and that he became the first Christian bishop of Malta. Interestingly, catacombs on Salina Bay have burials dating to the early Christian centuries. Musgrave notes Harrison Lewis's claim that pottery shards found in the cata-

combs date as early as the second to the fourth centuries A.D.[4] The location of these catacombs on the east side of Salina Bay not far from San Pawl Milqi may or may not have something to do with the identification of the shipwreck site.

The Geography of Malta

Malta is an arid, rocky island 58 miles south of Sicily, 149 miles south of the European mainland, and 180 miles north of Cape Bon in Tunisia. A little over 17 miles long, 9 miles wide, and 60 miles in circumference, it is the chief island of the Maltese group—which also includes Gozo and Comino islands. Gozo is 9 miles long by 4.5 miles wide, for a total area of 26 square miles, while Comino is only one square mile. The three islands together total 122 square miles, approximately one-tenth the size of Rhode Island.

The island of Malta is of limestone formation with thin but fertile soil. Agriculture was always its chief occupation in earlier centuries, but uncertain rainfall made farming a rather risky business. With an average rainfall of twenty-two inches per year, it actually has a rainfall that varies from ten to forty inches; and periods of drought have extended over three years. There are no rivers or rivulets on the island. Springs flow, but the largest part of the water supply is pumped from strata just above sea

The soil of Malta is thin but fertile. The generous sprinkling of rocks is commonly gathered into fences at the edge of the fields.

The Holy of Holies in the Hypogeum.

Dalam cave in the southeast of the island near Marsaxlokk Bay. There remains of elephants and hippopotami have been preserved.

Maltese History

Neolithic Beginnings

A brave group of Sicilian farmers must have looked out to the south on a clear day in about 5000 B.C. to see land on the horizon about sixty miles away. Sending out a scouting team, they learned of a group of small but habitable islands—the Maltese. Some of them proceeded to migrate.

level. Today only about 2 percent of the population work in agriculture, about 25 percent in industry, 20 percent in trade and finance, and the rest in a variety of other occupations.

The climate is healthful and temperate, with an average daytime temperature of 65° F in January to March and 90° F in July and August. There are no high mountains on the island. The hills are nowhere higher than 850 feet; the Bingemma Range in the west rises to 786 feet. Sheer cliffs 400 feet in height stand along the southwest coast.

Malta is a fragment of an old land bridge that once united Italy and Africa. Its connection with Africa may be seen in the Ghar

These early settlers brought with them a characteristic pottery—known as Impressed Ware—so similar in style to the pottery of southeast Sicily as to demonstrate that these settlers came from there. The geometric designs were impressed or incised in the wet surface before firing. The decorations were produced with the use of the edge of sea shells, pointed sticks, or fingernails.

These Neolithic people were food producers before they arrived on Malta. And they had domesticated numerous animals. Bones of sheep or goat, cow, pig, and dog were found in the early levels, as were carbonized grains of barley, wheat, and lentils. The discovery of slingstones suggests that they varied their diet by hunting birds or animals.

Though Malta had plenty of limestone, the inhabitants found it necessary to import harder stone for use as cutting tools: flint from Sicily; and obsidian (a natural glass found in volcanic deposits) for sharp knives, especially from the Lipari Islands north of Sicily. Lava was also brought in, probably from the area of Mount Etna in Sicily, for making such things as querns or handmills for grinding grain. The source of their obsidian has been confirmed by scientific analysis.

metres

The Ggantija complex. A common outer wall encloses two temple units, one with five apses and the other with four apses and a niche at the far end.

Main altar in the Tarxien temple.

Scholars identify five subdivisions of this period, each marked by distinctive types of pottery.Tombs built at the beginning of the period indicate that the dead were now being buried collectively in rock-cut tombs. The most outstanding of these tombs is the Hypogeum, located at Hal Saflieni, directly south of Valletta in the middle of the island of Malta. Dating to the general period of 3300–3000 B.C., it was a collection of halls and chambers cut out of the limestone on three levels. There at least six thousand people were buried with possessions of pottery or personal ornaments. While archaeologists are left to wonder at the purpose of the structure, at the minimum it was a place of burial and had some religious uses. Some of its features resemble temples built above ground.

These early inhabitants apparently lived in caves, such as the Ghar Dalam cave in the south of the island of Malta. But they also lived in village sites, as at Skorba in the northwest of the island. There they built houses of wattle and daub or mudbrick on stone foundations and two larger structures that must have been used as shrines. Clay figurines representing female figures may have been fertility goddesses.

Age of the Temple Builders

Some have called this the Copper Age, and occasionally the older books do, but the period is not marked by copper technology. It is better to call it the Age of Temple Builders because of the many impressive stone temples built at that time. This age lasted from about 4100 to 2500 B.C., by which time the entire population seems to have deserted Malta, perhaps because of extended drought.

There appears to have been a sharp cultural break in the civilization of Malta around 4100 B.C. Some assume that this resulted from the entrance of a new people from Sicily. But others observe that changes could have occurred from internal developments in the culture.

The ancient temples of Malta (remarkable structures known world wide) seem to have been built in the middle period (Ggantija, on Gozo, 3600–3300 B.C.) or later. Temple construction reached its climax during the Tarxien phase (c. 3000–2000 B.C.). Temples of this period have been found especially at Tarxien, Hagar Qim, Mnajdra, and Tas-Silg, all located in the southern third of the island of Malta. How these religious structures functioned is unknown. There were altars for sacrifice and pictures of sheep, rams, and pigs on blocks of stone in them. There were also large fleshy headless figures which local

Hagar Qim

tourist guides and others call "fat ladies." But in fact, they are asexual figures, and we should not conclude that they had something to do with a female fertility cult (see picture). One headless figurine of a standing nude woman with opulent features was found at Hagar Qim.

These temple units had a combination of apses which are better seen in diagram than explained (see accompanying plans). Generally large, nicely dressed stones were used in construction (again, see illustration). Numerous small stones, a little larger than large marbles, served as a sort of ball bearings on which stones could be moved about.

A "fat lady" from Hagar Qim.

Bronze and Iron Ages (c. 2500–900 B.C.)

What brought to an end the great temple age on Malta can only be guessed. As noted, the suggestion that an extended drought was responsible for a general exodus of the population is as good as any. What followed culturally in the Bronze and Iron ages is fundamentally different and culturally inferior. During the first phase (2500–1500 B.C.), that of the Tarxien Cemetery people, cremation was introduced and the ashes put in large urns with clothing, ornaments, tools, weapons, and pottery. Metal objects appear for the first time, such as copper awls and daggers. But the discovery of metal is not common because it was valuable and resmelted for further use. The discovery of obsidian

arrowheads presumes the use of the bow. Where the Tarxien people came from is uncertain, but some discoveries lead to the supposition that they came from Greece and may have spent some time in Italy before going to Malta.

What happened to the Tarxien peoples is as much of a mystery as their origin. In any case, the second phase of the Bronze Age and the whole Iron Age (1500–800 B.C.) was characterized by an effort to deal with the insecurity of the times. Villages were now built on hills with a couple of steep sides and a formidable stone wall on the flatter side. Inside the fortified enclosures stood villages of oval huts. Under them were shallow bottle-shaped pits for storage of grain or water. The discovery of numerous spindle whorls and loom weights suggests an extensive production of textiles, some of which must have been destined for export. The existence of numerous fortified towns suggests an effort to protect against pirate raids from abroad or against ambitious and warlike neighbors locally, perhaps both.

The Phoenician-Punic Era

The Phoenicians apparently used the harbors of Malta as a safe haven or for commercial purposes as early as the ninth century B.C. Then in the following century they colonized there—along the coast and also inland. Evidently they founded at least one large city, on the site of modern Rabat-Medina. Since the modern city covers the presumed site, archaeological confirmation is impossible. The Phoenicians prospered, and from Malta in about the seventh century founded a colony of their own at Acholla, opposite Malta on the east coast of Tunisia.[5] Though Phoenician cities on Malta cannot be excavated because they are occupied by modern urban areas, numerous eighth-seventh century B.C. burials of a Phoenician type have been found.

And at the sacred area of Tas Silg, near the harbor of Marsaxlokk, there was a Phoenician-Punic phase. There the

Modern Medina (Mdina), the Roman capital, refortified by the Muslims during the Middle Ages.
Courtesy Import & Export House, Valletta.

Phoenicians incorporated a third millennium temple into a temple of their own about 700 B.C. This Phoenician-Punic phase continued to the second century B.C. It consisted of an acropolis surrounded by a thick limestone wall, with a paved ramp leading up to it. Dedications were found there to Astarte in Phoenician and to Hera in Greek. Melqart (Heracles), the patron of seafarers, also had a temple nearby.

As Phoenicia's colony of Carthage expanded in the western Mediterranean, it occupied Malta in the sixth century B.C. This Punic period, as it is called, has been documented in various places, including in an excavation in the middle of Victoria on the island of Gozo. The Phoenician-Punic culture and institutions established themselves firmly on Malta and were slow to disappear, in spite of the Roman conquest, when Greek became the common language of the Mediterranean and Latin the official language. When Paul arrived about A.D. 60, Luke says in his writing of Acts that the "natives [barbarians] showed us unusual kindness" (Acts 28:2 NKJV). The *barbarians* should not be considered as uncultured but were to be thought of as non-Greek or non-Roman in their culture or language. Several modern Bible versions properly translate

"natives" here instead of the KJV "barbarous people." The Maltese language today is basically Semitic—Phoenician, Carthaginian, and Arabic, with modern words mixed in. A celebrated textile industry (producing women's clothing and cushions) developed on Malta during the Phoenician-Punic period and apparently guaranteed Malta a place in the Mediterranean trade. This industry continued on into the Roman period.

The Roman Era

As Rome slugged it out with Carthage for control of the western Mediterranean, what Carthage controlled was fair game for Rome. During the first Punic War, in 257 B.C. Rome thoroughly devastated and plundered Malta. Then at the beginning of the Second Punic War, in 218 B.C., Rome invaded and annexed the island, without a struggle with the Carthaginian garrison.

Malta was later joined to the province of Sicily, which was governed by a propraetor from 122 B.C. Sicily became a senatorial province in 27 B.C., which means that the Senate rather than the emperor appointed the governor. Syracuse, in eastern Sicily, was the seat of government. Melite (modern Rabat-Medina), in the center of Malta,

A first century villa, incorporated into the Museum of Roman Antiquities, Rabat. Hellenistic in style, the house had a central courtyard surrounded by sixteen columns of the Doric order. The floors of the courtyard (peristyle) and the surrounding rooms were decorated with magnificent mosaics with geometric designs. Measurements of the peristyle were about 22 by 21 feet. One of the rooms next to it was about 11 by 11. A reception room off the peristyle was somewhat larger than the peristyle itself.

market passed most of the delicate fabrics of adjacent Malta, only some sixty miles south of Sicily. In fact, production houses of Syracuse sometimes had Maltese weavers working for them.[6]

Some people worked as stone cutters and in the building trades. Geologically Malta consists of Upper Coralline limestone and Lower Coralline limestone with Globigerina limestone and clay in between. The Globigerina is soft and easily quarried and hardens on exposure to the atmosphere. The beautiful buildings of Malta are generally built of this limestone.

Most of the Maltese worked in agriculture in New Testament times. Outside the two Roman towns at Melita (Rabat-Medina) on Malta and Gaudos on Gozo, the population was largely spread over the countryside, raising sheep and cattle, wheat and barley, and olives, and producing honey. Shipping interests in Syracuse were probably largely responsible for transporting goods into and out of Malta.

About twenty-five first century villas scattered on the islands' countryside have

A statue of Paul in the Grotto of St. Paul, a cave beneath St. Paul's Church in Rabat. The traditional site of the villa where Paul converted Publius.

was the Roman capital of the islands and the headquarters of Publius, the "chief man" or "leading citizen" or Roman administrator. Gaudos (modern Victoria) was the chief town of Gozo. The modern town of LaValletta was not founded until A.D. 1566.

As a result of continued contacts with the Greek city of Syracuse and other Greek cities of Sicily, Greek culture and language became widespread on Malta. Latin also made inroads, but a great many of the people were still Semitic in culture and spoke a dialect of Phoenician when Paul landed there.

Malta was prosperous in the Roman period. Reference has already been made to the lucrative textile industry there. Syracuse on Sicily was the center of the textile industry of that island. Through that come to light. These tend to be farmsteads attached to large country estates, not designed as residences only. Part of the building, usually much of the first floor, was intended for agricultural activities, such as the processing of olive oil, or for the production of cloth. Rooms opened off open courtyards. A stairway led to the second floor, where most of the family rooms were located. The house connected with the church of San Pawl Milqi is of this type. These houses have cisterns for the collection of water (usually under the central courtyard) in this land with slim water resources.

Recent Political Developments

After Napoleon's capture of Malta in A.D. 1798 and looting of the island's treasure, the encouraging news reached Malta of Nelson's victory over the French at the Battle of the Nile. Malta then fell under the protection of the British, and British possession was confirmed by the Treaty of Paris in 1814. Finally in September, 1964 Malta achieved independence from Britain and became a republic in 1974. Its population in 2003 is close to 400,000.

On to Rome

After three months in Malta and it was safe to sail again, Paul and his companions boarded ship for Italy (Acts 28:11). The vessel on which they traveled, "a ship of Alexandria," was almost certainly another of the large ships of the grain fleet supplying Rome. This one had spent the winter in the island (Acts 28:11), probably at the southern port of Marsaxlokk. Where the company of 276 had spent the winter is not stated. Probably they had found quarters in Melite (Rabat-Medina) and now went south to the port.

NOTES

1. James Smith, *The Voyage and Shipwreck of St. Paul,* 4th ed. (Reprint, Grand Rapids: Baker Book House, 1978), p. 142.

2. George H. Musgrave, *Friendly Refuge.* Privately published in Malta, pp. 19–32. ISBN 09506480 0 0 (given to help readers trace copies).

3. Michelangelo Cagiano de Azevedo, *Testimonianze Archeologiche Della Tradizione Paolina A Malta* (Rome: University of Rome, 1966), p. 55.

4. Musgrave, *Friendly Refuge,* 94, 100, noting Harrison Lewis, *Ancient Malta,* (Bucks, England: Colin Smythe, 1977. See also, Jack Finegan, *The Archaeology of the New Testament* (Boulder, CO: Westview Press, 1981), p. 103.

5. Sabatino Moscati, *The World of the Phoenicians* (New York: Praeger, 1970), p. 189.

6. V. M. Scramuzza, "Roman Sicily," *An Economic survey of Ancient Rome,* ed. Tenney Frank (New York: Octagon Books, 1974), III, p. 290.

BIBLIOGRAPHY

Blouet, Brian. *The Story of Matla.* London: Faber and Faber, 1967.

De Azevedo, Michelangelo. *Testimonianze Archeologiche Della Tradizione Paolina A Malta.* Rome: University of Rome, 1966.

Ellul, Joseph S. *Malta's Prediluvian Culture at the Stone Age Temples.* Malta: Printwell, 1988.

Finegan, Jack. *The Archaeology of the New Testament: The Mediterranean World of the Early Christian Apostles.* Boulder, CO: Westview Press, 1981.

Gouder, Tancred C. *The Mosaic Pavements in the Museum of Roman Antiquities.* Malta: Department of Museums, 1983.

Musgrave, George H. *Friendly Refuge.* Privately published in Malta, n.d. (after 1977).

Rossiter, Stuart. *The Blue Guides: Malta.* London: Ernest Benn, 1968.

Smith, James. *The Voyage and Shipwreck of St. Paul.* Grand Rapids: Baker Book House reprint, 1978 (from the 1880 ed.).

A model of Rome from the Museum of the Civilization of Rome. In the foreground extends the great Circus Maximus. Behind that on the Palatine Hill stand the places of the Caesars. At the left foot of the Palatine Hill in the left center is the Roman Forum. In the center of the picture is the great temple of Venus and of Rome, the largest and most splendid temple in the city, to the right of which stands the Colosseum, and to the right of that the camp of the Praetoria Guard.

11

ITALY

When Paul landed at Puteoli (modern Pozzuoli), on the Bay of Naples, and traveled north along the Appian Way to Rome, he was headed for the city that for decades had controlled the Mediterranean world. To say, as some carelessly do, that Rome ruled the then-known world is untrue. The Romans knew of many lands beyond their borders in Europe, Africa, and Asia (including both India and China), which they either did not choose to conquer or were not able to subdue. And the Empire did not reach its greatest extent until A.D. 117.

The reference in Luke 2:1 to a Roman decree that all the "world" should be taxed or enrolled in a census (the decree that sent Joseph and Mary to Bethlehem for census taking) of course meant the Roman world.[1] The Romans were under no illusion about world control. However, they did sufficiently control the Mediterranean and its environs to call it *mare nostrum* (our sea).

Geography of Italy

Slashing diagonally across the center of the Mediterranean, Italy was strategically located for control of that sea. After Rome had annexed Sicily, she was in a position to dominate the east-west sea lanes. Not only is it significant that the peninsula is centrally located in the Mediterranean basin, but it

was also important for the development of the Roman Empire that nature had brought certain forces to bear to form that basin into a unified area. The uniform character of the Mediterranean basin is evident in a similar climate, a likeness of geological structure, and a similar distinctive type of vegetation. Moreover, the Mediterranean lands, while sharing a common seafront, are rather clearly separated from inland areas by an almost unbroken ring of mountains and deserts. Modern Bible students, influenced by the current divisive religious and political views in conflict there and the impact of the world power struggle on the area, lose sight of the factors that were so significant in unifying the Mediterranean world in antiquity.

Roman military power made the Mediterranean a Roman lake, surrounded on all sides by Roman territory. In that territory unity was enhanced by a single Greco-Roman culture with a universal language—Greek. The sea (some 2,300 miles from east to west), not the lands around it, was the center of the Empire. The sea routes were the arteries through which the trade of the Empire flowed, and Mediterranean ports were the chief cities of the Roman world.

While Italy was strategically located for controlling the Mediterranean, Rome was strategically located for controlling the

peninsula of Italy. Situated in the center of the peninsula, she could meet her enemies one by one and could prevent them from effectively uniting against her. If such a union should be formed, she could move against it with the advantage of a central base and short lines of communication. Early in her career of expansion, Rome developed the practice of building military roads to all parts of her domain.

Moreover, Rome was located at the lowest point of the Tiber River where firm abutments for a bridge could be found. So Rome controlled the main line of communication along the western and more populous side of the peninsula.

As is well known, Rome was built on seven hills.[2] None of these exceeded two hundred feet above sea level, but most of them rose for the most part in steep slopes above the surrounding valleys and at some points formed sheer cliffs towering over those valleys. The Tiber flowed past and later through the city and was navigable for the fifteen-mile distance between the coast and the capital. Ships docked at the foot of the

Rome was located at the lowest point of the Tiber where firm abutments for a bridge could be found. Here the ancient Roman Fabrician Bridge is about 190 feet long and extends from the bank of the Tiber to the island. The bridge from the island to the other bank of the Tiber was removed in 1888.

Aventine Hill. Her days as a leading center of trade did not come until the reign of Claudius (A.D. 41–54), however, when her port of Ostia was developed. Even then, port facilities were such that it was common for travelers to disembark at Puteoli and take the long land route to the capital. Paul's journey to Rome reflects this practice.

The area of Italy comprises approximately 90,000 square miles, almost the size of Oregon. It divides into two regions: the continental on the north and the peninsular on the south. The northern region measures roughly 320 miles east to west and about 70 miles north to south. The boot-shaped peninsula stretches some 700 miles toward the continent of Africa and is never more than 125 miles wide. In the toe and the heel of the "boot," the peninsula is only about 25 miles wide.

THE FLOW OF CULTURE TO ITALY

The Apennine Mountains extend almost the full length of the Italian peninsula in a great bow-shape. The eastern face of the Apennines approaches closely to the Adriatic shore and hinders communication there.

On the east side of the Adriatic the mountains of Greece block the flow of

communication to Italy. The open face of Greece—the good ports—lie on the east side of that country. And the open face of Asia Minor—the accessible river valleys—lie on the west side of the peninsula.

Thus, in ancient times culture flowed from western Asia Minor to eastern Greece and around the southern coasts of Greece and Italy to Italy's west coast.

So the placement of mountains in Italy slowed the flow of culture from the East (because it had to come around the south of Greece and Italy) and resulted in a high cultural development much later than in Asia Minor and Greece.

Mountains

Mountains dominate much of the landscape of Italy. The Alps form an irregular 1,200-mile arc across the north. While they arise rather abruptly on the Italian side and impede expansion, they slope more gently on the European side and did not prevent migration into Italy. The Apennines extend the full length of the peninsula in a bow-shaped range about 800 miles long and 25 to 85 miles wide. Since the average height

Rome brought a political unity to the whole Mediterranean world by the time of Christ.

of these mountains is only about four thousand feet and since the passes through them are not generally difficult, they did not pose the problem to the untiy of the country that the mountains of Greece did.

The Apennines approach closely to the Adriatic Sea, permitting little more than a coastal road in many places along the eastern coast, while on the western coast leaving room for arable lands that are carved up into plains by spurs extending from the main Apennine Range. Thus, Italy faced west. Because she did, the flow of culture from the more highly developed civilizations of the East was slowed in its journey to her shores. Along the west coast of the peninsula, both north and south of the Tiber and on adjacent islands, are extinct volcanoes. Volcanoes active since ancient times include Vesuvius near Naples, Stromboli (an island north of Sicily), and Etna in eastern Sicily.

Rivers

Several rivers originate in the mountains of Italy. Longest of these is the Po, which rises in the western Alps and flows eastward for 360 miles to the Adriatic Sea. The Po is the only one of the Italian rivers that can be classified as navigable. Along the Adriatic, rushing mountain torrents punctuate the rocky coastline. Flowing into the Tyrrhenian Sea on the west and navigable by small craft are the Volturno, the Liri (Liris), the Tiber, and the Arno rivers.

The Apennine Mountains stand in a great bow shape across the length of the peninsula of Italy.

The Travertine quarries.

Not only did the rivers of Italy fail to give the desired highway to much of the land but they presented a unique health problem. The sill at the Straits of Gibraltar breaks the force of the ocean tides flowing into the Mediterranean. This lack of brisk tidal movement prevents a daily scouring of the coast. Consequently, the accumulation of silt at the river mouths creates marshy areas that serve as breeding grounds for malarial mosquitoes. Both in ancient and modern times, Italy has suffered much from this dreaded disease.

In fact, in the first century B.C. a very severe type of malaria appeared in the agricultural districts around Rome. The gardens of the Campagna that supplied the city with fresh vegetables went out of cultivation. And the farmers who had lived and worked there moved to the city, adding to the overcrowding and bringing the infection with them. The live-birth rate of the Italo-Romans fell steeply during that time.[3]

Harbors

The silting up of the river mouths prevented Italian rivers from providing much in the way of harbor facilities. So extensive was this silting that in the days of the Emperor Claudius (A.D. 41–54), it was necessary to

The Tiber River as it flows into the sea at Ostia.

make a new cut for the discharge of the Tiber into the sea. Moreover, throughout a coastal length of over two thousand miles, Italy has few deep bays or good harbors. Almost all of those that do exist are located on the southern and western shores. The chief harbor on the Adriatic was Brundisium, located far down on the heel of Italy; in the instep of the boot in the south was Tarentum (Taranto) on the gulf of that name; on the west was Puteoli (Pozzuoli) on the Bay of Naples. Genoa and Lunae Portus (La Spezia) became important only in late Roman times. Ostia, which assumed importance as the port of Rome during the first century A.D., was a man-made harbor.

Climate

The climate of Italy differs in the northern and southern regions. The Po valley climate is similar to the continental climate of central Europe, with marked differences between summer and winter temperatures and clearly defined periods of spring and fall. There are frequent winter snows, copious spring and fall rains, and moderate rains in the summer. The climate of peninsular Italy is more typically Mediterranean with boisterous rain-washed winters, during which the Apennines lie heavily mantled with snow, and with summers of deficient rain. On most of the peninsula the drought extends over three or four months; at Rome it is of two months' duration. Land

and sea breezes temper the heat. In general, the climate of the western and southern coasts is subtropical. It is now generally believed that the climate of Italy has not changed much since New Testament times, though it may have been a little colder and wetter then.

The Plains of Italy

The large, level and fertile Po valley was the best grainland, but it was never an important source of supply for Rome. Since bulky goods had to be transported by water, Romans found it cheaper to obtain their food supply from a closer source. The distance from the mouth of the Po to Rome is longer than the distance from Sicily or North Africa and slightly shorter than that from Egypt.

Etruria is rough and broken by stone and better suited for pasture than for cultivation. Latium and Campania are small; their rich but shallow surface soil was soon exhausted, leaving a volcanic subsoil better for orchards and vineyards than for grain. But Campania was for a long time the chief granary of peninsular Italy and produced large amounts of fruits and vegetables.

Resources

Italy's primary source of wealth was always agricultural and pastoral. As some of the grain-producing soil became exhausted, farmers turned more to viniculture and pastoral pursuits. In fact, the name "Italia" was derived from the Oscan word *vitelliu*, meaning "calf-land." There were also notable mineral resources in ancient times, especially the copper and iron beds of Etruria and Elba. The marble quarries of Carrara in Liguria were first exploited in the last days of the Republic. Limestone was used for building purposes, the best being travertine from Tibur (Tivoli) near Rome. Large stands of timber still covered the mountainous areas and some of

A sculpture of the second century A.D., an allegorical work of a man recumbent, holding an oar in one hand and a cornucopia in the other, representing the prosperity that the Tiber provided Rome.

The travertine quarries near Tivoli, where stone for the Colosseum and other important buildings was cut.

the lowlands in the first centuries of the Christian Era. Italy also had abundant supplies of good clay for pottery, bricks, and tile.

The Peoples of Italy

Exactly when the first peoples arrived in Italy and where they came from is uncertain. In fact, no evidence connects the culture of these early inhabitants with what followed.

About 5000 B.C. Neolithic farmers began to arrive in the heel of Italy, apparently from across the Adriatic. They brought seed-grain, sheep, and cows, made pottery vessels, and built huts. They grouped their huts into compounds and surrounded them with ditches for protection. Skeletal remains indicate that they belonged to the Mediterranean branch of the Caucasian race and were characterized by dark complexions, dark hair, narrow heads, and medium to short stature. They have remained dominant in Italy to the present, assimilating both the Alpine and Nordic peoples introduced by subsequent migrations. As with other Neolithic peoples, their weapons and implements were of polished stone.

By around 3500 B.C. these Neolithic peoples had spread northward and westward in the peninsula. Their wares, especially their pottery, appeared in northwest Italy and even across the waters in Malta. And external influences from France, Spain, and North Africa began to appear on the peninsula. The knowledge of spinning and weaving was also acquired.

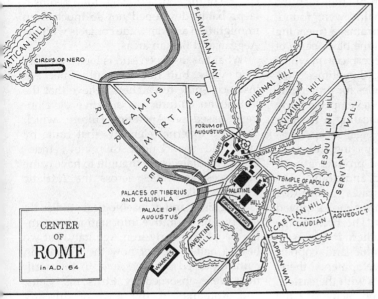

During the first millennium B.C. Rome gradually occupied her seven hills, identified here.

The Copper-Stone Age

Between about 3000 and 2000 B.C. Italy passed through the Chalcolithic or Copper-Stone Age. The knowledge of how to work copper came in from the areas of Bohemia and Hungary, and Alpine warrior immigrants from central Europe appeared on the scene. Copper-working was especially extensive in three centers: the Po valley, around Florence in the northwest, and south of Naples. The use of metal was of course expensive and limited. A great many continued to use stone tools and weapons in everyday activity.

The Bronze Age

Around 1800 B.C. metal workers discovered that by adding tin to copper they could produce stronger and more durable weapons and tools, and Italy passed into the Bronze Age. Some of these people, who established themselves in the Po valley, are known as the Palafitte. Partly Indo-European, who came in from the north, and partly native stock, they got their name from the Italian *palafitta* (meaning "row of stakes or piles") because they built their villages on piles over the northern Italian lakes and swampy areas of the Po valley.

A few hundred years later, after 1500 B.C., another group of people, known as the Terramare, came in from the Danube region. When their remains were found, they were called the Terramare (meaning "black earth") because of the black earth of their house walls and the terraces on which they built their houses. Sometimes they erected their houses on piles for protection, as did the Palafitte. They developed a fairly high civilization, domesticating a number of animals (cows, goats, pigs, sheep, horses), cultivating several crops (including flax as a source of linen), and producing commodities in bronze, wood, and cloth.

Current evidence indicates that neither the Palafitte nor Terramare peoples moved south into the peninsula. The Bronze Age culture in central and southern Italy was an outgrowth of the Neolithic and copper-stone (Chalcolithic) developments there, given impetus by contacts with the eastern shores of the Adriatic and Sicily and the Aegean world through a Mycenaean trading post on the Bay of Tarentum in the south. Probably a few settlers migrated into the Apennine region from the Aegean world.

The mountain peoples of the south were in part semi-nomadic pastoralists who had by the twelfth century B.C. become more sedentary and were engaging more extensively in farming. They lacked the knowledge of metal production of the northern Bronze Age peoples and were also different in that they buried their dead. By 1200 or shortly thereafter the north and the Apennine cultures had drawn much closer together, and cremation of the dead was becoming common in the south.

The Iron Age

About 1000 B.C. another wave of Indo-European people came into Italy, settling in the Po valley and in the northern and central parts of the peninsula, bringing the Iron Age with them. They are called Villanovans because their culture was first discovered at the site of Villanova, five miles from modern Bologna. In their irregular villages of round huts, these people used swords, spears, and axes of iron; clothing of wool; and helmets, shields, body armor, and utensils of bronze, the working of which at that time was greatly improved. The Iron Age culture of the southern half of the peninsula probably developed not so much from immigration as from trade contacts with the Aegean and Balkan areas.

What has just been said is the commonly held view but not the only one. For instance, some researchers believe that the Villanovan culture was a native development based on Apennine culture, which absorbed external elements that came by land and sea. Under this view, Indo-European dialects are thought to have come in successive waves across the Adriatic from the Balkans.

Linguistic and archaeological studies do not give us definitive information concerning peoples of early Iron Age Italy. But we have a better idea of how the Villanovan culture passed off the scene. In the north they were absorbed by Etruscans, Celts, and Romans. In the area of Tuscany (around Florence, and Siena,) the Etruscans

A seated Etruscan woman of the seventh century B.C.
British Museum

and wielded no enduring influence on its early civilization except for their indirect gift of the alphabet. In Sicily they were later to come into conflict with the Romans, and the wars that followed greatly affected the course of Roman history.

Around 775, or a little later, Greeks began to move into Italy. In the second half of the eighth century and for the next hundred years at least they established colonies in Sicily and on the southern and western coast of Italy from Tarentum to the Bay of Naples. And between 750 and 500 Italy became an important market for the Greek export trade. Greek settlers introduced the cultivation of grapes and olives and an alphabetic system of writing, which they learned from the Phoenicians. They also made an impact on pottery making and other crafts.

In the third century B.C. the Romans came face to face with the Greek settlements and fell under the spell of Greek culture. Thereafter their culture became a Greco-Roman culture which the Romans spread all over the Mediterranean world. This Greco-Roman culture was passed on into Medieval Europe and has become the basis of modern European and American civilization.

The towns the Greeks developed in the West showed a high level of city planning. For example, at Megara Hyblaea, just north of Syracuse on the eastern shore of Sicily, back in the eighth century B.C. houses were laid out on a grid of streets, as in Manhattan today. Various sectors of the city served specified functions. Urban planning did not originate in the Piraeus of Athens in the 430s B.C., as is commonly thought, but three centuries earlier in the western colonies of Greece.[4]

Who the Etruscans were is a subject of great debate among historians. And the debate began hundreds of years before Christ. Herodotus in his *Histories* in the fifth century B.C. said that they came from western Asia Minor and that they were an offshoot of the Lydians. Roman writers tended to accept that conclusion. But another Greek author, Dionysus of Halicarnassus (c. 30 B.C.), argued that they were of Italian origin and that they developed their unique

became dominant culturally and linguistically. In Latium and Rome they survived as Latins.

Within a few generations the population of Italy had become largely Italic. Various Italic tribes—the Umbrians (north central peninsula), Sabellians or Samnites (south central peninsula), and the Latins (central Italy around Rome)—were among the most important. The latter ultimately were to occupy the center of the stage of history. They formed the nucleus of Roman stock—their language developed into classical Latin—and their geographical position and innate abilities enabled them to become masters of the peninsula.

Around 800 B.C. three other peoples made their way to Italy: the Phoenicians, the Etruscans, and the Greeks.

The Phoenicians settled colonies in North Africa and Sicily and probably made trading visits to the coast of Tuscany. But they left little trace of their visits to Italy civilization on location in Western Italy. Under this view, their culture would have evolved from the Villanovan.

A third Greek historian, the astute fifth century B.C. Thucydides, commented that the pre-Greek population of Lemnos (west of Troy in the north Aegean) was Tyrrhenian (the Greek name for the Etruscans).[5] Thus he seemed to link the Etruscans with western Asia Minor. This indication, taken in conjunction with the fact that the Etruscan language is not Indo-European and Etruscan civilization seemed more Eastern than Italic, appeared to tip the balance in favor of Etruscan immigration from the East.

That did not settle the matter, however. As a result of archaeological and linguistic studies since World War II, it is now generally agreed that Etruscans did not invade Italy at all but evolved from the earlier Villanovan culture. Etruscan culture developed as a result of contacts with the Greeks and other peoples of the eastern Mediterranean—especially of Egypt and the eastern shores of the Mediterranean (the Levant), rather than Asia Minor. In this way Oriental elements crept in.

Gradually, by superior military prowess, the Etruscans conquered the surrounding natives and formed the ruling class in a new society characterized by urbanization and an economy based on commerce, superior craftsmanship in metalworking, and agriculture. From about 700 to 400 B.C. the Etruscans were the most important people in Italy. At the height of their power they controlled Etruria and Campania, as well as most of the Po valley.

Latecomers to Italy were the Celts, or that branch of Celts known as Gauls. During the fifth century B.C. they were pushed from their homeland in the upper Danubian region by Germanic peoples farther north. Swarming over the Alps, they defeated the Etruscans and occupied much of the Po valley. A barbarous people who supported themselves by cattle raising and primitive agriculture, they nevertheless showed considerable skill and artistic ability in metalworking, their chief industry.

Though the Gauls were formidable warriors, they failed to achieve greater domi-

nance because of internal dissension. They formed eight tribes, which were often at war with one another, and even within the tribes there was "schismatic infighting."

History of Rome and the Empire

Roman Beginnings

Generations of students have been treated to a glorious tradition of the founding and early history of Rome. Actually the account goes back to the days of Caesar Augustus (27 B.C.–A.D. 14), when Livy, Dionysius of Halicarnassus, and Virgil (70–19 B.C.), among others, wove together the account on the basis of tradition and scraps of information available to them.

According to the story, Romulus founded the famous city in 753 B.C. on the Palatine Hill. Then seven kings ruled Rome between 753 and 509 B.C., the traditional date of the overthrow of the monarchy and the establishment of the Republic. The first four kings (Romulus, Numa Pompilius, Tullus Hostilius, and Ancus Marcius) were Latin or Sabine, and the last three (Tarquinius Priscus, Servius Tullius, and Tarquinius Superbus) were Etruscan.

Then during the nineteenth century higher criticism attacked the traditional history of Rome, as it did the Bible, Shakespeare, and much else. In the view of nineteenth century critics, the early history of Rome was largely a fabrication, a romanticizing of tradition that catered to the vanity of the great families of the late Republic.

But during the twentieth century, archaeology has increasingly made its contribution and has helped to confirm at least some of the traditional history. Discoveries have shown that in the tenth century B.C. a colony of Latins established themselves on the twenty-five acre flat-topped Palatine Hill, and that during succeeding generations several other Latin villages were founded on adjacent hills. At least some of the names of the seven kings appear to be historical, and some of their supposed activities evidently occurred. But we have more confirmation of activities or developments than we do of some of the names.

Though the date 753 B.C. probably has no special significance, Rome was certainly in

An Etruscan tumulus tomb at Caere.

existence by that time. In fact, it had been developing for a couple of centuries prior to B.C. 753. Rome also made the transition from the monarchy to the Republic about 500 B.C. Evidence also suggests that there were more kings than the traditional seven.

While Rome was gradually occupying her hills along the Tiber, the Etruscans were expanding their holdings in Italy. They established a number of city-states along the coast of Etruria by the seventh century B.C. Eventually they organized a league of twelve cities (the more important including, Tarquinii, Vulci, Caere, and Veii in the south; and Clusium, Cortona, and Perusia in the north). But Etruscan cities were autonomous and failed to develop a national purpose or loyalty that enabled them to stand together against Rome. Moreover, geographical barriers got in the way of effective unity.

During the sixth century the Etruscans moved into Campania and the Po valley and were at their height a little after 500 B.C. Their control of Campania did not result from any military invasion but from migration of Etruscans from some of the cities of Etruria. In addition to their landholdings along the west coast of Italy and in the Po region, the Etruscans were an effective sea power, ably contesting with the Greeks and Carthaginians for control of the western

Mediterranean. Formidable warriors and possessors of superior weapons, the Etruscans also built massive walls and fortifications around their cities. They became the ruling aristocracy in a society they effectively marshaled.

The basis of their economy was agricultural, but they also exploited the mineral wealth of the country, especially its copper and iron. Their temples had a wide and deep frontage. The front half was a colonnaded portico; the back comprised three shrines for three deities. The foundations were of stone, and the main framework of wood, which was covered with multicolored terracotta ornamentation. In the later centuries of Etruscan development tombs were built in rows of streets—as tumuli (as at Caere) or underground houses of the dead, (as at Caere and Tarquinii). At Tarquinii the walls were covered with gaily colored wall paintings showing scenes of banqueting, dancing, wrestling, hunting, fishing, and more.

The Etruscans were important to the urbanization of Italy and encouraged a movement from villages to towns. But they were unable to achieve an effective political unity. A collection of cities and their colonies held together by commercial, religious, and cultural ties, they were politically and militarily incapable of meeting their

Wall paintings in Etruscan shaft graves at Tarquinii. The Tomb of the Leopards (above) depicts a farewell scene. The Tomb of the Baron (below) shows an entertainment at a funeral banquet.

foes with a united front. In spite of rigid organization, the aristocracies were unable to prevent armed uprisings of the under-privileged or the artisan class. After their navy was severely defeated by the Greeks of Syracuse in 474 B.C., they became increasingly vulnerable to Roman offensives on their southern flank and pressures of the Gauls in the Po valley.

The Etruscans did not take control of Rome about 600 B.C., as formerly widely believed, but the city developed independently during the following century (600–500) under the leadership of its kings. The kings were responsible for the urban-ization of Rome, the training of an efficient army, for promoting economic advance-ment—especially in a robust commerce with Etruscans and Greeks and others, for improving Roman cultural life, and in short, for making Rome the leading state in Laium.

Of the last three kings, Tarquinius Priscus was not an Etruscan but the son of a Corinthian aristocrat who migrated to Tarquinii. Tauquinius found that his non-Etruscan parentage (Greek father and Tarquinian mother) was a hindrance to his political advancement in Tarquinii, so he moved to Rome where he was accepted and had a chance to make his fortune. He did not come with an Etruscan force to conquer the city, however.

Servius Tullius, the son of a slave, was brought up in the palace and succeeded to the kingship on the death of Tarquinius. Tarquinius Superbus was the son (or possibly grandson) of Priscus. Superbus openly persecuted the aristocracy, and they, rather than the proletariat, organized the revolution to overthrow him. And in fact the last two kings were anti-aristocratic and tried to break the aristocracy's hold on Rome—thus the revolution and the institution of the Republic—in which the aristocrats dominated. In their efforts to break the power of the aristocracy, the last kings resembled contemporary Greek tyrants who were trying to do the same in Greece.

While there is not much of a case to be made for Etruscan rule in Latium, the Romans did have extensive contact with them in commercial and other ways and extensively borrowed from them. From the Etruscans came such conventionally "Roman" items as the purple-embroidered toga, the eagle-headed scepter, and the use of the fasces (bundles of rods enclosing a double-edged ax—see the 1916–1945 American dime) as a symbol of political power. But the worship of the triad Jupiter, Juno, and Minerva apparently came from Greek rather than Etruscan influence, as formerly believed.

In short, though Rome was an independent Latin community with a cosmopolitan population and a sophisticated culture, its ways were similar to nearby Etruscan cities. Rome and the Etruscan cities shared a combination of Greek, oriental, and native Italic elements.[6]

Rome under the monarchy was ruled by a king-council-assembly type of government. The king, who was commander of the army as well as judge and priest, had immense power, especially under the Tarquins. Neither quite hereditary nor elective, the monarchal candidate was chosen by the senate and approved by the popular assembly. The Senate was the king's council. According to tradition, Romulus appointed a senate of a hundred to assist him in government. Whenever it began, the

senate certainly consisted of the leaders of Roman society; and the number increased to three hundred by the end of the monarchy or the beginning of the Republic.

As men of wealth and prestige in the community, the senators exercised considerable influence over the king. But the resolutions they passed were not binding on the monarch, nor did they have the force of law in the state. The king, however, could not afford to flout their wishes consistently. In addition to the power of *consultum*, the Senate had the right to nominate candidates for king.

The popular assembly (*Comitia Curiata*) was composed of all citizens capable of bearing arms. They voted by *curiae* (a political subdivision), which seemingly consisted of groups of related families organized for religious, political, and military purposes. Supposedly the assembly was the sovereign power in the state, but whatever power it had was largely passive. It met on call of the king, listened to debates held before it, and voted on issues submitted to it. It was present at the king's inauguration, and its members swore an oath of loyalty to him and participated in religious festivals at which the monarch presided. Whatever the political incapacity of the assembly, wise kings were careful not to ignore it, and they used its meetings as a propaganda platform to win support for their policies.

The Republic

Roman tradition concocted a glorious patriotic tale of the origin of the Republic. The story recounts the tyranny of Tarquinius Superbus, a violent revolution against the monarchy, and successful expulsion of the king and the Etruscans, against whom the Romans fought with remarkable valor. Almost immediately thereafter a Republic was established under the rule of two consuls and a firmly entrenched Latin nobility. All of this is supposed to have occurred in the year 509 or 508 B.C. There is considerable dispute among scholars as to how much of this story to accept.

It has become traditional to date the fall of the monarchy and Etruscan rule over Rome about 509/508 B.C. and to conclude that this change was revolutionary.

Moreover, most scholars have put the beginnings of the republican form of government near this time. Those who dispute this traditional view feel that the transition from the monarchy to the Republic was evolutionary rather than revolutionary, that the rule of consuls and other elected officials came as a result of trial and error over a number of decades, and that Etruscan power over Rome disintegrated in connection with their general economic and military decline early in the fifth century B.C. The present state of knowledge seems to require belief that the constitution of the Republic came about through a long and complicated process.

Actually it appears that the downfall of the kingship (Roman, not Etruscan, as noted elsewhere) resulted from a movement by nobility against centralizing measures undertaken by the king to curb their power. As it turned out, the power of the nobility was weakened anyway by changes in military tactics instituted by the kings. The dominant cavalry units drawn from the top class had diminished clout when the role of heavily-armed foot soldiers as shock troops increased. These troops fought in solid formation, or phalanx. And commoners wealthy enough to outfit themselves with body armor, shields, iron swords, and spears, fought the battles of the State. With their ability to defend the State came increased rights to rule the State. The reform of the military made Rome the leading military power in Latium, in a position to dominate ever-increasing chunks of real estate.

SIGNIFICANT RESULTS OF ROMAN CONQUESTS

In order to defeat the Etruscans, Rome had to establish a standing army—hence the beginnings of her powerful military machine.

As she sought to conquer the Italic tribes in the south of Italy, she began her famous highway system. By the end of the first Christian century she had built 250,000 miles of improved roads.

When she conquered the Greeks in the south, she fell under the cultural influence of the Greeks. Thus began the development of the Greco-Roman culture, which is at the basis of our own culture.

When she fought the Carthaginians overseas, she was forced to begin her famous navy.

When she took Gaul and Romanized that country, she laid the basis for a new civilization in the West.

Conquests involve more than merely fighting wars.

Unification of the Peninsula

Struggle with Etruscans. Around 500 B.C. Rome began a struggle with the Etruscans that was to last some two centuries. Around the same time must be dated the beginning of the Republic, during which Rome managed to dominate the entire Italian peninsula, to expand on three continents, and to democratize her constitution to some extent. Rome, however, never really wanted a democracy, nor did she achieve such a form of government. As has been said, apparently all the Romans were interested in was a "government of law rather than of men."

The generation of American leaders who wrote the Constitution of the United States, classically educated, were greatly influenced by Roman ideas and practices. They, too, wanted a Republic rather than a democracy. In the original document, as unamended or unmodified, the Senate held immense power (and still does) with its right to control appointments to the Supreme Court, the Cabinet, and more. And electors, not the people, voted for president. As in ancient Rome, senators may still pass a *Senatus Consultum*, a resolution showing the President their will but not binding on him.

Early in their struggle with the Etruscans, the Latins of Rome made a league with nearby Latin tribes against the common enemy. This league fell under the domination of Rome. The provisions of this alliance were extremely significant for the future development of Rome and the Empire. In addition to the expected arrangements concerning equal responsibility for providing troops in wartime and equal privileges in dividing spoils taken, there were important provisions relating to peacetime rights.

Citizens of every city in the league had the right to own property, to trade, and to enjoy the rights of the law in every other city of the league. Moreover, rights of intermarriage were guaranteed by the treaty. Therefore, if a Roman married a woman from a nearby Latin town, his children would enjoy full Roman citizenship and could vote in Rome if they moved there. In this way a bond of union was established that would serve as a pattern for the ultimate establishment of an Italian nationalism and imperial citizenship.

During the fifth century, Rome and the Latins were busy securing the borders of Latium against frequent attacks of the Italian tribes (of the Sabellian group). At the end of the century Rome fought a war to the death with Veii, an important Etruscan citadel a dozen miles north of Rome. At Veii's fall, Rome almost doubled her territory. During this war Rome learned that the maintenance of an effective force for siege purposes demanded the payment of troops and the establishment of a professional army. Here were the real beginnings of Roman military power.

Gallic threat. Hardly had Rome beaten the Veientes when sudden disaster swept down on them from the north. The Gauls, having dispossessed the Etruscans in the Po valley, broke into Etruria and Latium on a massive plundering expedition. Fierce, reckless warriors, the Gauls were able to break the ranks of even the disciplined Roman soldiers. While the remains of the Roman army holed up in the ruined fortifications of Veii, the rest of the population of unwalled Rome fled to nearby towns. And while a brave contingent of Romans held out on the fortified Capitoline Hill. the Gauls descend-

ed like vultures on the unoccupied city, thoroughly plundering it. It was at this time (c. 390 B.C.) that the records of early Rome were destroyed, a fact that has led to much uncertainty in the reconstruction of the city's early history.

Not interested in the annexation of Roman territory, the Gauls accepted a ransom, collected their souvenirs, and went home. The Romans promptly reoccupied and rebuilt their city, providing it with more adequate defenses. Though Gallic raiders again moved into the peninsula subsequently, they did not come as far south as Rome. A show of Roman force sent them home on the double in 349 B.C., and the Romans concluded a peace treaty with them in 331.

Latin League in rebellion. Meanwhile, Rome was having more serious trouble closer to home. Taking advantage of Rome's weakness, conquered Etruscan and Italic cities revolted. Some of the Latin towns, fearing loss of their independence, broke their alliance with Rome. Rome was eventually successful on every front. First she toppled the resistance of the Italic towns. By 350 B.C. she had soundly defeated the Etruscans. But by 340 the whole Latin League was in arms against Rome and had made an alliance with some of the cities of Campania.

During the subsequent Latin War, Rome first succeeded in detaching the Campanian cities from their Latin alliance and secured with them a favorable peace. Three of them, including the important town of Capua, received the Roman private rights enjoyed by the Latin cities (but not the right of franchise). Then Rome defeated the Latin League and dissolved it. Several of the Latin cities were incorporated into the Roman state with full citizenship rights. The rest were returned to their position as Latin allies. While they retained the rights of trade and intermarriage with Rome, they lost the privilege of exercising those rights with each other.

Roman conquest was not planned. Every time the Romans made a new conquest, their frontiers faced a new enemy. There was no logical stopping place until the Romans controlled the entire peninsula. By that time they faced new enemies beyond their shores and conquered them also. The process continued until they had mastered the entire Mediterranean world and penetrated some distance into the interior. It should be added that sometimes Rome became involved in areas beyond her frontiers because some power had appealed to her for armed intervention or to arbitrate a dispute.

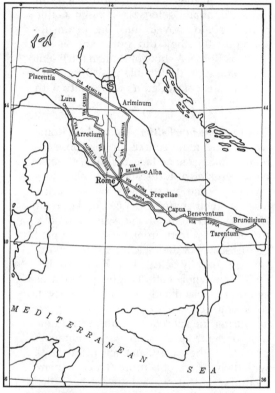

Major Roads in Italy. Rome began her famous highway system during the Samnite wars. The Appian Way (Via Appia) was the first road built.

Samnite attacks. One of the main reasons why the Campanian cities joined the Roman Republic was that they were periodically plagued by attacks of Samnite bands as they made sorties from their Apennine homeland. Not having sufficient land for expansion in their mountain valleys, the Samnites sought new homes among the rich acres of Campanian farmland. Rome found the task of defense against the Samnites to be costly indeed.

She fought two long and bitter wars with them: 326–304, 298–290 B.C.

To help them in fighting the first war, the Romans began their famous highway system. The first part of the Appian Way was laid in 312 B.C. and was completed as far as Capua in its initial stage. The Samnites were only slightly inferior to Rome in population size, and they were more adept at the kind of warfare that the rugged terrain demanded—at least in the early years of the war. At the end of the first war, which was bitterly fought, the Samnites retained nearly all of their territory in central Italy; but Rome was much stronger, having made several new allies during those years.

The second Samnite war was not to be won easily, however. The Samnites made joint cause with disaffected Etruscan cities of Etruria and with the Gauls, who had once more grown restless and were making sorties from their base in the Po valley. After hard fighting, Rome brought the Samnites to their knees in 290 B.C. Part of their land was added to the Roman public domain, and the Samnites became Roman allies. Rome now controlled the central part of the peninsula. But war was not over. Costly defeats stood between the Romans and their ultimate victory over the Etruscans and Gauls. When it finally came (in 280), Rome had annexed a considerable tract of Gallic territory in northwest Italy and forced Etruscan cities to resume their alliance with her.

Struggle with the Greeks. Hardly had the Romans concluded peace in the North when war clouds blew in from the South. During the latter half of the fourth century B.C., Greek cities in southern Italy suffered increasing attacks from the mountain peoples of that area. Tarentum, located on a gulf by the same name in the instep of the boot of Italy, was the largest and most powerful of the Greek cities and assumed a position of leader and protector of those cities. She was aided in this effort by mercenaries from Greece. Jealous of her own leadership over the other Greek cities, Tarentum had extracted treaties from Rome in 334 and 303 B.C. which guaranteed that Roman ships would not enter the Gulf of Tarentum.

In 282 Rome answered the appeal of Thurii in the upper part of the toe of Italy for help against attackers from the mountains. Winning a land battle, the Roman army left garrisons at Thurii and at Locri and Rhegium (in the toe of Italy), all of which had now allied themselves with Rome and received Roman protection. Tarentum was disturbed that her sphere of influence had been invaded. And when Roman warships entered the Bay of Tarentum, she attacked posthaste, sinking the ships.

Rome and the Greeks were now at war. Tarentum counted on the help of the mountain peoples of south Italy and, more especially, on some twenty-five thousand Greek troops from Epirus under the expert generalship of Pyrrhus. The forces of Pyrrhus included three thousand cavalry, two thousand archers, and twenty war elephants—a sort of armored tank of the times. Pyrrhus won the first engagement in 280—but with losses so heavy as to originate the expression "a Pyrrhic victory." The Greeks were now able to move up into Latium itself. Pyrrhus won another hard-fought battle in 279 B.C., he himself being wounded.

At a strategic moment, when Rome had entered into negotiations with the Greeks, Carthage threw in her weight on the side of Rome in an effort to keep Pyrrhus out of Sicily. But the Greek army decided to answer an appeal of Sicilian Greeks anyway and soon virtually drove the Carthaginians from the island. As Pyrrhus attempted to return to Italy, he lost part of his fleet to the Carthaginians. When the Romans subsequently defeated him, he decided to take most of his army back to Greece, where chances now seemed good for conquering Macedonia. Soon Tarentum and other Greek cities of southern Italy were subjugated and became Roman allies. After sporadic fighting elsewhere in Italy, Rome became mistress of the entire peninsula by 265.

Roman victory over the Greeks involved more than the glory of military success and the addition of territory in Italy. The Romans came upon the Greeks at a time in Roman history when they were beginning to develop their own cultural self-aware-ness. At that juncture the Romans fell under the spell of mature Greek culture and to a large degree adopted it as their own. In time what developed was a Greco-Roman culture that blanketed the entire Roman Empire. And the *lingua franca* (common language) of the Empire was Greek, though Latin was the language of government affairs.

Thus, during New Testament times there was a universal culture that dominated the whole Mediterranean world. As a result, those who spread the gospel in faraway places did not have to learn a new language or become familiar with a new culture (or suffer culture shock), as modern missionaries do. And of importance to all peoples of the Western World is the fact that this Greco-Roman culture was passed on through the Middle Ages and forms the basis of modern European and American culture.

Political Developments

As Rome conquered the peninsula, she developed a program of organizing and controlling the area. In general it may be said that this was a system of confederation. At the center was Rome and its surrounding territory where the citizen body, divided into thirty-five tribes, possessed full rights of every type. Then there were Latin and Italian allies, bound to Rome by treaty. The Latin allies enjoyed the privilege of intermarriage with Romans, had rights of trade with Rome, the protection of Roman law, the right of inheriting property, and, if they moved to Rome, the chance of voting as full citizens.

The Italian allies did not enjoy the rights of trade, marriage privileges, and protection of Roman law that the Latin allies possessed. But they did benefit, along with the Latin allies, from a new peace, security, and prosperity in Italy and exercised the prerogatives of government in their own communities, where a large measure of local autonomy existed. Both of these categories of allies were responsible for supplying troops or ships to the Roman military establishment.

In addition there were both Roman and Latin colonies established at strategic points throughout Italy. Roman colonies possessed full citizenship rights while Latin colonies possessed rights other than suffrage.

Thus defeated foes were not brought to extinction or mercilessly flattened. Rome imposed on them treaties of alliance providing for mutual defense and requiring troop contributions. Some of these alliances were entered voluntarily by tribal groups that sought to benefit from Roman protection. With every victory came a swelling of forces on which Rome could draw for further expansion. With each alliance Rome augmented her reservoir of manpower and with it came a self-perpetuating stimulus for imperialism.

The military and administrative successes of Rome were augmented or enhanced by a unique and generous expansion of the franchise. Beginning with the mutual interchange of citizenships in the Latin League, there was a steady expansion of private and civil rights of Roman citizens. Eventually all free persons on the peninsula gained Roman citizenship. Then emperors began to extend this privilege to the provinces. Finally in A.D. 212 all free persons in the Empire had access to Roman citizenship.

Constitutional changes. It is to be expected that a change from a monarchy to a republic and the expansion and internal development of Rome would bring about significant changes in the constitution. In the executive branch of the government, six groups of officials existed in 265 B.C.—consul, quaestor, rex, tribune, aedile, censor. All of these except the last were elected annually. Chiefs of state were the two consuls who also served as generals of the army. During periods of crisis a dictator might be chosen to rule for a six-month period. Quaestors supervised finance, and aediles administered public welfare. The rex (king) now presided over religious affairs. Tribunes had the responsibility of protecting plebians, or commoners. Censors, elected every five years for an eighteen-month term, took the census, supervised public morals, and arranged for important public construction.

Two praetors served—one in the judicial branch to supervise legal affairs of Romans and another to try cases of non-Romans carrying on business in the city.

In the legislative branch of the government, there were now three popular assemblies in addition to the Senate. The power of the old Assembly of the *Curiae* had dwindled to mere formality involving the right to install magistrates after their election. The Assembly of the Centuries—based on an organization of society according to ability to provide armor in time of war—elected consuls, praetors, and censors, declared war, and voted on laws submitted to it. The Assembly of the Tribes elected tribunes and quaestors and voted on laws presented by tribunes or consuls. It was perhaps the most important lawmaking body in the state.

The Senate possessed the power of consultation with consuls, who were reluctant to act contrary to the Senate's advice. This body also initiated and formulated legislation submitted to the assemblies. Senators served for life and were appointed by the consuls—who came mostly from certain patrician families. If a consul was not already a senator before taking office, he automatically became one at the end of his term of office.

Social conflicts. The changes in the Roman constitution between 500 and 265 B.C. were accompanied by and often caused by conflicts on the social scene. The patrician nobility held strong control over social, economic, and political affairs of state. Gradually the plebians (commoners) were able to force the patricians to relax that hold. It should not be concluded, however, that the plebians consisted only of the poor masses. Among them was quite a social graduation: there were rural and urban poor, merchants, craftsmen, and laborers.

The first great political victory of the plebians came about 471 B.C. At that time the Assembly of the Tribes won the right to pass laws binding on the plebians. About the same time they elected the first tribunes, who had the power of protecting any plebian against an act of some magistrate being enforced against him. A century later the consulate—and therefore the senate— was opened to plebians. By the Ogulnian Law of 300 B.C., all offices were opened to commoners. And in 287, by virtue of the Hortensian Law, legislation passed by the Assembly of the Tribes became binding on all without consent of the senate.

About twenty years after the plebians won the right to pass legislation binding on themselves, they reaped a judicial victory. The Valerio-Horatian Laws of 451–449 B.C. provided for codification of the Twelve Tables of the law and made legal provisions, previously known only to the nobility, available to all. Once familiar with those provisions, commoners had more adequate recourse to the law.

Some five years later the plebians obtained the right to marry into the patrician class. Subsequently society was grouped in three classes: the Optimates (landed aristocracy); the Equites (those with money wealth); and the plebians. Supposedly the plebians won an economic victory in the passage of the Licinian-Sextian Laws (367–362 B.C.); but that legislation, designed to limit the amount of land a man right hold, was never effective. Soon those statutes were dead.

Actually the plebians gained their rights on more than one occasion by withholding their services from the state until their demands were met. Those services were basically military. As Rome's military needs increased, larger numbers of conscripts were required. Therefore the plebs could exercise greater leverage politically. The ruling classes did not yield to a sense of social justice but to the momentum of territorial growth and its requirements. Moreover, the patrician families simply did not have enough personnel to fill the increasing numbers of government posts and to monopolize all the civil and military functions of a growing society. So they had to allow plebian leaders to participate in Rome's expansionist activities. The resulting compromises and the political and social stability they brought helps to explain Rome's success in Italy and later abroad. When a sufficiently large percentage of the population has a stake in the state, there is greater health in the body politic.

The Punic Wars

The Romans had hardly completed the conquest of peninsular Italy when they became embroiled in a series of foreign wars with Carthage. The immediate cause of these wars was an appeal from Messana (Messina) in Sicily. The background for the appeal was this. The Carthaginians occupied the western part of Sicily, and Greek colonists held the eastern part. Chief of the Greek cities was Syracuse, located in the southeastern part of the island. A considerable number of Campanian mercenaries had contracted to serve in the army of the king of Syracuse and later defected and shut themselves up in the town of Messana, just across the straits from the toe of Italy. Fearing certain defeat by Syracuse, the Messanians looked to Carthage for help. The latter, eager to give any assistance that would prevent Syracusan expansion, sent a garrison to Messana.

At this point the Messanians decided they did not want to be ruled by Carthage and sought alliance with Rome. Although the Senate recognized that Carthaginian control of Messana would put this North African power in a position to dominate the narrow sea-lanes[7] between Sicily and Italy and endanger the Italian mainland, they were loath to answer the appeal. Therefore, the Senate sent the request to one of the popular assemblies, probably the Centuriate. Though war-weary, the people were persuaded by their leaders to accept Messanian alliance, thereby beginning a devastating war to the death between the two great powers of the western Mediterranean.

Historians argue that the causes of the Punic Wars involved the question of who was to control Sicily, the basic ethnic difference between the two peoples (Carthage—Semitic; Rome—Indo-European), and a growing economic and national rivalry between Rome and Carthage in the western basin of the Mediterranean. So it seemed only a question of time before they locked horns.

But none of this seems to provide the real reason for Roman involvement. Rome acted on a specific appeal. And she had numerous Greek allies in southern Italy who were worried about Carthaginian control of the straits between Italy and Sicily, Carthaginian control of the trade routes

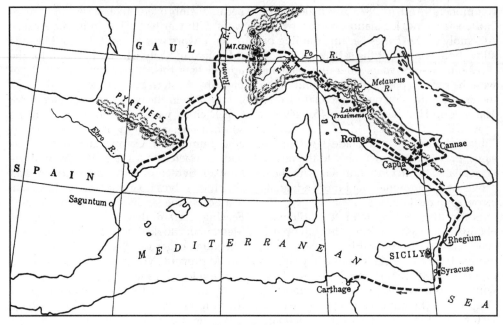

Hannibal's March

that provided the economic lifeblood of those allies, and the Carthaginian control of Sicily that threatened those allies. It was the Roman alliance system that led Rome to act. Some show of force on Rome's part was necessary in order to retain the allegiance of her allies in Italy.

The First Punic War. Whatever Rome's initial intent, for almost a quarter century she engaged Carthage on land and sea in the First Punic War (264–241 B.C.). The war was fought very largely for control of Sicily and was waged principally on the sea. At the beginning of the war, Carthage was a naval power, but Rome was not. In constructing her navy, Rome could count on Greek naval allies of southern Italy to supply her with ships already built, with some knowledge of shipbuilding, and with crews for new ships under construction. But primarily Rome built a navy from scratch on the model of a captured Carthaginian galley. And men trained on dry land while the ships were under construction. Rome made effective use of the quinquereme (fives), probably a ship with five men on each oar—to achieve considerable speed. In this case only one of the rowers needed to be

experienced, important to Rome which was working largely with raw recruits.

The Roman method of fighting involved simply a transferal of land warfare to the sea. To aid them in this transfer, they employed the corvus principle, which involved the use of a gangplank with a huge iron spike at the end of it. When a Roman ship came close enough to a Carthaginian man-of-war, it simply lowered this gangplank. The two ships were locked together by the huge spike, and Roman soldiers poured onto the enemy ship and captured it.

After a hard-fought struggle, Rome won the first Punic conflict in 241 B.C. It has been estimated that Rome's losses were about six hundred ships and two hundred thousand men. She lost whole fleets as a result of storms or military action. At one point, as Rome was faced with a crash program of rebuilding the fleet, the public treasury was nearly empty and wealthy families made large contributions to the war effort. Rome was so drained financially by the war effort that in the terms of the peace treaty she imposed a large indemnity on Carthage. The treaty also gave her Sicily and some smaller islands.

The scene at Lake Trasimene where Hannibal trapped a Roman army between the lake and the hills.

During the next few years, contrary to the terms of the treaty, Rome found an excuse for taking Corsica and Sardinia, and the Tyrrhenian Sea became a Roman lake. Next, Rome got involved in protecting Greek allies in southern Italy against pirates operating from Illyria (modern Yugoslavia) and the area of modern Albania. In dealing with this menace, she established a protectorate over part of the Illyrian coast. This action alarmed Macedonia (who felt that Rome was invading her sphere of influence) and led to Rome's friendship with the Aetolian and Achaean leagues, enemies of Macedon.

In the midst of dealing with the threat from Illyria, Rome had to meet the Gauls on the battlefield once more. They were being pushed into Roman territory by new migrations from north of the Alps. In squelching the Gallic threat, Rome advanced her frontier to the southern foothills of the Alps.

In retaliation or compensation for her losses, Carthage moved farther north into Spain, establishing her border at the Ebro River, which flows into the Mediterranean south of Barcelona. Carthage got much silver, copper, iron, foodstuffs, and fish from Spain. The income provided resources to pay off Carthage's indemnity to Rome.

Second Punic War. It soon became clear that the peace of 241 B.C. was merely a truce. The western Mediterranean apparently was not big enough for the two powers. So war started again in 218. The immediate issue involved Saguntum (Sagunto) in Spain. Carthaginian expansion northward had been limited by treaty to the Ebro River in Spain. Saguntum was a Roman ally south of the river. Tensions around the Spanish town developed to the point that Carthaginian forces under the leadership of Hannibal attacked it in 218. At that point Rome did nothing to rescue her ally. This inactivity led Hannibal to believe that he could advance the Carthaginian border all the way to the Pyrenees Mountains and get away with it. As he did so Rome decided to act.

Rome's strategy was to send an army to Spain to detain the great Hannibal there, while she prepared an army for an African campaign. Since she controlled the seas (Carthage had never rebuilt her fleet), Rome thought she could effectively take the offensive. However, she planned without the genius of Hannibal, who determined to cross the Pyrenees Mountains, cut through southern Gaul, traverse the Alps, and invade Italy. The Carthaginian general counted heavily on Gallic and Italian defections to enable him to destroy the Roman confederation and bring Rome to her knees.

Hannibal made the difficult crossing of the Alps—but at the cost of almost half of his forces and nearly all his war elephants. He arrived in Italy with about twenty-five thousand infantry and six thousand cavalry. After a brief rest, Hannibal faced a Roman attack in northwestern Italy. A Roman army of about forty thousand crossed the swollen Trebia River (a tributary of the Po) in December of 218 and launched a frontal attack on Hannibal's forces. Almost immediately Hannibal attacked the Roman flank and rear with troops held in concealment and mowed down the Romans. With their retreat cut off by the flooded stream, they had no choice but to try to hack their way through the Carthaginian center. Only about ten thousand of the forty thousand managed to escape. After this disaster the Romans withdrew their forces from northern Italy and Hannibal wintered in the Po valley. There he welcomed recruits, especially from the recently-defeated Gauls, and built his force to about fifty thousand.

In the spring of 217 the Romans were ready to try again. But so was Hannibal. He slipped through an unguarded Apennine pass into Etruria and then drew a Roman defense force of twenty-five thousand under the command of Flaminius after him to Lake Trasimene. When the Romans, careless about reconnaissance, marched between the lake and the adjacent hills, Hannibal attacked their flank and their rear from behind the foothills. Almost the entire Roman army perished along the shore or in the waters of the lake.

The invaders now had an open road to Rome, but were without equipment and supplies for a long siege. Moreover, not a single town of central Italy threw open its gates to the Carthaginians. Therefore Hannibal decided to try his luck in southern Italy. There in 216, in Apulia near the Adriatic, he fought the great battle of Cannae. This time Hannibal fought in an open position, so the Romans had nothing to fear from hidden reserves. But Hannibal was the superior strategist. He threw his center well forward and then permitted it to retreat under Roman attack. Meanwhile his wings held firm until the line resembled a huge crescent with the Romans crowded between its encircling horns. To complete the encirclement, the Carthaginian cavalry defeated the Roman cavalry on the wings

and then proceeded to attack the Roman legions from the rear. Surrounded on all sides, the Roman army was cut to pieces. Depending on which ancient Roman historian we follow, the Romans lost fifty thousand or sixty thousand, or possibly even seventy thousand men on the field that day. The real figure was probably under fifty thousand.

The terrible loss of life in terms of sheer numbers was bad enough. But at that point in time Roman recruitment concentrated on citizens from the propertied classes. So, many of the leaders in society were lost, including eighty senators and other officials. Worse, several of Rome's important allies defected—including Syracuse and Capua. Worse yet, Philip V of Macedon sensed a chance to bring Rome down, so he made an alliance with Hannibal. This, like Rome's earlier involvement in Illyria, contributed to Rome's later military involvement in the Greek East. In fact, on this occasion the Aetolian League, Sparta, and Pergamum joined the war on the side of Rome, keeping Philip occupied and making Roman sending of an expeditionary force unnecessary.

Rome fought on doggedly, harassing but not fighting Hannibal, reconquering defecting allies in Italy, and taking Spain and thus depriving Carthage of its recruiting ground. Moreover, and very significantly, a Roman army defeated Hasdrubal, Hannibal's brother, in 207 at the Battle of the Metaurus River in northeast Italy. Hasdrubal had courageously managed to bring Carthaginian reinforcements over the Pyrenees and Alps to aid Hannibal. Rome cut the army to pieces, depriving Hannibal of help when he desperately needed it, and thus doomed Carthage ultimately to defeat. Interestingly, Edward S. Cressy in his *Fifteen Decisive Battles of the World* (covering the beginnings to Waterloo) includes the battle of the Metaurus River. The battle certainly was pivotal in determining whether Rome or Carthage was to control the western Mediterranean. From this point on Carthage knew she was doomed to defeat.

Finally, in 204 B.C., the Roman general Scipio crossed over into Africa and won victories that caused Carthage to sue for peace. With a preliminary peace treaty drawn up and the war nearly over, Hannibal embarked for home, having maintained himself in enemy territory for almost fifteen years and having effected great destruction in Italy.

On the return of Hannibal, Carthage received a transfusion of valor and confidence which caused her to break the truce and prepare for one last major battle with Rome. The battle took place at Zama in North Africa in 202 B.C. The two skilled generals, Hannibal and Scipio, pitted all their skill against each other. Scipio introduced the tactic of the long line, sending reserves from behind the lines to the right and left to prevent encirclement. But what helped to clinch Hannibal's defeat was the fact that at the crucial moment a contingent of Carthaginian mercenaries mutinied.

Scipio's triumph was complete. By terms of the peace treaty, Rome was granted both a huge reparation and Spain. The Carthaginian army and navy were disbanded. Yet in spite of her apparent triumph, Rome never quite recovered from the ravages of Hannibal's fifteen years in Italy. Thousands of small farmers lost their livestock, their farm buildings, and their homes. After the war they sold out to the large landholders. The virility of the lower middle class in Italy was greatly affected. Many moved to Rome where they constituted part of the unemployed mob depending on the largess of the state.

Third Punic War. The end of Carthage was not yet. During the next fifty years she achieved a certain amount of recovery through raising olives and grapes and through successful mercantile activity. Finally Rome waged another war against her (149–146 B.C.) and utterly destroyed the city. A particularly bloodthirsty element was dominant in Rome in 146 B.C., and it dictated the obliteration of both Carthage and Corinth in Greece, for reasons that are hard to discover at this distance. Rome sowed Carthage with salt. The land controlled by the once proud metropolis became the province of Africa.

Conquest of the East

A significant international effect of the Punic Wars was to involve Rome in affairs of the Hellenistic East. This involvement led ultimately to Roman control of the eastern basin of the Mediterranean.

It is important to note that Pyrrhus of Epirus had provided effective help for the Greeks of southern Italy in their struggle against Rome early in the third century B.C. Between the First and Second Punic Wars, Rome found it necessary to protect her shores against Illyrian pirates. Her activity in the East at that time led to favorable relations with Aetolian and Achaean leagues in Greece and to the hostility of Macedon. During the Second Punic War, Philip V of Macedon made an alliance with Hannibal, so by then Rome had been involved in warfare in the East for some ten years (215–205 B.C.). During those years Rome's command of the sea made it difficult for Philip to bring effective aid to Hannibal in Italy. Moreover, Rome's allies in the East —the Aetolian League, Athens, Sparta, and Pergamum—kept Macedon and the Achaean League so busy that it was unnecessary for Rome to become very directly involved. Philip was forced to make peace with the Roman Senate in 205.

The eastern Mediterranean faced changing conditions in the aftermath of the Second Punic War with its accompanying Macedonian War. Earlier there had been a relative balance of power between Macedonia, Ptolemaic Egypt, and Seleucid Syria. But now there was a boy king on the throne of Egypt, and Macedonia and Syria sought to take advantage of Egypt's weakness. The two made a secret treaty in 203 B.C. according to which they would take Egypt's overseas possessions. Syria took Palestine from Egypt and soon introduced conditions that led to the Maccabean revolt there, and Macedonia moved against Egyptian possessions in the Aegean region. Rome might have looked at the breakdown of the balance of power in the East and have gotten involved out of fear of what that might mean to her. Actually, they did not take that larger view but responded instead to appeals from her friends in the region.

Rhodes was upset over Macedonian advances in the Aegean and her treatment of subject Greek states. Pergamum joined Rhodes in its opposition to Macedonia and was suffering military defeat at the hands of Macedonia, so the two appealed to Rome for help and presumably told Rome about the Syro-Macedonian pact. Meanwhile Athens had suffered an attack from Philip's allies and called on Rome for protection. In addition, Philip was trying to woo Illyria from its alliance with Rome. The Senate responded with a call for war, but the Centuriate Assembly initially refused—the people were too exhausted from the Second Punic War. At length Rome demanded that Philip refrain from war with any Greek state and that he submit his conflict with Attalus of Pergamum to arbitration. In effect they were reducing Philip to the status of a client prince and Greece to a Roman protectorate. The details of negotiations and of the war are beyond the scope of this book.

It is enough to say that the Second Macedonian War lasted from 200 to 196 B.C. and that it ended with a Roman victory. Rome recognized the value of Macedonia as a bulwark against the Celts along the Danube and so did not seek the destruction of the Macedonian state. Rome exacted an indemnity from Macedonia, the dissolution of the Macedonian navy, the autonomy of all Greek states that had been dominated by Philip, and an alliance between Philip and Rome.

While Rome was busy with Philip, the Seleucid Antiochus III conquered Palestine, Ephesus, and other Greek cities held by the Ptolemies. By 195 B.C. Antiochus had crossed the Hellespont (Dardanelles) into Europe and had begun the conquest of Thrace. As the Syrians moved farther into Greece, Rome issued an ultimatum demanding that they turn back. The result of this demand was the establishment of spheres of influence. Rome was not to interfere in Asia Minor, and Antiochus was to stay out of Greece.

The arrangement was quite satisfactory until the Aetolians staged a revolt against Rome and tried to set up alliances, calling upon Antiochus for help. Then began the Third Macedonian War (192–189 B.C.), sometimes called an Asiatic war. At the battle of Thermopylae in 191, the Romans drove Antiochus from Greece and the following year at Magnesia (southeast of Ephesus) brought the Syrian to his knees, forcing him to pay an indemnity, to surrender his navy, and to give up most of Asia Minor. Rome did not annex this territory but followed her old policy of curbing the strong and strengthening the weak, leaving a group of mutually jealous states to check each other.

The Greek world remained outwardly quiet for about two decades, but there was much agitation under the surface. The Greek states were very discontent at finding themselves subject allies of Rome. Finally Perseus of Macedon resolved to free his country from Rome's dictation. Inheriting from his father an army of over thirty thousand, a full treasury, and an anti-Roman policy, he exhibited unwarranted confidence in his ability to stand up to Rome. A Roman ultimatum to come to terms was refused and war broke out in 171 B.C. For some two years the Romans "muddled through," but in 168 their victory at the Battle of Pydna ended the kingdom of Macedon and the country was divided into four states under Roman direction. Royal mines and domains became Roman property and other Greek states were dealt with sternly. Rome took a thousand hostages from the Achaean League, among them the great historian Polybius. These hostages were important for the process of Hellenization at Rome.

But Rome was still not ready to assume the responsibility of direct government. She made an occasional display of force but was not ready to annex territory and make it part of her empire. Twenty years later, however, this situation was to change. In 149 B.C. another Macedonian rebellion occurred, which was crushed after initial successes by the rebels. During the following year Rome organized the country as a Roman province.

However, troubles in Greece were not yet over; rebellion erupted among states of the Achaean League in 147. Of course the rebels were no match for Roman legions. The League was disbanded, and Corinth was made a terrible object lesson. In 146 it was sacked and burned. Carthage was destroyed in the same year—both under the stern new policies of Cato.

Though Macedonia was organized as a Roman province in 148 B.C. with Thessalonica as capital, it is unclear what happened to the rest of Greece. The New Testament speaks of two provinces there: Macedonia and Achaia (Acts 19:21; Romans 15:26; 1 Thessalonians 1:7–8), and generally of Macedonia and Greece (Acts 20:1–2). It does not appear that Achaia was constituted as a separate province after the suppression of the Achaean revolt in 146 B.C. Probably it was for some purposes subjected to the governor of Macedonia. Then in 27 B.C. Achaia became a senatorial province and included Achaia, Thessaly, and Epirus. Its capital was Corinth. Between A.D. 15 and 44 Achaia was ruled by the emperor as an imperial province. But in A.D. 44 (under Claudius) it again became a senatorial province and was ruled by a proconsul. So when Paul went there in 50 or 51, Gallio was the proconsul (Acts 18:12), appointed by the Senate. At that time the province excluded an important group of free cities, notably Athens, Sparta, and Delphi.

A Century of Revolution

A nation always purchases an empire at an enormous price. The cost to Rome of acquisition of lands abroad was frightful indeed and was most effectively related to the tragedy of the Second Punic War. During the fifteen years that Hannibal stalked the Italian countryside, it was often impossible for the citizen assemblies to meet. The Senate gradually assumed the powers of the purse, of handling foreign affairs, and of exercising the normal legislative functions of state. Because of these developments, the constitutional balance was upset.

Also, Hannibal's living off the countryside had ruined a large percentage of the class of citizen farmers. Unable to restock their pilfered farms, they sold their holdings to wealthy landlords who worked their estates largely with slave labor or who converted the land to the raising of sheep, olives, or grapes, which required less help. Changes in agriculture resulted in problems in food production and an increase in the price of food. Grains increasingly had to be imported from Sicily and later from Egypt. The gradual depopulation of the countryside reduced considerably the number of men from whom military levies could be drawn, for to this point in time only Roman citizens with a stipulated amount of property could be drafted into the Roman legions. Moreover, those who left the farms generally drifted to Rome, where they swelled the unemployed mass that was such a burden to the State.

All of the small farmers of Italy who left their lands did not do so because of the depredations of Hannibal, however. In earlier years Roman military service normally lasted only a few months at a time. Now, many men, finding it necessary to be away from home for years at a time on active duty, mortgaged their property heavily to support their families and finally went bankrupt. Too, they often found farm life rather dull after life in service. Also, the slow gains won from the soil required much more patience than the fast gains through spoils of war available to the successful soldier.

Another problem that Rome faced as a result of imperialism was class conflict. The middle class that was rising before the wars benefited greatly from the wars because of the peculiar way in which Rome attempted to supply her wartime needs. Rather than attempting to supply the military directly, the government contracted with private concerns to deliver goods to the army and navy. The rising middle class also became rich by exploiting the provinces. This new class of men with money wealth (Equites) soon contested with the old aristocracy with wealth in lands (Optimates) for political power, which the latter then effectively held.

SLAVERY IN THE ROMAN EMPIRE

Slavery was extensive in Rome and the empire. In fact, hundreds of thousands of new slaves were needed every year. Wealthy people in the towns kept large numbers of them, often more for show than for needed services. The large farms of southern Italy required many to work the land and to watch the flocks and herds.

Source of Slaves

Slaves became available especially as captives in war. Claudius' conquests in Britain and Vespasian's and Titus' capture of a hundred thousand Jews during the revolt that resulted in the destruction of Jerusalem in A.D. 70 are examples in point. Others were captured in border skirmishes or were obtained in trade with peoples just beyond the borders of empire. Some were born in slavery. Unwanted infants were sometimes brought up in slavery. Kidnapping and piracy netted many slaves.

Condition of Slaves

The lot of slaves in the empire was not as bad as often has been the case in slave-holding societies. They had no identifying mark and were the same color as freemen. Though slaves couldn't wear togas, any citizen engaged in a variety of tasks didn't either. So slaves could not be differentiated from freemen on the streets. Though presumably slaves and all their possessions belonged to their masters, owners generally allowed them to keep any tips or other funds they could accumulate. Sometimes they could even buy their freedom. Finally, slaves were generally regarded as human beings, who might even become citizens.

Economic Results of Slavery

The existence of slaves tended to reduce the wages free laborers could expect, since wages were determined by the cost of buying and maintaining slaves. Slavery on the large farms tended to drive the small free farmer out of agriculture. Then, when such dispossessed farmers moved to town, they could not find employment because of the competition of slave labor. The fact that slaves performed most labor tended to cause upper classes to look on all labor as servile and beneath the dignity of a free person.

Moral Results of Slavery

The fact that upper-class people had at their command individuals over which they had absolute control and could order them around as they wished had terrible effects on them. It tended to make the upper classes immune to any consideration of the rights of lower-class citizens or of human rights in general. Slavery also had terrible effects on the slaves themselves. Torn from the inhibitions of their settled societies (family bonds, laws, public opinion, etc.), and made to live under conditions where they were not supposed to have any moral judgments of their own, they tended to lose all sense of right and wrong. The only control was force or fear of force. Worse, hundreds of these slaves were freed every year. What had made them good slaves made them terrible citizens.

Freeing of Slaves

Slaves could be freed fairly easily in Rome. Loyal service sometimes brought the reward of freedom. Or it might come through the provisions of the last will of their masters. Occasionally slaves bought their freedom. In Rome itself freedmen and their descendants far outnumbered citizens of Roman and Italian stock during the first century A.D.

In acquiring an empire, Rome had found a new and unhealthy basis for her economy. She was now living too largely from the exploitation of the Empire. Benefits from such exploitation went into the pockets of the Optimates and the Equites, not the common people. And an increasing percentage of Rome's labor force consisted of slaves taken in war. These competed with the free labor force, to the detriment of the latter. On occasion slave rebellions threatened the very peace and safety of the State. A number of such revolts occurred in the years just prior to 133 B.C.

Revolts of other kinds occurred during those years too. Especially fierce were the rebellions in Spain 154–133 B.C. Roman reverses there made Tiberius Gracchus determined to return the Italian peasants to their lands and thereby provide new military strength for the state by restoring a basic source of manpower.

Yet another area where Rome experienced rising tension in 133 was in her relations with the Italian allies. Rome used them but did not give them booty. Their citizenship rights were limited. And the Equites kept allied merchants from the profits of war.

In these times of stress the Senate failed to give the necessary leadership to the State. Accepting privileges without the corresponding responsibilities, this body failed to discover a satisfactory solution to the problems that threatened to bring the Republic down in a heap. The senatorial class was bitterly opposed to any changes of the existing order that would affect their position in government and society. So adamant was their stand and so rapidly did the problems increase that revolution seemed inevitable. Opponents within the senatorial class often were not much less selfish or less responsible in their statesmanship than senatorials as a group, and it must be borne in mind that much of the leadership for the reform movements did come from the senatorial class.

The Gracchi. The lid blew off the political caldron in 133 B.C. In that year Tiberius Sempronius Gracchus, newly elected tribune, submitted to the Assembly of the Tribes a land law designed to limit the estates of the wealthy. The head of a house might own as much as 350 acres, and two sons might possess an equal amount, for a total of 700 acres for a household. Initially Tiberius seems to have been concerned about restoring the peasants to their land in order to provide a source of military manpower and to solve some of the food problem of Italy. While Italians had traditionally grown grain, owners of the large estates raised cattle, sheep, olives, and grapes, and there was now an actual shortage of food in Rome. Parenthetically, it should be noted that agricultural changes in southern Italy had especially come about because of over-pasturage and deforestation. Moreover, extensive naval expansion had resulted in denuding the hillsides of trees, allowing widespread erosion. Therefore, olive orchards and vineyards began to replace grain farms.

There was nothing particularly new or revolutionary about a land bill. Rome had had such for centuries. But this bill challenged the social and economic position of the Optimates, and it forecast a change in the political control which the Senate had enjoyed since the days of the Second Punic War. Putting legislation through the Assembly of the Tribes was something of a revolution in itself. Worse than that, Tiberius introduced an unconstitutional election of recall when his fellow tribune threatened to veto the land bill, at the instigation of the Senate. When the recall failed, Tiberius simply overrode the veto.

Then the Senate threatened to render the land reform ineffective by failing to appropriate sufficient funds for its operation. At that juncture, Attalus III (Philometor), King of Pergamum, conveniently died and left his kingdom (which became the province of Asia) to the Roman people. Tiberius proposed to use Attalus' treasury to finance his program, thereby challenging the Senate's power of the purse. However, Tiberius' term of office was ending. When he stood for an unprecedented second term, the Senate provoked a riot in which he was assassinated.

Tiberius Gracchus was no rabble-rousing demagogue. He himself was an aristocrat with a conservative aim: restoration of the dislocated rural poor to the land. He did resort to unconventional methods, but his reform was as much in the interests of the aristocracy as the commoners. We cannot know his personal ambitions because his career was cut short. With the passage of time he might have gotten stars in his eyes and sought high office.

After the death of Tiberius, his younger brother Gaius continued active on the agrarian commission. In 124 B.C., on return from a quaestorship in Sardinia, Gaius offered himself for the tribunate, with the hope of making the land distribution program more effective. More politically astute than Tiberius, he tried to organize a political party, composed of political "outs"—Equites (wealthy business magnates outside the ranks of the senatorial class) and the plebians. He converted the tribuneship, previously an agency of the Senate, into an instrument of almost absolute power. His example was followed by others in the future, notably Julius Caesar, who rose to power through the tribunate.

Gaius appealed to the Equites by making them jurymen to try senators who misgoverned provinces, by indemnifying them for war losses sustained while executing State contracts, and by giving them the right to contract for tax collection in the wealthy province of Asia. He appealed to the masses with a program of cheap grain and an increase of acreage available in the land distribution program. The grain made available inexpensively to the Roman masses at this time was later given to them, and the dole was continued until the fall of Rome. Gaius attempted to placate the senators by declaring off limits for land distribution certain areas where their holdings were most extensive.

Although Tiberius had been unsuccessful at reelection, Gaius did manage a second term. But during his second term he made a dual proposal that was very dangerous to his political career: citizenship for the Latin allies and promotion of Italian allies to the status of Latin allies. Whether he was a courageous statesman risking his life on a piece of enlightened legislation, as some historians claim, or whether he turned to the Latins for support as he saw his political clientele being eroded by his opponents, is something of a question.

At any rate, he made the proposal, and the Senate determined to rid itself of him. Passing a decree of martial law, they dispatched a senatorial posse that routed and killed some 250 Gracchans and executed thousands more after farcical trials. Thus ended the period of her reformers. Apparently Rome's problems were not to be solved by legislative means.

As was true of Tiberius, Gaius' program was not revolutionary. It proposed a broadening of the political base, a sharing of power with groups outside the ruling oligarchy, some relief for the lower classes, and more generous treatment of Rome's allies in Italy. The senatorial oligarchy was not yet ready to make such extensive concessions. But the Gracchan legacy could not be so easily swept away.

Marius. Marius was one of the few politicians of the period to come from a class other then the senatorial nobility. An equestrian, he rose to fame through a military career. After service in the cavalry in Spain, he held the office of tribune in 119 B.C., of praetor in 116, and of propraetor in Spain in 115. He next appeared during the Jugurthine war in North Africa (111–105). Dissatisfaction in Rome with the progress of the war and with senatorial bungling in the conduct of the war effort led a coalition of Equites and popular leaders to elect Marius to the consulship for the year 107 and thus to the command of the troops in Africa.

In recruiting troops for the Jugurthine War, Marius broke all precedents by accepting as volunteers all who were physically fit, regardless of property qualifications. He created a professional long-term army for which men volunteered for sixteen to twenty years. He introduced improvements in weapons and organization and developed an army with a loyalty often greater to its commander than to the State. From then on, Rome was faced with the problems of a personal army in the State and the provision of rewards for veterans, especially land, when they were mustered out of service.

With his new army behind him, Marius prosecuted the war with vigor. As this war and other threats plaguing the state required more than a one-year consulship, Marius was elected for an unprecedented seven-term consulship, in a day when a ten-year interval was supposed to elapse between consulships. These many reelections came as a result of a menace from north European tribes along the Alpine border and the fear of a repetition of the Gallic sack of Rome in 390 B.C. Marius' success was phenomenal. The invaders were virtually annihilated.

Mithridates, king of Pontus

Rome: The Latin allies remained loyal, as did a number of municipalities and rural areas throughout Italy. But the two-year war (90–88 B.C.) was a bloody one, especially because so many veterans of Roman wars fought in the rebel army, and the havoc created must have approximated that of the Second Punic War in many communities.

Although Rome commanded the seas and could bring in troops and supplies from the provinces, what really broke the rebellion was the *lex Julia,* which conferred citizenship on all Latins and Italians still loyal to Rome and to those who would at once lay down their arms. Subsequent legislation granted full citizenship to all free persons living south of the Po River.

The Mithridatic War. As Italy counted her dead and set her house in order after the civil war, a new threat loomed in the East. Mithridates VI, the Great, king of Pontus in Asia Minor, took the offensive and swept all Roman opposition before him. As he advanced into the province of Asia, the inhabitants welcomed the chance to make the Romans pay for their forty years of oppression. The whole province rebelled, slaughtering (on order of Mithridates) seventy-five thousand Italians in one day (mostly tax agents, moneylenders, and merchants), according to some. Next Mithridates advanced into Greece, taking most of the southern part of the country and massacring the merchant and slave-trading population of Delos. The island never recovered. The people of Athens seized control of the state and joined Mithridates.

Having won his victories and having served his consulships, Marius dropped out of sight for several years. Although he had the power to become a dictator, he refused to use his army to attain that position.

Civil War. While Marius was in retirement, Marcus Livius Drusus the Younger, an idealistic senator who had been elected tribune, attempted a reform program, including citizenship for Italians. Italian veterans sought citizenship so they could gain land distribution given to Roman legionnaires, and Italian business and commercial classes wanted the same kind of economic opportunities available to their Roman counterparts. Some Italians wanted the chance to pursue political careers in Rome. Drusus did not try to stir the proverbial hornet's nest but attempted to avoid the civil war that would certainly come if Rome failed to let the Italians have their way. For his efforts he was stabbed by an unknown assailant.

Almost immediately the flames of rebellion swept like a prairie fire from the Gulf of Tarentum to the Po. The insurgents established a confederacy they called "Italia," with a government modeled on that of

Two generals were particularly eager for the appointment to the Mithridatic command: Marius and Sulla. Marius wanted to recover his lost popularity, and Sulla desired a road to power and fame. The Senate awarded the command to Sulla. All might have gone well, if it had not been for the actions of a tribune named Rufus who managed to force passage in the Assembly of the Tribes of an omnibus bill that replaced Sulla with Marius in the command against Mithridates.

Sulla returned to Rome at the head of an army and instituted a reign of terror.

Marius escaped to Africa. Hardly had Sulla made an about-face and started for the front once more when a consul, Cinna, annulled the Sullan laws and recalled Marius from Africa. Marius, enraged at the treatment he had received after having been the savior of the state, roamed the streets of the capital, striking down nobles and senators he hated. After arranging election to the consulship, he fell ill and died within a few days.

Sulla proceeded to the East this time, postponing the squaring of accounts with his enemies in the capital. Marching east from Epirus, he defeated a Pontic force sent against him. Then he invaded Attica and besieged Athens, which held out for several months. When it did fall, his soldiers killed every tenth Athenian, looted the town and destroyed the docks and harbor installations at the Piraeus. Athens never recovered from the devastation. Next he defeated a force of a hundred thousand sent against him in eastern Greece by Mithridates.

Crossing the Hellespont, Sulla had to fight little to persuade Mithridates that the end had come. And Sulla, eager to return to Rome to deal with his enemies there, offered the softest terms of any Roman victor: surrender of conquests in Asia Minor, the payment of an indemnity, and the relinquishment of eighty warships. The cities of Asia did not fare so well. Forced to pay a huge indemnity for the slaughter of the Italians and to provide quarters and pay for the upkeep of Sulla's troops during the winter of 85/84 B.C., they fell victims to a crushing burden of debt.

When Sulla landed in Italy, he brought with him some thirty-five thousand men, more loyal to himself than to the state. Among those who subsequently joined his forces were Pompey and Crassus, who would soon be heard from again. His opponents proved incapable of turning him back, and he entered Rome in 82 B.C. Proclaimed dictator with authority to revise the constitution, he ordered a bloodbath which in many ways surpassed the worst days of the French Revolution. Shortly after he entered Rome, he tortured to death six thousand captives from the army that had

opposed his entry into the capital. Thousands of others were exiled or had their property confiscated, many of them only for the crime of possessing property that Sulla needed to reward his veterans. Among those killed were ninety senators and twenty-six hundred Equites.

Next Sulla revised the constitution. He increased the Senate by three hundred, adding many from the equestrian class; reformed the courts, initiating trial by jury in many instances where it did not exist; established an orderly progression of office-holding, establishing minimum age limits for each office; and reorganized the provinces. He designed his whole program to restore to power the senatorial class, which by that time had completely lost its control of the state, and had proved itself as incapable of ruling in the past as it would in the future.

Sulla had been a dictator, but he used his power to restore the constitution, not to rule for the rest of his life. His design for government was to bring into government leaders of groups responsible for dissension in the past. Many new members of the Senate were from the equestrian order. In the civil magistracies there was to be a steady and regular progression that would give experience to those who reached the top. All classes—the Optimates, the equestrian order, the urban populace, new citizens, and the army—would have a piece of the action. Having accomplished his aims, Sulla retired to private life in 78 B.C. and died soon thereafter. Before the ashes of his funeral pyre had cooled, forces were at work to demolish the house of cards he had erected.

Pompey. From this time on it became increasingly clear that the Senate could not control affairs and that the important man in Rome was the man with the army. Such men would bypass the Sullan system or manipulate it for their own purposes. The important man with the army in the 70s and 60s was Pompey. Having been a general in the army of Sulla, he was one of the military leaders called on by the State to suppress the rebellion of Marcus Aemilius Lepidus in 78 B.C. When he subsequently

Pompey

miles wide around the entire Mediterranean. This command, bestowed upon Pompey, was to last for three years. He completed the task in about three months.

Meanwhile, Rome was fighting another fierce war with Mithridates VI of Pontus in Asia Minor. After rather brilliant initial victories, Lucius Licinius Lucullus was not able to lead the Roman forces to ultimate victory. "Like a buzzard come to enjoy another's kill," Pompey, already in the East with a large army, was appointed to succeed Lucullus. Pompey vigorously prosecuted the war during the years 66–62 B.C. He conquered much of Asia Minor and pacified it, dividing it into the provinces familiar to the student of the New Testament. He brought Syria into the Empire in 64 B.C., terminating the Seleucid

refused to disband his army and demanded to be sent to Spain to quell the revolt of Quintus Sertorius there, the Senate reluctantly granted his wish. Although he was not the best general on the field, he had the best public relations staff. When the war was over, the populace believed he was the real victor. On his way home from Spain, he was able to share in the glory of Marcus Crassus' victory over the slave revolt of Spartacus in Southern Italy. Pompey and Crassus shared the consulate for the year 70 and both thereafter retired from public life.

Pompey did not have long to wait for a new assignment. Pirates were racing all over the Mediterranean with hundreds of fast ships. They stormed dozens of cities around the Mediterranean, including coastal cities in Italy itself, destroyed a large Roman fleet, and prevented much of the grain supply from reaching the capital. With their food prices skyrocketing and food increasingly scarce, the people of Rome determined to clear the seas. To this end the Gabinian Law was put through the Assembly of the Tribes in spite of senatorial opposition. It provided for a fleet of 500 ships, an infantry force of 120,000 men, and power superior to that of the provincial governors over a strip of territory fifty

Julius Caesar

dynasty there; and Palestine the following year, bringing to an end the Maccabean or Hasmonean dynasty.

When Pompey landed at Brundisium (modern Brindisi) in 62, he disbanded his army, rather than attempting to become ruler of the Empire by force. As soon as he did so, he lost his bargaining power with the Senate, which opposed the political settlement he had made in the East. Thus his veterans went without the grant of homesteads that they expected at the time of mustering out.

While Pompey was engaged in his conquests, two new figures came in from the wings and began to stride across the Roman stage: Marcus Licinius Crassus and Gaius Julius Caesar (Caesar was the surname of the Julian family). Their political alignment was with the radical popular element and to some extent with the Equites. Their advance was somewhat impeded by Cicero, who defended the interests of Pompey. Cicero earned much of his fame by quashing two conspiracies against the state by Cataline, who seems to have been connected in some way with Crassus. Cicero then tried to effect an alignment between the senators and the Equites in order to give proper direction to the politics of the State. His efforts were never successful.

Three Against the State. In 60 B.C., the interests of Pompey, Crassus, and Caesar all seemed to coincide. At least, all of them wanted something, and none by himself was strong enough to get what he wanted. Caesar, returning from a governorship in Farther Spain, sought a consulship, commission, and army to conquer new lands for Rome. Crassus was interested in a modification of contracts that he and some of his friends had made with the government for the collection of taxes in the province of Asia. Harvests had been particularly bad there, and the Equites stood to lose heavily. As has been stated, Pompey wanted a recognition of his political settlement in the East and land for his veterans. The three made an informal agreement to pool their resources—an arrangement known as the First Triumvirate. Caesar was to be elected con-

sul and was to push through legislation to satisfy the needs of all. He did just that.

Crassus and his friends got their rebate. Pompey's eastern settlement was approved and he received land for his veterans. Caesar won the proconsulship of Gaul for five years and the right to raise and lead an army into battle in the conquest of this very rich province. Cicero was banished because of his opposition to Caesar and Crassus.

While Caesar was off in Gaul winning battles, the political situation in Rome deteriorated rapidly; Pompey and Crassus began to quarrel. With the Triumvirate about to collapse, Caesar called for its renewal in 55 B.C. The terms of the new agreement dictated that Pompey and Crassus should stand for the consulship in 55, that Pompey should thereafter be governor of the two Spains and Cyrenaica for five years with six legions, that Crassus for an equal period should be governor of Syria with the right to wage war against Parthia, and that Caesar's proconsulship should be renewed for another five years. Apparently what happened was that both Crassus and Pompey had become increasingly disturbed over Caesar's military successes and demanded positions in the State that would permit them to command armies with which to protect themselves.

Caesar did conquer Gaul, ended the Gallic danger to Rome, and provided Italy with another market. Moreover, his conquest of the area is important to the history of western civilization because the effective beginnings of the Romanization of Gaul were to lead ultimately to a cultural difference between France and Germany that has been disastrous in modern history. Then, too, the Romanization of Gaul led ultimately to the development of the Holy Roman Empire and of a new civilization in the West.

The Triumvirate soon began to disintegrate. In the spring of 53 B.C. Crassus was killed in battle against the Parthians. Pompey had for some time been blowing hot and cold toward the Senate and toward Caesar and Crassus. As an impossibly vain man, it seems that he could not bear to be anything but first. As Caesar's star rose, Pompey became more difficult. Although he had renewed his governorship of Spain for five years, he had never gone there. In the breakdown of civil government in Rome in 52, Pompey obtained a third consulship—this time without a colleague—and thereby ruled as a virtual dictator. Determined to check Caesar's rise to power, he demanded that all military personnel in Italy take their oath to him personally and obtained from the Senate a third five-year proconsulship in Spain.

Supporters of Caesar and Pompey parried legal blows in the Senate. Finally, on December 1, 50 B.C., that body voted to strip Caesar of his command in Gaul. Subsequently they passed a motion calling for Pompey to step down. A short time afterward the Senate declared Caesar a public enemy and proclaimed martial law.

JULIUS CAESAR'S HISTORICAL SIGNIFICANCE

Julius Caesar was a great conqueror, and his military tactics of speed, mobility, and surprise have influenced many military strategists down through the ages. But he is significant in history for many other reasons.

He conquered Gaul and contributed to the Romanization of the province, from which was to rise a new civilization in the West.

But, his success in conquering Gaul and his failure to take control of the Germans has led to a cultural and political division in Europe that has had disastrous results. The lack of understanding and trust between the French and Germans has become a source of animosity for centuries and led to two world wars during the twentieth century.

For Rome politically, Caesar was important in bringing an end to the Republic and instituting one-man rule.

A good writer, as a historian Caesar provided primary source materials on the Gallic Wars and the Germans.

For all of us Caesar is significant for his reform and refinement of the calendar. The calendar we follow with its leap year every fourth year is essentially his doing.

On hearing of the Senate's action, Caesar decided to act without further delay. Crossing the Rubicon River, which separated Italy from Cisalpine Gaul, he provoked a civil war. Pompey, of course, was the only leader in Italy capable of opposing him. Caesar had few troops, but he counted on speed and surprise tactics to win the day. Pompey had not yet been able to mobilize his troops; and some that he had under arms had fought under Caesar's command and might possibly desert to his side. With lightning thrusts Caesar took the entire peninsula; Pompey escaped with his army to Greece. The task before Caesar would have made a lesser man quail. His opponent had forces in Spain, had tremendous resources in the East, and controlled the sea.

In setting the Italian house in order, Caesar apparently won over few senators, but he did win the support of the rising Equites. This backing was to stand loyally behind the Empire when it was established at the end of the first century B.C. His efforts to draw Cicero into his entourage were disappointing. Having established control of Italy, Caesar led an army overland to Spain and subdued the Iberian Peninsula in forty days. But the victory was not without hard-fought and almost disastrous battles.

Meanwhile, Pompey was amassing a large force in Greece for the invasion of Italy. Again counting on the value of speed and the element of surprise, Caesar managed to slip past Pompey's naval patrols on the night of January 4, 48 B.C., and land his troops in western Greece. Although later reinforced by Mark Antony, he lost initial battles to Pompey. At Pharsalus the story was different. Outnumbered more than two to one, Caesar won a tremendous victory by superior generalship, and Pompey fled. As he landed in Egypt, a Roman living there assassinated him. Caesar arrived three days later.

Caesar Alone. Caesar wintered in Egypt, conquering the kingdom for Rome and marrying Cleopatra, which he could do under Macedonian or Ptolemaic law but not Roman, for the Romans did not permit bigamy. Returning to Italy the next year, he was confronted with the task of considerable economic and political reform before he could embark for Africa to destroy the last pocket of resistance. There, at Thapsus, in Tunisia, Caesar again outgeneraled his opposition and became the undisputed master of the Roman world.

Caesar was now faced with reconstruction of the Roman State. For this he had sufficient power. From 48 B.C. on, he was steadily a consul. In 46 he was named dictator for ten years and the following year dictator for life. In 46 he was also made censor and given the power and inviolability of a tribune.

As Caesar began to reform the government, he stood peculiarly alone. He did have a few of the old nobility, such as the Julians and Claudians, on his side; but the great families of the last century of the Republic were conspicuously absent from his train. The bulk of his following was the new middle class. So he made deliberate use of men with talent, rather than men with family connections. Mark Antony illustrates his practice. Subsequent rulers would follow him in this course of action.

The overall effect of Caesar's reforms was to start Rome toward true imperial organization and to stake out paths in which later emperors would walk. The importance of Rome and the Roman Senate was gradually reduced. To begin with, the Senate was increased from six hundred to seven hundred. A large percentage came from the equestrian class, and some came from Gaul. Meanwhile, a process of development had been evolving in the Italian towns whereby these municipalities were achieving a political and social structure similar to that of the capital. Caesar's Julian Municipal Law was something of a culmination of that process. The burghers of the "downstate" towns were satisfied to participate in their local senates and aspired less to membership in the Roman Senate or other departments of government.

As a second aspect of his reforms, Caesar conferred full Roman citizenship on many cities of Spain and Gaul, and Latin rights on others. In a further effort to Romanize the Mediterranean world and at the same time to relieve the problem of the poor in Italy, he established numerous colonies of Roman citizens in the Empire. Reportedly, eighty thousand of Rome's population alone were sent to such places as Sinope on the Black Sea, and Corinth and Carthage. In attacking the problem of the poor and establishing colonies abroad he cut the grain dole in Rome from about 320,000 to 150,000.

Third, he rebuilt the strategically important cities of Carthage and Corinth. Fourth, as dictator he could control the provincial governors and bring an end to the confusion and corruption of the previous century. This objective was not fully accomplished until the days of Augustus, however. Fifth, Caesar improved the administration of Rome by increasing the number of magistrates and reforming the lawcourts. And sixth, one of his most enduring acts was the reform of the calendar, which, after that, had a year of 365 days and a leap year in which February had 29 days.

He proposed other changes, such as a census of the Empire, a codification of Roman law, a new highway across the Apennines to the Adriatic, improvement of the harbor at Ostia, and draining the Pomptine Marshes in Latium, but these were not carried out. This list is by no means complete, but it shows that Julius Caesar was more than merely the conqueror of Gaul, the writer of a famous work on the Gallic wars (that won him rank among the famous historians of the world), and a character immortalized by Shakespeare.

Demise of the Republic. But Caesar did not have a chance to pursue his statesmanlike program. As most of us know, he was struck down by the knives of assassins on the Ides of March (March 15), 44 B.C. The conspiracy involved a combination of supporters of Pompey, jealous members of his own camp, and Republicans opposed to dictatorship. While he had not destroyed

The Senate building in the Roman forum, where Caesar was assassinated.

Triumvirate. This one was not as informal as the first had been but was recognized by the Senate. Before the triumvirs took office on January 1, 43 B.C., they engaged in a cold-blooded proscription in which some two thousand senators and Equites lost their lives. As in the case of Sulla's proscription, many were executed merely to get their property. Some, however, were political enemies of the triumvirs. Most distinguished of the expendables was Cicero. After squelching all opposition in Italy, the triumvirs set out to dispose of Brutus and Cassius, who had been ransacking the treasuries of eastern provinces to raise a formidable military force. The story of the defeat and death of the two assassins on the plains of Philippi in the fall of 42 has become one of the best-known events of military history, thanks to the pen of William Shakespeare.

With their Republican enemies eliminated, the triumvirs started to dispose of each other. Lepidus, the weakest of the three, was the first casualty. The other two shunt-

the forms of the Republic, he had sapped the life out of them. Elections had become empty political acts because Caesar had determined their results in advance. For many the sacrifice of the old Republican political structure for an apparent achievement of peace and security in the Empire was too costly.

Unfortunately for Caesar's conspirators, they had not come to terms ahead of time with Caesar's supporters: Lepidus, the master of the cavalry, who gained control of the army; with Mark Antony, who got Caesar's money and his papers; and Octavius (or Octavian), Caesar's grandnephew and adopted heir. Octavius, then eighteen, was waiting in Epirus to join Caesar in prosecuting the Parthian War. On receiving the news, he came to Rome with his friend Agrippa. During the succeeding months there was a jockeying for power by these three and Brutus and Cassius, the leaders of Caesar's assassins.

Finally Antony, Octavius, and Lepidus formed the Second

The interior of the Senate building, where Caesar was assassinated. Chairs of the senators stood on the risers. The president of the Senate sat or stood on the platform at the far end. The floor is inlaid marble.

ed him off to the province of Africa, of which he became governor. Eventually he died a natural death on his estate in 13 B.C. Antony was much better off than Octavius for the moment; he had control of the entire East and the provinces of Gaul. Octavius was not even undisputed master of Italy, and he was plagued by Sextus Pompey, who enjoyed naval superiority over much of the Mediterranean, as well as Sicily and Sardinia. Pompey was able to harass the grain supplies of Italy and incite considerable unrest in the peninsula.

Before long, Gaul came over to Octavius, and in 40 B.C. the triumvirs arranged a peace with Pompey. Later, with the help of Antony, Octavius managed to destroy Pompey and to become more fully master of the West. Meanwhile, Antony was busy fighting the Parthians and enjoying the feminine graces of Cleopatra. Octavius' hope was to bide his time and effectively propagandize the areas under his control.

Of great value to his propaganda machine were Roman fears of the loss to the Empire of the rich kingdoms of the East and/or the threat of a divided empire. Then there was Roman dislike of an Oriental queen and Roman revulsion against orientalization of the government. Octavius' greatest propaganda victory came as a result of the publication of Antony's will. (Whether it was real or forged is debated.) One of Antony's supporters defected to Octavius and reported that his will had been deposited with the vestal virgins in Rome. Octavius promptly found it and read it to the Senate. Supposedly it confirmed the disposition of eastern lands to the children of Cleopatra and acknowledged Caesarion, her son by Julius Caesar, as the true son and successor of Julius Caesar. A shudder swept across Italy, and Octavius capitalized on it by fomenting opposition to Antony.

Both antagonists headed toward the final showdown in 32 B.C. Antony gathered his forces at Ephesus and sailed for Greece, taking up battle stations at Actium on the Ambracian Gulf in northwestern Greece. Octavius massed his forces across the Adriatic Sea. When Octavius' troops attacked on September 2, 31 B.C. their victo-

ry was complete. Antony's ships were too heavy and slow, and the morale of his troops was low. When in the middle of the battle Cleopatra broke away with several ships and the treasure, Antony panicked and followed her to Egypt.

There Octavius pursued them the following year. After a brief battle Antony committed suicide and Cleopatra followed suit a few days later. Though Julius Caesar had in a sense conquered Egypt for Rome, Cleopatra had continued to rule there. Now Octavius definitely took the kingdom for Rome and became the undisputed master of the Empire. He had established his claim to the political inheritance of Julius Caesar.

The Empire

THE EMPIRE AND THE EMPERORS

Rome had a growing empire from the third century B.C., when she started to conquer overseas territories (Sicily, Corsica, Sardinia, Spain, etc.). And it is proper to speak of the empire from that time on. But the empire period politically (as distinct from the earlier monarchy and Republic) began with Octavius (later known by his title of Augustus).

The term "emperor" comes from the Latin *Imperator* (literally *commander*). During the Republic *Imperator* was an honorary title bestowed upon a general after an important victory and was placed after his name. With Augustus it became a permanent title of the Roman emperors and was placed before the proper name. The word signified *commander, chief, leader, head, master, lord.*

Augustus. In the late summer of 29 B.C. Octavius returned to Rome in triumph. His victory ended a century of civil war. With the cessation of hostilities, the great *Pax Romana* (Roman Peace) began. This peace was to last for about two centuries. The term *Pax Romana* does not indicate a lack of warfare, but that Roman power was so

Augustus as a military commander.

During the year 28 B.C., Augustus conducted something of a sociopolitical reformation. He purged from the Senate some two hundred unworthies who had come there under the administration of the triumvirs, and he established property qualifications for senators and equestrians.

In a very dramatic move, Octavius appeared before the Senate on January 30, 27 B.C., surrendered the extraordinary powers that he had exercised during the civil war, and handed the commonwealth back to the Senate and the Roman people, retaining the consulship that he had enjoyed continuously since 33. But the Senate did not want the responsibility of governing the state; nor did they quite know what to do with it. They first delegated to Augustus proconsular power for ten years (later renewed) over the provinces of Spain, Gaul,

Augustus as a Pontifex Maximus, the head of the state religion.

overwhelming as to enforce a general peace and stability in the Mediterranean world. Interestingly, the Han Dynasty dominated most of Asia from about 200 B.C. to A.D. 200 and maintained a Chinese Peace (*Pax Sinica*) there. Between them Rome and China maintained a general stability from Western Europe throughout the Mediterranean and North Africa and East Asia—from the Atlantic eastward to the Pacific. The trade routes across the Middle East were relatively secure. Goods flowed between the Orient and the West to the enrichment of both.

Everywhere Octavius was hailed as the savior of the Empire and founder of a new golden age. And he spared no effort to make that hope a reality. Piracy virtually disappeared from the high seas, and brigandage markedly declined on land. He brought a general stability to the frontiers. Because of settled conditions, commerce flourished throughout the Empire.

and Syria. Since these were the provinces where most of the troops were stationed, this power gave him command of the real power in the state, the army. Three days later they conferred upon him the title of "Augustus," meaning "the revered or respected one." Actually the whole proceeding was carefully stage-managed by his agents.

During subsequent years the Senate conferred many other powers on Augustus. He was never a dictator but princeps (first citizen) of the Empire. His proconsular power gave him control over the army and an authority superior to that of governors of the provinces; his office of *pontifex maximus* gave him power over the religion of the state; as *princeps senatus* (president of the Senate) he was in a position to direct the affairs of that body; and his tribunican power gave him control over the assembly.

As the first citizen of the Empire, Augustus exercised actual control over all phases of government. But he tried to operate within the framework of a dyarchy (rule of two units) in which he cooperated with the Senate in running the government of Rome and the Empire. Elections of Roman magistrates continued. By monopolizing what amounted to a spoils system, he was able to manipulate the social and political structure of the state. While men rose to places of prominence through the army or the magistracies, he had final control over their advancement to the highest positions. Those whom he wished to reward he admitted to senatorial rank. As chief executive, he created boards or commissions to dispense governmental functions. He also organized a sort of cabinet or council to aid him in shaping policies.

AUGUSTUS CAESAR

Augustus Caesar (the grand-nephew of Julius Caesar and adopted as his son) brought in a new era of peace, security, stability and prosperity for Rome and the Empire. With him began the Roman Peace (the *Pax Romana*), especially welcome after about a century of civil war and instability. The *Pax Romana* was to last for about two hundred years.

As Rome's first emperor he tried to avoid a military dictatorship and cooperated with the Senate in administering Rome, Italy, and the Empire. To perpetuate the form of rule that he created, he adopted his successor and associated him with himself in the government. Thus, that individual would be prepared to rule effectively when he took the reins of government.

To gain and maintain the loyalty of the populace he instituted the ruler cult and extended citizenship rights. He used the army to protect the borders of the empire, not to maintain his position in the state.

He built extensively in Rome. One of his best-known buildings was the Pantheon. In connection with his highway construction, he set up the golden milestone in the Forum at Rome (20 B.C.) to measure distances to various cities of the Empire—hence the saying "all roads lead to

The Pantheon as it stands in Rome today.

Rome." His literary patronage helped to launch the golden age of Roman literature. One of his stars was Vergil (Virgil), who composed the *Aenid.*

Augustus' earlier conquests had brought Egypt into the Empire (with the demise of Cleopatra's line).

His first empire-wide census involved the birth of Jesus Christ in Bethlehem (Luke 2).

As early as 27 B.C., he secured appointment of a committee of the Senate to work with him in preparing an agenda for meetings of the Senate. Later this became a sort of cabinet, consisting of other topflight administrators outside the Senate. He also had the authority to issue executive edicts; these became more and more important with successive emperors and gradually replaced the legislative functions of the Senate and became an important source of judicial principles.

Just as Augustus shared the administration of Rome with the Senate, so he also shared the rule of the provinces with them. In general, senatorial provinces (such as Sicily) were those most thoroughly Romanized and, therefore, needed only a few local police or militia to keep order. Imperial provinces, on the other hand, required legionary forces to keep order. Since the emperor commanded the troops, such provinces were assigned to him. Especially subjugation of the warlike and restless peoples of the newly conquered provinces along the Rhine and Danube frontiers required a show of military force.

The division of the provinces between Senate and emperor was not fixed. As unruly provinces became settled, they were turned over to the Senate; and occasionally the emperor took control of one that needed a demonstration of Roman might. The Senate appointed governors of the senatorial provinces and the emperor of the imperial provinces.

Governors of the senatorial provinces usually serve for one year. In the imperial provinces term of service depended on ability of the governor or the emperor's need for his services elsewhere. In all provinces, governors and other officials received a salary in Augustus' day, thereby removing one of the great causes of extortion during the days of the Republic.

In addition to these two classes of provinces, a number of client kingdoms existed within the Empire. While the foreign relations of these principalities were controlled by Rome, they enjoyed a great deal of local autonomy. Judaea and Galatia, among others, fell in this category in Augustus' day. Before the end of his reign he transformed them into provinces. Egypt was in a special category, treated as a private possession of the emperor, very important to him as a source of wealth and a supply of grain for the army and the people of Rome.

At home, Augustus turned his attention to problems that the Senate had never been successful in handling during the days of the Republic. To provide adequate police protection for the capital, he organized three cohorts of fifteen hundred men each. For general administrative purposes, he divided Rome into fourteen districts and in turn subdivided

Fragments of the golden milestone in the Roman Forum.

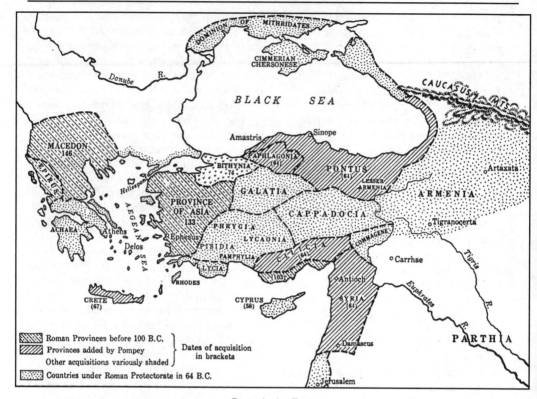

Rome in the East

these into 265 precincts. These precincts developed into little worlds of their own with officials of various sorts. Thus, those with a desire for political or social recognition could get it on the local level, even though government generally, at higher levels, was becoming increasingly dictatorial. There they could enjoy being "a big frog in a little puddle."

After trying other ineffective measures to solve the problem of fighting fires in Rome, Augustus organized a corps of seven thousand men to serve as a fire brigade and as night police. This force was divided into one thousand-man cohorts, each cohort serving two of the fourteen districts. To solve the problem of the grain supply and the needs of the large number on public dole (some 150,000 or more), the Senate turned over to Augustus the responsibility of maintaining the grain fleet and obtaining adequate grain stores—from Egypt and elsewhere.

Of special interest to Bible students is Augustus' census-taking activities.

Censuses were nothing new to Rome, for censuses of citizens had been taken regularly at five-year intervals for centuries. But now that Rome had an empire, was free from civil strife, and had a ruler who wanted to set in order the administrative machinery, empire-wide censuses were in order. Augustus tallied up the citizen roster in 28 B.C., 8 B.C., and A.D. 14. Exactly how far beyond the boundaries of Italy the census-takers operated in 28 B.C. is unclear.

There must have been a degree of irregularity in the Empire—at least in the early days of Augustus when the emperor was getting administrative details organized. For instance, censuses were taken in Gaul in 27 and 13 B.C. In Egypt they were apparently taken at fourteen-year intervals for some centuries thereafter. A record exists of a census in Egypt during the year A.D. 20. Assuming that the fourteen-year cycle was followed, a census could have occurred there about 8 B.C. Possibly censuses were taken in Palestine about the same time as in Egypt.

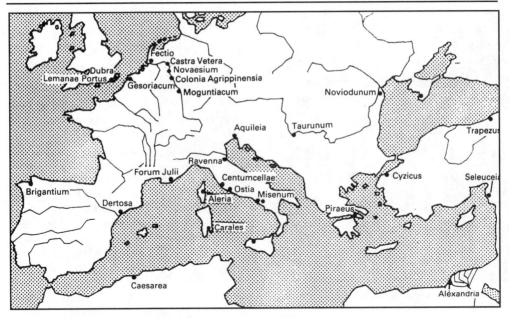

Naval Bases of the Roman Empire

According to Luke 2:2, the imperial census was first taken in Palestine at the time of Christ's birth. It is known that the Gregorian calendar (the one now in use) is several years in error. For instance, Herod the Great, who ruled Judea at the time of Christ's birth, actually died in 4 B.C. Christ may well have been born a couple of years or more before that. On the basis of this and other evidence, it is possible to push the date of the birth of Christ back to 6 or 7 or possibly even the end of 8 B.C.[8]

Population estimates based on the imperial census and other evidence vary greatly, but some useful approximations can be noted. Italy in Augustus' day probably had about fourteen million people; by the end of Nero's reign the figure likely reached twenty million. The city of Rome seems to have had a population of about one million in Augustus' day. Jerome Carcopino's long discussion in the first chapter of his *Daily Life in Ancient Rome* gives us about as reliable a basis as we can find for reaching such a conclusion. The population of the Empire as a whole during the first century A.D. was presumably about eighty million.

It was one thing for Augustus to work out an administration of the Empire. It was quite another to devise means of keeping it

loyal. There was always the way of military subjection. But neither Augustus nor his successors chose that method. The usual number of legionnaires kept under arms during the first century was 150,000, of which about one-third was stationed along the Rhine, another third along the Danube, and the remaining scattered in Syria, Egypt, and Africa. Clearly the troops were primarily for protecting the frontiers. Other ways of keeping the Empire in line were through a process of extension of Roman citizenship, through ruler worship, and through creation of urban centers as a means of controlling the countryside. All of these paths Augustus followed.

First, Augustus tried to create an Italian nation out of the Empire through urbanization and extension of Roman citizenship. Much of the East was already urbanized with a culture different from that of Rome. In the West the population lived mainly in tribal communities. As Augustus' successors followed his lead, the entire Empire was urbanized within a couple of centuries, and the citizenship was gradually extended. Finally in A.D. 212 Caracalla granted citizenship to all freemen of the Empire.

During the latter days of the Republic, colonies of Roman citizens—civilians and

Temple to the Divine Julius in the Forum at Rome.

provinces imitated the language, religion, and customs of the citizens in their presence.

A second means that Augustus used to maintain support for his regime and of keeping the Empire in line was through the ruler cult. This concept had at its background the god-king ideal of the ancient Near East, and the efforts of the successors of Alexander the Great in Egypt and Seleucid territories to link worship of the ruler with loyalty to the state. During his rise to power Augustus had arranged the deification of Julius Caesar in an effort to win the loyalty of Julius' troops. The eastern provinces were quick to seek permission to worship the living ruler, whom many hailed as a divine savior responsible for the peace, prosperity, and security of the Empire. (Many had already deified Julius Caesar and Mark Antony.) Augustus himself refused divine honors but styled himself "Divi filius," son of the deified Julius Caesar.

veterans—were settled in various places in the Empire. Augustus continued and augmented this policy. Other municipalities, as they became Romanized, were granted full citizenship. A third category had Latin rights (of trade and intermarriage with Rome). A fourth category consisted merely of native municipalities without Roman or Latin rights.

There was a regular process of promoting these towns to higher categories. Naturally, since Roman citizenship carried with it legal and political rights and since it opened the way to important careers, it was highly prized. The process of voluntary Romanization was steady as natives in the

Traces of Augustus worship can be seen in the East as early as 29 B.C., when Nicaea, Ephesus, Pergamum, and Nicomedia erected temples to him and the goddess Roma. Soon thereafter Herod the Great built temples to Augustus at Caesarea and Samaria.

Emperor worship was not at home in the West and was established there more slowly. In 12 B.C. an altar to Augustus was erected in Gaul near the modern city of Lyons (ancient Lugdunum), in order to prevent revolt there. Augustus himself erected a temple to the divine Julius in the Forum in Rome. And in each of the 265 precincts of Rome he set up shrines dedicated to the genius of Augustus—the divine spirit that watched

Center for the worship of the ruler cult in the firemen's barracks at Ostia.

A coin issued during Augustus' reign. Note that he is accorded divinity (Divus) and is described as father of the Fatherland (Pater).
Courtesy Gleason Archer

over his fortunes. Gradually the ruler cult was established; by A.D. 100 the whole Empire was blanketed with ruler cult establishments.

While emperors encouraged this worship, they did not demand it until the days of Domitian, at the end of the first century. Emperor worship unified patriotism and religion and made support of the state a religious duty. It created a very serious problem for Christians, for refusal to worship the emperor and the goddess Roma constituted treason or at least a question of disloyalty to the state. Treason has never been lightly handled by the state. Thus the persecution of Christians came about. The harassment waxed and waned until Constantine declared Christianity a legal religion early in the fourth century A.D. It should be noted, however, that persecution was commonly instigated on the local level and for reasons other than refusal to worship the emperor. The ruckus in Ephesus during Paul's ministry there is one example (see Acts 19).

One of the chief difficulties of Augustus' administration was how to arrange for a successor. Theoretically, since the Senate had conferred his powers on him, those powers reverted to the Senate on his death. But with Augustus' reconstruction of the State, it was impossible for the Senate to take over again. In solving this problem,

Augustus (like Julius, who had adopted him) chose the plan of selecting his successor, adopting him as his heir, and associating his heir with him in a coregency. Thereby an orderly succession would be assured, with the Senate later ratifying the successor.

This became the solution used by Augustus' successors during the next two centuries of the principate. From A.D. 14 to 68 the Julio-Claudian line held the reins of government; from 69 to 96 the Flavians; and after them what are known as the five good emperors (Nerva, Trajan, Hadrian, Antoninus Pius, and Marcus Aurelius), who broke the dynastic principle but continued the fiction of a line by adopting their successors.

During the next two centuries, the political arrangements which Augustus inaugurated were generally continued. There was,

Augustus tried to bolster his regime by a vast patronage system—in construction, literary production, and more. Head of much of this system was his son-in-law and adviser, Agrippa, pictured here. Note that Agrippa's name appears on the Pantheon (see preceding illustration).

As the expansion of the empire demanded the expansion of the Roman Forum, Julius Caesar, Augustus Caesar, and later emperors added forums of their own. Here is a model of Augustus' Forum.

however, a gradual usurpation of senatorial and assembly rights and a decline in the value of elections. Eventually the functions of the magistrates were assumed by individuals appointed by the princeps.

Although there were times when the state was in danger of losing its civilian character and becoming a military monarchy, that did not happen until after A.D. 180. So the first two centuries of the Christian Era were for Rome a time of peace and prosperity and political stability.

Augustus' wife Livia

Of course Augustus had to deal with more than political and military concerns. The city of Rome needed a massive face-lift. He restored or rebuilt dozens of temples, and built the Pantheon, the Altar of Peace, the Theater of Marcellus, the Forum of Augustus, his own tomb, as well as other structures. He himself claimed that he had found Rome a city of brick and left it a city of marble. The great architect of the period was Vitruvius, whose treatise on architecture, *De Architectura,* for many centuries was accepted as the final authority in the field. Palladio rediscovered him in the Renaissance, and Thomas Jefferson rediscovered Vitruvius and Palladio and used their principles as he designed, among other things, the University of Virginia, the Virginia capitol in Richmond, and his home at Monticello.

ROMAN EMPERORS OF THE NEW TESTAMENT PERIOD

Augustus, 27 B.C.–A.D. 14
Tiberius, A.D. 14–37
Caligula, A.D. 37–41
Claudius, A.D. 41–54
Nero, A.D. 54–68
Vespasian, A.D. 69–79
Titus, A.D. 79–81
Domitian, A.D. 81–96

The tomb of Agustus in Rome, also used by several successive emperors.

Augustus also gave attention to the production of literature, especially as it served to promote and glorify his regime. In fact, his was the golden age of Roman literature. His friend Maecenas was the great literary patron of the period and Virgil (*Eclogues, Georgics*, the *Aeneid*), Horace (*Satires, Odes, Epistles*), Ovid (*Metamorphoses, et al.*), and Livy (*History*) were four of the leading literary giants of the Augustan golden age. Karl Galinsky surveys the whole field of Augustan culture admirably in his *Augustan Culture* (1996).

Augustus lived long enough to outlast most of his candidates for the imperial office. He had no children of his own by his wife Livia, though he had a daughter Julia by his previous marriage to Scribonia. So his dynastic plans focused on Julia's husbands and children, but none of these lived long enough to become a viable heir. Finally he was forced to settle on Tiberius, the eldest son of Livia by a previous marriage.

Tiberius. Before his death, Augustus adopted Tiberius as his son and associated Tiberius with himself in ruling the State. Upon Augustus' death in A.D. 14, the Senate and assembly voted Augustus' powers and prerogatives upon his successor. The new emperor was by birth a member of the Claudian family, by adoption a member of the Julian family. Therefore, in him these two great houses were united and from this Julio-Claudian line came the first four successors of Augustus in the principate. The Julio-Claudians maintained themselves because of the personal power and prestige of Augustus and the strong bond of allegiance by which the Roman army was attached to his family.

Tiberius (who ruled A.D. 14–37) had become embittered by the knowledge that he had been chosen the heir of Augustus by necessity rather than by choice. After all the other preferable candidates for the imperial office had passed off the scene, he was the only viable candidate left. Though he enjoyed a good reputation as a soldier and

A reconstruction of the tomb of Augustus.

Tiberius

Caligula

administrator, his standing was undercut by an overly-stern sense of duty, a cold and reserved manner, and a suspicious nature. Entering office with no enthusiasm for the position, he ultimately came to loathe it. In fact, he found his job so unpleasant that he retired to his villa on the island of Capri in A.D. 26 (the year he appointed Pilate procurator of Judea), leaving the rule of Rome to Sejanus, commander of the Praetorian Guard.

While he was on Capri, a crop of stories represented him as sunk in a condition of debauchery, especially of a homosexual sort. But the gossip remains unsupported by any first-century evidence. He did spend his time, however, enjoying the company of scholars, jurists, and men of letters. When Sejanus was found to be plotting to take over the imperial office, he was removed and executed. Tiberius had a moderate financial policy with economy in expenditures and liberality when necessary. At his death he left a full treasury. He was a blessing to the provincials, to whose welfare he directed particular attention and whom he governed ably and conscientiously. Of prime significance for the Christian move-

ment is the fact that Christ was crucified during Tiberius' reign.

Increasingly during the first century a bureaucracy ran the day-to-day affairs of government. So ships were built for the navy, roads and bridges were built on land, governors of the provinces maintained oversight there, the army received supplies of food and equipment, taxes were collected, and a host of other governmental functions went forward on a regular basis. If emperors proved to be incompetent or were assassinated or even if there was a brief civil war (as after the death of Nero), the basic stability and prosperity of the Empire continued during the first and second centuries. The *Pax Romana* was not jeopardized.

Caligula. Unfortunately Tiberius did not adopt his successor before his death. But clearly he had in mind that Caligula, grandson of Augustus' daughter Julia, would be the next emperor. At the age of eighteen Caligula went to live with Tiberius on Capri and gained the favor of Macro, the new commander of the Praetorian Guard after the fall of Sejanus. Macro submitted

Caligula's name to the Senate and they accepted the imperial nominee without debate in A.D. 37.

Caligula began his reign with a brilliant political honeymoon. After the stern and efficient rule of Tiberius, the lavishness of Caligula's public entertainments, his donations, his reduction of taxes, and his pardoning of political offenders imprisoned by Tiberius, brought him great popularity. But then after a few months he suffered a serious illness. He recovered, but the usual interpretation is that he then emerged as a megalomaniac and a tyrant.

It is easy to dismiss Caligula merely as a madman, but Anthony Barrett in his 1989 definitive biography *Caligula the Corruption of Power* puts a different spin on the emperor. He points out that Caligula may have suffered a nervous breakdown, but after his recovery there was no dramatic change in his behavior. In fact, his serious excesses and clashes with the Senate did not begin until A.D. 39. His thesis is that Caligula could behave sensibly throughout his reign, that he made some excellent administrative appointments, and was capable of statesmanlike acts. But he had a "self-centered view of the world" and a "grimly ironical sense of humour." He was "indifferent to the consequences of his actions on others." He was self-indulgent and unpredictable, devoid of any sense of moral responsibility. And the Roman political system of the time did not provide any checks on willful autocrats.

Barrett describes Caligula as a "frightening Stalinesque figure." There have been rulers like that in history—like Stalin or Pol Pot of Cambodia, or Mao Zedong of China, who could liquidate their opponents by the millions without any qualms of conscience. At least Caligula had no Gulag. His executions totaled about thirty.

In any case, Caligula finally reached the limits that leaders in government and society were willing to endure. A plot against his life, carried out by a member of the Praetorian Guard, was successful on January 24, A.D. 41.

Caligula had alienated not only the Romans but the Jews as well. Their monotheistic beliefs prevented them from

Claudius

worshiping images of the princeps, and his statues were forcibly erected in the synagogues in Alexandria. But before the order to set up his statue in the temple in Jerusalem could be carried out, news of the emperor's death arrived.

Claudius. In the Senate's enthusiasm over the death of the tyrant, it began to entertain heady ideas of restoring the Republic. However, the senators failed to realize how completely the reins of government had passed from their hands. Some soldiers of the Praetorian Guard, while they were plundering the palace after the murder of Caligula, saw two feet sticking out from under a curtain. They belonged to Claudius, Caligula's uncle. The frightened captive evidently feared that the governmental purge would include him too. But the soldiers took him to the Praetorian camp, where he was hailed as emperor. The transaction involved a handsome bribe for each member of the Guard, and the Senate had no choice but to confer the imperial powers upon Claudius.

Claudius was plagued all his life by a deformed and somewhat incapacitated

Nero at age sixteen, when he was under the
supervision of Seneca and others.
The Capitoline Museum, Rome

body—some say as a result of a birth injury; others, as a result of poliomyelitis. This incapacity had turned him into a student and something of a recluse. He produced books on both Etruscan and Carthaginian history. His enemies presented him as a much more grotesque figure than he probably was. He was no Hunchback of Notre Dame. They have also portrayed him as under the domination of members of his household rather than the real leader of the state.

Whatever the real situation, it seems that the emperor Claudius provided a high quality of administration for the Empire. He adjusted tax burdens and inaugurated an extensive program of public works. This involved building new aqueducts, roads, and canals; swamp drainage; and especially the development of Ostia as a harbor for Rome.

In foreign policy, Claudius followed more in the train of Julius than Augustus. He annexed Thrace and spread Roman influence around much of the Black Sea. In the Near East he reestablished the Roman

protectorate over Armenia and restored Judea to its position as an imperial province after its brief experience as a client kingdom under Herod Agrippa I (A.D. 41–44).

His forces invaded and conquered Britain in A.D. 43 and the years following. Though Julius Caesar had invaded the island long before, he had never completed the conquest and added it to the Empire. Exactly why Claudius determined to undertake this conquest is uncertain. There were appeals to Rome by British tribes for help against other tribes of the island; there was a threat to the peace and security of Gaul by British tribes; but possibly of greater importance was an exaggerated estimate of the resources of the island. Claudius extended Roman citizenship in the provinces and advanced the process of urbanization there.

At home Claudius, like Augustus, tried to give a large share of the responsibility of the state to the Senate and returned to that body some powers it had lost under Tiberius and Caligula. And he introduced Gallic members into the Senate. On the other hand, he dealt the Senate a mortal blow in his effective organization of the departments of government (treasury department, justice department, records department, etc.), each with a head who was a member of the imperial cabinet—an organization composed largely of freedmen loyal to the emperor.

Whether or not Claudius was dominated by his freedmen and his adulterous wives in his governmental policies, as is frequently charged, he was dominated by his fourth wife Agrippina to the point that he adopted Nero, her son by a previous marriage, as his son and successor, in preference to his own natural son. Subsequently Nero married Claudius' daughter Octavia and succeeded to the imperial chair when Claudius died in 54. Evidently Agrippina had him poisoned after she had arranged for her son to become emperor.

Apparently Claudius had some trouble with the Jews in Rome. The early historian Suetonius observed in his *Life of Claudius,* "Since the Jews were continually making disturbances at the instigation of Chrestus, he [Claudius] expelled them from Rome."[9]

This is a corroboration of Luke's statement in Acts 18:2: "Claudius had commanded all Jews to depart from Rome." And it may be early evidence for the existence of Christ too. Many believe that these disturbances were struggles between Jewish followers and opponents of Jesus Christ (Christus).

Nero. Nero was the last of the Julio-Claudians. Coming to the imperial chair at sixteen, he was during the first five years of his rule largely dominated by his mother, Agrippina, and the very capable heads of the executive departments of government that had been instituted by Claudius. Chief of this circle of leaders was Nero's tutor, the Stoic philosopher Seneca—greatest of the literary figures of the Julio-Claudian period. During those early years, administration of the Empire was generally efficient and peaceful, and prosperity continued. In fact, the Empire as a whole was not seriously affected by Nero's inadequacies until the rebellion at the end of his life.

As Nero grew into manhood, he attempted to assert his independence; in so doing he clashed with his domineering mother. This conflict, involving as it did the threats of his mother, led Nero to fear plots against the throne. This fear, coupled with the ambitions of his mistress and later wife, Poppaea Sabina, proved to be his undoing. Ultimately his mother, his wife (Octavia), and his stepbrother, (Germanicus, son of Claudius), were all disposed of. Increasingly Nero's rule became a reign of terror as plots against the throne were ruthlessly tracked down. As money began to run short, estates of the wealthy were confiscated as sources of easy revenue.

One hot July night in A.D. 64, fire broke out in Rome in the slums east of the Circus Maximus and burned with unabated force for nine days, gutting or severely damaging almost three-fourths of the city. No effort to check it succeeded. Even Nero's palace lay a charred mass, with its priceless art treasures forever lost to posterity. In spite of the emperor's measures to alleviate the suffer-

General view of the Golden House of Nero.

ings of the homeless, he could not allay the people's suspicion that he had started the fire in order to have the glory of rebuilding Rome along grander lines. Rebuild it he did, and he spared no expense in the process. In the middle of the new capital he built his great Golden House, which with its gardens and lakes covered 120 acres.

According to Tacitus,[10] Nero tried to lay the blame for this holocaust on Christians in order to divert suspicion from himself. This view has been generally accepted. Moreover, it was widely asserted that Nero was actually to blame for the fire. On the other hand, some have doubted that Nero persecuted Christians or that he blamed the fire on them. For instance Heichelheim and Yeo[11] observe that none of the contemporary writers mention the Neronian persecution and that Suetonius mentions the Neronian persecution without relating it to the fire. Tacitus, we should note, wrote about A.D. 120 and Suetonius about 150.

What is the modern student to think of all this? To begin with, likely no one will ever know whether Nero had anything to do with starting the fire—very likely he did not. Moreover, apparently Christians were considered to be enemies of society in Nero's day. Increasingly numerous, they strongly opposed many social and religious practices that acted as something of a cement for the pagan society of which they

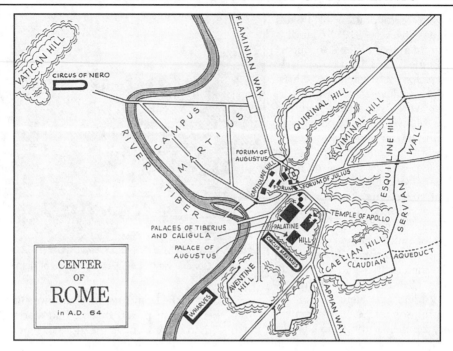

were a part. Therefore, they cold be regarded as enemies of that society. In such a hostile atmosphere it was possible to charge them with incendiarism. And finally, it seems that the testimonies of Tacitus and Suetonius are reliable and that a severe persecution of Christians did occur in Rome, instigated by Nero and related to the charge of incendiarism, and that it began in the latter part of 64 and lasted until 66 when Nero went abroad. William Ramsay has given a helpful and detailed discussion of the whole question.[12]

In 66 Nero embarked on a grand concert tour of Greece. Having pursued his musical interests for many years, he now invaded the land of the muses, accompanied by numerous musicians, actors, and soldiers. He won hundreds of prizes for his singing and acting. Whether he had much real ability is unknown. The judges at any contest awarded first prize to another at the peril of their lives. One historian writing some seventy-five years after Nero's death described his voice as "weak and husky." But whether he knew what his voice was really like or was trying to discredit the emperor we cannot say.

While Nero "fiddled," or rather sang and played his lyre, Rome not only burned

but plots against his rule thickened in back rooms at the Senate, in barrooms around the city, and especially in barracks on the frontiers. Nero made the fatal mistake of not paying enough attention to the troops which were, after all, the basis of the emperor's power. Not only did he finally allow their pay to fall in arrears because of worsening financial conditions, but he had not even bothered to become acquainted with the commanders. Worse, the full effects of long-term service of men at one location on the frontier were now being felt. Men in the ranks became more attached to their commander than to the emperor or the state. They were willing to fight to raise their officers to the imperial chair. Moreover, Nero's failure to engage in any military action left the troops without a means of rapport with him, their commander-in-chief.

Despite Nero's disregard for the military, however, his primary opposition came from the senatorial class. The enormous expenditures of his later years led him to confiscate property—naturally from the rich. And they were the ones who most strongly disapproved of his "concerts" and his love of Greek culture. Moreover, as plots hatched against him proved to be

Vespasian

engineered by members of the senatorial class, his estrangement from them grew. As a matter of fact, he had wide popular support to the end.

Civil War. Not long after Nero's return from Greece, a rebellion broke out in Gaul and spread to Rome, where it was supported by the Praetorian Guard and the Senate. Nero fled from the capital and committed suicide. Whether or not he was really insane, as some writers have suggested, is open to question. His intense interest in music and drama need not be considered evidence of madness, and his suspicious nature may in part be attributed to his conflicts with his mother and the resultant insecurity of his office. Some of his executions or exiles were more for the purpose of obtaining funds for such projects as the rebuilding of Rome than for the thwarting of plots. A few of the contempo-

rary writers who tried to discredit him did so because of the Hellenistic or Oriental or other non-Roman tendencies of his political and cultural pursuits.

With Nero, the last of the Julio-Claudians, removed from the scene, with armies on the frontiers determined to advance their particular candidates for the imperial chair, and with the Praetorian Guard interfering in affairs closer home, Rome was in trouble. The year 68/69 is sometimes known as the year of the four emperors. The first, Galba, who had been governor of the province of Hither Spain, was able to buy the support of the Praetorian Guard, and the Senate followed their lead.

Galba ruled during the latter part of 68, but the lukewarm support of the Praetorians and his failure to win support of the Rhine legions were his undoing. A greater problem was the corruption among the officials he appointed. Otho (a former husband of Nero's wife Poppaea) next bought the support of the Guard, which slew Galba. Otho ruled from January to April 69, then was defeated by the legions from the Rhine and committed suicide. The victorious army set up their commander, Vitellius, who lasted from April to December.

At that point the army of the East went into action under Vespasian. The Danubian legions soon declared for Vespasian too.

A catapult like those used to besiege Jerusalem (now located at the tomb of Hadrian in Rome).

The Arch of Titus in the Forum at Rome.

Next the fleet sided with Vespasian. But hard battles were fought in Italy before the incumbent, Vitellius, was slain and Vespasian was recognized as emperor. In this way was inaugurated a dynasty that was to last through three imperial administrations.

Vespasian. Vespasian's rule (69–79) was faced with numerous problems. The entire Empire was in a disheveled state after the civil wars. Rebellions were still in progress in Germany, Gaul, and Judea. Finances were in disarray, and his political position was not effectively established. However, the new emperor met the challenges. He had served in eight different provinces in various capacities and knew the Empire better than most of those who occupied its highest office.

The rebellions were all suppressed in A.D. 70. Perhaps the most fiercely fought was the insurrection in Judea, which had begun in 66. Friction existed between the Jews and Hellenized inhabitants of the cities of Palestine. The Jews also opposed the pressure of Roman taxation. But the greatest cause of the rebellion lay in the monotheistic religion of the Jews, which would naturally be opposed to Greco-Roman polytheism and which identified national loyalty with uncompromising devotion to monotheistic faith.

Vespasian was battering the Jewish rebels when he made his bid for power in 69. He had conquered the countryside and was ready to begin the siege of Jerusalem when he left for Rome. The conquest of the capital he left to his son Titus. After a protracted siege Titus destroyed the city and temple in 70, slaughtered many thousands, and sold many more into slavery. To commemorate this victory, Titus erected a triumphal arch at the east end of the Forum in Rome. One of the reliefs of this arch shows plunder from the temple, including the golden candelabra and the silver trumpets.

A panel from the Arch of Titus, showing plunder from the Temple, including the golden lampstand and the silver trumpets. *E. Richter, Rome.*

The Colosseum, reconstructed

Next Vespasian reformed the army by developing legions and auxiliary troops of men of mixed nationalities, instead of recruiting them from the frontier regions in which they served. Thus they would not likely give their loyalty to a local province in its struggle against the state. He also sought legionary enlistment in the provinces, thereby contributing to the broader policy of Romanizing the provinces. This process of Romanization and urbanization he effectively pushed, extending the benefits of citizenship to many communities and enrolling senatorial members from Spain and Gaul.

To insure greater stability of the frontiers, he established extensive fortifications, strengthened defense lines, extended conquests in Britain, and came to terms with the Parthians in the East.

At home, Vespasian treated the Senate with respect but not in any sense as an equal partner. They obviously had less power now than earlier in the principate. Part of this decline resulted from an expansion of the civil service, which at that time was largely managed by equestrians rather than freedman.

Vespasian showed tremendous ability in the fiscal affairs of the Empire. Frugality, good business procedures, and sufficient control over the bureaucracy to prevent embezzlement—all contributed to his success. Of special importance was his firm control over the military—he did not have to bribe them to do what he wanted.

THE COLOSSEUM

Colosseum is a word familiar to modern Americans and Europeans as a large structure built for recreational purposes. Actually it apes the original Colosseum, or Flavian Amphitheater, that Vespasian began and his son Titus (destroyer of Jerusalem and the Temple in A.D. 70) completed in A.D. 80, with one hundred days of festival and celebration.

A cross section of the Colosseum.

ing room above, for a total capacity of about fifty thousand. The arena was separated from these tiers by a high platform carrying marble chairs for officials and a box for the emperor. The arena was floored in timber, covering cages for beasts, mechanical elevators, and storage.

Spectators held tickets corresponding to the seventy-six marked arcades on the bottom level. Most of the Roman numerals above these arcades are still plainly visible. An elaborate system of staircases serviced all parts of the auditorium.[12a]

Through thrifty, Vespasian managed to find large sums for construction of defenses in the provinces and for public buildings and education in the capital. His most famous structure, which he was unable to finish, was the great Colosseum, built on the site of one of the lakes on the grounds of Nero's palace. On the whole he used much restraint in the treatment of his opposition in the Senate and the city of Rome. For some time he even allowed the Cynics and Stoics to continue their open-air tirades against him, but finally banished them from the city.

It was built in central Rome on the site of the lake of Nero's Golden House.

The great structure measures 617 by 512 feet along its axes, with an arena measuring 289 by 180 feet. The exterior stands to a height of 170 feet in four stories or levels (faced with Travertine) of superimposed arcades framed by half columns of the Doric order on the first level, Ionic on the second, and Corinthian on the third. These are surmounted by a masonry attic decorated with Corinthian pilasters (rectangular piers) and poles around the roof for attaching awnings to cover the seating arrangement. Thus it was possible to protect spectators from being broiled in a hot Roman sun.

The seating was supported by concrete vaults in three tiers, with stand-

Titus. Before he died in A.D. 79, Vespasian had effectively linked his son Titus with him in the government, allowing for smooth transition to the new administration. Titus lasted only twenty-six months and died with the goodwill of the populace and the Senate. He showed great moderation in the treatment of political enemies and promoted the general welfare. He delighted the public with his splendid games and shows, and on the occasion of the dedication of the Colosseum held a one-hundred-day festival.

Three major catastrophes marred Titus' reign. In August of 79 Mount Vesuvius erupted, burying Pompeii, Herculaneum, and Stabiae. Then a plague descended on Campania. And in Rome another great fire burned for three days, destroying thousands of homes and several important public structures, including the Pantheon.

Titus

of his nights partying with disreputable characters. He also stirred criticism because of his affairs with the Jewish Queen Berenice. (This Berenice was the sister of Agrippa II who had an incestuous affair with Agrippa that lasted into the time when Agrippa heard the apostle Paul's defense in Caesarea; cf. Acts 25:23 ff.) During the Jewish War Berenice became Titus' mistress and later went to live with him in Rome. Oriental monarchs were so disliked in Rome that Vespasian forced Titus to send her back to Palestine.

When Titus became emperor he made a complete about-face. His goodness became legendary. When Vesuvius erupted he poured disaster relief into the stricken area. The same was true after the fire of Rome in 80. But attention to needs at home did not mean neglect of the provinces. He also sought to meet the needs there. Titus became a well-loved emperor.

Though Titus had a good reputation as a soldier, leading Rome to victory in the Jewish war, almost everything else about him was negative in the years before he became emperor. He was regarded as callous and cruel and the type that spent many

Domitian. Dying without an adult heir, Titus was succeeded by his younger brother Domitian (A.D. 81–96), who was received without opposition by the Praetorian Guard and the Senate. Very soon he won the undying hostility of the Senate by his autocratic ways, which indicated his intention of absolute dictatorship. After A.D. 86

The Temple of Zeus in the excavated Forum of Pompeii.

Domitian. *The Capitoline Museum*

suspicious and inaugurated something of a reign of terror in Rome. Many prominent persons (including about a dozen ex-consuls) were executed on trumped-up charges of treason, or "atheism" for refusing to accept his deity.

A persecution of Christians broke out in the Empire about A.D. 90, originally directed against Jews who refused to pay a tax to Jupiter Capitolinus. Being associated with Judaism in the minds of many, Christians also suffered during this persecution. Upon refusal to participate in emperor worship, Christians were charged with treason. Some were martyred, some dispossessed of property, and others banished. It was during this persecution that the apostle John was exiled to the Isle of Patmos, where he received the vision of the Revelation. Today biographers of Domitian tend to conclude that the tradition of Domitian the persecutor has been greatly exaggerated.

But Domitian cannot be dismissed as a mere tyrant. In Rome he was an able administrator and built extensively in an effort to erase the scars left by the great fire of 80. His finest public structure was the Temple of Jupiter on the Capitoline Hill, with columns of Greek marble, gold-plated doors, and a roof overlaid with gold leaf.

he seems to have required officials of his household to address him as "Lord and God." After the rebellion of Saturninus, legate of Upper Germany, during the winter of 88/89, Domitian grew increasingly

· THE ROMAN EMPIRE ·
44 B.C. TO 234 A.D.

▨ TERRITORY IN 44 B.C.
▧ ACQUIRED - 44 B.C.-14 A.D.
▦ ACQUIRED - 14 A.D.-117 A.D.
▩ TERRITORY HELD TEMPORARILY

He kept the populace happy with bread and games and the soldiers content with higher pay. He pushed Romanization in the provinces and saw to it that they were governed by men of ability, with the result that they flourished under his rule. Along the frontiers he built numerous fortresses and garrison camps. And after costly battles in Dacia (modern Romania), he managed to stabilize the situation there. Roman territory in Britain was increased.

Though Domitian demonstrated his abilities, he is more often remembered for his tyranny and his reign of terror. Ultimately it seemed that no one was safe. His wife Domitia, believing she was to be the next victim, conspired with two members of the Praetorian Guard and others. When the emperor fell a victim to the assassin's dagger on September 16, A.D. 96, his memory was cursed by the exultant Senate. Nerva, who succeeded him, was the first of the group known as the five good emperors.[13]

ROMAN TERRITORIAL GROWTH

(dates of most annexations)

Control of Italy by 265 B.C.

Sicily, 241 B.C.

Sardinia and Corsica, 238–31 B.C.

Spain, 206 B.C.

Illyricum (modern Yugoslavia), 167 B.C.

Macedonia, Greece, Carthage, 146 B.C.

Asia, 133 B.C.

Numidia, 106 B.C.

Cilicia, 103 B.C.

Cyrenaica, 96 B.C.

Bithynia, 74 B.C.

Crete, 67 B.C.

Syria, 64 B.C.

Palestine, 63 B.C.

Cyprus, 58 B.C.

Gaul, 51 B.C.

Egypt, 30 B.C.

Galatia, 25 B.C.

Britain, A.D. 43

Thrace, A.D. 46

Dacia (Modern Romania), A.D. 106

Armenia and Mesopotamia, A.D. 114

Demise of the Empire. In the first decades of the second century A.D. wars added territory north of the Danube and in the Mesopotamian valley and brought the Empire to its largest extent in A.D. 117, but these conflicts did not upset the general peace and security.

WHY ROME FELL

Scores of books have been written on the subject of why Rome fell. And as historians have studied the issue, they have constructed widely differing schools of interpretation. But some comments on the subject may prove useful.

And at the outset it is important to note that we are only dealing with the question of why Rome fell in the West. After the capital was moved from Rome to Constantinople (A.D. 330), the empire (the Byzantine) continued for more than 1100 years until Byzantium (Constantinople) fell to the Ottoman Turks in A.D. 1453.

Some Suggestions on Why Rome Fell in the West

1. Lack of a proper method of succession for leadership gave the army a chance to get control. Augustus and his successors adopted their own successors and associated those adopted persons with them. But if an emperor had not yet adopted his successor before his death or if he was assassinated, there was trouble. For example, with the assassination of Caligula, the army stepped in and chose Claudius as emperor. With the suicide of Nero

there was civil war, and the army brought Vespasian to power.

2. There was increasing centralization under the need to solve problems. Increasing despotism dried up individual ability, making the system more rigid or less flexible.

3. There was an increasing barbarization of the army and the civil service. That is, both were staffed by non-Romans and it was impossible to get the same success with them as with Roman or Italian stock. Such persons were not as familiar with Roman ways nor were they as dedicated to them.

4. A gradual breakdown of discipline and control of the army led to chaotic conditions during the third century A.D., when for some decades the army was on average putting forth a new emperor every couple of years. In fact, studies have been conducted on the loss of Roman military effectiveness and inability to meet the barbarians successfully in the field.

5. The development of large estates in Italy at least, where the workers were slaves or serfs, without much incentive to produce resulted in a decline in productivity.

6. A decrease of morality and spirituality, especially among the upper classes, eroded the moral fiber of the state.

7. A loss of population through numerous wars and plagues produced a serious manpower shortage.

8. Continued invasions by the Barbarians, who set up their separate states in Europe during the fifth century A.D. (the Franks, Visigoths, Ostrogoths, Vandals, Burgundians) and destroyed the very existence of Rome in the West.

The emperor Trajan brought the Roman Empire to its greatest extent.

Toward the end of the second century A.D., however, the principate was on its way out. The economic base of the municipalities began to show increasing signs of strain; this was coupled with the militarization of the state. Militarization was largely the work of Lucius Septimius Severus (A.D. 193–211), who was put into power by the army of the Danube and therefore felt that he had to favor the military. He increased its size and improved its conditions of service and discharge benefits. From that time on, officers moved directly into important positions in the civil service on retirement from army life. The effects of this militarization were soon felt.

The years 235–283 constituted a period of anarchy, of barrack-room emperors, many of whom bought their position from the armies. Some forty of them were put forward by the armies during those years. At last Diocletian established order out of confusion and effected a reorganization of the State. His reorganization was ineffective and civil war started again at the end of his reign. Peace was restored when Constantine

Constantine stopped persecution of Christians and moved the capital of the empire to Constantinople.

established himself as sole ruler and moved the capital of the Empire to Constantinople.

During the decades just before Diocletian took office, barbarian tribes moved against the northern frontiers of the Empire, especially in the Danubian region. Some of these had been permitted to move into the Empire and to settle along the frontiers where they would serve as a buffer against other barbarians. Before these tribes were completely Romanized, a new wave of barbarian infiltration began in the fourth century during the days of Constantine. This was too much of a strain for the Empire, and it began to disintegrate into semi-barbarian states. Although Rome was no longer the seat of power after A.D. 476, the Empire continued on in the East with its capital at Constantinople until 1453.[14]

The Apostle Paul in Italy

The Italy to which Paul came as a prisoner was fully enjoying the *Pax Romana* and had not yet reached the height of her prosperity. Her most magnificent structures had not yet been built and the limits of her territorial expansion had not been reached. Moreover, cracks had not yet begun to appear in the hull of the ship of state, and there were no evident signs that the ship would one day break apart and sink. Romans were still quite confident, and their rule of the Empire was still effective. As we remember, the apostle Paul was brought to Italy because he had appealed to Caesar for the adjudication of a case that had not been satisfactorily handled in Palestine. On the way he had been shipwrecked on Malta.

After three months on Malta, Paul and his companions boarded ship for Italy (Acts 28:11). Very likely the month was March because the closed season for sailing in the Mediterranean was roughly November 10 to March 10. The year may have been A.D. 59.[15] The vessel on which they traveled, "a ship of Alexandria" (Acts 28:11), was almost certainly one of the large ships of the grain fleet supplying the city of Rome. Some of these ships must have been approximately as large as modern merchantmen. The grain ship on which Paul sailed to Malta carried 276 passengers besides its cargo of wheat (Acts 27:37). For purposes of comparison, the ship on which Josephus came to Italy later in the century had a passenger list of 600.[16] A grain ship on which Lucian of Antioch sailed late in the second century was 180 feet in length and 45 feet in breadth. Smith estimates the tonnage of that ship at between eleven and twelve hundred tons.[17] But Columbus' three ships had a combined tonnage of only about two hundred, and a combined crew of about ninety.

Ancient ships were sailed mainly by one large sail on a single mast. The leverage of this sail exercised a tremendous disruptive power on the hull of the vessel. Sometimes there was a topsail above the mainsail. Also, there might be one or more small storm sails that could be substituted for the great sail when the wind was too strong. In addition, there was frequently a small sail on the bow.

Syracuse

After leaving Malta, Paul's ship next docked at Syracuse, about a hundred miles

A Roman merchantman. *Courtesy of the Department of Classics New York University*

away. Located on the east coast of Sicily, Syracuse was the principal city of the island. Originally a Corinthian colony founded in the eighth century B.C. (about 734), Syracuse became one of the most magnificent Greek states. Her ancient power was well demonstrated by her naval victory over the Carthaginians in 474 that gave her control over the southern basin of the Mediterranean, and by her defeat of the great Athenian flotilla of 415 B.C. At the end of the First Punic War in 241 B.C., Syracuse fell with the rest of Sicily to the Romans.

During the Second Punic War she sided with Carthage; and Rome was forced to conquer her, which Rome did in 212. The city was thoroughly plundered and tremendous booty was taken.

From that time Syracuse sank into the condition of an ordinary Roman provincial town. Sicily suffered terribly during the Roman civil wars of the last part of the first century B.C. Syracuse was so decayed that Augustus tried to restore the city by sending a Roman colony there in 21 B.C. Strabo, writing around the time of Christ, described the whole island of Sicily as in a state of decay, some of the cities having disappeared and others declining. The interior to a large extent was given over to grazing and horse breeding. Syracuse rapidly regained its prosperity during the first century A.D. and continued to be one of the most important cities of Sicily throughout the Roman Empire. She was destroyed by Muslims in A.D. 878 and never fully recovered the greatness she had once enjoyed. Today the city has a population of about 125,000.

Paul's ship lay at anchor there for about three days on his way to Rome (Acts 28:12). Nothing is said about his preaching in the city, but he may have done so. Some believe there was a Christian community there when Paul arrived. Others conclude that Christianity spread to Sicily from the mainland at a later time.

Syracuse as Paul could have experienced the city was an impressive place. His ship would have headed straight for the small island of Ortygia (about a mile long by a half mile wide), where the Corinthians had planted the original settlement. Very close to the mainland, this island was joined to land by a bridge. The city sprawled out in four other quarters from the island. It was blessed with two natural ports, a small one to the south and a large one on the great bay to the north of Ortygia. Paul's ship probably put in at the larger harbor.

A dominant structure on the island was the temple of Athena, a

SYRACUSE

0 — 1 — 2 Kilometres

Leontini

Walls of Dionysius I

EURYALUS

EPIPOLAE

Walls of Dionysius I

Walls of Dionysius I

Quarries

Theatre *Quarries*
Altar of Hieron II *Roman Amphitheatre* TYCHE
TEMENITES
NEAPOLIS ACHRADINA

Acrae

Helorus

Great

R. *Anapus*

Harbour

Olympieum

Agora *Little Harbour*

Temple of Apollo
ORTYGIA

Arethusa fountain

Temple of Athena

Courtesy of Margaret Guido

The northern harbor of Syracuse .

Doric temple of the fifth century B.C. (approximately 90 by 225 feet), with six columns across the front and fourteen along the sides and having doors of gold and ivory. On the summit of the pediment stood a statue of Athena with a gold shield visible from far out at sea. This temple is now incorporated into the Cathedral of Syracuse.

A temple of Apollo (sixth century B.C.) stood at the entrance to the island from the mainland. This Doric temple measured about 75 by 180 feet and had six columns at the end and seventeen on the sides, with a double row at the entrance. On the mainland adjacent to the island sprawled the agora, now a public park. A little to the west of the city on a small elevation overlooking the great harbor rose the temple of Zeus (sixth century B.C.). Like the temple of Apollo it had six columns on the ends and seventeen on the sides, with a double row of columns at the entrance. It measured about 80 by 200 feet.

North of Ortygia island, at the northern edge of the Neapolis section of Syracuse, rose the Greek theater. Constructed in the fifth century B.C. and modified in the third century, it was largely carved from the living rock, at least in the lower courses of the cavea. The largest ancient theater in Sicily and one of the largest in the Mediterranean world, it had an outer diameter of 454 feet and accommodated about twenty-two thousand spectators.[18] By comparison, the famous Theater of Dionysus in Athens held about 17,000. Adjacent to the theater were the quarries from which much of the building stone of the city was cut. This was the place where in the fifth century B.C. seven thousand Athenian prisoners had been kept.

The temple of Apollo, Syracuse.

The Greek Theater, Syracuse.

Commentators have sometimes suggested that the ship actually sailed around the island. The Greek term *perielthontes* of Acts 28:13 is difficult; but James Smith, a practical yachtsman, provides a satisfactory explanation. To him the term signifies that the wind was so unfavorable that the ship could not run a straight course but had to tack northeastward toward Italy and then back to the Sicilian coast.[19] J. B. Phillips in *The New Testament in Modern English,* supports this viewpoint with his translation: "from there we tacked round to Rhegium."

A short distance southeast of the theater sprawled the third century B.C. altar of Hieron II. An enormous rock-cut podium 650 feet long, it had ramps leading up to the central part where public sacrifices were offered by the city. West of the city stood the Euryalus fort, which enclosed the Epipolae ridge, one of the most remarkable complexes of Greek fortifications still in existence.

Rhegium

From Syracuse the grain ship on which Paul made his way to Rome sailed northeastward to Rhegium (modern Reggio). The King James Version says the sailors "fetched a compass" (Acts 28:13). The New King James Version has "circled round."

Rhegium was close to the narrowest point of the Straits of Messina, separating Sicily and Italy, just opposite the Sicilian town of Messana (formerly Zancle). The actual point of crossing from Sicily was at Columna, six miles or more north of Rhegium. The straits were very dangerous in ancient times—more so than now. Some miles north of Rhegium was the dangerous rock Scylla (Scilla) and north of Messana was the whirlpool of Charybdis (Galofalo). Ships often had to lie at Rhegium waiting for a suitable wind so that they might avoid these dangers and also navigate the periodically swift currents in the straits.

As a result, the twin gods Castor and Pollux, the patrons and protectors of sailors, were much worshiped at Rhegium

The altar of Hieron, Syracuse

The Puteoli harbor, with the Roman wharf on the far side of the picture.

and were represented on its coins. Mariners of the ships that put in there often discharged their vows to the twin gods in the town. The ship on which Paul traveled sailed under the sign of Castor and Pollux (Acts 28:11).

Rhegium, a Greek town founded by Chalcis about 720 B.C., was destroyed by Syracuse in 387 B.C., and the inhabitants were sold as slaves. Rebuilt, it was destroyed again between 280 and 270 by Campanian troops. When her army captured it, Rome gave the town back to the remnant of the former population. From that time on, Rhegium was allied with Rome and successfully withstood attacks by Rome's enemies, including Hannibal. The inhabitants received Roman citizenship in 88 B.C. at the end of the social war. Despite frequent earthquakes, it remained a populous Greek-speaking city throughout imperial times. The ship in which Paul sailed from Malta to Puteoli (Pozzuoli) lay for a day in the harbor of Rhegium waiting for a south wind. The Rhegium-to-Puteoli run, a distance of 180 miles, probably took about twenty-six hours (Acts 28:13).

Puteoli

Puteoli was the great commercial port of Italy, located on what is now called the Bay of Naples. The name is of doubtful origin but is attributed either to the putrid odor of the sulphurous springs close by or to the wells (*putei*) of the place. A colony of the nearby Greek town of Cumae, which it served as a port, Puteoli was in existence at least by the sixth century B.C. During and after the Second Punic War it rose to a high degree of commercial importance, which it subsequently retained.

Puteoli became the chief port of Rome, though it was 150 miles away. It won that distinction because of the safety of its harbor and the inhospitality of the coast near Rome. Although Claudius created an artificial harbor at Ostia (near Rome), Puteoli's trade had not markedly declined in the days of Nero. But the southern port decayed rapidly early in the second century B.C. after Trajan made the harbor at Ostia adequate. The city never recovered from the Barbarian invasions of A.D. 410, 455, and 545.

While a great part of the goods handled at Puteoli were Alexandrian grain supplies for Rome, that was only one branch of its extensive commerce. The iron of Elba, after being smelted in Populonium (Populonia) was brought to Puteoli for manufacture into a variety of implements; these formed an important element in the brisk trade with Africa and Spain. The port also profited from an extensive copper and bronze industry. Bronze from the adjacent plain of Campania was used all over Europe in the form of utensils and

The Roman amphitheater of Puteoli.

weapons. Work in gold also went on there, as did production of Surrentine pottery (a red ware).

Campania was also famous for its wines, and it produced olive oil and perfumes from its rose gardens. Luxury goods from the Orient formed an important part of the trade of Puteoli in value, though not in bulk. Trade with Tyre was of such importance that the Tyrians had a merchant colony there. Several merchants of Berytus (Beirut) also lived at Puteoli. Travelers from the East frequently landed there; the disembarkation of Paul and that of Cicero before him are cases in point. The neighborhood of Puteoli became a favorite resort of the Roman upper classes, many of whom had villas there.

As already indicated, Puteoli had an excellent port. It was well sheltered by its natural situation and was further protected by an extensive mole or pier built in the days of Augustus. Extensive docks were constructed to care for the city's widespread maritime interests. A great boon for construction of dock works was the city's good supply of volcanic sand that formed a waterproof mortar or cement of extreme hardness and durability and was also waterproof.

Into this bustling port of some one hundred thousand came the apostle Paul, probably on one of the first grain ships to dock that spring. The smoke of Mount Vesuvius was something he did not see as his ship glided across the Gulf of Puteoli. The volcano was at that time a harmless-looking mountain whose southern slopes were covered with vines. Less than twenty years were to elapse before the lava flowed and hot cinders fell on Pompeii and nearby towns on that terrible August night in A.D. 79.

As the apostle's ship pulled into the harbor, it no doubt docked at the great pier, at least to let the passengers disembark. The ship later may have moved to another dock to unload the grain. The great pier was fully 1,150 feet long and almost 50 feet wide. It was decorated with columns topped by statues, a triumphal arch, and a lighthouse and it ended in an architectural ship's prow. Hovering over the harbor on a low hill about one hundred feet high stood a temple to Augustus.

Near the harbor lay a great market. This consisted of a rectangular courtyard about 118 by 125 feet surrounded by a portico which opened into shops on the east and west. The grand entrance was in the center of the south side. In the center of the courtyard stood a circular structure supported by sixteen columns. Statues stood between the columns, and a fountain adorned the center. Stairs led to an upper story. The entire market was surrounded by a one-story enclosure with additional shops. And as with modern malls, there were latrines in the northeast and northwest corners.

In the upper town stood an amphitheater dating to Augustus' day. Its axes were about 312 by 427 feet. After Paul's time in the days of Vespasian (A.D. 69–79) a great amphitheater was built, accommodating some forty thousand spectators.

Today it is impossible to see all this. Remains of the Augustan pier are embedded in the modern breakwater. The temple of Augustus is gone; a few pieces of it appear in the modern cathedral. The amphitheater of Augustus' day was located under the modern Rome-Naples railway line. The great market is almost entirely under water; a few pillars stand out of the water. These have commonly been called the Temple of Serapis. Over time much of the lower town has sunk and risen again, and since the eighteenth century has again been slowly sinking. The great amphitheater of the later first century A.D. is in a fair state of preservation.

There seems to have been a Jewish colony at Puteoli,[20] and this may possibly account for the presence of Christians in the town. At any rate, believers there desired Paul to stay with them for a week (Acts 28:14). Exactly how this was possible when the apostle was a prisoner is unclear. Possibly the commander in charge had some business to do in town anyway. Or he may have needed to wait for instructions.

The Roman Roads

From Puteoli, the apostolic company took the tomb-lined Via Consularis to Capua (twenty miles away), where it joined the main line of the Appian Way. The distance from Puteoli to Rome was 155 Roman miles or 142 English miles (a Roman mile was 1,614.6 yards). From Capua to Rome (131 Roman miles) was considered to be a journey of five days for an active traveler. William Ramsay concluded that travelers on foot seem to have accomplished sixteen to twenty miles a day on an average Roman road, the ordinary rate being about seventeen. Travelers driving wagons or other vehicles moved at the rate of four Roman miles an hour or about twenty-five Roman miles a day. The imperial post could travel as fast as fifty miles a day.[21] It is impossible to know whether Paul and his companions walked or rode.

Rome took great pride in her road system which she flung in every direction from the capital throughout Italy and the Empire. In those days it was literally true that all roads led to Rome. Initially designed as military highways, they served also as arteries for commerce and the backbone of a communications network. Special officials of praetorian or even consular rank were entrusted with the maintenance of the roads. And at important points permanent military guards in special guardhouses were stationed. These guards had responsibility not only for care of the roads but even more for keeping the roads and the public in the surrounding region safe from robbers.

Rome not only exercised great care in the maintenance of her roads but she built them to last. Some modern roads in Italy and elsewhere in the Mediterranean world are merely blacktopped Roman roads. Naturally the type of construction varied with expected traffic, terrain, and available materials. Mountain roads might be only five or six feet wide (with wider places for passing) and surfaced with gravel, while the main roads were fifteen to twenty feet wide and paved with stone.

ALL ROADS LEAD TO ROME

The familiar saying that "all roads lead to Rome" originated with a milestone that stood in the Forum at Rome recording distances by road from Rome to the chief cities of the empire. Augustus Caesar set up that milestone in 20 B.C. By the end of the first Christian century about 250,000 miles of improved roads, ten times the circumference of the earth at the equator, crisscrossed the empire.

The Appian Way near Rome.

Before the Romans built a road, they conducted a survey. Though they have not left much information about how they ran the survey or what instruments they used, they were evidently very competent. They could calculate distances to inaccessible points, run levels with accuracy, measure angles, and lay out tunnels and dig them from both ends. Surveyors preferred straight lines, plotted from ridge to ridge, but they took into consideration the slope of the land and questions of defense. Across a plain they tried to take a straight course, constructing bridges and paved fords to cross rivers, and viaducts to span marshes. Because Romans tried to build straight roads, often over hills rather than around them, slopes frequently were steep; 10 percent grades were common.

After the survey was complete, construction could begin. When building an important road, Roman engineers dug a trench the full width of the road and four or five feet deep. The roadbed was then built up with successive layers of large and small stone and rammed gravel; sometimes there was a layer of concrete. Normally roads were surfaced with gravel, which might rest on a bed of mortar. In the neighborhood of cities,

in places where traffic was heavy, or in the construction of a very important road, engineers paved the surface with large carefully fitted stone (without the use of mortar or metal), about twelve inches thick and eighteen inches across.

Naturally the type of construction varied with expected traffic, terrain, and available materials. Mountain roads might be only five or six feet wide (with wider places for passing) and surfaced with gravel, while the main roads could be fifteen to twenty feet wide and sometimes paved with stone. Unfortunately we do not know how long it took to build the Roman roads or the size of road gangs.

When constructing an important road, Roman engineers dug a trench the full width of the road four to five feet deep. The roadbed was then built up with successive layers of large and small stone and rammed gravel. The surface paving was made of large, carefully fitted stone (without the use of mortar or metal), about twelve inches thick and eighteen inches across. Generally the roads were straight, going over hills rather than around them. Therefore, slopes might be steep; 10 percent grades were common. Where roads crossed streams, stone bridges were usually built, resting on

As Paul neared Rome, he would have passed the Claudian Aqueduct.

a series of arches based on piers of masonry. Some Roman bridges are still in use.

The Appian Way, the principal road to southern Italy, was begun in 312 B.C. as a military road by the famous censor Appius Claudius Caecus and ultimately was extended to Tarentum and Brundisium. Paving of the road was begun in 295 B.C. and was certainly completed by Gracchan times (late second century B.C.). Its width was about eighteen feet, wide enough for two wagons to pass abreast; and it was paved with blocks of basaltic lava (silex).

As on the other great roads, inns, taverns, and places of refreshment existed in abundance along the Appian Way. Little is known about them and what is known gives no favorable picture. Inns offered wretched accommodations and equally wretched food. Persons of higher social standing usually arranged to spend the nights at the homes of friends or relatives. Military personnel, such as those who accompanied Paul, could have lodged at military, police, or government installations along the way. The Antonine Itinerary lists eight main stations on the Appian Way between Capua and Rome, two of which are mentioned in Luke's narrative—Appii Forum and Tres Tabernae (Three Taverns).

Appii Forum

When Christians in Rome received word that Paul was coming, they came as far south as Appii Forum and Three Taverns to meet him (Acts 28:15). Appii Forum, or Forum of Appius, apparently named for the builder of the Appian Way, was located forty-three Roman miles from Rome, in the middle of the Pomptine Marshes. As an alternate means of transportation, a canal ran alongside the road from there to the sixty-second milestone, and it was used chiefly at night for conveying passengers in barges towed by mules. Horace (68–65 B.C.), not long before the birth of Christ, told of his experience of spending the night at Appii Forum. Apparently conditions did not change much before Paul's arrival.

Horace said that the water was so bad it made him sick. And when night descended, a "hideous clatter" arose as the bargemen along the canal prepared to move their human cargo downstream. Then there was the confusion of stuffing three hundred passengers on one barge and collecting their fares. All hope of sleep fled because of croaking bullfrogs, buzzing mosquitoes, and the singing of drunken bargemen and passengers. And so the hours of a romantic Italian evening wore on.[22] We have no way of knowing whether Paul was treated to the

The tomb of Caecilia Metella.

along the main roads, especially the Appian Way.

Some three miles from the Porta Capena, which led through the old Servian Wall and into the main part of the city, Paul would have passed the famous Claudian aqueduct, though it was obscured from his view by the contour of the land. This great water channel rested on 110-foot arches which strode across the landscape to bring water to Rome from a distance of forty-five miles. Begun by Caligula in A.D. 38 and completed by Claudius in 52, it brought a total of nearly fifty million gallons of water per day to the city.[23] There were at least seven other aqueducts supplying the capital in Nero's day.

With the Claudian aqueduct far off to his right over the hill, the tomb of Caecilia Metella stood almost in front of Paul to the right of the road. The woman for whom the tomb was built was the wife of M. Crassus, evidently the son of the triumvir of the same name, who had shared power in Rome with Julius Caesar and Pompey. Decorations of the tomb date it to the beginning of the Augustan period. The tomb is a huge drum of concrete on a square base. Faced with travertine, it is sixty feet in its outside diameter. The roof probably originally consisted of a conical vault. In the Middle Ages the tomb was transformed into a fortress and the crenellation (battlements) added around the top. The elegant frieze of ox heads and garlands remains as a memento of its former grandeur.

About a mile farther down the road was the Campus Rediculi, where, according to Pliny the Elder, a pet crow of Tiberius was buried.[24] A little beyond that, still on the right, were the columbaria (burial vaults) of the slaves and freedmen of Livia, wife of Augustus. A mile farther down the road, again on the apostle's right, would have been a celebrated temple of Mars, god of war. And about a half mile beyond stood the third century B.C. tomb of the celebrated Scipio family. After another five or six blocks, Paul found himself at the Porta Capena, the gate through the old Servian Wall into the main part of the city. This seven-mile-long wall, built during the first half of the fourth century

luxury of the boat ride or whether he walked, but likely he walked.

Three Taverns

Ten Roman miles closer to Rome was Three Taverns (Tres Tabernae). The location of this place, long in doubt, has now been determined with some degree of certainty at a point near the beginning of the Pomptine Marshes, about three miles from modern Cisterna. The Latin *tabernae* signifies booths, huts, or shops of various kinds. Here it probably refers to inns for travelers. From Tres Tabernae the apostolic party traveled the seventeen miles to Aricia and then moved along the last sixteen miles between Aricia and Rome.

The Last Leg of the Journey

About eleven miles from the capital stood the ancient village of Bovillae. Here was the center of the ancestor cult of the Julian family, and here Augustus' body lay for a night on its way to Rome in A.D. 14. Tiberius reconstructed the shrine, in which a statue of the deified Augustus was placed. He also instituted games in the nearby circus, a few of the arches of which may still be seen among the vineyards. Probably tombs lined most of the way between Bovillae and Rome. Since Roman law forbade burial of the dead inside the city, it became the practice to build tombs along the principal roads. By the time of Nero, tombs extended for many miles

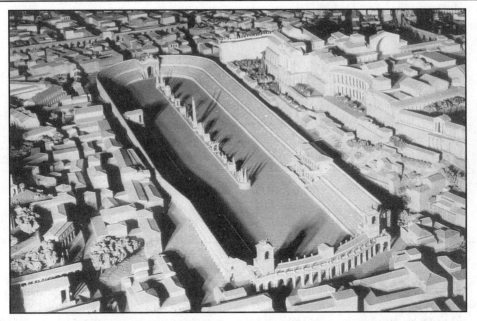

The Circus Maximus. The Palatine Hill: the palaces of the Caesars rose to the right.

B.C., was now deep within the expanding city of the first century A.D. No longer needed for defense, the wall had been allowed to fall into decay.

Arrival in Rome

It is hard to imagine what the Apostle Paul's thoughts may have been as he stood there at the Porta Capena. If he had been a poor provincial from rural Palestine, we might picture him as overawed with the great metropolis. But such was not the case. Paul had been born in the proud city of Tarsus. His missionary activities had taken him to most of the important cities of the East—to Antioch, Ephesus, Corinth, Athens, Thessalonica, and Jerusalem. Certainly he did not come with the curiosity of a tourist or the acquisitiveness of a businessman. No doubt there was some trepidation as he realized that the moment when he would stand trial for his life was drawing closer. And probably he had enthusiasm as an evangelist who longed for a means of winning some in this strategic center to faith in the Lord Jesus.

The Circus Maximus

As the apostolic company passed through the gate, before them stood the great Circus Maximus, and overhanging it on the right were the palaces of the Caesars on the Palatine Hill. As modern visitors to Rome stroll across the great grassy area where once stood the circus Maximus and glance up at the massive ruined substructures of the imperial palaces, they have a hard time visualizing the sight that greeted the apostle's eyes.

Between the parallel slopes of the Aventine and Palatine lay a valley some 600 yards long and 150 yards broad. Here the great circus had evolved through a process of repeated destruction and rebuilding. And it was destined to be almost completely rebuilt by Nero after the fire of A.D. 64.

In Paul's day the total length of the circus was about 600 yards and the total width not over 200 yards. The width was achieved by building out over the streets on the north and south sides. The size of the arena was about 570 yards long by about 85 yards wide. In the middle of it stood the spina (the central barrier around which chariots raced), 345 yards in length. On the spina were fountains, statues of dignitaries, an obelisk from Egypt, and bronze dolphins and large egg-shaped blocks

The substructures of the palace of Domitian on the Palatine Hill.

of wood to help spectators keep track of the number of laps run in a given race.

At the west end were the twelve *carceres*, or starting places for chariots. These were set on a curve so the distance was the same from each to the starting line, and they were closed by rope barriers that were dropped simultaneously at the start. The east end of the circus was curved, with a gate in the center. A raised platform surrounded the arena, on which chairs of high officials were placed. From this platform rose three tiers of seats, the lower of stone and the upper and perhaps the middle of wood. Estimates of seating capacity vary greatly, but perhaps two hundred thousand is not far from wrong. The exterior consisted of a three-story arcade with engaged columns, like the Colosseum,

and all was covered with travertine, limestone from the quarries near Tivoli.

The circus was by no means the only place a Roman could go to be entertained in Paul's day. There were also amphitheaters, theaters, and baths. It was the emperor who took the lead in building most of the structures for public entertainment, and it was usually he who paid for the entertainment provided in these structures once they were finished.

Palaces of the Emperors

As already noted, the palaces of the emperors stood on the Palatine Hill overlooking the Circus Maximus. Today virtually all one can see on the Palatine is great masses of brickwork with arched roofs. In Paul's day these structures were encased in marble or at least travertine. On the Palatine, Augustus had a villa and Tiberius and Claudius had built their palaces; these eventually covered the hill.

Connected with the villa of Augustus (he never built an ostentatious palace) was a beautiful temple of Apollo constructed of white marble and surrounded by porticoes with columns of yellow marble. Of the images within—of Apollo, Artemis, and Latona (mother of Apollo and Artemis), the first was sculptured by Scopas. This temple lasted throughout the imperial period.

The inlaid marble floor in the dining room of Domitian's palace.

Members of the Praetorian Guard in full regalia.

The location of neither the temple nor Augustus' villa can be identified with certainty today. But one can still see part of the house of Livia, Augustus' wife, and its wall paintings that are reminiscent of those in Pompeii. On the northwest part of the hill Tiberius built his palace, the site of which is today almost covered by the Farnese Gardens. Only a little of the southern and western sides of the palace can be seen, and little is known of it. Caligula extended the palace of Tiberius toward the Forum, and it seems that there were stairs leading from the palace down into the Forum in Paul's day. At that time too there were temples to Jupiter and Magna Mater (Cybele) on the Palatine.

The entire Palatine was modified by new buildings of Domitian, who demolished earlier buildings of the whole central part of the hill. The palace of his day consisted of two great complexes of rooms, each surrounding an open courtyard. One of these complexes is known as the *Domus Flavia* and the other, the *Domus Augustana*. Adjacent was the "stadium," which was probably used for minor games or entertainments; it was not big enough for chariot racing.

Although Nero is probably responsible for some of the construction on the Palatine, he built his palace on the Esquiline Hill, northeast of where the Colosseum now stands. The palace was destroyed by the great fire of 64. It was not in the palace but probably in one of the public buildings in the Forum that Paul would appear before Nero.

Appeal to Caesar

But Paul was not destined to be granted a hearing for a long time. After a stay of two whole years in the capital, his case still had not been adjudicated (Acts 28:30). Reasons for the delay can only be conjectured. Perhaps there was a large backlog of cases; perhaps the court did not meet often to deal with cases of this type; conceivably the prosecution failed to present its case; or possibly the settlement of such cases depended on the whim of the emperor or more likely of one of his top assistants. At any rate, there was a delay; and meanwhile the apostle lived "at his own expense," the preferred translation of "his own hired house" (Acts 28:30).

So Paul was in Rome. He had appealed to Caesar. Exactly why is unclear. He may have been afraid that authorities in Judea would keep him in prison indefinitely with the hope of obtaining handsome bribes (Acts 24:26) and that the only way to escape was to appeal to Caesar, and in this way guaranteeing a hearing. Or he may have felt that to submit to another trial in Judea would result in his ultimate conviction and execution. Festus, the new procurator, apparently was interested in buying the goodwill of the Jews by tokens of that sort (Acts 24:27). Then too the Jews seemed rather determined to destroy him (Acts 23:12). Or perhaps Paul may have actually felt that an appeal to Caesar would win him an opportunity to go to Italy to engage in missionary work and that he could reasonably hope for acquittal in the pagan capital on the mere charge of propagating the Christian faith among the Jews.

Whatever the reason, Paul had appealed; and Festus, after discussing the case with his council, decided to send him to Rome (Acts 25:10–12). He delivered him and other prisoners to Julius, "a centurion of Augustus' band" (Acts 27:1). Probably by this we are to understand that Julius was captain of a cohort of the Praetorian Guard responsible for communication service between the emperor and his provincial armies and authorities. When he arrived in Rome, Paul was delivered to the "captain of the guard" (Acts 28:16), which Sherwin-White understands to be the head of the organizational command of the Praetorian Guard.[25]

The opportunity for provincials to appeal to Caesar presumably arose early in Augustus' reign. When he appeared before the Senate in 27 B.C. to turn over control of the state, that venerable body conferred upon Augustus the proconsular imperium by which he had full authority to rule the imperial provinces. Generally speaking, imperial provinces were those not fully Romanized and therefore requiring a body of soldiers to keep order. Senatorial provinces on the other hand were pacified and did not require troops. Gradually Caesar became the supreme court for provincials in imperial provinces. Since Judea was ruled directly by the emperor through his procurators,[26] appeals would early have been sent from there.

Subsequently, in 23 B.C., the Senate conferred upon Augustus the *maius,* or greater, imperium, which gave him the right to interfere in any province. Thus all provincials came to look upon the emperor as the final court of appeal. What began with Augustus was continued to an increasing degree under successive rulers.

When the emperor acted as judge, he called a council of about six of his advisers to consult with him on how to deal with the case at hand. Usually the Praetorian prefect (commander of the Praetorian Guard, who might be almost a second ruler, as was Sejanus during Tiberius' reign) judged *vice principis.* And probably in the case of lesser individuals like Paul, the Praetorian prefect handled the entire case as president of the emperor's court, without consulting his superior.

Certainly it was impossible for the emperor to handle all the details that called for his attention. During periods when the chief executive was out of the city, much work had to be deputized. It seems that under Nero the trial of capital cases on appeal was delegated to other persons and the sentences were confirmed by him afterward.[27] Thus it is likely that Paul never appeared before Nero at all.

Paul's Freedom and the Appearance of Rome

So Paul had appealed and now he waited for his case to be heard. In what part of the city he was confined is unknown, and how much freedom he had to move about is unknown: "Paul was permitted to dwell by himself with the soldier who guarded him" (Acts 28:16 NKJV). The Romans didn't have a prison system like ours where individuals were locked away for a period of time to pay their debt to society. Rather, someone sat in jail awaiting trial or execution or sentence. Individuals were rarely chained, except when they were moved, to keep them from escaping.[28] But Paul had not even been chained on the voyage from Caesarea to Rome. He talks about being chained while in Rome (Acts 28:20; Ephesians 6:20; Philippians 1:7, 13–14; Col. 4:3, 18; Philemon 10, 13), but this could be a figure of speech to describe his confinement. Or he, like others, may have been chained temporarily to prevent his escape when receiving visitors.

In any case, Paul had a considerable amount of freedom during his first Roman imprisonment, receiving numerous visitors (cf. Acts 28:30). During that time he wrote the Prison Epistles and sent them to the respective churches (cf. Ephesians 3:1; 4:1; Philippians 1:7; Colossians 4:3, 10; Philemon 9). Evidently he had to pay for his keep during the two years in Rome (Acts 28:30), so he would have been delighted with gifts from the church at Philippi (cf. Philippians 4:10; cf. 4:16, 17) and any other church that was moved to send one.

If Paul could have gone for a walk in Rome, he would not have found it to be very impressive. True, the city had its palaces, some fine temples, recreational establishments, and the like. And there were parks (perhaps as much as one-eighth

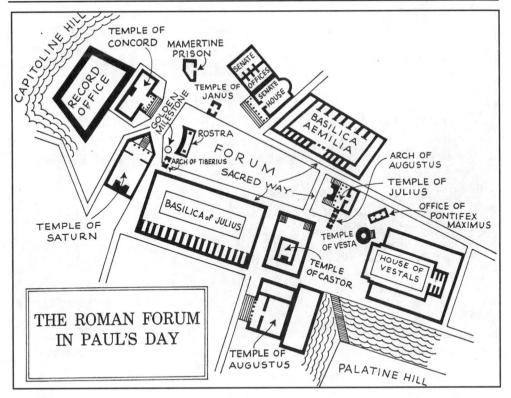

THE ROMAN FORUM
IN PAUL'S DAY

of the city was reserved for this purpose) and homes of the wealthy.

But in much of the old city the streets were narrow, steep, and crooked—often not more than ten feet wide. They were frequently littered with garbage and were unlighted at night. In the poorer sections of the city, wooden tenement houses (*insulae*) rose to a height of as many as six stories, each one covering a block. Often these were poorly constructed, and sometimes they collapsed. Running water from the aqueducts was available only on the first floors, and light and heat were inadequate. These huge tinderboxes provided abundant fuel when the fire of Rome roared through the city in A.D. 64.

The wider streets, the great baths, and many of the finest buildings of Rome were to come during the rebuilding after the fire and as Rome with her imperial income was able to finance more beautiful and imposing structures in later centuries. Though reportedly Augustus had bragged that he had found Rome a city of brick and left it a city of marble, there was much lacking

when Paul arrived close to a half century later.

THE ROMAN FORUM

The Roman Forum functioned as the hub of the life of the city from earliest times. Especially was this possible after the construction of the great sewer, early in the Republic, that drained this marshy area at the feet of the Palatine and Capitoline hills.

Temples, a public record office, the Senate building and offices, a court building, a currency exchange, the golden milestone, and a podium where officials could address assembled crowds, were among the many structures erected there. Of course, as the city and empire grew, the area proved to be inadequate to handle all the crowds that converged upon it.

To alleviate crowding and provide for additional public functions, Julius Caesar added an adjacent forum of his own. Augustus followed his

Ruins of the west end of the Roman Forum, showing the Basilica Julia on the left and columns of the Temple of Saturn on the right.

example, and so did Nerva and Trajan a hundred years later. As a result of archaeological activity, much of the ancient city center has now emerged from the accumulated debris of the centuries. But enough is still covered by modern roads and buildings that we find it difficult to visualize how the area appeared when Rome ruled the Mediterranean world.

We can make some visual comparison of a Roman forum by a visit to Pompeii, where the city center is fully excavated. But then Pompeii had a population of only about twenty thousand, while Rome's population exceeded a million.

The Forum Area

At last the day for Paul's trial came; exactly when and where it was held is unknown. Very possibly it occurred in the Basilica Julia at the southwest end of the Forum. There is no way of knowing from which direction Paul came to the Forum. Let us suppose it was from the east. And let us remember that the Roman Forum no longer served as the scene for as much business as it had in the days of the Republic. To the northwest Julius Caesar had begun a new forum of his own. Augustus had finished it and added one of his own alongside that of Julius. After Paul's day Vespasian, Domitian, Nerva, and Trajan would continue the expansion.

If Paul entered the Forum[29] area from the east down the Sacred Way, the first building he would have passed was the house of the vestal virgins. He might have observed that the house was rather large for a sisterhood of only six priestesses. But such an objection is erased with the observation that the vestals were held in high esteem and that their house was chosen by private citizens and by the State as a safe deposit for documents.

Adjacent to this house was the Temple of Vesta. Vesta was the goddess of the hearth and was considered the patron of the fire that symbolized the perpetuity of the state. It was the responsibility of the priestesses to

A reconstruction of the Basilica Julia.

maintain this sacred fire and to renew it each January 1.

Just in front of the Temple of Vesta was the Regia, office of the Pontifex Maximus, head of the religion of the State and repository of the acts of the college of pontiffs concerning the religious life of Rome and the sacred law. As Paul continued westward, he passed the Temple of Caesar, or Temple of the Divine Julius, which is supposed to have stood on the very site where the dictator's body was burned on a pyre improvised by the crowds after Mark Antony's famous speech.

At the corner of the Temple of Caesar, the Sacred Way turned left, and passed in front of the temple, and led straight to the steps of the Temple of Castor and Pollux, the sanctuary of horsemen and of travelers in general. The temple had eleven Corinthian columns about thirty-eight feet high (three of which may be seen today). The Arch of Augustus was located to the left.

Following the Sacred Way to the right, Paul found himself alongside the Basilica Julia. Straight before him in the center of the Forum would have stood the Rostra, where orators held forth and officials made public speeches. At one corner of the Rostra was the *miliarum aureum,* or golden milestone, a marble column covered with gilt bronze, on which the distances from Rome to the principal towns of Italy and the Empire were marked. This is the basis for the oft-repeated statement, "All roads lead to Rome." Rome kept building great highways all during the first centuryA.D., so that by the time the Revelation was written (90–100) there were some 250,000 miles of roads—ten times the circumference of the earth at the equator.

Next to the golden milestone stood the Arch of Tiberius. Behind that a portion of the Temple of Saturn was visible. The Saturnalia, in honor of the god, was held each December. With its parties and exchanges of gifts, it was later incorporated into Christmas festivities. Beyond, at the edge of the Capitoline Hill was the Temple of Concord, behind which rose the Public Record Office, still relatively intact.

Across the Forum from the Basilica Julia stood the Basilica Aemilia, a great commercial center about three hundred by eighty feet, especially used for money changing. Next to that stood the Senate House and the Senate Office Building.

Paul's main interest would have been the Basilica Julia. This great structure was probably begun in 54 B.C. and completed by

Rome under the emperors

themselves while public business was conducted.

Paul's Release?

The conviction that Paul left the emperor's court a free man has gained support over the years for several reasons.[31] First, the charges of infraction of Jewish law brought against Paul would not have been serious in the eyes of a Roman. Apparently the case against him was weak anyway. In this connection Acts 26:32 is quite revealing: "Then said Agrippa unto Festus, 'This man might have been set at liberty, if he had not appealed unto Caesar.'" Moreover, when the apostle arrived in Rome, he learned from Jews there that no documents from his opposition had reached the Jews of Rome (Acts 28:21). If his prosecutors did not carry the case to Rome, Paul might have won by default.

Second, it seems Paul left as a free man because his attitude while in prison was that he would be released (cf. Philemon 22; Philippians 1:25–26; 2: 23–24). He had also planned to go to Spain, where he had not gone before his imprisonment (Romans 15:24, 28). Early church writers indicate that Paul did go to Spain, that his ministry there came after his first Roman imprisonment, and that he was imprisoned a second time in Rome and martyred.[32]

Third, there are several other biblical references that may indicate a fourth missionary journey. One such is 2 Timothy 4:20, where Paul mentions that he left Trophimus sick at Miletus. This could not have happened during Paul's last journey to Jerusalem, because Trophimus was not left behind (Acts 20:4; 21:29), nor on the journey to Rome, because he did not touch at Miletus then. This reference seems to presuppose another voyage.

If Paul made a fourth missionary journey, he probably went first to Spain and then to the East once more. Very likely he spent some time in Crete winning converts—hence the necessity to leave Titus there to organize the church on the island

Augustus. It burned down soon thereafter, but was rebuilt and enlarged by Augustus and dedicated in A.D. 12 in the names of Gaius and Lucius Caesar, his two young grandsons. The structure was 312 feet long by 156 feet wide with a great central hall measuring 234 by 85 feet.[30] The latter was surrounded on all sides by a double row of brick pillars faced with marble, which formed aisles that were vaulted and stuccoed. Above the aisles were galleries.

The central hall was covered with a wooden roof, which rose above the side aisles on a clerestory. Through the clerestory light was admitted into the great hall. The floor was paved with slabs of marble, colored in the central court and white in the aisles. The structure was abundantly beautified with sculpture, mostly in the form of freestanding statues.

The Julian Basilica was the seat of the tribunal of the *Centumviri*, who judged civil cases, especially inheritance disputes. Therefore, large and curious crowds frequented the place. Like crowds that gathered in Hadrian's Forum in Jerusalem and along the edge of the Forum at Philippi and elsewhere in the Roman world, they carved diagrams of games on the floor and amused

Entrance to the Mamertine Prison.

false charges—perhaps devised by the men he berated in the references just noted.

When Paul arrived in Rome the second time, perhaps about A.D. 66, the city had a very different appearance than during his earlier visit. The fire had made possible some extensive changes. Many streets had been widened and straightened, the Circus Maximus had been rebuilt and embellished, and many other public structures had been built or rebuilt. At that time much still lay in ruins. Nero had reserved the entire center of the city for his grand new palace, which justly deserved the name *Domus Aurea*, or "Golden House."

Built between A.D. 64 and 68, the entire complex covered 125 acres, which reached from the Palatine Hill, across the Forum and the Velia as far as the Oppian Hill. Besides the palace, the grounds included parks, groves, pastures, a zoo, and a lake. It was a kind of first century Versailles in the center of an earlier teeming metropolis. Later emperors did their best to destroy the memory of this monstrosity of Nero. The Flavians filled in the lake and built the Colosseum on it, and Trajan built his baths on top of the palace on the Oppian Hill. These and others built temples and other public buildings over the monumental approach to the grounds along one side of the Forum.

Since 1907, when the German archaeologist F. Weege wormed his way through a hole in the wall of the Baths of Trajan and began to explore the *Domus Aurea*, modern archaeologists have been working on the site. So far eighty-eight rooms of the palace complex have been worked on; much more is to be done there. A description of one room serves as a sample of what the *Domus Aurea* was like:.

"Room 70 is a vaulted corridor 227 feet long . . . painted sky-blue . . . seabeasts, candelabra, and arabesques, sphinxes with shrubs growing out of their backs, griffins, centaurs, acanthus-leaves, Cupids, gorgons' heads, lions' heads with rings in their mouths, dolphins holding horns of plenty, winged horses, eagles, tritons, swags of flowers make up the riotous décor. In recesses in the walls, impressionistically painted landscapes

and for penning an epistle to him there later (Titus 1:5). Probably he was arrested in Asia, possibly at Ephesus. He had left books, parchments, and clothes at Troas expecting to return for them. The particular wrong that Phygellus, Hermogenes, and Alexander had done him in Asia may have been misrepresenting him to the authorities and securing his arrest (2 Timothy 1:15; 4:14).

Rome Again

If Paul was arrested a second time later on and martyred in Rome, that arrest would have occurred after the fire of Rome, when Christians could no longer enjoy the freedom they once had. It is not necessary to hold, however, that Paul was arrested because of his faith. Some of his enemies may have hauled him into the courts on and seascapes attempt the illusion of the out-of-doors."[33]

The Mamertine

Tradition has it that during his second imprisonment Paul was detained in the Mamertine Prison in Rome. The name *Mamertinus* is postclassical—during the Empire the place was known simply as the *Carcer* (the prison). This was the ancient state prison of Rome at the foot of the Capitoline Hill. It was used as a place of detention, not of penal servitude, although executions occurred there.

The upper room is a vaulted trapezoid, the sides varying in length from eleven to sixteen feet. Below lies a subterranean chamber, originally accessible only by a hole in the roof, through which food or prisoners might be lowered. This lower chamber, the Tullianum was nearly twenty-one feet in diameter and, according to Sallust, twelve feet high.[34] All who wrote of the place describe it with horror. Sallust (86–34 B.C.) described it as "exceeding dark, unsavory, and able to craze any man's senses."[35] Under such circumstances the apostle would indeed have felt the need of the cloak and the books he had left behind at Troas (2 Timothy 4:13).

But the present condition of the prison does not seem to help much in visualizing Paul's last days. As I have visited the prison on several occasions, I could not imagine Paul's writing Second Timothy or anything else under such conditions. Apparently what now exists is only a small part of the first century prison, only one of a number of cells. It's possible that Paul may have had somewhat better conditions in another part of the facility.[36] Visitors to the Mamertine today should be careful not to assume that it looked the same in the days of Peter and Paul.

In any case, Paul knew he could not expect release this time. As he wrote Second Timothy, he had none of the optimism expressed in his earlier letters, when he expected release. He had obtained a preliminary hearing, and it had been a dismal failure (2 Timothy 4:16). Though he found himself in dire circumstances, Paul delivered what sometimes has been called his valedictory, for he was about to "graduate." "The time of my departure is at hand" (2 Timothy 4:6), he said. The English is so bland. The Greek for "departure" here is both a military and a nautical term. As a military expression it was used for taking down a tent and departing. As a nautical term it had to do with the hoisting of an anchor and sailing a ship. The Greek may be literally translated "Loosing away upward" and has a wonderful connotation for us. As a dirigible or balloon strains at its holding cables waiting to be released, so Paul's soul was straining to be loosed away upward to join his Maker and Redeemer.

But he was not merely longing to go. He made a declaration of triumph: "I have fought a good fight, I have finished my course, I have kept the faith: Henceforth there is laid up for me a crown of righteousness, which the Lord, the righteous Judge, shall give me at that day (2 Timothy 4:8, KJV)."

But Paul did not go alone. He had all of the church on his mind and heart: "and not to me only, but unto all them also that love his appearing" (2 Timothy 4:6–8 KJV). And we end this book on that note of triumph.

In this book we have followed the biblical narrative from Abraham in Mesopotamia through the experiences of the Israelites in the rest of the Old Testament (in Egypt, Palestine, and elsewhere) and the life of Christ and the establishment and growth of the church in the New Testament. The story of the development of the church has led us through Syria, Cyprus, Asia Minor, Greece, and Italy. This has not been merely a historical geography of Bible lands. Hopefully it has enriched the reader's faith and provided a meaningful context for the biblical message, while providing a greater sense of the reality of the Biblical narrative.

NOTES

1. Though one or two modern versions read *Roman world, Roman* is not in the Greek original and therefore should not appear in the English.

2. Capitoline, Palatine, Aventine, Caelian, Esquiline, Viminal, Quirinal. Eventually it expanded onto other hills, including the Pincio and Janiculum.

3. Frederick F. Cartwright and Michael D. Biddiss, *Disease and History* (New York: Dorset, 1972), 11.

4. Rick Gore, "When the Greeks Went West," *National Geographic,* Nov. 1994, 16.

5. M. Cary and H. H. Scullard, *A History of Rome,* 3rd ed. (New York: St. Martins, 1975), 19.

6. For an up-to-date discussion of the Etruscan question and the early legendary history of Rome, and documentation for much of the point of view expressed here, see T. J. Cornell, *The Beginnings of Rome* (New York: Routledge, 1995), 45–47, 119–172.

7. The straits were about one mile wide in ancient times, but today they have widened to about two miles.

8. For discussion of Luke 2:2 and Quirinius as governor, see Harold W. Hoehner, *Chronological Aspects of the Life of Christ* (Grand Rapids: Zondervan, 1977), Chap. 1.

9. Suetonius, "Life of Claudius," *The Twelve Caesars,* Chap. XXV, Section 4.

10. Tacitus, *The Annals,* Chap. XV, Section 44.

11. Fritz M. Heichelheim and Cedric A. Yeo, *A History of the Roman People* (Englewood Cliffs, NJ: Prentice-Hall, 1962), 326–7.

12. William M. Ramsay, *The Church in the Roman Empire Before A.D. 170.* 5th ed. (Grand Rapids: Baker reprint, 1979), 226–51.

12a. Louis H. Feldman has suggested, on the basis of an inscription found at the Colosseum, that its construction was financed by booty from Jerusalem and the temple at the time of the destruction of Jerusalem in A.D. 70. See Louis H. Feldman, "Financing the Colosseum," *Biblical Archeology Review,* July/ August 2001, 20–31.

13. In keeping with the general plan of this work, the history of an area is not carried in detail beyond the end of the first century, about which time the Revelation, last book of the New Testament to be composed, was written.

14. This historical treatment is somewhat elongated and seemingly throws this work out of balance. However, it is inserted here because it provides historical background for the New Testament period, since the Roman Empire at that time controlled the whole Mediterranean world. Moreover, this survey provides a wider historical context for several of the other sections of this book: Greece, Asia Minor, Cyprus, Phoenicia, Syria, Palestine, and Egypt.

15. Paul apparently appeared before Festus shortly after he took office, probably in 58. The apostle would then have been sent to Rome late in the same year. After wintering in Malta, he would have resumed his journey in 59. There are many problems involved in establishing the Pauline chronology. On the basis of a different calculation, the apostle may have come to Rome in 61.

16. Josephus, *Life,* Section 3.

17. James Smith, *The Voyage and Shipwreck of St. Paul*, 4th ed. (Grand Rapids: Baker, 1978 reprint), 129–47.

18. William B. Dinsmoor, *The Architecture of Ancient Greece* (New York: W. W. Norton, 1975), 317.

19. Smith, Ibid., p. 156.

20. Josephus, *Antiquities of the Jews*, XVIII.XI.3.

21. William M. Ramsay, "Roads and Travel in the New Testament," *A Dictionary of the Bible*, ed. By James Hastings (New York: Charles Scribner's Sons, 1904), Extra Volume, 386–87.

22. Horace, *Satires*, Chap. I, Section 5, 87.

23. Samuel B. Platner, *A Topographical Dictionary of Ancient Rome*, completed and revised by Thomas Ashby (London: Oxford University Press, 1929), 22.

24. Thomas Ashby, *The Roman Campagna in Classical Times* (New York: Macmillan, 1927), 178.

25. A. N. Sherwin-White, *Roman Society and Roman Law in the New Testament* (Oxford: Clarendon Press, 1963), Baker reprint, 110.

26. The first procurator, Coponius, was appointed in A.D. 6 when Herod Archelaus was deposed. Procurators then ruled Judea continuously until the fall of Jerusalem in A.D. 70 except for the brief reign of Herod Agrippa I (41–44).

27. Sherwin-White, Ibid., 111.

28. Albert A. Bell, *A Guide to the New Testament World* (Scottsdale, PA: Herald Press, 1993), 29.

29. It is very difficult for the modern visitor to Rome to visualize the Forum as Paul knew it because of the constant rebuilding carried on subsequently. Many of the ruins to be seen are of buildings dating to the rebuilding by Septimius Severus (193–211).

30. Authorities differ slightly on the measurements of this building and its parts. The figures given here are from Pietro Romanelli, *The Roman Forum* (Rome: Instituto Poligrafico Dello Stato, 1959), 36.

31. While Sherwin-White does not hold that there is any necessity to conclude that Paul was released, he notes that emperors might cancel outstanding cases on the judicial docket to shorten the list of cases in arrears or engage in acts of clemency. He notes that there were numerous known acts of clemency during the first five years of Nero's reign, encouraged by his tutor Seneca. Sherwin-White, Ibid., 119.

32. Clement, *Epistle to the Corinthians*, Chap. V, Eusebius, *Ecclesiastical History*, ii, 22; and the Muratori Canon.

33. Paul MacKendrick, *The Mute Stones Speak*, 2nd ed. (New York: W. W. Norton, 1983), 239.

34. Platner, Ibid., 99–100.

35. Sallust, *Conspiracy of Cataline*, 55.

36. Brian Rapske, *The Book of Acts and Paul in Roman Custody* (Grand Rapids: Eerdmans, 1994), 3, 20–22.

BIBLIOGRAPHY

Alfoldy, Geza, *The Social History of Rome*, Baltimore: John Hopkins, Rev. Ed. , 1988

Adkins, Lesley, and Roy A. Adkins. *Dictionary of Roman Religion.* New York: Facts on File, 1996.

Adkins, Lesley, and R. A. Adkins. *Handbook to Life in Ancient Rome.* New York: Facts on File, 1994.

Alston, Richard. *Aspects of Roman History, AD 14-117.* London: Routledge, 1998.

Anderson, William J., and R. Phene Spiers. *The Architecture of Ancient Rome.* Revised by Thomas Ashby. London: B. T. Batsford, 1927

Arnold, W. T. *Roman Provincial Administration*, Rev. E. S. Bouchier. 3rd ed., Chicago: Ares, 1974.

Ashby, Thomas. *The Roman Campagna in Classical Times.* New York: Macmillian,1965.

Auguet, Roland. *Cruelty and Civilization: The Roman Games.* London: George Allen & Unwin, 1972.

Austin, N. J. E., and N. B. Rankov. *Exploratio: Military and Political Intelligence in the Roman World.* New York: Routledge, 1995.

Banti, Luisa. *The Etruscan Cities and Their Culture.* Berkeley: University of California Press, 1973.

Barrett, Anthony A. *Caligula, The Corruption of Power.* New Haven: Yale University Press, 1989.

Barrow, R. H. *Slavery in the Roman Empire.* New York: Barnes & Noble, 1996.

Bell, Albert A., Jr. *Exploring the New Testament World.* Nashville: Thomas Nelson, 1998.

Benko, Stephen. *Pagan Rome and the Early Christians.* Bloomington: Indiana University Press, 1986.

Boatwright, Mary T. *Hadrian and the Cities of the Roman Empire.* Princeton: Princeton University Press, 2000.

Boethius, Axel. *The Golden House of Nero.* Ann Arbor: University of Michigan Press, 1961.

Boak, Arthur E. R. *A History of Rome to 565 AD.*, 5th ed., New York: Macmillan Co., 1965.

Bohec, Yann Le. *The Imperial Roman Army.* New York: Routledge, 1994.

Bowersock, G. W. *Martyrdom and Rome.* Cambridge: Cambridge University Press, 1995.

Bradley, Keith R. *Discovering the Roman Family.* New York: Oxford University Press, 1991.

Bradley, Keith R. *Slavery and Society at Rome.* Cambridge: Cambridge University Press, 1994.

Bradley, Keith R. *Slaves and Masters in the Roman Empire.* New York: Oxford University Press, 1987.

Branick, Vincent. *The House Church in the Writings of Paul.* Collegeville: The Liturgical Press, 1989.

Buckland, W. W. *A Text-Book of Roman Law from Augustus to Justinian.* Cambridge: Cambridge University Press, 1921.

Bunson, Matthew. *Encyclopedia of the Roman Empire.* New York: Facts on File, 1994.

Campbell, Brian. *The Roman Army 31 B.C.–A.D. 337.* New York: Routledge, 1994.

Carcopino, Jerome. *Daily Life in Ancient Rome.* New Haven: Yale University Press, 1940.

Cary, M. *The Geographic Background of Greek and Roman History.* Oxford: Clarendon Press, 1949.

Cary M., and H. H. Scullard. *A History of Rome.* 3rd ed., New York: St. Martin's, 1975.

Casson, Lionel. *Everyday Life in Ancient Rome*. Rev. ed., Baltimore: Johns Hopkins University Press, 1998.

Clauss, Manfred. *The Roman Cult of Mithras*. New York: Routledge, 2001.

Collis, John. *The European Iron Age*. London: Routledge, 1984.

Cornell, T. J. *The Beginnings of Rome*. New York: Routledge, 1995.

Cornell, Tim and John Matthews. *Atlas of the Roman World*. New York: Facts on File, 1981.

Croom, A.T. , *Roman Clothing and Fashion*, Charleston, SC: Tempus, 2002

Cunliffe, Barry, *Rome and Her Empire*. New York: McGraw-Hill, 1978.

David, Jean-Michel. *The Roman Conquest of Italy*. Oxford: Blackwell, 1996.

Deiss, Joseph Jay. *Herculaneum, Italy's Buried Treasure*. New York: Thomas Y. Crowell, 1966.

Deiss, Joseph J. *The Town of Hercules*. Malibu, CA: The J. Paul Getty Museum, rev. ed., 1995.

Dersin, Denise, ed. *When Rome Ruled the World*. New York: Time-Life, 1997.

Dill, Samuel. *Roman Society from Nero to Marcus Aurelius*. New York: Meridian Books, 1956.

Dixon, Suzanne. *The Roman Family*. Baltimore: Johns Hopkins University Press, 1992.

Duncan-Jones, Richard. *The Economy of the Roman Empire*. 2nd ed., Cambridge: Cambridge University Press, 1982.

Earl, Donald. *The Age of Augustus*. New York: Exeter Books, 1968.

Edelstein, Ludwig. *Ancient Medicine*. Baltimore: Johns Hopkins University Press, 1967.

Evans, Harry B. *Water Distribution in Ancient Rome*. Ann Arbor: University of Michigan Press, 1994.

Everitt, Anthony, *Cicero*, NY: Random House, 2001

Fasola, Umberto M. *Peter and Paul in Rome*. Rome: Vision Editrice, 1980.

Ferrero, Guglielmo, *The Women of the Caesars*. Williamstown, MA: Corner House Publishers, 1978.

Finer, S. E. *The History of Government From the Earliest Times*. Vol. I, Oxford: Oxford University Press, 1997.

Frank, Tenney. *An Economic Survey of Ancient Rome*. Vol. 1, New York: Octagon Books, 1975.

Frazer, Alred, ed. *The Roman Villa*. Philadelphia: University Museum, 1998.

Friedlander, Ludwig. *Roman Life and Manners Under the Early Empire*. Trans. J. J. Freese and Leonard A. Magnus. 3 vols. London: George Routledge & Sons, 1936.

Galinsky, Karl. *Augustan Culture*. Princeton: Princeton University Press, 1996.

Goldsworthy, Adrian K. *The Punic Wars*. London: Cassell, 2000.

Goldsworthy, Adrian K. *The Roman Army at War 100 B.C.–A.D. 200*. Oxford: Clarendon Press, 1996.

Goldsworthy, Adrian K. *Roman Warfare*. London: Cassell, 2000.

Goodman, Martin. *The Roman World 44 B.C.–A.D. 180*. London: Routledge, 1997.

Grant, Michael. *The Army of the Caesars*. New York: M. Evans & Company, 1974.

Grant, Michael. *Augustus to Constantine: The Rise and Triumph of Christianity*. San Francisco: Harper & Row, 1990.

Grant, Michael. *Cities of Vesuvius*. New York: Penguin Books, 1976.

Grant, Michael. *Gladiators*. New York: Barnes & Noble, 1967.

Grant, Michael. *The Jews in the Roman World*. New York: Dorset Press, 1970.

Grant, Michael. *Nero*. New York: Dorset Press, 1970.

Grant, Michael. *The Roman Emperors*. New York: Charles Scribner's Sons, 1985.

Grant, Michael. *The Twelve Caesars*. New York: Charles Scribner's Sons, 1975.

Greene, Kevin. *The Archaeology of the Roman Economy*. Berkeley: University of California Press, 1986.

Griffin, Miriam T. *Nero, the End of a Dynasty*. New Haven: Yale University Press, 1985.

Gurval, Robert A. *Actium and Augustus*. Ann Armor: University Michigan Press, 1995.

Gwynn, Aubrey. *Roman Education*. New York: Russell & Russell, 1964.

Hacket, John. *Warfare in the Ancient World*. New York: Facts on File, 1989.

Hamey, L. A. and J. A. *The Roman Engineers*. Cambridge: Cambridge University Press, 1981.

Hammond, M. *The Augustan Principate in Theory and Practice During the Julio-Claudian Period*. Cambridge: Hardvard University Press, 1933.

Henderson, Bernard. *Five Roman Emperors*. Cambridge: Cambridge University Press, 1927.

Halloway, R. Ross. *The Archaeology of Ancient Sicily*. London: Routledge, 1991.

Holland, Richard, *Nero*, Phoenix Mill, England: Sutton, 2000

Jackson, Ralph. *Doctors and Diseases in the Roman Empire*. London: British Museum, 1988.

Jeffers, James S. *The Greco-Roman World of the New Testament Era*. Downers Grove: InterVarsity, 1999.

Jiménez, Ramon L. *Caesar Against Rome*. Westport, CT: Praeger, 2000.

Jones, Brian W. *The Emperor Domitian*. New York: Routledge, 1992.

Keppie, Lawrence. *The Making of the Roman Army*. New York: Barnes & Noble, 1994.

Kern, Paul B. *Ancient Siege Warfare*. Bloomington: Indiana University Press, 1999.

Kiefer, Otto. *Sexual Life in Ancient Rome*. New York: Dorset Press, 1993.

Kirschenbaum, A. *Sons, Slaves and Freedmen in Roman Commerce*. Jerusalem: The Hebrew University, 1987.

Koloski - Ostrow, Ann O., Ed., *Water Use and Hydraulics in the Roman City*, Boston Archeological Institute of America, 2001

Lanciani, Rodolfo. *The Ruins and Excavations of Ancient Rome*. Reprint. New York: Bell Publishing Co., 1979.

Landels, J. G. *Engineering in the Ancient World*. Berkeley: University of California Press, 1979.

Levick, Barbara. *Claudius*. New Haven: Yale University Press, 1990.

Levick, Barbara. *Tiberius the Politician*. 2nd ed., New York: Routledge, 1999.

Levick, Barbara. *Vespasian*. New York: Routledge, 1999.

Lieu, Judith, and others, eds. *The Jews Among Pagans and Christians in the Roman Empire*. London: Routledge, 1992.

Luttwak, Edward N. *The Grand Strategy of the Roman Empire*. Baltimore: Johns Hopkins University Press, 1976.

Laurence, Ray. *Roman Pompeii*. New York: Routledge, 1994.

MacKendrick, Paul. *The Mute Stones Speak*. 2nd ed., New York: Norton, 1960.

Mackinnon, Albert G. *The Rome of Saint Paul*. Philadelphia: John C. Winston Co., 1930.

MacMullen, Ramsay. *Christianizing the Roman Empire*. New Haven: Yale University Press, 1984.

MacMullen, Ramsay. *Roman Social Relations*. New Haven: Yale University Press, 1974.

Macnamara, Ellen, *The Etruscans*, Cambridge Harvard, 1991

Maiuri, Amedeo. *Pompeii*. Rome: Instituto Poligrafico Dello Stato, 1959.

Martin, Ronald. *Tacitus*. London: B. T. Batsford, 1981.

Mattern, Susan P. *Rome and the Enemy.* Berkeley: University of California Press, 1999.

McKay, Alexander G. *Houses, Villas, and Palaces in the Roman World.* Baltimore: Johns Hopkins University Press, 1975.

Meeks, Wayne A. *The First Urban Christians: The Social World of the Apostle Paul.* New Haven: Yale University Press, 1983.

Meeks, Wayne A. *The Moral World of the First Christians.* Philadelphia: Westminster, 1986.

Meier, Christian. *Caesar.* New York: Basic Books, 1995.

Meiggs, Russell. *Roman Ostia.* 2nd ed., New York: Oxford University Press, 1997.

Meinardus, Otto F. A. *St. Paul's Last Journey.* New Rochelle, NY: Caratzas Brothers, 1979.

Mellor, Ronald, ed. *The Historians of Ancient Rome.* New York: Routledge, 1998.

Mellor, Ronald. *Tacitus.* Nw York: Routledge, 1993.

Millar, Fergus. *The Emperor in the Roman World.* Ithaca: Cornell University Press, 1977.

Millar, Fergus. *The Roman Near East.* Cambridge: Harvard University Press, 1993.

Mommsen, Theodor. *The Provinces of the Roman Empire. From Caesar to Diocletion.* 2 vols., reprint, New York: Barnes & Noble, 1996.

Mommsen, Theodor. *The Provinces of the Roman Empire. The European Provinces.* Chicago: University of Chicago Press, 1968.

Montagu, John D. *Battles of the Greek & Roman Worlds.* London: Greenhill Books, 2000.

Nash, Ernest. *Roman Towns.* New York: J. J. Augustin, 1944.

Paget, Robert F. *Central Italy: An Archaeological Guide.* Park Ridge, NJ: Noyes Press, 1973.

Pallottino, Massimo. *The Etruscans.* Bloomington, IN: Indiana University Press, 1975.

Parker, Geoffrey, ed. *Cambridge Illustrated History of Warfare.* Cambridge: Cambridge University Press, 1995.

Perrottet, Tony, *Route 66 A.D.*, NY: Random House, 2002

Platner, Samuel B. *A Topographical Dictionary of Ancient Rome.* Completed and revised by Thomas Ashby. London: Oxford University Press, 1929.

Portella, Ivana D. *Subterranean Rome.* Venice: Arsenale Editrice, 1999.

Potter, T. W. *Roman Italy.* Berkeley: University of California Press, 1987.

Ramsay, William M. *The Church in the Roman Empire Before A.D. 170.* 5th ed., London: Hodder and Stoughton, 1897; Baker Book House reprint 1979.

Ramsay, William M. "Roads and Travel in the New Testament," *A Dictionary of the Bible.* Edited by James Hastings. Extra Vol. 1904.

Rapske, Brian. *The Book of Acts and Paul in Roman Custody.* Vol. 3, Grand Rapids: Eerdmans, 1994.

Richardson Emeline. *The Etruscans.* Chicago: University of Chicago Press, 1964.

Richardson, Lawrence, Jr. *A New Topographical Dictionary of Ancient Rome.* Baltimore: Johns Hopkins University Press, 1992.

Richardson, Lawrence, Jr. *Pompeii: An Architectural History.* Baltimore: Johns Hopkins University Press, 1988.

Rivoira, G. T. *Roman Architecture.* Oxford: Clarendon Press, 1925.

Roberts, J.M., *Rome and the Classical West*, NY: Oxford University Press, 1999

Robertson, D. S. *Greek and Roman Architecture.* 2nd ed., Cambridge: Cambridge University Press, 1943.

Robinson, O. F. *Ancient Rome: City Planning and Administration.* New York: Routledge, 1992.

Robinson, O. F. *The Criminal Law of Ancient Rome.* Baltimore: Johns Hopkins University Press, 1995.

Roebuck, Carl. *The World of Ancient Times.* New York: Scribner's, 1966.

Romanelli, Pietro. *The Palatine.* 2nd ed., Rome: Istituto Poligrafico Dello Stato, 1956.

Romanelli, Pietro. *The Roman Forum.* 3rd ed., Rome: Istituto Poligrafico Dello Stato, 1959.

Rostovtsev, Mikhail. *The Social and Economic History of the Roman Empire.* 3 vols., 2nd ed., Oxford: The Clarendon Press, 1957.

Salmon, E. T. *A History of the Roman World 30 B.C.–A.D. 138.* London: Methuen & Co., 1950.

Scarre, Chris. *Chronicle of the Roman Emperors.* London: Thames & Hudson, 1995.

Scullard, H. H. *From the Grachi to Nero.* London: Methuen & Co., 1959.

Schullard, H. H. *Roman Politics 220–150 B.C.* Oxford: Clarendon Press, 1951.

Setzer, Claudia. *Jewish Responses to Early Christians.* Minneapolis: Fortress, 1994.

Shelton, Jo-Ann. *As the Romans Did.* New York: Oxford University Press, 1988.

Sherwin-White, A. N. *The Roman Citizenship.* 2nd ed., Oxford: The Clarendon Press, 1973.

Sherwin-White, A.N. *Roman Law and Roman Society in the New Testament.* Reprint, Grand Rapids: Baker, 1992.

Shotter, David. *Nero.* New York: Routledge, 1997.

Shuckburgh, E. S. *Augustus Caesar.* New York: Barnes & Noble, 1995.

Smith, William. *A Dictionary of Greek and Roman Geography.* 2 vols., reprint, New York: AMS Press, 1966.

Sinnigen, William G. and Arthur E. R. Boak. *A History of Rome to A.D. 565.* 6th ed., New York: Macmillan, 1977.

Sordi, Marta. *The Christians and the Roman Empire.* Norman: University of Oklahoma Press, 1986.

Southern, Pat. *Augustus.* New York: Routledge, 1998.

Southern, Pat. *Domitian, Tragic Tyrant.* Bloomington: Indiana University Press, 1997.

Stark, Rodney. *The Rise of Christianity.* Princeton: Princeton University Press, 1996.

Starr, Chester G. *A History of the Ancient World.* 4th ed., New York: Oxford University Press, 1991.

Starr, Chester G. *The Roman Imperial Navy.* Westport, CT: Greenwood, 1979.

Stowers, Stanley K. *Letter Writing in Greco-Roman Antiquity.* Philadelphia: Westminster Press, 1986.

Syme, Ronald. *The Augustan Aristocracy.* Oxford: Clarendon Press, 1986.

Syme, Ronald. *The Roman Revolution.* Oxford: Oxford Univesity Press, 1939.

Taplin, Oliver, ed. *Literature in the Greek World.* Oxford University Press, 2000.

Thomas, Carol G. and Craig Conant. *Citadel to City–State.* Bloomington: Indiana University Press, 1999.

Toppin, Elizabeth, ed. *The World of the Romans.* New York: Oxford University Press, 1993.

Toynbee, J. M. C. *Death and Burial in the Roman World.* Baltimore: Johns Hopkins University Press, 1996.

Treggiari, Susan. *Roman Marriage.* New York: Oxford University Press, 1991.

Turcan, Robert. *The Cults of the Roman Empire.* Oxford: Blackwell, 1996.

Turcan, Robert. *The Gods of Ancient Rome.* New York: Routledge, 2001.

Ulansey, David. *The Origins of the Mithraic Mysteries.* New York: Oxford University Press, 1989.

Vehling, Joseph D., ed. and trans. *Apicus: Cookery and Dining in Imperial Rome.* New York: Dover, 1977.

Wallace-Handrill, Andrew. *Houses and Society in Pompeii and Herculaneum.* Princeton: Princeton University Press, 1994.

Ward-Perkins, J. B. *Roman Imperial Architecture.* 2nd ed., New Haven: Yale University Press, 1981.

Warmington, B. H. *Nero: Reality and Legend.* New York: W. W. Norton, 1969.

Watson, G. R. *The Roman Soldier.* Ithaca, NY: Cornell University Press, 1969.

Webster, Graham. *The Roman Imperial Army.* 3rd ed., Totowa, NJ: Barnes & Noble, 1985.

Wedeck, Harry E. *Roman Morals.* Lawrence, KS: Coronado Press, 1980.

Wellesley, Kenneth. *The Year of the Four Emperors.* 3rd. ed. London: Routledge, 2000.

Wheeler, Mortimer. *Rome Beyond the Imperial Frontiers.* Harmondsworth, England: Penguin Books, Inc., 1955.

White, K. G. *Roman Farming.* Ithaca, NY: Cornell University Press, 1970.

Wiedemann, Thomas. *The Roman Household, A Sourcebook.* London: Routledge, 1991.

Wilken, Robert L. *The Christians as the Romans Saw Them.* New Haven: Yale University Press, 1984.

Wilkes, J.J., *Diocletian's Palace, Split,* Oxford, Oxbow Books, 1986

Williams, Margaret H. *The Jews Among the Greeks and Romans.* Baltimore: John Hopkins University Press, 1998.

Zanker, Paul. *Pompeii Public and Private Life.* Cambridge: Harvard University Press, 1998.

GENERAL BIBLIOGRAPHY

The literature on the Bible lands is now incredibly vast. It grows every day. But it is possible to construct a meaningful general bibliography for this book.

In doing so we may first eliminate the older books that are now somewhat dated in their conclusions. Then we may leave out the more technical materials designed for the advanced student, such as the *Journal of Cuneiform Studies*, or *Hesperia*, or Oriental Institute publications of the University of Chicago. Publications in foreign languages have not been included, in part because they are not usually readily available to the general reader, in part because of the language barrier, and in part because so many of the best ones have been translated into English. Further, it is not necessary to repeat the books and articles appearing in the endnotes and bibliographies of individual chapters of this book. What remains, then, is a limited number of periodicals, atlases, encyclopedias, and dictionaries, and various background study books.

Periodicals:

American Journal of Archaeology (almost every issue has a summary of recent work in one of the major Bible lands)

Archaeology

Archaeology Odyssey

Bible Review

Biblical Archaeology Review

Bulletin of the American Schools of Oriental Research

Expedition (published by the University of Pennsylvania Museum)

Journal of Biblical Literature

Journal of Near Eastern Studies

Near Eastern Archaeology (formerly *Biblical Archaeologist*)

Atlases:

Aharoni, Yohanan, and Michael Avi-Yonah. *The Macmillan Bible Atlas*. New York: Macmillan, 1968

Atlas of Israel. 3rd ed., New York: Free Press, 1985.

Baines, John, and Jaromir Malek. *Atlas of Ancient Egypt*. New York: Facts on File, 1980.

Beek, Martin A. *Atlas of Mesopotamia*. London: Thomas Nelson, 1962.

Beitzel, Barry J. *The Moody Atlas of Bible Lands*. Chicago: Moody Press, 1985.

Cornell, Tim, and John Matthews. *Atlas of the Roman World*. New York: Facts on File, 1982.

Levi, Peter. *Atlas of the Greek World*. New York: Facts on File, 1980.

May, Herbert G. *Oxford Bible Atlas*. Revised by John Day. New York: Oxford University Press, 1985.

Oliphant, Margaret. *The Atlas of the Ancient World*. New York: Simon & Schuster, 1992.

Pritchard, James B., ed. *The Harper Atlas of the Bible*. New York: Harper & Brothers, 1987.

Rasmussen, Carl G. *The Zondervan NIV Atlas of the Bible*. Grand Rapids: Zondervan, 1989.

Roaf, Michael. *Cultural Atlas of Mesopotamia*. New York: Facts on File, 1990

Wiseman, Donald J., and others. *New Bible Atlas*. Downers Grove, Ill.: InterVarsity Press, 1994.

Wright, George Ernest, and Floyd V. Filson. *The Westminster Historical Atlas*. Philadelphia: Westminster Press, 1956

Dictionaries and Encyclopedias:

Avi-Yonah, Michael, ed. *Encyclopedia of Archaeological Excavations in the Holy Land*. Englewood Cliffs, N.J.: Prentice-Hall. Vol. 1, 1975; vol. 2, 1976; vol. 3, 1977; vol. 4, 1978.

Bienkowski, Piotr, and Alan, Millard, eds. *Dictionary of the Ancient Near East*. Philadelphia: University of Pennsylvania Press, 2000.

Bimson, John J., ed. *Baker Encyclopedia of Bible Places*. Grand Rapids: Baker, 1995.

Bromiley, Geoffrey, revising editor. *International Standard Bible Encyclopedia*. Grand Rapids: Eerdmans. Vol. 1, 1979; Vol. 2, 1982; Vol. 3, 1986;Vol. 4, 1988.

Butler, Trent C., ed. *Holman Bible Dictionary*. Nashville: Broadman & Holman, 1991.

Buttrick, George A., and Keith R. Crim, eds. 5 vols., *Interpreter's Dictionary of the Bible*. Nashville: Abingdon, 1976.

Elwell, Walter A., ed. *Baker Encyclopedia of the Bible*. 2 vols., Grand Rapids: Baker, 1988.

Grant, Michael. *A Guide to the Ancient World*. New York: Barnes & Noble, 1986.

Harrison, R. K., ed. *The New Unger's Bible Dictionary*. Chicago: Moody Press, 1988.

Hastings, James, ed. *A Dictionary of the Bible*. 4 vols. plus Supplement, Peabody, Mass.: Hendrickson Publishers, reprinted 1988.

Hillyer, N., ed. *The Illustrated Bible Dictionary*. 3 vols., rev. ed., Wheaton, Ill.: Tyndale House, 1980.

Hillyer, N., ed. *New Bible Dictionary*. rev. ed., Wheaton, Ill.: Tyndale House, 1982.

Hopkins, Daniel J., ed. *Merriam Webster's Geographical Dictionary*. 3rd ed., Springfield, MA: Merriam-Webster, 1997.

Hornblower, Simon, and Anthony Spawforth, eds. *The Oxford Classical Dictionary*. 3rd ed., New York: Oxford University Press, 1996.

Meyers, Eric M., ed. *Oxford Encyclopedia of Archaeology in the Near East*. 5 vols., New York: Oxford University Press, 1997.

Miller, Madeleine S., and J. Lane. *Harper's Encyclopedia of Bible Life*. Revised by Boyce M. Bennett, Jr. and Daniel H. Scott. New York: Harper & Row, 1978.

Neilson, William A., ed. Webster's Biographical Dictionary. Springfield, MA: Merriam-Webster, 1980.

Packer, J. I., ed. *Nelson's Illustrated Encyclopedia of Bible Facts*. Nashville: Thomas Nelson, 1995.

Pfeiffer, Charles F., and others, eds. *The Wycliffe Bible Encyclopedia*. 2 vols., Chicago: Moody Press, 1975; reissued by Hendrickson Publishers, Peabody, MA, as the Wycliffe Bible Dictionary, one vol., 1998.

Richards, Lawrence O., ed. *Revell Bible Dictionary*. 2nd deluxe ed., 1994. Revell is now a division of Baker Book House, Grand Rapids, Michigan.

Sasson, Jack M., ed. *Civilizations of the Ancient Near East*. 4 vols., New York: Charles Scribner's Sons, 1995.

Schiffman, Lawrence H., and James C. VanderKam, eds. *Encyclopedia of the Dead Sea Scrolls*. 2 vols., New York: Oxford University Press, 2000.

Stern, Ephraim, ed. *The New Encyclopedia of Archaeological Excavations in the Holy Land*. 4 vols., New York: Simon & Schuster, 1993.

Stillwell, Richard, ed. *The Princeton Encyclopedia of Classical Sites*. Princeton: Princeton University Press, 1976.

Tenney, Merrill C., ed. *The Zondervan Pictorial Bible Dictionary*. Grand Rapids: Zondervan, 1988.

Tenney, Merrill C., ed. *The Zondervan Pictorial Encyclopedia of the Bible*. 5 vols., Grand Rapids: Zondervan, 1975.

Youngblood, Ronald F., ed. *Nelson's New Illustrated Bible Dictionary*. rev. ed., Nashville: Thomas Nelson, 1986.

Background Study Books:

Angus, S. *The Mystery Religions*. New York: Dover, 1975.

Archer, Gleason, L. *A Survey of Old Testament Introduction*. 3rd ed., Chicago: Moody Press, 1994.

Aylen., Leo. *The Greek Theater*. Cranbury, N.J.: Associated University Presses, 1985.

Baigent, Michael, and Richard Leigh. *The Dead Sea Scrolls Deception*. New York: Summit Books, 1991.

Barber, Elizabeth W. *Women's Work, The First 20,000 Years*. New York: W. W. Norton, 1994.

Beacham, Richard C. *The Roman Theatre and Its Audience*. Cambridge: Harvard University Press, 1991.

Becker, Jurgen. *Paul, Apostle to the Gentiles*. Louisville: Westminster John Knox Press, 1993.

Bickerman, Elias J. *The Jews in the Greek Age*. Cambridge: Harvard University Press, 1988.

Boardman, John, and others, eds. *The Oxford History of the Classical World*. New York: Oxford University Press, 1986.

Borowski, Oded. *Agriculture in Iron Age Israel*. Winona Lake, IN.: Eisenbrauns, 1987.

Bremer, J. M., and others, eds. *Hidden Futures, Death and Immortality in the . . . Biblical World*. Amsterdam: Amsterdam University Press, 1994.

Brothwell, Don, and Patricia Brothwell. *Food in Antiquity*. Expanded ed., Baltimore: Johns Hopkins University Press, 1998.

Bruce, F. F. *Second Thoughts on the Dead Sea Scrolls*. rev. ed., Grand Rapids: Eerdmans, 1961.

Burkert, Walter. *Ancient Mystery Cults*. Cambridge: Harvard University Press, 1987.

Burrows, Millar. *The Dead Sea Scrolls*. New York: Viking, 1955.

Burrows, Millar. *More Light on the Dead Sea Scrolls*. New York: Viking, 1958.

Casson, Lionel. *The Ancient Mariners*. 2nd ed., Princeton: Princeton University Press, 1991.

Casson, Lionel. *Libraries in the Ancient World*. New Haven: Yale University Press, 2001.

Casson, Lionel. *Ships and Seamanship in the Ancient World*. Princeton: Princeton University Press, 1971.

Casson, Lionel. *Travel in the Ancient World*. Toronto: Hakkert, 1974.

Clements, R. A., ed. *The World of Ancient Israel*. Cambridge: Cambridge University Press, 1989.

Collis, John. *The European Iron Age*. New York: Routledge, 1984.

Coogan, Michael D. *Oxford History of the Biblical World*. New York: Oxford University Press, 1988.

Cross, Frank Moore, Jr. *The Ancient Library of Qumran and Modern Biblical Studies*. Grand Rapids: Baker, 1961, reprinted 1980.

Culican, William. *The First Merchant Venturers*. London: Thames & Hudson, 1966.

deCamp, L. Sprague. *Great Cities of the Ancient World*. New York: Dorset, 1972.

DeVaux, Roland. *The Bible and the Ancient Near East*. Garden City, N.Y.: Doubleday, 1971.

Drinkwater, J. F. and Andrew Drummond, eds. *The World of the Romans*. Oxford: Oxford University Press, 1993.

Edelstein, Ludwig. *Ancient Medicine*. Baltimore: Johns Hopkins, 1967.

Engberg-Pedersen, Troels. *Paul in His Hellenistic Context*. Minneapolis: Fortress, 1995.

Feldman, Louis H. *Jew and Gentile in the Ancient World*. Princeton: Princeton University Press, 1993.

Freeman, Charles. *Egypt, Greece and Rome*. New York: Oxford University Press, 1996.

Gordon, Cyrus H., and Gary A. Rendsburg. *The Bible and the Ancient Near East*. 4th ed., New York: W. W. Norton, 1997.

Gower, Ralph, and Fred H. Wight. *The New Manners and Customs of Bible Times*. Chicago: Moody Press, 1987.

Grant, Michael. *A Guide to the Ancient World*. New York: Barnes & Noble, 1986.

Harris, H. A. *Sport in Greece and Rome*. Ithaca: Cornell University Press, 1972.

Harris, Roberta L. *The World of the Bible*. London: Thames & Hudson, 1995.

Harrison, R. K., ed. *Major Cities of the Biblical World*. Nashville: Thomas Nelson, 1985.

Hoerth, Alfred J., and others, eds. *Peoples of the Old Testament World*. Grand Rapids: Baker, 1994.

Humphrey, John H. *Roman Circus*. Berkeley: University of California Press, 1986.

Keener, Craig S. *The IVP Bible Background Commentary: New Testament*. Downers Grove: InterVarsity Press, 1993.

LLamsa, George M. *Old Testament Light*. New York: Harper & Row, 1964.

LaSor, William S. *The Dead Sea Scrolls and the Christian Faith*. Rev. ed., Chicago: Moody, 1960.

LaSor, William S. *The Dead Sea Scrolls and the New Testament*. Grand Rapids: Eerdmans, 1972.

Leick, Gwendolyn. *Who's Who in the Ancient Near East*. London: Routledge, 1999.

Malamat, Abraham. *Mari and the Early Israelite Experience*. Oxford: Oxford University Press, 1989.

Marclay, John M. *Jews in the Mediterranean Diaspora: From Alexander to Trajan*. Edinburgh: T & T Clark, 1996.

Matthews, Victor H. *Manners and Customs in the Bible*. Peabody, Mass.: Hendrickson Publishers, 1988.

Matthews, Victor H., and Don C. Benjamin. *Social World of Ancient Israel 1250-587 BCE*. Peabody: Hendrickson Publishers, 1993.

Meiggs, Russell. *Trees and Timber in the Ancient Mediterranean World*. Oxford: Clarendon Press, 1998.

Meijer, Fik. *A History of Seafaring in the Classical World*. New York: St. Martin's, 1986.

Meijer, Fik, and Onno van Nijf. *Trade, Transport and Society in the Ancient World*. London: Routledge, 1992.

Millard, Alan. *Discoveries from the Time of Jesus*. Batavia, Ill.: Lion Publishers, 1990.

Millard, Alan. *Treasures from Bible Times*. Batavia, Ill.: Lion Publishers, 1985.

Modrzjewski, Joseph M. *The Jews of Egypt from Rameses II to Emperor Hadrian*. Princeton: Princeton University Press, 1995.

Murphy-O'Connor, Jerome. *Paul the Letter Writer; His World, His Options, His Skills*. Collegeville, Minn.: The Liturgical Press, 1995.

Niditch, Susan. *Ancient Israelite Religion*. New York: Oxford University Press, 1997.

Niswonger, Richard L. *New Testament History*. Grand Rapids: Zondervan, 1988.

Osiek, Carolyn, and David L. Balch. *Families in the New Testament World*. Louisville: Westminster John Knox Press, 1997.

Owens, E. J. *The City in the Greek and Roman World*. London: Routledge, 1991.

Patai, Raphael. *The Children of Noah, Jewish Seafaring in Ancient Times*. Princeton: Princeton University Press, 1998.

Peters, F. E. *The Harvest of Hellenism: _A History of the Near East from Alexander the Great to the Triumph of Christianity*. New York: Barnes & Noble, 1970.

Pritchard, James B., ed. *Ancient Near Eastern Texts*. 2nd ed., Princeton: Princeton University Press, 1955.

Porten, Bezalel. *Archives from Elephantine*. Berkeley: University of California Press, 1968.

Rainey, Anson F., ed. *Egypt, Israel, Sinai*. Tel Aviv: Tel Aviv University, 1987.

Redford, Donald B. *Egypt, Canaan, and Israel in Ancient Times*. Princeton: Princeton University Press, 1992.

Reicke, Bo. *The New Testament Era*. Philadelphia: Fortress Press, 1968.

Richards, Lawrence O. *The Victor Bible Background Commentary: New Testament*. Colorado Springs:Victor Books/SP Publications, 1994.

Romer, John. *Testament: The Bible and History*. New York: Henry Holt, 1988.

Schiffman, Lawrence H. *Reclaiming the Dead Sea Scrolls*. New York: Doubleday, 1994.

Seltzer, Robert M., ed. *Religions of Antiquity*. New York: Macmillan, 1987.

Shanks, Hershel. *The Mystery and Meaning of the Dead Sea Scrolls*. New York: Random House, 1998.

Shanks, Hershel, ed. *Understanding the Dead Sea Scrolls*. New York: Random House, 1992.

Sinnigen, William G. and Arthur E. R. Boak. *A History of Rome to A.D. 565*. 6th ed., New York: Macmillan, 1977.

Sussmann, Ayala, ed. *Excavations and Surveys gin Israel*. Vol. 19, 1999. Published almost annually by the Israel Antiquities Authority. Distributed in the United States by Eisenbrauns, Winona Lake, Indiana.

Thompson, J. A. *Handbook of Life in Bible Times*.

Downers Grove: InterVarsity Press, 1986.

Torr, Cecil. *Ancient Ships*. Chicago: Argonaut, 1964.

VanderKam, James C. *The Dead Sea Scrolls Today*. Grand Rapids: Eerdmans, 1994.

Van Der Woude, A. S., ed. *The World of the Bible*. Grand Rapids: Eerdmans, 1986.

Van Der Woude, A. S., ed. *The World of the Old Testament*. Grand Rapids: Eerdmans, 1989.

Vermes, Geza. *The Complete Dead Sea Scrolls in English*. New York Penguin Press, 1997.

Von Rad, Gerhard. *Holy War in Ancient Israel*. Grand Rapids: Eerdmans, 1991.

Von Soden, Wolfram. *The Ancient Orient*. Grand Rapids: Eerdmans, 1994.

Vos Howard F. *Nelson's New Illustrated Bible Manners & Customs*. Nashville: Thomas Nelson, 1999.

Watts, John H., and Victor H. Matthews. *The IVP Bible Background Commentary: Genesis-Deuteronomy*. Downers Grove: InterVarsity Press, 1997.

Young, Gordon D., ed. *Mari in Retrospect*. Winona Lake, IN: Eisenbrauns, 1992.

Young, Gordon D., ed. *Ugarit in Retrospect*. Winona Lake, IN: Eisenbrauns, 1981

Scripture Index

OLD TESTAMENT

9	183	17:2	150	15-18	226
9:3-4	183	18:25	33	15:7-10	218
9:46	183	18:27	33	15:18	201
11:26	116	19:1-17	215	15:30	157
13:1-16:31	203	19:18-24	215	17:11	168
14-15	198	20:1-42	215	17:28	263
14:8-18	265	21	216	18:6-17	237
14:19	200	21:10-15	201	18:19-33	84
16:4	150	23:7-13	215	19-20	226
16:21	198	23:15-29	215	19:8	210
16:25-31	204	24:1	225	20:8	182
16:27	202	24:1-4	172	20:23-26	228
16:28-30	198	24:1-22	215	22	225
17:6	198	25:18	263, 264	23:1	221
18	241	26:1-25	215	24	225
20:1	144, 168, 241	26:6	390	24:15	225
20:18-28	240	27	201	24:17	226
		27:6	217		
Ruth		28:4	216	**1 Kings**	
4:1-11	242	28:7-25	215	1-2	223
4:11	210	29	206	1:1-2:9	227
		30:14	177	2:3-4	227
1 Samuel		31	167	3:1	233
2:10	211	31:1-8	216	3:4-15	181
3:20	144, 168, 209	31:10	218	3:9	228
4	206	31:12	218	3:16-28	228
4:3	207, 284			3:28-29	228
4:4	208	**2 Samuel**		4:1-6	228
4:5	208	1:21	216	4:5	224
4:15	208	2:1-4	218	4:11	148
4:18	202, 205, 209	2:12-17	181	4:20-28	229
5	202	3:2-5	226	4:24	198, 456
5:1-5	199	3:10	168	4:25	229
5:10-6:12	201	5	221	4:26	229
6:17	200	5:1-3	240	4:29-34	228
7:2	209, 209	5:3	220	5:1-12	349
7:3	208, 210	5:4-5	220	5:11	350
7:5	210	5:5	212	5:22	209
7:5-6	209	5:6	220	6:1	20, 21, 115, 195, 233, 348
7:12	207	5:8	220	6:2-10	233
7:13	211	5:11	337	6:4	234
7:15-17	209	5:11-12	348, 349	6:4-7	232
7:16	240	5:17-25	220	6:5-10	234
8:2	169	6:17	221	6:8	233
8:4	211	7	221	6:14-38	234-35
8:5	212	7:2	337	6:18	337
8:11-17	212	8	221	6:20-22	236
8:19	212	8:3-6	392	6:30	236
8:22	211	8:6	222	6:31	349
9:12-13	209	8:9-11	392	6:31-36	236
10:1-10	213	8:14	222	6:38	233
10:3	240	8:15	223	7	337
10:17	209	8:16	223	7:1-12	231
10:23	212	8:16-18	228	7:2-8	233
10:26	213	8:17	223	7:3-4	232
11:4	213	8:18	223, 224	7:9	233
13:2	213	10-12	221	7:13-14	349
13:8-13	209	10:1-5	222	7:13-51	236
13:13-14	214	10:1-7	391	7:23	236
13:14	227	10:8	391	7:27-29	236
13:19	207	11	503	7:46	237
14:25-29	265	11-12	225	7:48-50	237
15:34	213	11:1	222	8:1-66	237
17	201	11:3	390	9:10-14	350
17:1	261	11:3ff	508	9:15	159

NEW TESTAMENT

GENERAL INDEX

A-bar-gi , 17
Aamu. *See* Asiatics
Abana, 375
Abd-Astartus, 348
Abdi-Ashirta, 344
Abi-Baal, 348
Abi-Milki, 345
Abiathar, 215, 223, 226, 227
Abigail, 263
Abijan, 251
Abimelech, 168, 178, 183
Abner, 220
Abradates, 599
Abraham, 1, 2, 5, 17, 20-24, 59, 60,
    110, 121, 143, 150, 157, 168,
    170, 175, 177, 179, 183, 218,
    240, 430, 502, 503
Absalom, 157, 181, 201, 218, 222,
    226, 237
Abu Hureyra, 9, 377
Abu Simbel, 115
Abydos, 454
Abydos Seti, 113
Accho, 335, 363, 392
                see also Acre
Acco, 313
Achaea, 614, 621-22, 624, 626, 667
Achaean League, 521, 622, 664-66,
    667, 702, 755, 757, 758
Achaean Revolt, 759
Achaeans, 511
Achaemenes, 396, 434
Achaia, 519, 558, 703, 759
Achaicus, 709
Achan, 194
Achelous River, 615
Achilles, 517
Achish, 201, 216-17
Achmetha. *See* Ecbatana
Acholla, 728
Aclepius, 357
Acra, 156, 275
Acragas, 630
Acre, 146-47, 335, 398
Acrocorinth, 701
Acropolis, 232, 613, 640, 652, 683,
    684, 686-90, 703
Actium, 129, 404, 666-67, 671, 770
Adad, 379
Adad-Nirari I, 30
Adad-Nirari III, 34-35, 394
Adada, 533

Adam, 189
Adana, 390, 524, 525, 530, 542
Adar, 270
Adonijah, 226-27
Adonis, 358, 384
Adonizedek, 218
Adriatic Sea, 616, 617, 737-38,
    740, 768, 770
Aegae, 617, 657
Aegean Islands, 596, 613
Aegean Sea, 127, 352, 364, 387, .
    473, 491, 494, 497, 585, 615-16,
    742
Aegina, 642, 648, 708
Aelius Aristides, 587, 591
Aeneid, 773, 779
Aeolians, 514, 558, 560, 586
Aeschylus, 447, 652, 687
Aesop, 514
Aetokremnos, 470
Aetolian League, 520, 621, 755,
    756-57
Aetolians, 621, 664, 665, 758
Africa, 83-84, 305, 352, 741, 743,
    756-57, 762, 764, 768, 770, 775,
    797
Afrocentrism, 83
Agade, 18, 378
Agamemnon, 560, 627, 635, 637
Agapenor, 481
Agbatana, 437
Agora, 683, 684, 685-86, 690-95,
    702-4
Agrippa, 688, 694, 769, 810
                see also Herod
    Agrippa I, Herod Agrippa II
Agrippina, 782-83
Ahab, 34, 44, 149, 150, 154, 160,
    167, 168, 192, 204, 244, 245-46,
    247, 252, 292, 337, 349, 353,
    356-57, 393
Aharoni, Yohanan, 169, 255
Ahasuerus, 270, 428, 444
Ahaz, 35, 250, 254, 256, 395
Ahaziah, 202, 247, 248, 252
Ahhiyawa, 506, 507
Ahijah, 240
Ahikan, 263
Ahimelech, 223, 390
Ahiram, 356
Ahmose, 94, 95-96, 385
Ahmose I, 185, 343

Ahuramazda, 270, 436, 441-42,
    445, 452
Ai, 118, 181, 188-89, 194, 197
Ain Feshka, 302
Ain Ghazal, 171
Ain Hawara, 107
´Ain-es Sultan, 191
Ajalon, 122, 229, 251
Akanthou, 468
Akhenaton, 109
Akkad, Akkadians, 6, 17-18, 21,
    28
Akko, 335
Akromandra, 468
Akrotiri Peninsula, 468, 470
Akserai, 579
Akurgal, Ekrem, 587
Al Mina, 391
Alabanda, 594
Alalakh, 177, 347, 379, 381-82, 391
Alambra, 472
Alaric the Visigoth, 697, 702
Alasehir, 600
Alashiya, 470, 472, 473, 474
Alastos, Doros, 472
Albania, 617, 755
Albright Institute, 202
Albright, William F., 116, 213-14,
    240, 348
Alcaeus, 560
Alcibiades, 655
Alcimus, 274
Alcman, 643
Aleppo, 9, 177, 377, 378, 379, 381,
    382, 390, 412, 456, 505
Alexander the Great, 14, 50, 69,
    73, 121, 125, 126, 127, 184, 198,
    270, 271-73, 360-62, 397, 445,
    450, 454-58, 476, 496, 517-19,
    526, 527, 531, 533, 545, 547-62,
    563, 569, 586, 597, 617, 642,
    656, 675, 776, 881
Alexander Jannaeus, 276, 290, 307
Alexandretta, 374, 397
Alexandria, 60, 61, 71, 83, 84, 125,
    127-29, 130, 456, 582, 590, 662,
    682, 781, 793
Alexandria Troas, 545, 668
Alishar, 501, 504
Alishar Hüyük, 500
Alma Dag, 335
Alon, D., 178

834

Gangas River, 673
Gangites River, 673
Garden of Eden, 1
Garden of Gethsemane, 157
Garden Tomb, 317-19
Garrod, Dorothy, 149, 170
Garstang, John, 116, 148, 161, 192-93
Gate of All Nations, 453
Gate of the Lions, 636
Gath, 149, 198, 201, 216, 221, 394
Gaudos, 730
Gaugamela, 450-51, 456, 457
Gaul, 518, 542, 592, 663, 744, 748, 749, 755, 766, 767, 768, 770, 774, 776, 782, 786, 787
Gaulanitis, 165, 313
Gaulus, 589
Gaumata, 439
Gavdos, 625
Gaza, 5, 114, 122, 126, 145, 149, 176, 198-99, 272, 303, 305, 376, 395
Gazara, 275
Gebal, 335, 339-40, 341, 355, 358
Gedaliah, 182, 209, 263
Gediz, 495, 596
Gedrosia, 429
Gelb, I. J., 504
Genghis Khan, 50
Gennasaret, 161
Genoa, 740
Gentiles, 402, 556, 679, 706
George Cross, 721
Georges VI, 721
Geraneia Ridge, 699
Gerar, 178
Gerasa, 279, 298
Gerizim, 154
Germa, 595
German Oriental Society, 13, 46, 314, 504
German Society for Scientific Research, 183
Germanicus, 783
Germany, 766, 786, 790
Gesher, 389
Gezer, 121, 160, 187, 188, 198, 229-31, 275, 356
Ggantija, 727
Ghajn Tuffieha Bay, 721
Ghar Dalam, 726-27
Ghûtah, 375, 395
Gibeah, 213, 215
Gibeon, 122, 181-82, 188, 228, 251
Gibson, McGuire, 20
Gichon, 222
Gideon, 152, 204, 216

Gihon, 227
Gilead, 165, 203, 229, 247, 249
Gilgal, 211, 213
Gilgamesh Epic, 43
Gitin, Seymour, 202
Gittites, 222
Giza, 76, 78, 336, 341
Globigerina, 730
Glueck, Nelson, 116, 164, 350
Gobryas, 396
Gog, 514
Golan Heights, 165, 172, 279
Golden Bay, 721
Golden House, 783, 788, 811
Goldman, Hetty, 504, 530
Goldmann, Zeev, 146
Golgotha, 319
Goliath, 150, 201, 214, 261
Gomer, 37
Gomme, A. W., 653-54
Gomorrah, 24, 50-51
Gordion, 455, 513
Gordium, 513, 517, 542
Gordius, 518
Gordon, Cyrus H., 387
Gordon's Calvary, 317-19
Goshen, 64, 65, 103
Goths, 548, 551
Götze, Albrecht, 504
Gozo, 725, 729, 730
Gracchi, 761-62
Granicus River, 360, 397, 454, 517
Great Pyramid, 76-78
Great Zab, 2
Greater Europe Mission, 710
Greco-Persian War, 646
Greece, 83, 129, 238, 346, 359, 444, 446, 474, 510, 519, 522, 545, 552, 613-710, 737, 758, 767, 784
Greek Evangelical Church, 710
Greek Orthodox Church of St. Gabriel, 309
Greek Period, 360-62
Greeks, 71, 123, 271, 297, 347, 352, 360, 361, 371, 403, 439, 440, 444, 446-47, 451, 475-76, 491, 496, 512, 516, 517, 521, 527, 528, 534, 535, 542, 552, 562, 567, 570, 595, 597, 743, 745, 751
Green, Peter, 661-62
Greenewalt, C. H., Jr., 597-98
Gregory of Nazianzus, 582
Gregory of Nyssa, 582
Grittites, 201
Grotefend, Georg, 433
Gubaru, 396
Gudelisin, 540

Gugu, 514
Gulf of Adramyttium, 558
Gulf of Aqaba, 106, 170, 247, 376
Gulf of Astacus, 583
Gulf of Cius, 583
Gulf of Iskenderun, 494
Gulf of Puteoli, 798
Gulf of Suez, 5, 106
Gulf of Volos, 617
Gulf War, 51
Gurney, O. R., 505
Guti, 18, 19, 175
Gütterbock, Hans, 504
Gyges, 514, 597

Habakkuk, 258
Habiru. See Apiru
Hachilah, 215
Hacilar, 499
Hadad, 181, 238, 379, 414
Hadadezer of Damascus , 34
Hadadezer of Zobah, 222
Hades, 698
Hadet, 337
Hadrian, 298, 310, 316-18, 460, 536, 538, 548, 555, 560, 570, 592, 667, 683, 685, 697, 699
Hagar, 25-26, 59, 60, 106
Hagar Qim, 727-28
Haggai, 270, 427, 428, 442, 448
Haibre, 124
Haifa, 147, 149
Hal Saflieni, 727
Hala Sultan Tekke, 473
Halab, 505
Halaf, 10
Haleb, 377, 412
Haliacmon River, 618
Halicarnassus, 455, 514, 517
Halys River, 431, 434, 494, 498, 515, 542, 579, 581
Ham, 14-15, 59, 176, 339
Hama, 374, 377, 389, 390, 413, 504
Hamadan, 429, 431, 457
Hamath, 374, 390, 392, 393, 394, 395, 396, 413
Hammond, N. G. L., 661
Hammond, Philip C., 219
Hammurabi, 7, 14, 26-27, 31, 45, 177, 346, 371, 381, 430
Hammurabi's Code, 19, 25-29, 389, 510
Han Dynasty, 771
Hanani, 252
Hanfmann, George M. A., 597
Hannah, 150
Hannibal, 398, 520, 665, 755-57, 797

594, 614, 758
Magnesian Gate, 549, 554
Mahanaim, 226
Makkedah, 188
Malachi, 428, 448
Malatya, 508
Malek, Jaromir, 95
Malian Gulf, 648
Malkart, 357
Mallia, 629
Mallory, J. P., 626
Mallowan, Max, 33
Mallus, 525
Malta, 85, 351, 721-31, 793, 797
Mamertine Prison, 812
Mamre, 219, 293
Manasseh, 152, 203, 258, 355
Manetho, 68-69, 84, 92, 93
Manhattan Island, 286
Manisa, 596
Mansel, Arif, 532
Manzikert, 491
Maon, 215
Marah, 68, 107
Marathon, 125, 271, 440, 516, 613, 647, 684
Marble Street, 555-56
Marcellus, 529
Marcus Aemilius Lepidus, 764-65
Marcus Aurelius, 587, 674
Marcus Cato, 477
Marcus Licinius Crassus, 765-66
Marcus Livius Drusus the Younger, 763
Mardonius, 447, 649
Marduk, 27, 41, 46, 47, 268, 434, 435, 436
Mareshah, 150
Margueron, Jean Claude, 381-82
Mari, 27, 177, 180, 378, 379-83
Mariamne, 284, 287
Marisa, 273
Marius, 762-63
Mark (apostle), 338, 484
Mark Antony, 129, 277-79, 418, 460, 524, 534, 538, 543, 548, 580, 666-67, 671, 767-70, 809
Marneptah, 345
Marquet-Krause, Judith, 194
Mars, 693, 802
Mars Hill, 613, 695
Marsascirocco Bay, 722
Marsaxlokk Bay, 722, 726, 728, 731
Martu, 379
Martyrium of St. Philip, 577
Mary (mother of Jesus), 60, 130, 307-11, 492, 735

Mary Magdalene, 315
Mary's Well, 308
Masada, 279, 280, 287-90, 310
Masoretic, 20
Massagetai, 436
Massoretes, 316
Matgenus, 349
Mattaniah, 260
Mattathias, 273-74, 275
Matthew, 312, 314, 338
Matthiae, Paolo, 378
Mazaeus, 457
Mazar, Amihar, 171, 202
Medes, 34, 35, 41, 45, 50, 123, 269, 395, 431-32, 434, 515, 527
Media, 427, 429, 459
Medinet Habu, 121
Mediterranean Sea, 5, 123, 125, 144, 347, 350, 351, 352, 355, 361, 364, 373, 374, 467, 494, 497, 615-16, 735, 745, 751, 765
Mediterranean Riviera, 495
Megara, 616, 642, 645, 648, 699, 743
Megiddo, 97, 122, 149, 160, 166-67, 182, 185, 188, 229, 230, 251, 258, 336-37, 385, 395
Mekal, 383
Meleda, 722
Melid, 508
Melita, 722, 729-31
Melkart, 348, 357-58, 475, 729
Mellaart, James, 499-501
Melos, 626, 630
Memmius, 555
Memnon, 455
Memphis, 41, 67, 71, 72, 84, 113, 123, 128, 130
Men, 534-35, 536, 573, 576, 578
Men-nefru-Mine. See Menfe
Menahem, 35, 246, 249, 354, 394
Menderes, 495, 497
Menelaus, 273, 274
Menes, 69, 72
Menfe, 71-72
Menkaure, 78
Mentuhotep, 84
Mercury, 555
Meriç, Recip, 601
Meriggi, P., 504
Merimda, 69
Merneptah, 117, 120, 187, 230
Merodach-Baladan, 37, 39, 40, 45
Mersin, 499
Merytre, 96
Mesaoria, 468
Meskalumdug, 17
Mesopotamia, 1-51, 73, 83, 91,

143, 171, 175, 184, 377, 378, 385, 386, 389, 430, 458, 459, 460
Messana, 753, 796
Messara Plain, 625
Messenia, 623, 643
Messogis Range, 495, 546, 573
Metroon, 692
Metropolitan Museum of Art, 407
Micah, 253
Michal, 215
Midas, 513-14
Middle Kingdom, 64, 69, 80, 82, 83, 84-91, 97, 125
Midianites, 204, 216
Migdal, 315
Migdal Nuna. See Magdala
Miletus, 407, 440, 455, 512-13, 514, 515, 516, 517, 548, 552, 562, 563-66, 586, 630, 646, 676, 810
Miltner, F., 551
Minerva, 747
Minet el-Beida, 382
Minoan Pompeii, 630
Minoans, 352, 626, 627-33, 638
Minos, 627
Minotaur, 484
Mishnah, 316
Misrayim. See Egypt
Mita, 513
Mitanni, 30-31, 344, 381, 385-86, 501, 505, 506
Mithraism, 664
Mithridates I, 459
Mithridates II, 459, 548, 560, 561, 573, 579
Mithridates IV Philopater Philadelphus, 521
Mithridates V Euergetes, 521
Mithridates VI, 521-23, 580, 666, 763-65
Mithridatic Wars, 511, 521-24, 543, 581, 666, 763-64
Mitylene, 559-60
Mizpah, 207, 209-12, 213, 263
Mizraim, 59, 176
Mnajdra, 727
Mnevis, 102
Moab, 165-66, 214, 222, 229, 243, 244, 247, 248, 252, 392
Modin, 273
Mohammed, 460
Mommsen, Theodor, 362, 582
Monastery of St. John, 601
Mongol, 50
Montet, Pierre, 346
Mordechai, 451
Moriah, 156

CAANAN IN THE BRONZE AGE

- City
- *Moab* Kingdom
- *Aram* Region
- *Esdraelon Plain* Geographic feature

0 — 10 — 20 Miles
0 — 10 — 20 Kilometers

THE MEDITERRANEAN SEA

PHOENICIA

Sidon

Tyre

Achzib

Acco

Mt. Carmel
Achshaph?
Jokneam

Dor

Hannathon

Megiddo
Aruna
Ibleam
Mt. Gilboa

Socoh

Dothan

Tirzah
(Tell el-Far'ah North)

Mt. Ebal
Mt. Gerazim Shechem

Aphek

Joppa
Ono

Lod

Gezer
Ekron(Tel Miqne)
Ashdod
Ashkelon
Beth-shemesh
Gath(Tell
es- Safi)
Timnah
Adullam
Keilah?
Eglon?
Lachish Mamre
Hebron

Gaza
Sharuhen(Tell el-`Ajjul?)
Gerar
(Tel Haror?)
Ziklag
(Tel Sera`?)

Besor Brook

Beer-sheba Moladah

Hormah(Tel Masos?)

Rehoboth

The Negeb

ARABAH

Valley of Jezreel
Esdraelon Plain

Plain of Sharon

The Shephelah

PHILISTIA

Debir

ARAD
Arad
Hormah(Tel `Ira)

Ijon
Abel Beth-rehob
Dan/Laish

Mt. Hermon

Kedesh

MAACAH

Hazor
Merom? Aduru

Chinnereth

Hammath
Mt. Tabor
Shunem En-dor
Anaharath

Taanach

Lake Huleh

Sea of Galilee

Yanoam

Beth-shean
Rehob
Pehel (Pella)

Shiloh

Bethel Ai
Gibeon Jericho
Gilgal
Jerusalem/
Salem
Bethlehem

Valley of Aijalon
Valley of Sorek
Aijalon

Jordan River

Succoth
(Deir `Alla?)
Penuel

Jabbok R.
Mahanaim

Jazer

Shittim

Mt. Pisgah
Mt. Nebo
Medeba

Ataroth

Dibon
Aroer

Bab ed-Dra' Ar

MOAB

Numeira

Zoar

Arnon R.

The Dead Sea

GESHUR
BASHAN

ARGOB
Karnaim
Golan Ashtaroth

Yarmuk R.

HAVVOTH-JAIR

Edrei

Ramoth-gilead

GILEAD

AMMON
Rabbah

Elealeh
Heshbon

Mattanah

AMORITES

**ARAM
(SYRIA)**

Damascus

Abana R.

Pharpar R.

EDOM

Zered Brook

©2003 CHK AMERICA WWW.MAPSUSA.COM

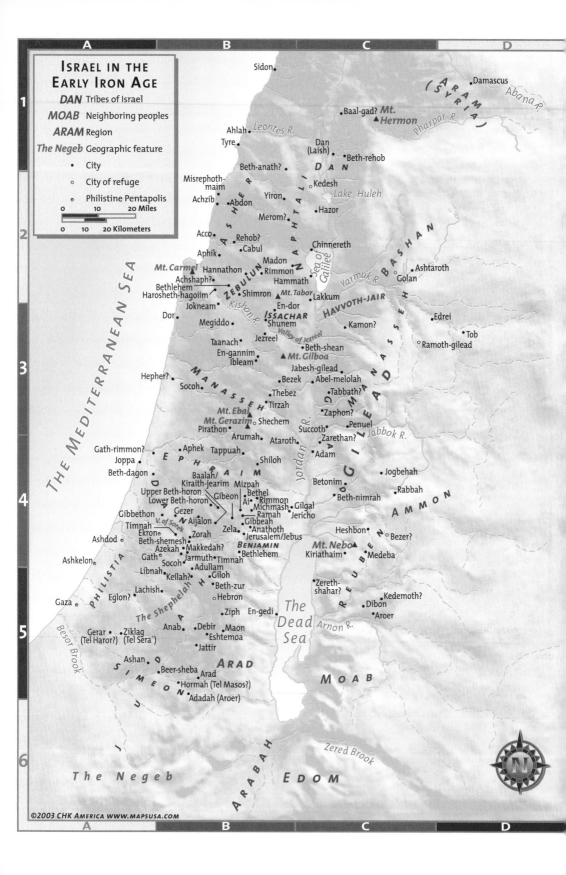

ISRAEL IN THE EARLY IRON AGE

DAN Tribes of Israel
MOAB Neighboring peoples
ARAM Region
The Negeb Geographic feature

- • City
- ○ City of refuge
- ⊙ Philistine Pentapolis

0   10   20 Miles
0   10   20 Kilometers

©2003 CHK AMERICA WWW.MAPSUSA.COM

Kingdoms of Israel and Judah During the Divided Monarchy

JUDAH Hebrew kingdoms
MOAB Neighboring peoples
GILEAD Region
THE NEGEB Geographic feature

- Israel
- Judah
- City

0 10 20 Miles
0 10 20 Kilometers

A B C D

1

Sidon
Zarephath
Ijon
Damascus
Abana R.
PHOENICIA
VALLEY OF LEBANON
Leontes R.
Mt. Hermon
Pharpar R.
Tyre
Abel-beth-maacah
Dan
(A R A M
(SYRIA))
Kedesh
Lake Huleh
BASHAN
Yiron
Hazor
Merom?
Janoah
Acco
Karnaim
Ashtaroth
Chinnereth
Sea of Galilee
Aphek
HAURAN
Rumah
Mt. Carmel
Hannathon
Gath-hepher
Yarmuk R.
Edrei
Jokneam
Kishon R.
Mt. Tabor
HAVVOTH-JAIR
Dor
Shunem
Beth-arbel
Megiddo
Jezreel
Taanach
VALLEY OF JEZREEL
Ramoth-gilead
Beth-haggan
Ibleam
Mt. Gilboa
Borim
Dothan
Tishbe
I S R A E L
Socoh
Yazith
Abel-meholah
Samaria
Tirzah
G
Mt. Ebal
Pirathon
Shechem
Lo-debar?
Penuel
Mt. Gerazim
Jabbok R.
Baal-shalishnah
Jordan R.
Mahanaim
I L E A D
Tappuah
Shiloh
A M M O N
Joppa
Jeshanah
Zeredah
Ephron
Gimzo
Bethel
Rabbah
Gibbethon
Zemaraim
Beth-horon
Mizpah
PLAIN OF SHARON
Jabneel
Ramah
Gebah
Gezer
Aijalon
Gilgal
THE MEDITERRANEAN SEA
Baalath?
Anathoth
Jericho
Ekron
Timnah
Zorah
Jerusalem
Heshbon
Ashdod
Beth-shemesh
Nebo
Bezer?
Azekah
Bethlehem
Mt. Nebo
Ashkelon
Gath
Etam
Kiriathaim
Medeba
Socoh
Adullam
Tekoa
Beth-meon/Baal-meon
Libnah
Beth-zur
Beth-diblathaim
Sharuhen (Tell el-Ajjul?)
Gaza
Mareshah
Zair
The
Ataroth
Jahaz?
Lachish
Hebron
Adoraim
Dibon
PHILISTIA
Yurza
Ziph
En-gedi
Dead
Aroer
Gerar (Tel Haror?)
Carmel
Arnon R.
Raphia
WILDERNESS OF JUDAH
Sea
Besor Brook
THE SHEPHELAH
JUDAH
Beer-sheba
Gurbaal
M O A B
Kir-hareseth
Waters of Nimrim
ARABAH
THE NEGEB
Tamar?
Zoar
Zered Brook
E D O M

2

3

4

5

6

N

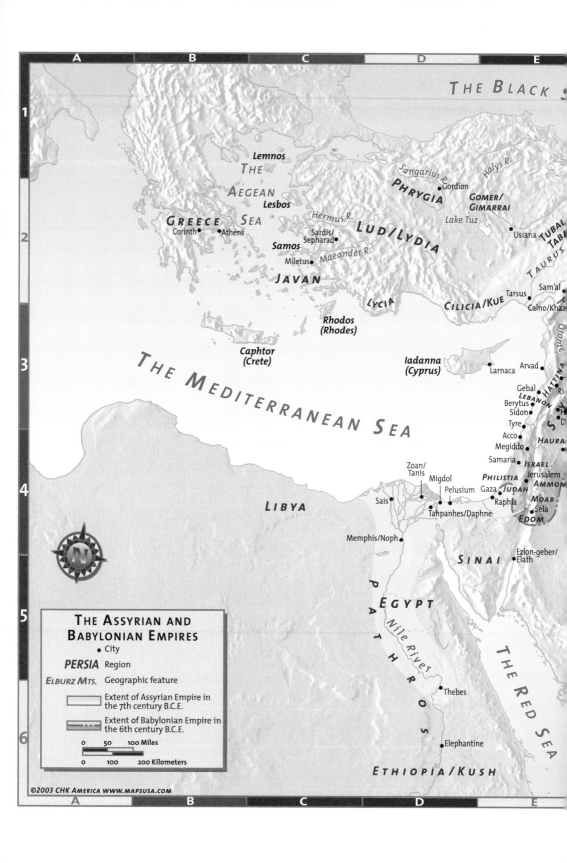

A B C D E

1

THE BLACK S

Lemnos

Sangarius R. *Halys R.*

THE PHRYGIA ● Gordion

AEGEAN GOMER/
GIMARRAI

Lesbos Lake Tuz Usiana ● TUBAL
TABA
GREECE SEA Hermus R. LUD/LYDIA
Corinth ● ● Athens Sardis/ TAURUS
Sepharad ●

2 Samos Sam'al ●
Miletus ● Maeander R. Tarsus ● Calno/Khaz ●

JAVAN

LYCIA CILICIA/KUE

Rhodos
(Rhodes) Iadanna Arvad ●
(Cyprus) ● Larnaca

3 Caphtor Gebal ● Ri
(Crete) LEBANON
Berytus ● H
Sidon ● D

THE MEDITERRANEAN SEA Tyre ● SY
Acco ● HAURA
Megiddo ●
Samaria ● ISRAEL
Zoan/ Jerusalem
Tanis PHILISTIA AMMON
Migdol ● Gaza ● JUDAH
4 Pelusium ● Raphia ● MOAB
LIBYA Sais ● Sela ●
Tahpanhes/Daphne EDOM

Memphis/Noph ● Ezion-geber/
● Elath
SINAI

P
A
5 T
H
THE ASSYRIAN AND R
BABYLONIAN EMPIRES O EGYPT
● City S
Nile River
PERSIA Region
ELBURZ MTS. Geographic feature
Extent of Assyrian Empire in Thebes ●
the 7th century B.C.E. THE RED SEA
Extent of Babylonian Empire in
the 6th century B.C.E.
0 50 100 Miles
Elephantine ●
6 0 100 200 Kilometers

©2003 CHK AMERICA WWW.MAPSUSA.COM ETHIOPIA/KUSH

A B C D E

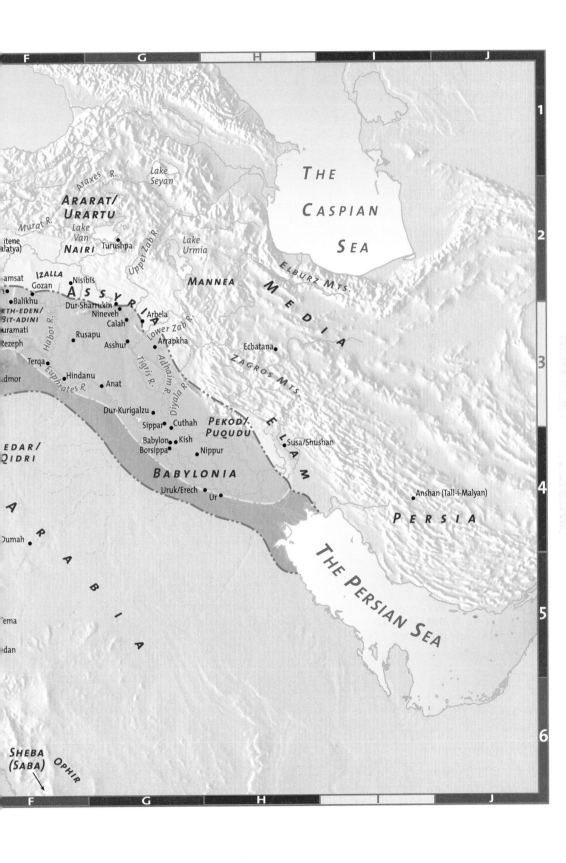

F **G** **H** **I** **J**

1

Araxes R.

Lake Seyan

THE

ARARAT/ URARTU

CASPIAN

Murat R.

itene alatya)

Lake Van

NAIRI Turushpa

Lake Urmia

SEA

2

MANNEA

ELBURZ MTS.

amsat

IZALLA

• Nisibis

Gozan •

ASSYRIA

M

Balikhu •

Dur-Sharrukin •

• Arbela

E

ETH-EDEN/ BIT-ADINI•

Nineveh •

Calah •

Upper Zab R.

D

uramati

• Rusapu

Asshur •

Lower Zab R.

Arrapkha •

Ecbatana •

I

Rezeph •

Terqa •

• Anat

Hindanu •

Tigris R.

Adhaim R.

ZAGROS MTS.

A

dmor

Euphrates R.

Habor R.

Diyala R.

3

Dur-Kurigalzu •

E

PEKOD/ PUQUDU

L

EDAR/ QIDRI

Sippar •

• Cuthah

A

Babylon •

• Kish

Susa/Shushan •

Borsippa •

• Nippur

M

BABYLONIA

4

Uruk/Erech •

• Ur

Anshan (Tall-i-Malyan) •

A

Dumah •

PERSIA

R

A

B

I

A

THE

Tema •

dan

PERSIAN SEA

5

SHEBA (SABA)

OPHIR

6

F **G** **H** **I** **J**

THE ROMAN EMPIRE
Paul's Journeys

First Missionary Journey (46-48 C.E.)
Second Missionary Journey (49-52 C.E.)
Third Missionary Journey (53-57 C.E.)
Journey to Rome (59-60 C.E.)
Laodicea ● "Seven Churches of Asia" (Rev. 1-3)
● City
THRACE Roman province
Boundary of Roman Empire 65 C.E.
Roman road

0   100   200 Miles
0   100   200 Kilometers

©2003 CHK AMERICA WWW.MAPSUSA.COM

F G H I J

1

BOSPORUS
Chersonesus

SARMATIA ASIATICA

COLCHIS

THE BLACK SEA

THE CASPIAN SEA

2

Ionopolis Sinope
Amastris
a BITHYNIA & PONTUS Amisus
Gangra Amasea Side Trapezus
Comana
GALATIA Ancyra Tavium
aeum Gordium
Pessinus Lake Tuz
LYCAONIA Halys R.
Antioch CAPPADOCIA Caesarea (Mazaca)
in Pisidia Archelais Malatya
Iconium Derbe Samsat
Lystra COMMAGENE Edessa
MPHYLIA Tarsus Issus Zeugma Carrhae
erga CILICIA Europus (Harran)
Seleucia (Carchemish) OSROENE
Antioch
Seleucia Pieria
Apamea
CYPRUS Salamis Epiphania
Tripolis SYRIA Emesa Palmyra
Paphos Berytus
Sidon PHOENICIA
Tyre ABILENE Damascus
Ptolemais Caesarea Philipi
Caesarea Tiberias
Sebaste Scythopolis
Joppa JUDEA Jordan R.
Gaza Jerusalem
Dead Sea

KINGDOM OF ARMENIA
Cyrus R.
Lake Seyan
Artaxata
Araxes R.
Lake Van
Tigranocerta
Lake Urmia
MEDIA ATROPATENE

GORDYENE ADIABENE
Nisibis Ninus Arbela

MEDIA

PARTHIAN EMPIRE

Dura-Europos

MESOPOTAMIA
Tigris R.
Euphrates R.
Seleucia Ctesiphon
Babylon

ELAM

3

4

s Sais
Pelusium
Heliopolis
Babylon
YPT
Nile R.

Petra
NABATEAN KINGDOM
Aila (Aelana)

Dumah

THE PERSIAN SEA

5

THE RED SEA

ARABIA

Tema

N

6

F G H I J

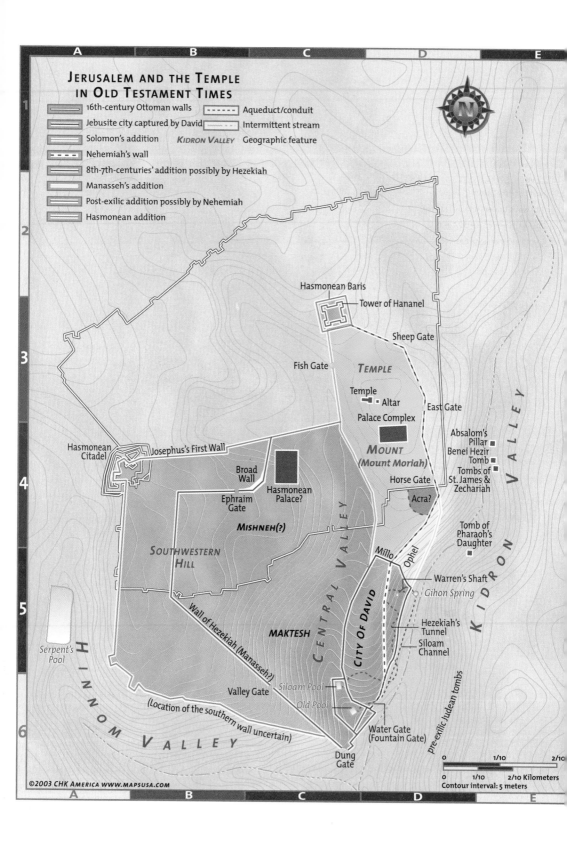

JERUSALEM AND THE TEMPLE IN OLD TESTAMENT TIMES

16th-century Ottoman walls
Jebusite city captured by David
Solomon's addition
Nehemiah's wall
8th-7th-centuries' addition possibly by Hezekiah
Manasseh's addition
Post-exilic addition possibly by Nehemiah
Hasmonean addition

Aqueduct/conduit
Intermittent stream
KIDRON VALLEY Geographic feature

Hasmonean Baris
Tower of Hananel
Sheep Gate
Fish Gate
TEMPLE
Temple
Altar
East Gate
Palace Complex
MOUNT (Mount Moriah)
Hasmonean Citadel
Josephus's First Wall
Broad Wall
Ephraim Gate
Hasmonean Palace?
Horse Gate
Acra?
Absalom's Pillar
Benei Hezir Tomb
Tombs of St. James & Zechariah
Tomb of Pharaoh's Daughter
MISHNEH(?)
SOUTHWESTERN HILL
Millo
Ophel
Warren's Shaft
Gihon Spring
Wall of Hezekiah (Manasseh?)
MAKTESH
CENTRAL VALLEY
CITY OF DAVID
Hezekiah's Tunnel
Siloam Channel
Serpent's Pool
Siloam Pool
Old Pool
Valley Gate
(Location of the southern wall uncertain)
HINNOM VALLEY
Water Gate (Fountain Gate)
pre-exilic Judean tombs
Dung Gate
KIDRON VALLEY

©2003 CHK AMERICA WWW.MAPSUSA.COM

0   1/10   2/10 Kilometers
0   1/10   2/10
Contour interval: 5 meters

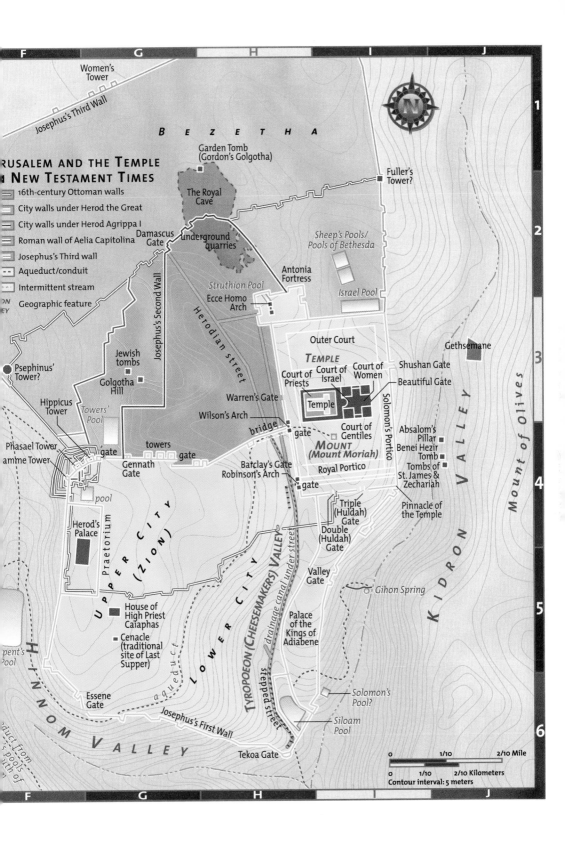

JERUSALEM AND THE TEMPLE IN NEW TESTAMENT TIMES

Legend:
- 16th-century Ottoman walls
- City walls under Herod the Great
- City walls under Herod Agrippa I
- Roman wall of Aelia Capitolina
- Josephus's Third wall
- Aqueduct/conduit
- Intermittent stream
- Geographic feature

Women's Tower

Josephus's Third Wall

B E Z E T H A

Garden Tomb
(Gordon's Golgotha)

The Royal Cave

Damascus Gate

underground quarries

Fuller's Tower?

Sheep's Pools/
Pools of Bethesda

Josephus's Second Wall

Struthion Pool

Antonia Fortress

Ecce Homo Arch

Israel Pool

Herodian street

Outer Court

TEMPLE

Gethsemane

Jewish tombs

Golgotha Hill

Court of Priests

Court of Israel

Court of Women

Shushan Gate

Beautiful Gate

Psephinus' Tower?

Warren's Gate

Temple

Hippicus Tower

Wilson's Arch

bridge

Court of Gentiles

Solomon's Portico

Absalom's Pillar

Benei Hezir Tomb

Tombs of St. James & Zechariah

Phasael Tower

Mariamme Tower

gate

towers

gate

gate

MOUNT
(Mount Moriah)

Gennath Gate

Barclay's Gate

Robinson's Arch

gate

Royal Portico

Pinnacle of the Temple

K I D R O N   V A L L E Y

M o u n t   o f   O l i v e s

pool

Triple (Huldah) Gate

Double (Huldah) Gate

Herod's Palace

U P P E R   C I T Y   (Z I O N)

Praetorium

Valley Gate

Gihon Spring

House of High Priest Caiaphas

L O W E R   C I T Y

T Y R O P O E O N   (C H E E S E M A K E R S)   V A L L E Y

drainage canal under street

Palace of the Kings of Adiabene

Cenacle (traditional site of Last Supper)

aqueduct

stepped street

Solomon's Pool?

Serpent's Pool

H I N N O M   V A L L E Y

Essene Gate

Josephus's First Wall

Siloam Pool

Tekoa Gate

aqueduct from pools of Etham

Gihon Spring

Scale:
0   1/10   2/10 Mile
0   1/10   2/10 Kilometers
Contour interval: 5 meters

THE LAND OF ISRAEL/ PALESTINE IN THE FIRST CENTURY OF THE COMMON ERA

- • City
- *Mt. Nebo* Geographic feature
- GALILEE Region
- *NABATEAN* Kingdom/province

  Boundary of Herod's kingdom – greatest extent

  Province boundaries

  0   10   20 Miles
  0   10   20 Kilometers

Sidon
Sarepta
Damascus

PHOENICIA
ITUREA
ABILENE
Abana R.
Pharpar R.

Mt. Hermon
PROVINCE OF SYRIA

Tyre
Panias
Dan (Caesarea Philippi)
Kedesh

Lake Huleh
Gischala
Merom?
GAULANITIS
BATANEA
TRACHONITIS

Ptolemais (Akko)
Chorazin
Capernaum
Beth-saida
Raphana

Gennesaret
Magdala/ Taricheae
Hippos
Gamala
Dion?

Mt. Carmel
GALILEE
Sepphoris
Sea of Galilee
Yarmuk R.

Geba/Hippeum
Nazareth
Abila
Gedor (Gadara)
AURANITIS

Mt. Tabor

Dor

Caesarea (Strato's Tower)
Scythopolis (Beth-shan)
Mt. Gilboa
Pella

DECAPOLIS

THE MEDITERRANEAN SEA

Sebaste (Samaria)
Gerasa (Jerash)

Plain of Sharon
HEROD
Amathus

Apollonia
Mt. Ebal
Neapolis (Nablus)
Jordan River

Mt. Gerazim
Jabbok R.

Antipatris (Aphek)
Joppa
SAMARIA
Alexandrium
Gadara

Yarkon R.
Thamna
Phasaelis
Philadelphia (Amman)

Lydda (Lod)
Gophna
Archelais

Gazara (Gezer)
Modein
PEREA

Jamnia (Jabneh)
Emmaus
Jericho
Cyprus
Betharamphtha

Azotus (Ashdod)
Jerusalem
Bethany
Esbus (Heshbon)

Ascalon (Ashkelon) (free city)
JUDEA
Hyrcania
Qumran
Mt. Nebo

Bethlehem
Medeba

Anthedon
KINGDOM
Herodium
Callirrhoe

Gaza
Betogabri (Beth-guvrin)
Machaerus

Marisa (Maresha)
Adora
Hebron

En-gedi
The Dead Sea
Arnon R.

IDUMEA

Besor Brook
Masada

Raphia

Bersabe (Beer-sheba)
Malatha

THE NEGEB
Mampsis
NABATEAN KINGDOM

Khirbet Tannur
Zered Brook

Nessana

N

A   B   C   D

Map of The Assyrian and Babylonian Empires

Map of The Land of Israel/ Palestine in the First Century of the Common Era

Map of The Roman Empire